The Napoleonic Wars

The Napoleonic Wars

ALEXANDER
MIKABERIDZE

A Global History

OXFORD
UNIVERSITY PRESS

OXFORD
UNIVERSITY PRESS

Oxford University Press is a department of the University of Oxford.
It furthers the University's objective of excellence in research, scholarship,
and education by publishing worldwide. Oxford is a registered trade mark of
Oxford University Press in the UK and certain other countries.

Published in the United States of America by Oxford University Press
198 Madison Avenue, New York, NY 10016, United States of America

© Alexander Mikaberidze 2020

Library of Congress Cataloging-in-Publication Data
Names: Mikaberidze, Alexander, author.
Title: The Napoleonic Wars: a global history/Alexander Mikaberidze.
Description: New York: Oxford University Press, [2020]
Identifiers: LCCN 2019019279 | ISBN 9780199951062 (hardback: alk. paper)
Subjects: LCSH: Napoleonic Wars, 1800–1815. | Napoleonic Wars,
1800–1815—Influence. | Geopolitics—History—19th century. | Military
history, Modern—19th century.
Classification: LCC DC226.3 .M54 2020 | DDC 940.2/7—dc23
LC record available at https://lccn.loc.gov/2019019279

9 8 7
Printed by LSC Communications, Inc.
United States of America

For Anna

I am called to change the world.
—Napoleon to his brother Joseph

We have won an empire by armed might, and it must continue to rest on armed might, otherwise it will fall by the same means, to a superior power.

—Secret Committee of the British East India Company

Now Napoleon, there was a fellow! His life was the stride of a demigod from battle to battle and from victory to victory.... It can be said that he was in a permanent state of enlightenment, which is why his fate was more brilliant than the world has ever seen or is likely to see after him.

—Johann Wolfgang von Goethe

One man alone was then alive in Europe; everyone else tried to fill their lungs with the air he had breathed. Every year France made him a gift of three hundred thousand young men; and, with a smile, he took this new fiber pulled from the heart of humanity, twisted it in his hands, and made a new string for his bow; he then took one of his arrows and sent it flying across the world, until it fell into a vale on a deserted island under a weeping willow.

—Alfred de Musset

History is not the soil in which happiness grows. The periods of happiness in it are the blank pages of history.

—Georg Wilhelm Friedrich Hegel

CONTENTS

LIST OF MAPS

PREFACE

IT HAS LONG BEEN ACCEPTED that, together with the French Revolutionary Wars, the Napoleonic Wars constitute a single conflict, lasting some twenty-three years, that ranged France against shifting alliances of European powers and produced a short-lived French hegemony over most of Europe. Between 1792 and 1815 Europe was plunged into turmoil and transformation. The French Revolution unleashed a torrent of political, social, cultural, and military changes. Napoleon extended them beyond the country's frontiers. The ensuing struggle was immense in its scale and intensity. Never before had European states resorted to a mobilization of civilian and military resources as total as during this period. What's more, this was a contest of great powers on a truly global scale. The Napoleonic Wars were not the first conflict to span the globe—such a distinction probably belongs to the Seven Years' War, which Winston Churchill famously labeled as the first "world war." But this was a war that in its scale and impact dwarfed all other European conflicts; for nineteenth-century contemporaries, it came to be known as the "Great War." Though provoked by the rivalries within Europe, the Napoleonic Wars involved worldwide struggles for colonies and trade, and in scale, reach, and intensity they represent one of the largest conflicts in history. In his efforts to achieve French hegemony, Napoleon indirectly became the architect of independent South America, reshaped the Middle East, strengthened British imperial ambitions, and contributed to the rise of American power.

Starting in the spring of 1792, revolutionary France became embroiled in a war. At first the French aspired to defend their revolutionary gains, but as the war progressed, their armies spread the effects of the Revolution to the neighboring states. With General Napoleon Bonaparte's rise to power, France's war aims reverted to more traditional policies of territorial expansion and continental hegemony seen under the Bourbon kings. Born on the island of Corsica into a noble but impoverished family of Italian descent, Bonaparte studied at French military schools and was commissioned as a lieutenant in the French artillery in 1785. The Revolution, which he welcomed despite his aristocratic roots, opened career prospects that would have been unimaginable to a young captain from a remote outpost of the French Empire. Rising rapidly in the new revolutionary armies, he was given command of French forces to invade Italy in 1796 and won brilliant victories that not only secured northern Italy for France but also helped to end the War of the First Coalition, as is called the first attempt to stop French expansion beyond its borders. Bonaparte's next campaign, in Egypt, was a military fiasco that failed to achieve its goals and ultimately resulted in the departure of the French. But it did enhance Bonaparte's reputation as a decisive leader, which helped him overthrow the French government in November 1799. By that point, a decade of revolutionary upheaval and uncertainty had made firm rule, and the order and stability that it promised, more enticing than the ideas and promises of radical revolutionaries.

Though youthful (he turned thirty in 1799), the gifted General Bonaparte proved to be a figure of authority. After seizing power in a coup, he assumed the title of First Consul of the Republic and pursued an ambitious domestic policy to stabilize France. The reforms of 1800–1804 consolidated revolutionary gains, with the famed Napoleonic Code reasserting fundamental principles of the Revolution: equality of all citizens before the law and security of wealth and private property. Neither a revolutionary nor a power-hungry maniac, Bonaparte instead gave France a form of enlightened despotism masked by a façade of democratic ideals. Sovereign power resided only with the ruler, not with the people. Though some scholars describe him as a "child of the Revolution," it would be more appropriate to refer to him as a child of the Enlightenment. Bonaparte had little patience for the chaos, confusion, and radical socioeconomic changes that revolutions tend to produce; on several occasions he had openly expressed his disdain for the crowds that played a decisive role in shaping the course of the French Revolution. Instead, Bonaparte felt more comfortable within the traditions that emphasized rationalism and strong political authority as well as tolerance and equality before the law. True to the tenets of enlightened despotism, he strove to build a strong French state by giving the people what he believed they needed, yet never holding out the prospect of embracing republican democracy or surrendering sovereignty to the will of the people.

Bonaparte, who was proclaimed Emperor Napoleon of the French in 1804, is widely recognized as one of the greatest military commanders in history, but he made few original contributions to the theory of war. His genius lay in his ability to synthesize prior innovations and ideas and to implement them in an effective and consistent manner. Between 1805 and 1810, having crushed three European coalitions, Napoleonic France emerged as the dominant continental power, extending its imperium from the Atlantic coastline of Spain to the rolling plains of Poland. Along the way, the French armies prompted important changes in Europe. In this regard Napoleon might be perceived as "the revolution incarnate," as the Austrian statesman Klemens Wenzel von Metternich once described him, but the title must be viewed in practical rather than ideological terms. After coming to power, Napoleon lost the radical ideological zeal that had characterized his earlier years. But to defeat France, European monarchies were compelled to pursue the path of reforms and to incorporate select elements of France's revolutionary legacy, such as greater centralization of bureaucracy, military reforms, transformation of royal subjects into citizens, and arousing people's sense of rights while deflecting their patriotic energies and passions toward defeat of a foreign enemy. In short, they needed to employ French ideas against France.

The Napoleonic Wars should not be perceived merely as the continuation of the revolutionary struggles. It is more appropriate to view them within the context of the wars of the eighteenth century. Between 1803 and 1815 European powers repeatedly pursued traditional national objectives. There were two main constants. One was France's determination to create a new international order that would in turn produce hegemonic power. From this point of view, Napoleon's policies and Europe's response to them echo Louis XIV's reign and the efforts of the Grand Alliance to contain expansionist France and to preserve the fragile balance of power in Europe. The French Revolution added an important ideological element to the Napoleonic Wars but did not erase geopolitical issues that stemmed from earlier rivalries.

The other constant was the long-standing Franco-British rivalry, which exerted considerable influence on the course of events. France remained officially at war with Britain for twenty years (240 months, starting in 1793), far longer than the period France spent at war with Austria (108 months, starting in 1792), Prussia (58 months, also starting in 1792), or Russia (55 months, starting in 1798). Furthermore, between 1792 and 1814 Britain more than tripled its national debt and spent the staggering sum of £65 million on subsidizing wars against Napoleon. Indeed, one may argue that the Revolutionary and Napoleonic Wars constituted a new phase of what has been sometimes described as the Second Hundred Years' War, one that France and Britain waged between 1689, in the wake of the Glorious Revolution and France's support for the overthrown King James II, and 1815, when French imperial dreams ended at Waterloo. As in the earlier conflicts (in addition to the War of the Spanish Succession, there was the War of the Austrian Succession and the Seven Years' War), these two powers struggled for dominance not only in Europe but also in the Americas, Africa, the Ottoman Empire, Iran, India, Indonesia, the Philippines, the Mediterranean Sea, and the Indian Ocean.

Such was the determination (and capacity) of Britain that the British government continued its steadfast opposition to Napoleon even when it found itself acting alone for many of those years. More often than not, however, Britain was at the heart of a wide array of coalitions that sought to contain the French emperor's efforts to build a Europe-wide empire. As soon as one coalition collapsed, London made efforts to create another, financed from the profits of rapidly expanding trade networks and growing industrial development. The contest between Britain and France was, in effect, the struggle between two societies in the process of building empires. France threatened, cajoled, and browbeat its neighboring governments on the continent, but so did Britain, using its economic and naval might to build and protect a global commercial empire. As one senior British official opined in 1799, "It is laid down as an axiom applicable to the conduct of an extensive warfare by this country that our principal effort should be to deprive our Enemies of their Colonial possessions. By so doing we weaken their power while at the same time we augment those commercial resources which are the sole Bases of our maritime strength."[1]

The French Revolutionary and Napoleonic Wars have kept historians busy for the past two hundred years. Thousands of books have been written on Napoleon himself, and when related titles—on the Napoleonic campaigns, politics, and diplomacy, as well as his opponents and allies—are added to the pile, the total number of books would certainly be in the hundreds of thousands. The last decade in particular has seen the publication of a number of new titles, including more than a dozen biographies of Napoleon. The shelves of any decent library groan under the weight of works on the Napoleonic Wars.

Yet it is my firm belief that the story of the French Revolutionary and Napoleonic Wars is far more complex than has been dealt with by the traditional approach, which views the era either as a backdrop for Napoleon's life or as a means to study the intermittent coalition wars within Europe. There is, of course, a vast body of scholarship about Napoleonic-age militaries and diplomacy—Paul Schroeder's *The Transformation of European Politics* serves as one of the finest examples of this genre—but it remains restricted in coverage to Europe. The few studies that extend beyond European coverage tend to unfold entirely within the framework of Franco-British rivalry, with little consideration of events outside it. Most recently, for example, the British historian Charles Esdaile wrote the masterly *Napoleon's Wars: An International*

History, "a history of the Napoleonic Wars that reflects their pan-European dimension and is not just Franco-centric."[2] Again, though, his focus remains firmly on Europe,

My intention is to add to the history of these wars by showing that between 1792 and 1815 European affairs did not unfold in isolation from the rest of the globe. Indeed, the tremors that spread from France starting in 1789 tend to overshadow the fact that the Revolutionary and Napoleonic Wars had truly global repercussions. Austerlitz, Trafalgar, Leipzig, and Waterloo all hold prominent places in the standard histories of the Napoleonic Wars, but alongside them we must also discuss Buenos Aires, New Orleans, Queenston Heights, Ruse, Aslanduz, Assaye, Macao, Oravais, and Alexandria. We cannot fully understand the significance of this period without involving the British expeditions to Argentina and South Africa, the Franco-British diplomatic intrigues in Iran and the Indian Ocean, the Franco-Russian maneuvering in the Ottoman Empire, and the Russo-Swedish struggles for Finland. Rather than remaining at the periphery of the story, they go to the core of its significance.

Offering a global context to the Napoleonic Wars reveals that they had far greater long-term impact overseas than within the European continent itself. Napoleon was, after all, defeated and his empire erased from the map of Europe. Yet this same period saw the consolidation of British imperial power in India, a crucial development that allowed Britain to emerge as a global hegemon in the nineteenth century. This empire-building process required immense commitments in terms of men and resources. More Britons died during the years of sporadic campaigns in the West and East Indies than during the Peninsular War in Spain and Portugal.[3] And it was not merely Britain's expansion that gives global relevance to these years. The early nineteenth century witnessed Russia pursuing its colonial designs in Finland, Poland, and the Pacific Northwest while seeking to expand at the expense of the Ottoman Empire and Iran in the Balkan Peninsula and the Caucasus. In the Atlantic world alone, the Napoleonic Wars saw three established European empires and the young American republic actively competing, with each determined to preserve its territory and attempting to enlarge it at the expense of its competitors. The United States more than doubled in extent after the purchase from the French of the Louisiana Territory and challenged Britain during the War of 1812. In the Caribbean, the French Revolution produced the Haitian rebellion, the most consequential of all slave revolts on the Atlantic rim. In Latin America, Napoleon's occupation of Spain in 1808 spurred independence movements that ended the Spanish colonial empire and created a new political reality in the region. Momentous changes were also unfolding in the Islamic world, where the political, economic, and social upheavals in the Ottoman Empire and Iran laid the foundation for the "Eastern Question" dilemma. In Egypt, the French and British invasions of 1798–1807 led to the rise of Mehmet Ali and the eventual emergence of a powerful Egyptian state that would shape Middle Eastern affairs for the rest of the century. Nor did South Africa, Japan, China, and Indonesia escape the effects of the European power struggles.

On a more personal level, having studied and taught Napoleonic history for well over two decades, I believe that there is a pressing need for an international perspective. History teaches the inexorable truth that actions have consequences that reverberate long after the events themselves end, a fact clearly illustrated in the period in question. The Napoleonic Wars set many parts of the world on a separate course of development, and without them, the Revolution itself might have remained largely a European affair and with limited influence on the outside world. But France's ambitions and European efforts to thwart them meant that the war spread to far-flung corners of the world. As one American historian observed, "In part deliberately, in part despite himself, Napoleon made the Revolution a crucial event in European and world history."[4]

What follows is divided into three parts. The first provides an overview of the revolutionary period from the start of the French Revolution in 1789 to General Napoleon Bonaparte's ascent to power in 1799. It contains contextual background to the subsequent events, for it would be impossible to understand the Napoleonic Wars without looking at the decade that preceded them. The second part is organized both chronologically and geographically, making allowance for the fact that events were unfolding simultaneously worldwide. It starts with Europe at peace in 1801–1802 and explores Napoleon's efforts to consolidate French gains in the aftermath of the French Revolutionary Wars and Europe's response to them. Chapters 8 and 9 concentrate on the Franco-British tensions that ultimately erupted into a conflict that went on to consume the rest of the continent. In the subsequent chapters, the narrative moves away from the traditional focus on western and central Europe to consider other areas of conflict, such as Scandinavia, the Balkan Peninsula, Egypt, Iran, China, Japan, and the Americas, demonstrating how far the Napoleonic Wars reached. The third and final part of the book traces the fall of the Napoleonic Empire. By this point the Napoleonic Wars had been all but resolved in Asia, so the narrative shifts to Europe and North America and culminates in the defeat of Napoleon and the convocation of the Congress of Vienna. The concluding chapter casts a broad look at the world in the aftermath of the war.

In undertaking this task, I have inevitably had to be highly selective and there is much that was not included or discussed at length in this work. I hope nonetheless that my choices will not detract from the book's message and will still reveal how and why the Napoleonic Wars, and those who fought them, influenced the course of events across the globe.

ACKNOWLEDGMENTS

LIKE MOST PEOPLE, I learned about Napoleon in early childhood. This initial interest turned into a genuine passion when during a regular visit to a bookstore in my hometown of Tbilisi, Georgia, I discovered a dusty volume of the French emperor's biography written by the great Soviet historian Albert Manfred. I was so mesmerized by Napoleon's exploits that I searched high and low for more books, not an easy task amid the political and economic turmoil that followed the collapse of the Soviet Union. Since then I have devoted more than two decades to studying Napoleon, and it has become one of the defining experiences of my life. It is because of this fascination with the emperor that I was able to leave my war-ravaged homeland to pursue a new academic career, traveled widely around the world, met my wife, and pursued an "American dream." In so many ways, Napoleon changed my life.

Over the years, my views of Napoleon have evolved from the unbridled admiration of my youth to a much more circumspect appreciation of the man and his talents. His personality is crucial to understanding the turbulent years that shaped Europe at the start of the nineteenth century. Napoleon was a consummate reader whose prodigious memory, analytical mind, and ability to select relevant details made him a highly effective administrator. One of the greatest military minds, he was a stirring visionary, and the scale of his ambitions continues to capture people's imagination. But his other traits are distinctly unpleasant to contemplate. He was a climber and double-dealer who exploited others for his own gain. He was egotistical and prone to nepotism, richly rewarding his relatives even when confronted with their continued incompetence; his demands for efficiency often blurred lines between lawfulness and criminality; and he cynically exploited human weaknesses whenever the occasion arose. He was not the "Corsican Ogre" that he is often made out to be, but neither was he the romantic figure of the Napoleonic legend.

He was a man whose many talents are incontestable but whose role and place in history require a more nuanced evaluation; within his unquestionable genius lurk many flaws. But whatever view one takes of him, whatever aspect of his accomplishment is discussed, whether one admires him as a superb military leader or condemns him as the precursor of latter-day dictators, one cannot deny that he was a self-made man who dominated his age like no other individual, a fact that his die-hard enemies grudgingly admitted as well.

This book is the product of years of research and contemplation. Throughout this time, I have received support, guidance, and encouragement from numerous friends, colleagues, and family members. I would like to thank all of them, especially those who were there when I first embarked on this project a decade ago and who continued to encourage me when common sense might have inclined them to impatience. My family has lived with Napoleon for a very long time; in the case of my children, for the whole of their young lives. My sons, Luka and Sergi, have become *les marie-louises,* frequently playing underneath the office desk waiting for their father to finish writing yet another page; they merrily ask me to convey their regards to "Uncle Napo" every time I travel to France. I am grateful to my family—Levan, Marina, Levan Jr., and Aleko Mikaberidze, and Tsiuri, Jemal and Koka Kankia —for tolerating my Napoleonic passion as well as heaps of Napoleonic books and documents scattered around the house for so many few years. This book would not have been possible without their love, patience, and support.

I first came up with the idea of producing an international history of the Napoleonic Wars while still in graduate school at the Institute on Napoleon and the French Revolution at Florida State University. I was very fortunate to work under the guidance of Professor Donald D. Horward, an eminent Napoleonic scholar who directed more than one hundred graduate students and turned FSU into one of the most prolific centers for the study of the revolutionary era. His decision to respond to a simple inquiry from an aspiring student from a war-torn country had profound ramifications for my life. Whatever accomplishments I have as a scholar are entirely due to his unwearied mentorship and guidance. Equally important to me is the support of J. David Markham, without whom I probably would not have embarked on a career of the Napoleonic historian.

Michael V. Leggiere and Frederick Schneid have taught me much through their friendship and scholarship. Michael's meticulous studies on the collapse of the French Empire in 1813–1814 have shaped my own understanding of this momentous event. Rick continues to amaze me with the breadth of his knowledge and his willingness to share and assist. Despite being deeply involved in their own research, Michael and Rick have been generous with their time, read many parts of this manuscript and shared their criticisms, corrections, and suggestions.

My editor at Oxford University Press, Timothy Bent, has been both extremely patient and kind in working with me, putting up with numerous delays and accepting a manuscript that was far larger than the one he had commissioned. With his warm sense of humor, he gently guided me through the editing and helped me refine the book, for which I will be eternally thankful. I am much indebted to the guidance and dedication of my agent, Dan Green. It has been a genuine pleasure to work with the remarkable staff at Oxford University Press: Mariah White, Joellyn Ausanka, and especially my copyeditor, Sue Warga, for her meticulous scrutiny of the text. George Chakvetadze did a splendid job designing maps for this book. I would also like to thank anonymous readers who provided valuable criticism that made the book much stronger.

Over the years I have been privileged to get to know and work with a remarkable group of scholars: Katherine Aaslestad, Frederick Black, Jeremy Black, Rafe Blaufarb, Michael Bonura, Alexander Burns, Sam Cavell, Philip Cuccia, Brian DeToy, Charles Esdaile, Karen Greene (Reid), Wolf Gruner, Wayne Hanley, Doina Harsanyi, Christine Haynes, Jordan Hayworth, Marc H. Lerner, Dominic Lieven, Darrin McMahon, Kevin D. McCranie, Rory Muir, Jason Musteen, Erwin Muilwijk, Ciro Paoletti, Christy Pichichero, Andrew Roberts, John Severn, Geoffrey Wawro, and Martijn Wink. I have learned much from them and am grateful to each of them for their continued support and encouragement. I have benefited immensely from the expertise and astute judgment of Alexander Grab, Sam Mustafa, Bruno Colson, Marco Cabrera Geserick, Michael Neiberg, Virginia H. Aksan, Jonathan Abel, Mark Gerges, John H. Gill, and Morten Nordhagen Ottosen, who have taken time from their busy schedules to read parts of this manuscript and provide invaluable feedback. Nathaniel Jarrett generously shared a treasure trove of documents that he has mined in the British archives; Heidrun Riedl helped me research Austrian war efforts at the Kriegsarchiv in Vienna. I will miss wonderful discussions about the impact of the Napoleonic Wars on the Middle East with the late Jack Sigler, a Foreign Service officer who had spent decades serving in the region and generously shared his knowledge and experience with me. Much of what I know about French naval history is the result of my close friendship with Kenneth Johnson, which started back in graduate school when we were still dreamers riding around in a 1976 Buick LeSabre, a genuine warship on wheels.

Away from the United States, I am thankful to Huw Davies for an opportunity to discuss this project at the international conference "Waterloo: The Battle That Forged a Century" at King's College London in 2013. Two years later Peter Hicks extended a similar invitation to a symposium at the Fondation Napoléon in Paris. Through the years Thierry Lentz, François Houdecek and Pierre Branda, of the Fondation Napoléon, have generously shared their time to discuss with me aspects of the Napoleonic history; I still hope to see an English-language history of the Napoleonic Empire that can match Lentz's superb multivolume *Nouvelle histoire du Premier Empire*. I have benefited from the help and counsel of many individuals from across Europe, among them Yves Martin, Dimitri Khocholava, and Jovita Suslonova in France; Nika Khoperia, Beka Kobakhidze, Shalva Lazariashvili, Paata Buchukuri, and George Zabakhidze in Georgia; Ciro Paoletti in Italy; Alexander Tchudinov, Dimitri Gorchkoff, and Vladimir Zemtsov in Russia; Michael Bregnsbo in Denmark; and Alan Forest and Jonathan North in Great Britain. The Napoleon Series project, where I have been involved for many years, remains an immensely useful place for discussion and exchange of ideas. I owe a great debt to many its members but especially to Robert Burnham, Tom Holmberg, and Steven Smith.

I have benefited in too many ways to mention from the wonderful atmosphere provided at Louisiana State University–Shreveport by my colleagues, especially Gary J. Joiner, Cheryl White, Helen Wise, Helen Taylor, John Vassar, Blake Dunnavent, and the late Bernadette Palombo. My sincerest thanks go to Larry Clark, Chancellor of LSUS, and Laura Perdue, Executive Director of LSUS Foundation, for their continued support and encouragement. This book has improved greatly from the discussions I have had with students in my French Revolution and the Age of Napoleon courses, especially Ben Haines, Autumn Cuddy, Ethan Puckett, Art Edwards, Zachary Favrot, Mitchell Williams, Douglas Smith, and Aaron Kadkhodai.

At the Noel Foundation, I am indebted to Robert Leitz, Shelby Smith, Delton Smith, Gilbert Shanley, Merritt B. Chastain Jr., Steven Walker, Laura McLemore, Stacy Williams, Dick Bremer and Richard Lamb for their bighearted support, which allowed me to undertake research trips to European archives and to acquire many titles for the growing Napoleonic collection at the James Smith Noel Collection. Similarly, I am appreciative of the Patten family, whose endowment of the Sybil T. and J. Frederick Patten Professorship helped me conduct research in the French diplomatic archives. Beyond the confines of academia, I have discussed the Napoleonic Wars with more people than I can remember but I owe a particular debt for the advice and encouragement to Martha Lawler, Janie Richardson, Jerard R. Martin, Sara Herrington, Ernest Blakeney, Ray Branton, Dmitry and Svitlana Ostanin, and Mikhail and Nataly Khoretonenko. Needless to say, despite all this support, I alone bear the responsibility for any mistakes that remain in this book.

The book would not have been done were it not for the loving support and care of my wife, Anna Kankia, who has stoically endured all my absences, travels and obsessions. I dedicate this work to her with these words from Catullus 51: *Nam simul te aspexi, nihil est super mi*. These words are as true today as they were twenty years ago when we first met.

Alexander Mikaberidze

Shreveport, Louisiana

August 15, 2019 (Napoleon's 250th birthday)

The Napoleonic Wars

Map 1: Europe in 1789

CHAPTER I | The Revolutionary Prelude

ON FEBRUARY 17, 1792, British prime minister William Pitt (the Younger) delivered his regular budget speech in the House of Commons. Discussing Britain's circumstances, Pitt uttered the famous prophecy that while the country's prosperity was not ensured, "there never was a time in the history of this country, when, from the situation of Europe, we might more reasonably expect fifteen years of peace than we may at the present moment."[1] Two months later began a war that dragged Britain into a two-decade-long quagmire.

Reading Pitt's speech, one cannot but wonder how the prime minister could have been so wrong and why, instead of fifteen years of peace, Britain experienced twenty-three years of war. The role of the French Revolution can hardly be overestimated. The revolutionary decade ushered in by the events of 1789 brought institutional, social, economic, cultural, and political transformation to France and served equally as a source of inspiration and as a source of abhorrence across Europe and beyond. The wars it inspired, which are generally seen as lasting from 1792 to 1802, were the first general European war since the Seven Years' War a half century earlier. Revolutionary ideals and institutions were spread by force and by emulation, and the language and practices to which they gave rise have helped to forge modern political culture.

———◦◦◦❧◦◦◦———

Discussion of the origins of the French Revolution involves a paradox. Both participants and later commentators recognized it as a global event, yet almost none of them sought global causes for it. Indeed, much of the existing scholarship on it falls into the category of "internalism," which operates on the premise that France's domestic circumstances provide the only relevant frame of reference for the revolutionary events. The traditional narrative of the Revolutionary Wars follow a specific pattern: it starts around 1792 and focuses on events in western Europe, including France's efforts to safeguard its revolution from neighboring monarchies, which, one by one, were eventually forced to accept peace with the French. But such an approach offers too narrow a perspective and ignores a number of important developments in other parts of the world, developments that were made possible by France's political and military vulnerability. The Revolution and the Revolutionary Wars took place amid existing political tensions that exposed the weakness of French power and in turn encouraged the imperial ambitions of European powers elsewhere in the world. Indeed, events in eastern and southeastern Europe, the Pacific Northeast, and the Caribbean had important consequences for international politics and the situation back in Europe on the eve of the Revolution.

In the last few decades two different approaches have emerged in considering the French Revolution in a broader context. Following the paths of Robert R. Palmer and Jacques Godechot, historians began to focus on the shared experiences and connections within the Atlantic world, exploring the circulation of ideas, people, and goods around the Atlantic Ocean.[2] More recently this "Atlantic model" underwent a significant transformation to account for the global nature of eighteenth-century commerce, finance, and colonization. This new model operates within a far wider geographic frame and describes the period between 1770 and 1830 as an era of "Imperial Revolutions"—rather than the "Age of Democratic Revolution," as Palmer famously put it—that were precipitated by colonial competition and warfare waged by the colonizing European nations.[3]

Irrespective of which model one chooses, one thing remains clear: the Revolution was precipitated by a host of complex political, financial, intellectual, and social problems, many of them with origins outside France itself. Among the most crucial developments were the establishment of ocean trade linkages between Asia, Africa, Europe, and the Americas in the sixteenth century and the emergence of worldwide commercial circuits in the seventeenth. Both occurred within the context of fierce European competition for diplomatic, military, and economic hegemony. By the mid-eighteenth century, participation in the fast-developing global economy was of paramount importance to rival European powers, which sought access to and control over transcontinental commerce by building formidable fleets, chartering trading companies, fostering colonial expansion overseas, and engaging in the transatlantic slave trade.[4] Despite political and military setbacks suffered during the Seven Years' War (1756–1763), France not only retained its share in the Atlantic slave trade and Indian Ocean commerce during the 1760s and 1770s but considerably increased it. The French slave trade reached its height on the eve of the Revolution, with the French transporting more than 283,897 slaves between 1781 and 1790, compared to 277,276 slaves for the British and 254,899 for the Portuguese.[5] Between 1787 and 1792 the largest share of vessels sailing around the Cape of Good Hope to India belonged not to Britain but to France.[6] Despite the setback of the Seven Years' War, the French continued to possess a veritable commercial empire, one that resided on the American, Indian Ocean, and African networks and was sustained by a banking system that rapidly assumed global dimensions to accommodate the rising volume of international trade.[7]

This proved to be a double-edged sword. France depended on Spanish silver, which was imported in large quantities to satisfy the demands of the French mints and, in turn, to sustain the entire fiscal-political system in place at the time.[8] But developments threatened its continuing access to this bullion. In the 1780s the newly established Spanish Banco Nacional put in place tighter controls over currency exports in order to maintain Spain's position in international markets, and the Spanish government began to reconsider France's long-standing most-favored-nation trade status. This in turn affected French manufacturing, which faced higher import duties and stiffer competition from European rivals.[9] The signing of the Anglo-French commercial treaty of 1786, which called for a mutual lowering of import duties, also proved damaging to the French economy, as it allowed British textiles and industrial goods to enter the French market, causing considerable damage to the country's manufacturing.[10]

The French trade in India left much to be desired. The vessels sailing to India were, on average, smaller than those of their competitors. Unlike the British East India Company, which brought home goods with a value of at least three times the amount of specie shipped to India, the French balance of trade barely broke even. More broadly, between 1785 and 1789 the French East India Company exported some 58 million livres' worth of goods and specie and imported only 50 million livres' worth.[11] Imported goods posed additional challenges, and the French monarchy's efforts to establish a tobacco monopoly and to protect its textile industry from Asian cloth imports actually contributed to the growth of an underground economy that soon assumed vast dimensions and had important political implications.[12] To suppress this parallel shadow economy, the French had to introduce institutional changes, including expanding the General Farm, a private financial company that, beginning in 1726, leased the right to collect indirect taxes (on tobacco, salt, beer, wine, and a variety of other goods) in exchange for advancing enormous loans to the French crown.[13] By the late eighteenth century, the General Farm maintained a veritable army of some twenty thousand agents, assisted by a reorganized criminal justice commission (funded by the Farm) that dealt harshly with contraband cases, especially those involving salt and tobacco. Efforts to suppress this parallel economy resulted in the prosecution of tens of thousands of people and the expansion of the French penitentiary system.[14] Recent scholarship demonstrates that the vast majority (some 65 percent) of tax rebellions, the most common form of French protest in the eighteenth century, were caused by the government's efforts to suppress contraband.[15]

The ongoing contraband rebellion exerted considerable pressure on a state already troubled by its inability to balance income and expenses. French monarchs presided over an elaborate welfare system that maintained roads, undertook public works, and provided justice, education, and medical services, all of which required substantial expenditures. The royal court further drained considerable sums as the king underwrote the expenses of courtiers and granted lavish awards and pensions. To make up for its inadequate sources of revenue, the king sold government posts, which reduced their efficiency and created independent (and usually venal) officeholders who could not be easily removed.[16]

Furthermore, to maintain their position relative to other states, especially during the long rivalry with Britain, the Bourbons incurred increasingly high expenses that lay a heavy burden on the economy. France remained on a permanent war footing for much of the eighteenth century. This dramatically increased military expenditures whether the country was at peace or war. In 1694 (a year of war), they amounted to some 125 million livres. In 1788 (a year of peace), they were 145 million livres. On the eve of the Revolution, more than half of the French budget, some 310 million livres, went to cover interest on the money borrowed during the previous century of wars. Between 1665 and 1789, France was at war for fifty-four years, or almost one year out of every two. The wars of King Louis XIV (r. 1643–1715), especially the War of the Spanish Succession (1701–1714), which produced no tangible gains, significantly weakened the French economy, leaving the state with debts estimated at 2 billion livres.[17] These economic problems were exacerbated by a series of costly wars waged after 1733. The defeat in the Seven Years' War (1756–1763), which cost a total of 1.2 billion livres and saw France lose many of its colonial possessions in Canada, India, and the Caribbean to the British, had a profound economic impact on the kingdom and helped set in motion events that ultimately led to the revolutions on both sides of the Atlantic.[18] Though inheriting a financially and militarily weakened realm,

King Louis XVI (r. 1774–1792) went on to intervene in North America, where French expeditionary forces played an important role in helping the American colonies secure independence from Britain in 1783. However, this success required a great deal of investment and delivered no tangible rewards that could have rectified France's dire financial condition.[19] To the contrary, participation in the American Revolution resulted in France borrowing more than 1 billion livres, which drove the government to the brink of bankruptcy.[20]

France's wars were only partly financed by taxes due to inherent problems with tax collection (a rather slow and tangled process) and a system of privileges that saw the wealthiest groups largely exempt from paying them. In fact, the money sustaining French colonial ambitions had its origins in global finance. Throughout the eighteenth century France found itself increasingly dependent on an international capital market on which it could borrow vast sums from foreign creditors. Yet unlike Britain and the Dutch Republic, which had more transparent management of public debt, France's byzantine financial accounting meant that it was forced to borrow at an interest rate of 4.8 to 6.5 percent, compared to just 2.5 percent for the Dutch or 3.0 to 3.5 percent for the British.[21] Furthermore, starting in 1694, the British managed their debt through the Bank of England—investors bought stock in the bank, which in turn provided loans to the government. France had a publicly funded debt too, but it was not managed or guaranteed by a national bank (which was only established in 1804), and the French monarchy's long history of financial difficulties and partial defaults was one reason interest rates on its loans were higher than the market rate.[22] The growth in international trade and capital markets proved too great a temptation for the French monarchy, which in the late 1780s encouraged speculative investment in its credit instruments, including the disastrous speculation on the value of the newly reestablished French East India Company, which ended up costing the government more than 20 million livres.[23]

France might have managed these financial strains if not for the government's inability to implement much-needed reforms. Any change to the status quo implied an attack on those with tax exemptions, particularly the clergy and nobility, and on trade guilds, municipal corporations, and provincial estates, which had some role in allocating the tax burden in the lands under their authority. Furthermore, the French kings, although popularly envisioned as absolutist monarchs, were in reality far from exercising unlimited authority and were obliged to rule according to laws and customs developed over the ages. In this respect, the provincial Estates General and royal courts of appeal—the thirteen *parlements*—represented an important check on royal authority.[24] Although nominally royal courts, the *parlements* were, in essence, independent bodies, given that their members purchased their seats from the monarchy. The *parlements*, especially the powerful Parlement of Paris, emerged as a potent check to the crown, claiming the right to review and approve all royal laws to ensure that they conformed to the traditional laws of the kingdom. In the absence of representative institutions, the *parlements* (though representing the nobility and protecting its interests) claimed to defend the interests of the entire nation against arbitrary royal authority, and to the public they represented the last barrier against the "despotic" tendencies of the monarchy.[25] Thus, in the final decades of the Old Regime, the French state had to contend with two kinds of "pre-revolutions": a plebeian one involving pervasive and intractable contraband rebellion, and its elite counterpart, which sought to limit royal authority.

The prevalent social organization in most European countries was one of orders that were arranged in a religiously sanctioned and legally determined hierarchy. The groups, and the individuals who belonged to them, were explicitly unequal in their status, rights, and obligations. France represented a classical form of this hierarchy, in which one's function defined one's place. At its simplest, this corporate society consisted of three orders, or estates, that corresponded to the medieval notion that some prayed, some fought, and the rest farmed or worked in some other capacity. The First Estate consisted of the clergy, who were subject to their own church court system and were entitled to collect tithes. Over the course of hundreds of years, the Catholic church had become a wealthy institution, owning large tracts of land and real estate; in some cases, such as the Electorate of Bavaria (in southeastern Germany), the church was the largest landlord. In parts of central Europe, bishops and abbots were simultaneously secular princes, presiding over both a diocese and secular government. While bishops and abbots enjoyed a relatively lavish lifestyle, the parish clergy lived much more modestly, often in poverty.

The Second Estate consisted of the nobility, whose status granted it the right to collect taxes from the peasantry and to enjoy many privileges, including exemptions from most if not all forms of direct taxation. Furthermore, top positions in the church, army, and royal administration were traditionally limited to nobles. They were the largest landowners in most European countries, and in parts of eastern Europe they generally possessed people (serfs) as well as land. The nobility was not a monolithic bloc, however, and most nobles in the ancien régime would have struggled to demonstrate the antiquity of their titles. Indeed, few families could trace them through multiple generations. Alongside the grand nobles who monopolized court positions and enjoyed enormous wealth, there was the vast multitude of the lesser nobility, such as the *noblesse de robe* and the *noblesse de cloche*, which had titles by virtue of holding certain government or municipal positions, and the *noblesse militaire*, which earned its titles through military service. In France, there was considerable flexibility in entering the ranks of the nobility since the government sold certain government offices that conferred titles.

The top two estates thus enjoyed most of the privileges, and they perceived government reforms as a threat to their respective positions. In France, among the sharpest opponents of reform were many members of the traditional nobility who had fallen on hard times and clung anxiously to any and all privileges as a way of maintaining their status.[26]

The Third Estate consisted of unprivileged commoners, which represented the vast majority of the population. It was a loose group, lacking common interests, since it included the wealthiest bourgeoisie, who mixed easily with the nobility, as well as the poorest peasants. In France, the number of wealthy commoners (merchants, manufacturers, and professionals), often called the "bourgeoisie," grew significantly in the eighteenth century, and merchants in Bordeaux, Marseille, and Nantes exploited overseas trade with colonies in the Caribbean and the Indian Ocean to reap sometimes tremendous profits. These wealthy commoners were, naturally, dissatisfied with the social and political system in France, which placed a heavy tax burden on their shoulders yet failed to provide them with proper representation in government.

The role of the bourgeoisie at the start of the French Revolution has been hotly debated through the years and provides the basis for the so-called bourgeois revolution thesis, which views revolutionary upheaval as the inevitable result of the commoners' struggle for class equality. Recent historical research has downplayed such an explanation, since the boundary between the nobility and the wealthy bourgeoisie was fluid and the classes had common interests. As has been mentioned, the French nobility was not a closed caste and was constantly renewed with the infusion of "new blood" from below. As the British historian William Doyle points out, the nobility was "an open elite," and remained so throughout the eighteenth century.[27] Similarly, some argue that the bourgeoisie aspired to noble status, and many nobles were involved in business enterprises (mining, textiles, overseas trading, etc.) that traditionally have been considered the province of the bourgeoisie. These nobles abandoned traditional aristocratic disdain for commerce and business and gradually acquired the capitalist mentality associated with the middle class. In fact, by 1789, this line of thought runs, the line between aristocracy and prosperous bourgeoisie was no longer clearly marked, and the destruction of the aristocracy and its privileges, which was accomplished in the opening stage of the Revolution, was not part of a preconceived bourgeois program. Instead, it was an improvised response to the violent turmoil (known as the Great Fear) that spread throughout the countryside in July and August 1789.

Of the groups constituting the Third Estate, the peasantry was the largest and yet the least empowered. Unlike their brethren in eastern or central Europe, the majority of French peasants enjoyed legal freedoms, and some even owned land, but most rented land from local seigneurs or bourgeois landowners. Rural conditions differed depending on the region, and such differences later influenced peasants' reactions to revolutionary events. In general, the peasantry had to perform the corvée (labor service), tithe, pay royal taxes, and bear the numerous seigneurial rights and dues owed to their landlords, who included both nobles and wealthy non-nobles. By the late eighteenth century, the heavily taxed peasants were acutely aware of their situation and less willing to support the antiquated and inefficient feudal system, even as landlords sought to revive old rights that had fallen into disuse, seeking to squeeze as much profit out of their estates as possible to redress the rising cost of living. Such practices, however, stoked tensions in the French countryside, which was a much more populous place than just a century earlier. The population of France grew rapidly, from around 20 million in 1715 to 28 million in 1789. For many, such an increase brought with it greater misery and hardship, particularly during the bad harvests of the 1780s, brought about by changing climatic conditions during the 1770s. Food production could not keep pace with population growth, contributing to rapid inflation as prices outstripped wages. Secular attitudes become prominent in the countryside, and tolerance for the existing social order began to wear thin.

Revolutionary movements, one prominent French historian has observed, require "some unifying body of ideas, a common vocabulary of hope and protest, something, in short, like a common 'revolutionary psychology.'"[28] The Enlightenment movement provided such a "unifying body of ideas," and the ideological origins of the French Revolution can be directly linked to the activities of the Enlightenment philosophes, who championed radical ideas and called for social and political reform. The intellectual arguments of the Enlightenment had been read and discussed more widely in the educated circles in France than anywhere else. Applying a rational approach, the philosophes criticized the existing political and social system. In his *Spirit of the Laws* (1748), Charles-Louis de Secondat, baron de La Brède et de Montesquieu, provided a fresh study of politics and called for a constitutional monarchy that would operate with a system of checks and balances between its branches. Many philosophes participated in a monumental undertaking to produce the

Encyclopédie, edited by Jean d'Alembert and Denis Diderot, which applied a rational and critical approach to a wide range of subjects and became a best-seller that, in part, shaped the newly emerging public opinion.

The works of Jean-Jacques Rousseau proved to be especially influential. In *The Social Contract* (1762), Rousseau explained the rise of modern societies as a result of complex social contracts between individuals, who were equal and possessed a common interest—what he called "the general will." If the government failed to live up to its "contractual" obligations, Rousseau maintained, citizens had the right to rebel and replace it. His ideas would eventually nourish the radical democratic section of the revolutionary movement. But Rousseau also believed that though each citizen had an equal stake in the body politic, he who broke the laws agreed upon by the general will was no longer a member of the state and could be treated "less as a citizen than as an enemy"—a rather ominous idea in light of the Terror and later totalitarian regimes.[29]

One of the major outcomes of the Enlightenment was the growth of public opinion, which was formulated in an informal network of groups. In 1715 the average literacy rate in France stood at 29 percent for men and at 14 percent for women. By 1789 it was 47 percent for men and 27 percent for women, and in Paris it may have been as high as 90 and 80 percent, respectively. This expansion in literacy presented writers and publicists with the opportunity to spread political, religious, and social concepts among a wider audience than ever before. Above all, the very notion of a "public opinion," independent of church and state, to which one could appeal for legitimacy evolved in the eighteenth century. In Paris, this public opinion manifested itself in salons, informal regular meetings of artists, writers, nobles, and other members of the cultural elite that became forums for discussion of a variety of ideas. Essays and various literary works presented in these salons eventually appeared in the growing number of newspapers and journals that further disseminated information.[30]

The spread of the Masonic movement, which was introduced from Britain in the early eighteenth century, stimulated discussion as well, since it advocated an ideology of equality and moral improvement, irrespective of social rank. The spread of freethinking accelerated after 1750 and affected people from various social groups. Cafés in Paris and other cities established reading rooms where patrons could peruse and discuss a wide range of literature, notably the works of the philosophes. The late eighteenth century also saw the rapid growth of pamphleteering, which was largely directed against the government and provided ample criticism of the royal family, particularly the widely unpopular queen, Marie Antoinette. Some pamphleteers eventually emerged as leading revolutionary orators and journalists.

The ideas that the European philosophes espoused were not limited to the intellectual sphere. The start of the American Revolutionary War in the 1770s, with the subsequent Declaration of Independence and the US Constitution, strongly influenced European opinion, demonstrating that it was possible to create a system of self-government with elected representatives and without a monarch. France was particularly exposed to these ideas since the French government actively supported the American colonies (after 1778) and contributed substantially to their ultimate victory. Parisian salons and drawing rooms were animated by talk about North America. A number of French officers had served there, and upon returning home they served as an effective propaganda apparatus (together with the Americans in Paris, such as Benjamin Franklin and Thomas Jefferson) to spread the word about American experiences.[31] Jefferson's draft of the Declaration of Independence was deeply rooted in Enlightenment thought and reflected a belief in the universality of natural rights. This represented a break with the existing practice of legitimizing politics by relying on divine power or on "ancient rights and liberties," as was the case with the English Bill of Rights in 1689.[32] This universalist attitude was prevalent among French revolutionaries, whether in 1789 or in 1793 during the Terror, who repeatedly expressed their conviction that they were acting on a stage that transcended the boundaries of France and dealt with the future of mankind as a whole.

The mid-1780s witnessed the development of the French monarchy's fiscal crisis.[33] As the ancien régime confronted its shortage of funds, it was naturally compelled to consider the ways governments normally raised money: conquests, loans, and taxes. France was in no position to embark on a war of conquest, which required funding to mobilize and field forces, and would have been prohibitively expensive to wage. In fact, France was struggling to protect its interest in neighboring territories, as the Prussian intervention in the Netherlands in 1787 revealed. Neither could France obtain any additional loans, since foreign banks were increasingly reluctant to take on the risk. The last option—raising taxes—thus seemed a practical choice, but the Bourbon monarchy's attempt to do just that met with resistance from the *parlements*, which hoped to use the country's financial predicament to restore some of the nobility's influence. In 1787, King Louis XVI was compelled to call the Assembly of Notables, consisting of high-ranking nobles as well as senior members of the royal bureaucracy and of the Provincial Estates, to support him in facing down the *parlements* and proceeding with some changes. But he found little support, since even those sympathetic to reform were reluctant to allow the monarchy free rein. Instead they called for the convocation of the Estates General, a general assembly representing French estates of the realm, which had not been called since 1614, to address the state's financial predicament. In 1788, bowing to mounting pressure, the king summoned the Estates General. Louis's decision unleashed a vociferous political debate in France, one that eventually contributed to the outbreak of revolution.

After the Estates General convened on May 5, 1789, it became deadlocked over the question of procedure. The first two estates, seeking to control the assembly, insisted that traditional practice stipulated that each estate meet separately and vote as a corporate body. Such an arrangement naturally offered great advantages to the two privileged orders (clergy and nobility), since the Third Estate, small farmers and commoners, would always be outvoted. The representatives of the Third Estate refused to accept such an arrangement and instead called for a change of procedure that would have given it greater influence. On June 17, after weeks of futile attempts to have all three estates sit in a common assembly, the Third Estate made a revolutionary move, declaring itself the National Assembly.

The persistence of the Third Estate delegates and the growing unrest in Paris, where residents supported the National Assembly, forced the French monarchy to yield and order the other two orders to join with the Third Estate in the National Assembly. This was a momentous decision, one that marked a successful challenge to the traditional political order and provided an opening for subsequent reforms, including the drawing up of a constitution that limited the king's power. The court's later attempt to use army to put down the National Assembly led to the famous storming of the Bastille fortress in Paris on July 14, 1789, an event that had far-reaching consequences since it frightened the court into withdrawing the troops. The fall of the Bastille, a symbol of the ancien régime's despotism, served as a powerful inspiration for the supporters of reforms.

The reform cause was further strengthened by the peasant upheavals (the so-called Great Fear) in late July and early August, which provided the National Assembly with an opportunity to start the transformation process. In August 1789 it abolished the special privileges of the nobility and the clergy, effectively undermining the entire aristocratic structure. The Declaration of the Rights of Man and of the Citizen embraced the universal ideals of the Enlightenment and proclaimed inalienable rights and freedoms, including popular sovereignty and equal treatment under the law. The Great Fear and the effective abolition of feudalism induced sporadic emigration, particularly among nobles, to neighboring German and Italian cities.[34]

The fall of 1789 witnessed the National Assembly's assault on the First Estate and the privileges of the Roman Catholic church, whose lands were confiscated and put up for sale. In 1790, the Civil Constitution of the Clergy sought to reorganize the church and transform the clergy into government officials, who were required to take an oath to uphold the Civil Constitution. Such treatment quickly alienated the church and devout Catholics, divided French society, and gave opponents of the Revolution a powerful issue to rally around. The assembly also launched far-reaching administrative and judicial reforms that swept aside the traditional institutions of the ancien régime. The process of transformation reached its primary goal in September 1791, when the National Assembly adopted the first written constitution. This document turned France into a constitutional monarchy, guaranteeing parliamentary government, equal treatment under the law, and careers open to talent, while limiting suffrage on the part of propertied groups. Such changes consolidated the rule of the bourgeoisie, which broke the power of the aristocracy yet kept the common masses from asserting power.

The bourgeoisie's desire to go no further, however, was rendered moot by two divergent forces. On one side, a counterrevolutionary movement driven by nobility, churchmen, and large segments of the peasantry sought to reverse revolutionary changes. On the opposite side, a large part of the urban population—small shopkeepers, artisans, and wage earners—was dissatisfied with the limited nature of reforms introduced by the National Assembly. Exasperated by economic and social hardships, they perceived the bourgeoisie as the successor to the aristocracy as the ruling class. Whereas the bourgeoisie sought equality of rights, basic liberties, and opportunities, the "sans-culottes," as the urban masses became known, called for social equality and more far-reaching political reforms that would give the common man a voice in the government. King Louis's attempt to flee France (the so-called Flight to Varennes in June 1791) to solicit foreign support against the Revolution proved to be a major political blunder, one that turned many against the monarchy and strengthened the position of those who favored a democratic republic.[35]

Despite its tensions, the international situation in 1789–1790 did not make an outbreak of war inevitable. While relations between European powers were marked by various degree of rivalry—as was the case in Holland, for example—these powers were also preoccupied with internal affairs and more pressing questions of their foreign policy. Thus, Austria was more worried about the Prussian threat, unrest in Belgium, and the ongoing war against the Turks, which brought about the near collapse of the Austrian state's finances. For many European leaders, the French Revolution represented an opportunity, not a threat. It meant that—for a while, at least—France could be counted out of the grand game of European politics, given that its internal difficulties would incapacitate its foreign endeavors. Indeed, some European statesmen simply did not see the revolutionary contagion to be a danger. In November 1791 Wenzel Anton, prince of Kaunitz-Rietberg, Austria's minister of foreign affairs, submitted an official memorandum on "the pretended dangers of contagion" of the French Revolution, while Russian empress Catherine II argued in a memorandum in 1792 that a small corps, with just 10,000 men, would suffice to put an end to the revolutionary menace.[36]

The arrest of the Bourbon royal family following the Flight to Varennes convinced some European monarchs that it was time to interfere in French affairs. The thousands who had fled France and concentrated in Koblenz and other towns along the border added fuel to the war fervor by urging European rulers to intervene and suppress the Revolution; the revolutionaries were naturally annoyed at the warm reception given to émigrés at some of these courts. Threats of French action against neighboring German states that harbored royalist émigrés prompted Austrian emperor Leopold II, brother of Marie Antoinette, to urge European monarchs "to restore the liberty and honor of the [monarchy] and to limit the dangerous extremes of the revolution."[37] The only ruler who responded to Leopold's initiative was King Frederick William II of Prussia; Russia and Sweden were not in a position to act, while Spain and other European states were too weak militarily. The Prussian and Austrian monarchs then issued the Pillnitz Declaration (1791) denouncing events in France and declaring them to be against the common interests of all Europe. They asserted their willingness to interfere to protect the Bourbon dynasty only if agreement was obtained from their fellow European sovereigns. Leopold's qualifying *if*—"alors et dans ce cas"—made this declaration a largely empty gesture. A pan-European agreement among rulers was impossible because of existing disagreements, and both Leopold and Frederick William II knew that only too well.[38]

Yet whatever its authors' intentions, the language of this declaration was provocative and contributed to the growing war temper. In France, the king, for one, welcomed the prospect of war. He anticipated that the French armies would suffer defeats and that his disillusioned countrymen would then throw themselves into his arms and beg to be saved from the Revolution. Meanwhile, the declaration triggered a fierce nationalist and revolutionary fury among the patriots, propelling them to action. Some revolutionaries portrayed the declaration as an unmitigated threat by foreign powers to intervene and crush the revolutionary process in France.[39] Fired up by revolutionary enthusiasm, the Legislative Assembly, the lawmaking body that replaced the National Assembly in October 1791, debated the extent of France's response. Some deputies called for an immediate war against Austria, which was harboring many of the émigrés and threatening to invade. They also saw war as a means of uniting the country behind them, and regarded themselves as crusaders against tyranny, desiring to spread revolutionary ideals to other lands as well.[40] "A people who, after ten centuries of slavery, have re-conquered liberty, have need of war. War is necessary to consolidate liberty," thundered Jacques-Pierre Brissot, one of the revolutionary leaders.[41] In December 1791 the newspaper Le patriote français reported a speech by Anacharsis Cloots, a wealthy Prussian nobleman who had left his homeland to dive passionately into the revolutionary turmoil, in which he urged the Legislative Assembly to adopt war, as it "would renew the face of the world and plant the standard of liberty over the palaces of kings, the harems of Sultans, the chateaux of petty feudal tyrants, the temples of popes and muftis."[42] Young, patriotic, and idealistic, the revolutionaries believed in full sincerity that France faced an immense foreign conspiracy that could be dismantled only through the means of war. Many revolutionaries shared Brissot's view that the "enslaved" multitudes of other nations would rise up in arms to welcome the French liberators.[43]

As much as European powers might have been concerned about revolutionary upheaval, the declarations of war did not come from them. Instead, following a ten-day debate, the deputies of the Legislative Assembly voted in favor of sending an ultimatum to Austria, demanding formal assurances of peaceful intentions and renunciation of all agreements directed against France. These demands meant war, for Austria had no intention of accepting any of them, especially after Emperor Leopold passed away on March 1, 1792, and was replaced by his more combative brother Francis II. With no response forthcoming from Austria, on April 20 the Legislative Assembly declared war on Austria (soon followed by declarations against Prussia and Holland). It was, the assembly declared, a "just defense of a free people against the unjust aggression of a king." There would be no conquests, the declaration said, and French forces would never be used against the liberty of another people.[44]

When discussing the French Revolutionary Wars, heavy emphasis has been placed on the changing nature of military conflict. In reality, the armies involved still utilized eighteenth-century technology and weaponry, while tactical and strategic developments that are often thought of as French "breakthroughs" were in fact far less innovative than commonly perceived.

As historian Peter Paret has noted, the turmoil in France coincided with a "revolution in war" that had started earlier, but now the two "meshed."[45] Indeed, the army was in many respects the beneficiary of the traumatic shock that France experienced in the Seven Years' War (1756–1763). That defeat had prompted the army to reform and innovate, and it placed reformers such as Jean-Baptiste Vaquette, comte de Gribeauval, and Jacques Antoine Hippolyte, comte de Guibert, at the vanguard of the military change.[46] Many reforms introduced in the French army during the Revolution had their origins in the pre-1789 army.

Yet the French Revolutionary Wars did mark a new turn in warfare. For the first time in European history the conflict unleashed ideological forces whose power and appeal called into question the very notions that underpinned the European political and social system. The French revolutionary armies carried with them the abstract notions of "nation," "people," "equality," and "freedom" that directly challenged the existing monarchical regimes based on privilege and inequality. Wars that had been the affairs of kings were now the affairs of nations. "The tremendous effects of the French Revolution abroad," commented Karl von Clausewitz, "were not caused so much by new military methods and concepts as by radical changes in policies and administration, by the new character of government, the altered conditions of the French people." Unlike earlier conflicts, the wars turned "the people" into active participants, throwing "the full weight of the nation" into the balance.[47] They also engendered remarkable popular enthusiasm and a scale of mobilization that other states were compelled to match.[48]

The almost continuous fighting between 1792 and 1815 witnessed national resources engaged and expended to an unprecedented degree, making possible the continuation and expansion of the conflicts. Threat to existing power structures formed the social backdrop of the revolutionary ideology of this conflict. In the occupied territories, the French usually pursued what we now call "regime change," with far-reaching political, economic, social, and cultural consequences. The revolutionaries convinced themselves that the Revolution would be welcome with open arms across Europe. If European monarchies tried to launch a "war of kings," asserted one revolutionary, "we shall raise a war of peoples . . . who will embrace each other in the face of their dethroned tyrants." Humanity would doubtless suffer in the impending conflict, but it was a price the revolutionaries were ready to pay to bring liberty to the entire world.[49]

CHAPTER 2 | The Eighteenth-Century International Order

WHEN THE LEGISLATIVE ASSEMBLY voted to declare war, it acted in expectation of a short conflict from which it would emerge triumphant. In the event, this initial conflict between France and Austria turned out to be the first stage of a twenty-three-year conflagration that engulfed all of the European states and expanded overseas to the Americas, Caribbean, Africa, and Asia. It is wrong to attribute the global expansion of European squabbles to the French Revolutionary Wars alone, since the process can be traced to earlier centuries. But political turmoil in Europe between 1792 and 1815 certainly provided some European states with greater freedom of action to pursue their expansionist policies while depriving their historical rivals of the resources and political will needed to challenge them.

The French Revolutionary Wars must therefore be considered within the context of contemporary international politics, given that existing state rivalries played a critical role in shaping both the short-term calculations and long-term assumptions of individual states. During the first few years of the Revolution, the response of European monarchies was shaped not as much by the threat of revolutionary ideology as by what was made possible by France in turmoil.

The eighteenth century was in general a period of major transformation in the international order, and the system of international relations it established survived until the start of World War I.[1] At the heart of this transformation lay the balance of power maintained by a select group of states.[2] Early modern Europe was a rather contentious part of the world, one in which states constantly clashed with one another and repeatedly sought to achieve political equilibrium by forming successive coalitions, mainly to restrain the

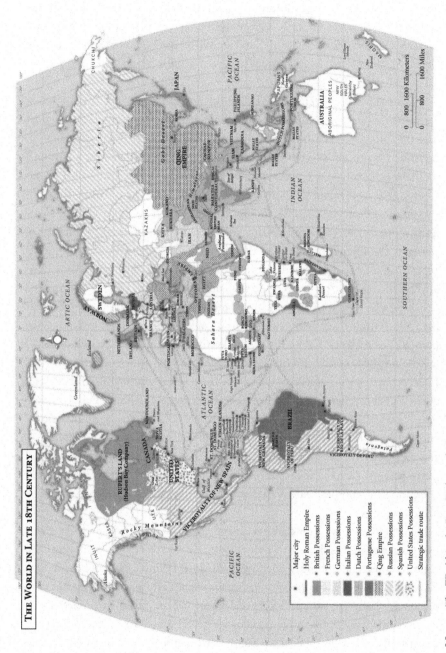

Map 2: The World in the Late Eighteenth Century

ambitions of the larger powers. In the seventeenth century such coalitions were aimed at Spain and France, but these conflicts gradually changed European politics, creating localized balances, such as the ones that emerged between France and Austria in the Italian peninsula, among Denmark, Sweden, and Russia in the Baltic, and among France, Prussia, and Austria in Germany. These localized balances then gradually merged into a general balance that extended to the entire continent.[3]

At the start of the century, the continental equilibrium was envisaged as France (supported occasionally by Spain and a few German states) against Austria (joined by Britain and the Dutch Republic). After the War of Austrian Succession (1740–1748) and the Seven Years' War (1756–1763), the balance involved a greater number of powerful states and covered a far greater geographical area. These wars established British maritime and colonial dominance at the expense of France and Spain and developed a clear pattern of operation: the Royal Navy, with more than double the number of warships the French had, denied the French fleet the ability to gain crucial experience offshore, cut them off from naval supplies, and generally locked up French military manpower on the continent, where the British secured alliances while establishing military and commercial supremacy overseas. By 1789 Britain was clearly the leading commercial and colonial power in Europe. The meteoric rise of Prussia under the leadership of King Frederick II (r. 1740–1786) and the emergence of Russia as a great power under Empresses Elizabeth (r. 1740–1762) and Catherine II (r. 1762–1796) shifted the center of the European balance away from the West, where it had remained for so long, and brought to the fore new "questions"—the "Northern Question," on the fate of the Baltic region and the Polish-Lithuanian Commonwealth, and the "Eastern Question," on the future of the Ottoman Empire. Traditional great powers Austria and France, by contrast, had suffered repeated setbacks in the conflicts and experienced significant financial and political difficulties.[4]

On the eve of the French Revolution, a well-defined group of five states had thus emerged as the "great powers," recognized to be much stronger than their European neighbors. Collectively, Austria, Britain, France, Prussia, and Russia shaped European politics, using war as the arbiter once the niceties of diplomacy had been exhausted. As one eminent historian aptly observed, "To be predator or prey: that was the choice" in early modern Europe.[5] This was particularly relevant in central Europe, which remained fragmented into hundreds of minor principalities, ecclesiastical cities, and minor states, contained within the Holy Roman Empire but susceptible to external threats. The Italian peninsula contained several small kingdoms and principalities, some independent and others controlled by Austria. Austrian statesman Klemens von Metternich was very near the truth when he remarked that Italy was no more than a geographical expression.

Yet any discussion of the "great powers system" must consider that these individual states were also part of separate political universes that shaped their political goals and aspirations. The Europe of this period can be divided into three broad categories of states, each with its own set of imperial pretensions and challenges.[6]

In the first category are the "continental powers" Austria and Prussia, primarily focused on maintaining their authority within Europe. The former, with its capital at Berlin, comprised the core provinces of Brandenburg, Pomerania, East Prussia, and Silesia, as well as enclaves in western Germany and substantial territories in the east, which Prussia had gained during the Partitions of Poland at the end of the eighteenth century. Ruled by the House of Hohenzollern, Prussia had established itself as Europe's newest great power just a generation before the French Revolution, having won two major conflicts despite seemingly impossible odds.[7] Under Frederick II (known as Frederick the Great), the kingdom had been the model state of the Enlightenment philosophes but in actuality faced considerable challenges in the international arena. It was in a precarious position due to its relatively small territory (some 76,000 square miles vs. France's 277,200 square miles) and population (over 6 million vs. France's 28 million and Russia's 35 million). By the start of the French Revolutionary Wars, Prussia remained a comparatively necessitous power, without much industrial development or colonial possessions, yet it heavily taxed its population to maintain its recently acquired status as a great power.[8] This explains Prussia's desire for territorial aggrandizement at the expense of Poland in the concluding decades of the eighteenth century and its grander ambitions in Germany. The Berlin court was conspicuous among European courts as a center of intrigue, embracing various schemes with the avowed purpose of despoiling its neighbors to the east and south. Placed between three potentially hostile powers—Russia, France, and Austria—Prussia traditionally sought to be on good terms with at least one of them. In practical terms, its almost constant rivalry with Austria over the German states meant that Prussia had to turn either to France or to Russia for support.

Austria, which traditionally dominated central Europe through its control of the Holy Roman Empire, was also insecure about its position.[9] The Austrian state lacked the linguistic, ethnic, and institutional unity of some of its European neighbors, and attempts by Joseph II (r. 1780–1790) to establish a unified administration had largely failed. Having suffered two defeats at the hands of Prussia in 1748 and 1763, the Austrian Habsburgs had begrudgingly accepted that their province, Silesia, so rich in people, trade, and resources, was now part of Prussia, at least for the duration of Frederick the Great's reign. But tensions between the two German rivals remained, and in fact they had risen in the 1780s when a series of revolts broke out across the Habsburg territories (Belgium, Tyrol, Galicia, Lombardy, and Hungary). Prussia did its best to exploit them to further diminish Austrian power in Germany; at one point the Hohenzollern court even encouraged the Hungarians to rise up against Vienna and create an independent state ruled by a Prussian prince.[10]

Austria's alliance with France was a recent phenomenon (formed in 1756) and was marked by a mutual distrust underpinned by the previous two and a half centuries of hostility. Thus, Austrian attempts to acquire Bavaria demonstrated the tenuous nature of the Franco-Austrian alliance, since France refused any assistance to Austria (even if the latter was attacked), and in the subsequent War of the Bavarian Succession (1778–1779) the Saxon-Prussian alliance successfully prevented Austria from acquiring the Electorate of Bavaria. Yet despite continued frictions and disagreements, neither Austria nor France wanted or expected war in the 1790s. Austria was keen to use its alliance with France to safeguard its western borders and recoup its losses through further expansion into Poland and the Balkans, where the Habsburgs had waged a war against the Turks in 1787–1791. In fact, these seemingly unrelated events—the Austro-Ottoman War in the Balkans and political power struggles in Poland—had an important influence on the course of the French Revolution. As France, the greatest continental power, descended into political turmoil, the other major powers were preoccupied with their own affairs and schemes for aggrandizement, giving the newly founded French revolutionary government two years of respite.

In the second category of European powers were those whose interests were not confined solely to Europe. These powers—France and Britain in the first place, but also Russia, Portugal, and Spain—exploited their geographical situation and their possession of colonies to secure a large share of international trade, which in turn sustained their political and military aspirations. Visitors to Britain and France were struck by the evident signs of prosperity of their great Atlantic port towns, generated by the vast profits made through colonial trade.[11] On the eve of the French Revolution, the value of French trade with America amounted to a quarter of the value of all French commercial operations; the share was even higher in the case of Britain's foreign trade. Portugal had overseas possessions that included Brazil and numerous trading posts in Africa, India, and China. But the Portuguese were so dependent on their trade with Britain that, economically speaking, the country was a British dependency in all but name. The Portuguese government—formally ruled by Queen Maria, whose insanity made her incapable of governing and forced her to delegate her authority to Prince Dom João—was weak and inefficient. It persistently feared Spain, which had once briefly consumed its smaller neighbor and undoubtedly would have attempted to do so again had Britain not been determined to keep Portugal's all-weather ports in friendlier hands. If Portugal felt threatened by Spain, it was the only country that did. Spain possessed the largest colonial empire in the world, with its dominions straddling much of the Americas and extending to the Philippines in the Pacific Ocean. But by 1789 the once-proud nation of the conquistadors had suffered continued economic decline and political stagnation that affected its ability to properly defend its interests.[12]

In the century before 1789, France had exercised a pervasive influence over the rest of Europe. Its literature, art, and fashion were in demand everywhere, and French was the language of the elites across Europe. France was *la Grande Nation*, with a vast population, considerable natural resources, and immense possessions overseas, the nation that frequently transcended its continental interests to pursue a more comprehensive policy spanning continents and oceans.[13] In the Americas alone, France had formed and settled fourteen colonies, stretching from Canada to French Guiana.[14] The range and pace of its activities in Asia and the Americas only increased throughout the eighteenth century, with France seeking alliances with North American tribes, negotiating with rulers of Burma and Cochin China, and pursuing its interests in India and the Indian Ocean islands. The French made overtures to Iran and Muscat (Oman), where they hoped to develop trade and limit British influence. They also had a better understanding of the strategic importance of Egypt, where they pursued closer relations with the ruling Mamluk elite. By the 1780s, France was reaping the benefits of its longstanding alliance with the Ottomans, enjoying a dominant position in foreign trade with the Levant and eastern Mediterranean and seeking to make inroads into the Black Sea.

But such global aspirations also carried immense liabilities. The middle of the century saw the devastating defeat in the Seven Years' War, which resulted in the loss of colonies and unleashed a prolonged financial crisis that led to an international eclipse that would last until the 1790s. France could only stand by helplessly as its traditional ally, the Kingdom of Poland, was partitioned by Austria, Russia, and Prussia in 1772, while a popular (and Francophile) revolt in the Dutch Republic was put down by Prussian forces in 1787. Just three years later France could not provide support to a short-lived revolt in the Austrian Netherlands (present-day Belgium) and failed to honor the Bourbon family alliance when disagreements over the Pacific Northwest brought Britain and Spain to the brink of war.[15] Despite having the second-largest navy in Europe, France was unable to scrape together enough funds to sustain naval operational activity befitting a great power.[16]

France's longtime rival was also not limiting its interests to Europe. In fact, British military intervention on the continent was traditionally unpopular domestically and unlikely to be undertaken except to defend the country's paramount interests, most notably the status of the estuary of the Scheldt River (in northern Belgium and southwestern Netherlands). Britain exploited its naval and commercial capabilities to project its interests into far-flung regions of the world. Such aspirations, however, meant military confrontations with rival powers. Britain emerged from these wars with heavy financial burdens and faced major challenges at home, including the intractable "Irish problem." Just six years before the French Revolution, the British had been humiliated by the loss of their American colonies, the result of a coalition that included France, Spain, and the Dutch Republic. Its poor military showing in America might have dented Britain's reputation, but the country had strengths that its rivals lacked. Its first advantage was being an island nation, which protected it against invasion. This was guaranteed by the maintenance of the largest and most efficient fleet in the world. Thus, despite losing some of its overseas possessions, Britain was able to build a new empire upon the remains of the old, and economics regained the trade that politics had lost.[17] A flexible financial and political system allowed Britain, which Prime Minister George Grenville (r. 1763–1765) claimed to be in deep distress in 1763, to survive the loss of colonies and a doubling of national debt and emerge stronger than before. Colonial possessions brought it wealth, but of even greater importance were the resources available immediately on the British islands. The Industrial Revolution, which began in earnest in Britain in the 1760s, exploited Britain's abundance in coal and iron to an extent undreamed of on the continent and gave tremendous strength to the nation, so even the long war that began in 1793 did not reduce Britain to bankruptcy.[18]

The French Revolution was initially welcomed in Britain. At the very least, it was thought, it would weaken the old enemy; at best, it would create another constitutional state in Europe. But the initial enthusiasm quickly subsided, and the British government became increasingly alarmed over the contagion of radical ideas streaming out of France. Following the French declaration of war in February 1793, Britain became the target for three invasion attempts (once through Wales and twice via Ireland) and responded with a blockade of French ports and attacks on its colonial trade.

Russia emerged as a great power in the second half of the eighteenth century, when it persistently pursued—and achieved—rapid and vast territorial expansion; no other state in Europe added as much territory in such a short period of time. This can be partly explained by the fact that, compared to other European powers, Russia had greater opportunity for success due to its geographic location and the relative weakness of its immediate neighbors. The dramatic territorial changes of 1772–1775, when Russian empress Catherine II skillfully exploited Polish weakness to carry out the first Polish Partition, not only greatly expanded Russian territory but also served as the catalyst for a major diplomatic realignment in Europe. Russia's dominant position in the eastern half of Europe was further strengthened in the subsequent decades as Catherine pursued aggressive policies in the Balkans, the Caucasus, the Caspian littoral, and eastern Siberia. The Russo-Ottoman War of 1767–1774 resulted in Russian annexation of lands along the northern coastline of the Black Sea, while the Treaty of Georgievsk (1783) with the Kingdom of Kartli-Kakheti (eastern Georgia) extended Russian military presence across the Caucasus Mountains. The Turks had hoped to stem Russian expansion into the Crimea in 1783, and by declaring war they gained the initiative, only to lose it in a series of military setbacks. In 1796 Russian troops campaigned in Daghestan, threatening Iranian interests along the Caspian shoreline. At the same time, Russian authority had been consolidated in Siberia, where the former tsardom of Siberia was reorganized into three provinces led by Russian governors.[19] As impressive and persistent as its success was elsewhere, Russia showed no such steadiness of policy or level of accomplishment in Europe, and perhaps to a greater degree than elsewhere it began to reflect the sensibility of whoever ruled it.[20] With each change of monarch—the death of Empress Catherine II in 1796, and the death of Emperor Paul I and the rise of Alexander I in 1801—Russian domestic and foreign policy experienced major changes.

The last category of European states included weaker polities that could not effectively compete on the international level, frequently served as subsidiaries to greater powers, and occasionally turned into conflict zones. Until the late nineteenth century central Europe was occupied by the Holy Roman Empire, one of the most irrational institutions in what was proudly described as the Age of Reason.[21] This was hardly an empire in the traditional sense of the word, but rather a patchwork of more than three hundred polities owing allegiance to the Holy Roman Emperor. The empire was ethnically, religiously, and politically fragmented; as the French philosopher Voltaire famously remarked, it was "neither holy, nor Roman, nor an Empire."[22]

Although the majority of the Holy Roman Empire's inhabitants were Germans, there were also significant non-German communities in Bohemia and the Spanish Netherlands; the empire included numerous lay and ecclesiastical princes, free cities, and imperial knights, who all owed formal allegiance to the emperor, but the more powerful ones were almost entirely beyond his control. Ever since the Thirty Years' War (1618–1648), imperial authority had been backed neither by a permanent army nor by a centralized bureaucracy. The emperor's authority, which was not inherited but was subject to election by the most powerful princes of the empire, was largely restricted to arbitrating disputes between the German states, which were considered independent and capable of conducting their own foreign policy. The imperial assembly, the Imperial Diet, to which the German states sent their representatives, was a quarrelsome, ineffective institution that lacked legislative authority.[23]

Like the Holy Roman Empire, Switzerland was also a disunited conglomeration of cantons, but it combined a burgeoning banking business with the equally lucrative hiring out of mercenaries to European powers.[24] Italy remained divided into more than a half dozen states and subject to the domination of foreign powers. Lombardy remained firmly under Austrian control, though the thousand-year-old Venetian Republic, in the northeastern corner of the Italian peninsula, defended its interests. Meanwhile, the Kingdom of Piedmont-Sardinia jealously guarded its position in the northwest and on the island of Sardinia, while the popes still controlled a broad swath of central Italy. The largest state in Italy was the Kingdom of the Two Sicilies, a rather confusing name for a realm that centered around the city of Naples but straddled the island of Sicily and all of southern Italy.

The once-mighty Polish kingdom had degenerated into a feeble political entity that became, as we've seen, the target of Russian, Austrian, and Prussian ambitions before ceasing to exist entirely in 1795. The Dutch Republic drew vast wealth from its East Indian possessions and the Cape of Good Hope, but of even greater importance were its great financial centers, to which all of Europe came to borrow money. Although affluent, the Dutch state was also torn by internal dissent, politically weak, and dominated by its neighbors. Defeated in the Fourth Anglo-Dutch War (1780–1784), the Dutch experienced domestic turmoil that resulted in the Prussian invasion in 1787. In the meantime, Scandinavia comprised just two states. After enjoying its golden age in the seventeenth century, the Swedish Empire (which included Finland) had gradually turned into a regional power whose influence in the Baltic was continually contested by Russia and Britain. Which is why Sweden was anxious to acquire Norway, then linked by a common crown to Denmark, Sweden's perennial rival.

This broad categorization of European states during the revolutionary era is useful when discussing the variety of interests and conflicts present in this period. Though the Revolution added a significant ideological dimension, there was a clear continuity of interests from before the revolutionary era, and European powers continued to be guided by traditional factors, such as long-standing rivalries and territorial interests. So while the execution of the French king caused the Spanish Bourbons to join the First Coalition against France in 1793, it did not prevent the same Spanish monarchy from allying itself to the French republic in 1796. The Polish Partitions of 1792 and 1795 reflected the continental powers' sense of opportunity created by the outbreak of political turmoil in France as well as their concern about one another's expansionism.

By the late eighteenth century, commerce was the lifeblood of the great nations, and control of the seas and the international trade lanes that ran between the continents became one of the central elements of rivalry among the European powers. The resources of the New World and the hugely profitably trade with Asia were crucial to the financial stability and growth of European states, and the desire to protect and exploit these sources of wealth was closely tied to the growth of European naval power. Indeed, control of the seas protected friendly merchant shipping (with all the benefits stemming from it) and colonies, thwarted enemy trade, and projected a nation's authority overseas. France increased the value of its exports from 120 million livres in 1716 to more than 500 million livres in 1789, and the growth of British commerce was only slightly higher. The dominant political economic theory, mercantilism, required that a nation establish a favorable balance of trade and amass bullion. Backed by their own and crown troops, European trade companies, most famously the British and French East India Companies, gained control of trade with Asia, importing spices, indigo, textiles, tea, and other items to Europe and making considerable profits in the process. Maritime trade was thus crucial to securing the wealth necessary to sustain a war-making capability.[25]

Britain's commercial gains came largely at the expense of traditional French markets. Despite its global aspirations, France's preoccupation with European affairs was partly a matter of necessity. Unlike its main rival, which was protected by the sea, the French kingdom suffered from "amphibious geography," as it was located near the western extremity of the Eurasian supercontinent and was therefore tempted to strive after supremacy on both sea and land.[26] This entailed dealing with the troublesome Dutch and English as well as its traditional adversaries, including Austria and—ultimately the more dangerous ones—Prussia and Russia. The French kings thus maintained a peacetime standing army of at least 150,000 men, which consumed enormous resources and hampered the development of French naval power. By comparison, Britain's army was one-third that size (and most of it was deployed in India and other colonies), while the Royal Navy steadily expanded throughout the eighteenth century. In 1715 Britain had some 120 ships-of-the-line versus 39 for France; in 1783 the Royal Navy could deploy 174 ships-of-the-line and almost 300 other warships, while France had about 70 line vessels and some 150 others. The desire to avenge the humiliation of the Seven Years' War sustained France's program of naval reform and investment in the 1770s and 1780s, but the French navy suffered greatly during the Revolutionary Wars because of officer emigration, mounting strikes, and mutinies by seamen.

But one must bear in mind that a powerful navy was not as essential to France's national survival during the Revolutionary Wars as it was to Britain's. Attacked from almost all sides, France concentrated on building up its land forces, and consequently the demands and expectations placed upon the French fleet were drastically different from those of the British. The turmoil in the French navy as well as economic, administrative, and technical innovations had combined to give Britain a distinct superiority over its French, Spanish, and Russian rivals. Britain had a far larger ocean trade than any of its principal enemies, which provided it with a bigger reserve of professional seamen from which to man its warships. Long deployments at sea, whether on blockade or on convoy escort, gave British captains plenty of opportunities to train their crews, who typically achieved a higher rate of fire than their opponents. The global nature of British power meant that its resources had to be stretched around the world, though British naval commanders demonstrated great flexibility and a tendency to adopt bolder methods in confrontations with their enemies.

The naval struggle during the Revolutionary and Napoleonic Wars can be divided into two interrelated but markedly different periods. The first twelve years of the war, from 1793 to 1805, witnessed British efforts to obtain command of the seas over its enemies, the much-weakened French and Spanish navies. Although these fleets did engage in a number of decisive battles, most of the British naval effort involved expeditionary warfare, which saw British troops deployed on both sides of the Atlantic, and the blockade of coastlines and ports. The second period, inaugurated by the British triumph over the French and Spanish at Trafalgar in 1805, was marked by the Royal Navy's consolidation of its command of the sea and French efforts to rebuild its naval capacity and challenge the post-Trafalgar status quo on the sea.

———∞∞⊗∞∞———

The most convenient starting point for an overview of the competition between European powers is the beginning of the Austro-Russo-Ottoman War in 1787. It not only showcased the existing rivalries among the great powers—the Austro-Prussian rivalry in the center of Europe, the Russo-Prussian rivalry in the east, and the Anglo-Russian rivalry in the south—but also intensified them. Events in southeastern Europe represented the beginning of one of the most challenging diplomatic problems of the nineteenth century, the Eastern Question, which centered on the European contest against the weakening Ottoman Empire.

At its greatest extent the Ottoman Empire held suzerainty over all of Asia Minor, the Balkan Peninsula, Hungary, the Black Sea littoral, south Caucasia, Syria-Palestine, Egypt and the coastal states of North Africa. Furthermore, in his capacity as caliph or spiritual leader of the world's Muslims, the Ottoman sultan held nominal leadership over the entire Islamic world, stretching from the Atlantic coast of Africa to India. Yet by the late eighteenth century the Ottomans were confronted with a host of domestic and foreign challenges that contributed to internal turmoil and loss of provinces, weakened Ottoman finances, and encouraged the European powers' ambitions. While the Ottoman sultans maintained nominal claims to Algeria, Libya, and Egypt, actual power there resided in the hands of local elites, who often defied the sultan's authority. In the Balkans and Caucasus, the Ottomans faced the resurgent aspirations of local peoples (Greeks, Serbs, Georgians, etc.) and the growing ambitions of Russia and Austria, which showed interest in ever-larger parts of the Ottoman realm. Between 1745 and 1768 the Ottoman Empire experienced a period of relative peace and stability; moderate reforms were introduced, but they failed to resolve the empire's economic problems or curb administrative corruption, nor did they succeed in establishing a modernized standing army, one of the key assets of the contemporary European states.[27]

This failure proved to be consequential in 1768, when the Russo-Ottoman conflict entered a new stage. The Russian armies scored decisive victories over the Ottomans in the Danubian principalities, forcing Sultan Abduhamid I to negotiate a peace at the village of Küçük Kaynarca in Bulgaria in July 1774. The subsequent treaty was one of the most pivotal in the history of European diplomacy and marked a turning point in Ottoman history. The loss of territories was limited but politically damaging to the sultan. The Ottoman defeat encouraged provincial elites to contemplate breaking away from the empire, and the sultan's authority was openly defied by Mamluk beys in Egypt and powerful notables in Anatolia, Syria, and Arabia. Furthermore, the treaty recognized Russian merchantmen's freedom to navigate on the Black Sea and in the Turkish Straits (the Bosporus and the Dardanelles), leading to the growth of a Russian merchant marine in the region and, consequently, a more powerful Russian naval presence to protect commerce. Equally significant was the Ottoman sultan's decision to grant Russia the right to build an Eastern Orthodox church in Pera, the diplomatic quarter of Constantinople, and to accept a rather vaguely phrased provision that allowed Russia to make representations on behalf of this church and "those who serve it." Russia exploited the ambiguous nature of this provision to claim representation on behalf of all the Eastern Orthodox subjects of the Porte, thereby justifying interference into the Ottomans' domestic affairs. Henceforth, in both time of war and peacetime, Russia sought to extend its privileges and interference in the Ottoman realm.

The Treaty of Küçük Kaynarca had, in effect, laid the foundation for the Eastern Question by turning the Ottoman Empire into the object of the European powers' political and territorial aspirations. The commercial concession to Russia whetted appetites in France, Britain, and the Dutch Republic, all of which sought similar concessions for their own merchants. Furthermore, the treaty revealed the scope of Ottoman weakness. A sultan whose armies once used to threaten the heartland of Europe thus turned into an increasingly irrelevant ruler at the margins of European diplomatic rivalries, with his territories subject to diplomatic maneuverings by Russia, Britain, Austria, and France.

The Ottomans spent the decade after the treaty reorganizing their military. They achieved some success in modernizing their navy, while the army was restored to its prewar status, although it continued to lag behind its European counterparts. Throughout these years both Russia and the Ottoman Empire complained of infringements of the Treaty of Küçük Kaynarca. The sultan's only hope was international support, but this did not materialize. Meanwhile, a secret Russo-Austrian alliance of 1781 proved essential in Russia's continued expansionist policy in the Balkans. In agreeing to this alliance, Austria was forced to deal with the fundamental problem of its late eighteenth-century foreign policy: that of reconciling its need for Russia's support against Prussia with its fundamental opposition to further Russian expansion in southeastern Europe. By joining with Russia, Austria hoped both to strengthen its hand vis-à-vis Prussia and to limit Catherine's gains in the Ottoman domains.[28]

In 1783, to the deep resentment and humiliation of the Ottomans, Russia annexed the Crimea, the most significant territorial change in southeastern

Europe since the Seven Years' War.[29] It was a major accomplishment on Russia's part, made possible by strong Austrian support in exchanges with the Ottoman government. The Crimea provided Russia with adequate naval bases and ports on the Black Sea—and an ability to launch a seaborne attack directly against Constantinople. The threat of further Russian expansion at Ottoman expense should have provoked a response from other great powers, but it never materialized, for the reason that no single power could provide effective logistical support to the Turks. Britain was still recovering from its defeat in the American Revolutionary War, while France, already weakened by economic crisis, was further neutralized by the revelation of the Russo-Austrian alliance. In the spring of 1787 Empress Catherine II's triumphal procession through the southern part of the Ukraine and Crimea caused new concerns about Russian intentions and exacerbated tensions between the Ottoman Empire and Russia. In August of the same year, Sultan Abduhamid I, influenced by the vociferous pro-war political factions and *ulama* (religious leaders), as well as by British prodding, declared war on Russia in an effort to reclaim territories lost in preceding conflicts.

Catherine II welcomed this new conflict. France was still mired in its financial crisis and unable to support its traditional ally, so the Russian empress had an opportunity to take on the Ottomans, with an eye toward expanding influence in the Black Sea littoral and possibly fulfilling her cherished "Greek Project"—the reestablishment of a Byzantine state on Ottoman territory with Constantinople as its capital.[30] Once the war began, Austria joined it on the side of Russia.[31] The Turks were ill-prepared. Although they successfully dealt with the Austrians in the Banat (parts of present-day Romania, Serbia, and Hungary), they could not stop the Russian advance. His army in disarray and lacking supplies and quality recruits, the new sultan, Selim III, was forced to sue for peace.[32] By the Treaty of Jassy (1792), Russia acquired the remaining parts of the Crimea and the lands between the Bug and Dniester Rivers, consolidating its control over the northern shore of the Black Sea. The Ottomans were forced to recognize the Russian annexation of the Crimea and to reconfirm the provisions of the Treaty of Küçük Kaynarca.[33] The end of the war with Russia and the start of the French Revolution distracted the European powers, giving the Ottomans a few years of respite from Western imperialism. Selim III used this moment to initiate a period of limited reforms in the Ottoman state and sought to centralize his authority, modernize the army, and improve finances.

The events in the Balkans had ramifications beyond southeastern Europe, of course. Just as Russia and Austria became embroiled in the war, a crisis erupted in the Dutch Republic, which had experienced an economic decline in the wake of the devastating Anglo-Dutch Wars. It centered around the ongoing conflict between the Orangists, who supported the authoritarian policies of stadtholder (chief magistrate) William V, Prince of Orange, and the so-called Patriots, representing the middling orders, who were inspired by the ideals of the Enlightenment and sought a more democratic government and society. Relying on their militias, the Patriots took control of several cities and regions and in May 1787 defeated the stadtholder himself near Vreeswijk in the Dutch province of Utrecht.

What made the Dutch turmoil more than just another case of civil strife was that both sides enjoyed significant foreign support. France sided with the Patriots, and Britain and Prussia had deep ties with the House of Orange. The arrest and brief (but humiliating) detention of the stadtholder's wife, who was the sister of King Frederick William II of Prussia, provoked Prussian intervention, though not before Berlin secured promises of assistance from Britain. The Patriots' appeals to France for assistance touched the greatest of British concerns: French maritime and colonial intentions. Alarmed by the prospect of French influence over the Dutch navy and colonies, Britain supported a Prussian invasion of the Dutch Republic in September 1787; despite its threats to act, France was thwarted not only by its financial crisis and internal divisions in the royal government but also by the lack of any meaningful involvement from Austria or Russia, both of which were preoccupied with the Turks. The Prussian army, under the command of the Duke of Brunswick, quickly overran Dutch cities—the last Patriot stronghold, Amsterdam, surrendered in early October—and restored the stadtholder to power. Many of the Patriots fled to France, where during the Revolution they actively lobbied for French action against the House of Orange and later supported establishment of a revolutionary government. After the suppression of the Dutch revolt, the Anglo-Dutch-Prussian alliance of 1788 all but confirmed that French influence had been eclipsed in the Low Countries. Moreover, France's inability to prevent Prussian intervention so close to its borders signaled its diplomatic (and military) nullity.[34] Austria and Russia paid no heed to French efforts to mediate peace in the Balkans, and Britain took a more active role in Ottoman affairs, a role that France traditionally had reserved for itself. In short, the Dutch crisis and its aftereffects were a humiliating experience for the French monarchy, as they revealed to Europe that France could no longer be ranked among the first-rate powers.

Meanwhile, Russian preoccupation with the Turks prompted Sweden to launch a surprise attack in July 1788. The two-year Russo-Swedish War was inconclusive and ended with a treaty that confirmed the *status quo ante bellum* with respect to the borders. But Russian involvement in these wars galvanized a movement for domestic political reform among the Poles, who detested the growth of Russian influence. Once a powerful state, the Polish-Lithuanian Commonwealth possessed but a shadow of its former glory by the late eighteenth century. It was dominated by a powerful aristocracy, exercising its authority through the Sejm (an elected parliament) that limited royal executive power, often preventing effective governing of the state. A single deputy to the Sejm could end its proceedings, declaring *liberum veto* (meaning "I am free to say no") and dissolving it. Growing corruption and foreign interference by powerful and greedy neighbors only further exacerbated political chaos in Poland. It was this form of government, which has been aptly described by one historian as "a constitutional anarchy tempered by civil war," that European powers exploited at the end of the eighteenth century.[35] In 1772 Catherine II had engineered the First Partition of Poland, claiming much of the eastern Polish kingdom and placing her favorite, Stanislaw August Poniatowski, on the Polish throne.[36] Political struggles between Europe's great powers played a large role in Catherine's choice. Austria was alarmed by Russian successes against the Turks in the Danubian region. Prussia was willing to accept the partition of Poland as a way to satisfy Russia's expansionist ambitions, to provide compensation for Austria, and to secure for itself the long-covered Polish province of West Prussia, which separated East Prussia from Brandenburg. In all, Poland lost about one-third of its territory and population.[37]

This First Partition had demonstrated the dangers the Polish state was facing, helping nurture public opinion favorable to reform. Russo-Prussian relations, already tense in the last years of Frederick II's reign, further deteriorated after Frederick William II's accession to the Prussian throne in 1786; Catherine II's anti-Prussian sentiments meant that a pro-Austrian party in Russia soon outshone its pro-Prussian rivals and led to the Russo-Austrian rapprochement.[38] The signing of the 1781 alliance between St. Petersburg and Vienna left Berlin isolated in Europe, a gratifying turn of events in the eyes of Austria's emperor, Joseph. Although Prussia remained Russia's ally (if only a nominal one), Frederick William II was keen to acquire more Polish territory, and waited for an opportune moment to do it.

That opportunity arrived during the period 1786–1789, when Europe descended into turmoil. France, rapidly drifting toward revolution and deprived of Charles Gravier, comte de Vergennes, the talented French foreign minister who died in February 1787, was timid and irresolute. Austria and Russia were at war with the Ottoman Turks, while Gustavus III of Sweden was attempting to regain from Russia the provinces of Finland and Carelia. The Prussians quickly moved to exploit the situation, hoping to make the most of the Austrian and Russian predicaments and to compel Austria to make concessions in central and eastern Europe as compensation for any gains Russia might achieve at the expense of the Turks. In 1788 Frederick William II joined the Triple Alliance of Prussia, Britain, and the Dutch Republic, which was designed, in the eyes of its chief architect, British prime minister William Pitt, to lay the foundation for a collective security federation in Europe. Frederick William scored another diplomatic triumph in January 1790 when he negotiated an alliance with the Ottomans, raising the prospect of a joint Prusso-Ottoman action against Austria just when it was struggling to suppress internal unrest in Hungary and the Austrian Netherlands (Belgium).[39] Only two months later Berlin concluded a pact with King Stanislaw II Augustus of Poland, pledging Prussia to stand by the Poles against Russia in exchange for the Polish cession of the fortified town of Thorn (Toruń) on the Vistula (Wisła) River and the great port city of Danzig on the Baltic Sea.

Having received Prussian assurances of support, the Poles set out to reform their country's debilitating political institutions and to restore Poland's political vitality. On October 22, 1788, the Four Years' Parliament (Sejm Czteroletni) opened its sessions and introduced a series of reforms that culminated in the constitution of May 1791, which made a first step toward overthrowing the Russian protectorate and reestablishing the Polish monarchy. The constitution proclaimed a hereditary, limited monarchy that could raise enough taxes to provide for defense of the country, and it abolished many of the domestic causes of Polish impotence, including the *liberum veto*, which had incapacitated the previous Polish government. It also reformed state finances and modernized and enlarged the royal army.[40] Remarkable as these political changes were, their success ultimately depended on Poland's neighbors, which had vested interests in keeping the Polish realm weak. Preoccupied with Sweden and the Ottoman Empire, Russia could not initially react to the loss of its influence in Poland. This created a situation favorable to Prussia, one that encouraged a Polish reform movement as a way of weakening Russian influence and solidified Prussia's own hegemony in the region.

The international situation had soon changed. Alarmed by the turmoil in Hungary, the Austrian Netherlands, and France, Holy Roman Emperor Leopold, who replaced his brother Joseph II in February 1790, tried repairing relations with the Hohenzollerns of Prussia. In July 1790 he and Frederick William II negotiated the Convention of Reichenbach, settling their differences (at least for the moment). The convention allowed the Austrian ruler to end the war with the Turks and to concentrate on restoring control over his domains, with both Belgium and Hungary pacified by the summer of 1791. Furthermore, by fostering more amicable relations between the two German powers, the Convention of Reichenbach led Prussia to support Austria over the intervention in France and eventual participation in the Revolutionary Wars, as well as to the Second and Third Partitions of Poland.

After Empress Catherine II ended her wars against Sweden and the Ottoman Empire in 1792, she turned her attention to Poland. The adoption of a constitution prompted a backlash by Polish nobility who felt threatened by the new ideals. Upon receiving assurances of Russian support, a group of Polish aristocrats signed the Act of Confederation against the constitution on April 27, 1792, just seven days after France declared war on Austria. The act, announced on May 14 in the town of Targowica, declared the constitution void and called for military intervention from Russia. In the subsequent War in Defense of the Constitution, Russian troops crossed the Polish-Lithuanian border, aiming to support the Confederation of Targowica and restore the old form of government. The smaller and less experienced Polish-Lithuanian army struggled to contain internal revolt and resist the Russian invasion; Prussia had earlier pledged to come to Poland's help but failed to do so. The Battle of Dubienka on July 18, 1792, effectively marked the end of the war. The Polish king, Stanislaw, hoping to preserve his royal prerogatives, decided to join the Confederation of Targowica and cease military operations.[41]

In its handling of Polish affairs, Russia exploited the growing European preoccupation with the French Revolution to increase its own freedom of maneuver. Empress Catherine encouraged her Austrian and Prussian counterparts to deal with France and promised support in combatting the French ideological menace. For her, though, events in France had always been less important than the fate of neighboring Poland. Austria had a vested interest in Poland and supported the Polish reform movement as a safeguard against Prussia's aggrandizement, but it could do little at that time to prevent a second partitioning, as it was absorbed in the developments in France. Furthermore, Austria's inability to contain Russian-Prussian ambitions in Poland was compounded by the sudden death of Emperor Leopold II in March 1792. Leopold had always opposed any further reduction of the Polish state and tried to uphold the status quo in the region. His passing, however, removed this moderating influence on Russia, and Leopold's successor, Francis II, agreed to the Russo-Prussian partition of Poland provided that Austria was allowed to exchange the Austrian Netherlands for Bavaria. Remarkably, the anti-Prussian principles that had shaped Austrian policy since 1740 were abandoned almost overnight, and the new generation of Austrian diplomats hoped to exploit cooperation with Berlin against France to create an enduring Austro-Prussian alliance that would replace the nebulous alliances Austria kept with Russia and France.[42] This shift in foreign policy came at a high price. The defeats at Valmy (September 20) and Jemappes (November 6, 1792) forced Vienna to accept that the war with France had to be its main priority and stimulated Prussian desires for Polish lands that would compensate for the failures in the west. In January 1793 a formal Russo-Prussian treaty was signed in St. Petersburg, deciding Poland's future. The ensuing Second Partition dramatically reduced Polish territory and turned this once proud realm into a rump state dominated by its neighbors.[43]

The partition marked a triumph for Russian diplomacy, which skillfully manipulated the international situation. It was also a serious diplomatic defeat for Austria and Britain, which strongly advocated maintaining the balance of power in northeastern Europe. Yet the British-conceived collective security federation required a corresponding willingness to provide the necessary funding, which was nowhere to be found. Consequently, Britain's standing in Europe was undermined, and in 1793 it joined the war not as a member of a multilateral coalition but as an isolated power.[44]

The international impact of European squabbles stemmed from the fact that European powers were colonial empires. By the late eighteenth century just four European states held control over two-thirds of the Western Hemisphere.[45] Portugal was the weakest of the European colonial powers but still retained control over the vast Amazonia region, where twelve royal colonies (captaincies) coalesced into the Governorate General of Brazil. The colonies were initially governed from São Salvador da Bahia de Todos os Santos, in northeastern Brazil, but in 1763 the center of the Portuguese colonial administration shifted to Rio de Janeiro, which served as a colonial capital until 1808. Portugal's historic rival, Spain, controlled a wide belt of territory from Chile to what is now the southwestern United States, the legacy of the Spanish conquests of the sixteenth and seventeenth centuries. In the Gulf of Mexico and the Caribbean, Spain controlled nearly the entire coast, with the significant exception of French-ruled Louisiana, and many islands, including Cuba and half of Hispaniola. Most of France's colonial possessions dated back to the seventeenth century, when the French monarchy actively explored and colonized parts of the New World. By the mid-eighteenth century France owned parts of present-day Canada (Acadia, Canada, Louisiana, Newfoundland, Île Royale) and the Caribbean (Saint-Domingue, Tobago, etc.), only to lose most of them in the disastrous conflict with Britain.

At the end of the Seven Years' War Britain had become the world's greatest colonial power, gaining vast territories in eastern North America, including most of Canada and the lands east of the Mississippi River. Yet its efforts to obtain new revenues from its American colonies to help pay for the war sparked the American Revolution, which led to the establishment of a new nation. Receiving considerable French support, the thirteen American colonies gained their independence in 1783. The conflict that helped create the United States also set in motion the formation of a second nation, although achieving Canadian nationhood took more than seven decades. After the American Revolutionary War, Britain still retained a considerable presence, exerting control over the northeastern half of North America, where the colonies of Quebec, Nova Scotia, and Prince Edward Island remained staunchly loyal.

Because of the challenges created by the influx of tens of thousands of Loyalist migrants from the newly independent United States, the British government was forced to reorganize its North American colonies. In 1784 New Brunswick was formed from the western shore of the Bay of Fundy, previously part of Nova Scotia. And in 1791 Quebec was divided into two colonies, Upper Canada (present-day Ontario) and Lower Canada (present-day Quebec). Together, the five colonies of Upper Canada, Lower Canada, Nova Scotia, New Brunswick, and Prince Edward Island constituted British North America.

At the start of the Revolutionary Wars, the fledgling American republic found its sympathies divided between Britain and France. Americans remained concerned about the continuing British presence in Canada. Under the provisions of the 1783 Treaty of Paris, the British retained Canada but surrendered their claims to the Ohio Country, then called the Old Northwest Territory, which lay north of the Ohio River and south of the Great Lakes. Yet the British still carried on trade in furs with the many tribes living there and even refused to give up major frontier outposts in the region, such as Fort Detroit, until the matter of colonial-era debts was resolved. British officers who had fought in the Revolutionary War and continued to serve in Canada openly spoke of a day when the United States would again belong to Great Britain. Thus John Graves Simcoe, the first lieutenant governor of Upper Canada (1791–1796), spoke of a future war with the American republic and did his best to prepare his province for it. In the mid-1780s George Washington's administration attempted to establish friendly relations with Britain, making several diplomatic overtures that were all declined. Only when the Nootka Sound Crisis threatened to produce a war between Britain and Spain did the British government lend a receptive ear to the American offers.

The Nootka Sound Crisis highlights the global nature of the claims that European powers were making by the end of the eighteenth century.

Traditional discussion of the crisis focuses on Anglo-Spanish relations and points to the British attempt to establish a base on Vancouver Island, on the Pacific coast of North America, as a precipitating factor. Spain had claimed this region since the sixteenth century and never admitted the right of any foreign power to sail or trade within its waters or land.[46] Yet British vessels frequently encroached on the Spanish claims. In 1789 the Spanish navy seized British ships operating in the area, imprisoned the crews, and asserted exclusive Spanish sovereignty over the entire Pacific coast of North America.

This discussion overlooks one more increasingly expansion-minded European power that had interests in the Northeast Pacific and whose actions, in fact, contributed to the start of the Nootka Sound Crisis. Russians had reached the Pacific Ocean in the mid-seventeenth century. Over the next decades, various Russian pioneers discovered and explored the vast expanses of Northeast Asia and the Pacific. It was a Russian expedition, led by the Danish explorer Vitus Jonassen Bering, that explored the northeastern coast of Asia and the western coastline of North America, including the straits (named in Bering's honor) separating the two continents.[47] Continuing this tradition of exploration, Russian fur hunters (*promyshleniki*) and seafarers explored the entire chain of the Aleutian Islands, reached the Alaska Peninsula in the early 1760s, and began to explore the northeast coastline of modern-day Canada. These discoveries were of great commercial importance, as the newly encountered regions gave access to a vast quantity of furs, which were sold at exorbitant prices in China.[48]

The British explorations of the Pacific, especially British captain James Cook's final expedition in 1776–1780, played a role in fostering the Russian presence in the Northeast Pacific.[49] The appearance of the British in the Aleutian Islands and then in the Russian port of Petropavlovsk, in the Kamchatka Peninsula, in 1779 served as a clear and forceful reminder of both the economic value of this region and its relative defenselessness (Russia had no warships in the far northeast); Russian anxieties were exacerbated by news of the arrival of the French expedition of Jean-François de Galaup, comte de Lapérouse, at Kamchatka in the mid-1780s.

Russia's response to the news of British, Spanish, and French activity in the Pacific was to prepare its own expeditions. During the five years following Cook's final voyage, news of which reverberated from Kamchatka to St. Petersburg, the Russian government considered at least half a dozen projects for exploring the North Pacific Ocean and exploiting its latent wealth. Catherine II gave her consent to two, a scientific expedition led by Joseph Billings, a former British merchantman who was accepted into the Russian service, in 1785 and a military one led by G. Mulovskii a year later.[50] Both received expansive instructions that outlined their scientific, commercial, and political objectives. Mulovskii's instructions included a section on the question of Russian sovereignty in the North Pacific area.[51] These reflected the Russian official position that it was "indisputable" that Russia held sovereignty over the American coast from 55° 21′ N and extending thence northward, including all islands lying off the mainland of America and by the Alaska Peninsula, as well as the Kurile Islands of Japan.[52] Catherine II's December 1786 decree specified that Russian warships, "armed in the same manner as those used by the English Captain Cook," should be dispatched around the Cape of Good Hope to protect Russian possessions in the North Pacific.

Mulovskii's expedition was cancelled due to the outbreak of war with the Ottoman Empire in 1787, but it caused considerable apprehension at the Spanish court in particular because of the longtime Spanish presence on the Pacific coast of North America. Pedro Normande, the Spanish ambassador in St. Petersburg, produced a steady stream of reports on Russian discoveries and colonization in the North Pacific, which, although containing mistakes and exaggerations, painted a frightening picture of impending Russian expansion into North America.[53] It was in response to such reports that the Spanish government felt compelled to send out a new set of instructions to the colonial authorities in Mexico and lost no time in dispatching warships to establish a post in Nootka Sound to enforce its claims in the region. One of these ships was commanded by Esteban José Martínez, who, upon his arrival at Nootka on May 4, 1789, found not Russians but British and American ships there. In the ensuing confrontation Martínez quickly moved to stop foreign activities in the region and ordered the seizure of the British ships.

British prime minister William Pitt, determined to revive British power following the American War of Independence, demanded reparations and insisted upon access for British commerce and colonization along the Pacific Northwest coast. Spain agreed only to the first demand, and both sides prepared for war.[54] The Nootka Sound Crisis placed the United States and France in a difficult position. The United States was alarmed about the prospect of British invasion and occupation of Spanish territories in Florida and Louisiana, which would result in the encirclement of the United States in the east and west of the country. Equally troublesome was that France, an ally of Spain, was already caught up in revolutionary turmoil and unable to extend a helping hand to the Spaniards. The United States was thus concerned that the Franco-US alliance of 1778 might oblige it to come to Spain's aid. President Washington sought the advice of his cabinet in dealing with a potential British threat. His new administration recognized the relative weakness of the United States and the need to avoid war, but Secretary of State Thomas Jefferson and Treasury Secretary Alexander Hamilton offered conflicting counsel. The former argued that the United States should extract concessions either from Britain (withdrawal from northwestern posts and a commercial treaty) or from Spain (acquiring New Orleans, Florida, and the right to navigate the Mississippi River) as the price for American neutrality in the pending conflict.[55] Hamilton, who sought peace with Britain at any cost to protect his economic system, favored war against a weaker Spain and recommended that the British be allowed to cross US soil because the United States could neither stop them nor afford to fight another war against them.

The Nootka Sound Crisis ended when Spain chose to negotiate. According to the terms of the Nootka Sound Convention (1790), Spain permitted British trade and settlement in unoccupied areas along the Pacific coast above San Francisco. It signaled the effective end of Spain's claim to monopolize trade and colonization in the region. The Spanish concessions strengthened British claims to sovereignty in what became known as the Oregon Country.

Yet Britain was unable to exploit this concession fully because of the French Revolutionary Wars, in which it became involved in 1793. This allowed the United States to expand in later years without British opposition. The Nootka Sound incident showed the Washington administration that the United States would not be immune from European struggles and that Britain constituted the chief threat to US security. The crisis shaped two fundamental principles of American foreign policy: opposition to European colonization in the Americas (later declared in the Monroe Doctrine) and avoidance of "entangling alliances," as President Jefferson put it in his inaugural address. American leaders realized the perils caused by European rivalry in areas around the Mississippi River. Finally, this crisis led to the establishment of permanent diplomatic ties between the United States and Britain. The British government, concerned over congressional threats to impose discriminatory tariff and tonnage duties against British goods and fearful that the United States would take advantage of the crisis to expand its territory, sent its first minister to the United States, George Hammond, in 1791.

The wider significance of the Nootka Sound Crisis, however, was its demonstration of France's weakness in the international arena and the opportunity for its rivals to benefit. It also revealed the influence the French Revolution was to have in global events.

The Caribbean basin was first to experience a large-scale armed struggle that was directly provoked by the Revolution, and it later served as a vital theater of the Revolutionary Wars. Six European powers—Britain, Spain,

France, the Dutch Republic, Denmark, and Sweden—were actively vying for the Caribbean. Of these, Britain and France were particularly attentive to the region in the wake of the Seven Years' War, after which the focus of the rivalry had largely shifted away from North America and India to the Caribbean colonies.[56] France was especially sensitive to any threats to its Caribbean interests because of its growing reliance on colonial commerce. By 1787 commodities from the colonies accounted for almost 40 percent of imports, while more than a third of the French exports went to the Caribbean.[57] One contemporary warned that "in the turmoil currently sweeping through the European trading system, for France to lose sight of its [Caribbean] colonies would make it England's slave."[58]

The French Saint-Domingue (present-day Haiti) was the single richest colony in the Americas and played the leading role in sugar production. In 1789 it counted some eight thousand plantations that employed half a million slaves, who represented 89 percent of the colony's population; there were just thirty thousand white inhabitants, slightly more than the number of free people of color (*gens de couleur*).[59] Saint-Domingue was at the center both of a global commercial system that successfully circulated people, commodities, and ideas and of a complex web of diplomatic intrigues. Traditional colonial competition between European powers in the Caribbean was complicated by the outbreak of slave uprisings following the French Revolution.

Spanish domination of the Caribbean basin had kept the British and French from founding colonies there until the early seventeenth century. As the sugar, tobacco, and other plantations, which relied on slave labor, turned into a lucrative source of revenue, European powers regularly organized expeditions to try to capture rival colonies or to protect their own.[60] Due to the geography of the Caribbean, such military operations largely involved naval forces, but they were complicated by disease (most notably yellow fever) and weather. During the War of the League of Augsburg (1688–1697), the War of the Spanish Succession, and the War of the Austrian Succession, Spain, Britain, and France clashed over control of the islands, but these wars produced little effect on the balance of power in the Caribbean. The Seven Years' War, however, ended differently. The French navy was unable to protect French islands because of a stifling British blockade, and the Royal Navy swept through the region, capturing Guadeloupe, Martinique, and most other French Caribbean islands. The Treaty of Paris (1763) confirmed British possession of Dominica, St. Vincent, and Tobago, but Martinique and Guadeloupe were returned to the French in exchange for Canada.

Thirsting for revenge, France got its opportunity during the American Revolutionary War. After secretly helping the Americans, the French formally entered the war in 1778, and major fighting at sea took place in the Caribbean, with the French capturing Dominica, St. Vincent, Grenada, Tobago, St. Eustatius, and St. Kitts between 1778 and 1781 but suffering a major defeat in the Battle of the Saints (April 12, 1782), which salvaged British positions in the Caribbean. The Peace of Paris of 1783 restored most of the British islands to them, including the Bahamas, which had been captured by the Spanish in 1782. Surprisingly, the profound upheaval produced by the American Revolution had limited impact on the Caribbean colonies, and recent scholarship assigns no significant role to the American struggle against Britain in the Haitian uprising against the French masters.[61]

The French Revolution was different. It led to the start of a new conflict between Britain and France over the Caribbean because the economic importance of colonial production to European commerce ensured that there would be intense efforts to secure control of the West Indian islands. The traditional colonial rivalry, however, was complicated by slave uprisings unleashed by the Revolution. Revolutionary events in France, especially the Declaration of the Rights of Man and of the Citizen (August 1789), had an immediate effect in the French colonies, especially Saint-Domingue; there was a slave insurrection in Saint-Pierre, Martinique, in late August 1789, another in the south of Saint-Domingue in early October, and a new wave of major disturbances in the south of Martinique in November.[62] Honoré Mirabeau, one of the most prominent leaders at this early stage of the Revolution and an active member of the Société des Amis des Noirs, publicly argued that the Declaration implied that "there are not, and cannot be, either in France or in any country under French laws, any other men than free men, men equal to one another."[63] Wealthy white planters hoped to gain autonomy for themselves without risking the abolition of slavery, while free men of color desired to gain the rights listed in the Declaration of the Rights of Man and of the Citizen. White planters insisted that the Declaration did not apply to people of color, and debates over mulatto citizenship increasingly turned violent.

In September 1790 civil strife broke out between aristocratic planters and patriots of the towns of Saint-Pierre and Fort Royal on the island of Martinique. In December there were attempted insurrections in French Guiana and on the island of St. Lucia, and in April 1791 slave unrest erupted in Guadeloupe.[64] The French National Assembly's decision in May 1791 to grant full citizenship to all financially qualified men born of free fathers and mothers led to open street battles in Port-au-Prince in Saint-Domingue, and by early November 1791 several parishes in Martinique were roiled by slave revolts.[65] The question of freedom and citizenship as well as the ongoing political turmoil incited slaves to rise up against their masters in the densely settled plains and hills of Saint-Domingue's northern provinces.[66] Nonetheless, this strife in the French colonies did not immediately divide plantation owners and their slaves. Throughout 1790 and 1791 the former successfully employed the latter to bolster their military strength and to overcome their revolutionary rivals. Between 1790 and 1792 the royalists triumphed in Guadeloupe and Martinique, but in both cases they owed their victories to having armed the slaves. Indeed, throughout this period both the patriots and the royalists competed in their efforts to attract the rebel slaves to their side.[67] By the summer of 1791, however, the revolutionary turmoil began to be felt outside the French colonies as well. Within a month of the initial uprising, British authorities were able to contain threats of slave uprisings in Jamaica.[68] The British sent a delegation to the French plantation owners with an offer of aid against slaves. The Spanish in the eastern half of the island, meanwhile, exploited an opportunity to enrich themselves by selling arms and supplies to the insurgent slaves. Though relations between whites and mulattos remained tense, the free colored militia were key in fighting the slave rebels and in the process accelerated recognition of their civil rights. On April 4, 1792, the French National Assembly extended citizenship to all free men of color, hoping this measure would win their loyalty and support.[69] Just sixteen days later started a war that changed the world.

CHAPTER 3 | The War of the First Coalition, 1792–1797

THE WAR THAT BEGAN in April 1792 was France's first conflict against a continental power since the end of the Seven Years' War thirty years earlier. And it began abysmally for the French, whose armies had already been affected by the pre-revolutionary financial crisis and then crippled by the mass emigration of noble-born officers, the breakdown of discipline and attendant mutinies, and an overall lack of equipment and supplies. France was isolated diplomatically as well. And, despite the revolutionaries' claims, there was no immediate similar revolutionary response in the rest of Europe. Distance, aristocratic control, and state constraints kept the news out of northern, southern, and eastern Europe, where the established order held fast; only in Poland were the reformers able to act upon their enthusiasm, but even there success proved short-lived.

Fighting began when French forces invaded the Austrian Netherlands (modern Belgium) and gained some success in the border regions. This proved to be the extent of the French success at this stage of the war. In the spring and summer of 1792 French troops suffered a series of setbacks as Austro-Prussian forces under Charles William Ferdinand, duke of Brunswick-Wolfenbüttel, invaded France and slowly advanced toward Paris. On July 25, 1792, the Allies issued a warning—the so-called Brunswick Manifesto—threatening to "exact an exemplary and forever memorable vengeance by giving Paris over to martial law and complete destruction" if the French royal family was harmed. The manifesto, one of the most notorious documents in modern European history, represented a rather peculiar ultimatum—it started somewhat conciliatorily and stressed that Allies had no desire "to meddle in internal politics of France" before employing direct threats if the

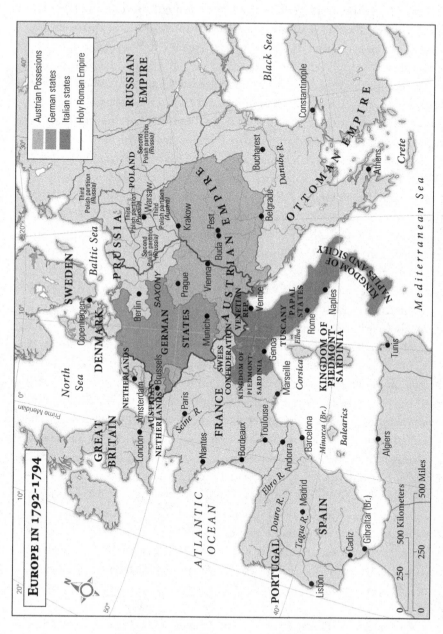

Map 3: Europe in 1792–1794

French failed to meet its demands. As so often in the time of conflict, the manifesto produced precisely the opposite effect from the one intended and merely fanned the flames of revolutionary fervor in Paris. The Allies intended it as a warning, but it played into the hands of French revolutionary propagandists, who presented it as a direct threat to the nation's existence and contributed to a new round of revolutionary violence in Paris. On August 10, 1792, crowds stormed the Tuileries palace and imprisoned the royal family. In September the new legislature, the National Convention, abolished the French monarchy, proclaimed a republic, and turned to the challenging task of defending France. "La Patrie en danger!" was the rallying cry that the French revolutionaries used to mobilize forces to defend the nation.

Not without cause. A Prussian army (with some Austrian support) was already beyond Longwy, some two hundred miles from Paris, with nothing to stop them from marching directly on Paris except for the unwillingness of their commander, the duke of Brunswick. For all the ferocity expressed in his manifesto, Charles William Ferdinand disapproved of his mission, and having reached the Meuse River, he halted, claiming further advance impossible; only the unexpected surrender of the fortress of Verdun shamed him to move forward. At the small town of Valmy, about 150 miles from Paris, Brunswick encountered a hastily reorganized French army under the command of Generals Charles Dumouriez and François Kellermann. On September 20, 1792, he marched out to attack what seemed to be ill-disciplined throngs of Frenchmen but came under fire from French guns. The artillery was the branch of service least affected by the Revolution and therefore still staffed with professionals. Deployed on the rolling hills of Valmy, the French gunners refused to be silenced by the Prussian counterfire and kept targeting the advancing enemy infantry with what soon came to be called "the cannonade of Valmy." As the Prussians wavered, Kellermann raised his hat and cried, "Vive la Nation!"—a sentiment picked up again and again by almost the entire French army. With the French soldiers cheering and eager to fight, the duke of Brunswick seized his chance to break off the campaign, declaring the French position impregnable and calling back his men.

The Battle of Valmy, such as it was, constituted a crucial French strategic and political victory, for it stopped the Austro-Prussian advance and protected the revolutionary government. The patriotic emotions stirred by the cries of "La Patrie en danger!" were bolstered by the national pride in defeating the veterans of Frederick the Great. Moreover, the French forces seized the initiative to more vigorously prosecute the war: General Adam Custine crossed the Rhine from Alsace and occupied Mainz and Frankfurt in October, while Dumouriez moved into the Austrian Netherlands, defeating the

Austrians at Jemappes on November 6. This battle marked one of the turning points in the war. as the French followed up by occupying much of the Austrian Netherlands and sending a squadron up the Scheldt to besiege Antwerp. Simultaneously, French troops also occupied Savoy and Nice, on the Italian front line. The victories in the fall of 1792 seemed in many respects a miraculous deliverance for France, but their root causes lay in several factors, including internal disagreements between the coalition partners and their preoccupation with events in Poland; the growing numerical superiority of the French troops, who had demonstrated a rousing spirit to fight (*élan*) that surprised their opponents; and adoption of military reforms long advocated by great French military theorists such as Jacques Antoine Hippolyte, comte de Guibert.[1]

Despite these victories, 1793 started badly for France. European monarchies were incensed by the execution of King Louis XVI on January 21 and the National Convention's proclamation that it was waging a popular crusade against privilege and tyranny. The revolutionaries' desire to establish direct relations with peoples, going over the heads of their monarchs, posed a direct challenge to existing regimes. The so-called Edict of Fraternity, issued by the National Convention on November 19, gave further alarm to monarchical states; revolutionary France promised "fraternity and assistance to all peoples who wish to recover their liberty," in effect offering an open invitation for the overthrow of existing regimes. The Edict of Fraternity did indeed inspire would-be revolutionaries in other parts of Europe, even those countries not at war with France, to challenge their existing governments. In Britain, for example, the French embassy held receptions for deputations from the local radical societies, including the Norwich Revolutionary Society and the Manchester Constitutional Society, which expressed their joy at seeing France "fulfilling its great destinies," as one public declaration stated, and welcomed donations in money and armaments that the English radicals offered to the revolutionary armies in Belgium.[2]

The edict reinforced belief among many French revolutionaries (and the public in general) that continued French expansion was a moral imperative. This was, in the words of the great French historian Albert Mathiez, "the apogee of the cosmopolitan and humanitarian policy" of the Revolution as "the emancipatory propaganda took the form of tutelage, almost of a dictatorship. Revolutionary France recognized that free peoples left to themselves were incapable of imitating its example on their own." The French revolutionaries had to assist these peoples in carrying out revolution for them, without them, and if need be against them.[3] French expansion into the neighboring territories soon revealed a more sinister side. The Edict of

Fraternity's idealism was largely subverted by the law of December 15, 1792, that decreed how the "liberated" peoples would defray the costs of French military occupation. European radicals soon discovered that protesting against the excesses of French occupation brought harassment, fines, and imprisonment. Already in January 1793, Georg Forster, a German radical who initially welcomed the French troops into the Rhineland, bitterly complained that the lofty ideals of the Revolution were compromised on a daily basis and "the brigandage of troops has succeeded all too well in alienating souls and diverting them from the project of giving themselves to France.... The inhabitants would been less cruelly deceived if the [French] troops had told them upon arrival, 'We have come to take everything from you.'"[4]

The Revolution posed a threat not because it was impelled by powerful ideas but because those ideas carried guns. The other countries of Europe were quite capable of suppressing their own revolutionaries. When accused of making war on revolutionary "opinion," the British prime minister famously replied, "It is not so. We are not in arms against the opinions of the closet, nor the speculations of the schools. We are at war with *armed* opinions."[5] It was the power of the reformed French armies that made revolution dangerous. Early on, the French revolutionary government did reveal plenty of sincere idealism in its foreign policy and even passed a decree repudiating conquests and territorial aggrandizement.[6] But by late 1792, having experienced a first taste of success, the Revolution's "war for liberty" had evolved into a conflict for more traditional objectives. The French conquests in the Rhineland threatened Austrian interests, while the invasion of the Austrian Netherlands and the opening of the Scheldt estuary—which had been closed by the Treaty of Westphalia in 1648 but was opened by the French in mid-November 1792, providing them with direct access to the North Sea—struck at the heart of British security and trade, which rested on the premise that no other great maritime power held control of any Channel ports.

The revolution thus threatened the status quo. The intensity of Europe's response to the revolution was, in part, caused by a clear contrast between France's self-proclaimed mission to "free" the continent and the military occupation that this entailed. The Revolution's universal principles were indeed welcomed by many in neighboring countries, but the French occupation bred resentment and hostility among the larger populations, as the supposed beneficiaries of emancipation began to feel very much like the victims of what one British observer dubbed "the homicidal philanthropy of France."[7]

In the spring of 1793, most European states, including Britain, Prussia, Austria, Spain, and Naples, joined their efforts in the First Coalition against

France; the pope lent his moral support to the coalition. By declaring war on Britain the French republic had introduced a new dimension into the struggle: the sea. Neither Austria nor Prussia had significant naval resources, but Britain, of course, was indisputably the supreme naval power, and now it used its vast naval resources to pursue French commercial and military targets. The Allies opened a new offensive, with the British attacking French merchantmen and interdicting maritime shipments, the Prussians besieging Mainz in the Rhineland, and the Austrians seeking to reclaim the Austrian Netherlands. The French were defeated at Neerwinden on March 18, and Brussels was retaken by the Austrians.

Bad news kept coming for the French.[8] Army commander General Dumouriez, fearful for his own life after the success of his political rivals in Paris, defected to the coalition.[9] General Custine suffered a defeat against the Austrian, Hanoverian, and British forces of Prince Josias of Saxe-Coburg-Saalfeld near Valenciennes on May 21–23 and was unable to relieve the besieged fortress of Condé; recalled to Paris, Custine was charged with treason and prosecuted by the Revolutionary Tribunal, which found him guilty on August 27 and had him guillotined the following day. By the end of the summer of 1793, the Austrians and Prussians had pushed the French out of all of Belgium and the Rhineland, the Spanish army threatened France from the south, and the British continued to blockade much of the French coastline. Counterrevolutionary insurrections raged in the west of France; meanwhile, acrimonious struggle among the various revolutionary groups and the resulting civil and political instability and administrative impasse left the armies of the Republic lacking in supplies and pay and suffering from low morale. In late August the city of Toulon, on the Mediterranean coastline, became a symbol of France's political problems. First, the city's moderate republicans rebelled against the radical policies of the Jacobins, but they were soon supplanted by the royalists, who invited Anglo-Spanish forces to take over the city. Admiral Sir Samuel Hood of the Royal Navy and Spanish admiral Juan de Langara could hardly believe the opportunity they had been handed. In just one stroke, they had seized one of France's key naval arsenals along with twenty-six ships-of-the-line (about one-third of France's entire fleet).[10]

As the Republic faltered in the face of foreign invasion, internal insurrection, and economic crisis, the revolutionary leadership grew more radical. In June 1793, the Jacobin faction seized control of the government. Facing an extremely volatile domestic and international situation, the Jacobins called for extraordinary measures to protect the nation and the revolutionary ideals. They believed that only strong and centralized leadership could save the

Republic. Such was provided by the twelve-member Committee of Public Safety (CPS), which introduced radical reforms to achieve greater social equality and political democracy and began imposing the government's authority throughout the nation through violent repression and terror.

In the interest of the nation's defense, the CPS launched a *levée en masse*—the masterwork of minister of war Lazare Carnot—that mobilized the resources of the entire nation. "From this moment until that in which the enemy shall have been driven from the soil of the Republic," stated the National Convention's decree of August 23, "all Frenchmen are in permanent requisition for the service of the armies." In a remarkable administrative feat, the revolutionary government had raised an astonishing fourteen new armies and equipped some 800,000 men within a year. The CPS introduced universal conscription of all single men ages eighteen to twenty-five, requisitioned supplies from individual citizens, and ensured that factories and mines produced at full capacity. The success of this mass mobilization was aided by a vast state propaganda campaign that touted the *levée en masse* as a patriotic duty aimed at defending *la patrie* against tyranny and foreign threats. Citizens not privileged to bear arms and fight on the front line were encouraged to work harder to make up for it. These messages were spread via posters, broadsides, leaflets, and newspapers, while speakers and decorated veterans toured the country to rouse the masses. In creating the "nation in arms," the Jacobins heralded the emergence of modern warfare.[11]

The citizen soldiers of the Republic proved their worth on the battlefields. In September 1793 General Jean Nicolas Houchard defeated the Anglo-Hanoverian army at Hondschoote, in Flanders, while Jean-Baptiste Jourdan routed the Austrians at Wattignies on October 15–16, thus turning the tide of war against the First Coalition. Two months later the French army drove the Anglo-Spanish force out of the strategically important port of Toulon, where an obscure artillery major named Napoleon Bonaparte first distinguished himself. In the west of France, the revolutionary armies brutally suppressed the royalist revolt in the Vendée.[12] After General Jourdan's victory at Fleurus on June 26, 1794, the French pushed back the coalition forces along the northern frontier and reclaimed Belgium and the Rhineland; in January 1795 the Dutch Texel fleet of fourteen ships-of-the-line was trapped in ice and captured by a French squadron of hussars and an infantry company riding pillion behind them—the only example in history of a cavalry capturing a fleet.

In the south, the French revolutionary armies occupied Savoy and kept the Spaniards at bay on the Pyrenean front. The French naval campaign was less successful, largely due to the loss of the officer corps and partly as a result of losses sustained at Toulon, where a significant part of its fleet was captured or destroyed by the British. In the months following, the British Royal Navy carried out a successful offensive in the Canadian Maritime Provinces and the West Indies, seizing the islands of St. Pierre, Miquelon, and Tobago, and invading Martinique and Saint-Domingue (though the French managed to recover them later). Meanwhile, in European waters, the Royal Navy extended His Britannic Majesty's protection to the island of Corsica and celebrated victory at the Battle of the Glorious First of June.[13] However, it failed to attain the larger strategic goal of intercepting the grain convoy delivering supplies for the starving French population.[14]

French naval setbacks, however, were more than compensated for on land, where a war that begun in defense of the Revolution and for the liberation of oppressed people had turned into one of conquest and plunder. French military successes were facilitated by political rivalries between the Allied powers. Prussia, Austria, and Russia were preoccupied with the Partitions of Poland, diverting considerable resources and political will away from France. Furthermore, financial exhaustion and two years of campaigning with no tangible results sapped any enthusiasm for war in some countries. The favorable progression of the war made the excesses of the Jacobins seem increasingly unnecessary. Indeed, the excesses caused moderates in the Convention to overthrow the CPS in July 1794 and reverse some of the more radical reforms it had introduced. After the dismantling of the CPS, more moderate leaders took control. The Reign of Terror came to a halt, and the National Convention adopted a new constitution that reflected the desire for stability without sacrificing, so it announced, the ideals of 1789. The new French government—the five-member Executive Directory and two legislative councils—was battered from all sides: on the right, royalists sought to restore the monarchy, while on the left, Jacobin hopes of reclaiming power were revived by continuing economic problems.[15]

Despite these challenges, the Directory proved to be the longest-lived of all the revolutionary governments, though its politics were a seesaw: in the first two years the Directory moved to the right until it was threatened by the resurgence of royalism, whereupon it veered back to the left, which in turn encouraged the revival of Jacobinism. Historians have long condemned the Directory for its weakness, corruption, inept domestic and foreign policy, and financial incompetence, which in turn seemingly justified its overthrow by General Bonaparte. However, it is clear now that the essential institutions of the Consulate and Empire were already in working order under the Directory, which earnestly pursued the centralization and consolidation of government administration. Nonetheless, the Directory also lacked public confidence from its inception. Emotionally exhausted by years of economic, social, and political turmoil, many French citizens fell into a mood of indifference or cynicism.

Despite the successive coups aimed at strengthening its position, the Directory grew weaker and increasingly had to appeal to the military for support.

By the opening months of 1795, France had control of Belgium, Luxembourg, and the left (west) bank of the Rhine, which had now become integral parts of the French Republic.[16] The spring campaign brought new victories to the French arms as an invasion across the Pyrenees and victories in the Rhineland caused the First Coalition to crumble. Tuscany withdrew its unofficial support, and it was quickly followed by the new Batavian (Dutch) Republic in May. On July 22, 1795, Spain, which two years earlier had declared war on revolutionary France to stave off the threatening ideology of liberty, equality, and fraternity, was forced to sue for peace after continued military setbacks.[17] Peace offered a poor alternative for Spain given that Britain now targeted Spanish shipping, which compelled Madrid to sign a treaty of alliance (the Treaty of Ildefonso) with France, bringing Spain into the war against England. Thus, within a year of signing a peace with France, Spain found itself once more at war, with Britain blockading Spanish ports and attacking the Spanish arsenal at Ferrol.

Equally critical was France's success with Prussia, which had hinted at its withdrawal from war in 1794. During negotiations held in the Swiss city of Basle, Prussian diplomats were left in no doubt of French determination to carry on the war—"We shall trace with a sure hand the natural limits of the Republic. We shall make sure of the rivers which, after watering several of our departments, take their course towards the sea, and limit the countries now subject to our arms," declared one French delegate—but were more concerned about the events in the east, where Russia was preparing for the final partitioning of Poland.[18] According to the terms of the Treaty of Basle, signed on April 5, 1795, Prussia withdrew from war and recognized French control of the left bank of the Rhine, while France returned all of the lands east of the Rhine captured during the war.

The Treaty of Basle marked a crucial moment in German history and was, at least according to one historian, a "death certificate" of the Holy Roman Empire, since Prussia "rejected *Reich* [empire] in favor of *raison d'état.*"[19] The treaty not only consolidated French control of the Rhineland but divided Germany into two spheres of influence, drawing a virtual line at the Main River, north of which the German states—Hesse-Cassel, Nassau, and the states of the Swabian Circle (*Reichkreis*)—soon followed Prussia in deserting the imperial cause and accepting neutrality agreements with France. The treaty aroused loud criticism in Germany, and anti-Prussian attitudes were felt very deeply in many southern German states, helping shape their policies in the decades ahead.

With key coalition partners Prussia and Spain out of the war, France still faced Britain on the seas and Austria and its Italian allies on the continent. In the Mediterranean, French and British navies fought inconclusive actions in the Gulf of Genoa (March 13–14, 1795) and at Hyères (July 13). Elsewhere, the British narrowly escaped being trounced at the hands of a larger French force off Belle Isle on June 17, while Admiral Alexander Hood (Lord Bridport) captured several French vessels in a naval engagement off Île de Groix (June 23) but squandered a unique opportunity to incapacitate the entire French Atlantic fleet.[20]

On the continent, French military operations were confined to two key front lines: the Rhineland and northwestern Italy. In the former, four years of incessant warfare had left the region completely despoiled; one French general recalled that by the spring of 1796 parts of the Rhineland were so "exhausted that it was virtually impossible to make war there before the next harvest came in."[21] Nevertheless, France had its largest armies—General Jourdan's Sambre-et-Meuse (78,000 men) and General Jean Moreau's Rhin-et-Moselle (80,000 men)—deployed here. Facing them was the newly appointed Austrian commander, Archduke Charles, brother of the Austrian emperor, who commanded some 90,000 men.[22] Jourdan's offensive across the Rhine, which opened on June 10, enabled Moreau to cross the river at Strasbourg, but the French offensive soon ground to a halt. Archduke Charles soundly defeated Jourdan at Amberg (August 24) and Würzburg (September 3), forcing the French back along the Rhine and leading to an armistice. Meanwhile, Moreau had defeated an Austrian force at Friedberg on August 23, but after hearing of Jourdan's repulse, he recrossed the Rhine on October 26.[23]

The French war effort was saved by Napoleon Bonaparte, who took command of the Armée d'Italie in April 1796, at the age of twenty-seven.[24] Facing slightly larger Austrian-Piedmontese armies, commanded by septuagenarian Feldzeugmeister Johann Peter Beaulieu, Napoleon attacked the junction between the two forces on early April, and after scoring a victory at Montenotte (April 12), he interposed his forces between the Piedmontese and the Austrians, thus introducing one of the key traits of his later campaigns—dividing separate elements of a numerically superior enemy in order to defeat their smaller, constituent parts. Holding a central position, Bonaparte proceeded to engage the Piedmontese and Austrians, driving them farther apart and defeating them piecemeal. Within two weeks of the start of the war, Bonaparte occupied the Piedmontese capital city of Turin and forced the Piedmontese to sue for peace.[25] He then pursued the retreating Austrian forces, scoring an important victory over the Austrian rear guard at Lodi, a battle that came to establish his destiny as a hero both to his men and to the nation—not without reason. Throughout the summer and fall of 1796

Bonaparte outmaneuvered his Austrian opponents, scoring major victories at Castiglione (August 5) and Bassano (September 8) and besieging the great fortress of Mantua, where half the Austrian troops were penned up.[26] Reinforcements from Germany, led by Feldzeugmeister Joseph Alvinczi von Borberek, enabled the Austrians to attempt to relieve besieged Mantua, but after a three-day battle at Arcola (November 15–17), Bonaparte forced them to retreat. After another Austrian attempt at relieving the fortress suffered a decisive defeat at Rivoli in January 1797, the Austrian garrison at Mantua capitulated, bringing to an end all Austrian resistance in Italy.[27] Bonaparte's subsequent crossing of the Alps and invasion of Austria prompted the Viennese court to request an armistice.

The Treaty of Campo Formio, concluded on October 17, marked a critical moment in the Revolutionary Wars. The War of the First Coalition was effectively over, and France was triumphant. Lands ceded to the French Republic included the Austrian Netherlands; although the treaty did not contain any major provisions relevant to the Batavian (Dutch) Republic, it effectively recognized the republic's existence under the French sphere of influence.[28] Austria was forced to recognize French satellite republics in northern and central Italy, and consented to the French claims on the left bank of the Rhine River, including the strategic cities of Mannheim and Mainz.[29] Austria received compensation in the form of Venice, but France was to keep the Venetian dominions in the Adriatic Sea and Eastern Mediterranean, including the island of Corfu.[30]

The Treaty of Campo Formio effectively placed the Low Countries and northern Italy under French control, rendering France a hegemonic power in Western Europe, with Britain its only remaining major rival. Bonaparte's insistence on the occupation of the Ionian Islands, former Venetian possessions, brought the French interest to the Adriatic shores, significantly improved its position in the eastern Mediterranean, and introduced revolutionary ideals to the Balkan peninsula, especially in Greece. The treaty, which Bonaparte settled largely without reference to Paris for instructions, demonstrated his elevation from a mere soldier of the Republic to a statesman who harbored great political ambitions. Yet as advantageous as the treaty was, it still faced resistance from the Directory, which insisted on even better terms, especially with respect to the Rhineland, where the frontier was not formally secured. Considering public enthusiasm for the peace, however, the Directory and the legislative councils felt compelled to accept it.[31]

British spirits, dampened by the steady reports of the French triumphs on the continent, received a much-needed tonic with the news of the Royal Navy's triumphs on the seas. In 1795, the French takeover of the Dutch Republic had given Britain a unique opportunity to penetrate the Dutch colonial empire. A year later, after the Treaty of San Ildefonso allied France and Spain, Britain feared the prospects of facing a combined Franco-Spanish fleet that could harass its trade and impair communications with its colonies. Indeed, the Spanish declaration of war and Bonaparte's victories in Italy made the Royal Navy's position in much of the western Mediterranean untenable. Its ships could no longer easily replenish their supplies, and it faced a Franco-Spanish fleet that was more than twice its size. The British were therefore forced to evacuate the islands of Corsica and Elba and consolidate their positions around Gibraltar and Sicily, while seeking to defeat their opponents piecemeal.

The British got their opportunity in early 1797, when the British squadron (fifteen ships-of-the-line) commanded by Admiral Sir John Jervis learned about the Spanish fleet sailing near Cadiz, attempting to join with the French fleet at Brest for a possible invasion of Ireland. Unaware of the enemy fleet's size, Jervis quickly sailed to intercept it. As a thick fog enveloped the choppy seas of Cape St. Vincent on February 14, the British engaged the Spanish fleet, commanded by Admiral Don José de Córdoba y Ramos. The start of the battle led to a memorable exchange between Jervis, who was unaware that he was outnumbered two to one, and his captains, who counted the Spanish warships as they emerged through the mist:

> "There are eight sail-of-the-line, Sir John."—"Very well, Sir."
> "There are twenty sail-of-the-line, Sir John."—"Very well, Sir."
> "There are twenty-five sail-of-the-line, Sir John"—"Very well, Sir."
> "There are twenty-seven sail, Sir John!"...—"Enough, Sir, no more of that: the die is cast; and if there are fifty sail, I will go through them."[32]

Go through them he did. Jervis cut the Spanish line in two, while his better-trained and better-commanded crews outclassed their foes, killing or wounding more than 3,500 Spaniards. Captain Horatio Nelson, commanding HMS *Captain*, distinguished himself by a daring and unconventional maneuver that resulted in the capture of two Spanish warships.

The Battle of Cape St. Vincent was a major strategic victory for Britain. Although in the end Spain's losses in ships were slight (four ships captured), its fleet took refuge in Cadiz, where it was blockaded by the British. The battle thus put an end to any French plans for an invasion of Ireland and, more important, demoralized the Spanish navy and made it reluctant to join France in future operations.[33]

The memories of victory at St. Vincent were still fresh when the British celebrated another triumph, this time nearer to home. After occupying the Dutch Republic, France sought to utilize Dutch naval resources to replenish its ravaged fleet but was unable to move Dutch warships due to the ongoing British blockade. In the fall of 1797, taking advantage of a number of mutinies that hampered Britain's Channel Fleet, the Dutch fleet (eleven ships-of-the-line and more than a dozen other warships) under Vice Admiral Jan de Winter sailed out into the North Sea but was intercepted by the British squadron under Admiral Adam Duncan, who commanded fourteen ships-of-the-line and ten other warships. The ensuing battle at Camperdown resulted in a decisive British victory. The Dutch fleet attacked in two loose formations and got overwhelmed by the far superior British warships. With a desperate final effort, the Dutch tried to escape into shallower waters but were pursued and forced to surrender by the British, who claimed eleven warships, including seven ships-of-the-line.

The Battle of Camperdown was rightly celebrated as one of the greatest victories of the British fleet to date. Its effects were immediate and widespread: it struck a severe blow to Dutch and French ambitions, further consolidated the Royal Navy's positions in the northern Atlantic, and eased the pressure of Britain's naval resources.[34]

Perhaps the most obvious victim of the First Coalition War was the Polish state. As previously noted, French military successes in Italy, the Low Countries, and the Rhineland had been facilitated by Prussia, Austria, and Russia's preoccupation with the fate of Poland. As we've seen, the Second Partition of Poland (1792–1793) produced decisive results, though it also created an inherently unstable situation. Russia's position on the Polish issue was unambiguously in favor of further expansion; Austria clearly resented exclusion from the Second Partition; and Prussia openly desired additional lands as well. The establishment of Russian hegemony promoted resentment and indignation within what was left of Poland. Indeed, Russo-Polish relations rapidly deteriorated, reaching a nadir on March 12, 1794, when General Antoni Madalinski rejected Russian demands to disband the Polish-Lithuanian army. This sparked a general outbreak of anti-Russian riots throughout the country.

The uprising quickly spread through the Polish lands, and Tadeusz Kościuszko (Thaddeus Kosciusko), a veteran of the American Revolutionary War, was invited to lead the insurrection. Kościuszko returned to Poland in late March 1794 and called the Poles to arms. The Polish army, undermanned and poorly trained (some peasants were armed with scythes), achieved a surprising victory over the numerically and technically superior Russian force at

Raclawice on April 4, 1794. The initial Polish success greatly alarmed Catherine II, who called on Frederick William II of Prussia for military support. In May 1794 the Russian army, supported by Prussian troops in the west, began a counteroffensive. During the summer Polish armies suffered major defeats at Szczekociny and Chelm; Prussian troops occupied Kraków and, together with Russian forces, began a siege of Warsaw. Kościuszko's troops managed to win several minor clashes and lift the siege of Warsaw but soon suffered a crucial defeat at Maciejowice on October 10; Kościuszko himself was wounded and taken prisoner by the Russians, depriving the Poles of their charismatic and capable leader. Between November 4 and 9, the Russian army under General Alexander Suvorov stormed the Warsaw suburb of Praga, where thousands of residents were massacred by the Russian troops. The last Polish troops surrendered to the Russian army at Radoszyce on November 17.

These Russian military victories gave Catherine II the political initiative in postwar settlement talks, though she also recognized the need to gratify other powers: Prussia was not going to evacuate the occupied Polish territory, and Austria, disgruntled at its exclusion in 1793, would not allow itself to be excluded once again. The three powers, therefore, had to agree to jointly carry out the Third Partition, which eliminated the Polish-Lithuanian Commonwealth. The negotiations turned out to be prolonged and complex, reflecting increased tensions between Austria and Prussia due to their unsuccessful campaigns against France. Russia exploited these divisions to consolidate its gains. Catherine II quickly negotiated an agreement with Austria and, seeking to restrain Prussia's territorial appetite, supported Vienna over Berlin. The Prussian intransigence led to the secret Russo-Austrian treaty (January 1795) directed against Frederick William II, who, fearing a potential war, hurried to conclude a peace with France at Basle in April so he could deal with the Russo-Austrian maneuvering in Poland in October 1795. Under the agreement, which was further modified in 1796–1797 and became known as the Third Partition of Poland, Russia received some 46,000 square miles (120,000 square kilometers) of the Polish territory and 1.2 million inhabitants, Prussia claimed over 18,000 square miles (48,000 square kilometers) and just over 1 million new subjects, and Austria gained about 18,000 square miles (47,000 square kilometers) and 1.5 million inhabitants.

The three partitions of Poland were a genuine tour de force of imperial expansion. Poland had effectively ceased to exist, and to underline how momentous this outcome was, all three powers agreed to never use the name Poland in any official documentation. The Poles would not see an independent state until after World War I. The third-largest continental state had been wiped off the map of Europe, and the balance of power in eastern Europe was profoundly changed. Poland paid a dear price for the absence of outside support. France, a traditional ally of the Poles, was consumed by revolutionary turmoil and unable to offer anything. Britain also had its hands tied due to the nature of the conflict in Poland. Diplomatic representations alone were unlikely to have any impact as long as Britain could not afford military intervention; the English man of letters Horace Walpole remarked that the British fleet would have to "be towed overland to Warsaw" to have any effect on the partitioning powers.[35]

The limitations of British power in Poland were more than offset when it came to the overseas regions. While the war began in Europe and would be primarily fought there, Britain had understood from the outset that this would be a global conflict, one that could deal another severe blow to France (after its defeat in the Seven Years' War), consolidate British command of the seas, and underpin the growing British economy. The West and East Indies represented major commercial hubs, accounting for a large share of British and French overseas trade, so controlling these regions offered immense financial benefits. Furthermore, the British government was concerned about the spread of republican ideals to the Caribbean, where just 50,000 British colonists maintained almost half a million slaves. The British entry into the war in 1793 meant that the War of the First Coalition acquired a global dimension, one that, as we will see, kept expanding with each passing year. Yet implementing a successful global strategy would prove to be hard.

The British presence in the West Indies was concentrated at Jamaica and Barbados. Given the vagaries of wind and weather, the Royal Navy made the decision to split its forces into two commands: Vice Admiral Sir John Laforey commanded a small squadron at Barbados, while Commodore John Ford stationed his ships at Jamaica. Neither squadron was particularly strong; the largest Royal Navy ships were the fifty-gun *Trusty* and *Europa*. Therefore, upon the start of the war, the most pressing need was to reinforce these two commands with additional vessels. Accordingly, Rear Admiral Gardner sailed with seven ships-of-the-line (and two infantry regiments) to the West Indies in late March 1793.[36]

The outbreak of a general European war in 1793 had of course weakened France's hold on its colonies. Spain threatened Saint-Domingue from Santo Domingo (modern-day Dominican Republic), while the slave rebels also had to contend with the United States, which supported the white settler community with approximately $400,000 in aid until 1804.[37] Britain—exploiting this occasion to take control of Saint-Domingue outright, thereby securing its holdings in the Caribbean against slave rebellion, and laying claim to the lucrative sugar and coffee plantations—dispatched considerable forces to the region. The British involvement began in the spring of 1793 when Vice Admiral Sir John Laforey's squadron transported British forces to capture the island of Tobago, which the British lost to the French during the American Revolution; the island surrendered on April 15 after the British landed a small force, attacked the fort of Scarborough, and forced the island's French garrison to capitulate.

After his arrival at Barbados, Rear Admiral Alan Gardner unsuccessfully attempted to take the island of Martinique. The French governor of Martinique, General Donatien Rochambeau, was in the midst of putting down a royalist revolt when a British expedition arrived in June. Despite being supported by several hundred royalists, the British attack on St. Pierre on June 18 failed after running into stiff republican resistance. The British withdrew and evacuated more than five thousand royalist refugees.[38] More successful was Commodore John Ford, commander of the Jamaica station, who in September 1793 captured Môle-Saint-Nicolas, one of the best harbors in the Caribbean, with the support of planters who had become wary of the French revolutionaries' radicalism.

In late 1793 British secretary of war Henry Dundas drew up plans for a large expedition to the Caribbean to be commanded by Lieutenant General Sir Charles Grey and Vice Admiral Sir John Jervis. Events in Europe postponed the dispatch of this expedition until November, and despite being promised more than 16,000 men, Jervis and Grey received just over 7,000 men because of Britain's increased European commitments. It was only in the early spring of 1794 that Jervis and Grey undertook large-scale operations against French colonies in the West Indies. They first targeted—again—Martinique, which was attacked in February 1794. Despite possessing detailed plans of the French defenses, provided by the royalists, the British attack stalled at the forts protecting Fort-de-France, where Rochambeau was able to hold out until March 25, thereby costing the British nearly a month and half of the campaign season.

Nevertheless, the eventual British capture of Martinique was a major strategic success because it denied France its major naval and commercial base in the region. The British followed up on this victory with a quick sweep of the West Indies, capturing the islands of St. Lucia and Guadeloupe in April 1794 and occupying Port-au-Prince, the capital of Saint-Domingue, in June. Yet these victories also proved to be costly to British manpower, which found itself stretched between far-flung islands and suffering greatly from yellow fever. The unexpected arrival of a small French force of two frigates and transports resulted in the expulsion of the British from Guadeloupe by December 1794. Grey and Jervis tried to strike back but were repelled in July 1795.

With the French firmly in control of Guadeloupe, the British faced the daunting challenge of containing a wave of slave revolts that spread across the islands of the West Indies. In 1796 the British government conceived a new campaign in the Caribbean, preparing to dispatch some 30,000 soldiers. Severe storms prevented these forces from leaving European waters until late 1795, but in early spring 1796, once the weather improved, Rear Admiral Hugh Christian and Major General Ralph Abercromby crossed the Atlantic. Abercromby landed on St. Lucia in late April; the French garrison put up stiff resistance but was forced to surrender after a month-long siege. Leaving a strong garrison on this island, Abercromby then sailed to St. Vincent and Grenada, both of which were quickly secured.

During the summer of 1796 the British made little progress in the West Indies, as disease claimed some 6,500 troops and confined another 4,000 to the hospitals; barely a third of the original forces were fit for duty by January 1797. Meanwhile, in Europe, France had by this point forced Prussia and Spain out of the war, the latter power switching sides to oppose Britain, as we've seen, and thus forcing the Pitt government to end its offensive in the Caribbean. When Spain declared war on Britain on October 8, 1796, Britain decided to target the vulnerable Spanish colonial possessions, starting with the Rio de la Plata and Trinidad. The former expedition was cancelled due to lack of available ships, while the mission to Trinidad was delayed until early 1797 because of difficulty in obtaining shipping and the news of General Louis Lazare Hoche's expedition to Ireland. In mid-February 1797 Admiral Henry Harvey and General Abercromby finally set course for Trinidad, which was captured after brief resistance. In April, the British commanders proceeded to Puerto Rico, landing east of San Juan on April 18. The Spanish governor, Don Ramón de Castro, refused the British demand to surrender, instead reinforcing the island's defenses. After several failed attempts to advance on the formidable fortifications of San Juan, Abercromby abandoned his plans and evacuated his forces during the night of April 30.[39] With hurricane season approaching, Harvey then chose to end the entire campaign.

The naval operations of 1795–1797 constituted some of the largest overseas expeditions ever mounted by Britain and involved more than 25,000 troops; combined with the forces already in the West Indies, this accounted for almost half of the British army. Yet, considering the vast resources in manpower and funds that they required, they produced limited results. In the words of one British naval historian, with the failure of the British attack on Puerto Rico, "the heyday of Caribbean warfare was over."[40] Britain instead focused on retaining key conquests rather than continuing its offensives.

The French-held Saint-Domingue served as a center for the revolutionary tumult in the Caribbean. Jacobin commissioners sent from Paris to Saint-Domingue emancipated all the slaves in the French colonies (a move confirmed by the National Convention in Paris in February 1794) and enlisted the support of free men of color against foreign invaders.[41] One such new ally was Toussaint Bréda Louverture, a former slave coachman who had fought in Spanish ranks before joining the French.[42] An effective leader and capable commander, Louverture contributed to a French victory and the withdrawal of Spanish troops in 1795 and then British troops in 1798. Even though the British retained control of Martinique, the third major French colony in the Caribbean, the French successes in Saint-Domingue and Guadeloupe, made possible by the black troops led by Louverture, ensured the survival of a considerable French presence in the region. By 1798 Louverture had emerged as the leading figure on the island and was eager to consolidate his power by removing his former allies. He expelled French commissioners, defeated rival mulatto generals (including André Rigaud in the War of the South in 1799), and extended his control to Spanish Santo Domingo in 1800. Though France was at war with Britain, Louverture pursued the best possible relations with the British, recognizing that they were the only ones capable of ensuring Haiti's eventual independence. In 1801 he issued a constitution that made him governor-general for life (with the right to name his successor) and spoke of racial reconciliation and economic recovery. Yet in practice Louverture pursued a different agenda, creating a repressive regime that kept former slaves, now nominally free, as forced laborers (*cultivateurs*) on plantations. His actions laid the foundation for what modern Haitian historians have called the "Louverturian state," based on centralized authoritarian government and repression, whose legacy can be felt in Haiti today.[43]

———◇◦◦◦◦———

The impact of the Revolutionary Wars reached Africa and the Indian Ocean, although it was not as profound due to limited European influence in these regions. When the news of the war in Europe reached Calcutta on June 1, 1793, the British quickly moved to seize French commercial possessions; most of them fell without a fight, although Pondicherry, the crucial French colony in India, required an almost month-long siege.[44] The French possessions, however, were not limited to the Indian mainland; they extended to the far-flung islands of Isle de France (Mauritius) and Bourbon (Réunion), which served as the bases for French privateering operations in the Indian Ocean. Supported by French warships, the privateers posed a major threat to

East Indiamen plying their trade between Europe and India. To deal with this threat, the British dispatched Commodore Peter Rainier to Madras in the fall of 1794. Rainier was a seasoned naval commander who had excellent knowledge of the Indian Ocean, having fought there against the French, led by the famed Admiral Pierre Andre de Suffren, during the American Revolutionary War. Rainier was given the impossible task of ensuring the maritime security of British interests in the vast region that stretched from the southern tip of Africa to China and encompassed the entire Indian Ocean, including the Persian Gulf and the Bay of Bengal. Upon reaching Madras, Rainier clearly understood the challenges he faced and chose to pursue a defensive strategy, seeking to protect the lucrative British East India trade. But European development soon provided him the opportunity to pursue more vigorous actions to extend the British presence in the Indian Ocean.

After the French occupation of the Dutch Republic in 1794–1795, Britain considered it vital to secure the former Dutch possessions in the East, both to safeguard the route to India and the East Indies for the Royal Navy and British trade and to disrupt the French connection to Asia. In August 1795 Rainier, now promoted to rear admiral and supported by Colonel James Stuart's troops, attacked Ceylon, forcing the Dutch garrison to surrender the island, which would remain a part of the British Empire for the next 153 years.[45] He then proceeded to seize the remaining Dutch possessions in the Indian Ocean, capturing Malacca, Amboyna, and the surrounding Spice Islands.[46] The year 1796 also witnessed the British reduction of the Dutch colonies of Demerara, Essequibo, and Berbice in South America, although Surinam and the island of Curaçao, where a major slave rebellion raged in 1795, were not taken till four years later.[47] Of greater significance, however, was the Dutch colony at the southern tip of the African continent. Capture of the Cape Colony could offer a strategic position on the sea line of communication between Britain and India and counter the potential danger from French privateers, who had established a base at Mauritius, harassing British merchant shipping in the Indian Ocean.

Sir Francis Baring, chairman of the British East India Company, believed the Cape Colony was as important to the exercise of British naval power in the East as Gibraltar was in the Mediterranean.[48] The prospect of a French presence at the cape was too threatening for the British not to act. As Captain John Blankett observed, "What was a feather in the hands of Holland will become a sword in the hands of France."[49] Consequently, the British government, claiming to act under mandate of the exiled Dutch prince of Orange and as part of its strategy of taking the war to enemy colonies and disrupting enemy trade, organized an expedition to the Cape of Good Hope. Departing from Britain in March 1795, the British expedition, led by Vice Admiral Sir

George Elphinstone and Major General James Craig, arrived at Simon's Town in June and easily overwhelmed the small Dutch garrison. Coming ashore, Craig then led his troops to Cape Town; after a month-long series of skirmishes with the Dutch forces, he captured the town in mid-September 1795. A Dutch attempt to retake the colony in August 1796 failed, and the cape remained in British hands until it was returned to the Batavian Republic under the Treaty of Amiens in 1802.

Geographically separate from Europe but closely aligned in terms of culture and politics, the newly independent United States of America pursued neutrality in an effort to safeguard its hard-won freedoms. In his Farewell Address upon declining a third term as president, George Washington had left a solemn legacy to his countrymen to "observe good faith and justice towards all Nations" and to avoid foreign entanglements, holding it to be "the true American policy to steer clear of permanent alliances with any portion of the foreign world."[50] In pursuance of this policy, the United States had not hesitated to break with its long-standing ally France and adopt a proclamation of neutrality, sparing the fledgling American republic from a costly war at a moment when it needed to establish firm footing. Nevertheless, the United States could not avoid the impact of the Revolutionary Wars. Europe's suffering worked to America's advantage. Occupied with fierce and deadly struggle in Europe, the great powers had no forces to spare for North America, where the new republic proceeded to consolidate its position and to settle its critical frontier issues with Spain and Britain.

At the start of the War of the First Coalition in 1792, the Franco-American Treaty of Alliance and the Treaty of Amity and Commerce (1778) were still in effect and raised some awkward questions, such as whether the United States was obliged to help defend French possessions in the West Indies or to deny ports and supplies to the British. President George Washington consulted his cabinet before declaring American neutrality and seeking the warring parties' acknowledgment of this fact. The declaration, made on April 22, 1793, greatly disappointed the French government, which expected support out of republican solidarity, mutual hatred of Britain, and gratitude for aid during the War of Independence. But it was the Anglo-American rapprochement that marked the turning point in relations between the United States and France. Following independence, there remained nagging problems in America's relationship with the former metropole. Despite pledges made in the Treaty of Paris in 1783, the British had retained a string of forts along the Canadian border, arguing that their presence was justified by the Americans' failure to pay their prewar debts to British creditors. In 1790

Gouverneur Morris, an American political figure who was engaged in private business in France, was dispatched across the English Channel to sound out the British government on the subject of establishing formal diplomatic relations and negotiating a settlement of outstanding disputes. Morris had several meetings with William Pitt, the prime minister, and Lord Grenville, the secretary for foreign affairs, but they remained noncommittal. Only when the Nootka Sound Crisis brought Britain close to a war with Spain did the British government become more cordial to Morris and consider the possibility of diplomatic relations between the United States and Britain.

The prospects of an Anglo-Spanish confrontation alarmed President Washington and his advisors, who feared Britain might request permission to march troops through American territory to threaten Spanish-held regions. This is in turn could be exploited by the British to tighten their hold on the trans-Appalachian territory. The American government was divided on the best course of action to follow.[51] Some members, most notably Treasury Secretary Alexander Hamilton, favored granting passage rights and exploiting the opportunity to secure American interests along the whole of the Mississippi River.[52] But others, including Vice President John Adams, Secretary of State Thomas Jefferson, and Chief Justice John Jay, called for refusal of such passage rights, believing that the United States should exploit its power over commerce to compel the British government to settle the outstanding issues. These differences were at the core of the growing struggle between the Hamilton-led Federalists, who controlled the Senate and called for a strong centralized government, national bank, and good relations with Britain, and their political opponents, the Jefferson-led Democratic-Republicans, who denounced most of the Federalists' policies. The Democratic-Republican efforts to introduce a national navigation act to prohibit imports from countries that refused the import of American products in American vessels facilitated the British decision to dispatch to Philadelphia the twenty-eight-year-old George Hammond, who despite his youth was already a seasoned diplomat. Arriving in October 1791, Hammond did his best to prevent Congress from passing a navigation act that would have been detrimental to British interests. The British government was willing to consider a treaty of commerce with the United States, but only if payment of prewar debts was secured and if a neutral Indian barrier state, under British protection, was set up along the northern frontier near the Great Lakes. The American government naturally rejected these conditions as an infringement of its sovereignty, so Hammond's mission produced limited results.

News of the French declaration of war on Britain reached the United States in April and took the government by complete surprise. According to the 1778 Treaty of Alliance, the United States was a perpetual ally of France and therefore obligated to assist that nation. Yet despite considerable Francophile sentiment among the American public, few wanted to dive into the morass of European wars, especially when the fledgling republic still lacked a navy. Neutrality was the only sensible policy; even such bitter rivals as Hamilton and Jefferson agreed on it. The former favored declaring the French alliance invalid because it had been made with the French monarchy, which no longer existed. Jefferson, on the other hand, urged avoiding entanglement in the war and using the alliance as a bargaining point with Britain. President Washington chose neither. On April 22, 1793, he signed a neutrality proclamation that declared the United States "friendly and impartial toward the belligerent powers" and warned US citizens that they might be prosecuted for "aiding or abetting hostilities" or taking part in other non-neutral acts.[53] Washington did, however, accept Jefferson's advice that the United States should recognize the new French republic. In the spring of 1793 Citizen Edmond-Charles-Edouard Genet, France's new ambassador to the United States, landed at Charleston, South Carolina, and was enthusiastically welcomed throughout his journey to Philadelphia. Yet Genet's actions and the growing radicalism of the French government soon dissipated this goodwill; for many Americans, what was occurring in France resembled their worst nightmares of anarchy and ochlocracy (mob rule). Discourse on the French and British causes galvanized and divided American public opinion. In July 1793, unable to maintain his political influence in Washington's administration and embittered by his own ideological struggles with Hamilton, Jefferson resigned as secretary of state.

At the beginning of the war Britain informed the American government that it would take enemy property wherever it could find it, including on neutral ships on the high seas. Thus an order-in-council of June 8, 1793, instructed British naval commanders to detain all neutral ships bound for French ports with cargoes of corn, flour, or meal.[54] In early November an even harsher order-in-council was issued, ordering the British fleet to "stop and detain all ships laden with goods the produce of any colony belonging to France, or carrying provisions or other supplies for the use of any such colony."[55] Arriving in the Caribbean, the British captains thus targeted the American merchant fleet trading with the French islands; several hundred American ships in the West Indies had been confiscated by early 1794. News of the British attacks on American shipping reached Philadelphia in March 1794, just as a report that British troops in the Ohio River Valley were arming Indians, who in turn attacked American settlers. A crisis was growing between Britain and the United States.

In April 1794 Washington appointed Chief Justice John Jay special envoy to Britain with instructions to negotiate and settle all major disputes.[56] Over the next six months Jay conducted wide-ranging negotiations with the British that resulted in the conclusion of the Treaty of Amity, Commerce, and Navigation, commonly known as the Jay Treaty, on November 19, 1794. The treaty secured some American goals, including limited rights for American merchants to trade with the British West Indies, withdrawal of British military from forts in the Old Northwest Territory (the area west of Pennsylvania and north of the Ohio River), and reparations for the seizures of American ships and cargo in 1793–1794. The parties agreed to submit disputes over wartime debts and the US-Canada boundary to arbitration. But the American side also made important concessions, including accepting the more limited British definition of neutral rights and granting Britain most-favored-nation status in American commerce.[57] The treaty was one-sided in Britain's favor but, in the words of American historian Joseph Ellis, it was also "a shrewd bargain for the United States. It bet, in effect, on England rather than France as the hegemonic European power of the future, which proved prophetic."[58]

The terms of the Jay Treaty caused public outrage in the United States and engendered such intense debate that some feared an outbreak of civil strife. The Democratic-Republicans, who favored France, denounced the treaty and called for "a direct system of commercial hostility with Great Britain," even at the risk of war.[59] The Federalists were much more receptive to the treaty, but even they were disappointed by the limitations on their trading rights in the British West Indies. The Senate debated the treaty in secret and consented to it on June 24, 1795. The news of the Jay Treaty prompted the French government to suspend diplomatic relations with the United States. This decision was further buttressed when in October 1795 the American minister in Spain, Thomas Pinckney, negotiated the Treaty of San Lorenzo (Pinckney's Treaty), securing the American boundary at the 31st parallel, strengthening US commercial rights to use New Orleans in Spanish Louisiana, and opening access to the Caribbean from the Mississippi River.[60] In response, France began seizing American ships trading with Britain, reasoning that American cargo heading for British ports could be interpreted as contraband subject to seizure. By summer 1797 French privateers and naval vessels operating in the Caribbean and along the American coast had seized more than three hundred ships.

Following his inauguration as the second president of the United States, John Adams quickly moved to restore relations with France. Yet an American attempt at diplomatic settlement with France led to the infamous XYZ Affair, when French diplomats requested a $6 million loan to France and a

$250,000 bribe as prerequisites for serious discussions. The French demands aroused a public outcry, with Representative Robert Goodloe Harper of South Carolina famously proclaiming, "Millions for defense, but not a penny for tribute."[61] But American outrage did not lead to an all-out war between the United States and France. Instead, Congress suspended commerce with France and authorized the capture of armed French ships, creating a separate Department of the Navy to pursue this mission. The fledgling American navy and privateers became involved in an undeclared war with French ships, mainly off the American coast and in the Caribbean. This conflict, known as the Quasi-War, saw numerous privateer actions but few significant naval engagements.[62] By 1799 French ships had been driven from the American coast and French privateering largely eliminated from the Caribbean. In part this result was owing to France's recognition of its naval limitations following the defeats at the hands of the Royal Navy. In 1800 First Consul Napoleon Bonaparte initiated a change in French policy, opening negotiations with the United States. The Treaty of Mortefontaine (September 1800) ended the Quasi-War and restored normal diplomatic and commercial relations between the United States and France. Probably more crucially, it paved the way for the Louisiana Purchase less than three years later.[63]

CHAPTER 4 | The Making of *La Grande Nation*, 1797–1802

T HE FIVE YEARS BETWEEN 1797 and 1802 were crucial in shaping the course of European history. France emerged triumphant and embarked on a rapid territorial expansion in Europe, initially under the guise of liberation. Just as the defeats of 1793–1794 had exerted a profound influence on the direction of the revolutionary turmoil in France, the exhilaration of victories in 1797–1802 shaped the outlook of revolutionary leaders and the French public, causing them to look beyond France's borders. This marked a turning point in the process of redefining the "new world order," one that was not based on relationships between sovereign rulers.[1] French foreign policy during these five years was not "discreet, specialized, and secondary to the internal issues of the period," as one French historian has put it, but rather the result of highly public discussion.[2] There was a vigorous debate in the French press about what to do with the recently conquered territories, especially Italy, and the legitimacy of French actions there.[3] Such discussions revealed divisions of opinion within France, with some calling for a return to older boundaries while others insisted on extending French sovereignty to what was increasingly described as the country's "natural frontiers"—that is, the Rhine, the Alps, and the Pyrenees.[4]

As we saw in Chapter 3, General Bonaparte's Italian Campaign ended the War of the First Coalition on terms highly advantageous to France. The government naturally exploited this moment of triumph to pursue a more aggressive foreign policy, believing that war had become essential to sustaining army and state, as well as providing occupation for commanders whose ambitions were clearly not limited to military matters alone.[5] The French occupied Rome and the Papal States in February 1798 and Switzerland in

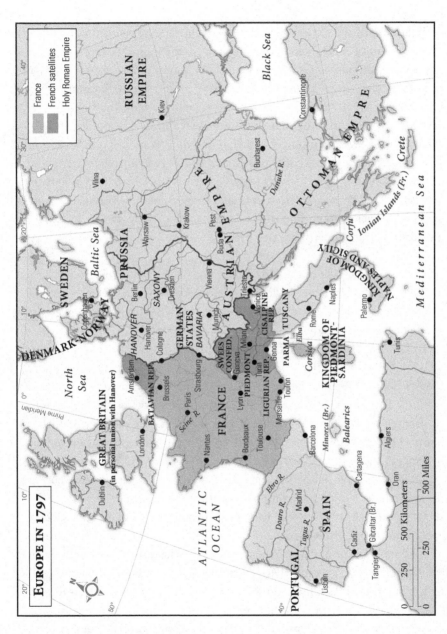

Map 4: Europe in 1797

April. The decision to reorganize these satellite states into *républiques soeurs* (sister republics) created new ground for redefining French political discourse and for justifying continued French expansion and interference in neighboring states.[6]

France's military victories and financial exigencies, as well as local politics in the newly occupied territories, all helped to nudge its foreign policy toward the notion of *la Grande Nation*, which sought to reconcile the idea of liberating other peoples from "tyranny" with preserving the interests of the French state, even if those increasingly diverged from the aspirations of local patriots. This was an important shift, because it implicitly implied the subversion of earlier revolutionary principles of liberty and republicanism, as well as support for the claims of France's wider geopolitical interests and imperial *machtpolitik*. As early as 1797 General Louis Desaix jotted down in his journal that Bonaparte "has a great and shrewd policy, which is to give all of these peoples a grand idea of the French nation."[7] He would do so on a global scale, starting with France's greatest enemy.

————•◦◦❊◦◦•————

At the end of the War of the First Coalition, the French revolutionary government, for the first time, could contemplate invading Britain, a threat that would occupy considerable British military and naval resources over the course of the next decade.

In late 1796 the French Directory organized the Expédition d'Irlande, which involved more than forty ships and some 15,000 soldiers, all under the command of General Lazare Hoche, to support the United Irishmen and drive the British out of Ireland. This "unhappy country," as the French official newspaper described Ireland, had long served as "the experimental laboratory of British colonization" and suffered greatly from the Anglo-Protestant hegemony that had been firmly established in the wake of the Cromwellian conquest of Ireland in the mid-seventeenth century.[8] Despite representing the vast majority of the population and outnumbering Anglo Protestants by about five to one, the Catholic Irish were dispossessed of their land, denied entry into certain professions, and disallowed from political participation. The French Revolution had a major impact on Ireland. In 1791 Presbyterian and Catholic Irish came together to form the Society of United Irishmen, led by the Dublin Protestant lawyer Wolfe Tone.[9] Influenced by French revolutionary ideals, the United Irishmen called for Catholic emancipation and major political and economic reforms, though some radical members also envisioned an independent Irish republic free from English control.[10]

During the first three years of the French Revolution, the United Irishmen published newspapers and hundreds of pamphlets expressing clear sympathies for the French revolutionaries. The British government was naturally perturbed by the organization, especially after the outbreak of war between Britain and France in February 1793, when it came to see the United Irishmen as potentially treasonous. In 1793 the British authorities adopted several laws targeting the society before outlawing it entirely in 1794. The United Irishmen, forced underground, continued their struggle. The crackdown only radicalized its members, and over the next three years they reorganized the society, turning it into a militarized organization that made preparations for rebellion, which France was eager to exploit.[11]

After mobilizing at Brest on the Brittany coast, the French launched the operation in December 1796, amid what proved to be one of the roughest winters of the eighteenth century. Sailing toward Bantry Bay, the French fleet suffered greatly and was unable to make amphibious landings in Ireland. Within a week the entire expedition was recalled, with a dozen French ships captured or wrecked and more than 2,000 men lost. The invasion was defeated not by the Royal Navy but rather by a combination of bad weather, poor seamanship, and poor French decision-making. It did, however, reveal weaknesses in the British defenses, especially in light of continued mutinies over pay and conditions in the Royal Navy.

A year and a half later France organized an expedition in support of a local rebellion in Ireland. The uprising first began around Dublin but quickly spread to County Wexford, in southeast Ireland. On May 29 the United Irishmen stormed the town of Enniscothy and then succeeded in taking the town of Wexford. The rebellion soon spread to other areas as well, including Antrim and County Down, where rebel forces assembled under the leadership of Henry McCracken and Henry Monro. The Irish hoped for French military support, but it failed to materialize. British victories at Ballynahinch (near Belfast), New Ross and Bunclody (in County Wexford), and Arklow (in County Wicklow) effectively neutralized the rebellion. Both McCracken and Monro were captured and executed without proper trial. Tone, also captured, committed suicide in jail.[12]

The Irish rebellion seemed over when on August 22, 1798, a French expeditionary force, led by General Jean Joseph Humbert, landed at Kilcummin. The French continued to see Ireland as Britain's weak point, while the Irishmen still hoped for French support in their struggle against British rule. Upon their arrival the French forces occupied the town of Killala, where they hoisted a green flag with the slogan "Erin go Bragh" (Ireland forever) and a harp without a crown, inviting the Irish rebels to "assert their freedom" from the British monarchy and join the free Frenchmen, who had "come for no other purpose but to make them independent and happy."[13] The French scored a minor victory over the British at Castlebar, which encouraged many Irishmen to renew their resistance. Humbert called for further French reinforcements, but these did not arrive, owing yet again to poor weather in the Atlantic. Meanwhile, British troops led by Lord Charles Cornwallis, the lord lieutenant of Ireland, converged on Humbert, who suffered defeats at Ballinamuck (September 8) and Killala (September 23) and was forced to surrender. Humbert's defeat marked the end of the rebellion, which had led to the death of some 20,000 Irishmen, and dashed Irish hopes for independence from British rule.

----◦◦◦※◦◦◦----

Ireland was just one target among several in France's strategy to seek a way to solve the conundrum of how to defeat Britain without achieving command of the sea. Another was Egypt. Straddling the isthmus connecting Africa and Asia, Egypt constituted an axis of France's global interests. With the loss of India and North Africa during the Seven Years' War, France's presence in the eastern Mediterranean assumed much greater importance. Egypt could serve as a crucial link between France's Levantine interests and its imperial aspirations in Asia, as well as provide further connections with Arabia, North Africa, and East Africa. The idea of establishing a French presence in Egypt and the Levant had informed French strategic thinking since the time of Louis XV, but it was during the Revolutionary Wars that France made a tangible effort to carry it out.[14]

Egypt had been under Ottoman sovereignty since the early sixteenth century, but it was not completely immune to French interests. French merchants had had a strong presence there since the fifteenth century, and France enjoyed a relationship with the Ottomans that could be traced back to the sixteenth century, when the two states united in their struggle against the Holy Roman Empire.[15] While many European nations had, over the centuries, made agreements and sent ambassadors to the Turkish court, the French had been one of the most highly favored nations. The French were the first to conclude a commercial treaty with the Ottomans; French merchants actively traded and invested heavily in the Ottoman economy; and by the late eighteenth century Roman Catholics in the Ottoman Empire were placed under French protection. During the Russo-Ottoman War of 1768–1774 France took a pro-Ottoman stand. Though France could not provide any material help, it was the only European power on which the sultan thought he could rely.

Egypt felt the reverberations of the French Revolution even before French troops landed on its shores. Within a year of the start of the Revolution, the French consul in Alexandria was lamenting the spread of a "plague of insubordination and licentiousness" that visiting French sailors had brought to the French community in Egypt.[16] In 1790 the sailors even organized a major mutiny against their captains and demanded the introduction of revolutionary reforms; the more radical among them organized a "national guard" in Cairo and approached local authorities for permission to build a Temple of Reason.[17] But Ismael Bey, the Mamluk *sheikh al-balad* who governed Egypt on behalf of the Ottomans and had been well disposed toward the French, died during an epidemic in Cairo in 1791.[18] His rivals, Georgian Mamluks Ibrahim Bey and Murad Bey, seized power in Egypt and targeted the French for their earlier involvement in the Ottoman intervention that had driven them from power.[19] In 1795 the French bemoaned the fact that "since the beginning of the French Revolution, and particularly since the overthrow of the monarchy, the enemies of the French people have worked in Egypt with the same ferocity as in all parts of Europe."[20] With the French monarchy overthrown, some had argued that the French no longer possessed protections and privileges granted under former agreements. The French merchants in Egypt produced a steady flow of complaints to Paris, asking for intervention. "Could we remain in Egypt in such a humiliating position? Should the French Republic, so accustomed to victories, submit to such humiliation? Could she forget what is owed to national dignity, as much as to the interests of trade?"[21]

French merchants' denunciations of Mamluk despotism and demands for forceful intervention played a significant role in shaping official French policy toward Egypt. French consul Charles Magallon inundated the foreign ministry with demands for compensation of losses suffered in Egypt, and among his various suggestions was a plan for a military takeover of Egypt and the establishment of "armed trading posts" in Alexandria and Cairo to project and protect French interests. Although Magallon's project was quickly shelved, it eventually found its champions in French foreign minister Charles Maurice de Talleyrand and General Napoleon Bonaparte.[22] During his triumphant campaign in Italy in 1796–1797, Bonaparte had already begun looking eastward: besides occupying the Ionian Islands, he had dispatched a mission to the Maniots (Peloponnesian Greeks) and another agent to the ambitious Ali Pasha of Janina, who increasingly defied the Ottoman central authorities.

There was also a separate issue of the French struggle against Britain. With the French navy too weak to challenge the British navy openly, and a direct invasion of Britain out of the question in the wake of British triumphs at St. Vincent and Camperdown, the French government continued to look for other methods of attacking British interests. In the summer of 1797 the

French foreign ministry prepared three reports on possible cooperation with Indian princes against the British.[23] Egypt featured prominently in these various proposals, with Bonaparte telling the Directory in August 1797 that "to destroy England thoroughly, the time is coming when we must seize Egypt."[24] A French occupation of Egypt could strengthen the French presence in the eastern Mediterranean and serve as a jumping-off point for greater ambitions in Asia. In the spring of 1798 the Directory seriously considered mounting an expedition to Egypt, which appeared vulnerable and could confer considerable advantages. With its rich and fertile soil, Egypt might prove to be a valuable source of commodities—a worthy replacement for the loss of Saint-Domingue.[25] Such proposals were framed within the notion of a "recivilizing" mission that would restore Egypt to its ancient splendor. They represented a continuation of the Enlightenment-era debates on "Oriental despotism" and the revolutionary ethos against dictatorship and tyranny.[26] In his memorandum to the Directory, Talleyrand expressed this ideology of benign colonialism when he explained that "Egypt was once a province of the Roman republic; it must now become that of the French Republic. The Roman conquest was the era of decadence for that great country; the French conquest will be the era of its prosperity."

In March 1798 the Directory made a formal decision to launch the expedition to Egypt and appointed Bonaparte commander in chief of the Armée d'Orient. Bonaparte was instructed to first occupy Malta and then proceed with the conquest of Egypt. Once the occupation was complete, he was to establish communications with India and secure "exclusive possession of the Red Sea for the French Republic," which would then facilitate "the expulsion of the English from the Orient" and a future French expedition to India.[27]

With remarkable speed and secrecy, Bonaparte threw himself into the preparations for the expedition.[28] The entire Armée d'Orient was ready to depart in less than eleven weeks, instead of the months usually required to muster an army. Bonaparte had at his disposal a force of some 36,000 soldiers, the majority of them veterans of the Armée d'Italie. The fleet gathered to transport the army was equally large: about 13,000 sailors on some three hundred ships, including thirteen ships-of-the-line under the command of Admiral François Paul, comte de Brueys.[29] Several ports of embarkation—Toulon, Marseilles, Genoa, Ajaccio, and Civitavecchia—would launch the enormous operation. A unique feature of this campaign was the large contingent of *savants* Bonaparte invited to accompany the expedition. Among these scientists were mathematicians Gaspard Monge and Étienne-Louis Malus, chemists Jacques Conte and Claude Berthollet, geologist Déodat Gratet de Dolomieu, and naturalist Étienne Geoffroy Saint-Hilaire.

French activity at Toulon had caught the attention of the British, whose naval squadron under Rear Admiral Sir Horatio Nelson was deployed in the western Mediterranean. It was a stroke of luck for the French that a strong gale scattered and damaged the British ships in mid-May. By the time they recovered, the French had already departed for Egypt. Bonaparte's first objective was Malta, a strategically located island just south of Sicily that was essential for the French to have a presence in the Mediterranean.

Bonaparte arrived at Malta on June 9 and secured the island without much resistance from the Knights of Malta (formally the Order of St. John of Jerusalem, also called the Knights Hospitaller), which had ruled the island since 1530.[30] The swiftness of the French conquest was ensured not only by the superior force at Bonaparte's disposal but also by a conspiracy among the knights that the French general helped bring about even before leaving French soil; by the time the French anchored off Malta's shores, the conspirators (all of them French knights) had helped undermine the order's resistance. On June 11 the order capitulated, and the knights were expelled from the island; their leader, Ferdinand von Hompesch zu Bolheim, was offered a German principality and a lucrative pension.

After his forces had secured the island, Bonaparte reorganized the local government, turned the holdings of the knights into national lands, abolished slavery and all remnants of feudalism, reorganized the local Catholic church, and established new education and taxation systems.[31] The French also seized the enormous treasury of the knights, which was supposed to defray the costs of the expedition.[32] Yet the French occupation of Malta also demonstrated an abject failure to consider the mentality of the Maltese, who regarded the occupying force with suspicion and complained, as one knight reported, that "such an outrage was not even committed by the [Ottomans] at Rhodes."[33] The local population was particularly upset by enforced contributions and higher taxes, as well as the changed terms of leaseholds and mistreatment of the Catholic church. Within three months of Bonaparte's departure, much of Malta was in revolt and the French garrison was driven into Valetta, where it remained, besieged, for the next two years.[34]

The French capture of Malta only strengthened the determination of Russian emperor Paul, who inherited the imperial crown in November 1796. As a young man Paul had studied the history of the Knights of Malta and romanticized them; to him, the knights represented an ideal union that could instill the qualities of duty, piety, obedience, and service to God and sovereign, all in counterbalance to the new ideas emanating from revolutionary France. Paul's first move was to convince the Russian priory of the Order of St. John to depose Hompesch zu Bolheim, the order's leader, and elect Paul the new grand master. Assuming the mantle of protector of Malta, Paul then proceeded to negotiate an alliance with the Ottomans, which secured Russian entry into the war against France.[35]

Bonaparte departed from Malta for Alexandria on June 18, narrowly missing interception by Nelson's pursuing ships on the night of June 22–23. On July 1, after six weeks at sea, the Armée d'Orient arrived off the Egyptian coast and began disembarking a few miles west of Alexandria.

By the late eighteenth century, Egypt had been ruled by the Mamluks for more than five hundred years. The Mamluks were a warrior caste created from non-Muslim boys who had been kidnapped at an early age, sold at slave markets, converted to Islam, and trained as mounted warriors. Although nominal vassals of the Ottoman Empire since 1517, they took advantage of the Ottoman decline in the mid-eighteenth century to achieve a considerable degree of autonomy under the leadership of the Georgian Mamluks, first Ali Bey al-Kabir and later Murad Bey and Ibrahim Bey.[36]

The French army landed at Alexandria on July 2, 1798, and easily overwhelmed the Mamluk cavalry, which was still essentially a medieval fighting force. After capturing Alexandria, Bonaparte engaged the Mamluks at Shubra Khit on July 13 and then routed the main army under Murad Bey in the Battle of the Pyramids near the village of Embabeh, just across the Nile River from Cairo, on July 21. Bonaparte entered Cairo on the twenty-fourth and dispatched General Louis Desaix to pursue Murad Bey, who had fled into Upper Egypt.

The French successes on land were countered by a decisive British triumph at sea. On August 1 Nelson located the French fleet, which was anchored in line in the shallows of Aboukir Bay near Alexandria. In the ensuing engagement, known as the Battle of the Nile, eleven French ships-of-the-line and most of the frigates were captured or sunk. The French army was stranded in Egypt, and the British fleet had reasserted its control of the Mediterranean.

Notwithstanding his predicament, Bonaparte set about reorganizing Egyptian society, just as he had on Malta, by introducing French-style administrative and judicial systems. He sought to abolish remnants of the feudal system, proclaim freedom of religion and equality before the law, establish the rule of law, and create the institution of an elected government—all, needless to say, under French tutelage. One of his most significant acts was the establishment of the Institute of Egypt in Cairo, which both propagated European culture and ideas in the East and undertook research in Egyptian culture and history, vastly expanding European knowledge of the East. Bonaparte also discussed with Muslim clerics the possibility of converting his army to Islam, though this and other efforts to garner popular support failed to achieve their goal.

Following the Battle of the Nile, Bonaparte found himself in a perilous situation. Although he had defeated the Mamluks, he had not destroyed them: Ibrahim Bey had withdrawn across the Sinai Peninsula to Palestine, while Murad Bey had retreated southward to Upper Egypt, where he tied down the French troops under Desaix. On September 9 the Ottoman Empire declared war on France and began preparing two large armies for the invasion of Egypt.[37] The French also had trouble controlling Cairo, where a revolt against the occupation broke out on October 21 but was brutally suppressed, with approximately 2,000 Egyptians and 300 French killed. In this precarious situation, Bonaparte made a new plan: to force the sultan to make peace. He decided to march on Acre (at the time located in the Ottoman province of Syria, now Akko in Israel), where the Turks were raising an army under the local governor, Ahmad Pasha al-Jazzar (Djezzar Pasha). Still thinking of a wider, anti-British strategy, Bonaparte wrote a letter to the ruler of Mysore, Tippu Sultan, at Seringapatam in India, offering to cooperate against the British.

In late 1798 Bonaparte organized an expeditionary force for the invasion of Syria. He left Cairo on February 10, 1799, and on the twentieth he seized El Arish, where he captured several hundred Turks and Mamluks, who were later freed on parole. Bonaparte entered Gaza on February 25 and stormed Jaffa on March 7. At Jaffa some 2,500 Turks, many of them former prisoners from El Arish, surrendered on the understanding that their lives would be spared. Bonaparte, believing he could spare neither troops to escort the prisoners to Egypt nor the rations to feed them, ordered every one of the captives executed.

On March 17 Bonaparte reached Haifa and began besieging the stronghold of Acre, just across the bay. The odds were against the French: they lacked heavy artillery, and many of the troops had contracted bubonic plague in Jaffa. (Bonaparte had visited the plague hospital on March 11, an incident later commemorated in a painting by Antoine-Jean Gros.) A British squadron under Commodore Sir Sidney Smith supported the Ottoman garrison under Ahmad Pasha, while French émigré officers directed the Turkish artillery.

While the siege of Acre dragged on, the Turkish pasha of Damascus dispatched a large army to attack the French from the rear. Between April 8 and 15 the French defeated the Turkish detachments near Nazareth, near Canaan, and on the Jordan River north of Lake Tiberias. On April 16 General Jean-Baptiste Kléber's 2,000 men engaged a Turkish army of 25,000 men at Mount Tabor and resisted for ten hours, until Bonaparte arrived with reinforcements to rout the Turks. The French made repeated assaults on Acre but were repulsed each time. Bonaparte finally decided to abandon the siege and return to Egypt.

The retreat began on May 20, and the demoralized French forces reached Cairo on June 14. One month later, another Turkish army of some 20,000 men arrived on the Egyptian coast. The Turks landed near Aboukir on July 25 but were routed by Bonaparte's troops, who drove them into the sea.

Despite his victories, Bonaparte knew that the expedition was doomed. The British controlled the Mediterranean, preventing the Directory from sending any reinforcements to Egypt. After receiving the news of the setbacks France had suffered in the War of the Second Coalition, Bonaparte became convinced that he should return to France. On August 22, with only the handful of men selected to accompany him, he boarded a frigate and left the army in Kléber's hands. After an uneventful voyage of forty-seven days, he landed at St. Raphael in France on October 9 and was given a hero's welcome by French citizens anxious for a turn in their country's fortunes.

————∘∘∘※∘∘∘————

The arrival of the French troops on the shores of North Africa just nine years after the storming of the Bastille reveals how quickly the revolution transcended not only French borders but also those of Europe. The expedition left a lasting legacy in science and culture—and was instrumental in establishing the entire field of Egyptology—but was essentially a military and political defeat. It cut straight through the traditional policies of France in the Levant, and instead of striking a blow at the colonial power of Britain, it drove France's traditional ally (the Ottomans) into an alliance with its long-standing enemies, Russia and Britain. Politically, the expedition served to showcase the Directory's aggressive foreign policy and facilitated the formation of the Second Coalition in late 1798. It demonstrated the failure of the project to combine republican ideals with colonialism and territorial expansion.[38] Bonaparte's expedition to Egypt also transformed the nature of Franco-British rivalry in the East. French forays into India, for example, had been made from island bases in the Indian Ocean, relying on French naval power, which the British could counter with their own fleet. Bonaparte's attempt to conquer Egypt by land profoundly altered this equation, however, forcing the British government to consider not just maritime approaches to India but also paths through territories adjacent to the subcontinent, drawing Britain into a lasting endeavor to secure its Indian dominions against an overland attack.

Historians often identify the French invasion as a watershed event, one that ushered in the modern era in Egypt. But this is not entirely accurate. The occupation itself did little to "modernize" Egyptian society, as the principles that the French had introduced were too radical and foreign, and faced bitter resistance. It did, however, create a political vacuum that was soon

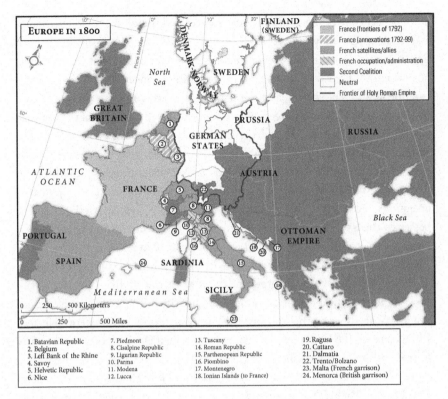

Map 5: Europe in 1800

filled by Kavalali Mehmet Ali Pasha, who within a decade of the French departure defeated the Ottomans and the Mamluks and began laying the foundation for a modernized and strong Egypt that would play an important role in later Middle Eastern history.

Equally far-reaching is the campaign's impact on the development of Orientalism, the study of non-European cultures and languages that became an important element of European colonialism. The Egyptian campaign represented the first (albeit not the last) modern attempt to incorporate an Islamic society into a European empire and, in the words of Edward Said, constituted the formative moment for the discourse of Orientalism, the moment when all its ideological components converged and a full arsenal of instruments of Western domination was employed to project it.[39]

———◇◇◇❈◇◇◇———

Bonaparte's decision to abandon his army in Egypt and return to France was prompted by news that a new alliance had formed against *la Grande Nation*. By now France had extended its military authority far beyond its traditional sphere of influence, controlling much of Italy, Switzerland, Belgium, the Netherlands, and southern Germany, and it had launched expeditions overseas to Ireland and Egypt. It was clear that the French victory in the War of the First Coalition was not the end of French expansion, and that military convenience and opportunism, ideological conviction, and the political and economic advantages of continued expansion all encouraged aggressive behavior. By the end of the year, the Second Coalition already included Britain, Austria, Russia, Naples, Portugal, and the Ottoman Empire. The Directory made preparations for offensive operations in Naples, northern Italy, Switzerland, and the Rhineland, while additional forces were to defend Holland against expected Anglo-Russian amphibious operations. Yet French armies had been considerably understrength, and none possessed the level of morale so characteristic of the earlier revolutionary armies. France faced a challenge that would prove difficult to overcome.

The Kingdom of Naples, which had so far avoided becoming embroiled in the revolutionary wars, threw in its lot with the coalition in late 1798. Soon thereafter the Neapolitan army marched into Roman territory. France lost no time in avenging the insult. The Neapolitan forces were defeated, while back in Naples a popular insurrection forced the Bourbon royal family to seek refuge on a British warship, which evacuated them to Sicily. In late 1799, after brushing aside the local defenses, the French army under General Jean Étienne Vachier Championnet entered the city and began setting up yet another French satellite state, known as the Parthenopean Republic.

The French offensive stalled elsewhere, allowing the coalition to score a string of major victories in the spring of 1799. Archduke Carl's Austrians drove the French back beyond Zurich in Switzerland and defeated a French offensive in southern Germany. A popular uprising in Calabria, led by a charismatic cleric, Cardinal Fabrizio Ruffo, challenged French control of southern Italy. Austria, Russia, and Britain launched a major campaign against the French. The Russian and British navies achieved considerable success in the Mediterranean, capturing the Ionian Islands and the island of Corfu and besieging Malta.[40] More crucially, the Russo-Austrian forces, led by Russian field marshal Alexander Suvorov, invaded northern Italy and routed the French in a series of battles—Magnano (April 5, 1799), Cassano (April 27), the Trebbia (June 17–19), and Novi (August 15)—reclaiming virtually everything that Bonaparte had conquered just two years prior. In late August an Anglo-Russian expedition invaded the North Holland Peninsula in the Batavian Republic, seeking to incite a popular uprising and challenge French control of the Low Countries.[41]

Thus, in the span of just six months, the Second Coalition had reversed almost all of France's achievements in Italy and seriously threatened French positions in the Low Countries and Switzerland. The French setbacks were partly the result of their own poorly conceived military operations. As the Allies approached the republic's borders, their strategic and logistic position significantly improved. The Jourdan Law (September 5, 1798), which instituted "universal and obligatory conscription" of all French men ages twenty to twenty-five, raised some 400,000 new soldiers, something the Allies simply could not match. The impending Allied invasion was averted after General André Masséna scored a decisive victory over the Allies at Zurich (September 25–26), while General Guillaume Brune defeated an Anglo-Russian amphibious invasion of Holland at Bergen and Castricum (September-October).

The French successes were greatly facilitated by tensions and political disagreements between the Allied powers. Russian commanders, for example, became increasingly frustrated by what they believed was British failure to exploit an initial advantage. The most important fissure in the coalition involved Austria and Russia. After expelling the French from Italy, the Russian emperor expected restoration of the legitimate rulers of Tuscany and Sardinia, but Austria demurred, preferring to pursue its imperial designs in Italy instead.[42] Paul felt betrayed and informed his Austrian counterpart of his decision to no longer participate in the war for Austrian aggrandizement.[43] Less acrimonious but still significant was the quarrel between Russia and Britain over the island of Malta and the failure of the joint expedition to Holland.

Back from Egypt, Bonaparte quickly exploited political instability in France to seize power. Assuming the title of First Consul in the three-member Consulate that had replaced the Directory, Bonaparte offered peace to the European monarchs and, upon their rejection, renewed his campaign in northern Italy against the Austrians in 1800.[44] Following his crossing of the St. Bernard Pass, he won a victory, albeit narrowly, over the Austrians at Marengo on June 14, driving them out of Italy and accepting their offer of armistice. Despite its subsequent renown, the Battle of Marengo did not end the war; Austria had not been beaten so decisively as to be forced to sue for peace. A preliminary peace treaty (generally confirming the provisions of the Treaty of Campo Formio, with some changes) was agreed upon in Paris in late July, but Vienna refused to ratify it, choosing the continuation of war.[45] The Austrian decision is often explained as a consequence of Vienna's determination that only a victorious war could guarantee its territorial ambitions in Italy. But Austrian actions were shaped by a far greater consideration: to accept French demands implicitly meant to surrender Austria's status as a great power.[46] On July 23, 1800, Britain and Austria negotiated a new alliance that included two key terms: the British agreed to provide a financial subsidy to sustain the Austrian war effort, while Austria pledged not to make a separate peace with France.[47] Assured of British support (and gold), the Austrian government was eager to pursue the war to its conclusion and used the armistice to rally its military. Yet when hostilities resumed, Austrian and British military cooperation failed and Austria found itself teetering on a political precipice. In the fall the French seized Philippsburg, Ingolstadt, and Ulm before General Jean Moreau scored a crushing victory over Archduke John at Hohenlinden (southern Germany) on December 3, 1800. With the enemy cavalry outposts set up forty miles from Vienna, the Austrian monarchy requested armistice on Christmas Day. The war was over, and now it was a matter of trying to preserve a peace commensurate with it.

| The Second Coalition War and the
Origins of the "Great Game"

FOR MUCH OF the nineteenth century Europeans keenly followed the "Great Game," a term for the strategic rivalry and conflict between the British Empire and the Russian Empire for supremacy in Central Asia and India. Alarmed by the expansion of the Russian Empire in Asia, Britain feared that whenever its interests opposed Russia's in Europe, the Russians would threaten to invade their most precious colonial possession. It therefore determined both to contain Russian expansion and to counter any possible invasion.

Yet such geopolitical machinations had in fact begun much earlier and the original "great game" involved Britain, Russia, and France. The British government and the British East India Company (BEIC)—an English joint-stock trading company formed in 1600 to conduct commerce in Asia—had long been engaged in a war of diplomatic intrigue against Britain's European rivals in Asia, and in India in particular. The Revolutionary and Napoleonic Wars saw this European enmity extending to much of Western Asia, most notably Iran, Egypt, and the Arab states of the Red Sea and the Persian Gulf.

The Indian subcontinent was one of the focal points of European—especially Franco-British—struggles in the early modern era. France had lost most of its positions on the subcontinent following the Seven Years' War. Victory allowed the BEIC to consolidate its presence in India. Thus, in addition to native states, there was considerable European presence on the subcontinent. The British possessions were grouped around the three presidencies, which were politically and geographically distinct entities. The Madras presidency, centered at Fort St. George, included various scattered territories in southern India. On the eastern coastline of India, the British also controlled

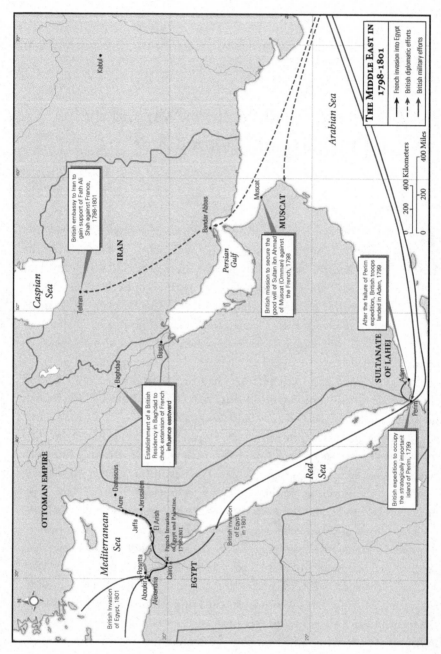

Map 6: The Middle East in 1798–1801

Within the map:

THE MIDDLE EAST IN 1798-1801
→ French invasion into Egypt
⇢ British diplomatic efforts
→ British military efforts

OTTOMAN EMPIRE

IRAN

EGYPT

Mediterranean Sea

Caspian Sea

Persian Gulf

Red Sea

Arabian Sea

MUSCAT

SULTANATE OF LAHEJ

British embassy to Iran to gain support of Fath Ali Shah against France, 1798-1801

Establishment of a British Residency in Baghdad to check extension of French influence eastward

British mission to secure the good will of Sultan ibn Ahmad of Muscat (Ommani) against the French, 1798

After the failure of Perim expedition, British troops landed in Aden, 1799

British expedition to occupy the strategically important island of Perim, 1799

British Invasion of Egypt, 1801

French Invasion of Egypt and Palestine, 1798-1801

British invasion of Egypt in 1801

Kabul

Tehran

Bandar Abbas

Muscat

Baghdad

Basra

Aden

Perim

Damascus
Acre
Jerusalem
Jaffa
El Arish
Rosetta
Aboukir
Alexandria
Cairo

0   200   400 Kilometers
0   200   400 Miles

a large territory north of Masulipatam, called the Northern Circars, on a lease from Hyderabad. The Bengal presidency, centered at Fort William, included Bengal, Benares, Ghazipur, Bihar, Chittagong, and parts of Orissa. The Bombay presidency covered the islands of Bombay and Salsette as well as a few hundred miles of the Malabar coastline. To the northwest of the Bengal presidency was Oudh, which the British undertook to protect; much of this state's income was spent on a British subsidiary force.

The eighteenth-century India witnessed the gradual erosion of Mughal imperial power through factional conflicts in Delhi and ineffectiveness. By 1800 there had emerged several powerful regional states.[1] The Marathas Confederation, whose chieftains descended from the ancient Hindu dynasties of northwestern Deccan, controlled vast territories in central India and held the Mughal emperor as a virtual captive. Yet the confederacy was in disarray, with its powerful *sardars* often bickering with each other.[2] To the south of it was the dominion of Hyderabad, which lost much of its power in the wake of a crushing defeat by the Marathas at Khardla in 1795. Its ruler (known as the *nizam*) thus found himself crammed between two powerful native states— the Marathas in the north and west, and the dominion of Mysore to the south. Like the Sindhia (Scindias) Maratha, the *nizam* relied heavily on the military commanded by French.[3]

The BEIC, especially the Madras presidency, was actively involved in shaping Indian politics. Facing opposition from Hyder Ali (1722–1782) of Mysore, the BEIC struck an uneasy alliance with the Marathas and Hyderabad, and defeated Mysore forces in the First Mysore War (1767–1769). The BEIC's position in India, however, remained delicate, especially in the late 1770s and early 1780s, when Britain was preoccupied with the American War of Independence. The French had reestablished their presence in India and supported local Indian rulers, most notably Hyder Ali, who was dissatisfied with the BEIC. In 1780 Hyder Ali launched the Second Mysore War and, with French military assistance, scored a major victory over the British at Perambakam (Pollilur) on September 10. Hyder overran Karnataka and menaced the British stronghold of Madras before being defeated at Porto Novo, Pollilur, and Sholingarh in the fall of 1781. However, French naval forces intervened with the capture of Trincomalee on the coast of Ceylon (Sri Lanka) in 1782 and were able to send aid and arms to Hyder, as well as inflict a defeat on the British at Cuddalore. Despite this victory, the 1783 Treaty of Paris, which ended the American Revolution, mandated the withdrawal of French support from Mysore, and the following year the Mysoris had little choice but to make peace.

Hyder's successor, Tippu Sultan, continued Mysori opposition to the hegemony of the BEIC, prompting the outbreak of the Third Mysore War in 1790. The BEIC forces under Lord Cornwallis invaded the territory controlled by Tippu, capturing the Mysore stronghold of Bangalore in 1791. Maintaining the momentum, Cornwallis defeated the Mysoris at Carigat (Arikera) and conducted a wide-ranging campaign that culminated in the storming of Seringapatam, Tippu's stronghold, considered one of the most formidable fortresses on the subcontinent. The subsequent Treaty of Seringapatam forced Tippu to surrender much of his dominion to the BEIC and its allies. The astringent terms of peace kept Mysore antagonistic to the British.[4] Tippu used the truce that commenced in March 1792 to regroup for a new war, which came seven years later.

When war broke out between France and Britain in 1793, Cornwallis, governor-general of the BEIC, had ordered the seizure of all French establishments in the subcontinent. The continuing Franco-British conflict did not directly involve India again for another five years, though European political turmoil frequently echoed on the subcontinent. By the late 1790s the fear of a revival of French power was instrumental in driving British expansion in India, especially under Richard Colley Wellesley, who succeeded Cornwallis and became governor-general of the BEIC in 1798.[5] A talented and ambitious man, Wellesley was the first of the great nineteenth-century imperialists who believed that territorial power in India would give Britain an insurmountable advantage over its European rivals. He took advantage of the degree of freedom he had from London—it took four months for an action in India to become known in England and as many months for official reaction to reach his headquarters at Calcutta (Kolkata)—to pursue his own policies. Wellesley formulated many of his conclusions about the state of India as he was on his way to Bengal. During a long stay at the Cape of Good Hope, he perused available materials, including BEIC correspondence, and interviewed BEIC officials to satisfy, as he put it in a letter, his "anxious desire to learn the actual states of affairs in India from the most authentic source."[6]

There was much to learn. The French expedition to Egypt (1798) and its professed goal of threatening British interests in India caused considerable apprehension in British political circles. Furthermore, in the spring of 1799 the French fleet broke through the British blockade of Brest on the Atlantic coastline, freed the Spanish fleet at Cadiz, and proceeded to attack small isolated British squadrons across the Mediterranean. The French soon surrendered the initiative by returning to their Atlantic ports, but their actions shook the British. In the Indian Ocean, the French expedition to Egypt prompted redeployment of the British fleet into the Arabian Sea, exposing trade routes. A British convoy barely escaped destruction by the Spanish at Macao in January 1799, while French privateers operated with great success in the Bay of Bengal.

To the authorities in London, these actions vividly illustrated that British superiority on the seas could be challenged at any moment and that the British presence in India could not be taken for granted. Wellesley and Henry Dundas, the secretary of state for war and president of the Board of Control responsible for overseeing the British East India Company, were concerned both by the immediate prospect of a French invasion and by continued French intrigues with local Indian rulers. They were therefore aware of communications between the French and Tippu Sultan of Mysore, who had requested military help from the French administration of Mauritius. With General Bonaparte in Egypt, French soldiers of fortune training the armies of several Indian rulers, and Zaman Shah of Afghanistan (with whom the British thought Tippu and the French had some understanding) encroaching on India from the northwest, the BEIC felt its interests in India were threatened, and it acted accordingly.[7]

Wellesley first dealt with Hyderabad, whose ruler, Nizam Ali, had recruited French officers to train his troops and thus allowed for "a French state in the peninsula," to use Wellington's phrase.[8] In September 1798, with the support of a pro-British faction at the *nizam*'s court, Wellesley compelled Nizam Ali to disband his French-trained forces and replace them with a British-officered force of sepoys. Nizam Ali may have gained security, but he essentially lost control of foreign affairs. Pleased with this arrangement, the BEIC Board of Control urged Wellesley to push for similar deals with other Indian states.[9]

Next on the list of Wellesley's targets was Mysore, which, despite the loss in the last Anglo-Mysore War, still remained a formidable military power and avowedly hostile to the BEIC. The news that Tippu Sultan had welcomed French republican envoys, planted a tree of liberty at Seringapatam, and made overtures to the French in Mauritius only further strengthened British suspicions of the French threat to their position in India and made the BEIC governor-general determined to act at once.[10] In the spring of 1799 Wellesley went to war against Tippu Sultan, and the ensuing Fourth Mysore War was short and decisive. British forces swept through Mysore and stormed its capital, Seringapatam, on May 4, 1799. With Tippu killed, Wellesley kept part of Mysore under control of the BEIC and used the rest to reward his Indian allies.

So far Governor-General Wellesley had been carried along on the premise of securing British interests against a French attack. But in 1800 he turned his attention to the Marathas, believing that so long as they remained outside his system, there could be no British supremacy in India. Had the Maratha chiefs united, the BEIC could have accomplished little, but the Maratha confederacy was never an organized or tightly controlled polity, suffering from a succession of inexperienced *peshwas* (chief ministers; the young Baji Rao II since 1795) and their infighting with military chiefs, who were increasingly asserting their independence. The two leading contenders for the Maratha leadership were Daulat Rao Sindhia, who had inherited a capable military force but lacked the necessary ability and determination, and the brilliant Jaswant Rao of Holkar, "a man cast in the mould of an Italian *condottiere,* [who] moved across the north Indian scene like a blazing and erratic comet."[11] The squabbling facilitated British intervention, especially considering the BEIC's suspicions of French influence with the Marathas. Wellesley was particularly concerned by French military adventurers Charles Benoit de Boigne and General Pierre Perron, who had played an important role in setting up armies for the Sindhia.[12]

Exploiting the ongoing power struggle between the Maratha contenders, Wellesley negotiated the Treaty of Bassein with the Maratha *peshwa* Baji Rao II, who accepted a subsidiary alliance, guaranteeing his security but forsaking his control of foreign affairs.[13] This was Wellesley's master stroke, for while the treaty ostensibly called for the protection of the "peace, union, and friendship" between the Marathas and the BEIC, in reality it paved the way for British supremacy in the Deccan because the terms effectively turned the Maratha Confederacy into a virtual protectorate of the British. The Maratha lords of Holkar, Sindhia, and Bhonsle naturally refused to recognize this agreement and went to war with the BEIC, which made great use of its subsidiary alliances to shore up support for the war.[14] Hence, when Arthur Wellesley, younger brother to Richard and the future Duke of Wellington, marched to fight the Marathas, the bulk of his forces were, in fact, troops from Mysore, consisting of five sepoy infantry battalions of the Madras Native Infantry and three squadrons of Madras Native Cavalry. Equally effective was the BEIC's use of political intrigue and bribery to split up the Maratha Confederacy (Holkar chose not to fight at the start of the war) and to encourage desertion among the Sindhia's European officers (many British or Anglo-Indian), who took up offers of generous rewards if they switched sides.

The Second Maratha War was fought on several fronts across a sizable area. Despite serious logistical challenges, the British were able to overcome their opponents, with Arthur Wellesley defeating the Sindhia-Bhonsle coalition at Assaye in west-central India. This "most brilliant and important victory," as the Duke of Wellington put it, actually involved just one brigade of Sindhia's forces, with almost 50,000 men taking no part in the fighting.[15]

Still, Wellesley's victory at Assaye, followed by victories at Argaon and Gawilghur, resulted in the defeat of Sindhia's and Berar's armies in the Deccan. Simultaneously, General Gerard Lake (future 1st Viscount Lake) pushed on to Delhi (where the British took the aged emperor Shah ʿAlam II under protection), Agra, and lands north of the Chambal River, all of which fell after Lake defeated Sindhia's French-trained army at Delhi and Laswari.[16] These victories allowed Richard Wellesley to negotiate the Treaties of Deogaon and Surji-Arjungaon (December 1803), which forced the Marathas (except for Holkar) to enter into subsidiary alliances with the BEIC, to recognize the earlier Treaty of Bassein, to permit the company political access through the stationing of a British resident at court, to cede territory, and to banish Europeans other than the British from their service; in exchange they would receive military and financial support in the case of internal conflict or external threats.[17]

The Anglo-Maratha wars were not over, however. In 1804 Jaswant Rao of Holkar, realizing his mistake of not supporting the neighboring Marathas, intervened and scored quick victories that allowed him to besiege Delhi by the end of the year. The fall of Delhi would have been unquestionably calamitous to British prestige and interests, but the city's garrison gallantly defended it. The intervention of Holkar served as a signal for the exasperated BEIC directors, and the British cabinet, to seek an end to the conflict, which placed enormous financial strains on the Company.

British colonial expansion elsewhere followed a similar pattern. Southeast Asia, particularly the area around the Straits of Malacca, became significant to the British because it controlled the route to and from Canton (Guangzhou), the only port the Manchu dynasty of China opened to the British. This region, however, had been under control of the (Dutch) United East India Company (VOC) since the seventeenth century. Before the French Revolution, Britain's concern for the security of its Indian possessions put a premium on friendly relations with the Dutch Republic. Once the republic came under French influence in May 1795, however, the British moved against the Dutch in the East Indies.[18] The British government ordered all Dutch property seized and launched general reprisals against Dutch colonial possessions. A squadron under Rear Admiral George Elphinstone, the future 1st Viscount Keith, was dispatched to take possession of the Dutch settlement at the Cape of Good Hope, while Commodore Peter Rainier, commanding the East India Squadron, deployed his forces to Ceylon. Acting out of the concern that French control of the Dutch Republic might deliver the Kandyan kingdom of Ceylon to the French, Rainier occupied the coastal areas of the island in 1796. Five years later, at the outbreak of war between Britain and Denmark, the BEIC took control of the Danish colonies of Frederiksnagore (Serampore) and Tranquebar (Tharangambadi), consolidating its possessions in India.

Initially, British interests in the Persian Gulf were exclusively commercial. In the seventeenth century the BEIC supported the Safavid dynasty of Iran against the Portuguese, which allowed the British to reap handsome rewards in regional trade. At the same time, in 1661 the East India Company gained capitulations from the Ottoman sultan, who sanctioned British trade in the Ottoman provinces adjacent to the Persian Gulf and fixed customs duties on English trade at 3 percent. A BEIC factory opened at Basra in 1725 and soon forced rival Dutch merchants to move their station to Kharg Island. By the 1750s, during the Seven Years' War, French agents (with consular rank) attempted to challenge the British in the region, but the BEIC's interests rapidly became dominant. The company kept a resident (*baleos*) with consular rank at Basra until 1798, when the office was moved to Baghdad. More important, the company fully exploited its economic power to support regional authorities even when they conflicted with the Ottoman government. Thus the BEIC played an important role in supporting the Georgian Mamluks who governed Baghdad until 1831 and increasingly drew their main supplies, particularly ammunition, from India, making them heavily dependent on the BEIC's goodwill.

By 1800 the BEIC considered withdrawing from the Gulf coast because of declining trade. But French political rhetoric and overtures to the Near East made such a withdrawal unacceptable. Some French diplomats called for expansion into the Levant as a springboard to eventual conquest of India. "Once we are masters of the Red Sea," explained Charles Magallon, the French consul in Cairo, in a memorandum in 1795, "we shall soon control the English and drive them out of India, if an operation of the kind is envisaged by our government."[19] Only a year later the British were alarmed by news of a scientific expedition undertaken by the distinguished French naturalists Jean Guillaume Bruguière and Guillaume Antoine Olivier to the Ottoman Empire, an expedition the British suspected was in fact a reconnaissance mission. Indeed, the naturalists' expedition was not purely scientific—it was intended to assess the situation in the Near East, to revive the 1708 and 1715 commercial treaties with Iran, and to entice the new Iranian government to ally with France.[20] Bruguière and Olivier spent more than three years traveling in the Middle East and eventually made it to Tehran, where they were received at the Qajar court. The shah of Iran, Agha Muhammad, was not impressed by the humble appearance of the French envoys (to allay British and Ottoman suspicions, they traveled without an entourage) and therefore showed little interest in Bruguière and Olivier's offers, especially since he was preoccupied at the time with political problems in the Caucasus and northeastern Iran. In 1798 the French envoys returned back home empty-handed.[21] By then the French invasion of Egypt was already under way, with Bonaparte informing the members of the Executive Directory that "as soon as he became master of Egypt, he would establish relations with the Indian princes, and, together with them, attack the British in their possessions."[22]

The French activities revived British interest in the Near East, but the British government found itself in disagreement on what to do next. The Foreign Office, led by Foreign Secretary William Wyndham Grenville, down-played the importance of the French invasion of Egypt; he was more anxious to shore up the anti-French coalition back in Europe, which wanted France expelled from the Low Countries.[23] Henry Dundas, Secretary of State for War and President of the Board of Control of the BEIC, strongly disagreed with this approach. He believed that Britain was an imperial state and must focus on defending its strategic and commercial interests, leaving the task of restraining France in Europe for the continental powers.[24] The Board of Control argued that once the French had consolidated their control of Egypt, they would inevitably threaten British interests in Asia. They could do that by choosing one of four lines of advance to India: (1) through Constantinople, along the Black Sea, and through Iran and Herat; (2) through Egypt to the Red Sea and then straight to India; (3) through Hejaz, Yemen, and Muscat to the Indian Ocean; or (4) through Syria into southern Iraq, then across the Persian Gulf to India. Dundas and his supporters believed the ultimate purpose for the French expedition was the overthrow of British power in India. The French must therefore be dealt with vigorously. "We have won an empire by armed might, and it must continue to rest on armed might, otherwise it will fall by the same means, to a superior power," one BEIC official noted. Another argued that "we cannot doubt for a moment that the French Republic would try to exploit this situation to introduce into India the revolutionary machinations she has successfully employed in almost all parts of Europe."[25]

Horatio Nelson's victory at Abukir Bay on August 1, 1798, meant that the French lines of communication were severed, hampering Bonaparte in his future movements. However, the threat of a French attack via the Red Sea or the Persian Gulf prompted Dundas to send reinforcements to India and to request that the British Admiralty increase the naval presence in the Arabian Sea. In 1798 Jonathan Duncan, the British governor of Bombay, sought to secure the goodwill of Sultan ibn Ahmad of Muscat (Oman), who ruled a state whose political influence extended to most of the lower Persian Gulf and the coastline of East Africa and southern Arabia—all very suitable staging points for a potential French expedition to India.[26] In fact, Bonaparte had already dispatched a letter to the sultan, informing him of the French occupation of Egypt and asking for assistance in establishing communications with Tippu Sultan in India. The letter was intercepted by the British navy at Mocha and forwarded to the BEIC, where it only increased apprehensions about French designs. In mid-October 1798 the BEIC envoy convinced the sultan to accept the first written British treaty of friendship with an Arab ruler in the Gulf. In exchange for preferential treatment of his merchants in India, the sultan pledged to deny the French access to his territory and to assist the British in their naval operations.[27]

The BEIC remained concerned about a possible French excursion from Egypt. To guard against such a possibility, the BEIC government of Bombay sent an expedition, under command of Lieutenant Colonel John Murray of the 84th Regiment, to occupy the island of Perim, which controlled the Straits of Bab al-Mandab, in April and May 1799.[28] This expedition, however, proved to be a fiasco, since the island was inhospitable and unable to support a garrison. After wasting away for more than five months on what was effectively a barren rock, Murray suggested occupation of neighboring Aden, which offered better conditions for troops and still allowed for control of the entrance into the Red Sea. His force of some 300 men moved to Aden, where Ahmed bin Abdul Karim, sultan of Lahej, received them hospitably and even offered Aden to the British. As one modern historian justly noted, Murray's decision to occupy Aden was not as simple as it seems. It implied that the British had permanent interests in the region and that they were important enough to warrant a military base in Arabia. In effect, Murray was asking the BEIC leadership to "consider for the first time, how far west and in what form should be the farthest outposts of British India."[29] Ultimately the British withdrew from both Perim and Aden, considering them dispensable in their defense of India. But the debate within the British government and the BEIC over occupation of these remote locations offers revealing insight into the factors that shaped British policies. The involvement of so many different government bodies often resulted in perplexing and contradictory policy.[30] Commercial and political factors naturally played lead roles, but so did the interests of individuals who sought independent command and expected rewards and promotions.

The threat posed by the French presence in Egypt was alleviated in the summer of 1799. As previously discussed, Bonaparte's campaign in Palestine ended in a defeat at the siege of Acre (Akko), effectively putting an end to the possibility that the French would attempt passage to India through the Persian Gulf or Red Sea. Meanwhile, Britain concluded an alliance with the Ottoman Empire. General Kléber, whom Bonaparte designated as his successor upon abandoning the army, had to negotiate with the British and Turks and agreed in the Convention of El Arish of January 24, 1800, to evacuate Egypt. However, after the French surrendered several key fortresses, the British vice admiral Viscount Keith renounced the convention and the Turkish army seized Cairo. In response, Kléber destroyed Ottoman forces at Heliopolis on March 29 and then promptly recaptured Cairo. Alas, this was his last success - a Muslim zealot assassinated him on June 14. The command of the French army transferred to General Jacques-François Menou, who was both less capable and unpopular with the troops.

In its concern for India, the Board of Control was not assuaged by the military successes the anti-French coalition had scored in 1799. The Allies had reclaimed most of Italy and had driven the French behind the Rhine, an Anglo-Russian army had invaded Holland, and the fourth Anglo-Mysore War had resulted in the defeat of pro-French Tippu Sultan of Mysore and further reduction in Mysorean territory. Dundas was pleased to hear of these successes, of course, but his concern continued to revolve around the possible threats to India.[31] The Franco-Spanish threats against Portugal, for example, raised the prospect of the French securing control of Portugal's outposts at Diu and Goa. A French army could break out of Egypt, sail along the coastline, land at the estuary of the Indus, and link up with the Marathas or Zaman Shah Durrani, who had thrice descended upon northern India between 1792 and 1797 and advanced as far as Lahore.[32] British authorities were also disturbed by the growing understanding between Paris and St. Petersburg and reports that they were planning a joint invasion of India.

To protect British interests in India, the Board of Control desired to establish a new frontier zone in northwestern India and in the process inserted the issue of the North-West Frontier into British political discourse. Dundas argued that defending British India required acquiring the island of Diu from the Portuguese, who would be unable to defend themselves against a French attack, and establishing control over the Maratha territory in Gujarat, where the British could maintain a subsidiary force at the expense of the Marathas.[33] This was easier said than done, for the British victory over Mysore created yet new challenges.[34] Sir James Craig, the senior BEIC officer in Bengal, argued that the British triumph over Tippu Sultan had alarmed local rulers across much of India and caused them to rally around the Marathas and Zaman Shah. Other BEIC officers contended that though a French invasion was no longer an immediate threat, the prospect of such an invasion would endure as long as the French stayed in Egypt.

The French army might have suffered losses during its two-year occupation of Egypt, but in the minds of the British officers it was still a formidable opponent, especially when it came to fighting non-Western forces, a point of view reinforced by the French victory over the Ottomans at Heliopolis. In an act of desperation, they might break out of Egypt and fight their way to India, where local dissatisfaction with Britain's recent victories would have created fertile ground for supporting a French invasion. "The preservation of our Indian empire absolutely requires…the destruction of the French army in Egypt," declared a senior BEIC officer in 1799.

———◇◇◯§◯◇◇———

Such wider geopolitical considerations set the ground for the final British efforts against the French presence in Egypt.[35] This undertaking consisted of a multi-pronged strategy to secure their interests in the Mediterranean and Red Seas, although key British officials disagreed on where precisely efforts should be concentrated.[36] Ultimately it was agreed that one force, under Sir Ralph Abercromby, would attack the French from the Mediterranean, while another, under Sir David Baird, would sail from Bombay to attack from the Red Sea.[37] In early 1801 Abercromby's men were conveyed by the British Mediterranean Fleet to the north coast of Egypt, where they landed on March 1. The British proceeded to inflict a serious blow on their opponents at Alexandria on March 20–21. The two-day engagement claimed as many as 3,000 French and 1,400 British casualties, including Abercromby himself.

Their defeat left the French severely demoralized, and disagreements between Menou and his generals only exacerbated the situation. French troops were isolated from each other and confined to the major cities of Alexandria and Cairo. General John Hely-Hutchinson, who replaced Abercromby, pushed deeper into Egypt, capturing Cairo in late May. At this time the second British force, under Sir David Baird, was still at sea, detained by contrary winds. Not until July did it land in Egypt, at Kosseir on the western coast of the Red Sea. Thence Baird's men marched across the desert due westward to the banks of the Nile and northward to Cairo, where they arrived in August 1801 only to find that the French had already been vanquished by Abercromby's expeditionary force. Beset by the Anglo-Ottoman forces, struggling to contain worsening plague, and despairing of ever receiving reinforcements from France, the French capitulated on August 31, 1801, on the promise of repatriation to France.[38]

———◇◇◯§◯◇◇———

British efforts to protect their Indian possessions were not limited only to Egypt and Arabia. Of equally grave concern was the threat emanating from Afghanistan, where Zaman Shah Durrani had consolidated his power and repeatedly threatened to invade northern India. In the autumn of 1798 the Afghan leader was once more menacing the Punjab from his staging grounds at Peshawar. For the British, restraining Zaman Shah posed a crucial challenge, one they sought to accomplish with the help of Iran.

Iran had a long history of relations with the West, though its knowledge of Europe (and vice versa) had long bordered on the fantastic and even whimsical. This situation improved in the sixteenth century when the Safavid monarchy established close contacts with European powers, employing many Westerners (especially Englishmen) to improve its military and pursuing commercial ties with a host of European merchants. Western travelers frequented Iran, increasing European knowledge of this faraway land as well as shaping Iranian perceptions of Europe, which were based on convictions of Iranian civilizational and religious superiority. Indeed, the Iranian *Weltanschauung* reflected a deeply held conviction that Iran was at the center of the known world and that its rulers were the most exalted of sovereigns.[39] Petrus Bedik, a Catholic Armenian missionary cum Austrian diplomat who visited Iran in the 1670s, wrote at length of Iranian society's growing acquaintance with the *farangians* (Westerners), even if this understanding was marked by a deep sense of superiority. The Persians saw the "Russians as uncultured, the Poles as bellicose, the French as quarrelsome, the Spanish as noble, the Italians as sagacious, the English as politically inclined, and the Dutch as mercantile."[40]

The eighteenth century saw Iran gradually awakening to the reality of growing European power. The once-glorious Safavid dynasty fell to the Afghan invasion in 1722, causing the state to disintegrate. Although the military adventurer Nadir Shah briefly reunited Iran, neither he nor his successors were able to put an end to the widespread anarchy that afflicted Iran and Central Asia. The final phase of this prolonged civil strife took place in the 1780s when Qajar tribesmen conducted a successful campaign against their rivals and made their leader, Agha Muhammad Khan, undisputed master of Iran.

Although his reign proved to be rather brief—he was proclaimed shah in 1796 and murdered by his servants just a year later—Agha Muhammad Shah (and his successor) benefited from the turmoil in Europe. The start of the Revolutionary Wars drew the attention of European powers away from Iran and Central Asia, albeit temporarily. Russian and British preoccupation with events in France and the resulting absence of their militaries in the East meant that the Iranian armies were the strongest military force in the region and the Qajar ruler practically an unimpeded master of the fast-resurgent Iranian state. Before his death, Agha Muhammad could afford to reject French offers of military cooperation and joint assistance to Tippu Sultan in India.

The shah's chosen successor was his nephew Fath Ali Shah, who had ambitions to expand his realm westward into the Caucasus, as we'll see, and eastward into Khurasan and Afghanistan to recover the former Safavid territories held by Zaman Shah, amir of Kabul, whom the BEIC governor-general of Bengal, Lord Wellesley, had invited to cooperate against Tippu Sultan—only to have second thoughts about his offer. Tippu was killed in battle in 1798, and with the Afghan assistance no longer needed, Zaman Shah's appearance in India could pose serious problems for the BEIC; Wellesley was aware of negotiations the Afghan amir was conducting with the powerful Indian princes. The Afghan menace was made even more formidable in Wellesley's eyes by the French invasion of Egypt and their professed interest in driving the British out of India. Thus Fath Ali's intention to reclaim former Safavid territories presented the British with the opportunity to conclude a mutually profitable arrangement that would both constrain the Afghan lord and, potentially, strengthen British interests in Tehran to prevent the spread of French influence.

In late 1798 Wellesley made his first attempt to negotiate with Fath Ali, but it fell short of expectations, with the shah being irritated by the BEIC's intercession and simply promising to detain any Frenchman found along the Iranian coastline.[41] Fresh reports about Zaman Shah's preparations to invade Punjab prompted Wellesley to launch a more robust diplomatic effort to Iran. In January, at Wellesley's orders, Captain John Malcolm traveled to the Persian Gulf, where he was instructed to solicit Iranian support to contain Zaman Shah as well as to "counteract the possible attempts of those villainous but active democrats, the French."[42]

The Iranian court tended to determine the status of visiting European embassies in light of a particular country's usefulness as well as by the splendor of its mission and gifts. Malcolm, a shrewd and perceptive man, understood that "the two great necessities of diplomacy in Iran were the giving of presents and the stickling for forms," and he was determined to make his visit a memorable one.[43] He was accompanied by an enormous entourage: "six European gentlemen, two European servants, two surveying boys, forty-two troopers of the Madras native Cavalry, forty-nine Bombay Grenadiers, sixty-eight Indian servants and followers, a hundred and three Persian attendants, and two hundred and thirty-six servants and followers belonging to the gentlemen of the Mission."[44] The British mission was received by Fath Ali Shah in Tehran on November 16, 1800.

Malcolm's efforts soon paid off. He was able to proceed rapidly with negotiations for commercial and political treaties, which were signed on January 28, 1801. Fath Ali agreed to attack Afghanistan should the Afghan ruler threaten India, while Britain undertook to supply the shah with military support if he was attacked by the Afghans or if a French army attempted to establish itself "on any of the islands or shores of Persia."[45] Although signed, the Anglo-Iranian treaty could not be enforced until it was ratified by the respective parties. In early 1802 Fath Ali sent his ambassador Hajji Khalil Khan to secure formal ratification, but this mission suffered a dramatic setback early on when, upon reaching Bombay, the Iranian ambassador was mistakenly killed in an altercation between his retinue and British troops. The BEIC authorities hastened to make amends for this incident and sent such lavish gifts to the shah that he is said to have quipped that more ambassadors could be killed on the same terms. The threatened break in Anglo-Iranian relations did not materialize.[46] Yet by then the treaty was already obsolete: Zaman Shah, who had struggled to contain internal dissensions within his own realm, was deposed and blinded by his rivals in late 1800.

For Fath Ali Shah, these diplomatic overtures with Britain presented an opportunity to deal with a threat far more serious than Afghani tribesmen: the Russian Empire. Prior to the eighteenth century Iran and Russia had had sporadic contacts, although commercial activity between them increased following Tsar Ivan IV's conquest of Kazan and Astrakhan in the late sixteenth century and the Russian expansion to the Caspian littoral in the seventeenth century. The reign of Peter the Great saw a major transformation in the nature of Russo-Iranian relations. Despite Russia's exhaustion after the Great Northern War (1700–1721), Peter turned his attention to the Caspian Sea, where he campaigned (with partial success) in 1722–1723.[47] Russian involvement in Iranian affairs faded away after the tsar's death. In 1732–1735 Nadir Khan, the maverick warlord who restored Iranian power after the political turmoil of the 1720s, forced Peter's successors to give up previous conquests and by the Treaties of Rasht (1732) and Ganja (1735) to withdraw the Russian presence in the former Iranian provinces. Following the death of Nadir Shah in 1747, Iran descended into political chaos, while Russia remained preoccupied with the Ottomans and European affairs.

By the 1780s Russia showed growing interest in the southern Caucasus, especially in eastern Georgia, where King Erekle (Heraclius) of Kartli-Kakheti sought Russian help against the Ottomans and Iran. The Russian government considered a foothold in southern Caucasia valuable for a number of reasons. For starters, expansion fit well into Russian statecraft because it had long been a feature of Moscow's policy, with the process of "gathering the Russian lands" extending back at least four centuries.[48] Indeed, this "gathering" was later expanded to include non-Russian principalities, with Russia exploiting a rather fortuitous circumstance: that it was so much stronger than its immediate neighbors. Russian expansion in the Caucasus raised the prospect of accessing regional trade networks, which Russia aspired to dominate. The Caucasus also offered a position from which to exert additional pressure on the Ottoman Empire, Russia's historical rival, and to project authority into Iran, where political turmoil created favorable conditions. Furthermore, many in the Russian government believed that local Caucasian states—whether the Christian Georgian kingdom or its neighboring Muslim khanates—possessed vast natural resources that Russia could utilize, and that those states would welcome the arrival of the "benevolent" northern power to counterbalance Iran's presence in the region. Thus in 1781 a Russian expedition, led by Count Voinovich, landed near Astrabad with the goal of establishing a fortified base and facilitating the subsequent conquest of Persia's northern provinces. Agha Muhammad Khan, the new leading contender in Persia's power struggle, quickly realized the threat and had the members of the expedition arrested and deported. Although Agha Muhammad then tried to smooth over relations with Russia, Catherine II felt slighted by the incident and refused to accept the Iranian envoys. The relations between two powers continued to deteriorate, with the Russians supporting Agha Muhammad's opponents and Agha Muhammad imposing tariffs on Russian products.[49]

The turning point in Russo-Iranian relations took place in 1783, when the eastern Georgian kingdom of Kartli-Kakheti and Russia signed the Treaty of Georgievsk, which placed much of eastern Caucasia under Russian protection.[50] The arrival of Russian troops in Georgia was of major importance. Not only did it challenge Iranian and Ottoman influences in the Caucasus, but it served notice to rival European powers, most notably France, that the balance of power in the Near East was shifting in Russia's favor. Yet this promising start to the Russo-Georgian relationship proved to be brief, as Russian implementation of the treaty guarantees proved sorely inadequate. In 1787, as Russia became embroiled in yet another conflict with the Ottomans, Catherine II recalled her troops from Georgia, effectively leaving King Erekle II of Kartli-Kakheti to look after his own defense.[51]

Russia spent the next decade preoccupied with Polish and Balkan affairs, not the Caucasus. This allowed Iran to attempt to restore its authority over southern Caucasia. In 1795 Agha Muhammad Shah led an invasion of eastern Georgia, unleashing the full force of his wrath on the Georgian capital city, Tiflis (present-day Tbilisi), where thousands of local residents were massacred or taken into captivity.[52] Russia provided no military help against the Iranian invasion, but the news of the sack of Tiflis did outrage Catherine II, who understood that the Persians had dealt a major blow to Russia's status in the region. In response, she sanctioned an invasion of Iran to overthrow Agha

Muhammad and replace him with a more favorable (from Russia's perspective) candidate. The Russian troops, led by Count Valerian Zubov, set out in April 1796, capturing Derbent and obtaining nominal submission of most of the east Caucasian khanates.[53]

The deaths of Catherine II in 1796 and of Agha Muhammad Shah in 1797 created an opportunity for rapprochement between the two powers. As we've seen, Russian emperor Paul shared Catherine's general outlook on the nature of Russia's interest in Western Asia and India but distanced himself from her methods and showed reluctance to project Russian interests in the East through force. Rather, seeking to resolve the ongoing conflict with Iran through diplomatic means, Paul pursued, in the words of one historian, "a pragmatic diplomacy," one that was based on rational evaluation of local circumstances and conciliatory, if also forceful, policy toward Iran.[54]

The new Iranian ruler, Fath Ali Shah, also sought improved relations with Russia, and his efforts were well received by Emperor Paul, who agreed to limit the Russian presence in the Caspian Sea. However, Russia's refusal to withdraw from Georgia proved to be the most divisive issue, since no Iranian ruler could seriously consider abandoning a region that for so many generations had been under the influence of the Iranian state. In the summer of 1798 Fath Ali urged unsuccessfully Giorgi XII, who would be the last king of Kartli-Kakheti, to abandon his alliance with Russia and rally to the Iranian banner.

Although Russian actions in 1787–1796 effectively invalidated the Treaty of Georgievsk, Giorgi XII felt that he had no recourse but to seek Russian protection.[55] Aside from Iranian encroachments, he was beset by court intrigue and challenges from his own brothers for the crown. In September 1799 the king sent an embassy to St. Petersburg with instructions to surrender his realm into the care of Emperor Paul—"not under his protection, but into his full authority"—provided that his throne was guaranteed and the royal dignity was preserved forever in the royal family of Bagration (Bagrationi); in effect, Giorgi XII was seeking a status comparable to that of native rajahs under the British Empire in India. The Russian imperial government showed interest in the request because the French invasion of Egypt had highlighted the possibility of European encroachment into the Middle East. Furthermore, Giorgi's health was rapidly declining, and considering the hard-nosed nature of the Georgian court struggles, it was natural to expect that claimants would seek help not only from Russia but from the Ottoman Empire and Iran, a prospect that clearly was alarming to the Russian court.

Keen to secure his position in the region, Emperor Paul agreed to guarantee royal dignity and privileges to King Giorgi, but he also took measures to ensure greater Russian control over the eastern Georgian realm. In November 1799 a small Russian force arrived in Tiflis, and in November 1800 Paul instructed the Russian general in command of the Caucasian front to pre-empt any Georgian efforts to nominate an heir to the Georgian throne in the event of King Giorgi's death. Peter Kovalenskii, the Russian ambassador to Kartli-Kakheti, gradually assumed control of Georgia's foreign relations. The Russian and Iranian courts soon exchanged fiery notes reaffirming each court's determination to keep eastern Georgia under its control and threatening to defend its interests by force.

Despite Iranian protestations, on December 18, 1800, in further violation of the Treaty of Georgievsk, Russia unilaterally abolished the Georgian kingdom of Kartli-Kakheti and had it annexed to the empire as a province.[56] Giorgi XII passed away ten days later, still unaware of the Russian imperial manifesto. The Russian military authorities quickly moved to prevent the Bagration claimants from acceding to the crown and to set up a temporary administration, just as Paul's instructions required of them. Yet before he could tackle this succession problem, Paul was himself assassinated in St. Petersburg in March 1801, leaving the Georgian question to his successor to resolve.

Russia drew several lessons from its involvement in the Caucasus and Iran. Its political, commercial, and intellectual circles found such involvement highly desirable because it fostered perception of Russia as the equal of the great Western powers. Having missed out on European colonialism in the sixteenth and seventeenth centuries, Russia could now lay claim to membership in the circle of great powers by securing colonies on its periphery. This was especially important in light of Bonaparte's expedition to Egypt. The Iranian sack of Tiflis in 1795 was a turning point in Russian involvement in the Caucasus and directly contributed to Russia's permanent involvement in the wider region, as it was a blow to Russia's prestige and encouraged the Russian monarchy to play a more direct and active role in eastern Georgia and beyond.

———◇◇◇◇◇———

The start of the French Revolutionary Wars in April 1792 was one of the most decisive events in modern European history—a watershed, to use an overused word, in the development of the international system. The conflicts that resulted from it established a new political reality, with France hegemonic in western Europe, Russia dominant in eastern Europe, and Britain remaining supreme on the seas. War had an immediate and direct impact on France and its neighbors: revolutionary ideology shaped hearts and minds (to employ another overused phrase), while revolutionary arms ravaged the countryside and required the mobilization of human and material resources on an unprecedented scale.

Several factors contributed to the failure of the continental powers to contain France and prevent political realignment. The first decade of the war was the result of a general breakdown of the existing balance of power system rather than of a French revolutionary challenge to it. Indeed, the threat posed by revolutionary France did not immediately dominate European politics. In the early stages of the war, France faced monarchies that were preoccupied by their own concerns. Britain initially welcomed revolutionary upheaval in France because it weakened its traditional rival and, at least at first, seemed similar to what England itself had experienced slightly more than a century prior. The two German powers, Prussia and Austria, continued to look at each other with a deep antipathy that often complicated their military cooperation. Russia remained on the sidelines for much of the revolutionary decade, exploiting Austrian-Prussian preoccupation with France to seek territorial aggrandizement in eastern Europe and the Caucasus. In Germany, some princes of the Holy Roman Empire supported the French revolutionary armies, hoping to expand at the expense of their neighbors. The fates of Poland and the Ottoman Empire remained overriding issues.

During the War of the First Coalition European monarchies did not necessarily view revolutionary France as an irreconcilable foe, and were ready to negotiate and conclude separate treaties with it; Austrian foreign minister Johann Amadeus von Thugut, who loathed the Revolution, nevertheless argued that there was no need to destroy the revolutionary regime.[57] But the turmoil in Paris meant that France was not a stable negotiating partner, and it seemed keen on shaping Europe into its new image. The First Coalition finally collapsed because of its members' conflicting political aspirations as well as France's ability to exploit this disunity while mobilizing its own resources.

The Revolutionary Wars also proved to be very different from what either side had initially expected. Despite suffering early setbacks, the French revolutionaries responded by waging war *à outrance*, which was contrary to the established practices of the Old Regime. French civilian and military authorities cooperated, albeit grudgingly and oftentimes hostilely, in forging a new army that was at its heart the old royal army, though one that had eliminated most of its deficiencies and retained many of its strengths. The meritocracy ushered in by the Revolution revealed a new cadre of commanders whose talents and abilities proved to be of great service to the revolutionary cause, and the ruthlessness with which the revolutionary government dealt with unsuccessful generals made the French commanders more zealous to win. The European powers, on the other hand, struggled to adapt their military establishments in such a way as to allow them similarly to maximize their resources.

With the war, the French Revolution spread beyond France, threatening traditional order and ushering in radical change. Its famous motto—"Liberté, egalité, fraternité"—offers a concise summary of the decade that followed 1789. In France and its colonies overseas, the dismantling of the Old Regime was rapid. The Revolution began as a patriotic reform movement championed by reform-minded ministers and aristocrats, but its failure to bring about effective change turned it into a rather confused and incoherent effort to replace the traditional political order with a more democratic one. This desire to create a new society, one in which law and authority sprang from below rather than from above, was genuinely revolutionary. It espoused the cause of liberty and the Declaration of the Rights of Man and of Citizen, which proudly declared that "men are born and remain free and equal in rights."

Between 1789 and 1799 the remnants of feudalism were swept aside in France, clerical privileges were curtailed, the French middle class won its freedom from obsolete restraints, and Protestants, Jews, and freethinkers gained the equality and toleration that had been denied them for so long. The Revolution made all men equal in the eyes of the law and advanced fraternity in a broader sense by encouraging nationalism, which had existed before 1789 but became a powerful creed in the concluding decade of the eighteenth century. The *levée en masse* of August 23, 1793, served as a clear manifestation of this new nationalist creed, as it called for total mobilization of the French population in the name of defending *la patrie* and gave various sections of the population a stake in their country and its wars.

Emboldened by their unexpected military successes, the revolutionaries promised "fraternity and assistance to all peoples who want to recover their liberty," and the French armies that swept through neighboring territories often met with shouts of revolutionary slogans in Italian, German, Dutch, and other languages.[58] But the initial enthusiasm soon became more subdued when the harsh realities of the occupation became clear and the benefits brought by the "liberators" seemed increasingly outweighed by the price exacted for them. The liberationist rhetoric of the French was belied by their exploitative practices, especially after September 1793, when the National Convention decreed that its generals should "renounce from henceforth every philanthropic idea previously adopted by the French people with the intention of making foreign nationals appreciate the value and benefits of liberty." The generals were instructed to "exercise with regard to the countries and individuals conquered by their armies the customary rights of war."[59] This decree effectively sanctioned spoliation of the occupied territories, where the French forces levied massive war contributions. As one French historian justly noted, these levies were "nothing more than well-organized looting."[60]

The armies expropriated not only monies but anything else that could benefit the republic. Cultural artifacts—paintings, sculptures, manuscripts, and so on—were at the top of expropriation lists, and the art treasures of Italian, Belgian, Dutch, and German cities soon found their way to France, which, as the official newspaper *Le Moniteur* brazenly declared, "by virtue of its power and the superiority of its culture and its artists is the only country in the world that can provide a secure refuge for these masterpieces."[61]

The revolutionary decade should not be perceived as a triumphant march, for it also revitalized the old traditions of absolutism and centralization. The quest for revolutionary change proved to be convoluted, and oftentimes it produced not liberty, equality, and fraternity but rather disillusionment, oppression, and civil strife. In France itself, this path led to the establishment of a government structure that was more centralized than had been the case under the Old Regime, while the Reign of Terror showed the terrifying power of the state, far eclipsing the supposedly absolutist monarchy of the Bourbon dynasty.

The war played a crucial role in this process, and French historian François Furet once observed that "the war conducted revolution far more than the Revolution conducted the war."[62] Indeed, international relations profoundly affected the domestic development of the Revolution, and after 1792 it was increasingly driven leftward as the war contributed to the rapid radicalization of French political discourse. The great revolutionary *journées* that defined the course of the Revolution—the revolt of August 10, 1792; the September 1792 massacres; the revolts of May 31 and June 2, 1793; even the coup of the Ninth of Thermidor in year II (July 27, 1794)—were all responses to developments in foreign affairs. Similarly, the war produced a new generation of military commanders that came to play increasingly greater role in French politics. Battered from all sides, unable to solve the country's economic problems, and still carrying on the wars inherited from the Committee of Public Safety, the Executive Directory increasingly relied on its military commanders to maintain its power. The most successful of France's conquering generals, Bonaparte was quick to understand the facts of the political situation. He had defended the government against a royalist uprising in 1795, successfully prosecuted war in Italy in 1796–1797, and again saved the government from another attempted coup in 1797. Newly returned from his seemingly victorious campaign in Egypt, Bonaparte plotted with some of its leaders to take over the state in a coup d'état that was successfully implemented in November 1799.

CHAPTER 6

The Rites of Peace, 1801–1802

WHILE THE WARFARE from 1792 to 1815 can be viewed as a single drama—the rise and fall of French hegemony in Europe, fueled by the energy of the Revolution—the starting point for the Napoleonic Wars is usually dated to the breakdown of the Peace of Amiens in May 1803. The ensuing twelve years of warfare were nevertheless a continuation of the Revolutionary Wars and produced major political, economic, and social changes throughout Europe. Ideological differences are often viewed as a major source of the conflict, but after Bonaparte's self-coronation as the emperor of the French in 1804, Europe was less sharply divided along ideological lines than by geopolitical considerations that predated the revolutionary era and were similar to those existing during the Wars of Louis XIV. France's military successes threatened the balance of power in Europe and led to the creation of broad coalitions of European powers to prevent the French from achieving complete dominance. The long-standing colonial and commercial rivalry between France and Britain served as a crucial backdrop to the Napoleonic Wars.

When General Bonaparte returned from Egypt to France in October 1799, he found the nation still in the grip of economic malaise and recovering from the last round of the War of the Second Coalition, in which the French experienced major setbacks in Italy and the Rhineland. The governing Directory struggled to cope with internal and external threats, including rebellions in the stubbornly royalist Vendée and Brittany regions, renewed hostilities with Austria and its allies, the rapid drop in value of government securities and paper money, and widespread banditry. But the Directory was not as incompetent or hapless as Bonaparte and his admirers long claimed. A more balanced reassessment reveals that it had a better record on domestic

France (frontiers of 1801)
France (annexations 1800-3)
French satellites
French occupation/administration
Frontier of Holy Roman Empire

1. Hanover/Hamburg
2. Batavian Republic
3. Neuchâtel
4. Helvetic Confederation
5. Republic of the Valais
6. Piedmont
7. Ligurian Republic
8. Parma
9. Italian Republic (showing territory gained since 1799)
10. Kingdom of Etruria
11. Papal States
12. Montenegro
13. Republic of the Seven Islands
14. Piombino (French occupied)
15. Lucca
16. Ragusa
17. Cattaro
18. Dalmatia
19. Malta (British garrison)

Map 7: Europe in 1803

policies than most of the revolutionary governments that preceded it. The seeds of a number of reforms that Bonaparte later claimed credit for had in fact been planted by the Directory. But most acknowledge that the Directory had lost the people's trust by failing to end what seemed to be interminable turmoil and to restore order and stability. It was unpopular and, therefore, vulnerable.[1]

Bonaparte did not have a well-defined plan of action when he reached Paris, but he was soon approached by a group of statesmen conspiring against the current French government. Led by Emmanuel Sieyès (himself a member of the Directory), these men thought they could control a simple military man like Bonaparte and were eager to exploit his status as a war hero for their political gain. Yet Bonaparte was anything but simple. On his arrival in Paris, he adopted the role of the modest and studious citizen, meeting with *savants*, delivering speeches on the scientific work of the Egyptian expedition at the Institut de France, and in general portraying himself as eager for knowledge and respectful of intellect. But deep in his heart he knew that "change here is indispensable," and he closely observed political undercurrents, exploring every party and faction—there may have been more than half a dozen active plots against the Directory—before committing to one.[2] Sieyès and his co-conspirators would soon realize that they had misjudged this man. They envisioned a manipulable "sword" that they could use to see the conspiracy through and then quietly "sheathe" in the aftermath. None foresaw that after effectively putting him in power they would be on the outside looking in.

On November 9–10 (Brumaire 18–19), 1799, the conspirators put their plans in motion. Claiming an imminent threat of a Jacobin plot, they induced both legislative councils to transfer their sessions to the relative safety (and isolation) of the former royal palace at St. Cloud, where their security would be ensured by Bonaparte and his troops. At the same time, the whole Directory resigned, starting with Sieyès himself; some members did so under pressure, and for others the process was sweetened with a bribe. Despite success on the eighteenth of Brumaire, matters did not go smoothly the following day, when the legislative council demanded explanations. Bonaparte's intervention only heightened tensions as he was mobbed and manhandled in the Council of Five Hundred, with some deputies denouncing him as an "outlaw." His brother Lucien Bonaparte, who served as president of the Council of Five Hundred, saved the day. Maintaining a cool head, he declared to the troops outside that an assassination attempt had been made on his brother and called upon them to restore order. In the highly charged atmosphere, this claim was enough to sway the troops and induce them to obey orders to dissolve the councils. Later the same night a compliant rump of the legislative councils was reassembled to formally vote on the dissolution.[3]

The ease with which the conspirators seized power demonstrated that after ten years of revolutionary turmoil and violence, the French people had become numbed to political upheaval and willing to accept yet another change in the government as long as it promised order and stability. The government that emerged from the Brumaire coup was provisional, tasked with providing France with a new constitution and a stable government. "Constitutions should be short and obscure," Bonaparte is credited with saying. The new constitution of France was both, and it demonstrated how deeply Sieyès and his colleagues had miscalculated. In the newly established three-man Consulate, Bonaparte, not Sieyès, was chosen as First Consul, with the authority to exercise full executive power; the Second and Third Consuls were given limited authority and could only advise the First Consul. The new constitution provided for a three-part legislature, but one that was closely controlled by the executive branch. It granted universal male suffrage but also created a mechanism to constrain electoral freedoms and negate the doctrine of popular sovereignty. The primary electorate, about six million men, was the largest in Europe, but they could exercise their right only by choosing communal electors, who in turn selected departmental electors. Furthermore, it was the consuls who decided who got into the three legislative institutions, the Legislative Corps, the Tribunate, and the Senate; they named a majority of the Senate, which in turn selected members of the remaining two legislative bodies. More important, the legislative process itself was designed in such a way as to emasculate the legislative bodies and make them incapable of challenging the executive branch. None of the legislative bodies could initiate laws, which was the prerogative of the State Council, a body of chosen experts presided over by the First Consul. The Tribunate could only discuss legislation, the Legislative Corps could only vote on proposed laws, and the Senate merely considered matters of constitutional interpretation. Between 1801 and 1803 Bonaparte effectively wielded his authority to purge these legislative bodies of any individuals who created difficulties for him. He also exploited existing loopholes in the constitution to bypass the legislature, relying on the Senate's privilege of issuing decrees (*senatus consulta*) to avoid any parliamentary opposition.[4]

For France, the Consulate (1800–1804) was one of the most dynamic periods of the entire nineteenth century.[5] The Revolution was now at an end. Its radical vestiges were swept aside, churches reopened, and émigrés were allowed to return home if they wished. Reconciliation and restoration of order became paramount. These policies helped secure public confidence in the new government and allowed Bonaparte to embark on a series of reforms that, taken together, constituted the most constructive and enduring legacy of his career. The key elements of these reforms combined preservation of the Revolution's gains with restoration of order. Stability of the nation's finances came as the result of vigorously applied centralization. Bonaparte replaced elected officials and local self-government, the hallmarks of the Revolution, with centrally appointed bureaucrats—prefects for the departments, sub-prefects for the districts, and mayors for towns and communes—who have remained at the heart of France's administrative system ever since.[6] To remove limitations to his power, Bonaparte resorted to various stratagems that exploited the uncritical approbation that the majority of the French people extended to the new head of state. He was the first political leader to make effective use of plebiscitary democracy to legitimize and sustain his authority, a practice that would become ubiquitous in the twentieth century.[7] Behind the façade of universal male suffrage and popular involvement in politics, Bonaparte's regime gave no actual power to the governed masses and instead skillfully shaped and control political process. Thus, a nationwide plebiscite of all French citizens, held in January-February 1800, on the establishment of the Consulate showed more than 3 million votes in favor of the new constitution and 1,562 votes against. The results of later plebiscites also suggested massive popular support, with the 1802 poll, which made Bonaparte a consul for life, showing more than 3.5 million votes in favor and just 9,074 against.[8] Of course, these figures should not be taken at face value—abstention rates were substantial, and the voting was not secret and therefore subject to intimidation and manipulation, especially on the part of Minister of Interior Lucien Bonaparte, who probably had forged as many as half of the "yes" votes.[9] Yet given that turnout was much higher than during the revolutionary era (see Table 6.1), the plebiscites represented, in the words of French historian Claude Langlois, "a relative success."[10] They suggested growing support for the new government, reflected in comments many voters wrote about Bonaparte on their ballots. "The man who has given us peace, religion and order in such a short space of time," declared one Parisian, "is the most capable of perpetuating these achievements." "A hero is needed to save France by bringing back joy and hope to our hearts and restoring liberty, justice, and peace," observed a voter in Lesmont (Department of the Aube).[11]

Bonaparte relied heavily on censorship and secret police to tame opposition. The first two years after the Eighteenth of Brumaire coup witnessed several conspiracies, the most threatening of which occurred on Christmas Eve of 1800. An "infernal machine"—a carriage loaded with gunpowder barrels—exploded in the street just as the First Consul was traveling to the Opéra. The explosion claimed at least twelve innocent bystanders and wounded twice as many. Bonaparte, unhurt, took this opportunity to suppress

Table 6.1: Constitutional Plebiscites in France

Year	Plebiscite	Estimated electorate	Abstention rate	Yes	No
1793	Adoption of the Constitution	7,000,000	73%	1,866,000	12,766
1795	Adoption of the Constitution	7,200,000	74%	957,000	915,000
1795	The "Two-Thirds" Laws	7,200,000	94%	263,000	168,000
1800	Adoption of the Constitution	7,900,000	62%	3,011,000	1,562
1802	Making Bonaparte First Consul for life	7,900,000	55%	3,568,000	9,074
1804	Proclamation of Empire	8,900,000	60%	3,524,000	2,579

Sources: Based on Thierry Lentz, *La France et l'Europe de Napoléon, 1804–1814* (Paris: Fayard, 2007); Claude Langlois, "Le plébiscite de l'an VIII ou le coup d'état du 18 Pluviôse an VIII," *Annales historiques de la Révolution française*, 1972; Malcolm Crook, *Elections in the French Revolution: An Apprenticeship in Democracy, 1789–1799* (Cambridge: Cambridge University Press, 1996).

domestic opposition. He first targeted his opponents on the left and, overcoming considerable reluctance on the part of his associates, insisted on introducing extraordinary measures to suppress "Jacobin agitation." One hundred and thirty well-known republicans were branded as terrorists and either interned or deported to Guiana, where climate and disease claimed many of them. With the left neutralized, Bonaparte then revealed "new" evidence that pointed toward the real perpetrators of the crime—his right-wing opponents, royalists and Chouans, led by Georges Cadoudal, who had received support from the British government. Although Cadoudal escaped to London, his co-conspirators were arrested, found guilty, and executed in 1801. The events of 1800–1801 revealed that Bonaparte troubled himself little about unorthodox methods provided they helped him suppress dissent and consolidate power.

This emphasis on centralization extended to public finances, which were tightened up and put upon a sound footing after years of mismanagement and disarray. In 1800 Bonaparte decreed the establishment of the Bank of France as the central financial institution, tasked with stabilizing the currency and facilitating government borrowing.[12] The same emphasis on centralization can be seen in Bonaparte's approach to education. He kept most of the revolutionary reforms that had offered free elementary education for all children (though in practice their implementation proved to be problematic). More important, Bonaparte reorganized secondary education, establishing the famed lycées, which were placed under close government supervision. In 1808 the French educational system was even further centralized and a single system (Université impériale), incorporating the entire range of public schools, was established.[13]

One of the most significant achievements of the Consulate was the codification of laws, the Code civil des Français, which ultimately became known as the Napoleonic Code. The French Revolution had swept away many of the statutes and law of the Old Regime and adopted myriad new laws, but it failed to reconcile them within a coherent legal structure. Bonaparte addressed this problem by setting up a committee to draft a new legal code. He regularly attended its meetings. In 1804 the new code was published and was later augmented by the Code of Civil Procedure (1806), the Code of Criminal Procedure (1808), and the Penal Code (1810). Together they represent a remarkable achievement, one based upon three innovative principles whose influence would transcend the codes' actual legal application: clarity, so that all citizens could understand their rights if they could read, without needing recourse to jurists steeped in customary law, with its hundreds of exemptions and eccentricities; secularism, which insisted on separating religion from the affairs of the state, recognized marriage as a secular civil contract, and permitted divorce, thereby paving the way for an entirely new form of individual and civic existence; and, finally, the right to individual ownership of property, which was declared absolute and inviolable. The new codes reflect the duality of Bonaparte's legacy. The Civil Code retained the main legal victories of the Revolution—equality before the law, the rights of citizens, abolition of manorial privileges—but it also marked a retreat to patriarchy in the realm of family life. The sanctity of private property, which the code upheld to the great benefit of the property-owning middle class, bedeviled French labor for much of the nineteenth century.[14]

The civil achievements of the Consulate occupied but part of Bonaparte's energy. The new century dawned amid unremitting hostility in Europe. As we have seen in earlier chapters, Austria and Prussia had conflicts of interest in Germany; Russia and Austria were at odds in the Balkans; Prussia, Austria, and Russia had designs on Poland; and all of them looked ravenously at the Ottoman Empire. For France, the most serious threats emanated from Britain and Austria, which were in a wearyingly prolonged struggle.

The start of the New Year (1801) had been elaborately celebrated in Britain and France, but for different reasons. On the British Islands, the first day of the nineteenth century was noteworthy for the final arrangements of the Act of Union, the defining event in modern Irish history and a focal point for the interlacing issues of nationalism and political identity. The act was the last stage—after the incorporation of Wales in 1535 and the amalgamation of Scotland in 1707—of a political process that brought about the establishment of the United Kingdom of Great Britain and Ireland. Some one hundred Irish members had been admitted into the House of Commons, and free trade between England and Ireland was formalized. The government of William Pitt had also promised to remove the laws against Roman Catholics that had driven so many Irish to rebel in 1798.[15] The Act of Union was ostensibly based on "fair, just and equitable principles," as described by its architects, but in practice it meant very different things to different people. For the British government, which celebrated it with salutes of gunfire and the hoisting of the new imperial standard over the Tower of London, the act represented the fulfillment of Britain's "civilizing mission," as Pitt put it, and was justified in the interests of the "power, stability, and the general welfare of the Empire."[16] Yet for many Irish the act sanctioned continued colonialism and exploitation by the Protestant minority of the Catholic majority.[17]

Across the English Channel, France was celebrating as well. The cause was the opening ceremonies of the Franco-Austrian peace conference at Lunéville, where a peace treaty was signed on February 9, 1801.[18] The Treaty of Lunéville ended nine years of enmity between the two powers and changed the map of Europe materially. With the French armies within striking distance of Vienna and Russia posturing menacingly in the east, Austria had little room for diplomatic maneuver.[19] The final treaty required Austria to confirm territorial concessions it had made in the Treaty of Campo Formio, starting with the loss of the entire left bank of the Rhine, which meant the net loss of more than 25,000 square miles and nearly 3.5 million residents. Austria was stripped of much of the territorial concessions it had received in Italy four years prior, and the treaty recognized the Helvetian (Swiss), Batavian (Dutch), Ligurian (Genoese), and Cisalpine (Lombardy) Republics, which became French dependencies. In addition, Vienna also agreed to give up the Grand Duchy of Tuscany and, more important, committed itself to the principle of secularization in Germany, which produced profound results within just two years.[20]

The Peace of Lunéville accomplished a major change in European affairs. It pacified continental Europe for the first time in a decade and provided a larger backdrop for France's negotiations with other states. The peace settlement was accepted, if grudgingly, by all continental powers. Even Austria considered Lunéville a decisive settlement, much to the chagrin of the hawkish Austrian foreign minister, Amadeus Frans de Paula Thugut, who understood that the treaty made Austria's decline as a great power irreversible.[21] France emerged as a hegemonic state in western Europe, with its power acknowledged in the Low Countries, Bavaria, Baden, Switzerland, and the Italian states.

No wonder, then, that the treaty was greeted with great relief and celebration in France; the public especially cheered the news of army demobilization and the return of thousands of conscripts who were about to be called up for service. On February 13, in his address to the Senate, Bonaparte celebrated the conclusion of the Treaty of Lunéville and declared that the French government would continue to "fight only to secure the peace and happiness of the world."[22]

Within weeks Bonaparte seemingly delivered on his promise, as he achieved two more diplomatic successes. On March 21, 1801, France and Spain signed the Treaty of Aranjuez, which was part of a larger diplomatic agreement between the two states: Ferdinand, duke of Parma, relinquished his ducal claims, and in return his son, Louis I, was granted the Kingdom of Etruria, which was created from the Grand Duchy of Tuscany vacated by Grand Duke Ferdinand III under the terms of the Treaty of Lunéville. The island of Elba passed from Tuscany into French possession, but in compensation Bonaparte agreed to transfer the Principality of Piombino and the State of Presidi (even though he did not control either of them) to Etruria. The treaty also laid the grounds for the cession by Spain of the vast territories of Louisiana to France.[23] Just a week later, on March 28, 1801, Bonaparte turned to Naples forcing it to accept the Treaty of Florence with Naples which made it possible for Bonaparte to fulfill provisions of the Franco-Spanish Treaty. The Neapolitan kingdom was saved from a French invasion by the intercession of Russia, but the terms of the treaty were predictably harsh.[24] Naples was compelled to cede the Principality of Piombino and the State of Presidi to France, withdraw troops from the Papal States, and close Neapolitan ports to British and Ottoman shipping. Naples also consented to the stationing of French troops, with Neapolitan financial support, on its territory.[25]

Continuing his peaceful outreach, Bonaparte negotiated with the leaders of the revolt in La Vendée, which had festered in western France for almost seven years. These negotiations were greatly facilitated by Bonaparte's conclusion of the Concordat with the papacy on July 15, 1801.[26] Although he himself was not *croyant*, Bonaparte understood that the vast majority of the French people were still devout Catholics and desired the return of organized religion to France. He spent weeks negotiating with the Vatican, with discussions kept secret because of potential hostility from liberal intellectuals and from the Jacobin elements still to be found in the military and many ministries.[27] "The Government of the Republic acknowledges that the Catholic, Apostolic and Roman religion is the religion of the great majority of French citizens," read the opening lines of the Concordat. This was one of the key passages of the document, as it included acknowledgment that while Catholicism might be the faith of "the great majority of the French," it was not the official state religion, thus establishing religious freedom in France. The treaty reorganized church dioceses and parishes, and it gave the papacy the right to depose bishops, although this made little difference because the French government nominated them and paid clerical salaries. The most significant provision of the treaty required the Roman Catholic church to give up all its claims to church lands that had been confiscated and nationalized since 1790.[28] The Concordat was welcomed in rural (and conservative) areas of France, but it was unpopular in the army, where many still retained revolutionary ideals and expressed their disappointment, if not outright anger, at the return of organized religion. When a Te Deum mass, the first in many years, was celebrated at Notre Dame on Easter Sunday (April 18), 1802, one of the generals was heard to remark, "*Quelle capucinade!* The only thing missing is one million men who died to get rid of all this!"[29]

The Concordat, however, had a lasting legacy. It helped to end the decade-long religious strife in France and remained the basis for relations between the French state and the papacy for a century.[30] Despite making a number of concessions, Bonaparte secured all the major points of contention—although the Catholic church returned to France, it did so under close supervision by the state. This became especially obvious after Bonaparte issued *Les Articles organiques*, a law that further strengthened the state control over the church. Bonaparte's goal of restoring law and order was much aided by the Concordat, for the church became a pillar of the state.

Bonaparte's peace offensive of 1801–1802 proved to be very successful. Each treaty was aimed at producing immediate, tangible results, bolstering Bonaparte's credentials abroad and consolidating his power at home. The First Consul preferred short negotiations to achieve deals with individual states and avoided getting involved in prolonged discussions on a general political settlement in Europe. Furthermore, he skillfully exploited circumstances to build upon each treaty negotiation. At Lunéville, for example, Bonaparte forced Austria to give up Tuscany and then used it as compensation to Spain for turning over Louisiana to France by the Treaty of Aranjuez; the same can be said about Franco-Neapolitan treaty that effectively subsidized France's arrangements with Spain. Yet Bonaparte's diplomatic overtures proved less successful in Russia, where he genuinely hoped to establish closer relations with the Romanov court,.

Russia seemed bereft of allies as the War of the Second Coalition produced considerable fissures in its relations with European powers. By the end of 1799 Emperor Paul I had become convinced that Russia's sacrifices had proved a futile expedient and that his Austrian and British allies could no longer be relied on as partners, a conclusion that would recur frequently in Russian military and political circles throughout the Napoleonic Wars. Annoyed by what he believed was the perfidy of the Austrian and British governments, Paul began to move away from his former allies. He recalled his troops from Switzerland, expelled the Austrian and British envoys from St. Petersburg, recalled his own ambassador from London (who refused to leave), and disgraced his Anglophile ministers.[31] More important, he embargoed British trade and began working toward reviving the League of Armed Neutrality in the Baltic. Emperor Paul's foreign policy has long been misrepresented. Though grandiose, it was not inconsistent.[32] For Paul, the overarching goals remained the same as those of his predecessors—to protect Russian interests in Germany and Italy and expand them in the Balkans and the Caucasus—but he made significant changes in tactics. Paul had been very hostile to the Revolution and one of the prime movers of the Second Coalition. He saw Bonaparte as an upstart, but one who could stabilize France and serve as a potential partner in pacifying the whole of Europe.[33] The French government took immediate notice of the changing Russian attitude and pursued an ambitious goal of aligning France and Russia against Britain and Austria; even if such an alliance did not materialize, its very prospect would cause considerable anxiety in London and Vienna. Already in the early summer of 1800 First Consul Bonaparte insisted that "it is necessary to give Paul some proof of our esteem, to let him know that we want to negotiate with him."[34]

Bonaparte was well aware of Paul's penchant for chivalric gestures—Paul once considered resolving international disputes by challenging the sovereigns of Europe to a knightly tournament—and sought to entice the Russian ruler by playing upon such sentiments.[35] First, the French government presented Paul, who was the de facto grand master of the Order of St. John of Jerusalem (Knights of Malta or Knights Hospitaller) and entertained idealistic notions of chivalry, with the sword of Jean Parisot de La Valette, the famed grand master of the Knights of Malta who had valiantly defended the island from the Ottoman Turks in the sixteenth century. Next Bonaparte offered to return Malta itself—an offer that was clearly a ploy, considering the ongoing British blockade of the island and the imminent surrender of the French garrison. The final element in this charm offensive was the French decision to liberate, without reciprocal exchanges and with full military honors, about 6,000 Russian prisoners of war taken in recent campaigns.[36]

The flattery was transparent but effective. Paul was touched by what he regarded as acts of true chivalry on the part of the French leader and responded positively to the overtures. Anglophile deputy chancellor Nikita Panin was disgraced and ousted, and Louis XVIII—brother of the executed Louis XVI—and his followers were told to leave the Russian province where they had safely resided for the past few years.[37] More important, in October 1800 the Russian foreign minister, Count Fedor Rostopchin, informed France of Russia's readiness to make peace on reasonable terms, which included recognition of the Russian interest in Germany and the Mediterranean: Russia required the restoration of the island of Malta to the Maltese Knights and a mutual guarantee of the integrity of Sardinia, Naples, Bavaria, and Wurttemberg, which had close ties to Russia.[38]

The French agreed to these preliminary terms, and by the end of the year both sides designated diplomats to conduct formal negotiations. The Russian foreign ministry prepared a lengthy memorandum surveying the European situation and urging Russian realignment with France. The document, approved by Paul, is noteworthy for its focus on the Eastern Question, describing the Ottoman Empire as a "hopelessly sick man"—probably the first use of this well-known political expression—and outlining an ambitious plan for a grand realignment and territorial redistribution in Europe. Under the proposal (a copy of which the French government had acquired), Russia would have gained Romania, Bulgaria, and Moldavia, and France would have gotten Egypt.[39] To appease other continental powers, Rostopchin suggested compensating Austria with parts of Bosnia, Serbia, and Wallachia, and giving Prussia Hanover and a few North Germanic bishoprics.[40] Russia was to convince Sweden and Denmark to restore the League of Armed Neutrality, which would then be extended to include France and Spain.[41]

Rostopchin's proposal was unmistakably expansionist, but in sharing the spoils of the Ottoman Empire with Austria and France, it also revealed Russia's awareness of its own limitations. The essence of the Russian proposal was clear: the Franco-Russian alliance would pacify and realign Europe and challenge British domination on the seas. This anti-British thrust of the Franco-Russian rapprochement involved several crucial elements, not the least of which were discussions for a joint expedition to India.[42] Whether an actual plan had ever been devised remains unclear, since no original text of the plan has ever been located in either French or Russian archives and the published versions contain enough inaccuracies to raise suspicions about their veracity.[43] What is more revealing is that the Russian emperor was willing to act alone. In January 1801 he dispatched a corps of Cossacks to India, instructing its commander, General Vasilii Orlov, to make common cause with Indian princes against the British and to secure favorable conditions for Russian trade and industry, displacing those of Britain.[44]

Paul's decision to launch this expedition has been frequently depicted as an example of his folly or madness, but the plan was conceived not from mental derangement or megalomania (incidentally, charges made against Bonaparte as well) but from a widely shared strategic assumption that India represented Britain's weakest point. It was an extension of Anglo-Russian hostilities in Europe. A direct attack on this island nation, with its formidable navy, seemed futile. India could be reached by land, and the political and military circumstances there did not favor the British. Paul followed this reasoning when he justified an attack on India by noting that "it is necessary to attack [the British] where the blow will be [most] felt by them and where they least expect it. Their establishments in India are the best for this."[45] Invading India was not necessarily a mad scheme. Invasion through Iran or Central Asia was not inherently impossible, as testified to most recently by the campaigns waged by Nadir Shah and Ahmad Shah Durrani, not to mention those by Babur, Timur, Mahmud of Ghazneh, and Alexander the Great before them. Yet even if a campaign to India was not in itself an irrational undertaking, it was certainly not a judicious choice for projecting Russian power. Zubov's Persian campaign of 1796 had clearly shown the logistical challenges of campaigning in Eastern realms, and the Indian project was far more challenging.

Thus Britain again found itself standing alone against France. Not only had its allies been defeated, but some had even become hostile to its interests. Outraged by British searches of neutral shipping for contraband cargo destined for France, northern European states took concrete steps to protect their interests.[46] The years of measures taken by Britain against Denmark, which pursued a typical policy of neutrality, was the tipping point. The decline of Denmark's traditional competitor (the Netherlands) and the commercial difficulties of other continental powers (such as France) offered the Danes a unique opportunity to grow their share of international shipping and commerce; by 1805 Denmark had a mercantile marine eight times larger than it had been forty years earlier.[47] For much of the Revolutionary Wars, Denmark steadfastly maintained its neutrality and even allowed ships from belligerent powers to sail under its flag. Britain's policy of arbitrary searches and seizures forced the Danes to start using naval convoys to defend their merchant vessels.[48] There were several small-scale confrontations when Danish warships in charge of convoys resisted British search. Danish frustrations culminated in the summer of 1800 when British cruisers seized a small convoy protected by a Danish frigate. The Danish crown saw this as an insult to its honor and appealed to Russia and other neutrals for support. This, in turn, prompted Britain to dispatch its fleet to Danish shores.[49]

The entry of the British fleet into the Baltic Sea and its refusal to accept Russian mediation infuriated Emperor Paul, who was already lending a willing ear to French diplomatic overtures. Now he adopted a distinctly anti-British position.[50] He placed an embargo on all English ships and goods in the ports of Russia; payments to British merchants were stopped and their goods and warehouses seized. More than three hundred British ships were trapped in Russian ports and their crews detained.[51] Paul then ordered mobilization of 120,000 soldiers "for the protection of the shores of the Baltic Sea and for operations against England" and invited Sweden, Denmark, and Prussia to join him in protecting neutral shipping by reviving the League of Armed Neutrality; he made it clear to them that he would view any unwillingness to support him as an affront. The league, which was formed on December 16–18, 1800, embraced the principle of "free ships, free goods" and agreed to take adequate measures to protect it.[52]

By December 1800 Britain and Russia were effectively in a state of war. But more was still to come. In early 1801 Denmark embargoed all British goods and occupied Hamburg and Lubeck, major entrepôts for British commerce, while Bonaparte pressured Naples to close its ports to the English.

British trade was also threatened in Hanover, where the interests of France, Russia, and Prussia converged.[53] Prussia was a keen participant, hoping in the process to acquire Hanover and consolidate its control of the five great river systems (the Vistula, Oder, Ems, Weser, and Elbe) that bore the bulk of north European commerce.[54] On March 30 Prussia sent more than 20,000 men to occupy the city.[55]

The combined effects of French and Russian policies produced a virtual continental blockade, one that placed almost the entire coastline of Europe, from the Arctic shorelines of Norway to the ports of Naples, beyond the reach of British commerce. Even Britain's erstwhile ally Portugal was forced to close its ports in the aftermath of what became known as the War of Oranges. The Continental System of 1801 presaged that of 1806–1807 but suffered from a lack of careful planning and execution. It revealed Britain's acute dependence on naval supplies, grain, hemp, and other resources imported from other parts of Europe but did not last long enough to have long-term consequences for British commerce.[56]

Britain responded to these threats with a combination of vigorous diplomacy and brute force.[57] In the summer of 1800 it launched an expedition to Spain, with British troops landing at Ferrol in northwest Spain; after finding the defenses there to be too formidable, the expedition then proceeded to Cadiz, another major Spanish naval base. Neither attack produced tangible benefits, but they did showcase Britain's ability to threaten at will. By the end of 1800, British attention switched to the Baltic region, where the League of Armed Neutrality was gathering steam. In January 1801 Britain issued an order-in-council placing an embargo on Russian, Danish, and Swedish ships. A British squadron under Admiral John Thomas Duckworth raided the Swedish colony of St. Bartholomew and the Danish islands of St. Martin, St. Thomas, St. John, and St. Croix between March and June 1801, defeating the Swedish and Danish forces stationed there.[58] In mid-April the French evacuated the Dutch colonies of St. Eustatius and Saba, which were quickly seized by the British. At the same time the British fleet, led by Sir Hyde Parker and Lord Horatio Nelson, arrived at the Danish capital, Copenhagen, attacking its defenses and forcing the Danes to suspend participation in the league.[59] As Nelson sailed to Riga, a likely Anglo-Russian confrontation was averted by the news of Emperor Paul's death in a palace coup.[60] At about midnight on March 23, 1801, a group of Russian noblemen, concerned that the emperor's unpredictable behavior and drastic policies might prove threatening to Russia's domestic order and external security, carried out an assassination plot that put an end to Paul's life and, with it, to the profound political realignment in Europe.

The Russian emperor's assassination was a major blow for the French government. During his short reign Paul had nudged Russia toward an alliance with France and a war with Britain, coercing Denmark, Sweden, and Prussia into an anti-British coalition. In Paris, the Prussian envoy recorded the consternation with which Bonaparte received the news of the palace coup in St. Petersburg: "The news of the death of the Emperor has been a veritable thunderbolt for Bonaparte. In receiving it from Talleyrand, he uttered a cry of despair.... He thinks that he has lost his strongest support against [Britain] and, having counted on finding in Paul I what Frederick found in Peter III, he does not expect to find the same in Paul's successor."[61] The new Russian emperor, Alexander I, put an end to his father's ventures, forcing the League of Armed Neutrality to dissolve, lifting the embargo on British commerce, renouncing the grand mastership of Malta, and recalling the Cossack expedition. More crucially, on June 17, 1801, he signed the Russo-British Convention, which normalized relations between the two nations and destroyed France's anti-British policies in northern Europe.

France was not the only nation exasperated by Alexander's decision. Prussia, which had been able to count on Paul I, more or less, to support it in north German and Baltic affairs, feared abandonment. The Hanover affair had already soured relations between Berlin and London, where many believed that the Prussians were aspiring to seize the British king's "electoral dominions." This explains King Frederick William III's insistence on neutrality and the evacuation of Hanover in 1801, but such an approach also marked Prussia's failure to exploit Hanover as a bargaining chip in negotiations with Britain.[62] Involvement in the League of Armed Neutrality and subsequent wrangling over Hanover damaged Prussia's position internationally, raising suspicions in Vienna, London, and St. Petersburg.[63] This compelled Prussia to seek closer relations with Paris, which soon resulted in an advantageous agreement on territorial compensation. On May 23, 1802, Paris and Berlin agreed on the terms of a treaty that brought about changes in southern Germany. Prussia secured the possession of a number of former imperial cities and secularized ecclesiastical principalities in exchange for ceding the left bank of the Rhine River to France and formal recognition of the changes Bonaparte had made in Italy. In compensation, the stadtholder of Holland received from France a share of German territory, consisting of a bishopric and several abbeys.

With the French navy blockaded in ports and the Royal Navy concentrating its efforts on the English Channel, the Mediterranean witnessed increased pirate activity. The pirates, mainly based in the Barbary States (comprising the territories of Morocco, Algiers, Tunis, and Tripoli, along the North African coast), actively preyed upon the merchant shipping of Western nations. Depredations by the Barbary pirates were exacerbated by the start of the wars of the French Revolution, which diverted British, Spanish, and Italian naval resources to the struggle against France. After coming to power, Bonaparte received a steady stream of reports on the despoliation of French trade and the mistreatment of French fishermen by the Barbary States. He was able to conclude a treaty with the pasha of Tripoli (1801) and the bey of Tunis (1802), ensuring the relative safety of French fishermen and merchantmen in Mediterranean waters. But Mustafa Pasha, the dey of Algiers, demanded that France offer a tribute, as Spain and the Italian states did.[64] Incensed, Bonaparte wrote to the dey reminding him that France "destroyed the Mamelukes because they dared to demand money after having insulted the French flag. I have never paid anything to anyone, and I have imposed the law upon all of my enemies." Bonaparte instructed his minister of marine to dispatch a flotilla of three ships-of-the-line (reinforced by ten ships-of-the-line and five frigates if needed) to ensure that the French flag was treated with due respect in Barbary waters. The arrival of the French warships compelled the dey to accede to French wishes. On August 28 the First Consul was pleased to inform the pope that he had "just obtained from the dey of Algiers the release of a great number of Christians."[65]

While French merchantmen could seek the protection of France's navy, their American counterparts were more vulnerable to pirate activity after the protection provided by the Royal Navy was lost after the American Revolutionary War. The fledgling American republic lacked warships and was unable to defend its citizens in the faraway Mediterranean and eastern Atlantic. Throughout the 1780s and 1790s, the United States followed an expedient policy of paying tribute to the Barbary States in exchange for the safety of its commercial vessels, or on some occasions delivering a ransom for the release of captured sailors. American shipping suffered even more depredation when fighting between France and Britain extended to the American merchant ships, as each side tried to deny the other access to goods and supplies. In 1794 the US Congress passed and President George Washington signed the Act to Provide a Naval Armament, authorizing acquisition (by purchase or construction) of six frigates, marking the birth of the US Navy.[66]

This proved to be a difficult birth. Construction on the frigates was slow; more important, there was considerable domestic opposition to the establishment of an American naval force, which was perceived as expensive, imperialistic, and provocative. To placate these dissenters, the bill stipulated (in its Article 9) that in the event of a treaty between the United States and a Barbary state, the construction work on the ships would be halted at once. In March 1796, much to the chagrin of the proponents of American naval power, Congress approved a peace treaty with Algiers in which the United States agreed to pay more than $500,000 to the dey of Algiers to ransom a hundred American captives and pledged an annual tribute of more than $20,000; the total costs of the agreement ultimately reached over $1 million, a sum that amounted to one-sixth of the entire US budget.[67] The ratification of the treaty with Algiers resulted in the cessation of frigate construction; only three frigates—the *United States*, *Constitution*, and *Constellation*—were commissioned. In 1796–1797 the United States negotiated additional agreements with Tripoli, Algiers, and Tunis, pledging to provide tribute in return for protection for its citizens.[68]

With European countries preoccupied with the War of the Second Coalition, and despite the agreements it had signed with the Americans, the Barbary corsairs continued to harass the European and American merchant marine, capturing hundreds of sailors who were pressed into hard labor and mistreated. This prompted the United States to form the Department of the Navy, tasked with putting an end to tribute payments to the Barbary States and preventing attacks on American shipping. In 1801, just as Thomas Jefferson was inaugurated as the third president of the American republic, Pasha Yusuf Karamanli of Tripoli threatened the United States with war unless it paid tribute commensurate with the one the Americans were paying to the neighboring state of Algiers.[69] Yet the new administration under Jefferson, bolstered by its recent successes in the undeclared Quasi-War against France (1798–1800) and the addition of several powerful frigates to its naval force, rejected Tripoli's demands. In May 1801 the pasha declared war, ordering the cutting down of the flagstaff in front of the American consulate and sending out warships to take American vessels. The United States responded by dispatching a small squadron of three frigates and a schooner to the Mediterranean with orders to blockade Tripoli's coastline. The Americans scored their first success over the Tripolitans on August 1, 1801, but the meager size of their squadron prevented them from maintaining a close watch on the coast.

The Tripolitan War dragged on for four years with little effect on pirate activities. This compelled Jefferson to alter his naval policies and seek greater engagement in the Mediterranean. The American squadron visited Sicily, where its commanders sought help from King Ferdinand IV of Naples, who agreed to supply them with men and resources and allowed them to use the ports of Messina, Syracuse, and Palermo as naval bases to launch operations against Tripoli. Under the command of Commodore Edward Preble, the American squadron performed creditably in the Mediterranean, including the famed raid by Lieutenant Stephen Decatur to destroy the captured 36-gun frigate *Philadelphia* in Tripoli harbor on February 16, 1804. Decatur's exploit, performed without the loss of a single man, boosted the American public's morale and raised the prestige of the nascent US Navy.[70] American warships launched several seaborne attacks against Tripoli in 1804, but none produced results decisive enough to end the war. Only after the United States supported internal Tripolitan opposition to Pasha Yusuf Karamanli and launched a land invasion across the Libyan Desert in March 1805 did the four-year-long conflict come to an end; in June 1805 the pasha agreed to release the American prisoners for $60,000 in ransom.[71]

The Tripolitan War may seem a minor episode in the larger context of the Napoleonic Wars, but it was a reflection of the reality where European powers were preoccupied with their own affairs and unwilling (or unable) to devote much attentions and resources to the Barbary coastline. The war was certainly of considerable political and military significance for the United States. It marked the first instance of the American republic extending its power well beyond its shores and raising its flag in victory on foreign soil, demonstrating that, if necessary, it would not be content with a defensive policy and could reach out well beyond its territorial waters. The war stimulated American warship construction and trained a new generation of officers who, just seven years later, took on the mightiest naval force in the world during the War of 1812.[72] Still, the war failed to resolve the underlying problem. Distracted by the Franco-British hostilities in the Atlantic, the United States was unable to resolve the corsair problem until after the end of the Napoleonic Wars.

CHAPTER 7 | The Road to War, 1802–1803

O N MARCH 25, 1802, France and Britain signed the Peace of Amiens, the culmination of almost two years of negotiations that began soon after Bonaparte came to power.[1] The immediate impetus for it had come on Christmas Day in 1799, when Bonaparte wrote a letter to King George III of Great Britain lamenting the ongoing war between the two nations: "The war which, for eight years, has ravaged the four quarters of the world, must it be eternal? Are there no means of coming to an understanding? How can the two most enlightened nations of Europe, powerful and strong beyond what their safety and independence require, sacrifice to ideas of vain greatness, the benefits of commerce, internal prosperity, and the happiness of families? How is it that they do not feel that peace is of the first necessity, as well as of the first glory?"[2]

Bonaparte's olive branch produced no immediate results. George III was known for scathingly anti-French views that had been shaped by the century-long conflict between Britain and France. The revolution had only further sharpened them, and George's correspondence is filled with xenophobic sentiments. The king believed that if the Revolution was not contained, it would end up "destroying all religion, law, and subordination . . . without the smallest inclination after this destruction to build up anything."[3] France and the French were "those savages," "that perfidious nation," and "that unprincipled country."[4] Treating with Bonaparte, the Revolution incarnate to many contemporaries, was out of question. Writing to his foreign secretary, Lord Grenville, George described the "Corsican tyrant's letter" with contempt and declared that it was "impossible to treat with a new, impious, self-created aristocracy."[5] With the king refusing to reply in person, Grenville was compelled to compose a formal response to the French, addressed not to Bonaparte but to his foreign minister.

King George went further than a snub of Bonaparte. In February 1800 he informed both houses of the British Parliament that further subsidies were required to make arrangements with the continental allies, including Austria, to counter the French threat. The news that he was asking for more than £2 million for continuation of the war caused considerable debate in Parliament, where the opposition attacked the government's whole policy. One opposition leader, George Tierney, argued that Britain's original aims for going to war with France had been achieved by Bonaparte's destruction of revolutionary radicalism. "I would demand of the Minister [Pitt]," Tierney added, "to state in one sentence what is the object of the war." Pitt famously replied, "Sir, I will do in a single word. The object, I tell him, is Security!" He then proceeded to explain that revolutionary radicalism was not dead and that Britain's security had not been achieved. Rather, "Jacobinism" was embodied in one individual, "who was reared and nursed in its bosom; whose celebrity was gained under its auspices, and who was at once the child and the champion of all its atrocities."[6] There would be no peace with France. Instead, the king's cabinet urged Austria to continue its war and promised hefty subsidies in return.

In late August 1800, following Bonaparte's victory over the Austrians at Marengo, Louis Guillaume Otto, the French diplomat and commissioner in matters regarding prisoners of war, conveyed Bonaparte's second peace offer to the British. Otto's letter to Grenville discussed the official announcement of the Anglo-Austrian treaty of alliance and suggested expanding it to include France "with respect to the places which are besieged and blockaded."[7] Bonaparte's immediate goal was to rescue the French forces in Malta and Egypt, which had been cut off from France for almost two years.[8] Knowing that he was asking too much, Bonaparte linked his proposed naval armistice to the continental armistice with Austria. If Austria, Britain's ally, was to have the opportunity to resupply and reinforce its forces in the Rhineland, France should receive similar concessions.

Pitt's personal preference was for peace, but the cabinet was divided, with hawks, led by Secretary of War Henry Dundas, counseling against accepting the armistice, which would have negated many advantages that Britain had gained since its entry into the war. In the end, Britain chose to reject the French offer. Instead, as we saw earlier, it made final arrangements for the expedition to Egypt and proceeded with its new treaty of alliance with Austria, one that provided it with a financial subsidy to the sustain war effort.

The Anglo-Austrian cooperation did not last long, however. In early December the French defeated the Austrians at Hohenlinden, and Vienna had to sue for peace. After the loss of its key ally, British felt compelled to enter into diplomatic negotiations with France. It was forced to recognize that in spite of its great naval successes in the Atlantic, the Baltic, and the Mediterranean, and despite all the effort and money it had expended on coalitions, France was still the strongest nation on the continent. Without support, Britain had reached the limits of what it could accomplish, particularly since many parts of Europe had become increasingly anti-British. Continental hostility toward Britain was summarized by Prussian diplomat Friedrich von Gentz. "The dominant principle of European politics," he wrote in a memo that was quoted in a letter to Grenville in November 1800, "and the dominant principle of all thinkers and political writers currently is the jealousy of Britain's power." The hatred toward Britain derived from two convictions, Gentz argued: that British wealth was generated by impoverishing the rest of Europe, and that Britain exploited the war to further its interests.[9] Indeed, the events of the last coalition war had left ill will among British allies, who felt that they were being used to do all the fighting.

Domestic changes also contributed to the British decision to consider peace, including the fall of William Pitt's government in 1801 and the formation of a new ministry under Prime Minister Henry Addington, a candid but unimaginative statesman who was hardly cut out to deal with Bonaparte.[10] Addington was keen on ending a war that had now entered its eighth year and was both draining the economy and having deleterious social effects. The country was moving from its agricultural phase to industrialization, and this was causing upheaval at every level. The rapidly growing manufacturing capacity meant finding new outlets for goods; it was becoming increasingly indispensable for Britain to have access to European markets, which had been closed to it in recent years. Even after the collapse of the League of Armed Neutrality, British was still excluded from many continental markets, while French diplomatic efforts continued to score important victories. To further isolate Britain on the continent, Bonaparte turned his attention to Portugal, Britain's longtime ally. After a year-long negotiation, he persuaded Spain's King Charles IV and his influential minister Manuel de Godoy y Álvarez de Faria to sign the Convention of Madrid, which threatened Portugal with war unless Lisbon closed its ports to the British and agreed to an immediate peace with France.[11] Spain was promised one-fourth of Portugal's territory as a guarantee for the return of its colonies by Britain in the eventual general peace treaty.

In the summer of 1801 Spanish troops invaded northern Portugal and, after a quick campaign, forced the Portuguese court to accept the terms of the

Treaty of Badajoz, which ceded the province of Olivenza to Spain and closed Portuguese ports to Britain.[12] Although it was a victory for Spain and France, the war fell short of Bonaparte's expectations. He was furious upon receiving the news of the Spanish-Portuguese armistice. That Portugal would be defeated was a foregone conclusion, he argued. The actual goal of the Franco-Spanish alliance was to strike at Britain and deny it its last continental ally. For this, key Portuguese areas, including Lisbon and Porto, had to be occupied. Spain's failure to share and implement this vision led Bonaparte to suspect either Spanish ignorance or outright duplicity. His initial reaction was to threaten the Spanish monarchy with direct intervention unless it rejected the Treaty of Badajoz and pushed on with the occupation of Portugal. But this was 1801, not 1808, and Bonaparte was not yet emperor of France nor the conqueror of Europe, merely a French general who had been in power for just a year and a half.[13] Spain refused the French demands, arguing that it had met its contractual obligations and that there was no tangible reason for further escalation of the conflict. Facing Spanish intransigence, Bonaparte had no choice but to compromise. In late September 1801 France and Portugal signed a treaty ending their hostilities and compelling Lisbon to cede territory in South America and to pay a heavy indemnity in favor of France.

The War of Oranges—so called for a branch of an orange tree that the Spanish generalissimo had sent to the queen of Spain as proof of his victory— reverberated not only within Europe but also in South America, where Spanish and Portuguese forces clashed over the Paraguayan borderlands. Despite its brevity, the war marked an end to Spain's northward expansion, setting the boundaries of what eventually became the independent state of Paraguay.[14] Portugal's defeat also caused alarm among British ministers, who worried that the French (or Spanish) might be able to take control of the Portuguese island of Madeira, which lay astride the vital Atlantic trade routes. To prevent this, a British expedition preemptively invaded and seized the island.[15]

France's success in Portugal was balanced by its setbacks in Egypt, where the French army, after holding out for more than a year after Bonaparte's departure in 1799, was forced to capitulate to the British in August 1801. The question of Egypt had been one of the principal obstacles to a cessation of hostilities, and its fall paved the way for an Anglo-French compromise. In October 1801 British and French envoys agreed upon a preliminary peace that called for a halt to the long conflict. Later that year new negotiators— Lord Charles Cornwallis for Britain and Joseph Bonaparte, the First Consul's brother, for France—met at Amiens to draft the formal peace treaty.[16] Throughout the negotiations, the French side was firmly resolved to make no concessions that would admit that the advantage in the war had been on the

British side. France refused to discuss any issue related to its continental conquests in the previous six years, and given that Britain acquiesced to this, the
treaty that was produced tacitly accepted and endorsed two crucial outcomes
of the French Revolutionary Wars: France's domination of western Europe
and Britain's maritime supremacy. The negotiations instead focused on two
main issues: overseas colonies and the Mediterranean region. Britain agreed
to return all of its colonial conquests, except for Trinidad (formerly Spanish)
and Ceylon (Dutch), to restore Malta to the Knights of Malta (under nominal
Neapolitan suzerainty), and to evacuate "generally all the ports and islands
that they occupy in the Mediterranean or the Adriatic." In return, France
pledged to evacuate its troops from Naples, Taranto, and those parts of
the Papal States that were not in the Italian Republic, the successor to the
Cisalpine Republic, which Bonaparte had established in 1797. Britain also
pledged to withdraw from Egypt, which was to be restored to the Ottoman
Empire, and supported the independence (under a Russian protectorate) of
the Septinsular Republic on the Ionian Islands. The Amiens treaty provided
for "an equivalent compensation" (Article XVIII) to the exiled House of
Nassau for the loss of its Dutch estates, but it made no mention of the futures
of Holland, Switzerland, and northern Italy, which in itself was an important
attainment for French diplomacy.[17] Bonaparte ensured that no explicit provision safeguarding British trade interests on the continent had been included
in the treaty, although he agreed to respect the independence of Portugal and
the Batavian Republic (the Netherlands), which in practice would have
meant that the ports of these states would be open to British trade.[18]

The Treaty of Amiens brought a formal end to the French Revolutionary
Wars. With the Second Coalition now in tatters, the British recognized that
they had little prospect of bringing down the resurgent France, so they grit-
ted their teeth and largely accepted the continental status quo, allowing
France to retain conquests in the Low Countries, Rhineland, and Italy.[19]
Amiens had produced a complete transformation in the European balance of
power, and William Pitt had to acknowledge that the international system
established since the Peace of Westphalia in 1648 "had been so completely
done away . . . that it was idle to consider [it] as in force."[20]

It has been traditional to argue that the Peace of Amiens, together with
the Treaty of Lunéville, could have been the basis for a durable peace in
Europe—had Bonaparte only chosen to uphold it. This argument seems disingenuous. French military successes had created a new European balance of
power, with France restored to the position of primacy it had not enjoyed
since the height of King Louis XIV's reign a century earlier. At the same time
Britain's naval power, already predominant before the war, had been further

strengthened. Even had Bonaparte fallen from power after Amiens, France still would have sought to consolidate its position in western Europe and to revive its colonial ambitions. This would have placed it on a collision course with Britain. More important, the Peace of Amiens was inherently flawed. Britain's extensive cessions—the abandonment of the Mediterranean and the routes to India, the surrender of almost all French and Dutch overseas colonies, and a promise to evacuate Egypt—caused domestic alarm and despondency, as it seemed to be surrendering strategic advantages acquired in eight years of warfare. "We have yielded every point and every principle," said one member of Parliament.[21] Many contemporaries denounced the treaty terms as too favorable to France. One senior British politician fumed that "to have [retro]ceded to France, Martinique, Malta, Minorca, the Cape, the Dutch settlements both in the East and West Indies and even Cochin, and to have obtained nothing in return but the name of peace, is such an act of weakness and humiliation as nothing in my opinion can justify."[22] Britain had joined the war in 1793 out of security concerns and yet nine years later was faced with "a peace which gives us no security for the future."[23] Prime Minister Addington was, in essence, relying on France to renounce the use of aggression to consolidate its gains, but there was no evidence that it would actually do so. In the words of a contemporary, "If ever peace was precarious, this was that peace. If ever precarious peace was dangerous, this is that precarious peace."[24]

Why, then, was the Treaty of Amiens even signed? Part of the answer lies in the fact that the French diplomats outclassed their British counterparts.[25] Assisted by a talented staff of diplomats and negotiators, Bonaparte showed here his talent for discerning and exploiting his opponents' inexperience and weaknesses.[26] But it would be wrong to portray Prime Minister Addington and his foreign secretary, Robert Banks Jenkinson, Lord Hawkesbury, as shortsighted and incapable statesmen.[27] Patriotic histories of Britain tend to compare Addington and Hawkesbury unfavorably to Pitt and Grenville. Yet Pitt's government was largely responsible for the difficult situation that Addington and his ministers faced in 1801. Pitt's war policies, often based on false assumptions, and their haphazard implementation undermined British strategy, alienated the country's key allies, and left Britain in an unenviable position of fighting alone against France.[28]

Equally important was the worsening domestic situation in Britain. In 1799–1800, as mentioned, the country was in the midst of economic turmoil made worse by hard winters that had produced poor harvests. The price of wheat and other grains steadily rose, hitting the lower ranks of society hardest. In September 1800 food riots erupted in many parts of Britain. The League of Armed Neutrality's embargo of British commerce in the Baltic caused the price of grain to rise even higher, creating shortages in some areas. The war-weariness was increased by the direct taxation that Pitt introduced to finance the conflict against France. In short, fears of social unrest and even possible revolution naturally weighed heavily on Addington's government. Although the harvest of 1801 was good, the average price of wheat increased by some 200 percent between 1798 and 1801 before falling precipitously after news of the peace broke. The coincidence of the fall in grain prices with the arrival of peace was popularly interpreted as proof that war had been the cause of the dearth.[29] When on October 10, 1801, French envoy General Lauriston arrived in London to conduct negotiations, a large crowd unhitched the horses from his carriage and drew him through the streets themselves. The British elite got the point.[30] Peace was necessary to grow the economy and stem the prospects of social unrest. Furthermore, with the coalition in tatters, there was nothing for Britain to gain by fighting on.

The Treaties of Lunéville and Amiens appeared to have stabilized the situation on the continent, even though they created, as British politician William Eden, Lord Auckland, had noted, "the inordinate and frightfully overgrown power of France."[31] Britain alone could not change that reality. What it needed was time—time to deal with its domestic challenges and time to allow Austria, Russia, and Prussia to come to the realization, as British admiral George Keith Elphinstone put it, that "with France as strong as she now is, Europe can never be secure; perhaps the great continental powers will be at length convinced of this and heartily join their forces to reduce her within reasonable bounds."[32] As it was, the Peace of Amiens proved to be short-lived and was already showing clear signs of stress by the end of 1802. The circumstances and factors that contributed to the outbreak of conflict the following spring are worth examining in detail.

The success of the revolutionary government in advancing the French frontier into the Low Countries, the Rhine, and Italy set the framework for Napoleonic policies. In 1796 British philosopher and statesman Edmund Burke had lamented that the French were aspiring "to erect themselves into a new description of Empire, which is not grounded on any balance, but forms a sort of impious hierarchy, of which France is to be the head and the guardian."[33] Bonaparte's unique impact on the European international system was his ability to consolidate power within the politically volatile French realm and then achieve decisive military victories. By 1802 France's foreign policy had come to rely to several key elements: continuing struggle against Britain; maintaining control of the Low Countries, German states, and Italy; and reviving colonial power overseas. Over the next decade one or another of these three aims always remained uppermost, sustained by continued French triumphs on the battlefield. Needless to say, Bonaparte's tremendous capacity for work, attention to detail, and unique energy and spirit—not to mention his vast ambition—all played an important role in shaping international affairs and doomed Amiens.

As soon as he secured power in 1800, Bonaparte began planning for the reduction of British economic power. His vision of a France to rival Britain extended to his colonial projects. This was not an unusual ambition; earlier French governments had also at intervals concerned themselves with overseas colonies. For Bonaparte, the pursuit of colonies afforded several advantages, including keeping his generals and troops occupied and shaping public opinion through a sustained narrative of military victories that further empowered and enriched France. Throughout 1802 and 1803 the First Consul received comprehensive reports on the situation in various colonies as well as numerous memorandums on colonial projects that France could pursue, some envisioning France taking over administration of parts of the Spanish colonial empire.[34]

The recovery of the French outposts in India provided Bonaparte with an opportunity to send troops there. The peace of Amiens allowed France to, as the former minister of marine put it, "h[o]ld just enough of India to be able to say that she was not excluded."[35] In June 1802 General Charles Mathieu Isidore Decaen, a high-spirited and impetuous man who had distinguished himself under General Jean Moreau in the Rhineland and was well known for his hostility to Britain, was appointed *capitaine général des Indes* and ordered to lead an expedition to restore French authority in Pondicherry, one of the crucial French possessions in India since the seventeenth century. His instructions required him to behave "with softness, dissimulation, and simplicity," to cultivate relations with the Indian princes, and to sound the depths of Indian antagonism to British rule. "The mission of the captain general is primarily one of observation," the instructions noted. But the First Consul also advised him that "the punctual execution of the preceding observations may give the opportunity of one day acquiring the glory which prolongs the memory of man beyond the duration of centuries."[36]

The expedition actually did not set sail until March 1803.[37] On his journey to India, Decaen visited the Cape of Good Hope, which the British had restored to the Dutch in the wake of Amiens.[38] He was disappointed to find public opinion there more favorable to Britain than to the Batavian Republic, and it was clear that in case of hostilities the colony would revert to Britain unless measures were at once taken to fortify it, which he urged in his dispatches.[39] Another disillusionment awaited Decaen upon his arrival at Pondicherry, in southwestern India, in July 1803. To his dismay he found that the British had not yet evacuated the city and the Union Jack was still proudly waving over its ramparts; a large British squadron was ostentatiously anchored close to the French ships. Negotiation on the landing of the French troops and the British cession of local settlements was still under way when news of the rupture of the Treaty of Amiens (which had happened in May) reached India. Although the British detained some of his troops as prisoners of war, Decaen slipped away with the larger part of them to Mauritius, which he turned into the chief French naval and military station in the Indian Ocean and which for the next eight years served as a thorn in the side of British commerce.[40]

The first year of the Consulate, 1799, also witnessed the dispatch of the scientific expedition of Captain Nicholas Baudin. Conceived during the Directory, Baudin's expedition spent four years exploring the Indian and Pacific Oceans, reaching southern Australia in April 1802, exploring the region christened Terre Napoléon, and stopping by the British settlement at Port Jackson in Sydney Harbor.[41] Baudin's instructions had been explicit about the expedition's scientific and exploratory aims, but questions about its political character were raised almost from the very beginning; François Péron, one of the naturalists who accompanied Baudin, later submitted a memo outlining a French imperial vision of Australia comparable to the contemporary idea of a "British Pacific," though it remains to be seen if he did so under any formal orders.[42] Be that as it may, the French exploration caused concerns in Britain, where it was believed that its true object was to assess the possibility of the French conquest of eastern Australia.[43]

Bonaparte's visions of French colonial empire may have floundered in the East, but it began to take more definite form in the West. The Treaty of San Ildefonso (October 1800) had compelled Spain to retrocede Louisiana to France. For the development of that colony, the recovery of French colonies and trade in the Caribbean was an absolute essential. The First Consul hoped to knit the French possessions of the Antilles and Louisiana into a firm commercial, social, and political union that would safeguard French interests in the region and cut the United States out of the region's lucrative trade and commerce. This vision of the revived French Empire in the west hinged on the recovery of Saint-Domingue.

Taking prompt advantage of the maritime truce with Britain, Bonaparte also sent an expedition to assert France's authority over Saint-Domingue, which had been in rebellion since the early 1790s and was controlled by the government of Toussaint Louverture. The relations between the colony and metropole had been strained by Louverture's increasingly authoritarian policies, which alienated many French republicans; even some of the black deputies

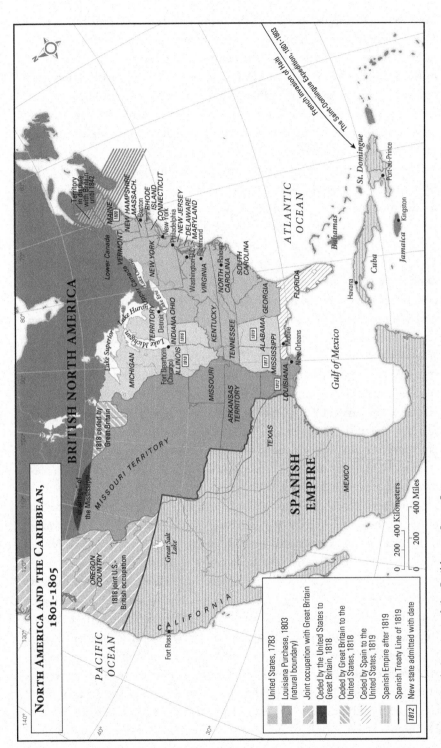

Map 8: North America and the Caribbean, 1801–1805

from Saint-Domingue, as well as the members of the Société des Amis des Noirs, turned against him, urging the French government to intervene. Louverture increasingly defied the central authorities, leading a takeover of the Spanish territory of Santo Domingo and drafting a constitution without any consultation with the French government. Such news was not well received in Paris since it underlined Louverture's tendency to make his own decisions and stoked fears that he would lead Saint-Domingue to complete independence from France.[44]

Louverture had reason to be suspicious of Bonaparte's intentions. The Constitution of the Year VIII, which Bonaparte and his co-conspirators imposed on the country in 1800, did not include an explicit declaration of rights, a provision that the earlier constitutional documents had contained, and in Article 91 it specified that colonies would be governed by "special laws."[45] Thus the colonies could no longer presume that they were guaranteed the same rights as in metropolitan France, and it was possible that the "special laws" might facilitate the restoration of slavery on the islands; the latter prospect seemed likely after Bonaparte gave up on his efforts to apply the emancipation law of 1794 to the French colonies in the Indian Ocean, where white colonists vigorously contested the Directory's attempt to emancipate slaves in 1796–1797. Bonaparte also made it clear that he would not grant freedom to the slaves in Martinique. This naturally raised concerns among the recently emancipated slaves of Saint-Domingue; Louverture himself cited Bonaparte's decision about Martinique as one of the reasons for his distrust of the French government's intentions. Among other factors were Bonaparte's overtures to former colonial officials and his tolerance of the public efforts of former slave owners and slave traders to defend the institution of slavery.[46]

Contrary to some scholars' claims, Bonaparte had not decided from the outset on the restoration of slavery in Saint-Domingue, and the French expedition had not been prompted by lobbying on the part of exiled planters.[47] Recent scholarship reveals that Bonaparte's thinking on colonial matters, including slavery, was contradictory and shifting. He did espouse racist views that were prevalent in early modern Europe, but he was also a pragmatist willing to adjust his positions whenever it was beneficial.[48] After coming to power, Bonaparte encountered three major factions that did their best to shape France's colonial policy. The most radical group comprised established abolitionists, including Bishop Henri Grégoire, who wanted to preserve revolutionary achievements, including the emancipation of slaves; they urged the First Consul to seek an understanding with the rebel leadership in Saint-Domingue and to employ black troops in consolidating French positions in the Caribbean. The second, more moderate faction comprised a diverse group of people who had previously served in Saint-Domingue but had been forced to flee the island due to conflicts with Louverture and his supporters. These men, including François-Marie de Kerversau and André Rigaud, believed that Louverture could not be trusted and should be removed from power; they did, however, support emancipation and advised against restoring slavery in the colonies. The third and the most conservative camp was that of planters and colonial officials who sought not only restoration of French authority in the colonies but also return of white rule and slavery.

Bonaparte thus found himself caught between conflicting lobbying efforts. His views underwent a gradual but drastic change within two years of his coming to power. Bonaparte initially espoused a pro-abolitionist stance and sought good relations with Louverture, who was not only confirmed in his rank but also promoted to lieutenant general. Bonaparte publicly expressed his support for the emancipation of slaves and assured the "citizens of Saint-Domingue" that "the sacred principles of the liberty and equality of the blacks will never be attacked or modified."[49] He also instructed that a special statement—"Brave blacks, remember that only the French people recognize your liberty and the equality of your rights"—be sewn in gold lettering on all of the National Guard's battalion flags in Saint-Domingue.[50] Informed of Louverture's talks with the British, Bonaparte argued that Saint-Domingue "might go for England if the blacks were not attached to us by their interest in liberty."[51]

By the fall of 1801 Bonaparte's view had evolved into a far more conservative position that sought not only to remove Louverture from power but also to restore slavery. Such a shift was facilitated not just by the presence of former colonial officials in senior positions of the Consulate government but also by Bonaparte's own exasperation with the steady flow of reports that Louverture was asserting his authority. The expulsion of French civilian agents, invasion of the Spanish-held part of the island in contravention of direct orders, and publication of a new constitution that proclaimed Louverture governor-general for life made it clear that Saint-Domingue was breaking away from the mainland. "From this moment, there was no point deliberating," Bonaparte later reminisced.[52]

Peace with Britain made it possible to prepare a major expedition to the Caribbean. Commanded by Bonaparte's brother-in-law General Charles Victor Emmanuel Leclerc, it was to proceed in three phases. First, the French commander had to reassure the populace of his intentions, promising anything "in order to take possessions of the strongholds and to get ourselves into the country." Once this was accomplished, the French authorities would make further demands, forcing Louverture to surrender his authority and taking control over the black army, which would be used to suppress any rebellious activities. Once the island was pacified, Leclerc was to embark on the final phase of his mission, which included the arrest of Louverture and other black generals and officers so as to deny leadership to the black population, which was to be completely disarmed. Bonaparte's instructions may not have explicitly called for the restoration of slavery in Saint-Domingue, but the net effect of the French activities would have been an imposition of white military control over the island and subjugation of the black populace.[53]

Even before the Treaty of Amiens was fully ratified, Bonaparte had ordered Leclerc with some 27,000 men and Admiral Louis Thomas Villaret-Joyeuse with a fleet of twenty-one frigates and thirty-five ships-of-the-line to Saint-Domingue; counting later reinforcements, France had committed two-thirds of its navy and more than 40,000 men to the reconquest of the Caribbean. The French expeditionary force—one of the largest overseas military efforts any European power had undertaken in this age—reached Saint-Domingue in January 1802. The fleet divided into smaller squadrons, each sent out to capture one of the coastal towns of Saint-Domingue. While some black commanders defected to the French, Louverture called on the entire population to rise up against the invaders, and he withdrew into the interior of the island. Fierce fighting raged in the island's two major cities, Cap Français and Port-Républicain (Port-au-Prince), as well as in the mountains between the West Province and the North Province. Entrenched in steep-sided valleys, the black troops fought with incredible valor and determination against superior French forces. "Deprived of water and food in this overwhelming heat," described an eyewitness, "the [black] troops had to chew on balls of lead in the hope of quenching their unbearable thirst. They suffered without complaint, out of hope for vengeance."[54] Yet their sacrifices proved to be in vain. Leclerc gradually persuaded most black leaders to return to the service of France by promising that they would keep their rank, position, and property. By May 1802 Jean-Jacques Dessalines and other black leaders were forced to end their resistance and accept Leclerc's authority. The French quickly moved to neutralize these leaders. In early June, Louverture was lured into a trap and captured by French troops. He was shipped to France, where "the most unhappy man of men," as William Wordsworth famously described him, was subjected to harsh treatment during solitary confinement at Fort de Joux and died less than a year later.

The successful start of the Caribbean expedition was continued by General Antoine Richepanse, who led some 3,500 troops to the island of Guadeloupe in the spring of 1802. The French overcame fierce local resistance led by Louis Delgrès, who made his last stand at Matouba, where on May 28 he and more than three hundred followers blew themselves up rather than surrender.

The reconquest of Saint-Domingue and Guadeloupe coincided with the conclusion of the Peace of Amiens, which restored to France all of its lost colonies. These included the islands of Martinique, St. Lucia, Tobago, and Réunion, where slavery had never been abolished in practice since they were in British hands. To clarify the legal status of the black populations on these and other French colonies, on May 20, 1802, the French government approved a new law that specified that slavery (and the slave trade) remained legal in the islands captured by the British during the war, while the status quo prevailed in colonies where slavery had previously been abolished. The law also authorized the First Consul to reconsider the latter's status at some point in the future. Bonaparte did not wait long to act. In July 1802 he secretly instructed his colonial officials to restore slavery in Guadeloupe, Guiana, and Saint-Domingue at the earliest opportunity. This was accomplished relatively easily in small colonies such as Guadeloupe and Guiana but faced significantly greater obstacles in the much larger Saint-Domingue, where the French position rapidly deteriorated as yellow fever decimated the troops and news of the restoration of slavery in Guadeloupe and Martinique reinvigorated black resistance.[55] Moreover, the collapse of the Peace of Amiens in May led to the resumption of hostilities with Britain, whose navy blockaded the island, preventing badly needed reinforcements and supplies from reaching the besieged French garrison, portions of which soon began surrendering to the British in order to escape from black forces.

Fighting ravaged Saint-Domingue until November 1803 in what was among the most violent conflicts of the entire revolutionary period. Soldiers on both sides used brutal tactics, including the French use of a makeshift gas chamber (*étouffier*) on board ship in which volcanic sulfur was burned to suffocate prisoners.[56] In a letter to Bonaparte, Leclerc advocated what would now be considered a genocidal massacre: "We must destroy all the negroes in the mountains, men and women, sparing only children younger than twelve, destroy half of those who live in the plains, and not leave in the colony a single man of color who has worn an officer's epaulette."[57] Bonaparte may not have known the details, but he was certainly aware of the savage nature of the war in Saint-Domingue and did nothing to restrain it. On November 2 Leclerc died from yellow fever, and command of the troops in Saint-Domingue passed to General Donatien Rochambeau, who fought in vain to maintain control of the island. French atrocities convinced many black officers, including Dessalines, to leave the French ranks and join the rebels. On November 18 Dessalines routed the French at the Battle of Vertières and threatened the last remaining French stronghold at Cap Français. Rochambeau had no choice but to negotiate the French evacuation. On leaving the island, he and his troops were intercepted by a British squadron and remained in captivity for most of the Napoleonic Wars.[58]

More than 50,000 French soldiers, sailors, and civilians and a far greater number of black troops and civilians perished in Bonaparte's attempt to reclaim Saint-Domingue.[59] This marked one of the worst defeats a French army suffered during the entire revolutionary era and had profound consequences for both the island and the metropole. After their victory over the French, the black military leaders elected Dessalines "governor-general for life" and proclaimed Haitian independence on January 1, 1804. Haiti was the only nation in the world established as a result of a successful slave revolt and the first independent nation of Latin America and the Caribbean. The Haitian Declaration of Independence was only the second such act (after the American Declaration of Independence), but it was the first to assert the right of a nonwhite population to govern itself.

Dessalines's short tenure as Haiti's first emperor, a title he took in October 1804, was notable for his attempts to establish the new nation through a combination of revolutionary reforms, virulent xenophobia, and forced plantation labor.[60] The new constitution proclaimed slavery "abolished forever" and asserted that all citizens, regardless of skin color, were equal in their rights. Yet the new regime also ordered the execution of Haiti's remaining French residents and prohibited whites from owning land. Most controversially, Dessalines sought to create a militarized state, with no provisions for any legislative body to limit the power of the emperor. He retained Toussaint Louverture's forced-labor system of agriculture, which had caused widespread grievances on the island.

That Haiti succeeded in ending slavery and establishing a struggling but independent state sent shock waves throughout the Caribbean and helped usher in a counterrevolutionary reaction. On the neighboring islands, especially Cuba, planters exploiting the devastation of the once-thriving French colony quickly moved to fill the void left in the world market for sugar. They did so by reinforcing institutions of slavery and colonial rule, so the success of a slave revolt in Haiti meant violent entrenchment of slavery elsewhere in the region.[61]

The failure of the Saint-Domingue expedition had immediate consequences for France, which was now deprived of its most lucrative colony and a commercial hub in the Caribbean. Furthermore, the Saint-Domingue fiasco dashed Bonaparte's grand vision for a French colonial empire in the Atlantic. With a new war against Britain nearly unavoidable, the French government was concerned about its ability to protect its newly reclaimed Louisiana territory, a vast (and vaguely defined) area stretching from the Mississippi River to the Rocky Mountains. Originally a French colony, Louisiana, including the port of New Orleans, had been ceded to Spain by secret treaty in 1762, near the end of the Seven Years' War. In 1795 the United States and Spain concluded the Treaty of San Lorenzo (also known as Pinckney's Treaty), which granted the United States the right to transport and deposit goods originating in American ports through the mouth of the Mississippi without paying duty. These concessions were crucial to ensuring American economic interests west of the Appalachians as well as the survival of thousands of settlers who founded settlements in the Ohio River Valley in the decade after independence.

France had been seeking the return of Louisiana for some time, and this increasingly worried the Americans, who believed that Spain, a proud but militarily ineffective power, would be unable to stem the spread of the expanding American populace into its territories. Spanish military officials had long tried to block American advances and repeatedly (but in vain) asked for military reinforcements from Spain. France was a more formidable opponent, and with French control of the Mississippi Valley and the British presence in Canada the United States faced the prospect of being hemmed in between two great powers. As early as 1798 some American leaders advocated a preventive takeover of Louisiana and even secured a statement from Britain that it would welcome American control of the Mississippi estuary.[62]

The news of the Treaty of San Ildefonso (October 1800), by which Spain returned Louisiana to France in exchange for the newly created Kingdom of Etruria in Italy, caused great anxiety in Britain.[63] Some feared that it would facilitate French efforts to destroy, in the words of British editor William Cobbett, "the commercial and naval preponderance of England."[64] It was also a source of concern in the United States, which considered its commercial interests threatened. The United States had no agreements with the French on its continued use of the Mississippi and New Orleans, and the Treaty of Amiens had deprived American shippers of the windfall profits they had earned by dominating trade while England and France were at war. Of far greater concern was the French expedition to Saint-Domingue, which indicated an assertive French imperial policy in the Western Hemisphere. American political leaders were thus keen on finding a way to prevent France from excluding the United States from New Orleans and to secure the Mississippi River for American commerce.

With this goal in mind, the American government pursued a two-pronged policy: threatening France with a conflict while offering to settle the problem by diplomacy. President Thomas Jefferson sent special commissioner James Monroe to Paris to negotiate with the French government the purchase of

New Orleans and surrounding territory, or at the very least to gain perpetual rights of navigation and deposit.[65] If France refused and threatened American commerce, the United States was willing to consider forceful resolution of this problem, including an Anglo-American alliance to drive the French out of the region. Bonaparte's efforts to reclaim Louisiana, Jefferson warned in a letter to Pierre S. du Pont de Nemours, "will cost France…a war which will annihilate her on the ocean, and place that element under the despotism of two nations, which I am not reconciled to the more because my own would be one of them."[66]

Bonaparte realized that given the lack of firm control of Saint-Domingue, the American threats and the prospect of a renewed war with Britain meant that possession of Louisiana could become a huge liability for France. If he could sell Louisiana to the Americans, he could deny the British a potential prize in the Western Hemisphere, and not only avoid conflict with the Americans but, more important, enable the United States to be a future rival power to Britain. Bonaparte was therefore receptive to American inquiries about purchasing New Orleans. In 1803, surprising American negotiators, he instructed his minister of the treasury, François Barbé-Marbois, to offer the entire Louisiana Territory, an area of more than 800,000 square miles, for the price of $15 million ($11.25 million in cash and the cancellation of $3.75 million in debts owed by the French government). Formal negotiations commenced upon Monroe's arrival on April 12, 1803, and continued until the signing of the agreement on May 2.[67] The final transfer of Louisiana came on December 20, 1803.

The Louisiana Purchase called for the transfer of American bonds to France, but the French government had no desire to hold these securities as an investment, and it could not simply float such a huge bond issue in Europe. Needing cash, Bonaparte therefore decided to exploit the British and Dutch banking systems, even though Britain and France were back at war. The Dutch banking house Hope and Company of Amsterdam and the British banking house Francis Baring and Company of London were approached with an offer to sell the stock in Britain and Holland and then transfer cash to France. These banking houses were among the largest in Europe, had close connections in the British government, and had previous experience handling American securities, all of which allowed them to successfully (and profitably) implement the scheme.[68]

To Bonaparte, it seemed clear that the Louisiana Purchase would turn the United States into a maritime rival of Britain, one that might in time challenge British ascendancy on the seas or at least counterbalance it. That he ceded not a part but the whole of the Louisiana Territory, thereby breaking his promise to Spain, testifies to his determination to prevent British control of the Gulf, as he preferred to see it in American hands during the coming struggle. For the United States, the Louisiana Purchase marked a watershed moment "ranked in historical importance next to the Declaration of Independence and the adoption of the Constitution."[69] It doubled the size of the American republic and gave it the ability to control the whole of the Mississippi River and much of the Gulf Coast; it was the making of part or all of fifteen new states. The purchase created the conditions for Americans to limit the influence of foreign powers in the region, and it set into motion a pattern of expansion that radically altered the demographics of North America. The boundaries of the Louisiana Purchase were so vague that it made Manifest Destiny—the idea that the United States had both a right and a duty to own and settle these vast open spaces—almost inevitable.

American territorial aggrandizement, however, proved catastrophic for the Native American tribes, which were increasingly dislodged from huge tracts of land destined for future settlement by Americans. Equally important was the impact of the Louisiana Purchase on the development of the American West through the expansion of cotton production and slavery. Within months of the signing of the Louisiana Purchase, South Carolina, which had banned the slave trade in 1792 and repeatedly upheld the ban for the next ten years, sanctioned the importation of slaves, which rapidly increased over the next five years.[70] Indeed, the Louisiana Purchase caused considerable headaches in American political circles.[71] The American emissaries knew well that by signing the final agreement they were going far beyond their original authorization. The Louisiana Purchase generated considerable debate about the constitutionality of the decision Jefferson's government made to incorporate new territory into the Union, which in turn raised still more thorny questions about the relations between states and the Union. The acquisition of such vast frontier lands came with a corresponding increase in the responsibility for governing it, even if the precise boundaries remained in dispute and the loyalty of its inhabitants was questionable at best.[72] Yet for every policymaker who challenged the constitutionality of purchasing the Louisiana Territory, there was another who complained that the agreement did not go far enough because it failed to deliver the Floridas too.

The disappointment felt in British political and business circles about France's colonial policies sharpened upon their realization that Amiens had brought not a halt to French power in Europe but an expansion of it. Indeed, more than anything else it was France's continental policy that undermined its relations with Britain and caused Amiens to fall apart. Bonaparte, who was declared consul for life in August 1802, chose to impose French hegemony in

western Europe. In the Batavian Republic, Bonaparte suppressed a local legislature, imposed a new constitution, and exacted financial contributions.[73]
This policy was motivated partly by his intention to send an expedition to
Louisiana but largely by the financial expediency of maintaining French
troops at Dutch expense.[74]

In September 1802 France reasserted its authority in Switzerland, which
French troops had evacuated in the wake of the Treaty of Lunéville. The Swiss
Confederation, a loose union of thirteen cantons (sovereign regions), lacked
strong central government, uniform administration, and a national armed
force; instead, each region had its own government, legal system, administrative structure, and military. Cantonal governments were dominated by oli-
garchies composed either of aristocratic families (as in Bern, Lucerne, and
Fribourg) or of urban elites (as in the cantons of Uri, Schwyz, and Zug), while
the vast majority of the Swiss resided in rural communities, still subject to
feudal privileges. Swiss neutrality, which can be traced back to the sixteenth
century but was formally established by the Peace of Westphalia in 1648,
helped France survive the economic blockades of the 1790s, when the French
imported goods and provisions through Swiss intermediaries; the revolutionaries spoke in glowing terms of the important service rendered by the Swiss.
Yet as the French revolutionary armies gained victories, Swiss neutrality ceased
to be of value to France, and "our necessary allies" came to be described as "oli-
garchs, vassals of princes, and friends of England."[75] In February 1798 French
troops invaded Swiss cantons, and in April they helped establish the Helvetic
Republic. As in other areas, the French occupation meant sudden and profound
changes. The new, French-drafted constitution ignored centuries of cantonal
autonomy when it proclaimed the Helvetic Republic as "one and indivisible."
Despite its progressive provisions, the constitution was not welcomed by a
large number of Swiss. The document was doctrinaire in character, and the
ham-fisted nature of its introduction only stoked hostility and resistance.
Furthermore, the heavy-handed policies that the French implemented in order
to raise monies and resources in Switzerland contributed to social and economic
suffering, which soon engendered popular resistance. The French withdrawal
in 1801 had led to the rapid deterioration of political stability between
the Unitarians, who favored maintaining a strong central republic, and the
Federalists, who championed traditional cantonal sovereignty. Rejection of the
French-offered constitution, repeated coups d'état (in August 1800, October
1801, and April 1802), and the Swiss decision to conclude treaties of friendship
with Britain, Austria, and Russia without consulting the French aroused the
anger of the First Consul. Political turmoil between the Unitarians and the
Federalists soon spilled into a civil war—the War of Sticks (Stecklikrieg), as it

came to be known—that seemingly proved Bonaparte's contention that the Swiss could not resolve their differences and required outside intervention. The First Consul lamented that the Swiss provided "a distressing spectacle" and that their "history proves above all that your domestic wars could never have been ended without the active intervention of France."[76] In October 1802, responding to Swiss requests for help, Bonaparte dispatched a military force under General Michel Ney into Switzerland. Less than two months later he hosted a gathering of dozens of Swiss notables and deputies—the so-called Helvetic Consulta—which, under the close guidance of and mediation by the French government, developed the Mediationsakte (the Act of Mediation), a new constitution for the Swiss Confederation.[77]

A landmark in the constitutional development of Switzerland, the Act of Mediation stabilized the country without sacrificing its tradition of cantonal independence. It reestablished thirteen cantons as near-sovereign states and formed another six cantons with full rights. The new federal government had limited powers and had to defer on most questions to the cantons. In a partial reversal of the revolutionary reforms, the act allowed some cantons to revive their earlier patrician-aristocratic styles of government, though all privileges of place and birth were disallowed. For Bonaparte, the Swiss reorganization was not just a means of bringing peace and order to a neighboring state but also a way of ensuring Swiss isolation and continuing French authority in the region. As Bonaparte envisioned it, the Swiss confederation was to be weak and ever dependent upon France.[78] Freedom of commerce and industry was granted in name only, since both were tied closely to French economic and commercial interests. The Swiss army was kept small, while cantons were obliged to place their troops at the disposal of the French.

France's actions in Switzerland produced muted reactions among the continental powers that were keen on gaining France's favor in the impending reorganization of Germany (discussed later). But in Britain it produced a vocal outcry. Despite the fact that Britain had barely any national interest in Switzerland, politicians vehemently denounced the Act of Mediation, claiming that the political turmoil in the confederation was merely the "lawful efforts of a brave and generous people to recover their ancient Laws and government," as Sir Arthur Paget put it.[79] The reality was more complex than that. After the French withdrawal from Switzerland in 1801, Britain had intervened in Swiss affairs and dispatched agents with money and instructions to encourage local unrest and pledge British "pecuniary assistance" in case the Swiss were willing to resist the French.[80] In the words of Bonaparte, Britain sought to turn Switzerland into "a new Jersey [island] from which troubles against France would be fomented."[81]

Another nail in the coffin of the Treaty of Amiens was France's annexation of Piedmont in February 1803. This decision—which the French authorities claimed was "made due to the abdication of the sovereign and the wishes of the people"—was in line with Bonaparte's overall policy in Italy, which aimed at securing French supremacy in the Italian peninsula and facilitating financial exploitation of the entire region.[82] Austrian hopes of preventing French domination of Italy had been dashed on the fields of Marengo and Hohenlinden as well as by Russian acquiescence to the French presence in the peninsula and by British reluctance to include Italian affairs in the Treaty of Amiens. Yet the French also faced growing opposition in Italy, where after five years of intermittent occupation even the warmest of their supporters were beginning to find the French presence exasperating. In Piedmont a strong royalist base demanded the restoration of the House of Savoy. Elsewhere Italian patriots had grown tired of waiting for the French to deliver on their promises of Italian independence. Yet France, whether led by the Directory or by Bonaparte, had no interest in seeing an independent Italian state that could restrain French interests and play a role between France and Austria.

Instead, the French government sought to become the master of northern Italy. In early 1802 the assembly (*consulta*) of northern Italian notables finalized the constitution of the Italian (formerly Cisalpine) Republic, electing Bonaparte as its president; in his absence, his vice president, Francesco Melzi d'Eril, exercised authority and played a crucial role in the shaping of the new republic.[83] The Ligurian Republic was also given a new constitution and though Bonaparte was not elected its president, he still received the authority to nominate the doge and chief magistrates of the republic. The newly established Kingdom of Etruria, formed on the basis of the Franco-Spanish Treaty of Aranjuez, was formally independent, but with French troops present on its territory, the Etrurian king's authority was nominal indeed.

Bonaparte's actions constituted a clear step toward the consolidation of French control in northern Italy. While French rule was accomplished by means of coercive methods, it helped develop the north of Italy, which, compared to central and southern Italian states, did enjoy comparatively better conditions. Swiss historian Anton Guilland pointed out that "her citizens, if they did not enjoy liberty, possessed at all events equality and equitable laws. If Bonaparte did not give the country its independence, he developed its wealth by undertaking works of public utility....Consequently, among the Venetians, the Romans, and the Neapolitans there were many who would have welcomed French rule or annexation to the Italian republic."[84]

European courts had been alarmed by France's actions in Italy, but none made any demonstration, understanding that they lacked the means to back up their protests. Moreover, as in the case of French intervention in Switzerland, European response to the French moves in Italy was moderated by the ongoing events in Germany. Britain refused to recognize the new Italian states (Etruria and the Ligurian and Italian Republics) but was unwilling to jeopardize its others interests by pressing this issue too far. Thus the fate of Italy was not discussed at Amiens.

By late 1802 Bonaparte deemed the time ripe for resolving the fate of Piedmont. Until then the French leader had bided his time in his relations with the region, mainly because he was anxious to placate Emperor Paul of Russia, who had supported the House of Savoy. In fact, in the fall of 1800 Bonaparte had actually considered the restoration of the larger part of Piedmont (except for the territory east of Sesia, which was transferred to the Cisalpine Republic) to the House of Savoy. The French government had invited a Piedmontese envoy to Paris for negotiations, but these quickly stalled: King Charles Emmanuel demanded restoration of all of Piedmont before any discussion could take place, while the First Consul argued that the king first had to close his harbors to the British. In the spring of 1802 Bonaparte took steps to consolidate his control over Piedmont, first by deploying a military garrison and then by formally annexing it to France.[85]

France's actions in Italy played a key role in rekindling war tensions in Europe and undoing Amiens. Unlike Germany, where he pursued a skillful diplomacy, Bonaparte was far more openly forceful in his dealings with Italian states, annexing some and imposing his will on others. There is no doubt that such policies violated provisions of the Treaty of Lunéville, and although Bonaparte got away with this, his activities undermined the chances for political stability in Europe. Russia was displeased with how its Piedmontese ally had been treated by the French, and Britain refused to recognize changes in the Italian peninsula because they threatened general political equilibrium in Europe.

The tacit recognition by Prussia, Austria, and Russia of the French consolidation in Switzerland and northern Italy was a consequence of the *Reichsdeputationshauptschluss*, or Imperial Recess, which was made necessary by French territorial expansion during the late 1790s. The Revolutionary Wars had fractured the power of the Holy Roman Empire, which had shaped German history for the better part of eight hundred years. In 1795 the Treaty of Basle, by which Prussia recognized French control of the left bank of the Rhine while France returned all of the lands east of the Rhine captured during the war, marked a crucial moment in German history. It consolidated French control of the Rhineland and divided Germany into spheres of influence, with the northern one, dominated by Prussia, effectively deserting the imperial cause. Despite his pledges to defend southern German polities, including dozens of imperial counts and knights, Emperor Francis II was unable to stem the tide of French aggression, and this effectively undermined his leadership among the German states. More important, French expansion into the Rhineland resulted in the dispossession of the many German secular and ecclesiastical princes, and according to Article VII of the Treaty of Lunéville, German princes who had incurred losses during the coalition wars, had to be compensated.[86] In practice this meant mediatization and secularization, with the former signifying "the subjugation of lesser territorial units to stronger states, while the latter meant the annexation of ecclesiastical principalities by larger secular states."[87]

In October 1801 the Diet of the Holy Roman Empire had formed a committee to discuss plans for such reorganization. Composed of representatives of Mainz, Bohemia, Brandenburg, Saxony, Bavaria, Württemberg, Hesse-Cassel, and the Hoch- und Deutschmeister (grand master of the Teutonic Order), this deputation largely accepted decisions already made in a series of bilateral agreements between France, Austria, Prussia, Russia, and the German states.[88] In a revival of the traditional French policy of Austrian containment, Bonaparte sought to weaken the Habsburgs both territorially and politically in Germany, where he wanted to create a group of middle-sized German states (dependent on France) as a counterweight to Austria. He conveyed the central tenets of his Germany policy in a letter to Foreign Minister Talleyrand. Bonaparte's intention was "not to compromise in any way France's position in German affairs" but also "not to take even the hundredth of a chance that could break the peace." Above all, the future of German rearrangement depended on ensuring that "more than ever a disunion exists between Berlin and Vienna."[89]

———◦◦◦❀◦◦◦———

France's aims echoed in Russia, which had secured the right to intervene in German affairs with the Treaty of Teschen, which ended the War of the Bavarian Succession in 1779. Russian Emperor Alexander I was keenly interested in strengthening the German states of Württemberg, Baden, and Hesse-Darmstadt, all of which were dynastically linked to the House of Romanov. Bonaparte understood this, writing to his brother that "it [would be] difficult to negotiate respecting Germany without cooperation of [Russia]."[90] Consequently, in June 1802 Russia and France had reached an agreement outlining key elements of the indemnification on the right bank of the Rhine and paving the way for the transformation of German states.[91]

Austrian efforts to counter French (and Russian) designs by seeking closer relations with France or developing an alliance with Prussia and Bavaria and offering the latter some territorial compensation proved to be in vain.[92] Upon learning of Austrian advances toward Bavaria, Bonaparte wrote directly to Maximilian Joseph, elector of Bavaria, assuring him that "the proposition made to Your Highness by the House of Austria conforms so perfectly to the constant aims of that august House that it appears to me to be contrary to the interest of your own."[93] More important, France successfully divided the German states and secured Bavarian and Prussian support by offering them far more generous compensations than Austria was willing to consider; once it became known that Russia would join France in a common mediation, many secondary German states scrambled to seek the favor of the French government, thereby further weakening Austria's position.

The Imperial Recess represented one of the most extensive redistributions of property in European history. This process directly affected the smaller states of the imperial knights and ecclesiastic princes, whose territories were designated for absorption by larger states. The Imperial Recess eliminated 112 sovereign estates, including 66 ecclesiastical principalities and dozens of estates belonging to imperial knights; of the ten electoral states that existed in 1792, four now became part of France. Some three million German subjects had to change their allegiance, which largely benefited Bavaria (which gained a third more subjects than it had lost), Württemberg (which gained four times more), Prussia (which gained five times what it had lost, mainly in the northwest), and Baden (which gained 7.5 times what it had lost). Although Austria gained some land in the south to compensate for the loss of imperial possessions in the west, the overall settlement further undermined the Habsburg position in Germany by eliminating ecclesiastical states that traditionally had supported them and by strengthening Prussia and other German states that traditionally had challenged the Viennese court.

With the elimination of the secularized archbishops of Cologne and Trier and the selection of the new electors of Württemberg, Baden, Hesse-Cassel, and Salzburg, six Protestants and four Catholics now sat in the Imperial Electoral College, which meant the next Holy Roman Emperor could very well be Protestant. Furthermore, the Imperial Recess meant not only the end of the ecclesiastical principalities' political independence but also the outright confiscation of church property, which effectively destroyed the church's position within Germany. This, in turn, had significant social consequences in terms of education and welfare, traditionally the responsibility of the church. Of approximately fifty free cities, only six remained—Frankfurt, Augsburg, Nuremberg, and the three Hanseatic cities of Lübeck, Bremen, and Hamburg—and some of these did not survive the next wave of restructuring that France would undertake three years later.

Together with the further reorganization of Germany into the Confederation of the Rhine in 1806, the Imperial Recess determined the geopolitical structure of Germany for much of the nineteenth century. It greatly simplified the political map of Germany and turned the Holy Roman Empire into an obsolescent entity whose dissolution was all but inevitable, as the leading German states were keen to profit from its growing weakness.[94] The *Reichsdeputationshauptschluss* was perhaps beneficial for Germany in the long term, but in the short term it effectively undermined the existing international order in Europe. While an indirect threat to Britain, French intervention in Germany was a direct challenge to Austrian and Russian interests in the region. That France could bring about a revolution so effortlessly (at least it seemed so to many contemporaries) can be explained by several factors. The great-power rivalries abetted the French. Britain could do little to stop these processes, while Russia participated in them and accepted *faits accomplis*. Prussia also collaborated with the French, as it sought to ensure peace in Europe though a triple alliance of Russia, France, and Prussia that would have partitioned Europe into spheres of influence and guaranteed the neutrality of the states within each sphere. Prussia, naturally, expected to reserve for itself the hegemony of northern Germany and was willing to overlook French transgressions in Italy and southern Germany in exchange for rich bounty elsewhere. Prussia's gain, however, would have been Austria's loss. Vienna had vested interests in Germany and should have resisted more forcefully, but it did not; its armies were defeated, its allies indifferent, its revenues declining, and its state debt growing. From an Austrian point of view, Prussia could not be trusted because of existing enmity, while Russia's support inevitably would have resulted in the sacrifice of some Austrian interests and strengthening of the Russian position in the region, and because of the close relations between Russia and Prussia, that would have meant gains for Prussia as well.

The establishment of French hegemony over the southern German states was the result of both military and diplomatic victories. Throughout 1801 and 1802 Bonaparte outmaneuvered his rivals by exploiting existing squabbles among the Germanic states and the great powers; when Austria tried to use force to discourage territorial changes in Germany, Bonaparte quickly sided with Prussia and Bavaria, offering them generous compensation. The Franco-Russian accords of 1801 further strengthened France's hand in southern Germany. Bonaparte did not ignore Russian interests but rather sought common cause with them. If there was one thing France, Russia, and Prussia agreed on, it was the desirability of seeing Austrian power reduced in central Europe. Without any allies, Austria had no choice but to back down. Bonaparte's diplomacy, centered on gaining the cooperation of Prussia and Russia and decreasing Austrian influence by attracting to France's orbit a group of middle-sized German states, thus proved to be decisive in determining the fate of Germany. As radical as the change may seem, there was considerable support for secularization and reorganization within the Holy Roman Empire, as many of those middle states were keenly interested in profiting from it. The French claim that German states would be better protected in this new arrangement was widely accepted, and states like Bavaria, Baden, and Wurttemberg were delighted to see their territories enlarged. Britain was not.

CHAPTER 8 | The Rupture, 1803

T HE TREATY OF AMIENS lasted 420 days before it collapsed amid mutual
recriminations. The end came as no surprise. Just a few months into the
peace, the Franco-British amity was already under stress for the reasons outlined in Chapter 7, and it was becoming increasingly clear that the treaty left
too many questions unresolved, including France's territorial ambitions in
Europe and commercial and colonial rivalry with Britain. These were not
new causes of disagreement but rather old issues that had bedeviled these two
nations for the preceding 150 years (at least). As it was, the Treaty of Amiens
was incapable of resolving them.

The main reason behind the collapse of Amiens was, to paraphrase
Thucydides and the Peloponnesian War, the rising power of one state and the
fear it inspired in another. France's colonial power had been decimated during the Seven Years' War and then again during the Revolutionary Wars,
when the remaining colonies had been either lost to slave revolts or taken by
the British. On the conclusion of peace, Britain pledged to restore the seized
colonies, but it quickly became clear that France had changed. Its colonial
holdings had increased, as Bonaparte extracted major concessions from his
neighbors—Portugal ceded a part of Brazil, allowing the French possession
in Guiana to extend toward the estuary of the Amazon River, while Spain
returned the entire territory of Louisiana. Furthermore, France's dominance
over the Spanish and Dutch colonies was almost certain in light of the weakened state of their metropoles. The return of the Cape of Good Hope to the
Batavian Republic implied that this crucial station on the maritime route to
India would come under indirect but nonetheless strong French influence. It
was also quite clear that Bonaparte had not given up on his ambitions in the
Mediterranean, where Britain enjoyed a strong position due to its control of

Gibraltar, Egypt, and the islands of Minorca, Elba, and Malta. Yet under the terms of Amiens, the last four of those places were supposed to be evacuated, leaving Britain with just Gibraltar as a base of its operations in the vast sea.

France's colonial ambitions could not be fulfilled without building a strong navy, a prospect that naturally alarmed Britain. Contrary to popular perception of Bonaparte as having a poor grasp of naval power, he in fact possessed incisive nautical knowledge and gradually developed an astute understanding of sea power.[1] Upon coming to power, the First Consul inherited a navy that suffered from a decade-long political, military, and financial crisis. He knew well that it would take a long time to put France's fleet in order. "To pretend that France can equal England's navy in less than ten years is nothing but a fantasy," he wrote Denis Decrès, minister of the navy and colonies. "This would cause us expenses great enough to compromise our position on the continent without, however, giving us any surety of gaining ascendancy on the sea."[2] Bonaparte had a much longer game in mind and envisioned a gradual expansion of French naval forces that would be augmented with those of neighboring nations that France controlled. In 1802–1803, while Amiens was still holding, Bonaparte increased the marine budget (in part by diverting monies he had received from the Louisiana Purchase), made contracts for the purchase of timber (for the construction of ships) from Etruria, Sicily, and Russia, and pressured Spain, Naples, and the Batavian Republic to keep up and increase their navies. For Britain, it was clear that France, utilizing the resources of almost all of western and southern Europe, would progressively strengthen its navy, whether at peace or at war.

After Amiens, France was keen on restoring its commercial interests. However, it found its foreign trade impeded by British competition nearly everywhere, competition that was bolstered by the increased output of the nascent Industrial Revolution. This industrial rivalry remained a principal cause of hostility between France and Britain.[3] The Treaty of Amiens was incapable of resolving it and called for the sacrifice of too many of Britain's interests to be durable. The British negotiators were negligent enough to leave the matter of trade untouched by the treaty—the word "trade" appears nowhere in the text, while "commerce" is discussed only within the context of the future of the island of Malta (Article X, Section 8). This was a remarkable omission, considering that the key reason for Britain's entry into the Revolutionary Wars in 1793 had been the French occupation of Belgium and the opening of the Scheldt, which directly threatened British commercial interests. In 1802 London was willing to accept the peace, assuming that its old commercial relations would no longer be endangered. With its manufacturing rapidly industrializing and the costs of producing goods steadily falling, Britain was keen to open up continental markets to export its wares. British statesmen had "little doubt," as one put it, "of our trade penetrating deep into France herself and thriving at Paris."[4]

Such hopes were dashed soon after the peace was signed. The most important coastal areas in western Europe remained under French control and closed to British commerce.[5] The absence of any commercial agreement in the Treaty of Amiens meant that the peace not only failed to reopen the continental markets but deprived Britain of the monopoly of overseas commerce after the captured colonies were restored to France and the Batavian Republic. After two decades of consistent growth, Britain's outgoing tonnage actually decreased during the peace interval, from 2 million tons in 1801 to 1.7 million in 1803.[6] This may seem a small decline, but it was sufficient to cause some to wonder whether war was not indeed preferable to such a peace. The evacuation of Malta was highly unpopular in British business circles because it would have further jeopardized British trade in the Mediterranean and the Levant. Nor was anyone pleased with Bonaparte's efforts to restore relations with the Ottoman Empire, which included signing a commercial treaty that granted France most-favored-nation status in the Black Sea ports. It is not surprising, then, that influential British merchants were quick to denounce the peace. In the summer of 1802 a French agent reported about widespread dissatisfaction among the merchants in the City of London: "I am persuaded that tomorrow all voices will be for war, if the English people, finally conscious of our power, realize that they cannot obtain a treaty of commerce from us except by force of arms."[7]

At first France was willing to consider some sort of commercial arrangement with Britain. In the summer of 1802 a French delegation visited London to discuss a possible agreement. Such an agreement would have been limited in nature, since Bonaparte had no intention of signing another free trade treaty that could have had effects similar to the Anglo-French Free Trade Treaty of 1786, which had been a major French mistake and partly precipitated the outbreak of the Revolution.[8] In 1802 the conditions for an agreement were even less favorable than in 1786. France had just endured a decade of political and military turmoil that prevented its commerce and industry from keeping up with their rivals across the Channel. French commerce and industry were not prepared to engage in a free competition. Bonaparte understood that and had no desire to alienate some of his key support groups just as he was consolidating his power. He wished to encourage and protect French industry and trade, which meant keeping them insulated from British competitors. With this in mind, Bonaparte sought limited trade with Britain, but this went nowhere. His request that Britain open its markets open to

French silks and wines was ignored because of Britain's desire to shield its own emerging silk industry and to honor existing agreements with Portugal.[9] For its part, Britain suggested returning to the 1786 treaty with new safeguards that would have permitted France to take temporary measures to protect its home industry.[10] This Bonaparte could not accept since it would have eventually opened the French market to British goods. Forced to choose between free trade and protectionism, he instinctively chose the latter.[11]

Napoleon's refusal to agree to a commercial treaty aroused resentment among the British, who could not understand how any country could seek good relations with them while treating British goods as if they were plague-ridden. They could see little value in a peace treaty that produced neither a lessening of commercial duties nor the suspension of French colonial designs that could be detrimental to British trade. Britain came to believe that Bonaparte's sole purpose in signing the Treaty of Amiens was to wrest back lost colonies, rebuild French naval capacity, and humiliate Britain on its own shores. The news of French interventions in the Rhineland, Switzerland, and Italy, not to mention French advances in the West Indies and Egypt, as described in Chapter 7, only reinforced their worst suspicions about Bonaparte's designs.

The immediate cause for the collapse of the Treaty of Amiens involved the future of the island of Malta. Of the twenty-two provisions of the treaty, the longest (Article X) dealt with the island, indicating the degree of importance both sides attached to it. France had a long connection to the island. For more than two centuries prior to Bonaparte's conquest of Malta, its trade was closely tied to France, helped by the fact that many of the knights who were its governors were of French descent. In 1788 almost half of the ships calling upon the island were French; only a small percentage were British. Still, Bonaparte's Egyptian campaign revealed Malta's strategic value. The island was a gateway to the East, where any French conquests would directly affect British interests. To Britain, preoccupied above all with India, preventing French control of the island, with is picturesque harbor and splendid fortress, seemed a vital necessity. "If we retire beyond the Mediterranean," argued one senior British diplomat, "we can exercise no effectual interference either to prevent or to modify such events.... If, however, we retain Malta, Great Britain will be able, under all probable occurrences in the Levant, to adopt that line of conduct respecting them, which may at the time best suit her situation."[12]

At Amiens, France and Britain agreed that Malta and its two sister islands of Gozo and Comino would be restored to the Maltese knights under specific provisions. British forces would be evacuated within three months of the treaty's ratification, the islands would be proclaimed neutral, and their independence would be guaranteed by France, Britain, Austria, Spain, Russia, and Prussia; the Neapolitan kingdom, which had claimed nominal sovereignty over Malta, would furnish garrison forces. The knights would restore a general chapter and elect a grand master from among the natives of those nations that preserved their *langues* (administrative divisions of the order); to ensure the island's independence with respect to themselves, France and Britain would both abolish their respective *langues*.[13]

Implementation of Article X proved to be contentious.[14] Several of the subsidiary clauses presented particular challenges—the grand master was to be elected in Malta by a vote of the *langues*, but his headquarters was formally in St. Petersburg because the Russian tsar was officially the protector of the order. The tsar resented that he had no say in the framing of the provisions and that in the list of guaranteeing powers Russia was placed after Austria, a non-player as far as Mediterranean affairs were concerned. For Bonaparte, any further vacillation on this issue meant "adding further provisions to the treaty," which he could not accept.[15]

The real stumbling block was the fact that both sides had woken to the value of Malta. As one British officer put it, "Situated nearly at an equal distance from the entrance of the Straits and the coasts of Syria, the whole trade of the Mediterranean and Levant in time of war must be at the mercy of its possessors."[16] Malta could easily command the trade in the Mediterranean Sea, which is what both Paris and London feared. For the latter, the surrender of the Cape of Good Hope to the Batavian Republic, France's dependency, meant that it had lost access to a key position on the route to India. Were the British to evacuate Malta, they would have no control over an alternative route.

Three months after the treaty had been concluded, Malta was still occupied by British troops, and naturally the French government protested.[17] The British response—that the island could not be evacuated until the provisions of Article X had been fulfilled and the island's independence was guaranteed—did nothing to mollify the French. The reluctance of Russia, Prussia, and Spain to provide their guarantees only further hardened the British position. By the end of 1802, as the scale of Bonaparte's foreign policy was becoming clear, the British government clearly regretted agreeing to the island's evacuation and sought to find ways to avoid fulfilling its commitments. In November 1802 Prime Minister Addington's foreign secretary, Lord Hawkesbury, instructed the British ambassador to France "to avoid saying anything which may engage His Majesty to restore the island, even if these arrangements should be completed according to the true intent and spirit of the tenth article of the Treaty of Amiens." Hawkesbury believed that Britain "would certainly be justified in claiming the possession of Malta, as some counterpoise to the acquisitions of France since the conclusion of the definitive treaty."[18] Thus some members of the British government considered it conceivable to violate the treaty even before the first reports of French overtures to North Africa and Egypt hastened a change in the attitudes of both the British public and the government as a whole.

The publication on January 30, 1803, of General Horace Sebastiani's lengthy report on his tour of North Africa, Egypt, and Levant in the official French newspaper *Le Moniteur* gave the British cabinet a plausible excuse for the retention of Malta. Sebastiani's mission sought to revive French commercial interests in the Ottoman realms, but it also served as an excellent opportunity to reconnoiter the area for future military ventures.[19] Sebastiani's observations were doubtless designed to appeal to Bonaparte. He wrote of the enthusiastic reception he had enjoyed in Egypt and Syria, hinting that the French would be welcomed in the region; he even claimed that a French expedition might involve fewer than 10,000 men. The report was mainly intended to warn Britain that if it did not honor its obligations and evacuate Malta, France would consider renewing its efforts in the East. Sebastiani showed just how fragile the political situation was in Egypt. The Mamluk chiefs were disunited, the Turks were too weak to take control over the region, and there was bad feeling between both of them and the British, who, the report alleged, were openly detested in Cairo. Furthermore, during his meeting with Sebastiani, the British commander, General John Stuart, nonchalantly declared that he had no orders to evacuate Egypt and expected to spend the winter in Alexandria. This seemed to fly in the face of commitments that Britain had undertaken at Amiens, and it encouraged Bonaparte's bellicose attitude. On February 5, 1803, the French foreign ministry instructed the French embassy in London to point out to the British public the wider context in which Sebastiani's report had been produced: Britain's failure to evacuate Egypt and Malta, "despite the stipulations of the Treaty of Amiens, is an act that can provoke the renewal of war."[20]

Yet the publication of Sebastiani's report was a major mistake.[21] It was an inept attempt to apply pressure on the British, and it backfired. Bonaparte himself seems to have realized this belatedly and tried to soften its impact, but the damage was done.[22] From St. Petersburg to London and Constantinople, the report provoked unfavorable reactions. For Britain, the report proved that France was still contemplating a return to the Orient, which would be catastrophic to British interests in the Mediterranean in general, in the Levant and Egypt specifically, and by extension in India. Sebastiani's report, together with the news of Bonaparte's order (issued in mid-January) to General Decaen to lead a colonial expedition to Isle de France in the Indian Ocean, further reinforced prevailing views within British political and public circles that

Bonaparte's ambitions were boundless and had to be contained. Appreciating the full importance of Malta and realizing their mistake in pledging to surrender it, the British ministers began, in the words of a former British secret agent, to "catch at anything like a fair pretext for retaining Malta. It seems...as if ministers, ashamed of the cession, were unwilling to let it slip through their fingers, and were anxious to withhold it, if they could, without committing the honour of the nation by a violent breach of its plighted faith."[23] Sebastiani's report, in effect, provided Addington's government with an excuse to halt to all further withdrawals from Malta and India until France fulfilled its commitments under the Treaty of Amiens.[24]

In late February, in light of the continued British recalcitrance on the issue of Malta, the French government hardened its position. Bonaparte invited British ambassador Lord Whitworth to the Tuileries, where they conversed for more than two hours. The First Consul denied having any designs on Egypt in the near future, complained about the British failure to evacuate Egypt, and warned that war would be inevitable if Britain did not follow through on the obligations it had assumed at Amiens.[25] He buttressed his message two days later when his "Consular Exposé" on the state of the French republic was delivered to the legislative bodies. Bonaparte wrote of Britain's "implacable hatred of France" and warned that "five hundred thousand men ought to be, and shall be, ready to defend" the nation in case of war.[26] New instructions to the French embassy in London called for pressing for the expulsion of leading French émigrés, counteracting anti-French sentiments in the press, and, most important, demanding that the British evacuate Malta.[27] It was clear that Franco-British relations were fast approaching a point of no return.

On March 8, before the houses of Parliament, King George III read a speech that effectively decided the fate of the peace. Denouncing "very considerable military preparations" in the ports of France and Holland, the king "judged it expedient to adopt additional measures of precaution for the security of his dominions."[28] He proposed the mobilization of militia forces and an additional levy of 10,000 men for the navy, all approved by Parliament three days later. The king's speech further strained Franco-British relations. "The argument of contemporaries and certain historians that this action was on a par with the Consular Exposé is unconvincing," observed eminent American historian Harold C. Deutsch. "While the First Consul had played with indirect threats, England here made a move, which, according to diplomatic usage, was a preliminary step to war."[29]

Although the British foreign ministry tried to portray these measures as "precautionary," Paris reacted angrily to them.[30] The French foreign ministry declared that the British decision was an inexcusable hostile act that was made based on false information—military preparations under way in the French and Dutch port towns were not aimed at Britain but were, as officially declared, part of an expedition to Louisiana. Furthermore, Bonaparte had the British ambassador informed that in light of the king's speech France might be forced to start mobilizing as well and might consider reoccupying all of Holland.[31] On March 11, writing to Emperor Alexander of Russia, Bonaparte complained that Britain was coming up with new excuses to avoid treaty obligations: "How can one conclude treaties if they are so explicitly violated in spirit and letter?" He urged the tsar to intervene, or at least rebuke the British for their illegal retention of Malta.[32] Two days later, at a diplomatic reception at the Tuileries on March 13, Bonaparte held an audience with Lord Whitworth at which he lost his patience and publicly derided George III's speech and the British failure to honor its treaty obligations. It was clear, he exclaimed, that the British "do not respect treaties" and wanted another decade of war. "If they are the first to draw the sword, I will be the last to sheathe it," Bonaparte famously concluded before storming from the room.[33]

The First Consul's behavior may have violated diplomatic courtesy, but its importance has been exaggerated by historians. It was a deliberate display of rage.[34] Over the next few days Bonaparte tried to be conciliatory toward Britain, seeking to show that he had "no desire to go to war [and] that he has nothing to gain from [war] and that the whole country is against it."[35] Still, he pointed out that France's honor demanded that Britain fulfill its obligations or risk war. Upon receiving a new dispatch from the British government, the First Consul personally drafted a detailed response that analyzed (and refuted) British charges and posited French offers. The note shows that Bonaparte was willing to compromise on Egypt as long as Britain fulfilled its obligation with regard to Malta. Even Lord Whitworth admitted that "the tenor of this note" showed that France was not "desirous to proceed to extremities."[36] The deliberate nature of Bonaparte's bluster is underscored by a series of reports concerning French naval forces that he had received in March. These revealed that the French navy was in desperate need of repair and expansion; even the most optimistic forecasts suggested that by September 1803 the French navy would have only twenty-two ships and twenty-eight frigates ready for service, hardly enough to confront the Royal Navy, which had almost four times as many ships-of-the-line. Furthermore, to complete the necessary repairs, refitting, and construction, the navy would require a staggering four million cubic feet of wood, an unattainable amount. And even if the supplies were available, the French naval arsenals lacked a sufficient workforce, as hundreds of trained workers had been previously dismissed. Bonaparte was well aware that France was not ready for a war with Britain.[37]

On April 3 the British foreign ministry responded to the French overtures by demanding further concessions. France was to apologize for the publication of Sebastiani's report, accept British control of Malta, evacuate Holland and Switzerland, and indemnify the king of Sardinia; in return, Britain was willing to recognize the Kingdom of Etruria and the Italian and Ligurian Republics.[38] The French government was taken aback by the tone and content of the note but showed willingness to consider some concessions—although not on the issue of Malta, on which it felt honor-bound to insist. As a compromise, Bonaparte proposed that upon evacuation of Malta the British be allowed a Mediterranean base on Candia (Crete) or Corfu that would serve well to defend British interests. France was also prepared to sign a formal convention to reassure Britain with respect to its aspirations in the East.[39]

If Addington's cabinet had truly desired to maintain peace, the French offer represented the opportunity to do so. The British reply amounted to an ultimatum, rejecting the French offer and insisting not only on British possession of Malta but also on French withdrawal from Holland and Switzerland.[40] France had just one week to consider these terms or face a break in diplomatic relations.[41]

Bonaparte was, predictably, furious at the British demands, yet he still made a counteroffer.[42] The British could stay in Malta for up to four years, he proposed, and then transfer the island into the care of a guaranteeing power (i.e., Russia).[43] The French foreign minister's letter to his ambassador in London reveals the extent to which Bonaparte's position had evolved in an attempt to avoid war: "We will never consent to a formal requirement providing for a single day of the English occupation of Malta but we will not raise any obstacles to the [temporary] occupation...that can become a very extended one."[44] The French offer seemed so appealing that Lord Whitworth chose to disregard his government's earlier instruction to depart from Paris, since the French proposal could offer "an honorable and advantageous adjustment of the present differences."[45]

The British government, however, failed to see it that way, declining the French offer as "loose, indefinite and unsatisfactory," as Lord Hawkesbury wrote to Lord Whitworth, and rejecting the guardianship of Russia on the grounds that St. Petersburg was certain to refuse it.[46] In vain did Talleyrand assure Lord Whitworth that Russia had, in fact, reversed its stance and was now keenly interested in resolving differences between the two powers. He even revealed that in late April Emperor Alexander had accepted Bonaparte's request for mediation and had now offered his services. The change in position was occasioned by the growing belief in Russia that the prospect of war was "particularly undesirable" because an "inconsistent and very weak government" ruled over Britain. The goal of offering mediation was, in the words of the Russian chancellor, to "constrain France within her current boundaries" by seeking the territorial integrity of the Ottoman Empire and "new guarantees for the Italian states, the German Empire, Holland and Switzerland, ensuring the neutrality of these states."[47] Bonaparte accepted this offer. Whether this was a ploy to gain time or not, he had shown a willingness to negotiate before the British forced his hand. On the evening of May 12 Whitworth, though surprised by the unexpected revelation of Russian mediation, requested his passports and departed from Paris.

The extent of Bonaparte's anxiety to repair the fast-crumbling edifice of Amiens is revealed in his final offer, which Whitworth received as he was already traveling toward the coast. France offered Britain the right to stay on Malta for ten years if the French could occupy parts of the Neapolitan kingdom for a similar period; France was even willing to concede Britain's control of Malta until such time as an international guarantee of neutrality had been agreed upon.[48] This proposal represented a real and clear opportunity to safeguard peace. Again, though, Britain rejected it, making the excuse that its obligations to Naples made such an arrangement impossible.

On May 18, 1803, Britain made a formal declaration of war against France, launching a conflict that would last for more than a decade.[49] Despite some authors' claims that the British government declared war with a united country at its back, there was in fact considerable anti-war sentiment, and support for war was never either unanimous or continuous. While anti-war liberals did agree that Britain stood for the cause of liberty and supported the government's declaration of war against France, this support was also conditional on the war remaining a defensive one. Yet as the war lengthened, British actions could hardly be styled as defensive, and anti-war sentiments rapidly increased. Some 150,000 people from Yorkshire and Lancashire alone signed a peace petition in 1808.[50] The British government did its best to cajole the nation into action, using the threat of compulsory training and turning to Scotland and Ireland to recruit men primarily from Catholic areas, as it was by "no means desirable... to bring away any of the Protestants of the North," as the historian Jenny Uglow has noted.[51]

———◦◦◦❖◦◦◦———

At the start of the twentieth century German historian Otto Brandt highlighted the role the shifting Russian sympathies had played in the start of Franco-British War. "On this relationship between England and Russia," he wrote, "hinged all the later developments of the Amiens question."[52] Indeed, the court of St. Petersburg played a crucial if often overlooked role in the crisis between the two powers, both of whom had sought Russian military and diplomatic support against the other. As we have seen, while the relations between St. Petersburg and Paris remained lukewarm in the wake of Emperor Paul's assassination in March 1801, they did undergo major change with the accession of his son Alexander to the throne. Bonaparte tried to ensure continued Russian support for his policies by dispatching his trusted aide-de-camp Michel Duroc to St. Petersburg with instructions to outline French designs for Germany and Russia's possible role in them.

Duroc arrived at the Russian capital at a rather opportune moment, given that the Francophobe faction was on the wane. Russia was keenly interested in German affairs, since the Russian imperial family had close family connections to many Germany princely houses. Alexander appears to have been interested in gathering the help of other great powers so as to dilute France's influence in German affairs. Such Russian sentiments had been reinforced by Austrian overtures suggesting a new Russo-Austrian alliance. The arrival of Duroc, however, changed the Russian position.[53] The French revealed that the Austrians, while sounding out Russia on the question of a new alliance, were also eagerly pushing proposals for reviving the old alliance with France. Unpleased by this double game, the Russian court was willing to consider French offers. On October 8, 1801, five months before Amiens, a formal peace treaty between Russia and France was signed in Paris. The treaty consisted of two parts, with the public section containing formal declarations of amity and peace between the two nations, while the second part contained secret articles in which the real conditions of Franco-Russian relations were outlined. In the second set of provisions, the two powers agreed to achieve a common accord in respect to Germany, where a "just equilibrium between the Houses of Austria and Brandenburg [Prussia]" was desired.[54]

The Treaty of Paris showed that Alexander was not against changes in Germany; in fact, he hoped to work jointly with Bonaparte on German reorganization as long as it satisfied Russian interests. Furthermore, Alexander, unlike the British statesmen, differentiated between a balance of security and a balance of power, and sought to establish the former. This could be accomplished not through building a coalition against France, as Britain intended to do, but rather through forming a restraining alliance with France, so that Paris and St. Petersburg could become "mediating arbiters" of Europe. The Anglophile faction at the Russian court warned, however, that France was becoming too powerful for a stable European system and that Franco-Russian relations would be fragile. Such arguments gained in strength when it became clear that the czar had been outmaneuvered on the question of German indemnities and had in fact contributed materially to the establishment of French hegemony in southern Germany. Alexander naturally refused to see

Germany transformed into a French protectorate and wanted to ensure that Russia continued to have a say in the region.[55]

Russian protestations routinely elicited the French foreign ministry's response that France's actions in Germany were no different from Russia's in Poland. Exasperated by this, the Russian government instructed its ambassador in Paris to respond that the Polish partition was "already a thing of the past and it was pointless to bring it up." More concerning to Russia was the fact that "when France incorporated the Netherlands and gave herself the Rhine and the Alps as frontiers, her governments designated these as a compensation for what others had taken in Poland. Yet, these acquisitions already surpass those which we made then."[56]

Upset at France, the Russian government was also mindful of British unreliability. Memories of the failed joint expedition to Holland in 1799 and of British haggling over the financial and diplomatic price necessary for Russian support were still fresh. With the League of Armed Neutrality formed and Britain denied access to Baltic trade in grain and naval stores, Russia seemed to pose a greater problem to Britain than France did. Addington's government understood well that repairing relations with Russia was key to strengthening Britain's political and military position in Europe.[57] Its first foreign policy overtures were, therefore, directed toward St. Petersburg, and the manner in which they were conducted reveals British preoccupation with a Russian alliance as much as with a war against France. On March 24, 1801, Lord Hawkesbury sent special instructions to the British minister in Berlin granting him full powers to restore diplomatic ties with Russia. These instructions are revealing not only for the concessions that Britain was ready to make—fulfilling the terms of the 1799 Anglo-Russian agreement on Malta, by which Britain accepted Russian garrisons on the island—but also for their date of composition. On March 24 Hawkesbury didn't yet know that Emperor Paul, the driving force behind Russia's recent Anglophobia, had just been murdered. The new Russian sovereign was more favorably disposed to Britain and wished to settle all outstanding Anglo-Russian disputes.

Learning of the change in the Russian government in mid-April, Prime Minister Addington focused his diplomatic efforts on Russia, even postponing the negotiations that would lead to the Treaty of Amiens with France. The appointment of a new ambassador reflected Britain's desire to flatter Russian sensibilities, given that Lord St. Helens was one of its most experienced and esteemed diplomats—he had participated in diplomatic negotiations ending the Seven Years' War and had served as a minister plenipotentiary to Spain in the 1790s. St. Helens was instructed to "propose an arrangement," as Hawkesbury wrote him in a letter, "which shall place everything between the two countries on the same footing on which it was."[58] This included abandoning the League of Armed Neutrality, opening the Baltic trade to the British, and acknowledging Britain's right to search neutral shipping. On June 17, after several weeks of negotiations, St. Helens and Russian foreign secretary Nikita Panin signed an agreement that granted Britain those terms while temporarily setting aside the question of Malta.[59]

This was a major accomplishment by Addington's cabinet, one that is often overshadowed by the failure of the Treaty of Amiens. Already in the spring of 1801 the British ministers envisioned joint defense plans designed to restore political equilibrium in Europe.[60] They clearly hoped that once relations were restored, Russia would rejoin their struggle against France and serve as a focal point for any anti-French coalition. Unfortunately for the British, Emperor Paul's successor, Emperor Alexander, Anglophile though he was, sought to avoid foreign entanglements at the start of his reign. While recognizing that Britain was one of Russia's "natural allies," he wanted to avoid any hostilities with France. "I intend to follow a national policy that is based on the benefits of [my] state and not, as is often the case, on predilections of this or that power," he confided to one of his diplomats.[61]

Alexander believed that Russia required major reforms in administration, agriculture, and industry, all of which needed peace to succeed.[62] His country would therefore remain on the sidelines of the Franco-British peace negotiations. Disappointed, Britain continued efforts to promote Anglo-Russian rapprochement. During diplomatic negotiations with France, British ministers sought to consider Russian positions on a number of issues and regularly shared intelligence with Russia, causing one senior Russian diplomat to acknowledge that this was a "grand sign of trust."[63] Yet the court of St. Petersburg refused to openly support Britain. With Bonaparte reorganizing Germany, Russia feared alienating the French, even if Bonaparte's designs for Germany and the Ottoman Empire were clearly of great concern. Thus Russian diplomats regularly reminded their British colleagues that St. Petersburg could never allow them (or the French) to annex Malta, but neither did it want to get involved in resolving the fate of the island.[64] Britain was naturally irritated by the Russian vacillations, and its annoyance only increased when in June 1802 Russia and France reached an agreement paving the way for the reorganization of German states and calling for Russian mediation between the French and the Turks.[65] This agreement was a major accomplishment of French diplomacy, for it was a key element in Bonaparte's efforts to keep Britain at bay, reconcile Russia and Prussia, and form a coalition to isolate Austria.

Addington's cabinet felt betrayed by Russia's actions. Hawkesbury bitterly complained that in light of Britain's exertions "for the purpose of rescuing

Egypt from the hands of the French and of restoring it to its lawful sovereign, it would be impossible . . . to regard the endeavors of the Russian government to mediate a separate peace between France and the Ottoman Porte in any other light than as a most unfriendly act."[66] Addington's cabinet nonetheless persevered, and its diplomatic correspondence in 1802–1803 clearly shows that Britain was eager to make use of peacetime to build a new coalition against France.[67] As German, Italian, and Swiss reorganizations progressed, Britain exploited Russia's growing concern about French aggrandizement to renew its efforts to establish an alliance against France. Addington understood that any anti-French coalition had to include Russia but he also knew that bringing both Austria and Prussia into the coalition would prove to be a daunting task because of their long-standing rivalry in Germany, as well as French success in mollifying the Prussian court.

Britain's eagerness to secure Russia's support overshadowed its relations with Vienna. Addington was puzzled by Austria's reluctance to become a partner in a new continental alliance. The reason lay in its fear that in light of recent defeats it would have to act as a junior partner and that any future settlement would be dictated by Britain and Russia. Matters were further complicated by the fact that during the German reorganization Russia had aligned itself more closely with Prussia, while Britain, reversing an earlier pro-Prussian stance, staked its interests on closer relations with Austria. In September and October 1802 the British foreign ministry urged its diplomats to find a way to detach Russia from Prussia and promote Russo-Austrian cooperation. One such opportunity arose when Prussia recognized France's annexation of Piedmont without requesting compensation for the Piedmontese king, a request that Russia had made repeatedly. The British Foreign Office quickly sent out new instructions to its embassy in St. Petersburg "to take advantage of this and of every other circumstance of the same nature which may arise to estrange as much as possible" Russia from Prussia and to connect it with Austria. The British embassy was asked to remind the Russian government that Austria, whose ambitions lay in Italy and Germany, posed a much smaller threat than did Prussia, which faced them across the Baltic.[68] By late October Hawkesbury envisioned, as he noted in a letter, "a system of defensive alliance" between Britain, Russia, and Austria designed to contain resurgent France and prevent "further innovations in the system of Europe."[69]

British efforts once again proved to be in vain. Russia refused to jeopardize its positions. It was clearly concerned by Bonaparte's actions and claimed that British efforts to form a coalition would only provoke French countermeasures that could lead to hostilities. Russia's finances could not sustain another war. "The wisest policy for Russia is to stay calm and take care of her inner prosperity," insisted Emperor Alexander as late as January 20, 1803.[70] Declining British offers of a formal alliance, Russian senior diplomats also argued that "the interests of Russia and those of England have so many points in common between them that the two powers can consider themselves as allies without having any need of writing it on paper."[71]

Unable to convince Russia to join a coalition with Austria, the British government tried to play on Russia's concerns over the Ottoman Empire, where Bonaparte was pursuing two major goals. First, he sought to mend France's relations with its former Ottoman ally. In October 1802 Bonaparte dispatched General Guillaume Brune as the French ambassador to Constantinople with instructions to restore French standing at the Ottoman court and to protect French commercial interests in the region. A Franco-Ottoman treaty, signed in 1802, mutually guaranteed the integrity of the French and Ottoman possessions and restored France's former privileges (commercial capitulations and the right to serve as protector of the sultan's Catholic subjects); furthermore, for the first time, the Porte gave French merchant vessels the right to trade freely on the Black Sea, where Russians had long sought to establish their trade (Article 2 of the treaty).[72] With this agreement, Bonaparte largely reversed the diplomatic revolution of 1799 that had united Russia and the Ottomans against France, and set the Ottoman Empire and France on the road to rebuilding their diplomatic relations. It was not a complete victory for the French, though. Sultan Selim III remained highly suspicious of French designs and secretly urged Britain to keep Malta. As British ambassador Lord Elgin reported (with clear hyperbole), "The Porte does estimate the duration of its independence by the period of our continuance in possession of this island."[73]

While improving his relations with the Turks, Bonaparte also desired to exploit Russian interests in the Near East. In detailed instructions to Michel Duroc in St. Petersburg, Bonaparte urged his envoy to make every effort to divert Russian attention from French actions in Italy by raising the possibility of Russian aggrandizement in the Near East: "Speak of [Russian empress] Catherine II as of a princess who foresaw the fall of the Turkish Empire and who realized that there would be no prosperity for Russian commerce until it found an outlet in the south."[74] During his conversations with the Russian ambassador, Bonaparte also frequently hinted at the dissolution of the Ottoman Empire and the possibility of the Franco-Russian partition of its land. Bonaparte thus pursued a double game with the Turks, wooing them while conspiring against them. His Ottoman policy served as "a means of diversion and transaction," observed French historian Albert Vandal. "It was on this terrain that he hoped to divide [his] enemies, dissolve the coalition by stealing away one of its members, attach one of the principal courts to himself, whichever it might be, [and] finally conquer the grand alliance, which he needed in order to master the continent and vanquish England."[75]

Russia rebuffed France's suggestion, with Russian chancellor Alexander Vorontsov stressing that it could not "participate in any hostile projects directed against Turkey."[76] This statement is noteworthy for its duplicity because at the very moment that it was declining France's offer Russia was actively expanding its influence into the traditional Ottoman domains. Russia had long sought to gain security, power, and prestige in the Middle East against the much weaker Ottoman and Persian Empires, something that in turn would further enhance its standing in Europe. Russia therefore had no interest in accepting the French offer, which represented an intrusion into what Russia already considered its sphere of influence. The frequency with which the First Consul hinted at the dissolution of the Ottoman power only alarmed Russia and made it more quietly attentive to British overtures.[77]

Russia's perception of the French threat in the East naturally extended to the question of Malta, which was, as we've seen, so central to the rupture of Amiens. In their negotiations with Bonaparte, the British had insisted on the neutrality of the island, which could be ensured by a third power; to the British this power was Russia, and in their efforts to convince Alexander to get involved, Hawkesbury went as far as to offer to pay the costs of the Russian garrison on the island.[78] St. Petersburg was not pleased; Britain chose to overlook the Russian protectorate over the Maltese knights, complained one senior Russian diplomat, and so Russia could not provide guarantees for the island's independence, as required by Article X of Amiens.[79] By the end of 1802, however, the Russian position had evolved, and this shift played an important role in the ongoing tensions between Britain and France. In December 1802 Vorontsov suggested to the British envoy that Russia might be willing to accept temporary British occupation of the island. A month later Prince Adam Czartoryski, who assumed the functions of the Russian foreign minister, informed the British embassy that the British should not evacuate Malta, a message that was reinforced two days later when Czartoryski openly stated that Emperor Alexander wished Britain to keep Malta.[80]

The news of the change in Russia's position reached London on February 8, just as debate was raging over the publication of Sebastiani's report on Egypt, and played an important role in solidifying the British position on Malta. On February 9, just a day after learning about Russia's shift, the British foreign minister sent new instructions to Lord Whitworth explaining that Britain was also entitled to compensation, which should involve British occupation of Malta.[81] Thus while Lord Whitworth envisioned "a system of observation on the part of Great Britain and Russia... to check the ambitious career of the First Consul," his superiors at the Foreign Office were more ambitious and desired a secret defensive alliance with Russia, arguing that Sebastiani's report demonstrated that the Ottoman Empire had to be defended against renewed French aggression.[82] Again the Russians demurred, downplaying France's threat to the Ottoman Empire and arguing that any efforts to form a coalition could directly provoke a war in Europe. However, the Russian government was not convinced that Franco-British tensions would lead to an actual war. Reports by the Russian ambassador to Paris suggested that France had every reason to avoid war, which in turn caused senior Russian officials to believe that somehow the crisis between Paris and London would be resolved peacefully. Russia did, however, promise to act in concert with Britain in the event of any threat to the Porte and on the subject of Malta, promises that probably contributed to the intransigence of the British government in the last stages of its negotiations with France.[83]

Assured of Russian support (even if it was not formalized), Addington's government was willing to exert greater pressure on Bonaparte.[84] At the same time, unaware of the Russian diplomatic overtures to Britain, Bonaparte sought help from Alexander, hoping that Russian mediation would compel the British to compromise and leave Malta.[85] He had realized belatedly that his talk of an Eastern partition could strain relations with Russia, and so he made sure to include in his new state-of-the-republic speech an implicit rejection of any aggressive action against the Ottomans.[86] The French foreign ministry agreed to act on the long-standing Russian requests for compensation for the Sardinian monarchy and even submitted a draft convention for that purpose.[87] It was clear that Bonaparte was doing his best to appease Russia and use its intercession to preserve peace. Emperor Alexander I thus found himself trapped: if he refused to mediate, war would most certainly break out between France and Britain, but getting involved would mean endangering relations with one of the sides. The Russian emperor vacillated throughout March and April before making a last-minute decision to accept the French proposal and offer mediation. The Russian offer reached Paris on May 12, by which time it was "too late" to convince Britain to accept it.[88] Still, the Russian intervention put the British "in a very embarrassing situation" of having to reject it and pursue the course for war.[89]

The collapse of the Treaty of Amiens is one of the turning points in modern history. It unleashed twelve years of war and misery and shaped the destinies of Europe and the world beyond. The question of responsibility for the collapse of the Peace of Amiens has been the subject of endless discussion, much of it centered on the extent to which Bonaparte personally contributed to the outbreak of the war. For many historians, responsibility for the resumption of war lies squarely on the shoulders of the French leader, whose very name is now associated with the conflict. They say that Bonaparte was driven by insatiable imperial lust and megalomania. He was "not in the least interested in peace" and was "looking for any excuse to renew the war," charges one of these historians.[90] "All the faults were on the French side," notes another.[91] This concurs with American scholar Paul W. Schroeder's view that "all the wars after 1802 were Bonaparte's wars."[92]

———◦◦◦◦◦———

There is no doubt that Bonaparte displayed Anglophobia (just as many Europeans did) and that his continental and colonial policies contributed to the British decision for war.[93] But it seems disingenuous to hold him solely responsible for the turmoil that unfolded between 1800 and 1815. As in the case with any debate about the causes of war, evidence is often made to fit one's point of view. The fact is that no actor in this global conflagration is completely innocent. Without getting too deeply into counterfactuals, perhaps one thought experiment offers some perspective here. Had Bonaparte died in Italy or Egypt, the first decade of the nineteenth century almost certainly would have witnessed a period of warfare in Europe nonetheless. Looking at a general pattern of war causation in Europe in the eighteenth and nineteenth centuries, we can clearly see that the defense and extension of a state power—driven by domestic pressures, external affairs, and long-standing interests and rivalries—was the most significant systemic factor in a decision to fight a war. Attempts to assign blame for war to the inner dimensions of Bonaparte's character seem to miss a key aspect: namely, his acute geopolitical mindset, which understood France's position within the wider international system. Bonaparte's policies in 1800–1802, though they did contribute to war, were not radically new. They originated in the objectives formulated by the Bourbon monarchy earlier in the century and represented a direct and natural progression of the Revolutionary Wars.[94] The revolutionary conflict, now a decade old, resulted, in the words of one German historian, in "Germany's helplessness, Prussia's resignation, Russia's retirement, Austria's defeat and England's exhaustion."[95] By contrast, France had achieved its grand goal of hegemony in western Europe and secured a cordon sanitaire of Switzerland, northern Italy, and the Low Countries, where Bonaparte was now seeking to consolidate French rule. Moreover, Bonaparte believed that France was losing its struggle with Britain for the domination of global trade, industry, and colonies. During the wars of the eighteenth century Britain had used its superior naval power to defend and enlarge its economic dominion, which even the loss of its American colonies did not hamper. By 1800 France was clearly losing. Between 1750 and 1800 its share of total

European manufacturing fell from 17.2 percent to 14.9 percent, while Britain's rose from 8.2 percent to 15.3 percent; furthermore, during the same period British industrialization (on a per capita basis) far outpaced that of France, its overall trade volume tripled, and its merchant marine doubled in size.[96] Given all this, it is hard to envision any French leadership that could have pursued a docile foreign policy, as is sometimes suggested, and one that would not have been eager to exploit circumstances to reclaim French influence on the continent. Bonaparte's policies in the period 1800–1803 followed a geopolitical rationale that was rooted in French fears for their position in the global economic system against their traditional rival. Britain's rapid industrialization, growing share of international trade, closed colonial system, and superior naval power meant that France faced the prospect of being shut off from markets and raw materials and unable to maintain its position in the wider international system. The French elite shared such concerns, which meant, as historian Steven Englund correctly pointed out, that Bonaparte's expansionist policies enjoyed considerable support at home, and "the evidence suggests wide popular and elite pride in . . . French aggrandizement."[97] The need to challenge and confront Britain had been recognized by French leaders before Bonaparte came to power. Bonaparte's predecessors in the revolutionary governments pursued policies that were no less belligerent, because they realized that after the defeat of the First Coalition France was in a unique position to realize hitherto undreamed-of opportunities; such sentiments only strengthened after the overthrow of the Second Coalition. France's economy had come to depend on resources extracted from neighboring states, and any French government would have found it difficult to compromise its standing in the Low Countries, the Rhineland, and Italy. The army had tasted glory and welcomed the opportunities for exploitation afforded by conquered or occupied territories. In January 1802 George Jackson, the brother of the British envoy involved in the Amiens negotiations, noted in his diary that the French officers "have become dissatisfied with Bonaparte on account of the 'premature peace' [and] have sought to alienate the affections of his guards; and many well-informed persons think the army is not be relied upon."[98]

Those who put the burden of blame on Bonaparte make the error of assuming that France's interests were unnatural and worthy of condemnation while those of Britain or its continental allies were natural and commendable.[99] But as French historian Albert Sorel pointed out more than a century ago, virtually every crime in international relations with which Bonaparte has been charged could be found in the repertoire of the ancien régime states that all too often practiced predatory behavior toward their neighbors. In the absence of an international system regulating the behavior of states, such as exists today, why should France of the early 1800s be considered more "rogue," as one modern historian put it, than Russia of the 1790s or Prussia of the 1740s?[100] Were Russia and Austria more justified in their partitioning of Poland than France in annexing the Rhineland and Piedmont? Were Bonaparte's apparent ambitions for colonial expansion inherently so different from British aspirations?

No European power was in a position to condemn France for changing the official status of other areas of Europe. British, Austrian, and Russian accusations that France disregarded the will of neighboring peoples should be considered within the context of, for example, the British incorporation of Ireland into the United Kingdom, Austrian policies in the Balkan borderlands, and Russian actions in Poland and Georgia, none of which represented an exercise in free will by the affected populations. Was Britain more justified in bombing Copenhagen in 1801 to defend its interests in the Baltic than France was in sending troops into Switzerland in 1802? Condemning French actions in Switzerland, Russian chancellor Vorontsov claimed that Bonaparte was ignoring that "every free nation has the right to choose a form of government that best suits its circumstances, roots and traditions of its people." Yet when the French reminded him of what the Russians had done in Poland just six years prior, Vorontsov could only respond that it was already "a thing of the past" and it was "pointless to bring it up."[101] Pursuing a policy of aggrandizement, France was not the only one willing to risk a resumption of conflict. European capitals had plenty of hawks who desired to exploit political and military turmoil to their advantage. Russia clearly nurtured grand imperial ambitions, and we have already discussed Rostopchin's memorandum regarding political realignment of Europe. No less ambitious was the memorandum prepared by Henry Dundas, Britain's secretary of war, advocating colonial conquests in the Americas.[102] Austria had not lost hope of reclaiming its lost territories and of forcing France back within its ancient limits. But France was unique among these countries in enjoying a steady record of military and political successes, and so it could attempt to pursue policies to which others could only aspire.

Despite claims that Bonaparte had violated the terms of the Treaty of Amiens, he had not, at least from a legal point of view.[103] French activities in Piedmont and Switzerland were not in breach of the Anglo-French peace treaty, nor were they as threatening as the British made them out to be. None of these regions posed a direct threat to British interests or were in the traditional British sphere of influence; both had already been under French influence at the end of the Revolutionary Wars, and Bonaparte's actions were aimed at consolidating power that France had already wielded there.[104] It must be noted that Britain showed little interest in Piedmont-Sardinia until 1803, as evidenced by the British rejection of the Sardinian request to have its representative present at peace negotiations, which allowed French ambitions to influence the kingdom's fate.[105] The British were on firmer ground in their criticisms of Bonaparte's violations of the Treaty of Lunéville by failing to fully evacuate his troops from the Batavian and Italian Republics.[106]

None of this is to say that Bonaparte bears no responsibility for the twelve years of bloodshed that started in March 1803. The First Consul's actions and words indicated a drive for power, not the qualities of prudence and conciliation that might have maintained continental peace. He was not a "builder in love with peace," as some of his defenders continue to claim.[107] And he did consider war to be "merely the continuation of policy by other means," to use Prussian military theorist Carl von Clausewitz's famed formulation—one that was drawn from observations of the Napoleonic era.[108] Bonaparte wanted to take advantage of every opportunity that his opponents provided him. He prodded and nudged his neighbors as much as he could to secure what he wanted, sowing seeds of resentment that eventually bore the fruits of war. Considered individually, France's actions were provocative but not *casus belli*. Still, as a whole they created a new international reality wherein France was a hegemonic power that aggressively pursued imperial designs in Europe and overseas. This Britain could not tolerate, and it felt compelled to resist.[109]

This slide toward war was facilitated by Bonaparte's misconceptions about Britain's economic difficulties and what he perceived as its eagerness to make peace even on disadvantageous terms. He believed that Britain was war-weary and would not be willing to risk a new war, especially when lacking allies on the continent. He was wrong and the war came too soon for Bonaparte, who in 1803 rattled his saber but did not actually intend to use it.[110] He knew well that his domestic consolidation was not finished, that the country was still economically weakened, and that his forces, especially his navy, had not reached the point where they could seriously challenge Britain's. He had every reason to wish for amity. In peacetime, commerce and industry could be revived, colonies developed, and the military strengthened. That Bonaparte was not *yet* ready to fight is clear from the last-ditch efforts, noted earlier, to find a compromise with Britain on the issue of Malta, on which he had shown willingness to accept terms that would have constrained his policies in the eastern Mediterranean.

Historians tend to discount these efforts by questioning their sincerity, but they deserve to be given proper acknowledgment and consideration. One may argue that in 1803 Bonaparte should have done more to maintain peace, but this argument cuts both ways. British newspapers, journals, and gazettes continued to explicitly express hope for the demise of the French leader, who was portrayed as a yellow-skinned pygmy or a monstrous hybrid of, according to a period tabloid, " 'an unclassifiable being, half-African, half-European, a Mediterranean mulatto."[111] His family members were not spared either, with his wife, Josephine, portrayed as a harlot and his stepdaughter, Hortense, accused of incestuous relations. A statesman of Bonaparte's magnitude might have been better advised to ignore such attacks but, always acutely sensitive to his portrayal in the press, the First Consul was furious at such characterizations; in the words of State Councilor Joseph Pelet de la Lozère, they drove him "into a fury that resembled the lion in the fable stung to madness by a swarm of gnats."[112] When the French envoy presented a formal list of six key grievances to the British government in August 1802, the issue of newspaper articles hostile to France was at the top. To prevent the spread of British newspapers in France, Bonaparte violated the agreement made between the French and British post offices, instructing his officials to disregard certain clauses that related to customs duties and the conveyance of passengers.[113] In the summer of 1802 he personally wrote at least five articles for the French official newspaper *Le Moniteur* complaining about the British failure to restrain the press. "Does freedom of the press reach so far," read his August 8 article, "as to permit a newspaper to say of a friendly nation, newly reconciled with England, things one would not dare to say of a government with whom one was at war?"

The continued publication of diatribes in Britain only reinforced Bonaparte's belief that the British government was guilty of bad faith; he could never quite accept that it was as uninvolved or powerless as it claimed. Members of the British government had stakes in many newspapers, and British explanations that the government could not interfere with traditional English freedoms rang hollow to the French. The repressive Treasonable Practices Act and the Seditious Meetings Acts of 1795, which had silenced all pro-French newspaper opinion, had shown that the British government could, if need be, restrict English press liberties. Naturally, any such action on behalf of Bonaparte would have incited a political firestorm that could have consumed the Addington government. Hence, despite the French complaining in the bitterest terms, the British government did nothing to curtail activities of the most vociferous émigrés, and the libelous activity of the British press continued to exercise its destructive influence upon Anglo-French relations.[114]

The issue of the press was directly related to another thorny issue in the relationship between France and Britain. Ever since the Revolution started in 1789, Britain had served as a refuge for hundreds of émigrés who actively conspired against France. The British funded many royalist agents who infiltrated back into France and incited disturbances or targeted government members. In 1798–1799 British agents supported a French royalist plot to assassinate the entire membership of the Directory.[115] Bonaparte himself was the target of several assassination attempts, and in the most infamous of them, he and Josephine narrowly escaped death after the royalist agents detonated a large bomb—*la machine infernale*—on the rue Saint-Nicaise on Christmas Eve of 1800. The royalist circles continued to operate in Britain after the signing of the Treaty of Amiens, and Bonaparte was justified in his objections to their continued presence on British soil. It would have cost the British government little to enforce provisions of the 1793 Alien Act to deport some seditious writers in the French émigré community who were particularly vociferous in their denunciations of Bonaparte.[116]

Britain did not go to war in 1803 out of "an irrational anxiety" about Bonaparte's motives and intentions, as some have suggested.[117] In choosing this course, it acted out of a clear sense that while at peace it had no ready means to contain France in continental or colonial affairs, the reality that Bonaparte so successfully exploited. Having occupied Holland, Piedmont, and Naples and forced the Spaniards to send troops into Portugal, France had effectively closed western and southern Europe to British commerce, a situation that was ratified at Amiens. The British government's conduct during the peace negotiations—where, in the words of Russian chancellor Vorontsov, it "first gave everything away in the preliminaries, and then again in the Treaty of Amiens"—placed Britain in an unenviable position because the peace treaty made it rather easy for France to exploit its advantages and hard for Britain to react without violating the treaty.[118]

That Britain was not sincere in its efforts to uphold peace was manifest during the three months after the rupture of the Treaty of Amiens. In May-July 1803 France repeatedly made concessions only to see them rejected. It is often forgotten that Bonaparte offered (and Russia agreed to) conditions that went far beyond what he had been willing to concede at the start of the year. He agreed to transfer to Britain the island of Lampedusa, which could have ensured a permanent British naval and commercial presence in the Mediterranean. He also pledged to evacuate Holland, Switzerland, and Naples if the British did the same for Malta; even then, Bonaparte, who preferred to see the island in the hands of Russia, was willing to close his eyes if Russia later decided to transfer it to Britain. France promised to compensate Sardinia for its losses in northern Italy, while the remaining international issues would have been resolved at a specially summoned congress. This was truly a startling offer, and it should have been seriously considered. If Bonaparte was insincere in his intentions, as the British government claimed (and as many historians continue to assert), it would have been very easy to unmask him. Considering the French proposals would not have required much effort or time and would not have jeopardized British security, given that France was not in a position to threaten it directly—as Britain well knew. If anything, considering those proposals would have strengthened the British position: Bonaparte would have been forced to either follow through with his pledge or renege and thereby compromise himself.

But the British foreign ministry demanded more general and extended bases upon which a possible peace agreement might be concluded. This dismayed the French government, which earlier had offered to discuss provisions of Whitworth's "ultimatum" of April but was now concerned that Britain's reference to a broader base for peace settlement might involve greater concessions. Since France had already offered to discuss the affairs of Switzerland, Holland, and Italy, the French foreign ministry questioned the extent of the new British demands, which seemingly extended to French control of the Rhineland and Belgium. If so, this would have amounted to conceding almost all French territorial acquisitions since 1793 and accepting restrictions on its foreign policy, something that no French government would have been willing to accept.

In August Bonaparte finally gave up on his mediation efforts. "A mediation must have bases," noted Talleyrand in one of his letters. "The English do not wish any.... We realize very well that in this [mediation offer] the interests of England are well protected, and they have gone even further in this regard than Lord Whitworth in his ultimatum, but we would have to undergo terrible defeats before we would accept such a dishonor."[119] Bonaparte's correspondence in the summer of 1803 reveals his growing concern for his prestige and how he would be perceived by the public if he backed down in this showdown with Britain. Both nations, he argued, had critical political and commercial interests. Unless Britain was willing to voluntarily limit its power, France had no choice but to confront it. The British refusal to evacuate Malta, Bonaparte argued, "made clear its intention to add the Mediterranean to its almost exclusive commercial sphere of the Indies, America, and the Baltic." Of all the calamities that could arise for France, "there is none comparable to this [British economic hegemony]." War was therefore necessary. France could not bow down before a nation that "makes a game of all that is sacred on the earth, and that has, especially in the last twenty years, assumed an ascendancy and temerity which threaten the existence of all nations in their industry and commerce, the very lifeblood of states." Consenting to British demands would have meant opening a pathway to a peace that would have negated everything France had striven for in the previous ten years. As Lord Grenville observed in March 1803, "Our government [has] so contrived things, that it is hardly possible for Bonaparte himself to recede, had he the wish to do so. The only real support of his power in France is the influence he possesses with a part of the army and the opinion in the country that he is powerful and respected in Europe. If he now suffers himself to be intimidated by our preparations, he must lose all consideration at home and abroad."[120]

War had its own clear rationale. It could provide Britain with the means to restrain France by exploiting its superiority on the seas and rallying anti-French sentiment on the continent to revise the existing international order. Some British statesmen, who had just recently condemned France for depriving "brave and generous people" of their "ancient laws and government," now spoke of inciting "three great continental powers to act, either by large subsidies or by large offer—the Low Countries, and even Holland, to Prussia, all Lombardy to Austria, to Russia whatever she might ask."[121] The extensive shipbuilding program that Bonaparte initiated in 1802–1803 could have in a few years made its navy large enough to challenge Britain's mastery of the seas, which was an additional incentive for Britain to deal with France while the latter's naval capabilities were still underdeveloped. War could be also beneficial to British merchant shipping, since any trade with those countries that were not altogether dependent on France would almost exclusively be carried on by Britain. The case for war was facilitated by British memories of France's economic woes from the previous decades, not to mention the social and political turmoil of the revolutionary era; the new French government itself could still prove to be as short-lived as many of its predecessors had been.[122] Furthermore, the Addington government faced acute domestic pressure. If in October 1801 "the existence of the government seemed to be firmly linked with the preservation of peace," two years later "a vociferous demand in the country" was in favor of a more assertive policy toward the resurgent France.[123]

It seems unwise entirely to dismiss, as some have, the Anglo-French rivalry over the balance of power in Europe as having nothing to do with provoking this war.[124] It did, in many ways. The conflict between France and Britain was one between two imperialisms, each of which sought to safeguard its national interests by manipulating international circumstances to its advantage. This applied not only to Europe, where France held an upper hand, but also on the seas and beyond, where Britain jealously guarded its positions, particularly in India. Another imperial power, Russia, could have played a decisive role in the Franco-British relations, but the inexperience of its young ruler, his ambiguous aspirations, and the country's internal interests combined to make Russia more content to concentrate on domestic challenges than to try to shape the course of events in Europe.[125] This, in turn, played a major role in the final breakdown of peace in Europe.

CHAPTER 9

The Elephant Against the Whale

France and Britain at War, 1803–1804

T HE PAN-EUROPEAN CONFLICT that eventually became known as the Napoleonic Wars started as a conflict between France and Britain, the familiar spectacle of the great land power at grips with the great sea power— the elephant versus the whale. With the largest and most powerful navy in Europe, there was little doubt that Britain was supreme at sea. France, meanwhile, had an imposing land army led by an industrious leader. Neither side was positioned to enter the other's turf: the French navy was still struggling to recover from the deplorable condition it had found itself in during the revolutionary era, while the British army could hardly hope to overcome the French veterans who had gone through the forging kilns of the coalitional wars. How one of the two powers was to prevail over the other remained to be seen.

During the short peacetime afforded by Amiens, French businesses invested heavily in shipbuilding to take advantage of the opening of overseas trade. After the collapse of Amiens they suffered heavy losses, as British squadrons began to seize French merchantmen wherever they came across them. This in turn threatened French banks that had provided loans to these businesses or were directly involved with maritime trade. In May-June 1803, as banks lost millions of francs' worth of investments, stocks plummeted on the French exchange. To stabilize the financial sector Bonaparte turned to the Bank of France, which had been officially formed in February 1800 but was not yet fully capitalized. He quickly raised the bank's capital to 45 million francs, gave it the exclusive rights to issue paper money, and tasked it with supervising the country's finances.

The Bank of France was successful in mitigating the impact on the French economy in the short term but could do nothing about the French overseas trade, which came to a virtual standstill as the British attacked French colonial holdings. For Britain, the war was first and foremost a naval conflict; the two primary goals were to safeguard the island nation against an invasion and to protect the imperial and maritime trading networks, which offered the prospect of acquiring wealth and empire.[1] One British newspaper observed that "by a judicious exertion of our naval force, seconded perhaps by some occasional expeditions, the advantage of the war may be on our side, and the enemy may feel himself so straitened and distressed, as to wish for peace."[2] It was no surprise, then, that as soon as the war commenced, the Royal Navy targeted French overseas possessions. A British squadron blockaded Saint-Domingue, preventing badly needed reinforcements and supplies from reaching the besieged French garrison, portions of which began surrendering to the British in order to escape retribution by the black forces. In the Windward Islands (in the Lesser Antilles), Lieutenant General William Grinfield and Commodore Samuel Hood attacked the island of St. Lucia in late June 1803, forcing the outnumbered French garrison to surrender. The British followed up this success with an attack on Tobago, which fell on June 30. Next were the Dutch colonies in South America, some of which were already in turmoil. In April 1803 the garrison in Berbice (modern-day Guyana) mutinied after the start of the Franco-British war deprived it of supplies from the Batavian Republic; the revolt was suppressed with the help of troops from other Dutch colonies, but it further undermined the already weakened defenses of those colonies. In September 1803 a British expeditionary force appeared off the coastline of the Dutch colonies of Berbice, Demerara, and Essequibo, leaving the Dutch colonial authorities no choice but to submit; Suriname resisted the initial British invasion but fell to a stronger British force led by Hood and Major General Charles Green on May 4, 1804. Thus by late spring of 1804 the Dutch colonies in South America were already in the hands of the British.[3]

The Franco-British hostilities also extended to the coastline of Senegal, where France had claimed possession of St. Louis (at the mouth of the Senegal River) and Gorée Island (adjacent to Cape Martin) since the seventeenth century. Principally slave trading posts, these colonies had been target of British attacks during the Seven Years' War and the War of the American Revolution, though France recovered them on both occasions.[4] During the Revolutionary Wars, French privateers used both locations as staging grounds for their raids on British shipping, compelling the British government to take measures to check their activities. In 1800 a British squadron under Sir Charles Hamilton had seized Gorée, but the island was supposed to be restored to France upon the conclusion of Amiens. The British never did so, regarding French control of Gorée as "a thorn in our side" as far as their interests in West Africa were concerned. Henri Dundas's order to the British governor of Gorée to evacuate the island was soon countermanded by his successor. For more than a year the French patiently awaited the British withdrawal, which kept being deferred due to an alleged lack of transports. By the summer of 1803 the two nations were of course already at war, and evacuation was out of the question. With the Royal Navy in firm control of European waters, British control of Gorée would have seemed ensured were it not for a network of French privateers that stretched between West Africa and French Guiana in South America. These privateers harassed British interests on both sides of the ocean, and in January 1804 they helped a small French force launch a transatlantic attack on Gorée. The French arrival surprised the British garrison, which had to capitulate after a brief but valiant defense. The French success proved to be short-lived. In March of the same year the British recaptured the island and commenced an occupation that would last the next thirteen years.[5]

To challenge the British on the seas, Bonaparte focused his energies on pursuing three main goals: denying Britain any commerce in Europe, consolidating control over a larger portion of Europe, and preparing for an invasion of the British islands. For the first, the French government confiscated British goods and made their importation illegal in any regions controlled by the French; furthermore, Bonaparte ordered the incarceration of any British subjects found within French-controlled territories. Although he justified his actions in light of the British seizures of French merchantmen, their scale and vindictiveness were considered outrageous and only served to portray Bonaparte as the demonic tyrant he was painted to be in England. To compete with the British on the seas and, when the time came, to invade the British Isles, Bonaparte also undertook large-scale naval construction, urging his Ministère de la Marine to build as many vessels as possible and noting that "money is no object."[6] Bonaparte expected that by 1804 he would have more than 1,600 flat-bottomed boats—critical to bringing troops to the shore—supported by another 1,000 fishing vessels that could be converted into transports.[7]

While its navy was expanding, France moved quickly to consolidate control of as much of western Europe as possible. The Dutch were pressured to accept a treaty of alliance and provide troops and warships, as well as material support for the French armies.[8] By fall, the Swiss Confederation had also pledged to send more than 15,000 soldiers, with another 10,000 if France was attacked.[9] French troops, meanwhile, reoccupied Neapolitan ports, including Taranto, Otranto, and Brindisi, all located on the heel of the Italian "boot."[10] In northern Europe, Bonaparte sought to embarrass his British foe by occupying the state of Hanover, which had been in a personal union with Britain since the death of Queen Anne in 1714, when the Hanoverian rulers ascended the British throne while maintaining control over their ancestral city-state.[11] The arrangement was quite advantageous to Britain, since Hanover served as a commercial emporium and could be turned into a base of operations in Europe. Seizing Hanover would be of considerable advantage to France, and in late March 1803 Bonaparte warned Prussia that in the event of hostilities with Britain, French troops would enter Hanover to secure the North Sea coast and cut off British commerce from the continent; the city-state could also serve as a useful bargaining chip in future negotiations with Britain.

A French presence in Hanover, however, would undoubtedly provoke resistance from Prussia, which could not accept French expansion so close to its borders. When a French envoy delivered Bonaparte's letter warning of the impending occupation of Hanover, the court of Berlin was seized with fright and consternation.[12] Prussia had no interest in participating in the Franco-British war and wanted to maintain the neutrality that had served it well over the previous seven years.[13] Furthermore, French intervention in Hanover would have effectively killed the Prussian dream of north German hegemony and affected its regional commerce. Prussian foreign minister Christian August Heinrich Graf von Haugwitz argued that allowing the French seizure of Hanover would be the beginning of the end for Prussia, whose "sole advantage would consist in seeing itself the last victim" of Bonaparte's "boundless ambition." "When England exercises supremacy [*despotisme*] on the seas, it is of great inconvenience. But [France's] supremacy on the continent is infinitely more dangerous."[14] Berlin initially offered mediation between Britain and France, coupled with a threat that if the offer was declined, Prussia would occupy Hanover as compensation for the damage likely to be suffered by Prussian commerce in case of Franco-British hostilities.[15]

The Prussian threat was hollow, however. Unlike 1801, when it was able to occupy Hanover with French support, Berlin now faced a very different set of circumstances. Most crucially, it lacked the support of great powers. Britain refused Prussian mediation and, in fact, showed a certain indifference to the fate of Hanover, which some British officials considered immaterial, considering what was at stake in any Franco-British conflict.[16] The French response was also unequivocal: either Prussia supported the French occupation of Hanover or France would have to reconsider its relations with that state. "Our inclinations are for Prussia," observed one senior French diplomat. "May she not force us to court Austria."[17]

As with other issues, Russia could have made a difference through more vigorous intervention, especially since Prussia, Hanover, and Britain had all solicited Russian guarantees for the neutrality of northern Germany. A more assertive Russian stance might have allowed Prussia (or Hanover) to resist French designs, even in the face of the Army of Hanover that Bonaparte was already mustering. But yet again the Russian government chose to remain on the sidelines. Although Emperor Alexander I harbored personal goodwill toward Frederick William III, his senior advisors expressed annoyance over recent Prussian policies, including the decision to offer mediation without first consulting with Russia. They remembered well how keen Prussia had been to keep Hanover in 1801 and how willingly it had supported the French reorganization of southern Germany.[18] Although in June 1802 Alexander and Frederick William had met to mend fences at Memel (present-day Klaipeda), Russian officials still had doubts about Prussian motives and suspected a Franco-Prussian collusion to recast the balance of power in northern Germany, which would have been contrary to Russian aspirations to maintain regional equilibrium.[19] Thus, with Austria rejoicing, Britain indifferent, and Russia disapproving, Prussia found itself unsupported and unable to act on its earlier threat to occupy Hanover. Frederick William could not afford to place himself in a predicament similar to the one in 1801 when he had been obliged to recall his troops under threat from Britain and Russia. Despite the calls of his foreign minister, Haugwitz, and senior military figures for a unilateral action, Frederick William sided with the voices of moderation, who argued that Prussia was neither financially or militarily in a position to resist the French. With no help coming from other powers, Prussia had a stark choice: either allow the French to invade Hanover or fight them alone.[20] It chose the former. At the end of May 1803 General Édouard Mortier led 25,000 French troops from Holland into the electorate, which capitulated without a fight and signed the Convention of Suhlingen on June 3.[21]

The French occupation of Hanover was a key marker in European affairs during the Franco-British war. The electorate found itself under a decade of submission to foreign rule and required to provide vast indemnities to France; in 1803 alone, the French extracted more than 17 million francs before forcing Hanover to secure millions more in loans from neighboring states.[22] More important, the Hanoverian crisis illustrates well the attitudes prevalent among the European powers—mutual suspicion, lack of cooperation, preoccupation with regional interests—which would allow France to dominate the continent for the next decade. Even though northern Germany was of concern to all the European powers, they proved unable to cooperate to prevent France from invading Hanover and gaining a position of predominance in northern Germany. Russia pursued an equivocal policy throughout the spring of 1803, and its failure to stand by Prussia had made the French occupation of Hanover possible in the first place. Interestingly, Russia belatedly realized what was about to transpire and drastically changed its position. Just as the French force was crossing the Hanoverian border, Russia invited Prussia to launch a joint intervention in Hanover to protect the neutrality of northern Germany.[23] But this change of alignment occurred too late to be of any consequence, especially after Bonaparte rushed to soothe the ruffled feelings of the Hohenzollern court.[24]

The outcome of the Hanoverian affair affected Prussia more profoundly than the others. Frederick William had failed to deal with the first great crisis of his reign and proved that he was, to borrow an apt expression from William Shakespeare, "a lamb that carried anger as a flint bears fire."[25] Surrounded by a group of his favorite councilors—meaning those who followed his inclinations—the king did everything he could to avoid giving Bonaparte cause for a confrontation and ignored suggestions that he should mobilize troops. Instead he insisted on peace at any price even as the French occupation of Hanover directly challenged Prussian hegemony in northern Germany and resulted in the British blockade of the Elbe, Weser, and Ems Rivers, all crucial outlets for Prussia's commerce. Furthermore, this crisis forced Prussia to rethink its notion of "neutrality zone": instead of applying it to the northern German states, the Prussians embraced a more restrictive definition that involved only their own territory. Under this new policy, Prussia would not take up arms unless its own territory was attacked by the French.[26] All of this meant that Prussia's standing in Europe had been undermined. Its failure to defend a neighboring region from aggression naturally raised questions about its ability to protect itself. Throughout the fall of 1803 Bonaparte continued to extract additional concessions from Prussia, pushing hard for a Franco-Prussian alliance while refusing to accept any of the Prussian conditions.[27] Bonaparte's intransigence ultimately resulted in the collapse of these negotiations. This was a clear failure on his part. Although France had extended its influence to northern Germany, it had done so by sowing the seeds of deep discord with a state that sought to remain neutral above all else and forcing it to seek participation in an anti-French coalition. It was only due to its monarch's customary indecision that Prussia did not join the Third Coalition in 1805.

—◦◦◦⊱❀⊰◦◦◦—

"What a lesson we here receive regarding the slightest respect we enjoy abroad," lamented Johann Ludwig Cobenzl, vice chancellor of the Austrian Empire. "Respect that alone constitutes the security of states."[28] After the Peace of Lunéville, Austria indeed got no respect from continental powers, and its political and military influence waned. The Habsburg court was isolated diplomatically and unable to stem the tide of French expansion or the growing influence of Prussia and Russia. The seemingly close relations between the Russian and Prussian sovereigns served as a source of significant concern for Vienna, which distrusted both. Of particular concern for Austria was Russia's interference in Italy—either from the neighboring Ionian Islands, where the Septinsular Republic existed as a Russian protectorate, or more directly through the Kingdom of Piedmont, which had come to rely heavily on Russian support.

Piedmont had long posed obstacles to the Habsburg interests in Italy, successfully exploiting the Franco-Austrian rivalry to maintain its position as the strongest of the Italian states. The kingdom fared poorly during the Revolutionary Wars, having been defeated and occupied by the French in 1796. Three years later, however, as we saw, the French were driven out by the joint forces of Russia and Austria. Yet the two powers soon clashed over the issue of Piedmont, whose influence in the Italian peninsula the Habsburgs had tried to limit. In 1799–1800 Austria opposed Russia's plans for restoring King Victor Amadeus III to his throne, one of the fundamental issues in the Russo-Austrian rupture. Three years later, even with its survival put into question by the nascent French empire, Austria was still aspiring to weaken Russia-supported Piedmont. The Austrians' reluctance to support British coalition-building efforts after Amiens should be considered in light of their concern that such a coalition would ultimately benefit Russia and its dependencies, including Piedmont. The news of Anglo-Russian negotiations seemingly confirmed the worst of the Austrians' fears, because it envisioned restoration of the Piedmontese kingdom—and, if circumstances allowed, expansion.[29] Thus the Habsburgs faced a major dilemma: needing to solicit Russian support to contain France while seeking to deny Russia an opportunity to extend its influence in Germany and Italy.

Spain was France's partner—a crucial partnership, but one skewed in France's favor. Paris viewed the Spanish possessions as an opportunity to reestablish its own overseas empire. With a vast empire encompassing most of Central and South America, Spain had immense resources that Paris wanted to utilize in its war against Britain. The Second Treaty of San Ildefonso (1800) had stipulated a defensive arrangement between France and Spain and obliged the latter to furnish France with six ships-of-the-line, 74 guns each.[30] In 1800 seventeen Spanish warships arrived at Brest for a coordinated effort against Britain, and although the plan ultimately failed, the Treaty of Ildefonso seemingly reinvigorated the Franco-Spanish cooperation.

Spain's alliance with France, however, became increasingly a one-sided arrangement, since France rarely treated its ally equitably or fairly. Bonaparte did not conceal his disdain for Spain's performance in the War of Oranges. Equally revealing was Bonaparte's decision to sell Louisiana to the United States in 1801. The sale violated the terms of the Franco-Spanish agreement specifying that the retrocession of Louisiana would take place six months after territorial exchanges in Italy; yet barely two months after Ildefonso Bonaparte sold the territory. The sale had profound implications for Spain, which had long strived to contain American expansionist designs in North America but now faced a newly empowered country eager to consolidate its positions in the Gulf of Mexico. Soon after the Louisiana Purchase, the United States insisted on an adjustment of the newly acquired territory's eastern boundaries, which in practice meant taking over West Florida, the strip of Spanish land between the Mississippi and Perdido Rivers. In 1804 senior American officials, including Robert Livingston, the US ambassador to France, urged President Jefferson to seize West Florida by force and present the European powers, which were already preoccupied with the preliminaries to the War of the Third Coalition, with a fait accompli. The American claims were thwarted (temporarily) only when France and Spain signed an agreement on January 4, 1805, by which Bonaparte pledged to guarantee the return of any colonies that Spain lost during the war. The French diplomatic maneuvering exasperated the United States, with one American diplomat complaining that to Napoleon Spain and the United States were "a couple of oranges... which [he] will squeeze at pleasure, and against each other, and that which yields the most will be the best served or rather the best injured."[31]

For Bonaparte, the War of Oranges between Spain and Portugal demonstrated "Spain's resolve to act in their own interests" in spite of continued threats emanating from Paris.[32] Indeed, in 1801–1802 Madrid attempted to assert its independence from Bonaparte and French foreign policy.[33] As upsetting as it was for Bonaparte to deal with his independent-minded ally, he still could not forsake it. As long as Spain remained well disposed toward France, the combined French and Spanish navies could pose an acute threat to Britain. Spanish colonial holdings offered a huge area for France's future territorial aggrandizement, while the vast quantities of bullion that Spain mined in Mexico and Bolivia could be used to subsidize the French war effort.

Spain had welcomed the Peace of Amiens because it provided an opportunity to revive its commerce and to reform an economy that had stagnated as the result of the British blockade. The value of Spanish exports skyrocketed, from just 80 million reales de vellón in 1801 to almost 400 million in 1802, while imports jumped by an even higher margin.[34] Just as Spain was harvesting the profits of the peace and seeing its economy steadily improve, the war broke out. And just as it had in 1793, Madrid faced a strategic dilemma—either turn away from France by declaring neutrality or continue to support its brash ally.[35] Spain's position was complicated by the fact that it had not only signed a peace with France in 1795 but then gone on to establish a military alliance that, in effect, contributed to the establishment of French hegemony in western Europe. European monarchies found it hard to forgive Spain, which in 1803 found itself isolated in the international arena.

Striving to maintain a middle ground, Spain went so far as to suggest to Russia that they form a new League of Armed Neutrality that would shun the war.[36] The Russian response was tepid, supporting the idea in general but offering no tangible help.[37] By now France had asked Spain for support in its war against Britain, to which Spanish prime minister Godoy demurred, noting that war was in France's interests, not Spain's. Bonaparte was increasingly annoyed by Madrid's delay in responding to French demands for funds as well as by its failure to prevent the Royal Navy from attacking French shipping in the Spanish waters. The news of Spanish militia forces mobilizing near the French borders and speculation that the British had offered a generous bribe to Godoy only further complicated matters. Exasperated, Bonaparte instructed his ambassador, General Pierre Riel de Beurnonville, to exert pressure on the recalcitrant Spaniards, who faced a stark choice: either declare for France, demobilize their forces, and provide a generous subsidy of more than 70 million francs, or face an army of some 80,000 men forming on the Spanish border and preparing to invade.[38] Spain had until September 7, 1803, to decide.[39]

The French ultimatum—or "the insolent French note," as King Charles IV described it—was a bluff. Bonaparte knew well that he could not afford a conflict with Spain just as he was gearing up for a war with Britain; the nation's finances were already stretched. The army that Bonaparte used to menace Spain existed only on paper, and the camp at Bayonne included fewer than 6,000 men.[40] Bonaparte desperately needed Spain and all that it could offer. He therefore had to force Spain's hand. For this purpose he both threatened and cajoled the Bourbon court, demanding Godoy's dismissal and warning Charles IV that his prime minister was leading the kingdom into the embrace of the British, which could produce dire consequences.[41] Beurnonville, a career officer, delivered these warning with the appropriate directness and brusqueness. His "conduct at Madrid lacked any finesse and was pure power politics," notes his biographer.[42]

The Spanish court refused to buckle. The September 7 deadline came and went without Madrid addressing any of the French demands. This was partly because of the British ambassador, Sir John Hookham Frere, who worked diligently to buttress Spain's position with regard to France.[43] Bonaparte was at an impasse: with each passing day the potency of the French ultimatum seemed to be losing its strength, yet the French army at Bayonne was still woefully inadequate to enforce the threat behind it. The French government therefore adjusted its tactics. In September it asked Charles IV for a sign of friendship by allowing passage of French troops through Spain to reinforce Admiral Jacques Bedout's squadron, which had sought refuge from the Royal Navy at Ferrol, in northwestern Spain. The Bourbon monarchy faced a difficult choice. If Spain denied passage, that could be considered a *casus belli* by France; granting it, however, would inevitably cause concern in British circles. The latter was exactly what Bonaparte and his foreign minister, Talleyrand, hoped for, as they expected that a seemingly minor event such as this would be misconstrued by Britain and cause serious repercussions in its relations with Spain.

Godoy responded by assuring the British of Spain's neutrality and by offering France the opportunity to negotiate a treaty that would preserve Spain's neutral status in exchange for significant subsidies. On October 19, 1803, Spanish ambassador Joseph-Nicolas Chevalier de Azara and French foreign minister Talleyrand signed the Convention of Neutrality and Subsidy, which allowed Spain to remain neutral in exchange for an annual subsidy of 72 million francs to France for the duration of its war with Britain; the first payment was backdated to the outbreak of the war in May 1803, which meant Spain owed five months' worth of subsidies.[44]

Spain's decision to accept these humiliating conditions should be considered in light of the enormous challenges it was facing. The Basques were, as always, defiant in the north, while a plague epidemic raged in the east and south of Spain. The kingdom was heavily in debt, its troubles further compounded by a severe earthquake that struck at Málaga on January 13, 1804. Negotiations leading up to the convention demonstrate Bonaparte's belief that, to paraphrase Mao Zedong's famous quote, diplomatic power grows out of the barrel of a gun. France's diplomatic overtures were always accompanied by threats to utilize the country's military might. Lacking resources or allies to defend itself from either France or Britain, the court of Madrid faced the prospect of a financial despoilment by the French or the dissipation of its economy by the British. In the end, Madrid chose the former but could not avoid the latter.

Britain was understandably distraught by the developments in Spain. Despite Spanish assurances to the contrary, the British government came to believe that Spain's subordination to France was now almost complete: its subsidies would certainly bolster the French war effort, while French privateers could successfully harass British shipping from the safety of Spanish ports. Remembering the lessons of 1796–1797, when Spain's entry into the war on the side of France posed a major threat to Britain's security, William Pitt, who returned to the premiership on May 10, 1804, called for a more forceful stance in relations with Madrid. He ordered the Royal Navy to blockade the Spanish coastline and target Spanish shipping. On October 5, 1804, the Royal Navy intercepted a large bullion shipment from the Río de la Plata, destroying one Spanish warship and capturing the rest, which were carrying some 2 million pounds' worth of silver. The seizure caused furious political debate both in London and in Madrid. On December 14, 1804, Spain declared war on Britain.[45]

Spain's entry into the war was of course welcome news for Bonaparte, who was busy preparing for the invasion of Britain. Success in this endeavor depended on three major factors: a well-trained and well-equipped invasion force, an adequate system of transports, and a fleet capable of safeguarding the passage and disembarkation. France already possessed one of the most formidable armies in Europe, but Britain's superior fleet meant that the French government could not simply invade the enemy homeland and end the war in triumph. Any invasion attempt depended on wresting control of the English Channel from the Royal Navy. With characteristic energy, Bonaparte began working toward that goal. This was not the first time France had attempted to invade Britain, but the scale and intensity of the effort were certainly new, as Bonaparte hoped to utilize experiences and resources from the previous endeavors.[46]

Starting in the spring of 1803 Bonaparte supervised a massive mobilization for the invasion of England, one of the largest state-sponsored projects of the nineteenth century. He sought to create a flotilla of more than two thousand vessels capable of transporting his troops, horses, and artillery over the twenty miles of open water that separated France from its historical rival.[47] This was easier said than done. Flotillas that had been built for previous attempted invasions in 1798 and 1801 were in the worst possible state. Many of the ships had rotted away in ports over the years, and in March 1803 there were only 28 flat-bottomed boats (*chaloupes*) and 193 gunboats surviving from the invasion flotilla constructed just two years earlier.[48] Thus hundreds of new transports and warships had to be constructed, purchased, or procured in some other way. The magnitude of Bonaparte's vision was truly bewildering. A decree of May 24, 1803, established a new government institution, the *Inspection générale de la flottille nationale*, whose task it was to coordinate the creation of this new flotilla.[49] The French naval officials requisitioned vessels and demanded deliveries of ships from as far away as Spain, which only exasperated local populations whose sentiments were already running high from earlier French expropriations. The Dutch were expected to provide five ships-of-the-line and an equal number of frigates, along with a sufficient number of transports for the embarkation of 25,000 men and 2,500 horses; an additional 350 transport vessels capable of transporting 36,000 men were requisitioned. Six naval military districts were tasked with handling the logistical details of purchasing ships and placing orders for new ones, their operations financed by millions of francs loaned by French banks as well as by contributions from businesses, municipalities, and departments, not to mention millions extracted from the occupied countries.[50] The ports of Antwerp, Ostend, Dunkirk, Calais, Boulogne, Dieppe, Le Havre, Rouen, Cherbourg, Granville, and Saint-Malo were tasked with constructing new vessels. To ensure uninterrupted movement of supplies and troops, Bonaparte made major investments in improving roads in coastal areas as well as between Paris and naval bases at Brest, Cherbourg, and Boulogne. Almost all major ports on the Atlantic coastline underwent renovation and expansion to meet the ambitious demands that the First Consul had made. Overall, these naval preparations cost France more than 40 million francs just for the construction and purchase of vessels, along with millions more spent on improving port facilities.[51] Costly as these measures were, they serve as a testament to Bonaparte's ability to supervise such an immense project and to harness the resources of several nations. By August 1805 the improved French naval infrastructure and more than 2,300 vessels of all types were ready to attempt a crossing of the Channel.

The army Bonaparte had inherited from the Revolution continued to benefit from the qualities that had brought it victory over the first two coalitions, and it had gained invaluable battle experience over more than a decade of warfare. Nevertheless, what Bonaparte did with that army in 1803–1804 was truly remarkable. On June 14, 1803, Bonaparte ordered the establishment of six military camps along the Atlantic coast of France from Bayonne to Holland, where he embarked on a major transformation of the French military forces. He sought centralization of authority and a streamlined chain of command. At the top, he formed the General Staff (État-Major), responsible for elaborating and transmitting orders, preparing maps for Bonaparte, and coordinating movements, intelligence, military finances, logistics, medical services, and so on.[52] This reorganization combined with the strength of his own personality, his leadership, and his understanding of the men he commanded made the French army seemingly invincible.

Bonaparte—or, rather, Napoleon, as he should be known after the French Senate elevated him to the rank of emperor in 1804—retained all the authority to make decisions and preferred to supervise everything himself. "The Emperor...needs neither advice nor plans of campaign," wrote Marshal Alexander Berthier, his chief of staff from 1796 through 1814. "Our duty is to obey."[53] Combining the authority of head of state and supreme commander had clear advantages: Napoleon could set objectives and pursue diplomacy and strategy more effectively than his opponents, whose hands were often tied by military councils or royal sovereigns—not to mention the complications of coalition warfare. The advantages of having a single person firmly in charge of all aspects of the war effort were magnified by the fact that the one person at the helm was arguably the most capable human being who ever lived. His mastery of the details of political, military, logistical, and numerous other factors was prodigious. But the extreme concentration of decision-making authority had costs as well as benefits. In an era when communications could usually move no faster than a trotting horse, it sometimes proved impossible for a single man, no matter how competent, to coordinate forces operating over vast distances, often in widely separated theaters of war.

In the Boulogne camps, as the cantonments along the Channel coast are now collectively known, the French army spent almost two years preparing for war.[54] Ineffectual officers were weeded out and talented men promoted. Troops received systematic training not only in new tactics and maneuvers but also in coordination between various service branches and in making amphibious landings.[55] Each camp eventually coalesced into a *corps d'armée*, composed of infantry, cavalry, and artillery, and capable of fighting independently. This corps system turned the French army into a stronger, faster, and more flexible military force, and contributed greatly to the long streak of French victories after 1804. The concept was not an entirely new one; it was essentially a scaling up of the all-arms divisions created by Lazare Carnot in his reorganization of French forces in 1794; other French generals, including Jean-Baptiste Kléber and Jean-Baptiste Jourdan, experimented with *corps d'armée*, though none honed it to the same degree as Napoleon. Each corps contained two to four infantry divisions, a brigade of light cavalry, and several batteries of artillery attached to the corps headquarters (in addition to the light artillery attached to each regiment). Each corps commander also had at his disposal a staff, a medical detachment, and a unit of engineers. Napoleon's achievement, then, was not that he invented the corps system but that he implemented it as the standard structural unit for the French army. Over time, the strength of individual corps varied widely depending on their intended purpose. Napoleon's *Grande Armée*, as the newly reformed French army became known on August 26, 1805, consisted of seven corps, the army cavalry reserve, the army artillery reserve, and the imperial guard.[56]

The corps system offered Napoleon a more mobile and manageable system of control over military forces by enabling him to issue orders to a relatively small number of subordinate corps commanders. Being smaller than a full army, a corps could travel faster and forage more easily. The ability to march over multiple routes, change front when encountering an enemy, and concentrate against that enemy greatly accelerated the pace of war and made it difficult for the opposing force to avoid combat. This, in turn, allowed Napoleon to gain the decisive battle he always sought and to bring the campaign to a quick conclusion. As Napoleon later explained to his stepson Eugène de Beauharnais in an 1809 letter, "Here is the general principle of war—a corps of 25,000–30,000 men can be left on its own. Well handled, it can fight or avoid action depending on circumstances, and maneuver without any harm coming to it because an opponent cannot force it to accept an engagement but if it chooses to do so it can fight alone for a long time. A division of 9,000–12,000 men can be left for an hour on its own without inconvenience. It will contain a foe, however numerous he might be, and will win time for the arrival for the army. Therefore, it is useful to form an advance guard of no less than 9,000 men and to place it more than one hour away from the army."[57]

However, the key to a "march divided, fight united" approach was the ability of each separately marching element to survive contact with an enemy force long enough for its supports to arrive. While all-arms divisions already existed, Napoleon's organization of the permanent corps system offered further advantages. The bigger the unit, the longer it could hold out against a superior enemy, so the farther away the next element could be. Organization into corps therefore facilitated marching on a broader operational front, making use of more roads and providing access to the food resources of a larger area. Such a system allowed large armies (like the Grande Armée of 1805) to operate with speed and flexibility similar to what could be achieved for smaller armies (like those of the Revolutionary Wars) with the divisional system. The corps system allowed Napoleon to operate with greater adaptability in what Clausewitz famously called the "fog of war," when the exact location of the enemy remained vague.[58] Being a combined-arms unit, a corps could temporarily engage a larger enemy force and hold it in place until reinforcements arrived. This procedure eventually became standard practice, employing a formation military historians call the "battalion square" (*bataillon carré*), borrowing Napoleon's metaphor for an arrangement of corps that could respond equally well to a threat from any direction, just as a literal battalion square of infantry could on a battlefield.

All of this relied heavily on well-trained soldiery—which is where the high quality of the French command and staff system, as well as individual commanders' improvisation, came into play. The corps system gave the French almost infinite capacity to change direction at once and concentrate anywhere within twenty-four hours, making warfare much more fluid. "Thanks to the superb flexibility of the Napoleonic system of moving corps over vast distances in a loosely drawn but carefully coordinated formation," in the assessment of British historian David Chandler, "it mattered little on what point of the compass the foe was discovered."[59] The new system quickly showed its superiority. Napoleon's Grande Armée scored a series of decisive victories between 1805 and 1807, forcing other European armies to reevaluate their tactics and adopt elements of the French system. Austria began reorganizing after its defeat in 1805, while Prussia and Russia began reforming in the wake of their setbacks in 1806–1807.

By August 1805 Emperor Napoleon had enough landing craft to transport more than 150,000 troops across the Channel to various points in southern England. Yet the invasion was still far from realistic. The vast flotilla faced logistical and technical challenges, not the least of which was the need to coordinate the departure of hundreds of ships and subsequent disembarkation of troops on the other side of the Channel. Britain had responded to the threat of French invasion with vast defensive preparations. Existing systems of signal communication were repaired and extended, to allow for a fast delivery of news from the coastlines. Britain's coastal defenses were organized into several districts, where recruitment for local militias was increased while new defensive works were hurriedly constructed. These measures reduced the possibility of success for a French invasion force.

A far greater obstacle for the French was the Royal Navy, which still exercised control over the English Channel and could easily devastate an invading force. With their navy qualitatively and quantitatively inferior to the British, the French had to find a way to negate this advantage. There were rumors of using balloons to transport troops to Britain or building a tunnel under the English Channel, though all those ideas were utterly unfeasible and mainly fodder for the British press.[60] As anxiety gripped the entire southern coastline of England, newspapers asked readers to "be on the alert" and reassured them that "your native courage, acknowledged proficiency and military discipline, and the recollections of the glorious deeds performed by your illustrious predecessors in former times, will stimulate you to imitate their noble example."[61]

So despite Napoleon's having turned the French army into a fearsome fighting machine, the problem of overcoming the Royal Navy remained; the elephant still could not best the whale. Napoleon seems to have considered slipping across the Channel on some dark, still night with little or no support from a protecting fleet, but he quickly realized the futility of such a daring enterprise. Instead, by the summer of 1804 Napoleon developed a grand strategy that, despite at least half a dozen revisions, pursued the following basic objectives: a French fleet would break through the British blockades, link with a Spanish fleet, and then jointly sail to threaten British imperial possessions in the Caribbean, thus forcing the Royal Navy to redeploy. The Franco-Spanish fleet would then swiftly return to Europe, overwhelm the British naval force in the English Channel, and escort an invasion flotilla to Britain's shores. But as the French admirals began to implement this plan in the summer of 1805, Napoleon received more distressing news: Britain, Austria, and Russia were forming a new coalition against him.

| The Emperor's Conquest, 1805–1807

L ATE AT NIGHT on August 21, 1803, a British frigate approached the coastline of France. On board were eight Frenchmen led by Georges Cadoudal, one of the leaders of the irreconcilable French royalists.[1] The group landed on rock-strewn cliffs in Normandy and quickly disappeared into the night. Over the next few weeks additional groups of royalist émigrés crossed the Channel from Britain, all plotting to overthrow the Consulate and restore the Bourbon monarchy. The conspirators gradually made their way to the French capital, where they were concealed in safe houses while waiting for an opportunity. Believing reports on the fragility of the Consular government, the British government extended support to these conspirators, helping them cross over to France and providing them with funds to sustain the conspiracy.

These reports had been written by British ambassador Lord Whitworth and, exaggerated as they were, they did contain kernels of truth about political and social tensions. Bonaparte's increased authoritarianism and efforts to suppress dissent had caused particular disgruntlement in the army, where many senior officials and generals were eager to see him gone. General Anne Jean Marie René Savary, who commanded a special unit of gendarmes tasked with guarding the First Consul, lamented "envious, mischief-making, and for the most part narrow-minded men," including General Jean-Baptiste Bernadotte, who were "busy in stirring up the people" and seeking to assassinate Bonaparte.[2] Anne-Louise-Germaine de Staël (Madame de Staël), whom Bonaparte later exiled from France, also spoke of "a party of generals and senators" who wished to find means "to stop the progress of the usurpation."[3]

Unfortunately for the conspirators, Minister of Police Joseph Fouché's agents easily infiltrated conspiracies and maintained tight supervision of

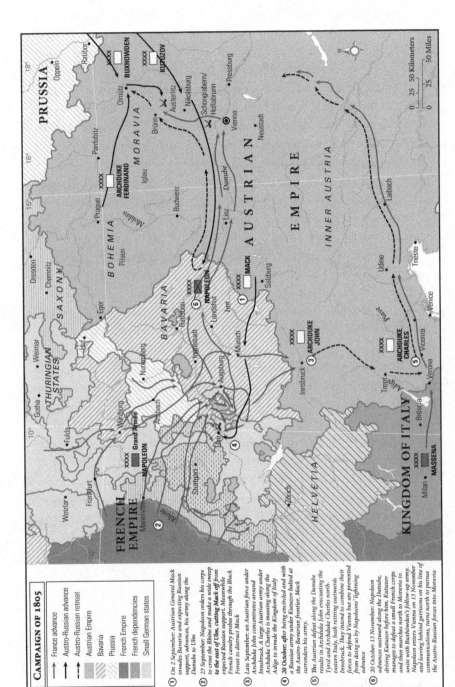

CAMPAIGN OF 1805

↑	France advance
↑	Austro-Russian advance
↑	Austro-Russian retreat
	Austrian Empire
	Bavaria
	Prussia
	French Empire
	French dependencies
	Small German states

① On 2 September: Austrian General Mack invades Bavaria and expecting Russian support, advances, his army along the Danube to Ulm

② 23 September: Napoleon orders his corps to cross the Rhine and make a wide sweep to the east of Ulm, cutting Mack off from expected Russian support. Meanwhile French cavalry probes through the Black Forest to distract Mack

③ Late September: an Austrian force under Archduke John concentrates around Innsbruck. A large Austrian army under Archduke Charles is massing along the Adige to invade the Kingdom of Italy

④ 20 October: after being encircled and with a Russian army under Kutuzov halted at the Austro-Bavarian frontier, Mack surrenders his army.

⑤ The Austrian defeat along the Danube results in Archduke John evacuating the Tyrol and Archduke Charles north-eastern Italy, both retiring eastwards. They intend to combine their forces to defend Vienna but are prevented from doing so by Napoleon's lightning advance

⑥ 20 October–13 November: Napoleon advances eastward along the Danube, driving Kutuzov before him. Kutuzov manages to defeat a small French corps and then marches north to Moravia to unite with Buxhöwden's follow-up army. Napoleon enters Vienna on 13 November and leaving behind garrisons on his line of communications, turns north to pursue the Austro-Russian forces into Moravia

Map 9: Campaign of 1805

them. Cadoudal's group had been detected soon after it landed in France and police agents followed them to Paris, where they were arrested in February 1804. Cadoudal and his companions were tried, convicted, and guillotined, while General Jean Charles Pichegru, who after a distinguished career during the War of the First Coalition ran afoul of the Directory and now conspired against the Consulate, died in prison under suspicious circumstances.[4] General Jean Moreau, the hero of Hohenlinden and a clear rival to Bonaparte, was arrested, convicted, and banished from France.[5] During interrogation, one of Cadoudal's lieutenants confessed about the participation of "a prince of the house of Bourbon." Talleyrand and Fouché both suspected Louis-Antoine-Henri de Bourbon-Condé, duc d'Enghien, who resided in the neighboring Principality of Baden.[6] Wanting to send a forceful message, Bonaparte ordered the arrest of the duke. D'Enghien was abducted from his house in Baden on the night of March 14–15, 1804, in violation of that principality's neutrality, and brought to Vincennes, where he was tried for treason before a military tribunal. Despite the lack of evidence or of any witnesses, d'Enghien was found guilty and executed shortly after midnight on March 21. He was buried in a grave that had been dug that evening in the moat of the fortress.[7] Fouché, a keen observer, remarked of the execution, "It is worse than a crime, it is a blunder."[8]

He was right. Governments all across Europe were outraged at Bonaparte's role in what amounted to the murder of the last prince of the illustrious house of Condé. Even for many of his supporters, it left a stain on his reputation that could not be erased by his subsequent successes. "It would be difficult to describe the sensation which this occurrence produced in Paris. Disturbance, dismay and consternation prevailed," lamented a member of the Council of State.[9] That Bonaparte was misinformed by his advisors (especially Talleyrand, who had his own reasons for wanting d'Enghien done away with) and subordinates is undeniable but does not lessen his own responsibility for this crime. Like all important state decisions, this came directly from the Consul. Bonaparte never hesitated to take full responsibility for the act, claiming that his decision was firmly grounded on *raison d'état*. The execution of the Bourbon prince sent an unmistakable signal to Bonaparte's opponents, royalist or Jacobin, that he was willing to use any means necessary to protect his power. "My veins run with blood, not water," he sternly declared in a lengthy speech at the Council of State before confiding to Second Consul Jean-Jacques Régis de Cambacérès that "the House of Bourbon must learn that the attacks it directs against others can come down on itself."[10] During a lengthy conversation with Senator Jean-Barthélemy Le Couteulx de Canteleu, Bonaparte remarked that he could have saved d'Enghien but that "it has been necessary to show the Bourbons, the cabinet of London, and all the courts of Europe that it was not child's play to plot his assassination."[11] In this respect, the d'Enghien affair had accomplished its goal. No further royalist plots were made against the French leader.

Although its importance in the formation of the Third Coalition is sometimes exaggerated, the affair did provoke an adverse reaction in Europe and cost Bonaparte goodwill outside France. Initially, the most vocal protest came from the Swedish king, Gustavus IV, who was traveling in Germany when he heard the news of d'Enghien's execution. The king immediately broke off negotiations on the Franco-Swedish alliance and vocally condemned the French action. In many other European states, however, the reaction was far more muted, guided by more pragmatic considerations and fear of the powerful French neighbor.[12] King Charles IV of Spain, for example, showed no compassion for his distant relative, and his minister Godoy bluntly told the French ambassador that "spoilt blood had to be blotted out wherever one found it."[13] Prussia and Austria also showed little interest in the affair, and the latter even welcomed this tough measure to put an end to conspiracies.[14] Britain initially ignored the matter, but after French revelations involving the collusion of British diplomats and agents, it was forced to defend itself.

It was in Russia that the affair's true impact could be seen. Franco-Russian relations, already strained since the death of Emperor Paul, took on an air of hostility after the collapse of the Peace of Amiens. Anti-French sentiments rapidly increased in the wake of France's reoccupation of Italian states and its seizure of Hanover, though Russian indecision facilitated the latter. The Russian ambassador to France, Arkadii Markov, was known for his Francophobia and discourteous, if not outright belligerent, attitude; his reports made the most of Bonaparte's bellicose rhetoric, while his conduct often exceeded imperial instructions.[15] Even more provocative were the actions of the Russian envoy to Saxony, Emmanuel Henri Louis Alexandre de Launay, comte d'Antraigues, a French émigré and political adventurer who published libelous articles about the French head of state.[16] Bonaparte's resentment at the Russian diplomatic snubs erupted at one of the state dinners at the Tuileries Palace, where he berated the Russian ambassador in the presence of numerous officials and diplomats. Shortly thereafter Markov was permitted to resign his embassy, but not before receiving from St. Petersburg the Order of St. Andrew, one of the highest imperial awards, as a reward for his services.

The Russian court was infuriated by the execution of a prince of royal blood but even more so by the French invasion of German territory and the violation of sovereignty of Baden, whose ruler was Alexander's father-in-law.[17]

The violation did not occur in isolation; rather, it took place within a wider context of French actions that belied a lack of respect for Russia's status in Europe. To many in the Russian government, it was time to make a public stand against Napoleon. The court responded by going into mourning for the duke and sending notes of loud protest to Paris and to the Imperial Diet, the general assembly of the Imperial Estates of the Holy Roman Empire, of which Baden was part. The latter caused considerable consternation among the German states, which could not ignore the Russian sovereign's demand but also did not want to alienate their powerful French neighbor. Ultimately, the German states reached a compromise, by which the elector of Baden claimed that the French had given him satisfactory explanations for their actions and asked that the matter be dropped in light of possible repercussions. The Diet quickly approved this request.[18]

Russia was naturally displeased by this decision, and its anger only grew upon receiving Bonaparte's response to its note of protest. Rejecting Russian protests, Bonaparte advised Alexander to mind his own business. "The complaint which Russia presents today leads one to ask," Bonaparte declared, "whether if, when England was planning the assassination of Paul I, one had known that the authors of the plot were to be found within a few leagues of the frontier, one would not have hastened to seize them."[19] This was a blunt answer, and its allusion to Alexander's involvement in the murder of his father was too hard for the proud sovereign of "all Russias" to swallow. He rejected French requests for d'Antraigues's recall, arguing that it was his prerogative, not France's, to choose his diplomatic representatives.

In April 1804 Alexander made Vienna a secret offer of alliance against France, promising to contribute some 100,000 men if Austria mobilized against Napoleon, The Austrian government, having learned from prior experiences, questioned the Russian offer, fearing that once it had committed to the alliance Russia might make an advantageous deal with France, leaving it in the lurch.[20] Alexander was a bit more successful in his overtures to Prussia, entering into an understanding with Frederick William on preserving north German neutrality in case of French aggression; yet in what one historian has described as a policy of "the hedgehog and the possum," Prussia continued to vacillate on its position vis-à-vis France, and what Russians considered a defensive alliance was anything but that for the Prussians.[21] Russian efforts to organize some semblance of opposition to Napoleon were of course heartily welcomed in Britain, where the fall of Addington's cabinet in May 1804 brought William Pitt back to power and a more assertive policy on the continent. In June Pitt could not but rejoice upon receiving the news of the French ambassador's departure from St. Petersburg, marking an effective rupture in Franco-Russian relations and opening a door for a possible European alliance against France.

———◦◦◦❈◦◦◦———

The discovery of Cadoudal's royalist plot hastened the completion of a project that had been on Bonaparte's mind for some time. The First Consul had long pushed for constitutional changes to consolidate his power. He was successful in obtaining the consulship for life, and in August 1802 he claimed the right to name his own successor. It was becoming increasingly clear to many contemporaries that the palaces of Tuileries and St. Cloud were no longer the seat of a republican government but rather the court of a new sovereign. "Severe etiquette prevailed there," observed André François Miot de Mélito, a senior official at the ministry of war. "Officers attached to the person, prescribed honors paid to the ladies, a privileged family; in short, everything except the name of Consul was monarchical, and that name was destined soon to disappear." For a Prussian envoy, it was becoming clear that Bonaparte wanted to be "a second Charlemagne," and that there was "no doubt that he has a plan, it is just the timing that has yet to be decided." Bonaparte's decision to establish the Légion d'Honneur, the highest civil and military award France could bestow on its citizens, caused consternation among the republicans, who accused him of creating a new nobility. As early as June 1802 the Russian ambassador was convinced that the French republic was on its last breath and that Bonaparte would soon take the title of "Emperor of the Gauls."[22]

The plots to kill Bonaparte stirred public fears that his death might lead to political turmoil or even the restoration of the Bourbon monarchy. Bonaparte used the Cadoudal conspiracy to impress upon the French that his life, and consequently their well-being, was in perpetual danger, which in turn helped him attain general consent for the transformation of the life consulate into a hereditary empire.[23] His earlier efforts to solidify power had provoked considerable resistance, but in the wake of Cadoudal's conspiracy and the duke's execution, public protest was negligible, as the timid feared Bonaparte's wrath and the ambitious sought to benefit from the new regime.[24] On May 2, 1804, the legislative bodies passed three motions that proclaimed Bonaparte emperor of the French republic, recognized this title as hereditary within the Bonaparte family, and called for protection of "Equality, Liberty and the rights of the people in their entirety." On May 18 the Senate officially proclaimed empire in a *senatus consultum*.[25] Four days later, registered voters took part in a plebiscite designed to create an illusion of popular support for imperial rule and, casting individually signed ballots, approved—with a vote of 3,524,000 to 2,579—what was already a fait accompli.[26] Georges Cadoudal, upon being told about these developments, remarked from a prison cell,

"We have done more than we hoped to do. We meant to give France a king, but we have given her an emperor."[27]

On December 2, 1804, an imperial coronation ceremony was held at the great Cathedral of Notre Dame in Paris.[28] Napoleon, as we shall henceforth refer to Bonaparte, had made careful preparations for this event, studying in detail and adapting rituals of the ancien régime. Pope Pius VII, whom Napoleon compelled to travel from Rome to Paris to attend the ceremony, occupied a seat of honor but was otherwise relegated to the sideline. Though he appeared to bless the emperor, he did not, in fact, crown him. In a prearranged move, Napoleon took the crown from the hands of the pope and crowned himself. With one hand holding a crown and another resting on his sword, the new ruler of France was intent on demonstrating that he was a self-made man who owed his powers to no one but himself. Napoleon's choice of imperial regalia—his crown, scepter, and hand of justice were styled after symbols that were believed to be Emperor Charlemagne's—also underscored his desire to show that he was not the successor of the Bourbons but an emperor in his own right.

The newly revised Constitution of the Year XII removed from France the last vestiges of parliamentarism and created a unique dichotomy of a republic ruled by an emperor, reflected in French currency, which featured the emperor's profile and the title "Napoléon Empereur" on the front and "République Française" on the back. Reminiscent of senatorial practices under the Roman Empire, the French legislative bodies continued their obscure existence before dying a quiet death; the Tribunate was abolished in 1807, while the Legislative Corps, deprived of real authority, lingered in the shadows until the empire collapsed. Napoleon himself no longer referred to the French people as "citizens," calling them "subjects" instead, and expected greater deference from his courtiers and ministers.[29]

Napoleon's coronation had created a brief diplomatic crisis, as the other powers were compelled to adjust to the new political reality in Europe. Smaller states had little choice but to recognize the French emperor. For the great powers, Napoleon's decision seemed to reveal a grand design for the revival of the empire of Charlemagne, which had covered much of western and central Europe. Napoleon's decision caused great consternation in Austria, where it was perceived as a clear challenge to Austria's own imperial aspirations. For Emperor Alexander, already embittered by the d'Enghien affair, the proclamation elevated the impudent French upstart while threatening to further undermine Russian interests in Germany. Yet neither power acted. Holy Roman Emperor Francis felt compelled to recognize Napoleon in this new capacity, though only after receiving assurances from France that he would be recognized as hereditary emperor of Austria and that his imperial title would take precedence over the French one.[30] Austria's decision to once again compromise with France greatly annoyed Russia, whose ruler perceived Napoleon's new title as a "new usurpation" that demonstrated his "boundless ambition to extend his domination still further beyond its current limits."[31] Alexander, joined by the king of Sweden, refused to recognize the new emperor, pressuring the Ottoman Empire to do likewise.

Just a month after his coronation, Napoleon wrote letters to the rulers of Britain, Spain, Naples, and Austria, offering to settle their differences and establish peace on the continent.[32] In a letter to King George dated January 1805, he noted that neither nation would gain much by prolonging the war. "Peace is the desire of my heart, but war has never been contrary to my glory," Napoleon noted in a veiled threat. Britain was at "the highest point of prosperity, so what does she hope to gain from war? To coalesce some continental powers? But the continent remains peaceful and a coalition would only increase the preponderance and greatness of France." Napoleon then pointed out that "the world is big enough so that our two nations can live in peace."[33] He had good reasons for desiring peace, given that the two years of Franco-British conflict had brought hardly any advantages to France. The British blockade confined French fleets to their ports and had driven French trade off the sea. France had effectively lost its foothold in the Western Hemisphere, with Louisiana sold to the United States, Haiti proclaiming its independence, and the British targeting the remaining French colonies in the West Indies. Back at home, France faced a growing financial crisis, with public credit about to reach its nadir and the burden of taxation provoking considerable unrest.

As much as Napoleon desired peace, he sought it on his own terms, terms that would have ensured continued French hegemony in western Europe. With France controlling the coastlines of Holland, Belgium, and Italy, Napoleon could exercise immense control over trade and commerce on the continent. Furthermore, Napoleon's peaceful professions contrasted sharply with his actions, which revolved around plans for colonial expansion, especially in the East. These considerations led the British to dismiss Napoleon's offer as disingenuous, merely designed to portray the British as irreconcilable enemies of France and disturbers of peace on the continent. Equally dismissive of Napoleon's overtures was the Russian government, where the deputy foreign minister, Prince Adam Czartoryski, a Polish nobleman who had embraced Russian imperialism with the zeal of a recent convert, urged Alexander to oppose a man who posed an acute danger to European peace and stability: "Napoleon had cast aside everything that could have led people to believe that he had a high and generous mission. He was a Hercules abandoning his task of succoring the oppressed and thinking only how to employ his strength in order to subjugate the world for his own advantage. His sole idea was to re-establish absolute power everywhere...he seemed like a sinister and devouring flame rising above all Europe."[34]

Throughout the fall of 1804 and the spring of 1805, diplomats from European powers shuttled back and forth to forge a new alliance against France.[35] Such coalition-building, however, was a difficult process, with the principal powers—Britain, Russia, and Austria—distrusting one another's ambitions and some states expressing reservations about reviving a coalition that had already been twice defeated by France. Nevertheless, the process began with Russia negotiating an agreement with Sweden (which was already allied to Britain) in January 1805, followed by the Convention of St. Petersburg, which Britain and Russia signed in April to "reestablish the peace and equilibrium in Europe." By August the Convention of Helsingfors ensured Swedish involvement in the war and allowed the use of Swedish Pomerania as a base of operations against France, in exchange for British subsidies.[36]

The Neapolitan kingdom, meanwhile, played a dangerous double game. On one hand, it maintained the outward appearance of friendship with France and accepted a treaty of neutrality (September 21, 1805) that resulted in the French withdrawing from Neapolitan territory. Yet at the same time King Ferdinand and his consort, Queen Maria Caroline, were alarmed by Napoleon's ambitions on the Apennine Peninsula. After the proclamation of the French Empire, it seemed incongruous that Napoleon should hold the imperial crown in France while serving as president of the Italian Republic. Consequently, in March 1805 the republic was transformed into a kingdom, and in May Napoleon was crowned at the Duomo in Milan with the Iron Crown of Lombardy and assumed the title of "Emperor of the French and King of Italy," underscoring the central role Italy was to play in his imperial designs; Napoleon's twenty-four-year-old stepson Eugène de Beauharnais was named as a viceroy of Italy. The kingdom encompassed much of northern Italy, including the former Duchies of Milan, Mantua, and Modena and parts of the Republic of Venice and the Papal States. Facing this French encroachment, the Neapolitan Bourbons felt that they had no choice but to join the coalition. On September 8, 1805, they signed a secret treaty of alliance with Russia and Britain, agreeing to a joint Anglo-Russian invasion through southern Italy.

The Austrian court, still reeling from military setbacks in the period 1796–1800, was reluctant to enroll in a new coalition. Since 1801 Vienna had showed that it was ready to swallow many humiliations before it would be drawn into another potentially disastrous war with France. Thus it accepted, with passive indignation, French annexation of Piedmont, Swiss submission to a French protectorate, and the violation of Badenese sovereignty in the d'Enghien affair. Even when Napoleon assumed the imperial title, Austria acquiesced, though Napoleon's decision to accept Austrian letters acknowledging his new dignity at Aix-La-Chapelle, the old capital of Charlemagne, only further humiliated the Habsburgs. It was Napoleon's policies in Italy that prompted Austria to break out of its state of passive acquiescence. Austrian sentiments were enflamed by the French decision to reorganize parts of northern Italy, annexing the Ligurian Republic (Genoa) to France and forming an imperial fief of Piombino for Napoleon's sister Elisa. Austrian anxiety and suspicion over this were all the greater because it took place in spite of Napoleon's solemn proclamations that the period of French annexations had ended with the takeover of Piedmont in 1802. The French encroachments made it clear that the Treaty of Lunéville had no longer had any bearing since it had been so flagrantly ignored. Russia and Britain pointed out to Austria that if it did not act promptly, it stood to lose its standing and could not hope to get any support from the other powers. In June 1805 Emperor Francis therefore joined the Anglo-Russian-Swedish coalition and began to mobilize his forces. Of the remaining powers, only Prussia, pursuing a steady policy of neutrality, refused to join the coalition, although even Prussian patience had limits, and unrelenting French depredations would soon force King Frederick William to leave his cocoon.

The coalition identified a number of concrete objectives it hoped to achieve. Many of these dealt with reversing territorial changes France had made over the previous decade. The coalition wanted French withdrawal from Hanover and northern Germany, the reestablishment of Swiss and Dutch independence, restoration of Piedmont-Sardinia, and complete removal of French forces from Italy. These were daunting goals, but the Allies did not stop there. They also sought, according to the terms of the treaty, "the establishment of an order of things in Europe that effectively guarantees the security and independence of the different states and present a solid barrier against future usurpations."[37] Indeed, the treaty contained many references to "tranquility," "peace," "security," and other high-minded concepts that the powers believed were needed to set up a "federative system" that would maintain peace and stability in Europe.

However, the coalition did not seek to conquer or implement a regime change in France. The treaty explicitly stated that the Allies did not wish "to interfere in any way with the national wish in France relative to the form of her Government."[38] The coalition members believed that with Napoleon's coronation, French revolutionary radicalism (and thus ideological threat) was over and in time the French people would choose to replace Napoleon with another monarch.

The coalition plans for the campaign called for unprecedented Europe-wide coordination of operations. Its members expected Napoleon to go on the offensive in northern Italy, and they planned to mobilize some 580,000 soldiers, identifying four major theaters of war.[39] In southern Germany, Archduke Ferdinand and General Karl Leiberich Mack commanded an army of some 60,000 men with instructions to invade Bavaria, whether its ruler, Maximilian Joseph, remained allied with the French or not.[40] Ferdinand would then remain on the defensive, sustaining his troops with Bavaria's resources, until a Russian army of 50,000 troops under Field Marshal Mikhail Kutusov arrived to launch a joint offensive. Another Russian army, this one with 40,000 men, under Friedrich Wilhelm Buxhöwden was to join them at a later time. Meanwhile, in northern Italy, Archduke Charles (with some 95,000 men) was to reclaim Austria's lost Italian provinces. Archduke John (with 23,000 men) was in Tyrol to maintain communications between the Austrian forces in Italy and southern Germany. The coalition's operations were not limited to Bavaria and northern Italy alone. The plan also called for some 45,000 Russian, British, and Neapolitan troops to land in Naples, where they would have overpowered the 20,000 French soldiers stationed there and restored the country's independence. At the same time, some 70,000 Russians and Swedes (with British help) were to land in northern Germany and recover Hanover for Britain.[41]

This strategy contained several major flaws. First, it completely neglected the principle of concentration, an especially grave problem because coordinating operations over such vast distances was beyond contemporary capabilities. Second, it mistakenly presumed Napoleon's main attack would be against northern Italy, and so it committed the largest Austrian army (under the best Austrian general) to that region. Third, it was based on a drastic underestimation of how long it would take for the French army operating in Germany to reach the Danube. To make matters worse, the Austrian leadership remained badly divided about the army's readiness for war and the strategy to be employed. Prussia's initial refusal to join the coalition denied the Allies many of the troops they had hoped for. Nor could the coalition hope to gain the advantages of surprise: organizing military operations on such a grand scale could not escape the keen eyes of Napoleon's spies.

As he followed his enemies' intentions and tallied up their potential strength, Napoleon realized that to meet the coalition's threat he must move swiftly and seize the initiative. He quickly identified his main target. With the Austrian forces already forming on the Danube front, Napoleon decided to march to the Rhine with an army of 200,000 men, then push into Swabia, gathering his south German allies, and defeat the enemy before they could concentrate their forces. A relatively small army would pin down Austrian forces in Italy; Hanover and Naples would not be reinforced. Any losses there would be easy to recover if Austria and Russia were defeated in the main theater. In late August Napoleon instructed his officers to travel to southern Germany, making notes of everything of military value, including the nature of roads and bridges, the width of rivers, and the condition of fortifications. On the twenty-fifth, Napoleon issued orders for the Grande Armée to march to the Rhine. The various corps were assigned to widely separated roads so that they would not interfere with each other and would have no difficulties with billets or supplies. Napoleon had personally calculated the march of his army and expected to have his forces on the Rhine by September 23, with some units covering three hundred miles in twenty-nine days. In Italy, Napoleon expected the combined Franco-Italian forces (68,000 men, under Marshal André Masséna) to keep the main Austrian army fully occupied.

Napoleon maintained secrecy surrounding the army's movements. He ordered some corps commanders to announce that they were simply returning to France so that their movements did not raise suspicions in the enemy camp. He prohibited newspapers from reporting on military operations and maintained a tight cavalry screen to cover his advance. To expedite marching to the Danube, Napoleon also made the most of his relationship with those German princes whose territories lay in the path of the Grande Armée. French diplomats assured the princes that Napoleon would guarantee their lands and sovereignty in return for their political and military support. The German princes thus found themselves between a rock and a hard place: they felt terribly uncomfortable siding with the French against the coalition, but they were also in no position to reject Napoleon's demands. Seeking a way out, the rulers of Baden, Württemberg, and Bavaria sought Prussian guarantees for German neutrality. However, the Prussian king, unwilling as yet to get embroiled in a war, ignored this plea, compelling Baden to accept the French offer of alliance while Württemberg announced its neutrality, causing the Austrians to think Napoleon would not violate its territory.

In early September the Austrian army under Mack invaded Bavaria, hoping to coerce the Bavarians (and other German states) into an alliance or disarmament before the French arrived. Expecting the French to attack from the vicinity of Strasbourg in November, Mack calculated that the Russian army would have ample time to reach him before he engaged the enemy. This move backfired, however—the Bavarians threw their support firmly behind the French, while Austrian aggression provided Napoleon with both a casus belli and a suitable target to engage. Mack thus found himself isolated in Bavaria. The Russian army under Kutuzov was still far away and not expected to arrive before mid-October.[42]

Traditional histories of the 1805 campaign focus on political and military aspects and usually discuss the formation of the Grande Armée and Napoleon's diplomatic maneuvering on the eve of the war. Yet one crucial element is often overlooked: financing it all. Military reforms and preparations for war proved to be very taxing for France. By late September 1805 the French capital was jittery as the prospects of a new war combined with a disappointing harvest to produce an economic downturn. François Nicolas Mollien, minister of public treasury, later recalled that the economic fatigue was such that Napoleon was able to provide only several million francs for the Grande Armée, with "the greater part coming from his own personal savings." Military contractors, who tried claiming payments for their deliveries in advance, had threatened to suspend their deliveries, forcing Napoleon to give them 10 million francs' worth of state-owned land in payment. Furthermore, the Treasury had pledged part of the revenues of 1806 by negotiating the obligations against the payments of that year.[43] Miot de Mélito, a member of the Council of State, spoke of the Bank of France being assailed with demands for the payment of its notes. As soon as Napoleon departed from the capital, financial circles were seized with fears of liquidity problems, as the Bank of France could only "give cash to the amount of 300,000 francs, accepting only one note for 1000 francs from each creditor who presented himself." This caused widespread dissatisfaction. "The Bank, or at least the principal shareholders, were accused of trading in the specie and of having exported a large quantity. Others laid the scarcity of money on the shoulders of the Government and on the loans made by it to the Bank."[44] Traveling in the streets of Paris, one would have seen how gloomy the popular mood was. Napoleon's call-up of tens of thousands of conscripts for a contingency reserve only worsened it. Even in the seemingly docile Senate, the emperor's speech explaining the causes of the new war elicited little support and revealed the profundity of the financial problems Napoleon faced as he embarked on a campaign. As he departed for Strasbourg, the emperor knew it was imperative to bring a quick end to the war.

As the Allies advanced, Napoleon raced to the critical point, exploiting the superior mobility of his corps, which had billets and supplies arranged by local authorities waiting for them. The smooth and rapid movement of such a large army was unprecedented: the French troops averaged some twenty miles per day. The Grande Armée reached the Rhine River by late September, and after crossing at various locations between September 26 and October 2, it advanced toward the Danube.[45] This speedy advance once again revealed a key feature of Napoleon's character: his willingness to accept long-term political risks for immediate strategic and operational advantages. To threaten the enemy position, Napoleon pushed his I and II Corps through the Prussian territory of Ansbach, flagrantly violating its neutrality. This was a politically perilous decision, but in Napoleon's mind it was justified by military need.

It took the Austrians by surprise, as they had received assurances that Prussia would oppose any such move, and so they were convinced of the security of their rear. Napoleon's gamble paid off, but it caused considerable outrage in Prussia and led to calls for war.

Napoleon needed to act quickly, and act quickly he did. With his spies reporting that Mack had concentrated his forces around Ulm, he issued a new set of orders designed to cut the Austrians off from the Russians and destroy them piecemeal. By early October Napoleon's forces were advancing in six great columns in a wide arc around to the north and then east of Mack's position. An important element in Napoleon's plan was his use of intelligence to deceive his enemy, with French agents Charles (Karl) Louis Schulmeister and Édouard Fetny well placed inside Austrian headquarters to supply misinformation to the Austrian command while transmitting crucial Austrian military plans to Napoleon.[46]

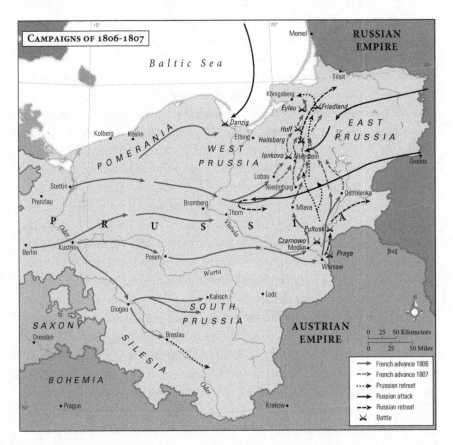

Map 10: Campaigns of 1806–1807

By September 30 Mack had realized that he was in danger of being encircled, and he tried to break out of the trap and open a line of retreat toward Vienna. In the first two weeks of October the Austrians suffered a series of major defeats: at Wertingen (October 8), Marshals Joachim Murat and Jean Lannes mauled the Austrian forces under Franz Auffenberg; at Haslach (October 11), some 4,000 French troops commanded by General Pierre Dupont managed to withstand an assault by 25,000 Austrians; at Elchingen (October 14), Marshal Michel Ney routed the Austrians and prevented them from escaping north of the Danube while most of Napoleon's forces were south of the river. By then, the French had two corps in the vicinity of Munich, eighty miles east of Mack, severing his line of communication and closing off his more southerly routes of escape. Napoleon's swift advance and victories demoralized the Austrian army. With the Russians still over a hundred miles away, Mack surrendered his forces, consisting of some 23,500 men and sixty-five pieces of artillery, at Ulm on October 19–20.[47]

The victory at Ulm was a remarkable success. In less than two months Napoleon had marched some 200,000 men from the Atlantic coast into Bavaria and achieved his major objective of annihilating the enemy army without even needing to fight a major battle. It was this success, achieved at the operational level rather than the tactical, that led his men to joke that Napoleon had found a new way to make war: with their legs rather than their arms.[48]

Napoleon moved quickly to follow up on his success. He pushed his main forces toward Vienna while André Masséna successfully engaged Archduke Charles to prevent him from supporting the Austrian war effort in Bavaria. Kutuzov's Russian army had just reached Braunau after marching at a breakneck pace for the last three hundred miles and losing thousands of stragglers along the way.[49] With Mack's army gone, Kutuzov's primary objective was to save his own forces, which he did not hesitate to do in light of the odds he faced. Pursuing the retreating Russians, Marshal Murat marched on the Austrian capital on November 13.[50] On the same day a small party of French generals captured the principal bridge over the Danube without firing a shot, and they did so by means of a superb bluff.[51] As the Austrians on the far bank were preparing to destroy the bridge, two French generals rode onto the structure and announced that they were coming to meet a senior Austrian general who had requested a conference. While the Austrians dithered, Marshal Lannes also crossed over, warning the Austrians that destroying the bridge would violate a just-signed armistice. Murat then sent a column of grenadiers forward. Lannes's lies and the force of his personality deterred the Austrian gunners from opening fire, and the French took possession of the bridge. The French marshals, however, failed to build upon their success. Encouraged by the success of this ruse, Murat tried it once more just two days later when he came upon the Russian army. The Russians feigned knowledge of the negotiations and amused the French marshal with fine words and negotiations; Murat, caught in his own snare, even dispatched a messenger to Napoleon informing him of the conditions of the armistice that the Russians pretended to offer. Meanwhile, Kutuzov's army marched toward Moravia, leaving behind a small rear guard commanded by his ablest general, the fiery Prince Peter Bagration. On November 16, upon receiving blazing criticism from the emperor, who accused the marshal of "wasting the fruits of the entire campaign," Murat attacked the Russian detachment with more than 30,000 men. The Russians lost more than half of their men but were able to hold off the French long enough to enable the main body of the Russian army to escape to safety.[52]

As Napoleon advanced deeper into Austria, his army became progressively weaker, a phenomenon known as "strategic consumption." Aside from battle losses, the French had to detach troops to protect their ever-lengthening line of communication back to France and to engage the remaining Austrian forces. In late November, as he began concentrating his forces near Brünn, Napoleon expected to marshal only about 73,000 men, and that with great difficulty.

The Allies, meanwhile, regrouped as well. Emperors Alexander of Russia and Francis of Austria gathered some 90,000 men near Olmütz. Archduke Ferdinand was with 18,000 men at Prague, while Archdukes Charles, with 85,000 men, was about to break out of Italy. It was clear that the Allies sought to concentrate their superior forces and engage the Grande Armée while it was far from home.

Moreover, the French advance through Prussian territory on the way to Ulm had so infuriated Frederick William that on November 3, 1805, he signed the Convention of Potsdam with Emperor Alexander, granting permission to the Russian forces to pass through Prussian territory. More important, Frederick William agreed to serve as mediator for Russia and Austria with regard to France, and he pledged that should the mediation fail, he would join the coalition with an army of 180,000 men.[53] Napoleon therefore desperately needed to win a decisive battle before the Allied armies could combine to overwhelm him.

Common prudence should have suggested to the coalition that it would be better to delay their operations until the Prussian army had taken the field. But the Allies were deeply divided over strategy. Many senior officers, including General Kutuzov, emphasized the importance of not engaging Napoleon in battle and argued that everything was to be gained by delay.

A precipitate engagement could lead to a disaster. Instead of giving battle, they proposed to gain time by withdrawing toward the Carpathian Mountains, to allow reinforcements time to arrive from Italy and Prussia. However, Alexander and Francis disregarded these arguments. According to Russian military regulations, Alexander assumed command of the army while he stayed with the troops, and although he officially kept Kutuzov in charge of the army, his presence limited the general's actions. The Russian emperor was surrounded by a group of young noblemen, most notably Prince Peter Dolgorukov, who urged him to lead the army against Napoleon notwithstanding the strategic circumstances. These princelings persuaded the emperor that he had the necessary qualities for military command and that his presence in the army would turn the tide of war.

Still reeling from their Ulm disaster, the Austrians also opposed withdrawal, arguing that it would prolong French depredation of Austrian lands. They wanted to use the Russian army to drive the French out of Moravia.[54] These arguments for an offensive fell on willing ears, since Alexander was eager to lead the army and defeat Napoleon on the battlefield.[55] After much debate, Alexander and Francis agreed to an offensive, and the Austrian major general Franz Weyrother prepared a plan of operations.[56] Under this plan, the main Allied forces would turn Napoleon's right flank and cut his communications with Vienna.[57] However, Weyrother's disposition was so complex that when the hour of advance came, many officers had not yet sufficiently studied their own. One of the Russian participants complained that because of Weyrother's "confusing" marching orders "our columns always crossed each other's path, in some cases as much as several times, and some columns wasted time waiting for others."[58]

The Russo-Austrian army slowly moved in five columns from Olmütz to Wischau, where its advance guard under Bagration successfully engaged the French troops. Emperor Alexander witnessed combat for the first time. He was initially thrilled by the action but soon came across the dead and wounded, which shocked him; he retired to the rear and refused to eat for the rest of the day.[59] The main army, meanwhile, continued its advance in almost complete ignorance of the French location or strength.[60] The Russian emperor's confidant Czartoryski recalled that "it was here that Emperor Alexander and his advisers were in fault. They imagined that Napoleon was in a dangerous position, and that he was on the point of retreating. The French outposts had an appearance of hesitation and timidity which nourished these illusions, and reports came at every moment from our outposts announcing an imminent movement of the French army to the rear."[61]

The Allied success at Wischau was actually orchestrated by Napoleon, who sought to entice the Allies into positions of his choice; he persuaded many at coalition headquarters that the French were indeed weak and wanted to avoid a decisive battle.[62] The Russo-Austrian commanders nonetheless vacillated over their next step. Kutuzov still argued that Napoleon was simply luring the Allies into a favorable position, where he would engage them.[63] Other senior officers wanted to remain in their present positions and await reinforcements marching from Silesia. However, the young Russian adjutants who claimed Napoleon was too frightened to fight finally swayed Alexander. In late November Prince Peter Dolgorukov was sent to meet Napoleon to discuss terms for negotiations, but he acted with incredible haughtiness.[64] Napoleon, infuriated though he was by Dolgorukov's behavior, took advantage of him to convey the impression of French weakness and induce the Allies to attack. He succeeded in this: upon his return, Dolgorukov "stated all around that Napoleon trembled, and that even our advance guard would be sufficient to defeat him."[65] As Alexander vacillated, Dolgorukov bluntly told him that any indecision would brand the Russians as "cowards." Alexander responded, "Cowards? Then, it is better for us to die."[66]

As it advanced, the Allied army passed through Austerlitz on the morning of December 1 and slowly climbed the slope to the Pratzen plateau, which the French had just evacuated. That the French had surrendered what seemed to be key ground without a fight added to the impression of weakness that Napoleon was cultivating. Though the Allied troops marched in good order, the columns still became entangled, with some columns halting farther along than intended.[67] Bagration bivouacked his forces around Posoritz, on the extreme right flank of the Allied position.[68]

In fact, the arrival of coalition forces at Austerlitz was part of Napoleon's operational plan. The French emperor initially had placed his men on the Pratzen heights, just east of the village, for he recognized that this position would be a critical point for the battle. He then moved his men westward to lower ground, deliberately weakening and overextending his right flank in order to make his opponents concentrate their attention on this apparent vulnerability and to fix in their minds an impression of weakness of the overall French position. The French right wing seemed an irresistible target, for if the combined Austro-Russian army could break it, the Allies could sever the French line of retreat to Vienna (and to France) and trap Napoleon for the winter in Bohemia. Napoleon, on the other hand, was betting that Marshal Davout's late-arriving reinforcements would strengthen his right flank sufficiently to enable it to hold while he delivered the decisive blow elsewhere.

The coalition attack began early on December 2, when the battlefield was still shrouded in mist, concealing the main French army. By midmorning, the coalition forces had gained some ground on the French right flank, which was steadfastly defended by Davout's troops. At the critical moment, around 9:30 a.m., as the mist burned off and the "Sun of Austerlitz" lit the battlefield, Napoleon ordered Marshal Nicolas Soult to launch an assault on the Pratzen Heights. The French attack surprised the Allied forces, splitting their army into two and spreading disorder among their ranks. The French attack pressed hard against the disintegrating Allies' left flank, with French artillery firing at the frozen ponds to break through the ice and thus make any retreat more difficult. By 6:00 p.m. the battle was largely over.

Austerlitz was the masterpiece of Napoleon's military strategy. Despite their numerical superiority, the Russo-Austrian army was decisively defeated. The French lost some 9,000 men, of whom 1,300 were killed, but the coalition army suffered around 27,000 casualties. The Russians sustained most of the losses, with over 21,000 killed, wounded, and captured and 133 guns lost. Looking at the flower of the Russian military lying scattered across the bloodstained fields, Napoleon is said to have remarked, "Many fine ladies will weep tomorrow in St. Petersburg!"

Austerlitz was a blow that Austria could not recover from. With his armies defeated and his capital occupied, Emperor Francis of the Holy Roman Empire had no choice but to sue for peace on December 4. Emperor Alexander of Russia, despite his defiant rhetoric, was compelled to lead the battered remnants of his army back home. The moral and political impact on Russia of the Battle of Austerlitz was profound. On the morning of the battle, Napoleon famously welcomed the "Sun of Austerlitz" as it rose above the December mists. But for Russia, it could truly be said to have been the "Eclipse of Austerlitz." For a hundred years Russian society had been accustomed to seeing its army victorious, whether over the Turks, Swedes, Poles, or French, and believed it was unbeatable. Austerlitz shattered such illusions. Alexander was the first tsar to command the field army since Peter the Great, which only further heightened the Russian sense of defeat on the fields of Moravia. Indeed, the disastrous conclusion of the battle shocked Russian society. Writing from St. Petersburg, Joseph de Maistre commented that the "Battle of Austerlitz had a magical effect on the public opinion...and it seems that the defeat in a single battle had paralyzed the entire empire."[69] The Russian nobility initially refused to believe the extent of the loss. But as more details arrived and the size of the defeat became clear, a strong upsurge of nationalism led to calls to continue the war in order to recover the honor of Russia.

The triumph of 1805 gave Napoleon unchallenged mastery of western and central Europe, where through persuasion and pressure he secured the active cooperation of the key southern German states (Bavaria, Baden, and Wurttemberg). The other European powers were stunned by the scale and briskness of his victories. The campaign demonstrated their inability to form and lead a coalition strong enough to defeat a resurgent France. As in 1798–1801, Anglo-Russian military and political cooperation was badly strained, while relations between St. Petersburg and Vienna reached a new low, with each side holding the other responsible for the defeat. Although Alexander did not openly blame Austrian "treachery and imbecility," to borrow one British statesman's expression, anti-Austrian sentiments, already rampant among the Russian officers since their joint campaigns in Italy and Switzerland in 1799, became only more pronounced.[70] "As for the [Austrians]," one Russian general grumbled to his wife, "you cannot imagine what a misfortune it is to be with these scoundrels.... This bloody campaign should teach us not to trust these Germans, who are greater enemies to us than the French."[71]

———⊶⊱✦⊰⊷———

Yet French victories on the continent barely had any effect on Britain itself. In fact, France's triumph at Ulm coincided almost to the day with the crushing defeat at Trafalgar, where Horatio Nelson eliminated two-thirds of the Franco-Spanish fleet and consolidated British mastery of the seas. As discussed in Chapter 9, in 1804 Napoleon developed a strategic plan for his invasion of Britain. It called for Admiral Pierre de Villeneuve, in command of the French fleet at Toulon, to slip out of the port, join a Spanish squadron, and sail for the West Indies, thereby drawing the British Mediterranean fleet, under the command of Nelson, away from Europe in pursuit. Once in the Caribbean, Villeneuve was to elude the British forces, sail back to Europe, and rendezvous with French fleets from Brest and Rochefort and Spanish ships from the ports of Cadiz and Ferrol. This combined force would then sail into the English Channel in early August in order to escort the invasion force and protect it against the remaining British warships.

Villeneuve indeed set sail for the West Indies on March 30, 1805. He successfully eluded the British blockade and met up with a Spanish fleet under Admiral Don Federico Gravina at Cadiz. Thus reinforced, Villeneuve led the combined fleet to the West Indies, both to divert the attention of the British fleet keeping watch in the Channel and to rendezvous with other Franco-Spanish naval forces. He reached the West Indies in mid-May and waited at Martinique for other French fleets to join him. On June 11, realizing that no reinforcements were forthcoming, he sailed back to Europe, having failed to achieve any major objectives in the Caribbean. Nelson, who set off in pursuit a couple of weeks later, reached the Caribbean in early June only to learn of Villeneuve's departure. He immediately dispatched a frigate to inform the Admiralty in London that the Franco-Spanish forces were returning to European waters. This information allowed the Channel fleet commanders to be more vigilant in their blockades of French harbors. As a result, the French fleet at Brest failed to break through the cordon of enemy vessels. Although the Rochefort fleet had earlier managed to get out to sea, it could not rendezvous with Villeneuve and so it returned to port, effectively dooming the entire enterprise. On July 22 Villeneuve's fleet, weakened by the back-to-back crossings of the Atlantic Ocean and sailing to break the blockade at Brest, stumbled upon Admiral Sir Robert Calder's British fleet off Cape Finisterre (northwestern Spain). The ensuing battle gave neither side an outright victory—the British admiral was, in fact, later court-martialed for his performance—but this in itself constituted a strategic victory for the British. Despite suffering limited losses, Villeneuve despaired of reaching Brest, where his fleet could have joined with other French forces to clear the English Channel for an invasion of Great Britain. Instead he turned to Cadiz, where he was soon blockaded by the Royal Navy. Villeneuve was blamed for the failure of the invasion plan, but Napoleon had in fact decided to abandon it even before he learned about the failure of Villeneuve's operations. By the time Villeneuve docked at Cadiz, Napoleon had already broken up his camps at Boulogne and begun the march to the Danube, where Austria and Russia were preparing to confront him. He ordered Villeneuve to steer for the Mediterranean to provide protection and logistical support for the French forces in Italy. Villeneuve followed the imperial writ but, informed of Nelson's presence at Gibraltar, decided to reverse course and return north to Cadiz. His British pursuers, however, intercepted him on October 21 near Cape Trafalgar.

The Battle of Trafalgar was one of the largest naval battles of the nineteenth century, featuring sixty ships-of-the-line engaged. On sighting his opponents early on the morning of October 21, Nelson gave the signal from his flagship, HMS *Victory*, to his twenty-seven ships-of-the-line, carrying 17,000 men and 2,148 guns, plus four frigates and two auxiliary vessels, to prepare for battle. The Franco-Spanish fleet of thirty-three ships-of-the-line and five frigates, carrying 30,000 officers and men and 2,632 guns, was larger in size but could not match its opponents in terms of training and morale.[72] While Villeneuve arranged his fleet in a customary single file, Nelson chose a bolder approach, deploying his smaller fleet in two squadrons. It was a dangerous maneuver, since a weak wind could have hindered British movement and allowed the French and Spanish to pummel the lead British ships. Nelson reckoned that in piercing the enemy's line, he would be able to break its formation and turn the battle into a series of small engagements between individual ships (or groups of ships), where British superior gunnery, seamanship, and morale could overcome the numerical superiority enjoyed by their adversaries.[73] In true Napoleonic fashion, Nelson was seeking a decisive victory:

"It is...annihilation that the country wants, and not merely a splendid victory," he wrote shortly before the battle.[74]

Just before noon, Nelson hoisted the famous signal, "England expects that every man will do his duty," and the British fleet commenced attack. Despite heavy enemy fire, the British warships held their course and the two columns drove into the long line of Franco-Spanish ships. As each British warship passed through the line, its broadsides enfiladed the enemy vessels, to devastating effect. "I thought [our ship] was shattered to pieces, pulverized," recalled a French participant. "The storm of projectiles that hurled themselves against and through the hull on the port side made the ship heel to starboard. Most of the sails and the rigging were cut to pieces, while the upper deck was swept clear of the greater number of seamen working there."[75] The battle raged for five hours before resulting in one of the most decisive and consequential British naval victories in history. Seventeen ships of the Franco-Spanish fleet were captured and one was destroyed. Not a single British ship was lost. The Spaniards lost approximately 1,000 killed and wounded, while the French casualties exceeded 4,000 killed and wounded; approximately 7,000 French and Spaniards became prisoners. British losses were remarkably small—just 449 officers and men killed and 1,214 wounded, or approximately 10 percent of the total force. The greatest loss for the British, of course, was that of Admiral Nelson, who was mortally wounded by one of the French marines firing onto the decks of the *Victory*. He died around 4:00 p.m., but not before learning that victory was ensured.[76]

Trafalgar, like Ulm and Austerlitz, had profound consequences. However, its importance tends to be exaggerated and colored by patriotic sentiment, and it is important to distinguish between what appeared to have been won and what in fact had been accomplished. Nelson had indeed scored a brilliant victory, one that removed the immediate threat of a French invasion. It certainly helped to shore up the role of the Royal Navy in the forthcoming Peninsular War, as the fight for Spain came to be called. The battle also demonstrated the inability of sea power to affect the outcome of a war being fought on the continent: victories at sea might gain momentary respites but could not make up for inherent limits when dealing with land-based powers. Trafalgar did not produce, as some historians suggest, "decisive consequences"—Napoleon went on to destroy the Third and Fourth Coalitions and engineered a geopolitical shift in the Near East, where the Ottoman Empire and Iran aligned with France.[77] For the next seven years the British made little progress in their efforts to bring about the downfall of Napoleon and his empire. Neither did the battle secure British command of the sea or crush Napoleon's maritime aspirations. Until recently, the general tendency among historians was to conclude that the maritime struggle had ended in 1805, without much thought given to the six years of naval warfare that followed.[78] Contrary to popular perception, French naval power was not completely destroyed at Trafalgar, and despite the losses suffered, French admirals continued to conduct wide-ranging operations in the Atlantic and the Indian Ocean in 1806–1807. Furthermore, Napoleon continued to replenish his naval forces by either building new fleets or acquiring them by conquest, forcing the British to challenge him again at Copenhagen and Lisbon in 1807, Walcheren and Aix (Basque) Roads in 1809, and the Mascarene Islands in 1810.

———◦◦◦❀◦◦◦———

Victory over the Third Coalition in December 1805 offered Napoleon an opportunity to turn his attention to the Italian peninsula, where he had encountered significant problems. The heavy-handed introduction of French administration (especially the more effective tax collection and conscription systems) had provoked an uprising in Parma that Napoleon had to suppress in early 1806.[79] His instructions to General Andoche Junot demanded severe punishment of the local populace, revealing not the slightest interest in understanding the particulars surrounding the origins of the revolt. "I do not share your opinion on the innocence of the people of Parma," the emperor told the general, who urged a more restrained treatment of the rebels. "Punishments should be numerous and severe; spare no one.... Burn one or two large villages so that no traces remain. Say that I have ordered it. Large states can only be maintained by acts of severity."[80] The revolt was put down in just a few weeks, but it did reveal the nature of Napoleonic rule, which not only offered reforms but also exacted severe punishment for any resistance. Meanwhile, Pope Pius VII found himself on the receiving end of Napoleon's wrath for protesting the French occupation of Ancona during the war. Troops occupied the whole of the Adriatic and Tyrrhenian coastlines, which represented the first step toward the incorporation of the Papal States into the French Empire.[81]

More important, after ending the War of the Third Coalition, Napoleon announced his intentions to chasten the Bourbon monarchy in Naples, whose king, Ferdinand, had allied himself with Napoleon by the Treaty of Florence in 1801 and pledged to remain neutral in the ongoing conflict, only to break his agreement with France, join the Third Coalition, and invite the coalition forces to land at Naples, as we've seen.[82] The Allies responded to Ferdinand's invitation with the dispatch of two expeditionary forces: Lieutenant General James Henry Craig left Malta with some 6,000 British soldiers, while General Maurice Lacy's 7,000 Russian troops sailed from the island of Corfu. The two expeditions converged on Naples on November 20, 1805. The timing could not have been worse. The Austrian army had been demolished at Ulm, and the

French were already in control of the Austrian capital. In northern Italy, Marshal André Masséna, with his Armée d'Italie, prevailed over the Austrian army under Archduke Charles at Caldiero and pursued it toward Vicenza and then Venice, which was soon blockaded by French forces under General Saint Cyr.[83] Furthermore, upon landing in Naples, Craig and Lacy found the Neapolitan kingdom's defenses in a woeful state and its army in disarray. Unable to launch an offensive as it was originally envisioned, they decided to hold a defensive line along the northern border of the Neapolitan kingdom, with the Russians near the Apennine Mountains and the British on the Garigliano River.[84]

In the wake of Napoleon's triumph at Austerlitz, however, General Lacy received orders to withdraw from Italy, and his departure made the British position untenable. The prospect of the Allies' departure threw the Neapolitan monarchy into turmoil. King Ferdinand knew well what to expect from Napoleon for his perfidy: in January 1805 the French emperor had warned the Neapolitan Bourbons that "at the first sound of a war that you cause, you and your posterity will have ceased to reign, and your children will wander like mendicants through the different countries of Europe, begging help off their relatives."[85] King Ferdinand's desperate appeals caused Lacy to consider interpreting his orders with some latitude, but after a disagreement with Neapolitan officials, he decided to sail back for the Ionian Islands in January 1806. His departure was followed shortly by the evacuation of the British forces to Malta.

King Ferdinand thus found himself effectively abandoned by the Allies and facing down the French Empire with only his poorly trained army. Now, with the Austrian army in tatters and northern Italy firmly under his control, the French emperor could turn to the double-crossing Neapolitans. At the start of the New Year Marshal Masséna prepared his Franco-Italian army of some 41,000 men for the invasion of Naples. Ferdinand, never known for valor, fled with his court to the safety of Sicily and the "wooden walls" of the British navy. The Neapolitan army, left to defend the kingdom under the command of Marshal von Rosenheim and General Roger de Damas, was dolefully unprepared for the task, with its troops demoralized by their king's flight and hardly cherishing the prospect of engaging the far superior French army. Consequently, the French invasion of Naples proved to be a brief affair. The newly designated Armée de Naples, nominally under the command of Napoleon's brother Joseph but actually commanded by Marshal Masséna, crossed the Neapolitan border on February 8 and, routing the Neapolitan armies at Campo Tenese on March 10, occupied Naples and much of the kingdom by the end of the month. Joseph Bonaparte was installed as the new king of Naples on March 30 and began introducing reforms intended to modernize the kingdom's administration and economy.[86]

The ease with which the French occupied the kingdom proved to be deceptive. Southern Italy in the early nineteenth century was among the poorest regions in Europe, with its residents still recovering from the devastating Calabrian earthquakes that claimed as many as 100,000 lives in February and March 1783. The arrival of the French only increased their misery, as Joseph Bonaparte proceeded to set up French-style administration, conscript troops, and introduce efficient taxation to support them; numerous cases of abuses and mistreatment perpetrated by the French troops further alienated the local population. Many young men refused to report for conscription (or deserted from their units) and fled into the mountains, where they turned to brigandage that soon evolved into an open revolt against the French authority.

The British were happy to lend support to this uprising. In late June 1806 a small British expeditionary force of 5,200 men (many of them veterans of the Egyptian campaign) led by Major General Sir John Stuart crossed the Strait of Messina and landed unopposed in the Gulf of St. Euphemia on the Italian mainland.[87] On learning of the landing, General Jean Reynier advanced with about 6,500 men toward the gulf and took up a position overlooking a plain and the small village of Maida.[88] Here, on July 4, 1806, the two sides fought a battle that resulted in a French defeat that claimed almost half of Reynier's force. The Battle of Maida is often held up as an example of the superiority of the British line over the French column, something that would come to feature prominently during the Peninsular War, but recent scholarship has questioned the veracity of this claim.[89]

When considered within the wider scope of the War of the Third Coalition, the Neapolitan engagement loses its significance; the British, had they been bolder, could have caused serious problems for the French in southern Italy. Instead they chose to retreat to Reggio before quitting the mainland in August 1806. Still, the British intervention in Calabria had a significant regional impact. It weakened French control over Calabria, an area that was geographically, linguistically, and culturally isolated from the rest of Italy and well suited for a partisan uprising. The local anti-French resistance raged for the next five years and constituted the most serious challenge to Napoleon's control of the Italian peninsula. The *masse*, as the rebels became known, spread across the "toe" of Italy and quickly assumed a viciously murderous nature, with little mercy shown by either side. The French found themselves attacked by an "invisible" foe that operated under the cover of darkness and disappeared as soon as the attack was over; the brigands were encouraged by the British reward in gold for every captured live Frenchman they brought in, but as Stuart lamented in a report, the "locals prefer butchering to gold...their reward is blood. Not even the Turks are as abominable."[90]

Struggling to suppress this "most monstrous of wars," as Reynier described it, the French authorities diverted additional forces to the region, and in August 1806 some 6,000 men under Marshal André Masséna engaged in anti-insurgency operations, resorting to collective punishments and executions. Masséna decreed that any peasant found with arms would be executed, and in just three days in mid-August he had more than six hundred put to death. By the end of the year the French had reestablished control over most of the interior Calabrian towns but still struggled to control the countryside, a forewarning of things to come in Spain. For the next few years the French authority in southern Italy rested squarely on military force, repression, and exploitation, especially after the summer of 1809, when the Calabrians rose in another full-scale revolt.[91]

British victories at Trafalgar and Maida did not change the fact that by 1806 the Third Coalition lay in tatters and Napoleon dominated the European continent. When William Pitt received the news of Austerlitz, he pointed to a map of Europe hanging on a wall of his cabinet room and asked for it to be removed. "Roll up that map," he supposedly said. "It will not be wanted these ten years."[92] Pitt was right. The triumphs at Ulm and Austerlitz made Napoleon supreme in Italy and southern Germany and gave him a free hand to redraw the political map of Europe. On December 26, 1805, Austria signed a new peace at Pressburg (present-day Bratislava). In addition to confirming French gains made in the previous Treaties of Campo Formio and Lunéville, the Habsburgs were required to surrender all remaining Austrian possessions in Italy, including Venice and its hinterlands, and pay a vast war indemnity. France's allies, Bavaria, Baden, and Wurttemberg, were all rewarded for their loyalty and support with Austrian territories in the Tyrol and southern Germany.[93] Thus the Treaty of Pressburg marked an end to the Habsburg influence in Germany and henceforth completely excluded them from Italy. The Holy Roman Emperor, Francis II, helplessly watched the demise of the political institution that his predecessors had toiled so hard to maintain.

The French emperor could have concentrated on consolidating his vast gains. Instead he pursued even more grandiose plans. The French army was kept intact in Germany at German expense while Napoleon busied himself with extracting contributions from Austria, Spain, Switzerland, and German and Italian states, reorganizing the Batavian Republic into a monarchy, placing his brothers on royal thrones (Joseph in Naples, Louis in Holland), and rewarding his loyal officers with new titles and fiefs in Germany and Italy. Furthermore, even in peace, the emperor was keen on expanding his realm, redrawing borders in northeast Italy and directing French intrusions into Istria and Dalmatia.

As had been the case in 1800–1801, the most profound changes occurred in Germany. In the aftermath of the Third Coalition's demise, the Imperial Reichstag was abolished (January 20, 1806), enabling Napoleon to launch a new wave of reorganization of German states. In March he established the first of a new set of minor German states, to be ruled by members of his family; the newly formed Grand Duchy of Berg was given to his brother-in-law Marshal Murat. More important, the emperor made steps toward a wholesale transformation of the Holy Roman Empire into a French-dominated German political entity that could serve as a buffer against Prussia and Austria, a market for French goods, and a source of military manpower for the empire. The Confederation of the Rhine (Rheinbund/Confédération du Rhin) came into formal being in July 1806 when German princes (*Fürsten*) accepted the Treaty of Paris and recognized Karl Theodor von Dalberg as "prince-primate" (*Fürstenprimas*) and Napoleon as the "protector" (*Protektor*). Among the original sixteen German states of the confederation were Bavaria, Württemberg, Hesse-Darmstadt, Baden, and Berg, all of which withdrew from the Holy Roman Empire on August 1, marking the effective end of the empire; five days later, the Holy Roman Emperor, Francis II, had no choice but to surrender the Habsburgs' ancient imperial dignity and proclaimed himself Emperor Francis I of Austria in its place.[94] Almost a thousand years after its inception, the German *Reich*, in the words of historian Sam Mustafa, "died with a whimper."[95] Twenty-three additional German states would eventually join the Confederation of the Rhine, with only Prussia and Austria, alongside the much smaller Danish Holstein and Swedish Pomerania, remaining outside it.

The establishment of the confederation was not just a product of Napoleon's ambition. It also reflected the fact that the south German states were deeply apprehensive of Austrian and Prussian ambitions and willing to support France in exchange for lands and titles. As an inducement for their support (though, in practice, that support was often effectively coerced), Napoleon generously rewarded his Bavarian, Wurttembergian, Badenese, and other allies. Austria was forced to recognize the elevation of the electors of Bavaria (Maximilian Joseph) and Württemberg (Frederick II) to the rank of kings, releasing them as well as the newly minted grand dukes of Baden (Charles Frederick), Hesse-Darmstadt (Louis I), and Würzburg (Ferdinand I) from all feudal ties. Furthermore, these states were made larger by incorporating *Kleinstaaten*, the smaller imperial member states that the Imperial Recess had swept aside.

Yet such aggrandizement did not come cheaply for the German states, which had exchanged benevolent Austrian leadership for the far more constricting and effective hegemony of France. The confederation was, at its heart, a political-military alliance, and France extracted vast contributions in men and matériel from individual members. And the Rheinbund had a deep, long-term impact on Germany. With its establishment, Napoleon had unwittingly placed the first brick in the foundation of the future united Germany. The French interventions in Germany in 1801 and 1806 profoundly changed the German political reality, reducing the approximately three hundred duchies, ecclesiastical cities, electorates, principalities, and duchies to just three dozen states that were ultimately united in 1871. The formation of the Confederation of the Rhine was a crucial moment in the development of modern Germany.

If Austria's dominance in Germany had all but vanished, the same may be said of Prussia too. Berlin could have had a decisive effect on the outcome of the War of the Third Coalition in 1805. King Frederick William III, a man of good intentions but characterized by weakness of will and vacillation, had, as we've noted, dithered about declaring war, and by the time he finally decided to intervene, it was too late.[96] In November Prussia signed a convention with Russia, placing some 180,000 troops on a war footing and dispatching its envoy Christian Graf von Haugwitz to offer armed mediation to Napoleon under the threat of Prussian entry into the war. Napoleon kept the Prussian envoy at arm's length until after his victory at Austerlitz on December 2, by which time the geopolitical situation in central Europe had profoundly changed. Rather than present his ultimatum, Haugwitz was forced to sign the Treaty of Schönbrunn (December 5, 1805), which created a Franco-Prussian alliance. As a reward for Prussian acceptance of the treaty, Napoleon agreed to transfer Hanover to Prussia in exchange for ceding the Margravate of Ansbach to the French ally Bavaria, and the Principality of Neuchâtel (a Prussian enclave in Switzerland) to France.

The transfer of Hanover was designed to cause frictions, if not outright rupture, in relations between Prussia and its only potential ally in Europe, Britain. The Prussians understood this, but the French offer was too tempting to turn down.[97] Berlin initially refused to ratify the Treaty of Schönbrunn without modifications and then made an unwise decision to demobilize its forces. Napoleon, annoyed by the Prussian demands for revisions, at once raised the price of peace. In February and March 1806 France rejected the Prussian requests and instead imposed a new agreement on Berlin, requiring it to close all north German ports to British commerce. Facing a choice between accepting this humbling treaty and fighting a war with France, Frederick William III chose the former, thereby bringing Prussia into even greater dependence on France. Britain responded by declaring war and the Royal Navy blockaded the Prussian coastline, causing considerable harm to Prussia's maritime trade, which in the preceding decades had contributed so much to Prussian prosperity.

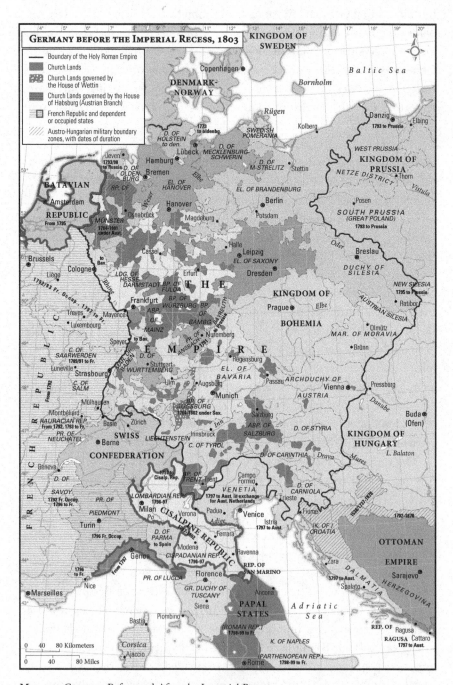

Map 11: Germany Before and After the Imperial Recess

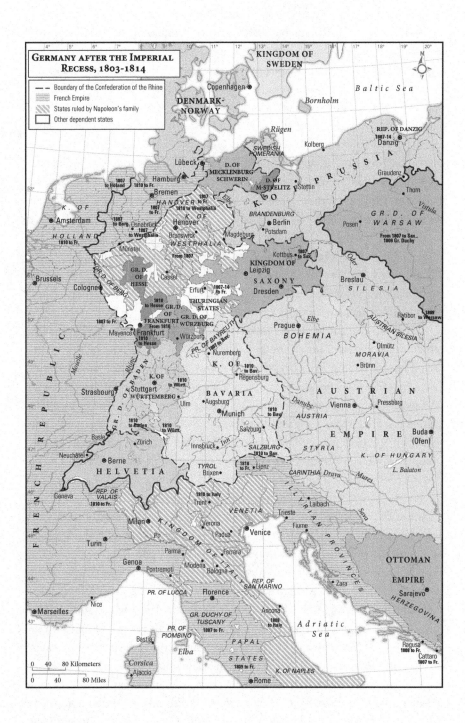

GERMANY AFTER THE IMPERIAL RECESS, 1803-1814

- - - Boundary of the Confederation of the Rhine
French Empire
States ruled by Napoleon's family
Other dependent states

KINGDOM OF SWEDEN

Baltic Sea

DENMARK-NORWAY

Copenhagen

Bornholm

REP. OF DANZIG
1807-14
Danzig

Rügen

Kolberg

Graudenz

SWEDISH POMERANIA

Lübeck

D. OF MECKLENBURG-SCHWERIN

Stettin

Thorn

Hamburg

1807 to Holland

1810 to Fr.

Bremen

D. OF M-STRELITZ

Vistula

GR. D. OF WARSAW
From 1807 to Sax., 1809 Gr. Duchy

Posen

P R U S S I A

K. OF

HANOVER

1807 to Fr.

1807 to Fr.

K. O

BRANDENBURG

Berlin

Amsterdam

1807 to Berg

Osnabrück

1807 to Westphalia

Hanover

K. OF

Potsdam

HOLLAND
1810 to Fr.

Münster

WESTPHALIA
From 1807

Brunswick

Magdeburg

Breslau

SILESIA

Brussels

GR. D. OF BERG

Cassel

Kottbus

1807 to Sax.

1809 to Warsaw

Cologne

GR. D. OF HESSE

Leipzig

KINGDOM OF SAXONY

Dresden

Erfurt

1807-14

AUSTRIAN SILESIA

Ratibor

1810 to Hesse

THURINGIAN STATES

GR. D. OF FRANKFURT
From 1810

GR. D. OF WÜRZBURG

Elbe

Prague

BOHEMIA

Olmütz

MORAVIA

1807 to Fr.

Mayence

Frankfurt

1810 to Hesse

Würzburg

PR. OF BAYREUTH
1807 to Bav.

Brünn

Strasbourg

GR. D. OF BADEN

Nuremberg

K. OF

1810 to Bav.

Regensburg

A U S T R I A N

K. OF WÜRTTEMBERG

Stuttgart

1810 to Württ.

BAVARIA

Danube

Vienna

Pressburg

Augsburg

Ulm

Munich

1810 to Bav.

AUSTRIA

E M P I R E

Buda (Ofen)

1810 to Baden

1810 to Württ.

Salzburg

Zürich

Innsbruck

Inn

SALZBURG
1810 to Bav.

STYRIA

K. OF HUNGARY

Basle

Neuchâtel

Berne

HELVETIA

TYROL

Brixen

1810 to Fr.

Lienz

CARINTHIA

Drava

Mures

L. Balaton

Geneva

REP. OF VALAIS
1810 to Fr.

1810 to Italy

Trent

VENETIA

Trieste

Laibach

ILLYRIAN PROVINCES

Sava

FRENCH REPUBLIC

Moselle

Rhine

Po

Milan

KINGDOM OF ITALY

Verona

Padua

Venice

Fiume

Zara

OTTOMAN EMPIRE

Turin

Parma

Genoa

Pontremoli

Modena

Ferrara

REP. OF SAN MARINO

Sarajevo

HERZEGOVINA

Nice

PR. OF LUCCA

Bologna

Florence

Ancona

1808 to Italy

Adriatic Sea

Marseilles

GR. DUCHY OF TUSCANY
1807 to Fr.

PR. OF PIOMBINO

PAPAL

Ragusa
1808 to Fr.

Cattaro
1807 to Fr.

Bastia

Elba

STATES
1809 to Fr.

K. OF NAPLES

Corsica

Ajaccio

Rome

0   40   80 Kilometers

0   40   80 Miles

Never had Prussia been so humiliated and isolated as it was in 1805–1806. Not only had it conceded to French demands, it stood by helplessly as Napoleon increased his power in Europe. During the summer of 1806 the steady stream of news about Napoleon's reorganization of Germany and the conversion of the Batavian Republic into the Kingdom of Holland exasperated the Prussian government, which could see its standing in northwestern Europe rapidly evaporating. The Prussian monarch was therefore particularly incensed to discover that the confederation would include several regions formerly held by Prussia and presumably still within its sphere of influence. Napoleon further aroused Prussian resentment by sanctioning the execution of Johann Philipp Palm, a Nuremberg bookseller who had been arrested for selling a brochure condemning Napoleon and calling for German resistance to France.[98] Tried by a military commission, Palm refused to divulge the name of the pamphlet's author and was shot at Braunau on August 26, 1806. The disparity between the relative paltriness of the crime and the severity of the punishment angered many Germans and helped to arouse Prussian (and German in general) sentiment against France.[99]

But even in light of these humiliations, the Prussian monarchy seemed reluctant to be drawn into a conflict. The events of the Third Coalition reinforced long-standing Prussian opinions about Britain and Russia. The latter had a history of encouraging Prussia to oppose France before leaving it to deal with the consequences by itself. As for Britain, the Prussians found British naval supremacy as troublesome as French continental hegemony, and Frederick William pledged not to be used by the British, who, as he put it, "dangled a purse in the air" to make other powers to do their bidding.[100] The British preoccupation with South American schemes, as we will see, only further reinforced such sentiments in some European capitals.

It was the news that Napoleon, in his abortive negotiations with the British government, had actually offered to restore Hanover to Britain in exchange for peace that pushed Prussia toward war. The Treaty of Schönbrunn gave the state of Hanover to Prussia in return for territories on the right bank of the Rhine, which Prussia ceded to France. Berlin viewed the news of Napoleon now offering the region to London as a betrayal of the worst sort, hardly diminished by the fact that the Anglo-French negotiations quickly broke down. Although Napoleon's duplicity over Hanover was the immediate cause for war, the Prussian decision to confront France had already been made as early as July 1806 and was provoked by a clear realization that French aggrandizement posed an existential threat to the vital Prussian interests in northern Germany.[101] It was an "offensive strategy out of desperation," as the eminent American historian Paul Schroeder aptly put it, developed on the basis of rational calculation that "unless it broke through French encirclement by its own offensive, [Prussia] would not be able to fight at all."[102]

By the summer of 1806 anti-Gallican spirits ran high in Prussian society. A French officer who visited Berlin in August found "evidence of the frenzy to which their hatred of Napoleon carried the Prussian nation, usually so calm . . . The officers whom I knew ventured no longer to speak to me or salute me; many Frenchmen were insulted by the populace; the men-at-arms of the Noble Guard pushed their swagger to the point of whetting their sword-blades on the stone steps of the French ambassador's house."[103] Open criticism of the submissiveness of Frederick William's foreign policy was voiced among the high bureaucracy and the royal family, many of whom shared, in the words of a contemporary, "a great thirst for war" and "certain hope of victory."[104]

Strongly influenced by Queen Louise and the war party that still cherished proud memories of Frederick the Great, Frederick William finally agreed to send an ultimatum to Napoleon, demanding the immediate withdrawal of the French armies across the Rhine and France's acceptance of the formation of the North German Confederation under Prussian leadership. Napoleon, finding these demands ludicrous, did not respond. On October 9 Prussia declared war—joining in a war against France for the first time since 1795.

Yet Prussia was not prepared for the type of war that Napoleon unleashed. Despite being a member of a new coalition (Britain, Prussia, Sweden, Saxony, and Russia), Prussia was in a weak position strategically and politically. The decision to declare war was not done in concert with Emperor Alexander, with whom the king concluded a secret agreement of support in the event of an attack by France, and consequently no Russian troops were readily available to support Prussia. Britain's financial subsidies were certainly welcome but could not replace actual boots on the ground. Sweden's involvement produced few tangible benefits. The indigence of Prussia's foreign policy was equaled only by the ineptitude of its military high command. The Prussian army enjoyed a reputation far in excess of its actual merits. Long gone were the glory days of Frederick the Great. The Prussian military of 1806 was much inferior to the army that was responsible for the brilliant successes of the 1740s and 1750s. While the Prussian soldiers continued to display admirable courage, their aging superiors failed to fully account for changes that had taken place in the art of war during the Revolutionary Wars.[105] In the words of a Prussian observer, they demonstrated not just "a style of fighting which had outlived its usefulness but the most extreme poverty of the imagination to which routine has ever led."[106] On the eve of its war with France, Prussia could rely only on its own forces and on small contingents from Hesse and Saxony, the latter being rather reluctant to fight on behalf of their northern neighbor. The main part of the Prussian forces, around 65,000 men, was commanded by Charles William Ferdinand, Duke of Brunswick, while Friedrich Ludwig Fürst Hohenlohe-Ingelfingen took charge of a Prusso-Saxon corps of around 45,000 men; another 34,000 men were left to protect Westphalia and Hesse, and 18,000 West Prussians were kept in reserve.[107]

Napoleon was better prepared for the war. He commanded a well-honed army that had been fully trained in the camps of Boulogne and tested on the battlefields of 1805. The Grande Armée, which had not returned to France following the last campaign but instead remained quartered in southern Germany, had some 180,000 men on the river Main, determined to strike at Berlin before help could arrive from Russia. On October 6 the French invaded Saxony and, taking advantage of the Prussian failure to block passage through the Thüringian Forest, scored a first victory at Saalfeld (October 10), where Marshal Jean Lannes routed an exposed Prussian-Saxon corps under Prince Louis Ferdinand of Prussia, who was killed in action.[108] The defeat dazed the Prussian commanders, who decided to fall back to the Elbe and Berlin. It was too late. Four days later, on October 14, Napoleon caught up with them. Assuming that the main Prussian army was at Jena, the French emperor divided his forces, sending Marshal Louis Nicolas Davout with the III Corps some ten miles north to strike the enemy's rear. When the battle commenced at Jena, Napoleon was able to quickly concentrate some 95,000 men against just 38,000 Prussians commanded by Frederick Louis, Prince of Hohenlohe-Ingelfingen. The Prussian commander hoped to have the support of another 15,000 men deployed about ten miles away at Weimar, but they arrived only in the afternoon, when the outcome of the battle was no longer in doubt. The Prussians fought valiantly but were no match for the French troops, superbly commanded by Napoleon and his marshals. By afternoon the Prussians were already in a retreat that soon turned into a rout.[109]

While Napoleon smashed what he believed was the main Prussian army at Jena, Davout's III Corps of just 28,000 men stumbled across the bulk of the enemy forces at Auerstädt, where Brunswick had concentrated more than 60,000 men with 230 cannon. Realizing the danger he was facing, the French "Iron Marshal" exploited the terrain of the Saale Valley—hilly, with deep ravines cutting into the various plateaus—to fight a resolute action. He formed his divisions into huge squares whenever the Prussian cavalry charged, and he demonstrated an ability to coordinate the actions of his infantry, artillery, and cavalry. Despite losing a quarter of its men, the French corps not only held its ground but seized the initiative and pushed forward, threatening to envelop the Prussian flanks. The death of the Prussian commander in chief, Brunswick, disheartened the Prussian army, which began to break up even though its reserves had not yet been committed. A disorderly retreat degenerated into chaos when the fleeing masses of Brunswick's force crossed paths with the Prussian survivors from Jena, whom Hohenlohe was leading into Pomerania.[110]

The destruction of the Prussian forces in the twin battles of Jena and Auerstädt caused profound demoralization in Prussia. And, in what became one of the most thorough and rapid pursuits in history, French forces scattered across the Prussian kingdom, capturing cities, fortresses, and thousands of prisoners. The great Prussian fortresses of Spandau, Stettin, Küstrin, and Magdeburg, with garrisons counting thousands of men, could have checked the French advance and gained precious time for the army to reorganize. Instead they capitulated without so much as firing a shot, effectively breaking Prussia's military backbone.[111] Some detachments of Prussian forces held out for another month before capitulating one by one. Hohenlohe's 14,000 men surrendered to Marshal Joachim Murat at Prenzlau on October 28.[112] Murat then joined Soult and Bernadotte in pursuit of some 12,000 Prussians who had shown much spirit under the fiery Gebhard Lebrecht Blücher von Wahlstatt as they retreated to the Hanseatic port of Lübeck, hoping to unite with a Swedish army that was reported to be there. But upon arriving on November 5 Blücher found that the Swedes had landed only a small brigade of fewer than 2,000 men. The following day, the French forces stormed and sacked Lübeck, forcing Blücher to capitulate; the Prussian general's last stand quickly entered Prussian lore, turning him into a symbol of heroism and steadfast resistance for the defeated nation.[113] However, in just one month Prussia had effectively been knocked out of the war, apart from a force under General Anton William Lestocq, which moved east to link up with the Russians, and another under General Friedrich Adolf Graf von Kalkreuth, which was besieged in Danzig.[114]

On October 25, because of its valiant performance at Auerstädt, Davout's III Corps was given the honor of being the first to enter the Prussian capital, Berlin, followed a day later by Napoleon, who visited the tomb of Frederick the Great and supposedly stood in silence for a minute before remarking, "If you were still alive, I would not be standing here."[115]

The Franco-Prussian war was brief, lasting just four weeks, but the military and political collapse of Prussia had enormous ramifications. In contrast to his victory over Austria in 1805, Napoleon insisted on organizing a victory parade in Berlin, where the prisoners from the Noble Guard, who just weeks before had sharpened their swords on the French embassy's steps, were prominently featured. The war not only destroyed Prussia's martial reputation but ended the country's claims to the status of a great power. Napoleon demanded vast concessions from Frederick William: all Prussian territory, except for Magdeburg and Altmark, on the left bank of the Elbe was to be surrendered; Prussia could make no alliances with any other German state and had to pay a war indemnity. The king had a week to comply. As more and more Prussian cities and fortresses surrendered, Napoleon revised his demands, adding the requirement that Prussia surrender all its territory up to the Vistula. Frederick William rejected the terms and fled, along with his family and court, to the fortress of Königsberg in East Prussia, where he desperately grasped at the straw of salvation proffered by Russia.

Napoleon, joined by Saxony (which had signed the Treaty of Posen on December 11, 1806), was now free to take on these Russian forces, which, under the command of Levin Bennigsen, marched to support their Prussian allies. Russia had learned indelible lessons at Austerlitz and in 1806 began rapidly reorganizing its military forces. New levies were called up and more than 600,000 men recruited from thirty-one provinces.[116] These vast human resources allowed Alexander I to form three new armies, including two under Bennigsen and Buxhöwden with a total of 120,000 men, to contain Napoleon's attempts to expand his sphere of influence into northeastern Europe.[117]

Hostilities resumed in November 1806, when Bennigsen maneuvered with his 70,000 men in central Poland. Yet lack of unity of command hampered Russian operations; Buxhöwden and Bennigsen were on bad terms and refused to cooperate. Exasperated by squabbles among his generals, Alexander lamented that "there is not a single one with the talent of the commander in chief."[118] In worsening weather—"snow, rain, and thaw . . . we sunk down up to our knees . . . and our shoes would stick in the wet mud," as one participant described it—the Grande Armée marched into Poland to engage the Russians, who hastily withdrew beyond the Vistula.[119] The French cavalry occupied the former Polish capital city, Warsaw, on November 28. A second Russian army, under Buxhöwden, advanced to confront the French.

On December 26, at Golymin, the French caught up with the Russian rear guard, under General Prince Dmitry Golitsyn, whose troops were too exhausted to march further. Golitsyn desperately held on to the town of Golymin to help General Fabian von der Osten-Sacken's troops, who were in danger of being cut off. With a total of about 16,000–18,000 men facing the corps of 38,000 men under Marshals Augereau and Murat, the Russians held out until nightfall and then withdrew. On the same day, about twelve miles away, General Bennigsen decided to attack Marshal Jean Lannes's corps of 20,000 men with his 40,000–45,000 men at Pultusk. Both sides claimed a victory, but Bennigsen, who claimed that he had defeated Napoleon himself, left the field to Lannes.

The battles at Pultusk and Golymin demonstrated that Napoleon could no longer hope for the swiftness of the previous campaigns. In Poland, one of the poorest regions in Europe, there were scarce supplies, and both the French and Russian armies starved. Bad roads and cold weather further complicated the movement of supplies to the armies. With the Russians retreating northward, Napoleon decided to move his army into winter quarters north of Warsaw.[120] Meanwhile, confusion reigned in the Russian army, as Count Mikhail Kamensky, a field marshal Alexander appointed to lead the Russian armies, left his post just a few days after reaching headquarters.[121] Bennigsen was then appointed to lead the Russian forces and decided to launch a surprise offensive against the French left wing, scattered in bivouacs in northern Poland. Its main objective was to protect Königsberg, where the Prussian court and huge Russian supply magazines were established.

The Russian offensive began successfully and Marshal Ney's corps was forced to give ground. However, as the Russian army moved farther away from its bases, Napoleon saw a chance to encircle his opponent. In January he conceived of a maneuver that would have turned the enemy flank and destroyed Bennigsen's army.[122] Yet, as one Russian officer observed, "the Russian God was too great" to let that happen.[123] A dispatch sent to Marshal Bernadotte detailing the emperor's plans was captured by a Cossack patrol. Bennigsen, realizing he was, in the words of French officer Henri Jomini, "rushing blindly on to his destruction," immediately ordered his army to withdraw.[124] Napoleon's forces vigorously pursued him, and after a series of rearguard actions, the two sides met near the small town of Preussisch-Eylau, where the Russians drew up a position that stretched from northwest to east behind the town.[125]

The battle commenced on February 7, 1807, when the French attacked the Russian rear guard, commanded by Prince Peter Bagration, who fought his way back through the streets of Eylau as darkness descended. The following morning the massed Russian artillery opened the battle with a bombardment that set Eylau ablaze. A daylong battle, fought in a blizzard, proved to be exceptionally bloody, but the steadfast Russian resistance sapped French attacks and the arrival of the Prussian corps under General Lestocq helped bolster the beleaguered Russians, who held their positions until nightfall.[126] By the end of February 8, the frozen fields around Eylau were covered with tens of thousands of corpses, causing one participant to describe it as "the bloodiest day, the most horrible butchery of men that had taken place since the beginning of the Revolutionary wars."[127] Despite Napoleon's subsequent claims, the Battle of Eylau was far from a great victory, and it is now generally viewed by historians as a costly draw at best, with losses estimated at more than 25,000 Russian casualties and as many as 30,000 French; the exhausted state of the French forces rendered pursuit impossible. Both sides went back into winter quarters to recover from this bloodletting, but with the certain expectation of renewed fighting in the spring.[128]

In late March 1807 Emperor Alexander personally visited his troops in Poland, boosting their morale in expectation of a new campaign. He held military reviews and brought strong reinforcements, including the Russian Imperial Guard.[129] Alexander and Frederick William of Prussia visited Heilsberg, where Bennigsen had constructed strong defensive positions and had concentrated his army.[130] On May 30, Russian headquarters received news of the surrender of Danzig, which allowed Napoleon to divert his forces from the fortress to the Passarge River, where the Russian army was deployed. Ahead of the anticipated French offensive, Bennigsen decided to attack the seemingly isolated VI Corps of Marshal Ney before the main French forces arrived. The Russian plan failed: Ney's 16,000 men succeeded in escaping the superior Russian army because of the tactical skill of the French troops and, more important, ineffectual leadership of the Allied generals, who acted disjointedly, even insubordinately.[131]

Late on June 6 Bennigsen received intelligence that Napoleon was rapidly concentrating his forces for a counterattack, and so he withdrew the Russian army to Heilsberg, where another sanguine but inconclusive battle was fought on June 10. Concerned about Napoleon's possible flanking maneuvers, Russians left the battlefield and retreated to the town of Friedland, on the Alle River.[132] Wearied and in poor health, Bennigsen, who suffered from kidney stones and had passed out from exhaustion during the Battle of Heilsberg, had barely gotten any rest before he was informed about the French outposts appearing in the woods near the town. The fighting rapidly intensified as both sides committed additional forces, and by dawn a major battle was already raging.[133] Upon receiving news of the battle, Napoleon rapidly concentrated his army at Friedland and, noticing how disadvantageous the Russian positions were, made quick adjustments to the French dispositions. Around 5:30 p.m. a salvo of twenty French guns signaled the renewal of the battle.[134] The French attack against the Russian left flank proved to be unstoppable, as the advancing French skillfully employed their artillery to maintain devastating fire at the tightly packed masses of the Russian infantry.[135] By 8:00 p.m., with its flanks threatened, the Russian army had begun to withdraw through the narrow streets of Friedland and across the congested bridges over the Alle River.

Friedland was a decisive military and diplomatic victory for Napoleon. It revealed his ability to quickly size up a situation and exploit the enemy's mistake, tailoring his tactics according to circumstances. The battered

Russian army, which lost some 20,000 killed and wounded, retreated toward the Niemen River, which marked the boundary of the Russian Empire. On June 19, Marshal Murat received Bennigsen's letter seeking an armistice. "After the torrents of blood which have lately flowed in battles as sanguinary as frequent," the letter read, "[Russians] desire to assuage the evils of this destructive war, by proposing an armistice before we enter upon a conflict, a fresh war, perhaps more terrible than the first." The offer was accepted, and Alexander agreed to meet Napoleon to discuss peace. The Russian military defeats would have lain heavily on Alexander's mind as he traveled to this meeting. But so would have his bitterness at Britain, which seemed to be more interested in consolidating its interests in the wider world than in supporting its allies in Europe. Talking to British ambassador Granville Leveson-Gower, Alexander vented his frustration that "the whole burden of the war [had] fallen upon his armies...that hopes had been held out that a British force would be sent to...Germany—month after month however passed, and no troops were even embarked."[136]

The negotiations between Napoleon and Alexander at the end of June 1807 constituted one of the most dramatic episodes of the Napoleonic era. The meeting between the leaders took place in the early afternoon of June 25 on a specially built raft in the Niemen River. The two emperors, accompanied by their retinues, approached the banks of the river and boarded the vessels that were to take them to the raft. As the boats reached the raft, the two emperors embraced each other; it was said that Alexander greeted Napoleon with "Sire, I hate the English as much as you do." To which Napoleon replied, "In that case, the peace is made."[137]

Over the next few days, the two emperors conducted a series of conferences in which they appear to have divided the continent. As if to heighten the drama, Frederick William of Prussia was left on the riverbank, riding anxiously up and down the shore in expectation of the outcome of the meeting, which could determine the future of his entire state. After almost two weeks of meetings, fêtes, and military reviews, on July 7 Alexander and Napoleon concluded the Treaty of Tilsit, one of the most comprehensive treaties of the Napoleonic Wars. The agreement proclaimed an alliance between the French and Russian empires and effectively divided Europe into western and eastern spheres of influence dominated by the respective powers. Alexander gave his formal recognition to the Confederation of the Rhine, firmly establishing Napoleon's control in central Europe while greatly weakening Prussia, which lost the port of Danzig after the Treaty of Tilsit established it as a free city.[138] Russia also recognized the creation of the Kingdom of Westphalia under Napoleon's youngest brother, Jérôme, and accepted the rule of other Bonapartes: Joseph in

Naples and Louis in Holland. In what constituted one of most substantial concessions, the Russian sovereign agreed to the reorganization of the formerly Prussian-controlled Polish lands into the Duchy of Warsaw under formal control of King Frederick Augustus of Saxony, Napoleon's close ally.[139]

The treaty did not stop there. Alexander agreed to offer his services in negotiating peace between France and Britain, and he pledged that if this measure did not produce positive results by the first day of November 1807, he would declare war against Britain and join Napoleon's efforts to eliminate British commerce on the continent; Russia would also force Denmark and Sweden to close their ports to the British and use its naval power against British trade in the Mediterranean. Napoleon led Alexander to believe that in return for these concessions, he was acknowledging Russia's claim to an east European empire. Specifically, Napoleon agreed not to impede Russian ambitions in Swedish-controlled Finland and offered to mediate for peace between Russia and the Ottoman Empire; if the Ottomans refused to negotiate, Napoleon pledged to "make common cause with Russia against the Ottoman Porte" and help Russia expand into the European portion of the Ottoman Empire, with the exception of Constantinople and the province of Rumelia (on the Balkan Peninsula).

Two days after concluding this agreement with Russia, Napoleon signed a separate treaty with Frederick William III, one that was disastrously harsh for Prussia. It effectively eviscerated the Prussian kingdom, forcing it to cede all its lands west of the river Elbe and to accept territorial changes stipulated in the Franco-Russian treaty. This meant forsaking most of the Prussian-controlled Polish lands and the port city of Danzig. These changes resulted in a net loss of half of the Prussian territory, from about 89,000 square miles to just over 46,000 square miles. Prussia was required to formally recognize all of Napoleon's reorganizations in Germany, to enter into a military alliance with France and Russia in the event of war against Britain, and to support the blockade of British goods. A separate military convention reduced the strength of the Prussian army to a minimal force (no more than 42,000 men for ten years) while prohibiting any additional recruitment of militias or guards. On July 12, to add insult to injury, Frederick William was coerced to accept the occupation of all of his remaining territory by French troops pending the payment of a vast war indemnity, which was set at 140 million francs in 1808.

Tilsit marked the culmination of Napoleon's campaigns, which in just two years had reshaped the European balance of power. These wars "inordinately extended the range of Napoleon's enterprises, and so made the French Empire merely the core of the 'Grand Empire' which itself began to evolve," notes the French historian George Lefebvre.[140] Indeed, French hegemony now stretched from the snowy fields of Poland to the rugged Pyrenees and from the sun-swept hills of Calabria to the misty shores of Prussia. For the first time in millennia all of the German-speaking lands were under some degree of French control, either annexed, allied, occupied, or recently defeated.

Returning to Paris in late July, Napoleon was greeted with almost universal public acclaim. The French capital celebrated his birthday with a splendor that evoked Louis XIV's era.[141] The emperor's speech at the opening session of the Legislative Corps was one of his proudest: it spoke of the humiliating defeats of Austria and Prussia, the collapse of the Holy Roman Empire, and a profound territorial and structural reorganization of central Europe. France's "new triumphs and peace treaties have redrawn the political map of Europe," Napoleon informed the legislators.[142] Not since the days of Charlemagne had a ruler exercised such vast power over the continent, deciding the fates of rulers and millions of their subjects.[143] France's triumph over ancien régime Europe was a crucial moment in what German historian Reinhart Koselleck called a *Sattelzeit*, an epochal threshold that marked the transition from the early modern age to modernity, a moment that facilitated the rise of nationalism, modernization, and state creation.[144]

CHAPTER 11 | # "War Through Other Means"
Europe and the Continental System

A S THE RESULT of the French triumphs at Austerlitz, Jena, and Friedland, the mounting economic confrontation between France and Britain acquired such dimensions that it engulfed almost all of continental Europe. As noted elsewhere, the two nations had been engaged in almost continuous conflict since the War of the Grand Alliance (1688–1697) and employed a wide range of restrictions on trade, including tariffs and blockades, against each other as well as against other nations, belligerent or neutral.[1] As the preeminent commercial (and rapidly industrializing) power, Britain understood that seaborne commerce was the lifeblood of much of Europe, including France, and sought to employ it to its advantage by instituting an economic blockade. Napoleon's continued victories made this task progressively more challenging as they brought new territories under French control and expanded the coastline the British needed to guard. While the French were dominant on land but lacked a navy to challenge the British sea power, Britain found itself in a reverse situation, resulting in a military standoff between the two great powers.

Considered by many to be one of Napoleon's biggest mistakes, the Continental System was not as irrational as it is sometimes alleged. It was, at its simplest, "war by other means," to use Prussian military theorist Carl von Clausewitz's famous phrase—an attempt to utilize economic means to resolve existing military/political problems. In this, it represented no more than a continuation of traditional policies that had been attempted in the past, long before Napoleon took power. The dominant economic doctrine of mercantilism held that in order to gain wealth, a country had to take it from another by achieving a more favorable balance of trade. Both Britain and France pursued mercantilist policies and worked aggressively to contain the export trade of their rivals and to promote their own. The long succession of Anglo-French economic and military rivalries was briefly interrupted by the signing of the Eden Treaty (promoting free trade) in 1786, but it was widely believed to be more beneficial to the British, and in any case it was soon rendered irrelevant by the outbreak of the Revolution. With the start of the Revolutionary Wars, both France and Britain not only reverted to their earlier policies of trade control but expanded them to restrict the trade with neutral nations as well.[2] Between 1793 and 1799 Britain implemented a traditional type of naval blockade, obstructing trade at major French ports and closely observing and limiting French maritime activities.[3] France's countermeasures were of limited nature until 1800, when, as discussed in Chapter 6, French diplomacy was able to encourage the establishment of a virtual continental blockade of British trade along much of the European coastline from Norway to southern Italy.

The Treaty of Amiens ended this first continental system. However, it was revived at the start of the Napoleonic Wars, when the belligerent powers

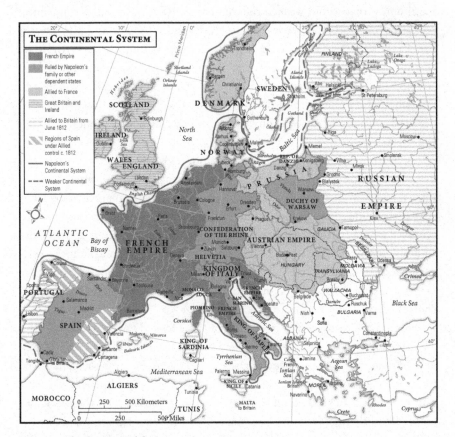

Map 12: The Continental System

began to impose blockades designed to limit trade and constrain naval activities. Britain took the lead in this. When hostilities began, the British seized all French vessels in British ports (May 1803), began to regulate neutral trade with the French colonies (June 1803), established a blockade of the Elbe and Weser Rivers (June-July 1803), and eventually extended it to all French ports along the Atlantic coastline (August 1804).[4] France responded with a similar range of policies, including prohibiting the import of British goods and raising tariffs. These efforts were only partially successful. With so many French ships lying at the bottom of Trafalgar Bay, French colonial ambitions unfulfilled in the Americas, the steady decline of the French merchant marine, and the marked inability of French industrialists to compete successfully with their British counterparts, Napoleon became convinced that only the effective isolation of the British Isles from continental Europe could bring Britain to its knees.[5] He envisioned France uniting the continent behind a barrier past which no British products could pass. The resulting loss of markets would be devastating to the British economy and might cause domestic political and social unrest that would weaken the country. Conversely, by subjecting continental Europe to French economic interests, the system would also greatly benefit the empire. "You should never forget that if English trade triumphs at sea, it is because the British are the strongest there," Napoleon advised his stepson. "So it is fitting, since France is stronger on land, that she will ensure the triumph of her own trade."[6]

Three successive decrees provided the basic structure underlying the Continental System. The first of these, the Berlin Decree of November 21, 1806, was prompted by the British decision, on May 16, 1806, to launch a naval blockade of France's ports and those in French-occupied Europe, spanning the area from Brest to the Elbe River. In response, Napoleon declared that Britain "does not recognize the system of international law universally observed by all civilized nations" and perpetrated a "monstrous abuse of the right of blockade."[7] Therefore he was placing the British islands under a continental blockade that would prevent any ship sailing from Britain from reaching a port of destination in Europe. Any British goods found in French-controlled areas were subject to seizure as prizes.

From the British perspective, the initial blockade approved by Prime Minister Grenville's Whig government was relatively mild because it targeted France but allowed neutral trade to continue. So after the collapse of Grenville's government in March 1807, the new Tory government of William Cavendish-Bentinck, Duke of Portland, sought to strengthen the blockade, especially in the wake of the Chesapeake-Leopard Affair that strained Anglo-American relations, as we'll later see. Starting on November 11, 1807, the

Portland government issued new orders-in-council that were intended to restrict neutral trade with the Napoleonic empire and deprive French-controlled areas of colonial goods (cotton, sugar, coffee, etc.).[8] The orders did allow for a neutral ship to stop in a British port and then sail to a French or allied port with British goods; the neutral trade of the United States was to be limited but not eliminated. Napoleon responded to these new British measures by further tightening the Continental System through two Milan Decrees of November 23 and December 17, 1807. Because the British actions had "denationalized the vessels of all the nations of Europe" and "no government may compromise in any degree its independence or its rights," Napoleon's new decrees targeted neutral ships that stopped at a British port or consented to being searched by British vessels, mandating that they could be seized at sea as lawful prizes when captured by the French or their allies.[9]

The resulting Continental System thus had three interrelated parts: the use of military victory to reduce Britain's economic power through blockade of British goods, the formation of an economic sphere to foster economic development on the continent, and the consolidation of French hegemony on the continent. The terms "Continental Blockade" and "Continental System," which are habitually used as if they are interchangeable, reflect these different intents. The former comprised a wide range of political, economic, and military measures directed against British trade. The latter reflected Napoleon's notion of a new political, institutional, and economic organization for Europe, in which France enjoyed economic preeminence.[10] These two concepts are not identical. The Continental Blockade was an economic policy implemented by a land power that sought to undermine a maritime rival; Napoleon's decrees tacitly admitted British superiority at sea and the French inability to attempt a classical naval blockade British ports. The Continental System, on the other hand, was conceptually about creating new political and economic reality in Europe and involved far greater restructuring on the continent.

By the end of 1807, the basic contours of the Continental System were in place. This was the most important policy initiative that Napoleon had launched as emperor. Although it would survive for just six years, the system served as the cornerstone for Napoleon's policies and had a dramatic effect on the European and Atlantic economies. The prohibition of British goods had been enforced in France since the 1790s, but the system created after 1806 was unparalleled in its scale and scope. It was designed to encompass not only Britain's relations with France but also its interactions with the rest of the European continent. In effect, it sought Europe-wide integration into a new French-dominated economic sphere. Thus, extending control of the European coastline became a crucial element of French foreign policy, causing Napoleon to embark on geopolitical schemes that sought to reshape the continent and consolidate his imperial hegemony. No one was spared in this drive: former adversaries, close allies, and neutral states all found themselves bound to the system. In 1807 Denmark, Prussia, Russia, and Spain joined it, while Austria did so three years later. It was Napoleon's desire to expand and enhance this system that led to his decision to invade Portugal and Spain in 1807–1808, to quarrel with Pope Pius and annex the Papal States in 1809, to take over the Illyrian Provinces in 1809, to extend direct French control to Holland and the Hanseatic cities in 1810, and, most crucially, to go to war against Russia in 1812. It is hard to underestimate the importance of the Continental System in Napoleon's imperial vision for Europe, as well as its role in the eventual collapse of the French Empire.

Though the Napoleonic Empire would turn out to be transient, Napoleon had always had a political vision for the continent. "I wished to found a European system, a European code of laws, a European judiciary. There would be but one people in Europe," he claimed in his exile. But this vision of "the United States of Europe," which was later popularized by generations of authors and writers, should not be construed as an early version of the European Union. It did not entail equality of its members or the creation of an economic union with free trade and unrestricted movement. To the contrary, Napoleon envisioned a tiered economic system that would put the interests of France above all others—"La France avant tout," as he noted—and protect French commerce and industry by reviving old tariffs that constrained the movement of goods.[11] He hoped that French exports would fill the vacuum left by the exclusion of British goods and that French industry would seize this historic opportunity to establish a dominant industrial presence on the continent.[12] Napoleon was little inclined to facilitate the industrial development of other parts of Europe and refused proposals to establish a customs union among the member states of the Confederation of the Rhine (an idea later championed by Prussia in the Zollverein) and made no effort to economically incorporate Italy with the rest of the continent.[13] He was well aware that the Continental System would cause hardship, admitting to his brother Louis that "the blockade will ruin many commercial towns: Lyons, Amsterdam, Rotterdam," and he could have added many other coastal ports to this list.[14] But Napoleon was convinced that short-term hardship would be more than offset by the ultimate demise of the British economy and future economic growth under French economic hegemony.

Another peculiar aspect of the Continental System was that it did not envision the complete economic isolation of Britain. France could not actually impose a blockade to halt British shipping entirely or deny imports from elsewhere into the British Isles. Instead, the aim was to constrain British ability to export manufactured goods and acquire resources that could be used for consumption and production, an approach that one historian compared to a "self-blockade." From an economic point of view, the system resembled more a traditional tariff and quota restrictions than a customary maritime blockade. Indeed, unlike other historical examples of blockades that sought to reduce the enemy's military and economic power by depriving it of critical commodities, Napoleon was quite ready to trade with the "nation of shopkeepers" in order to sell his own goods and to create a balance-of-payments deficit for Britain that would ultimately lead to an outflow of specie, consequently reducing British wealth and productive capacity.[15] Writing to his brother Louis, the King of Holland, in April 1808, Napoleon specified, "If you need to sell your country's *genièvre* [Dutch gin], the English will buy it. Designate locations where the English smugglers can pick it up, and make them pay in money, never in commodities."[16] Reducing the British specie reserve would not only have an impact on Britain's financial health but also, to Napoleon's thinking, weaken its ability to subsidize continental nations' struggle against France.

The French effort to reduce Britain's supply of specie was partly successful, with bullion at the Bank of England declining from £6.9 million in 1808 to just £2.2 million in 1814.[17] The peculiar nature of the French "blockade" was further revealed during the British grain crisis of 1809–1810, when harvest failures resulted in an acute shortage of wheat. Rather than seeking to impose costs by limiting the amount of grain Britain could import, Napoleon encouraged grain export to Britain as a way of generating an increased trade deficit and assisting French farmers; in 1810 almost two-thirds of the wheat imported to Britain came from France.[18]

During its existence, the Continental System therefore produced mixed results. It certainly was not "little more than a theatrical gesture," as one eminent historian assessed it.[19] The system was never simply about blockading the exports of one particular nation, but rather encompassed economic, military, and political policies that were subject to constant changes due to internal and external factors; changing weather conditions and resulting fluctuations in the size of harvests could (and did) affect the success or failure of the blockade. Moreover, the system was not implemented with the same zeal and vigor throughout its existence, and consequently its impact varied greatly depending on year, geographical location, and particular industry. Industries dependent on imports naturally suffered from a lack of access to critical raw materials (especially colonial products), poor land transportation infrastructure, and weak demand from European trading partners, who were also suffering from the effects of prolonged warfare and economic isolation. On the other hand, there were areas that had seen a positive impact from the system. In northern France, Belgium, and southern Germany, some industries (especially textiles) prospered because the blockade protected them from British competition and paved the way for their future industrial growth. In the Kingdom of Italy, agriculture experienced a period of major growth.[20]

The Napoleonic regime was generally business-friendly, and its policies helped create an environment for development: political stability, relatively stable currency, regulation of commercial credit through the Bank of France, favorable tax treatment, and development of infrastructure and communications means. The protectionist nature of the Continental System helped some French industries by increasing domestic consumption of manufactured goods and fostering expansion and mechanization; in the period 1807–1810 the most dynamic sector of French industrial development was cotton spinning.[21] Though French industries had limited success in the rest of the continent (German competition was especially strong), their exports still steadily increased.[22] Even the shortage of raw materials proved to have a silver lining. To compensate for the loss of sugar, coffee, indigo, and other colonial products, the Napoleonic Empire provided incentives for innovations and new development. To replace cotton, Napoleon turned to wool production and sought to expand the number of merino sheep farmed in France. The shortage of indigo prompted research (encouraged by government prizes) into new methods of dyeing wool and silk, which soon resulted in innovations, most notably by Jean Michel Raymond-Latour, professor of chemistry at Lyons, who won a prize for developing new methods for dyeing textiles with Prussian blue.[23] Most famously, Napoleon supported chemical industry (especially the making of soda ash from sea salt according to the Leblanc process) and invested in the cultivation of sugar beets as a replacement for cane sugar from the colonies.[24]

The Continental System existed for just six years, which was not long enough to bring Britain to its knees. Those who argue that Napoleon had failed because British goods were smuggled into the continent on a large scale should be reminded that between July 1807 and July 1808, and again from the spring of 1810 to late 1812, the Continental System was strictly enforced, drastically reducing illicit trading and exerting severe pressure on the British economy. Napoleon's failure lay in his inability to maintain this system rigorously for a sufficiently long period to ensure its success. In this regard, several factors played a particularly important role. First, Napoleon's blunders in Spain and, more important, in Russia delivered decisive blows to the system. Second, British national and economic security was never truly threatened due to the flexibility of the British financial system, which adjusted to the blockade.

Finally, the French navy was not large enough to either threaten British control of the seas or to effectively enforce a blockade capable of excluding British goods from the European continent.

Even more significant to undermining the Continental System was Britain's ability to deny France access to overseas markets and partially compensate for the loss of European markets by increasing sales elsewhere. British merchants seized every opportunity—in Buenos Aires in 1806, in Brazil in 1808, in the Baltic in 1810—to open up new markets. Between 1806 and 1810 exports to South America steadily increased, rising from just 1.8 million pounds to 6 million pounds, and the region would remain an important export market for the British goods for years to come. In 1808 the establishment of the South America Station of the Royal Navy served the dual purpose of protecting the exiled Portuguese monarchy in Brazil and securing British economic interests in the region. Thus British government members literally laughed off the French blockade and questioned the value of Napoleon's policy, which in their eyes "was worth no more than the paper on which it was written. What was the use of talking of blockading Great Britain, when [Napoleon] had scarcely a ship on the ocean to enforce his order? He might as well have talked of blockading the moon, and possessing himself of all the lunar influence."[25]

Yet we should not be as cavalier in underestimating the Continental System's impact on Britain, as it was partly successful in its central goal of causing economic hardship. Continental Europe accounted for 40 percent of Britain's total exports, and the loss of this important market had serious repercussions for British industry and commerce. By 1810–1811 Britain faced a crisis that was compounded by bad harvests and the government's discordant policy toward the United States, a policy that hurt British interests in North America. The worst period for British economy occurred when both Europe and the United States were closed to British exports. In 1811–1812 a depression struck British industry, resulting in high unemployment and hardship. How critical the economic situation was in 1812 can be glimpsed in the major campaign by provincial economic interests for the repeal of the orders-in-council.[26]

Similarly, the traditional claim that British commerce successfully replaced the European market with the Latin American market belies the fact that one of the factors in the 1810–1811 economic crisis was large-scale British speculation in the newly opened Portuguese and Spanish colonies. With European markets closed, many British entrepreneurs, despite lacking trading and financial knowledge of Latin America, rushed to make massive and mostly unprofitable exports to Brazil and Spanish colonies. As these business ventures failed, a financial crisis hit the very heart of the British economy. In July

1810 Brickwood & Co., one of the leading banks in London, collapsed with debts of over £600,000 due to the failure of its merchant clients in the Western Hemisphere. The public shock at the loss of a bank that was, in the words of a contemporary British observer, "as solid a house as any one in the City" was augmented by the bankruptcy later that month of another London bank, Devaynes, Noble and Co., regarded as one of the "West End" or premier banking institutions.[27] Bank failures naturally caused subsequent damage to their merchant clients, causing many of them to collapse (most notably John Leigh and Co., one of the leading British transatlantic trade companies) or suffer from acute credit contraction.[28] Growing hostilities with the United States and the strangling of British exports by the Non-Importation Act added yet another layer of complexity.

Ultimately, the causes of the Continental System's failure were deeply rooted in its internal contradictions. The fact was that it was impossible to prevent British goods from reaching European markets because they were highly sought after and France was simply incapable of replacing them. Furthermore, Napoleon's policies naturally provoked much resentment and anger from those who were forced to endure it. The economies of many previously prosperous areas, especially the great commercial centers in Holland and the Hanseatic cities, suffered heavily under the blockade. The initial effect of the system was to run up prices on sugar, indigo, tobacco, chocolate, cotton, and other colonial products. Businesses dependent on overseas trade were nearly wiped out, and bankruptcies of merchant and shipping companies, as well as manufacturing enterprises, were rampant across the French Empire and its satellites. To satisfy demands for manufactured and colonial goods, many Europeans encouraged smuggling, undermining the system. Even members of the imperial family participated in it, with Louis Bonaparte largely ignoring his brother's dictates when it came to the Kingdom of Holland and Murat oftentimes turning a blind eye to smuggling in Naples. That Empress Josephine herself bought smuggled goods on the black market only further highlighted the nature of the problem.

Smuggling was done on a continental scale, with contraband centers emerging at key locations along European coastline. Thus the Danish archipelago Heligoland served as a major transit point for contraband destined for northern European ports, while the Ottoman Thessaloniki served as an entrepôt for southeast Europe; in 1809 alone, Britain exported more than £10 million worth of goods to southern Europe, almost four times as much as just three years earlier, while its exports to northern Europe were at the highest point since the start of the war.[29] By 1811, with British blessing, more than eight hundred vessels were engaged in smuggling operations between Malta and southern Mediterranean ports.[30] Although Napoleon formed a vast network of customs officers to supervise trade at continental ports, endemic corruption encouraged them to turn a blind eye to the contraband. In an ingenious ploy to circumvent the blockade, English vessels loaded with forbidden merchandise were sent out by arrangement to be captured by French privateers and taken into a French-controlled port whose commanding officer sold the goods at a profit. While deployed in Naples, Marshal André Masséna made a lucrative business out of such trade, though this came to Napoleon's ears and he confiscated some 3 million francs of the marshal's profit.[31] Napoleon tried to stamp out corrupt administrators by replacing them with his personal choices, creating a new customs court, and increasing penalties, but these changes rarely produced meaningful results. Instead, French imperial customs revenues declined from 51 million francs in 1806 to less than 12 million in 1809.[32]

Despite Napoleon's best efforts to suppress it, smuggling reached such magnitude that the emperor had no choice but to become personally involved.[33] In 1810–1811 he softened some aspects of the Continental System, with the Saint-Cloud Decrees (July 1810) allowing specially licensed ships to trade with Britain in exchange for the payment of a fee, effectively providing a legal cover for the already existing smuggling operations; the Decree of Trianon (August 1810) permitted the importation of strategic commodities upon payment of tariffs as high as 50 percent. Napoleon thus undermined the very system he had created to combat his British nemesis, because blockading British commerce was clearly incompatible with admitting British goods (even if only colonial produce). The new decrees meant that the object was no longer to exclude British goods but to resort to conventional tariff mechanisms to produce revenue, which in turn continued to benefit British manufacturers.

In sum, the Continental System proved to be more detrimental than advantageous to the Napoleonic Empire. It fostered the development of a "hothouse" economy that relied heavily upon the resources of the conquered territories but offered little incentive for technological development, despite the best efforts of the Napoleonic regime.[34] The loss of neutral and overseas trade was damaging to France's great port towns, including Nantes, Bordeaux, and La Rochelle, which had flourished on colonial trade but after the implementation of the Colonial System saw their commerce virtually dry up. In March 1808 the American consul at Bordeaux reported, "Grass is growing in the streets of this city; its beautiful port is deserted except by two...schooners and three or four empty vessels which still swing to the tide."[35] Tonneins, a small town east of Bordeaux, employed two hundred rope makers in 1801 and none ten years later, while the number of sugar refineries in Bordeaux dropped from forty in 1789 to just eight in 1809.[36] The licensing system that Napoleon introduced in later years was of limited success because licenses were costly, bureaucratically complicated, and conducive to corruption.[37]

Nor was the Continental System beneficial to French industry. The cotton industry, which did enjoy a fast expansion when it was sheltered from the British competition in the first three years of the blockade, ultimately could not escape the irremediable challenge of the blockade: an insufficient supply of raw cotton.[38] The French wool and silk industries, which also experienced short-term gains, later suffered from trade dislocations; by 1809, for example, Rheims lost its most important markets for woolens in Spain and Portugal because of the ongoing war there.[39] French silk manufacturers in the Rhône, Isère, and Lyons were hurt not only by a poor harvest of silkworm cocoons in 1810–1811 but also by the market dislocation caused by war.[40] The creation of special councils for manufactures and commerce was an important step toward addressing the serious problems facing French commerce and industry. Still, they had little influence over the economic policy and produced meager results, instead fostering a sense of disillusionment and resentment toward the imperial regime.[41]

The crisis of 1810–1811 was therefore the culmination of a long list of problems fostered by the blockade. In Paris, the number of bankruptcies reached a record high—more than sixty—in January 1811, while more than two-thirds of 1,700 textile enterprises stopped operating and laid off their workers. The burden of empire had stretched the French economy to the breaking point, and in the coming years, when France's military fortunes waned, so did the Continental System.

The situation was even more dire in the rest of Europe. Merchants and manufacturers faced shortages of raw materials, which they either had to buy at prohibitive prices sanctioned by imperial tariffs or try to smuggle, which was both risky and costly. Furthermore, unlike their French counterparts, European merchants and manufacturers could not fully access markets in some parts of Europe, where Napoleon restricted local manufacturing capacity and established a tariff system to the benefit of French commerce and industry. Thus Italian maritime trade came to a virtual standstill, and some Italian industries—tanneries, tobacco factories, corn mills, distilleries, breweries, glassworks, cotton printing, and the silk and linen industries—came close to collapsing. In the Kingdom of Naples, Murat struggled to impose the blockade, unable to overcome corruption, passive resistance to the new central administration, and incessant guerrilla outbreaks in regions such as Calabria. Even the mild version of the Continental System introduced by the

Dutch king, Louis Bonaparte, proved to be devastating for Holland, which lived almost entirely by trade. The Continental System also had a disastrous effect on northern German states, where its effects combined with Napoleon's continued demands for contributions to sustain his forces. In the Iberian Peninsula, the industrial progress that Portugal had achieved in the late eighteenth century was all but lost in 1808; by the end of the Napoleonic Wars, one-third of Portuguese establishments were closed or in a state of utter decay. Far worse was the impact in Spain, where the loss of the colonial empire and the desolation caused by the war destroyed any remaining vestiges of the industrial revival achieved during the preceding decades. Even in faraway Norway, the Continental System brought about a sharp decline in the timber and iron industries.

The Continental System contributed to profound trade dislocations, a major shift of capital from trade and industry toward agriculture, and deindustrialization of some areas of Europe, which had already experienced social anxiety, loss of manpower, and capital destruction due to the wars and the upheavals they brought about. The system also caused the permanent decline of some industries and slowed the progress of others, as it isolated much of continental Europe from active interaction with Britain and hindered the flow of new technologies and methods. Even in France, which enjoyed the most preferential treatment in the system, the combined volume of industrial production at the height of the empire was not much higher than in the twilight of the Bourbon monarchy, while some parts of France experienced what the French historian François Crouzet called a process of pastoralization from which they never really recovered.[42] The protective barrier put in place by the Continental System did not last long enough to allow for the maturation of continental industries, and so when the peace was restored in 1814–1815, the removal of tariffs and opening of markets produced an acute economic crisis, as these industries were hit hard by British competitors. As a whole, the continental powers lost economic ground to Britain, and about a twenty-year lag in technological development persisted for some time after the Napoleonic Wars ended. It would not be until the end of the century that British factories and mills would encounter viable competitors.[43]

One of the most enduring legacies of the Continental System was the shift in the location of continental industries. In the eighteenth century the European economy was geared to overseas markets, and important industries tended to congregate in seaboard districts to exploit vibrant maritime trade. After 1815 the center of the continental economy shifted away from the Atlantic seaboard toward the Rhine, as many industries turned inward and reoriented themselves toward national markets. The economic reorganization asked of European states was enormous, matched only by the resentment it produced against the system and its originator. Contemplating what was necessary to satisfy Napoleon's demands, one German writer wondered how any nation could simply close its ports, abandon its foreign trade, and treat all those residing on the coasts as criminals because, having no other sustenance, they engaged in smuggling. Yet "such are the sacrifices, which Napoleon would exact...for an indefinite term, without holding out the hope of any other return than, now and then, a majestic token of approbation. So revolting are these pretensions that...a sense of national dignity alone, ought, at once, to determine their rejection."[44] The economic distress was one of the crucial causes of the nationalistic revival that eventually ended Napoleon's dream of complete European domination. Across the continent, people blamed the system for creating shortages, forcing up prices, and contributing to overall social misery. This burning sense of bitterness and anger at being exploited for the benefit of a foreign ruler was both profound and justified. It helped radicalize public opinion in many parts of Europe and made Britain's economic ascendancy, which had been equally resented, seem a less oppressive, if not preferable, alternative.

In enforcing their economic policies, Britain and France both pursued an "either you're with us or against us" approach. They trampled the rights of neutral nations, tried to control their trade, and made neutral vessels fair prizes. These policies soon brought about a significant response by the largest of the neutral powers, the United States of America. I will discuss the details of the American response more fully later, but suffice it to state here that American displeasure with the Anglo-French policies resulted in the Embargo Act, which was passed by Congress and signed by President Jefferson in 1807. Directed against trade with both belligerent powers, it ultimately contributed to a war between the United States and Britain.

Meanwhile, back in Europe, Napoleon's policies toward the hitherto neutral nations produced important results. To ensure that the continent remained united in cordoning off British commerce, Napoleon needed to control the entire coastline, which he recognized early on would be an enormous challenge. The Treaties of Tilsit helped France to consolidate control over northern Germany and to extend the blockade to Russia's Baltic coastlines. Napoleon next turned to minor states, pressuring them to join the system and enforce the blockade against Britain: the Confederation of the Rhine joined by the fall of 1807, while the Papal States, despite initial protests, signed on in December. If states proved unwilling to enforce the system, the emperor did not hesitate to cajole and/or threaten them; the north German territories—Hamburg, Lübeck, Bremen, and the Duchy of

Oldenburg—were ultimately incorporated into France in order to tighten the blockade. Napoleon's own family members were not spared, as revealed by his spat with his brother Louis, King of Holland, who was ultimately removed from the throne while his kingdom annexed to France. Most sequential of all was Portugal's refusal to embrace Napoleon's economic policies, as it resulted in the French invasion that marked the start of the Peninsular War.

CHAPTER 12 | The Struggle for Portugal and Spain, 1807–1812

IN THE SUMMER OF 1807 Napoleon informed the Bragança monarchy of Portugal that it must close its ports to British commerce. Portugal thus faced an intolerable dilemma. It was naturally reluctant to join the French-led Continental Blockade, which would jeopardize its colonial holdings (Brazil in particular) and commercial prosperity. Yet defying Napoleon would mean a French invasion, occupation, and loss of overseas trade. In either case Portugal would face immense harm, if not ruin.

Closely allied to Britain since 1373, Portugal became a virtual part of Britain's informal empire in 1703 when the Treaty of Methuen opened Portuguese markets to British textiles in exchange for a privileged position for Portuguese port wine on the British market. Over the next century British trade so came to dominate Portugal that beneath the veneer of cooperation and trade lurked genuine Portuguese fears of British commercial hegemony. Thus in the mid-eighteenth century Sebastião José de Carvalho e Melo, marqués de Pombal, initiated a series of major reforms to revive the Portuguese economy and control the flow of British goods without breaking the valuable Anglo-Portuguese alliance. Pombal pursued a vigorous colonial policy, one that sought to increase mining taxes and establish protective barriers for Portuguese commerce and manufacturing by keeping the British out of the colonial markets.[1] The Pombaline reforms represented "defensive modernization," as some historians described them, and sought to increase state revenue in order to finance Portuguese industrialization, which would in turn free Portugal from British tutelage.[2]

However, their effect proved quite different. Colonists resented the new system of taxation, while affected local and foreign merchants reacted bitterly

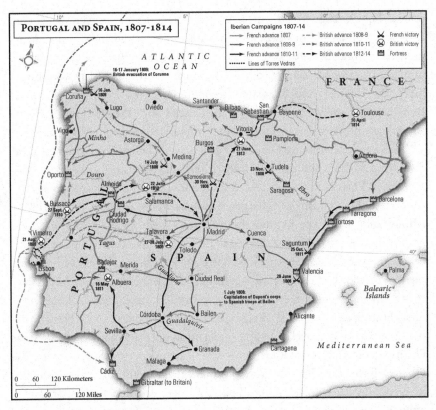

Map 13: Portugal and Spain, 1807–1814

to the creation of Portuguese monopoly companies. Though after Pombal's fall in 1777 his successors abandoned many of his economic policies, their own policies still increased tensions within Portuguese economic and administrative circles and caused considerable discontent in Brazil. In 1789 the first in a series of uprisings, the Inconfidência Mineira, saw the magnates of Minas Gerais (in southeastern Brazil) embracing nativist sentiments and seeking to create an independent state. The Portuguese authorities suppressed this revolt, but a more powerful factor in reducing the colonists' thirst for independence was the outbreak of revolutionary turmoil in France and the Caribbean colonies. In 1798 the failed revolt of the Bahia mulattoes, whose aim was not only to establish a separate state but to level the society so that, in the words of the rebel leader João de Deos, "all Brazilians would become Frenchmen...to live in equality and abundance," played a decisive role in abating well-to-do Brazilians' desire for change.[3] In a slave-based plantation society, a political change could easily turn into a social revolution. Although these uprisings failed, they did bring about changes in Portugal's colonial policy. The Portuguese crown's new, more liberal policies were welcomed in Brazil but faced considerable criticism at home, where the merchant-industrial oligarchy refused to accept the federative project proposed by the minister of colonial affairs, Rodrigo de Souza Coutinho, which would have given the colonists much greater freedom. However, by 1807 almost all Brazilian ports showed a favorable trade balance with the metropolis, gradually relegating Portugal to a secondary position in the colonial system.[4]

The execution of King Louis XVI of France in January 1793 caused great dismay in Lisbon but did not lead to outright rupture between the two nations, as Portugal still considered it desirable to maintain diplomatic relations with France. But the Bragança monarchy found itself pressured by Britain and Spain into joining the military expedition to invade southern France in late 1794. When Portugal took up arms against France, which never posed an immediate threat to Portuguese territory, it was the first time the two nations had gone to war against each other, and it marked a distinct change in Portuguese policy, one that proved to have great consequences. First, Luso-Spanish military campaign resulted in a defeat—the French won the "War in the Pyrenees" in 1795—and created a diplomatic quandary that Portugal could not escape for more than a decade. After Spain signed the Peace of Basle with France, Portugal found itself having to choose between its erstwhile allies: Spain, now allied to France, declared war on Britain in 1796, placing Portugal's national security in greater danger than at any other moment since the Restoration War (1640–1668).[5] Long at odds with its more powerful neighbor, Portugal historically preferred alliance with Britain but sought to avoid further entanglement in the conflict by announcing its neutrality and declaring Lisbon a free port in 1796.[6] Portugal's decision failed to satisfy either Madrid or Paris. The former accused its neighbor of providing support for British warships (which often victualed in Portuguese waters) while they were targeting Spanish shipping. France, noting that the Portuguese government had been the first to declare war and had not negotiated peace at Basle, exploited the existing state of war to target Portuguese commerce, which suffered considerably from French privateers.[7] Furthermore, the French Directory demanded that Portugal close its ports to the British, something that Lisbon—so heavily dependent on maritime trade, especially in wheat—could not accept.

We saw earlier how Bonaparte, continuing the Directory's policy, sought to uphold a blockade of British commerce. In November 1800 he confided to his brother that "the greatest damage we could inflict upon English commerce would be to seize upon Portugal."[8] Napoleon believed that Portugal was Britain's Achilles heel. Thus France orchestrated a Spanish invasion in

1801, and in the ensuing War of Oranges, Portugal was defeated and forced to cede the province of Olivenza to Spain, close its ports to Britain, and pay a war indemnity to France. Portugal accepted the Madrid agreement with France in September 1801, and the new French ambassador, General Jean Lannes, arrived in Lisbon in the spring of 1802, just as France and Britain concluded the Treaty of Amiens. The Anglo-French amity rapidly deteriorated, of course, making life difficult for Dom João (John), the Portuguese prince regent who governed on behalf of his incapacitated mother and tried to remain neutral in this new European conflict. For six years, exploiting Portugal's relative geographic isolation, João maintained political neutrality despite the efforts of British and French diplomats. In 1802–1803 he came under heavy pressure from the French ambassador, who denounced the presence of royalist émigrés in Lisbon and sought to limit British influence at the Bragança court.

A talented officer, Lannes lacked diplomatic finesse and acted, in the words of his biographer, like a "military bull in a diplomatic china shop."[9] He became involved in a "vitriolic diplomatic pas-de-deux" with the British ambassador, Lord Robert Fitzgerald, and clashed repeatedly with members of the Portuguese government, raising the diplomatic stakes by forcefully demanding their dismissal.[10] When war resumed between France and Britain in May 1803, Lannes demanded that the prince regent sign a treaty of alliance with France, closing Portuguese ports to British commerce and paying a substantial subsidy to France. Heavy as this demand was, Dom João might have considered it if not for Fitzgerald's warning that any such payment would be considered by London as a hostile act. To appease the French, the prince regent dismissed several ministers known to be pro-British, declared neutrality, and accepted the new Franco-Portuguese treaty (March 1804), granting generous commercial favors to the French imports and promising to pay a $16 million subsidy to France for its guarantee of neutrality.[11]

Over the next two years the Portuguese monarchy watched with apprehension as the Anglo-French conflict spilled across the continent. The destruction of the Franco-Spanish fleet at Trafalgar secured Britain's dominance of the seas, while Napoleon's triumphs at Austerlitz, Jena, and Friedland made France's hegemony on the continent indisputable. Portugal continued to maintain its neutrality but irritated the French emperor by permitting ships of the Royal Navy to use the Tagus estuary, near Lisbon, for provisioning. In early 1805 the French foreign ministry prepared a diplomatic mission (led by General Andoche Junot) to Lisbon with the overt goal of breaking Portugal's relations with Britain and creating a new political reality that would have been more suitable for French interests in the peninsula.[12] Junot's mission failed, and Napoleon's designs toward Portugal now took a more definite form. He considered it imperative to bring Portugal under his control to close the last remaining gap in the Continental System.[13] Equally important, however, was Napoleon's desire to replenish the war-scarred French navy with warships from the Iberian nations; Portugal may have had a small navy, but its warships were of excellent quality. As one of the leading historians of the Napoleonic navy pointed out, "In nearly every order issued to the commander of the invasion of Portugal, General Jean-Andoche Junot, Napoleon stressed the need to secure the Portuguese fleet."[14]

On July 19, 1807, the French government formally issued the following demands to the Portuguese government: close its ports to British trade, confiscate all British goods, arrest all British subjects on its territory, join its fleet to the French, and declare war on Britain. The official notification was accompanied by the threat of force in case of refusal.[15] On August 12, 1807, as the Portuguese monarchy vacillated, a French envoy delivered an ultimatum stating in part that "the liberties taken by the English government constitute a veritable outrage against [Portuguese] independence." If Napoleon had tolerated Portugal's relations with Britain before, he was now intent on declaring that "if Portugal should suffer any longer the oppression of which she is the victim, he would have to consider this as the renunciation of all sovereignty and independence." The Portuguese crown thus had to accede to France's demands or face the consequences.[16] France's requirements naturally frightened Dom João and his ministers, who complained that it was unjust to require Portugal, which had steadfastly observed neutrality, to declare war upon an ally against whom it had no complaint and whose support was indispensable both economically and militarily.[17] The Portuguese played for time, but their failure to provide a direct response caused the French envoy to quit Lisbon by October 1.[18]

Throughout September and October, the Portuguese monarchy had found itself between a Scylla and Charybdis: whether to pursue a policy of French appeasement or adhere to its alliance with Britain. Neither option promised peace and stability; both would embroil Portugal in a conflict. In the words of British historian Alan Manchester, the Bragança monarchy was "caught like a shellfish in a tempest between the waves of England's sea power and the rock of Napoleon's armies."[19] Furthermore, the shadow of a possible reunification with Spain also hovered in the air, as it was clear that Spanish minister Godoy's policy sought to secure a free hand in the peninsula and possibly to rebuild the Iberian unity lost in 1640. The Portuguese decision-making was greatly hampered by the struggle between a pro-British faction led by Rodrigo de Souza Coutinho and a Francophile faction of Portugal's chief minister, Antonio d'Araujo e Azevedo. The prince regent tried to steer a middle course but, in the words of an eminent Portuguese scholar, he was "characterized by indecision, fear, and awkwardness, influenced only by whims and pressures from favorites."[20]

Britain was well aware of the threat to the sovereignty of its Portuguese ally. Foreign Secretary George Canning had dispatched diplomat Percy Clinton Sydney Smythe, Viscount Strangford, to Lisbon to urge the Portuguese prince regent to hold fast to the English alliance, and then conducted negotiations with the Portuguese ambassador in London that culminated in the conclusion of a secret convention of friendship and alliance. The treaty specified that if the Portuguese regent was forced by the French to leave his state, the British government would facilitate his departure to Brazil; once established there, the Portuguese government would negotiate a further agreement with Britain concerning aid and commerce.[21]

Dom João hesitated to ratify the treaty, still nurturing a hope that war with France could be avoided. He sought to appease Napoleon by making gradual concessions to his demands, and on November 8, in a frantic effort to safeguard his kingdom, Dom João even declared war on the British and ordered the sequestering of British property.[22] A week later a British squadron, commanded by Rear Admiral Sidney Smith, arrived off Lisbon and proceeded to institute a blockade of the Lisbon harbor "so long as the present state of misunderstanding exists."[23]

The Portuguese concessions to the French were of no avail. Unbeknownst to them, on October 27, 1807, France and Spain had signed a secret treaty at Fontainebleau agreeing on the invasion and military occupation of Portugal, which would be subsequently split up into three parts.[24] The country's southeastern provinces of Alentejo and Algarve were assigned to Godoy, who had long desired his own personal fiefdom; the central regions, from Douro to the Tagus, would be placed under military rule until the end of the war; northern Portugal was to be transferred as compensation to the king of Etruria, a minor Italian potentate whose territory Napoleon wanted to annex in an effort to secure complete domination in Italy.[25]

On October 18, 1807, ten days before the treaty at Fontainebleau was finalized, General Andoche Junot, a close associate of Napoleon—he had first taken note of the young officer at Toulon in 1793—led his Army of Portugal into Spain and began his march to Lisbon.[26] The French were initially well received by the Spaniards, whose goodwill enabled them to quickly progress across the peninsula.[27] On November 23, as his troops approached the Portuguese border, Napoleon announced the dethronement of the Braganças and the impending French invasion of Portugal.[28] The news forced the prince regent to cast his die. The next day, November 24, Dom João and his ministers finally decided to implement the Brazil option, starting the evacuation of the entire Portuguese government and court. In a remarkable logistical achievement, the Portuguese prepared the embarkation of some fifteen thousand evacuees in just five days, loading personal possessions, government records, works of art, and the contents of the royal treasury onto Portuguese ships anchored in the Tagus.[29] The evacuation was completed on November 29 when the Portuguese fleet, under protection of the British squadron, embarked on a long journey across the Atlantic.[30] The following day, the French troops entered Lisbon.[31]

The French occupation of Portugal faced only feeble Portuguese resistance, partly due to the lack of central leadership and partly due to the reputation of the French armies. Except for a brief riot that broke out in mid-December, when the French organized a ceremony to replace the Portuguese flag with the tricolor, both civil and the military authorities submitted to Junot's orders.[32] This was nonetheless a somewhat hollow victory for Napoleon, who had sent repeated orders to Junot to get to Lisbon as soon as possible.[33] The French did take the Portuguese capital, but the great prize—the Portuguese government, state treasures, and fleet—had escaped; in fact, the French occupation of Lisbon strengthened the British presence in the waters off the coast of Portugal since, under the terms of an Anglo-Portuguese treaty, the British occupied the islands of Madeira and Azores and turned them into bases of operations.[34] Still, the fall of Lisbon was a success because it achieved the termination of trade between the British and Portuguese home ports. Napoleon had effectively shut every major port in Europe (except those of Sweden) to British trade. The French quickly moved to consolidate their authority, reminding the Portuguese that their government had abandoned them and warning them against resisting the occupation.[35] Although a five-men regency council was set up by the Portuguese government, Junot quickly moved to oust it and ruled the country as a conquered territory subject to a military occupation. New imperial instructions ordered Junot to disarm Portugal and to send the Portuguese troops to France along with "all princes, ministers and other men who might serve as rallying points for resistance."[36] The Portuguese army was partly demobilized and partly converted unto a special legion that was first sent to Spain before being deployed elsewhere to fight under the French banner. Many nobles and key officials were removed to France under various pretexts. The French then proceeded to levy an extortionate tax of 100 million francs on the kingdom.[37]

The crisis of 1807 was a watershed event in Portuguese history. Portugal's personal and public wealth, most of its political leaders, and virtually all of the country's maritime strength were drained out. The departure of the royal court, which would remain in Brazil for thirteen years, marked the demise of Portugal's ancien régime and a transatlantic shift of profound political, cultural, and economic consequences. For the first time, a ruling European royal house established itself in overseas colonies, highlighting the crucial role colonial holdings played in the life of the metropole. Upon its arrival in Brazil in January 1808, the royal family was greeted with an enthusiastic welcome by its colonial subjects in Bahia. One of the first orders of business that Dom João addressed was the inability of Brazilian merchants to export their goods due to the French capture of Lisbon and Oporto. On January 28 the prince regent announced his decision to open the ports of Brazil to commerce with other nations, a decision that, in hindsight, turned out to be the first step toward Brazil's independence. The substantial British financial and material aid to Portugal meant that from 1808 to 1821, in the words of Portuguese historian A. H. de Oliveira Marques, the country turned into an "English protectorate."[38]

The French invasion of Portugal had depended on Spanish cooperation. This swift and practically bloodless conquest suggested that the French would face but minor difficulties in establishing control in the Iberian Peninsula. To understand what happened next, it is necessary to consider how weak Spain's position actually was at the start of the nineteenth century.

The great epoch of Spanish revival and reform largely ended with the death of King Charles III in 1788.[39] Historians tend to agree that the Spanish monarchy struggled in its efforts to modernize and nationalize, and the thirty years or so after the passing of Charles III constituted the most decisive period in the history of modern Spain since the era of discoveries and conquests in the Americas in the sixteenth century. The new king, Charles IV, though rich in good intentions, lacked the necessary intellect and willpower to build on his father's legacy and govern effectively. Censuses showed that some 27 million people resided in the Spanish Empire, with 10 million of them residing in Spain itself. The remaining 17 million inhabitants of the Spanish colonies enjoyed unprecedented prosperity that was the result of relaxation of commercial restrictions under Charles III.[40] The comparative prosperity of the earlier reign, however, had given way to an economic stagnation that was exacerbated by failures in foreign policy. At war with France in 1793–1795, Spain reversed its position in 1796 when it joined France's war against Britain. The results of this decision, however, were the opposite of those anticipated by Charles IV and his ministers. The first naval battle of the war, fought near Cape St. Vincent in 1797, was a decisive victory for the British over a larger Spanish fleet, and resulted in a tight blockade of Spanish ports and the harassment of Spanish trade. The Bourbon monarchy found itself so hamstrung that it was compelled to reverse its long-standing policy and grant unprecedented permission for neutral vessels to trade with Spanish ports in the Americas, a move that largely benefited the United States and Britain.[41] Alliance with France had cost Spain the loss of Trinidad, while Spanish colonies that were not actually seized by Britain began to edge toward independence because of strained contacts across the Atlantic. The lull in the war in 1802–1803 brought Spain some respite and allowed Madrid to briefly reassert its authority in the colonies. The renewal of the war in 1804 brought only new disasters. The Battle of Trafalgar finished off what had begun at Cape St. Vincent, with Spain all but eliminated as a serious maritime power. Throughout these years the Bourbon kingdom had gone to every length in its efforts to appease its demanding ally—transferring parts of its empire, furnishing considerable subsidies, ships, and troops—while enjoying little if any benefit in return. Not surprisingly, after 1805 Spain showed signs of wanting to break free of the heavy-handed French embrace.

Despite maintaining the appearance of an absolute monarch, King Charles IV left government responsibilities to his ministers—José Moñino y Redondo, conde de Floridablanca, Don Pedro Pablo Abarca de Bolea y Jiménez de Urrea, conde de Aranda, and Manuel de Godoy y Alvarez de Faria, encountered earlier—who had struggled to resolve Spain's growing economic, social, and political problems. Their effort to strengthen the monarchy's authority and reform privileged corporations (the church, the nobility) caused much resentment and social unrest, which only undermined the reform movement.[42] The Spanish nobility and the church, which together owned almost two-thirds of the land, showed little interest in agrarian improvements, leaving Spanish agriculture to suffer from low productivity. Military setbacks had caused much economic stagnation, which was further compounded by a series of natural disasters.[43] Some ten thousand people perished when a newly constructed dam on the Segura River burst in April 1802. Just two years later, a major earthquake shook south and central Spain, causing considerable damage. The outbreak of a yellow fever epidemic was worsened by unseasonable weather and harvest failures that in turn caused social discontent.[44]

Public bitterness focused on the person of Manuel de Godoy, the Spanish prime minister, as we have seen. A scion of the petty nobility who had made a remarkable career at the Spanish court and was rumored to have been the queen's lover, Godoy was generally seen as narcissistic, venal, and corrupt. While he considered himself a man of the Enlightenment and tried to sustain limited reforms, this won him little support from the nobility, the church, or old royal officialdom, which resented his meteoric rise to power and the influence that he wielded over the monarchy. For many ordinary Spaniards, Godoy's insistence on dead bodies being interred in new municipal cemeteries (instead of traditional church ones) and his prohibition of bullfighting (because it was ostensibly economically wasteful and a threat to public order) went one step too far. Popular mistrust was fueled by the reality that Godoy had neither an adequate education nor political or administrative experience and committed his share of missteps that seriously harmed the Spanish kingdom and made it subordinate to French interests. In 1806, during Napoleon's campaign against Prussia, Godoy came to believe that the Prussians would win, and he made a blundering effort to assert Spain's sovereignty by launching military preparations and calling upon the Spaniards to rouse themselves for military service to defeat an "enemy" and thereby save the country through a lasting peace; the "enemy" was not named, but everyone assumed it to be France.[45]

A faint hope that Spain would turn against its French ally flickered to life, only to be extinguished by the French triumph at Jena-Auerstadt just nine days later. Godoy was forced into a swift and humiliating volte-face: he withdrew his proclamation, agreed to join the Continental System, and dispatched some of the best Spanish troops to the Baltic region. Even so, the imbroglio reinforced Napoleon's loathing of Godoy and reminded him that the weak Bourbon leadership could harm his interests by reducing the value of Spain as an ally.[46] More important, Spain's chief minister struggled to deal with two warring parties—the liberals, who insisted on further reforms, and their conservative opponents, led by the heir apparent, Prince Ferdinand. Ferdinand despised Godoy, whom he suspected of seeking to become the next king of Spain. Powerful elements in the church and aristocracy had used the dull and malleable crown prince to oppose Bourbon attempts at reform and hoped that Godoy's rise to the Spanish throne would shore up their privileged status.[47]

By the late fall of 1807 matters had reached a crisis point in Spain. Public disillusionment became ubiquitous, as the government's economic, administrative, and military policies had alienated so many. The Spanish royal army was poorly equipped and trained, with the best of its soldiers on their way to northern Germany. Continued court intrigues only further complicated the situation and served as a crucial backdrop to the French intervention. The supporters of Prince Ferdinand, known as the *grupo fernandino*, hoped to exploit the current turmoil to ensure the succession of their figurehead. Some of them became involved in secret negotiations with the French ambassador, while

Prince Ferdinand himself appealed to Napoleon for protection and wrote obsequious letters to Paris. Ferdinand's schemes were vague and futile, largely limited to denunciations of the hated "Prince of the Peace" (Príncipe de la Paz), as Godoy had been styled ever since negotiating a peace treaty with France in 1795. But rumors of possible conspiracy spurred Godoy to action. On October 27, after a dramatic confrontation at the royal palace of El Escorial, Charles IV accused his son of having plotted to dethrone him and to murder his mother and Godoy.[48] A search of the princely apartments uncovered only drafts of a manifesto denouncing Godoy's influence and papers indicating that the prince had considered possible scenarios in the case of his father's death or permanent incapacity. This was enough, however, to convince Charles to place his son under arrest and imprison his alleged co-conspirators.[49] This episode, known as the Escorial affair, boosted Ferdinand's popularity while further undermining the position of Godoy, who was widely believed to have been behind this effort to discredit the prince. Probably nothing could have suited Napoleon's design better than the scandalous revelations of domestic quarrels within the royal family. The Escorial affair demonstrated the weakness of the Spanish monarchy and played an important part in Napoleon's subsequent decision to intervene. Observing events in Spain, he came to believe that the Bourbon government was incompetent and corrupt, a realization that, in the words of historian Pieter Geyl, would have "offended Napoleon in what one might call his professional self-respect."[50] The emperor was convinced that what Spain truly needed was the strong and efficient hand of France.

However, the roots of this thinking went deeper. Napoleon's foreign policy borrowed many elements from the ancien régime, and when it came to Spain, as one Spanish observer justly noted, it drew inspirations from "the foreign policy of Louis XIV, and, in particular, his attempts to harness the Spanish nation to the wagon of his fortune."[51] Spain had much to offer in terms of money, resources, and manpower. Napoleon was well aware of this potential because of the scale of the transatlantic commerce with Spanish America. During the Peace of Amiens, as noted, Spanish commerce revived and silver remittances arrived in vast quantities from the colonies. In fact, the period between 1802 and 1804 had marked the height of American silver transfers over the three hundred years of Spanish colonial history; in less than three years, more than 114 million pesos' worth of silver and gold were shipped to Spain.[52] Napoleon quickly moved to tap this source of revenue, forcing King Charles IV to sign the Subsidy Treaty, which guaranteed annual payment of some 6 million francs a month to the French treasury.

The outbreak of the Anglo-French War in 1803 threatened the delivery of subsidies, since Britain refused to consider Spain neutral and targeted the

Spanish merchant fleet and convoys returning from the colonies. Trade with Spanish America all but collapsed after December 1804.[53] Ever resourceful, Napoleon still found a way to collect "his" monies. To prevent the British from seizing Spanish silver convoys, he resorted to other means: beginning in 1805, the payment of Spanish subsidies was handled by French merchant par excellence Gabriel Julian Ouvrard, who acted in a dual capacity: as war profiteer and as agent of the French Treasury. In a remarkable example of commercial collaboration in the midst of major military conflict, Ouvrard helped organize a mercantile network involving French, Dutch, and British merchant bankers and traders who engaged in an extraordinary endeavor to carry Mexican treasure in neutral ships (even, on several occasions, on British warships) from the New World on behalf of the Spanish king—but, in practice, for Napoleon.[54]

The French emperor was thus keen to exploit Spain's political turmoil and prevailing anti-Godoy sentiments to exert greater control over Spain, which, with her vast colonial holdings and long Atlantic and Mediterranean coastlines, could become an essential partner in France's ongoing war against Britain. With memories of Godoy's Prussian imbroglio still fresh, Paris noted that despite Charles IV's acceptance of the Continental System, British goods continued to make their way into the peninsula through smuggling and corruption of provincial officials. Ferdinand's sycophantic letters, which referred to the French emperor as "that hero who effaces all those who preceded him" and urged him to intervene in Spanish affairs, only further reinforced Napoleon's intention to act.[55]

The decision to overthrow the Spanish monarchy was not made spontaneously but rather evolved.[56] As late as January 1808 Napoleon still considered a matrimonial alliance with Spain, asking his brother Lucien to send his daughter to Paris as a prospective bride for the Spanish prince. But Napoleon's indecision over the future of the Bourbon monarchy did not stop him from making preparations for direct intervention. As Junot's troops crossed Spain on their way to Portugal, Napoleon instructed his general to document routes and settlements. "Let me see the distances of the villages, the nature of the country, and its resources," he requested in one of his October letters, suggesting that he was already contemplating invasion.[57] By the end of 1807 Napoleon used the French invasion of Portugal to occupy key points and fortresses in the northern Spanish provinces, including San Sebastian, Figueras, Pamplona, and Barcelona, where the French resorted to simple but ingenious ruses to seize citadels.[58] In February 1808 additional army corps began to cross the Franco-Spanish border and spread out across Navarre, Biscay, and Old Castile.[59] To lull Spanish suspicions, Napoleon ordered word spread that the troop movements were part of a plan to lay siege to British-held Gibraltar and to prepare for an expedition to North Africa.[60]

Napoleon formally unveiled his plan to intervene in the Bourbon kingdom on February 16 with the announcement that France, as Spain's ally, could not ignore what was happening at the Spanish court and felt obliged to mediate between the rival political factions. Four days later Napoleon appointed his brother-in-law Marshal Joachim Murat as "lieutenant of the Emperor in Spain" and tasked him with leading the intervention. Marshal Murat crossed into Spain on March 10 and quickly progressed toward the Spanish capital.[61] The Spanish government, predictably, had failed to respond to the news of the French incursion; even after the French seizure of the border fortresses, Charles IV could not bring himself to make a stand, apparently refusing to believe that Napoleon could turn against him. As late as early April, the king kept assuring his people that they could "breathe freely" and that the intentions of "my dear Ally the Emperor of the French" were not to be feared.[62] Still, anxious about these developments, the king and his court left Madrid for Aranjuez.

The news of French intervention spurred a popular reaction that focused mainly on Godoy, who had been accused of ruining the realm by virtually handing it over to the French emperor. There were also rumors that Godoy planned to take the royal family to Andalusia and the Balearic Islands, and if necessary to Spanish America, just as the Portuguese royal family had escaped to Brazil. On the evening of March 17 a mob of soldiers, peasants, and citizens gathered at Aranjuez to prevent a royal flight. Shortly after midnight, as passions flared, the people broke into Godoy's quarters and sacked it, furious at not capturing the minister, who was hiding in a roll of matting in the attic.

The events at Aranjuez, reminiscent of the great *journées* of the French Revolution, terrified the Spanish royal couple, with the queen beseeching her son to parley with the mob. Ferdinand exploited the moment, announcing that Godoy had been removed from office and banished from the court; thirst and hunger forced Godoy to come out of his hiding place a day later, but he was captured, beaten, and nearly blinded in one eye before being rescued through the intervention of his nemesis, Prince Ferdinand. With his property confiscated, the formerly all-powerful minister found himself imprisoned at the castle of Villaviciosa de Odón.[63] Ferdinand told his parents that their personal safety (and Godoy's life) could only be secured through an outright abdication. Surrounded by mutinous crowds, Charles IV had no choice but to issue a proclamation announcing that his age and infirmities compelled him to resign the crown to his very "dear son and heir."[64] Ferdinand was hailed as king amid almost universal rejoicing, and the troops took the oath to him as sovereign. On March 24 he made an entry into Madrid, acclaimed by an immense crowd that was elated that Fernando *el deseado* (the desired one) would solve all their troubles.[65]

The new king faced considerable challenges. The country was full of unrest, and the public violence that had helped bring down Godoy also caused considerable anxiety among well-to-do Spaniards, who dreaded the prospects of popular fury and civil strife. Charles IV himself regretted abdicating even before the ink was dry on the paper, and he sought to reverse it, writing secretly to Napoleon to deny the validity of his resignation and claiming it had been done under duress. Thus the events at Aranjuez provided Napoleon with a perfect opportunity to attempt a takeover of Spain.[66] Ferdinand's decision to travel to Madrid was rather unwise considering that Murat and the French troops had already arrived there. The French ambassador refused to acknowledge him as king, and Murat treated him with open disdain. Ferdinand's timidity further played into the situation, as he wrote another sycophantic letter to Napoleon assuring him of his loyalty and renewing his request for a bride from the imperial house.

The revolution of Aranjuez surprised Napoleon, whose earlier designs involved presenting himself as delivering Spain from the tyranny of Godoy.[67] This was no longer possible because of Ferdinand's accession to power. Napoleon resolved to exploit the new political situation. Using as a pretext the secret protest against abdication that Charles IV had sent him, the French emperor refused to recognize Ferdinand as king and invited both father and son to the city of Bayonne in France, where they became part of an infamous tragicomedy. Threatened and cajoled by Napoleon, Ferdinand resisted demands to resign until May 6, when (under threat of being tried for high treason and executed) he agreed to return the crown to his father. Only then did he discover that Charles IV had already transferred his throne and all his rights to Napoleon. With their kingdom snatched from them, the Spanish royals were conveyed to separate estates—Ferdinand to Valençay and Charles IV to Compiègne, then Marseille—where they remained until the end of the Napoleonic Wars.

The Bayonne abdications seemed to represent yet another of Napoleon's masterstrokes. But it involved an odious combination of force and deception, which does justify one eminent historian's conclusion that "in talents, Napoleon was a great military captain; in character and methods, a great capo mafioso."[68] Events in Bayonne marked a point of no return, a moment when the emperor had fully committed himself to what soon turned into an impossible situation. The sheer size of Spain, its varied geography and climate, and its lack of proper transportation and communication infrastructure meant that the French faced challenges they had rarely encountered before. Moreover, Napoleon had a limited understanding of the Spanish people, their rich history and traditions, the vaunted Spanish pride and sense of dignity, and people's resilience and willingness to fight for their fundamental beliefs. José Canga Argüelles, a Spanish statesman who witnessed these turbulent years and later published one of the first studies of this period, was correct when he contended that the war in Spain cannot be grasped without understanding the very nature of the Spanish national character. In a lengthy discussion of the constituent elements of "true national character," he pointed to people's strong attachment to traditions, disdain of foreign customs, resistance to innovations, loyalty to the king, "imperturbable constancy in misfortunes," and "extreme sensitivity to impulses of honor."[69] A voracious and inquiring reader such as Napoleon should have known more about the country he was invading, especially since French diplomats in Spain warned him that the Spaniards "do not resemble any other nation . . . They have a noble and generous character but which tends in the direction of ferocity and they could not stand being treated as a conquered nation. Once driven to despair, they would be capable of the most valiant decisions and could commit the worst excesses."[70] Napoleon's confidant General Anne Jean Marie René Savary later admitted that "we did not show enough consideration for Spanish national self-esteem."[71]

In many respects, the occupation of Spain was one of Napoleon's most fundamental miscalculations, a mistake for which he would pay a heavy price. He could have pursued a much safer course by marrying one of his relatives to Prince Ferdinand (as the latter had repeatedly asked), establishing a matrimonial alliance with Spain that he would have been able to dominate. Instead, the emperor chose the more radical course of getting rid of the Spanish Bourbons and taking direct charge over their realm. In doing so, Napoleon had failed to recognize that the animosity shown by the Spaniards toward their royal family did not necessarily imply a corresponding enthusiasm for rule by a foreign power. Furthermore, he had failed to make proper preparations. The 100,000 troops that he had assembled in Spain were hardly the finest of the Grande Armée, with only a third of them belonging to reputable units and the rest lacking esprit de corps, adequate training, and equipment. The emperor did not want to redeploy his veteran forces because they were to stay in Germany to watch Austria. The ad hoc nature of the Armée d'Espagne would be one of the reasons behind the French occupation's initial failures. Its principal asset—its reputation for invincibility—turned into a major liability as soon as the French started to suffer setbacks. Napoleon's decision to divide the French forces and dispatch them against various scattered objectives was foolhardy at best; Marshal Bon Adrien Jeannot de

Moncey's weakened corps of less than 10,000 men, with no siege train, hardly stood any chance of capturing the fortified city of Valencia, while General Pierre-Antoine, comte Dupont de l'Étang, with some 20,000 Swiss and German auxiliaries and fresh conscripts, never should have been sent unsupported to faraway Cadiz.

Napoleon's attempt to create a vassal monarchy in Spain touched off a revolution that unleashed a tremendous force of provincial centrifugalism, which had long been dormant under the surface of Spain's national fabric. Shortly after King Ferdinand was arrested at Bayonne, popular discontent erupted into open revolt. On May 2, as rumors spread that the French were pressuring the Junta de Gobierno, the governing council left behind by Ferdinand, into sending the last members of the royal family to Bayonne, the citizens of Madrid took the streets and massacred some 150 French troops. The following day, Murat brought in reinforcements that suppressed what became known as Dos de Mayo Uprising, so vividly immortalized by the great Spanish artist Goya. In retaliation for the killings of May 2, the French army executed hundreds of Spaniards but still failed to quell the revolt, which triggered a groundswell of resistance across Spain as locally organized groups defied French authority and began attacking foreign troops.[72] Though the Junta de Gobierno submitted to French authority and accepted Napoleon's decision on June 4, 1808, to place his brother Joseph on the throne of Spain, provincial and municipal authorities rejected the new ruler and incited violent risings in different parts of Spain.[73] Inspired partly by the writings of the great Spanish scholar Francisco Suárez, these local governments argued that the authority of the state was not derived from the divine monarchy but was based on a social contract between the monarch and the people.[74] With Spain's legitimate monarch in French captivity, the local governments felt justified in transforming themselves into ad hoc governmental juntas consisting of leading local figures.[75] These juntas fostered nationalist sentiments, rejected the Junta de Gobierno's pronouncements, and called for organized resistance to the French occupation. As early as the end of May the juntas of Valencia and Seville decreed the mass mobilization of adult men and recruited more than 20,000 men who swore their allegiance to Ferdinand and pledged to fight the common enemy.[76] Equally important was the fact that the juntas made claims to speak for the entire Spanish nation, declaring null the Bourbon renunciation of the crown in favor of Napoleon not only because it had been done under duress but also because it lacked the consent of the nation, a more crucial factor.[77]

In late May 1808 Napoleon convoked in Bayonne an assembly of representatives of the Spanish nobility, clergy, and commoners to ratify a new constitution that had been prepared for them.[78] The Constitution of Bayonne, publicized in late July 1808, was the first written constitution of the Spanish world. Modeled after earlier French constitutions, it sought to introduce revolutionary ideals into Spain while accommodating the particularities of Spanish culture. The constitution turned Spain into a constitutional monarchy and introduced significant changes in the government, abolishing feudal privileges (but not nobility), recognizing certain individual liberties, and calling for the establishment of an independent judiciary and a tricameral national assembly (*cortes*) of the representatives of the three estates.

These liberal provisions of the constitution were designed to appeal to the *afrancesados*, the supporters of the French, who can be grouped into three broad categories: those who had long struggled against the corruption and incompetence of the ancien régime and saw the French dominion as the continuance of the enlightened reforms pioneered by Charles III between 1759 and 1789; those who saw collaboration with the French as more profitable than confrontation; and those who were alarmed by the popular violence that erupted in May 1808 and felt their own interests threatened by it. These Francophiles made up only a small minority of the population, the vast majority of which was rural, devoutly Catholic, and conservative. Furthermore, the Constitution of Bayonne reflected Napoleon's authoritarian approach to governance. It denied legislative power to the assembly, which could only discuss and approve legislation initiated by the king. In a clear concession to Spanish sensibilities and the power of the Catholic church in Spain, the constitution failed to recognize freedom of religion and proclaimed Catholicism as the official religion of the country, with none other tolerated.[79] Thus the constitution hardly won the hearts and minds of the Spanish. It was received, in the words of one contemporary, with "a silent and equivocal indifference" in the French-occupied cities and with "bitter contempt" in the countryside.[80]

The Constitution of Bayonne was also never fully implemented. By the time King Joseph reached Madrid in late July 1808, he had a full-blown war on his hands. The provincial juntas were busy raising troops, while the Spanish royal army was already fighting the French. On June 14, 1808, the Spanish fleet attacked the French squadron of Admiral François Rosily and after five days of fighting forced it to surrender, capturing six French warships and almost 4,000 men. Almost equally disastrous was the French campaign on land. On Napoleon's orders, the French corps moved to secure key areas across Spain, with Marshal Jean-Baptiste Bessières moving to occupy Aragon and Old Castile, Moncey proceeding to Valencia, General Guillaume Philibert Duhesme to Catalonia, and Dupont south toward Seville and Cadiz. The French advance soon ground to a halt. In the two successive Battles of the Bruch on July 6–14, the Spanish forces defeated a French detachment marching toward Zaragoza, where General José Rebolledo de Palafox y Melzi defied the French throughout the summer. Equally unsuccessful was Moncey, whose assault on Valencia came to naught. The French strategic standing in northern Spain was briefly salvaged by Bessières, who exploited poor coordination between the Spanish royal generals Gregorio García de la Cuesta y Fernández de Celis and Joaquín Blake y Joyes and defeated them at Medina del Rio Seco on July 14, 1808.[81] A week later Joseph entered Madrid and was crowned king of Spain.[82]

Bessières's success proved to be the solitary French triumph, and it was soon overshadowed by an outright disaster at Bailén. On his way to Cadiz, General Dupont was alarmed by the news of the Spanish capture of Rosily's squadron and the spreading popular revolt. He decided to cut short his march and turn back northward. Surrounded by hostile population and the Spanish Army of Andalusia under the command of Generals Francisco Castaños and Theodor von Reding, Dupont's troops found themselves attacked at several points as they attempted in vain to break through to the north. Dupont, who despite his considerable experience and long record of service acted with surprising incompetence, asked for a truce and signed the Convention of Andujar, which stipulated the surrender of his entire corps of 18,000 men on July 21, 1808.[83]

Bailén was the worst French military performance of the Napoleonic Wars, made more humiliating by the fact that it was a triumph of the same Spanish royal army that Napoleon had derided as the worst in Europe. The defeat mortified the emperor, who considered Dupont's capitulation both a personal insult and a stain on French arms.[84] Yet the emperor bears responsibility for it. Dupont's detachment was too weak and inexperienced to successfully operate without support in a hostile region. This was Napoleon's mistake and a clear indication that he had underestimated of the gravity of the challenges he was facing in Spain. Bailén's repercussions were felt both within the peninsula and across Europe. Stunned by this defeat, King Joseph fled Madrid and ordered a general retreat to the Ebro River, which meant abandoning most of Spain. From his headquarters at Vitoria, Joseph clashed with his brother, whom he accused of violating the Constitution of Bayonne and seeking to conquer Spain. He tried giving up his crown, arguing that he had no desire to impose himself on a people that did not want him: "Becoming the conqueror amid all the horrors of a war against all the Spanish, I would become an object of terror and execration. I am too old to live long enough to atone for all that evil."[85] Napoleon rejected his brother's entreaties and instead demanded he take charge of the situation. Time was of the essence.

The defeat of the hitherto invincible imperial armies caused elation in many parts of the continent, given the state of deep despair into which Napoleon's successive victories had plunged so much of Europe. Briefly obscured at Eylau, Napoleon's star had been shining more brightly than ever, and his power seemed unassailable. Yet Bailén dealt a major blow to this reputation and gave new sustenance to anti-French sentiments across Europe. In Austria, the buoyed "war party"—those in favor of an open conflict with the French—thought the moment was opportune for a renewed challenge to the French Empire. And Bailén catalyzed resistance all across the Iberian Peninsula. In June and July 1808 the Portuguese rose in revolt after the Spanish garrisons left the Portuguese cities to aid the insurrection back home. The city of Oporto rebelled in early June, followed by Braga, Bragança, and Viena, where provincial juntas were formed. These soon recognized the authority of the Portuguese Supreme Junta formed in Oporto and headed by local bishop Antonio de Castro, whose enthusiasm for revolt far exceeded his leadership abilities. Throughout the summer, the central and northern provinces of Portugal were the scene of armed conflict between newly formed Portuguese militias and French troops. In July the Supreme Junta dispatched representatives to seek aid from Britain. Simultaneously the Spanish provincial juntas of Asturia, Galicia, and Seville also appealed to London for help, urging the British to end hostilities and instead support the Spaniards in their struggle against the French.

Keen on exploiting the situation in the peninsula, the British government sent envoys to establish relations with the Iberian authorities. Britain's immediate goal was to neutralize Spanish centrifugalism and convince the Spaniards to join in some provisional national government that would be strong enough to resist Napoleon and lead efforts to liberate the country. The Spanish victory over Dupont at Bailén caused many in the British government to overestimate the capabilities of the Spanish forces. To them it appeared that Spain was a nation that would rise up against Napoleon and pay no attention to its historical animus with Britain. In the summer of 1808, British foreign secretary George Canning dispatched Charles Stuart as special diplomatic agent to the juntas at Corunna. Stuart spent weeks generously distributing money and arms to the Spanish insurgents in northern provinces, all the while trying to direct them toward union with other provinces to form a central junta. The Supreme Central Governing Junta of the Kingdom was finally formed at Aranjuez in September, though in practice many local juntas paid only nominal attention to it.[86] The Anglo-Spanish war union, in the formation of which Stuart played an important role, was to endure throughout the Napoleonic Wars despite many setbacks, disappointments, and accusations between the allies, which were often driven apart by old jealousies and resentments.[87]

While its agents delivered monies and arms to Spain, the British government also made preparations for a military expedition to the peninsula. In August 1808 the British army landed in Portugal under the command of Lieutenant General Sir Arthur Wellesley. The British defeated General Henri François Delaborde at the Battle of Roliça on August 17 and, four days later, engaged Junot's main forces at Vimeiro, where the thin red line under Wellesley's superb leadership repelled poorly coordinated French assaults and garnered a major victory.[88] Despite his victories, Wellesley was still a junior in command, and he was soon superseded by more senior officers Sir Harry Burrard and Sir Hew Dalrymple. On August 30 Dalrymple, a cautious man who had seen little fighting and was eager to exploit circumstances without further resort to violence, signed the Convention of Cintra, which granted the French very favorable armistice terms, including unmolested departure from Portugal. Remarkably, over the next few weeks the Royal Navy evacuated more than 20,000 French soldiers, with all their equipment and "personal property," which included plenty of looted Portuguese valuables, to France.

The news of the Convention of Cintra, which had effectively negated Wellesley's earlier victories, arrived in Britain in the wake of reports of the British triumph at Vimeiro and caused a political scandal in Britain.[89] Dalrymple, Burrard, and Wellesley were execrated, and all three of them were swiftly relieved of command in the peninsula. A specially formed commission recalled the three commanders from Portugal and subjected them to an official inquiry. In the end all three were cleared. Burrard and Dalrymple were quietly pushed into retirement, while Wellesley moved on to greater things.[90]

The British army in Portugal was, meanwhile, placed under command of Sir John Moore, a general who while serving at Shorncliffe Army Camp had demonstrated an innovative approach to military training and produced Britain's first permanent light infantry regiments.[91] In October 1808 Moore decided to leave Portugal to join the Spanish forces, while Sir David Baird was dispatched with reinforcements (and 150 transports) out of Falmouth to Corunna to provide support on the British left wing. Furthermore, in a daring operation, the Royal Navy evacuated a division of 9,000 Spanish troops under Pedro Caro y Sureda, marqués de la Romana, from Denmark and transferred them to Santander in northern Spain, where they arrived just as the first British troops crossed the Spanish border from Portugal.[92] It would have been sensible for the British and the Supreme Central Governing Junta to coordinate their military operations. Yet the new campaign plan, which Moore described rather harshly as "a sort of gibberish," called for the northern

Spanish armies to launch a double envelopment of the French forces around Burgos and in Navarre, while Blake's Army of Galicia was to march east to support Moore.[93] The plan thus divided the Spanish forces and failed to consider how bad the Portuguese roads were, making it doubtful whether a combined Anglo-Spanish force could indeed conduct joint operations.

Napoleon watched events in the Iberian Peninsula closely. He knew well that the French setbacks in Spain had enlivened public opinion across Europe and stirred some European states to consider challenging his imperium. He also knew that it was essential to repair his prestige with a decisive campaign in Spain. That his commitments were elsewhere made it a very challenging decision. It would require the transfer of troops from occupied German states to the peninsula while maintaining sufficient forces to keep Austrian belligerence at bay. Furthermore, the fifteen months since the Treaty of Tilsit had witnessed major changes in European geopolitics.

In fact, the early euphoria of Tilsit had by now evaporated and cold realism had set in on both sides. Russia was clearly weighing the cons and pros of an alliance with Napoleon, who in turn was regretting his concessions with regard to the Ottoman Empire, which was still an important ally of France in its struggle against Britain. Far from evacuating its forces from the Danubian Principalities, as called for by Article 22 of the Treaty of Tilsit, Russia revealed its intention to annex these realms.[94] For the Romanov court, earlier hopes of French support for the Russian acquisition of the Ottoman provinces of Moldavia and Wallachia, not to mention the prospect of eventual partition of the Ottoman Empire, had dissipated. Napoleon had clearly turned his back on pledges he had made at Tilsit and now claimed that the Russian takeover of Moldavia and Wallachia must be accompanied by the French acquisition of Prussian Silesia. Napoleon even expressed a desire to take control of Constantinople and the Straits, informing the incredulous Russians that while this move would pose no threat to Russia, Russian control of these locations would directly threaten France.[95] Napoleon's changing position on what Russia considered modest concessions in northern and southern Europe embittered the Russian court, where some urged the emperor to show greater steadfastness in his dealings with Napoleon.[96] In August 1808 Russia refused to ratify an armistice that the French had mediated with the Turks and made preparations for the resumption of hostilities. Napoleon was unnerved by the prospect of a partition of the Ottoman realm, though he did not rule it out as long as Russia acquiesced to the French takeover of Morea, Albania, or Egypt in exchange for acquiring the Danubian provinces. In short, the situation was precarious, and both Alexander and Napoleon were motivated to arrange a face-to-face meeting to review European politics and address any ambiguities that had remained from Tilsit.

On September 27 the two emperors gathered at Erfurt in Thüringen (central Germany). Greeting each other on the road between Weimar and Erfurt, they embraced with what one French historian caustically described as "that air of perfect cordiality of which kings alone possess the secret, especially when their intention is rather to stifle than to embrace."[97] Surrounded by immense crowds of soldiers and civilians, Napoleon and Alexander then made their entry into the town, where they were joined by dozens of German kings, princes, and *hommes de lettres*, among them Johann Wolfgang von Goethe, who had a memorable meeting with Napoleon.[98] As the host of the conference, Napoleon spared no expense, noting that he wanted "Germany to be overawed by my magnificence."[99] For the next two and a half weeks the guests were treated to a remarkable spectacle of military parades, banquets, and balls.[100] Against the background of this amiability and proclamations of friendship, Napoleon and Alexander conducted negotiations on several major issues, starting with the situation in Spain, where the insurgency was already under way. Napoleon wanted Alexander to exert pressure on Austria to prevent it from attacking France while he was in Spain. Alexander refused to commit himself. Unbeknown to the French emperor, the Russian ruler had met with the French foreign minister, who urged him to resist the French demands. Talleyrand's behavior has long been debated, with some accusing him of treason and others pointing to higher ideals that motivated the minister. His behavior was not so much a betrayal of France as infidelity to its ruler, a distinction that Talleyrand always maintained. Even in Paris, the minister kept up a vocal public criticism of the imperial government and welcomed opposition elements gathering around him, hoping that this would compel Napoleon to restrain his ambitions.[101] Talleyrand was not yet actively trying to overthrow the emperor, but he was already convinced that France's national interest required that imperial ambitions be curbed before it was too late. To accomplish this, Talleyrand wanted the continental powers to stand their ground and to cooperate with each other.[102] It was during one of his meetings with Emperor Alexander that Talleyrand supposedly told him: "Sire, what have you come to do here? It is up to you to save Europe and you will only succeed by standing up to Napoleon. The French people are civilized, its ruler is not; the ruler of Russia is civilized, his people are not. It is thus up to the Russian ruler to be the ally of the French people."[103] Talleyrand made a fundamental distinction between working for Napoleon and serving the French nation, choosing the latter.

Alexander, stunned though he was to hear such counsel from Napoleon's own foreign minister, understood the value of cultivating his relations with Talleyrand, who kept urging the Russian emperor to abstain from supporting Napoleon's projects, especially against Austria. Night after night, in casual social encounters as well as in a secret meeting in the ladies' drawing room, Talleyrand unraveled the web that he helped Napoleon weave during the day. He urged the Russian emperor to stand strong in the face of Napoleon's bluster, understanding that the more challenges Napoleon created for himself in Spain, the more he would require Russian cooperation, and therefore he would be forced to make concessions. Talleyrand even went as far as to instruct Alexander on how to negotiate with the French emperor. Irritated by the unexpectedly strong Russian pushback, Napoleon complained that Alexander was "defiant and unspeakably obstinate. He wanted to treat with me as between equals."[104] Talleyrand's disloyalty continued even after he returned to Paris; he became, in effect a Russian agent, code-named "Anna Ivanovna," and provided Russia with sound advice and information for years to come.[105]

Austria remained at the center of the Franco-Russian negotiations at Erfurt. Napoleon wanted to see Austria disarmed but, failing this, he hoped to secure Russian commitment for a joint war against Vienna. Alexander initially resisted Napoleon's demands but ultimately compromised: Russia would not join France in an attack on Austria but would stand by France if it was attacked by Austria.[106] Russian cooperation, however, would not come free, and Alexander sought to exact significant concessions, including acceptance of Russian annexation of the Danubian Principalities and Finland. Russia also insisted on the withdrawal of French troops from Prussia and the Duchy of Warsaw, the latter being too close to the Russian frontier for Alexander's comfort. In exchange for Russian recognition of French claims to Spain and continued cooperation in the war against Britain, Napoleon acceded to the Russian demands on the Danubian Principalities and Finland, but he refused to remove French troops from Prussia, arguing that they were needed to threaten Austria's northern flank in the event of an Austrian attack on France. As for the Eastern Question, in secret provisions of the Convention of Erfurt, Napoleon recognized the Russian imperial frontier along the Danube River and pledged not to intervene in case the Russo-Ottoman conflict rekindled, unless Austria sided with the Turks against Russia.[107]

As soon as the Erfurt Congress ended, Napoleon hurried south. Taking the helm of the French forces in the Pyrenees, he swiftly launched a campaign that saw the Spaniards suffer major defeats at Espinosa de los Monteros (November 10), Gamonal (November 10), Tudela (November 23), and Somosierra (November 29–30). In the last of these battles, the gallant Polish *chevau-légers* of the Imperial Guard made a memorable charge up the mountain slopes to clear the road to Madrid.[108] With the Spanish armies in tatters, on December 4 the emperor entered Madrid, where he reestablished French authority and initiated major reforms. Over the next few days the imperial rescripts reorganized Spanish administration, nationalized church property, removed internal customs barriers, and abolished feudal rights and the Inquisition. "I did not invade Spain in order to put one of my own family on the throne," he later claimed, "but to revolutionize her."[109] Napoleon clearly intended to use the modernization approach, which he had honed so well in central Europe, to transform Spain and benefit from her "revenue of more than 150 million francs, not counting the immense colonial revenues and the possession of 'All the Americas.'"[110] He genuinely believed that this process of regeneration would be popular with many Spaniards. But to convey the seriousness of his intention, the emperor also warned the Spaniards that they had been misled and misinformed earlier. "I have abolished everything that was opposed to your prosperity and grandeur," he proclaimed. "If all my endeavors are in vain and you do not respond to my confidence, I shall have no alternative but to treat you as conquered provinces. In that case I shall set the crown of Spain on my head and I shall know how to make the wicked [*méchants*] respect my authority, for God has given me the force and the will to surmount all obstacles."[111] This proclamation shows both Napoleon's modernizing intention and his willingness to resort to brute force to accomplish it. It also reveals how little he understood the Spanish nature; unsurprisingly, this document had no impact on the Spanish resistance. But it did increase anxiety in Vienna, where Napoleon's threat to assume the crown of Spain and move his brother to a different throne was interpreted as meaning that the Napoleonic regime could possibly target the Habsburgs. While not a decisive factor by itself, the declaration did play an important role in shaping the thinking of Austrian political leaders as they pondered their options on the eve of the war with France.[112]

Napoleon's offensive may have been swift and triumphant, but it failed to resolve the underlying challenges: Spanish regular forces continued to fight, and resistance endured (if not increased) among the guerrillas and in towns, of which Saragossa soon become the symbol. Furthermore, the French faced a new threat—the British expeditionary force under the command of Lieutenant General Sir John Moore.

After assuming command of his army on October 6, Moore left some 10,000 men in Lisbon and ordered his 23,000 men to advance to Spain, where he hoped to join Lieutenant General Sir David Baird, whose 12,000 troops had disembarked at Corunna (La Coruña). The British advance had been, as noted, delayed by poor roads, and it was only in early December that Moore's men finally reached Salamanca, exhausted. They barely had time to rest before the news of Napoleon's capture of Madrid arrived. Realizing the danger he was facing, Moore made the decision to withdraw his force back to Lisbon. But when he learned that Marshal Nicolas Soult's corps lay isolated north of Madrid, the British general decided to launch a quick strike and gain a victory that would serve well in justifying the whole campaign back home.[113]

Napoleon was overjoyed at hearing the news of the advance of the British expeditionary force: at last he could meet his enemies on *terra firma*.[114] He diverted part of his army to catch the British between the main French force and that of Soult. But Moore anticipated this move and led his army toward the relative safety of Corunna, where he could rendezvous with Baird and have the Royal Navy extricate his troops. At first Napoleon personally led the pursuit, traveling on foot at the head of a column as a blizzard raged in the Sierra de Guadarrama.[115] As eager as he was to engage the British, shortly after the New Year (1809) Napoleon received alarming news about Austrian movements that raised the prospect of a new conflict. He relinquished direct command of his army to Soult and departed for France, leaving orders to pursue the British to the coast and destroy as much of their force as possible.

Hurrying to Corunna, Moore left behind a rear guard under Major General Edward Paget, who fought off the French cavalry and destroyed bridges to delay the enemy advance. Still, the British retreat soon turned into a disaster, as soldiers and camp followers dropped from exhaustion and cold; ultimately, as many as 5,000 men out of 25,000 died during the retreat, while another 3,000 were sick or wounded.[116] On January 11, Moore's frostbitten and tattered troops finally reached Corunna, where warmer weather and sufficient supplies helped them recover. But the menace remained immediate and grave. As at Dunkirk in May 1940, the British found themselves trapped on the shore with their backs to the sea, while the enemy formed an arch around them. At an anxious moment when the very survival of his expeditionary corps was in doubt, Moore received news of the arrival of the long-expected Royal Navy squadron and transports, which had been hastily dispatched from Britain to rescue the troops. As the evacuation was under way the French attacked Corunna, which Moore skillfully defended before being fatally wounded when a French round carried away his left shoulder and collarbone. Despite their commander's death, the British held their ground and completed their evacuation, boarding all their troops and cannon and destroying vast quantities of ammunition that they could not remove.[117]

The Battle of Corunna was a success in terms of extricating a British army. But it could not conceal the fact that the expedition sent to Spain to help expel the French from the peninsula had itself been forced into a humiliating retreat that claimed thousands of lives. As the London *Times* noted, "The fact must not be disguised that we have suffered a shameful disaster. It was all very well to talk of the courage and endurance of the troops but of what use were these virtues alone when pitted against the genius of Napoleon? 35,000 men had crossed the Spanish frontier against him; 8000 had not returned. We were unworthy of our great past."[118] Even more damaging than the physical losses were the deep fissures that emerged in Anglo-Spanish relations, as both sides accused each other of not doing enough, if not of outright betrayal and bad faith.[119]

Yet Moore's decision to retreat to Corunna instead of Portugal proved to be a blessing in disguise. It diverted French attention and protected the British base in Lisbon, allowing London to pour in reinforcements, now commanded once again by Arthur Wellesley, and plan for the next stage of the war. Having been called away from Spain by the prospect of a new war with Austria (as well as by rumors of intrigues by Talleyrand and Fouché that hinted at possible conspiracy), Napoleon never returned to the peninsula.[120] Even after the victory at Wagram, Napoleon showed no inclination to go back to Spain and finish what he had started. Instead, he continued to direct his brother Joseph and various commanders, most notably marshals André Masséna, Nicolas Soult, Michel Ney, and Claude Perrin Victor—to consolidate French authority in Spain. The results of his brief fall campaign skewed Napoleon's perceptions of the war in the peninsula. Over the course of the next five years, he consistently underestimated the challenges of local terrain, logistics, and popular resistance, and frequently gave his generals instructions that were physically impossible to comply with. In hindsight, one can see that it would have been prudent for the emperor to learn lessons from the first year of fighting in Spain and adjust accordingly—that is, to restore Ferdinand to the throne and seek a political compromise that would have secured French interests in the peninsula. As it was, Napoleon had committed himself to the continuance of a war that consumed his best troops, weakened his military hold in central Europe, and bolstered his enemies across the continent.

The events of 1808–1809 had an important impact on the course of war in Spain. After Napoleon's campaign, the French regained control of most of central and northern Spain but continued to face an uphill struggle in many areas. Parts of Catalonia, Andalusia, and Extremadura strongly resisted them, and the valiant defense of the cities only further galvanized Spanish resistance. The most visible example of this defiance came from the city of Saragossa, which was first unsuccessfully besieged from June through August 1808.

The French returned in December when Marshal Jean Lannes brought some 44,000 men (with more than 140 cannon) to the city's walls. The Spanish garrison of 34,000 men, commanded by General José Palafox, refused to surrender and was actively supported by some 60,000 civilians. The ensuing siege, lasting until February 20, represented one of the worst urban combats ever seen in Europe before the twentieth century and redefined the contemporary notions of siege warfare. Men, women, and children armed with knives, swords, pikes, muskets, or stones fought alongside Spanish soldiers, transforming buildings into fortlets and repelling French assaults in spite of their own appalling losses. Ultimately the French did succeed in taking the city, but only after they had systematically mined and destroyed a large portion of it and killed an estimated 54,000 Spaniards, two-thirds of them civilians.[121]

At least in Saragossa the French prevailed; in large parts of the Spanish countryside they could not. The guerrilla war, with its emphasis on surprise and shock, posed a major challenge to the French, who lamented the fact that "an invisible army spread itself over nearly the whole of Spain, like a net from whose meshes there was no escape for the French soldier who for a moment left his column or his garrison." Without uniform and seemingly without weapons, the *guerilleros* easily avoided patrols or ambushed troops sent against them. The task of finding them was insurmountable, since "men at work in the fields would seize on the gun hidden in the earth, on catching sight of a solitary Frenchman, while to the detachment crossing the field in which they laboured they were but peaceful peasants."[122]

This was a war of frightening totality, inhumaneness, and fervor, so graphically portrayed in Goya's unforgettable series of etchings entitled *Los desastres de la guerra* (*The Disasters of War*). It posed challenges that Napoleon could not overcome despite his continued efforts. The French relied on a traditional mixture of reform, occupation, collaboration, and repression that had worked elsewhere. But in Spain they were confronted by an opponent that was willing to bear the terrible costs of war, "bleeding France more than France could bleed Spain."[123] The intrepid guerrillas absorbed the greater part of the French army's energy, as the French were constantly forced to skirmish and engage in punitive expeditions and searches.[124] In December the Supreme Central Governing Junta attempted to bring some order to the guerrillas, authorizing the creation of *partidas* and *cuadrillas* of a hundred volunteers each, led by a *comandante* and subject to the same military discipline as in the regular army; the *partidas* were considered as forming part of the regular army and had to follow orders from the generals commanding army units in areas where the bands operated.[125] On April 17, 1809, in a decree on so-called land privateering (*el corso terrestre*), the government declared that "all inhabitants of the provinces occupied by French troops who are capable of bearing arms are authorized to do so, even to the extent of using forbidden weapons, to attack and despoil...French soldiers, seize the provisions which are earmarked for them, and to do them as much harm as possible." Article 13 instructed the authorities of occupied towns and villages to furnish irregular detachments with all possible information on the strength and disposition of the enemy, and to deliver to them the necessary provisions. In short, the decree called for a total war in which the guerrillas played the role of the population in arms.[126]

The actual nature of the guerrilla movement has been misunderstood for a long time. Traditional narrative tended to portray it as a Spanish uprising for "God, king, and country." Recent scholarship, most notably by British historian Charles J. Esdaile, has revealed major problems with such an approach. It has shown that the primary concern for many rebels was not the preservation of the Bourbon (or, for that matter, Bragança) monarchy. Instead it was a fight for land, bread, and, in many cases, revenge on the propertied classes. The guerrillas did attack French convoys, intercept French communications, and harass enemy rears, but they also engaged in predatory activities against Spanish towns and villages and were routinely heavy-handed in extracting food and supplies from their own compatriots. Neither were the leaders of this insurgence united by common goals or ideology. To the contrary, they entertained a variety of conflicting interests, though they did share a common desire to resist French occupation.

Consequently, any history of the Peninsular War must take into account a great complexity, where the infamous "little war" (*guerrilla*) can no longer merit the description of a "people's war." The guerrillas were characterized by regionalism, fluidity of affiliation, banditry, and agrarian unrest, not to mention military desertion, tax evasion, and resistance to the junta authority and, later, to the Anglo-Spanish forces. Indeed, as Esdaile correctly argues, discussion of the Spanish guerrilla war must consider the distinction between the small units of regular troops who adopted guerrilla-style irregular tactics and the civilian (and in many cases quasi-brigand) *partidas*, many of whose members had fled to avoid conscription into the Spanish army or had deserted after being called up. Some of the *partida* members were motivated by patriotism and a desire to avenge the abuse (and atrocities) committed by the French; others were driven by sheer opportunism and preyed on their fellow Spaniards as much as they did on the French.[127]

Drawing this distinction does not minimize the impact that the guerrillas had on the war against the French or on the subsequent history of Spain. The guerrillas signaled a new period of politicization that demonstrated that the populace had to be reckoned with rather than simply discounted. The damage inflicted by the guerrillas on the French was immense: the French forces were constantly harassed, their attempts to requisition supplies encountered obstacles at every step, and King Joseph's officials trying to carry out instructions were either killed or living in constant fear of being killed.[128] In July 1810 the French ambassador in Madrid lamented the fact that the guerrillas "shrink the circumference of occupied towns and reduce the exercise of royal authority to a very limited area. It is an evil that demands a special treatment and which will not be destroyed until it is attacked everywhere by units specifically set up for this sort of service."[129] The war in Spain was undoubtedly among the worst experiences French soldiers had during the revolutionary era. They were well aware of this and expressed their frustrations in numerous letters home, diaries, and, later on, memoirs. A common saying among the troops that was scrawled in many places proclaimed, "War in Spain . . . death for soldiers, ruin for officers, fortune for generals."[130]

The Spanish armies may have survived Napoleon's onslaught in 1808, but so serious had been their losses that they struggled to recruit and equip new forces. Resistance to conscription among the populace was greater than ever, and not even generous British supplies of arms and uniforms could replace the need for actual soldiers. The outbreak of revolutions in Latin America only further emasculated the Spanish war effort. Still, the British decision to keep a small force (some 9,000 men under Sir John Cradock) in Portugal proved to be vital. The British presence, even if it was confined to the Lisbon area, meant that the British government remained committed to the struggle in the peninsula and that both Portuguese and Spanish resistance could receive much-needed succor. In February 1809 General William Carr Beresford was given the task of rebuilding the Portuguese army with the help of a small cadre of British officers and a great deal of money and arms. Perhaps of greater significance, in April Sir Arthur Wellesley, the hero of the first British invasion of Portugal, was named commander of the British forces in Portugal. Contrary to Sir Moore's claim that Portugal was untenable, Wellesley argued that if granted 20,000–30,000 men and given authority over local forces, he would be able to establish a British bridgehead in the peninsula and fight off any French invasions.[131] Wellesley landed at Lisbon in April 1809 and lost no time in engaging the French.

Before leaving Spain, Napoleon had laid down the general lines of the plan that his marshals were ordered to follow. While Ney was told to remain in Galicia, Soult was instructed to march with his corps from Corunna into Portugal, seizing Oporto and then Lisbon. Soult duly advanced with some 23,000 men, overcoming disorganized Portuguese resistance and forcing his way into Oporto by the end of March. Here Soult's initiative petered out. His corps was exhausted and hardly strong enough to sustain further offensive operations without receiving reinforcements, but none were forthcoming.

Such was the state of affairs when Wellesley landed in Portugal. Born into an aristocratic Anglo-Irish family, Wellesley first rose to prominence as the victor of several major battles in India, where he served under his brother, Richard Wellesley. Having in the process acquired much useful experience, particularly in regard to logistics and alliance diplomacy, in 1805 he returned to Britain and received an army command. Notorious for his stern countenance and acerbic temper—he frequently reduced grown men to tears— Wellesley was, like Napoleon, a man of contrasts: of modest personal tastes yet with vigorous sexual appetites; possessing a keen mind yet displaying intellectual arrogance; having a pronounced sense of duty yet tending toward great injustice and shifting responsibility for mistakes on to others. He was instantly recognizable for his aquiline nose and for a peculiar laugh that some wit likened to a horse with whooping cough. To later cartoonists, these characteristics made him a figure of fun, but to his soldiers he was "Old Nosey," a leader who was notorious for his insistence on the harshest discipline yet inspired undying trust on account of his unerring ability to win battles without excessive cost to his men's lives.[132]

Returning to Portugal, Wellesley at once grasped the situation: Soult's corps was isolated and vulnerable. Marching with some 16,000 men to the Douro River, the British commander made a surprise crossing of the river in broad daylight, under the nose of the French patrols, and scored a decisive victory over Soult at the Second Battle of Oporto on May 12. The battle ended the second French invasion of Portugal; Soult was forced to retreat to Spain, losing some 5,000 men and much of his artillery and baggage. Thus, just four weeks after landing in Lisbon, Wellesley had driven the French army out of Portugal and established a firm British presence in the region. His success only further encouraged Spanish resistance in the neighboring region of Galicia, where the French faced Romana's army and local guerrillas. To Soult's and Ney's credit, they were able to meet up at Lugo and regroup their forces within just a few short weeks, taking the field once more.

Wellesley did not expect the French to recover so soon and hoped to exploit France's preoccupation with the war in Austria to invade Spain. With Soult and Ney tied down in northwestern Spain, the British crossed into Spain and joined some 30,000 Spanish troops under General Gregorio García de la Cuesta y Fernández de Celis. However, before the joint Anglo-Spanish force, under Wellesley's overall command, could figure out what to do next, French Marshal Claude Victor advanced. On July 27 at Talavera, a small town some seventy-five miles southwest of Madrid, Wellesley engaged some 46,000 Frenchmen that Victor had amassed by using up the last reserves from Madrid. There followed a bloody battle that lasted two days. The French were the first to attack, directing their assault at the Spanish right and the British left, but were unable to make headway. At daybreak on July 28, the French resumed their attacks on British positions but were repulsed with heavy losses, with fighting turning into a heavy exchange of cannon fire in the afternoon. Unable to break through at any point, the French chose to leave the battlefield, after suffering more than 7,000 casualties.[133]

Talavera was a British victory, but it came at a heavy price, with the British losing a quarter of their force (over 6,000 men) in two days of fighting. Wellesley, who was ennobled as Viscount Wellington for this battle, understood the pyrrhic nature of his success and, with Soult threatening his communication lines, had no choice but to retreat hastily back to Portugal. His experiences during the Battle of Talavera turned Wellington against cooperation with the Spaniards, and he became determined to ignore Spanish affairs in order to concentrate on one essential point of his new plan: the security of Lisbon. Anticipating a French invasion, he hoped to make himself so strong at Lisbon that the French would exhaust themselves trying to break through. Just weeks after returning from Spain, he gave orders for a vast system of defensive works across the entire Lisbon peninsula—the Lines of Torres Vedras. In what constituted the greatest single engineering feat in the entire Napoleonic era, the Portuguese military and civilians constructed three strong lines of mutually supporting forts, blockhouses, redoubts, and ravelins with fortified artillery positions.

The lines were a reflection of Wellington's comprehensive approach to the defense of Portugal. In case of French invasion, Wellington desired that their path be subjected to deliberate total devastation—local residents evacuated, villages abandoned, supplies removed or destroyed, livestock slaughtered or driven off. The enemy would find itself in a man-made wasteland in which they would struggle to secure supplies while being harassed by specially raised irregular home guards (the *ordenança*). The British army itself, with the bulk of the Portuguese civilian population (ultimately some 200,000 inhabitants would be relocated), would weather the invasion behind the Lines of Torres Vedras. Once the French forces were sufficiently weakened, Wellington intended to bring them to battle, to which end he intended to utilize the Portuguese army, which had been completely rebuilt under the direction of Sir William Beresford.[134]

The Royal Navy was instrumental to the success of this grand strategy. Although it was not immediately clear, control of the sea meant victory on land, because the navy provided crucial logistical support. With an army of some 40,000 British and German soldiers, 26,000 Portuguese regulars, and 45,000 Portuguese militia and untrained local *ordenança* militia, as well as numerous Portuguese refugees, behind the Lines of Torres Vedras, maintaining a steady stream of supplies quickly became a matter of tremendous importance. This was the task that Admiral George Berkeley's squadron of eleven ships-of-the-line, three frigates, eight other vessels, and nearly three hundred transports undertook, ensuring the conveyance of reinforcements and resources from Britain and North Africa.[135] This logistical effort proved so successful that Wellington's Anglo-Portuguese army could have theoretically resisted indefinitely. Furthermore, British sea power would provide a route of escape in the event of some catastrophic failure of Wellington's operation, thereby sufficiently allaying fears and enabling the entire endeavor to take place at all.[136] As Wellington admitted privately, "If anyone wishes to know the history of this war, I will tell him that it is our maritime superiority [that] gives me the power of maintaining my army while the enemy are unable to do so."[137]

Wellington's massive preparations were soon justified. With Austria defeated in the summer of 1809, Napoleon poured reinforcements into the Iberian Peninsula and instructed his marshals to conduct offensive operations to reestablish French authority. Over the next few months the French seized the initiative, launching a massive offensive that overran Seville, Granada, Córdoba, Málaga, and Jaén, followed by successes at Oviedo, Astorga, Ciudad Rodrigo, Lérida, Tortosa, Badajoz, and Tarragona. In Aragon, Suchet had already defeated the Spanish forces of General Blake at Maria and Belchite on June 15–18, 1809, and now moved to further consolidate his authority across the Aragonese plains. He initially took a more conciliatory attitude toward the population and, aware of cultural differences between the French and the Aragonese, sought to minimize the disruption his troops caused to the local population. In 1809–1810 he was probably the most successful of the French commanders in dealing with guerrilla war, demonstrating a keen understanding of social dynamics and leveraging local elites and the strong Aragonese regionalism.[138] In Catalonia, Saint-Cyr faced a far greater challenge as he tried in vain for six months to capture the fortress of Gerona, which was defended by the resourceful Spanish general Mariano Alvarez. Gerona was ultimately captured on December 10, 1809, but it cost some 14,000 French casualties and was undoubtedly one of the most brilliant actions performed by the Spaniards during the entire Peninsular War.[139]

In Castille, the Supreme Central Governing Junta's decision to launch offensives in the fall of 1809 led to disastrous results. The Spaniards suffered crushing defeats at Ocaña (November 19) and Alba de Tormes (November 26); the French victory at Ocaña was of particular significance because it destroyed the only force capable of defending southern Spain, which was overrun by the French during the winter of 1810. These successes marked the high tide of French operations in the Peninsular War: much of the Iberian Peninsula was now under French control. The Spanish juntas were reduced to controlling the island city of Cadiz, where the Supreme Central Governing Junta was besieged by the French, and parts of Galicia and the Levante.[140] The Spanish guerrillas, while still effective in harassing the enemy, found themselves coming under more and more pressure.

By the summer of 1810 Napoleon was already preparing for the third invasion of Portugal, which, he hoped, would result in the destruction of the British army. Many observers, both in France and in Britain, thought that the end to organized resistance in the Iberian Peninsula was at hand. Britain, which had to use specie to pay its own forces and provide subsidies to the peninsular allies, suffered from economic problems stemming from the Continental System and worsening relations with the United States, and some in the British government doubted whether British involvement in the peninsula was worth the cost. Relations between Spain and Britain remained strained, with the Spaniards expressing profound suspicion of British motives and aims in the war and resisting British commercial penetration of Spanish overseas possessions. These tensions undermined military cooperation between British and Spanish forces; Wellington frequently expressed frustration with his Spanish counterparts.[141]

There was a six-month gap in the French offensive operations between the conquest of Andalusia and the commencement of the third invasion of Portugal as Napoleon moved nearly 100,000 more troops across the Pyrenees to consolidate his authority in Spain. By the summer of 1810 there were no fewer than 350,000 French troops in the peninsula, the highest number ever seen.[142] Napoleon nominated Marshal André Masséna to lead the new Army of Portugal. Masséna was one of the most talented French commanders, probably more capable of conducting such an important campaign than any other marshal. Napoleon pledged 100,000 men, with whom Masséna was to destroy the British and take Lisbon. That promise never fully materialized. The French marshal ultimately received 65,000 men and faced continued logistical challenges when he embarked on an invasion of Portugal. He did everything he could do to succeed, but in light of the limited resources at his disposal and the substantial opposition he faced, his task was clearly challenging, if attainable at all.[143]

Delayed by the siege of the fortress of Ciudad Rodrigo (April–July), Masséna didn't cross into Portugal until late in August and first laid siege to

Almeida, the fortress that protected northeastern Portugal. Defended by a strong and well-supplied garrison, Wellington expected Almeida to offer stiff resistance to the French, but just three days into the siege a shell exploded the main powder magazine, causing such massive destruction that it forced the British to surrender the very next day. After two weeks of regrouping, Masséna resumed his advance but suffered a defeat at Busaco (Buçaco) (September 27), where Wellington defended a dominating ridge with some 25,000 British troops as well as an equal number of the newly reformed Portuguese troops, who played such a prominent part in attaining victory that it served as a great morale boost to these inexperienced forces.[144] Nevertheless, the French marshal soon found a path around Wellington's front, forcing the Anglo-Portuguese army to steadily fall back to the pre-pared positions in the Lines of Torres Vedras.

On entering the interior of Portugal, the French were surprised to find the entire countryside stripped of supplies and inhabitants, while Portuguese irregulars closed round their rear. By mid-October the French outposts were within twenty miles of Lisbon when they came across the astounding sight of the fortified lines cutting across the Portuguese countryside. For Masséna, one look was sufficient to understand the scope of the challenge he now faced. Reporting to the emperor, he concluded that he would compromise his army if he were to attack in force such formidable lines.[145]

With neither side willing to compromise its position by attacking, Masséna did his best to ensure his army's survival for four long months. The British and their allies "could have everything [they] desired from London, freely and with great certainty," lamented a French officer, Jean Jacques Pelet, "while we needed more than a month and a half to obtain a very simple answer from Paris, if one arrived at all."[146] Surprised by the French army's resilience in the desert-like conditions of Portugal, Wellington later acknowl-edged that "it is astonishing that the enemy have been able to remain in this country so long; and it is an extraordinary instance of what a French army can do.... With all our money and having in our favour the good inclinations of the country, I assure you that I could not maintain one division in the district in which they have maintained not less than 60,000 men and 20,000 animals for more than two months."[147] In mid-November, lacking siege equipment, his army outnumbered, starving, and disgruntled, and fully aware of the strength of the lines in front of him, Masséna made the decision to withdraw his army to Santarem, some forty miles up the Tagus.[148] He remained there for another four months before realizing that his position in Portugal was no longer tenable, and he returned to Spain in March 1811. This effectively marked the end of the French campaign and the twilight of the marshal's glorious career. "Masséna had grown old," bemoaned Napoleon as he replaced him with the young and ambitious Marshal August Marmont.

The Torres Vedras campaign proved a deciding factor in the Peninsular War. The British had achieved a great victory with minimal losses, although Wellington came under great criticism. The British public was not pleased with the methodical, Fabian nature of Wellington's strategy, which did not produce decisive battles and triumphs. In November 1810 Grenville bewailed Wellington's tactic as "desperate and wicked; it puts to hazard our safety, failure may involve us in ruin, [while] the utmost success cannot...insure to us the least permanent advantage."[149] Such criticisms stung Wellington, who complained clamorously about the government's handling of the war and failure to wholly support him.[150] The Portuguese decried what they perceived as the British willingness to sacrifice Portugal, its people, and its resources; the French success in advancing deep into Portugal raised the fear of the British embarking on the waiting fleet and sailing home while leaving the Portuguese to deal with the stark reality. Nonetheless, Wellington's strategy, as destructive as it was to the Portuguese countryside, was pragmatic, perceptive, and, most important, successful. It signaled the beginning of a new phase of the war. The French found it impossible to mount another invasion of Portugal, and the British built upon their success to counterattack into Spain. Equally important was the fact that Anglo-Portuguese alliance survived this harsh test. With the French sweeping through Portugal's countryside, no pro-French group emerged in Lisbon, and the Portuguese remained determined to endure the heavy burden of war and to support the British army.[151]

Wellington soon discovered that guarding the Lines of Torres Vedras was one thing and invading Spain quite another. The French-controlled border fortresses of Ciudad Rodrigo and Badajoz thwarted British progress and helped lay the ground for major French counteroffensives, though none of them succeeded. On May 16, 1811, the small town of Albuera, in southern Spain, became the setting for one of the bloodiest battles of the Napoleonic Wars as a combined Spanish, British, and Portuguese force led by Beresford blocked the march of the French marshal Soult, who was trying to reach Badajoz. In just four hours of fighting Beresford held on to his position but lost five colors and some 6,000 men, with the British contingent losing 40 percent of its men and one of its brigades entirely destroyed in a French cavalry charge.[152] Along with an earlier battle at Fuentes de Oñoro (May 3–5), Albuera was a tactical victory for the British but failed to change the strategic situation in the Iberian peninsula. The French continued to exercise authority in the larger part of Spain, while the British remained able to exert only marginal influence outside Portugal. The campaign in many respects reflected the evolving nature of Wellington's mission in the peninsula. For the first three years he had been defending Portugal, and his force, particularly the cavalry, was sized for warfare in the mountainous Portuguese countryside. But the weakening of French positions in Spain allowed Wellington to become bolder and grander in his plans. Still, the battles and sieges of the fall of 1810 and spring of 1811 cost Wellington heavy losses and discouraged him from attempting another invasion until he had procured cavalry reinforcements suitable for the more open terrain of Spain and an adequate siege train.

With the support of the Royal Navy, Wellington worked to address these challenges. In the autumn of 1811 he received a powerful siege train, one that allowed him to strike across the border and quickly capture the fortresses of Ciudad Rodrigo (January 20, 1812) and Badajoz (April 7), opening pathways into Spain. The arrival of five cavalry regiments further buttressed prospects for a successful strike deeper into the Iberian Peninsula. But equally decisive in changing the strategic situation in the peninsula was Napoleon's determination to invade Russia in June 1812. This massive conflict dried up the supply of men and resources for Spain, making the spectacular gains achieved by Wellington during the first half of the year even more significant. The beleaguered Armée d'Espagne had seen tens of thousands of troops recalled for the campaign in Russia. Meanwhile, Soult's 54,000-man Army of the South, deployed in Andalusia, continued to be tied down in the siege of Cadiz, while the Army of the North was hunting down guerrillas in Navarre. Marshal Suchet did have sizable forces (some 60,000 men) in Catalonia and Aragon but had rarely shown interest in supporting his fellow marshals.

It was Marshal Auguste de Marmont's Army of Portugal, some 52,000 strong, that posed the more immediate problem for Wellington, who in the late spring of 1812 decided to launch another invasion of Spain. In engaging Marmont, Wellington hoped to secure several major goals at once—defeating a major enemy force, threatening the main French communications, and forcing Soult to abandon the siege of Cadiz and withdraw from southern Spain or risk being isolated. After spending the month of May procuring sufficient food, ammunition, and fodder, Wellington launched his campaign with almost 50,000 men and 54 cannon; the bulk of his forces were British, but there were also the fast-improving Portuguese troops, who had proven themselves at Busaco and were fully integrated with the British forces. In addition, Wellington's command included a Spanish division and regiments of the famed King's German Legion.

The Allied army began its advance from Ciudad Rodrigo on June 13, and four days later its troops entered Salamanca unopposed, laying siege to small French garrisons that Marmont had left in neighboring forts.[153] For the next several weeks, the two armies remained in close proximity to each other, cautiously maneuvering into position. Neither was willing to attack; in fact, at one point they moved parallel with each other on opposite sides of the river Guarena, the martial music of their bands blaring loudly as they marched.

In late July, despite stormy weather, both armies continued their march across flat and rolling countryside before deploying on the southern side of the Tormes River, not far from the town of Salamanca. Here, on July 22, 1812, Wellington surprised Marmont with a succession of flanking maneuvers in oblique order that resulted in a rout of the French left wing. With senior French officers, including Marmont, wounded, confusion reigned among the French command, creating an opportunity that Wellington successfully exploited. In just a few hours of fighting the British smashed through the French positions and gained a decisive victory.[154] Six days after the battle, General Maximilien-Sebastien Foy wrote in his diary that the Battle of Salamanca was the most skillfully fought, the largest in scale, and the most important in results of any that the British had fought in recent times. "It elevates Lord Wellington's reputation almost to the level of that of Marlborough," he observed. "We knew about his prudence, his eye for choosing good positions, and the skill with which he used them. But at Salamanca he has shown himself a great and capable master of maneuvering."[155] Salamanca thus demolished the belief that Wellington was merely a defensive-minded and overly cautious commander. Instead, it secured his reputation as a British war hero and one of the great military leaders in Europe. This was undeniably Wellington's best-fought battle, and in its conception and skillful execution it compares to Napoleon's great victory at Austerlitz. This "beating of forty thousand men in forty minutes," as one French officer put it, stunned the French, who were forced not only to lift their siege of Cadiz and abandon the entire province of Andalusia but also to evacuate the royal capital city of Madrid, which irreparably damaged King Joseph's government.[156]

Despite his triumph at Salamanca, Wellington found himself in a precarious position between Soult's Army of the South marching from Andalusia, Soult's Army of Aragon in Catalonia, and King Joseph's Army of the Center in Toledo; even the battered Army of Portugal remained anything but inactive under the leadership of General Bertrand Clausel, who had rallied and reequipped his troops with remarkable speed. The failure of British siege operations at Burgos (with its masterly defense by General Jean Louis Dubreton) in September and October was accompanied by a sudden counteroffensive by the supposedly beaten French forces, which forced Wellington to retreat to Portugal lest he be crushed. By November the British had abandoned

Madrid to the counterattacking French forces under King Joseph's command and retreated westward.[157]

Thus the glory Wellington had gained in July petered out in the snow and rain of a peninsular winter and was dimmed by his subsequent setbacks and his withdrawal to Portugal, exposing him to bitter complaints in the British newspapers and criticism in Parliament. The condition of the British army was deplorable: well over 15,000 men were on the sick list, and a large amount of equipment had been lost during the retreat. The state of the Portuguese and Spanish forces was little better, and there was a growing Spanish animosity toward the British commander in chief. Nonetheless, generally the campaign of 1812 turned out in the Allies' favor. The victory at Salamanca and the liberation (if temporary) of Madrid boosted morale and helped expel the French from much of southern Spain. The Spanish guerrillas were again rampaging across much of the peninsula, hampering French operations.

But the fate of the Napoleonic Empire was not decided in the rolling hills of Spain, even if Napoleon himself later claimed that "it was the Spanish ulcer that destroyed me." In reality, events in Spain, as important as they were, did not threaten the survival of the French Empire, and Napoleon continued to dominate the rest of the continent. The future of Europe was instead decided in the snowy fields of Russia and on the green plains of Germany, where Napoleon's inability to score a decisive victory and impose his will on the coalition leaders had, as we shall see, profound repercussions. One cannot but wonder what would have happened if, instead of leading the invasion of Russia, Napoleon had chosen to return to Spain in 1812 and, utilizing his vast resources from across the entire continent (just as he did in Russia), confronted the peninsular problems before dealing with his Russian adversaries.

As important as it was militarily, the year 1812 also left a profound political legacy, for it was in this year that the Spanish Cortes laid the cornerstone of the Spanish liberal tradition. The Cortes was the successor to the Supreme Central Governing Junta, which had led the Spanish resistance to Napoleon for two years but was compelled to summon an assembly in order to legitimize the situation created by the continued absence of the Bourbon monarchy. In 1810, guarded by British ships and besieged by French troops at the Isla de León in Cadiz, the Cortes opened its meetings to deputies from across the Spanish-speaking world.[158] This was the first parliamentary body to feature representatives of both the metropole and the colonies. Amid the din of gunfire, the deputies embarked on vociferous debates on the nature of government, citizenship, and representation that ultimately resulted in the adoption of a new constitution.

Three main groups shaped the proceedings of the Cortes. The first included liberals who had been influenced by the French Revolution, embraced many of its ideals, and wished to go beyond the mere support of the war effort against France and draft a constitution that would introduce profound changes in the state and society. Their opponents were the realists (*realistas*), who had remained loyal to Bourbon authority and believed that sovereignty should be shared between the king and the nation; they backed modest reforms, including a constitutional government that had to be rooted in Spanish history and tradition and would not jeopardize the "ancient fundamental laws." The third group, the *americanos*, consisted of deputies from the American colonies who had campaigned on issues relevant to the overseas territories. Their ideas reflected a mix of traditional Bourbon reformism, ideals of the Enlightenment, and principles from the early years of the French Revolution, and they promoted the introduction of universal male suffrage (based on proportional representation), which would have benefited the colonial populations.[159]

The liberals dominated the drafting of the constitution throughout the entire process, insisting on a centralized government, an efficient civil service, equality before the law, property rights, and a wide range of socioeconomic reforms that were reminiscent of the reforms that Napoleon had introduced in France less than a decade prior. The new constitution's 384 articles were finalized in March 1812 and reflected an underlying liberal triad of "liberty, property and all other legitimate rights."[160] The constitution was deeply rooted in Ehlightenment principles as well as concepts derived from the American and French Revolutions. Much to realists' chagrin, Article 3 explicitly declared that "sovereignty belongs to the nation" and that the people had "exclusive" rights to "to establish fundamental laws." The issue of constitutional balance served as another crucial point of disagreement between liberals and the realists, with the former ultimately prevailing in their insistence on a stronger legislative branch.

The constitution thus gave Spain a strictly limited monarchy with a single-chamber parliament that contained no special representation for the church or the nobility. Although the deputies did their best to steer clear of any accusations that they were borrowing from the French revolutionary legacy, the final document clearly reflected the revolutionary ideals of the 1791 French Constitution, as it enshrined civil liberty (Art. 4), property (Arts. 4, 172.10, 294, and 304), personal freedom (Art. 172.11), freedom of the press (Arts. 131.24 and 371), tax equality (Art. 339), inviolability of the home (Art. 306), the right to a public trial (Art. 302), habeas corpus (Arts. 291 et seq.), and so on.[161] Grappling with the issue of what to do with colonies that were already in the grips of political turmoil, the Cadiz liberals sought to resolve the matter by making the colonies constitutionally part of metropolitan Spain, putting the colonists—except for those of African descent (slave or free) but inclusive of Indians and mestizos—on equal footing with regard to political representation and taxation.[162]

The Constitution of 1812 was the major success for Spanish liberalism and represented a rupture with Spain's Old Regime in numerous ways. But it is also a clear example of the global impact of the Napoleonic Wars. The Cortes deputies were far more liberal than the Spanish population as a whole, and they produced a document that was far more liberal than would have been possible were it not for the exceptional circumstances created by war. As a blueprint for governing a heterogeneous empire, the Constitution of 1812 went on to became the "sacred codex" of Latin liberalism, the first constitution implemented across the world, from Florida to New Spain and from Peru to the Philippines. It offered a seemingly "viable alternative to both continued imperial rule from a disconnected metropole and to the separatist aspirations that emerged in the early nineteenth century across the diverse territories of Spanish America."[163]

The nascent struggle between loyalists and liberals prevented the constitution from taking full effect in the colonies—in fact, it barely had an impact in some areas, such as Peru—but it did have an enormous impact on the formation of a generation of political leaders in Latin America and Europe.[164] The constitution's lofty liberal ideals outraged the more conservative and traditional elements of the Spanish society and army, who just two short years later joined the newly restored King Ferdinand in decrying the constitution as reflecting French influences designed to undermine Spain's monarchy and tradition.

CHAPTER 13 | The Grand Empire, 1807–1812

HISTORIAN THOMAS NIPPERDAY'S acclaimed history of nineteenth-century Germany opens with the sentence "In the beginning was Napoleon."[1] The idea goes to the very heart of the issue of Napoleon's place in European history. His victories were dramatic and even inspiring, but they did far more than achieve military success. After Austerlitz, Jena, and Friedland, Napoleon began to speak openly of the grand empire that he hoped to construct in Europe to replace the now-defunct Holy Roman Empire. His empire marked a pivotal episode in the story of state-making in Europe, for Napoleon's military victories were followed by an effort to transform, for better or for worse, European governments and societies. As French historian Louis Bergeron observed, "Paradoxically, Napoleon was both behind and ahead of his time, the last of the enlightened despots, and a prophet of the modern State."[2]

For Europe, the Napoleonic regime meant both a fresh outlook on the modern world and the act of a power draining its resources and treasuries. His "influence upon the history of the German people, their lives and experiences," wrote one German historian, whose assessment can be applied to other parts of Europe, "was overwhelming at a time when the initial foundations of a modern German state were being laid. The destiny of a nation is its politics, and those politics were Napoleon's—the politics of war and conquest, of exploitation and repression, of imperialism and reform."[3]

The key question remains: what aims did Napoleon's empire serve? The claims of a familial affinity (first for his siblings, then for his son) as a legitimate motivating force behind this empire building seem too simplistic. Equally spurious are claims, greatly shaped by British propaganda, of Napoleon's megalomania for world domination. Meanwhile, admirers of

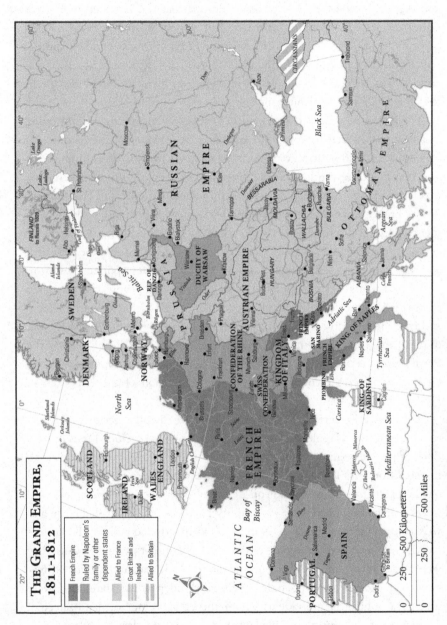

Map 14: The Grand Empire, 1811–1812

Napoleon saw (and continue to see) him as man of action, a revolutionary who brought down obsolete and repressive institutions, abolished centuries-old customs and traditions, retooled educational and judicial systems, and laid the foundation for a new, modern Europe that was based on individual rights and the championing of merit. But a more nuanced answer to this question is that Napoleon replaced one form of tyranny with another, spreading reforms but also undermining civil liberties and exploiting occupied territories. This remains, in the words of American historian Alexander Grab, the "Janus face of Napoleon's rule."[4]

The Napoleonic Empire had France at its heart, but its borders continued to change with each passing year, spreading reforms, along with conscription, taxation, and political repression, to virtually every corner of Europe. In 1790 the French revolutionaries divided France into eighty-three departments; in subsequent years that number steadily increased, reflecting the ebb and flow of French territorial expansion. By 1800 there were ninety-eight departments, including fourteen that comprised the former Austrian Netherlands and parts of the Rhineland and Switzerland. Over the course of the next decade the Napoleonic conquests increased the size of metropolitan France to 130 departments (with a population of some 44 million people) that stretched from the Adriatic coastline to the North Sea. These included France proper and the lands directly annexed to it at different times: the German left bank of the Rhine (1802), Piedmont (1802), Liguria (1805), Tuscany (1808), the Papal States (1809), the Illyrian Provinces (1809), and the Dutch and north German territories incorporated after the dissolution of the Kingdom of Holland in 1810.

The French Empire, however, was much more than the territory administered directly by Napoleon. The informal empire also included tens of millions of people residing in the subject and allied states beyond the French imperial frontiers. These territories can be categorized into three groups based on the extent of control Napoleon exercised over them. The first included states that had retained their sovereignty but became "allies" of France and were compelled to acquiesce to Napoleonic demands and policies. For a time Austria, Prussia, and Denmark-Norway all fell into this category, as they were forced to submit to Napoleon's economic, political, and military directives. The second group included nominally independent states that were under the control of individuals whom the French emperor hand-selected. These tended to be primarily his family members and close confidants, who became great beneficiaries of the imperial largesse. Napoleon possessed a strong sense of family and rewarded his brothers and sisters, believing that they shared a blood bond of loyalty that would help him consolidate control over the vast realm. In 1806, as the French troops occupied southern Italy, Napoleon's elder brother, Joseph, who had served him reasonably well in diplomatic negotiations with Austria, United States and Britain, became king of Naples. The same year Napoleon's brother Louis became king of Holland, while the youngest brother, Jérôme, took the reins in the newly created kingdom of Westphalia in 1807. As we have seen, just as Joseph was trying to win over the loyalty of his Neapolitan subjects, the emperor moved him to the throne of Spain and granted the Neapolitan crown to his brother-in-law Marshal Joachim Murat, while his stepson Eugène de Beauharnais became viceroy of the Kingdom of Italy. Nor did the emperor forget his sisters— Elisa became the princess of Piombino and Lucca in 1805 and grand duchess of Tuscany in 1809. Pauline was given the Duchy of Guastalla in 1806, though she soon sold the duchy to Parma and kept only the title. Caroline, the most ambitious of Napoleon's sisters, married Marshal Murat and was lavished with the titles of grand duchess of Berg (1806) and queen of Naples and Sicily (1808). In addition, Napoleon rewarded many of his generals and senior officials with "sovereign" states, including Benevento (given to Talleyrand), Pontecorvo (Marshal Bernadotte), Siewierz (Marshal Lannes), and Neuchâtel (Marshal Berthier). Finally, the third category was of satellite states that were nominally independent but closely supervised and managed by the emperor from Paris. These included the Grand Duchies of Warsaw and Frankfurt, the Swiss Confederation, and some of the states in the Confederation of the Rhine (most notably Westphalia and Berg). For the last two categories of states Napoleon laid down policy and expected complete subordination of their interests to those of France. These satellites were agents of political and social Napoleonic reforms: reorganization of local authorities into a centrally controlled bureaucratic government manned by professional bureaucrats and supported by bourgeois notables; creation of new legal systems (based on the Napoleonic Code) that reflected the French revolutionary ideals of secularism, equality before law, religious tolerance, and reaffirmation of individuals' private property rights; introduction of more efficient systems of tax collection and military recruitment; establishment of a police force and gendarmerie to maintain a close watch over the population; and a change in church-state relations that frequently meant the sale of property confiscated from the Catholic church.

Taken as a whole, this "Napoleonic system" represented a definitive challenge to the *ancien régime* societies, bringing about the abolition of the remnants of feudalism in the French-controlled territories and the assertion of revolutionary principles. It eradicated some polities and created new ones, expanding middle-sized German states while consuming small secular polities, ecclesiastical states, and free cities. Between 1803 and 1808, some 60 percent of the German population had changed rulers.[5] Napoleon's correspondence is littered with letters that reveal his desire to dismantle the old order and install a new one. In 1807, for example, he penned the following instructions for his brother Jérôme, whom he had placed on the throne of the newly formed kingdom of Westphalia:

> My concern is for the well-being of your people, not only as it affects your standing and my own, but also because of the impact it has on the whole condition of Europe. Do not listen to anyone who says that your subjects, being so long accustomed to servitude, will fail to feel gratitude for the freedoms you bring to them. The common people of Westphalia are more enlightened than such individuals would have you believe, and your rule will never have a secure basis without the people's complete trust and affection. What the people of Germany impatiently desire is that men without nobility but of genuine ability will have an equal claim upon your favor and advancement, and that every trace of serfdom and feudal privilege... be completely done away with. Let the blessings of the Code Napoleon, open procedures and use of juries be the centerpiece of your administration.... I want all your peoples to enjoy liberty, equality, and prosperity alike and to such a degree as no German people has yet known.... Everywhere in Europe—in Germany, France, Italy, Spain—people are longing for equality and liberal government.... So govern according to your new constitution. Even if reason and the enlightened ideas of our age did not suffice to justify this call, it still would be a smart policy for anyone in your position—for you will find that the genuine support of the people is a source of strength to you that none of the absolutist monarchs neighboring you will ever have.[6]

This letter (and many others like it) evokes the idealism and reforming aspirations that made Napoleon such an appealing figure. French historian Louis Madelin was rather fond of a story of the 1820 visit the Habsburg emperor Francis made to the Illyrian Provinces, which had been under French rule from 1809 to 1814. The kaiser was shown many interesting places— palaces, schools, roads, and so on—and when he would ask who built them, the answer would invariably be "The French, Sire." By contrast, he noted the air of neglect and disrepair caused by Austrian administrative mismanagement of the last few years. "Those French devils would have done well to have remained here a few years longer," he is said to have remarked to his adjutant.[7]

There is a certain truth in the emperor's quip. In the long term, many parts of Europe benefited from the French introduction of more efficient administrative institutions, more equitable laws, fairer distribution of the burden of taxation, careers based on merit, the destruction of some of the nobility's privileges and seigniorial structures, and the removal of discriminatory practices (including special taxes and occupational restrictions placed on Jews). In the Grand Duchies of Berg and Frankfurt, for example, the French authorities modernized political and administrative institutions, abolished the nobility's tax exemptions, and nationalized ecclesiastical lands.[8] Wurttemberg, Baden, Hesse-Darmstadt, and Nassau all followed suit, launching extensive reforms that reorganized their governments and finances. In Bavaria, the indomitable chief minister Count Maximilian von Montgelas played a crucial role in restructuring the Bavarian royal administration and creating a French-style centrally controlled bureaucracy that was staffed with professionally trained officials drawn from the middle class and nobility.[9] In all of these states, the governments, with little French intervention, adopted legislation that proclaimed equality before the law and freedom of religion, emancipated Jews (though denied them full equality), and retooled the educational system. The Rheinbund states embraced Napoleonic-style reforms, especially those establishing a rational state bureaucracy and efficient taxation, because they clearly enhanced state authority.

It would nonetheless be disingenuous to claim that Napoleon had a master plan for the development of Europe or that he introduced such reforms for the sake of revolutionary ideology or principle. In fact, when considering Napoleon's political schemes, it is not always easy to determine what was end and what was means, whether a specific policy was carried out merely for its own sake and short-term gain or intended as a step toward some long-term goal. The emperor's legacy in France is undeniably immense, but beyond French borders, his social, political, and legal impact is much more mixed. The French emperor is often perceived as a "builder of Europe" or the "real father" of modern European unity, or so many of his admirers continue to claim. During an exile on St. Helena, Napoleon himself claimed that he had planned to create a federation of Europe with a shared currency, market, and law. Some would credit Napoleon with laying the foundation for the key features of the present-day European Union—equality before the law, a common legal system, a single economic market, dismantling of borders, and so on.[10]

These assertions are open to question. The emperor's devotees fail to mention that France would have unequivocally dominated this European federation and that its political, economic, fiscal, and other needs would have trumped those of other states. The present-day European Union's monetary union and common economic and foreign policy are based on equality of its member states (even if recent political-economic developments have somewhat dented this image). Napoleon would have been incapable of accepting such a model, since his vision of Europe revolved intrinsically around France's strength. He genuinely believed that France had a superior administrative and legal system and that extending it to the rest of Europe would benefit peoples elsewhere; there was also a self-serving incentive, since transforming countries along French lines would greatly facilitate Napoleon's own rule over them and exploitation of their resources. The Napoleonic regime never offered a vision of a "European" identity and by no means did it ever transcend its very essence, which remained soundly French; at the end of the day, the very survival of the empire depended on the enduring superiority of French arms, not popular support for the imperial rule.[11] If Napoleon was motivated by any transcendent ideal, it was the ideal not of a federation of equal nations but rather of a universal empire, closer in its spirit to that of Charlemagne than to the European Union. He could have aspired toward a multinational common economic market—maybe similar to the latter-day Zollverein that helped German states prosper—that would have opened borders and allowed his various subject territories to trade unhindered across continental Europe. Instead, he did the opposite. His insistence on agricultural protectionism for France meant that many satellite states, especially in northern Europe, experienced a deepening depression in agricultural prices due to their inability to trade with Britain and to France's refusal to fill the resulting gap. While the cotton industry of Saxony benefited from the Continental Blockade, the rest of Germany's industry groaned under the Napoleonic restrictions and experienced dramatic declines. Furthermore, the imperial decrees of 1806–1810 turned the entire Kingdom of Italy into a "reserved market" for French textile goods, to the detriment of both Italy and its neighboring states; it is worth noting that this in turn weakened their purchasing power and reduced their demand for French imperial exports.[12]

The radical nature of the Napoleonic system, therefore, must be qualified. Napoleon's main interest in the occupied territories lay more in their material resources—soldiers, money, and supplies—than in their political and socioeconomic transformation. So even though the French-imposed constitutions of German states promised representative assemblies, few were actually summoned—in Wurttemberg, in fact, King Frederick II used the reform movement to suppress the existing Landtag and assert supreme leadership of the state while remaining the emperor's loyal ally. Moreover, the effects of the Napoleonic reforms were not uniform across continental Europe. One of the key determinants was the length of a given region's exposure to the French occupation. The closer to France a region was, the longer it would have stayed under the French rule, and the more enduring the reforms that this entailed. Beyond France, the territories where the reforms had their most enduring impact were Belgium, the Rhineland, Piedmont, Liguria, and Lombardy, all of them occupied during the Revolutionary Wars and staying under French influence for more than a decade. By contrast, the Duchy of Warsaw and the Illyrian Provinces had seen only four years of Napoleonic rule before the empire collapsed in 1813–1814.[13]

The Napoleonic impact depended to a great degree to the extent to which a given region's own social and economic development made it receptive to transformation. For example, the Napoleonic reforms were more successful in Belgium and the Rhineland because these regions already possessed the necessary structural elements that made them responsive to those reforms; in fact, many of the reforms that are traditionally ascribed to Napoleon had already been in place, and local elites usually cooperated with the Napoleonic regime in order to defend and further their own interests. In lands where aristocratic and clerical influences were deeply entrenched—Spain, Poland, and southern Italy, to name just a few—the Napoleonic impact was far less pronounced and lack of cooperation from the local elites made the reforms virtually unachievable.

Even within France proper, the Napoleonic regime struggled to fully impose its will on some parts of the country, as the example of Vendée, perennially resistant to state demands for more taxes and recruits, amply illustrates. In the Duchy of Warsaw, serfdom was abolished in theory but not in practice, and the ideal of civic equality could not overcome deep-seated prejudices and traditions.[14] And while the Napoleonic Code is usually credited with the "de-feudalization" of central Europe, the reality is far more complex. The code did introduce the concept of equality before the law, but its impact on the Confederation of the Rhine was subverted in practice when local elites simply ignored it; the lack of French officials (or French-trained local jurists) made it difficult to enforce the code's legal provisions.[15] Plus in those places where the code was enforced, the gendered consequences, which stabilized paternal power within the family and society, had lasting negative effects for the rest of the nineteenth century.[16] The reforms affecting the Jews were likewise conditional and were associated with new obligations that the Jewish community actually came to resent.

The Napoleonic system represented a sort of cultural imperialism. Its exponents—military governors and/or civilian prefects and auditors—were convinced of the superiority of the Napoleonic system, which in their minds represented the most rational and efficient (and therefore better) organization of its day. To a certain degree, they saw themselves as agents of the *mission civilisatrice* that entailed exporting these changes for the benefit of the peoples who had found themselves under French rule. "I have come to occupy your land," announced a French marshal to the residents of Kassel in 1806. "You have nothing to expect but improvements."[17] Westphalia makes for a particularly interesting case study since it represents both the strengths and weaknesses of the Napoleonic regime in Europe. Napoleon, who saw Westphalia as a "model state," imposed the first written modern constitution in Germany, established an effective central administration, and promoted progressive reforms. Yet the kingdom was never a "German" state per se. Its establishment enabled French cultural imperialism, as the French culture and language came to dominate Westphalian society, and many key civil and military posts, especially those dealing with control of the population (i.e., high police, interior ministry, censorship) remained in the control of Frenchmen who reported to Paris, not their local governments. The French-dominated government sought to suppress local dissent, turned to heavy taxation and government control to support Napoleon's war efforts, and imposed conscription that mobilized thousands of Westphalians.[18]

The benefits of the Napoleonic system, therefore, must also be considered within the context of the demands that France made on territories under its control. Napoleon believed that war should support war, which in practice meant that the French occupation brought not only the high ideals of equality before the law and freedom of religion but increased troop recruitments and material exploitation, given that the presence of French troops invariably imposed a heavy burden on the local population to satisfy all of their military needs. Napoleon's "Grand Empire" was, at its heart, one gigantic military system that required each member state to provide troops and financial support, without which Napoleon would have been unable to maintain his hegemony in Europe. On top of fiscal contributions, the Napoleonic regime demanded conscripts to sustain its military might. Overall, more than 2 million men were conscripted into the Grande Armée between 1803 and 1814. Belgium alone provided more than 216,000 troops between 1798 and 1813.[19] Once it was established in 1806, the Confederation of the Rhine was expected to supply more than 100,000 men—Berg alone was required to furnish 5,000 men, a number that increased steadily until 1811, when it reached 10,000, or 1 percent of its population. Westphalia was obliged to provide a military contingent of at least 25,000 men, while the Grand Duchy of Frankfurt provided some 7,000 men (2 percent of its population).[20] The Swiss Confederation was coerced into supplying 12,000 men, who served alongside tens of thousands of conscripts from the Duchy of Warsaw and the Kingdom of Italy; it has been estimated that 125,000 Italian soldiers out of the 200,000 who served in the Napoleonic Wars perished from disease, the elements, or combat.[21] The size and scope of Napoleon's conscription mechanism were most evident during his preparations for the invasion of Russia, when he relied on his satellite states and allies to provide more than half of his 600,000-man-strong army; among these were 5,000 Neapolitans, 9,000 Swiss, 17,000 Westphalians, more than 25,000 Italians, 90,000 Poles, and some 100,000 Germans, not counting Prussians and Austrians, who formed separate contingents.

Napoleon's continued demand for conscripts was undeniably one of the core reasons for popular opposition to his regime across the continent. Reflecting on the impact of the conscription, Neapolitan writer Vincenzo Cuoco observed that "of all the ideas, projected, executed, abandoned and amended in the last decade, maybe the one that will most greatly influence the future destiny of Europe will be the system of conscription."[22] Indeed, a regular conscription system was a new experience for many Europeans, who found their traditional lives disrupted by the central government's demand for soldiers. Recruits detested being separated from their families and used a variety of means to avoid it; draft-dodging and desertion remained widespread and unabated through the Napoleonic period, causing central authorities, be it in France, Italy, or German states, to resort to a growing centralization and repressive apparatus. Recent scholarship has clearly shown that conscription was the focal point of power struggles between the central state and local communities and contributed to their mounting estrangement. It created a profound collision between the traditional and modern and made people choose sides, thereby placing the very governability of the state at risk.[23]

Yet it would be wrong to think that Napoleon forcibly imposed French-style conscription on other states. Conscription may have been a necessary measure to meet Napoleon's military requirements, but many governments clearly perceived it as a useful way of centralizing their authority. Conscription was one of the key elements in the process of modern state- and nation-building, since it brought peoples from diverse ethnic, cultural, and/or socioeconomic background into the same barracks and helped break down traditional identities or loyalties. The Napoleonic Wars played a decisive role in this ongoing tug-of-war between a centralizing state that demanded recruits and local communities that were hesitant to see their sons shipped off. By the end of the wars, the former had clearly won.[24]

Another crucial element of Napoleon's imperial policy was making occupied territories and satellite states useful to the empire through increased exploitation of their markets and resources. As historian Alexander Grab notes, an "efficient and lucrative financial system was indispensable for...imperial expansion."[25] Elimination of traditional fiscal privileges and establishment of efficient tax collection through centralized and uniform financial administration was at the core of the Napoleonic financial restructuring, which in turn sustained the French war machine. The Napoleonic regime did not simply introduce new or heavier taxes; it became highly adept at collecting existing ones. Throughout the Napoleonic Wars, military costs represented the largest state expenses, expenses that France alone would not have been able to support. Instead, the emperor exacted the necessary resources from his defeated enemies and satellite states.[26] Resentment against the relentless cash levies and requisitioning for the French army's needs was amplified by the Continental Blockade, which hurt many of France's subject states not only because it denied them access to British commerce but also because of its "France comes first" nature.[27]

The Napoleonic regime siphoned off resources from satellite kingdoms to the benefit of the imperial metropole and produced considerable economic disparities across Europe. Throughout history, of course, armies have plundered and confiscated resources. The French originality lay in developing a truly institutionalized system of confiscation. "You must make it your guiding principle that the war must feed the war," the emperor advised one of his marshals.[28] After each military conquest, Napoleon imposed vast indemnities to pay for his war expenses, such that between 1804 and 1814 at least half of French military expenditures were paid through contributions from conquered territories. In those territories French officers equipped with specially preprinted forms required local authorities to provide *argent* (money) and *fournitures* (matériel), all of which was carefully documented. In 1807 alone Prussia and its allies (Saxony, Hanseatic cities, and others) were subjected to heavy demands that ultimately exceeded 500 million francs, while the Kingdom of Italy provided close to 300 million lire in order to maintain a French army in the Italian peninsula.[29] For much of its existence, the Westphalian state experienced deep financial problems because, as historian Sam Mustafa has recently shown, for every franc a Westphalian paid in taxes to his own state, he paid an additional 1.5 francs, either in cash or in confiscated goods, to France. To meet French demands, the Westphalian government also resorted to several forced bonds (*Zwangsanleihe*) that became popularly known as the "French taxes" because all monies collected went directly to France. Local authorities were required to maintain separate record books to keep track of individuals who had not paid for the bond issue.[30] Although Westphalia represented in many respects a unique and extreme case, other German (and Dutch and Italian) satellites were obliged to provide fiscal contributions to the French state and to grant crucial economic concessions to France, opening their markets to its commerce and industry. While the prevailing picture of Napoleon's campaigns is that thanks to conquests and permanent war contributions France was able to balance its economy and keep deficits moderate, recent studies, most notably by French historian Pierre Branda, paint a more nuanced picture of Napoleon trying to pay for war with war but ultimately failing at this. From 1805 to 1813 Napoleon collected close to 1.8 billion francs, including over 600 million francs' worth of "extraordinary contributions," from the occupied territories. Yet his war expenditures amounted to some 3 billion francs, forcing him to resort to tax increases, sale of national and communal property, and loans; at one point the emperor himself lent money he had received from the civil list to the French Treasury. In the end, the French state bore hundreds of millions of francs' worth of deficit until the end of the war.[31]

Increased taxation, forced contributions, conscription, and repression were core reasons the Napoleonic regime failed to maintain popular support across Europe. Whether in Germany, Italy, or the Low Countries, the aristocracy was, naturally, irked by what the French reforms had entailed, but the bourgeoisie, which stood to benefit the most from these changes, struggled to reconcile its delight at its newly acquired rights and status with annoyance at being repressed, censored, and made to suffer from heavy taxes and the Continental Blockade. The peasants tended to bear the brunt of the Napoleonic presence in paying higher taxes and supplying armies with food and men. For all the talk of the French emperor being a revolution incarnate, this former Jacobin did not embody the principles of 1793–1794, and his reforms were never aimed at achieving socioeconomic equality. Neither did he fully represent the principles of 1789. In France and the conquered territories, Napoleon suppressed all means of organized influence or expression of opinion.

Even when it comes to feudalism, the remnants of which Napoleon is usually credited with removing, the situation is more complicated than usually suggested. The modernizing vision that the French troops so confidently professed in the early years of the empire was soon replaced by *la politique de grandeur*, which sought to consolidate imperial rule and embellish its luster. In the later imperial years (1809–1812), Napoleon increasingly resorted to military administration and its heavy-handed interventions to ensure prompt payment of indemnities. Those who advocate Napoleon as a modernizing reformer, for example, rarely mention the *domaine extraordinaire* that the emperor established between 1805 and 1810. This was a special financial mechanism that accumulated spoils of war and siphoned off formerly feudal revenues from occupied territories; these funds were not subject to any law and were managed at Napoleon's complete discretion. French historian Michel Brugière was correct when he described "the profoundly archaic character of this institution, which in its nature and its profits reflected only the right of conquest of the emperor, 'exercising the right of peace and of war.'"[32] Indeed, in Westphalia, where the Constitution of 1807 was supposed to abolish all feudal revenues, King Jérôme's bureaucrats kept and repurposed much of them in order to sustain the *domaine extraordinaire*.[33] Similar problems existed in southern Italy, where the early modernizing impetus of the reforms was hindered by the exploitative nature of the imperial regime.[34]

While espousing equality before the law, Napoleon proceeded with the establishment of an imperial nobility and the granting of imperial fiefs that seriously hampered the implementation of reforms. In 1804–1805 he created imperial dignitaries and grand officers, which included the new marshals of the empire. As the empire grew in size, so did the number of imperial titles and the complexity of the imperial hierarchy. The French marshals and generals—sons of grocers, tanners, merchants, wigmakers, innkeepers, and coopers—became princes, dukes, counts, and barons, with each title supported by a considerable land endowment. To woo talented men who could serve him loyally in exchange for a stake in the new regime, the emperor resorted to distributing *dotations* that were derived from his claim to as much as half of the income of the domain lands seized from the feudal lords and nationalized royal lands. The *donataire* (recipient) had to swear an oath of allegiance to Napoleon and was entitled to steady revenue from designated fiefs in the conquered territories of the Grand Empire, most notably Westphalia and the Duchy of Warsaw. The scale of the *dotation* system was vast, and by the end of the empire it counted nearly six thousand individuals who together received some 30 million francs a year; in Westphalia alone, nearly 20 percent of public revenues went to satisfy the needs of the *donataires*, greatly hampering efforts to develop the Westphalian state and preventing it from ever being fiscally solvent. As expected, the largest number of *dotations* was given to the military. There were more than fifteen *duchés grands-fiefs* that granted their holders vast tracts of lands but no rights of sovereignty. Thus Marshal Bessières became duke of Istria, Macdonald duke of Tarento, Soult duke of Dalmatia, Oudinot duke of Reggio. Some generals were granted victory titles in recognition of their martial exploits. Marshal Davout became prince of Eckmuhl and duke of Auerstaedt, Berthier prince of Wagram, Masséna prince of Essling and duke of Rivoli, and Ney duke of Elchingen (and later prince of Moskowa). These ducal and prince titles all provided considerable annual incomes to their holders. Although the system was not a form of feudalism, it still defied revolutionary precepts, including provisions of the Napoleonic Code. In theory, these endowments were sustained by land rents drawn from confiscated lands of nobles. In practice this meant that the Napoleonic bureaucrats exploited legal loopholes to convert existing feudal dues into steady incomes for the *donataires*, who never resided in or visited their "fiefs." The system underscores an important element of the Napoleonic regime: reliance on traditional landed interests that gained economic security and social prestige through collaborating with the imperial regime. As historian Stuart Woolf once noted, "No better example could be given of the unresolvable contradictions between the modernizing ideals of integration of the French administrative class and the practice of exploitation that accompanied the expansion of the Empire."[35]

Napoleon had a special relationship with the Italian Peninsula, where his ancestors had originated and where he had first earned his laurels. A great student of Italian history, he clearly drew inspiration from the Roman imperial legacy. But he also remained rather critical of Italians' character, describing them as "unworthy" of the sacrifices that France had made for them. "Do not let the Italians forget that I am master to do as I like," he told his Italian viceroy. "This is necessary for all peoples, but especially for the Italians, who obey only a voice of command."[36] Napoleon's 1796–1797 campaigns brought major political transformations in northern parts of the peninsula. Over the next few years, abolishing or annexing some existing polities, the French split up Austria's holdings and set up a series of new republics, complete with French-inspired bureaucracies and legal codes.

In 1802 Napoleon established the Republic of Italy and was elected its president. Three years later, after his triumph over the Third Coalition, he transformed the republic into the Kingdom of Italy, with himself as king and his stepson Eugène de Beauharnais as viceroy. The kingdom gradually expanded with the addition of Venice in 1806, the Marches in 1808, and the Italian Tyrol in 1810.[37] At its height, the kingdom covered an area of 35,000 square miles and had more than 6.5 million inhabitants, about one-third of the peninsula's population; Dalmatia, where the Republic of Ragusa fell to the French in 1806, was briefly ceded to the Kingdom of Italy before Napoleon annexed it directly to France. Meanwhile, Napoleon also actively intervened into affairs of other Italian states, installing members of his family as rulers in Naples, Tuscany, and Guastalla.

"French Italy" steadily expanded in the northwestern corner of the peninsula, where Piedmont was replaced by six departments that were administered as French provinces. In later years the French-governed areas extended to Parma and Piacenza; the Kingdom of Etruria survived until 1807, when Napoleon dissolved it and established three new departments. In the Papal States, Pope Pius VII frequently clashed with Napoleon over continued inter-ference in central Italy and the extent of papal involvement in the Continental System. The French insistence on the Italian states signing a concordat with the pope only further strained relations, for while the treaty recognized Catholicism as the state religion, it also confirmed freedom of religion, intro-duced civil marriage and divorce, authorized the republic to nominate bish-ops, and confirmed the new owners of church land that had been confiscated and sold. Pope Pius VII, unsurprisingly, opposed these changes and fought to preserve the traditions of his office, including the spiritual and temporal independence of the Holy See; neither was he keen on participating in the Continental System, which would have had a profound impact on the local economy. These frictions with the imperial government culminated in a papal humiliation in 1809, when Napoleon occupied and annexed the Papal States while the pope, who excommunicated anyone who participated in this spolia-tion, was made prisoner and transported to Savona and later to France, where he remained under house arrest for the next five years.[38]

In all of these Italian territories, Napoleonic rule followed a rather famil-iar pattern. The French administrators, alongside a core group of Italian officeholders, supervised the introduction of administrative, economic, and social reforms. The cooperation of the local elites as well as the legacy of local reform movements played crucial roles in the extent to which these efforts succeeded; their absence, as in southern Italy, not only undermined those efforts but engendered popular resistance. Furthermore, the French reforms were not necessarily creating a better system. Tuscany already had an excel-lent judicial system and a relatively humane penal system—the legacy of its enlightened Habsburg-Lorraine dukes—and was forced to accept harsher French laws.

Overall, Napoleon did succeed in unifying these diverse regions into just three polities—"French Italy" in the northwest, the Kingdom of Italy in the northeast, and the Kingdom of Naples in the south—that featured uniform legal, administrative, and financial structures modeled on the French system. In northern Italy, French rule forged a successful amalgam between the tradi-tional nobility and the wealthy bourgeoisie, creating a new elite that would shape Italian destiny throughout the nineteenth century. The period saw greater centralization of power, which made the administration more effec-tive, professional, and reliable: prefects supervised the departments, vice pre-fects ran the smaller districts, and mayors managed the cities. The government laid the foundation for a modern secular secondary school (licei) system with a uniform curriculum, and it expanded the number of elementary schools, though the educational system as a whole continued to suffer from a shortage of resources and qualified staff. In the Papal States, the government launched major public works, agricultural improvements, and a new system of poor relief, all the while drafting imposing plans for the restoration of the ancient monuments of Rome.[39] Taken as a whole, Napoleonic reforms modified the political structure of Italy more than anywhere else. For the first time since the fall of the Roman Empire, the Italian peninsula, with its great diversity of spoken languages (as many as twenty different dialects), customs barriers, differing legal systems, currencies, and systems of weights and measures, came under control of a centralizing and standardizing authority.

All this could not efface the resentment that Napoleon's fiscal and military policies aroused all across Italy. The government was thoroughly authoritarian, and modernization went hand in hand with occupation and exploitation. The increasing efficiency of the tax system meant a rising fiscal burden, particularly on the lower classes. The resulting doubling of state revenues did benefit the local population—some of these monies were spent on the construction of roads and waterways, the retirement of public debt, and administrative costs, not to mention embellishments in almost every major town as well as the clearing of the Po River to make it navigable by night—but a large share of the revenues went for pay for France's military expenses. Francesco Melzi d'Eril, the vice president of the Italian Republic from 1802 to 1805, had repeatedly warned Napoleon that the costs of the military establishment were too heavy for the republic to bear; of the 12 million francs that the republic sent to France annually, less than half ever came back to cover the costs of provisioning the French troops deployed in the region. On top of their fiscal contributions, Italian polities, as Napoleonic satellites, were required to pay for the upkeep of French troops, who numbered over 75,000 in the Kingdom of Italy alone, and to provide tens of thousands of men between the ages of twenty and twenty-five, who were drafted for four years. Despite widespread opposition, desertion, and draft-dodging, the Italian authorities drafted more than 150,000 men between 1802 and 1814. Italian troops fought in every campaign that Napoleon waged.[40]

When it came to the economy, the Italian states were brought under tighter control and the Kingdom of Italy formed a national market by eliminating internal tariffs and adopting a uniform commercial code and a single currency (the lira). But these changes were overshadowed by Napoleon's rejection of Italian demands for economic freedom and his insistence on a special tariff system with France. The emperor was not just mercantilist; he was also a firm proponent of bullionism who defined wealth by the amount of precious metals he had. On many occasions he remarked that his object was to export French manufacturing and import foreign specie as a way of promoting France's economic growth. Such an approach hamstrung Italian manufacturing and commerce, as the tariffs promoted the sale of French manufactures and the export of raw materials to France. By 1810 Italians were prohibited from importing any but French linen, cotton, wool, and other textiles. Silk, the Italian kingdom's main export, was the exception, allowed to enter France for the benefit of the French silk industry. In the last few years of the Napoleonic Empire, Italy had in effect been turned into a colony, one that supplied raw materials to French manufacturers, whose products were then imported into Italy and undersold local merchandise. During the same period, the Italian economy suffered from the adverse effects of the Continental System, which all but paralyzed coastal ports, including those of Venice and Ancona, and caused shortages of colonial materials.[41]

———— ◦◦◦※◦◦◦ ————

The Neapolitan decision to break neutrality and join the Third Coalition in 1805 was an act of bad faith that Napoleon could never forgive. The French invasion ended Bourbon rule in Naples and installed the Napoleonic regime, first presided over by Joseph Bonaparte and later by Joachim Murat. Both Joseph and Murat sought to reform the Neapolitan state along French patterns, which included reorganizing and centralizing administration, initiating tax and judicial reforms, and introducing new, French-style legal codes and educational reforms.[42] One of the most crucial French reforms involved redeeming and consolidating public debt, which was done through expropriating church properties and turning crown and church lands into *beni nazionali* that were then sold off; between 1806 and 1811, some thirteen hundred monasteries, convents, and other religious institutions were abolished and their lands sold by auction.[43]

Several factors constrained the new regime's modernizing spirit. Both Joseph and Murat struggled with the effects of a prolonged economic recession, which deprived them of much-needed funds. Thus, public works projects rarely received sufficient funding and continued to languish; this problem routinely topped lists of local grievances. Naples had few manufacturing industries, yet even those suffered from the economic downturn, especially after the start of the Continental System. Murat's efforts in 1808–1810 to protect local industries by imposing duties on imports (primarily French) and seeking relaxation of the embargo on British goods ended after imperial outrage in Paris. French administrative reforms did establish a more efficient bureaucracy, as noted elsewhere, and naturally this produced deep resentment against its intrusive nature, not to mention heavy financial burdens that local communities were asked to shoulder to maintain it. While modernizing reforms were welcomed by some urban Neapolitans, the rest of the population was reticent to embrace them. The Calabrian provinces remained in open revolt, while in other areas public discontent was sustained by conscription quotas that the government had set after initially favoring voluntary conscription.[44] The conscription issue became especially important after 1809, when Murat doubled quotas, provoking unrest and resistance in and around Rome in 1810 and 1811. French efforts to consolidate public debt resulted in creditors (mostly private banks and charitable foundations) losing a significant share of their investments.[45] As one eminent historian of the Neapolitan kingdom aptly observed, these French reforms were designed to secure political gains for the Napoleonic regime and benefited only "groups of senior administrators, wealthy nobles, and foreign financiers." But these changes also meant vast losses for what French officials described as the "patrimony of the idle"—"the religious houses and corporations whose assets had gone to pay off the debts of the ancient régime."[46]

The success of the Napoleonic regime in Naples was greatly dependent on the goodwill of the imperial government. Yet relations between Paris and Naples were often strained due to ongoing disputes over commercial matters, enforcement of the Continental Blockade, and contribution of troops. Equally significant were Murat's long-nurtured dynastic ambitions. The Neapolitan king and his wife, Caroline, were alarmed by Napoleon's decision to marry Austrian archduchess Marie Louise not only because it raised the prospect of Napoleon producing an heir but also because the new empress was a favorite granddaughter of the Neapolitan Bourbons who resided on the island of Sicily under the protection of the British arms. Murat feared a possible rapprochement between Napoleon and the Bourbons—Queen Maria Carolina was rumored to be secretly negotiating with the emperor—that could cost him a crown. Shortly after the imperial wedding, Murat sought to shore up his dynastic claims by insisting on an invasion of Sicily. By late spring 1810 he had mobilized some 20,000 Neapolitan troops for the expedition and expected to have another 15,000 French troops at his disposal. His aspirations suffered a heavy blow when he learned that the French contingent would be placed under a separate French command, and he realized that Napoleon had never seriously considered invading the island; he had seen it purely as a diversion that would compel the British to shift resources away from the Iberian peninsula. It worked—the British lifted the blockade of Corfu and suspended the transfer of troops from Sicily to Spain.

Obviously this was hardly any consolation to Murat, who had spent the summer of 1810 on the shores of the Strait of Messina. With expedition costs mounting and relations between French and Neapolitan officers worsening, Murat gambled, launching an invasion. The first troops crossed the strait during the night of September 17. As soon as they landed near Messina, they came under heavy fire and quickly reembarked. Disheartened by this setback, Murat disbanded the expedition. Napoleon was enraged when he got this news, accusing his marshal of canceling the invasion without orders and thereby contributing to the defeat of Marshal André Masséna's forces in Portugal, which was not the case.[47]

Murat's failed expedition underscored that Sicily had become a British stronghold in the Mediterranean basin, offering, along with Gibraltar and Malta, an advantageous point of departure for harassing the French in Italy and elsewhere.[48] Still, relations between the exiled Bourbon monarchy and the British authorities were hardly amicable. Queen Caroline, who dominated her hapless husband, King Ferdinand, believed that while the French were open enemies, the British were little better and could put an end to Bourbon sovereignty, which they had already reduced to a shadow. The Bourbons also suspected that Britain might use them as a bartering piece in diplomatic discussions with France. Indeed, British and French diplomats had discussed such an arrangement in 1806, and only the untimely death of British foreign secretary Charles Fox put an end to such considerations.

Nor for their part were the British pleased with their Neapolitan allies. The treaty of commerce that they signed with King Ferdinand in 1808 required them to defend the Sicilian strongholds of Messina and Augusta, where they had to deploy a garrison of at least 1,000 men. In addition, Britain was obliged to pay the Bourbon court an annual subsidy of £300,000, backdated to September 1805, and later increased by another £100,000. Notwithstanding the size of this subsidy, Queen Caroline continued to demand further pecuniary aid from her ally. The Treaty of Schönbrunn, which ended the Franco-Austrian war in 1809, only further strained Anglo-Neapolitan relations. With Napoleon's marriage to Archduchess Marie Louise, whose mother was the daughter of the Neapolitan ruling couple, Queen Maria Caroline had effectively become the grandmother to the French emperor. In itself, this meant little to the queen, though she hoped to exploit Austrian connections to better position herself vis-à-vis Britain. In early 1811 the British envoy Lord Amherst wrote exasperatingly about a diplomatic intrigue that Queen Caroline was engaged in with the court of Vienna, which involved restoring King Ferdinand in Naples while placing a Habsburg prince on the throne in Sicily.

Caroline's preoccupation with the recovery of Naples and Ferdinand's profligate lifestyle made them both ignorant of Sicilian culture and politics. The island had a long history of representative assemblies composed of the barons, the clergy, and the tenants of the crown. The assembly met every four years, and its new session opened in the great hall of the royal palace at Palermo on January 25, 1810. The Bourbon monarchy demanded a sharp increase in taxes as well as a special donation to the royal family, all of which considerably affected the barons' finances. The assembly debated the matter for more than three weeks but could agree only on a little more than half the sum the Bourbon crown demanded. Enraged by this tardiness, King Ferdinand dissolved the assembly on June 13 and announced the summoning of a new one, which he hoped would be more willing to toe the line. To appease local sensibilities, the king promised not to appoint foreigners to key positions and to employ the Sicilian ministers.

When the new assembly convened, it proved to be even less willing to extend a blank check to the king, who had failed to keep his earlier promise, appointing Neapolitans instead of Sicilians to key positions. Among the new appointments was Marchese Donato Tommasi, who, as the minister of finance, sought to fill royal coffers through the sale of religious property and the more vigorous collection of increased taxes. These measures elicited an angry response from the new assembly, which perceived them as an exercise of arbitrary power by the monarch.[49] The Sicilian barons, who controlled some 160 votes out of the 275 in the assembly, vociferously opposed the measure but were unable to convince the king to reverse it. Instead, Ferdinand, at the urging of his wife, issued a royal decree to arrest five of the leading barons who had signed a letter of protest against the royal measures.[50]

Matters were coming to a crisis when Lord William Bentinck, the new British envoy who was to act as civil and military governor of Sicily, reached Palermo in July 1811. Capable and experienced though just thirty-six years old, he had already had served as an officer in several military campaigns and had governed Madras in India for four years. Bentinck's main weakness was that, in the words of an esteemed British historian, "he was too much of an Englishman and was apt to consider narrow English remedies as a panacea for all political diseases whenever they might arise."[51] Bentinck initially sought to defuse the conflict between the barons and the Bourbon court, fearing that further escalation of tensions could threaten British control of the island. His effort to convince the Bourbon rulers to revoke the problematic edicts and instead compromise with the barons was met by a robust rejection. Nor was he successful with the barons—politically a Whig, Bentinck caused growing concern among the local elites by challenging feudal rights of the nobility and corporate privileges.

After traveling for consultation to London in the fall of 1811, Bentinck returned with a new set of instructions that called for treating Sicily like "a refractory Indian ally."[52] For that purpose, Bentinck was authorized to use British subsidies as the chief means of political pressure on the Bourbon court. He wielded this authority with a heavy hand, demanding major concessions from the crown. The ensuing power struggle with the royal family went on for over a year, with one showdown between Queen Caroline and the British envoy followed by another amid a flurry of accusations, letters, and notes.[53] Bentinck believed that Queen Caroline's actions posed a significant threat to British interests in the region and that she was in clandestine contact with the enemy. Many in the British government agreed with him and hoped to see the island of Sicily placed under firmer British control, if not annexed outright. Bentinck himself was sympathetic to the plight of the Sicilians and was convinced of the need for British intervention, not so much for Britain's sake as for the well-being of the Sicilians themselves.

Between 1811 and 1814 Bentick exploited the barons' opposition to cajole the Bourbon monarchy into accepting political reforms that resulted in the summoning of a new assembly and the drafting of a liberal constitution in 1812. The new constitution, which was composed with the English constitutional framework in mind, was concise but far-reaching: it reorganized the monarchy, affirmed the sovereign independence of Sicily, and granted the island a far greater degree of political and fiscal autonomy than it had previously enjoyed. It also established a constitutional monarchy that recognized the legislative authority of the parliament (a two-chamber assembly styled after the British Parliament) while granting veto power to the king; the legislature had the authority to impeach ministers and public functionaries. The judicial branch was formed as distinct from and independent of the executive and legislative authority. Most significantly, the constitution abolished the feudalistic privileges and practices that had been recognized for the past several hundred years, and outlined basic rights and freedoms that Sicilians could henceforth exercise; this was a rather paradoxical conclusion to a process that had begun with the nobility's claim of constitutional rights in defense of those very feudal privileges.[54]

Naturally, the sudden changes to existing laws and customary rights provoked great dissatisfaction among those most negatively affected by them. "To copy a [British] law verbatim and to apply it to a people in totally different circumstances is to counteract and spoil the very effect we intended," lamented one Englishman in August 1812. "In one moment is overturned the whole fabric of an ancient government which has existed nearly ten centuries, without opening one of its records nor examining the foundations on which it rested."[55] Even reform-minded Sicilians were alarmed at the fast-paced nature of these political changes, with one of them warning Bentinck,

"Too much liberty is for the Sicilians, what would be a pistol, or a stiletto, in the hands of a boy or a madman."[56]

Such fears were soon realized. With the long-standing traditional bonds ruptured and no clear sense of higher collective good prevailing over private interests, a series of rancorous power struggles broke out between the crown, the nobility, and the burgeoning middle class. Less than two weeks after the constitution was approved, the parliament was prorogued, with Bentinck lamenting that the Sicilian nation was still in its "infancy and weakness" and that the island had to be governed with "bonbons in one hand and *il bastone* [a baton] in the other."[57] Frustrated, Bentinck sought more power to effect the change. For nine months starting in the autumn of 1813 he ruled Sicily as a virtual dictator. Queen Caroline, who fought these changes every step of the way, was forced into exile, with the British obligingly supplying a warship that transported her to Russia so she could safely travel to the Austrian capital city.[58] Bentinck hoped that the liberal reforms he shepherded on the island would inspire mainland Italians to challenge the Napoleonic regime. Bentinck's experiment in establishing a constitutional government in Sicily lasted only a few years. With the end of the Napoleonic Wars, Ferdinand IV returned to the throne of the Kingdom of the Two Sicilies and, in one of his first decisions, abolished the constitution. Still, the constitutional experiment was not a complete failure: the ideas found therein lingered in the memories of the Sicilians and had an influence on the desire for autonomy that was at the base of the subsequent Sicilian revolutions in 1820 and 1848.

Napoleon's long-term impact varied considerably across Europe. Nonetheless, even in those territories where the French could not directly intervene, the shocks of military defeat and foreign occupation had profound repercussions, forcing local elites to accept internal reforms in an effort to deal with France. The best example of this comes from Prussia. The post-1807 years were marked by economic devastation caused by mounting state debts, unrelenting French demands for indemnity payments, and the costs of supplying an army of occupation. The government was forced to increase taxes, debase the coinage, and issue paper money. The financial health of the state continued to deteriorate, with the state debt, which stood at 53 million gulden before 1806, increasing to 112 million gulden in 1811 and over 200 million by the end of the Napoleonic Wars.[59]

The effects of the French occupation stirred national sentiments among many Germans. The plight of German states inspired Johann Fichte, a professor at the University of Erlangen, to deliver his famous fourteen "Addresses to the German Nation" (1808), one of the first expressions of budding

German nationalism. Selfishness and division, Fichte argued, had ruined German states, which now faced the daunting task of surviving French domination. Evoking distinctiveness in language, tradition, and literature, he called upon the German people to free themselves from Napoleon.[60] These sentiments echoed in patriots such as Karl August Fürst von Hardenberg, Heinrich Freiherr vom und zum Stein, Gebhard von Blücher, Gerhard von Scharnhorst, and August von Gneisenau, who did their best to rebuild the country's economy and military in the wake of the shattering defeat.

Foremost among the men to whom Prussia owed its national regeneration were Stein, Hardenberg, and Scharnhorst. The first, the scion of an old family of *Freiherr* (imperial knights), was appointed Prussia's chief minister in October 1807. Although Stein stayed in power for just one year, his name is closely associated with key reforms in the system of government, social structures, local government, the army, and education. One was the Emancipation Edict, which freed Prussian peasants from the last vestiges of serfdom. His reforms granted a considerable degree of self-government to cities and towns, abolished feudal restrictions on land ownership, and sanctioned free trade in land. This in turn swept away the caste system that had underpinned occupations, facilitating the rise of talented commoners to the higher ranks of society. Later the same year Stein was able to push through a new central government that replaced a rather convoluted dual system under which power was divided in varying and confusing proportions between the king's ministers and the king's cabinet. Stein's efforts, however, were interrupted in late November 1808 when a letter in which he expressed his belief that the French should be expelled was intercepted by the French authorities.[61] Napoleon demanded his dismissal. Frederick William tried to delay complying with the demand but was informed in no uncertain terms that the French would not evacuate the country as long as Stein remained in the government. In December 1808 Napoleon declared Stein an enemy of France, sequestered all of his possessions, and ordered Stein seized wherever he could be found. Informed of this danger, Stein escaped to Bohemia, then part of the Austrian Empire, from where he continued to plot Napoleon's overthrow.

Stein's fellow advocate of change, Hardenberg, was also not a Prussian. Hanoverian by birth, he served in Hanover and Brunswick before entering the Prussian service in 1790s. After years on the margins, Hardenberg got his opportunity when Frederick William II appointed him *Staatskanzler* and tasked him with leading the ministries of finance and the interior. He was instrumental in the total reorganization of Prussia's finances, which included ending tax exemptions (though some were later reinstated), introducing freedom of enterprise, and reforming the tariff and toll systems. Gerhard von

Scharnhorst, an officer of considerable intellect and talents, played a decisive role in modernizing the Prussian military and developing new and influential concepts in military theory and practice. As Prussia abolished serfdom, Scharnhorst and his fellow reformers appealed to the common Prussian's sense of patriotism as a means to create an army of citizen-soldiers. In July 1807 King Frederick William III established a Commission for Military Reorganization, with Scharnhorst as president. The commission conducted a veritable purge of the Prussian army in light of its performance in the 1806 debacle, dismissing incapable officers, promoting worthy ones, and ending the custom of recruiting foreigners. The harsh discipline of the Frederickian army was abolished, while the stifling power of the *Junkers* (landowning nobility) was relaxed, to allow for the rise of men of talent and merit. The reforms reorganized the Prussian army into effective combined-arms brigades along the French model, improved its drill and tactics, and developed the Landwehr, a national militia. Equally important was the *Krümpersystem* (shrinking system), which was designed to quickly train army recruits and move them into the reserves so that more men could be trained while keeping the size of the standing army at the 42,000 limit imposed by Napoleon in the Peace of Tilsit (1807). Furthermore, the Prussian monarchy gave its consent to the establishment of the famed Berlin Kriegsakademie (War College), where Prussian officers began laying the foundation for a truly modern general staff.[62]

Fichte's appeals for an enlightened system of education had a noteworthy effect. The Prussian education system was reformed and placed under the leadership of the distinguished Prussian philosopher and linguist Wilhelm von Humboldt (brother of the famed geographer and naturalist Alexander von Humboldt), who used his learning and enthusiasm to lay the foundation for what became the *Humboldtisches Bildungsideal* (Humboldtian education ideal), integrating the arts and sciences with research to achieve comprehensive general learning and cultural knowledge.[63] Prussian universities—at Königsberg, Frankfort on the Oder, and Halle, augmented by the newly established ones at Berlin and Breslau—played a key role in the national revival, kindling the patriotic spirit and training a new generation of men to lead the Prussian state. The Prussian patriots also formed a number of secret societies to encourage the country's rebirth, the most prominent of them being the Tugendbund (League of Virtue), founded in Königsberg (now Kaliningrad) in 1808. Members of the Tugendbund were army officers, men of letters, and sons of landowners who burned with a desire to end the French occupation of their country and bring about, as the royal order that licensed it stated, "the revival of morality, religion, serious taste, and public spirit."[64]

The Tugendbund did not last long enough to see its members' dreams fulfilled. In 1809 it was blamed for instigating an anti-French rebellion. Frederick William III, fearing Napoleon's reaction, issued a decree dissolving this group. Nevertheless, the Tugendbund was soon replaced by new groups such as the Deutsche Gesellschaften (German Patriotic Societies), the Burschenschaften (German Students Associations), and the Turngesellschaft (Fitness Society), which all strove to prepare Germans in both body and mind for the forthcoming war against France.

CHAPTER 14

The Emperor's Last Triumph

IN 1809, AUSTRIA DECIDED to exploit Napoleon's preoccupation in Spain to redress its position in central Europe. Many key leaders in the Habsburg court shared Foreign Minister Johann Philipp Stadion's belief that "Napoleon wants to destroy us because our principles and size are incompatible with a single universal hegemony."[1] In light of Napoleon's dethronement of the Spanish Bourbons, the Austrian war party—those advocating open conflict with the French—concluded that the survival of the Habsburg monarchy could be ensured only through a forceful challenge to Napoleon. When Napoleon sent tens of thousands of his troops across the Pyrenees in 1808, such an opportunity presented itself. Austrian aspirations were bolstered by the initial setbacks French had suffered in Spain, and particularly the defeat at Bailén, the first capitulation of a major French force since 1801. The steady stream of reports about the problems Napoleon faced in Spain, and even back in France, seemed to suggest that he was losing his energy and fighting ability, while the news (if exaggerated) of Spanish guerrillas excited talk of a similar popular resistance in Germany. "The French army is preoccupied in Spain. France is at odds with the Porte, it has enemies in Italy and is hated in Germany," the Prussian foreign minister told an Austrian envoy. "A single victory and the universe will rise against Napoleon."[2]

Austria had learned valuable lessons from the previous defeats, and the four years since the 1805 Treaty of Pressburg had been devoted to reforms. Archduke Charles spearheaded structural and tactical reforms inside the Austrian military, with many of these changes directly borrowed from the French. Artillery was reorganized, new infantry regulations were introduced, and corps formations—nine line and two reserve—were established. In 1808, imitating the French *levée en masse*, Austria established the Landwehr, a militia

Map 15: Europe in 1809

force that enrolled all males ages eighteen to forty-five and could muster, at least on paper, up to 180,000 men. These reforms did improve the Austrian army's capabilities, but their scope should not be exaggerated: tactics remained antiquated, and the corps system suffered from a lack of common doctrine and a properly trained officer corps.[3]

Stadion thus embarked on the path to direct confrontation with France, which, in case of victory, would have allowed Vienna to forestall Napoleon's presumed plans to destroy the Habsburg Empire as well as to redress injustices that Austria had suffered in the preceding two decades. In the autumn of 1808, the war party succeeded in overcoming Archduke Charles's opposition and secured Emperor Francis's approval for a new conflict with France that came to be known as the War of the Fifth Coalition.[4] Austrians discussed commencing wide-ranging operations against Napoleon in southern Germany, Poland, Italy, Tyrol, and Dalmatia, and they rather belatedly urged Britain to launch a diversionary attack either in southern Italy (to help Archduke John [Johann]) or in northern Germany, where the British could land at the mouth of the Weser River and raise a German insurrection. Compared with conditions in 1796 or 1805, Austria seemed to be in a stronger position; France was perceived to be financially weaker and militarily overextended. As one senior Austrian official proudly declared, earlier defeats had been the result of a lack of vision and leadership, but they had learned from those previous mistakes: "Let us fight the enemy with his own weapons, let us send him back his own bullets." Austria must challenge French prestige and either destroy it or "cease to exist."[5]

Although the impending conflict formally involved a new coalition of Austria, Britain, Spain, Sicily, and Sardinia, the contributions of the last four states were rather nominal. Throughout late 1808 and early 1809, communications between the coalition members were slow, and the Austrians themselves did a very poor job of approaching the British and securing firm commitments from them. In fact, London balked at the immense subsidy Austria requested, the largest sum ever demanded and, in the words of a British statesman, "utterly beyond the power of this Country to furnish."[6] Besides, Austria was not the only one seeking British support. Prussia also explored the possibility of challenging Napoleon while he was preoccupied with Spain and Austria. In the spring of 1809, a Prussian envoy secretly asked the British cabinet to set up an arms depot in Heligoland and provide £50,000 to support a Prussian insurrection.

In early April 1809 the British foreign ministry responded to both Prussian and Austrian requests. The former received £20,000 in a letter of credit, with more promised if the Prussian insurrection materialized. Far more substantial was the British response to Austria. London agreed to deliver £250,000 in silver to an Austrian port in the Adriatic, while an additional £1 million would be deposited on Malta for use by Austria once it went to war against Napoleon.[7] Britain refused to launch a diversionary attack in Germany but promised to exert some pressure in the Iberian Peninsula, where a British force was already present in Portugal, and, more important, to launch an expedition to the Scheldt (in the Low Countries), where Britain had long wanted to establish a presence.[8]

Austria hoped to secure the support of Prussia, which had seethed since its military defeat in 1806. A French officer visiting Berlin reported to his superiors that "there is not one of [the Prussian officers] who would not like to resume the war with France. This bellicose mood, which meets well with the hatred for the French, is pleasing to some townsmen and the greater part of the common people, and thus influences popular opinion."[9] The Prussian monarch was apprehensive about supporting Austria, Prussia's longtime rival, and feared that another failed conflict would physically eradicate his realm. Frederick William III therefore abstained from participating in the new coalition even though some of his senior advisors urged him to support the Austrian challenge to Napoleon. Aware of bellicose attitudes among his officers and senior officials, the king tried to contain them, warning of the "disadvantageous and unpredictable consequences" that their actions might produce.[10] In early March the Prussian foreign minister's formal note reiterating the nation's neutrality and existing obligations to France dispelled any hopes the Austrians had about Prussian support.

The Austrian desire to reclaim its lands and its status as a first-rate power placed Russia in the difficult position of having to choose between its new and old allies. Legally, Russia was bound to France by the Treaties of Tilsit and Erfurt, the latter agreement specifying that "in case Austria should engage in war against France, the Emperor of Russia agrees to declare himself against Austria and to make common cause with France, that case being likewise one of those to which the alliance that unites the two Empires applies."[11] Considering the long-standing tradition of Russo-Austrian alliance, this provision represented a drastic change in Russian foreign policy. The court at first rationalized it by accepting Napoleon's accusations that "perfidious Albion's" hand was stirring the pot in central Europe. During his meetings with the Russian diplomats Napoleon regularly referred to Anglo-Austrian collusion and claimed existence of "a certain agreement concluded between England and Austria."[12] The Russian ambassador to Paris, Alexander Kurakin, noted that Napoleon was claiming that "it is England's money that allows [Austrians] to cover their expenses, which are so incompatible with her [current] possibilities. Austria imagines that she is still in the same position that she held two hundred years ago, forgetting what she has become since then and what France has accomplished."[13] In February Napoleon continued to vent his anger during his meetings with the Russian envoys, telling them, "Austria needs a slap in the face, and I will give it to her on both cheeks, and you will see how she would thank me and ask for my orders on what to do next."[14]

Russian high society, despite its cultural and linguistic bonds with France, was hostile toward the Franco-Russian alliance and was concerned about both the revolutionary ideas that French soldiers spread and French expansion into central and eastern Europe. In their opinion, this alliance simply made Russia subservient to French interests. An Austrian diplomat who visited St. Petersburg in early 1809 was astonished at the welcome he received, writing, "Everyone wants to show through outpourings of friendliness how attached they are to the [Austrian] cause.... I cannot express how pronounced the opinion is against the French. There are very few houses where they are received, and only two or three where they are welcomed."[15] The army particularly represented a hotbed of anti-French sentiment, and many prominent Russian generals, including Field Marshal Alexander Prozorovsky and Generals Peter Bagration, Mikhail Vorontsov, and Sergei Golitsyn, were against the war with Austria.[16] Many of Emperor Alexander's ministers and advisers not only were against war with Austria but even urged mobilization against France. Few Russian statesmen, Foreign Minister Nikolai Rumyantsev being the most prominent one, supported a pro-French policy. Rumyantsev was certainly apprehensive about French hegemony in Europe, but he also understood the importance of alliance with Napoleon. For him, Napoleon was no longer "the abominable creature of the revolution," but rather the man who by crowning himself emperor had put an end to the Revolution.[17]

Alexander also believed that Russia stood to benefit from its closer relations with France. Writing to his mother, he argued that "it is in Russia's interests to be on friendly relations with this colossus [Napoleon], the most dangerous enemy of Russia. To prevent any French hostile actions, it is essential to arouse his interests in Russia that would be the driving factor in the political life of our states. Russia has no other means to secure alliance with France but to share... French interests and to convince [Napoleon] to trust Russian intentions. All our efforts, therefore, must be directed to achieve this goal and gain time to increase our forces and resources."[18] When Frederick William of Prussia proposed the formation of "a triple defensive alliance of Prussia, Russia, and Austria" against France, Alexander quickly refused it, urging the king to pursue a more sagacious policy toward France.[19]

Assessing the situation in Europe and the military potentials of France and Austria, Alexander believed that the Austrian army was unprepared for the war, while Russia, already at war with the Ottoman Empire and Sweden, could not afford to jeopardize its relations with France. Yet Alexander was unwilling to forsake his former German allies completely. King Frederick William III spent the first three weeks of the new year in Russia, where his very presence reminded Alexander of earlier agreements and promises. As the Prussian monarch departed from Russia in late January 1809, Alexander received the Austrian special envoy, Prince Karl zu Schwarzenberg, who arrived in St. Petersburg to secure Russian neutrality in case of war against France.[20] Schwarzenberg faced the challenging task of convincing Russia to support Austria, though his superiors were willing to exploit Russia's conflicts with Sweden and the Ottoman

Empire to bring about a change in the Russian attitude; Stadion considered providing support to either of these states, as well as threatening Russia with the restoration of Poland, should it refuse to cooperate.[21]

During his two-hour meeting with Schwarzenberg, Alexander accused Austria of bellicose conduct toward France and warned that if the Viennese court attacked first, he would fulfill his alliance obligations to Napoleon. He also tried to assure the Austrian envoy that Napoleon had no hostile intentions toward Austria and that a war would only lead to "inevitable defeat." Schwarzenberg, for his part, reassured Alexander that "as late as at the time of his departure, there was no discussion [in Austria] about provoking a rupture with France." Austria armed itself in defense, the prince argued, concerned that Napoleon would threaten its monarchy once he had secured Spain. Alexander rejected these arguments, repeating that he knew "from the most dependable" source that France was most concerned about "restoring a general peace in Europe," and claiming that Austria's behavior only strengthened Napoleon's conviction that Britain was inciting another war on the continent.[22] Alexander was convinced that Russia's goal should be to maintain "balance of power in Europe whose intrinsic condition is, in my mind, the existence and integrity of three great monarchies: Austria, France and Russia." Therefore, Russia should "side with France in her efforts to set reasonable limits on Austria's ambition if the latter continued to maintain offensive posturing, but [Russia] should also be ready to side with Austria anytime it faces unjustified aggression from France."[23]

These two principles—the preservation of peace and the integrity of the Austrian empire—guided Russian behavior during the Franco-Austrian war. Austria's decision to launch war, and therefore became an aggressor, compelled Alexander to honor his responsibilities to France, but he was naturally unwilling to help the French in destroying one of the cornerstones of European equilibrium as he had perceived it. "Although this situation imposed on him an obligation to send his troops into Galicia," Alexander told Schwarzenberg he would delay his entry into the war for as much as possible and instruct his commanders to "avoid every collision and every act of hostility" with Austrian forces.[24]

The Franco-Austrian war started on April 10, 1809, when Charles and the main Austrian army invaded Bavaria, Napoleon's stalwart ally, as another Austrian army under Archduke John marched into northern Italy; several days later, Archduke Ferdinand's corps threatened the Duchy of Warsaw, while smaller Austrian forces invaded Dalmatia.[25] The French forces in Italy, commanded by Eugène de Beauharnais, confronted Archduke John on April 16 at Sacile, where the Austrians mounted a flank attack that threatened to cut the French line of communication. Beauharnais recalled his troops and made a fighting retreat, first to the Piave River and later to the Adige, thereby conceding northeastern Italy.[26] But Italy was just a sideshow, and the change in the fortunes of the main Austrian army soon compelled Archduke John to suspend his offensive.

The decisive theater of operations was in Germany, in the valley of the Danube River, where the Austrians hoped to exploit Napoleon's preoccupation in Spain to catch the French forces unaware, score early victories, and provoke a popular insurrection in Germany. Archduke Charles led the Austrian army of some 200,000 men into Bavaria, a French ally and the principal member of the Confederation of the Rhine, informing the Bavarian authorities that he intended to advance through their territory and would treat as an enemy anyone who opposed him. A war manifesto called upon the Austrian soldiers to fight for freedom: "Europe looks for freedom under your banners.... Your German brethren wait for redemption at your hands."[27] Austrian hopes for a popular uprising quickly faded as most Germans remained unmoved by these appeals or patriotic agitators. Furthermore, Austrian assumptions about the French war in Spain proved to be misplaced, as Napoleon routed the Spanish forces, captured Madrid, and sent the British army fleeing headlong from the peninsula.

Napoleon had received reports of increased belligerency in Austria while campaigning in Spain and spent several months rebuilding his forces in Germany. In January 1809 he had instructed the Confederation states to mobilize their contingents, and he combined these with the remaining French forces east of the Rhine as the Army of Germany to deter Austria. Eugène de Beauharnais and Prince Jozef Poniatowski both received detailed instructions on preparing defenses of Italy and the Grand Duchy of Warsaw. Napoleon then recalled his stalwart commanders—Lannes, Lefebvre, and Bessières—from Spain but, not willing to provoke Vienna, he remained in Paris, appointing Marshal Alexander Berthier, his redoubtable chief of staff, as acting commander of the French forces in Germany. Napoleon thus expected war but did not think the Austrians would start it before May. Charles's attack therefore caught the French army unprepared. Berthier, as masterly as he was under Napoleon's supervision, struggled in the absence of the emperor. His aide was distressed to see this man, "so calm in the midst of fire, whom no danger could intimidate, trembling and bending under the weight of his [new] responsibility."[28] Berthier's confused directives, compounded by bad weather and subsequent interruption in optical telegraph transmissions from Napoleon, failed to concentrate the French army, which, on the eve of the war, was split into two groups, with some corps still proceeding to their designated locations. Three French corps were scattered in the region between Munich, Augsburg, and Ratisbon (Regensburg), while Marshal Masséna with

IV Corps was still on the march from Frankfurt to Bavaria. More significant, Marshal Davout's III Corps at Ratisbon was far ahead of the remaining French forces and vulnerable to Austrian encirclement.

Had the Austrians struck in March or carried out their April offensive with greater vigor, they perhaps could have gained victories that might have induced Prussia to act. Instead, they dithered. And once the offensive began, the Austrian army, even after four years of reforms, performed lethargically and failed to exploit its advantages. As his opponent wasted precious time, Napoleon swiftly reacted to the new threat. Leaving Paris on April 13, he reached the front and took personal command of the army on the seventeenth. His presence and leadership roused the army and filled his subordinates with a sense of duty and urgency. Napoleon responded to the Austrian offensive by launching a counterstrike that used the corps of Davout and Lefebvre as a holding force upon which the rest of the French army pivoted to engage the enemy. On April 21, in a series of encounters that collectively became known as the Battle of Abensberg, Napoleon engaged what he believed to be the larger portion of the now divided Austrian army and directed most of his troops against just 36,000 men of Feldmarschalleutnant Johann Hiller, which formed the left flank of the Austrian army. The French overwhelmed Hiller, driving his men across the Isar River at Landshut and seizing a quarter of his men and most of his artillery and transports.[29] It was then that Napoleon learned that the bulk of Archduke Charles's army was, in fact, in the north, attacking Davout and Lefebvre at Eggmühl. The Austrians might have scored a victory here had it not been for Davout, the "Iron Marshal," who doggedly defended the town. On April 22, with Davout's men having almost exhausted their ammunition and dropping from fatigue, the reinforcements that Napoleon had dispatched came rushing in, forcing Charles's army to retreat toward Bohemia in some confusion. With the road to Vienna open, the French entered the Austrian capital on May 13; as in 1805, the Austrian imperial court and government had long been evacuated, but the French still secured vast quantities of supplies that had remained in the city.[30]

The first week of the campaign demonstrated Napoleon's operational improvisation, which the Austrians simply could not match. The French triumphed in five successive battles in as many days, inflicting more than 500,000 casualties on the Austrians. Napoleon had wrested the initiative from the enemy, which could have gained victories but displayed little initiative and revealed grave shortcomings in command and control. The Austrian commander, who before the war had cautioned Emperor Francis that "the first lost battle [will] be the death sentence of the [Habsburg] monarchy," was so demoralized by these setbacks that he urged his government to sue for peace and offered to meet Napoleon with an "olive branch" in hand.[31]

Still, victories at Abensberg and Eggmühl, significant as they were, were not on par with Austerlitz or Jena. The Austrian army, despite its poor performance, escaped destruction and retreated to the safety of the eastern bank of the Danube, where Charles soon rallied it and took a defensive position on the far side of the Danube to the north and east of Vienna. With bridges across the Danube destroyed, the only feasible way to cross the river and engage the Austrians was by way of the floodplain of Lobau, south of Vienna, where islands divided the Danube into three distinct channels. The French quickly seized the islands and by May 20 had built a series of pontoon bridges over the raging Danube, which was flooding due to melting snow and spring rains. Emboldened by his victories and knowing that Austria would gain much from delay, Napoleon ordered his men across the river. By dawn on May 21, Marshal Masséna, with four infantry and two cavalry divisions, took positions on the far bank, occupying the small villages of Aspern and Essling.[32]

This was a major mistake. With the French forces astride the river, Archduke Charles counterattacked, bringing his vast army (over 95,000 men) to bear on Masséna's 25,000. As the French prepared to mount a counterattack, the raging Danube washed away one of the bridges, interrupting communications between Masséna and Napoleon. The Austrian briefly captured the village of Aspern, but the French managed to cling to their positions throughout the day.[33] Still, the heroism of Masséna's men could not conceal the fact that Napoleon had suffered a major setback, potentially more damaging than the near disaster at Eylau. Napoleon's position, far from France, with fragile bridges over the rising river behind him and the enemy on three sides, was one of extreme peril.

Fortunately for Napoleon, the bridge was repaired at midnight and remained open till dawn, allowing for the transfer of reinforcements. By sunup Marshal Lannes's corps was safely across the river and posted to hold the central sector of the French position. The fighting resumed at first daylight, when the Austrian I and VI Corps launched a full-scale assault on Aspern. Throughout May 22, a fierce battle raged over the control of the villages of Aspern and Essling, but neither side could prevail. The Austrians were unable to push the French into the river, and the French couldn't break through the Austrian positions; Napoleon's efforts to reinforce his troops were interrupted by continued collapses of the bridges due to the ingenuity of the Austrians, who floated blazing barges and debris down the river. When nightfall brought an end to the fighting, Napoleon recalled his troops to the island of Lobau, leaving behind nearly 7,000 killed; among the 16,000 who were wounded was Lannes, who died of his injuries a week later.[34]

The news of the Austrian victory provoked shock and excitement in Europe, with many welcoming the dimming of Napoleon's star. At long last the French emperor had been thwarted and the Austrian army had gained a victory over Napoleon, the first in more than a decade. Despite its poor performance at the start of the campaign, it showed its stronger side at Aspern-Essling, demonstrating that the military reforms instituted prior to the war were bearing fruit. The tactical performance of the Austrian infantry was impressive, and when Archduke Charles was present, coordination between units notably improved. But there were major problems as well, and the Austrian army remained, in the words of historian John H. Gill, "an inept offensive instrument, cumbersome in movement, difficult to coordinate, and inflexible once engaged."[35] Amid the euphoria that spread in Austria, many conveniently overlooked the fact that the army had failed to destroy the French, though it enjoyed numerical superiority and a better tactical situation. Furthermore, rather than build on the victory, Archduke Charles decided to stand down, keeping his troops concentrated on the eastern bank of the Danube and hoping that the logistical challenge of maintaining his troops in the Danube valley would soon force Napoleon to withdraw.

Napoleon was clearly stung by the defeat at Aspern-Essling. He also learned from his overconfidence and hasty preparations. The battle had showed him that he was facing an army that deserved respect. For seven weeks thereafter, he methodically prepared, strengthening his position on the island of Lobau and biding his time until he could once more cross the river and renew the fight against Charles. Time served him well, for his troops gained the upper hand in other theaters. Eugène de Beauharnais launched an offensive in northern Italy and defeated Archduke John on the Piave, forcing him to retreat into Inner Austria, where he received the news of the Austrian success at Aspern-Essling and, feeling emboldened, took up a position at the town of Raab, some seventy miles southeast of Vienna. On June 14 Beauharnais attacked and, after a heated engagement, forced the Austrians to retreat; thereafter he marched to Vienna to join Napoleon. Meanwhile, in Dalmatia, Major General Andreas von Stoichevich's 8,000 Austrian troops gained initial success in crossing the Zrmanja River on April 26–30 and driving the scattered French forces toward Knin (Kurn) and Zadar (Zara). The news of Archduke Charles's defeat on the Danube and of Archduke John's retreat in Italy, however, thwarted Stoichevich's further advance. This allowed General Auguste Marmont, who commanded 10,000 French troops in Dalmatia, to counterattack, defeating the Austrians at Pribudic (May 16), Gračac (May 20), and Gospić (May 21). As the result of his victories Marmont was able to seize Triest on May 28 and Ljubljana (Laibach) six days later before continuing his march northward to Vienna, where he joined Napoleon just in time for the final showdown with the Austrians.[36]

By July Napoleon had concentrated nearly 190,000 men. He knew that a victory was imperative to reclaiming his reputation and ending the war before resistance movements, inspired by his setbacks, could spring up in other parts of Europe. There were already signs of agitation in Germany. In late April Friedrich von Katte, a former Prussian officer and member of the Tugendbund, led a brief revolt in Westphalia before fleeing to Prussia, where he was promptly arrested. The same month, another member of the Tugendbund, Wilhelm von Dörnberg, an infantry officer in King Jérôme's army, led a short-lived uprising that sought to seize the Westphalian capital, Kassel. It was suppressed, and Dörnberg fled to Austria before later entering Russian service.

Far more significant was the revolt of Major Ferdinand von Schill, a Prussian officer who led the men of the Brandenburg Hussar Regiment across northern Germany, seeking in vain to spark a popular uprising. Schill, one of the very few Prussians to emerge a hero from the debacle of 1806, was able to launch "a long ride," as historian Sam Mustafa aptly observed, through Germany and scored a minor success near Dodendorf; he was ultimately hunted down by the French-allied Dutch and Danish forces and defeated at Stralsund, where he was killed in battle. In death Schill accomplished what he had failed to do in life: he was transformed into a martyr for the cause of German liberation, with his stature only increasing as years passed and the German national awakening deepened.[37] The same can be said also of Duke Frederick William of Brunswick-Oels, who had been deposed from his duchy in the wake of Napoleon's triumph in 1807. Two years later the duke formed a volunteer corps in Bohemia and at the outbreak of the Franco-Austrian war joined the Austrian war effort. His "Black Brunswickers," featuring the infamous *Totenkopf* (death's head) badges on their shakos, gained the upper hand over the Saxon and Westphalian forces in several engagements; in June they helped the Austrians seize Dresden.[38]

As uprisings raged in northern Germany, the Tyroleans raised the banner of revolt in the south. The Tyrol region had been long part of the Habsburg domain, but the Treaty of Pressburg (1805) forced Austria to cede it to Bavaria. The Bavarian and French authorities introduced a number of changes in the region, including closing local assemblies and monasteries and imposing conscription and taxes, which caused much discontent among the Tyrolean peasants. By 1809 they were willing to take arms to defend their way of life. The rebellion began almost as soon as the Austrians commenced the invasion of Bavaria. On April 11–12 the rebels, led by Joseph Speckbacher and Andreas Hopfer, surprised their Bavarian overlords and captured Bavarian garrisons at Sterzing, Hall, and Innsbruck. Although the Bavarians, reinforced by the French, soon reclaimed Innsbruck, the Tyrolean rebels scored a major victory at Berg Isel (May 29) and retook the city. The rebellion soon spread to other parts of Tyrol, with Speckbacher besieging (but failing to capture) Castle Kufstein.[39] It even spilled over into Italy, where revolts erupted in the former Venetian provinces and the province of Emilia-Romagna, in central Italy, where the widespread detestation of the Napoleonic regime became outright revolt following the introduction of conscription to meet the demands of France's new war against Austria.[40]

The news of uprisings in Westphalia, Tyrol, and Italy alarmed Napoleon. Nonetheless, he concentrated on the far more important task of destroying the Austrian army. Headquartered at the island of Lobau, he had spent more than a month preparing for a new offensive, gathering troops, improving roads, and building solid bridges to secure links between the two sides of the Danube. Starting on June 30 he ordered his men to move across these bridges and into the plain, where the Austrian army had spent the last seven weeks largely idling. The Austrian high command seems to have entertained hopes of a general uprising in Germany that never materialized. Although French intentions to attack were clear by July 1, the Austrian headquarters failed to prepare and was divided as to the best countermeasures. Charles initially hoped that Napoleon would repeat his earlier mistakes of Aspern-Essling, though he quickly realized that the French emperor had no intention of attacking the well-defended Austrian positions there, instead bypassing them to threaten the Austrian left flank.

At dawn on July 5 the first three French corps to cross, under marshals Nicolas Oudinot (II Corps), André Masséna (IV Corps), and Louis Davout (III Corps), opened the battle, attacking the Austrian positions. The French drove back the Austrian corps of Feldmarschalleutnant Johann Graf Klenau and Feldmarschalleutnant Armand von Nordmann, and allowed Napoleon to pour additional forces—the Armée d'Italie under Eugène de Beauharnais and Marshal Jean-Baptiste Bernadotte's IX Corps (Saxons)—into the gap between Masséna and Oudinot. Facing this French onslaught, Archduke Charles recalled his forward troops behind the Russbach River, where he defended his main position. By day's end, he was content with the performance of his army, which had withstood the French attacks. Napoleon also was pleased with the first day of the fighting. He had successfully moved his troops across the river and Archduke Charles's army appeared prepared to fight instead of retreating northward. Both sides spent the night regrouping and readying for the final showdown.

The second day's fighting proved to be fierce. Charles discerned a weakness of the French left wing and intended to advance on his right with Klenau's VI Corps toward Aspern and into the French rear, seeking to cut Napoleon off from the river and the line of retreat. At the same time the Austrian left flank, consisting of Feldmarschalleutnant Franz Fürst von Rosenberg-Orsini's IV Corps, would attack the French right flank, where he hoped for the support of Archduke John, whom Charles implored to get to the battlefield as soon as possible. At dawn, the Austrians under Rosenberg pushed back the French outposts and engaged Davout's infantry divisions, which exploited the slow pace of the Austrian advance to inflict heavy losses on the attackers. Napoleon responded by sending the Imperial Guard and Marmont's XI Corps to Davout's support. By now it had become clear that Archduke John could not join the battle and that the Austrian commanders had failed to properly coordinate their attacks on the flanks. While Rosenberg's attack was in progress, the Austrian right flank under Klenau was not yet moving, forcing Archduke Charles to recall his unsupported attack on the left wing.

It was at this moment that Napoleon receiving the alarming news of the departure of Bernadotte's Saxon corps from the village of Aderklaa, allowing the Austrians to threaten the French center-right. He ordered Masséna to reclaim this position, but the marshal was unable to do it because of the vast firepower the Austrians concentrated there. By late morning the Austrians had secured Aderklaa, while Klenau's corps belatedly launched an attack on the French left flank, defended by General Jean Boudet's single division of Masséna's corps. As the Austrian assaults developed, Napoleon responded by redeploying his forces. Davout and Oudinot were ordered to attack along the Russbach, where their unrelenting attacks soon allowed the French to secure the plateau behind Markgrafneusiedl. Masséna was told to redeploy across the battlefield to Aspern to defend the French left flank, and to facilitate such a risky maneuver, the emperor ordered Marshal Jean-Baptiste Bessières to attack with his cavalry. The French cavalry charge was supported by a grand battery of more than a hundred guns that maintained such ferocious fire that the Austrians were forced to retreat. As soon as he noticed this, Napoleon ordered a general advance, with the assault led at the center by Jacques Étienne Macdonald, at the helm of three divisions of the Armée d'Italie, which formed into a massive square.

By 3:00 p.m., after suffering more than 40,000 casualties and giving up hope of receiving support from Archduke John, Archduke Charles withdrew his army from the field, beaten but not broken. The French, having lost some 34,000 men, were too exhausted to pursue him. The Austrians retreated for four days and, after suffering a setback at Znaim, asked for an armistice on July 10, which Napoleon accepted.[41] Turned into a scapegoat, Archduke Charles was stripped of his rank and forced to resign from the command. His replacement could do little to repair the damage, both moral and physical, that the defeat at Wagram had caused. After three months of discussions, Austria realized that it was in no position to continue war and accepted Napoleon's conditions for peace.

They were harsh. Signed on October 14, the Treaty of Schönbrunn punished Austria for starting the war and imposed stringent restrictions. Austria recognized all the political changes in Italy and Spain and pledged to support Napoleon's Continental System against Britain. Napoleon also extracted an indemnity of 85 million francs and forced Vienna to reduce its army to 150,000 men. Far worse were his territorial demands. Austria ceded the provinces of Salzburg and Berchtesgaden, along with parts of Upper Austria, to France, which later transferred them to its devoted ally, Bavaria. In Italy, France secured further territorial concessions in Trieste and the Croatian Littoral and consolidated its hold over former Venetian possessions along the eastern Adriatic Sea, which were now transformed into the Illyrian Provinces of the French Empire. Austria also was forced to cede small Habsburg enclaves to Saxony and transferred its gains under the Partitions of Poland—western Galicia (except Kraków) and the district of Zamosc in eastern Galicia—to the Duchy of Warsaw. Russia, despite its unenthusiastic performance during the war, was rewarded with the Galician district of Tarnopol (around Brody).

The Franco-Austrian war of 1809 had a profound impact on contemporary European politics. It somewhat dimmed the aura of invincibility that had shrouded Napoleon since the heydays of the Italian campaigns. Though he had acquitted himself at Wagram, a careful observer could see that the Grande Armée was no longer the splendid and fearsome instrument of the 1805–1806 campaigns. The casualties sustained in the various campaigns, along with deployment across much of Europe, had left it with comparatively few veteran troops. Setbacks at Aspern-Essling and the limited victory at Wagram, which, as noted, paled in comparison to Austerlitz and Jena, suggested that future conflicts would be more difficult for Napoleon to win. Indeed, this was the last time he actually won a war. His earlier victories had been achieved over the armies of the Old Regime, which had struggled to keep up with dynamic warfare that the French Revolution unleashed and Napoleon perfected. But the War of the Fifth Coalition demonstrated that France's rivals had gained precious experience from those defeats, and their efforts to match Napoleon's prowess resulted in gradual modernization of their armies and diminishment of the qualitative advantage held by the

French troops.[42] Even more dramatic were the diplomatic and political consequences of the war. Another crushing defeat had forced Austria into a servile alliance with Napoleon, where it remained for the next few years. But this was not its biggest impact. The French victory compelled Austria, Britain, and Russia to adjust their expectations and laid the ground for future collaboration. The war thus helped pave the way for the great coalitions of 1813–1814 that ultimately brought down the Napoleonic Empire.

Meanwhile, in the late summer of 1809, the Austrians were forced to evacuate Tyrol. In August Marshal Lefebvre, with 40,000 Franco-Bavarian troops, launched a campaign to end the local revolt, though he faced an uphill struggle against the rebels, who skillfully exploited the region's mountainous terrain. They scored victories at Sterzing (August 6–9), Berg Isel (August 13), and Lofer (September 25) but suffered heavy losses. In October the Tyrolese suffered a heavy defeat at Melleck, which marked the effective end of the rebellion; many rebels accepted the amnesty the French offered them, while the recalcitrant ones were hunted down. In November, at the third engagement at Berg Isel, the rebel leader Hopfer was defeated; he was ultimately captured and, on the direct order of Napoleon, executed on February 10, 1810.

The Venetian revolts, which were sparked by the rebellion in Tyrol, raged until November 1809, when the French finally diverted sufficient resources to suppress them, though sporadic attacks on officials in Verona, Vicenza, and Belluno still occurred well into 1810. Equally unsuccessful were the rebels in Emilia-Romagna. At the same time a brutal insurgency restarted in Calabria, where the French success of 1806–1807 was undone by the new Neapolitan king, Joachim Murat, who insisted on showing leniency to the rebels; he reduced French military patrols in the countryside and released brigand leaders who had been awaiting execution. This proved to be a mistake. By the summer of 1809, Calabria was once again in a full-scale revolt. The rebels not only intercepted communications between Naples and Calabria but attacked and massacred armed convoys, including some 300 civic guards who were lured into the woods near Nicastro and butchered. Encouraged by their success, the rebels even raided towns, where they killed local officials and their entire families; women and children were publicly burned. Violence only begat violence, and the French response was swift and ruthless. The military governor of the province, General Charles Antoine Manhès, understood the communal nature of the revolt, which allowed the insurgents to survive in the mountains with the help of supplies from neighboring villages. In 1810 Manhès decreed that any peasant caught outside his village with any form of food would be executed on the spot, with no exceptions made for age or gender.

Indeed, during the summer the French shot men, women, and children who were caught with even a piece of fruit in hand outside their communes. The mercilessness of these measures worked, and the starving insurgents were forced to come out of the mountains and into the valleys, where they were hunted down by the French flying detachments. No leniency was shown; all captured brigands were executed, their bodies left by the side of the road as a warning. By early 1811, the last of the Calabrian bands was destroyed; their leader, Parafante, was killed and his head displayed in the public square of a neighboring town. Having executed hundreds, by the spring of 1811 Manhès could report that Calabria was once again at peace.[43]

⸻∘∘∘❀∘∘∘⸻

On the eve of its war with France, Austria had tried to secure British support and cautiously broached the subject of financial help, offering to mobilize 400,000 men in return for £7.5 million, with £2.5 million up front. Though it had earlier encouraged the Austrians to challenge France, London showed no interest in the offer this time around. Foreign Secretary George Canning replied that Austria would have to fight the war on its own with little if any help from the British; once the war was under way, London would decide how it might help.[44] Abandoning its former ally did not mean that Britain was not interested in exploiting any advantages the Franco-Austrian war might provide. This was a reflection of a more robust foreign policy advocated by the new British prime minister, William Henry Cavendish Bentinck, the Duke of Portland, and his hawkish ministers: Canning, Chancellor of the Exchequer Spencer Perceval, and Secretary for War and the Colonies Robert Stewart, Viscount Castlereagh.

Once the Franco-Austrian War was indeed under way, Portland decided to participate directly by launching an attack on the Low Countries. The British expedition to Walcheren, a vital island in the estuary of the Scheldt River, was not an attempt to support Austria militarily; in fact, British leaders were indifferent to Austria's fate and paid attention to its war with France only in the context of its diverting Napoleon's attention away from the Low Countries, making a British attack there possible. The Walcheren expedition was conceived for British national security reasons and reflected Britain's political and commercial interests.[45] An expedition to the Scheldt had been long on the mind of Viscount Castlereagh, who argued that the capture of this island would ensure British control over the trade in the Scheldt estuary and provide a convenient point for exerting influence over the Low Countries.[46] Furthermore, control of Walcheren would allow Britain to target naval installations where Napoleon's warships were being repaired and constructed. Napoleon had established the second-largest French naval arsenal in and around Antwerp and sought to rebuild his naval capabilities there in the wake of Trafalgar. Napoleon expected that British would threaten Antwerp and had made considerable investments in fortifying its port against a possible attack. However, as historian John Bew correctly pointed out, in 1809 "intelligence reports suggested that Antwerp and Flushing had been stripped of defenses as the French took the fight to the Austrians further south on the River Danube."[47] Thus a British attack could neutralize the threat of the revived French navy and possibly undermine the Continental System, which was starting to hurt the British economy. If successful, this would be another Copenhagen (which the British bombarded twice in 1801 and 1807), but on a grander scale.

Political maneuvering and logistical challenges prevented the British from completing their preparations until July. Sir David Dundas, who had been just appointed commander in chief of the forces, argued that the British army could not mount any expeditions since it was still recovering from the thrashing it had endured during a failed invasion of Spain.[48] Castlereagh prepared a special memorandum outlining the reasons for and scope of the expedition to Walcheren and solicited feedback from a number of senior officers, who all agreed on the importance of the campaign but also cautioned about its hazardous nature; success would be largely dependent on the speed and energy of its execution.[49] The British cabinet was still vacillating when news of the Austrian success at Aspern-Essling reached London, putting an end to any doubts as to the scheme's practicability. Preparations began in earnest in late May, and on June 22 Castlereagh requested (and received) the king's permission for the expedition.

The expedition was ready to be launched when the news of the Austrian defeat at the Battle of Wagram arrived. British officials should have realized that the battle probably meant that Austria would be forced to sue for peace, but they opted to continue with the expedition. On July 28 a fleet of more than 600 vessels, including more than 260 warships, sailed under command of Sir Richard Strachan, carrying a 37,000-man army led by John Pitt, 2nd Earl of Chatham, to the Dutch shores. One eyewitness recalled feeling a sense of immense pride as he watched "the departure of the grandest fleet that ever sailed from the shores of England. Above three hundred vessels spread their wings to the wind, and from North Foreland to South, the Channel was one cluster of moving vessels—a sight never to be forgotten, whilst memory holds a seat."[50]

British forces landed on Walcheren on July 30, just as the momentum on the continent had shifted back in favor of the French. Surprising local French and Dutch forces, the British quickly proceeded to seize neighboring cities: Middleburg and Veere on July 31 and the fortress of Batz on August 1.[51] The success of the expedition now depended on a rapid advance to Antwerp, where the British could have delivered a very serious blow to Napoleon's power. At this point, however, the British campaign began to flounder. Despite his instructions, Chatham decided to direct his efforts toward the city of Flushing, which was bombarded from the sea and occupied by the army on August 15.[52]

By now the French had recovered from their shock at the invasion. Their warships sailed upstream to Antwerp, where they were safely sheltered. Marshal Bernadotte, who had just been removed from command for his insubordination at Wagram, was sent to deal with the British expedition. He reinforced local defenses and brought reinforcements from St. Omer, Ecloo, Brussels, and Louvain. By the end of August he had some 40,000 French and Dutch forces in and between Bergen-op-Zoom and Antwerp, preventing the British from advancing up the Scheldt and threatening Antwerp. Furthermore, Chatham and Strachan could not agree on the future course of the campaign. As the days passed, the British soldiers found themselves stuck on the island in hot, swampy conditions, suffering terribly from "Walcheren fever," a malarial disease that quickly spread among the troops camped out in the low-lying areas of the island and incapacitated entire regiments.[53] On August 26 a British council of war decided that the expeditionary force (led by Sir Eyre Coote) should rally on Walcheren while the Royal Navy attempted to sail upstream. On September 2 the British warships made an attempt to reach Antwerp but were stopped by the French, who had spent the previous three weeks furiously working on improving coastal defenses. Relations between Chatham and Strachan broke down completely and on September 14 the former returned to England. By the end of the month the majority of the British force reembarked aboard the Royal Navy, though a garrison force of more than 16,000 men remained on Walcheren till the end of the year.[54]

The Walcheren campaign was one of the poorest-organized expeditions Britain conducted during the entire revolutionary era—a true debacle that sent many brave soldiers to a useless death.[55] While only approximately 100 British soldiers died in combat, a staggering 4,000 succumbed to disease, while thousands more suffered from the effects of malaria for years to come; a year later, more than 11,000 men were still listed on the rolls as sick.[56] The failure at Walcheren caused universal indignation in Britain, where public debate raged over who was to blame for this failure. The *Times* called it a national disaster, while other newspapers were even more strident in their condemnation. In Parliament the opposition railed against the government, which had been weakened after Prime Minister Cavendish-Bentinck suffered a paralytic stroke. Amid the political firestorm centered on the Walcheren expedition, some members of the Portland government indulged in intrigues, with Canning seeking the removal of Castlereagh. In September, both men resigned their respective positions. Their relations had become so acrimonious that on September 21, 1809, two days after resigning, they fought a duel over the affair; Canning missed, but Castlereagh wounded his opponent in the thigh.[57] Parliament convened a formal inquiry to examine the causes of the defeat of the expedition but failed to come to any conclusion except that there had been a lack of unanimity among the commanders. On April 5, 1810, the *Times* bitterly lamented, "If the Walcheren expedition is to pass unmarked by the general censure, then can no calamity happen on which the British nation will deserve to be heard?"

As devastating as the Walcheren expedition was, it needs to be considered within the larger context of British operations in 1809–1810. This was a period that witnessed British engagement in the Peninsular War and the colonial conquests that all but eliminated the French threat in the Atlantic and Indian Oceans. In the Caribbean, the British seized in quick succession the French islands of Saint-Domingue (taken by Spanish troops aided by the British), Martinique (captured in February 1809), and Guadeloupe (taken in February 1810 after a long blockade). Simultaneously, Fort Louis du Sénégal, the last French possession in Africa that served as a safe haven for French attacks on British commerce, was captured in the summer of 1809. Given that the French threat in the Atlantic had been largely neutralized, the British government could afford to draw down troops across the British colonies and utilize these newly released forces to conduct further operations. The fall of the French colonies in the Atlantic meant that the only remaining French bases outside Europe were the Mascarene Islands in the Indian Ocean and the Dutch East Indies, all of which British targeted in late 1809 and 1810, as will see.

This discussion of the War of the Fifth Coalition has not touched on events in the former Polish-Lithuanian lands, where Archduke Ferdinand conducted a half-spirited campaign against Jozef Poniatowski's Polish forces. At the start of the war Ferdinand advanced to Warsaw, only to be checked at Raszyn on April 19 and forced to abandon almost all of the occupied Polish territory. Poniatowski then went upstream on the Vistula, invaded Galicia, and raised a rebellion among the Polish population of the Austrian Empire. He forced the Austrian garrisons to surrender and began setting up a Polish administration, appealing to all Poles to unite in liberating their land. It was at this moment that the Polish plans were disrupted by the arrival of Russian troops.

Russia learned about the Austrian invasion of Bavaria on April 16. Emperor Alexander at once made it known that he would recall his ambassador from Vienna as well as demand that the Austrian envoy leave Russia. To Napoleon, the Russian emperor wrote, "Your Majesty can count on me; my means are not great, having already two wars on hand, but all that is possible will be done.... You will always find a faithful ally in me."[58] In reality, however, the Russian emperor had little desire to assist the French in dismantling the Austrian monarchy. Therefore, though Russia quickly mobilized an expeditionary corps under command of the sixty-year-old General Sergei Golitsyn, it delayed its dispatch for over a month.[59]

By late May, the principal Austrian army had already suffered a series of defeats in Bavaria and Napoleon was in possession of the Austrian capital. He was naturally displeased with the Russian foot-dragging, urging Alexander to act and lamenting that "compliments and phrases are not armies; it is armies which the circumstances demand."[60] This was especially imperative in light of the French reversal at Aspern-Essling on May 21–22 and the failed Austrian invasion of the Duchy of Warsaw that exposed Austrian weaknesses. Napoleon insisted on the *casus foederis* (case of the alliance), and Alexander felt compelled to act, ordering Golitsyn to support French operations against Austria. On May 18 the Russian emperor issued a set of decrees and instructions that shed light on Russian intentions. Golitsyn was told to avoid battle with the Austrian forces "by all means possible" and instead to secure key locations and "to entice [the Polish populace] to the Russian side" because "the stronger your position will be in the region, the more useful it will be to our interests" after the war.[61] Golitsyn, who vehemently opposed the Franco-Russian alliance, was in no hurry to act; neither were his subordinates, most of whom demonstrated pro-Austrian sympathies.[62] As early as June 6, Archduke Ferdinand was pleased to report that Golitsyn had promised "to avoid all hostilities against us and to arrange his marches as slowly as possible and leave my troops time for orderly withdrawal."[63] Poniatowski was exasperated by the Russian procrastination and complained to Napoleon about "delays that, according to all reports, [the Russians] seek to put on any active cooperation with us."[64]

Relations between Napoleon and Alexander were further exacerbated by the revelation of secret correspondence between Russian and Austrian commanders who sought to establish closer contacts, share intelligence, and coordinate their actions. The most egregious example of this was the affair involving a Russian lieutenant general, Andrei Gorchakov, in charge of the 18th Division, who corresponded with Archduke Ferdinand and expressed hope to "see our armies unite on the field of battle" against the French.[65] Gorchakov's letter was intercepted by Polish troops, who sent the original to Napoleon and a copy to Alexander, causing a scandal. Both emperors were infuriated, of course. Napoleon saw it as evidence of Russian duplicity. "The

Emperor's heart is wounded," the French ambassador to Russia, Armand de Caulaincourt, was informed by the French foreign minister. "This is the reason why he does not write to Emperor Alexander; he cannot show to him a confidence he no longer feels. He says nothing, he does not complain; he keeps to himself the displeasure he feels but he no longer appreciates the Russian alliance."[66]

For his part, Alexander demanded immediate investigation of this affair owing to "the grave nature of the accusation and in an effort to deflect false talk that it would produce." Gorchakov was quickly removed from command, court-martialed, and dismissed from military service.[67] Still, this affair made a major impression on Alexander, who was concerned about its impact on his relations with Napoleon as well as growing anti-French sentiment in the Russian officer corps. He was keen on dispelling any doubts as to the Russian commitment to the war, but his efforts to encourage Golitsyn to undertake more vigorous campaign failed.[68]

After the War of the Fifth Coalition, the Polish question emerged as one of the thorniest issues in Franco-Russian relations. Russia was the prime beneficiary of the eighteenth-century partitions of the Polish-Lithuanian Commonwealth, extending its territory deep into northeast Europe. The new lands were heavily populated and more advanced agriculturally and industrially than most of the other Russian provinces, proving to be an important economic asset for the Russian Empire. Napoleon's establishment of the Duchy of Warsaw in the summer of 1807 thus threatened Russian interests. Polish demands for eventual restoration of their kingdom only increased Russia's concerns that it would be obliged to cede territory acquired in the Polish partitions. Despite Napoleon's assurances that he had no intention of restoring Poland—"I have no desire to become the Don Quixote of Poland," Napoleon declared—Alexander remained greatly concerned by the existence of the Polish duchy, especially after 1809, when Napoleon further enlarged the duchy by retroceding to it the lands that Austria had claimed in the Partitions of Poland.[69]

The War of the Fifth Coalition revealed how strained relations between Russia and the Polish ducal authorities had become. Polish and Russian forces repeatedly confronted each other over control of the Galician lands. Poniatowski insisted on replacing the Austrian administration with Polish authorities and complained about Russian indolence, which allowed the Austrians to continue conducting operations. He was particularly upset by the Russian decision to abolish Polish authorities in the regions occupied by Russian troops. The Russians, on the other hand, disparaged the Poles for inciting unrest and spreading nationalistic propaganda, which, they felt, could spill over and cause unrest in the Russian provinces as well. "They already considered Galicia as their new conquest, their own property, and, through their speeches and appeals, were instilling a hope among the local residents in an eventual restoration of Poland," lamented the Russian court historian Alexander Mikhailovskii-Danilevskii.[70]

Russia was displeased with Poniatowski's declaration that he was "authorized by the Emperor of the French to occupy both Galicia, accept residents' oath of allegiance, conduct justice and punishment in [Napoleon's] name and replace Austrian symbols with the French eagles." In response, Golitsyn informed Poniatowski that that he considered "all locations occupied by Russian troops to belong to the Russian emperor" and demanded that Poniatowski withdraw his military forces from these territories and put an end to the recruitment of local residents.[71] An odd situation thus developed: Russians and Austrians, officially at war with each other, essentially tussled with the same enemy, the Poles, who were the formal allies of the Russians. The Russo-Polish enmity became especially pronounced in the wake of Archduke Charles's defeat at Wagram, when Archduke Ferdinand could no longer maintain his position in Galicia and had to abandon Krakow. Both Russians and Poles rushed to seize this venerable city, in which generations of Polish kings were buried. A Russian detachment rushed some forty miles in eighteen hours to beat the Poles on July 15. Yet later the same day, the much larger Polish force approached Krakow and forced its way into the city, creating an impasse that could easily have erupted into open warfare had the commanders on both sides not agreed to divide the city into two zones and occupy it jointly.[72] Just days later, the Russian commander in chief complained that "the insolence of the Warsaw troops exceeds all boundaries.... Mutual hatred reigns not only among officers but the rank and file as well.... I cannot describe all the humiliation that our troops suffer from the [Poles]."[73] The Russians were particularly incensed by the Polish decision to hang in the Krakow theater a stage curtain featuring a rising sun illuminating a coffin from which a Polish king was rising and on which the inscription outlined the borders of the former Polish kingdom. When Poniatowski began to identify himself as the "commander in chief of the Polish army," Golitsyn bluntly told him, "I do not recognize either Poland, which has long outlived itself, nor the Polish army or troops," and urged Emperor Alexander "to take immediate measures to put an end to the insolent behavior of the Warsaw troops and prevent the grave consequences that it could produce."[74]

Polish aspirations posed an acute threat to Russia and forced its government to devote considerable time and effort to the matter. Alexander had been urged to consider annexing the Austrian-held Polish territories, a prospect

Joseph Bonaparte, King of Spain (19th-century German gravure, The James S. Noel Collection).

The Spanish royal family, with King Charles IV and Queen Maria Louisa (19th-century Spanish gravure, The James S. Noel Collection).

Napoleon and his retinue during the Russian campaign (19th-century French print, author's collection).

Mehmed Ali, who took advantage of the turmoil unleashed by the Napoleonic Wars to seize power in Egypt (Portrait by Louis-Charles-Auguste Couder).

König Friedrich Wilhelm III. von Preußen.
Nach Stich von Bolt. 1813.

King Friedrich Wilhelm III of Prussia. A reserved and quiet man, he steered a careful political course in the wake of Prussian defeat in 1806 (19th-century German gravure, The James S. Noel Collection).

Simon Bolivar (19th-century Spanish print, The James S. Noel Collection). Nicknamed "The Liberator," he fought long and hard for the independence of Spanish colonies.

Admiral Edward Pellew, 1st Viscount Exmouth (Portrait by James Northcote, National Portrait Gallery, London). As commander-in-chief of the East Indies Station, he spent four years fighting the French in the Indian Ocean. His son, Fleetwood Pellew, was in command of the frigate HMS *Phaeton* that was involved in a raid on Nagasaki in 1808.

THOMAS JEFFERSON

Thomas Jefferson (19th-century American print, Author's collection). As the third president of the United States, Jefferson defended the nation's interests during the Napoleonic Wars, authorizing the first use of the American military force overseas, sanctioning the Louisiana Purchase and implementing the Embargo Act of 1807.

Kaiser Franz I. von Österreich.
Nach Stich von Longhi.

Emperor Francis I of Austria (19th-century German gravure, The James S. Noel Collection).

Sultan Selim III of the Ottoman Empire
(Portrait by Joseph Warnia-Zarzecki, Pera
Museum). A reform-minded ruler, he could not
avoid getting embroiled in the Napoleonic
Wars and was ultimately overthrown in a coup.

Gilbert Elliot-Murray-Kynynmound, 1st Earl of Minto (Portrait by James Atkinson, National Portrait Gallery, London). He served as the Governor General of the British East India Company in 1807–1813, the height of the Napoleonic Wars.

Fath Ali Shah of Iran (Portrait attributed to Mihr Ali, Louvre-Lens Museum, France). The Napoleonic Wars had a profound impact on his reign he sought to contain Russian imperial ambitions through alliances with France and Britain.

The R! Hon.ᵇˡᵉ WILLIAM PITT.

William Pitt, the Younger. His tenure as a prime minister of Britain was dominated by the French Revolutionary and Napoleonic Wars (19th-century British gravure, The James S. Noel Collection).

Richard Colley Wellesley, 1st Marquess Wellesley, the Governor General of the British East India Company (Portrait by Thomas Lawrence, Government Art Collection, Great Britain). He "found the East India Company a trading body, but left it an imperial power."

Admiral James Saumarez, 1st Baron de Saumarez (Portrait by Edwin Williams). He played an important role in protecting British interests in the Baltic region during the Napoleonic Wars.

Der Marsch auf Paris.
Nach Gemälde von f. Dietz.

"The March on Paris"—Gebhard Leberecht von Blucher, nicknamed Marschall Vorwärts ("Marshal Forward"), urging his men forward as they march toward the French borders (19th-century German print, The James S. Noel Collection).

Iranian Envoy Mirza Mohammed Reza-Qazvini meeting with Napoleon I at the Finckenstein
Palace to negotiate a Franco-Iranian alliance in April 1807 (19th-century gravure based on
painting by François Mulard, The James S. Noel Collection).

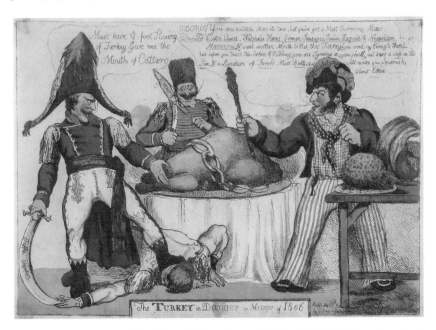

"The Turkey in Danger," declared this British caricature in May 1806. With Austria crushed,
France and Russia are preparing to carve up a "turkey" while the British sailor, proudly
wearing the "Trafalgar" and "Nile" ribbons in his hat, tries to stop them (Author's collection).

The Battle of Grand Port was one of the worst defeats of the British Royal Navy during the Napoleonic Wars. This painting by Pierre-Julien Gilbert shows HMS *Iphigenia* striking her colors and HMS *Magicienne* and HMS *Sirius* being scuttled by fire, while HMS *Nereide* is about to surrender to the French. Just four months later, the British returned with vengeance, defeating the French and capturing the Isle de France (Musée national de la Marine, Paris).

French troops repelling one of the Mamluk charges during battle of the Pyramids (Painting by Paul Dominique Philippoteaux). The French invasion had shattered the Mamluk power in Egypt and had caused major geopolitical repercussions for the rest of the Middle East.

Napoleon accepting the surrender of Madrid in the fall of 1808 (19th-century lithography based on the painting by Antoine-Jean Gros, The James S. Noel Collection). The French invasion marked a turning point not just for Spain but, more crucially, the vast empire it controlled in the Americas.

King Louis XVIII hastily departing the royal palace in March 1815 (19th-century lithography based on the painting by Antoine-Jean Gros, The James S. Noel Collection). Just hours later, Napoleon reclaimed his crown, completing one of the most daring and improbable invasions in history.

The Waterloo heroes assembled at Apsley House in London (19th-century British print, Anne S. K. Brown Military Collection).

A British attack on Buenos Aires, as seen by Madrid Martinez in 1807 (Casa Rosada Museum).

Probably one of the most recognizable Napoleonic print, this caricature by James Gillray shows Napoleon and British Prime Minister William Pitt carving up the world. The diminutive Napoleon, rising from his seat in order to reach the table, slices off Europe while Pitt carves half a globe and a large slice of ocean, illustrating the respective areas of power in the ongoing war between Britain and France (Author's collection).

Napoleon as "der Universalmonarch." Josiah Boydell's caricature, published in 1813, shows Napoleon sitting on a heap of human skulls while his feet rest on a pile of diplomatic documents. Marshal Alexander Berthier is kneeling before him in adoration while a court official on the right pours from a ewer marked "Tears" into a cup. Next to Napoleon, a Folly personified flings awards to soldiers as cities are burning in the distance. In the foreground are sacks inscribed "Hessian treasure," "Austrian contributions," "Domain monies," etc. In the sky, the eagles of Prussia, Austria, and Russia are hurling their thunderbolts at Napoleon (Author's collection).

One of the most iconic moments of the Napoleonic Era: the meeting of Emperors Napoleon and Alexander on the raft on the Nieman River in 1807. Tilsit marked the high-tide of Napoleon's power in Europe (19th-century French print, The James S. Noel Collection).

Napoleon entering Berlin at the head of his Grande Armée in the wake of Prussia's catastrophic defeat in 1806 (Painting by Charles Meynier).

The Battle of New Orleans, one of the decisive moments of the War of 1812, took place after the signing of Anglo-American peace but before the news could reach the United States. The battle featured many veteran British troops from the Peninsular War, including Major General Edward Pakenham (on the left) who was mortally wounded. (Print by John Landis, 1840, Anne S. K. Brown Military Collection).

One of the most famous naval battles in history, Trafalgar was a decisive British victory over the Franco-Spanish fleet that confirmed the naval supremacy of Britain. However, contrary to popular perceptions, the French naval power did not end there. Over the next nine years, Britain had much to fear from France when it came to command of the sea. (Painting by Clarkson Stanfield).

that clearly alarmed the Austrian monarchy.[75] Golitsyn advised the Russian emperor to annex Galicia, pointing to a group of Polish magnates who had approached him in secrecy with an offer of immediate allegiance should Alexander consent to restore Poland and place the country under his rule. In late June this question was considered in a top-secret memorandum written by Nikolai Rumyantsev that explored the pros and cons of annexing Polish lands. As enticing as it might have been to exploit Austrian weakness and seize new territories, the Russian government chose to reject it, arguing that such an act would violate agreements sanctioning the three Polish partitions. Furthermore, even if Russia annexed the new Polish lands, there was no guarantee that the Poles would not rally around the national cause and seek to detach themselves completely from Russia. Comparing the relations between Russia and Poland to those of Britain and Ireland, the imperial memorandum spoke of "popular unrests [that] present immediate advantages to the enemies of England in any conflicts and where the British government continues to struggle with administration despite the many centuries that have passed since England's annexation of this land."[76]

In the wake of the 1809 war, Alexander was very anxious over Polish behavior in Galicia and wanted "to be reassured at all costs" that Poland would not be restored. "The world is not large enough for us to settle the affairs of Poland if the question of the Polish restoration is raised."[77] The Russian government sent a special note to Napoleon clearly expressing its fears of a reestablished Poland and demanding assurances that this would not happen.[78] Throughout 1809–1810 France and Russia were engaged in protracted (and bitter) negotiations over the fate of the Polish polity, which revealed the degree of Russian trepidation over a possible Polish state. The Russian government urged Napoleon to accept a draft convention that would have prevented the restoration of Poland. The draft's very first article stated bluntly, "The Kingdom of Poland will never be reestablished," while subsequent articles prohibited the contracting parties from using the very terms "Poland," "Pole," or "Polish," so that these words could "disappear forever from all official or public acts of whatever nature."[79] Napoleon rejected these demands.[80] Furthermore, he was upset by continued Russian harping on the Polish subject: "What is Russia pretending? Does she want war? Why these perpetual complaints? Why these injurious worries? Had I wanted to reestablish Poland, I would have said so and would not have withdrawn my troops from Germany. Does Russia want to prepare me for her desertion? . . . Does she not get all the fruits from the alliance?"[81]

Napoleon failed to see that from the Russian perspective the "fruits" of the Franco-Russian alliance had already wilted and been replaced by more pragmatic considerations. The foremost of them was preservation of the balance of power. In 1808–1809 the Russian emperor sought to prevent hostilities in Europe; unable to achieve this, he hoped for a quick ending of the war that would have preserved Austria as a potential counterbalance to France. On June 20 Alexander approved a lengthy memorandum to Baron Bethmann, who represented Russian interests in the Confederation of the Rhine. The letter revealed that Alexander did not want to see either the Austrians or the French scoring a decisive victory. A major victory "would have given [Austrians] all the reasons to become overconfident and would have only postponed the conclusion of peace . . . Europe would have again found itself in political turmoil, and fresh and protracted efforts would have been needed to restore order everywhere." Yet the Russian emperor was also glad that Napoleon did not come out decisively on top at Aspern-Essling. "His power would have increased infinitely without having any effect on England's might. He would have forced Austria to accept all of his conditions but how would Europe have benefited from this?" Instead, Alexander hoped that France and Austria would realize how detrimental their war was to both of them and settle their difference through negotiations. The Russian emperor was concerned that the Austrian emperor, Francis, was captive to "illusions" of British support. "Where does he hope to find funds to continue this expensive war if England denies him subsidies? With what forces does he intend to pursue his futile plan of reigning in France if England denies him assistance?" The Russian government wanted to see if the Viennese court "was ready to acknowledge that the restoration of peace might be worth some sacrifices by Austria instead of gambling on continuing a war that may end up in the complete destruction of the monarchy that holds such a glorious place in the annals of European history."[82] On August 16, as Napoleon and Francis began negotiating peace, Alexander commented that the intercepted French letters revealed "certain irritation" at Russia's behavior at the French court. "But this is not important since in current circumstances I prefer this irritation to what could have been if we had actively assisted [Napoleon] in the destruction of Austria. Emperor Napoleon mentioned in one of his conversations, 'I conducted negotiations with Austria only because she still retains her army. If she had lost it, I would not have talked to her at all.' Therefore, we should be thrilled that we did not contribute to the destruction of the Austrian army."[83]

While Alexander may have wanted to project the image of a faithful ally to Napoleon, he faced a major obstacle at home, where the nobility "was as proud of Austrian victories as if there were our own, and everyone was enraged by [the Austrian defeat at] Wagram." The French ambassador was struck by "the state of agitation that spread in the Russian society. I have never seen anything like it." In the salons, Emperor Alexander was called "good but stupid" and the malcontents spoke openly about entrusting the destiny of the empire to firmer hands.[84] Senior military figures openly condemned the Franco-Russian alliance, which in their minds made Russia subservient to Napoleon, and predicted that France would soon restore Poland, the first step in the eventual decline of Russia. "Whoever might rule Russia in the future," one field marshal concluded, "we, the noblemen, would manage to preserve our property. But the [Romanov dynasty], if it continues its current policy, would lose everything it has."[85]

CHAPTER 15

The Northern Question, 1807–1811

T HE WARS OF THE THIRD and Fourth Coalitions were far more complex events than the traditional narratives suggest, with their focus on Napoleon's defeat of Austria, Prussia, and Russia. In addition to their profound impact on central Europe, these conflicts decisively changed the balance of power in the Baltic region with far-reaching ramifications for the Scandinavian countries.

At the start of the nineteenth century, Scandinavia consisted of just two states: the kingdoms of Denmark, whose domains extended to Schleswig, Holstein, Greenland, Iceland, and Norway, and of Sweden, whose kings also ruled over Finland, parts of Pomerania, and the city of Wismar. Once a dominant partner in the so-called Kalmar Union, which brought together the Scandinavian nations in 1397, Denmark was gradually eclipsed by its Swedish neighbors, especially in the wake of the Thirty Years' War, when King Gustavus Adolphus's intervention marked the rise of Sweden as the dominant regional power. The two states routinely went to war against each other, with the Swedes gaining the upper hand throughout the seventeenth century. Yet the eighteenth century had not been kind to the Swedish rulers, who had witnessed a gradual decline of their influence in the Baltic due to the rise of the Russian Empire. Sweden's defeat during the Great Northern War (1700–1721) meant that Denmark enjoyed a period of economic growth, with its agricultural expansion stimulating an increase in maritime activity, an important factor in Denmark's eventual involvement in the Napoleonic Wars. By contrast, Sweden's economic and military weakness after the Great Northern War did little to reduce its desire to revive past glories. The Swedish sovereigns still harbored hopes of acquiring Norway, linked by a common crown to Denmark since 1536.[1]

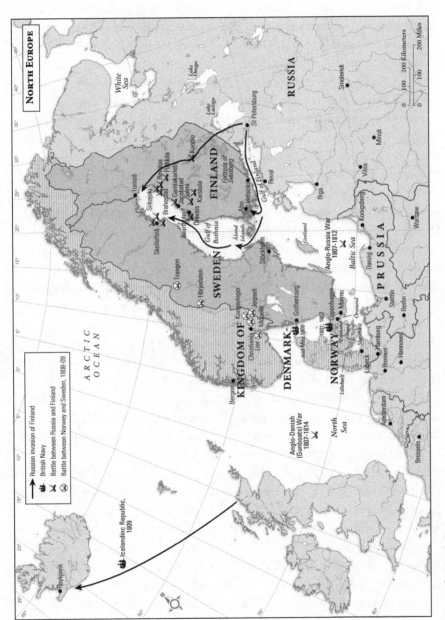

Map 16: North Europe

The already complex political situation in the Baltic was further complicated by the start of the French Revolution, which produced contrasting
reactions on either side of the Danish Straits. In the Danish realm, the middle
class tended to be sympathetic to the revolutionary changes unfolding in
France because of reforms that were already well under way under the aegis
of a benevolent absolutism in Denmark. Danish writer Knud Rahbek liked
to describe himself, half jokingly, as "'a Jacobin in France but a royalist in
Denmark," a description that many of his fellow Danes probably would have
accepted.[2] Denmark remained neutral throughout the Revolutionary Wars,
concerned more about British naval power than the spread of revolutionary
ideology. Britain was naturally concerned with maintaining trade with and
naval access to the Baltic region, elements crucial to its own naval power.
Should the Danes come under France's influence, British trade and access
would be imperiled because of the closure of the narrow Sound, the strait that
served as British shipping's only entry into the Baltic Sea. Moreover, the
Danish navy, considering its size and quality, could also pose a major threat,
since a possible union of the Danish, French-Dutch, and Spanish naval forces
would put British control of the North Sea, if not the rest of the Atlantic, in
jeopardy. It was these tensions that ultimately resulted in the British attack
on Denmark in 1801. Interestingly, the British aggression did not result in
a Franco-Danish alliance, partly because of Danish crown prince regent
Frederick's dislike for Bonaparte, and France in general. The Danish government instead strove to remain neutral, a policy reinforced by the reality of the
Danish economy's dependence on neutral trade and shipping.

In Sweden, where there had been a growing conflict between the aristoc-
racy and a monarchy that showed an autocratic streak. King Gustavus IV
Adolf's abhorrence of the French Revolution resulted in Sweden's direct
involvement in anti-French coalitions, which required considerable expense
and yet brought no tangible benefits.[3] In 1805 Gustavus's decision to join the
Third Coalition led to the Franco-Swedish War, which began with the
Swedish declaration of war on France in October 1805. A month later, an
Anglo-Russian-Swedish expeditionary force landed in Swedish Pomerania
but was unable to make headway against the French troops in Hanover.
Napoleon's triumph at Austerlitz in December forced the coalition partners
to withdraw their forces, leaving just Swedish troops to defend Pomerania.[4]
In 1806, during the War of the Fourth Coalition, Sweden was surprised by
the sudden collapse of Prussia and tried desperately to evacuate its forces but
was caught unprepared by the rapidly advancing French forces at Lübeck,
where, on November 6, 1806, the French routed the fleeing Prussian troops
of General Blucher and trapped the few remaining Swedish troops.[5] Although

of minor military importance, this event did have political ramifications—
Marshal Jean-Baptiste Bernadotte's respectful treatment of captive Swedish
officers earned him goodwill among the Swedes, who remembered his benev-
olence when the French marshal was considered as a possible candidate for an
heir to the Swedish throne four years later.

In early 1807, Napoleon ordered his troops to invade Swedish Pomerania
and seize its main port city, Stralsund. Marshal Édouard Mortier blockaded
the city after his efforts to capture it had been frustrated by the Swedish garrison under Hans Henric von Essen. The siege lasted throughout the spring
of 1807, with Essen scoring a brief success in late March when Napoleon's
decision to divert the bulk of Mortier's corps to the fortress of Kolberg in
Prussian Pomerania allowed the Swedes to push the remaining French troops
away from the city, briefly lifting the siege. The Swedish offensive, in fact,
captured more than 1,500 French prisoners and several towns, reviving King
Gustavus's hopes for a successful campaign against his French nemesis. The
unexpected nature of the Swedish success, however, proved its undoing, as
the French quickly responded to this new threat. Mortier returned in force to
Pomerania, defeated the Swedes at Belling on April 16, and compelled them
to seek a truce two days later. Napoleon, preoccupied with the military operations against the Russians and Prussians in Poland, agreed to accept the
terms of the Armistice of Schlatkow, which transferred the islands of Usedom
and Wolin (in the estuary of the Oder River) to France and allowed Swedish
troops to remain in Pomerania only north of the Peene River.[6]

The Armistice of Schlatkow threatened to undermine Anglo-Swedish
relations. The British government denounced it as a disgraceful capitulation
and warned the Swedish royal government against conducting formal peace
talks with France. Britain's fears that armistice might signal a change in
Swedish foreign policy were not entirely unfounded, given that many in the
Swedish government and army believed that the long-standing Anglo-Swedish
"Common Cause" was actually detrimental to Swedish interests.[7] Although
the two states entered into alliance in 1805, contemporary observers remem-
bered well that Sweden had joined the League of Armed Neutrality against
Britain just four years earlier and was in fact a much more eager partner than
Denmark. Furthermore, many Swedish officers opposed participation in the
Third Coalition and could not see any worth in their campaign in Pomerania,
a territory that their king had repeatedly tried to swap for Norway. But King
Gustavus nonetheless remained resolutely anti-French, still disgruntled by
the lack of French support for his Pomeranian-Norwegian exchange plan,
Napoleon's meddling in German affairs, and the Imperial Recess. The final
straw that led him to become resolutely anti-French was the publication of

scathing remarks about him in the French official newspaper *Le Moniteur* in the wake of his outspoken condemnation of the murder of the duc d'Enghien. For Gustavus, the spring armistice was just a respite that allowed him to negotiate with Prussia and Russia regarding a joint attack on the French. On April 20, just two days after the armistice was agreed upon, Sweden joined Russia and Prussia in the Convention of Bartenstein, in which they pledged to make no separate peace with Napoleon and agreed that Prussian troops should join the Swedes in Rügen for the purpose of driving the French from Pomerania.[8] After ratifying the convention, the Swedish king traveled to Stralsund, where he took personal charge of the Swedish forces and denounced the armistice on July 3. His decision was bolstered by the signing of two conventions (on June 17 and 23) with Britain, which in addition to its usual offer of subsidies also pledged to commit troops to the war in Pomerania.[9]

Gustavus's timing for the renewal of his alliance with Britain could not have been worse, since Prussia and Russia, militarily defeated and exhausted, were on the cusp of signing the Treaty of Tilsit, the news of which reached Gustavus only a few days after the rupture of the armistice. The Prussian troops were thus withdrawn, and although the British expeditionary force under Lord Cathcart arrived at Stralsund in mid-July, it failed to support Swedish troops in Pomerania. Instead the British force was recalled once news of the Treaty of Tilsit revealed the scale of Napoleon's triumph in northern Europe. Left alone to face the French, the Swedes crumbled. Napoleon responded to the Swedish bluster by sending Marshal Guillaume Brune into Swedish Pomerania, where the French, reinforced by their German, Italian, and Spanish allies, quickly overran Swedish defenses and laid siege yet again to Stralsund. Gustavus hastily departed from the city in late August, leaving to his hapless generals the task of fighting the French. The Swedish command quickly came to the conclusion that resistance was futile, and after spiking most of their cannon they evacuated the city, assisted in this by Brune's decision to allow them to depart when he could have easily annihilated the Swedish army at Rügen. By September, Stralsund and the neighboring island of Rügen were in French hands, while Sweden was driven out of Germany.[10]

In the wake of the Swedish defeat in Pomerania and the Franco-Russian rapprochement at Tilsit, Britain focused its attention on Denmark, which at the start of the nineteenth century faced two main challenges: the protection of its maritime commerce, which had been threatened by Britain, and the preservation of its own safety in the face of the rising power of France on the continent. We have already seen how incensed the Danes were by the British practice of stopping and examining neutral commerce, including Danish merchantmen, which caused Denmark to support the League of Armed Neutrality in 1800–1801. The British attack on Copenhagen dissuaded the Danish monarchy from participating in the league, but it also hardened Danish sentiments toward the British. During the Wars of the Third and Fourth Coalitions Denmark prudently adopted neutrality, though this did not spare it from the rigors of war.

In late 1806, in the wake of Jena-Auerstadt, Napoleon's forces approached Danish frontiers while pursuing the retreating Prussian troops. In November, during the fighting at Lübeck, French troops under Marshal Joachim Murat strayed into the Danish province of Holstein, where they were promptly engaged by the Danish border guards.[11] The Danish crown prince regent (*kronprinsregent*) Frederick, who acted as the regent for his mentally incapacitated father, King Christian VII, protested the French violation of neutral territory, and Murat immediately withdrew his troops, pledging to take "extreme measures to ensure respect for the neutrality" of the Danish realm.[12] However, just ten days after this exchange, the prince regent ordered his troops to redeploy to a new defensive line along the Eyder River, which meant that the province of Holstein had been all but abandoned by the Danes. The Danish decision was intended to show their commitment to neutrality as well as ensure the goodwill of Napoleon, who was anxious to protect his lines of communication. Yet the powers leagued in the Fourth Coalition were upset by these Danish "sympathies" for Napoleon, since neither Russia, Prussia, nor Britain could anticipate the lengths to which Prince Frederick was willing to go in his efforts to appease the French emperor. In December 1806 Britain considered organizing an alliance with Sweden and Denmark to defend northern Europe. Inspired by their experiences in Sicily, where the Royal Navy protected the Bourbon royal family of Naples, the British government offered to assist the Danish monarchy if it decided to leave Copenhagen for the safety of Norway, which could be well protected by a British squadron. Sweden expressed readiness to send troops to Denmark for a joint defense of the realm. The Danes rejected the offer, which went against their declared policy of neutrality and would have resulted in the French capture of the whole of Denmark or, worse still, the country's occupation by Swedish troops.[13] The Danish refusal to cooperate, however, upset coalition partners, who were determined to take whatever steps were necessary to make Denmark side with them. Thus, though the April 1807 Convention of Bartenstein contained provisions to force Denmark to join the coalition, the continental powers had no opportunity to put it into effect.

Britain, however, could act, and in the summer of 1807 it did. The British decision to launch a naval attack on a neutral (however tentatively) country caused a fierce public outcry and was condemned by many leading political and public figures at home. George Canning, foreign secretary in the government of Prime Minister William Henry Cavendish-Bentinck, Duke of Portland, claimed that the decision had been prompted by crucial intelligence gained about the Franco-Russian negotiations at Tilsit—involving Napoleon discussing the possible formation of a Franco-Russian maritime league against Britain, a league that Denmark, Portugal, and Sweden were to be forced to join.[14] Yet when challenged by the opposition, Canning could not produce any conclusive evidence of this, nor could he prove that Denmark would have placed its fleet at Napoleon's disposal.[15] In later years it emerged that some details of the Franco-Russian discussions came from a British agent, Colin Alexander Mackenzie, whose family claimed he had procured this information by disguising himself during the emperors' meeting on a raft, an exploit that can be safely rejected as preposterous.[16] The intelligence on the possible maritime league against Britain actually came from the comte d'Antraigues, a French royalist émigré in the Russian service who, in turn, received it from one of Alexander I's aides-de-camp. Recent analysis has shown that d'Antraigues's letter was full of inaccuracies and was most certainly written to secure for d'Antraigues a permanent refuge and pension in Britain.[17] Canning believed that he had received genuine intelligence from Tilsit, however, and his certainty would in turn have impressed other members of the government.

While d'Antraigues's letter may have provided an immediate cause for the expedition, the underlying reasons for the British expedition to Copenhagen were more complex. That the Portland government considered the situation in Denmark so key is reflective of the Baltic region's central role in Britain's notions of its security and trade. Britain's well-being was based on the strength and quality of its fleet. Yet with British forests all but depleted by the late eighteenth century, the Royal Navy had become largely dependent on foreign wood supplies. The Baltic was crucial because it was a source of Russian timber—the oak and fir used for masts, underwater planking, and decking. Britain could acquire these resources from other locations (in Germany or North America), but they tended to be inferior in some aspects and the Royal Navy frequently rejected them.[18] Equally important for the Navy was Russian hemp, which accounted for more than 90 percent of the British needs. Though successive British governments tried to diversify their sources by cultivating hemp in North America and elsewhere, their efforts produced paltry results, leaving Britain heavily dependent on Russia and the Baltic trade.[19] The Baltic region also served as an important trade emporium, one in which the value of British exports had increased sevenfold between 1793 and 1803, a clear consequence of the French policy of denying British trade access to continental ports.[20]

London was concerned not just with safeguarding its trade and naval supplies but also with denying Napoleon an opportunity to rebuild his naval capacity after Trafalgar. Denmark's alliance with Napoleon would furnish the latter with a means of closing the Sound, blocking Britain's access to the raw materials necessary to the upkeep of the Royal Navy, while the Danish fleet—fifth-largest in the world, with twenty ships-of-the-line (plus three under construction), twenty-seven frigates, and sixty smaller vessels—could, in combination with Napoleon's naval resources, pose a serious threat to British control of the North Sea.[21]

Thus from the British perspective the general situation in 1807 was far worse than that of 1800 because it came about in the wake of Napoleon's triumphs over Prussia and Russia, which had extended French control all the way to the Baltic shores. Danish withdrawal from Holstein, complaints against the British blockade of the Elbe (instituted in response to Napoleon's Berlin Decrees), new work on Danish coastal defenses, and, most important, British reports (that were far from accurate) that the Danish fleet was preparing to sail within a month all reinforced the British government's opinion that the Danes were hostile to Britain and were only waiting for an opportune moment to show their hand.[22] This threat touched Britain's most sensitive spot, and the reaction was immediate. For Canning and many other senior British statesmen, it was time for the Royal Navy to pay another "visit" to Copenhagen, and Denmark's supposed inability to defend itself against Napoleon gave Britain an excuse to portray its actions as a matter of self-preservation.[23] Danish historians might have a point when they argue that in the wake of Napoleon's string of victories on the continent, a forceful action against Denmark served the political purpose of showing the British public, and the world, that Britain had not been beaten yet.[24]

The British government chose to ignore (whether intentionally or not) Danish efforts to resist Napoleon. It is deeply ironic that had the British expedition been postponed, the Danish court still would have had to choose whether to side with or against Britain, because Napoleon was about to force its hand. On July 31 he ordered his foreign minister to warn the Danish government to take action against British violation of the Baltic Sea and to "choose either to make war on England or on me."[25] Talleyrand, who resigned from his post nine days later, did not convey his master's ultimatum during his meeting with the Danish emissary in Paris and instead assured him of Napoleon's readiness to let Denmark continue its existing policy of neutrality. The cause for Talleyrand's disobedience remains unknown, though a talented diplomat like him could have easily anticipated possible repercussions of the more aggressive approach that Napoleon tended to favor. He would have been well aware of the Danish government's announcement that should the French demand the closure of its ports to British ships, it would consider Britain as its "natural ally." Inexplicably, the British government paid no attention to such a declaration, just as it ignored the Danish refusal to comply with the French demand for the closure of the British mail route through Denmark.[26]

In any case, Britain proceeded with an attack. On July 26 Admiral James Gambier sailed from Yarmouth Roads for Copenhagen in command of twenty-five ships-of-the-line and forty frigates and other vessels. Accompanying him was Lieutenant General Lord Cathcart, in charge of an expeditionary force of more than 25,000 men in 377 transports. The British fleet anchored off Helsinger on August 3 and quickly moved to secure the Storebælt (Great Belt) Strait to blockade Copenhagen. At this point, the experience of the 1801 expedition played a decisive role—the Great Belt had been unnavigable for anyone but the Danes until the Royal Navy charted it in 1801. The Danes, surprised by the arrival of the British armada, rejected the British demand to hand over their entire fleet and enter into a defensive alliance.[27] They could have hardly done otherwise. Throughout 1806–1807 the Danish monarch hoped that by avoiding overt hostile acts and asserting neutrality, it would be able to maneuver between France and Britain.[28] The arrival of Gambier's fleet now left them no choice. As Danish diplomat Joachim Bernstorff lamented, "A war with England will be disastrous for us. Yet any compliance with England's demands must inevitably cause a rupture with France."[29] He was correct. While war with Britain entailed financial disruption and naval destruction for Denmark, a conflict with France certainly would have led to French occupation of Holstein and Schleswig, if not the Jutland Peninsula—in other words, a larger share of Denmark's most populated areas.

On August 15, with diplomatic negotiations called off, Gambier launched his attack on Copenhagen. The British troops landed at Vedbaek and Skodsborg, a few miles north of Copenhagen, and approached the Danish capital. On the sixteenth, Denmark formally declared war on Britain, a declaration followed by first skirmishes between the two sides. After the land attacks failed to coerce the Danes, on September 2 the British fleet commenced its bombardment of Copenhagen, one that was directed not only at the city defenses, a legitimate military target, but at the city itself. The British applied the valuable lessons they had learned six years earlier and organized one of the most intensive bombardments of the entire nineteenth century, launching hundreds of bombs, grenades, and incendiary rockets, which caused significant damage and set the central districts of Copenhagen, including its Latin quarter, on fire, though the loss of life was surprisingly low.[30] On September 6 the Danes capitulated, agreeing to the British demands, including the occupation of Heligoland and the Danish colonies in the West Indies, as well as the surrender of the entire Danish fleet. No less valuable was the seizure of supplies from the Danish naval dockyard, which included thousands of tons of naval stores, wood, hempen ropes, sails, and masts.[31] It took six weeks of hard work—proof of how wrongheaded earlier British promises had been—for the British to prepare as many Danish warships as they could for a journey to Britain; those that could not be readied were destroyed. On October 21 Admiral Gambier sailed back home, pleased at having successfully prevented augmentation of Napoleon's naval strength.

The Copenhagen expedition was a major British success, neutralizing a potential naval threat. It was also significant for the effect it had in Portugal, where just weeks later the Portuguese monarchy found itself faced with British and French demands. With events in Copenhagen undoubtedly fresh in his mind, the Portuguese king chose to accept the British offer to help him evacuate to Brazil. Nonetheless, success at Copenhagen came at a heavy price for Britain. Just ten days after the British departure, the Danes signed a treaty of alliance with Napoleon and on November 4 declared war on Britain. An unprovoked attack by a great power on a weaker neutral state had deprived Britain of any higher moral ground in its struggle against Napoleon, whom the British government routinely condemned for violating international law. "We shall henceforth be dubbed the Nation of Saracens instead of the Nation of Shopkeepers," observed one British general.[32] The bombardment of Copenhagen aggravated the resentment that coalition partners already felt toward Britain's perceived unfaithfulness; Russian, Swedish, and Prussian diplomats compared the swiftness and efficiency with which the British government organized this expedition to Denmark with the slothfulness of its actions when the allies needed British support.

Copenhagen echoed particularly strongly in St. Petersburg. Emperor Alexander had already agreed at Tilsit to go to war against Britain should his mediation fail. In August, just as the British fleet sailed to the Danish shores, the new Russian ambassador to London, Maximilian von Alopeus, offered the British government Russia's mediation and was told in clear terms that Britain was not interested; a similar response was also given to Prussian and Austrian overtures to discuss a general peace. British intransigence, viewed against the backdrop of bombardment of Copenhagen, did much to alienate European powers, especially in Russia, where there was a growing belief that the alliance with Britain no longer served Russian interests.[33] Thus in a declaration of November 5, 1807, the Russian government broke off all communication with Britain, reproaching it for revealing global imperial aspirations (as shown by the British invasions of Rio de La Plata and Egypt) and for failing to adequately support its allies.[34] Britain was now at war with all but three European states (Sweden, Portugal, and Sicily).

The British attack on Copenhagen also had far-reaching consequences for Scandinavian nations. Within Denmark, the attack caused a burst of patriotism that helped rally the people against Britain and sustained the Danish war effort for the next seven years. The government did its best to enflame public opinion against Britain, supporting publication of numerous articles and pamphlets in German, French, and English and commissioning special propaganda prints.[35] The attack on Copenhagen turned Denmark from a neutral power into a dependable ally of Napoleon for the duration of the Napoleonic Wars.[36] It also ignited a new conflict in Scandinavia, whose two halves were pulled in opposite directions, and involved both of them in the wider struggle between the supreme land powers (France and Russia) and the preeminent sea power (Britain), which now regarded the European coastline as a frontier zone.

The Danes may have lost their fleet but not their desire to fight back. In the immediate aftermath of the war, thousands of Danish and Norwegian seamen joined in Anglo-Danish hostilities that became known as the "gunboat war" and involved small operations in which shallow-draft vessels went after British shipping along the North Sea and Baltic coasts. Although a constant nuisance to the Royal Navy, the Danish gunboats never came close to challenging British control of the seas.[37] The fighting unfolded not only in the North Sea but also in the Caribbean and India; in December 1807 a Royal Navy squadron under Admiral Alexander Cochrane captured the Danish islands of St. Thomas (December 22) and Santa Cruz (December 25), which remained in British hands until the end of the Napoleonic Wars. Meanwhile, in February 1808, the British took control over the Danish possessions at Tranquebar (Tharangambadi, in south India) and Serampore (in northeast India). This marked an abrupt end to Denmark's lucrative trade in colonial wares. Denmark's finances suffered both from the heavy burden of financing the war and from the disruption of trade with Britain and its shipping industry; by 1811, the kingdom was forced to suspend capital payments on its foreign loans.

The Danish prince regent found himself between a rock and a hard place. Despite his opposition, a war against Sweden became one of the key provisions of the Franco-Danish alliance. Even though the decision to wage war was not his, this was obviously how it appeared to the Danish public, the Norwegians in particular. It drove a wedge between Denmark and Norway, which was highly dependent on the seas for its trade and food supplies and traditionally enjoyed close ties with the British Isles, which consumed Norwegian timber, iron, and other commodities. With Denmark's entry into the war, Norway found itself subjected to a British blockade that, combined with the bad harvests of 1807–1808, caused much hardship among its populace, some of whom were reduced to consuming bark bread for survival.[38] Also not spared was Iceland, which had remained one of Denmark's dependencies since the late fourteenth century. At the start of the Napoleonic Wars, it was a sparsely populated island (Reykjavik boasted a population of just 307 in 1801) that believed itself far enough from Europe to escape the ravages of wars and revolutions.[39] The British bombardment of Copenhagen proved otherwise. In its immediate aftermath the British navy began to intercept Icelandic ships, causing considerable misery.

At the same time, the British had revived earlier plans to seize the island from Denmark and either turn it into a penal colony, similar to the infamous Botany Bay colony in Australia, or exploit its famed cod fisheries.[40] The British government sought the advice of Sir Joseph Banks, the great British botanist and president of the Royal Society who had led the first scientific expedition to the island and had firsthand knowledge. Banks produced a lengthy memorandum supporting annexation plans—Iceland quite simply "ought to be a part of the British Empire," he argued—but advising against a military expedition, given that the local population lacked firearms. Banks was instrumental in convincing the British ministry to change its policy toward Iceland and secured the release of detained Icelandic vessels, which were allowed to resume trade with the continent. In return, British merchants were granted licenses to trade on the island.[41]

The first British trading expedition, led by soap merchant Samuel Phelps, sought to trade in wool, fish, and tallow, which were readily available in Iceland. However, the expedition caused political turmoil. Britain and Denmark were at war and the expedition could not hope to secure the support of the Danish governor of Iceland, Count Frederik Christopher Trampe, who remained loyal to the metropole and tried his best to obstruct trade with Britain by posting notices that any interaction would be a capital offense. Unable to comprehend how Trampe could refuse an offer to relieve the suffering of the starving Icelandic population, Phelps decided to impose "a free trade" on the islanders, soliciting Joseph Bank's help in securing the dispatch of a British warship to Iceland. Returning to the island in June 1809, Phelps found that Trampe was still intractable, and so Phelps resolved the matter by having him detained and deposed from his post. Realizing that he had overstepped the boundaries of his trading license, Phelps sought to distance himself from the incident and allowed his twenty-nine-year-old interpreter, Jørgen Jørgensen, a Dane who, as Phelps put it, "had imbibed all the quixotism of a petit Napoleon," to take over governance.[42] On June 26, 1809, Jørgensen assumed the role of the governor of Iceland.[43]

Born in Copenhagen in 1780, Jørgensen seemed an unlikely revolutionary.[44] He had spent most of his adult life in the British navy, crisscrossing the oceans to New Zealand, Tasmania, and South Africa. In 1807 he witnessed the British bombardment of Copenhagen and embarked on a new career as a privateer, attacking British vessels. This career lasted less than six months; the ship he had commanded was stumbled upon and captured by a British warship. and Jørgensen was put on parole. In 1809 he broke his parole by absconding from Britain as an interpreter for Phelps's trade expedition to Iceland, where he found himself in charge of the local government. Jørgensen proved to be a natural at it. He declared Iceland free and independent of Denmark.[45]

Taking advantage of the islanders' calm response to the overthrow of the royal governor, Jørgensen began to introduce Jacobin-like political and social reforms: the granting of basic rights and freedoms, equality before the law, voting rights, educational reform, and relief for the poor. All debts owed to the Danish monarchy or Danish merchants were forgiven, while taxes were slashed in half. Jørgensen's professed intentions were to form an Icelandic republic with a legislative assembly that was democratically elected from across the island. Facing pushback from certain groups within the island's community, Jørgensen declared himself "protector" and claimed absolute authority until the convocation of the legislative body, scheduled for July 1810. To enforce his reforms, he also formed a militia, mainly staffed by petty criminals, which he used to arrest dissenters. The arrival of a Danish merchant ship with 10,000 Danish *rigsdaler* of overdue wages proved a boon for the new government, which immediately seized it and used to sustain its reforms.

The Icelandic republic survived for just nine weeks before its existence was cut short by the arrival of HMS *Talbot*, which was dispatched to follow up on the success of Phelps's trading party. Instead, Captain Alexander Jones was astonished to find a fledgling republic governed by a former Danish prisoner of war. Jørgensen's political opponents exploited this opportunity to denounce him, prompting Captain Jones to arrest Jørgensen and declare all proclamations and decrees issued by the new government void. On August 25, 1809, two months after seizing power, Jørgensen left Iceland as a prisoner once again of the British.[46]

The brief life of the Icelandic republic highlights the impact of the Napoleonic Wars on even remote corners of Europe, but it also offers a clear indication of the absence of political nationalism or democratic ideas in many areas. Jørgensen's vision of a democratic and egalitarian Iceland was admirable, but its ephemeral nature was due to the passivity of ordinary islanders, who did not defend their newly acquired rights and freedoms. Wealthy islanders were more concerned about a possible British ban on navigation between Iceland and the European mainland, which would have been disastrous for the island's maritime economy. Indeed, some British officials were alarmed by the spread of the revolutionary spirit in Iceland and insisted on a more direct involvement in its affairs. In February 1810 the British government reaffirmed its recognition of Danish sovereignty over Iceland but announced that the island would remain a dependency for the remainder of the war.[47]

Though the Swedes were not privy to the British planning for the attack on Copenhagen, their alliance with Britain had exposed them to charges of being a co-conspirator. Senior Swedish officials openly expressed their complaints that the British preoccupation with Copenhagen contributed to the defeat of the Swedish campaign in Pomerania, and even those who had supported pro-British policies in the two years previous had become disillusioned by their ally's actions. They worried that the Copenhagen attack would provoke a direct confrontation between Britain and the Franco-Russian alliance, which would inevitably drag the Swedish kingdom into a ruinous war and undermine its international standing even further.[48] Sweden had already of course lost Pomerania, a major blow to its ambitions in northern Europe. In an effort to soften the impact and to retain control of the Sound, the British invited King Gustavus to participate in the occupation of Själland (the island of Zealand), which could economically benefit Sweden though the collection of fees on the traffic in the Sound. But Gustavus, disillusioned by Britain's failure to support him in Pomerania, declined to participate in a venture that would have further stoked suspicions of Swedish collusion in the British attack on Copenhagen and could have gotten him embroiled in a war with Denmark and Norway. Instead he urged Britain to ensure that Denmark would remain neutral and serve as a buffer zone for Sweden. This was entirely unrealistic in post-Copenhagen (and post-Tilsit) environment. The Danes fell into the waiting hands of Napoleon, who negotiated the Treaty of Fontainebleau on October 31, 1807. Denmark and France agreed to make common cause for the duration of the war and not to conclude a peace with Britain separately. Furthermore, Napoleon pledged to guarantee the territorial integrity of Denmark and promised to procure compensation for Danish losses during the war. Prince Regent Frederick committed himself to France's ongoing struggle against Britain and agreed to join the Continental System and participate in all efforts to force Sweden to join the trade war against Britain. Thus the two Scandinavian states found themselves in a unique situation: neither of them really desired to have a problem with the other, and least of all war, but were nevertheless drawn into the vortex of international affairs that forced them to choose sides (Britain or France) and find themselves at war with each other.

Denmark's lurch toward France spurred the British to secure the strategically important Danish Straits. Britain made at least two more offers to Sweden to protect the straits, by either occupying Zealand or deploying British troops in Scania, the southernmost province of Sweden; to sweeten the deal Canning even offered to transfer the Dutch colony of Surinam to Swedish control. These offers were met with lukewarm support at the Swedish court, which was concerned that the presence of British troops might undermine Swedish sovereignty and imperil a region that had served as a breadbasket for the entire kingdom. As enticing as the Surinam offer was, the Swedish ministers knew how challenging it would be to govern and protect the distant colony. The British offer only served to deepen divisions in the Swedish government, as the king and his ministers had already found themselves increasingly at odds over the future direction of the Swedish realm: Gustavus believed that an Anglo-Swedish alliance could serve as a deterrent against French or Russian aggression, while his ministers perceived this partnership as one of the main reasons Sweden was having problems with its neighbors.

Sweden's continued alliance with Britain caused restlessness in Russia, which was concerned about the growing British presence in the Baltic Sea. The Baltic was particularly critical to Russia, because the Russians had limited access to warm-water ports and were consequently deprived of a larger share of lucrative overseas trade. The Baltic Sea provided the shortest routes into western Europe; without access to it, Russia could not develop its economy or hope to project its status as a great European power. Russia's presence on the Baltic was closely intertwined with its imperial identity. In the seventeenth century Peter the Great spent much of his reign "opening a window into Europe" through the Baltic. The Great Northern War between Russia and Sweden resulted in Russia annexing territories in eastern Finland and along the southern Baltic coastline. A new capital of the empire, St. Petersburg, was built on the eastern coast of the Gulf of Finland, and the political center of the Russian Empire was shifted northwest.

The struggle between Sweden and Russia continued, however. In 1741 Sweden, supported by France and Turkey, declared war against Russia; within two years it was defeated and was forced to accept a new, more disadvantageous peace concluded at Åbo (Turku).[49] Forty-five years later, Sweden tried to recover its lost lands again, but the two-year-long conflict with Russia (1788–1790) turned out to be a draw, and the Peace of Wereloe confirmed Russia's previous territorial acquisitions. During the following decade, Russia consolidated its positions along the Baltic coastline, seeking to secure commercial routes into western Europe and to protect the imperial capital, St. Petersburg. This could have been partly achieved through the conquest of Finland, then in Swedish possession, but Russian involvement in the Polish partitions and the outbreak of the Revolutionary and Napoleonic Wars postponed any such designs Russia might have had. Defeats at the hands of Napoleon contributed to growing Russian disenchantment with its allies, especially Britain, which, as far as the Russians were concerned—as discussed earlier—had failed to live up to its promises.

At Tilsit in 1807, Emperor Alexander had agreed to exact a measure of "revenge" (in the words of a Swedish diplomat) on Britain by attacking one of its last remaining allies, Sweden, though just a few months prior St. Petersburg and Stockholm themselves had formed an anti-French coalition.[50] This diplomatic turn was not easy for the Russian sovereign to pull off, and he faced considerable opposition at court. Again, here is where the British attack on Copenhagen proved decisive. Alexander was infuriated by the British aggression against his Danish ally and believed that it violated the Russo-Swedish agreements of 1780 and 1800 regarding closing the Baltic harbors to British ships and "uniting the three Nordic States for the maintenance of the Baltic peace."[51] Concerned that the British squadron could sail into the Gulf of Finland and threaten the Russian Baltic fleet at Kronstadt, Alexander personally supervised the repair of the defensive works along the coastline in the fall of 1807. Russian diplomats expressed interest in reviving the League of Armed Neutrality and unequivocally warned the Swedes that a failure to join the league would force St. Petersburg to review its relationship with Stockholm.

Gustavus rejected the Russian proposition, arguing that it was designed to weaken Sweden and facilitate Russian expansion in the Baltic Sea and Finland.[52] The king complained about the Russian forces massing near the Finnish border and believed that a war with Russia was inevitable; he even considered a preemptive attack against the Russian base at Kronstadt, which his dismayed ministers quickly rejected, instead calling for a more peaceful line toward their eastern neighbor. Baron von Ehrenheim, Sweden's chancellor for foreign affairs and a great opponent of the Anglo-Swedish alliance, urged the king to abandon Britain and seek a rapprochement with Russia, which relied on Sweden as a conduit for its trade with Britain; Ehrenheim and his supporters believed that Sweden was not prepared for a direct confrontation with Russia and should instead adopt strict neutrality. The prospect of a war with Russia increased Swedish public sentiment against the king and the alliance with Britain. Visiting Stockholm in the fall of 1807, one British traveler was surprised to find "anti-English feeling so general in Sweden that I was advised to travel as a German through the country."[53] Indeed, passions ran so high among the members of the Swedish Riksdag (assembly) that some already considered overthrowing the king and ending the British alliance to avoid a war with Russia.

On November 10, 1807, Emperor Alexander forbade British ships from entering Russian ports and suspended the property rights of British subjects residing in Russia.[54] He then demanded that Sweden close the Baltic Sea to all foreign (i.e., British) warships. It took two months before the Swedish crown responded, and on December 30, 1807, Russia threatened that if Sweden continued to avoid giving a clear reply, it would be forced to act. Finally, in January 1808, Gustavus rejected Russian demands to honor the previous arrangements as long as French troops were present on the Baltic coast and Napoleon had German ports closed to Britain. Russia considered this rejection as *casus belli*.

Russian preparations for war had begun two months earlier, when a new corps of three infantry divisions was formed near the Finnish border.[55] General Fedor Buxhöwden assumed overall command, but his divisions were understrength and exhausted by the campaign in Poland; combined, they amounted to just 24,000 men. The initial Russian strategy called for the occupation of as much territory as possible before opening negotiations.[56] Despite Russian mobilization, the Swedes were not prepared for the campaign. Partly this was due to an earlier political decision made by Gustavus and his advisors to refrain from taking any measures that could provoke Russia into declaring war. While they all considered war with Russia inevitable, they assumed that hostilities would not happen until late spring of 1808, at which point the Royal Navy could provide assistance. One may forgive the king and his ministers for thinking that the Russians would not risk a grueling winter war in Finland. Yet this was exactly Russia's plan of action, and the desperate dispatches full of warnings that the Swedish envoy to St. Petersburg, Curt von Stedingk, had sent to Stockholm were all ignored.[57] Thus the Swedish military forces were not fully mobilized and remained dispersed in their winter quarters.[58] Matters were further complicated by Gustavus's quarrel with the Riksdag over war funding, which forced him to rely heavily on British subsidies. On February 8, 1808, two weeks before the war began, Sweden and

Britain renewed their subsidy treaty and London promised to pay £1.2 million a year.[59] In early February, Gustavus ordered Field Marshal Mauritz Klingspor to leave strong garrisons at Sveaborg and Svartholm and withdraw the remaining forces to Ostrobotnia. The Swedish forces, reinforced with troops from Sweden proper, would avoid any pitched battles and wait for an opportune moment when, aided by the Royal Navy, they could commence a counterattack.[60]

On February 21, 1808, without issuing a formal declaration of war, notification, or ultimatum (an omission that the Swedes condemned as a violation of international law), the Russian Army invaded Finland.[61] It spread proclamations urging the local populations not to oppose the occupation and promising to observe order and make payment for requisitions. Swedish soldiers were encouraged to surrender without a fight.[62] The initial Russian strategy called for the occupation of as much territory as possible before opening negotiations and ending the war. Russian forces, therefore, advanced quickly, capturing Kuopio, Tavastheus, Tammerfors, and Åbo, as well as the shoreline between Åbo and Vaasa in March. In addition, the Russian advance guard seized the Åland Islands and the island of Gotland, the latter success being particularly satisfying in light of Russian fears that the British might establish a naval base there that would directly threaten the Russian coastline.[63] As Swedish forces withdrew northward, the Russians added further territories, including Jacobstad, Gamlakarleby, and Brahestad.[64] The seizure of southern Finland without bloodshed convinced the Russians that the campaign was almost over. By April, Emperor Alexander had issued a manifesto requiring his new Finnish subjects to swear an oath of loyalty to him, another violation of international law.

The war was anything but over, however. The campaign was waged across the rough terrain of Finland, dissected by numerous streams, lakes, and fjords. Immense swamps made many regions impassable to troops. The terrain was more advantageous for defensive warfare than for offense; the Swedish army included Finnish troops, who were familiar with the terrain and knew how to exploit it. The climate of Finland constituted another problem for the Russian army. A cold and prolonged winter required an effective supply system to provide the army with provisions and warm clothes, but it limited operations of the Russian fleet in the Gulf of Finland, which was partly frozen. The spring thaw brought rains and sleet that further complicated troop movements. The Swedes concentrated their forces in the north, where they were better supplied and reinforced from the mainland. Russian columns, on the other hand, were extended along lengthy lines of communication, with significant numbers of forces tied up at the fortress of Sveaborg, pacifying a Finnish population that displayed increasing discontent with the Russian presence in the region.

The Swedish high command failed to exploit these advantages. Gustavus refused calls for reinforcements to be diverted from the Norwegian front and instead pinned his hopes on a general uprising in Finland and the great Swedish fortresses at Svartholm and Sveaborg that were expected to wear down Russian forces before the impending counterattack. Yet such hopes were soon dashed. First, on March 17, the fort at Svartholm capitulated to the Russians, who then turned their attention to Sveaborg, the largest and the most formidable of all fortresses in Finland, well supplied and supported by a naval squadron and defended by a strong Swedish garrison of some 6,700 men as well as more than 1,000 cannon under Vice Admiral Karl Olof Cronstedt. The Russians blockaded the fortress on March 19 and then attacked, but their attacks caused no serious damage. Unwilling to jeopardize their forces in an all-out assault, the Russians instead exploited anti-Gustavian sentiments in the Swedish officer corps, most notably Cronstedt himself, who was bitter over his earlier demotion. Through ruses and bribes, Russian representatives General Paul van Suchtelen and Göran Magnus Sprengtporten convinced the Swedish commander to surrender. On May 6 Cronstedt handed over Sveaborg with its depots and military installations intact, allowing the Russians to seize more than a hundred gunboats and some 1,200 cannon.[65] The fall of Sveaborg, which was the linchpin of the Swedish defenses in Finland, was joyously celebrated in St. Petersburg.[66] Unsurprisingly, the news startled and demoralized the Swedish side. Equally grave was the impact on British confidence in the Swedes' ability to successfully prosecute this war.

Sweden, meanwhile, faced a new international challenge. On March 13, 1808, as the Russians were invading Finland, the mentally deranged King Christian VII of Denmark passed away and was replaced by Frederick VI, who pursued a harder stance toward Sweden. Just a day later, the Danish envoy presented a declaration of war to the Swedish government.[67] Napoleon did his best to encourage Danish ambitions of exploiting Sweden's vulnerable position to reclaim territories lost in the preceding century, and so the Danes looked hopefully to the French promise, made in the Treaty of Fontainebleau, to provide some 30,000 Franco-Spanish troops under Marshal Bernadotte to invade Sweden.[68] Both Napoleon and Frederick VI expected that Sweden would be easily defeated in a war that would involve a Russian attack through Finland, a Norwegian thrust against Gothenburg, and the Danish invasion of southern Sweden from Zealand.

The surprise news of the Danish declaration of war naturally caused great alarm in Sweden, which now found itself threatened from almost every direction.[69] The Swedish public complained about the loss of Finnish territories, the obvious lack of preparation for the war, and the lack of strong military leadership. Even senior Swedish officials expressed their reservations over Sweden's situation. "The kingdom is completely exposed on the Norwegian border and disturbing rumors already are spreading," lamented Chancellor Ehrenheim in March 1808, "and yet no one here [in Stockholm], not even the most senior military officials, knows about our means to resist."[70] King Gustavus initially intended to launch an invasion of Denmark, but the Swedish setbacks in Finland and the prospect of fighting the French caused him to sideline this plan; instead, the Swedish forces in Götaland were placed in defensive positions and the focus shifted to Norway, which Sweden considered the weakest of its opponents and where it hoped to find compensation for the loss of Finland to Russia. The king ordered a reorganization of the Swedish forces to form a new army under command of General Gustaf Mauritz Armfelt to invade Norway, and he appealed to Britain for military support. "Now is the time to push England without fail since Sweden has never been in a more perilous position than the present and England should [therefore] send massive aid quickly, quickly, both troops and ships, and more money of course. This aid is imperative if Sweden is to survive at all."[71]

The British government well understood what was at stake in the impending war in the Baltic. Faced with the combined hostility of Russia and France, Sweden had little chance of prevailing, and Britain was unwilling to jeopardize its own war effort by supporting Sweden's. The British government found the Swedish demand to more than double the subsidy to £2.8 million impossible to satisfy, and it was also reluctant to organize another major expedition, like the one to Copenhagen, to the Baltic shore; it could find a better use for those military resources elsewhere. Throughout March and April 1808, the Swedes tried unsuccessfully to convince their British ally to land troops in Norway and conduct joint operations against Denmark.[72] The British foreign secretary, Canning, remained unconvinced of the feasibility of such plans and instead offered to maintain naval blockade of coastlines, a far cry from active British involvement. Even when the British finally agreed to commit an expeditionary force to Sweden, they stressed that it was to remain under British command, would be limited to coastal operations, and could be recalled at any moment.

By late March both the Danes and the Swedes were ready for military operations, but the presence of the British naval squadron under Hyde Parker, which had wintered in the Swedish port towns, hampered Franco-Danish actions. Despite heavy ice floes in the Baltic Sea, Parker made a show of force along the Danish shoreline, underscoring British control of the seas and prompting Bernadotte, whose troops were deployed in Själland just across from Sweden, to halt his plans to cross the Danish Straits (Storebælt, Lillebælt, and Öresund) to Sweden. The news of the revolt spreading in Spain only further complicated the Franco-Danish operations; Bernadotte's corps included some 14,000 Spaniards, whose loyalties could no longer be trusted. With the Royal Navy in the Sound, the original plan for a joint Franco-Danish invasion had to be scratched. Bernadotte's troops remained, much to the local population's chagrin, while the Danes placed their hopes on the Norwegians, whose forces, about 10,000 men strong, were under command of Prince Christian August of Augustenburg, the head of the Norwegian Government Commission (Regjeringskommisjon), an executive institution formed in the wake of the British attack on Denmark. This made it very difficult to administer Norwegian affairs from Copenhagen. Nonetheless, the establishment of the commission marked an important moment in Norwegian history, since it was only the second time in more than 270 years that Norway had gained self-government, however limited.[73]

Augustenburg initially intended to invade western Sweden, but slow mobilization, supply and equipment shortages, and the cancellation of the Danish invasion of Scania caused him to give up on this intention. This, in turn, allowed the Swedes to take up the offensive. In the first major operation of the war they advanced into Aurskog-Høland but were defeated and driven back. The Swedish commander General Armfelt then marched with 8,000 men toward the fortress of Kongsvinger, defeated the Norwegians at Lier (April 18), and invested the fortress.[74] Swedish elation at these successes was short-lived, as the situation soon changed drastically. The Norwegians scored minor but significant victories at Trangen (April 25), Mobekk (May 18), and Jerpset (May 24) that prevented Armfelt from advancing farther and ultimately contributed to his decision to lift his blockade of Kongsvinger due to logistical challenges and fall back to the Swedish borders.[75] Despite the arrival of the British expeditionary force (as we'll see), the Swedes were unable to regroup for counterattack. The Swedish high command failed to develop a coherent strategy, and the king and his generals frequently misunderstood each other's intentions. Furthermore, most of the Swedish resources had been committed to the war in Finland, where the Swedes tried to seize the initiative. In early April, the young and energetic Swedish general Karl Johan Adlerkreutz was appointed second in command to Marshal Klingspor in Finland. He urged an immediate counteroffensive against the dispersed Russian forces. His victories at Gamlakarleby, Brahestad, Siikajoki, and Revolax improved Swedish morale and resulted in a new general offensive in eastern and northern Finland, with the Swedes scoring another victory at Pulkkila (May 2) and seizing Kuopio and recapturing both Gotland and the Åland Islands after the Russian navy failed to support its land forces.[76]

The Swedish offensives triggered popular uprisings in parts of Finland, where local populations refused to pledge allegiance to the Russian sovereign and instead launched a guerrilla war, attacking isolated Russian detachments and lines of communication.[77] Although the Finnish guerrilla war never matched the Spanish one in intensity, it did pose serious challenges to the Russian military and forced the Russian authorities to compromise.[78] In June 1808, facing the prospect of a prolonged guerrilla warfare in Finland and an uncertain political situation in Europe, Alexander issued a manifesto pledging to uphold all existing liberties of the Finnish estates and people and later issued orders for the convocation of the Diet of Porvoo (Borgå Landtdag).[79]

Alexander's decision should not be perceived simply as a concession to the Finnish guerrillas. It was, in fact, rooted in Russia's long-standing policy. During the eighteenth century many members of the Swedo-Finnish official class and elite were frustrated with Sweden's ongoing wars with Russia, as they only proved Stockholm's inability to defend Finland and brought much misery to the region. Russia tried repeatedly to exploit such sentiments, offering support to the Finns in 1741–1743 if they broke away from Sweden. Although nothing came of this effort at the time, the plan was revived some forty years later during the Russo-Swedish War of 1788–1790. Russia welcomed disgruntled Finnish officers, most notably Colonel Göran Magnus Sprengtporten, who had left Swedish service and expressed willingness to support a Russian-supported autonomous Finland. By 1788, 113 officers had formed the Anjala League (Anjalaförbundet), which advocated the idea that Finland's future lay not with the declining Sweden but with the rising power of Russia; these officers believed that a Russian expansion was inevitable in the long term and that, rather than risking a war and forceful takeover, it would be better to seek a peaceful compromise with Russia that would entail transferring Finland to Russia on the best terms possible.[80] The end of the Russo-Swedish War in 1790 frustrated the Anjala League's aspirations, but eighteen years later its surviving members, led by Sprengtporten, were given a unique opportunity to resume their work. Sprengtporten actively promoted his plan for an autonomous Finland within the Russian Empire, and although his proposal for the early convocation of a Finnish diet was postponed until 1809, his arguments did play a role in convincing Emperor Alexander to treat the Finns differently than other recently acquired territories (i.e., Poland or Georgia).[81]

The Russian monarch believed that Finnish cooperation was essential to securing Russia's precarious position in the Baltic at a time when the political situation in Europe seemed volatile: with France displacing Russian interests in Germany and the Ottomans making preparations to renew hostilities against Russia in the Danubian Principalities, Russia now faced the menace of the Anglo-Swedish alliance in the Baltic. Britain had already committed to provide a subsidy of more than £1 million to support Sweden against France, but these monies would also sustain Swedish war efforts against Russia. As part of the second British commitment to the alliance with Sweden, a naval squadron under Admiral James Saumarez was dispatched to the Baltic in February. The squadron delayed its departure until late April because of the addition of Sir John Moore's 10,000-man expeditionary force, which, it was hoped, would deploy to protect southern Sweden and free up Swedish troops to undertake operations against the Russians.[82] Remarkably, Moore was specifically ordered not to operate under Swedish command, in order to avoid direct Anglo-Russian military conflict, but Saumarez received instructions to examine the possibility of attacking the Russian naval base at Kronstadt to prevent France from using the Russian Baltic Fleet.[83]

The British expeditionary force reached Gothenburg in mid-May. Moore was surprised to receive a rather cold reception from his Swedish allies, who distrusted Britain's intentions and, despite earlier promises, refused permission for the British troops to land until their future use was agreed upon.[84] Yet the news from Sweden was anything but reassuring, given the steady stream of reports of setbacks in Finland and Norway and public opinion turning against Gustavus. Moore grew especially annoyed by Gustavus's insistence on using British troops to consolidate control over neighboring territories. Had the king accepted the landing of the British troops in Skåne, it would have enabled him to move at least 10,000 soldiers to the Finnish theater, where they could have had a major impact. As it happened, the bulk of the Swedish army, including the best units, was kept out of the Finnish War as the king wrangled with the British over the next course of action. In a series of meetings Gustavus proposed several plans that involved either campaigns against Denmark and Norway or direct attacks on Russia in Finland or the Russian coastlines in the Baltic. These were plans that even Swedish generals considered unfeasible. The king's insistence on them only further antagonized Moore, who found all of them contrary to his own instructions; by June he had concluded that "if we undertook anything, or once placed ourselves under [Gustavus's] orders, it was impossible to say the absurdity to which we might be exposed."[85] Yet his attempts to point out the futility of such expeditions only resulted in a rupture with the king, who ordered that Moore be placed under house arrest, a move that provoked a diplomatic rift between Sweden and Britain.[86] Moore ultimately escaped and made his way back to his troops in Gothenburg, where he received a new set of orders from the

British War Office, which, having grown impatient with the lack of progress in the Baltic, had already shifted its attention to the Iberian Peninsula, where a wave of popular unrest against the French offered better prospects for a victorious campaign. On July 3, 1808, the British expedition left Gothenburg.[87]

Moore's departure from Sweden coincided with one of the most dramatic episodes of the Napoleonic Wars: the spiriting away of an entire Spanish division by the British Royal Navy. As we saw in Chapter 12, in late 1807 Napoleon had bullied and pressured the Spanish king, Charles IV, and prime minister, Godoy, into providing some of the best Spanish troops to bolster the French army in Germany; this demand also aimed to ensure Spain's continued loyalty and to weaken local resistance should Napoleon need to occupy Spain. Organized into the Division del Norte, some 15,000 Spanish troops were placed under command of Pedro Caro y Sureda, marqués de la Romana, a commander who participated in the American Revolutionary War and distinguished himself during the conquest of the British-controlled island of Minorca in 1781. Romana led his division to northern Germany, where he spent the winter of 1808 performing garrison duties in Hamburg, Mecklenburg, and towns of the old Hanseatic League before being assigned to Marshal Bernadotte's corps, which was sent to Denmark for a planned invasion of Sweden. Although the invasion never materialized, the Spanish troops remained in Denmark and were stationed in Jutland and on the island of Funen. In the spring of 1808, despite France's best efforts to intercept Spanish communications, Romana and his officers learned about the French occupation of Spain, the May uprising in Madrid, and the start of war in the Iberian Peninsula. Infuriated by the news, these officers made plans to repatriate to Spain, then realized that the French would never let them return home. French authorities tried to calm down the Spaniards by increasing the officers' pay and granting them certain privileges—Bernadotte used Spanish troops as his personal escort—but, as one Spanish officer observed, "the more the [French] tried to persuade us that Spain was tranquil, and had settled down to enjoy an age of felicity under Napoleon, the more clearly did we foresee the scenes of blood, strife, and disaster which were to follow these incredible events."[88]

In the summer of 1808, as the British sought for ways to bolster anti-French resistance in Spain, Romana's division began to feature prominently in government discussions.[89] A British agent, posing as a traveling merchant of exotic goods, successfully evaded French counterintelligence and visited Romana in Nyborg, where he shared details of the British plan: if the Spaniards could reach the coast, the British navy would pick them up and deliver them to any location in the Spanish Empire. Overcoming his initial reservations,

Romana consulted with his officers and agreed to the plan.[90] By late July, Admiral Richard Goodwin Keats, the commander of the Baltic Fleet, was busy gathering transport vessels from England for the Baltic in preparation for a daring evacuation.

For the plan to succeed, Romana needed to assemble his scattered troops and take control of the nearby ports. He initially wanted to concentrate the Spanish troops under a pretext of holding a grand review, but the plot almost unraveled when new orders arrived from France that all Spanish soldiers were required to swear an oath of loyalty to King Joseph Bonaparte. Spanish troops on Jutland and Funen took the oath "in a more or less farcical way," swearing allegiance to Prince Ferdinand rather than to Joseph. But those on the island of Sjælland, most of them unaware of the escape plans, mutinied on July 31 and were quickly surrounded and forced to surrender by the larger Danish forces. This incident naturally alarmed the French. However, before they could do anything, Romana learned that the British fleet was en route, and so he decided to act. On August 7 the Spaniards seized control of the port of Nyborg, on the island of Funen, where they were joined by the men of the Infante, Rey, and Zamora Regiments, who were stationed on the island of Jutland and commandeered small vessels to cross over to Funen; the Algarve regiment, however, had failed to break through, largely due to its colonel's vacillation. Between August 9 and 11, the Spanish troops on Funen, numbering some 9,000 men, crossed to Langeland, where they overcame the Danish garrison and waited for ten days for the arrival of the British fleet. Admiral Keats evacuated the Spanish division and transported it to Santander, in northern Spain, where Romana's troops landed by mid-October. The Division del Norte almost immediately joined the war against the French. Those Spanish soldiers who had been captured by the French and Danish forces were reorganized into the Joseph Napoleon Regiment and scattered through Italy, the Netherlands, Germany, and France before being called upon to participate in Napoleon's invasion of Russia, where many of them perished.[91]

———∽∾⊰⊱∾∽———

The British involvement in the Baltic affair did not end with the fiasco of Moore's expedition. In fact, a low-intensity Anglo-Russian war—a "smokeless war," as one Russian historian memorably called it—continued long after that.[92] The conflict tends to be lost in the traditional histories of the Napoleonic Wars, largely because it failed to produce large-scale battles and mainly involved isolated naval engagements between British and Russian warships in the Mediterranean, Barents, and Baltic Seas. Smokeless or not, it merits a look to reveal another aspect of the larger story of the Napoleonic Wars.[93]

Russia entered this war in a weakened position because its naval resources had been scattered across European waters; the Baltic Fleet, the jewel of the Russian navy, had had many of its ships (including eight ships-of-the-line) deployed to the Ionian Islands as part of the Archipelago expedition, commanded by Vice Admiral Dmitri Senyavin.[94] Recalled to Russia in 1807, Senyavin sailed with a larger party of his squadron (including five ships-of-the-line) to the Baltic Sea, but bad weather forced him to anchor in Lisbon in October 1807, just as the French invaded Portugal and forced the Portuguese court to flee. Because Russia was at war with Britain, Senyavin found himself trapped between the British navy blockading Lisbon and the French troops controlling the city. After the French were defeated by the British army at Vimeiro in August 1808, Senyavin's squadron came under greater pressure from the British, who now controlled both the sea and the coastline. The British avoided a direct attack on the Russians—Senyavin threatened to destroy his ships and set Lisbon ablaze—but pressured the Russian admiral to transfer his ships to British control. In August 1808, Senyavin agreed to have his ships escorted to Britain (without lowering their Russian flags). On arriving at Portsmouth in September, he was prevented from leaving under various pretexts until the weather made his return to Russia impossible. After another year of virtual captivity, the Russian admiral was allowed to leave Britain and his emaciated crewmen were delivered on British ships to Riga, but the Russian warships remained in Britain until 1813.[95]

The Russian fleet faced a more daunting challenge in the Baltic, where in the spring of 1808 Saumarez took charge of the reconstituted Baltic squadron.[96] He was ordered to conduct operations against the Russians in support of the Swedes and to provide protection to ships engaged in commerce; though the Baltic was largely closed to British shipping, the Royal Navy facilitated neutral trade (as well as smuggling) that involved British goods. The British squadron reached Gothenburg just as news of the Russian capture of Sveaborg arrived, causing great consternation among the British and the Swedes. Meeting with the Swedish officials, Saumarez (together with the British ambassador to Sweden, Edward Thornton) agreed to focus his efforts on protecting the coastline of Sweden and keeping the Danish Sound and entrance to the Baltic open to trade.

The first major engagement between Russian and British vessels took place on June 23, when the Russian cutter *Opyt* stumbled upon the HMS *Salsette* and, despite a valiant defense, was captured off Norgen Island near Revel. Two weeks later, the Russian Baltic Fleet, twenty warships (nine of them ships-of-the-line) under the command of Admiral Peter Khanykov, sailed out of Kronstadt to engage the Swedish navy, led by Admiral Rudolf

Cederström. Saumarez dispatched HMS *Centaur* and *Implacable*, the 74-gun ships-of-the-line, to support his Swedish ally. By late August both sides deployed fleets between Hango and Örö near the southern tip of Finland. On August 25, 1808, the Anglo-Swedish fleet sailed to engage the Russians, who chose to avoid the actions. As the Russians retreated, the British ships-of-the-line pulled ahead of the rest of the fleet and attacked the Russian warship *Vsevolod*, which was captured and burnt.[97]

The naval war continued in similar fashion for the next two years. In July 1809, several Russian gunboats were captured or destroyed off Hango Head (Hangöudde) and Aspö Head (near Fredrikshamn). In the Barents Sea, the Anglo-Russian hostilities unfolded parallel to the Anglo-Danish "gunboat war," which had caused the British to impose a wide-scale blockade on the coastline of Norway and conduct raids as far north as Hammerfest and Murmansk, disrupting trade between northwest Russia and northern Norway. The British warship *Najaden* (formerly the Danish frigate *Naiad*) was particularly active in these operations, capturing Russian merchant vessels and raiding Russian settlements in the Kola district in 1809–1810.[98] British control of the seas had limited impact on Russian operations against Sweden, since the Russian army's supply lines remained uninterrupted on land while much of the Gulfs of Bothnia and Finland froze in winter, constraining naval movements.

The Anglo-Russian War was unique in that both sides sought to avert major engagements. The Russian fleet consistently avoided open confrontation with the Royal Navy, while the British government, engaged in a war against France, repeatedly indicated its desire to find common ground with Russia. By late 1810, with Russia gradually withdrawing from the Continental System, the war had largely subsided, and trade between Britain and Russia grew. In fact, as Franco-Russian relations progressively worsened, Britain laid the groundwork for a possible alliance. After Napoleon invaded Russia in June 1812, the Anglo-Russian alliance finally materialized in the Treaty of Örebro (July 18), which formally ended the war and laid the foundation for the establishment of the sixth anti-French coalition.[99]

––––––∞∞∞§∞∞∞––––––

The departure of Moore's expedition and the evacuation of Romana's division left the Anglo-Swedish "common cause" in tatters. The Swedes perceived Britain as an unreliable partner and lamented British focus on the Iberian peninsula at the expense of Swedish interests. The Senyavin affair, described earlier, only further drove a wedge into Anglo-Swedish relations, as the Swedish court complained about the British decision to release Senyavin's detained sailors, who upon their return to Russia were expected to join the Russian Baltic Fleet, to the detriment of Sweden. Canning's assurances that the British would delay the Russian departure (which, as noted, they did for an entire year) did little to allay Swedish suspicions that Britain would readily sacrifice its ally's interest to safeguard its own. Indeed, Gustavus believed (wrongly) that the British fixation on Spain, where a British expeditionary force under General Moore was already under way, meant that a crucial opportunity for defeating the Russian fleet in the Baltic had been missed and that this, in turn, had hampered the Swedish war effort in Finland. Chancellor Ehrenheim openly expressed his view that British had "abandoned" Sweden because they hoped to gain more advantages in Spain, where "there are fleets to win, trade to revive, colonies to raise and a mass of power to direct against points far more sensitive to Bonaparte than Russia and Denmark."[100]

By 1809, Anglo-Swedish relations were characterized by mutual suspicion and recrimination.[101] Swedish demands for increased subsidies were met with continued British rejections, culminating in Gustavus's threat to close Swedish ports to British trade unless he was paid. During a meeting with a British envoy in late February 1809, Gustavus erupted in anger at what he described as the continuing British refusal to fully support him. "Is your trade to the Baltic and your intercourse with the Continent through Sweden of no consequence to you? Will you not feel the Sound being shut against you, or do you think that your commerce to the Spanish colonies will indemnify you for the loss of that in Europe? I am much reduced as to my means but I can still do much harm and you will feel it."[102] This was no idle threat. Gustavus quickly showed that he meant what he had said. Shortly after the meeting, he ordered the closure of the port of Gothenburg to British trade and placed British vessels under a forty-eight-hour embargo. This maladroit attempt at extortion infuriated Canning and other members of the British government, who believed that the Swedes should express greater appreciation for the support Britain had already shown them. They refused to budge on the issue of subsidies, compelling Gustavus to sign a new subsidy agreement based on older terms on March 1, 1809.

Further overshadowing Anglo-Swedish relations were fears of one side making a deal with their common enemies. London worried that the Swedish court was engaged in secret peace talks with the French and Russians, while Swedish anxiety that Britain might conclude a separate peace with Napoleon increased after learning about the new peace terms France had offered to Britain in October 1808: ending hostilities if the British accepted Spain under French control and Finland under Russian control. London immediately rejected the offer, and Canning assured the Swedish ambassador that Britain was committed to Sweden's security. Nonetheless, he was unable to dispel Swedish doubts that surfaced after he failed to include Finland's restoration as a precondition for any future peace settlement. In Stockholm, this was interpreted as yet another sign of Britain's willingness to sacrifice Swedish territorial integrity to gain Russian support.[103]

Meanwhile, war was still raging in Finland. Swedish vacillation in the summer of 1808 allowed the Russians to regroup and launch a new offensive that turned the tide of the war. As the Russian troops pushed toward Kuopio and Toivola, Major General Nikolay Kamenski routed the Swedish army under Lieutenant Colonel Otto von Fieandt at Karstula on August 21 and scored a quick succession of victories at Lappfjärd (August 29), Ruona and Salmi (September 1–2), and Oravais (September 14). Infuriated by these setbacks, Gustavus personally led a landing force on the southeast shore of the Gulf of Bothnia but was repelled by the Russian forces of General Peter Bagration in late September.[104] These defeats forced the Swedes to seek a cease-fire that the Russian commanders welcomed, because by this point they suffered from a lack of supplies, ammunition, and reinforcements. Although the armistice was concluded on September 29, 1808, Emperor Alexander, on his way to meeting Napoleon at Erfurt, refused to approve it and demanded an immediate resumption of hostilities. The armistice thus ended on October 27, and the Russian army advanced northward, capturing virtually all of Finland by the end of the year. On December 1, rejecting the advice of the powerful minister of war, Aleksey Arakcheyev, who called for outright annexation of Finland, Emperor Alexander appointed Sprengtporten as the new governor-general of Finland. This was a key decision because Sprengtporten was the only governor in Russia not subordinated to the Imperial Senate but responsible to the emperor himself, underscoring the special status of Finland within the Russian Empire.[105] In 1809 Alexander presided over the opening of the Diet of Porvoo, confirming the rights and privileges the Finns had traditionally enjoyed and granting them a degree of self-rule that Sweden had never permitted and that no other region of the Russian Empire enjoyed.[106] The diet welcomed Russian concessions and helped pacify the local population by disbanding Finnish militias and calling for collaboration with the Russian authorities.

Setbacks in Finland caused the Swedes to cede the initiative in Norway, where Danish-Norwegian forces launched a surprise attack and destroyed a Swedish detachment at Berby in mid-September. This defeat caused a public outcry in Sweden and forced the Swedish monarchy to send reinforcements to shore up the front line. The Swedish operations failed to produce results, however, so by the end of the year all of the Swedish troops were withdrawn from southern Norway and the war in this theater had reached a stalemate; in December the sides agreed to an armistice that lasted for the next six months.[107]

In the spring of 1809, Emperor Alexander, preoccupied with the Franco-Austrian conflict in central Europe and eager to bring a quick conclusion to the war with Sweden, appointed General Bogdan von Knorring to command Russian forces in Finland with orders to invade the Swedish mainland. The news of a Russian invasion spread confusion in Swedish coastline towns; meanwhile, dramatic events unfolded at the royal capital, Stockholm. Gustavus was unpopular even before the war against Denmark and Russia started, but the military defeats, which were largely blamed on his ineffective command and erratic policies, only further undermined his reputation. With Russian troops about to cross the Gulf of Bothnia, a group of Swedish army officers—still reeling from royal punishments for the failure of the fall offensive in Finland—organized a coup.[108] Lieutenant Colonel Georg Adlersparre, acting commander of the Western Army, took advantage of the armistice with the Norwegians to leave just 800 men to defend the Norwegian front and led the rest of his force to Stockholm.[109] Gustavus tried to solicit British military support in suppressing this insurrection, but whatever goodwill the British might have had toward him had dissipated during the acrimonious debate over subsidies and the king's decision to embargo British troops.[110] On March 13, 1809, the rebel officers deposed Gustavus and proclaimed his uncle, Duke Karl of Sudermania, the future Karl XIII, as the new head of state.[111]

The dethronement of King Gustavus might have resolved one problem, but it created another, as Sweden struggled with reestablishing the legitimacy of its government. The new government lost no time in emphasizing Gustavus's responsibility for the disastrous state of the Swedish kingdom, charges that have been frequently repeated by Swedish historians, some of whom accuse the king of being a warmonger who pursued a criminally irresponsible foreign policy.[112] One of the most pressing problems for the new government was that of succession. Karl XIII was already sixty years old and childless, while the decision to exclude Gustavus IV's son and rightful heir, Prince Gustavus, from the succession triggered a strong legitimist reaction that sought to increase royal authority. Thus, besides the obvious question of who would next occupy the Swedish throne, a greater problem lay in where the next king would lead Sweden. The new regime removed the so-called Gustavian group—members of the elite associated with both Gustavus III and Gustavus IV—from positions of power and replaced them with the more reform-minded "men of 1809,"[113] who were all members of the Swedish elite, though some, including Georg Adlersparre and Hans Järta, had shown considerable sympathy toward the French Revolution and were therefore suspected of radicalism and pro-French sympathies. The British envoy to

Stockholm thought that the new government would soon turn away from Britain and seek closer relations with France.[114] In light of Napoleon's continued ascendancy in Europe, a Francophile faction soon gained influence at the Swedish court and argued that the best course for Sweden was to make an alliance with France and to use Napoleon's mediation in the peace talks with Denmark and Russia. In March, the Swedish government approached Napoleon with a request for mediation with Russia.

However, Swedish hopes for a rapprochement with France were quickly dashed when Napoleon responded on April 12, declining to intervene in Sweden's affairs.[115] The timing was clearly not in Sweden's favor, because Napoleon had no wish to alienate Russia just when he needed its support against Austria, which had invaded Bavaria and opened the War of the Fifth Coalition. Sweden's overtures to Britain were no more successful, as the British government had grown disillusioned by Stockholm's erratic and unfriendly attitudes. Besides, Britain's political attention was focused on other parts of Europe: on the plains of Bavaria and Austria, where a new Franco-Austrian war was already under way; on the Portuguese countryside, where General Wellesley had launched a new (and victorious) campaign; and on the Dutch coastline, where the Walcheren expedition was under way by late July. In short, Sweden was hardly at the top of the British foreign agenda.

By late April 1809 the friendless and penniless Swedish government was in such a weakened position that some legitimists plotted to overthrow it and sought British aid for this purpose.[116] The government survived this threat but struggled to contain others. The most immediate and serious of them came from the Russian invasion. Since the Gulf of Bothnia was still frozen, hampering the Royal Navy's operations, the Russian plan involved a three-pronged offensive across the gulf, with General Bagration crossing to the Åland Islands and advancing directly to the virtually defenseless Swedish capital; General Barclay de Tolly proceeding with his corps across the frozen Östra Kvarken, the narrowest part of the gulf, to capture Umeå; and, further north, General Pavel Shuvalov leading his men along the gulf coast to capture Tornio (Torneå) and Kalix.[117] The crossing was an audacious operation, and the Russian troops braved cold weather and extreme conditions, marching in what one participant described as a "frozen snow wasteland" where "there were no signs of life...[and] no means of protecting oneself."[118] The exact number of losses the Russians suffered during the crossing remains unclear, but Barclay de Tolly later commented that there was "no longer any need to map the Kvarken because I have done it with the corpses of my troops."[119]

Amid continued political turmoil and commotion in the Swedish military, Karl XIII understood that Sweden was not in a position to resist the invasion, and so his first order was to dispatch an envoy proposing a truce and peace talks.[120] Despite clear imperial instructions to fight on, Russian commander-in-chief Knorring hesitated, realizing that his men had been exhausted by the crossing and lacked supplies and reinforcements. More important, the spring weather could soon thaw the ice in the gulf, leaving the Russian corps isolated from their bases in Finland. Fearing the Swedes would realize how perilous the Russian situation actually was, Knorring accepted armistice.[121] He ordered the immediate return of Russian forces to Finland, where the fatigued troops, who had twice crossed the gulf in the span of two weeks, arrived by March 31.[122] Emperor Alexander was infuriated by Knorring's decision and once again refused to accept the armistice. He traveled to Finland, where he praised his troops for bravery and castigated Knorring, who was dismissed from his post. The new Russian commander in chief, Barclay de Tolly, was given strict orders to end the cease-fire and resume the offensive into Sweden until the Swedes surrendered.

Thus the Russians spent next four weeks preparing for yet another crossing of the Gulf of Bothnia. By now the spring thaw had made it impossible to march across the gulf, while the presence of the British squadron under Saumarez kept the Russian fleet confined to Kronstadt.[123] Instead, the Russians launched an offensive in the north, where General Shuvalov could follow the coastline to descend upon central Sweden. Leaving Torneå, the Russian corps marched for more than two hundred miles, twenty-six of them up to their knees in the melting ice, to seize the Swedish town of Skellefteå.[124] The resumption of Russo-Swedish hostilities also revealed fissures within Denmark-Norway, whose king, Frederick, pushed for an invasion of Sweden. The new Swedish government had tried sounding out King Frederick on the question of the Swedish throne, and after being rebuffed they turned to Prince Christian August, whose popularity, the Swedes believed, could convince the Norwegians to join him if he was elected to the Swedish throne. Tensions between Frederick and Christian August became noticeable during the summer of 1809 when the latter refused to carry out the king's instructions to invade Sweden.[125] the Danish-Norwegian invasion of Sweden turned out to be a limited affair, carried out in July 1809 from Trondhjem, which remained under the northern Norwegian general command and not that of Christian August. In July a small Norwegian force crossed into Sweden and gained some early success before the Swedish counterattack routed them at Härjedalen on July 24.[126] An armistice, concluded the following day, eventually turned into the Treaty of Jönköping (December 10, 1809), which ended the Dano-Norwegian-Swedish War on the basis of the *status quo ante bellum*. Encouraged by this success, Karl XIII ordered a counterattack, made possible by Saumarez's continued naval cooperation, against the Russian forces in northern Sweden. But the last battles of the war—at Sävar and Ratan on August 19 and 20—failed to turn the course of the war and left the Swedes with no choice but to agree to diplomatic talks.

As the negotiations opened in Fredrikshamn (Hamina), it quickly became clear that even a partial restoration of Finland to Sweden was out of the question. Russia had won the war and insisted on its right to the spoils. For the Swedes, therefore, the most important task was to minimize further damage to their kingdom. From the outset Russia had insisted on three key preconditions for the peace: Sweden had to cede all of Finland (along with the Åland Islands), renounce its alliance with Britain, and make peace with France, Denmark, and Norway (which also meant joining the Continental System).[127] The Swedes balked at the vast territorial concessions that Russia was demanding, especially the Åland Islands—they were just twenty miles from the Swedish mainland, and Russian occupation there could pose a profound security threat. Yet Swedish attempts to negotiate a better deal proved futile; the Russians had already established effective control over the territories in question, and the Swedes had no trump cards to play. During the negotiations over the new frontiers in the north, the Swedish tamely responded to Russian demands by noting that "it behooves the honor of the [Russian] emperor not to demand a part of Sweden. It is enough that you have taken all of Finland."[128]

The peace treaty was signed after a month's negotiations on September 17, 1809, and incorporated the Russian demands in toto.[129] It marked a critical moment in the history of Scandinavia: Sweden had lost almost half of its entire territory, while Russia had firmly established itself in the region and secured its positions on the Baltic Sea.[130] Indeed, the Finnish population, after more than six hundred years of Swedish hegemony, now found itself under new imperial masters, though its status was safeguarded by special provisions that pledged to maintain traditional Finnish rights and freedoms, protect private property, and allow for continued economic activity between Finland and Sweden—all crucial factors in Russia's success in consolidating its authority in the newly acquired territories. In the long term, the separation of these two parts of the Swedish realm meant that different systems of government developed on either side of the Gulf of Bothnia. While the Finns fought to maintain the Gustavian constitutional arrangements within the newly established Grand Duchy of Finland, the Swedes themselves insisted on changing the old system and moved quickly to repeal the Gustavian laws and lay the foundation for a new political system that still survives to the present day.[131] The Treaty of Fredrikshamn also forced Sweden to recalibrate its foreign policy, as it was clear that any attempt to reclaim Finland would result in another devastating war with Russia. Instead, the Swedes chose to remove the "Finnish Question" from their strategic considerations and focus their attention on Norway as compensation for the losses in the east. This focus on Norway was owed in no small part to Georg Adlersparre, who believed that the selection of Prince Christian August for the Swedish throne could ensure a union of Sweden and Norway. Such aspirations were further buttressed by signals the Russian diplomats had given at Fredrikshamn that Russia would not necessarily oppose Sweden's takeover in Norway. Thus the peace at Fredrikshamn was the fulfillment of the long-standing Danish fear that a Russian conquest of Finland would render Denmark useless as Russia's ally and would embolden Swedish interest in Norway. As events would shows, the Danes' suspicions were well justified.

With the war against Russia over, Sweden could breathe a sigh of relief. On December 10 the Treaty of Jönköping restored relations with Denmark-Norway, while in January 1810 a separate peace treaty was signed with France. Yet the Swedes still faced political challenges. King Charles XIII was ailing and, as noted, childless; it was obvious that he was close to breathing his last and the Swedish branch of the House of Holstein-Gottorp would end. The election of the Danish prince Christian August as the heir to the Swedish throne allayed some of the worst fears and pointed toward a rather harmonious future for Denmark-Norway and Sweden. To contemporaries' great astonishment, the prince died suddenly just five months after arriving in Stockholm. While attending a military review at Scania on May 28, 1810, he suffered a stroke from which he did not recover. The sudden death of the forty-one-year-old prince, who had seemed to be in good physical condition, caused a huge public outcry, with many believing that the prince had been killed as a result of some insidious plot. On June 20, during Christian August's funeral, a crowd attacked those who were suspected of conspiracy and lynched Hans Axel von Fersen the Younger, the famed Swedish count who had been a close friend of Queen Marie-Antoinette of France and later served as the Swedish Marshal of the Realm.

The death of the crown prince created a crisis of succession that shaped the course of Scandinavian history. Christian Augustus had shown himself a mild-mannered and reasonable man who envisioned establishing a constitutional Scandinavian union and, had he lived, might have brought peace and stability to the region. As it was, his passing caused a domestic crisis. Various political factions at the royal court and within the Swedish Riksdag clashed over the possible candidates for the crown. Napoleon naturally paid close attention to these discussions, understanding that they would have ramifications far beyond Sweden's domestic affairs; a new king could possibly ensure Scandinavian union and strengthen the French position in northern Europe. At first, King Frederick VI of Denmark put forth his candidacy, which was ostensibly bolstered by the fact that Napoleon did not oppose it. Yet the vast majority of Swedes did, finding Frederick, who was notorious for his pedantry, intractability, and flashes of authoritarianism, unacceptable. Equally unacceptable was Prince Gustav of Vasa, the son of the deposed King Gustav IV Adolph and, technically, the rightful heir to the Swedish crown.

Instead, in the summer of 1810, the Swedes were considering inviting either the Danish king Frederick's son, the young and charismatic Prince Christian Frederick, or the deceased Prince Christian August's older brother, Duke Frederick Christian of Augustenburg, whose moderate character and liberal leanings were well known. By late July, the latter was increasingly considered a more suitable candidate, and attempts had been made to sound out Napoleon on the acceptability of this candidate. The French emperor supported the duke, with the prince as his second choice.[132] Neither choice was to the liking of Denmark's Frederick VI, who went as far as ordering a naval blockade of the island of Als, where the duke resided, an effort to prevent his departure to Sweden.

In August 1810, the Swedish Riksdag convened to discuss the candidates. As the debate raged, the earlier idealistic aspirations for a young, charismatic, and reform-minded ruler were soon replaced by the more pragmatic desire to have a candidate who was experienced in political and military matters and could help Sweden recover its position vis-à-vis Russia. These sentiments were particularly strong in Swedish military circles, which increasingly looked to France for candidates. Despite having no formal authorization to do it, they considered several prominent French political and military figures and ultimately settled on Marshal Jean-Baptiste-Jules Bernadotte, who had shown compassion for Swedish prisoners in 1807 and expressed genuine interest in the affairs of the Baltic nations. The matter was decided when Baron Karl Otto Mörner, entirely on his own initiative, offered the Swedish crown to Bernadotte, who replied that that he would not refuse the honor if he was elected. Although the Swedish political circles were stunned by the news of Bernadotte's entry into the royal race, they gradually rallied around him, helped by Mörner's publicity blitz, which assured his countrymen that Bernadotte enjoyed Napoleon's full support and was sufficiently wealthy, an important consideration considering Sweden's vast economic difficulties. On August 21, 1810, the Riksdag elected Bernadotte as the new crown prince of Sweden.[133] But Bernadotte, a French citizen, still needed to be released from his oath to Napoleon before he could accept the Swedish crown.

In spite of their earlier rivalry and Bernadotte's latter-day signs of insubordination, Napoleon did not oppose his selection, wishing "success and happiness to [Bernadotte] and to the Swedes."[134] He was hoping that Bernadotte would remain loyal to France, enhance French influence in northern Europe, and support war against Britain. In September he released the marshal from his oath of allegiance and allowed him to forswear his French nationality, famously asking him to agree never to take up arms against France. Bernadotte refused to make any such pledge, claiming that his new obligations to Sweden could not allow it, and prompting Napoleon to exclaim, "Go, and let our destinies be accomplished!"[135]

On November 2 Bernadotte made his solemn entry into Stockholm. Three days later he appeared in front of the Riksdag, converted to Lutheranism, and was formally adopted by King Charles XIII, changing his name to Charles John (Karl Johan). Though a newcomer at the Swedish court, Bernadotte soon emerged as the power behind the throne. He understood that his future depended entirely on embracing his newly adopted land and pursuing policies that defended its interests, not Napoleon's or France's. Over the next two years he gradually distanced himself from the Napoleonic imperial authority. To secure Sweden's eastern borders, he assured Russia that he would not make any attempt to retake Finland, and instead began to look westward to Norway, which he considered a fitting compensation for Sweden. He clearly understood that his crown depended entirely on him acquiring Norway, and his determination to achieve this played a decisive role during the War of the Sixth Coalition in 1813–1814.

CHAPTER 16

"An Empire Besieged"

The Ottomans and the Napoleonic Wars

T HE START OF THE FRENCH REVOLUTION coincided with the enthrone-
ment of a new Ottoman sultan who was keen on exploiting the few years
of respite from conflict with the West that resulted from European powers'
preoccupation with France. The son of Sultan Mustafa III and his Georgian
wife, Selim III was raised by his uncle, Sultan Abdulhamid I, who granted
him some degree of freedom in social interaction. Thus, besides his classical
Ottoman training, Selim III had also developed a fondness for the culture of
western Europe, his greatest interest being in European military institutions
and practices. Even before he became sultan, he had corresponded with King
Louis XVI of France concerning statecraft, social institutions, and the military arts. Selim III was surrounded by a small group of confidants who shared
his fascination with European customs, ideas, and institutions, and believed
there was an urgent need to introduce reforms that would restore the power
of the central government while preserving the territorial integrity of the
empire against internal and external threats.

The multi-ethnic, multi-linguistic, and multi-religious Ottoman Empire
was built on the principle of dividing the population into separate and
distinct religious communities, called *millets*. The system worked relatively
well, and also played a major role in preserving national cultures and distinct
ethnic and linguistic identities. The Ottoman state, centered around the idea
of religious identity, never developed a truly national identity, and instead
struggled to contain centrifugal forces that threatened it during the revolutionary era. But the challenges that the Ottomans faced went deeper than
this and involved several dynamics. First, and perhaps central to much of late
Ottoman history, was the enduring struggle between center and periphery.

The more the central government tried to assert its control, the more it faced resistance from the periphery, where local elites had gradually accumulated administrative, economic, and even diplomatic independence.[1] The process of gradual disintegration of the Ottoman central power culminated during the Napoleonic Wars when a political revolution claimed two sultans within a span of just one year. A second underlying factor was the need for an effective military and administrative system to maintain the empire, which in turn required an effective taxation system. In the Ottoman case, neither was up to the task, as they suffered from a weak central authority and a corrupt and inefficient bureaucracy. The growing national awakening among various peoples, especially in the Balkan peninsula, only further challenged Ottoman power, especially when considered in conjunction with external threats. Russia posed the greatest menace to the territorial integrity of the Ottoman state, but other European powers were keen on exploiting Ottoman weakness as well.[2] At the start of the nineteenth century, the Ottoman realm was truly, in the words of esteemed Ottomanist Virginia Aksan, "an empire besieged."

Selim III inherited the Ottoman throne in the middle of the Russo-Ottoman War, and since he was unable to turn the tide of the war, he decided to use it as a pretext for major military reforms.[3] Artillery (*topçu*), mortar (*hambaraci*), mining (*lağimci*), and cannon-wagon (*top arabaci*) were reorganized, discipline was restored, and units were placed under the command of officers trained by the French.[4] The Ottoman navy was also revitalized: state-of-the-art ships entered the service, older ones were modernized, and regulations were introduced that were designed to attract able seamen. The Imperial Naval Arsenal (Tersane) was enlarged, again with the help of the French naval experts, and new provincial arsenals were opened.[5] The unruly Janissaries—the elite military units that came to dominate the Ottoman government in the seventeenth century—did not escape reforms either. Their barracks were modernized, their rolls halved to about 30,000 men, wages were raised, and efforts were made to ensure that appointments were made according to ability. Selim III attempted to achieve a military transformation from the top down, the main idea being to establish a European-style infantry corps and later use it as a core around which to form a modern Ottoman military.

The name of this new Western-style corps, the Nizam-i Cedid (New Order), became the name of the entire reform package and indeed the era.[6] The first Nizam-i Cedid regiment was established in Levend in 1795, followed by the second unit in Üsküdar in 1799, and the third at Levend soon afterward. The size of the corps rose rapidly, from 9,300 in 1801 to 24,000 in 1806, though this swift expansion had affected its quality and training.[7] A system of conscription was introduced in Anatolia in 1802, and local authorities were required to send recruits to Constantinople for training; a similar effort failed in the Balkans because of strong opposition by local elites. The sultan soon recognized that he would not be able to achieve his objective without developing the wider technological and organizational support that a modern military structure required. Among the most enduring reforms of the Nizam-i Cedid period was the establishment of modern military schools. Technical and military books were translated into Turkish from Western languages, and recruits were trained based on French military manuals and by French instructors and trainers. By 1802, Selim III had combined the Mühendishane-i Cedide (New Engineering School) and Mimaran-i Hassa Ocag̃i (State Architecture Corps), and the resulting new institution produced both civil and military (except for naval) engineers, offering courses in drawing, geometry, algebra, astronomy, languages, and history. In 1806 the sultan introduced further changes to technical education: the Mühendishane-i Berri-i Hümayun (Imperial Military Engineering School) trained army engineers, and the Mühendishane-i Bahri-i Hümayun (Imperial School of Naval Engineering) provided a four-year education in naval engineering.[8]

These reforms required considerable funding at a time when the central government lacked the financial power to implement such ambitious restructuring. It derived its revenue from taxes but lacked the ability to collect them in the provinces, which were dominated by local notables who nominally accepted the suzerainty of the Ottoman sultan but in reality functioned as quasi-independent rulers, maintaining private armies and oftentimes conducting their own foreign policy. Thus the sultan could not generate revenue without the support and collaboration of the local elites, though securing this support also meant facing the very forces that opposed the sultan's centralizing reforms. To increase his revenue, Selim resorted to a series of policies—setting up a separate treasury, the Irad-ı cedid hazinesi (Treasury of New Revenues), debasing coinage, levying new taxes on basic consumer goods (textiles, tobacco, wine, coffee, etc.)—that made his reforms increasingly unpopular among an already overtaxed population.[9] There was stiff opposition to his reforms, especially to his Nizam-i Cedid, which represented a direct attack on the vested interests of traditional power groups, most notably the Janissaries.[10] Some Ottoman religious leaders (*ulamas*) condemned the spread of European practices that, they claimed, were incompatible with Islam. Meanwhile, the Janissaries refused to adopt any Western military practices and objected to serving alongside the new troops, whom they perceived as an open challenge to their traditionally dominant role.[11] These power groups, which also included members of local and inner governmental circles, feared that the sultan's reforms would result in the reimposition of state control over economic means. A crucial element in this was control of the land, the empire's chief economic asset. The Ottoman local elites (*ayans*) persistently tried to transform state lands (*miri*) into private fiefs (*mülk*) that would provide them with steady revenue and help achieve control over local communities. Hence the Nizam-i Cedid reforms engendered bitter opposition. The establishment of a modern military would have helped the sultan assert his authority and allowed him to free himself from dependence on traditional elites.

Sultan Selim's push to modernize his empire was hampered by a combination of internal and external challenges that occupied much of his attention and resources. He was unable to unite rival interest groups within his reformist camp, and their rivalry occasionally sabotaged reforms and was sometimes fatal to the leading reformers. The sultan also had to deal with numerous power groups—"entrenched beneficiaries of the old system," as historian Virginia Aksan put it—that challenged his authority and vied for political power.[12] Resistance by provincial notables in Anatolia, the Arab world, and parts of the Balkan Peninsula cost the Ottoman government heavily in revenue, prestige, and resources. Ali Pasha of Janina controlled most of Albania and northern Greece; the Mamluks under Murad Bey and Ibrahim Bey flouted the sultan in Egypt; Ahmet Cezzar Pasha was supreme in Syria, as was Suleyman Pasha the Great in Iraq. These local governors often openly defied the sultan, refusing to pay taxes or accept his reforms. Time and again the sultan had to overcome his antipathy for these seditious notables and cede them considerable authority, mainly to secure their military support against the external threats.

The end of the Austro-Russian-Ottoman War in 1791 marked the first major clash between the supporters and opponents of Ottoman reforms. During the war, the province of Serbia remained under the control of local Janissaries, who on a number of occasions demonstrated open disdain for central authority. Once the war ended, Selim III tried to reassert his authority in Serbia and instructed his new provincial governor to expel all unruly elements from the province.[13] The Ottoman authorities banished the Janissaries and replaced them with Serbs, who had been amnestied for their collaboration with Austria. The disgraced Janissaries did not simply vanish—they crossed to the neighboring province of Vidin, where the local governor, Pasvanoglu Osman Pasha, readily employed them to consolidate his power. By the turn of the nineteenth century Pasvanoglu emerged as one of the most powerful Ottoman notables, controlling vast amounts of territory in the northeastern Balkans and leading a growing opposition to the sultan's reform scheme. The governor claimed that the sultan's reforms were responsible for political and economic turmoil in the countryside, and gained considerable popularity by positioning himself as the people's guardian against government arbitrariness. The sultan's repeated orders to suppress the rebel governor remained ineffectual.[14]

In 1798, underscoring the threat of Pasvanoglu's power, Selim III launched his largest military campaign, sending some 80,000 men to Vidin.[15] The campaign failed, and Pasvanoglu successfully defended Vidin for eight months, gaining even greater prestige. Already disheartened by this turn of events, the sultan was forced to recall his troops upon receiving the news of the French invasion of Egypt. In early 1799, Pasvanoglu was not only pardoned and confirmed in his position but granted the titles of vizier and pasha.[16] Preoccupied with events in Egypt, Selim III hoped that these honors would keep the unruly governor appeased and loyal to the throne. Pasvanoglu quickly resumed his activities, however, knowing well that the sultan, already committed to the war against revolutionary France, could not send any troops to hinder him. Pasvanoglu's forces conducted wide-ranging raids across the northeastern Balkan Peninsula, spreading political chaos and causing considerable economic damage.[17]

In Arabia, the Ottomans faced a growing challenge from the Wahhabis, a religious sect founded by Muhammad ibn 'Abd al-Wahhab, a theologian from Najd, seeking return to pure Islam by removing any false beliefs and the regimes that support them. By 1800, the Wahhabist movement, led by Abd al-Aziz ibn Saud, extended its authority over parts of the Arabian Peninsula and displayed its growing confidence by attacking Iraq, Syria, and the Hejaz, and harassing Muslim pilgrims to the holy sites. In 1804 the Wahhabists scored their biggest victory to date when they seized Mecca and closed pilgrimage routes to the city for all non-Wahhabists. The Wahhabists went so far as to remove Sultan Selim III's name from Friday's prayers and replace it with that of the Sauds, usurping a privileged position in the Islamic world.

Meanwhile, Sultan Selim III faced a different kind of threat in the Caucasus, into which Russia had made considerable inroads in the late eighteenth century. We have already seen (in Chapter 5) that in 1800 the eastern Georgian kingdom of Kartli-Kakheti had been formally annexed by Emperor Paul I, who was assassinated in St. Petersburg in March 1801, leaving the resolution of the "Georgian Question" to his successor. The new emperor, Alexander, was at first uncertain about the issues; he strongly believed in the legitimate rights of monarchs and struggled with dispossessing the Bagrationi of their throne. He asked the State Council to decide whether by annexing the Georgian kingdom he would commit an offense against this royal dynasty. The debates in the State Council reveal the existing struggle between the doves and hawks of the Russian government and represented a crucial point in the shaping of Russian policies toward the Caucasian borderlands. Some of Emperor Alexander I's advisors—most notably Alexander Vorontsov and Victor Kochubei—urged him to repudiate his father's decision and cautioned against expanding into Georgia, which, they argued, offered limited economic and military advantages but would require considerable commitments in men and matériel to resolve domestic problems.[18] Alexander ultimately chose to ignore this sound advice and sided with the more hawkish members of the State Council, who claimed that, at the very least, countermanding Paul's decision to annex Georgia would dishonor Russia in the eyes of European and Islamic powers. They argued that the incorporation of Georgia into the Russian Empire was necessary because this was the supposed "wish" of the Georgian people, and because the failure to take such action would lead to Georgia's collapse due to both internal and external factors.[19] These council members believed—and Alexander concurred—that continued Georgian dynastic feuds offered Russia a precious opportunity to establish a foothold in south Caucasia, which could provide a springboard for further expansion into the Ottoman and/or Iranian realms and serve as a crucial commercial waypoint for trade with India. The emperor himself held that Iran would not pose a serious challenge to Russian expansion, and that the benefits of Russian rule in Georgia would soon convince neighboring Muslim state to place themselves under his protection.[20]

In late 1801 Alexander ordered the drafting of a manifesto announcing eastern Georgia's annexation. The manifesto rejected any suggestion of Russian self-interest and instead pointed to the continued bickering between and rivalry among the Bagrationi claimants to the throne, which left the realm on the verge of civil war. Alexander also underscored the responsibility of protecting fellow Christians against the Persians and Turks. The manifesto was published in Moscow on September 24, 1801, three days before Alexander's coronation, and was accompanied by instructions on how to form a new system of Russian administration in eastern Georgia. With the Georgian royal family removed from power, the commander in chief on Russia's Caucasian front assumed the leadership of the central government in Tbilisi and received the title of *pravitel*, or administrator, of Georgia. Alexander's September Manifesto was not published in Georgia until April 12, 1802, when the Russian commander in chief in the Caucasus, General Karl Knorring, publicly announced it at the Sioni Cathedral in Tbilisi and required the princes and notables of Georgia to swear an oath of allegiance to the Russian emperor. Although the announcement caused considerable outcry, the presence of armed Russian guards around the cathedral underscored the futility of protest.

Those who voiced their disapproval were quickly taken into custody; the rest were forced to pledge allegiance to the tsar.[21]

Alexander's decision to annex the eastern Georgian kingdom had profound ramifications for the Caucasus, the Ottoman Empire, and Iran. Already by the spring of 1802 the Russian emperor was arguing that it was essential for Russia to secure control over not only eastern Georgia but all of south Caucasia, as far south as the Aras River. He justified it in military terms, noting that Russia could defend its newly acquired territories only if it had established a border along the Kura and Aras Rivers.[22] This, however, meant intruding onto the traditional sphere of influence of the Ottoman Empire, which Russia had previously chosen not to do because of its commitments to anti-French coalitions in Europe.

While losing their foothold in southern Caucasia, the Ottomans faced an equally serious challenge in Serbia, which had been under Ottoman control for the previous four centuries. Here the Ottoman sultans pursued a dual policy: they sought to detach Serbs from Austrian leanings through the agency of the Patriarch at Constantinople, while also sending the Janissaries away from the capital into the provinces, including Serbia, which could be profitably plundered.[23] Sultan Selim III's reforms initially benefited the Serbs by curtailing the Janissaries and granting some concessions, including freedom of religion, to the local populace. Yet the Ottoman reform movement soon stalled, and the sultan was forced to compromise with his opponents. In 1799 Selim allowed the Janissaries to return to Serbia, where they murdered a popular local governor and took revenge on the Serbs by beheading some eighty Serbian notables (*knezes*) in what became known as the Slaughter of the Knezes (January 1804). The enraged Serbs united behind Djordje Petrović, known as Karadjordje (Karađorđe), in an armed revolt.[24]

Some scholars consider the Serbian revolt the first of the nationalist uprisings, but its actual causes and nature are more complicated than that. Within the Ottoman Empire's Christian communities, intellectuals were indeed drawn to the ideas of the Enlightenment, especially those of German philosopher Johann Gottfried Herder (1744–1803), who argued that language and literature constituted the distinct marks of a nation. The French Revolution embraced the idea of "nation" wholeheartedly and exported it to various parts of Europe, including the Ottoman provinces in the Balkans. However, the Serbian revolt sprang from a different set of circumstances. It was a protest by Serbian peasants against the usurpation of their land by the Janissaries, as well as the result of Serbian rejection of the Neobyzantinism championed by the powerful Phanariots (affluent and politically connected Greeks in the Phanar district of Constantinople). These Phanariots sought to revive Byzantine practices by empowering the Orthodox Patriarchate of Constantinople and reducing the relative antinomy of other Orthodox churches. Furthermore, the central Ottoman government initially did not oppose the revolt, since the Serbian rebels supported the sultan's suzerainty and targeted provincial notables (*sipâhis*) and Janissaries. Yet this approach allowed the revolt to accumulate momentum. As the Serbs gained an upper hand over the Janissaries, the Ottoman court belatedly realized the threat and tried to wrest back control over the region. It proved futile. The Serbs rejected the sultan's demands to disband and instead sought aid from foreign powers. Austria, with its hands tied in central Europe, chose not to support the rebels, favoring continuance of Ottoman rule instead of the establishment of a semi-autonomous (or fully independent) Serbia that might destabilize its southern border regions; Austrians advised the Serbs to resolve their differences with the Ottoman authorities through Austrian mediation.[25]

Serbian overtures, meanwhile, put the Russian emperor, Alexander, in an awkward position. Russia already enjoyed advantageous positions in Bessarabia, Moldavia, and Wallachia (commonly referred to as the Danubian Principalities) based on the Treaty of Küçük Kaynarca (1774), and recent operations against the French had further strengthened the Russian presence there through the Septinsular Republic (under joint Russian-Turkish control), which was formed in the Ionian Islands. Alexander, while desiring to exploit an opportunity to extend Russian influence to the Balkans, could not afford to alienate the Ottomans. His main concern lay with the increased French presence on the Adriatic shores, which could pose a threat to the integrity of the Ottoman Empire and undermine Russia's traditional goal of gaining an exclusive sphere of influence in the Balkan region. So a Serbian delegation to St. Petersburg received a tepid response: military aid was out of question, but Russia might consider providing diplomatic support.[26]

Encouraged by such prospects, the Serbs demanded self-government within the Ottoman Empire. In 1805–1806 they scored major victories over the Turks at Ivankovac and Mišar that allowed them to consolidate authority in northern Serbia. The newly established Narodna Skupština (People's Assembly), which shared political authority with the Ruling Council and Grand Leader Karadjordje, introduced major reforms, some of which drew inspiration from the French Revolution: all feudal obligations were abolished and the serfs were emancipated. The start of the Russo-Ottoman War in 1806 marked a key moment in the Serbian revolt, as demands for self-government within the Ottoman Empire evolved into a war for independence backed by the military support of the Russian Empire.

Upon ascending the throne in 1789, Selim had been anxious to keep out of European political complications, and so he pursued a cautious foreign policy. He was the first of the Ottoman sultans to develop the political tools of modern diplomacy. He appointed the first permanent Ottoman ambassadors to London (1793), Berlin (1795), Vienna (1795), and Paris (1795).[27] During the War of the First Coalition (1793–1797), the Ottoman Empire declared a formal neutrality for the first time in its history. As noted, Selim was determined to exploit European preoccupation with the complications arising from the French Revolution to carry forward his program of domestic reform. Ottoman neutrality did not last long, however, and the sultan soon found himself at the epicenter of European grand politics, which revolved around two interrelated issues concerning the fate of the Ottoman Empire.[28] The first was the continued viability of the empire. It faced mounting internal and external challenges, including economic woes, ongoing decentralization, and, by the late eighteenth century, the desire of subject peoples, especially in the Balkans, to assert greater self-governance, if not outright independence. The traditional narrative of Ottoman history—that starting in the 1600s the Ottomans entered a period of decline marked by steadily weakening military capacity and institutional corruption—has recently been supplanted by a more nuanced discussion of Ottoman resiliency and its ability to transform the empire during the eighteenth and nineteenth centuries.[29] The second issue involved the international situation, as the Ottomans faced the growing menace of imperial competitors who began steadily eroding the gains the empire had made in the fifteenth and sixteenth centuries. The question of what to do with the "sick man of Europe" was tightly bound up with the maintenance of the European balance of power. Though interested in partitioning the Ottoman realm, European powers were concerned that their "inheritance"—some 238,000 square miles in Europe alone in 1800—would not be equitably divided, empowering some at the expense of the others.

The origins of what would eventually be called the Eastern Question can be traced to Russia's continued military success against the Ottomans and the resulting territorial expansion of the Russian power along the Black Sea littoral. For European statesmen, the crucial question of the day was whether the Ottomans could fend off Russia's territorial and strategic aspirations, and if not, how the competing great powers should partition the Ottoman realm. On the eve of the French Revolutionary Wars, Austria closely cooperated with Russia and participated in wars against the Turks, hoping for a slice of the Ottoman-controlled Balkans. Austrian attitudes, however, began to change with the start of the revolutionary turmoil in Europe. After suffering setbacks in the Rhineland and Italy in the 1790s, Vienna's attention was, understandably, focused on events in central and western Europe, while the Ottoman borderlands remained in the background. Meanwhile, as the British presence in India increased, the British government became preoccupied with protecting the lines of communication to its most lucrative colonial and trading colony. Some of these routes ran across Ottoman lands, engendering British concern about possible encroachment by a European power. The French invasion of Egypt indicated that such fears were not groundless, but equally worrisome for the British was the prospect of Russia dealing a mortal blow to the Ottomans and seizing the Bosporus and Dardanelles, which would have established a Russian presence in the eastern Mediterranean. At the start of the Napoleonic Wars, therefore, Britain generally tried to prop up Ottoman power in order to maintain the balance of power in Europe as well as to bolster its Indian defenses.

So at the start of the nineteenth century the Russian government enjoyed a relatively free hand when it came to the Ottoman Empire and pursued three interlinked goals: expanding territorially, which involved unilateral annexations or partitions with other European powers of the Ottoman domains; securing great influence within the Ottoman Empire through the patronage of the sultan's Christian subjects and incitement of nationalist sentiments; and maintaining the rump of the Ottoman empire as a buffer zone. The last of these, occasionally referred to as the "weak neighbor" policy, implied rejection of Catherine's famed "Greek Project" because, in the words of one Russian minister in 1802, "Russia in its present expanse is no longer in need of enlargement, there is no neighbor more obedient than the Turk, and the preservation of this natural enemy of ours should be in the future the root of our policy."[30] According to this reasoning, once Russia had deprived the Ottomans of sufficient territory, the two empires could maintain friendly relations but would never be equals.

The Ottoman Empire enjoyed a long-standing relationship with France that can be traced back to the sixteenth century, when the two states united in their struggle against the Holy Roman Empire. While many European nations had made agreements and sent ambassadors to the Ottoman court over the centuries, the French had always enjoyed a particular status in Constantinople. They were the first to conclude a commercial treaty with the Turks, French merchants actively traded and invested heavily in the Ottoman economy, and in the late eighteenth century Roman Catholics in the Ottoman Empire were placed under French protection. During the Russo-Ottoman War of 1768–1774, France took a pro-Ottoman stand, and though it could not provide any material help, it was the only great power on which the sultan could rely. Indeed, the Ottoman Empire represented one point of France's "eastern trident" (along with Sweden and Poland), with which it sought to restrain the growth of the Habsburg power and later of the Russian Empire. The defeat

and humiliation of the Ottoman Empire in 1774 came as an unpleasant surprise for the French monarchy, which had begun to consider Russia as its
chief rival in northeast and southeast Europe. In the wake of the Treaty of
Küçük Kaynarca, France did its best to undermine the treaty's provisions,
thereby weakening Russia's influence and encouraging the Ottomans to
resist.

Franco-Ottoman relations deteriorated in the 1780s, however. France's
financial woes, followed by revolutionary turmoil, prevented it from providing any help to the Ottomans during the Russo-Ottoman War of 1787–
1791. The Ottoman sultan was well apprised of what was going on in France,
as his ambassador (and former tutor) to Vienna, Ebubekir Ratib Efendi, supplied him with a steady stream of dispatches on European affairs.[31] Selim III
hesitated to resume relations with the new regime in France and by now was
more interested in staying out of European affairs. Yet France's revolutionary
crisis also deprived the Ottomans of a major ally and the sultan was keen to
find a new one. In these circumstances, securing British support seemed to be
a viable and pragmatic solution. The Ottoman court appreciated British condemnation of Russian expansion in the Crimea and the Black Sea region,
which, in Ottoman eyes, elevated Britain to the status of a potential ally
while France was in turmoil.[32] It was no accident that Selim III dispatched
the first Ottoman resident mission to London rather than to Paris.[33]

By the mid-1790s the Ottomans were growing increasingly uncomfortable with French expansion, which brought the tricolor to the shores of
the Adriatic. General Bonaparte was looking eastward as early as 1797:
besides occupying the Ionian Islands, he had dispatched agents to the Maniots
(Peloponnesian Greeks) and cultivated relations with the ambitious Ali Pasha
of Janina, who demonstrated admirable diplomatic and military talents as he
exploited opportunities created by the weakening Ottoman central authority
and the outbreak of the French Revolutionary Wars.[34] The growing French
presence in the region was not welcomed by the Ottomans but, mindful of
long-standing amity between France and the Porte, they chose to maintain
cordial relations with their new neighbors.[35] The Turks agreed to lend money
and provide supplies to the French garrison on the island of Corfu and even
considered purchasing the Ionian Islands from France as a way to mitigate
the French menace there.

Franco-Ottoman relations took a turn for the worse in 1798, when the
French Republic decided to pursue its grand design of crippling Britain by
capturing Ottoman Egypt and threatening British trade. The French invasion of Egypt—extensively discussed earlier—cut right across France's traditional policies in the Levant, which included diplomatic support for the

Ottomans, protection for French merchants under the capitulations, and patronage of Latin Christians, especially in Syria and Palestine. The Ottomans naturally felt betrayed, and their anger was amplified by French claims that the expedition would not target their empire.[36] So instead of striking a blow at the colonial power of Britain, the French invasion had driven their traditional ally the Ottomans into an alliance with their enemy the British. In a major change in its long-standing policy, the Ottoman government allowed a Russian naval squadron to pass through the straits, where the residents of Constantinople greeted it in September 1798, declared war on France, and pledged to support Anglo-Russian fleets in the eastern Mediterranean.[37] The Sublime Porte signed treaties with Russia and Britain, joining their anti-French coalition—the first time the Ottomans had become a party to a European coalition.

The most important provision of the Russo-Ottoman treaty of alliance, signed in January 1799, was contained within a secret article granting Russia right of passage through the Dardanelles for the duration of the war. The Ottomans participated in operations against the French in Syria, Egypt, and the Adriatic, but that involvement only underscored Ottoman military weakness and demonstrated that the empire's alliances with Russia and Britain clearly lacked substance. The Ottoman defense of the fortress of Acre (where the Turks were supported by a British squadron) did thwart Napoleon's attempt to invade Syria. However, it was overshadowed by the Ottoman defeats at Mt. Tabor and Aboukir in 1799 and Heliopolis in 1800. More successful was the Ottoman policy in the Adriatic, where a joint Russo-Ottoman fleet under Admiral Fedor Ushakov was dispatched to the Ionian Islands, which were seized in the spring of 1799. By the Convention of 1800 the Russia and Ottoman government agreed to turn the islands into the Septinsular Republic under Ottoman suzerainty and Russian protection.[38]

The French occupation of Egypt ended in 1801, as we've seen, when the British launched a two-pronged invasion from the Mediterranean and the Red Seas. The French departure, however, left a political void that was quickly filled by feuding political factions. The British, as the occupying side, found themselves drawn into vicious power struggles between the Mamluks, who were decimated by the French invasion and had become divided into several factions, and the resurgent Ottomans, who aspired to reclaim their former authority in the region. This left the British in a bit of conundrum. While driving the French out, the British did not intend on claiming Egypt for themselves. Yet withdrawing troops would leave the region with an uncertain future. Letters written by John Hely-Hutchinson, who succeeded General Ralph Abercromby as commander in chief in Egypt, reveal the precarious situation in war-torn Egypt, where the Turks were in a "deplorable state... without money, without provisions, without resources of any kind." If the British departed, "the Mamelukes, Arabs and Greeks would be entirely overmatch for the Turks."[39]

The British thus struggled with the question of to whom Egypt should be delivered. Their withdrawal would very probably be followed by a descent into political turmoil and anarchy that would leave Egypt vulnerable to a European power, while the Ottomans might revert to their former cooperation with France. An official sent from the British embassy in Constantinople to study the situation on the ground painted a rather disheartening picture of a war-torn region that could not be simply left on its own.[40] His recommendations, which the British ambassador conveyed to London, called for a British military occupation, British indirect rule with Ottoman consent, or, if neither of those options was possible, the destruction of Egypt through inundation in order to "defeat the ambitious projects of a rival power who, by the possession of Egypt, would gain such immense commercial advantages."[41]

The British cabinet rejected all these recommendations and hoped to bring some semblance of peace and order in Egypt by restoring things to the way they had been in 1798; the Mamluks would have their rights and properties returned, while the sultan-appointed Ottoman governor would preside over the region. Such a proposition hardly appeased either side, especially after the Turks made an attempt to eliminate the Mamluk beys in late 1801.[42] With the enraged Mamluks retreating to Upper Egypt, the Turks refused to consider British offers, arguing that they had a historic opportunity to destroy the Mamluk regime and bring Egypt under greater control. As the Russian ambassador told his British counterpart, the Turks were "only waiting for the [British] evacuation of Egypt to act systematically against the beys, being resolved on their destruction."[43]

By 1802 the British were keen on departing from a region where no one welcomed them. During the peace negotiations with the French at Amiens, they pledged to evacuate Egypt and felt an increased sense of urgency to complete their commitment in order to deny the French any pretexts for complaint. Indeed, in the fall of 1802 Napoleon dispatched General Horace Sebastiani to examine the situation in Egypt, verify the British evacuation, and revive French commercial interests in the region. In his instructions Napoleon emphasized that Sebastiani was to assure everyone in Egypt that Napoleon "loved the Egyptians, and desired their happiness, that he often talked about them."[44] Sebastiani's report described a tenuous political stability in Egypt, where the Mamluks remained disunited, the Turks were too weak to take control over the region, and there was bad feeling between them and the British, who, the report alleged, were openly detested in Cairo. Sebastiani spoke of the enthusiastic reception he had enjoyed in Egypt and Syria and hinted that the French would be welcomed back in the region.

I have already discussed the role of Sebastiani's report in stoking tensions between France and Britain on the eve of the final rupture of Amiens. But the report had ramifications in the Ottoman world as well. The Turks were naturally alarmed by Sebastiani's mission and sought closer relations with the British, with the Ottoman vizier reassuring the British ambassadors of the sincerity of the sultan's friendly feelings toward Britain.[45] After the failure of Robert Lord Blantyre's last attempt to mediate in the long-protracted quarrel between the Ottomans and the Mamluks, the British evacuated the country in March 1803. Nonetheless General John Stuart, who supervised the withdrawal, also took steps to ensure a continued British presence. Agents were left in Cairo to protect British interests once the Turks and Mamluks "should no longer be overawed by the presence of [the British] army and when they should lose their recollection of the wholesome counsel of the British commander."[46] Stuart also provided secret supplies of monies and arms to the Mamluks to ensure their survival in Upper Egypt.

After seizing power in France in 1799, Napoleon embarked on rebuilding Franco-Ottoman ties, which, as we've seen, had unraveled in the previous two years. He understood that the Ottomans, despite their clear weakness, could play a key role in his European diplomatic maneuvering; friendship and alliance with the sultan could serve not only as a useful tool against the commercial interest of Britain but also as a means to bend Russia to his will. Napoleon took advantage of long-standing ties between France and the Ottoman Empire to approach the sultan with an offer of a peace treaty. In Constantinople, the end of the French occupation of Egypt revived old political alignments, and Britain and Russia sought to prevent an Ottoman-French rapprochement that could harm their interests. The Ottoman court was split into two major factions, with Grand Admiral Küçük Hüseyn leading the pro-French faction, which had been upset by Britain's continued presence in Egypt and British support for the Mamluks in a bid to secure their influence in the region; the admiral believed that an alliance with France would serve as a security guarantee against both Russia and Britain. Grand Vizier Yusuf Ziya Pasha, however, looked with suspicion at the French government and felt that an alliance with Britain could be used as a bulwark against France and Russia. Sultan Selim III played both factions to retain his freedom of action, unwilling to jeopardize his relations with any of European powers.

In 1801–1802 France negotiated two definitive treaties with Britain and the Ottoman Empire.[47] Article 8 of the Amiens treaty proclaimed that the territories, possessions, and rights of the Ottoman Empire were "maintained in their integrity, as they were before the war." A separate Franco-Ottoman treaty mutually guaranteed the integrity of the French and Ottoman posses- sions, while France regained its former privileges (such as capitulations and the right to act as protectors over the sultan's Catholic subjects) and, for the first time, the Porte gave French merchant vessels the right to trade freely on the Black Sea.[48] With this treaty, Napoleon reversed the diplomatic revolu- tion of 1799 and set the Ottoman Empire and France on the road to rebuild- ing their relations. In addition, Napoleon had opened up new markets by which France could trade with Russia, the Balkans, and even Iran. These new markets, he hoped, would rival and perhaps surpass British commercial inter- ests in the East.[49] The Peace of Amiens did not mean that Napoleon had abandoned all his plans to challenge Britain's commercial and naval interest, nor that he had given up on territorial ambitions for France in the Ottoman realm. He still desired to regain French control over the Ionian Islands (which he won in 1797, but which Russia captured in 1799) and set his sights on controlling key areas on the Adriatic Coast in the Balkans.

Napoleon pursued a multifaceted strategy toward the Ottoman Empire and frequently used the Eastern Question to facilitate his policies elsewhere. Thus, in 1801–1803 French diplomatic overtures to Austria and Russia reg- ularly mentioned the prospect of partitioning the Ottoman Empire in order to compensate them for losses suffered elsewhere in Europe; when the Austrians complained of the "paucity" of their compensations in Germany, Talleyrand consoled them with promises of "new acquisitions in Turkey at the time of its impending destruction."[50] One may agree with French historian Albert Vandal that Napoleon floated "the issue of partitioning of Turkey not to implement it but rather as a bait."[51] The goal was to sow discord among the European powers. Although Emperor Alexander ultimately declined France's offers, the British were alarmed by the fact that some senior Russian officials (espe- cially Prince Adam Czartoryski) found those offers enticing, favored taking action against the Turks, and rebuffed British offers for a collective engage- ment to provide for "security and integrity of Turkey."[52] Equally anxious were the Habsburgs, who were concerned that any Austrian aggrandizement in the Balkans would provoke Prussian demands for compensation, and that any Prussian acquisitions in Germany would far outweigh Austrian gains in the Ottoman realm. Above all, Austrian emperor Francis feared a repetition of the Partitions of Poland, into which, in his words, Austria had been "forced and duped." Unlike his grandmother Empress Maria Theresa, who, as Frederick the Great caustically observed, "wept but took [Polish lands] all the same," Emperor Francis felt that Austria should not be involved in the Ottoman partitions, as it would be saddled with more hard-to-govern territories in which "it would be necessary to shed too much blood for each step we make forward."[53]

In October 1802 Napoleon dispatched General Guillaume Brune as the new French ambassador to Constantinople, advising him to reclaim "the supremacy which France had enjoyed for two centuries in that capital." Brune was to safeguard French commerce and take under his protection the Roman Catholics across the empire; to showcase France's revival, Brune was instructed to stay put and keep the embassy fully illuminated on Muslim holidays. Napoleon underscored how beneficial alliance with France could be for the Turks. It would be based on reciprocal guarantee of territories, yet while the French Republic pledged to act in order to protect Ottoman territorial integrity, the sultan would assume no responsibility to take part in France's wars.[54]

Brune reached Constantinople in December 1802 and remained there for three years. Capitalizing on the anti-British feelings that resulted from Britain's continued occupation of Egypt, he largely succeeded in restoring France's position at the sultan's court (though his further efforts to gain Selim's confidence were stymied by the Russian and British envoys). Among Brune's accomplishments was revival of the French consular service, with consuls and agents posted in Greece, Crete, Cyprus, Syria, Wallachia, and Moldavia as well as the Russian and Ottoman ports on the Black Sea coast. This vast network provided Napoleon with a steady stream of information and insights into the Ottoman realms and shaped French foreign policy. As a result, as early as 1802–1803, Alexandre Romieu, French consul general in Corfu, urged action in Albania, where the growing power of the local governor suggested imminent rupture with the Ottoman sultan. Ali Pasha of Janina, who, in the words of the consul, "supremely detests the French," could pose serious threats to the French interests in the Balkans.[55]

Meanwhile, the quickly changing political situation in Europe threatened to embroil the Ottoman Empire in yet another conflict. After the Peace of Amiens collapsed in May 1803, Selim III was left to decide what do next. Any involvement in European squabbles would pose a grave threat to Ottoman interests. Despite Napoleon's assurances of amity, the Ottomans distrusted his intentions, remembering well how misleading French assurances had turned out to be in 1798. A French landing in Morea or Albania could mark the beginning of the dissolution of the Ottoman state. Yet the sultan could not afford to let his relations with France disintegrate, because he could never be sure what his Russian and British allies had in store for him; the latter had already resorted to the precautionary measure of anchoring a naval squadron at Tenedos, just outside the Dardanelles. Unwilling to

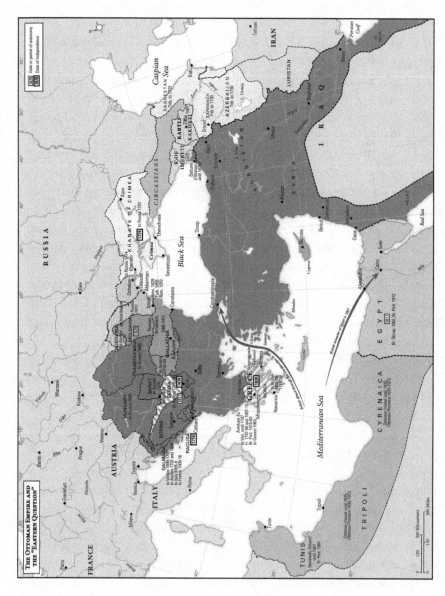

Map 17: The Ottoman Empire and the "Eastern Question"

get embroiled in European affairs, in September 1803 Selim III declared for neutrality, for the second time in ten years.[56] But Ottoman nonalignment did not exempt them from European rivalries.

France's Eastern policy was largely conditioned by European policies but was also characterized by the multipronged nature of Napoleon's design. In 1803 the French emperor was busy assuring both the sultan and the Mamluk chiefs, who of course defied Ottoman authority, of his friendship and support, all the while considering the prospect of partitioning the empire with other European powers. With Austria sitting on the proverbial fence, Russia and Britain were increasingly concerned about the possibility of French intervention inside the Ottoman Empire; Russia was even willing to forestall it through a "preventative" intervention of its own, which would "defend" the Ottoman domain and "improve" the condition of the Christian subjects of the sultan.[57] In early 1804, to prepare the ground for such an eventuality, Russia sent out feelers to Britain, but it was unable to secure any commitments to its projects; however, Britain did appoint consul generals in Morea and Egypt to counteract French intrigues. Still, it tended to rely on its naval power to forestall any French ambitions in the east.[58] Undeterred, the Russian government focused its efforts on shoring up support among the Christian population of the Balkan Peninsula and in August 1804 welcomed the news that the prince-bishop of Montenegro had made a formal appeal to place his principality under Russian protection.

Equally problematic was the situation in the Ionian Islands, which a joint Russo-Ottoman expedition had captured during the War of the Second Coalition. In April 1800 the two sides signed a convention that established the Septinsular Republic on the islands, which remained under the suzerainty of the Porte, paying the triennial tribute, while Russia guaranteed its administrative arrangement and continuity of its sovereignty against any foreign intervention.[59] Largely forgotten in the histories of the Revolutionary and Napoleonic Wars, this convention was a significant document, in that it established the first Greek state in the modern European history. The ink was hardly dry on the convention before both sides started to quibble over its interpretation, with Russia insisting that the republic was virtually independent of the Porte and placing it under de facto occupation.[60] Considering the strategic location of the islands, the Russian actions are hardly surprising.[61] The islands of Corfu, Zante, and Cefalonia provided convenient staging grounds for Russian naval forces and could serve as a strategic foothold for possible attack on Ottoman possessions in the Balkans.[62] Shortly after coming to power, however, Emperor Alexander made the decision to evacuate the islands, provided that no other foreign troops would be allowed there. The

Russian withdrawal revealed deep divisions within the Ionian population. The Septinsular Republic quickly collapsed, with its constituent islands rejecting Ottoman authority; some preferred to declare independence (as did Cephalonia and Ithaca), while others hoisted the British flag (like Zenta).

In light of Napoleon's aggressive policies in Italy, Russia feared that France might exploit the turmoil in the Ionian Islands and that the Ottomans would be unable to counter a potential French intervention. These concerns compelled Alexander to reverse his decision and send Russian troops back to the islands in late 1802.[63] Over the next two years the size of the Russian garrison increased sevenfold, reaching some 8,000 men, supported by a strong naval squadron. As instructions to its agents in the Septinsular Republic demonstrate, the Russian government used the islands as gateways into the Balkan Peninsula, where it sought to undermine any French influences while strengthening its own positions by highlighting the religious and cultural affinity between the Russians, the Greeks, and the southern Slavs. As Russian foreign minister Prince Adam Czartoryski observed, Russia "should carefully avoid anything that could discredit us in the eyes of the Porte, as it is important for us to be on friendly terms with it...[and] to prepare everything in such a way that it could be used for realization of any plan or decision that a turn of events might make us choose."[64]

Russian actions alarmed not only the Ottomans but also the Austrians and British. In the fall of 1804, as Britain and Russia discussed the prospects of forming a new coalition against France, the conversation also involved the future of the Ottoman Empire. Britain insisted on the territorial integrity of the Porte. Echoing elements of the "weak neighbor" policy, Czartoryski countered that if the Ottoman Empire did not side with France, it would "perhaps be best, after reestablishing her rights under old treaties, to leave her for the moment in her present condition," except for Serbia and the Ionian Republic, whose fate would have to be determined. However, if during the impending war the Turks showed any support for the French, "the question should arise of definitively settling the fate of the Ottoman Empire in Europe." Czartoryski envisioned the mass of Ottoman territories in Europe being divided into locally governed states within a Russian-led federation, while the eastern Ottoman possessions would be placed under a Russian protectorate; Austria would be appeased with Croatia, part of Bosnia, Wallachia, Belgrade, and Ragusa, while Russia would annex "Moldavia, Cattaro, Corfu and, above all, Constantinople and the Dardanelles, together with the neighboring ports, which would make us masters of the Straits." In exchange for accepting this arrangement, Britain and France would receive compensations in "Africa and Asia."[65]

The Russian delegation did its best to convince Britain that while France's territorial ambitions posed a threat, Russia's own expansion into the Ottoman realm would not be detrimental to British interests.[66] Surprised as he might have been to hear this, Prime Minister Pitt demurred, noting that "the realization of such plan would be highly ill-advised and damaging to our main goal [of containing France], and it would constitute a major breach of the law of nations [*droit des gens*]."[67] Nonetheless, on the eve of the War of the Third Coalition, neither Britain nor Russia could afford implacable hostility to each other's interests. The British cabinet decided to "try to adapt itself to the attitude of Russia as far as possible," while Czartoryski toned down his partition rhetoric and spoke of the common interests that Russia and Britain shared.[68] Britain and Russia thus chose to overlook their differences (for now) in favor of joining efforts against the growing French threat. The Declaration of Alliance, issued by Austria and Russia in November 1804, solemnly guaranteed the integrity of the sultan's domain.[69] In December Russia agreed to renew the treaty of alliance with the Ottoman Empire in order to "appease the concerns of Mr. Pitt, whose system, as far back as 1790, was based on the greatest jealousy of any new acquisitions on the part of Russia."[70]

The Russo-Ottoman negotiations revealed just how frustrated the Ottomans had become with their involvement in coalitions in which they increasingly felt like a junior partner. Russia made no effort to conceal its belief that the Ottoman Empire was declining and that it could no longer afford to bear "gratuitously" the burden of defending Ottoman territorial integrity.[71] Russia therefore insisted not only on the Ottoman confirmation of earlier concessions—notably, the right to intervene on behalf of Christian subjects and the right to move warships through the straits—but also on a new one that, in case of a conflict involving another European power, sanctioned "preventative" occupations of the Danubian Principalities by Russia and of Egypt and Morea by Britain.[72] Britain did not object to the Russian proposal because its cabinet had also considered occupying Alexandria should it become necessary in the course of war against France.[73] But for the Turks, the new demands rubbed salt into old wounds. They refused to accept the new provision, which conspicuously violated their sovereignty, and declared that "war would be preferable to an alliance founded on such principles."[74] The sultan broke off negotiations in September, though the British convinced him to return to the table once the unacceptable provision had been dropped.[75] Thus, finding themselves between the proverbial rock (Russia) and a hard place (France), the Ottomans chose the former and on September 24, 1805, signed a renewed alliance with Russia.[76] This experience left them humiliated and keen for a way out of the Russian embrace.

The renewal of the Russian-Ottoman alliance was a major setback for French diplomacy, which had worked so hard to drive a wedge between the sultan and the European powers. In March 1804 Napoleon sent a secret letter to the sultan, reassuring him of France's good intentions and friendship and denying any intention to invade Egypt or Greece. The emperor urged Selim III to reestablish his authority in Egypt and Syria and to deal quickly with the nascent Serbian revolt.[77] After Russia and France severed diplomatic relations in the wake of the execution of the duc d'Enghien, Napoleon continued to push the sultan to commit to the French cause. "I desire to support the [Ottoman] Empire [and] I desire that it recover a little energy," read his instructions to Brune.[78] The French emperor was willing to embellish some facts, and in an effort to impress the sultan he claimed the existence of special arrangements between France, Spain, and the United States against Britain.[79] His efforts seemed to have produced results, at least initially, for the sultan met France's special envoy, declared that "Napoleon is my friend," and agreed that there must be "perfect harmony" between the two states.[80]

Still, the sultan's pronouncements could not change the fact that Russia had gained a considerable naval presence in the eastern Mediterranean through its right to send warships through the straits and a continued presence in the Ionian Islands. This worried not only France but also Britain, which wanted to frustrate Russian ambitions but could not act openly because of its need for Russian support against France; instead, the British embassy to the Porte encouraged the sultan to continue modernizing his state and military. Though well aware of Russian designs, Selim III was unwilling to risk an open rupture, particularly at such a difficult moment for his empire, when it was beset with problems in the Balkans, Egypt, and Arabia. The St. Petersburg court exploited this situation to advance its interests in the Ottoman realm. Aside from the renewed alliance treaty, Russian also negotiated a new agreement that consolidated Russian positions in the Danubian Principalities and gave it the right to intervene on behalf of the *hospodars* (princes) of Wallachia and Moldavia, who were selected for a term of seven years and could not be deposed except in cases of misconduct and by *joint* Russian and Ottoman inquiry. As we shall see, the emphasis on "joint" proved to be very important, for the sultan's violation of this provision (at the behest of the French) in 1806 would serve as a casus belli for Russia. Simultaneously, Russia used provisions of the 1798 treaty with the Ottomans to move its warships through the Bosporus and Dardanelles, ostensibly to maintain communications with the Ionian Islands. France's opposition to the Russian naval movements and, more important, to Russian claims to exclusive control of the Black Sea—or, as the Russian ambassador told Brune, "a great lake belonging to Russia"—contributed to the growing Franco-Russian political rivalry on the eve of the War of the Third Coalition.[81]

In May 1804 Napoleon assumed the imperial title and the question of whether or not the Ottomans would grant him recognition became of paramount importance to him.[82] The Ottomans initially paid little attention to the change; the title of "emperor" meant little to them. In an effort to underscore its importance, Brune informed them that Napoleon had become "emperor and padishah," the latter being an Iranian title for a great king that combined Islamic perceptions of temporal and religious authority and came close to reflecting the sultan's own position. Yet Brune's effort backfired, given that the Ottomans had already conceded the title of "padishah" to the emperor of Russia, whose ambassador actively lobbied against extending a similar recognition to an upstart Corsican, whose activities in Italy and Greece pointed to his "perfidious designs against the Ottoman Empire." Britain shared the Russian position, stating that its new ambassador, then en route to Constantinople, would suspend his journey until the Turks provided assurances that they would not recognize Napoleon's emperorship.[83]

The recognition of Napoleon as the emperor of the French thus became the principal diplomatic question throughout the summer and fall of 1804, with the Ottomans skillfully avoiding using either term ("emperor" or "padishah") in official correspondence. The French continued to press for recognition but kept receiving vague responses that the sultan would not get involved in matters of Christian rulers and preferred to wait and see how other European powers acted on this issue.[84] The Ottomans were unmoved by Brune's arguments that the peace settlements had annulled the 1799 alliances or by his warning about Russian designs. In the fall of 1804 the French ambassador tried to force the sultan's hand on the issue of imperial recognition, threatening to leave Constantinople if Selim kept up his refusal and continued to allow Russian ships through the Straits. The French ambassador was given a perfectly vague answer: "This would be arranged, if God permits." As one French historian aptly observed, "God" in this affair was the Russian ambassador A. Italinskii, who immediately warned the Ottoman government that the slightest change in its policy would be an affront to Russia and Britain, and reminded it of the military dominance that the European powers enjoyed.[85] Brune therefore had no choice but to leave Constantinople while Russia went on to negotiate a new alliance treaty with the Turks in 1805.[86]

These were major setbacks for the French emperor, who lamented the growing Russian influence at Constantinople and reminded the sultan of Russia's traditional hostility toward the Porte. "Most high, most excellent, most powerful, most magnanimous and invincible prince, the great Emperor of the Muslims, Sultan Selim, in whom all honor and virtue abound," wrote Napoleon in January 1805. "You, the descendant of great Ottomans, Emperor of one of the greatest empires in the world, do you cease to reign? Why do you suffer the Russians to dictate to you?"[87] What Napoleon had failed to consider was that the sultan feared the military and naval power of Britain and Russia; he reasoned that they were far more capable at the time of backing up their threats and ambitions with force than was France.

Emperor Alexander understood that Sultan Selim III's commitment to the new Russo-Ottoman alliance depended on the outcome of the War of the Third Coalition. Napoleon's military triumph and the humiliation of Austria and Russia at Austerlitz naturally made a profound impression in Constantinople and paved the way for a more accommodating attitude toward France; the Ottomans "consider Bonaparte as an instrument in the hands of providence to punish the iniquities of an offending world," observed the British ambassador in February 1806.[88] Particular attention was paid to the 1805 Treaty of Pressburg, which recognized French territorial gains in the Adriatic (Istria and Dalmatia) and brought the French Empire into direct territorial contact with the Ottomans, thereby providing Napoleon with new leverage over the sultan. Thrilled by the "miraculous victories of our august emperor," the French chargé d'affaires, Pierre Ruffin, warned the Turks that any overt support of "the enemies of His Majesty, the Emperor of the French," would risk a direct confrontation.[89] Such veiled threats were entirely unnecessary. Sultan Selim III had quickly adjusted his policy by refusing to ratify the Russo-Ottoman alliance, restricting Russian movements through the straits, and suspending negotiations with Britain. In February 1806 the sultan officially recognized Napoleon's imperial title: "Having captured Vienna, conquered so many countries, and defeated [Austrian and Russian] emperors together, there can no longer be any question as to Bonaparte's imperial title," observed Sultan Selim in a note to his grand vizier.[90] Despite vigorous protests from the British and Russian ambassadors, the Ottomans justified their recognition by pointing to the new political reality in Europe, one that made France their next-door neighbor. Besides, the Ottomans felt emboldened to express their belief that after the defeats of 1805 Russia could no longer provide effective support.[91]

France responded to the changes in the Ottoman policies with alacrity, sending a special envoy and welcoming the dispatch of the new Ottoman ambassador, Seyyid Abdürrahim Muhib Efendi, who arrived with great pomp in June 1806.[92] In May 1806 Napoleon sent his new ambassador, Horace François Sébastiani, to Constantinople. His instructions reveal that he intended to use the Ottomans in his ongoing conflict with Russia, hoping to force Russia into a position whereby it had to choose whether to side with France against Britain or face multiple threats along its borders. To this purpose, the French hoped to render the Russo-Ottoman alliance ineffective and to make Russia's position in the Adriatic untenable by convincing the Ottomans to close the straits to Russian warships. If it came to it, an armed conflict between Russia and the Porte would be equally beneficial to France, diverting (and depleting) Russian resources away from central and eastern Europe.[93]

As the year 1806 progressed, it became clear that Selim III had firmly moved toward an alliance with France, declaring his intention to close the Bosporus and Dardanelles to Russian vessels, bolstering Ottoman defenses along the Russo-Ottoman frontier in Bessarabia and the Danube River, and, with French encouragement, mobilizing armed forces against the Serbs. The latter move is particular noteworthy because Napoleon made considerable use of the Serbian revolt, characterizing it as one of the most serious internal challenge that the Ottomans confronted. He blamed the revolt on Russian incitements and advised the sultan to deny Russia any participation in the Serbo-Ottoman negotiations, arguing that the establishment of Serbian autonomy, under Russian tutelage, would serve as a signal for other Balkan Christians to seek similar concessions, which in turn would precipitate the fragmentation of the Ottoman Empire.[94] Of equal importance to Napoleon was the prospect of Serbo-Russian military cooperation, which, along with British naval supremacy in the eastern Mediterranean, could have profound implications for French political and economic interests in the region. He therefore encouraged Selim III to subdue the Serbian rebels by force and without any foreign involvement. In February and March 1806 Ottoman military preparations against the Serbs gave Russia cause for grave concern, with Emperor Alexander instructing his ambassador to inform the sultan that he considered such preparations to be directed against the Russian interests and, further, that he was prepared to defend the Ottoman realm against any foreign interventions. Instead of the Serbs, the sultan should concentrate his attention on the Dalmatian borderlands, for that was where the danger of an external attack lay. These Russian efforts failed: in a suitably lukewarm letter to Alexander, Selim assured Alexander that he harbored no hostile intentions toward Russia.[95]

The French influence at the Ottoman court remained a source of growing alarm in Vienna and St. Petersburg. Austria, having seen its prestige shredded by the Treaties of Lunéville and Pressburg, felt justified in reversing its earlier stance on the Serbian issue, in the hope of gaining some grounds in the Balkans. A new appeal for help to Emperor Francis by Karadjordje offered the Austrians an opportunity to engage the Serbs. However, their offer of mediation was quickly spurned by the Ottomans, only further highlighting the decline of Austrian influence in a region that had become a proxy battle-ground for the Franco-Russian struggle.[96] Meanwhile, a special meeting of the Russian State Council examined the impact of Napoleon's victories and concluded that the French acquisition of Dalmatia posed a direct threat to existing Russo-Ottoman relations and provided Napoleon with the means of implementing his imperial designs in the Balkans. In order to forestall such eventualities, the State Council decided that Russia should both try to retain the confidence of the Ottoman government and pursue closer contacts with the Porte's Greek and Slav subjects.[97] Thus, when a new appeal from the Serbs arrived in the spring of 1806, the Russian government was already prepared to start reevaluating its earlier reservations about supporting them. Alexander I and his advisors believed that French agents were behind anti-Russian intrigues in the region, and they feared that another slight might force the Serbs to turn to France for help. Yet as long as the possibility of a mediated resolution existed, Alexander was reluctant to intervene in the affairs of the Belgrade *pashalik*, instead pursuing his interests in other Ottoman spheres of influence, most notably western Georgia, where Russians had moved to consolidate their authority in 1804–1806.

The growing Russo-Ottoman tensions, which soon erupted into a major war, must be set within the wider context of the geopolitical realignment that occurred during the Napoleonic Wars in Europe. After the War of the Third Coalition, France came to dominate central Europe and acquired the former Venetian territories that gave it access to the Balkans. French agents were sent to various regions of the Balkans with instructions to undermine Russian influence, while the French consulates in Moldavia and Wallachia became the principal centers of anti-Russian intrigue.[98] Furthermore, as the Russian ambassador to Constantinople noted in one of his reports, the per-ception of Russian weakness could tempt the Ottoman government to chal-lenge Russian positions in Georgia and on the eastern Black Sea coast.[99] Russia found it hard to accept the prospect of losing ground in regions where it had long sought to carve out its own place, and it was eager, in the words of a British ambassador to Russia, to "retrieve the glory of her arms, tarnished by the disasters of the late campaign, and to gratify the army by some important conquest."[100]

In early 1806 Russian foreign minister Czartoryski produced several mem-oranda that outlined Russia's new approaches to the Eastern Question. The overarching goal was to "have Turkey solely at our disposal. We must try to increase our influence on this state, having removed all rivals in such a way that the Porte would not follow anybody else's will or politics but ours."[101] Should the Ottomans continued to side with France, Russia, as a Slavic and Christian nation, had a moral obligation to support Slavic and Christian subjects of the Ottoman Empire and endeavor to create several Slavic states that "would enjoy independent administration in their internal affairs but would remain under supreme authority and protection of Russia."[102] Czartoryski believed that the Ottoman Empire would not be able to survive another major war and insisted that in the event of Ottoman dissolution the entire area between the Black Sea and the Adriatic must come under Russian influence. This could be accomplished through the incorporation of Moldavia, Wallachia, and Bessarabia directly into Russia, as well as the creation of separate, autonomous states under the exclusive protection of Russia in Serbia, Herzegovina, Montenegro, Greece, and other parts of the Balkan Peninsula.

These plans represented a marked departure from the benign Russian protectorate over the Balkan states that Czartoryski had advocated just three years earlier. Nonetheless, they conveniently fit in with Russia's long-term objective of creating autonomous Balkan states that would lean on Russia for support.[103] Aside from its political motives, Russia's policy in the Balkans was also influenced by economic considerations. Both Alexander I and his foreign minister recognized the commercial importance of the region to the Russian economy and saw in the growing French influence a definite threat to the establishment of Russian commerce. With the French already present in Dalmatia and the sultan's court seemingly falling under French sway, the Russian government felt the need to maintain its armed forces on a respectable footing, ready to oppose France should it threaten the Ottoman Empire. In this regard, the 12,000 soldiers and the Russian naval squadron under Admiral Dimitri Senyavin at Corfu remained a serious tool for Russian influence in the Mediterranean. In the spring of 1806 these forces further strengthened Russia's hold on the Adriatic coast by seizing Cattaro, Lissa, and Curzola, where local Austrian authorities had welcomed them after their emperor ceded these islands to France in the Treaty of Pressburg.[104]

In an effort to contain French influence in Constantinople, Emperor Alexander sought closer relations with Britain, both as an added means of influencing the Turks and as a way of securing an important ally in the ongoing struggle against France. A special Russian envoy, P. A. Stroganov, was dispatched to London to arrive at some understanding on the Eastern Question. Stroganov's instructions called for presenting any Russian acquisitions of the Ottoman territories under the guise of "compensation" necessary for restoring the balance of power in Europe and the eastern Mediterranean and for facilitating a general peace on the continent.[105] The Russian overture faced great hurdles almost from the very beginning. The death of Prime Minister Pitt in 1806 brought about a major change in British foreign policy, as we've seen, with the new cabinet pursuing a more defensive strategy and eager to conclude peace with France. Russian attempts thus failed to convince British foreign secretary Fox to support the plan for partitioning the Ottoman Empire. Even the Russian offer to allow the British to occupy Egypt, to prevent it from falling into French hands, could not produce the desired results; Fox denied that a French presence there would endanger British India in any way.[106] The British foreign secretary did, however, concede that should the Ottomans actively side with France by ceding territory or allowing French troops to pass through their realm, Britain would be ready to support Russia to "act vigorously against the Porte as well as against France," and "the further [Russia] can push her conquests the more [Britain] will be satisfied."[107]

More hawkish was the British ambassador to Constantinople, who lamented the decline of Russian influence at the Ottoman court and urged his government to send a Royal Navy squadron to cruise in Ottoman waters in order to support Russia and to deter the Ottomans from pursuing an overtly pro-French policy. The goal was "to unite a manifest disposition to conciliate with a marked determination to act with firmness." In practice this meant resorting to a combination of assurances and threats, an approach also typical of Napoleon's diplomacy.[108] Ultimately, no Anglo-Russian agreement was ever reached, leaving Russia to wait for the turn of events that might justify its intervention into Ottoman affairs.[109]

It did not have to wait long. By late spring 1806 the Ottoman government had clearly veered toward France. A special diplomatic mission, led by Abdürrahim Muhib Efendi, was sent to Paris, where it announced formal recognition of Napoleon's imperial title and, more crucially, outlined Ottoman objectives in the emerging Franco-Ottoman alliance.[110] The Ottomans argued that it was Napoleon, through his invasion of Egypt in 1798, who had brought about the existing state of affairs, and therefore it was appropriate for the French to exert themselves in addressing the situation. As part of any future settlement between France and Russia, the Ottoman government wanted the French to insist on several key conditions on its behalf. These included the annulment of the Russo-Ottoman alliance; the abrogation of the conditions concerning the principalities that Russia had earlier extorted; a new arrangement in the Ionian Islands that would protect Ottoman interests (in practice this would have meant the evacuation of the islands by Russia); an explicit statement prohibiting the passage of Russian warships through the Black Sea straits; and the return to their former condition of the areas Russia had captured in Georgia.[111] The Ottoman envoy was instructed to decline any French offers for a military alliance, noting as the main obstacle France's inability to defend the Porte against British naval power. At the same time the French had to be reassured about the existing Ottoman agreements with Russia and Britain, none of which, the Porte claimed, was directed against France. In short, Muhib Efendi's instructions clearly showed the Ottoman desire to remain neutral, avoid entanglements in the conflicts between European powers, and seize any opportunity to reduce Western influence within its realm.

Probably no other issue exasperated the Ottomans as much as did the *berats*, the passports granted by the foreign embassies and consulates to Ottoman subjects that offered exemption from Ottoman jurisdiction and taxes.[112] Part of the long-standing practice of capitulations, the *berats* had been abused by all the Western powers, especially Russia and France, depriving the Ottomans of much-needed revenue and fostering their sense of resentment against foreign interference. The scale of the misuse can be gleaned from the fact that by agreeing to revise its *berats*, the French embassy alone lost 1 million francs in revenue.[113] In May 1806, despite the opposition of the European missions, the Ottoman authorities began to vigorously check the legitimacy of the *berats* and reserved capitulary rights only to bona fide foreign representatives; among the measures they undertook was to order all Greeks, who had used the protection of the Russian flag, to surrender their *berats* within eight days or face the confiscation of their properties. Russia and Britain were vocal in denouncing these measures, which pointed to a more assertive Ottoman government, but ultimately chose to accept them in light of the much larger international issues at stake.

Far more worrisome for Russia was the Ottoman attitude toward the passage of Russian ships through the Dardanelles. When the Ottoman government declared that this jeopardized its neutrality and asked Russia to avoid using the straits for military purposes, the Russian response was immediate and vehement, rejecting any concessions on what the Russians considered a "right" derived from existing treaties.[114] The whole question of Russia's rights in the Ottoman Empire soon became a central issue in the ongoing Franco-Russian negotiations, which led to an agreement (the Clarke-d'Oubril Treaty, July 1806) that attempted to reconcile the two powers. Much of the agreement dealt with French and Russian interests in the Adriatic and the Balkans. Understanding that neither side would consent to any diminution of its influence in the region, the agreement vaguely stated that "the independence of the Ottoman Porte shall be acknowledged on both sides, and both the high contracting parties engage to protect it and the integrity of its possessions." Yet, in a major concession, the Russian envoy agreed to the

Russian evacuation of Cattaro and the reduction of the Russian garrison at Corfu, in exchange for French pledges to support the restoration of the Republic of Ragusa and to cease any hostile activities in the eastern Adriatic.[115] Emperor Alexander refused to ratify the agreement, regarding its provisions as too conciliatory and weakening Russian positions in the Adriatic, which he considered crucial to maintaining influence at the Porte and among the Ottoman subjects in the Balkans.

Furthermore, by August 1806 the Russians had achieved a major diplomatic success that made rejection of this agreement almost inevitable. Ever since the defeats of 1805, Russian diplomats had worked hard to negate Napoleon's influence by attaching Prussia to Russia through an agreement that would have made the maintenance of Ottoman territorial integrity its basis.[116] At first Napoleon blocked Russian efforts by negotiating the Treaty of Schönbrunn (December 15, 1805). But Prussia's frustration with French expansion created an opening that the Russians exploited in the summer of 1806. In July the Prussian and Russian negotiators agreed on a secret declaration at Charlottenburg. Prussia would agree to turn a blind eye to France and commit itself to guaranteeing, along with Russia, the Ottoman possessions (as well as those of Austria and Denmark).[117] The Charlottenburg Declaration in effect negated the Franco-Russian agreement, since Alexander no longer had any incentive to support its onerous provisions.

In August 1806 Sultan Selim III lent a willing ear to the newly arrived French ambassador, Sebastiani, whose instructions called for the closure of the straits to Russian ships, helping the Turks to strengthen fortifications along the borders with Russia, and restoring Ottoman authority over Moldavia and Wallachia.[118] Sebastiani started with the last of these, urging the sultan to replace the current *hospodars* of Moldavia and Wallachia, Princes Constantine Ipsilanti and Alexander Muruzi, because of their pro-Russian sympathies.[119] Despite repeated Russian warnings, Selim III indeed replaced these princes, on the grounds that they were abetting the Serbian rebels at the behest of their Russian patrons.[120] In their place he appointed pro-French *hospodars*, Alexander Suzzo and Scarlat Callimachi. But in doing so the sultan violated the existing agreement that required Russia's consent to dismiss or appoint the *hospodars*. Although the Ottomans quickly realized their mistake, the damage had been done.[121] Emperor Alexander considered the dismissals as the latest and clearest sign of growing French influence at Constantinople, which would justify his intervention into Ottoman affairs and compel Britain to act.[122] More significant was that the Russians felt their "weak neighbor" policy had failed—the Ottomans had proved just as likely to fall under the influence of a rival power. Therefore, only a forceful response could compel Constantinople to modify its positions; in the words of Czartoryski, "Fear is the only means that may have an effect on the Turks in these circumstances."[123] Alexander shared this sentiment and was determined to use the occasion to reaffirm Russian dominance in Constantinople. In fact, once the war began, the emperor gradually fell under the influence of his more hawkish advisors and reverted to the earlier expansionist aims of his grandmother.

The Ottomans thus faced the very situation that they had been studiously trying to avoid since war broke out in Europe thirteen years earlier: having to choose between France and its enemies. They initially sought a British mediation and, admitting their mistake, offered to remove the new *hospodars*, though they stopped short of reinstating the old ones. Yet that was precisely the demand that Russians considered sine qua non.[124] In mid-October, just as Napoleon routed the Prussians, the Ottoman state council (Encümen-i Şura) debated the issue, weighing the advantages of siding with France, maintaining neutrality, or redressing Russian and British grievances. Napoleon, preoccupied as he was in northern Europe, had limited means of threatening the empire, and the French military presence in the Adriatic, though ominous, could still be contained by Ottoman forces. Russia, on the other hand, could march to the Danube without much opposition, while Britain could attack the entire Ottoman coastline. In the end, Sultan Selim III yielded to pressure and decided to accommodate Russia's demands. On October 15 the Ottomans informed the Russian embassy of their decision to restore the dismissed *hospodars*, which they did over the following two days.[125] This was a major diplomatic setback for Napoleon, as the Ottomans had unmistakably revealed their low estimation of the French threat and their far greater concern over Anglo-Russian actions.

But Ottoman hopes of avoiding a war were soon dashed, as the Russian government pushed for a direct confrontation. On October 28, while the Russian armies prepared to fight Napoleon in Poland, Emperor Alexander ordered his troops to cross the imperial border with the Ottoman Empire and occupy Bessarabia, Moldavia, and Wallachia.[126] He justified this decision by pointing to uncertainty about Ottoman intentions. Constantinople had failed to provide any guarantees concerning Sebastiani's earlier threat to march French troops across Ottoman territory to the Dniester, which would have threatened the southern provinces of Russia. Besides, in the Russians' judgment, the Ottoman decision on the *hospodars* fell short of rectifying the situation.[127] Over the course of the next three months, a Russian army of over 40,000 men under General Ivan Michelson advanced through the Danubian Principalities, seized half a dozen Ottoman fortresses, and pushed Ottoman forces back to the Danube River, where the Turks repelled a Russian attempt to cross the river at Giurgiu (Giurgevo, located in present-day Romania).[128] The Ottomans, still hoping for a mediated resolution of this conflict, delayed their declaration of war until late December 1806.[129]

Napoleon, who, as noted, was fighting the Russians in Poland, welcomed the start of the Russo-Ottoman conflict, though the news of the rapid Russian advance into Wallachia could not have left him encouraged. He tried nevertheless to turn the events to his own advantage, publishing falsified news stories—containing a few grains of truth and dated from Bucharest and Tiflis—in French newspapers in order to "enlighten the public opinion." His goal was to showcase that by being threatened by the French in Poland, the Turks in Wallachia, and the Persians in southeastern Caucasia, "the Russian Empire is attacked on every side."[130] More pointedly, the emperor urged the sultan to declare war on Russia and resist the invasion with all his might.

The news of the French triumph over the Prussians at Jena (October 14) reached Constantinople in November and made Selim and his viziers more susceptible to French arguments. In November, as he informed Selim of his victories, Napoleon exhorted the sultan not make peace with Russia until he had taken possession of the Danubian Principalities, and he assured Selim that, owing to the French successes in Prussia, Russia had withdrawn some of its forces from the Dniester. On December 1, 1806, he authorized Sebastiani to conclude an offensive and defensive alliance with the Ottomans, pledging to guarantee the integrity of Moldavia, Wallachia, and Serbia. "The moment has arrived to restore the Ottoman Empire to her former grandeur," Napoleon encouraged Selim. "There is not a moment to waste; your frontiers are invaded. Your Highness must take vigorous measures offered by the loyalty of his people to leave our common enemies not a moment to rest. Call upon all your loyal subjects to defend what they hold most dear—their cities, mosques and everything Islamic the Russians wished to destroy."[131] In case the sultan needed help defending the Danube, Napoleon was ready to dispatch up to 25,000 men under General Marmont by way of Vidin (where a French agent was already stationed), and he thought the arrival of French troops would compel the Russians to divert more troops to Wallachia, thereby rendering his own campaign easier in Poland.

Napoleon's strategy against Russia was revealed in a series of instructions he sent to Marmont in Dalmatia and Sebastiani in Constantinople in January 1807. He argued that France had a unique opportunity to forge a tripartite alliance with the Porte and Iran and threaten Russian borders across a vast area between the Baltic and the Caspian Seas. He wanted the Ottomans to make better use of their naval resources and pledged to send six French warships (if they could escape the British blockade) to the Black Sea, where, with the help of the Ottoman fleet, they would attack the Russian fleet and harass Russian coastal regions. At the same time he hoped that the Iranian shah, with whom he was already negotiating (as we'll see), would increase his efforts to reclaim eastern Georgia and that the Ottomans would open a new front in western Georgia. "You must ensure that the Porte orders the pasha of Erzerum to march with all of his forces to [western] Georgia," Napoleon instructed his ambassador in Constantinople. "Also maintain good dispositions of the prince of Abkhazia [Kelesh Ahmed Bey] and instigate him to participate in a grand diversion against our common enemy. So that this prince, the pasha of Erzerum, the Persians, and the Porte all simultaneously attack Georgia, the Crimea, and Bessarabia."[132]

As conjectural as these plans may seem, some of them were in fact implemented—but with doleful results. The Ottoman spring counteroffensive of 1807, led by Grand Vizier Ibrahim Hilmi Pasha himself, showed some early promise, as the Turks attacked in two directions. They could not coordinate their actions, however, thereby allowing the Russians to defeat the Ottoman advance guard under Ali Pasha at Obilesti on June 13, 1807, and force the main Ottoman army to fall back beyond the Danube.[133] Even more disastrous was the Ottoman advance in southern Caucasus, an offensive so poorly planned by Yussuf Pasha, the *serasker* of Erzerum, that it was intercepted and routed by a smaller Russian force on the Arpaçay (Akhurian) River on June 18, 1807. This was a major Russian victory, for it effectively removed any threat of a major Ottoman invasion of Georgia and consolidated Russian positions in southern Caucasus.

Of even greater importance were the events that took place far away from the theater of war. First the British attacked the Dardanelles and Egypt, then a political revolution removed Sultan Selim III from power, and finally the Franco-Russian rapprochement at Tilsit profoundly affected the balance of power in Europe.

———◦◦◦✕◦◦◦———

The start of the Russo-Ottoman War, the French acquisitions in the Adriatic, and, most important, the growing French influence in Constantinople left Britain no choice but to act. Throughout the summer and fall of 1806 Britain remained completely committed to Russia's support of the Ottomans. As early as September 1806, the British ambassador Charles Arbuthnot demanded that the sultan curb French influence and allow Russian warships through the Bosphorus and the Dardanelles. Ottoman concessions in mid-October placed him in an awkward position, as he both urged conciliation toward the Porte and disapproved of Russia's conduct in invading the Danubian

Principalities. Nevertheless, Britain was committed to Russia, and Arbuthnot had no choice but to pressure the Ottoman government into further compromises. Although they were aware of the dangers posed by the Royal Navy, many in the Ottoman government, including the sultan himself, believed that Arbuthnot's pro-Russian sentiments did not represent the position of the British government.[134] They were mistaken. The British government believed that a strong show of force was necessary to compel the Ottomans to the negotiating table and had instructed Vice Admiral Sir Cuthbert Collingwood, who commanded the Royal Navy in the Mediterranean, to send a squadron under the command of Vice Admiral Sir John Duckworth to Constantinople.[135] Aside from supporting a Russian ally, this offered a unique opportunity to strengthen the British position in the eastern Mediterranean. Prime Minister Grenville envisioned several locations where the British might "want one or two important naval points, defensible by small garrisons, to shut up the road to the Dardanelles when the French shall have taken the Porte under their own protection."[136]

The British squadron left Cadiz in mid-January 1807, with Duckworth carrying orders to lead his eight warships to Constantinople and be "ready to act with vigour and promptitude, as circumstances and the state of affairs on his arrival may make necessary." He was to demand the surrender of the Ottoman fleet together with a supply of naval stores sufficient for its complete equipment, and to enforce the British ambassador's demands for the dismissal of the French ambassador and for concession of Russia's claims. Upon commencement of hostilities, a British expedition would be sent from Sicily for the occupation of Alexandria, in an effort to thwart French influence there.[137]

On February 10 Duckworth's fleet anchored at the island of Tenedos, near the entrance to the Dardanelles. A swift naval passage up the strait might have succeeded, but the British admiral encountered unexpected impediments.[138] For more than a week the wind blew directly down the Dardanelles, preventing him from sailing. The British appearance near the Ottoman shores both distressed and incensed the Turks, who were anxious to avoid a war with Britain. The British ambassador, aware of the Ottoman practice of taking hostages, as they had done against the Russians in 1768 and the French in 1798, fled from Constantinople.[139] This was a major blunder because, as one British statesman observed, it made the British naval expedition "assume the appearance of a mere military enterprise, not of a force destined to enforce the negotiations of the ambassador by placing before the eyes of the sultan an English fleet ready and able to bombard his capital."[140] In these circumstances, the Ottoman court refused to consider British demands until the fleet departed and its ambassador had returned to Constantinople.

On February 19, for the first time in its history, the Royal Navy began to force the Dardanelles. It continued to face challenges. Duckworth, as one British captain characterized him, was "a gallant, good seaman" but really only as "second-in-command to such a man as Lord Nelson."[141] He allowed the Turks to protract negotiations under various pretexts while unfavorable winds continued to prevent him from sailing further and saved Constantinople from the fate of Copenhagen. This delay gave the Ottoman government time to prepare its defenses. Civilians were mobilized to help build new fortifications, and the Ottoman fleet was brought in to defend the capital; more than a hundred fire ships were readied for action. The city's garrison, advised by Sébastiani and a small staff of French engineers began improving the sixteenth-century fortresses along the coastline.[142] Within days the Turks had mobilized tens of thousands of men and assembled more than three hundreds of pieces of heavy ordnance, "advantageously placed for flanking [the British fleet] in all directions."[143] Unable to overcome the Ottoman defenses, Duckworth became concerned that his squadron might be encircled in the Sea of Marmara, and thus he had no choice but to retreat back through the Dardanelles into the Mediterranean on March 1–3. His return trip proved costlier than the initial forcing of the straits, as the forts in the straits fired upon his ships, damaging several ships and killing or wounding some 160 men.[144]

Duckworth's expedition was a failure, both militarily and politically. "How a government could have asked an [Ottoman] empire to 'deliver up their fleet,' 'to renounce all connections with France,' and to make peace, and a disgraceful one, with Russia, with only seven ships of the line and not a single soldier to enforce their terms, is to me incomprehensible," lamented one expedition participant.[145] The British attack only further increased French influence at the Ottoman court and all but destroyed the British standing there; the sultan sanctioned the arrest of all Englishmen and confiscation of their property, and ordered the dey of Algeria to attack British commerce in the western Mediterranean. Selim showered rich gifts on Sebastiani and the French military mission, underscoring the high esteem and influence that the French now enjoyed. By May, upon his request, dozens of French troops arrived at the Ottoman capital, further augmenting the size of the French military mission. Furthermore, the defense of the Dardanelles boosted Ottoman morale, and shortly thereafter the Ottoman grand vizier left the capital in preparation for a new offensive against the Russians in the Danubian Principalities, while the Ottoman fleet prepared to do the same in the Aegean Sea.

Regrouping at Tenedos, Duckworth met Russian admiral Dimitri Senyavin, who suggested forcing the straits with a joint Anglo-Russian fleet. The British demurred—without any troops, there was no prospect of delivering a decisive blow, especially now that the Ottoman defenses had been strengthened. The allies parted ways. Senyavin remained in the Aegean Sea and in July defeated the Ottoman navy off the north Aegean island of Lemnos and blockaded the Dardanelles. Meanwhile, Duckworth proceeded to Malta to support the opening of another front against the Ottomans in Egypt.

In early March, just as Duckworth was sailing out of the Dardanelles, a separate expedition of 6,000 British soldiers was dispatched to Egypt. Ever since their success in 1801, the British had, as noted many times, grappled with the future of this strategically important place. The resumption of war with France in 1803 and the subsequent French triumphs increased British fears of the French threat to Egypt, which the British believed the Ottomans could not defend. The Franco-Ottoman rapprochement was interpreted as opening Egypt to the French. The British were keen to act at once.[146]

In the three years since the British evacuation, Egypt had witnessed a complete breakdown of law and order. The Ottoman-Mamluk power struggles resumed immediately, and a wide assortment of military forces, as well as the absence of effective central control, led to numerous abuses, harassment, and outright murder. The Mamluks, deprived of the military competence of Murad Bey, who had died, and of the political prudence of Ibrahim Bey, who was old and frail, fractured into quarreling factions led by Osman Bey al-Bardissi and Muhammed Bey al-Alfi, who demonstrated a tragic failure to learn from past mistakes and only further weakened their cause.

In the early summer of 1803, as part of his wider efforts to restore French positions in the east, Napoleon sent Mathieu de Lesseps as France's new "commissioner for commercial transactions" to Egypt. Although de Lesseps's instructions forbade him from getting involved in Egyptian politics, his arrival naturally led the Ottomans and the British, mindful as they were of Sebastiani's report, to conclude that he had been sent to form a "French party" in anticipation of another intervention. Such suspicions increased after Osman Bey al-Bardissi, who had maintained contacts with the French throughout the previous three years, approached de Lesseps with a request for help. The Mamluk chief was clearly trying to play European powers off against each other but was unable to get any commitments from the French.[147] Yet the Mamluk's contacts alarmed the British agent, Colonel Ernest Missett, who urged his superiors to redouble efforts to extirpate French influence in the region.[148] The opposing approaches of the British Foreign and War Offices, however, meant that British policy remained divided over the course of action to pursue. Missett, who was under the War Office, assiduously lobbied for British intervention, and at his urging, al-Bardissi's rival, Muhammed Bey al-Alfi, decided to travel to London with a view to securing some British assistance. At Malta, where Alfi had to spend some time before the British government agreed to receive him, the Mamluk chief also negotiated with the British commissioner Alexander Ball (also under the War Office) and broached the idea of restoring the Mamluk rule in Egypt under British protection.

In October 1803 al-Alfi arrived at London. Although his visit aroused enthusiastic interest in the British press, the British government proved less welcoming, with the Foreign Office clashing with the War Office and arguing against any British involvement in Egypt; Britain was the ally of the sultan and could not participate in what would effectively mean the partition of his realm.[149] Indeed, Alfi's visit was viewed with grave suspicion in Constantinople, and the British ambassador there was compelled to protest against his government receiving the Mamluk. On the other hand, Downing Street could not afford to ignore the Mamluks, out of concerns that this might drive them into Napoleon's hands. Consequently, it chose a middle course, making no tangible commitments to the Mamluks while promising to use its influence at Constantinople to bring about a lasting reconciliation between the Porte and the Mamluks. Al-Alfi could not have been thrilled by this response.

Meanwhile, the Ottomans struggled to restore their authority in Egypt. The troops that Sultan Selim III dispatched became part of the problem, not the solution. This body of troops included some newly established Nizam-i Cedid forces that had been trained and disciplined along European lines (with some European officers present) as well as other contingents, notably the 6,000-man-strong Albanian contingent. Upon arriving in Egypt, they found the country desolate and impoverished, with commerce and trade at a standstill, the population bled dry by heavy taxes, and money scarce. After not receiving pay for five months, the Albanian troops mutinied, assassinated the Ottoman commander Tahir Pasha, and chose his deputy Mehmet Ali (a fellow Albanian who fomented disorder as part of his bid for power) to lead them. The Ottoman viceroy (*wali*) Khusrav Pasha was unable to control the situation and fled from the Egyptian capital, which fell into the hands of Mehmet Ali and his Albanian troops, now the most powerful military force in the region.[150]

A shrewd and capable man, Mehmet Ali realized that he had been given a golden opportunity to fill the vacuum of power, and he moved to exploit it. As one French agent observed, the Albanian was a "man as ambitious as he was enterprising who, skillful in the art of intrigue, has for him the force of public opinion and arms. This astute man ... wishes to spread discontent and cut a path to the throne without seeming to want to do so."[151] First Mehmet Ali allied himself with the Mamluk beys to defeat Khusrav Pasha, who was captured and deported to Constantinople. When the sultan sent two more viceroys, they were defeated by the same Albanian-Mamluk coalition. By 1804, with the Mamluk usefulness over, Mehmet Ali exploited popular discontent against the heavy-handed treatment that the Mamluks had meted out to expel them from Cairo. He then moved swiftly to consolidate power and had Egyptian notables and religious leaders proclaim him a new governor in May 1805.[152] Learning what had transpired in Cairo, Sultan Selim III understood that the Albanian commander was a force to be reckoned with, especially while the empire faced threats on multiple fronts. So he acquiesced in Mehmet Ali's appointment as *wali* of Egypt in July 1805, a decision that he and his successors would come to regret on many occasions over the next four decades.

Regarded today as the founder of modern Egypt, Mehmet Ali faced daunting challenges at the start of his rule.[153] The troops that had brought him to power could just as easily turn against him if he failed to provide adequate pay and sustenance. The Mamluks, though defeated, still posed a serious threat to public security and were supported by British and French agents who believed that the Mamluk return to power would help increase their influence in the region. More important, the new *wali* was well aware of the precarious nature of his position, extracted as it had been from Sultan Selim III, who might try to depose him at the first opportunity.[154] All these concerns remained at the core of Mehmet Ali's long career, and the subsequent history of Egypt had been to a large degree shaped by his attempt to make his tenure more secure. Over the next year and a half Mehmet Ali demonstrated an ability to forge and break alliances in order to calm the situation in the country. In this he was assisted by the fortuitous deaths of the Mamluk leaders al-Bardissi and al-Alfi in 1806, leaving the Mamluk factions weak and vulnerable to the governor's political intrigues.

Mehmet Ali was still consolidating his authority when news of the British invasion arrived in mid-March 1807. Just as had happened six years earlier, the British expedition, this time led by General Alexander MacKenzie-Fraser, landed near Aboukir and captured Alexandria on March 21.[155] MacKenzie-Fraser's instructions confined his mission to capturing Alexandria; on no account was he to advance into the interior. Missett, who had lobbied so hard for the British intervention, was taken aback to learn of the limited scope of the British invasion. He had evidently envisaged a much larger undertaking, one that would have overthrown Mehmet Ali, whom he suspected of pro-French sentiments, and reinstated the Mamluk beys in Cairo.[156] MacKenzie-Fraser was, in fact, surprised by the extent of Missett's commitments to the Mamluks and initially refused to listen to his entreaties. But

Missett pointed out the impossibility of keeping Alexandria supplied with food or water for the British army without capturing neighboring Rosetta and Rahmaniya, which were reputed to have large granaries.[157] MacKenzie-Fraser's attempts to occupy the Delta region were nonetheless repulsed several times, with heavy British losses. Deprived of supplies, the British troops in Alexandria were facing a desperate situation. MacKenzie-Fraser and Missett blamed each other for the disaster and disagreed on the course of action to take; the former was in favor of evacuation, while the latter insisted on remaining in Egypt to prevent it from falling into the hands of the French.

Mehmet Ali, meanwhile, understood that he was not strong enough to drive the British out of Alexandria by force, and so he sought a diplomatic resolution to the conflict. He released one of the British prisoners and offered MacKenzie-Fraser an arrangement that would allow the British to evacuate with dignity. By September the negotiations produced an agreement that ended hostilities and released all prisoners of war. The British pledged to evacuated within two weeks and leave all fortification in their existing state to Mehmet Ali, whose troops occupied Alexandria as soon as the last British soldier departed.

"So ended this foolish and disastrous enterprise," observed a British historian.[158] The news of the defeat, arriving on the heels of earlier setbacks in Buenos Aires and the Dardanelles, caused considerable public consternation in Britain but otherwise had limited impact on the course of the British war effort in Europe. That the expedition had not been well thought through was obvious. If its main goal was to influence the sultan, Egypt was too far away to accomplish it. Of far greater importance was the effect the British expedition had in Egypt. Had it been successful, it would have undermined, if not entirely destroyed, the power of Mehmet Ali. As it was, this crisis only further strengthened his position. At the start of 1807 Mehmet Ali secured control over the great port of Alexandria, which offered tremendous commercial opportunities. British armies and fleets in the Mediterranean and the Iberian Peninsula required vast quantities of grain, which was in short supply in Europe. Mehmet Ali moved swiftly to satisfy British needs, and his monopoly over the export of grain reaped substantial profits that allowed him to further consolidate his power. Over the next four years he overhauled the revenue machinery and began modernizing his armed forces. At the same time the Mamluk question was also brought to a rapid and bloody denouement in 1811 when the Mamluk chiefs were massacred at a gathering in Cairo and the surviving Mamluks were hunted down and killed. Mehmet Ali was now the undisputed master of Egypt, paving the way for his modernizing reforms.[159]

Mehmet Ali's success was partly due to the fact that the Ottoman Empire was beset by too many problems at once. The war with Russia unfolded not just in Wallachia but also in southwestern Caucasia and on the Black Sea littoral, with the Ottomans unable to stem the tide of the Russian attacks. And the situation only got worse in 1808, when the unsettled political conditions of the empire led to the creation of a coalition of Balkan power brokers, Constantinople-based religious leaders (*ulama*), and the Janissaries, who challenged the sultan in one of the bloodiest episodes of modern Turkish history.

The sultan's push to modernize the empire's armed forces caused much grief among traditional power groups, who feared that they would lose their status and power. In 1806 the introduction of the new Nizam-i Cedid corps in Edirne provoked a revolt by local notables, Janissaries, and conservatives. The local government official was lynched by the Janissaries when he attempted to read out the imperial decree announcing the introduction of the Nizam-i Cedid troops. Sultan Selim refrained from immediately confronting the rebels and instead adopted a conciliatory approach toward them. He recalled the Nizam-i Cedid force to Constantinople and dismissed its capable commanders. In reaction to further threats by the notables, the sultan even placed the command of the Nizam-i Cedid forces in the hands of its enemies, hoping to mollify the conservatives.

The result was disastrous. In May 1807 the Janissary auxiliaries (*yamaks*) deployed in the forts along the Bosporus rebelled after a Nizam-i Cedid officer attempted to get them to wear new uniforms and undergo new training. Selim might have crushed this revolt but was convinced by his conservative advisors to compromise once more. The emboldened rebels marched on Constantinople, where they were joined by thousands of Janissaries, religious students, *ulama*, and others who condemned the sultan's modernization program. The demoralized sultan complied with all the demands of the rebels, including disbanding his Nizam-i Cedid army, removing his reform entourage, and appointing conservatives to key positions. But even such drastic concessions could not save his throne; they merely heartened the rebels, who dethroned and imprisoned Selim. Next in the line of succession were Selim's cousins Mustafa and Mahmud. However, given that Mahmud was suspected by the rebels of being close to the deposed sultan and sympathetic to his reforms, Mustafa was placed on the Ottoman throne as Mustafa IV on May 29, 1807.[160] These internal political crises severely hampered the Ottoman military capabilities and compelled the Ottoman forces, some of whom were commanded by provincial notables engaged in power struggles, to seek a defensive posture against the Russians and to maintain a defensive line on the Danube.

Weak and incompetent, Sultan Mustafa IV was merely a political puppet in the hands of the rebels, who embarked on demolishing the Nizam-i Cedid system that Selim had set up over the previous decade. They claimed that these Western-inspired reforms violated traditional principles of law and order and were what had caused all the turmoil and defeats. Although many local power groups opposed Selim's new army out of fear that a strong central government would undermine their power, there were also powerful notables who recognized the need to build a modern army capable of defending the empire; to them, supporting a stronger central government was the lesser evil when the alternative was being conquered by Christian European powers. As the new sultan and his anti-reform allies quickly realized, imperial rule was far from being unrestrained; in effect, it extended only to the capital and a number of its surrounding districts. The sultan could certainly project his authority beyond these territories, but that entailed bestowing favors on powerful notables and getting entangled in complex local rivalries. The most powerful of the provincial notables in southeast Europe was Bayraktar Mustafa Pasha of Ruse, who supported Selim III and opposed Mustafa IV. Rallying other powerful notables under his leadership, Bayraktar Mustafa Pasa marched to Constantinople in July 1808 to reinstate Selim. Mustafa ordered the assassination of Selim and Mahmud; the former was killed but the latter managed to escape. Bayraktar Mustafa Pasha deposed Mustafa and installed Mahmud as the new sultan on July 28, 1808.[161]

Like his predecessor, Mahmud II (1808–1839) was politically impotent and depended for his survival on Bayraktar Mustafa Pasha, the first provincial notable ever to become the grand vizier of the empire. To generate support for the new regime, Mustafa Pasha organized a meeting of powerful notables in Constantinople to discuss the political problems confronting the Ottoman Empire; although some power brokers, such as Ali Pasha of Janina and Mehmet Ali of Egypt, did not participate in this meeting, many others from all corners of the empire attended it. The gathering produced the Deed of Agreement (Sened-i Ittifak, October 7, 1808), in which both the sultan and the notables pledged to rule justly. They further promised to support reforms and the creation of a new army, declared their loyalty to the sultan, agreed to contribute military units to the sultan's army, and consented to implement the Ottoman tax system throughout the empire without diverting any revenue that belonged to the sultan. Finally, they promised to respect each other's territory and autonomy. In return, the sultan agreed to levy taxes justly and fairly. A remarkable document, the deed has sometimes been presented as a first attempt at constitutionalism, the "Magna Carta of the Ottomans." While far from being a formal constitutional document, it was indeed a pact between the ruler and his "barons," limiting the powers of the sultan and responsibilities of local authorities. Yet in the end the document failed to deliver—the sultan, not wishing to limit his own sovereign power, avoided signing it, and only four notables affixed their signature to it.[162]

Convinced that he had crushed the opposition, Bayraktar Mustafa Pasha turned to reviving the reforms of Selim III. With his army giving the reformers a kind of power that even the sultan had never had, the rebellious elements were killed or driven out of the capital. The grand vizier then revived the disbanded Nizam-i Cedid (under the new name of Segban-i Cedid) and reformed the Janissary corps. Nonetheless, he clearly underestimated the power of the Janissaries, the *ulama*, and conservative elements of the Ottoman society, which were not deceived by new names attached to old reforms, while the grand vizier's arrogant demeanor also alienated the sultan and government officials. When a revolt by a rival lord from Bulgaria forced Bayraktar Mustafa Pasha to dispatch most of his army from Constantinople, the opposition seized the opportunity to strike back. The Janissaries stormed the palace and trapped Bayraktar Mustafa Pasha in a powder magazine, where he blew himself up on November 15, 1808.[163] Having learned from the mistakes of his ill-fated cousin, Sultan Mahmud refused to concede to the rebels, understanding that concessions would only embolden the opposition. Instead, he reacted quickly, ordering his men to kill Mustafa IV, in order to deprive the rebels of the alternative candidate to the throne. He also rallied loyal commanders to his side and, rejecting the rebel demands, attacked them by land and sea.

The absence of an alternative to Mahmud and his ability to organize his forces against the Janissaries convinced the rebels that they could not depose the sultan and made them open to reconciliation. Mahmud agreed to end the reforms and disband the new Segban-i Cedid army, and in return the rebels agreed to recognize him as sultan. Although it initially seemed that the anti-reform forces had gained a major victory over the sultan, Mahmud had managed to survive, and he remained firmly committed to reform. The events of November 1808 provided him with valuable practical experience, which Selim III had lacked. The new sultan had witnessed his predecessor's weakness and indecision and drawn lessons from them. He understood that any future reforms had to be carefully planned, had to encompass the entire scope of state institutions, not just isolated elements of the military, and needed to be carried out through the destruction of traditional institutions, especially the Janissaries, who would do everything in their power to undermine the modernization of the Ottoman army.

Aside from daunting domestic challenges, the new Ottoman sultan had to confront the rapidly changing political environment in Europe. Austria had been defeated and forced to leave the anti-Napoleonic coalition while Prussia had been overrun. Britain continued to fight, but as far as continental powers were concerned, its help seemed to never materialize in time. These were considerations that weighed on the mind of Emperor Alexander of Russia as he stepped on the raft in the middle of the Nieman River and agreed to a peace treaty with France in July 1807. By the terms of the Treaty of Tilsit, Russia recognized Napoleon's conquests in central Europe, agreed to evacuate the Danubian Principalities, and transferred the Ionian Islands to France. However, this major diplomatic victory for France was gained by sacrificing the Ottomans. In this sense, Napoleon welcomed news of the political upheaval in Constantinople because, as he argued, the downfall of Selim III had negated any earlier commitments France had made to him. "This is a decree of Providence that just released me and told me that the Turkish empire can no longer exist," he told the Russian emperor.[164] At Tilsit, France effectively abandoned its alliance with the Porte and pledged to force the sultan to make a settlement satisfactory to Russia. In secret provisions of the treaty, Napoleon agreed that in the event of the sultan's refusing the offer of mediation or of the negotiations producing no agreement, "France will make common cause with Russia against the Ottoman Porte, and the two High Contracting Parties shall come to an agreement to remove all the provinces of the Ottoman Empire in Europe, the city of Constantinople and the Province of Roumalia excepted, from the yoke and the vexations of the Turks."[165]

France's agreement with Russia naturally riled the Turks, who felt betrayed by the fact that the French had concluded peace without consulting or involving them. Nonetheless, the Ottoman government also understood the short-term benefits of the treaty, which required Russia to evacuate Moldavia and Wallachia and to end their help to the Serbs. Sultan Mustafa entered into negotiations with the Russians under French mediation, eventually resulting in an armistice signed at Slobozia in late August 1807. The armistice, signed by the Russian commander in chief, General Ivan (Johann) von Michelsohnen, required Russian withdrawal from the Danubian Principalities within a month, while the Turks agreed to remain south of the Danube but in possession of Serbia. The armistice proved to be short-lived. Russia, using various specious pretexts, refused to accept the agreement and blamed the refusal on Michelsohnen, who, it was argued, was not authorized to conduct diplomatic negotiations, and on the Turks, who supposedly broke the armistice by moving toward strategic areas and oppressing the Christian population as soon as the Russians left.[166]

In reality, the culprit was Emperor Alexander, who had little desire to abide by the Tilsit commitments, especially at a moment when a revolution raged in Constantinople and the Ottoman government was in disarray. "The Ottoman Empire is dead," the Russian foreign minister Rumyantsev told the French ambassador, so why should not Russia keep the spoils of war?[167] Alexander increasingly thought in expansionist terms, echoing sentiments that Rostopchin had expressed six years earlier. Russia's future lay in expansion into the Balkans and the Caucasus, where it could hope to gain territories to compensate for the loss of positions in central Europe. Hence, imperial instructions to the Russian ambassador in Paris insisted on the Ottomans relinquishing Bessarabia and parts of western Georgia as well as the indefinite Russian occupation of Moldavia and Wallachia.[168] Napoleon was initially incensed by the Russian demands and responded by noting that should Alexander refuse to withdraw his troops from the Danubian Principalities, France would not evacuate Prussian Silesia.[169] But he also understood that he could not press Russia too much at a time when he was preoccupied with affairs in the Iberian Peninsula. Indeed, he needed Russian support to maintain political stability on the continent and if Russia demanded concessions in the Ottoman Empire, he was ready to make them, though of course only after they had been carefully vetted and discussed.

In the spring of 1808, as the Russian and French diplomats discussed details of a possible partition of the Ottoman Empire, the Serbian issue continued to feature prominently. Both sides understood that Austria's geographic interests entitled it to some territory in the event of the Ottoman partition. Russia's new foreign minister, Count Nikolay Rumyantsev, confirmed Russia's willingness to cede Serbia to Austria, provided that France accepted the Russian takeover of Bessarabia, Wallachia, Bulgaria, and southwestern Caucasia as well as control of Constantinople and the straits. Napoleon, meanwhile, could retain Albania—"it is close to you and offers valuable resources for your navy," as Rumyantsev observed—along with Greece proper, Thessaly, and Crete; the Russians were also willing to see the French acquire Egypt, Syria, and parts of Anatolia. However, Napoleon found the Russian claims to the Ottoman capital and the straits unacceptable.[170]

Through the fall of 1808 Emperor Alexander wavered between going along with Napoleon's halfhearted talk about partition of the Ottoman realm and pushing ahead with extending his influence in the Porte without French help, mainly by gaining the confidence of the Serbs and other potential allies from within. In October the French and Russian emperors met once again at Erfurt with the goal of consolidating their alliance. Alexander exacted a price for supporting France against Austria and insisted on the continued presence of the Russian forces in Wallachia and Moldavia because of "all the revolutions and changes which disturb the Ottoman Empire and which do not leave any possibility of giving, and in consequence any hope of obtaining, sufficient guarantees for the persons and goods of the inhabitants of Wallachia and Moldavia." Napoleon agreed to recognize Russian control of these territories but wanted to keep it secret "in order not to compromise the friendship existing between France and the Porte, nor the security of the French who reside in the Turkish dominions in order to prevent the Porte throwing itself into the arms of England." France also agreed that in the event a Russo-Ottoman war rekindled, it would not take any part therein, unless Austria or any other power made common cause with the Ottomans.[171] By December 1808 the French envoy in Constantinople, Florimond de Faÿ de La Tour-Maubourg, received a set of new instructions that tasked him with convincing the Ottomans to cede the Danubian Principalities to Russia.[172]

The situation changed the following year. The Franco-Austrian War of 1809 left no doubts in France that Russia had become an ally only in name. Napoleon understood this but felt that he had no choice but to stand by this alliance even as the fissures in Franco-Russian relations became visible. Britain, however, was only too eager to exploit them. Sir Robert Wilson was sent on two missions to St. Petersburg, assuring the Russians that Britain wanted to see Russian power augmented while France sought to curtail it; on the Eastern Question, London pledged that it "never would propose the partition of Turkey, but, nevertheless, if any arrangement could be made between Austria and Russia on the basis of occupying and exchanging [Danubian] provinces, which arrangement would secure the sincere alliance of both countries, [the British] never would make that a cause of quarrel."[173]

The failure of these missions prompted the British to make direct overtures to the Turks, who welcomed them in an effort to play European powers off against each other. In January 1809, after three months of negotiations during which the French repeatedly warned the Turks not to make peace with London, the Peace of Kala-i Sultaniye (the Dardanelles) restored Anglo-Ottoman relations.[174] The British government agreed to evacuate all occupied Ottoman territories, while the sultan restored capitulatory privileges to the British. London also agreed to mediate with Russia to obtain an Ottoman-Russian peace that would preserve the integrity of the sultan's territories and resist French designs. One of its most important provisions stipulated that the Bosporus and Dardanelles should be closed at all times to foreign warships of all nations, reflecting British concern about a possible union of the Russian and French fleets in the Mediterranean. For the next three years Britain pursued a complex strategy of putting a stop to the Russo-Ottoman

War, developing a triple alliance with the Ottomans and Austria, and containing both Russian and French influence in the Ottoman Empire. Thus when the War of the Fifth Coalition began, just four short months after the conclusion of the Anglo-Ottoman Treaty, Britain tried to convince the Turks to allow a British squadron into the Black Sea and to launch a joint Anglo-Ottoman attack on the Russian naval base at Sebastopol—a foreboding of things to come during the Crimean War a half century in the future—in order to "materially assist the conclusion of the Russian peace on fair terms and secure her neutrality."[175]

The Treaty of the Dardanelles was significant because it marked a turning point in Franco-Ottoman relations. It revealed a growing realization in Constantinople that alliance with Napoleon brought few tangible benefits. Still, France refused to let the Turks steer clear of their alliance. Napoleon assured them that he would not allow Russia to expand beyond the Danube and that he would guarantee their territorial integrity, save for Moldavia and Wallachia, which the Turks had to forsake as a price for peace. In December 1809, in a speech to the Legislative Corps, he warned the Turks of "the punishment if they let themselves be influenced by [Britain's] wily and perfidious advice." And to show that he meant what he said, Napoleon spoke with satisfaction about "my friend and ally, the Emperor of Russia" extending his authority to the Danubian Principalities.[176]

All this was just part of Napoleon's efforts to keep up at least the appearance of Franco-Russian amity. In reality he was feverishly exploring ways he could contain Russia. He tried to use the prospect of Russian expansion to secure Austrian cooperation. In early 1809, while meeting the Austrian ambassador Metternich to discuss ongoing Austrian military reforms and the threat they posed to France, Napoleon dangled before the Austrians' eyes a share in the spoils of the Ottoman Empire, threatening to make them helpless spectators as France and Russia partitioned the Ottoman lands. All the while the Ottoman ambassador stood just a few steps away, presumably with his eyes wide open—"conversation like this is probably unprecedented in the annals of diplomacy," Metternich observed in his subsequent report.[177]

It was about this time that Theodore Lascaris de Ventimille, a former Maltese knight and a descendant of the Byzantine emperors, traveled on a mission to the Levant. Upon arriving there, the French agent contacted Fathallah al-Sayegh, a Christian resident of Aleppo, with a request for help in exploring trade routes, stations, and water wells in the Syrian and Iraqi deserts. The two adventurers embarked on a dangerous venture in February 1810 and succeeded in visiting the most remote desert corners and interacting with various tribes. After months of traveling, Lascaris confided a remarkable secret to his Arab guide—he was not there to peddle goods but, in an incredible parallel to Lawrence of Arabia, to fulfill Napoleon's instructions to befriend local tribal leaders, unite them in a revolt against Ottoman power, and pave the way for the French return to the Levant. The mission, as Sayegh described it in his memoirs, was successful, and Arab tribal chiefs expressed readiness to challenge Ottoman power and ally themselves with Napoleon. Yet as Lascaris prepared for his journey back to France, he learned about Napoleon's disastrous invasion of Russia and understood its ramifications. He decided to travel to Egypt to see an old friend, the French consul in Alexandria, but died of dysentery shortly after his arrival.[178]

The strange story of Lascaris and Sayegh contains many inconsistencies and contradictions, and the lack of French consular or other official documents makes many elements impossible to verify.[179] Imaginary as it may be, the tale does touch upon a crucial historical fact—that Napoleon had long expressed his interest in returning to the East and threatening British interests in the Indian Ocean. In September 1810 he envisioned a general attack against Britain, which included an expedition to the Levant. A month later he instructed one of his agents to visit Syria and Egypt to examine the fortress of Saint-Jean-d'Acre, Jaffa, Rosette, Alexandria and Cairo and to report on local conditions; the same day, he also ordered French consuls in Syria and Egypt to submit regular memorandums on political, military, and financial conditions in both these regions.[180] These instructions seem to have been intended to lay the ground for an expedition that was to embark to the East after the end of the Russian campaign. Lascaris's mission would have fit well with Napoleon's ongoing efforts to explore conditions in the Levant, but further research is needed to make a definite conclusion about it.

———◦◦◦※◦◦◦———

At the start of the Russo-Ottoman war, a series of Serbian military victories, which resulted in the capture of Belgrade on December 29, 1806 and Šabac in February 1807, had left the Serbs in control of the former Belgrade *pashalik*. For the Russians, then, Serbia offered an important lever with which to crack the Ottoman resistance. Serbian leader Karadjordje openly sided with Russia and offered to accept Russian troops, thus paving the way for the Russo-Serbian military cooperation both on land and on the sea, with the Russian Army of Moldavia linking up with the rebels and the Mediterranean squadron of Vice Admiral Senyavin, stationed in Montenegro, providing further naval support.[181] Alarmed by the Russian intervention in Serbia, Sultan Selim III tried to negotiate an accommodation with Karadjordje, offering him terms that the Serbs themselves had earlier sought. Yet much had changed since then, and what would have been acceptable in 1804 was no longer sufficient in 1807. With the Russians speaking of common spiritual and ethnic bonds that linked them and Serbians, Karadjordje was naturally more inclined to accept their assurances of a future independent Serbia. In March 1807 the Serbian leaders rejected the Ottoman offer and declared the former *pashalik* independent of the Ottoman rule.

For the next several years the future of the Serbian state became intricately intertwined with the much larger power struggles of the Napoleonic Wars. Despite its promises, Russia was in fact not interested in a completely independent Serbia, preferring to maintain some type of patron-client relationship. Throughout this period the Russians endeavored to exert a considerable measure of control over Serbia's actions, and their overall policy was determined by the oscillations in relations with France and the Ottomans. Although the Franco-Russian Treaty of Tilsit made no mention of Serbia, the two nations did agree to "liberate" the Balkans in case the Turks spurned French efforts to mediate an end to the Russo-Ottoman War. A new round of Russo-Ottoman negotiations, which had been delayed by the political turmoil in Constantinople, commenced in Jassy in March 1809. The negotiations gridlocked almost immediately because Sultan Mahmud II refused to yield any territories to Russia, prompting the Russians to withdraw from the meeting and to resume military operations in the Danubian Principalities in the fall.[182]

By now, two years of military operations and the presence of tens of thousands of troops had caused severe socioeconomic dislocation in the region, which suffered from widespread looting, the exodus of thousands of peasants and the resultant sharp drop in in agricultural production, and, finally—just to top things off—regular outbreaks of the plague. The Russian army, which had increased to some 80,000 men, lacked adequate logistical support to conduct decisive military operations. Neither did it have capable leadership. Field Marshal Alexander Prozorovsky, appointed to command the Russian Army of the Danube in 1809 despite his age (he was seventy-six) and poor health, was a stalwart proponent of eighteenth-century positional warfare.[183] Instead of conducting a rapid campaign to engage and destroy enemy forces, he concentrated on capturing the fortresses of Giurgiu and Braila. Both assaults were badly organized and failed utterly; at the latter fortress alone, the Russian army lost almost 5,000 men.[184] Depressed by such failures, Prozorovsky refused to take any action for over two months.[185]

Meanwhile, the Turks exploited Russian idleness to launch a major offensive against the Serbs in the late spring of 1809. They defeated the Serbian army and seized control of the right bank of the Morava River, besieging the strategic fortress of Šabac on the left. The Ottoman gains prompted Karadjordje to issue a call for a general mobilization of all males between the ages of twelve and seventy, but even this desperate measure could not save the Serbs, who had been forced to abandon their positions and retreat northward.[186] The Serbs were particularly enraged by the Russian failure to support them after Prozorovsky promised to send troops but then recalled the Russian forces that had already been sent.

Annoyed by these setbacks, Emperor Alexander urged a new offensive and a quick victory over the Turks, one that would secure the Danubian regions, protect his Serbian allies, and free up Russian resources to deal with Napoleon elsewhere. A contemporary observed that Russian society expected quick victories over the Turks, but "the eighty-year-old half-dead Field Marshal Prince Prozorovsky" could not satisfy those ambitions.[187] Looking for a younger and more vigorous commander, Alexander turned to Prince Peter Bagration, one of the brightest stars in the Russian military pantheon, and someone who had had plenty of experience fighting the French. Sent to Wallachia in the summer of 1809, Bagration immediately launched an offensive across the Danube, defeating the Ottoman army at Rassevat (September 16) and Tataritsa (October 22) and capturing a number of fortresses. Although shortages of ammunition and supplies soon forced him to return to the northern bank of the Danube, his campaign had caused considerable harm to the Ottomans and forced them to divert resources from the Serbian front, where the Ottomans had been steadily gaining an upper hand. Still, Karadjordje was extremely upset by the Russian actions. "For God's sake, you have to help us because you named yourself our protectors, and if you will abandon us, all other states would disdain you.... I damn the soul of [Prozorovsky].... Oh, Lord, hold him accountable, for he deceived us and exposed us to the defeat" at the hands of the Turks.[188]

The events of 1809 revealed deep fissures in the Serbian leadership. While some Serbian leaders insisted on maintaining relations with Russia, other factions pointed to the Russian failure to protect them and urged seeking help from France or Austria; even the pro-Russian Serbs advised Karadjordje to be cautious in his relations with Emperor Alexander.[189] In the fall of 1809 Karadjordje summoned the national council (Skupština) to discuss the future of Serbia, its relations with Russia, and the Ottoman Empire. It concluded that the promise of Russian protection was not a sufficient guarantee without the actual presence of a strong Russian force in Serbia. The council's decision was conveyed to Prince Bagration, who met with the Serbian delegates and assured them of Russia's support in men and money.[190] A pragmatic man, Karadjordje put little faith in such promises and sought to lessen his dependence on Russia.[191] At the height of the military crisis, he appealed to Napoleon to become "the august defender and protector of the Serbian nation" and unite the peoples of Serbia, Bosnia, Herzegovina, Montenegro, Bulgaria, and Greece because "having all these peoples under the wings of France will make her enemies tremble." The Serbian leader hoped that the French troops would seize the fortress at Belgrade and Šabac and protect the region from the advancing Ottoman armies.[192] The Serbian emissary reached Vienna during the diplomatic negotiations on the Treaty of Schönbrunn, when Napoleon took little more than a cursory interest in Serbia and made no commitments.[193]

Karadjordje then appealed for help to the Austrian authorities, whose apprehensions over the future of Serbia only increased in the wake of the Treaty of Schönbrunn, which stripped them of all their Adriatic possessions. The prospect of Russian- or French-controlled Serbia brought an unpleasant realization that either country could easily sever key trade routes to the Near East that were of considerable value to the Austrian economy. In October 1809, just days after becoming Austria's new foreign minister, Metternich prepared a special memorandum on the Serbian issue, arguing that there were only two possible resolutions: either Serbia returned to being the Belgrade *pashalik* within the Ottoman Empire or it became an Austrian province. Austrians feared being excluded from a seemingly impending Franco-Russian partition of the Ottoman realm; these concerns increased after Alexander issued an imperial decree announcing his intention to annex the Danubian Principalities. France's silence appeared to confirm the worst of the Austrian fears.[194]

And yet when Metternich broached this subject with Napoleon, he realized that, far from being excluded, Austria could in fact play an important role in the Balkans. Napoleon hoped to exploit Austrian jealousy of Russian expansion in the Balkan Peninsula to block any further expansion in the area. "The Danube is of immense interest to you," he told the Austrians. "Look at the map. The [Danubian] principalities should belong to you, rather than Russia. And if the Russians should possess them, they would become a source of everlasting jealousy for you."[195] On the possibility of Russia taking control of Serbia, Napoleon expressed the following view to the Austrian minister: "The Danube serves as a great obstacle that has, up to the present, halted the progress of the Russian armies; but a single inch of land on the right bank in the hands of the Russians would be, in my opinion, equal to the complete destruction of the Ottoman Empire."[196]

The French assurances, however, had failed to convince the Viennese court, which had been simultaneously approached by St. Petersburg to accept a Russian takeover of the Danubian Principalities in exchange for comparable concessions in Bosnia and Serbia.[197] Amid this fluctuating international situation, Metternich came to believe that the best means of safeguarding Austria's economic and political interests was to ensure continued Ottoman rule in the Balkans. Only through restoring "legitimate" authority could the region's fragile balance of power be maintained. He therefore rejected the Serbs' offer to annex their country and instead tried to get all parties to accept Austrian arbitration, which might end the Russo-Ottoman War and bring some semblance of order to the Balkans.[198]

Metternich could not have chosen a worse moment. The Ottomans rejected the Austrian mediation, doubtful of its sincerity.[199] The memories of the recent Austrian rejection of the Ottoman request for mediation were still fresh: "When Austria was invited to mediate between Serbia and the Porte, she withheld her mediation; at the present moment she comes forward with offers of mediation and guarantee, equally unexpected and unsummoned," reported a British envoy in Constantinople, echoing Ottoman wariness of Austrian intention. "To what is the change to be attributed? Is Austria only influenced by a sudden apprehension, to which she was before insensible, of the profit likely to accrue to herself from the reconciliation of the Porte with its rebellious subjects; or is it that she is no longer afraid of incurring the hostility of Russia?"[200] The Turks were also well aware that the Habsburg court, while pledging to protect Ottoman territorial integrity, was turning a blind eye to vast shipments of supplies from Hungary to the Serbian rebels.[201] Even more disquieting to the Ottomans were the rumors, spread by the British, that the Franco-Austrian Peace of Schönbrunn contained secret arrangements to compensate Austria for territorial losses in central Europe at the expense of the Ottoman territories in the Balkans. "The intervention of Austria," wrote former British foreign minister Canning, "is objectionable to the Porte, who may reasonably suspect that she acts with the consent, and therefore under the direction of France, and to England, whose more extended views and liberal policy may foresee and apprehend the miserable consequences of her being engaged with Russia in a fruitless contest, profitable only to the common enemy of both."[202] As a consequence, the Ottoman government forcefully demanded that Vienna desist from any involvement in the affairs of the Belgrade *pashalik*.

The Austrian mediation offer was greeted with a similar aloofness in Belgrade. Having been spared imminent destruction thanks to the Russian intervention, Karadjordje could hardly afford alienating the only great power willing to support him against the Ottomans. Mistrusting the Austrians, he rejected their offer to negotiate: if Emperor Francis was sincere in his desire to help the Serbs, he should dispatch troops first.[203] The arrival of a Russian political resident, with Russian financial support, swung the Serbs back under Russian influence.[204] Aware of Karadjordje's double play, the Russian commander in chief, Bagration, criticized the Serbs for seeking foreign aid and expressed concerns over rumors of a peace offer that Hurshid Pasha, Ottoman governor of Rumelia, had extended to the Serbs; as part of this agreement, the Turks wanted to deploy up to 5,000 men at Belgrade to ensure peace and stability in the region.[205] Karadjordje promised to raise this offer with the national council, where the discussion of the Turkish proposal led to a division among the Serbs: one group demanding to continue the fight until full independence was achieved, the other preferring to sign a cease-fire and negotiate with Turkey.[206] The Russians, worried about losing their footing in the region, urged Karadjordje and other Serbian leaders to ignore the Ottoman offers and used money and rewards to ensure the council's rejection of the deal.[207]

With the Serbs appeased, Bagration then turned his attention to events in Bosnia, where the Christian population had started a rebellion against the Turks. He welcomed it as "useful for both the Serbians' and our interests" and wanted to encourage the Christian populace in other Ottoman territories to follow their example.[208] A special proclamation to the Serbian nation, which the Russian authorities drafted and spread, claimed, "This is the time when the Serbian people must be animated by their faith and love of motherland and armed with the spirit of courage. All Serbs must unanimously join the indomitable Russian army to overthrow arrogant tyrants of Serbia and establish security and peace in the country." Stressing the close ties between Russia and Serbia, then proclamation assured the Serbs that "your brothers, courageous warriors of Russia, are marching to defend you.... Meet them as brothers and fight the enemy together with them."[209] It is noteworthy that while pursuing imperial designs in the Balkans, Russian authorities sought to mask them under the guise of Serbian nationalism against the Turks. Bagration cautioned the Russian minister in Belgrade to choose "only such means that would not discredit" the Russians and Serbs in the eyes of other European states. Russian actions were supposed to create an "impression" that Serbian and other Balkan insurrections were caused by "aspirations of these Christian nations, not by an agitation by a foreign power."[210]

In 1810–1812, Emperor Alexander was eager for a resolution of the Russo-Ottoman War, which was now entering its fifth year. With Franco-Russian relations steadily worsening, he was genuinely concerned about the prospects of confronting the French while still engaged in a war against the Turks. Russian society, too, wanted immediate results, because "the war with Sweden made [it] accustomed to quick victories; Bagration's actions seemed rather unsatisfactory. 'So what that he crossed the Danube?' it was said.... 'Fifty years ago that might have surprised people, but not today. Now we need to cross the Balkan Mountains.'"[211] Demanding results, Alexander dismissed Bagration, who urged a more methodical preparation for the campaign, and replaced him with General Nikolay Kamenski. In late spring 1810 Kamenski moved the Russian army across the Danube once more, captured the fortresses of Silistra, Razgrad, and Bazardjik, and encircled the main Ottoman army of 40,000 men within the fortified camp at Shumla, which the Russians blockaded after unsuccessful initial assaults. Kamenski then wasted his time and men on a disastrous assault on Ruse (August 3) that resulted in almost 9,000 killed or wounded. The Russians regained momentum next month when Kamenski intercepted the Ottoman reinforcements marching to rescue the grand vizier's army in Shumla, and routed them at Batin on September 7–8.

Over the next six months, Russians swept through northern Bulgaria, capturing the fortresses of Ruse, Turnu, Plevna, Lovech, and Selvi. Yet despite these resounding victories, Kamenski still faced the same logistical challenges that had haunted his predecessors, and he had to withdraw his army to winter quarters north of the Danube.[212] One of his last decisions was to dispatch a small Russian detachment to Belgrade, where they arrived in January 1811 and precipitated a diplomatic crisis with Austria.[213] The Russian occupation of the Serbian capital was not dictated by military exigencies and was immediately condemned in Austrian military circles, which viewed it as a precursor to either Serbian independence or, worse, a Russian protectorate over Serbia, which would be more detrimental to Austria's international standing than "the loss of the Austrian Netherlands."[214] General Radetzky and other Austrian hawks had long called for a radical rethinking of Austria's Eastern policies and proposed seeking Austria's own "natural frontiers," which would have encompassed not only Bohemia, Moravia, Silesia, the Carpathians, and Bukovina in the north and east but also the entire area between the Adriatic Sea and the Black Sea in the south.[215] For Metternich, the Russian presence in Belgrade was worrisome because of the adverse effect it could produce on the millions of Slavs and Orthodox Christians residing in the Balkans, as well as within Hungary and Croatia, thereby jeopardizing the empire's internal stability. The Austrians demanded explanations of the motives behind the Russian occupation of Belgrade and ordered the strengthening of frontier defenses across the Danube from the Serbian capital. The Russian response, as expected, denied any ulterior intentions and sought to allay Austrian fears. A special envoy was dispatched to Vienna, where he assured Metternich that the deployment of Russian troops was undertaken by the Russian generals on their own judgment and "for purely military purpose."[216]

Austrians found these explanations unconvincing, and they were right. The Russian troops in Belgrade were of little military value but offered tremendous diplomatic leverage. As Franco-Russian relations continued to deteriorate (Napoleon interpreted the Russian action in Serbia as yet another breach of the Erfurt Agreement), Alexander understood that in case of war against France he stood little chance unless he was able to secure either the support or neutrality of Austria, which could otherwise threaten southwestern Russian provinces. During the winter and spring of 1811 Emperor Alexander tried to use the Serbian issue as a bargaining tool, to induce Austria to make commitments. Vienna refused to even consider them until Russia clarified its goals in the Balkans. "Finish this matter with the Turks, and then we will talk," Metternich bluntly told the Russian envoy in February 1811.[217] The Russian occupation of Belgrade was, therefore, designed to indicate to the Austrians the seriousness of Russia's intentions, and to prompt serious diplomatic discussions. The Russian sovereign was ready for unprecedented concessions. Writing directly to Emperor Francis, Alexander spoke of his readiness to cede all of Serbia and the Danubian Principalities up to the Sereth River, and to accept Austrian supremacy in Italy in return for Vienna's pledge of nonalignment.[218] As enticing as this offer was, Metternich understood that accepting it would have been tantamount to declaring war against the Ottoman Empire, if not France as well, given that Napoleon fully appreciated the strategic impact of the Russian advance to Belgrade. The Austrian government could not afford another war less than two years after the last disastrous one and had no choice but to reject the Russian offer.

Equally fruitless proved Russian overtures to Sultan Mahmud, who rejected the Russian offer to abandon the Serbian cause if he agreed to cede the Danubian Principalities. The Turks knew that time was of essence. A conflict between Russia and France was now becoming imminent. They therefore refused to open talks until Russia acknowledged the *status quo ante bellum*, giving up all the conquests of the previous five years.[219] Frustrated with these diplomatic setbacks, Emperor Alexander replaced Kamenski with General Mikhail Kutuzov in March 1811 and gave the new commander in chief strict orders to bring a victorious conclusion to the war as quickly as possible. Kutuzov withdrew Russian garrisons from most of the fortresses and concentrated his army near Ruse, on the right bank of the Danube. In June 1811 the Ottoman army, under Ahmed Pasha, launched an offensive against the Russians, but it was defeated near Ruse on July 4. However, concerned about the Ottoman forces at Vidin that could threaten his flank, Kutuzov abandoned Ruse and withdrew his army to the left bank of the river. In July and August Ottoman forces made several unsuccessful attempts to cross the Danube, which gave Kutuzov sufficient time to devise an operation to surround and destroy the entire Ottoman army. On September 10, 1811, he allowed Ahmed Pasha and his army to move across the river at Slobozea, near Ruse. He then dispatched a small corps of some 11,000 men to ford the river downstream and capture the Ottoman camp and the fortress of Ruse in the back of the Ottoman forces. Ahmed Pasha was thus surrounded and pushed against the river, where his men were gradually starved into submission before surrendering on December 5.[220]

The victory at Ruse was the stroke that broke Ottoman resistance. The sultan agreed to engage in diplomatic talks in October, hoping that the impending war between France and Russia would change the political situation in his favor. Hard pressed by the gathering threat of a French invasion, Russia finally chose to compromise with the Turks and signed the Treaty at Bucharest on May 28, 1812, just one month before the first French troops stepped onto Russian soil.[221] Emperor Alexander reluctantly agreed to restore Moldavia and Wallachia to the sultan and accept Bessarabia, a slice of land between the Dniester and Prut Rivers in eastern Moldavia, as compensation for Russian losses in the war. This was a far cry from the earlier Russian aspirations to the whole of the Danubian Principalities, but at this point Russia was more concerned about securing its southern frontiers and freeing up tens of thousands of troops in time for a war against France. The Treaty of Bucharest compelled the Turks to relinquish their claims to western Georgia, which had been under Russian influence for the better part of the previous decade. The Serbs suffered the most from this peace, as Russia coolly abandoned them. The treaty stipulated autonomy for Serbia, but Article 8 gave the Turks a free hand to suppress the Serbian rebellion. The treaty also confirmed earlier Russo-Ottoman agreements except those deemed obsolete, which included the treaty of alliance of 1805. This effectively meant that the Turkish straits would remain closed to Russian warships.

Europe's preoccupation with Napoleon in 1813–1815 provided a crucial respite for the Ottoman central authority; it declared its neutrality in the ongoing European conflict and refused Britain's suggestions to allow Russian warships to pass through the straits to launch an expedition to Italy. Sultan Mahmud used this window of opportunity to reassert his authority over rebellious provinces and to lay the groundwork for his eventual modernization program of defensive developmentalism. The end of war against Russia allowed him to divert military resources to Serbia, where in 1813 the Ottomans routed the Serbian forces and occupied Belgrade by December of that year. This effectively marked the end of the First Serbian Uprising, as Karadjordje and his supporters fled to Austria while some Serbian *knezes*, led by Karadjordje's rival Miloš Obrenoviç, accepted the restoration of Ottoman rule. However, Ottoman abuses and misrule soon alienated these Serbian collaborators. In September 1814 a revolt by Prodan Gligorijević (Hadži-Prodan) briefly threatened Ottoman rule in west-central Serbia before being suppressed. A more serious challenge came from Miloš Obrenoviç, who launched the Second Serbian Revolution on Palm Sunday, 1815. Napoleon's defeat at Waterloo and the end of the Napoleonic Wars greatly assisted the Serbs, as now the Russians were free to support the Serbs against the Ottomans. Sultan Mahmud acted with prudence, fearing the possibility of Russian intervention. He granted the Serbs limited autonomy and recognized Miloš Obrenoviç as the Prince of Serbia. It was a politic move, but in doing this, he had unwittingly taken the first step toward the political fragmentation of the Ottoman Empire.

CHAPTER 17 | The Qajar Connection

Iran and the European Powers, 1804–1814

THE QAJAR RULERS OF IRAN had initially benefited from the fast-changing international situation in Europe. As noted earlier, with European powers focused on revolutionary France, Agha Muhammed Khan and his successor Fath Ali Shah could contemplate wide-ranging campaigns to reassert Iranian influence in the region and consolidate their authority at home. Contemporary Europeans viewed the Qajar rulers as "Oriental despots" who wielded unlimited power, fusing the legislative, executive, and judicial functions of the state. In reality, the shah's authority was sharply curtailed due to the lack of a state bureaucracy or a standing army, as well as by powerful regional potentates whose collaboration was instrumental to implementing any royal decisions at the local level.

France's expedition to Egypt, and the geopolitical threat that it seemingly posed to British India, placed Iran in the limelight of European politics. The Qajars also profited from Empress Catherine II's unexpected death in November 1796. Paul I showed no interest in pursuing his mother's imperial policies in the Caucasus; indeed, he recalled Russian forces already there, thereby freeing the Qajar shahs to strengthen their power base. The sense of legitimacy and importance conferred by contacts with foreign delegations made the Iranians receptive to the approaches of European powers—in 1801, the Anglo-Iranian treaty established a tentative alliance between the two nations.[1]

Iran then had the benefit of just four years of respite. After the French departure from Egypt in late 1801, the British lost their interest in Iran—the British East India Company's Indian possessions were seemingly safe from French threat, and London was more preoccupied with the affairs in Europe.

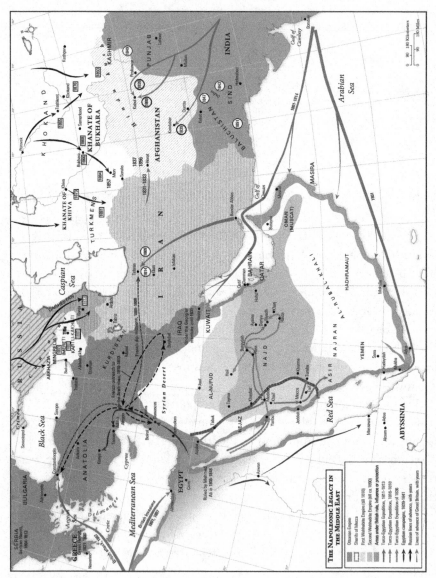

Map 18: The Napoleonic Legacy in the Middle East

British imperial priorities clearly did not include Iran—several Iranian embassies dispatched to the BEIC headquarters in Calcutta were received without much enthusiasm, and the treaty of 1801 remained unratified.[2] Furthermore, the death of Emperor Paul brought to power Alexander, whose views on the southern Caucasus differed dramatically from his father's and were more in line with his grandmother's. While Europe was preoccupied with the revolutionary turmoil, Alexander turned to southern Caucasia, which, again like his grandmother, he knew could serve as a conduit for Russian imperial ambitions in the Middle East. We have already seen that the eastern Georgian kingdom of Kartli-Kakheti sought an alliance with Russia as a means of protecting itself from Ottoman and Iranian encroachment. In 1801, in violation of the Treaty of Georgievsk, signed by his grandmother, Emperor Alexander issued a manifesto annexing the eastern Georgian kingdom to Russia, marking an unequivocal Russian involvement in Caucasian affairs that would endure. But within months of the decision it became clear that the region would not be easily acquired and the conquest would exact a high toll in men and resources.[3] Russian authorities were undeterred, confident of quick and easy success. Alexander, for his part, argued that the annexation of Georgia was done for the "benefit of the people"—by which he meant the Georgians—and not out of a desire to consolidate Russian interests in the region.[4]

The key figure in Russian efforts to pacify eastern Georgia and expand Russian rule in southern Caucasia was Prince Paul Tsitsianov, who was appointed Russian commander in chief in the Caucasus in 1802.[5] A scion of the powerful Tsitsishvili family of Georgian lords, Tsitsianov was nevertheless an uncompromising Russian imperialist who believed in Russia's *mission civilisatrice* in Asia.[6] The Russian plan of conquest for southeastern Caucasia envisioned a multi-step process, starting with the removal of the Bagration dynasty and the subjugation of the Georgian principalities. In 1802, after Prince Regent David Bagration was forced to step aside, Emperor Alexander ordered all members of the Georgian royal family to be resettled in Russia. The Georgian nobility protested the imposition of direct Russian rule and demanded implementation of the provisions of the Treaty of Georgievsk. When Russian authorities began to arrest and exile protesting nobles, a rebellion erupted in Kakheti (eastern Georgia) and the Bagration princes solicited support from Iran. Apprised of the uprising, Russian authorities under Karl Knorring took emergency measures to protect Tbilisi, brought reinforcements, and blocked strategic routes across the mountains. The Russian measures soon had an effect—the uprising withered away, the Georgian princes were forced to flee to Iran, and many Georgian nobles were made to reconsider their opposition to Russian rule. In the spring of 1804 another rebellion, sparked by the introduction of Russian customs and regulations, erupted in the highlands of Kartli (central Georgia), quickly spreading through the region before being suppressed later that same year.[7]

To ensure the safety of Georgia, the Russian authorities believed it was necessary to expand further west and south and to draw a border along the Aras River all the way to its estuary at the Caspian Sea. This frontier would be maintained from military bases at Yerevan and Nakhichevan, and be protected by a third forward base to the south in Talish, which would allow Russia to threaten the Iranian provinces of Ghilan and Mazendaran. Between 1802 and 1804 Tsitsianov proceeded to impose Russian rule on the western Georgian Kingdom of Imereti, the principalities of Mingrelia and Guria, and the khanates located south of Georgia. Some of the khanates submitted without a fight, but the khanate of Ganja resisted, prompting a Russian invasion that sacked the city of Ganja. Russian expansion into eastern Caucasia, which Iran considered part of its sphere of influence, posed a clear challenge to the Iranian regional hegemony.[8] Fath Ali Shah felt the need to enhance his legitimacy by asserting sovereignty over this region because, as a Qajar ruler, he understood that ideological justification for his dynasty's royal pretentions was that the Qajars had reunited the "breakaway" regions into the Guarded Domains of Iran (Mamalek-e Mahrusa-ye Iran) and had therefore restored the power of Shiite Islam. Russian expansion in eastern Caucasia posed a direct and grave threat to the pillar of ideological justification propping up the new Iranian monarchy.[9]

In May 1804 Iran demanded the Russians withdraw from Caucasia. They refused, and in June Iran declared war. This encounter with one of the great European powers proved to be a sobering experience for Iran, for it struggled to match the Russian army's firepower and discipline; the history of the nine-year-long Russo-Iranian War is peppered with examples of small Russian forces successfully fending off much greater numbers of Iranian troops. Fath Ali Shah sought British support to expel the Russians from the eastern Caucasus, but the Anglo-Iranian alliance failed this first major test. The Qajar shah interpreted provisions of the 1801 treaty as committing Britain to supporting Iran if it was threatened by any third party (i.e., Russia) in return for the Iranian guarantee to do the same for the British in India or wherever they might request his assistance. Throughout 1805–1806 he made several requests to the BEIC for military and financial assistance; all were denied. BEIC officials and the British government viewed the situation very differently, noting that the treaty had never been formally ratified and thus was nonbinding.[10] Furthermore, even if it had been ratified, the British argued, its provisions applied only to a threat from France, not Russia. Indeed, Britain had no interest in supporting Iran against Russia, a valuable ally in its war against

Map 19: Russian Expansion in the Caucasus

Napoleon in Europe; some senior British officials even condoned Russian expansion in the Caucasus. Fath Ali Shah was, naturally, exasperated by what he perceived to be Britain's reneging on its pledge of assistance. He believed he had made a treaty of equals. Now he realized that the British would not treat him as an equal, and he gradually began turning to France.

The Russian commander in chief in the Caucasus, Tsitsianov, was eager to fight Iran, claiming that war had to be waged quickly and decisively in order to establish a Russian foothold in the region.[11] The Russians seized the initiative at the very start of the war when Tsitsianov led some 3,000 troops to the khanate of Yerevan after its ruler, Muhammad Khan, refused to accept Russian sovereignty. In June the Russians besieged Yerevan and defeated Iranian forces at Gumry (Leninakan); the following month Tsitsianov scored a victory over the Qajar crown prince Abbas Mirza not far from Yerevan.[12] After these defeats, Iranian forces retreated to regroup, while Tsitsianov continued to exert pressure on local khanates. In 1805 Karabagh, Shakki, and Shirvan recognized Russian authority when Tsitsianov's troops conducted raids as far as Resht in northwestern Iran.[13] In February 1806 Tsitsianov reached Baku, intending to impose Russian authority on the local khan. But on February 20, 1806, during a meeting with the khan, Tsitsianov—who, with his characteristic bravado, arrived at the meeting with just two companions—was ambushed and murdered by the khan's guards, who then sent the Russian commander's head as a present to Iran's shah.[14]

Tsitsianov's death deprived the Russian Empire of a devoted and capable individual, someone who did much to determine the nature and character of the Russian conquest of the Caucasus. His tenure as commander in chief was marked by bluster, determination, energy, and, above all, a ferocious drive to remove any obstacles to Russian imperial power.[15] Iranian celebrations at the death of the "shedder of blood," as Tsitsianov became known in Iran, proved to be short-lived. Tsitsianov's successor, Ivan Gudovich, repelled an Iranian invasion in Karabagh in the summer of 1806 and pressed on with an offensive that soon conquered the khanates of Derbent and Kuba. In October the Russians stormed Baku, exacting harsh vengeance for the death of their commander.[16]

Despite early success in the war, before long Russia found its war efforts in the southern Caucasus hampered by a host of unforeseen challenges. The most important of these was the start of the War of the Fourth Coalition against Napoleon in 1806. Russia's political and military focus therefore shifted to northeastern Europe, where over 100,000 Russian troops were committed to fighting the French. Furthermore, in December 1806 Russia became embroiled in a new war against the Ottoman Empire, which tied down another 40,000 troops. The Russo-Ottoman War spilled over into western Caucasia, where the Ottoman sultans had long claimed suzerainty, forcing the Russian authorities to divert to the Ottoman frontier troops originally sent to fight Iran. The Russo-Swedish War, which began in February 1808, and the Russo-Austrian War of 1809 complicated matters still further. All these conflicts had direct repercussions in the Caucasus, since Russia could not commit any additional resources to its struggle against Iran. Thus Russia had no more than 50,000 men in the entire Caucasus region, and fewer than 10,000 troops could be committed to the theater of war in southeastern Caucasia; by 1811, there were fewer than 5,000 men deployed against the numerically far superior Iranian forces.[17] Aside from these military challenges, there were also financial problems. Russia's accession to the Continental Blockade and the ensuing Anglo-Russian hostilities disrupted Russian trade and constrained its ability to sustain war funding in the Caucasus. Contrary to their expectations, the Russians were unable to utilize their naval prowess in the Caspian Sea either for attacking Iranian coastlines or supplying Russian troops in eastern Caucasia. Aside from perilous weather, the Russian flotilla was woefully unprepared for the task and lacked the funds to improve the situation.[18]

All of this meant that Caucasian affairs became of secondary importance to Russia, at least for the moment. Emperor Alexander, preoccupied with European affairs, tried to end the war with Iran on several occasions between 1806 and 1808. Two years of military setbacks had made the Iranian government equally willing to seek a respite. The chief obstacle to peace was the Russian demand for Iranian cession of all territory north of the Aras River, though much of that region was under no more than nominal Russian authority. Showing a complete disregard for the seriousness of Iranian interests in the region, Alexander insisted that his troops establish the border on the Aras because, as Caulaincourt wrote to Napoleon, it was "necessary to prevent the incursions of barbarian peoples who inhabit the land."[19] Russian diplomats feared a possible rapprochement between Iran and France—which was indeed happening—while Russia was still burdened with commitments in Europe and the Danubian Principalities. To prevent this, it was ready to seek British intercession and to take advantage of friendly relations between Fath Ali Shah and the British East India Company. Reflecting the deep distrust the Russians felt toward the Iranians, a memorandum prepared in 1806 outlined three immediate priorities for Russian diplomacy in southeast Caucasia: "1. It is necessary to negotiate peace with Persia, without fully trusting their commitments, in order to prevent their union with the Porte; 2. To postpone, until a more advantageous time, the establishment of [the Russian imperial border] on the Kura and Aras Rivers; 3. To make military preparations in case of the union between the Turks and the Persians."[20]

In the summer of 1806 Britain missed a key opportunity. Both Russia and Iran were seeking a peaceful settlement, and Fath Ali Shah, strapped for cash and anxious to find an ally, made a request for British support. The British could have played a decisive role in mediating peace were it not for their preoccupation with European affairs, as well as the erroneous belief that as long as they maintained good relations with Russia and the Ottoman Empire, little if anything had to be done about possible French influence in Iran, which was not expected to have any tangible impact. Furthermore, London was concerned that any intervention in Iran would upset the Russians, whose support they were so keen on maintaining against Napoleon. This effectively opened the door for France to use Iran to threaten both Russian and British interests. As the British ambassador to the Ottoman Empire, Charles Arbuthnot, put it in August 1806, "To please the Emperor [of Russia], we have thrown away all our influence in Persia."[21]

In October 1806 Russia and Iran settled on the Uzun-Kilissa Armistice, which halted hostilities during the winter of 1807.[22] The negotiations that unfolded over the next several months revealed a chasm between Russian and Iranian conditions for peace. The Iranian hope that Russian aspirations in the south Caucasus might be moderated after the assassination of Tsitsianov were quickly dashed. His successor, Gudovich, insisted that the Iranian cession of Georgia and south Caucasian khanates was "necessary for the establishment of secure frontiers that make for amicable neighbors."[23] The Iranians, unsurprisingly, rejected such demands and instead insisted on a complete Russian withdrawal from the region and establishment of imperial frontiers in north Caucasus.[24] Despite the intransigent nature of the discussions, both sides were willing to continue them. For Russia, negotiations with Iran offered a crucial opportunity to regroup its forces and deal with the growing Ottoman threat in southwest Caucasia (discussed later). Meanwhile, with an Iranian embassy already on its way to meet Napoleon, Fath Ali Shah certainly hoped that by tying up the Russians in negotiations he would get a better bargaining position in forthcoming negotiations with the French, which is why the Russian emissary was, in the words of the French envoy General Claude Mathieu Gardane (Gardanne), "neither turned away nor completely rejected. The shah instead bid for time in expectation of the outcome of negotiations with France."[25]

The setbacks Iran experienced during the first two years of the war clearly demonstrated its need for an ally to overcome Russia, and the Qajar court was compelled to seek European help. Which meant they soon got caught up in the diplomatic maneuverings of the Napoleonic Wars. The shah, as noted, showed a preference for aid from Britain, but London's refusal to support Iran at this difficult hour opened doors for the French. Napoleon's ambitions in the East reflected elements of traditional French foreign policy and sought to uphold the Ottomans and Iran as a buffer for French interests in the region. Even as early as the Egyptian campaign, Napoleon—as we've seen—had envisioned Iran as a possible foothold for threatening British interests in India, and once Franco-Ottoman tensions had been resolved in 1802–1803, the French leader consistently demanded more information about Iran from his diplomats stationed in Constantinople.[26] In 1803–1804 Napoleon made diplomatic overtures to Iran through his ambassador at Constantinople as well as through Jean Rousseau, French consul at Baghdad (residing at Aleppo), and Louis Alexandre de Corancez, French commissary of commercial relations at Aleppo.[27] By 1806 he was contemplating using the Ottoman Empire and Iran against his principal enemies, Russia and Britain. "The unwavering aim of my policy is to make a triple alliance of myself," Napoleon wrote to Talleyrand in May 1804, "the Porte and Persia, aimed directly or by implication against Russia."[28] France's imperial strategy envisioned the Ottoman Empire (supported by France) as guarding French interests against Russia in southeastern Europe while Iran would help project Napoleon's influence further eastward and serve as a basis for the renewed French threat to India.

These efforts seemingly produced results when Fath Ali Shah, annoyed by the British ambivalence in the war against Russia, sought French help though his ambassador at Constantinople. The French welcomed the Iranian overture, and in March 1805 Napoleon dispatched the well-known Orientalist Pierre Amédée Jaubert to Tehran with instructions to inform himself of the situation in Iran, "province by province," and of the attitude of the governor there.[29] Just one month later, Napoleon sanctioned another mission, this one led by French diplomat Alexandre Romieu.[30] Both envoys traveled through Constantinople, where Pierre Ruffin, French chargé d'affaires there, provided them with the most recent information from Iran.[31] Their arrival caused great concern at the British embassy, which reported that "Romieu has the reputation of being a man of talents, of having a considerable sum of money at his disposal, and of being a great proficient in the science of intrigue."[32]

The French envoys' paths diverged at the Ottoman capital. Tracked by British agents, Romieu survived an assassination attempt—allegedly organized by a British consul in Aleppo—and reached Tehran in September 1805. He delivered to the shah Napoleon's letter praising him as the worthy successor of the great warrior ruler and urging him to defy the Russians and the British. "You will imitate and surpass the examples [your predecessors] have left behind. Like them you must distrust the counsels of a nation of shopkeepers, who, in India, traffic the lives and crowns of sovereigns; and you must oppose the valor of your people to the incursions of the Russians."[33] Romieu did not get to accomplish much because he suddenly became sick after attending a dinner at the shah's palace; he died on October 12, 1805 after three days of fever and vomiting. Although it could well have been dysentery, the French claimed that Romieu had been poisoned by the British, who steadfastly denied any involvement.[34] Before he died, Romieu submitted an insightful report on the state of affairs in Iran, noting the shah's desire to send an ambassador to France as well as emphasizing the shah's frustration with the British refusal to provide Iran with military assistance against Russia.[35]

France's second envoy, Jaubert, faced hurdles of his own. To deceive British agents, he changed his name and traveled incognito across Anatolia as far as Bayazid (modern Dogubeyazit), on the Turkish-Persian frontier, before being arrested by the covetous local governor, who kept him in an underground cell for several months.[36] In June 1806 Jaubert finally reached the Qajar capital and presented another letter from Napoleon expressing interest in a Franco-Iranian alliance.[37] Fath Ali Shah welcomed the offer and dispatched his envoy Mirza Mohammed-Reza Qazvini on a diplomatic mission to France. By November the Iranian mission had reached Constantinople, where it met the Ottoman grand vizier to discuss forming a joint front in south Caucasia. The Iranians also held brief discussion with the French ambassador Sebastiani, who, following Napoleon's instructions, dispatched several French officers to start advising the Iranian military.[38] After another two months of travel, Mirza Mohammed-Reza reached France, only to discover that Napoleon was no longer in Paris but in the snowy fields of Poland, where his Grand Armée was recovering from the bloody encounter with the Russians at Eylau. The Iranian envoy went to Poland, where he conducted negotiations that culminated in the Franco-Iranian Treaty, signed at the castle of Finckenstein on May 4, 1807.[39]

Set against the backdrop of the wars in Europe and the Russo-Iranian conflict in the Caucasia, the Treaty of Finckenstein reflected Napoleon's interest in forming a triple alliance with the Ottoman Empire and Iran to shore up France's positions in the east. In a rather flattering letter to the shah written on January 17, Napoleon announced his successes in the war against Prussia and Russia and raised the prospect of a joint Franco-Ottoman-Iranian front against a common enemy. "Let us all three join together and form an eternal alliance," he urged the shah.[40] The Treaty of Finckenstein was a manifestation of this ambition: it was designed to use Fath Ali Shah to carry out diversionary attacks against a common Russian enemy and, exploiting Iran's position as a western neighbor of India, to threaten British interests in the subcontinent. The treaty established a Franco-Iranian alliance that guaranteed the territorial integrity of Iran and recognized eastern Georgia and other south Caucasian polities as Qajar possessions (Articles 2–4). Napoleon pledged to "direct every effort to the ouster of the Russians" from these territories and, toward that end, to provide arms and military experts to modernize Iranian forces and "to organize it in accordance with principles of European military art" (Articles 6–7). The remaining articles were designed to stymie British influence in Iran, with the shah agreeing to declare war against Britain, expel all British presence from Iran, obtain Afghan cooperation in a French attack on India, and provide bases and supplies for a French naval squadron in the Persian Gulf.[41]

Almost immediately after concluding it, Napoleon tasked General Gardane, a man of considerable talent and resourcefulness who had family connections to Iran, with leading the French military mission to Iran.[42] Napoleon provided the general with detailed instructions that illustrate the scope and seriousness of Napoleon's ambitions in the East. He pointed out that Iran was important to France for two primary reasons: its enmity with Russia, France's rival, and as the means for a military passage to India, where France could challenge Britain. He urged Gardanne to obtain thorough information about Iran's military capabilities and to submit precise description of routes, fortresses, and ports throughout Iran and the Persian Gulf.[43]

Accompanied by an impressive staff of military and civilian assistants, Gardane left Poland on April 30.[44] While he was on his way to Iran—an arduous trip taking several months—momentous changes occurred both in the Caucasus and in Europe. As noted, Russo-Iranian hostilities were suspended during the winter of 1807. For Russia, in light of its continued commitments in Poland and the Danubian Principalities, this armistice served as a highly welcome respite, to regroup and, more important, to prevent the creation of an Irano-Ottoman alliance, which would have posed a serious threat to Russian positions in the Caucasus. Indeed, the Russian authorities took advantage of the negotiations with the Iranians to concentrate their efforts on waging war against the Turks, keeping only a small detachment to observe the Persian border, where no fighting (apart from occasional raids) took place.

Persian inactivity therefore allowed Gudovich to launch a three-pronged attack targeting the Ottoman garrisons at Akhalkalaki, Poti, and Kars, although the Turks repelled these attacks and, in the case of Akhalkalaki, inflicted heavy losses on the Russians.[45] Disheartened and facing bad weather, Gudovich had no choice but to end his campaign. Happily, from his perspective, a poorly planned Ottoman counteroffensive gave him an opportunity to make up for the earlier setbacks. In June Yussuf Pasha, the *serasker* of Erzerum, marched with some 20,000 men toward the Russian frontier, where they were intercepted and routed by a small Russian force on the Arpaçay (Akhurian) River on June 18, 1807. This was a significant Russian victory, for it effectively removed the threat of a major Ottoman invasion of Georgia and consolidated Russian positions in southern Caucasus.

Just a month later, in the wake of the Franco-Russian rapprochement at Tilsit, Gudovich was instructed to conclude an armistice with the Turks—on the condition that they were not to commence military operations without giving prior notification. While the Russians were fighting on the banks of the Arpaçay, Crown Prince Abbas Mirza, with almost 20,000 Iranian troops, was camped between Yerevan and the Algez Mountains. He could have exploited this moment to strike at the Russians. Instead he chose a more cautious approach, waiting for the outcome of the battle, hopeful that it would result in a Russian defeat. Gudovich's victory thus left him no choice but to congratulate the Russian commander on his victory and seek further negotiations.[46] Far more momentous were the changes going on in Europe. Four days before the Russian victory at the Arpaçay, Napoleon routed the Russian army at Friedland and forced Alexander to sue for peace. The resulting Franco-Russian treaty, as has been discussed, proved disastrous for Iran. Facing a choice between the Russian Empire and faraway Iran, Napoleon chose the former and ignored his earlier pledges to Iran. This all but destroyed the whole raison d'être for the

Eastern alliances that he had so carefully built over the previous two years. However, this need not have meant the end of Napoleon's interest in Iran, because in his betrayal of Iran's trust the French emperor turned out to be as skillful at reinterpreting words as Britain had been. Unwilling to support Iran against his newly acquired Russian ally, he was still keenly interested in using it as a doorway to India. In his mind, what remained operative of the Treaty of Finckenstein was Iran's obligation to defend French interests. Napoleon therefore chose to proceed with Gardane's mission. Informed of the change in Napoleon's policy, the French envoy was instructed to promote peace between Russia and Iran and to urge the Qajar ruler to act against British interests.[47]

Undercut by Napoleon's volte-face at Tilsit, Gardane tried to make the best of the circumstances. He negotiated a commercial treaty that confirmed concessions French had received in 1708 and 1715, and a military convention for the delivery of muskets.[48] He also dispatched French officers to survey the areas that might provide access to India. Exploiting the respite in Russo-Iranian hostilities, the French military mission became actively involved in the training of the Iranian military, the first major Westernizing reforms in Iran's history. The Iranian army, though much larger than its Russian counterpart, was a traditional force, relying on cavalry forces provided by tribal levies. The cavalry was better suited to operating in the eastern Caucasian terrain, so the Iranians employed tactics appropriate to it, such as raiding Russian settlements and isolated detachments and avoiding large-scale battles. British observers noted that Crown Prince Abbas Mirza frequently repeated his uncle Agha Muhammad Khan's saying, "Never come within reach of the Russians guns, and never, by the celerity of the cavalry, allow a Russian villager to sleep in peace."[49] In terms of discipline and gunpowder weapons, the Iranian infantry was a far cry from the Western soldiers, but what it lacked in armament it more than made up for in martial spirit; Western visitors frequently remarked on the Iranian soldiers' bravery and capacity to endure hardship.

The Qajar army's biggest problem stemmed less from the technological superiority of the Russian arms than from a fundamentally different approach to military organization and maintenance, and the prosecution of war. Tribal forces, which as noted dominated the Iranian military, were hard to control and coordinate. They naturally placed their tribal interests ahead of national ones and struggled to adjust to Western-style warfare. Fath Ali Shah and his advisors (most notably his son Abbas Mirza) were keenly interested in reforming their forces along Western lines. The shah was well aware, as he wrote Napoleon, that "the French troops, better drilled than those of the Orient in the handling of arms, are more accustomed to maneuver and are more coordinated in their movements. For this reason the soldiers of the West always have the advantage over Oriental irregulars."[50]

Despite the daunting challenges involved in introducing Westernizing reforms, the French officers spent more than a year forming, equipping, and training three battalions (about 4,000 men) of the Iranian recruits. These newly formed *sarbaz* units represented an amalgamation of Iranian and Western practices—their uniforms combined traditional sheepskin hats with European-style jackets. The French military mission also supervised construction of military barracks, arsenals, powder mills, and cannon foundries, which soon cast twenty cannon. French engineers taught their Iranian counterparts the basics of military engineering and tried improving existing fortifications in northwestern Iran.[51]

These were all important first steps in modernizing the Iranian military and remained only partially successful. The Qajar request that France send additional officers and artisans, along with promised weapons deliveries, was never fulfilled because of the Franco-Russian rapprochement. Financial problems prevented the Iranian government from maintaining all the *sarbaz* troops as a standing army, which meant that many of the reformed troops received only limited training. Thus when the hostilities with Russia resumed, the *sarbaz* were not fully prepared for fighting, as the Franco-Russian alliance prevented French officers from leading the troops in battle. More important, these reforms were highly unpopular; a good number of religious leaders denounced them as un-Islamic. The Qajar monarchy's efforts to portray these reforms as a revival of early Islamic practices—specific Quranic references were publicized to bolster these claims—fell flat. The sarbaz soldiers disliked the rigid discipline that their French officers subjected them to and resisted any efforts to erase their tribal solidarity.

As the French military mission progressed, Gardane sought to lessen the impact of the Treaty of Tilsit by making a number of promises that neither France nor Russia would have been able to accept or keep. In February 1808 he received instructions from Napoleon to serve as a mediator between Russia and Iran during the negotiations that were about to take place in Tehran. Napoleon framed his position as affirming a pledge he had made at Finckenstein to "make all effort to force Russia to evacuate Georgia and Persian territory."[52] He wanted to urge the shah to honor his part of the bargain by ending all commercial relations with Britain and by expelling British agents from Iran.[53] In conveying the imperial wishes, Gardane tried to convince Fath Ali Shah that Napoleon exerted a great deal of influence over Emperor Alexander and would be able to compel him to cede the disputed Caucasian territories. In fact, the French envoy urged the shah and his advisors to maximize their demands in their negotiations with Russia and tried to strengthen Iranian resolve in confronting the Russians.[54]

Such promises were doomed for failure. With his army entangled in Spain and facing growing discontent in central Europe, Napoleon could hardly afford to alienate Russia by insisting on concessions to Iran. In the larger scheme of things, Iran's interests were not as crucial to France as Russia's. Emperor Alexander knew this. During a private meeting with the French ambassador on August 12, 1808, Alexander rejected French mediation in Russo-Iranian affairs, comparing it to a hypothetical Russian mediation between France and Spain. "As the affairs of that country [Spain] do not concern me, those that I have with Persia [should be] of no interest to the Emperor," noted Alexander, before explaining that he would not "take any backward steps" in the Caucasus and had no intention to accept Iranian demands.[55] Indeed, Russia remained as intransigent as ever on the issue of the Caucasus. Russian officials misinterpreted Iranian intentions in an earlier diplomatic overture, which seemingly acknowledged the loss of Georgia to Russia, and continued to insist on the Iranian surrender of the entire territory north of the Aras River.[56] Such demands were bolstered by the Russian belief that the Qajar monarchy was in dire straits and that the shah, facing a number of domestic rebellions, was too weak to act forcefully. Therefore, Gudovich, the Russian commander in chief in the Caucasus, was instructed to pursue a hard line in his negotiations with the Iranians, insisting on a frontier that corresponded to the line occupied by the Russian troops.[57]

The presence of the French legation at Tehran caused great anxiety in the British government and the BEIC. The news of the Treaty of Finckenstein and Gardane's mission caused a stir in Calcutta, where the BEIC governor-general, Gilbert Elliot, Lord Minto, felt frustrated by France's "great diligence" in spreading "subversion" and "intrigues" to the borders of India.[58] His alarm increased after hearing of Gardane's success in signing Franco-Iranian treaties on commercial and military matters. As before, BEIC officials began to see the specter of a French invasion of India beginning to materialize. Early in 1808 Lord Minto dispatched John Malcolm, who had been promoted to brigadier general, on a second mission to Iran. Minto's first priority, as revealed in Malcolm's instructions, was to "detach the Court of Persia from the French alliance, and to prevail on that Court to refuse the passage of French troops through the territories subject to Persia."[59]

Malcolm arrived at Bushire (in southern Iran) in May 1808. Gardane threatened to leave Tehran if the British envoy was received there. Fath Ali Shah desired good relations with Britain but was keener still on preserving the French alliance, which seemed to offer greater advantages in Iran's conflict with

Russia. So, to appease Gardane, the shah refused to allow the British envoy to travel to the Qajar capital and instructed him to communicate only with the provincial authorities in Fars. Incensed by this treatment, Malcom returned to India, though not before scolding the Iranians for not upholding provisions of the 1801 treaty and threatening the shah with British intervention if he did not expel the French mission at once. Malcolm's contemptuous treatment of the Qajar monarchy elicited an angry response not only from Tehran but from his own superiors in the BEIC, with Lord Minto admonishing his envoy.[60]

Fath Ali Shah showed his continued interest in reviving his alliance with Napoleon against Russia by dispatching a new envoy, Askar Khan Afšar, to France and offering a new agreement that would have given France control of the island of Kharg (in the Persian Gulf) once it fulfilled commitments it had made in the Treaty of Finckenstein.[61] Gardane assured the Qajar officials that France would do its utmost to protect Iran and that Russia, now that it was allied to France, would avoid making any hostile actions—provided that the Iranians abstained from any provocations.[62] Yet French mediation failed to secure tangible gains for the Iranians. As negotiations between Russian and Iranian delegations stretched through the summer of 1808, it became progressively clear that Russia was paying no heed to French mediation and refused to consider any Iranian proposals, not even those offering to extend a truce and transfer negotiations to Paris (as Gardane suggested, in contravention to his own instructions). In fact, Gudovich bluntly told an Iranian envoy that the Qajar court was "wrong to count on the good offices" of Napoleon because the Treaty of Tilsit had effectively negated the Franco-Iranian alliance.[63]

The failure of his initiatives must have left Gardane feeling deeply humiliated, especially after Fath Ali Shah conveyed his exasperation that French mediation had not accomplished anything as of yet. Qajar officials reminded the French that they had fulfilled their commitments under the Treaty of Finckenstein by refusing to receive Malcolm's mission and limiting contacts with the BEIC. Understanding that the shah's goodwill would not last long, Gardane decided not to await instructions from Paris and made one last effort to mediate the Russo-Iranian conflict. In October 1808 he dispatched his secretary, Félix Lajard, to urge Gudovich to return to negotiations and warn him that "any attack" on Iran would be considered a provocation against its ally France. Gardane then assured the Qajar court that until both the French and Russian emperors weighed in on the negotiations, the Russians would make no hostile moves nor do anything to disrupt the relations between the two empires.[64]

Gardane's last gamble failed.[65] Instead of negotiating, Gudovich, hard pressed by Emperor Alexander and, at sixty-six years old, increasingly irascible and aware that he was not equal to the demands of his position, decided to force the Iranians into concessions by breaking the armistice and marching on Yerevan, which he did in October 1808. The Russian campaign, launched late in the season and poorly conceived, failed after a six-week siege of the Iranian fortress, where the Russians lost almost 1,000 men.[66] Gudovich tried to excuse his setback by claiming that the French officers had helped the Iranians defend the fortress, but his superiors knew better.[67] Alexander was furious when he learned how haphazardly the campaign had been planned. Gudovich was given no choice but to resign.[68]

Despite its failure, the Russian offensive had a major impact on Franco-Iranian relations. For starters, it revealed the tenuous nature of the alliance, which looked fine on paper but offered no tangible protection in practice. Compelled to tread a fine line between supporting Iran and honoring Napoleon's commitments to Russia, Gardane promised too much, and the Russian invasion of Yerevan made a mockery of his assurances. After spending much of the summer assuring the Iranians that Russia would not dare to defy Napoleon and resume hostilities while the French were mediating the negotiations, Gardane's response to the Russian offensive was to order the French officers attached to the Iranian army, who were expected to command the units they had trained, to withdraw and to avoid involvement in any hostile action against France's ally. This incensed many at the Qajar court, including Crown Prince Abbas Mirza and Qaim Maqam Mirza Issa Farahani, who lamented that Napoleon entertained such friendly relations with Emperor Alexander and ignored the bonds he had formed with Iran.[69]

A turning point in the relations between Napoleonic France and Iran occurred on November 23, 1808, when Fath Ali Shah held an audience with the French envoy. The shah complained that despite the guarantees that Gardane had given him, the war had been resumed. He was particularly irritated by the withdrawal of the French officers, which had hampered operations of the newly formed Iranian battalions. "Everything seems to have conspired against us," Fath Ali Shah told Gardane. "Emperor Napoleon has not yet informed us whether his feelings toward us correspond with what we expect from his loyalty and greatness, and the way in which he abandons us is more and more astonishing to us. We have not concealed from you the true situation in which things are, and everything has reached a point at which France may perhaps no longer come to our aid."[70] Gardane tried, feebly, to excuse Napoleon's inaction on the grounds of Russian perfidy. Once he realized "the strange behavior" of Russia, the French ambassador argued, Napoleon would demand heavy reparations and, "like a thunderbolt, he would fall on the enemies and destroy them." The "thunderbolt" line must have irked the Iranian shah, as he responded, "And what kept the thunderbolt from striking in the last ten months? ... Do you still think of Russia as an ally of France when it has a secret liking and an old friendship for England? Do you not see its contempt for your sovereign even in its current steps?"[71]

It was now clear that French influence at the Qajar court was on the wane. The shah gave Gardane just two months to clarify France's intention toward Iran.[72] Considering the distances involved, the French envoy could not have hoped to secure new instructions (the last instructions dated back to July 1808) within such a short period of time. His standing at the Qajar court was further undermined by the arrival of a British mission led by Sir Harford Jones, a longtime British resident in Basra and Baghdad who had formed personal connections with key Qajar figures. Unlike Malcolm, who represented the BEIC, Jones was the British king's envoy to Tehran and, in Qajar eyes, carried greater diplomatic weight. The shah, still nurturing hope for an alliance with France, initially commanded the British envoy be kept at the shores of the Persian Gulf. But as time passed Fath Ali Shah came to realize Napoleon's inability, if not unwillingness, to do anything for him, and once again weighed a British alternative. He knew full well that approaching Britain for help would entail major concessions since, unlike in 1801, Iran would now have to negotiate from a weaker position and Britain was upset about what it considered Iran's abandonment of the earlier treaty. In late 1808 the shah countermanded his earlier order and allowed Jones to travel to Tehran. On February 13, 1809, the day before the British emissary entered the Iranian capital, Gardane left the city, embarking on the long journey back home.[73] Writing to Paris, he noted that that the "state of affairs of this empire [Iran] is such that it will always be under the influence of and dependent on the nearest neighbor who has a greater force at his disposal. I do not believe France can hope to establish its influence here while her armies are so far away."[74]

Like Malcolm in 1800, Harford Jones arrived laden with rich gifts and promises, which greatly impressed the Qajar court. He showed sympathy for the Iranian cause and emphasized the advantages of Anglo-Iranian relations, urging Fath Ali Shah to break his alliance with France, which was already practically void, in exchange for an alliance with Britain against Russia, which had declared war on Britain in the wake of the Treaty of Tilsit. As an incentive, Jones offered British expertise in training Iranian troops and, most important, a hefty annual subsidy for as long as the war lasted. The second Anglo-Iranian treaty, signed in March 1809, remedied the key defects of the earlier treaties that the Qajars had signed with European powers. Britain pledged to train and equip the Iranian military and come to Iran's aid if it was attacked by a European power, as well as provide financial assistance. The price for all this was Iran's abrogation of all agreements and concessions made to France and a pledge to stop any European power that might attempt to cross Iranian territory to reach India.[75] The inclusion of the term "European" was an important Qajar victory, though the term was interpreted differently by the contracting sides: for Iran, it meant Russia, and for London, it meant only and always France. Britain had little interest in constraining Russian imperial designs in the Caucasus.

Despite Jones's success, Britain's interests in Iran had not yet been secured. The shah had tried to maintain some latitude to play the British against the French in order to obtain tangible help against Russia. Although Gardane was gone, members of his mission remained at the Qajar court, much to the chagrin of the British, and by cultivating relations with them Fath Ali Shah tried to pressure the British into increasing their subsidy. Interestingly, Jones's mission caused a rift between the British home government and the BEIC. Lord Minto, governor-general of the BEIC, understood the value of Jones's accomplishment—especially in light of his own setback with Malcolm's mission in 1808—and tried to sabotage Jones by ceasing to honor his bills, which raised questions about the British envoy's legitimacy.[76] Furthermore, Minto recalled Jones (despite lacking authority to do so) and dispatched John Malcolm on a third mission to Tehran. However, Minto's power play was thwarted by London, which confirmed Jones as the official envoy to Iran and demanded that Malcolm be recalled. Lord Minto complied but made sure that Jones was removed as well.

In February 1809 General Alexander Tormasov, sent as a replacement for Gudovich, took over command of the Russian forces in the Caucasus.[77] A capable and energetic man who had distinguished himself fighting the Turks and Poles in the 1790s, Tormasov found himself in an exceedingly difficult situation—that of having limited means to achieve ambitious goals set by the imperial government. The Russian forces in North Caucasus comprised 23,500 men, while just 18,500 troops were available to protect Georgia from possible attacks by the Turks or Iranians. More alarming was the situation in Georgia, Azerbaijan, and North Caucasus, where entire regions were in revolt. Russian authorities struggled to contain an insurrection in Daghestan, while in Abkhazia, a northwestern part of Georgia under Ottoman suzerainty, a power struggle raged between the sons of local ruler Çeles Bey (Shervashidze), who sought help from the Ottomans.[78]

Equally concerning was the threat posed by King Solomon of Imereti (western Georgia), the last independent Bagrationi monarch, whose opposition to the Russian presence in the Caucasus only hardened in the wake of the Russian overthrow of the Bagrationi dynasty in eastern Georgia. If some in the Georgian elite had once felt that the Orthodox Russians would save them from their traditional Muslim enemies, the events of the past few years had revealed that the Russians were interested not in Georgia's salvation but in its annexation. Solomon's court in Kutaisi became a center of opposition against the Russians, even after Tsitsianov forced Solomon to pledge an oath of fidelity to the Russian emperor in 1804.

In light of the political, economic, and social turmoil in southern Caucasia, Tormasov initially preferred to act cautiously, in order not to provoke any large-scale hostilities with the Turks or Iranians. He offered Iran a negotiated settlement of the war, though negotiations proved to be challenging, as both sides failed to agree on territorial claims. Furthermore, this time it was Britain that insisted that Iran should reject Russian offers and fight on. London did so out of concern over Russia's alliance with France and the prospect of growing Russian engagement in Europe should Russia end its war with Iran. The Qajar court reluctantly agreed, though one senior Qajar official noted presciently to Harford Jones that if the situation in Europe changed, Britain would probably leave Iran in a "tight spot." In fact, this is exactly what happened in the coming years. As the Russo-Iranian War progressed and the Franco-Russian alliance splintered, Britain found itself in the difficult position of having to assist Iran against Russia, which London was hoping to use to fight Napoleonic France in Europe.

The summer of 1809 turned out to be a frenetic one for Tormasov. Instructed to remain on the defensive, he watched as the Iranians mobilized forces along the frontier. However, Russian superiority in arms manifested itself once more and the Iranians were put to flight at Guymri and Ganja (Elisavetpol). Tormasov, meanwhile, pursued a tougher line with the Turks. With the Russo-Ottoman War continuing in the Danubian Principalities, he renewed hostilities in western Georgia and attacked Poti, a port town that could intercept communications between the Porte and the Caucasian mountaineers and secure an anchorage for the Russian fleet bringing supplies to the troops. A joint Russo-Georgian attack on Poti proved successful, and the port town was seized in mid-November.[79]

Simultaneously, Russian troops marched into Imereti, defeated the Georgian royal army, and captured King Solomon himself. Escaping from Russian captivity, Solomon tried launching a rebellion but was defeated and fled to Trebizond.[80] Unable to make much headway against the Russians, he turned for support to foreign powers. He traveled to Yerevan to enlist the shah's aid but was given only a small subsidy and advised to apply directly to the sultan for military help. Solomon sent a mission to Constantinople with letters to both the Ottoman sultan and the French embassy there. The latter packet contained the first of several letters that the Imeretian king wrote to Napoleon, asking him to put Georgia under his protectorate and liberate it from Russia.[81] Addressing Napoleon as "the most august of Caesars, the mightiest king," Solomon complained of the malicious actions of Russian sovereigns. "It is already twelve hundred years my family has ruled over this land; never before was our authority challenged... now only Your Excellency can rescue us.... I appeal [to you] to take my kingdom under your protection and liberate us from the Russians, either by war or peace." Napoleon never formally responded to these letters, but Georgia continued to figure in his plans. In 1812, on the eve of the Russian invasion, Napoleon seems to have nurtured an Oriental project of campaigning to India, and envisioned Georgia as a staging ground for it. "Imagine Moscow taken, Russia overthrown, [and] the tsar reconciled or murdered by a palace plot," he told his trusted aide-de-camp, "and tell me that it is impossible for a large army of Frenchmen and auxiliaries starting from Tiflis to reach the Ganges, where the mere touch of a French sword would be sufficient to bring down the framework of [Britain's] mercantile grandeur throughout India."[82]

Tormasov's victories in 1809 ensured that the following year was relatively peaceful. In late spring the Russian and Iranian negotiators met again near Askoran to discuss a possible cease-fire. Despite seventeen days of negotiations, the sides were unable to reach an agreement. Iran demanded Russian withdraw from the occupied eastern khanates. The Russian authorities were particularly incensed by the active role the British played in shoring up the Qajar resolve to continue war.[83] Hostilities therefore resumed at once. Crown Prince Abbas Mirza marched to Migri, on the Aras River, and was twice defeated by General Peter Kotlyarovskii's much smaller detachment. These defeats not only dampened the Iranian enthusiasm for war but raised concerns over the security of Iran's northwestern provinces, prompting the shah to reinforce Tabriz.

Unable to make headway against the Russians on the Aras, the Iranians discussed with the Turks the possibility of a joint operation—to combine their troops and invade Georgia from the southwest. In August Fath Ali Shah dispatched some 7,000 men under Huseyn Kuli (Hüseynkulu) Khan, *sardar* of Yerevan, to Akhaltsikhe, where they were joined by some 3,000 local Turkish troops under Sherif Pasha, and the combined force advanced to Akhalkalaki, with the intention of proceeding as far as Tiflis (Tbilisi). Upon learning of these movements, Tormasov swiftly counterattacked, a small detachment under Colonel Lisanevich leading the way. On September 17, 1810, after three days of marching in bad weather, Lisanevich came across the Turko-Iranian camp on the outskirts of Akhalkalaki and launched a nighttime attack. It was a complete rout. The Russian victory effectively ended Turko-Iranian cooperation, as each side blamed the other for the failure and retreated home. Tormasov followed up this success with a new offensive that aimed at the southern borderlands. The focal point of the attack was the Ottoman fortress of Akhaltsikhe, which the Russians besieged for ten days in late November 1810 but were unable to capture due to an outbreak of plague.[84]

The Qajar ability to successfully wage the war against Russia was hampered by the threats posed by the Wahhabists in Arabia and the Ottoman Kurds in Iraq. The former inflicted stinging defeats on the Iranians in 1811, while the latter's attacks in 1811–1812 meant that a Qajar army of some 30,000 men was tied down in Iran's western provinces. Fortunately for the Qajars, the British did provide officers and weapons for a Western-style army (along with the money to pay for it). Starting in 1809, British officers supervised a renewed restructuring of the Iranian army that, in its essence, was similar to the French one but on a larger scale. Over the next five years Britain supplied more than 15,000 muskets and 20 cannon, in addition to sabers, gunpowder, and gun carriages. Naturally, the British faced the same core problems that the French had confronted. Their efforts were further complicated by the existence of French-trained *sarbaz* units that resented their British-trained rivals and resisted any and all efforts to place them under British command.

At the start of 1811 Tormasov had fewer than 19,000 men at his disposal in Georgia. Facing renewed Ottoman and Iranian military preparations, he appealed for reinforcements from Russia so that he could launch preemptive strikes on strategically important positions at Derbent, Baku, and Sukhum Kale. His request was denied. More than that, Minister of War Mikhail Barclay de Tolly even inquired whether Tormasov couldn dispatch some of the Caucasian regiments to the western borders of Russia, where Napoleon's Grande Armée was already beginning to take shape. In the summer of 1811 the Turks and Iranians, having completed their preparations, agreed to concentrate their troops on the Arpaçay River. In June, the *serasker* of Erzurum, Emin Pasha, arrived with some 24,000 men at Kars, where he camped to await the Persians. Informed of what was happening, Tormasov once again gambled on the superiority of the Russian arms and decided to attack the Turks before the arrival of the Iranian army. This could have been a risky enterprise, but once again providence smiled on the Russians. During a hunt, a traditional pre-battle event, the Ottoman commander was shot by his longtime rival, thereby throwing the entire Ottoman campaign into disarray. Learning of the incident, the pasha of Trabzon, who had gathered more than 10,000 men at Batum in expectation of a joint Turko-Iranian attack, called off the campaign. The Iranian army, led by Huseyn Kuli Khan, had no choice but to turn back.[85]

This was Tormasov's last "success" in Georgia. He was soon recalled to command an army of observation that was forming in Volhynia (western

Ukraine) in expectation of a possible war with France.[86] Shortly after his departure, the Russian forces in the Caucasus were divided into two independent contingents. Lieutenant General Nikolay Rtischev was appointed to command troops in the north Caucasus, while Lieutenant General Marquis Philip Paulucci took charge of the troops in Georgia and began his tenure with a new offensive against Akhalkalaki, which the Russians (led by the intrepid Kotlyarovskii) captured in a daring raid on December 19, 1811.[87]

Several new developments strengthened Iranian resolve to continue fighting the Russians in the new year. The Anglo-Iranian treaty of 1809 proved of limited value, but the Qajar monarchy understood that it had no alternative to a British orientation now that France had proven itself incapable of providing sufficient military assistance. To deepen his ties with King George III's court, the shah dispatched his ambassador Abu'l-Hasan Khan to London. He returned with a new British envoy, Sir Gore Ouseley, a former BEIC official who was well acquainted with local affairs and instrumental in defending British interests at the Qajar court over the next few years. Under Ouseley's auspices, the 1809 preliminary treaty was renegotiated and formalized into the Definitive Treaty of Friendship and Alliance (March 1812). The treaty confirmed the earlier promises of military assistance and increased the amount of the British subsidy to £150,000.[88]

Bolstered by the new British commitment, Iran rejected Russian offers to negotiate and instead launched a major offensive, with Crown Prince Abbas Mirza leading more than 20,000 men into the khanate of Talysh (southern Azerbaijan).[89] This was an important campaign because Russia seemed to be weaker at this point than it had been since the start of the war in 1804. In early 1812 a major uprising erupted in Kakheti (eastern Georgia) in response to Russian authoritarianism and abuses. The weather in the first six months of the year was unusually bad, leading to poor harvests and rising food prices. The Russian authorities nevertheless insisted on quartering troops with households that were required to feed and house the soldiers, who frequently mistreated their hosts. Unsurprisingly, tempers flared, leading to a revolt.[90] The Qajars quickly moved to exploit the situation by providing help to Georgian prince Alexander Bagration (the son of King Erekle II), whose anti-Russian sentiments were widely known.[91] In the spring the Georgian rebels defeated the Russian detachments, massacred garrisons at Akhmeta and Tianeti, and took control of almost all of Kakheti, forcing the Russian authorities to seek a brief armistice. The Russian positions were further weakened in June 1812 when Napoleon led almost half a million men across the Niemen River and launched his fateful invasion of Russia. The scale and intensity of this assault meant that Russia had to devote all available resources to defending its heartland, leaving peripheries like south Caucasus to fend for themselves.

Napoleon's invasion of Russia produced a political realignment in Europe, but it also placed Britain in an ambiguous position in Iran. With France attacking Russia, London had formed a new alliance with St. Petersburg, pledging a joint front against the French. Yet in the Caucasus, the new Iranian offensive involved some 2,500 British-trained troops led by British military advisors, including Captain Charles Christie and Lieutenant Henry Lindesay, with Major D'Arcy directing artillery. When Ouseley learned of the Anglo-Russian rapprochement he tried recalling British officers from the Iranian army. This decision provoked anger at the Qajar court, and he was quickly compelled to keep some officers and drill sergeants with the troops. These British-led forces participated in a battle near Soltanbud, some fifty miles from Shusha, where the Russian detachment was soundly defeated. This was a rare Iranian victory over the Russian forces, and naturally it bolstered Iranian morale. It also revealed major deficiencies in the newly trained troops, including their failure to maintain discipline when victory was imminent and prisoners and booty beckoned.[92]

Paulucci understood that the Kakhetian uprising threatened Russia's entire war effort in the Caucasus. His conclusion was reinforced by the Russian defeat at Soltanbud. He responded by redeploying the few available forces from north Caucasia and the Ottoman front, including a detachment led by General Kotlyarovskii, the hero of earlier campaigns against the Turks. In October the Iranian army reached the Aras River, where it stumbled on Kotlyarovskii's small detachment (2,200 men) near Aslanduz. Confident of his success, Crown Prince Abbas Mirza rested his army on the left bank of the Aras River, with few outposts deployed to watch for Russian movements. On October 31, 1812, knowing that the Iranians avoided fighting in the dark, General Kotlyarovskii led his men in a forced march to the Iranian camp and launched a surprise nocturnal attack. The result was a stunning Russian victory. The British-led *sarbaz* troops did hold ground, but the rest of the army fled in disorder. Kotlyarovskii's men killed or captured more than 2,000 enemy troops (including Captain Christie) and more than three dozen cannon and falconets.[93] At the start of the New Year, the Russians seized the initiative, driving the Iranians back and storming Lenkoran (January 13, 1813), where the Russians took no prisoners.[94]

These Russian victories dealt a heavy blow to any remaining Iranian hopes of winning the war. The Qajars suffered heavy losses: some 10,000 men in just three months of campaigning. Iranian dreams of a successful uprising in Georgia also did not materialize. Prince Alexander Bagration, who tried to lead his detachments into eastern Georgia, was defeated at Sighnaghi and forced back across the border. The rebellion continued for another four months, though ultimately it gave way to superior Russian military might and was brutally suppressed in early 1813. Fath Ali Shah, who expected continued British support against Russia, was told by the British—and in no uncertain terms—that Iran must make peace with its enemy. With Napoleon defeated in Russia and a new European coalition formed against France, Britain was determined to support "our good friends and Allies the Russians even in this remote quarter" and to end a war that no longer served its imperial interests.[95] Threatening to withhold subsidy payments, the British ambassador Ouseley persuaded the shah to accept peace talks in the summer of 1813. Negotiations were held at Gulistan, a small village in northern Karabagh, where, on October 24, 1813, a British-mediated peace treaty was at long last signed between Russia and Iran.[96]

The treaty confirmed a Russian victory in the decade-long war against Iran and forced the Qajars to relinquish their claims to almost all territories north of the Aras River, including Daghestan, western and eastern Georgian kingdoms and principalities, and eastern Caucasian khanates (except for Nakhichevan and Yerevan).[97] These territorial concessions not only reflected an Iranian loss of sovereignty in the Caucasus but undercut Ottoman claims to some of these lands. Additionally, the loss of these territories meant the disappearance of considerable amount of revenue that had to be replaced by some other means. The unavoidable tax increase made the government quite unpopular and contributed to domestic instability.[98] Further, the shah surrendered Iranian rights to navigate the Caspian Sea and granted to Russia exclusive rights to maintain a military fleet in the Caspian, as well as to enjoy capitulatory rights to trade within Iran. Equally humiliating was the provision involving Russia in Iranian internal affairs, as Russian support would henceforth be required to guarantee the accession of the crown prince to the throne. The treaty provisions were worded so vaguely as to suggest that the Russians would be able to freely interfere in Iran in the future. Continued Russian encroachment into the southeastern Caucasian territories, as well as the mistreatment of Muslim populations, seriously strained Russo-Iranian relations. They also ultimately led to a second war, thirteen years later.

With Napoleonic France defeated, Britain no longer had any interest in supporting Fath Ali Shah, especially if it meant a possible showdown with the Russian Empire. The British government therefore pushed hard for a revision of the clauses of the Definitive Treaty of 1812 that bound Britain to aid Iran in the event its sovereignty was violated (as clearly it now was). Fath Ali Shah saw no alternative to a British orientation now that Napoleon was gone and Russia had become his principal and most dangerous enemy. A mere year after the Treaty of Gulistan, he accepted a watered-down version of the Definitive Treaty, which reiterated the shah's commitment to denounce all alliances with European nations hostile to Britain and resist any encroachment on his country by European armies hostile to Britain. The treaty's provisions dealing with British support of Iran were significantly revised. They specified that the purpose of the alliance was strictly defensive, and that British military assistance or an annual war subsidy, along with weapons, would be provided only in the event Iran was attacked by a foreign state. This provision, however, was effectively negated by Article 6, which stipulated that should any European state that was at peace with Britain attack Iran, Britain would not provide military aid and would instead "use its best endeavors" to mediate peace between the two side. The treaty cast a long shadow over Anglo-Iranian relations.

The Napoleonic Wars had a major impact on Iran, which, despite its glorious imperial past, found itself a pawn in the hands of European powers. Double-crossed by both France and Britain, it had suffered a humiliating defeat at the hands of Russia. The war revealed glaring inefficiencies in the Qajar state and convinced some leading Qajar statesmen of the need for military reforms. Herein lies one of the most enduring legacies of the Napoleonic Wars in Iran. Reform-minded men such as Crown Prince Abbas Mirza believed that the introduction of European-style military reforms would enable the shah to consolidate his power internally and to protect the state more effectively from outside threats. Inspired partly by the Ottoman reforms, Abbas Mirza set out to create an Iranian version of the Ottoman Nizam-i Cedid troops and reduce Qajar dependence on both tribal forces and foreign support. After the Russo-Iranian war, he began sending students to Europe to learn Western tactics and employed British and French officers (as well as a few renegade Russian officers) to raise and drill troops. The number of foreign instructors increased after the end of the Napoleonic Wars, when many unemployed European officers traveled far afield in search of positions.

For his part, Abbas Mirza built a gunpowder factory and an artillery foundry in Tabriz, established a printing press to translate and publish European military textbooks, and tried out a new recruitment system to create a steadier supply of manpower and to make himself independent of the local elite.[99] As with earlier reforms, Abbas Mirza had to overcome public resistance. And, as ever, the religious and traditional power groups disliked change—especially the European appearance of the new regiments and the presence of "infidel" instructors. The military reform did have some effect: by 1831 the army consisted of about 15,000 men who played a critical role in maintaining order and in defending the Qajar authority within Iran. What it failed to do was secure Iran from external threats.

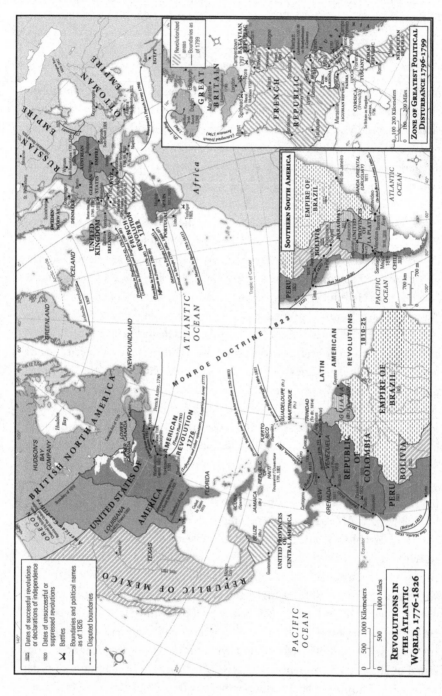

Map 20: Revolutions in the Atlantic World, 1776–1826

CHAPTER 18 | Britain's Expeditionary Warfare,
1805–1810

B Y THE LATE EIGHTEENTH CENTURY, gaining control of the seas and the
international trade lanes that ran through them became a central strategic element of the rivalries among European great powers. Yet during the
Revolutionary Wars, a powerful navy was not as essential to the survival of
France as it was to Britain. Attacked from almost all sides, France concentrated on building up its land forces, and the expectations placed upon the
French fleet were far less demanding than those on the British. Economic,
administrative, and technical innovations in Britain's Royal Navy had combined with the turmoil in France to give it a distinct military superiority at
sea over its French (and, after 1796, Spanish) rivals. Britain had a far more
extensive oceanic trade than its principal enemies. This provided a larger
reserve of professional seamen from which to man its growing fleet, which by
1805 was the largest in the world and exceeded the combined strength of the
next five naval powers.[1] British naval commanders adopted bold methods in
confronting their enemies, and their victories had laid the foundation for
naval hegemony of the Atlantic and the Mediterranean basins. In the fall of
1805 the British triumph at Trafalgar partly offset French military victories
on the continent, leaving Napoleon unable to contest British control of the
Atlantic. Consequently, Britain conducted naval operations across the entire
Atlantic basin, revealing ambitions that were as grand in design as those of
its main adversary.

To forestall Napoleon from strengthening French positions in South
Africa, the British government dispatched a major expedition under Admiral
Sir Home Riggs Popham and Lieutenant General Sir David Baird to seize the
Cape Colony. Originally formed by the Dutch East India Company (Vereenigde

Oost-Indische Compagnie, VOC), the Cape had a small settler population of about 14,000 people (and a slightly higher number of slaves) who frequently clashed with the local Xhosa and their allies for the control of the region. The *trekboers*—from the Dutch *boer*, meaning "farmer," and *trek*, meaning "to pull," as in a wagon—resorted to various means to seize ever-larger tracts of agricultural land.[2] The two sides fought several conflicts in the late eighteenth century. The most recent one had raged between 1799 and 1803, when the Xhosa threatened European settlers, who were experiencing internal divisions.

The invasion by a British force a few years earlier, in September 1795, had ended almost 150 years of VOC rule. The first British occupation lasted for eight years, until the Treaty of Amiens required the restoration of this colony to the Batavian Republic. The Dutch interlude that followed was brief but full of ambitious projects. A specially appointed commissioner general named Jacob Abraham de Mist tried to implement social and economic reforms that the Dutch hoped would make the Cape Colony prosperous and orderly. But neither the local settler population nor the available resources allowed for completion of these reforms.

More to the point, the Dutch had run out of time. The first British warships reached the Cape on Christmas Eve 1805 and immediately began blockading the colony, whose governor, Lieutenant General Jan Willem Janssens, could do little but watch as the British massed for the invasion. After a delay caused by rough seas, Baird landed at Melkbosstrand, north of Cape Town, on January 6–7 and, after easily defeating Janssens's small garrison forces at the Battle of Blaauwberg, he seized Cape Town on January 9. Janssens did continue resisting gallantly in the mountains for a week before being obliged to yield to superior numbers and accept the Articles of Capitulation on January 18.[3]

Like the Dutch before them, the British considered the Cape as a crucial midpoint on their route to India and the Far East. They made little structural change in the colony, seeking mostly to stimulate trade and the local economy. While not condoning the local slave-based economy, they became distinctly pro-settler and played a major role in the consolidation of white control in the South African countryside. A British commissioner appointed for the purpose examined the frontier situation and reported that lasting peace between the Xhosa and the European settlers could be achieved only by keeping these societies completely separated until the white population was strong enough to dominate the region. This report served as the blueprint for the eventual apartheid system, which encompassed the use of military force to dislodge black farming population in Southern Africa. It also fostered the development of a colonial society that would be well protected following the British military campaigns in 1811 and 1812. The Xhosa were ruthlessly expelled from their tribal territories, and thousands of European settlers began to acquire farmland along the west bank of the Fish River.[4]

The British government next explored prospects of appropriating Spanish America, hoping that even the possibility of a British attack might induce Spain to break its alliance with France. In early 1805 Henry Dundas, the First Lord of the Admiralty, who had a long track record of embracing revolutionary plans for Spanish America, examined new projects based on the argument that Britain should not wage a defensive war against France but rather go on the offensive outside Europe.[5] Since the Spanish monarchy had allied itself with France, Britain would be justified in targeting the vast Spanish domains in the Americas.[6] One such venture came from Sebastián Francisco de Miranda y Rodríguez de Espinoza, a Venezuelan adventurer who had spent the previous two decades trying, unsuccessfully, to incite a revolution in South America. In 1805 Miranda secured informal British support for an attempted invasion of the Captaincy General of Venezuela. Unfortunately for him, Guevara Vasconcelos, the captain general of Venezuela, had been alerted to the attack and had ample time to prepare for it.[7] On April 27–29, when Miranda attempted to disembark near Puerto Cabello, his efforts were thwarted by Spanish warships. This setback did not dampen the spirits of the would-be revolutionaries, who continued to enjoy unofficial British support. Miranda was allowed to regroup in the British colonies, and in August he set sail from Trinidad on his second expedition to Venezuela and this time was able to land at the port of La Vela, near Coro. This expedition failed as well, due to diligent Spanish defensive preparations and a propaganda effort that labeled Miranda a secret agent for Britain and a "traitor" who had committed heinous crimes. Landing on August 1, Miranda and his men found the nearby towns deserted, with most of the population fleeing at their approach. After ten exasperating days spent issuing decrees and appeals, Miranda understood that he would not secure popular support. When Spanish royal troops gathered near Coro, Miranda beat an ignominious retreat into exile.[8]

Miranda might have failed to incite a revolution in Venezuela, but his ideas and example had immediate effect elsewhere. Encouraged by his success at the Cape, Admiral Popham determined to take matters into his own hands and pursue greater glory (and financial reward) in South America.[9] His decision to invade Río de la Plata was not sanctioned in London, though it was clearly influenced not only by the exaggerated rumors of disaffection in Spanish colonies that Miranda had spread but also by long-standing British imperial aspirations to penetrate Spain's South American colonies with a view toward obtaining a position favorable to British trade; between 1702 and 1783, Spain had repelled no fewer than six such attempts by Britain. The Revolutionary Wars provided new opportunities for the British, who considered several plans, including one in which Nicholas Vansittart, Thomas Maitland, and, of course, Francisco de Miranda would seize Spanish colonies. Prime Minister William Pitt and other members of the British cabinet agreed that weakening Spanish authority in the region and opening new markets for the British economy would be of immense consequence. They were, however, not convinced that a military occupation was practical. Yet with the French and Spanish fleets depleted, the situation seemed ripe for a British attack on the Spanish colonies. That was why, without waiting for the orders from the Admiralty, Popham attacked the Río de la Plata where he hoped to replicate the success of the British invasion of the Cape Colony, conquer parts of South America, and open new large markets for British manufacture. The English commander explained that his project had "not arisen from any sudden impulse, or the immediate desires of gratifying an adventurous spirit." Rather, it was the outcome of a plan that he had previously framed at the request of senior government members for "a general emancipation in South America."[10]

The British fleet sailed for Río de la Plata in mid-April 1806. After a brief stop at St. Helena Island to pick up provisions and reinforcements, Popham reached his destination on June 8.[11] The lack of planning became quickly apparent. The British discovered that the estuary was too shallow for their warships to get close enough to lend support to the landing forces. Nevertheless, Popham pushed forward with a hastily drawn plan to capture Buenos Aires, which, new intelligence revealed, was poorly fortified; it was also weakly defended, because a part of the Spanish garrison had been dispatched to Upper Peru (today's Bolivia) to guard the frontiers from the remnants of Túpac Amaru II's indigenous uprising. More exciting was the news that the city was the repository of a large amount of bullion from Peru. On June 25–26 William Beresford, newly promoted to general, led 1,500 men onto the shore at Quilmes (near Buenos Aires) and, after defeating a small Spanish force, captured the city the next day; the Spanish viceroy, Marquis Rafael de Sobremonte, fled to Córdoba. Popham and his men were naturally thrilled by such an easy victory, which garnered them a sizable booty and, in the words of Popham, "open[ed] an extensive channel to the manufactures of Great Britain."[12]

Expecting to be welcomed as liberators, the British were surprised by the hostile reception they received from the locals. Although the members of the *cabildo,* the Spanish administrative council governing a municipality, collaborated with the British, the city's population was distraught by the British occupation and particularly displeased by the British decision to repeal the Spanish monopoly on commerce and to open the Río de la Plata to free trade, which harmed local economic interests.[13] By August the city's residents, who came to dislike the firm hand of British sea power more than the despotism of distant Spain, were resisting the British. Martín de Alzaga, one of the leading merchants and a member of the Buenos Aires *cabildo*, used his vast fortune to organize a group of conspirators, who were supported by Jacques de Liniers, a French officer in the Spanish military service who rallied a sizable local militia at Montevideo. On August 4 Liniers marched to Buenos Aires, where Alzaga and his men incited an uprising on August 10. While Popham sailed helplessly up and down the Río de la Plata looking on, General Beresford, outnumbered and unable to receive any reinforcements, was compelled to surrender his entire command on August 14, causing much joy and celebration in and around Buenos Aires. A newly published ode celebrated the liberation of "our beautiful capital city" from "the British brutes."[14]

Furious at this setback, Popham spent the next four months blockading the Río de la Plata before he was replaced by Rear Admiral Charles Stirling, who brought more troops under General Sir Samuel Auchmuty. In mid-January 1807 this new British invasion force landed near Montevideo, which fell on February 3, after a short siege. The local population, however, remained avowedly hostile, and British control over the city and its vicinity was tenuous. The situation improved somewhat later that spring when Admiral George Murray arrived with further reinforcements under Lieutenant General John Whitelocke. Whitelocke was determined to attack Buenos Aires, which served as the center of Spanish resistance. On June 28, with the Royal Navy's support, he landed with some 11,000 men near Buenos Aires and defeated Liniers's Spanish force on the outskirts of the city on July 1. It was a brutal fight. The British attack on the city led to ferocious resistance. House-to-house fighting claimed more than 2,500 British troops and forced Whitelocke to withdraw. A truce was negotiated with local authorities. The British agreed to evacuate all of their forces and end their blockade of the Río de la Plata.[15]

The failed British invasions had left an enduring legacy. Resistance to the British had involved nearly all of the Río de la Plata's residents, from the wealthiest merchants to the plebeian crowds of craftsmen, apprentices, and slaves, all of who saw their victory as affirming their community's unique destiny. A group of fourteen-year-olds who participated in the fighting even formed a military unit, Jóvenes de la Reconquista, with the permission of their parents and the approval of Liniers.[16] Having defeated a great power with little help from Spain, the local leaders were emboldened to assert themselves. Just two days after the British surrender in August 1806, the *cabildo* of Buenos Aires organized the Junta General, that asserted control over all regional military units, thereby challenging traditional colonial authorities and paving the way for a novel political discourse that involved popular participation. During the second British invasion, the streets of Buenos Aires were the scene of public demonstrations with people shouting, "Muera el virrey" (death to the viceroy), "Viva la libertad" (long live liberty)," and "Vamos a fijar la bandera republicana" (let's raise the republican flag). The newly formed Junta General then stripped the viceroy of his power and ordered his arrest.[17] This was the first salvo in the Latin American colonial independence movement, shattering the institutional status quo established in 1776 with the creation of the Viceroyalty of the Río de la Plata. Spain would never fully reclaim its positions in the viceroyalty. Existing colonial administrative structures (viceroy, *audiencia*, *cabildo*) struggled to adjust to new political realities on the ground, most crucially the emergence of an armed and politically active plebeian population.[18]

The events in Buenos Aires represented some of the largest British setbacks of the Napoleonic Wars; Admiral Popham, General Whitelocke, and other officers involved in them were court-martialed and censured. The invasions are also noteworthy for what they reveal about Britain's imperial thinking. The slowness of communications between South America and London and the precariousness of the situation in Europe, where Napoleon had already shattered Austria and Prussia and was on his way to defeating Russia, played key roles in shaping the frame of mind in British society and government. When news of the successful capture of Buenos Aires reached London in September 1806, for example, jubilant crowds thronged the streets, singing "Rule, Britannia" to mark the first great success in a year empty of victory. The fact that Popham and Beresford were British officers commanding British forces for clearly British ends meant that this expedition was treated differently than other forays into South America (such as Miranda's). The news was particularly welcomed in merchant circles, which had struggled to dispose of their ever-growing quantities of goods in France-dominated Europe and now perceived the fall of Buenos Aires as an opportunity to enter new markets. Britain's trade with South America was already running at well over £1 million a year. The news of the British capture of Buenos Aires provoked a speculative commercial boom as merchants anticipated vast profits to be made in newly opened markets, revealing frenzied expectations that were clearly outlandish.

The British government thus found itself in the awkward position of having to censure Popham for undertaking an unsanctioned expedition while also facing a growing tide of popular support for the action.[19] The "Ministry of All the Talents," as the coalition government formed by William Grenville in February 1806 was called for supposedly embracing "all the talents," was aware of the complicity of the previous administration but hesitated to support either an outright partition of the Spanish domains or efforts to instigate the very revolutionary turmoil that Britain was fighting against elsewhere. "How far shall we now countenance it or engage in it," wondered Prime Minister Grenville about Miranda's expedition to Venezuela.[20] The same could be said of the government's initial response to Popham's expedition. Foreign Secretary Charles Fox (and his allies), who had long castigated Pitt's war policy, opposed greater British engagement in South America before European affairs had been settled. Fox's death in September 1806 opened the way for more hawkish members of the cabinet. With public support for Popham's scheme swelling, the British government was keen on exploiting a conquest that it had earlier disapproved and, in doing so, made the same mistake as the leaders of the expedition who came as liberators but remained as conquerors. At the Board of Trade, William Eden, Lord Auckland, urged the government to do something to help British merchant houses because, as he put it, "the entire downfall of the Continental powers makes it more than ever necessary to advert to interests which are merely British. I feel strongly that in the actual predicament of Europe, the extension of our commerce is become the most efficient measure of war."[21] Such sentiments echoed in the Foreign Ministry, where Secretary Charles Grey, Lord Howick, had contended that it was time for Britain to abandon the European continent, where three coalitions had come and gone without much success against France, and to look after its own interests elsewhere.

Such thinking shaped British positions vis-à-vis European powers in the fall of 1806 and was the reason Prussia, for example, found Britain uninterested in another coalition against Napoleon. In responding to a Prussian plea for help against Napoleon, Lord Howick brusquely noted that "[Britain], having supported the great pressure of the contest against France during so many years in which Prussia has been at peace, has a right to expect that His Prussian Majesty should avail himself to the utmost of the resources of his own dominion before he can justly call upon [Britain] for pecuniary assistance."[22] William Windham, Britain's secretary of state for war and the colonies, filled with expansionist ideas, argued that since the current situation in Europe no longer afforded any scope for the deployment of British power, Britain must pivot to South America, where it should incite revolutionary upheaval and retain whatever territory it could in order to counterbalance France's continental hegemony. With British interests secured in South

America, Windham noted, "the period may not be far distant, nor exceed the term to which we can afford to wait, when the power of Bonaparte may begin to totter."[23]

Throughout the fall of 1806 the British cabinet drew up plans for the takeover of South America. One expedition was designed to navigate Cape Horn, seize the port of Valparaiso in Chile, and, after crossing the Andes, establish a chain of forts before conquering the whole southern half of the continent. Another envisioned separate attacks on Peru and Panama. Even Grenville, usually reserved when it came to overseas overtures, fell prey to this "imperial fever." In October he considered probably the most audacious of these plans: detaching several thousand men from the British force at Buenos Aires, transporting them across the Atlantic, and collecting 1,000 men from the garrison of the Cape of Good Hope; continuing to India, where they would be joined by 4,000 *sepoys*; invading the Philippines; and, finally, sailing across the Pacific to attack Mexico from the west. Another British expedition, from the West Indies, was to attack it at that precise moment from the east! The plan was presented to Wellington, who, fortunately, brought much-needed common sense to the discussion and pointed to the obvious impossibility of launching and coordinating such a global operation.[24] Noting that the proponents of this expedition called for the establishment of an independent Mexico (under one of the Bourbon princes), Wellesley pointed out that no consideration had been given to "in what manner the government recommended to be established in that country should be kept in existence, carried on, and supported after the revolution should have been effected, particularly against the attempts which might be made upon it by the United States."[25]

The news of the British defeats in the Río de la Plata made these plans moot. Still, they revealed that the British government was ready to pursue policies no less opportunistic and exploitative than those of Napoleon, whom it so often castigated for his imperial ambitions. After the fall of the Ministry of All the Talents in March 1807, the new cabinet of William Henry Cavendish, Duke of Portland, reexamined past plans and criticized its predecessor for the lack of a definitive policy toward South America. Further, it recognized that the conquest of such a vast region was hopeless unless the interests of the locals were taken into consideration. This marked a crucial change in British policy, one that had profound repercussions for the entire region.

———◦◦◦✕◦◦◦———

Between 1803 and 1810, the West Indies remained an important theater of the Napoleonic Wars, where operations were complicated by deadly diseases and the vast distances involved, as well as the necessity for cooperation between the army and navy and the continued threat of slave revolts.[26] Once hostilities against the French were resumed in May 1803, a British squadron blockaded Saint-Domingue, preventing badly needed reinforcements and supplies from reaching the besieged French garrison, which ultimately surrendered to the British. In the Windward Islands, Lieutenant General William Grinfeld and Commodore Samuel Hood attacked St. Lucia in late June 1803 and easily defeated the much smaller French garrison led by General Jean François Xavier Noguès. The British then followed up on this success with the capture of Tobago and the Dutch colonies of Demerara, Essequibo, Berbice, and Surinam, where conflicting interests between the French-influenced central government and the Dutch colonial authorities resulted in local efforts to safeguard trade and investments even at the price of supporting a British invasion.[27]

In 1805 Napoleon turned his attention to the Caribbean, where, as part of a larger plan for the invasion of Britain, he wanted his various fleets to rendezvous in order to harass the British commerce and to divert British naval forces from European waters. Admiral Édouard de Missiessy had sailed from Rochefort with five ships-of-the-line and three frigates. Arriving at Martinique in February 1805, Missiessy quickly proceeded to attack the nearby British island of Dominica, in expectation of Admiral Pierre de Villeneuve, who had avoided the British blockade fleet under Vice Admiral Lord Nelson at Toulon and sailed westward into the Atlantic, where he was joined by a Spanish squadron. After dropping off reinforcements at Guadeloupe, Missiessy raided St. Christopher (St. Kitts), Nevis, and Montserrat, where he collected hundreds of thousands of francs in contributions. In March, the French admiral received news that Villeneuve's initial attempt to break out of Toulon had failed. So he decided to complete his mission by reinforcing the French garrison of Saint-Domingue and returning to France.

Unbeknownst to Missiessy, however, Villeneuve had successfully crossed the Atlantic with the combined French and Spanish fleets and reached Martinique in mid-May. The French attacked and captured Diamond Rock, a little islet off the southern coast of Martinique that had been fortified by the British. Fresh from this success, Villeneuve learned that Missiessy had already returned to France and that the Brest fleet had not even left European waters. Realizing the planned rendezvous of the French fleet was no longer feasible, Villeneuve decided to attack Barbados in June. En route, he learned of the presence of a British fleet nearby, called off the attack, and sailed back to Europe.

This was to be the last French major offensive in the West Indies. In October 1805, Villeneuve's combined fleet was destroyed at Trafalgar, greatly

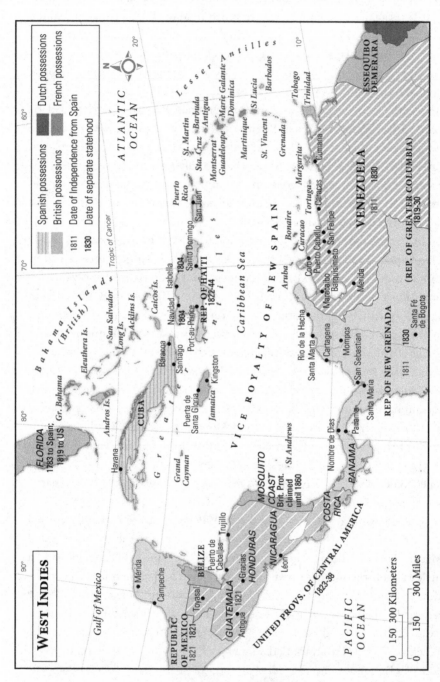

WEST INDIES

Spanish possessions

British possessions

Dutch possessions

French possessions

1811   Date of Independence from Spain

1830   Date of separate statehood

Tropic of Cancer

Gulf of Mexico

FLORIDA
1783 to Spain;
1819 to US

*Bahama Islands
(British)*

San Salvador
Long Is.
Eleuthera Is.
Acklins Is.
Caicos Is.

Andros Is.

Havana

Gr. Bahama

CUBA

*Grand
Cayman*

Santiago
Baracoa

Puerta de
Santa Gloria

Jamaica   Kingston

Navidad   Isabella
1804

Santo Domingo
1804

Port-au-Prince

REP. OF HAITI
1822-44

G r e a t e r   *A n t i l l e s*

L e s s e r   *A n t i l l e s*

Caribbean Sea

Puerto
Rico
San Juan

St. Martin
Sta. Cruz   Barbuda
Montserrat   Antigua
Guadeloupe   Marie Galante
Dominica

Martinique

St Lucia

St Vincent   Barbados

Grenada

Tobago
Trinidad

ATLANTIC
OCEAN

ESSEQUIBO
DEMERARA

REPUBLIC
OF MEXICO
1821   1821

Mérida
Campeche
Toyasal

Antigua
GUATEMALA
1821
Gracias
HONDURAS

Puerto de
Caballos   Trujillo

BELIZE

St Andrews

MOSQUITO
COAST
Brit. Prot.
claimed
until 1860

NICARAGUA
León

COSTA
RICA

UNITED PROVS. OF CENTRAL AMERICA
1823-38

PANAMA

Panama
Nombre de Dias

Santa Maria

San Sebastian

REP. OF NEW GRENADA
1811   1830
Santa Fé
de Bogota

Mompos
Cartagena

Rio de la Hacha
Santa Marta

Aruba
Curacao
Bonaire

Coro
Maracaibo
Barquisimeto   San Felipe
Puerto Cabello
Mérida

Tortuga
Margarita
Cumana
Caracas

VENEZUELA
1811   1830

(REP. OF GREATER COLUMBIA)
1819-30

VICE ROYALTY OF NEW SPAIN

PACIFIC
OCEAN

N

0   150   300 Kilometers
0   150   300 Miles

90°   80°   70°   60°

20°

10°

Map 21: West Indies

hampering French naval capability. The French had lost more than two dozen ships in the span of a few months, with the tattered remains of their squadrons sheltered at ports that were invested by the assiduous Collingwood. The end of the threat of French invasion was widely celebrated in Britain and caused some senior officials to reevaluate naval strategy: the First Lord of the Admiralty, Charles Middleton, Lord Barham, called for the withdrawal of the Atlantic blockade in order to reduce costs and damage to the Royal Navy.

Barham had clearly underestimated the French threat, however, and subsequent events demonstrated the enduring French threat to British interests in the West Indies. It is true that after 1805 the French were unwilling to risk their remaining capital ships in large fleet actions, which made the prospects of another general fleet-in-fleet battle unlikely. In 1811 the secretary of the British Admiralty lamented that "it is now six years since we had a general sea fight and we are growing impatient."[28] On the other hand, Napoleon, who had been encouraged by the success of Vice Admiral Charles-Alexandre Linois's squadron in the Indian Ocean and South China Sea in 1803–1804 and Rear Admiral Zacharie Allemand's "Invisible Squadron" in the Atlantic in 1805, concentrated his efforts on commerce-raiding campaigns and instructed Vice Admiral Honoré Ganteaume, in charge of the Brest fleet, to prepare strong squadrons for service in the Atlantic, where they were to target enemy merchant marine and inflict damage on the British economy.[29] These imperial orders set the stage for a series of transoceanic operations that have often been overlooked in the discussion of the Napoleonic Wars. They nonetheless qualify any claims that the victory at Trafalgar had secured British control of the seas.

French naval power did not end in October 1805. To the contrary, over the next nine years Britain had much to fear from France when it came to command of the sea. Napoleon did his best to unite the fleets of several nations, and had it not been for British countermeasures at Copenhagen and Lisbon, he could have taken control over the Danish and Portuguese fleets, which counted almost seventy warships. In addition, British operations also prevented the Swedish fleet from falling into French hands and bottled up the Russian Baltic Fleet (about twenty warships) in the Gulf of Finland. Napoleon then further weakened his hand through his intervention in Spain, which cost him the support of the Spanish fleet (over two dozen warships), which refused to acknowledge French authority. Traditional accounts overlook the fact that even in the post-Trafalgar period French admirals continued to cause plenty of trouble for their British counterparts. In 1806 alone the French launched several expeditions into the Atlantic basin. Captain Amand Leduc, with three frigates, raided British whaling and merchant vessels around Iceland and Greenland, inflicting some 2.5 million francs' worth of damage before his men succumbed to scurvy, forcing him to return to France.[30] Commodore Jean-Marthe-Adrien Lhermitte led an expedition to West Africa, where he conducted an effective raiding operation, capturing 10 million francs' worth of merchant ships before returning to France.[31] Despite the British blockade, Captain Louis-Charles-Auguste Delamarre de Lamellerie managed to escape with four frigates and spent the next six months cruising along the western coastline of Africa and in the West Indies before returning to the Bay of Biscay.[32]

Far more significant were two large squadrons that Ganteaume placed under command of Vice Admiral Corentin-Urbain Leissègues and Contre-Admiral Jean-Baptiste Willaumez. In December 1805 Leissègues broke out of Brest with five ships-of-the-line and two frigates, delivering reinforcements and supplies to the besieged garrison in Santo Domingo; he was then to spend two months blockading Jamaica before cruising along the American eastern seaboard and returning to France. After successfully accomplishing the first part of his mission, Leissègues decided to stay at Santo Domingo in order to finish the much-needed repairs on ships that had been ravaged by tropical storms. He never got his chance to complete his mission. Word of the French breakout reached Britain on Christmas Eve of 1805 and prompted an immediate response. Lord Barham ordered several additional squadrons to prepare for sea in search of the missing French squadrons and guarding the vital trade routes. One of them, under Rear Admiral Alexander Cochrane, crossed the Atlantic in early 1806 and joined Vice Admiral Sir John Duckworth's fleet anchored at Barbados. The British scouting frigates soon sighted Leissègues's squadron off the port of Santo Domingo, where Duckworth, leading a fleet of seven warships and two frigates, surprised and destroyed the French on February 6, 1806.[33] Napoleon was enraged by Leissègues's failure to follow his orders to reach Havana, where he would have completed the necessary repairs in the safety of the Spanish fortifications. "This is not bad luck but rather unparalleled stupidity and calamity," the emperor bemoaned.[34]

The other French squadron, under Willaumez, was tasked with raiding the shipping lanes of the South Atlantic before sailing to the Leeward Islands and supporting the French forces in Martinique, Guadeloupe, and Cayenne. Leading six ships-of-the-line and two frigates (with the emperor's younger brother, Jérôme Bonaparte, on one of them), Willaumez departed alongside Leissègues but steered for the South Atlantic, intending to pass into the Indian Ocean and cruise off the Cape of Good Hope, lying in wait for the British China Fleet, a large annual convoy of East Indiamen that carried lucrative Chinese goods. Willaumez encountered his first major obstacle when the crew of a captured merchant ship informed him of the British capture of the Cape Colony.

With this crucial supply base no longer available to him, the French admiral decided to remain in the South Atlantic, unaware that the British squadrons under Vice Admiral Sir John Borlase Warren and Rear Admiral Sir Richard Strachan were hunting for him hundreds of miles to the north. Warren spent the first three months of 1806 in the eastern Atlantic, hoping to find the elusive French squadron. Early at dawn on March 16, 1806, his lookouts reported sails to the northeast. Instead of Willaumez, these was the stragglers of Linois's squadron, which had spent the last three years sailing across the Indian Ocean and were greatly weakened by detachments and shipwreck. In the ensuing action of March 13, Linois tried desperately to escape but was attacked and captured by the superior British fleet.

Enthused by his success, Warren returned to Britain, leaving only Strachan still hunting for Willaumez's squadron in the vast ocean. After weeks of futile search, Strachan finally learned that Willaumez was in fact in the West Indies, where the French had raided British commercial shipping. As Strachan embarked on yet another transatlantic crossing, Rear Admiral Alexander Cochrane's squadron sighted the French off St. Thomas, where Willaumez intended to attack Britain's annual Jamaica convoy, which was preparing to sail out of Tortola. Cochrane's appearance forced the French to move to the Bahama Banks, where the French admiral still hoped to intercept the convoy, which counted nearly three hundred vessels laden with goods and monies. Yet with the British refusing to allow the convoy to sail until the whereabouts of the French squadron had been determined, Willaumez spent most of July in futile anticipation. By August, no longer able to delay the departure of the convoy, Cochrane allowed one part of the convoy—more than a hundred ships escorted by just one warship and two frigates—to depart. The convoy passed through the Bahama Banks just as Willaumez was frantically searching for Jérôme Bonaparte, who, on his own initiative and without informing the admiral, sailed his ship, *Vétéran*, northward in search of bounty. By the time Willaumez realized what was happening, the convoy was already on its way to Britain.

Meanwhile, Admiral Warren, having delivered Linois to Britain and refurbished his ships, had returned to the Atlantic in search of Willaumez. In August he explored the eastern Bahamas but missed the French, who at that time were further to the north. The Great Coastal Hurricane of 1806, which had ravaged much of the East Coast of the United States in August 1806, had badly damaged the French ships, scattering them across a large area and making some of them easy pickings for the British. One of them, *Impétueux*, tried to escape the British pursuers by steering closer to the American coastline but was still boarded and burnt. Ultimately, of Willaumez's original squadron only one ship—Jérôme Bonaparte's *Vétéran*, which had seized and destroyed several British merchant vessels from the Quebec convoy— returned back home as scheduled in 1806; three more ships had to undergo extensive repairs in the United States before eventually returning to France three years later.

The forays of 1806 left a mixed legacy. They resulted in the capture or destruction of some sixty British vessels, worth an estimated 27.5 million francs. However, these losses, as significant as they may seem, barely affected the overall volume of British commerce, which involved more than 19,000 vessels. Furthermore, the French paid dearly for these gains, and more than half of the vessels that ventured out on these cruises never returned to France.[35] Undaunted, Napoleon continued to plan large-scale commerce-raiding expeditions until his minister of marine made clear to him the dire straits of the French navy. "The difficulties of maritime operations have never been as great as on this occasion," wrote Denis Decrès. "The enemy has never had as many ships available and we have never had fewer ports of call and greater shortages in our distant ports. All of these expeditions...appear to me to have no chance of success, and especially no parity between their probable advantages and the nearly inevitable dangers that are associated with it."[36] Following Decrès's advice, Napoleon limited French naval operations to those involving only isolated frigates that were tasked with maintaining communications with the remaining French colonies. Aside from Allemand's expedition from Brest to Toulon in 1808, no other large-scale French naval campaigns were fought in the Atlantic Ocean during the rest of the Napoleonic Wars.

This does not mean that Napoleon had given up on the war at sea. To the contrary, starting in 1808, as we've seen, he concentrated his efforts on rebuilding the French fleet and pursuing a "fleet-in-being" strategy that involved a massive naval buildup across the entire French Empire. This change in French naval strategy coincided with several key developments. First, the Spanish imbroglio not only entangled Napoleon in a six-year war but deprived him of both the Spanish fleet and access to the Spanish colonies that had served as the bases for privateers against British trade; now these possessions could serve as a weapon against the remaining French outposts in the Caribbean. The Spanish fleet, despite its many problems, was of tremendous value to French naval operations. This it demonstrated on several occasions and even as late as the spring of 1808, when the British fleet searching for Admiral Ganteaume's French squadron near the tip of the Italian Peninsula was distracted by the news of the Spanish fleet sailing out to sea; as the British rushed to Minorca, Ganteaume safely returned to Toulon.[37]

Second, the French naval expeditions of 1806 had showed that the French maritime power, though weakened, could still pose a major threat, especially in light of the continued French triumphs on land. Indeed, by late 1807 the overall British position was far from satisfactory. With Russia, Prussia, and Austria defeated, London found itself almost entirely excluded from the European mainland and had no major continental ally except for the tepid Swedes in the north and the weak Neapolitan Bourbons in the south. In fact, the threat from Napoleon was so great and in so many different locations that the British government had no choice but to reassess its strategy. In the Mediterranean, where its invasion of southern Italy had failed in 1806, Britain decided to pursue a defensive strategy, reinforcing its forces in and around Sicily in anticipation of Napoleon's next move. British Secretary of War and the Colonies Castlereagh believed that if the war was to continue, colonial and maritime warfare were the only instruments at the disposal of Britain until new continental allies had been gained. Castlereagh sought to formulate a naval policy tied to this military urgency and concluded, "The more I have had time to reflect on our future prospects in this war, the more impressed I am with a conviction that neither peace nor independence can be the lot of this nation [Britain] till we...counteract at sea what [France] lawlessly inflicts and enforces on shore."[38]

Castlereagh's plan of operations consisted of two main parts. One was to take advantage of Britain's maritime superiority to effect an economic blockade of the enemy's harbors that might inflict on the French as much injury as possible. The other was to make full use of Britain's military force by transporting it from place to place by sea, compensating for its inferiority upon land. The orders-in-council discussed earlier were the result of the first proposition, while the great expeditions to the Iberian Peninsula, Scandinavia, and the West Indies were the result of the second. In 1807–1808 the Royal Navy conducted a wide-ranging sweep of the Caribbean, netting the Dutch colony of Curaçao and the Danish islands of St. Thomas, St. John, and St. Croix.[39] They stormed the French outposts of Marie-Galante and Désirade, thus denying safe anchorage to the remaining French privateers. In the fall of 1808 a new Anglo-Portuguese expedition was prepared to seize the colony of French Guiana. Commanded by Lieutenant Colonel Manoel Marques, the expedition involved some 550 men, who in December were carried aboard Portuguese transports escorted by a British frigate to Guiana. The Anglo-Portuguese forces quickly captured the districts of Oyapok and Approaque, and after just five days of fighting, the French authorities agreed to capitulate on January 12.[40] The fall of French Guiana was the last critical step in British preparations for an invasion of Martinique, the largest remaining French outpost in the Caribbean. After intercepted documents revealed the weakness of the French defenses there, the British launched the largest expedition—some 12,000 men aboard a fleet of six ships-of-the-line, nine frigates, five sloops, nine brigs, and dozens of transport ships—in more than a decade, landing on the island in January 1809. As in 1793, the British invasions unfolded along several axes and overwhelmed the French garrison of just 2,300 men, which fell back toward the fortifications around Fort-de-France, where they valiantly held out for a whole month before surrendering on February 24.[41] Building upon this success, the British then seized the remaining French dependency, the Îles des Saintes, and forced the remnants of the French garrison of Santo Domingo to capitulate by mid-July.[42]

Napoleon responded to these British successes with a vast program of shipbuilding. Despite frequent invocation of his supposed inability to comprehend naval warfare, the policy that he and naval minister Decrès followed between 1808 and 1813 was worthily conceived and conducted. Dozens of warships were constructed at Texel, Rotterdam, Amsterdam, Flushing, Antwerp, Cherbourg, Brest, L'Orient, Rochefort, Bordeaux, Toulon, Genoa, Naples, and Venice.[43] At many of these locations Napoleon expanded or built new harbors, docks, wharfs, and fortifications. The overarching aim can be gleaned from the emperor's annual *exposé* published in June 1811: "We shall be able to make peace with safety when we shall have 150 ships of the line; and, in spite of the obstacles of the war, such is the state of the Empire that we shall shortly have that number of vessels."[44]

As new warships were constructed, they were kept ready to set sail in various ports, forcing the British Royal Navy to spread itself over a vast area and to guard against possible breakouts. This inevitably caused significant wear and tear on men and ships. The fleet might remain at sea for months, consuming its victuals and enduring Atlantic or Mediterranean gales. Maintaining the fleet's efficiency was one of the greatest challenges the British Admiralty faced during the war, especially if one considers how few and far between were the dry-dock facilities necessary for major ship repairs.[45] The Royal Navy was unable to utilize Italian or Spanish dockyards, while the one on Malta was not completed. Thus, facing constant battering from wind and water, the British had no choice but to resort to trips back to home ports at Plymouth, Portsmouth, or Chatham. Shortages of materials (especially of timber) and of experienced seafaring men (by 1810 the British seafaring population had reached 145,000 men, or 2.7 percent of the total male population) meant that although the total size of the Royal Navy peaked at 728 vessels in 1809, it was never able to put more than 130 ships-of-the-line in service at any one time.[46] Napoleon's naval buildup therefore concentrated on ships-of-the-line, a significant share of them being the massive 130-gun warships.

Since ships-of-the-line underpinned the British mastery of the sea, they received priority in men and supplies at the expense of smaller vessels that could reconnoiter and, more crucially, target French coastal trade in waters too shallow for the larger warships. This coastal trade was of great importance to French imperial interests, made evident by the enormous efforts Napoleon took to protect it through construction of coastal defenses; in 1810 the French had more than 3,600 cannon mounted in some 900 places around the European coastline, manned by 13,000 gunners.

The lack of British cruisers that could be used to scout was one of the key reasons the French could launch excursions from their ports after 1805, including Allemand's successful departure from the Atlantic to the Mediterranean to join Ganteaume in 1808, Willaumez's sailing in 1809 from Brest to the Aix Roads, and Allemand's redeployment of warships from L'Orient to Brest in 1812 without any of their ships being intercepted. In fact, from 1807 to 1813, occasions on which the British were able to destroy French ships-of-the-line were few and far between, with the most significant occurring in 1809 at the Basque Roads.[47]

Alarmed by the British victories in the West Indies, Napoleon belatedly dispatched an expedition there. In late October 1808 he instructed the squadrons at Lorient and Rochefort to deliver reinforcements and supplies to Martinique, but the British blockade impeded their departure. In February 1809 Admiral Jean-Baptiste Philibert Willaumez was ordered to raise the blockade with the Brest fleet to allow smaller French squadrons to make their way to the Caribbean. Willaumez, with eight ships-of-the-line and two frigates, did chase off the British ships from Lorient. However, poor weather delayed the French squadron's departure until late February, and that would prove to be too late. As three French frigates tried to sail out, they were intercepted by a British squadron of three ships-of-the-line and forced to accept a fight at Les Sables-d'Olonne. Remarkably, the much smaller French frigates fought off the British warships and survived the battle, though at the cost of such irreparable damage that they were subsequently decommissioned.

Willaumez, meanwhile, sailed to Rochefort, where he found the local squadron ravaged by sickness and incapable of sailing out. The subsequent arrival of a large British fleet under James Gambier meant Willaumez was trapped in Rochefort. With General Moore's expedition already in Portugal and preparing for advance into Spain, the British Admiralty was very concerned that the concentration of the French fleet at Rochefort might affect military operations in the Iberian Peninsula. Consequently, the First Lord of the Admiralty, Lord Mulgrave, urged an attack on the French fleet by means of "fireships," which were packed tightly with explosives. Gambier opposed the plan, regarding fireships as "a horrible and anti-Christian mode of warfare."[48] His subordinate Thomas Lord Cochrane, a man of daredevil courage, embraced the plan and was given twenty-one such ships.[49] On the evening of April 11, 1809, despite hard winds and high seas, Cochrane sailed with his ships into Basque Roads, a sheltered bay northwest of Rochefort, where he attacked the French fleet. Although the French had been alerted to the British attack, Admiral Allemand, who had earlier replaced Willaumez, was unable to stop four of the British fireships from breaking the mile-long boom of heavy spars and chains that he had placed to protect the fleet. To Cochrane's consternation, however the fuses, which had been intended to burn for fifteen minutes, lasted little more than half that time, causing the fireships to blow up prematurely, filling the air with shells, grenades, and rockets but largely missing their targets. Still, they caused considerable indirect damage by spreading panic among the French crews, who attempted to escape the tight confines of the bay. In the ensuing confusion, most of the French ships drifted ashore, so that at daylight on the morning of April 12 the whole of their squadron, with the exception of two French warships, was helplessly aground.[50] Cochrane signaled Gambier to launch an attack, and by afternoon on that same day, the British warships joined him in capturing and destroying four French ships-of-the-line and one frigate—but Gambier's irresolution allowed the rest of the enemy fleet to survive.[51] The Battle of the Basque Roads was a key British victory, even if it fell far short of its intended goal, which was the destruction of the entire French fleet. In the words of British naval historian Noel Mostert, the battle revealed a dual nature of the Royal Navy: "Here one saw the old navy, never lacking valour, but deep set in its cautions, its imbued hesitation before the price and penalties of risk which might chance a national setback and a ruined reputation.... Here, too, was the entrenched permanence of acrimonious rivalry, the jealousies of opportunity and advancement, the ever-simmering hatred by one of being passed over by another, and on top of it all even a showing of the rising antipathy between the evangelical and the secular. But fortunately here, too, was Cochrane's example of Nelsonian daring and initiative."[52]

Building upon the naval successes of 1809, the British switched back to the West Indies, where in January 1810 they launched a full-scale invasion of Guadeloupe. The French general Manuel Ernouf held out for a couple of weeks before surrendering on February 6. From Guadeloupe, the British swept through the island of St. Martin and the Dutch colonies of St. Eustatius and Saba. By the end of 1810, the French and their allies had lost all their West Indian colonial possessions.

As excruciating as the loss of France's Caribbean colonies was, Napoleon focused on the far more important task of building up his navy. Losses that the French fleets had suffered in 1808-1810 were soon offset by new constructions. The French fleet at Toulon steadily increased to twenty-four ships-of-the-line (six of them 130-gun warships) that exploited local conditions to conduct almost daily exercises, often venturing as far as eight leagues from the port.[53] In late 1811 British admiral Edward Pellew, commander in chief of the Mediterranean Fleet, noted in a letter home that "I have never seen a French fleet in one half the order of the Toulon one is. They have, I am sorry to say, adopted too many of our arrangements.... They also keep everyone on board so that French officers are now of necessity obliged to find their amusement in their duty; and become acquainted with their people. Their ships are magnificent."[54] Shipbuilding continued at a fast pace at other ports, including Venice, where four 74-gun warships were built and five more were under construction, so by the end of the war France had thirty ships-of-the-line ready in the Mediterranean Sea, with another twelve or so nearing completion.

In the Atlantic, Napoleon prudently shifted the center of French naval operations away from Brest, where timber supplies had been largely exhausted and the British were in the best position to keep watch from Plymouth, to bases in the south (L'Orient and Rochefort) and the north (Cherbourg). Between 1808 and 1812 he embarked on a massive expansion of shipbuilding facilities at Antwerp, intending to establish a winter anchorage for no fewer than ninety warships (with Antwerp and Flushing holding fifty warships and Terneuse the remaining forty) and capable of departing twenty fully loaded ships on a single tide. The imperial authorities encountered many challenges in bringing such dreams to fruition. The work at Flushing had to be started all over in 1810 after the British expedition to Walcheren destroyed the newly built facilities. Meanwhile, the construction work at Terneuse was complicated by the local soil, which was poor and proved incapable of supporting the necessary foundations for shipbuilding. Nevertheless, by the end of the war Antwerp boasted some of the best naval facilities in Europe and was capable of building fifteen ships at one time. Further north Napoleon supervised the improvements at the Dutch ports of Rotterdam and Amsterdam, which collectively produced more than a dozen warships.

All this activity meant that in the foreseeable future Napoleon could hope for near parity with the Royal Navy, at least in the number of ships-of-the-line. This balance of force tilted in favor of the French when one accounted for firepower, since French had built at least half a dozen 130-gun warships and none that had fewer than 74 guns; Britain, on the other hand, had no ships of more than 120 guns and quite a few under 74.[55] Napoleon's decision to invade Russia therefore came at a fortunate hour for Britain. The Royal Navy was stretched to the limit, forced to undertake operations not only in the Baltic and Mediterranean Seas but also in the Atlantic, Indian and Pacific Oceans. Had Napoleon focused his efforts on the Peninsular affairs and gained sufficient superiority at sea, the struggle for Europe might have had a different outcome for France. By building up his navy in well-protected harbors, he could have prepared for a day when his fleet would be ready to challenge the Royal Navy on the sea. As it was, preparations for the invasion of Russia had first slowed and later completely stopped work in the French dockyards, as shipwrights and sailors were conscripted to reinforce the French army fighting for the survival of the empire.

CHAPTER 19

Britain's Eastern Empire, 1800–1815

INDIA HAS BEEN DESCRIBED by nineteenth-century contemporaries as the "jewel in the crown" of the British Empire. The vast subcontinent was the most valuable of British possessions, serving both as a source of seemingly inexhaustible natural resources and as an immense market for British goods. The growth of Britain's commerce with India and the enormous profits derived from it played a decisive role in Britain's emergence as the great power. Revenues transferred from India were reinvested in other economic enterprises, including the factories that later underpinned British economic might and sustained British military power, most famously the Royal Navy, which successfully defended the nation's interests around the globe. Without India there probably would have been no British Empire.[1]

Victorian historian J. R. Seeley famously argued that Britain's empire in India was acquired "in a fit of absence of mind," but there was nothing accidental about British conquests.[2] They were brought about by a potent mix of political hubris, "precautionary" occupations, direct intervention, and, above all, robust economic appetites.[3] Many of them were the result of the actions of the British East India Company, a monopolistic joint stock venture founded in London in 1600. The BEIC received trading concessions from the Mughal emperors of India and set up its first trading posts in the subcontinent at the start of the seventeenth century. During the course of the next century and a half, it exploited the weakening of the Mughal Empire and moved beyond its original commercial activities to pursue a political and military agenda that attempted to establish a strong polity in India. This entailed far more than the preservation of trade and marked the BEIC's gradual shift from a commercial focus to a military focus.[4] British historian Timothy H. Parsons rightly observes that "the Company's directors in London never planned to

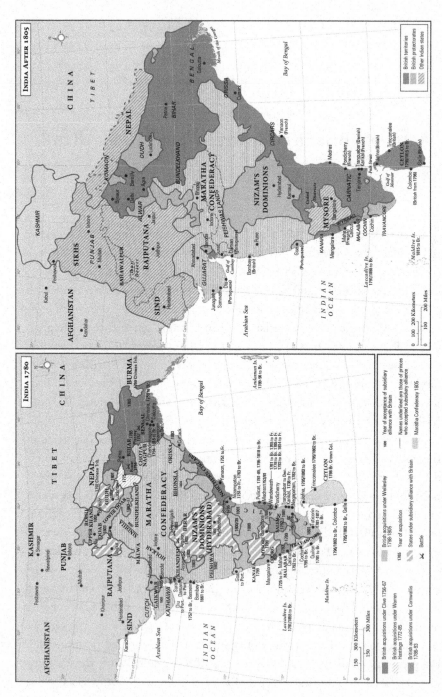

Map 22: India, 1780–1805

acquire an empire, but they were powerless to prevent their opportunistic employees from parasitizing Asian imperial systems."[5] By the second half of the eighteenth century, the BEIC, largely by force and subversion, dismantled and appropriated existing commercial relationships and political and cultural networks, preparing the way for the eventual conquest of India.[6]

Early modern India was a sophisticated civilization with some 150 million inhabitants, nearly a fifth of the world's population at the time. But it was not, in the Western sense at least, a single nation. The Mughal dynasty, which came to power in the sixteenth century, governed a vast array of states with a congeries of ethnic groups and religions. The empire reached its height in the seventeenth century and then, after the death of the last great emperor, Aurangzeb, in 1707, suffered from political turmoil, social unrest, and sectarian violence. The Mughal emperors continued to sit on the famed jewel-encrusted Peacock Throne, but their authority was increasingly circumscribed by the rival kingdoms and rebellious warlords that sprang up throughout the Indian subcontinent. At the same time, Europeans began to intervene more forcefully into Indian politics, manipulating and exploiting rivalries between Indian states and slowly building up alliances to secure their own political and commercial advantages.

The BEIC proved to be particularly adept at establishing and extending its presence in India. The turning point in this process was the Seven Years' War, during which Siraj-ud-Daula, the *nawab* of Bengal (in northeastern India), captured Calcutta, the key British outpost in India, and brought "an unwilling foreign trading company into the perilous game of Indian power politics."[7] Under the leadership of Governor General Robert Clive (1725–1774), the BEIC defeated Siraj-ud-Daula and his French allies at Plassey, laid the foundation for its rule in Bengal, and steadily expanded its authority to other parts of India.[8] The Company's increasing military commitments and concomitant financial strains soon compelled its leadership to solicit the help of the British state, which resulted in greater government involvement in and control over the entire organization. The Regulating Act of 1773 and the East India Company Act of 1784, occasioned by the company's misconduct in India, brought about British government's supervision over the BEIC and established a dual system of control.[9] The Company remained in charge of commerce and day-to-day administration, but important political matters were reserved to the Board of Control, which included members of the British government. The principal object of the 1784 reform was "to take from the Company the entire management of the territorial possessions and the political government of the country." The board was in a position to direct "what political objects the Company's servants were to pursue."[10]

Furthermore, the Declaratory Act of 1788 granted the Board of Control power to send Company troops to India without regard to the wishes of the directors. These developments were of great consequence because they effectively turned the BEIC into the main instrument of British imperial policy in India and transformed its Indian possessions from an enterprise that some Britons considered as morally questionable into the exact opposite—a civilizing mission. This change occurred concurrently with the British state's centralization, with industrialization, and with the consolidation of nationalism, all of which helped create a new narrative of imperialism, one that justified British sovereignty and economic domination in India.[11]

The American Revolutionary War briefly halted Britain's Indian overtures. Having lost an empire in the West, the British made up for it by gaining new domains in the East. Flush with profits and maintaining its own armed forces, the BEIC fought a series of wars—most notably the Anglo-Mysore Wars and the long Anglo-Maratha Wars—that extended its influence and administrative system to many parts of the Indian subcontinent. Success in these wars allowed the BEIC to bring new administrative order (as well as social and cultural changes) to a region that lacked strong central control. Still, the question remains: how did a few thousand foreigners from a small windswept island—Britain's territory was about 120,000 square miles, compared to over 1 million square miles under Mughal control—in northwestern Europe succeed in conquering and ruling this distant and vast subcontinent? The rise and growth of British power in India have been long debated. Early advocates of British colonialism in India credited it to character. Others ascribed Britain's success to the superiority of its arms. The reality, however, is more complex, and the reasons the British managed it can be explained by a combination of long- and short-term factors.

Compared to other parts of the world, European states were generally more mobilized for warfare and more ruthless in prosecuting it. Europe's close confines compelled all competing political units to innovate constantly in order to deal with different terrains and climates as well to ensure technological parity with their rivals. Over time more efficient financing and taxation emerged in Europe to deal with the endemic wars. In Asia, meanwhile, the great empires, such as the Mughal of India, felt less military pressure to adapt and could afford to remain indifferent to modernization. India was spared the vicious wars of religion and trade that afflicted Europe until the eighteenth century. As British historian C. A. Bayly astutely observed, "In some ways, Asia's relative peace in the seventeenth century was its undoing."[12]

It is sometimes argued that inadequate armies—that is, a lack of trained infantry and the weakness of indigenous artillery—placed the Indian states at a great disadvantage to the British.[13] While partly true, this argument ignores fairly significant military developments in India in the eighteenth and early-nineteenth centuries. Recent studies have shown that the technological gap between Indian and British forces narrowed considerably by the end of the eighteenth century. This was largely the result of India's borrowing European technology as well as recruitment of European (mostly French) officers and mercenaries to train its troops. A number of rulers, including Tippu Sultan of Mysore and Ranjit Singh of Punjab, made considerable progress in improving their armed forces and reforming supply and ammunition systems. Indeed, popular perceptions of the British expansion in India tend to overlook the fact that the British were not always successful on the battlefield. In 1779 a British army suffered a setback at the hands of the Marathas at Wadgaon, while a year later Haidar Ali of Mysore invaded the Carnatic and destroyed a British force under William Baillie at Pollilur (Pollilore).[14] The latter battle remains one of the most crushing British defeats in India, redressed only through skillful diplomacy that divided the BEIC's foes.

The late eighteenth century witnessed continued improvement in Indian infantry and artillery. British officers noted as much in the Battles of Buxar and Patna in 1764. Tippu Sultan launched a major military reorganization of the Mysore forces, which included a large number of light cavalry. This posed a serious threat to the British, who ultimately prevailed only after adapting their tactics and seeking help from the Maratha cavalry. The performance of the Maratha forces during the Second Anglo-Maratha War (1803–1805) had also revealed a high degree of infantry and artillery capability; after the Battle of Laswari in 1803, the British general Gerard Lake, who had fought the French in Flanders in 1793, was stunned by the viciousness of the Maratha fighting, commenting, "I never was in so severe a business in my life or anything like it, and pray to God, I never may be in such a situation again."[15]

Moreover, the British army did not operate alone, and its continued presence in the Indian subcontinent was dependent on the Royal Navy's control of the sea. The unquestioned supremacy of its sea power meant that the British could come and go as they wished, repair their losses, and attack the Indian coastline at will. The BEIC was naturally attentive to any threats to its naval dominance. For example, in February 1756, a British squadron under Rear Admiral Charles Watson raided Gheria, a small stronghold on the west coast of India, after it became clear that the local ruler was building up his fleet, one capable of posing some threat to the British naval presence. As British historian Jeremy Black points out, this victory largely put an end to the development of Indian naval power. For decades to come, British squadrons continued to patrol the seas around India, destroying native fleets, maintaining the imperial lifeline, and allowing for a sustained expansion in India.[16]

If there was any single factor decisive to British colonialism, it was sea power. Without it dominion in Asia would have been simply impossible. But sea power in itself could not guarantee that success. In the first half of the eighteenth century, India underwent a struggle for political power that all but destroyed central authority. The invasion by Nadir Shah of Iran in 1739 and incursions by the Afghani tribesmen of Ahmad Shah Abdali in the 1750s and 1760s sped up the breakup of the Mughal Empire and the assertion of autonomy (if not outright independence) by *subahdars* (provincial governors). Had the Mughal Empire overcome these difficulties and consolidated its authority, the BEIC would have faced a much more formidable enemy in the latter half of the century. As it was, the subcontinent was not a centralized state and lacked not only central political leadership but also the sense of a single identity and a common cause. Indian troops were devoted not to their nation (since there was no such concept as an Indian nation) but to their leaders, whose political ambitions, rivalries, and jealousies sustained continued civil strife in the subcontinent. This meant that the BEIC never faced a united front of Indian forces and could use coercive action, threats, and diplomacy to prevent local rulers from putting up a united struggle.

Equally valuable to the British was the civil discipline and talents of the BEIC's officials, both senior and secondary. Through their esprit de corps, pride of service, and dedication to a cause, they played a decisive role in shaping the British colonialism in India. This is not to say that there was no mismanagement, personal corruption, or abuses by BEIC officials—the trial of Governor-General Warren Hastings between 1788 and 1795 made abundantly clear that there was.[17] But BEIC leaders such as Clive, Cornwallis, and Wellesley skillfully exploited local rivalries within and between the Indian states to successfully advance the Company's economic and political interests in the region. They might have gone no farther their Portuguese, Dutch, or French counterparts had it not been for the military and financial resources at their disposal, the result of a flourishing British economy and the nascent Industrial Revolution. The BEIC exploited the fact that the Indian subcontinent, with its agricultural subsistence economy, could not contend with the burgeoning British capitalist system. The divided Indian states could never equal Britain's resources, which allowed the BEIC to maintain significant military forces, repair their losses, and, increasingly, to resort to raising armies of Indian sepoys trained in the European manner.[18] Such armed forces were sufficiently effective on the battlefield and, more important, cost less in pay than regular European troops. Consequently, the costs of expanding the company's domain remained relatively low.

The BEIC's use of subsidiary alliances—a type of alliance between a dominant nation and a nation that it dominates—underscores this point. In the mid-eighteenth century, Governor-General Clive sought to secure power in India while minimizing the responsibilities the BEIC had to shoulder. He preferred an indirect approach, one that secured actual power for the BEIC while leaving titular authority to native rulers. He began this policy by placing his ally Mir Jafar as the *nawab* of Bengal. In return, Mir Jafar pledged to provide financial support to the BEIC. As the BEIC's influence grew, more Indian states (especially those that were smaller and more vulnerable to indigenous warfare) entered into such subsidiary arrangements, which meant a growing loss of Indian autonomy. The essence of the system lay in the BEIC's pledge to protect a given state from any external dangers and internal disorders in return for control of its foreign relations. For this purpose, the local ruler agreed not to enter into alliance with any other power without the BEIC's permission, thus binding himself irrevocably to British power. Indian rulers also agreed to accept a subsidiary force of Company troops, who were usually stationed in a cantonment near the state capital, and to pay for their maintenance—providing, as it were, the means of their own coercion. Frequently, in lieu of payments, these rulers forfeited part of their territory to the BEIC, which further increased the company's hold over the region.

Naturally, one may wonder why the Muslim and Hindu rulers failed to foresee the risks they were running in becoming the Company's allies. Partly this was due to the BEIC's leaders, who, as noted, were generally capable, determined, and risk-taking, and who frequently ignored interference from distant Britain. Although there was considerable squabbling between the BEIC's offices in Bombay, Madras, and Bengal, the company nevertheless was a much more centralized and consolidated institution that any of the Indian states it faced, and at key moments its offices tended to cast their rivalries aside and mobilize necessary resources.

The Indian states, on the other hand, faced considerable challenges in effectively competing with the BEIC. Understanding the need for stronger armed forces, Indian rulers sought to increase revenues from every social group. This transition from traditional to European-style state forms was not smooth, however, and generated many frictions and conflicts—which, of course, the BEIC then exploited to its own advantage. Amid intermittent warfare between regional rulers, a subsidiary alliance with the BEIC could deliver a crucial advantage over a rival. They could do this and seem to save face, for while the company's governors-general might have had more political power than some Indian rulers, they made no display of royal trappings or behavior. Until 1857 the BEIC continued to recognize the sovereignty of the Mughal emperor and claimed to be acting in his interest. The Company made no claims to titular authority and did not interfere with native law, religion, and tradition, which made its authority more palatable to some indigenous elites.

In practice, all of this meant that the BEIC could use Indian resources and manpower to overcome Indian resistance. This was not always a straightforward process. In 1770s, the BEIC unsuccessfully meddled in the Maratha civil war and suffered setbacks in the First Anglo-Maratha War (1775–1782). Shortly afterward it allied itself with the Marathas but let this founder with the rise of Haidar Ali of Mysore, who allied with the French, the Marathas, and Hyderabad. To contain the British, Haidar Ali set out to beat the BEIC at its own game, improving his administration, reforming the army, and exploiting France's rivalry with Britain. He campaigned successfully in the Carnatic, but his death in 1784 led to the collapse of the alliance between Mysore, Hyderabad, and the Marathas. Charles Cornwallis, the new governor-general of the BEIC (1786–1793), formed an alliance against Mysore with Hyderabad, and after the Marathas joined the Tripartite Alliance of the British, Hyderabad, and the Marathas in 1790, the British position in India was greatly bolstered, since the BEIC could rely now on support from these two allies against Mysore. It took three sustained campaigns to bring Mysore to heel but ultimately half of its dominions ended up in the hands of the BEIC and its allies.

At this junction in history an important change occurred in British policy in India. There were two principal causes. First, there was a growing belief within the British government and the BEIC that only British control of India could end the constant wars on the subcontinent and create satisfactory conditions for commerce and trade. A greater cause was the transformation of European politics in the wake of the French Revolutionary Wars. The French invasion of Egypt raised the prospect of a direct threat to India, where the French could find many to welcome them, not least Tippu Sultan, who succeeded Haidar Ali in Mysore and was eager to see the British gone. The appointment of Richard Wellesley, the Duke of Wellington's elder brother, as the governor general of the BEIC marked the decisive moment in the rise of the British dominion in India. As discussed in Chapter 5, Wellesley closely followed the revolutionary turmoil that had tied down much of Europe, and he was convinced that this created a moment for the British to consolidate their position in India, whose vast resources could then serve British interests worldwide. Wellesley used the fear of the French as a cover for his own imperialist designs and as a justification for British expansion. His treatment of the Indian states marked a discernible change of attitude toward the subsidiary system. Earlier BEIC leaders had used it as a defensive instrument to safeguard the company's interests and possessions. But in the hands of

Wellesley, these subsidiary alliances became an offensive device with which to subject independent and even friendly states to British control.

The new political reality that emerged in India between 1798 and 1805 was the result of Wellesley's avowedly imperialistic aspirations.[19] Indeed, in his vigor, decisiveness, sense of purpose, and dynamism, along with his high-handedness, impatience, and pride that verged on insolence, Wellesley came close to being a British twin to Napoleon, and one cannot but wonder what he could have accomplished had he been placed in circumstances similar to those of the First Consul. His thoughts and actions revealed him to be an astute statesman rather than a mere administrator, and his chief accomplishment was the elevation of the BEIC to a position of paramount power in India.[20] The once-mighty Mughal empire was all but shattered as a political entity, though it had been a major part of Wellesley's policy to preserve and utilize its vestiges. The Mughal emperor, Shah Alam, was therefore established at Delhi under British protection, with considerable provision made for his dignity but none for his political authority.

Another central Wellesley legacy was a vast increase in the BEIC army, which expanded to more than 190,000 men during his tenure, making it the largest European-trained and -led army in Asia.[21] It constituted a military presence that no other European power could rival. Only 13 percent of its troops were European; the vast majority were sepoys, and these native soldiers remained the basis of British military power in the east for the rest of the nineteenth century. Equally important was the role of the Royal Navy, which was deployed in the "Eastern Seas" on a previously unprecedented scale. Led by capable and independent-minded captains such as Commodore Peter Rainier, the British fleet was instrumental in consolidating the British presence in Indian coastal waters as well as establishing it in new areas (the Dutch Spice Islands in 1796 and the Red Sea in 1801).[22]

Yet for all his successes, Wellesley was ultimately removed from his post. All of his major policies were directed at achieving two interrelated objects: securing British predominance in India and using India's vast resources in containing the menace of France's global ambitions. Whether or not he genuinely believed that the French would march overland to India, Wellesley exploited the threat of overland invasions to disguise his own empire-building. In the period 1798–1800 the British cabinet and the Company directors repeatedly acquiesced to Wellesley's aggressive policies because they believed that the French threat to India was real and immediate. But the situation changed dramatically over the next few years. When the war with France resumed in 1803, Napoleon was threatening Britain itself. "However jealous France is of our power in the East, and however steady she may be in her purpose of aiming at positions, from which she might one day hope to shake that power," wrote Lord Castlereagh, president of the Board of Control, to Wellesley in March 1803, "I cannot persuade myself that she has, or she can have for a length of time, the means to attempt any direct attack against possessions so defended as ours are."[23] By 1805, British cabinet members were dismayed that Wellesley's Indian policies required precious resources that they simply could not spare; as one British historian aptly noted, "Britain could not afford an indefinite Indian war in the year of Trafalgar and Austerlitz."[24] The BEIC was, first and foremost, a commercial organization that was expected to produce a profit. One can imagine how exasperated Company shareholders were to observe the mounting expenses associated with the Mysore and Maratha Wars, which almost doubled the Company's debt. The prospect of a prolonged war after British setbacks at the hands of Holkar prompted them to seek Wellesley's removal.

The BEIC spent the next decade dealing with Wellesley's legacy. The directors insisted on financial retrenchment—no further costly acquisitions of territory and no entanglements with states outside the existing borders of British India. Wellesley's immediate successor, Lord Cornwallis, was tasked with opening negotiations with Holkar to end the Maratha War, but he died after holding office for a little over two months. Still, as long as he could hold a quill, Cornwallis busied himself reversing his predecessor's gains, a policy that continued under Sir George Barlow, who succeeded provisionally to the post of governor-general in 1805. Understanding that the directors felt unprepared to undertake imperial responsibilities, Barlow sought a reduction of the company's commitments, and his tenure saw the BEIC's withdrawal from central India, where the Maratha rulers of Holkar and Sindhia enjoyed greater freedom in ravaging the Rajput states, which had been abandoned by the BEIC despite earlier commitments. Barlow's guarded policies and success in converting a financial deficit into a sizable surplus were welcomed by the Company shareholders. But they failed to satisfy the British government, which appointed a more dynamic governor-general, Gilbert Elliot-Murray-Kynynmound, Lord Minto, in 1807.

The state of India when Minto arrived in Calcutta on July 31, 1807, was precarious, not only because of continuing political turmoil in central India but also because of new challenges to British power. Napoleon's recent string of successes—military triumphs over Prussia in 1806 and Russia in 1807 and diplomatic overtures to the Ottomans and Persia—had made a renewed French threat to British India seem acute and immediate. The Continental System, inaugurated in late 1806, challenged Britain's economic interests on the continent, while French privateers were enjoying some success in

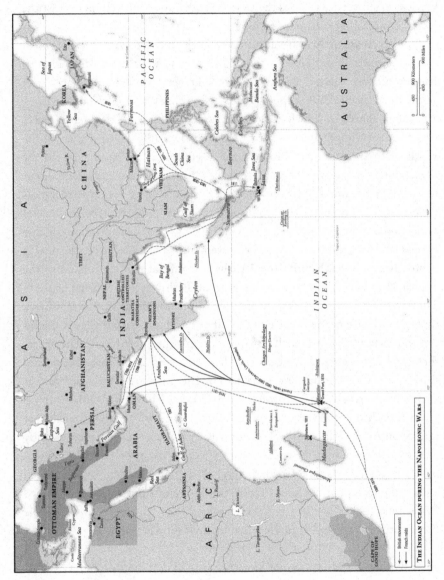

Map 23: The Indian Ocean During the Napoleonic Wars

disrupting British trade in the Indian Ocean. In India itself, the Vellore Mutiny of sepoy troops (1806) revealed deep-seated resentments toward the British, a foretaste of fifty years later, when the major rebellion took place.[25] A year later, the states of Travancore and Cochin, exasperated by the financial burdens of subsidiary treaties they had accepted, rose in rebellion against the BEIC, though they were suppressed.

The six years of Minto's administration coincided with the height of the Napoleonic Wars. The Treaty of Tilsit (1807) and the resulting Franco-Russian alliance revived British fears of a French-sponsored Russian attack across the Central Asian steppes. At the same time, with General Gardanne arriving in Tehran to deepen Franco-Persian cooperation and the French offices engaged in military surveys of Iran, many at the BEIC believed that, in the words of British diplomat Mountstuart Elphinstone, "it appeared as if the French intended to carry the war into Asia."[26] Consequently, Lord Minto spent next seven years working steadily to counter these threats. He pursued a multipronged foreign policy that combined diplomatic overtures with forceful projection of power across much of South Asia.[27] To guard against a possible French land attack, Minto dispatched several missions to secure northwestern approaches to India. Elphinstone led the first official British mission to the Afghan kingdom, where he met Shah Shuja at Peshawar in the spring of 1809. The two sides negotiated a treaty of "friendship and union" that established a defensive alliance between the British and the Afghans, with the latter pledging to block any joint French advance through their territories. The agreement proved to be short-lived; shortly thereafter the shah was overthrown and driven into exile.[28] At the same time, two British missions to Iran also brought some dividends. Sir John Malcolm and Sir Harford Jones were able to counteract French influence and sign a treaty of alliance with Fath Ali Shah that formed an Anglo-Iranian alliance against Russia, involving an annual subsidy of £120,000 for as long as that war lasted. Also in 1809, another BEIC diplomat, the young Charles Metcalfe, traveled to Punjab, where he negotiated with Ranjit Singh of the Sikh Empire the Treaty of Amritsar, which defined British and Sikh spheres of influence, secured Sikh support against possible French attack, and settled Anglo-Sikh relations for a generation.

———∞◦§◦∞———

Both Barlow and Minto sought to secure British dominion in India by neutralizing the remaining French outposts in the Indian Ocean and beyond. Scattered throughout the Eastern Seas, the British warships did their best to protect the merchant marine while hunting down the French and their allies. These efforts occasionally resulted in British intrusions into the Asian powers that had long been suspicious of European presence in the region.

By 1800 maritime commerce had connected much of the Indian Ocean and western Pacific basins into vibrant and fluid trade networks, with East Africa, India, China, Japan, Korea, and Southeast Asian states trading extensively with one another.[29] Having appeared in the sixteenth century, Europeans—first the Portuguese, next the Dutch, and then the British—had successfully penetrated this East Asian maritime world and were not averse to using force to gain access to trade routes. They faced serious hurdles. European products were not in demand in Asia, and European merchants were compelled to supply large quantities of bullion, which constrained European commerce. European trade often went hand in hand with missionary activity. Priests from the Jesuits and other religious orders sought new converts to the Christian faith overseas, activity that caused considerable anxiety in many parts of East Asia.

Japan became the first to limit interaction with Europeans. With a population of some 30 million people in 1800, Japan was three times larger than Britain. In the early seventeenth century, after prolonged feudal strife, the realm came under the government of the Tokugawa shoguns (*bakufu*), who brought some economic and agricultural prosperity but restricted contact with the outside world. Already suspicious of European missionary activities, the Tokugawas came to associate Christianity with domestic disorder after Christian samurai sided with the *bakufu*'s political opponents. In 1614 the government issued the Christian Expulsion Edict, which outlawed Christianity and expelled all Christians and foreigners except for the Dutch, who were allowed to maintain a small trading operation in Nagasaki. For more than two hundred years after that, the Dutch emporium served as Japan's window to the outside world. Once a year Dutch East India Company (DEIC) merchants arrived from Java to conduct business.[30] The Dutch struggled to develop their trade in Japan but continued to maintain it largely because of the earnings it yielded to individual participants rather than for any greater advantages it might provide.[31]

The British were well aware of this, which is why the BEIC did not attempt to penetrate the Japanese market. The Napoleonic Wars changed this rationale. The Dutch Republic was now under firm French control, and British warships therefore targeted Dutch shipping in East Asia. Between 1795 and 1806 the Royal Navy maintained a loose blockade around Dutch colonies and routinely captured merchant ships. The Dutch responded by chartering neutral ships to freight cargo between their possessions, but in 1807, as part of their larger struggle against Napoleon's Continental System, the British targeted neutral shipping and instituted an even tighter blockade of the Dutch colonies.[32] Although the Dutch did not own Dejima—a small fan-shaped man-made island built by local merchants in the Bay of Nagasaki in 1634—the British regarded it as a Dutch possession. In mid-August 1808 the residents of Dejima were thrilled to learn that a sail had been observed on the horizon. This arrival was later in the season than normal, but neither Japanese authorities nor DEIC representatives suspected anything.[33] As usual, Dutch representatives rowed out to welcome the visiting ship. Instead of finding their fellow compatriots, they were greeted by Fleetwood Pellew, the twenty-seven-year-old son of a British admiral and captain of the British frigate *Phaeton*, who had disguised his warship as a Dutch trading vessel in an attempt to seize any traders licensed to dock at Dejima, a stratagem that the British had already tried once in Manila (Philippines) in January 1798.[34] Pellew captured the Dutch representatives; their Japanese escorts managed to escape by jumping overboard. Not finding any Dutch vessels, Pellew demanded that water and provisions be delivered to his ship, threatening to hang his captives and set fire to all the Japanese vessels and Chinese junks.[35] Unable to do anything against the British warship, the Japanese authorities were forced to satisfy the British demands, and the *Phaeton* left two days later.

Although a minor incident, the Nagasaki affair had ramifications for Japan. The Japanese government was incensed at Britain's insolence, which at the very least violated a Japanese law prohibiting ships from leaving the port of Nagasaki without the approval of the local governor. Yet that paled in comparison to the humiliation that the *bakufu* felt at their inability to counter this intrusion. The Japanese coastal batteries had failed to identity a foreign vessel; in the event of a direct confrontation, their antiquated guns certainly would have been obliterated by a first-class British warship. Equally mishandled was the Japanese domainal defense system. Instead of the 1,000 soldiers that were required, fewer than 60 men were on duty as the result of complacency, fiscal difficulties, and the Japanese assumption that no ships would arrive in the off-season. The Nagasaki magistrate did call up some 8,000 troops and forty ships to confront the British, but they arrived long after the *Phaeton* had departed.[36]

The Nagasaki affair thus revealed the more broadly structural and organizational roots of Tokugawa military weakness. The main problem lay not so much in Japan's technological inadequacies as in fundamental problems in its civil and military administrations. Following the attack, the *bakufu* ordered the strengthening of coastal defenses and later issued a law, Muninen-uchikowashi-rei, that called for the use of force to drive foreign vessels from the Japanese coastal waters.[37] Perhaps equally significant was that the *Phaeton* incident made the Japanese government keen on learning about the outside world. The *bakufu* ordered the training of official interpreters in English and Russian; in 1814, the Dutch interpreter Motoki Shozaemon produced the first English-Japanese dictionary.[38]

This affair was not an isolated case of a European attack on Japan, as it occurred amid growing Russian pressures. Unlike other European powers, Russia was a latecomer to Japan, the first Russian ships appearing in the territorial waters of Japan only in the early 1700s.[39] The Russians had made several attempt to open trade with Japan but were habitually rebuffed. In the late eighteenth century, concerned by British voyages of exploration that seemed to threaten its interests in the Far East, Russia sought to shore up its "indisputable" sovereignty over not only Alaska but the islands lying off the Eurasian mainland.[40] In December 1786 Empress Catherine II decreed that Russian warships, "armed in the same manner as those used by the English Captain Cook," should be dispatched around the Cape of Good Hope to protect Russian possessions in the North Pacific.

Russia's encroachment on Japan entered a new stage when Emperor Alexander sent Nicholas Rezanov, a veteran of the Russian fur trade who avidly promoted Russian colonization in the Far East, to negotiate a commercial treaty with Japan. Rezanov reached Japan in late 1804. His abrasive and haughty character failed to endear him to his hosts.[41] After months of waiting, he left Japan empty-handed, enraged by his treatment by the Japanese and threatening that the Russian emperor would teach the Japanese proper respect for his personage.[42] Indeed, Rezanov returned with a vengeance in 1806, when he waged a self-declared war on Japan, raiding and burning Japanese settlements on the islands of Sakhalin and the Kuriles, and threatening to ravage all of northern Japan if the Japanese persisted in refusing Russian trade.[43]

The Russian attacks jolted the Japanese, who had become accustomed to the peace and stability of the Tokugawa regime. They reacted by increasing the number of soldiers defending the northern provinces, strengthening the central administration of Sakhalin and neighboring islands, and expanding the *uchi narai* system, which sanctioned firing on and driving away foreign vessels.[44] The *Phaeton* incident occurred while the Japanese government was still reeling from Rezanov's actions, and it responded to the event with some of the most substantive Japanese military reforms of the nineteenth century.[45] The Japanese reinforced their coastal defenses, revised the system for verifying incoming vessels, and established new signal networks to improve long-range communications and facilitate a faster response. These reforms, as promising as they were, proved ineffective in the long term because they focused primarily on improving infrastructure, instead of a more comprehensive overhaul of a defensive system that continued to suffer from a lack of codified procedures and a clear division of responsibility.

Despite being the primary source of trade in Asia, China, even more than Japan, was long reluctant to open up to the West. The imperial government carefully regulated foreign maritime trade through the special "Canton System," which required all foreign merchants to reside in the southern city of Canton, where they could only buy from and sell to the local merchant monopoly, the *cohong*, which was able to fix prices arbitrarily. Dissatisfied with these restrictions, Europeans sought to circumvent the system. Their requests for greater diplomatic engagement failed to make any impression on the Chinese emperors, who had long used trade as a political tool to reward or punish their satellite states. Europe was no exception. Europeans wanted Chinese products, while China wanted hardly anything from Europe, exporting more goods and inventions to Europe than it received. The imbalance of trade between East and West was made worse by Chinese insistence on being paid in bullion, which had been intermittently drained from the West since Roman times.

In the eighteenth century it was Britain's turn to endure the pains of a growing trade imbalance that was caused by its seemingly insatiable demand for tea, porcelain, and silk. To narrow this trade deficit, the British sought to find products that could be sold to the Chinese, an effort that contributed to the development of illegal traffic in the one commodity Chinese did want: opium. Starting in 1773 the BEIC had a monopoly on the manufacture of the drug, which was sold to various smugglers and merchants. By the start of the nineteenth century, vast quantities of the drug were sold over the sides of European ships in the Canton River.

British merchants, especially the influential supercargoes, continually lobbied the government to seek a new understanding with China, one that would revise the Canton System.[46] Many of them did not see why China should be able to dictate the terms of trade with Britain, which in their minds was the preeminent European power. In 1787 Charles Cathcart was instructed to negotiate with the Qianlong emperor (r. 1735–1799) for permission to use Macao (or Amoy, modern-day Ziamen) as the entrepôt for British commerce; the British envoy, however, died en route. Six years later King George III sanctioned a diplomatic mission led by George Macartney to negotiate the relaxation of trade restrictions on British merchants in Canton, to secure the opening of new ports for British trade in China, and to establish a permanent embassy in Beijing. On this first major British embassy to China, Macartney was accompanied by an entourage of more than eighty people, who brought with them hundreds of cases packed with British goods—clocks, telescopes, globes, plate glass, Wedgwood pottery, woolen cloth, carpets, and many other items—that they hoped would impress the Chinese and help open the vast Chinese market to British commerce. Yet the mission failed to achieve its objectives. Macartney refused to perform the kowtow—the traditional kneeling on both knees and bowing the head to the ground in front of the Chinese emperor—and the Qianlong emperor denied him a formal audience at the Forbidden City in Beijing. The British envoy was at last permitted to meet more informally with the emperor at a summer retreat, but no negotiations followed because the Chinese saw no merit in the British requests. As the Qianlong emperor pointed out in his formal reply, China "possesses all things in prolific abundance and lacks no product within its own borders."[47]

The British thus had no choice except to seek an arrangement with the Portuguese, who had a long-standing presence at Macao, the gateway to the great emporium of Canton (modern Guangzhou), which the British had had their eye on for decades. India's first governor-general, Warren Hastings, openly coveted Macao, which in his mind was mismanaged by Portugal: "Macao has been so neglected by the Government of Goa, that it is now the fit resort only of Vagabonds and Outcasts.... A place so little valued might perhaps be easily procured from the Court of Lisbon, and should it ever fall into the hands of an enterprising People, who knew how to extend all its advantages, we think, it would rise to a State of Splendor, never yet equaled by any Port in the East."[48] This was easier said than done. During the eighteenth century, the relations between British and Portuguese authorities in India evolved slowly. The Portuguese, unsurprisingly, resisted British penetration of the subcontinent and sought to protect their interests by supporting native powers against the BEIC. The British victories in India threatened Portuguese interests there and left them with no alternative but to forge stronger ties with the British. Francisco Antonio da Veiga Cabral, Portuguese viceroy of Goa, offered amity and cooperation to the BEIC and supported the British expedition against the French in the Red Sea in 1801.[49] The same could not be said about the Luso-British relationship in Macao, where the Portuguese were still keen on protecting their turf. Thus the Portuguese traders tended to support an Anglo-Portuguese alliance on national issues but were undeniably anti-British on local issues and commerce.[50] Even when the French invasion of Portugal left the Portuguese monarchy entirely dependent on Britain's goodwill, Portuguese authorities in Macao continued to act against British interests in China and refused to let the British use their harbor as a military anchorage.[51]

In 1801 France, supported by Spain, invaded Portugal, and the BEIC directors feared that this might lead to the French takeover of Portugal's overseas possessions. In an effort to forestall it, in March 1802 British warships delivered troops with the intention of "protecting" the small Portuguese garrison in Macao against a "possible" French invasion. When the British anchored their ships at Lintin, they discovered that the Portuguese governor of Macao, Jose Manuel Pinto, did not trust them and refused to let them in, leaving the expedition leaders in an awkward situation. The governor-general of India, Richard Wellesley, was in favor of a forceful takeover, arguing that "in the event of opposition on the part of the governor of Macao," the Portuguese colony had to be taken "by force of arms." But the Select Committee of the BEIC urged caution and a more diplomatic approach, in order to avoid confrontation with China. The Portuguese authorities of Macao understood this, and so their first decision was to protest both to the viceroy of the Liang-Guang and to the Portuguese bishop in the Chinese capital, who conveyed the news to the Jiaqing emperor (r. 1799–1820).[52] As expected, the Jiaqing emperor responded resolutely, rejecting British explanations—"We do not have to lend any credence to them because the intention of the English was no more than to take the town," was the imperial response—and demanding immediate withdrawal of British forces.[53] The British initially refused to comply, forcing the Chinese authorities to cut off their food supplies. A confrontation was averted only when the news of the signing of the Peace of Amiens reached Macao.[54]

As soon as the hostilities between France and Britain resumed in 1803, the question of what to do about the Portuguese colonies came back to the fore. For the first four years of the Napoleonic Wars, the British authorities in India "did not think Macao was in danger [of French takeover] because the Chinese would not allow the weak Portuguese to be replaced by a strong French presence."[55] But with the continued threats by French and Dutch privateers to Britain's trade, the BEIC increased patrols along the Chinese coastal areas and particularly near Canton, where the local Chinese magistrate actually requested British help in suppressing piracy.[56] This request posed a problem, since it went against the long-standing Chinese imperial injunction against any foreign military presence in Chinese coastal waters. Echoing this sentiment, one BEIC official noted that "the jealous and suspicious nature of the Chinese Government leads us to doubt whether the arrival of an English Naval Armament without the previous consent of the Chinese Government would not be highly offensive to that Government." Such healthy skepticism did not extend to Macao. Partly this was due to Napoleon's occupation of Portugal, which created a new sense of urgency in Britain to prevent the French takeover of the Portuguese colonies in Asia and led to the sending a military expedition to Macao in October 1808.[57]

Writing a few months after the expedition, the BEIC's Select Committee argued that "from the successes of the French in Europe, the exertions of their newly arrived capital force in Java, and possessing the control in Manilla, [the French threat to Macao] did not appear improbable...as this was to be accomplished with facility by the introduction of either officers or a garrison from Portugal."[58] By the late summer of 1808 the BEIC felt that the French threat to their China trade was direct and imminent; considering that it provided up to one-sixth of the entire income of the British crown, a forceful resolution was in order. Company officials were convinced that they had "no reason to apprehend any opposition on the part of the Portuguese Government but have every reason to believe that any objections or impediments on the part of the Chinese would be of a temporary nature."[59]

Lord Minto decided to act. Securing the support of the Portuguese viceroy of Goa, he dispatched a British squadron under Rear Admiral William O'Bryen Drury to East Asian waters with instructions to force Gia Long, the Nguyen emperor of Vietnam, to open his ports to British trade and then to proceed to Macao, where British troops were to be regarded as auxiliaries, assisting the Portuguese in defending this locale against French threat.[60] If the Portuguese refused, the town would have to be seized by force because of, as Drury was told, "the necessity . . . to prevent it falling into the hands of the French, which would involve in it the destruction of [British] commerce with China."[61] The British were well aware of possible Chinese resistance to their incursion but thought the prospect of cessation of the immensely lucrative trade through Canton would be worse, making the Chinese authorities more willing to compromise.[62]

Drury failed to fulfill his first task. What we presently call Vietnam has been historically divided into two: the Trinh lords ruled in the north, while the Nguyen were supreme in the south. In the late eighteenth century, during the Tay Son Rebellion, the two sides fought a prolonged conflict that ultimately brought the Nguyen to power. To prevail in this power struggle, a Nguyen prince, Nguyen Anh, sought an alliance with France, and in 1787, less than two years before the French Revolution, he signed a treaty of alliance with King Louis XVI of France, pledging to cede territory and grant concessions to the French in exchange for military support. The French monarchy collapsed before it could implement this treaty. Still, the agreement marked the starting point of French colonialism in Vietnam and the wider region. French missionary Pierre Pigneau de Behaine raised funds and organized a private venture of several French ships to sustain the Nguyen cause; French-trained military allowed Nguyen Anh to win the war and secure his power by 1802. He was the first to control the whole length of the Indochinese peninsula, and upon assuming imperial title he took the dynastic name Gia Long. The rise of the new dynasty in Vietnam coincided with the outbreak of the French Revolutionary and Napoleonic Wars in Europe. Considering the extent of French influence at the court of Gia Long, it is unsurprising that the

Royal Navy targeted the French-commanded Vietnamese merchant ships. In 1803–1804, two British envoys sought to convince Gia Long to abandon his alliance with France and open his realm to British trade; both missions failed. By 1808, the British were concerned that Napoleon might exploit Franco-Vietnamese ties to establish his presence in Southeast Asia, where he might help the Nguyen ruler build a navy that could threaten British trade in the South China Sea. Drury's mission was to prevent this from happening. Arriving in the Gulf of Tonkin, Drury tried to sail up the Red River to strike against the Vietnamese navy and force Gia Long to compromise. Yet the Vietnamese fought back, destroying several of Drury's ships and forcing the main body of the British squadron to sail on to Macao. After this setback, the British made no further attempt to intervene in Vietnam until 1822.[63]

Drury was even more unsuccessful with his second mission. He arrived in Macao in late September 1808 and immediately informed the Portuguese governor, Bernardo Aleixo de Lemos Faria, of his intention to occupy the town in order to protect it from the French. The Portuguese demurred, and the governor, having received no instructions from Lisbon, refused to accept the sanction of the Portuguese viceroy of Goa as sufficient authority for surrendering the place. He also explained that Macao's protection was the responsibility of the Chinese government, not Britain or the BEIC.[64]

Unsure whether he should call off the expedition or not, Drury sought the advice of the BEIC's Select Committee, which consisted of supercargoes and therefore possessed a better understanding of local circumstances. The committee argued in favor of a more forceful action. British supremacy on the seas ensured almost complete control of the Chinese export trade and offered the British a favorable moment to compel another round of negotiations with the Chinese imperial authorities, who might have granted more favorable terms to avoid any disruptions to their revenues. Drury consequently compelled Faria to assent to a British occupation—a Luso-British convention sanctioned the landing of some three hundred British troops in Macao on September 21.[65]

In occupying this territory, Drury ignored the fact that it belonged to China and that the Chinese had to be consulted. In effect, the British admiral was daring the Chinese, if they were serious about claiming ownership of Macao, to challenge the occupation.[66] China's response was swift and resolute. Provincial governor-general Wu Xiongguang asserted Chinese sovereignty over the region and rejected British explanations for the occupation of Macao, arguing that Drury could have easily protected the Portuguese from the alleged French threat by stationing his warships in the bay, without necessitating a military takeover. Drury refused to withdraw, claiming that his mission was to foster relations between Britain and China, "two great nations [that have] mutual interests in the friendship, peace and happiness of their people."[67] He also noted that should the mandarins foment hostilities, "nothing in his instructions prevented him from going to war with China." Infuriated by such audacious response, the Chinese provincial authorities halted all trade and negotiations until the British troops were removed.[68] In the face of what he considered temporary Chinese intransigence, Drury brought additional reinforcements to Macao, moving some 700 men to shore up the defenses and, in his words, "to pre-empt the Chinese from a feeling of success and save further embarrassments from their side."[69]

But the Chinese authorities were not bluffing. By November they had withdrawn Macao's Chinese inhabitants, closed all shops, gathered several thousand troops near Canton, and diverted dozens of junks to block the Pearl River against any movement upstream. On October 28, as the British ships tried to force their way to Canton, they encountered armed junks drawn across the river and were threatened by Chinese troops.[70] The situation remained very tense for the next few weeks, with Company commanders reporting that circumstances were so volatile that they could "place us in a most critical Situation and involved in a serious War" with China.[71]

Yet, barring immediate withdrawal of all British forces from Macao, the Chinese emperor refused to even consider negotiating, believing that only a forceful response would keep the British encroachment in check. "The ministers of England, full of deference for [our] dynasty, ordinarily send ambassadors bringing tribute," the imperial rescript declared. "But in these actual circumstances, they have no fear of offending us. In truth, they have exceeded the limits of permitted behavior. Therefore, it is extremely important to punish them." The emperor rejected British justifications for the attack: "Remember that the warships of China have never sailed overseas to land and quarter troops on your territory. However, the warships of your country dare to sail into Macao to land and live there! This is indeed a grievous and rash blunder. You say you fear that France might attack the Portuguese; do you not know that the Portuguese are living in Chinese territory?"[72] With the Chinese emperor threatening to send 80,000 men to drive the British out by force if they did not leave willingly, Drury had no choice but yield. On December 20–23, 1808, the British troops were evacuated and the fleet set sail for the Indies. "The most mysterious, extraordinary and scandalous affair that ever disgraced such an armament," as Drury described it in his final report, was over.

The British expeditions to Macao underscored a growing desire on the part of the BEIC to exploit the turmoil in Europe to secure its foothold in East Asia. The execution of it was poorly conceived and haphazardly carried out, with the "invade, then negotiate" attitude shaping British thinking.[73]

Neither expedition considered what the Chinese reaction might be to what effectively constituted the first hostile incursions into Chinese territory by a European power, and any hope that the Chinese would accept British troops in Macao was completely misplaced. Writing to the emperor, the provincial governor correctly noted that "the English nation is more powerful and more crafty than any other.... They have their views on and their eyes fixed on [Macao]...though they have so far not committed any act of violence and may mean to do any evil, it is possible if they possess Macao that they would pretend to the exclusive trade to the loss of all other nations."[74]

The French sinologist M. C. B. Maybon observed that the Macao affair showed that early nineteenth-century China was still capable, alongside its well-known overconfidence, of demonstrating "a spirit of defiance and a will of resistance against foreign intervention...[and] to force a great European power to back down."[75] From the Chinese perspective, the Macao affair was indeed an important victory against a formidable opponent, but this conclusion overlooks the wider international context of the British involvement in the Napoleonic Wars. With its military committed in Europe and the Royal Navy scattered across the oceans, Britain had no interest in entangling itself in yet another conflict, especially when it involved a crucial source of revenue. The affair allowed the British to gauge Chinese reaction to a possible territorial infringement and showed that the Qing court would not tolerate any such thing; this understanding shaped British policy toward China for years to come. For the rest of the Napoleonic Wars (and beyond) Britain preferred to maintain a neutral stance toward China and to continue to benefit from a trade that sustained its economy and war effort. The Canton trade continued to grow, especially after the BEIC began supplying opium shipments to its licensed traders, who then smuggled them into China; between 1805 and 1813 the company reaped profits as high as 900 percent, with opium replacing cotton as the chief British export to China. This contraband trade facilitated a massive currency drain and contributed to a financial hemorrhage that the Chinese government desperately tried to stop. When faced with Chinese "intransigence" over the opium trade in the late 1830s, Britain did not shy away from confrontation and used its naval and gunnery power to inflict a quick and decisive defeat on China.

By the late eighteenth century, the Indian Ocean formed an essential part of the vast network of trade routes that sustained the British economy. Each year, starting in the early 1600s, dozens of East Indiamen—ships sailing under charter or license of the BEIC—embarked on transoceanic journeys, carrying millions of pounds' worth of goods from Indian port cities such as Bombay or Calcutta to Britain.[76] Considering the immense value of this trade, it was natural that the BEIC and the British Admiralty made the security of these naval routes a priority during the Napoleonic Wars.[77] The capture of the Cape of Good Hope in 1806 was just the first step toward neutralizing the threat of the French raiders and privateers who used the surviving French possessions—principally Réunion and Mauritius in the Mascarene archipelago—as the bases for their operations in the in the Indian Ocean. British naval forces east of the Cape were divided between two command stations. Rear Admiral Sir Edward Pellew led the East Indies Station, tasked with protecting British shipping in the eastern half of the Indian Ocean, while his colleague Rear Admiral Thomas Troubridge was given command of the new Cape Station. Tragically, he perished with his entire crew in a cyclone in February 1807. His successor, Admiral Albemarle Bertie, was called upon to defend the western half of the Indian ocean from 1808 to 1811. Such a division compromised the effectiveness of the British war effort in the region; the British squadrons found themselves scattered over a vast area and struggled to coordinate their operations.

Napoleon had recognized the importance of the Mascarene Islands but had trouble keeping them supplied with troops, ammunition, and supplies due to the continued hemorrhaging of French naval power in the Atlantic. After General Decaen departed with a small force for the French East Indies in 1803 (see Chapter 7), Napoleon was able to allocate only a few frigates to reinforce him. Despite a lack of support from the metropole, the high-spirited but ill-tempered Decaen turned Mauritius into the chief French naval and military station in the Indian Ocean and for eight years harassed British commerce.[78]

Despite this, the French position in the Indian Ocean was precarious. There was little hope of receiving anything from the mother country. In June 1805 Napoleon announced that Decaen must "live from the product of [his] prices... All the money sent thither will be squandered." The French raiders were not unsuccessful, inflicting significant damages on the British shipping and capturing more than a dozen richly laden ships between 1807 and 1809. But there was the constant problem of procuring sufficient naval supplies to repair ships that suffered from the usual wear and tear as well as occasional hurricanes, such as the one in 1806 that wrought havoc on the islands. This was not simply a matter of local concern. Lack of provisions and supplies meant that when discussing his Eastern projects in 1803, 1805, 1807, 1808, and even as late as 1812, Napoleon faced a crucial question: that of whether the French islands could provide sufficient victuals for any large French expeditions dispatched to India.

Undaunted by the challenges he faced, Decaen threw himself into the struggle against the British. He tried to use diplomacy to strengthen the French presence in the Indian Ocean littoral and directed his attention to southern Arabia, where the Sultanate of Oman had emerged as a key regional player.

Franco-Omani relations became strained during the Revolutionary Wars, when French privateers targeted local shipping. Napoleon, who during his stay in Egypt had acquired a good understanding of the importance of Oman as a way-point on the path to India, sought to redress this situation, instructing Decaen to seek closer relations with Oman. A month after his arrival at Mauritius, the French governor dispatched an agent, M. de Cavaignac, to Muscat, with orders to convince Sultan ibn Ahmad to accept him as a French resident and to do his utmost to undermine British interests in the region.

De Cavaignac reached Muscat in October 1803 but was not allowed to disembark due to the absence of the Omani sultan, who was in the interior.[79] Conveniently, Captain David Seton, the BEIC's resident, was away on a cruise in the Persian Gulf, increasing French hopes for success. When the sultan finally returned, he refused even to meet with the French envoy, due to the just-received news of the collapse of the Treaty of Amiens and the resumption of hostilities between France and Britain; accepting a French resident would violate the agreement he had made with the British in 1798, and there were almost two dozen large Omani vessels at British-controlled ports that could become target of British reprisals. The British warning that "if the French obtain a footing at Muscat on any terms or in any situation, all communication between Muscat and India must cease" was clearly fresh in the sultan's mind.[80] Also a factor in the sultan's decision was his hope to secure British military support against the two great threats to his rule, the Wahhabis of central Arabia and the Qawasim of the Pirate Coast.[81]

The failure of the French mission demonstrated the BEIC's influence in southern Arabia. But it did not preclude the French from turning Muscat into a clearinghouse for the spoils of war. The Omani sultan argued that his agreement with the BEIC to form a formal alliance with the British still allowed him to continue to engage in commercial relations with the French.[82] The BEIC chose not to insist on a stricter interpretation of the treaty, as it would have deeply involved them in Muscat. This issue came to the fore in 1806, when Sultan ibn Ahmad's successor, Said ibn Sultan, allowed a French privateer to replenish its supplies and recruit seamen to do repair works in Muscat. The captain of a British frigate that also stopped by the Omani port denounced this as a violation of the Anglo-Omani Agreement of 1798 and demanded an immediate expulsion of the French ship. The sultan had no choice to comply. As soon as the French brig put to sea, it was captured by the British frigate, which had been patiently waiting for it just below the horizon. The French ship was towed to Bombay and sold as a lawful prize of war. This placed the Omani ruler in an awkward position vis-à-vis the French, one he tried to remedy by protesting the capture in a British court in Bombay.

By then it was too little too late. In late 1806 Decaen retaliated against the Omanis by attacking and capturing their merchant vessels. Said ibn Sultan thus found himself between a rock and a hard place when what he really desired was to be allowed to remain a neutral actor who could take advantage of French privateering spoils while simultaneously exploiting relations with the British government in India to deal with his domestic and external challenges.[83] Dispatching an envoy to Bombay, the sultan urged the BEIC either to return the captured French ship or to provide naval protection to Omani shipping, which was now harassed by the French. After weighing its options, the Company decided to reduce its commitments in southern Arabia and advised Said ibn Saud to assume a neutral position and to repair his relations with the French. To help the cause, the company restored the captured French brig. This meant the end of Oman's involvement in the Napoleonic Wars, for the sultan negotiated a commercial agreement with Decaen and accepted a French resident in late 1807.

Knowing that the Anglo-Maratha War had absorbed most of the BEIC's resources and that the British fleet could not effectively guard the vast Indian coastline, Decaen wanted to conduct more rigorous naval operations. The news of the sepoy mutiny at Vellore strengthened his belief that the situation was ripe for stirring up trouble. However, with Napoleon preoccupied with the War of the Fourth Coalition, Decaen could not hope to receive any reinforcements, and without them he lacked means to conduct any interventions in India. His greatest resource was the veteran Admiral Charles-Alexandre Léon Durand Linois's small squadron, which was tasked with raiding the British merchant marine. Linois excelled at this, capturing a few East Indiamen before he faced the chance of a lifetime at Pulo Aura on February 15, 1804, where he encountered the British China Fleet, consisting of almost thirty ships carrying trade goods worth the staggering sum of £8 million. Remarkably, the British convoy had no escort, making it vulnerable to a French attack. The convoy's commander, Commodore Nathaniel Dance, had disguised some of his merchant ships as warships to create the impression of a well-protected convoy; to further confuse his opponent, Dance made aggressive maneuvers to show his intention to engage enemy ships.

The stratagem worked. Linois, observing the enemy ships sailing in a line of battle, became convinced that the convoy was defended by more than half a dozen warships and quickly broke off the contact.[84] The escape of the China Fleet was widely celebrated in Britain, and Dance was rewarded with a knighthood and a general financial award. Linois, meanwhile, found himself the subject of ridicule, not to mention imperial disgrace—Napoleon raged against this abject failure to cause major harm to British trade. "My admirals see double and have discovered, I know not how or where, that war can be made without running risks," Napoleon seethed in a letter to his minister of marine. "Tell Linois that he has shown want of courage of mind, that kind of courage which I consider the highest quality in a leader."[85]

Linois spent the next two years conducting cruises across the Indian Ocean, but he was never able to escape the shadow of Pulo Aura. While his new raids did cause significant concern among the British authorities, the actual damage he inflicted on British shipping remained negligible and his operations became known more for their setbacks than their successes.[86] At no point did he cause any major disruption to British trade, and his decision to devote his flagship *Marengo*, a 74-gun ship-of-the-line, to chasing merchantmen was, in the words of a British historian, akin to "employing a steam-hammer to crack a nut."[87] While Linois's shortcomings did contribute to the overall failure of these operations (especially at Pulo Aura), he operated in very challenging circumstances, with meager naval resources, separated by vast distances from friendly ports, and, of course, facing a far superior British fleet that had acquired a new base of operations with the capture of the Cape of Good Hope in early 1806.[88] Equally problematic was the lack of stocks at naval stores. The French had no proper supply of masts, copper, and rope and were forced to utilize ships to find replacements. Prices for vital naval stocks skyrocketed and made ship repairs prohibitively expensive. Repairing just two frigates in the Indian Ocean in 1806 required more than 700,000 francs; constructing a brand-new one cost less back in France.[89] Frustrated and kept in the dark over events in Europe, Linois decided to return to France. He was intercepted and captured by a Royal Navy squadron in the Atlantic on March 13, 1806.

With Linois's ships gone, Decaen might have been forced to remain on the defensive if not for the mistakes the British themselves committed. The Royal Navy was concerned that Decaen might receive reinforcement from France and wage a more robust *guerre de course*, one that could wreak havoc with the East India Company merchantmen. A crucial element in disrupting any such plans was preventing the French from acquiring any bases close to Indian waters. In light of Napoleon's overtures to Fath Ali Shah, British attention was naturally drawn to Iran's coastline; rumors claimed that the French were already close to securing a base at Bandar Abbas, on the Persian Gulf. On receiving these reports, the BEIC ordered Admiral Pellew to lead his squadron to the Strait of Hormuz, where he could control the entrance into the Persian Gulf. Remarkably, the admiral refused the order; he was doubtful of the veracity of those reports on French movements and, more important, understood that he would have little opportunity to distinguish himself in the Iranian backwaters.

Still, the news from Iran was hardly encouraging. British political agents reported Franco-Iranian rapprochements and the discussion of a treaty of alliance, one article of which called for French control of Bandar Abbas and the island of Hormuz. For BEIC directors, this intelligence once again raised the prospect of a French invasion of India and made a blockade of the Persian Gulf a strategic necessity. Pellew disagreed once more, refusing to believe that the report was true. His continued refusal to sail into the Persian Gulf underscores an important element in British naval commanders' aspirations. "Like everybody in India," notes one eminent historian, "[Pellew] had gone out to make money [but] for two years the more profitable eastern half of [the Indian Ocean command] had been taken away from him." Instead of the Persian Gulf, Pellew was more keen on raiding Dutch colonies in the East Indies, where success and prize money could be easily had. Hence in late October 1807 he sailed to the East Indies, leaving behind just a couple of small warships while three more frigates were under repair at Bombay. BEIC officials were still concerned about the French threat in the Persian Gulf and hoped, in the words of Minto, that Pellew would soon share their belief that "the western side of India [was] the most important and immediate object of vigilance."[90] They insisted on dispatching a small squadron, led by Captain John Ferrier of HMS *Albion*, to Bandar Abbas, where the British arrived in early February.

Pellew's departure for the East Indies and Ferrier's to the Persian Gulf had exposed the Bay of Bengal to French privateers, who had raided local commerce so effectively as to cause merchants to complain to the BEIC governor-general. Minto had decided to dispatch a special mission to Tehran to sway the shah against supporting the French or granting them access to the Iranian coastline. As we have seen, he selected John Malcolm for this mission, but his initial intention to accompany the envoy with some 4,000 men and a strong British naval squadron—"the impression from the appearance of a British maritime force in the Gulf cannot be otherwise than salutary," he argued—drew the ire of Admiral Pellew, who refused to send his ships on such a mission.[91] He argued that the fleet could not be used as an offensive weapon and that his instructions were to defend India and the BEIC trade. Besides, what effect would a naval force have on a land power like Iran, which was not heavily dependent on maritime trade? Unable to compel the admiral to do his bidding, Minto had no choice but admit that "the line of battle ships are not necessary for any purpose connected with the designs or operation of the enemy by land."[92] Still believing that the French threat to India was imminent, the BEIC governor-general resorted to diplomacy, dispatching missions to Sind, Punjab, and Afghanistan in an effort to secure all possible overland routes the French might take.

Unbeknown to him, the French menace was about to emerge on the seas. Decaen made his next serious attempt at disrupting British trade in 1809.[93]

This was made possible by the arrival of Captain Jacques Félix Emmanuel Hamelin, who had sailed from Europe with a frigate squadron in late 1808. He reached Mauritius in March 1809, having already captured several prizes on the way. Over the next several months Hamelin conducted a masterful campaign, destroying the BEIC base at Tappanooly on Sumatra and capturing British ships. Impressed by these successes, Napoleon reinforced Hamelin with another frigate (the only one able to break through the British blockade), which arrived at Mauritius in early 1810. As the cyclone season ended, Hamelin launched a new campaign, raiding the Bay of Bengal and the east coast of Africa, where, in July 1810, his men defeated a convoy of East Indiamen.[94]

Concerned by Hamelin's operations, Admiral Albemarle Bertie at the Cape of Good Hope ordered Commodore Josias Rowley to hunt down the French frigates and blockade the Mascarene Islands in the Indian Ocean, to prevent their use as raiding bases. In August 1809 the British seized the island of Rodrigues, a success of great strategic consequence. The Cape of Good Hope and India were separated from the Mascarenes by more than 2,500 miles (in the case of Bombay, more than 3,000 miles) of open seas. Rodrigues, on the other hand, was just 380 miles away from Mauritius. Hence it could serve as both a forward station for the British frigates and as a staging ground for the invasions. As early as September 1809, unable to bring Hamelin's ships to battle, Rowley decided to raid the fortified anchorage of Saint-Paul on Réunion, where he captured one of Hamelin's frigates and rescued two East Indiamen. The success of this raid demonstrated the quality—or lack thereof—of French shore defenses and the British ability to strike at the French anchorages directly. It encouraged Rowley to consider a larger operation to seize the entire island.

Over the next several months Rowley made plans for the invasion with the support of Lieutenant Colonel Henry Keating, who commanded a contingent of British army regulars and BEIC sepoys. On July 7, 1810, the British expedition, numbering more than 3,500 men supported by five frigates, reached Réunion and landed at several locations. The British easily overwhelmed a small French garrison (less than 600 men, with some 2,500 militia) and seized the entire island.[95] This was a significant British victory because Réunion provided secure anchorages for the Royal Navy and allowed the British to concentrate their operations on the sole remaining French territory in the Indian Ocean, Mauritius. However, the ease with which the island had been captured had also left the British with an inflated sense of the possibilities. Just weeks after the capture of Réunion, Rowley was already busy planning the capture of Mauritius. As a preliminary stage for the impending invasion, he wanted to secure the smaller islands that controlled the passage of shipping through the coral reefs surrounding the island. In August, one of Rowley's subordinates, Captain Samuel Pym, seized Île de la Passe near Grand Port but was unable to prevent a French squadron under Captain Guy-Victor Duperré from passing into the harbor nine days later. The ensuing Battle of Grand Port (August 22–23) turned into a disaster, as two British frigates got irretrievably grounded in the shallow waters of the bay while the French captured two others along with their entire crews.[96]

Set against the great actions of the age, the Battle of Grand Port was a small-scale event, especially in the wake of the Battles of the Nile and Trafalgar. But it was, nonetheless, one of the worst defeats the Royal Navy suffered during the Revolutionary and Napoleonic Wars.[97] Rowley's five frigates had been reduced to just one while more than 2,000 British seamen (including four captains) were dead, wounded, or captured; the French lost barely 150 men. More disturbing to the British was the fact that their warships had failed to put up their usual fight, causing a contemporary British historian to lament that "no case which we are aware more deeply affects the character of the British Navy than the defeat it sustained at Grand Port."[98]

The Battle of Grand Port could have left Britain's vital trade convoys in the Indian Ocean exposed to attack from French frigates. However, its effects proved to be short-lived, failing to produce strategic consequences. With his squadron drastically weakened, Rowley made urgent requests for reinforcements from the British authorities in Cape Town and Madras. Hamelin tried to exploit the fact that any British reinforcements would arrive piecemeal and cruise in unfamiliar waters. In September he twice forced the surrender of British frigates, only to allow Rowley to recover his ships each time. On the second occasion, on September 18, the British not only liberated their warship but also netted Hamelin's flagship *Vénus*, bringing an end to the activities of his squadron. The loss of such a dynamic and capable French naval commander was a serious blow to the French, who all but ended their raiding operations and were forced to retreat to Mauritius, where Rowley blockaded them.

By now, the shock of the defeat at Grand Port had jolted the British into action, and available resources were quickly diverted to the region while preparations were made to invade and subdue Mauritius. In November 1810 Admiral Albemarle Bertie and General John Abercromby launched one of the largest British amphibious operations ever attempted in the Indian Ocean, involving more than 6,500 men and some seventy warships and transports traveling 3,000 miles of open seas. They all converged on the tiny fortified island in midocean. On November 29 the first troops landed on Mauritius unopposed by the French garrison, which counted just 1,300 regular troops. Just two days later the British invasion was under way, leaving Decaen no choice but to capitulate. He did so under advantageous conditions: he and his entire garrison were allowed to be repatriated with honors, retaining their personal arms and colors.[99]

The fall of Mauritius eliminated the last French outpost in the Indian Ocean. Britain not only seized the last remaining French frigates but acquired a key base for its further operations across the entire Indian Ocean. Renamed Mauritius, the island remained part of the British Empire until 1968. The news of the British capture of the Mascarene Islands did not reach France until after Napoleon, still thrilled by the French victory at Grand Port, had sanctioned Commodore François Roquebert to lead a small squadron to the Indian Ocean.[100] Roquebert reached the Mascarene Islands in February 1811 only to find them in British hands; a British squadron soon gave chase and captured all but one of the French warships near Tamatave (a trading post on Madagascar) on May 20, 1811.[101] The Battle at Tamatave marked the final French naval engagement in the Indian Ocean and all but ended any French threat to British merchant ships. Although Napoleon continued to plan various small expeditions to the Indian Ocean, only one—to the Dutch East Indies during the winter of 1811—materialized. In the end, the French efforts resulted in the loss of thirteen out of fourteen frigates sent to the Eastern Seas, while the their commerce-raiding campaign proved ineffective.[102]

———∘∞∘⊱❈⊰∘∞∘———

The fall of Réunion and Mauritius confirmed British dominance of the seas east of the Cape of Good Hope and allowed the British to turn their attention to the Dutch East Indies, the last remaining area where French influence still survived. Established by the Dutch East India Company in the seventeenth century, the Dutch East Indies centered around the city of Batavia (present-day Jakarta), which served as a center of the Dutch trading network in Asia.[103] The Dutch colonies gradually fell under French influence after France's occupation of the Dutch Republic in 1795. Four years later the Dutch East India Company's charter was not renewed, allowing the Dutch Republic to take over all of the DEIC's possessions (and debts). The Dutch authorities were well aware that acquiring these vast colonial holdings carried immense liabilities, including spreading the new sociopolitical system that had been established at home and defending possessions from the predatory activities of the British. The revolutionary changes were slow to appear in the colonies. In 1802, a new draft charter for the government of the East Indies called for "the greatest possible welfare of the inhabitants of the Indies, the greatest possible advantages for Dutch commerce, and the greatest possible profits for the finances of the Dutch state," but it was never implemented.[104]

In 1807, after reorganizing the Dutch Republic into the Kingdom of the Netherlands, Napoleon appointed Marshall Herman Willem Daendels as governor-general of the Dutch East Indies and granted him immense authority to administer and reform the colonies. Upon arriving at Java in 1808, Daendels, a thoroughly military man and admirer of Napoleon, had no connections with the clique that for the last twenty years had run the DEIC's affairs at Batavia. Hence he launched a series of major administrative and legal reforms that dismantled the old system of governance and laid the foundations for the new. The real object of Daendels's mission lay in the military realm. In the instructions he had received, twelve out of thirty-seven articles dealt with military affairs, with Article 14 specifying that military reorganization and the strengthening of defenses were to be the first of his duties.[105] Between 1808 and 1810, Daendels improved local defenses by building new fortifications, coastal batteries, military barracks, and arms factories; in a remarkable feat of engineering that cost a great many human lives, he constructed an almost six-hundred-mile-long road across northern Java, from Anjer to Panaroecan.

Daendels's willingness to ignore the advice of the old-timers and push through ambitious reforms was both his strength and his weakness. His authoritarianism alienated the Javanese nobility, with the result that many of them were willing to support the British against the Dutch and French. Daendels was also unable to bring his reforms to completion. He had made so many enemies that by 1811 they were strong enough to have him recalled and replaced with Jan Willem Janssens, who arrived in Java in April 1811, accompanied by several hundred French troops. Janssens had previously served as governor-general of the Cape Colony, where he had been forced to capitulate to the British in 1806. The same fate was about to befall him in Java.

After the success of the Mauritius expedition, the British knew that it was imperative for them to seize the Dutch East Indies before Daendels's projects were completed. In August 1810, the Board of Control wrote to Lord Minto, the governor-general of the BEIC, that it had no hesitation in supporting his plan of expelling the French from the island of Java and from any other place they still occupied in the Eastern Seas. "While the Dutch were independent, or at least nominally independence of France," the board concluded, "it was neither their interest nor their policy to give us much annoyance from Batavia or their other settlements in those seas. But the case is now materially altered. Holland is now incorporated with France and we must be prepared for the most active and inveterate hostility."[106]

In preparing for his expedition to Java, Lord Minto first targeted small Dutch colonies: Captain Edward Tucker seized the island of Amboyna and adjacent islets in the spring of 1810, while Captain Christopher Cole captured the Banda Islands, completing the conquest of the Dutch Spice (Maluku) Islands.[107] Minto now concentrated on a more challenging task:

invading Java itself. By late spring of 1811 the British force was ready to set sail. Commodore William Robert Broughton held the naval command.[108] The expeditionary corps of some 12,000 men was placed under command of Lieutenant General Sir Samuel Auchmuty. The expedition departed from various Indian ports in May and, after sailing through the Malacca Straits, arrived at the Dutch East Indies at the end of June.

On August 4 the British troops landed near the estuary of the Marandi River and immediately marched toward Batavia, which had been abandoned by Janssens on August 8. The Franco-Dutch force retreated into the newly built Fort Cornelis, where they were besieged by the British, who finally stormed it on August 26. In the words of Lord Minto, the French fortification was "most formidable in strength, and it really seems miraculous that mortal men could live in such a fire of round, grape, shells, and musketry... The slaughter was dreadful, both during the attack and in the pursuit."[109] Among the few who escaped from the fort was Janssens, who rallied the remaining defenders in a strong position south of Semarang and sought, in vain, help from the Javanese princes. Alas, only one remained loyal to the Dutch; the rest, embittered by their earlier experiences, embraced the British. On September 18 Janssens signed the capitulation treaty, which transferred Java, along with its dependencies of Timor, Macassar, and Palembank, to the British.[110]

The fall of Java marked the end of the war in the Eastern Seas. Every fresh gain France had made in Europe since 1803 was followed by a corresponding loss in the Eastern Seas. By 1812, Napoleon no longer had any bases east of the Cape, and so thoroughly had the fleets of France been swept from the Indian Ocean that the French emperor was forced to postpone any thoughts of naval operations there until after he had resolved his ongoing tensions with Russia. Between 1812 and 1815 the East Indies squadron of the British Royal Navy rested on its much-deserved laurels, consolidating its gains and standing guard against possible threats. British trade to India, China, and other parts of Asia flourished and supplied the government's coffers with the much-needed revenue that enabled continued war efforts in the Iberian Peninsula and coalition-building in central Europe. As Governor General Minto himself proudly informed the secretary of state for war, "The British nation has neither an enemy nor a rival left from the Cape of Good Hope to Cape Horn."[111] The British victories between 1803 and 1815 constituted a crucial step in the consolidation of a disparate collection of dependencies acquired at various times and in various ways into what became the British Empire.

CHAPTER 20

The Western Question?

Struggle for the Americas, 1808–1815

M ORE THAN ANY OTHER REGION, Spanish America demonstrates the global ramifications of the Napoleonic Wars. Largely ignored in traditional narratives of the war, the crisis and collapse of Spain's empire in the Americas were direct results of the political turmoil in Europe. If the Eastern Question revolved around the key question of the fate of the Ottoman Empire, there was a corresponding "Western Question," one that centered on Spain and its imperial domains. During the Napoleonic Wars, this vast empire got fragmented and was henceforth relegated to the sidelines of world politics. Spanish colonial elites, like their English-speaking counterparts in North America a generation earlier, seized upon the moment of European turmoil and political weakness to declare political regimes of their own, independent of colonial rule.

By the end of the eighteenth century, the Spanish colonial empire extended thousands of miles from modern-day California, Utah, and Colorado all the way down to the tip of present-day Argentina. Originally divided into two viceroyalties—New Spain, created in 1535, with its capital at Mexico City, and Peru, created in 1542, with its capital at Lima—the empire eventually came to include two additional viceroyalties: New Granada, with Bogotá as its administrative center; and Río de la Plata, with Buenos Aires as its capital. Within each territory, a viceroy exercised a broad military and civil authority as the direct representative of the king of Spain. He was advised by the *audiencia*, an advisory council and judicial body consisting of twelve to fifteen judges, and supported by the *cabildos*, administrative councils that governed municipalities.[1] By the late 1700s Spanish colonies had become fairly prosperous and were self-sufficient producers of provisions, textiles,

Map 24: South America, 1808–1815

and consumer goods. Although the silver mines of Peru had all but run dry, Mexico's silver mines were still the richest in the world, providing a steady stream of specie that accounted for at least 20 percent of Spanish revenue.[2]

The Spanish monarchy's decision to adopt free trade policies in the latter half of the eighteenth century stimulated trade, which grew rapidly between 1778 and 1788. This commercial growth could not cover up the stark reality of Spain's growing financial and industrial weakness, which the Bourbons, despite their best efforts, could not overcome. Spain's inability to keep sea-lanes to colonies open in time of war meant that Spain saw its Mexican silver remittances dwindle to almost zero, especially during the years from 1797 to 1799. Furthermore, colonial manufacturing suffered a heavy blow under free trade policies that involved opening colonial ports to foreign vessels of neutral origins—and which, in practice, meant those of the United States. This concession meant that during the Revolutionary Wars a spirited commerce developed between the United States, the Caribbean, and the South American colonies, resulting in a growing and prosperous colonial elite that increasingly drew its inspiration from Enlightenment thought and whose aspirations soon transcended the boundaries of their municipalities and viceroyalties.[3]

Spanish institutions had been grafted onto the Americas in the sixteenth century, but the resultant societies had by the end of the eighteenth century not yet evolved to the point of coalescing into national entities. Instead, colonial society reflected four distinct social groups. The *peninsulares*—numbering about 30,000, all of them born in Spain—were dominant, holding key leadership positions in the church and government through various arrangements with the Spanish crown. Their main contenders for power were the *criollos* (and their Portuguese counterparts, *crioulos*), some 3.2 million individuals of European descent who were born in the colonies. But terms like *criollos/crioulos* were more than just birthplace distinctions; they represented distinct social classes within an existing *casta* system. These were individuals who largely controlled the colony's commercial and economic life but struggled to break into the higher-level government and ecclesiastic positions filled by the *peninsulares*. Further down the socioeconomic ladder were about 2 million individuals of mixed background—*mestizos* (of Spanish and Indian parentage), *cholos* (of mestizo and Indian descent), *mulattos* (of Spanish and black parentage), *zambos* (of Indian and black origin), and others—who accounted for the larger part of artisans, farmers, soldiers, and small businessmen. Almost 8 million Indians, the descendants of the America's original inhabitants, and approximately 1 million African slaves occupied the lowest levels of the social ladder. Together, these social groups formed a vibrant colonial society of about 14 million people.

A growing sense of restlessness developed as racial, ethnic, and class privileges fueled discontent.[4] The *criollo* elite resented the patronizing attitudes and dominance of the *peninsulares,* and decried both the lack of political representation and the commercial restrictions imposed by the Spanish monarchy, which greatly benefited from the vast outward flow of riches through taxation and control of markets. For *mestizos* and Indians, lack of opportunity, overt racism, and widespread discrimination all sustained a growing sense of resentment toward *criollos* and *peninsulares*.[5]

As pronounced as these grievances might have been, any resort to a revolutionary transformation would have been difficult before 1789. The mid-eighteenth century did witness frequent Andean Indian rebellions, most notably the 1780–1782 massive uprising led by José Gabriel Condorcanqui, an Indian *cacique* (chief) who assumed the name of Tupac Amaru II. The causes of this revolt lay not in Enlightenment ideas of popular sovereignty, toward which the eighteenth-century Latin Americans were hostile, but in the rampant abuses of the Indian population by Spanish royal officials. The colonial government was strong enough to suppress this and other manifestations of dissent, offering only limited concessions in their wake. The Tupac Amaru revolt not only threatened to end the *repartimiento* system of forced labor imposed upon the indigenous population but raised the colonial elite's fears of racial and class warfare. Even the disaffected *criollos* did not wish to completely dismantle the existing system, one that granted them privileged positions; instead, they sought to reform it so that it would allow them greater participation. Despite the considerable wealth and sophistication found in such colonial cities as Buenos Aires, Lima, and Bogotá, very few intellectual or regional leaders entertained serious notions of radical reform or outright independence from Spain.

Events in Europe proved the catalyst that would change all this. We have already seen that the French Revolution unleashed an outpouring of violence in the French colony of Saint-Domingue, which affected the neighboring Spanish colonies as well.[6] During the Revolutionary Wars, Spain retained its possessions in the Americas and the Caribbean, although its hold on these territories was tenuous and subject to the vagaries of both colonial politics and international relations. In the early years of the French Revolution, the French government considered exporting its revolutionary ideology and welcomed overtures from the Spanish colonial revolutionaries such as Miranda, who had urged the French revolutionary leaders to free the Spanish Americas. At least one of them, Brissot, agreed that the "time has come to free the Spanish colonies."[7] Indeed, the Girondin leaders—Brissot, Jérôme Pétion de Villeneuve, Pierre-Henri-Hélène-Marie Lebrun-Tondu, and Charles Dumouriez—even considered forming an alliance with Britain to "free" and partition the Spanish colonies in the Americas. They were certain that the British would be enticed by the "immense benefits" that the emancipation of the Spanish colonies would give them.[8] But any British gains would be only temporary. After the French become "masters of the Dutch navy," they would be strong enough to take on and destroy England, possibly with the American help.[9]

In early 1793 the French government had considered sending an expedition to the Americas, but discussion of the plan was undercut by the entry of Britain and much of Europe into the War of the First Coalition.[10] Still, the instructions sent to the French ambassador to the United States, Edmond-Charles Genêt, called for securing American support for the liberation of the Spanish colonies by suggesting that it was in the Americans' interests to spread liberty and independence.[11] Although the American government remained lukewarm about the French offer, individual Americans did support plans for a revolution in the Spanish colonies. They rallied around George Rogers Clark, a veteran of the American Revolutionary War who had distinguished himself in the Northwest Territories and was now eager to see the United States expand southward as well. Like many living in the American West, he was upset by the continued Spanish control of Louisiana, which denied Americans free access to the Mississippi River. Given that President George Washington was unwilling to consider any forceful actions against Spain, Clark approached Genêt with a proposal to lead an expedition to capture St. Louis and New Orleans, then proceed to threaten other Spanish possessions. This "will be humbling Spain in its vital parts," he told the French, "and by conquering New Mexico and Louisiana, that of all Spanish America, with its mines, may soon after be easily achieved."[12] Genêt approved the plan and appointed Clark "Major General in the Armies of France and Commander-in-chief of the French Revolutionary Legion on the Mississippi River."[13] As Clark made preparations for a campaign, his efforts were undercut by Washington, who issued a proclamation forbidding Americans from violating US neutrality and threatened to dispatch troops to stop the expedition. Furthermore, the French government recalled Genêt and revoked the commissions he had granted to the Americans for the war against Spain. Clark's planned campaign thus came to naught.

Spain's decision to join the First Coalition in 1793 ensured that its colonial trade continued uninterrupted. Just two years later, by the terms of the Treaty of Basle, the Bourbon government unilaterally ended hostilities with the French and went to war with Britain. As the British attacked Spanish shipping, Spain's transatlantic trade collapsed and its connection with its South American colonies was weakened, encouraging foreign encroachments. The United States was keen on exploiting this opportunity, and its political leaders demonstrated an assertive attitude towards Spanish possessions. In 1796 the Treaty of San Lorenzo guaranteed Americans navigation rights on the Mississippi River, paving the path toward greater US influence in a region long dominated by Spain.[14] Indeed, the American leadership was keen to see that none of the European powers was permitted to secure any portion of Spanish dominions that shared borders with the United States.

The news of the French acquisition of Louisiana therefore provoked considerable apprehension in American political circles, which the British were eager to exploit. During his meetings with the American ambassador, Rufus King, British foreign minister Lord Hawkesbury had raised the issue of the Spanish secession of Louisiana as early as 1801, expressing his concern that such "acquisition might enable France to extend its influence up the Mississippi and thro' the lakes even to Canada." This would, the British argued, directly threaten their interests in North America, since "the facility with which the Trade ... might be interrupted and the [British West Indies] Islands even invaded, should the transfer be made, were strong reasons why England must be unwilling that this territory should pass under the dominion of France."[15] Consequently, Britain was only too pleased to see the American effort to contain French influence in North America; the British ambassador to the United States encouraged and supported plans of American senator William Blount of Tennessee and John Chisholm, veteran Indian agent, for joint Anglo-American actions against Spanish Florida and Louisiana as a way of preventing their falling into the hands of a nation that could menace British interests. Although the conspiracy ultimately collapsed, it is still revealing of the motives of British policy in the region.[16] Interestingly, the British government was not interested in acquiring the territory for itself. In 1803, in a conversation with an American ambassador, Prime Minister Addington noted that in case of war with France and its Spanish ally, one of the first British actions would be to occupy New Orleans but that "England would not accept the Country [Spanish Louisiana and Florida] were all agreed to give it up to her; that were she to occupy it, it would not be to keep it but to prevent another power from obtaining it."[17] Americans were pleased to hear such talk since they were "unwilling to see [Louisiana and Florida] transferred [to anyone] except to ourselves"; at the very least, they had "no objection to Spain continuing to possess it; they were quiet neighbors and we looked forward without impatience to events which ... must, at no distant day, annex this [region] to the United States."[18] A similar discussion took place between British ambassador Edward Thornton and President Thomas Jefferson in late May 1803 when the former, "half-jokingly," asked whether the United States would oppose British occupation of Florida and New Orleans "for the purpose of offering them on certain conditions to the Americans." Jefferson's response underscored a long-term American perspective on the Spanish possessions in North America: "the continuance of the Spaniards in the possession of these countries and their own [American] enjoyment of their present or greater privileges in the navigation and outlet of the Mississippi until acquiring greater strength and involved from whatever cause in a war, they [United States] could dispossess the latter entirely of [these territories]."[19]

Thus at the start of the nineteenth century Britain faced a dilemma: both France and the United States coveted Spanish possessions and the question was which to prefer. Throughout the period 1801–1803 British statesmen hesitated on what course of action to take. They were aware of Napoleon pressuring Spain to transfer the Louisiana territory but were unable to prevent it. Ultimately, they came to the conclusion that a US acquisition of the Spanish possessions in North America was the lesser of two evils and tried to entice America into a British alliance, painting a dire picture of Napoleon building a colonial empire that would threaten the young republic. In 1803 Prime Minister Addington informed the Americans that his government would be content with the addition of Louisiana to the US territorial domain in an effort to "prevent its going into the hands of France."[20] Hence, upon learning about the Louisiana Purchase, the British foreign secretary informed his American counterparts about "the pleasure with which His Majesty [King George III] has received this intelligence."[21] The sentiment was hardly genuine. The British were aware of the Americans' inflated expectations, including their interpretation that the newly acquired territory included everything that was not Canada. Nevertheless, for the next few years Britain paid little attention to these matters—even when some American statesmen solicited British support for establishing a sovereign state, under British protection, in the newly acquired territories—because of the ongoing war against Napoleon.[22]

In the wake of the Louisiana Purchase, the American desire for Spanish territory further intensified. The US government suspected Britain of coveting the Floridas, a suspicion that persisted well beyond the Napoleonic Wars. A more immediate goal was to exploit British maritime strength to thwart any French colonial aspirations. By 1807, the Americans were already considering joining the British, in order, as [James] Wilkinson wrote to Jefferson, "to preserve the western world from Napoleon and his unwilling ally, the king of Spain."[23] Some American proposals envisioned Anglo-American occupation of the Floridas and Cuba and independence for Mexico, Peru and other Spanish colonies.[24] At the same time, reflecting growing American frustration with British policies, the United States preferred not to see Britain's position strengthened in the New World. In April 1807, President Jefferson instructed the American ambassador to Spain to warn its colonial authorities against any political or commercial rapprochement with Britain, and noted that their continued existence depended on American goodwill. "Never did a nation act towards another with more perfidy and injustice than Spain has constantly practiced against us. And if we have kept our hands off it till now, it has been purely out of respect for France, and from the value we set on the friendship of France." Jefferson went on to express hope that Napoleon would compel Spain to make concessions for the United States or "abandon its to us." In the latter case, "we ask but one month to be in possession of the city of Mexico."[25]

The United States was not alone in their interest in the Spanish America. Political and economic tumult in Spain and Portugal created unique circumstances for the extension of Russian influence in the Western Hemisphere. As early as May 1806, Count Nikolai Rumyantsev, the Russian minister of commerce, argued that Russia could easily procure colonial goods of the finest quality directly from the Americas, circumventing the services of the Hanseatic merchants, and the money spent "on the commissions and profits of the Hamburg merchants," as he put it, could be used to promote domestic industry and expand the size of the Russian merchant marine. Such sentiments became especially widespread after Russia was forced to join the Continental System in the summer of 1807.

A distinctive symptom of economic malaise in post-Tilsit Russia was speculation in foreign goods and the rapid inflation that accompanied it. The lifestyle of the Russian upper classes, reported the governor-general of St. Petersburg, had made colonial goods essential articles of consumption, second only to the most rudimentary necessities of life. Effective measures to alleviate scarcities arising from Russia's accession to the Continental System were therefore demanded. Efforts to find solutions to the mounting crisis increased Russian interests in South America. In 1808, Russian officials pointed to the wealth of Portuguese colonies in South America as possible sources of commercial relief: with a vast array of colonial products (citrus, fruits, tobacco, coffee, sugar, spices, etc.) to offer, Brazil was increasingly perceived as a "land that awaits only human hands to yield up its precious gifts."[26]

Over the next three years the Russian government considered several proposals by the mercantile elite for expeditions to South America with the goal of establishing Russian commercial presence there.[27] These commercial ties faced a major obstacle: Russia remained part of the Continental System that banned British goods from the continent. With Spain and Portugal in alliance with Britain, the Russian government would have naturally faced French questions about admitting Spanish or Portuguese vessels (potentially carrying British goods) into its ports.

The Russian decision was simple but inspired. In December 1809 Rumyantsev informed his Portuguese counterpart that the government would ban any "Portuguese" ship from entering Russia but would not extend this restriction to "Brazilian" vessels, as long as the Portuguese court would offer reciprocal treatment to Russian merchants in Brazil. This decision reflected Emperor Alexander's desire to establish closer ties with Latin America. With Portugal and Spain in turmoil, he expected profound changes in the Americas, where, as he observed in a letter to the Russian envoy to the United States, several independent states might be soon established. "It is difficult to calculate just what changes such an event would produce in the political and commercial relations of Europe but it is easy to foresee that they will be of great importance."[28] In discussing Russo-Brazilian ties at the State Council in January 1810, Rumyantsev pointed out that Russia faced a unique moment, one in which it could expand its commercial interests overseas and undermine those of Britain.

The council accepted his arguments and approved the proposed Russo-Portuguese trade agreement, which was reached in May 1810 and revised in 1811–1812. Simultaneously the Russian government sought to establish its commercial presence in Spanish America. On receiving the news of revolt in Venezuela in 1811, it welcomed envoys from Caracas on several occasions, exploring possibilities of establishing direct trade relations.[29] However, Emperor Alexander ultimately chose not to pursue ties with the Spanish colonies. He found the prospects of extending recognition to the insurgent colonial authorities unappealing and, more important, his priorities had changed with the start of the Franco-Russian War of 1812. For the next few years Russia was preoccupied with the struggle over the future of Europe, devoting little (if any) attention to relations to the Spanish colonies. Nonetheless, the legacy of Russia's overtures to Latin America endured, and would play an important role in later decades.

The event that triggered Spanish-American power struggles and, ultimately, independence was the French takeover of Spain in 1808, when Napoleon removed King Charles IV of Spain and his son Ferdinand from power in Madrid and named his own brother, Joseph Bonaparte, king of Spain. The Spaniards refused to accept the new monarch and, in the words of a British historian, "their indignation rumbled hoarsely for a time, like a volcano in labour, and then burst forth in an explosion of fury."[30] The crisis of 1808 was unique in that it effectively truncated the existing government leadership by removing the entire royal family and breaking down central authority. Into this political void stepped the regional ruling councils (*juntas*), which rejected French rule and argued that, in the absence of a king, legitimate government devolved to the local level. The numerous *juntas*, which emerged across Spain and claimed sovereign powers, were not revolutionary in nature but rather acted like a collective sovereign still upholding the concept of monarchy and traditional privileges.[31]

The exodus of the Portuguese monarchy to Brazil and the turmoil at the Spanish Bourbon court were much talked about in the Spanish colonies. There was a spark of enthusiasm that accompanied the accession of Ferdinand VII in March 1808, when the colonial governments pledged their allegiance to the new king. Only weeks later they learned about the tragicomedy that unfolded at Bayonne—the capture of the Spanish royal family, the subsequent national uprising, and, most crucial, the Spanish victory at Bailén. Resistance to the Napoleonic regime sprang up across the Spanish American colonies, which turned a deaf ear to French promises of administrative reforms and modernization. In vain did French foreign minister Jean-Baptiste de Nompère de Champagny and Spain's new minister of the Indies, Miguel José de Azanza, assure colonial officials that the changes were limited to the ruling dynasty alone, that the Spanish nation has "preserved the integrity of its dominions and its independence" and that "such a splendid monarchy will not lose a single one of its precious possessions."[32] French emissaries who had slipped through the Royal Navy blockade to announce King Joseph's ascension in the Americas tried to convince colonial administrators to support a Napoleonic monarchy in Spain.[33] However, their arguments that this would "cure their homeland of evils that it has endured for so long" and that the convocation of the Bayonne Assembly was the first step towards "the regeneration of the country" were rejected out of hand, along with any suggestion of French influence.[34] As one emissary reported, the officials in Buenos Aires "had no desire whatsoever for any other king than Ferdinand VII. Many of them were of the opinion that they should take violent measures against me."[35]

The absence of a Bourbon monarch who could claim legitimate authority created a unique situation. Some colonial leaders insisted on continued loyalty to the Bourbon cause; others hoped to exploit the monarch's absence to secure greater independence. The latter argument was based on the premise that the Americas were joined with Spain in a personal union under a ruling sovereign, and that the deposition of Ferdinand VIII had destroyed the link that bound the colonies to the metropole. The Chilean Patriots, for example, later contended that the "Bourbons have abandoned the nation against the will of the people, and by this act they have lost even those obscure rights upon which their dynasty was raised. A nation left without a chief, on account of their domestic quarrels, could not belong to those emigrants. Ferdinand, from [the chateau of] Valençay, could not keep in his hand the extremity of the noose, or, speaking more properly, of the chain which fastens America."[36]

As early as mid-July 1808, there were attempts to establish representative institutions in Mexico City, in the Viceroyalty of New Spain, and in Caracas, in the Captaincy General of Venezuela.[37]

Furthermore, the Portuguese monarchy, which had fled to the safety of Brazil, tried to exploit all the tumult to extend its control in South America. Rodrigo de Sousa Coutinho, the Portuguese minister of war and foreign affairs, initially appealed to the "Cabildo and People" of Buenos Aires and the whole Viceroyalty of Río de la Plata to accept the Portuguese monarchy's protection against the French. When a British squadron commanded by Rear Admiral Sidney Smith visited Rio de Janeiro in May 1808, the Portuguese proposed a joint military operation into the neighboring Spanish viceroyalty, arguing that Infanta Carlota Joaquina (1775–1830), daughter of the deposed Spanish King Charles and wife of the Brazilian regent João VI, could, as a member of the Spanish royal family, act as a regent for the duration of the conflict.[38] Disregarding earlier British setbacks in Buenos Aires, Smith supported these plans.[39] This plan failed, partly as the result of the actions of the newly arrived Percy Clinton Sydney Smythe, Viscount Strangford, British ambassador in Rio de Janeiro, who, unlike Sidney Smith, was committed to upholding Spanish imperial integrity and opposed any Portuguese efforts to intervene into Spanish colonial affairs. Strangford believed that "the most effective way of retaining colonial friendships was by allowing the [Spanish] colonists to work out their situation in their own way, without external interference."[40] He therefore saw to it that Rear Admiral Smith was removed from command and recalled to England and that the infanta was admonished by her husband, who was told in no uncertain terms how important British support was for the Portuguese monarchy.

Strangford's position is noteworthy because it underscores a change in the British policy in South America. Britain had long sought to penetrate Spain's imperial possessions, and the two nations had gone to war on several occasions in the eighteenth century, including the memorably named War of Jenkins' Ear (1739–1748).[41] Starting in 1796, the Franco-Spanish alliance gave Britain the pretext it had been seeking to challenge Spanish hegemony in the Western Hemisphere. The threat of American intrusion into Spanish colonies also loomed large in British thought. While William Pitt was at the helm, the British cabinet seriously considered the emancipation of Spanish colonies as a part of its foreign policy; the economic advantage of such an event would have been tremendous, and the idea was popular with the mercantile classes. Although Pitt died in early 1806, his cohort continued to exercise influence, resulting in British attempts to force their way into Spanish American markets in 1806–1807, in the form of support for

Miranda's expedition to Venezuela and expeditions to Buenos Aires, the capital of the Viceroyalty of La Plata (modern Argentina) and the Atlantic gateway to the silver of the high Andes.[42]

This forceful "liberation policy" was effectively dead by 1807, with the new Portland cabinet preferring a subtler approach to the issue. As outlined by the new secretary for war and the colonies, Castlereagh, Britain was to ensure the success of its policies not through a military conquest but by offering support to the Spanish colonial populace. "In looking to any scheme for liberating South America, it seems indispensable that we should not present ourselves in any other light than as auxiliaries and protectors. In order to prove our sincerity in this respect, we should be prepared to pursue our object by a native force, to be created under our countenance; and the particular interest which we should be understood alone to propose to ourselves should be the depriving our enemy of one of his chief resources, and the opening to our manufactures the markets of that great Continent."[43]

Just as Castlereagh and other British statesmen explored what to do in South America, they were confronted with an event that forced a reevaluation of official policy. The envoys of the *juntas* of Asturias, Galicia, and Seville informed the British government of their decision to resist the French and requested British support. Britain's years-long hope of turning Spain against France had thus been fulfilled. The British reaction was immediate: members of Parliament famously declared that the British had to do better than merely "filching sugar islands" and "nibbling at the rind," while the newspapers wrote that "of plundering and marauding expeditions we have had quite enough." All agreed that Britain needed to devote itself to one great project and rescue the world.[44] As the British government pledged to support the *juntas*, all existing South American projects were put on hold. From now on, London would position itself as a protector rather than as a predator in South America, although its final goal of safeguarding Britain's economic interests in the Americas remained unchanged. This policy ensured that Britain would use its naval superiority to insulate Spanish colonies from any French threats while furtively encouraging them to seek greater independence. As the French sought to get Spanish American support against the British, the latter felt the "duty" to make, as Castlereagh noted in a letter, "every exertion for preventing the American provinces of Spain from falling into the hands of France by the same treachery which is subjugating Spain itself."[45]

By the end of 1810, events in South America had convinced British statesmen to work "toward increasing and stabilizing the Latin American trade and maintaining the fondness for England which the [Spanish] colonists had recently shown. The idea of conquest had vanished from ministerial minds;

even the prospect of abetting colonial independence by means of armed intervention had lost its appeal."[46] The British policy thus aimed at opening colonial markets to British commerce and ensuring that neither France nor the United States gained a foothold in the South America. The former goal was partly achieved when the Portuguese prince regent, upon his arrival in Rio de Janeiro, announced the opening of Brazilian ports to British commerce. Rio de Janeiro henceforth was to become, in the words of Foreign Secretary Canning, "Brazil's emporium for British manufactures destined for the consumption of whole of South America."[47] Fearful that Britain would support the revolutionaries in the colonies, the Spanish Council of Regency in Cadiz sought to appease the British by permitting them to trade directly with the colonies for the duration of the war.

Meanwhile, Napoleon continued his efforts in the Spanish colonies. Facing continued resistance from the Spanish royalist authorities, he adjusted his policy and sought to precipitate a formal break between Iberian and American Spain. "[I] will never oppose the independence of the continental nations of America," he declared in an address to the Legislative Corps on December 12, 1809. "That independence is in the natural course of events.... Whether the people of Mexico and of Peru should wish to elevate themselves to the height of a noble independence, France will never oppose their desires, provided that these peoples do not form any relations with England."[48] Throughout next few years, as relations between the colonial *juntas* and the Spanish *juntas* (and later the Regency Council) deteriorated, Napoleon dispatched dozens of agents to the Americas to foment rebellion and issue proclamations. He considered projects for military expeditions to South America, offered financial and military aid to the insurgents, and debated over recognizing Venezuelan independence in 1811–1812, only to be sidetracked by the preparations for the invasion of Russia.[49] Ultimately none of these efforts produced tangible benefits. Protected by the Royal Navy from any seaborne threats, the Spanish colonial government concentrated on internal challenges.

—◦◦◦※◦◦◦—

Starting in 1809, colonial *juntas*, styled after those in Spain, appeared in many Spanish American cities. They took it upon themselves to safeguard Spanish governance and interests against possible meddling by outside powers. On May 25, 1809, a *junta* was formed in Chuquisaca, Upper Peru; on July 16, in La Paz, Upper Peru; on August 10, in Quito, New Granada; on May 25, 1810, in Buenos Aires, Río de la Plata; and on September 18 a national *junta* was established in Chile.[50] Although these *juntas* were initially designed to support the Spanish king, Ferdinand VII, the power and autonomy they enjoyed soon emboldened their leaders to realize that in the absence of royal supervision and the concomitant drain of funds, their managerial efforts could not only sustain but enhance local conditions. Throughout the first year of the political tumult in the colonies, two key questions remained: whether these *juntas* should exist or not, and if they should exist, whether they were temporary organizations to be disbanded upon the restoration of the Bourbon monarchy or precursors to a permanent transfer of power from Madrid to the Americas. Loyalist/royalist *peninsulares* made the former argument, pointing out that the colonies had properly sanctioned royal bureaucracy in the persons of the governing viceroys and administrators, which made *juntas* redundant at best and seditious at worst. The more independent-minded *criollos*, however, argued that in the absence of the monarchy the colonies should follow the example of the Spanish *juntas* and form their own governing council, to rule until the return of Ferdinand VII. Furthermore, inspired by Enlightenment ideals as well the American and French revolutions, the *criollo* leaders were eager to exploit the turmoil in Europe in order to seek greater autonomy and a refashioning of colonial societies.[51]

Tensions between these groups quickly escalated into fighting that raged for almost two decades. The wars, initiated and driven by the *criollo* and *peninsulare* elites, were fought almost entirely independently within each of the four viceroyalties that made up Spanish America. Members from all levels of the *casta* system fought on both sides of the conflict, but the *criollos*, who liked to style themselves as the "Patriots," made up most of the revolutionary political and military leadership. They enjoyed significant advantages over the predominantly European-born royalists, whom they outnumbered. Being at the top of the economic and social pyramid, these groups stood to gain or lose much from the war's outcome and did their best to sway the lower groups, which represented the vast majority of the colonial population. Hence both sides made efforts to draw people of mixed background and Indians to their banner. Royalists, for example, made changes to Indian tributes, while Patriots spoke of legal equality and emancipation of slaves in exchange for service. Local support varied region to region; often, as happens in times of strife, loyalty was simply extended to existing local leaders.

Among the challenges the royalists faced was the ongoing war on the Iberian Peninsula. This made sending fresh royalist reinforcements extremely difficult. In later years, when the troops from Spain did arrive, royalists suffered from rivalries between the royal officers and veteran colonial officers, who found their new Spanish counterparts arrogant and ignorant of local people and customs. Furthermore, the royalist cause was also complicated by internal divisions between conservative absolutists, who wanted to restore the old monarchy without change, and liberal constitutionalists, who denounced the Bourbon abuses and corruption and preferred a constitutional monarchy. When the Supreme Central Governing Junta called for representatives from local provinces and overseas possessions to meet in an "Extraordinary and General Cortes of the Spanish Nation," it marked a major departure from the absolutist practices that had long shaped the Spanish colonies. This showed that a new government was shaping up in Spain, undermining royalist positions and encouraging demands for greater self-governance and representation for the colonies. This political debate over the nature of government was further affected by the dissolution of the central *junta* and establishment of the Regency Council, which, in an attempt to win support throughout the Hispanic world, pledged to extend political equality and representative government to the colonies.

The *criollos* suffered from internal splits and fighting as well. They disagreed over the territorial boundaries and constitutional issues, with the Federalists preferring to see weak central governments within a loose confederation of strong individual states and the Centralists preferring a strong federal government and limited states' rights. After initial success, the *criollos* sometimes turned against each other in rapidly escalating civil wars that left an enduring legacy of discord and conflict, one that shaped local societies long after the colonies had gained independence.[52]

The news of the situation in Spain first sparked a political crisis in the viceroyalty of New Spain. In July 1808, Viceroy José de Iturrigaray, who was upset at the downfall of his protector, Godoy, and warily pledged his allegiance to Ferdinand VII, was approached by the *criollo*-controlled city council with a suggestion to form an autonomous government of New Spain (with Iturrigaray at its head). It would govern the region until the Bourbon dynasty was fully restored in Spain. This incited a power struggle between the royalist *peninsulares*, who were convinced that Iturrigaray was attempting to a create a government that in no way depended on Spain, and the more-reform minded *criollos*, who pressured the viceroy to form a congress of representatives and to share power with the colonial notables.

The tensions culminated on September 16, 1808, when armed *peninsulares* charged into Mexico City's viceregal palace to depose the viceroy in favor of an octogenarian field marshal (*mariscal de campo*) named Pedro de Garibay, who was deemed more loyal to the old monarchy.[53] Political and social discontent continued to fester and reached its climax in 1810.[54] Distraught by widespread poverty and hardship, a priest in the small village of Dolores, Padre Miguel de Hidalgo y Costilla, took the first step toward righting what he considered injustices against the men and women of Mexico. On September

15, 1810, he delivered his "Grito de Dolores" ("Cry of Sorrows"), still known throughout South America, which urged the people to take arms and depose the *peninsulares*, all in the name of Ferdinand VII and the Virgin of Guadalupe. Just days later, Hidalgo led thousands of peasants and other supporters toward Mexico City. The rebellion remained entirely rural and failed to garner any support from urban areas, and the intensity of the rebels' anti-monarchical stance, along with their violence, horrified the creole elite, many of whom had initially supported the anti-colonial cause but now turned their backs on it.[55] The rebels initially defeated the royalist army under General Torcuato Trujillo in a battle at Monte de las Cruces on October 30. Yet Hidalgo turned his troops back; although they outnumbered the royal army, they lacked the discipline of trained soldiers and were armed only with machetes and crude homemade weapons. This proved to be a fateful mistake, for it allowed the royalist forces to regroup and counterattack. In January 1811 they crushed the rebels at the Bridge of Calderon (forty miles east of Guadalajara); the ferocity of the rebellion was matched only by the government's thirst for revenge. Thousands were executed, including Hidalgo himself.[56]

Hidalgo's death did not end the revolution, which rallied around the lieutenants he had dispatched to various parts of New Spain. The most prominent of these was the defrocked priest José María Morelos y Pavón, who was initially sent to take control of the port of Acapulco, on the Pacific coastline. Despite facing superior royalist forces and having no prior military experience, Morelos demonstrated considerable talents, leading his ragtag troops to consecutive victories. By the end of 1811 his forces had grown to some 9,000 men, allowing him to secure much of the southwestern coastal region.[57] Although defeated by the royalist army at Cuautla in May 1812, Morelos was able to rally his troops and launch a new offensive that netted him the cities of Huajuapan and Oaxaca.

Instead of attacking vulnerable Mexico City, he decided to lay the foundation for a new government. In 1813 Morelos convened the National Constituent Congress of Chilpancingo, which included representatives from the rebel-controlled provinces. The congress discussed and approved an ambitious program of political and social reforms, the Sentimientos de la Nación (Sentiments of the Nation), which drew its inspiration from the French Revolution. The delegates established a representative government, abolished slavery and racial social distinctions, prohibited torture and monopolies, and so forth. In one of his most radical reforms, Morelos called for the termination of the Catholic church's privileges and the compulsory tithe exacted from poor parishioners, and demanded nationalization of the large land estates.[58]

On November 6, 1813, the National Constituent Congress declared independence, producing the first official document of its kind in Spanish America. Yet as exhilarating as these developments were to Mexican reformers, their aspirations were ultimately thwarted by the failure to win the war. If Hidalgo's uprising had surprised wealthy *criollos*, Morelos's vision for a radical sociopolitical transformation increased their hostility and strengthened their resolve to fight. Morelos was defeated at Valladolid on December 23–24, 1813, and at Puruaran on January 5, 1814. By mid-spring the Patriots had lost all their gains in the south and the National Constituent Congress was forced to evacuate to a safer location. Guiding the legislature through royalist territory, Morelos came under a royalist attack at Tezmalaca (November 5, 1815), where he was decisively defeated, captured, and executed. His death marked a turning point for the revolution in New Spain. Deprived of capable and charismatic leaders, the rebels chose to accept the more conciliatory policies of the new viceroy, Juan Jose Ruiz de Apodaca, who offered amnesty to any Patriot who laid down his arms. The First Mexican Revolution came to an end.[59]

Meanwhile, more than a thousand miles farther south, in the Viceroyalty of Río de La Plata, the news of the French takeover of Spain had not only surprised the local authorities, which were still celebrating their victories over two British expeditions just two years earlier, but emboldened the *peninsulares* who wished to return to the old order. The revolutionary processes in Río de la Plata proved to be complex and multifaceted, involving not only outside interventions but regional disintegration within the viceroyalty itself. In this regard the conflict of two colonial centers—the viceregal capital city of Buenos Aires and Montevideo, the capital of the Banda Oriental province of Río de la Plata—is particularly central. In 1806–1807 both cities resisted British invasions, providing matériel and human resources to expel the invaders. Then their paths diverged. "The powerful merchants of Buenos Aires ... resented Montevideo's commercial autonomy, the need to maintain agents in the city and the required payment of taxes and fees to local authorities there."[60] During the British invasion of 1807, Montevideo served as a key commercial entrepôt for British goods in Río de la Plata and greatly benefited from trade with the United States and Portugal, much to the chagrin of the neighbors in Buenos Aires.[61]

During the political crisis triggered by the French occupation of Spain, the two cities found themselves increasingly at odds. In 1808 Napoleon's emissary Claude Henri Étienne Marquis de Sassenay arrived in Buenos Aires, requesting local authorities to pledge allegiance to Joseph Bonaparte. The French-born interim viceroy of Río de la Plata, Jacques de Liniers, vacillated over his response, leading the governor of Montevideo, Francisco Javier de Elío, and his *cabildo* to raise suspicions about the viceroy's loyalty and to challenge his legitimacy. After rejecting Napoleon's request and swearing loyalty to Spain's Supreme Junta, Liniers attempted to assert his authority over Montevideo, a popular move among the mercantile elites of Buenos Aires. However, Montevideo vigorously resisted Liniers's power grab. When Liniers's agent Juan Ángel de Michelena arrived in the city in late September 1808, he was greeted with a popular revolt that prevented the removal of Governor Elío and soon led to the formation of a *junta gubernativa* (governing council) that rejected the authority of Buenos Aires and swore loyalty to Ferdinand VII.[62]

In June 1809, the Supreme Central Junta in Seville (Spain) dispatched Admiral Baltasar Hidalgo de Cisneros y Latorre to restore order in Río de la Plata. On his arrival, Liniers relinquished office and Cisneros restored royalist control in the region, forming the Political Surveillance Court to root out the supporters of "French ideologies."[63] But he faced new challenges in Upper Peru, where juntas had been formed in Chuquisaca on May 25 and La Paz on July 16. In October Cisneros sent royalist forces to restore order in both places. In doing so, however, he inadvertently drew down the Spanish garrison in Buenos Aires and gave greater leverage to the *criollo*-controlled militias. In May 1810 news of the dissolution of the Seville *junta* and the establishment of the Regency Council of Spain convinced many *criollos* that with both the king and the *junta* now removed from power, Cisneros no longer had any legitimacy to govern. The viceroy tried to maintain the political status quo, but a group of *criollo* lawyers and military officials organized an open *cabildo*, which, after a weeklong (May 18–25) series of discussions, denied recognition to the Regency Council of Spain and declared the establishment of the United Provinces of the Río de la Plata under the control of the Primera Junta in Buenos Aires.[64]

This was the first successful revolution in South America. It also unleashed the Argentine War of Independence, which raged for the next eight years.[65] The Primera Junta claimed authority over the entire viceroyalty of Río de la Plata, generating political disputes with other regional centers. Thus just as Buenos Aires sought to break away from Spain, Montevideo rejected its authority and embraced royalism, becoming a bastion of Spanish loyalism and monarchism in South America. Furthermore, the Regency Council of Spain declared Buenos Aires a rogue city and moved the viceregal capital to Montevideo, where Elío was appointed the new viceroy. At the same time, the former viceroy, Liniers, organized a royalist uprising in Córdoba (about 450 miles from Buenos Aires) and expected reinforcements from the neighboring (and still royalist) Viceroyalty of Peru to suppress the revolution at Buenos Aires.

The Primera Junta's first decision was to suppress the uprising in Upper Peru. In early July a small expeditionary force, under Colonel Francisco Ortiz de Ocampo, was dispatched there. The expedition first stopped at Córdoba, where it defeated and captured Liniers and the other leaders of the Córdoba counterrevolution. After Ocampo balked at executing these prisoners, he was removed from command. A political commissioner, Juan José Castelli, put the Córdoba prisoners to death on August 26, 1810, while Antonio González Balcarce, who had replaced Ocampo as a military commander, moved to consolidate the Primera Junta's authority in Upper Peru. Despite being defeated at Cotagaita (October 27, 1810), the Patriots triumphed at the subsequent battle of Suipacha (November 7), which gave Buenos Aires control over the region; the royalist leaders, including generals Vicente Nieto, Francisco de Paula Sanz, and José de Córdoba y Rojas, were captured and executed. As Castelli considered crossing the Desaguadero River and invading the Viceroyalty of Peru, the royalist Captain General José Manuel de Goyeneche counterattacked with his Peruvian troops and crushed the Patriots at Huaqui (Guaqui) on June 20, 1811, opening the path for the royalist invasion of the Río de la Plata.[66]

The setbacks in Paraguay and Upper Peru resulted in the Primera Junta being replaced by an executive Triumvirate, comprising Manuel de Sarratea, Juan José Paso, and Feliciano Chiclana, in September 1811. The new government was convinced that if Peru remained in royalist hands, independence throughout South America would be threatened. To this end, the Triumvirate reorganized the Army of the North and appointed General Manuel Belgrano to lead it. Facing the far stronger royalist army of General Juan Pío de Tristán, Belgrano resorted to scorched-earth tactics and organized the Jujuy Exodus, evacuating thousands of inhabitants of Jujuy and Salta provinces while destroying the countryside. The stratagem worked. Belgrano was able to defeat the royalists at the decisive battle of Tucumán (September 24–25, 1812) before forcing the bulk of the royalist army to surrender at Salta on February 20, 1813. These victories not only safeguarded the Patriot government in Buenos Aires but ensured its authority over most of the northern territories of the former Viceroyalty of the Río de la Plata—although the royalist victories Vilcapugio (October 1, 1813) and Ayohuma (November 14) meant that the war continued here with intermittent success.

A civil war had also erupted in the Banda Oriental (modern Uruguay). Montevideo had long sought greater autonomy within the viceroyalty of Río de la Plata, but it was the political crisis caused by the Napoleonic Wars that allowed its mercantile elites to achieve their goal.[67] Their preferred political option was royalism and, throughout 1809–1810, the local royalists consolidated their power under the leadership of Viceroy Elío. Yet support for monarchism was not unanimous in the Banda Oriental and faced stiff resistance from republican factions led by José Gervasio Artigas Arnal. On February 28, 1811, the local republican patriots issued the famous "Grito de Asencio" (Cry of Asencio), urging their Argentine brethren to help them in their struggle against the royalists. The appeal opened a new, Uruguayan theater in the ongoing civil wars as the invading Argentine forces clashed with the royalists throughout April–June 1811. Victory at Las Piedras, on May 18, allowed the Patriots to march directly on Montevideo but the resultant siege failed in October. To resist the revolutionaries, Elio sought aid from the Portuguese queen, Carlota Joaquina. The Portuguese, who had long had aspirations to acquire the Banda Oriental, wasted no time in seizing the opportunity. The queen convinced her husband to intervene, and before British ambassador Strangford could do anything, the Brazilian Portuguese army, some 4,000 men strong, invaded the region and forced the Patriots to break their siege in July 1811.

As thrilled as Elío was by this success, he soon realized the grave mistake he had made in inviting the Portuguese. Portuguese commander Diego de Souza assured the local population that the Portuguese monarchy had no intention of conquering the region, but he also showed no intention to leave, claiming the continued need to defend this region from republican attacks. Thus small-scale hostilities persisted throughout 1812–1813 until a British mediation resulted in the conclusion of the Rademaker-Herrera Treaty between the United Provinces of the Río de la Plata and the Empire of Portugal (May 26, 1812) that ended the Portuguese intervention in the Banda Oriental.[68]

After the Portuguese departed in the summer of 1812, the Argentine Patriots, now led by Manuel de Sarratea, launched a new invasion of the Banda Oriental and besieged Montevideo for a second time. As in the previous year, they did not have the land strength to storm the walls or the navy to blockade the harbor. To address the latter problem, the United Provinces of the Río de la Plata acquired ships from the United States and formed its own squadron under command of William Brown, an Irishman who had formerly served in the Royal Navy against the French and now emerged as "the father of the Argentine navy." In June 1814 Brown's fleet, crewed by British and American sailors, conducted a methodical campaign in the Río de la Plata, and its naval blockade of Montevideo allowed the Argentine army to seize the city in June 1814, thus ending the royalist presence in the Banda Oriental.[69] Instead of joining Argentina in the United Provinces of Río de la

Plata, however, Artigas decided that the Banda Oriental would remain independent. In 1814 he organized the Unión de los Pueblos Libres (Union of the Free Peoples), of which he was declared protector. The following year he defeated the invading Argentine forces and reorganized the Union of the Free People into the Federal League, which stood independent of the United Provinces of the Río de la Plata as well as of Spain.[70]

Meanwhile, the Primera Junta was preoccupied with the Intendancy of Paraguay, which rejected its authority and prompted an invasion of the Patriot force under General Manuel Belgrano. Expecting little opposition, the Patriots gained an early victory at Campichuelo in December 1810, then were routed in the battles of Paraguari (January 19, 1811) and Tacuari (March 9, 1811) and forced to retreat. These victories emboldened many Paraguayan patriots, including José Gaspar Rodríguez de Francia, who had resisted the invasion but had no desire to see royalism prevail. Instead, flushed with victory earned without royal aid, they chose to turn the defeat of Belgrano into the launching pad for their own liberation. The Paraguayan campaign thus developed into a conflict between the *criollos* themselves. Those supporting the Primera Junta clashed with their Paraguayan counterparts who did not want to be controlled by Buenos Aires. On May 17, 1811, Paraguay broke its links with the Spanish crown and the Buenos Aires–based *junta* and declared its independence.[71]

------⋈⋈⋈⋈------

In New Granada (modern-day Colombia), Viceroy Antonio José Amar y Borbón, rejected the *criollos'* demands and opposed the *junta* movement. Upon learning that a *junta* was formed in Quito on August 10, 1809, he dispatched royalist troops to restore order but struggled to suppress new juntas appearing in other locations. By late July, however, he himself was deposed and a *junta* was formed in Bógota itself.[72] The viceroyalty was soon divided into regions that supported *juntas* and the royalist areas. The provinces of Guayana and Maracaibo, in the eastern and western portions of the viceroyalty, remained royalist and royalist forces continued to control of key areas in the south (including Popayán and Pasto) and the north (Santa Marta, near Cartagena). The juntas failed to form a common front and soon quarreled over contrasting visions for the future of the viceroyalty. Some championed a loose confederation of states that would pursue their own domestic policies while accepting the authority of the federal government, the United Provinces of New Granada. Other *juntas*, most notably that of Bógota, which had long served as a capital of the viceroyalty and therefore had much to lose in a decentralized system, insisted on a more centralized leadership. The Bógota leaders rejected the confederation plans and instead formed their own state of Cundinamarca, which fell under the "semi-dictatorial authority" of Antonio Nariño.[73] In the neighboring Venezuela captaincy general, the Caracas *junta* faced resistance from the royalist-leaning city of Coro, whose governor, José Ceballos, refused to accept its authority.[74] Denouncing Ceballos as an agent, the junta mobilized some 4,000 men against him but suffered a sudden defeat from the much smaller but more inspired royalist force at Toro, on the outskirts of Coro, on November 28, 1810. The defeat precipitated a political crisis in Caracas, where a special congress was convened to determine the future government.

The political debates at the congress reflected the growing appeal of radical voices, like those of Francisco de Miranda and Simón Bolívar, who had returned after unsuccessfully seeking British recognition and aid, and insisted on a complete break with the Spanish monarchy.[75] Although the First Venezuelan Republic was declared on July 5, 1811, it proved to be short-lived. A devastating earthquake hit republican provinces in March 1812, killing thousands and destroying much of existing infrastructure. Then a royalist counteroffensive under Domingo de Monteverde defeated the revolutionaries at the Battle of San Mateo (La Victoria, June 20 and 29, 1812) and brought the capital of Caracas back under Spanish control. Miranda's decision to accept a capitulation agreement on July 25, 1812, shocked his republican supporters, including Bolívar, who condemned it as a treasonous act and, along with other officers, arrested Miranda and then handed him over to the Spanish army. Once a great champion of colonial independence, Miranda spent the last five years of his life in a Spanish prison.

Bolívar assumed the mantle of leadership of the Venezuelan forces under the direction of the Congress of United Provinces of New Granada. In the summer of 1813 he launched his "Admirable Campaign" to free Venezuela from Spanish control. In late May, his forces entered the town of Merida, where he was proclaimed "El Libertador" (the Liberator), the sobriquet by which he would be known throughout South America. Two weeks later he seized Trujillo and issued his infamous decree "Guerra a Muerte" (War to the Death) decree on June 15, which ordered the extermination of all Spaniards who refused to change sides and support the revolution. This brutal measure represented a deliberate rejection of the rules of war in pursuit of the specific political goal of splitting the royalist opposition. It did produce short-term gains, as republican forces reclaimed Caracas and established the Second Venezuelan Republic, with Bolívar as its leader. But the republicans failed to secure the countryside, where the royalists continued to draw considerable support; neither could they prevent the landing of Spanish reinforcements at Puerto Cabello that further bolstered royalist forces.

Despite victories at Mosquiteros (October 14, 1813) and Araure (December 5), the republicans suffered from internal divisions and intrigues that prevented them from forming a common front. In 1814, the royalist general José Tomás Boves led a new counteroffensive, delivering a crushing defeat to Bolívar at La Puerta on June 15, 1814, and seizing control over much of Venezuela. With the second republic destroyed, Bolívar had no choice but to flee to New Granada, where he tried rallying his supporters only to find himself engaged in a fight with rival republicans. Frustrated, he fled the country in disgrace and sought shelter in Haiti, where he was welcomed by Alexandre Pétion, the president of the newly independent Haitian republic, who promised material and military support to him.[76] Bolívar's return to Venezuela in 1816 launched a new phase of the wars of independence that would continue for almost a decade.

While revolutions raged in New Granada, New Spain, and Río de la Plata, the viceroyalty of Peru remained solidly royalist. The viceroy of Peru José Fernando de Abascal y Sousa was a talented administrator who played a crucial role in organizing armies to suppress uprisings in Upper Peru and successfully containing the aspirations of the Argentine *junta*. He was unable to prevent the spread of the *junta* movement in his viceroyalty, however. The Captaincy General of Chile, an autonomous region since 1778, witnessed the establishment of a *junta* in Santiago in September 1810. The junta pledged allegiance to King Ferdinand VIII but also proclaimed Chile an autonomous republic within the Spanish monarchy and organized the first National Congress of Chile in 1811. By now, the more radical Patriots had called for Chile's complete independence from Spain and organized a coup that was led by José Miguel Carrera (a newly returned veteran of the Peninsular campaigns) and his two brothers Juan José and Luis Carrera. Yet the pro-independence camp was deeply split along lines of patronage and personality. In early 1813 Viceroy Abascal tried to restore the royalist authority in Chile, dispatching some 6,000 men under Antonio Pareja to Santiago. In the ensuing campaign, Carrera was outmaneuvered and outfought by his royalist opponent, resulting in his dismissal.

The Chilean criollos now rallied under the leadership of Bernardo O'Higgins, a prominent *criollo* of Spanish and Irish ancestry, who fought the royalists to a standstill and negotiated the Treaty of Lircay, which ended hostilities but also reaffirmed Chile as an integral part of the Spanish monarchy. Outraged by this concession, the Carreras and their supporters rejected the treaty and challenged O'Higgins's authority. The Patriots' descent into civil strife was halted by the news of a royalist offensive in the fall of 1814. Although Carrera and O'Higgins pledged to join forces against the common enemy, their eventual discord ensured a royalist victory at Rancagua on October 2, 1814.

This last battle was a crushing defeat for the Patriots. Of some 1,700 men, O'Higgins lost 600 killed, 300 wounded, and another 400 taken prisoner. With the royalists entering Santiago, he and the few remaining troops (along with their families) had no choice but to flee across the Andes to the United Province of Río de La Plata, where they welcomed by José de San Martín, the new governor of Cuyo Province. A veteran of the Peninsular campaigns against the French, San Martín had left Spain upon receiving news of political tumult in South America in 1812. Joining the Patriot forces, he distinguished himself by forming a regiment of horse grenadiers whose superb discipline and training made it one of the best units in all of South America. Appointed the governor of Cuyo, he reorganized local forces and put the entire region on a war economy of rations, forced loans and compulsory labor. With the Chilean patriots beseeching him for help, San Martin proposed a grand plan for winning the war. Instead of taking the usual path through Upper Peru, he suggested launching an attack across the snowy passes of the Gran Cordillera in the north-central Andes. Over the next two years, with crucial political and material support from Juan Martín de Pueyrredón, supreme director of the United Provinces, San Martín laid the groundwork for the eventual reconquest of royalist Chile.

CHAPTER 21 | The Turning Point, 1812

B Y THE START of the second decade of the nineteenth century, Napoleon had achieved what no one had been able to accomplish in a thousand years: supremacy over continental Europe. In terms of square miles of territory under French control, 1810 marked the height of the Napoleonic Empire. After Austria's defeat in the previous year, Napoleon extended his control southward along the Adriatic coast, and, because his brother Louis had shown himself more sympathetic to Dutch than to French interests, incorporated the Dutch kingdom directly into the French Empire. With new acquisitions along the North Sea coast, France proper now consisted of 130 departments (instead of the original 83), while its imperial authority stretched across a vast area—from the Baltic shores of the Danish Peninsula to the Adriatic coastlines of Italy and Dalmatia, from Andalusia in Spain to the borders of the Russian Empire. Napoleon was practically unchallenged on the continent.

Yet beneath the apparent strength and stability of the empire lurked a number of worrisome signs. The fall of the Mascarene Islands and Java in 1811 meant that Napoleon no longer had any overseas colonies left. The British victory was, in fact, so complete that it marked an end to more than two hundred years of European maritime imperial rivalry in Asia. Britain also, as we've seen now, enjoyed ascendancy in Iran and Arabia, while the Royal Navy controlled the seas. The situation was equally dire for the French interests in the Western Hemisphere, where Napoleon no longer had any footing whatever: the Louisiana Territory had become an American domain, Haiti was independent, the remaining French islands in the Caribbean had been seized by the British, and Spanish America, which Napoleon had hoped to sway, quickly descended into civil strife.

The question then arises: had Napoleon managed to sustain his authority in Europe, would the outcome of the Napoleonic Wars have been different in light of these global developments? France had lost a global war and now could only hope to win a regional one. But even in Europe Napoleon faced considerable challenges. His mistreatment of the pope earned him the bitter enmity of many Catholics. The war in Spain continued to sap financial and human resources with no tangible gains to show for it. The Ottoman Empire, war-fatigued as it was, did formally remain Napoleon's ally but was increasingly distancing itself from France. The Continental System had aroused widespread resentment, including in France, where the economic crisis of 1810–1811 revealed signs of growing discontent among the bourgeoisie, hitherto Napoleon's strongest supporter. The French model of government and administration may have stood for efficiency and uniformity but had little appeal for the common people, whether rural or urban, who resented increased taxation, conscription, and the efficient police forces that came with them. Reforms, no matter how enlightened and progressive, lost much of their appeal when they came from the barrel of a gun.

Indeed, French imperial power had awakened the force of the national spirit in Italy, Holland, and the German states, where French occupation aroused patriotic reaction on the part of educated elites and eventually common people. National sentiments were stirring in Prussia, where prominent German writers and philosophers who turned against Napoleon devoted their great talents to nationalist propaganda and fostering a new sense of freedom.[1] The earlier military defeats and resulting deep sense of embarrassment and humiliation helped change the very nature of the German Enlightenment thought, imparting it with romantic and nationalist traits at the expense of its earlier cosmopolitanism and rationalism. German and Austrian political leaders fostered this national spirit as a weapon against Napoleonic imperialism, with Prussian reforms exploiting the groundswell of patriotic feelings to strengthen the state and the Habsburg monarchy approving a national propaganda campaign.[2] Similarly, Italian writers and thinkers, even those who initially welcomed the French in 1796–1797, grew disillusioned with Napoleon and engaged in a fierce polemic in prose and verse whose call for Italian unity reverberated through a generation.[3]

Napoleon's decision to invade Russia in the summer of 1812 was his greatest effort to sustain the French imperium in Europe. It resulted in war on a colossal scale and produced results diametrically opposite to those the French emperor wished to attain. The six-month-long campaign furnished numerous episodes of triumph and hardship, transcendent courage and wanton depravity, but it offered many military lessons as well. In the grandeur of its conception, its execution, and its abysmal end, this war had no analogy until the German invasion of the USSR in June 1941.

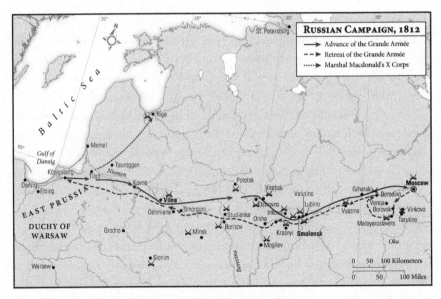

Map 25: Russian Campaign, 1812

The conflict between Russia and France began without formal declarations of war, but it did not come as a surprise to contemporaries. Relations
between the two empires had become increasingly tense in 1808–1811.[4]
Napoleon's Continental System, which Alexander had agreed to join under
the terms of Tilsit, proved highly disadvantageous to the Russian economy.
Russia was still a largely agrarian empire and heavily depended on exports of
its key raw materials. The number of manufacturing plants gradually grew
but, compared to Britain or France, Russia's industrial base lagged far behind.
To export its resources, it relied less on its merchant navy and more on a
foreign merchant marine, with Britain as the leading trade partner. The
Continental System thus caused considerable hardship due to the disappearance of trade with Britain, whose purchasing power was very hard to replace.
In 1802, during the Peace of Amiens, out of 986 merchant ships that visited
the Russian ports of St. Petersburg and Kronstadt 477 were British; only five
were French.[5]

The negative effects of the Continental System were augmented by the
start of the Russo-Swedish and Russo-Turkish Wars, which further limited
Russia's trading partners. Russian ports became stockpiled with raw materials (grain, hemp, tallow, flax, timber, leather, cattle, iron, etc.) that could not
be sold. Prices for exports fell precipitously, while prices of imports sharply
increased.[6] The Russian frustration with the Continental System culminated

in 1810 when Britain suffered from a poor harvest, whereas Russia had a bountiful one. Napoleon permitted (and heavily taxed) the export of grain from French control ports to Britain, but Russia could not sell any of its harvest to the British despite having the lowest prices anywhere on the continent. Needless to say, Russian landlords were fuming about this.

In 1807 French merchants had had high hopes of replacing their British rivals on the Russian market. Three years later they were facing the grim reality of losing their footing there. Due to the ongoing war with the British, they could not maintain direct maritime trade with Russia, which in 1808 received no French ships at all. This left land trade as the only alternative, though conveyance of goods across central and eastern Europe was significantly slower and more expensive, undercutting profits. The developing crisis in the Russian economy was of great concern for France, given that many of its own industries relied on the Russian market. Shortly after the start of the Continental System, the Lyon Chamber of Commerce, for example, warned Napoleon that the French silk industry was on the brink of devastation because of the loss of the Russian market. Aside from the vast distances involved, Franco-Russian commercial relations were hampered by a lack of credit and rapidly depreciating Russian money.[7] The termination of trade with Britain could not have hit Russia at a worse time: its economy was already saddled with a heavy foreign debt, while the national deficit, which stood at about 7 million rubles in 1801, reached 143 million rubles in 1809.[8] This contributed to the collapsing value of the paper ruble, made worse by the government's attempt to cover the growing deficit by printing more.[9] As a result, the value of the paper ruble plummeted from a high of 67 silver kopecks in June 1807 to just 25 kopecks in December 1810. This had a dramatic effect on the cost of maintaining Russian armies in far-flung regions of the empire and waging wars on several fronts. By 1812 Russia was facing economic calamity, as the actual value of the state's tax income was just two-thirds of what it had been prior to Tilsit.[10]

Starting in 1810, the Russian government took measures to stabilize the economy, reducing the amount of money printed, raising taxes, cutting spending, and restricting the import of luxury items through prohibitive tariffs. Alexander agreed to impose tariffs on luxury items (which were mostly French) and to relax restrictions for vessels under neutral flags, regardless of whose goods they carried. As trade rebounded at the Russian ports, Napoleon raged that "the Spanish, Portuguese, American, Swedish, and even French flags serve as a disguise for English trade. All these vessels are English; they are loaded for English commerce and with English merchandise." If Russia would only make serious efforts to counteract such trade, he believed, Britain would be on its knees within a year.[11] Instead, in 1811, Alexander's new decrees effectively took Russia out of the Continental System.

Poland was one of the crucial sources of friction between the two leaders. Napoleon's creation of the Grand Duchy of Warsaw, "a splinter in the body of Russia," as Emperor Alexander once described it, awakened Russian fears of a full reconstitution of Polish lands and national identity. Napoleon rebuffed Russian efforts to secure written guarantees that Poland would never be restored. He believed that the Duchy of Warsaw must endure as a strategic barrier against Russia: "The interests of France, those of Germany and Europe require it; the policy commands it...and honor demands it."[12] Franco-Russian interests also clashed over the future of the Ottoman Empire; Alexander's ambition of securing the Dardanelles appeared to be a move that Napoleon—fearing Russian interference in the Mediterranean—was determined to block. Neither could Russia and France agree on their designs to partition the Balkan Peninsula. Moreover, Napoleon's reorganization of the Confederation of the Rhine affected one of Russia's core interests in Europe. The Russian imperial house had long-standing familial connections with the German ruling princes, some of whom had seen their status affected by Napoleon. Alexander's own brother-in-law lost his domain when Napoleon annexed the Duchy of Oldenburg to France in 1810, a move that Alexander perceived as a deliberate insult, though the actual cause of it had been the Duke of Oldenburg's violation of the provisions of the Continental System, permitting British products to be smuggled into the duchy.[13]

It was apparent by the end of the first decade of the nineteenth century that the political settlement reached at Tilsit had outlived its course and that a new European war would soon ignite in Europe. French foreign minister Jean-Baptiste de Nompère de Champagny's "Report on Continental Affairs" (1810) argued that the alliance with Russia had served its purpose and that France should return to its traditional reliance on the Ottoman Empire, Sweden, and Poland to contain the "Russian imperial colossus."[14] Alexander and his advisors had also reached the conclusion that war with France was imminent, and therefore sought to entice Berlin and Vienna to turn against Napoleon. But the French presence in the Germanic states and the defeat of Austria in 1809 left little choice for these countries other than to submit to Napoleon.[15] According to a treaty signed on February 24, 1812, Prussia agreed to allow French and allied forces free passage through its territory and to supply 20,000 troops for a possible campaign against Russia; Prussia would also provide the French military with necessary supplies.[16]

France likewise negotiated an alliance with Austria. Having suffered four defeats at Napoleon's hands in the preceding fifteen years, Austria was not particularly interested in defying France, and the memories of Russia's support of France against Austria in 1809 remained fresh. In 1810–1812 Napoleon endeavored to tie Austria closer to France. His marriage to Austrian archduchess Marie Louise was the first step in this direction, followed by overtures to convince the Austrian emperor, Francis I, to accept an alliance. Austrian foreign minister Metternich exploited this opportunity to pursue a more conciliatory, yet pragmatic, policy of maintaining good relations with France—so long as Napoleon was on top of his game. In the new Treaty of Paris (March 14, 1812), France and Austria pledged mutual support and Austria agreed to raise an auxiliary corps of 30,000 men, under Karl Philipp, Fürst zu Schwarzenberg, that would report to Napoleon's supreme command in case of a war against Russia. Austria, however, played a duplicitous game. One month later Metternich assured Emperor Alexander that Austria would not pursue any war aggressively.[17]

Although Napoleon's overall strategy for any war against Russia considered the use of Sweden and the Ottoman Empire to form his extreme flanks, he was unable to exercise influence over either power. Sweden, though led by a former French marshal, Bernadotte, formed an alliance with Russia in April 1812. By the terms of the Treaty of St. Petersburg, the two nations pledged to "ensure safety of their possessions and the independence of the North, which are equally threatened by the ambitious and predatory plans of France." St. Petersburg and Stockholm agreed to create a combined force to land in Swedish Pomerania, which had been seized by France, and Russia agreed to aid Sweden in annexing Norway either by negotiations with Denmark or by rendering military assistance.[18] The treaty had immediate consequences as well, as it secured Russia's northern frontiers and freed up military forces deployed in Finland. As for the Ottomans, their traditional alliance with France made them a natural ally for Napoleon, but their six-year war against Russia had been disastrous. Their armies were defeated and their treasury exhausted. As noted, Russia achieved a significant diplomatic success in May 1812 when the Turks agreed to sign the Treaty of Bucharest. Although compelled to surrender most of its conquests in the Danubian Principalities, Russia did retain Bessarabia and western Georgia, and, most important, freed up the entire Army of the Danube to participate in military operations against Napoleon.[19]

Between the spring of 1810 and summer of 1812 Napoleon undertook preparations for war on a scale larger than any he had done before. The popular belief is that he underestimated the difficulties that lay before him. Actually, he was well aware of the challenges he would face in Russia, and the wide array of issues discussed in his correspondence during this period proves this. Together with a study of the history and geography of Russia, his previous campaigns in Poland had provided him with personal experience in fighting in underpopulated areas that lacked supplies and good roads.[20] He warned that war in Russia would "in no way resemble one in Austria; without means of transport, everything would become useless," and that "we can hope for nothing from the countryside and accordingly must take everything with us."[21] New levies of conscripts were called up, and French garrisons in northern Germany, particularly at Danzig and Hamburg, were reinforced.[22] Napoleon then coordinated the organization and redeployment of the twelve corps that made up his new Grande Armée, meticulously supervising the movements and outfitting of tens of thousands of troops and the establishment of a vast supply of ammunition depots to support them. The valley of the Vistula River became a logistical base for the Grande Armée. Supply and ammunition depots were set up at Danzig, Glogau, Küstrin, Stettin, Warsaw, Modlin, Thorn, and Marienburg, and an enormous number of supply trains were formed, tasked with transporting forty days' worth of supplies during the invasion.[23]

After the Russians scored a decisive victory over the Turks at Ruse in late 1811 and forced the sultan to sign an armistice, Napoleon fast-tracked his preparations. By the spring of 1812 the Grande Armée of some 600,000 men, with 1,372 guns and 180,000 horses, had assembled in northern Germany and the Duchy of Warsaw.[24] Approximately half of its manpower consisted of troops from Napoleon's allies, including Austria, Prussia, Saxony, Spain, Bavaria, Poland, and Italy. The army was divided into three primary commands deployed in an area ranging from Tilsit to Lublin, with the center and right wing remaining under direct command of the emperor, who, despite the vastness of the theater of war—his forces were scattered over a distance of some 250 miles—stayed true to his principle of unity of command. Russia fielded about 650,000 men in 1812, but they were scattered throughout Moldavia, the Crimea, the Caucasus, Finland, and other regions, leaving just 250,000 men with something over 900 guns in the western provinces to fend off Napoleon's invasion. These forces were organized in three major armies and several separate corps, with Mikhail Barclay de Tolly leading the First Western Army and Prince Peter Bagration in charge of the Second Western Army.

On June 23–24 the Grande Armée crossed the Nieman River. Knowing the scope of the Russian Empire, Napoleon planned to engage the Russians as soon as possible and had every confidence that he could achieve victory within three weeks by waging decisive battles in frontier regions. His first intent upon crossing the Nieman was to envelop the enemy in a sweeping flanking maneuver through Vilna.[25] If successfully executed, this operation would have defeated the Russian armies. Yet neither Napoleon's advance to Vilna to envelop the First Western Army nor his brother Jérôme's effort to pin down the Second Western Army succeeded. On June 28 Napoleon reached Vilna, where the Polish residents received him with acclamation. He knew better than to celebrate. The Vilna maneuver was Napoleon's first major operation of the war and it proved to be a failure, one that largely set the tone for the next two and half months. The First and Second Western Armies avoided direct confrontation with superior enemy forces and embarked on a continuous retreat that eventually brought them to the gates of Smolensk. As they withdrew, the Russians turned to a scorched-earth policy, destroying supplies and provisions to deny resources to the enemy. The searing heat and torrential rains further hampered Napoleon's plans and led to unexpectedly high losses for the Grande Armée. By July 1, hundreds of decomposing animal carcasses choked the road from Kovno to Vilna.

Events around Vilna showed how the sheer size of the Grande Armée sapped its leadership's ability to cope with challenges. The dramatic increase in the size of units produced vacancies for commissioned and noncommissioned officers, which were filled with less-than-suitable candidates; just eight days into the campaign, Napoleon himself complained about his staff officers and the fact that "nothing gets done."[26] Indeed, internal reports and correspondence reveal that Napoleon's headquarters operated in a fog of war. Despite having experienced military intelligence and a strong cavalry force, the French headquarters had rather limited knowledge about the enemy's location and virtually nothing about its intentions. Even simple tasks such as identifying villages and routes became difficult, causing Marshal Berthier to grumble that "the maps we currently use are not sufficiently detailed and we do not really know where [units] are located."[27] A day later it was Napoleon's turn to complain that "our maps are so deficient that they are practically unusable."[28]

Even more worrisome were the logistics. Almost as soon as it crossed into Russia, the Grande Armée began encountering problems that undermined its operations. In previous campaigns Napoleon's troops had dispersed to subsist off the land and frequently remained on the move to avoid exhausting a region's resources. This campaign should have been no exception to this practice, and the very timing of the invasion points to Napoleon's intention to take full advantage of the harvest cycle. The late summer would have provided fresh crops of hay and oats to replenish his stocks. However, Napoleon's earlier campaigns had been conducted in central Europe's densely populated and well-developed regions, places where the agricultural revolution and a

compact network of first-rate roads (in many cases, paved chaussées) had created a favorable environment for the mobile style of warfare that Napoleon
preferred. By comparison, Russia's western provinces were among the most
underdeveloped regions in Europe. Napoleon and his commanders quickly
realized that the heavy four-horse caissons could not, for the most part, be
used in Russia because of their weight and the condition of roads (especially
after heavy rains), forcing them to switch to smaller carts seized from the
locals. This, however, resulted in delays and disorder. Thus in the first few
weeks of the war it was not so much lack of supplies that affected Napoleon's
men as the inability to transport stocks to them in timely fashion.

The first month of the war also showed mixed results for the Russians.
On the diplomatic front they had negotiated treaties not only with Sweden
and the Ottoman Empire but also with Britain. The Treaties of Örebro,
signed between Russia, Sweden, and Britain on July 18, 1812, put an end to
the conflicts that these nations had been engaged in and paved the way for
their cooperation against France, effectively laying the foundation for the
establishment of the Sixth Coalition, which fought Napoleon in 1813–1814.[29]
Two days later, in the Treaty of Velikie Luki, Russia became the first great
power to officially recognize the representatives of the Spanish Cortes, which
was waging a bloody guerrilla war against Napoleon; both sides agreed to
coordinate their struggles against France.[30]

However, as key as these diplomatic successes were, they failed to deliver
what Russia needed the most—immediate military support against the invading Grande Armée. Sweden preferred to wait and see the outcome of the war
before openly confronting Napoleon.[31] Britain's position was more complex.
Though much has been made in the historical literature of British shipments of
weapons, the reality is that despite its promises to provide 150,000 muskets,
less than a third of that was actually delivered before the war was over. And even
then Britain sold, at inflated prices, older weaponry that turned out to be of
larger caliber than the existing Russian ammunition.[32] As a result, it had to be
retrofitted at the Russian arsenals at additional cost.[33] Neither was Britain willing to provide subsidies to alleviate Russian military expenses. Castlereagh
informed the Russian envoy that the war had distressed British finances.[34]
Britain's financial position had indeed been weakened by the effects of the
Continental System, the poor harvests of 1810–1811 (which contributed to
popular unrest in the Midlands and North of England), and the outbreak of
large-scale Luddite riots against new industrial technology.[35] Moreover, the
British were not fully convinced that Russia would be able to resist Napoleon
and were concerned that Emperor Alexander might be compelled to accept
another Tilsit-like agreement. Hence, their position was that should Russia

engage in a war with France, they were ready to help as far as they could without providing direct and immediate aid. British statesmen believed that their principal war efforts needed to be made in the Iberian Peninsula, where they could do more to undermine the French war effort and thus indirectly help Russia.

As their armies united at Smolensk, the Russians faced a crisis of command, one that stemmed from discord between the old Russian aristocracy and the foreign-born officers who had gained influence at the court and military headquarters. The immediate cause of friction lay in the contrasting strategic views evident among senior officers, who represented opposing parties. Barclay de Tolly, the nominal commander in chief, was surrounded by a group of officers (many of them of German descent) who supported the defensive strategy and urged a continued Russian withdrawal to weaken Napoleon. Opposing them was the much larger "Russian party," led by Prince Bagration (himself a Georgian), urging an immediate counteroffensive. Anti-Barclay sentiments were so strong among the senior officers that they called for the appointment of Bagration to the supreme command; some even encouraged Bagration to replace Barclay de Tolly by force.

Bending to this pressure, Barclay de Tolly agreed to an offensive at Smolensk, in an attempt to break through the French center and destroy the remaining French corps piecemeal. But due to differences among the commanders—made worse by Barclay de Tolly's indecision—precious time was lost in futile maneuvering, which allowed Napoleon to recognize Russian intentions and seize the initiative. In a maneuver that once again showcased his operational skill, Napoleon moved more than 100,000 men across the Dnieper River and, flanking the Russian forces, rapidly advanced on Smolensk. Yet a resolute stand by a small Russian rear guard at Krasnyi (August 14) halted the French movement and enabled the Russians to prepare Smolensk for defense. On August 15–16 the Russians repulsed the enemy assaults on Smolensk but were forced to abandon the city and withdraw east toward Moscow.

Napoleon spent several days at Smolensk and could not conceal his frustration. In the five weeks since crossing the Niemen, he had failed to bring the enemy to battle and succeeded only in occupying a few towns and villages. The supply system had already begun to collapse, and the lack of provisions caused significant disorder in the army, while bands of marauders who had abandoned their units roamed the countryside. The scarcity of drinking water during the hot midsummer season forced Napoleon's men to consume polluted water from swampy streams and lakes, which naturally resulted in the outbreak of dysentery and other diseases, affecting tens of thousands of troops.[36] A Württembergian physician lamented that diarrhea "assumed such violent scope that it was impossible to assure normal service, let alone indulge in any kind of drill. The houses were all filled with sick men, and in the camp itself there was such a continuous running back and forth behind the front that it was as though purgatives had been administered to entire regiments."[37] Attrition rates due to malnutrition, disease, and other factors were uncommonly high, and some units had already lost up to half of their strength.[38]

Napoleon seemed unsure about what course to take. He could halt his operations and regroup. He had already considered such an idea at Vilna and had told one of his officers that his intention was to advance as far as Smolensk and then return to Vilna and establish winter quarters closer to the border. But he based this plan on the assumption that the Russians would have been defeated by now. As it stood, Napoleon had little to show after almost two months of campaigning. Furthermore, several new factors had appeared to complicate his circumstances. He had thought the Russian forces on the flanks would follow the movements of their main armies, but the Third Western Army of General Alexander Tormasov held ground and even scored a major victory over Schwarzenberg in the south, while the Russian general Peter Wittgenstein held his own against Marshals Oudinot and Saint-Cyr. More important, the conclusion of peace between Russia and the Ottoman Empire released the Russian Army of the Danube under Admiral Pavel Vasilievich Chichagov, who clearly intended to move up from the Danubian Principalities and threaten the right wing of the Grande Armée. The Russo-Swedish negotiations promised to do the same in the north, where the Franco-Prussian corps was already bogged down near Riga. Battles and strategic consumption had reduced the strength of the central army group to fewer than 180,000 men.

Aside from logistical and operational concerns, Napoleon also had to account for the political aspect of the war. He was not just a commander in chief but also the head of state, presiding over a vast empire. In his mind, political considerations rendered any retrograde movement unthinkable, as it would appear tantamount to failure in the eyes of Europe and might jeopardize the French imperium. For Napoleon, the only course was to continue the advance in the hope of forcing the Russians to accept a decisive battle, which would allow him to dictate peace terms. With at least two months of good weather still ahead of him, he thought he had sufficient time to accomplish this.

The surrender of Smolensk created an uproar in the Russian army and in Russian society at large, and caused Emperor Alexander to replace Barclay de Tolly with General Mikhail Kutuzov, who had led the Russian troops at Austerlitz seven year earlier. Assuming command at the end of August,

Kutuzov withdrew the combined Russian armies still farther to the east, taking positions near the village of Borodino, about seventy miles west of Moscow. Here, on September 7, Napoleon finally got the decisive battle that he had sought for so long.

Borodino was neither Austerlitz nor Wagram. In a savage and bloody struggle involving close to 300,000 men, both sides displayed great bravery and steadfastness but suffered horrendous losses—upward of 35,000 French and 45,000 Russian killed or wounded in twelve hours of fighting.[39] The battle produced no decisive results militarily or politically. The Russian emperor was unshaken in his determination to fight, while his army remained unbroken and made an orderly retreat toward Moscow, which Napoleon expected the Russians to defend. Moscow was the largest Russian city, had served as the former capital, and was the very representation of the entire country, which Europeans had long referred to as "Muscovy."[40] He was mistaken about what the Russians would do, however: in a striking decision, the Russians ordered the evacuation of the entire city, a quarter million people—the first time such an evacuation had been attempted in the modern era—and abandoned it without a fight. On September 14, the French emperor rode down the deserted streets of the great Russian city, which would soon be completely destroyed in the ensuing conflagration. The fire was certainly not a deliberate action by Napoleon, who had every reason to preserve the city. Nor was it the outcome of long-term Russian planning, as has long been alleged: the fire began while the Russian army was still withdrawing through the city, and no Russian leader would have deliberately sanctioned such a potentially catastrophic action. The conflagration was caused by a combination of factors. Moscow governor Fedor Rostopchin contributed to it by ordering the destruction of a supply depot, as well as through his propaganda broadsheets, which in the preceding weeks had shaped the popular psyche and encouraged people to destroy their homes rather than see them despoiled by the enemy. The general evacuation of Moscow was an unprecedented move on the part of the Russian authorities, since no major European city had ever been completely evacuated in the face of the enemy. The invading army began its despoliation of the city almost immediately, providing the opportunity for fire to break out. And once the spark took hold, the spell of dry weather combined with strong winds and a lack of firefighting equipment (which had been evacuated) to spread the flames, which found plenty of fuel in the thousands of wooden buildings. The fiery devastation of the Russian capital had a profound effect on the troops of the Grande Armée, as they were forced to billet amid the ruins, lacking proper provisions and shelter. Discipline became lax; many turned to pillaging.[41]

Napoleon spent thirty-six days in Moscow. It is impossible to explain, one French general later observed, "this pertinacity in prolonging the stay of the army in the center of Russia, amidst the smoking ruins of the ancient capital, except by supposing that he was nearly certain of the speedy conclusion of peace."[42] Simply abandoning Moscow and retreating was, in Napoleon's opinion, tantamount to acknowledging defeat. Yet staying in the burnt-out city offered only bleak prospects for ending the war. Signing a peace treaty could have offered a way out of this situation, but Napoleon's repeated proposals were rejected. Like many of his contemporaries, Napoleon had misread Alexander's character and believed that the Russian emperor lacked strength of will.[43] He sustained his hopes for peace with the recollections of Tilsit and Erfurt, believing that the Francophiles in the Russian court would push Alexander in that direction.[44] Napoleon thus failed to understand how profoundly his relationship with Alexander, as well as the mood of Russian society, had changed. The tsar was well aware of the widespread displeasure that prevailed in Russia over his perceived subservience to Napoleon. Such sentiments only further intensified in the wake of the continual withdrawal of the Russian armies and loss of Russian provinces. Just days after the fall of Moscow, Grand Duchess Catherine warned her brother of people's exasperation. "Discontent is at its highest and your person is far from being spared," she noted. "If such news reaches me, you can imagine the rest. You are openly accused of having brought disaster upon your empire, of having caused general ruin and the ruin of private individuals, lastly, of having lost the honor of the country and your own personal honor. I leave it to you to judge the state of affairs in a country whose leader is so despised."[45] Even had he desired it, Alexander could not afford to compromise with the man who had invaded and despoiled his realm: public opinion was against it, and any sign of weakness on Alexander's part might have led to tragic consequences. A second Tilsit would have sealed the condemnation of his reign, and Alexander knew only too well what happened to unpopular monarchs in Russia—the preceding eighty years had witnessed a number of palace coups and murders of reigning sovereigns, including Alexander's own father.

With a Russian response to his peace offers not forthcoming, Napoleon had no choice but to leave Moscow. The sudden defeat of one of his corps on the river Chernishnya, north of Tarutino, on October 18 served a wake-up call for the emperor, who realized the urgency of the need to abandon the devastated ruins of Moscow before winter arrived and the Russians descended upon him. His forces had dwindled to just 100,000 men, accompanied by thousands of civilians and stragglers as well as an enormous baggage train laden with loot. "Anyone who did not see the French army leave Moscow," observed one eyewitness, "can only have a very weak impression of what the armies of Greece and Rome must have looked like when they marched back from Troy and Carthage."[46] Traffic on this scale not only slowed the army's movements but also distracted the troops, many of whom were more concerned about securing their portion of plunder than about maintaining discipline.

Burdened as it was, the Grande Armée ground along, gridlocking when encountering streams and defiles. To make matters worse, autumnal rains turned the roads into rivers of mud. Although Napoleon had gained a tactical victory at Maloyaroslavets on October 24, it was in fact a strategic defeat because the Russian army had prevented him from reaching the still-intact and abundant southern provinces. Instead, the Grande Armée had to retrace its steps along the devastated route via Smolensk.[47] This battle also signaled a change in the very nature of the campaign. Napoleon's strategic withdrawal from Moscow had by now turned into an outright retreat, with the Grande Armée ceasing offensive operations and seeking only to get out of the occupied provinces as fast as possible. The morale of the army plunged as the troops marched across the battlefield of Borodino, still covered with corpses half eaten by wolves or pecked at by carrion crows.

By early November Napoleon, beset everywhere by the Russian forces, had reached Smolensk, where his cold and hungry soldiers—many of whom had subsisted on horseflesh for the past few days—ravaged the magazines, leaving virtually no provisions to sustain the army. It was here that Napoleon received news from France that a false report of his death had led to a failed coup by General Claude François Malet in Paris. This event revealed the nature of the empire and deeply affected Napoleon, making him sensible to the necessity of quitting the army as soon as he could and returning to Paris to consolidate his control over the empire.[48]

Napoleon weighed his options. The strategic situation had clearly turned against him. During the fourteen days since departing from Moscow, the Grande Armée had suffered thousands of losses. With each passing day, the number of men under arms diminished, while the number of stragglers swelled. Remaining at Smolensk appeared pointless; the city was untenable and the stores were exhausted. With Russian forces closing from the north, south, and east, the French emperor believed his only chance of escape was to quit Smolensk, beat the converging Russian forces to the Berezina River, and seek better winter quarters farther west.

As the French army departed Smolensk, it came under attack from the Russian forces near Krasnyi, where the two sides fought a series of engagements on November 15–18. Individual French corps were temporarily cut off but kept fighting on, a testament to the enduring resilience of the French organization and leadership, especially on the part of Marshal Ney, who got separated from the main forces and made a heroic fighting retreat across the Dnieper River. Napoleon escaped the Russian encirclement but at the cost of losing some 30,000 men and almost all of his artillery. While the army still counted "corps" and "divisions," many were reduced to regimental strength, and the total number of combat-ready troops could not have exceeded 30,000 men, who were heavily burdened by tens of thousands of stragglers.

As Napoleon retreated westward the Russians had a unique chance of trapping him at the Berezina River. The main Russian army under Kutuzov pursued the Grande Armée from the east, while Wittgenstein's corps converged from the northeast and Chichagov's army marched from the southwest. They surrounded the enemy near the small town of Borisov on the Berezina. In the desperate fighting that took place on November 25–29, Napoleon crossed the river with a core of his army but lost up to 40,000 men, most of them stragglers. Napoleon's escape was due not to his own genius but to his dedicated and skilled troops, the sound leadership of the French officer corps, and, most crucially, the lack of Russian military initiative and coordination.[49]

The retreat from the Berezina to the Nieman River contains little of military interest. Much of the Grande Armée was now gone; although the chain of command remained relatively intact, relations between officers, especially corps commanders and marshals, deteriorated. Napoleon himself considered his job as a military leader largely done and decided to return to Paris to assume his mantle of political leader, which had been shaken by the recent coup attempt. On December 5 he appointed his brother-in-law Marshal Murat to take charge of what was left of the army and departed for France.[50]

So ended, in the words of a British eyewitness, the "severest campaign of six months on record in the annals of the world."[51] Indeed, there are few other examples of wars involving such enormous forces, vast distances, logistical challenges, and decisive outcomes within such a short period of time. The war had disastrous consequences for the Napoleonic Empire; it had been previously tested, but none of its earlier setbacks approached the scale of the defeat in Russia. The Grand Armée was almost entirely destroyed. The invasion ultimately involved some 600,000 men—450,000 men in the main thrust and about 150,000 reinforcements brought in later in the war—but fewer than 100,000 re-crossed the Niemen in December; of the half a million losses, probably as many as 100,000 deserted and more than 120,000 had been captured.[52] The rest perished from disease, battle wounds, or exposure to the elements. Equally catastrophic was the loss in matériel. Napoleon lost more than 920 of some 1,300 cannon and his cavalry was virtually wiped out—approximately 200,000 trained horses lay dead in the Russian countryside. Neither the artillery nor the cavalry fully recovered during the subsequent campaigns.

It has long been claimed that "General Winter" defeated Napoleon in Russia. Such claims are dubious. Contemporary data from meteorological stations reveal that the winter was in fact mild until late November, by which time Napoleon had already all but lost the war. The Grande Armée had lost almost half of its strength in the first eight weeks of the war, due to garrisoning, diseases, desertions, and casualties. It had neither the high standard of discipline nor the wholehearted devotion that it had demonstrated in previous campaigns. The troops included more than a dozen nationalities, so they were bound to lose cohesion and discipline under the vicissitudes of failure. Although Napoleon had made thorough logistical preparations, his supply system failed to function properly: major depots were established at too great a distance from the army, while lack of transport infrastructure within Russia prevented the timely delivery of available supplies to the troops. The Russian strategic plan of attrition through strategic withdrawal and a scorched-earth policy meant that the countryside provided the enemy with few provisions, especially in forage, which led to heavy losses in transport animals and war horses.

Napoleon did demonstrate glimpses of his military genius, and his operations at Vilna, Minsk, and Smolensk were well conceived and could have delivered a decisive victory. Yet time and again the emperor failed to bring them to fruition. His subordinates frequently showed lack of initiative or made poor tactical choices, which had effects on the operational level. Finally, Napoleon had initiated a vast campaign without a clear political strategy in mind. Hence we see him showing uncertainty and lingering too long at Vilna (eighteen days), Vitebsk (twelve days), and Moscow (thirty-five days) while he considered what to do next.

The Russian side must be given its share of credit as well. Its troops performed admirably and demonstrated fortitude and devotion, while their generals, despite frequent infighting and jealousy, acted with sufficient tactical, operational, and strategic foresight to win the war. Russian diplomats had successfully outsmarted their French counterparts, maintaining secret contacts with Prussia and Austria and negotiating treaties with the Ottoman Empire and Sweden, which in turn resulted in the ability of two Russian armies to operate on the wings of the Grande Armée.

Upon reaching the imperial border, the Russian leadership debated whether to cross it in pursuit of Napoleon or to remain at home and regroup. Some senior figures were against crossing the frontier, arguing that it was not for Russia to liberate the rest of Europe. Chief among them was Kutuzov, who looked beyond strictly military factors and believed that it was not in Russia's best interests to weaken Napoleon. "I am by no means sure that the total destruction of Napoleon and his army would be such a benefit to the world," Kutuzov noted. "His succession would not fall to Russia or any other Continental power, but to the power which already commands the sea [Britain], and whose domination would then be intolerable."[53] Besides, continuing war against France would involve additional losses at a time when it was important to preserve the army to ensure Russia's role in future political developments in Europe. "Our young hotheads are angry at me," the Russian commander in chief lamented, "for I restrain their frenzy; but they do not realize that...we cannot reach the frontiers with empty hands [i.e., without an army]."[54]

The Russian emperor, however, disagreed. As he stood on the frozen banks of the Nieman River, Alexander appreciated the momentous nature of the event he was witnessing. The French colossus was teetering, and the future of Europe was at stake.

———◦◦◦✕◦◦◦———

Napoleon's invasion of Russia commenced almost simultaneously with the American attack on Canada, an event often labeled as a "forgotten conflict."[55] Historian William Kingsford's observation at the end of the nineteenth century that the Anglo-American War of 1812 had not been forgotten in Britain because it has never been known there is largely true because the North American events remained, for a long time, overshadowed by the titanic struggles in Europe. Nevertheless, these events were of great significance to the fate of North America and had direct ramifications for the Napoleonic Wars.

Contrary to (often mythologized) public perceptions of the War of 1812, this was not a conflict between a peaceful American republic and an arrogant imperial power. Rather, the dispute sprang from several crucial circumstances. Britain was engaged in a decisive struggle against Napoleonic France and was prepared to go to any length to prevail over its rival, including by denying neutral trade, which was dominated by the United States. The American leaders had chosen to stay out of European squabbles in order to exploit the advantages that a neutral stance conferred. Furthermore, they had pursued aggrandizing policies and exploited events in Europe to challenge the imperial status quo in North America. In July 1805 the French ambassador to Washington, Louis Marie Turreau, noted that the United States was simply waiting for an opportune moment to pursue territorial claims against the Spanish Empire and quoted US secretary of state James Madison's statement that "when the pear is ripe it will fall of its own accord."[56] This conflict represented, as historian Troy Bickham observed recently, American assertion of national sovereignty against its former imperial master.[57]

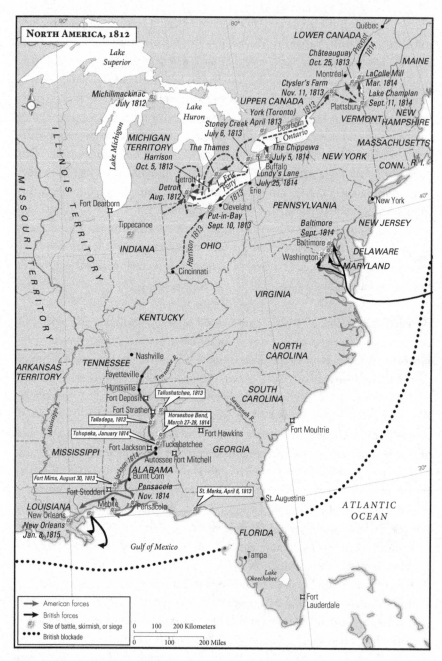

Map 26: North America, 1812

In a confidential address to the US Congress, President James Madison enumerated a long list of grievances, but the principal causes of the war can be distilled to three issues: British incitement of Native Americans, impressment of American seamen by the Royal Navy, and British interference with American trade.[58] Relations between the United States and Native Americans were tense, if not outright hostile; the problems were not new and predated the existence of the American republic. The growing white settler population meant increased demand for land that could be secured only at the expense of the native population; there was a mounting "land hunger," as some historians describe it, and many Americans openly embraced the idea of not only dispossessing native tribes but also targeting neighboring European possessions. In June 1812, Thomas Jefferson wrote to Madison that the young men of Virginia were eager to fight, and "the only enquiry they make is whether they are to go to Canada or Florida."[59] The Creeks, Cherokees, and other tribes faced heavy pressure to surrender their lands. In the 1790s the United States organized several military expeditions against the tribes that resisted white settlers' encroachment on their lands. The talented Miami chief Little Turtle successfully repelled some of them, inflicting one of the most disastrous defeats on the American forces in the Battle of the Wabash in November 1791. The young Shawnee warrior Tecumseh distinguished himself on this occasion and went on to become a leader of a Native American confederation that challenged US encroachments. In August 1810 he opposed US takeover of the lands that are present-day Illinois and Indiana, where the Shawnees and other tribes had long resided, and launched what became known as Tecumseh's War. Although the high point of this conflict occurred in the US victory at Tippecanoe in 1811, Tecumseh gained British allies in Canada and continued his resistance within the wider North American conflict that erupted in 1812. To restrain US ambitions, many Native Americans turned to Britain for help; unsurprisingly, the British welcomed these overtures and provided arms to the tribes, which they considered as "natural allies," as the London *Times* put it in 1812, against US expansionism.[60]

The other US grievances were interrelated since both dealt with maritime issues. Impressment, illegal in principle and unjust in practice, strained relations between Britain and the United States. It was occasioned by the continued demands of British operations against France between 1793 and 1812, when the size of the Royal Navy increased from 235 to 584 warships, with a corresponding increase in the number of seamen from 36,000 to 114,000. Britain was hard pressed for sailors to maintain its naval stations across the globe while blockading the French-controlled European ports. But this problem was not, as traditional historiography has long claimed, because of harsh working conditions, poor pay, or the image of a warship as a floating hell full of, in the apt description of Winston Churchill, "rum, sodomy, and the lash."[61] The Royal Navy, in fact, remained popular with experienced mariners and unskilled landsmen, who considered it a good opportunity for advancement. Nor was there a lack of volunteers; recent scholarship has shown that volunteers accounted for as many as 70 percent of seamen aboard British warships. Instead, manpower problems were caused by a shortage of available skilled sailors, many of whom turned their backs on the dangerous life aboard a British warship in favor of a more lucrative one on an American merchant ship; since the start of the French Revolutionary Wars in Europe, the American merchant navy had been steadily increasing in size, becoming, in terms of tonnage, second only to Britain's fleet. By 1812 the British government estimated that as many as 20,000 British sailors served on American ships. Hence the Royal Navy regularly intercepted and boarded American vessels in search of British subjects who could be impressed. The exact number of sailors impressed from American ships is hard to establish, but probably as many as 6,500 seamen were taken by the British during the Napoleonic Wars.[62]

The period of neutrality after 1793 had seen brisk economic activity and commercial growth for the United States, with benefits clearly visible in shipbuilding and export industries.[63] Both the British orders-in-council and Napoleon's Continental System dramatically changed the situation in 1806–1807, however. Neutral vessels, including American ones, were increasingly forced to enter British ports before proceeding to their destinations, which in turn exposed them to French retribution, as Napoleon authorized the capture of any vessels that submitted to British demands.

Britain's orders-in-council caused rapidly escalating frictions with the United States, and on June 22, 1807, the two countries were brought to the brink of war in the Chesapeake-Leopard affair. The American frigate Chesapeake, sailing from Norfolk, Virginia, to the Mediterranean Sea, was intercepted by HMS Leopard, which insisted on its right to examine the American ship for deserters. Upon the American refusal, the British warship opened fire, killing or wounding twenty-one American seamen. After inspecting the ship and impressing four men, Leopard sailed away, while Chesapeake limped back to Virginia.[64] The news of the incident triggered an explosion of indignation across the United States and inflamed national sentiment, with many clamoring for a war with Britain. Unwilling to risk a violent confrontation with London, President Thomas Jefferson preferred a more circumspect approach. In July he ordered all British warships from American waters.

Facing further depredations by France and Britain, Jefferson toughened his stance with the Embargo Act (December 28, 1807), which prohibited

US exports. The purpose of this embargo was to compel Britain and France to modify their decrees by denying them access to American commerce. The embargo hit Britain harder than France. It also proved to be quite detrimental to the United States. Rear Admiral Alfred Thayer Mahan, the American exponent of sea power, later observed that this embargo had all the deficiencies of a blockade by an enemy and none of the advantages of actual war, such as the opportunity to capture British ships or threaten British territory. This self-imposed blockade had a profound impact on American ports, undermining American economic prosperity and cutting into government revenues. British traveler John Lambert, who visited New York in the spring of 1808, described "the melancholy dejection that was painted upon the countenances of the people, whose seemed to have taken leave of all their former gaiety and cheerfulness." Grass was growing at the New York wharfs.[65] As in the case of Napoleon's Continental Blockade, Jefferson's embargo was impossible to fully enforce. It produced widespread smuggling that benefited British ports in Nova Scotia and generated considerable disgruntlement in New England.

With opposition to the embargo increasing, in March 1809 the US Congress repealed the Embargo Act, substituting for it the Non-Intercourse Act, which interdicted American waters to all British and French vessels but allowed American vessels to freely conduct trade. At the same time, George Canning, the British minister of foreign affairs, dispatched D. M. Erskine to negotiate with the United States. The resulting Erskine Agreement (April 18–19), which Erskine concluded in violation of his instructions, pledged to end the orders-in-council, establish free trade between Britain and the United States, and settle grievances stemming from the *Chesapeake-Leopard* affair; President Madison pledged to end the American non-intercourse stance as soon as the British orders-in-council were withdrawn. None of this came to be. The British government repudiated the agreement, given that Erskine had been unable to meet Canning's request to gain American acquiescence to British enforcement of orders-in-council and the acceptance of the colonial trade laws.[66] This setback only further soured Anglo-American relations. Napoleon exploited these circumstances to sanction the confiscation of more American vessels. His Vienna (August 4, 1809) and Rambouillet decrees (March 23, 1810) argued that since all American ships were banned from trading with France, any vessel claiming to be American while visiting French ports had to be engaged in smuggling. In May 1810 the United States adopted Macon's Bill No. 2, named after North Carolina congressman Nathaniel Macon, that was designed to discourage European belligerents from targeting American vessels. It repealed the Non-Intercourse Act of

1809 and proclaimed that the United States would resume trading with both belligerents. Macon's Bill had a direct and significant impact on the war in Europe. Over the next months, vast quantities of American wheat and flour—more than one million barrels of flour alone—were shipped to the Iberian Peninsula, where they sustained British military operations against the French.[67] This was a crucial moment in the Peninsular War. In the summer of 1810 French Marshal André Masséna had led some 70,000 men across the Portuguese frontier and pursued the Duke of Wellington to the Lines of Torres Vedras, where, as we have seen, the British and their Portuguese allies hunkered down while the French spent months eking out an existence in a devastated countryside. American supplies were crucial in sustaining Wellington's forces throughout this period.

Napoleon was alarmed by the prospects of revived commercial ties between Britain and the United States, as they would have undermined his Continental Blockade. Therefore, he quickly moved to exploit the Macon Bill's provision that should France repeal its decrees, the United States would renew its policy of non-importation against Britain, but that should Britain repeal its orders-in-council, the US would reimpose the non-importation policy on France. On August 5, 1810, the French foreign minister informed the American minister to France, John Armstrong, that Napoleon was revoking his earlier decrees, effectively preempting the British repeal of the orders-in-council.[68] Curiously, Napoleon had no intention of overhauling the Continental Blockade to suit American interests, nor could a simple note from the French foreign minister suspend such fundamental regulations. Madison nonetheless accepted the offer at face value, envisioning a diplomatic success. Britain refused to acknowledge France's revocation as valid and demanded more definitive proof before it would act. In response, the US Congress, still without proof that Napoleon had revoked his orders, declared that the non-intercourse provisions were in effect against Britain as of March 1, 1811, and forbade the entry of British ships and goods into the United States.[69]

Still in Portugal, the Duke of Wellington closely followed American economic policies, since they could have a direct impact on his war effort in the Iberian Peninsula. American supplies had become, as we've seen, crucial to the British war effort in Portugal and Spain: shipments of American grain increased from 80,000 bushels in 1807 to more than 230,000 in 1810 and an incredible 900,000 in 1812. On the eve of the War of 1812, a third of all ships arriving in Lisbon were American. One British observer noted that "if it was not for the supplies from America, the army here could not be maintained."[70] Unsurprisingly, in March 1811, Wellington was very concerned that closure of the American ports would cause significant food shortages for his troops and that it was "at all events desirable not to neglect any means which can be adopted to secure so desirable an object [grain]."[71] Bitter as it was at the US government for the non-importation policy, the British government understood that its options were limited. American supplies were too critical to its wartime economy, especially in the wake of the poor harvests in Britain in 1810. British business interests, especially in manufacturing, urged the government to take whatever steps were necessary to reopen trade with the United States. Following debate in Parliament, the British government repealed its orders-in-council restricting neutral trade on June 16, 1812. It would be weeks before this news became known in Washington, and by then it was too late. On June 18, 1812, the US Senate approved a declaration of war against Britain.[72]

The North American theater involved enormous geographical, operational and logistical challenges. George Prévost was the British governor-general of Canada and commander in chief, and the scope of his command was truly staggering. It stretched from Halifax, Nova Scotia, to Amherstburg in southwestern Upper Canada, an expanse of some 1,200 miles—a third greater than the distance from Paris to Warsaw. London, meanwhile, was 3,200 miles away from the seat of the British government in Canada. Prévost had just 10,000 British troops, supported by the Canadian militias and Native American allies, to defend this vast area. Unlike Europe, the region lacked a dense road network, but it did benefit from the presence of the Great Lakes and the oceanic coastline. Still, communications between various theaters of war in Upper Canada and the Niagara were laborious.[73]

The British war plans reveal that its focus was first and foremost on the struggle against Napoleon in Europe. "It must be needless for me to point out to you," wrote Lord Liverpool, secretary of state for war and colonies, to Prévost, "that the Exigencies of Public Service in Europe render it desirable that every Reduction of the British Force should be made in our distance possessions." Britain was engaged in a worldwide conflict against Napoleon, and resources were needed to "prosecute the contest with additional vigour in that quarter of the World, in which the Interests of the Country are...more immediately committed."[74] Liverpool's letter makes it clear that Canada was on its own and that the British strategy in Canada had to be defensive, designed to prevent any territorial gains by the Americans; even in later years, when the British launched attacks in the Gulf Coast and the Chesapeake, the overall aim of these campaigns was to ease pressure on the Canadian front line.[75] On the other side, American aims included not only concessions on the issues of impressment and maritime rights but also territorial aggrandizement at the expense of both Canada and the pro-British Native American tribes, like the great confederation established by the Shawnee chiefs Tecumseh and Tenskwatawa.[76]

On the eve of the war, Senator Henry Clay declared in a speech on the floor of the US Senate that "the militia of Kentucky are alone competent to place Montreal and Upper Canada at [our] feet."[77] He could not have been more wrong. But such sentiments prevailed in the minds of many American statesmen who, while itching for a war, refused to provide sufficient funding for it; they knew that the tax increases needed to sustain the war effort would be highly unpopular, especially during the election of 1811, when many seats in the US House of Representatives were at risk. Thus, the United States embarked on a war against one of the most powerful European powers having limited funding, a poorly prepared military, and a small navy. The American war plan envisioned a three-pronged invasion of Canada—principally around Lake Erie, near the Niagara River between Lake Erie and Lake Ontario, and near the St. Lawrence River and Lake Champlain—and the destruction of British naval forces on the Great Lakes. There was a general belief in the United States that, with their numerically superior forces and Britain deeply committed to the struggle against Napoleon in Europe, these objectives would be easily attained; there was also significant American immigration to the border areas, due to the offer of land grants to immigrants, raising the prospects that these settlers would favor the American cause. Invasion would be "a mere matter of marching," former president Thomas Jefferson noted optimistically in August 1812.[78]

It was not. The first five months of the war constituted a succession of American defeats as the more experienced and better-led British army prevailed over an untested opponent that struggled to implement an ill-conceived strategy and suffered from inadequate logistical support. "The best overall explanation for American defeat," concludes one American historian, "is that they had, from the start, ambitiously reached for all of Canada without the wherewithal to take and permanently hold any part of it."[79] In the middle of July the British captured Fort Mackinac, which controlled the strategic straits between Lake Michigan and Lake Huron, and by extension the fur trade on the Great Lakes. The American invasion under Brigadier General William Hull was thwarted by a vigorous British counterattack—under Major General Sir Isaac Brock, who had been actively supported by the Native American tribes under Tecumseh—that forced the Americans to retreat and abandon Fort Dearborn (present-day Chicago), leaving the entire Michigan Territory in British hands. On August 16 the British troops entered Detroit, sending shock waves across the entire American northwestern frontier.[80] In September the Seminole Indians and Black Seminoles, who had a long history of relations with the Spanish and British, launched raids into Georgia and defeated an American counterattack under Colonel Daniel Newnan in northern Florida. Indian attacks also occurred in the Indiana and Missouri territories.

Meanwhile, Major General Brock marched with his men to the eastern end of Lake Erie, where, in October, some 3,000 American troops (of whom just 900 were regulars) under New York militia leader Major General Stephen Van Rensselaer attempted to cross the Niagara River at Queenston Heights.[81] On October 13 Brock, despite being outnumbered, exploited divisions on the side of the Americans, whose militia contingent refused to leave the territorial limits of the United States, and attacked the small force of American regular troops as it was crossing over to the Canadian side. The ensuing battle led to a British victory, which was tempered by the death of Brock, a talented and charismatic officer who could have made a major impact in the war. Equally unsuccessful was the American attempt, under Major General Henry Dearborn, to invade Canada at Lacolle Mills near Champlain, Ontario. Defeated by a coalition of British regulars, Canadian militiamen, and Mohawk warriors, the Americans were forced to return to Plattsburgh, New York. Later the same month, US forces under Brigadier General Alexander Smyth made several poorly conceived and poorly implemented attempts to cross the Niagara River and invade Upper Canada, and were defeated at the battle of Frenchman's Creek (November 28).[82]

In bright contrast to the dismal performance of the US Army, the small but efficient American navy took on British sea power and celebrated successes in several single-ship actions.[83] Probably none was more famous than the destruction of HMS *Guerrière* by USS *Constitution* on August 19, 1812. The American frigate eluded a British blockade and, after making an epic three-day escape from a British squadron, encountered a British frigate, which it demolished in just a half-hour action. Throughout the fall of 1812 the US Navy demonstrated that, ship for ship, its seamanship and gunnery more than matched the vaunted British fleet and underscored the superiority of American ship designs—"superfrigates" powerful enough to engage any enemy frigate, yet fast enough to evade any ship-of-the-line. These dramatic ship-to-ship engagements, which Americans won, may not have threated British control of the seas but were still a disruptive factor that had wider repercussions for British commerce and the war effort. The impact of American commerce raiding was especially impressive: on one occasion the raiding sloop *Argus* captured twenty-one prizes in just a few months, throwing English merchants into a panic. Containing such attacks required substantial

British naval resources—for example, in the summer of 1813 the Royal Navy had more than fifteen men-of-war searching for Commodore John Rodgers and his *President*—and was made more difficult by communication problems between the Lords of the Admiralty and the various commanders of the North American station.[84]

A spate of American victories in 1812 shocked the British government, which rushed naval reinforcements to the western Atlantic, ensuring that after the summer of 1813 the Royal Navy dominated the war at sea. Furthermore, Britain's strategy came to include an economic blockade of almost the entire American coastline, which produced swift and severe effects. The Royal Navy interfered with American foreign trade, preventing export of agricultural goods and colonial commodities. As naval communications became more perilous, US commerce was forced inland, where the lack of cheap coastal shipping made it reliant on more expensive (and time-consuming) overland transportation. This meant that farmers had to dispose of their goods at neighboring markets, depressing prices locally while increasing them for distant urban customers. All of this in turn affected customs revenue, the principal source of tax income for the American republic, creating a major budget deficit and forcing the government to become more dependent on public credit, a rather perilous (and unreliable) development, considering the war-driven economic recession and the absence of a national bank that could coordinate the nation's fiscal policies.[85] Here lies one of the crucial consequences of the war: the lack of an effective banking system, which had been the subject of a bitter political debate so famously waged by Alexander Hamilton, Thomas Jefferson, and others, revealed the pitfalls of fiscal decentralization and unregulated currency, and was ultimately addressed (albeit temporarily) through the creation of a national bank in 1816.

The war in North America had a direct impact on the Napoleonic Wars. It diverted Britain's resources and prevented American trade from reaching Russian, Portuguese, and Spanish ports.[86] In April 1812, as it moved closer to declaring war, the US Congress passed a ninety-day embargo, stopping all exports from the United States. In Spain, Wellington was soon astonished to learn that "the Americans have laid a general embargo on all vessels. This is a measure of importance as all this part of the Peninsula has been living this year on American flour."[87] He immediately began considering other potential sources for supplies, including Brazil and Egypt, that could "keep the stores supplied with corn in the event then expected [March 1812] of the stoppage of the intercourse with America."[88] Fortunately for Wellington, the start of the Anglo-American hostilities did not affect his military operations, as the flow of American supplies continued for some time after the declaration of the war. Given that the shortages increased the price of grain in Portugal and Spain, many American merchants became willing to circumvent congressional restrictions to reap profits. The British sanctioned a licensed trade, permitting American vessels to deliver crucial supplies without interference from the Royal Navy.[89] This proved but a temporary measure, and by November 1812 the British government stopped this policy. The decision was partly reflective of an effort to exert greater economic pressure on the United States and partly the result of British confidence about securing sufficient supplies from the Barbary States and Mehmet Ali of Egypt.

CHAPTER 22

The Fall of the French Empire

T HE NEWS OF NAPOLEON'S DEFEAT in Russia sent shock waves throughout Europe, dramatically altering the balance of power and signaling an
opportunity to cast off French hegemony. The Convention of Tauroggen,
signed by Russian negotiators and Prussian general Johann von Yorck in
December 1812, had already marked the start of a new phase of the Napoleonic
Wars. The Prussian general's decision to declare his Prussian contingent of
the French army neutral was a clear act of defiance both against his French
superiors and against the Prussian king, Frederick William III, who had consistently discouraged the more patriotically minded Prussian officers and
statesmen from openly opposing Napoleon. Although Frederick William initially disowned the convention, the die had been cast.[1] Yorck's decision
altered the military situation, making it impossible for the French forces to
hold ground in East Prussia. Marshal Macdonald abandoned Königsberg
(present-day Kaliningrad) on January 4, 1813, and the Russians entered the
city later that same day.[2] Emperor Alexander, who reached Königsberg on
January 22, was beseeched by the local authorities to take control of the province and summon the local assembly. Once convened, the Estates of East
Prussia declared themselves against Napoleon without waiting for instructions from the Prussian king, and began raising armed forces for the forthcoming war. Despite Frederick William III's condemnation, similar acts were
repeated throughout Prussia, sparking off a wide-scale uprising that forced
the Prussian monarchy to switch sides.

Though often unheralded in Napoleonic histories, the Treaty of Kalisch
was of great consequence. Signed by Prussian chancellor Karl August Fürst
von Hardenberg and Russian field marshal Mikhail Kutuzov, the agreement's
fourteen provisions declared a cessation of hostilities between Russia and

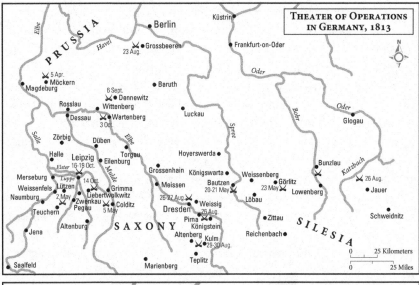

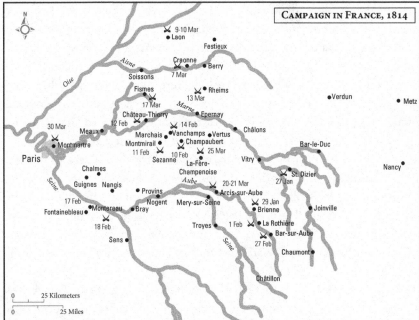

Map 27: Campaigns in Germany and France, 1813–1814

Prussia and established a military alliance between the two countries, with both sides pledging to deploy large military contingents (80,000 Prussians and 150,000 Russians) against France, and not to negotiate or sign unilaterally any agreements with Napoleon. From the start, the Russians made it very clear that they would be the senior partner in this alliance. The secret provisions of the treaty were particularly noteworthy because Russia pledged to restore Prussia to its "statistical, geographical, and financial" power and status as of 1806, but also permitted Prussia to retain only those Polish territories that it had received during the First Partition in 1772, together with a narrow strip of territory to connect it with Silesia. Thus Prussia was deprived of the territories it had gained in the Second and Third Partitions of Poland in 1793 and 1795 and had to acknowledge Russian hegemony in Poland. As a consolation, on March 19, 1813, Russia agreed in the separately signed Treaty of Breslau to compensate Prussia with territories taken from German states allied to France, with Saxony quickly becoming the target.[3]

The Russo-Prussian treaties served as the first steps toward the creation of the Sixth Coalition, which would go on to defeat Napoleon. They are also noteworthy for revealing Russia's pragmatic approach to the war. When the Prussians issued a proclamation calling for the Germans to rise up against Napoleon and participate in the war of liberation, the Russians objected, accusing their allies of acting "politically irresponsibly."[4] For Emperor Alexander and his advisors, this was more than a war of German liberation. Here was the chance to reorganize the continent and to extend Russian interests into eastern Europe (and maybe beyond), and they were keen on exploiting it. The Russo-Prussian treaties were silent about the liberation, freedom, or unity of Germany; neither did they reflect earlier diplomatic discussions, including that on the constitutional federation in Germany discussed in 1807. Instead, Emperor Alexander approved a harsh occupation statute that formed a central administrative council, the Zentralverwaltungsrat, with "unlimited" authority over the military and financial resources of the conquered areas in Germany.[5] When some German princes refused to support the Allies, as Prussia, Russia, and their partners will be called hereafter, they were denounced as tools of the French and forced to leave their states. Even the kings of Saxony and Bavaria had to seek the support and protection of Austria.

Both Alexander and Frederick William hoped that Emperor Francis I of Austria would join them, but their actions in Germany only raised concerns in Vienna. The Habsburg court welcomed the news of the French defeat in Russia, which raised the prospect of making changes to the imperial settlement that Napoleon had imposed on Europe. But would this necessarily be to Austria's advantage? If the French emperor was defeated decisively, it seemed all too likely that French hegemony would be supplanted by the dominance of Russia—hardly an appealing prospect for Austria. Consequently, Austrian foreign minister Metternich's national security objectives meant that Austria remained a wild card throughout the spring of 1813. Austrians might have loathed Napoleon, but neither were they enamored of the Russians. Metternich was well aware of Russian meddling in Austrian affairs, most recently in the conspiracy of Archduke John, who came close to inciting a major revolt in the Tyrol and Illyria; in late February Metternich's agents intercepted the conspirators' messages to the Russians, and with the evidence in hand, the foreign minister quickly suppressed the conspiracy. Equally worrisome for Vienna was the manifesto that the Russian high command issued in late March, calling upon the German princes to accept the protection of the Russian emperor, destroy the French-controlled Rheinbund, and build a new Germany. Should individual rulers fail to cooperate, they would be destroyed "by the force of public opinion and the power of the righteous arms."[6] For Austria, the key question was what kind of "new Germany" this would be. Metternich understood that the Russian manifesto, which had threatened the German princes, also created an opportunity for Austria to reclaim some of its lost standing by assuming the mantle of German protector.

Aware of Austria's precarious position, however, Metternich argued in favor of maintaining an armed neutrality to remove war from the Austrian borders and to seek mediation between Russia and France.[7] In keeping with this drive toward neutrality, Austria reached an armistice with Russia at Willenberg on January 30, 1813, and, much to the chagrin of the French, withdrew its forces to Galicia.[8] Throughout the spring of 1813, just as Prussia, Russia, and France clashed on the rolling hills near the Bohemian borders of Austria, Metternich slowly worked toward his grand project of reviving the Habsburg power. His overriding goal was to form a tripartite Germany, one that included Prussia, Austria, and, most crucially, neutral "Germany" in between. To accomplish this, the Austrian minister had to remove French control on the territories east of the Rhine and Russian influence west of the Vistula. Only through the revival of a European equilibrium could Austria and other smaller continental states maintain some semblance of independence and authority. In this regard, Austrian intentions coincided with British aspirations. By late 1812, Prime Minister Liverpool's cabinet had already been authorized to place £500,000 at Vienna's disposal should Austria be drawn into hostilities against Napoleon.[9] That attempt to turn Austria against Napoleon failed, but by April 1813 Austrians were firm in their intention to pursue armed meditation and, if Napoleon rejected negotiations, to join the Allies.[10]

Napoleon had returned to Paris on December 18, 1812, the day after the 29th Bulletin announced to the nation that the grandest army it had ever sent out was lying dead in the frozen fields of Russia. The news shocked the

French public and undermined Napoleon's prestige within the German Confederation, where the German nationalists made calls for *Befreiungskrieg*— a war of liberation. The situation in Spain was even more volatile. But Napoleon never lost countenance, and his public pronouncements and the explanations given to his allies and to the Senate showed the confidence of a victor. "My army has had some losses but it was due to the premature rigor of the season," he claimed in his address to the Senate on December 20.[11] A letter to the king of Denmark demonstrates his public attitude toward the Russian debacle, with Napoleon asserting that the Russians were "always beaten" and captured "neither an eagle nor a gun from my army." Any setbacks were due to the winter. "My army has suffered greatly, and suffers still, but this calamity will cease with the cold," the emperor concluded.[12]

Despite the terrible news coming daily to Paris, Napoleon began preparations for a new campaign. As noted in Chapter 21, out of the roughly 600,000 men who took part in the Russian campaign, fewer than 100,000 returned, and almost half of those were part of Austrian and Prussian contingents. So a new French army had to be built. Napoleon still had vast resources at his disposal, and few would have predicted in early 1813 that the year would witness the collapse of the Napoleonic Empire. The Russians had suffered nearly as much as their foes and reached the Niemen River with barely 40,000 effectives. What Napoleon needed was time. He urged Eugène de Beauharnais, who had assumed command of slightly over 100,000 men in Poland, to hold on to his positions for as long as he could, supported by French garrisons along the Elbe, Oder, and Vistula Rivers. To everyone Napoleon spoke of victory as certain. "You must always say," he instructed in one letter, "and yourself believe that in the next campaign I shall drive the Russian back across the Niemen."[13]

As Napoleon was dictating orders, the situation was rapidly changing in Poland. By the end of February, as the Russians advanced into East Prussia, Beauharnais had no choice but to fall back beyond the Vistula and the Oder. Napoleon pushed ahead with mobilization of new recruits and supplies in France, the Confederation of the Rhine, and Italy. The measures were hugely unpopular, but Napoleon was still in firm control in the west and could employ a range of effective methods against defiant satellites, including use of force. Besides, many of these princes owed their very political existence to him and had a vested interest in seeing him prevail.[14] By the end of April the French emperor had created a new army of over 140,000 men, with additional units finishing their mobilization by August. This new force could not compare in quality with the French armies of earlier years. It had a high proportion of young and inexperienced soldiers and was sorely lacking in artillery and cavalry. "I would be in a position to settle the affairs quickly if I had fifteen thousand more cavalry, but I am rather weak in this branch," the emperor complained to King Frederick of Württemburg.[15] Nevertheless, creation of such a massive army in a matter of just four months testifies to Napoleon's administrative genius and the effectiveness of the bureaucracy that he had forged over the last decade.

The campaign resumed in earnest in April as the Russo-Prussian forces liberated Berlin and invaded Saxony, whose king remained loyal to Napoleon. By late April the Allied armies had concentrated east of the Saale River near Leipzig, where Emperor Alexander appointed a new Allied commander in chief, General Peter Wittgenstein, after Field Marshal Kutuzov passed away of illness on April 28. By now Napoleon had led the newly formed Army of the Main into Germany to link up with remnants of his old Grande Armée. His plan was to defeat the Russo-Prussian allies as quickly as he could, push the Russians beyond the Vistula, and suppress the rapidly spreading national tumult in northern Germany.[16]

On May 1 the French crossed the Saale River and marched on Leipzig, seeking to threaten the Allies' interior lines. Yet the lack of cavalry prevented Napoleon from conducting a forceful reconnaissance, which left him unaware of almost 90,000 Allied troops under Wittgenstein massing on his right flank. It was while visiting the site of Swedish king Gustavus Adolphus's 1632 victory at Lützen that Napoleon heard the gunfire and learned of Marshal Ney stumbling upon the enemy. He immediately reinforced Ney and diverted his other corps toward Grossgörschen, near Lützen, where Napoleon first struck Wittgenstein with heavy artillery before sending in his Imperial Guard. With the guardsmen smashing through the Allied center, Napoleon threatened both Allied flanks with enveloping maneuvers that left Wittgenstein no choice but to beat a retreat.

The battle ended with a French victory, though it was far from a complete one. The lack of cavalry meant there was no French pursuit of the Allies, who withdrew in good order; in fact, the Allied officers and soldiers refused to accept that they had been beaten and pointed to, in the words of a senior Prussian officer, "the resoluteness and gallantry of the combined forces of two nations seized with ardent love for their Fatherlands."[17] The battle once again highlighted Napoleon's military talents and his ability, even with inexperienced troops, to respond to a new situation with an improvised but effective plan of action. If not for the lack of cavalry, Napoleon would have completed his double envelopment maneuver to shatter the Allied forces and possibly end the war before it got under way.

The defeat at Lützen created a brief rift in the Allied high command as Prussians and Russian laid the blame for it on the other. The former urged moving northward to guard Berlin, while the Russians wanted to march eastward to Breslau in order to remain closer to their home territory. The armies were about to separate when King Frederick William, understanding the disastrous results this would produce, gave in. Leaving the defense of Berlin to General Bülow's weak corps, the combined Prusso-Russian army moved to Bautzen, about thirty miles northeast of Dresden, and took up a position on the heights behind that town, where they were joined by reinforcements led by General Mikhail Barclay de Tolly. On May 16 the Prussian minister Hardenberg and Russian foreign minister Karl Robert von Nesselrode expanded the Kalisch-Breslau war aims to include the dissolution of the Confederation of the Rhine (Rheinbund) and the end of French rule in Spain, Holland, and Italy.

After regrouping at Dresden, Napoleon initially considered threatening Berlin in an effort to split the Allies. On learning of the Allied army bivouacked at Bautzen, however, he marched there with his main forces.[18] He once again successfully implemented his principle of concentration of superior forces, so the Russo-Prussian army of 96,000 men found itself face-to-face with some 144,000 men under Napoleon. The emperor sought the decisive victory that had eluded him at Lützen and devised a plan that called for Marshal Ney to perform a *manoeuvre sur les derrières* against the Allied right wing in order to cut off the Allies' line of retreat and deliver the decisive blow.

The first day of the Battle of Bautzen, May 20, unfolded as Napoleon expected: the French main army, deployed west and northwest of Bautzen, attacked the Russo-Prussian army, pinned it down frontally, and pretended to envelop the enemy's left flank, forcing Wittgenstein to commit most of his reserves there. Now all that was needed was for Ney to successfully complete his maneuver the following day. Yet the marshal lost sight of the strategic importance of his mission. Upon reaching the battlefield at noon on May 21, he misinterpreted imperial instructions to attack the enemy's line of communications and instead hurled his men upon the Kreckwitz heights near the village of Preititz, which he thought formed the key to the Allied position. For the next few hours he wasted precious time and men fighting the Prussians, who steadfastly defended their position.[19]

The Battle of Bautzen ended by nightfall. Although it was a French victory, it was, once again, an incomplete one. Had Ney continued his advance as Napoleon intended, the Allies would have been decisively defeated. But the moment was lost and the Allied forces, though mauled, were still intact and ready to fight again. Their high command, however, was again deeply divided. In the aftermath of two defeats, Wittgenstein's position as Allied commander in chief was untenable, and he was replaced by Barclay de Tolly, who suggested falling back to the Russian frontiers to rest troops and establish a proper supply system for the worn-out army. The Russian officer corps, who had spent almost a year campaigning, welcomed the prospects of a respite. The Prussians, naturally, objected. They could not afford to abandon Silesia and expose Berlin, both so crucial to the Prussian war effort, and risk another despoliation of Prussian territory by French troops. Ultimately, Emperor Alexander, understanding the importance of safeguarding his alliance with Prussia, ordered his armies to remain in Silesia. The northern provinces of Prussia were, however, abandoned to the French. Napoleon, still preoccupied with the enemy field armies, ordered Oudinot to seize the Prussian capital, but the marshal was unable to break through steadfast Prussian resistance under General Bülow at Luckau.[20]

For the Allies, the situation was fairly precarious. They had been defeated twice and in just one month's time driven back from the Salle to the Oder, a distance of 250 miles. Their armies had suffered from want of supplies; although the Allied soldiers fought magnificently, they were exhausted from marches; and wastage from sickness was quite high. Even more disheartening was the news from Hamburg, which the Allied troops, led by Lieutenant Colonel Friedrich Karl von Tettenborn, had initially seized on March 18.[21] This was the first time the Allies had invaded the territory of the French Empire itself—Hamburg was annexed to France in 1810—and the capture of this major port city was welcome news to the coalition partners, especially Britain, which could use it as a gateway to northern Europe. Just two weeks after the capture of Hamburg, Britain dispatched a small expeditionary force that landed at Cuxhaven, seventy miles to the northwest of the port, to secure its foothold in the region.[22] The Allied celebrations proved to be premature, however. Ordered by Napoleon to reclaim the city, Davout, the "Iron Marshal," drove the Allies out of Hamburg on May 30.

The continued difficulties pointed toward the Allied need for respite and especially for outside help. Although Bernadotte, the former French marshal turned Swedish crown prince, had supported Russia since 1812, no one expected him to produce sufficient military assistance. Britain pledged to provide a subsidy but little in terms of actual troops, committed as it was to Peninsular affairs. Thus only Austria could make a truly decisive impact on the course of the war. Yet the Habsburgs, having suffered four humiliating defeats in thirteen years, were not in a rush to challenge Napoleon. The French ruler was still a formidable foe with a large army, and Emperor Francis was not convinced that the Russo-Prussian coalition could defeat him. If Austria took the field against them and lost, the victorious French would be certain to wreak vengeance on the already reduced Habsburg dominion. Moreover, as noted, Austria had no desire to bring about Napoleon's defeat if this meant Russia becoming the arbiter of Europe. Nonetheless, staying out of the conflict was not an option either, since a Russo-Prussian victory (as remote as might have seemed in late May) would have left Austria on the political sidelines.

The news of a possible truce between France and the Allies was thus welcomed in Vienna, which quickly expressed a desire to serve as mediator. Both sides agreed, and an armistice was signed at Pleischwitz on June 4 and suspended hostilities until July 20, although the truce was eventually extended to mid-August.[23]

In hindsight, the Pleischwitz Armistice was one of Napoleon's greatest mistakes. He tried explaining that even though "this armistice interrupts the course of my victories, I decided on it for two reasons: the shortage of cavalry, which prevents me from striking decisive blows, and the hostile attitude of Austria."[24] There were other reasons for Napoleon's willingness to consider a truce. He might have won the first battles but they cost him up to 40,000 casualties, and twice as many men were sick and convalescing in hospitals. These losses had to be quickly replaced. His supply system was inadequate, and the enemy detachments bedeviled French lines of communication through Germany. In one particularly brazen incident, a Russian flying detachment had actually captured the city of Leipzig on June 7. Equally problematic was the uninspired leadership of corps commanders and marshals, many of whom were simply tired of war. "The turn of the wheel of Fortune has ravaged these souls of iron," was the despondent observation by Napoleon's first secretary, Baron Agathon Jean François Fain, as he listened to them talk at the camp.[25]

Political motivation was by far the decisive factor in Napoleon's acceptance of the armistice. He knew about Austria's increasingly hostile attitude and felt he had no choice but to negotiate. With his old confidence restored by recent victories, he hoped to use this respite to ensure that his Austrian father-in-law stayed by his side so that he could concentrate on crushing the Prussians and chasing the Russians back across the Niemen. These were all valid factors to consider, but they still do not hide the fact that the Allies had much more to gain from the respite than Napoleon. The Allied armies were exhausted and in a strategic cul-de-sac in Silesia, so another hard blow likely would have caused the coalition to collapse. For the Prussians and Russians, armistice was a godsend because they could use the much-needed respite to not only reorganize and reinforce their armies but also formalize the new coalition.

Austria played the decisive role in all of this. Metternich did his best to hold out the prospect of Austrian entry into the war on either side, hoping to convince Napoleon to negotiate while helping the Allies formulate peace terms that would bring about a general settlement in Europe. This required the Austrian foreign minister to pursue an intricate diplomatic campaign, one that occasionally stumbled in the face of Russian and French obduracy. Moreover, throughout the process, Austria, under the guise of neutrality, also carried out a covert mobilization of its forces, which was made public on June 14 with the calling up of the reservists and the Landwehr; by late July some 200,000 men had been gathered in Bohemia, while two more armies were mustered along the Danube.

The Allies, meanwhile, were preoccupied with diplomatic negotiations.[26] The British government had long acted as the paymaster for anti-French coalitions, and despite some handicaps, it endeavored once again to use its influence to bring the three continental powers together and push them toward the common end of defeating Napoleon.[27] Writing to the British envoy to Russia, Foreign Minister Castlereagh urged him to take advantage of any opportunity to advance the Allied war effort based on "the general principle of giving confidence to all powers which can be induced to take a part in reducing the power of France and restoring the independence of Germany."[28] To achieve this, London made the promise of British gold. Negotiating the finer details of subsidies, however, proved to be challenging. Emperor Alexander instructed his ambassador in London, Count Christoph Heinrich von Lieven, to request £7 million to maintain the 200,000 men of the Russian army but to be ready to reduce the sum to £4 million on the condition that half of it be given as weapons and ammunition.[29] Britain had already committed itself financially (to the tune of some £4 million) to Sweden, Portugal, and Spain and was negotiating separate subsidy offers with Prussia and Austria. So the British government balked at the magnitude of the Russian subsidy request, causing the Russian envoy to note that British ministers were "pleading to tears" when it came to the reduction of subsidies to Russia.[30] Castlereagh understood that subsidy treaties with individual powers were not enough; what Britain needed was a treaty combining all the powers at war into a coalition that Napoleon would be unable to break, whether by diplomacy or by brute force.

Forming a coalition was therefore a crucial element in the overall strategy that Britain pursued in 1813–1815. It consisted of three broad goals. First and foremost was Britain's desire to maintain its colonial and maritime supremacy. By now the British had already secured all of the French, Dutch, and Danish colonies, and the only overseas possessions still not under British control were those of its allies. Control of these vast dominions offered Britain a diplomatic weapon of great value, one that could be wielded to secure a continental settlement it desired. This was especially important with regard to the maritime rights that the British so jealously guarded not only against France but also against the United States and Russia. It was, therefore, a cardinal point of British policy to insist on excluding any mention of maritime issues from the negotiations. Second, Britain had to fulfill the obligations it had already undertaken under earlier agreements. These included promises to restore governments in Portugal, Spain, and Naples, as well as a pledge to support Swedish claims to Norway. Finally, the third task was to ensure an enduring political arrangement on the continent by reducing France to its pre-Napoleonic frontiers and constraining the rising Russian power. In this, London shared some common ground with Austria.[31]

On June 14–15, by the Treaties of Reichenbach, Britain pledged £2 million to Russia and Prussia and, renewing its earlier offer, offered £500,000 as an inducement for Austria to join the coalition. The latter was an interesting change for the British, who just a few short months earlier had provided tens of thousands of pounds to finance a revolt in the Austrian Tyrol. The Austrians again paid no heed to the British offer; Metternich was preoccupied with political wrangling with the Russians on the issues of Poland and Serbia. There was still a sizable gap between the Austrian and Russian positions. While Russia pledged to support restoration of Austria to its status as of 1805, this was far less than the Habsburg court expected, as by 1805 Austria had already lost most of its possessions in Italy. Equally divisive were the two powers' conflicting aims on Germany, where the Habsburgs looked with suspicion at the existing Russo-Prussian rapprochement as a sign of Austrian exclusion from German affairs. Metternich initially tried to position himself as the protector of smaller German states against the Russo-Prussian depredation, as mentioned earlier, and his efforts were partly successful: the Treaty of Prague (April 20) extended Austrian protection to Saxony, which was already threatened by Prussian territorial claims.[32] Still, this success proved fleeting—after Napoleon's victories in May, the German princes had flocked back to the French banners.

During the summer armistice, Metternich assumed a lead role in negotiations with both the Allies and France. His overall goal was to reduce French dominance and to prevent Russia from becoming dominant in its place. Toward this end, he pushed for Russia and France to retire behind their respective frontiers of the Vistula and the Rhine, and remain separated by an independent and strengthened central Europe. Under this plan, Napoleon would be forced to cede territory to restore Austria and Prussia to their statuses in 1805 and 1806, respectively, which, in turn, would ensure that there remained no territory to compensate either country for the cession of their Polish provinces to Russia. In his negotiations with the Allies, Metternich seemingly accepted Russo-Prussian demands on Poland and outlined the key elements of what he called a "good peace": the dissolution of the Duchy of Warsaw, as Russia had long wished; the restoration of Prussia to its former status; the reinstatement of all territories France had annexed east of the Rhine; the independence of Holland; the surrender of all Italian provinces seized by France; the restoration of the Papal States; the return to Austria of all territories lost in the Treaty of Lunéville; and the cessation of Napoleon's supremacy in Germany and Italy.[33] Metternich also believed that the Allies had to offer a minimum program in order to attract Napoleon to the peace table. Therefore, separate from the "good peace" proposals, Austrians also suggested two sets of minimal claims that would serve as grounds for the opening of preliminary negotiations. For Austria, these were the recovery of the Illyrian Provinces, the dissolution of the Duchy of Warsaw, and a new frontier with Bavaria. For the Russo-Prussian coalition, the terms included the restoration of Prussia to its former status, Napoleon's surrender of all German territory east of the Rhine, and, most crucial, the removal of French influence from the Confederation of the Rhine.[34]

Throughout May the Allies debated the final details of these terms, insisting, among other things, on adding the independence of Holland and Italy to the list of minimum demands. Further impediment appeared after the Treaties of Reichenbach were concluded in mid-June. As a price for its financial support, Britain insisted on the restoration of Hanover and a pledge that neither coalition member would sign a separate peace with Napoleon. British involvement meant that additional demands, most notably with regard to Spain, Portugal, and Naples, would be unavoidable in future negotiations with France. Still, amid deep mistrust and mutual suspicions, neither side could afford to go the distance alone: confronting Napoleon required a collective action.

On June 26, Metternich had a long interview with Napoleon in Dresden. It was a moment of truth for the entire war. The preliminary proposals that the Austrian minister delivered, and which were later discussed at the Peace Congress in Prague between July 12 and August 10, included the following: the dissolution of the Duchy of Warsaw, which would be divided among the Allied powers; the reorganization of the Confederation of the Rhine; return of the Illyrian Provinces to Austria; restoration of the Hanseatic cities, which France had annexed in 1810; and the reestablishment of Prussia to the position it had enjoyed before 1806.[35] Had Metternich convinced Napoleon to compromise and accept a diplomatic solution to the problem, history would have taken a rather different course. But Napoleon rejected them in the course of a heated conversation that underscored his sense of invulnerability even after the Russian catastrophe. "So you want war?" he told Metternich, "Well, you shall have it. I have already annihilated the Prussian army at Lützen; I have defeated the Russians at Bautzen; now you want to have your turn. Very well, we shall meet at Vienna."[36] Metternich left Dresden convinced that a genuine negotiation with the French ruler was no longer possible. One may say he knew this even before the meeting. As he set out for the interview in Dresden, he had already instructed his diplomats to sign, on June 27, the Treaty of Reichenbach, by which Austria joined the Allies—thereby completing the formation of the Sixth Coalition—and pledged to declare war on France if the peace conditions offered to Napoleon were not accepted.[37]

In hindsight, Napoleon's reaction to the Dresden Proposals is hardly surprising considering the scope of concessions demanded of him. Even after the French setbacks in Russia and Spain, these were hardly the lenient terms they are often argued to have been. Despite holding military advantages (at least in Germany) and still maintaining control over much of central Europe and Italy, Napoleon was told to give up twenty years' worth of French conquests and to surrender positions across the continent. Would any head of state, not to mention one in the mold of Napoleon, would have considered such massive concessions at a moment when he was buoyed by a string of recent victories? Would any of the Allied leaders themselves have considered comparable offers with regard to their own imperial interests, be it in India, the Caucasus, or the Danubian Principalities? Was Napoleon's attitude any different from Britain's, whose statesmen believed that the empires must be won and maintained by "armed might," otherwise they would fall by the same means to a superior power?[38]

There is no denying that Napoleon was reluctant to negotiate, but claims that he had no goal other than fighting or that the Allies had agreed to make peace with Napoleon on the basis of minimal conditions seem misplaced.[39] Like his opponents, the French emperor was seeking to achieve his own particular vision of a continental peace, and winning was a crucial element in this. The set of demands presented at Dresden were designed to start preliminary discussions only, and if the French had accepted them, the Allies would have raised new demands at the final negotiations. Napoleon knew that, and he clearly felt that he could not agree to the terms while he was in a relatively strong position militarily. His intransigence concealed two specific goals: to settle directly with Russia, the strongest of the coalition members, and to chastise Austria for breaking away from its alliance with France. Napoleon was explicit about this in the instructions he gave to Caulaincourt, who had been dispatched to negotiate in Prague.

The conference in Prague, however, produced no breakthroughs. It is often described as a farce, and Karl Nesselrode, the Russian representative, himself acknowledged that "neither side was particularly intent on a peace. The congress was just a sham."[40] There is a certain truth to this. Of the four sides involved, only Austria was keenly interested in organizing a general peace conference, and Metternich did his best—even at the cost of misleading his allies—to convince the French emperor of his peaceful intentions.[41] Napoleon remained suspicious, believing that the Austrians were offering an olive branch with one hand while readying a sword with the other. He was not mistaken in this, because the Habsburg court did take advantage of the armistice to complete its army mobilization. However, Napoleon's actions were based on other considerations. First, whether out of his sense of family loyalties or a patronizing view of Austrian military capabilities, he was genuinely convinced that Emperor Francis would not fight his own son-in-law; to emphasize these dynastic ties, Napoleon had conferred on Empress Marie-Louise—Francis's daughter—the position of regent during his absence from France.[42] Second, the prospect of accepting a "dishonorable" peace weighed heavily on the emperor's mind. He believed that the French people would not accept the loss of national glory that was, in the words of a British historian, "one of the vital four pillars—along with national property rights, low taxation and centralized authority—that bolstered his rule."[43] Napoleon was wrong. It is hard to imagine that he was unaware of the public expressions of joy that news of the armistice provoked across much of France; prefects' reports spoke of "the desire for peace [becoming] daily more intense, and if this hope appeared to have solid grounds, public jubilation and gratitude towards the Emperor would burst forth everywhere."[44]

The final set of demands that Napoleon received on August 9 (with the deadline on the tenth) represented his last major opportunity to negotiate from a position of relative strength.[45] Accepting the terms would have meant renouncing much of what he had achieved in the previous thirteen years and would have meant that the sacrifice of hundreds of thousands of lives had been in vain. Of course, the way was still open for Napoleon to deal with the situation through skillful diplomacy and timely concessions, exploiting the war-weariness of Europe, the mutual distrust and jealousies of the coalition members, and sovereigns' fear of the popular movements that the war could unleash. But such an approach also would have meant renouncing the Grand Empire, and that Napoleon simply could not bring himself to accept. He preferred the simpler but riskier path of war. Just a few months earlier he had observed grimly that "in this world, there are only two alternatives—to command or to obey."[46] Still, Napoleon did consider the Allied terms, accepting some and rejecting others. For example, he remained silent on renouncing his protectorate of the Confederation of the Rhine but agreed to the dissolution of the Duchy of Warsaw (which was to be partitioned by the Allied powers) and restoration of the Illyrian Provinces to Austria; he refused to give Danzig to Prussia but agreed to turn it into a free city. These were major concessions even if they fell far short of Allied expectations. Furthermore, had Napoleon conveyed them to Prague right away, the Allies might conceivably have accepted them as a basis for preliminary negotiations. Yet, whether out of his sense of pride or mere stalling, he delayed sending his counterterms, which reached Prague on August 11, after the deadline had passed.[47] The Russian and Prussian envoys, in the words of eminent American historian Enno Kraehe, with "their eyes fastened on the clock, their faces registering the smiles of vindicated prescience, did not wait a minute beyond the stroke of midnight to declare their powers expired."[48] The very next day, Austria declared war on France.[49] For the first time since the start of the Napoleonic Wars, France faced the combined efforts of Europe's great powers, whose armies were already in the field and ready to coordinate their actions.

The Pleischwitz Armistice was thus the turning point of the war. If at the start of the armistice Napoleon more than matched his foes and was indeed close to winning the campaign, by the time the truce ended the Allies were at least twice as strong as he was and united in their purpose to eject him once and for all from central Europe. They understood that even after recent setbacks, only an unprecedented cooperative effort could liberate Europe from Napoleon's control. Their sense of mission was further boosted by the news of continued British successes in the Iberian Peninsula.

———◇◇◇◈◇◇◇———

Wellington, who, as we have seen, had retreated to Portugal after his victory at Salamanca in the fall of 1812, had spent the winter regrouping his army, which increased to some 80,000 men, more than half of them British. Meanwhile, the French forces in Spain had been weakened by Napoleon's decision to recall thousands of troops for the campaign in Germany. To take full advantage of this, Wellington launched a fresh invasion of Spain in May 1813, sending Lieutenant General Sir Rowland Hill, with 30,000 men, as a diversion to Salamanca while the main Anglo-Allied force advanced across northern Portugal before coming down behind the French defensive lines. By early June his entire force was already on the northern side of the Douro River, much to the surprise of the French, who began to hastily redeploy to meet the new threat in the north. But such was the speed of the British advance that the French, under King Joseph, were forced to abandon Burgos on June 13 and were then caught unprepared near Vitoria a week later. The ensuing battle resulted in such a decisive defeat of the French army that as the troops fled they abandoned their entire baggage train, more than 400 caissons, and all but two of 153 guns. More incredible, however, was the sheer amount of treasure—the fruits of six years of plunder, which included paintings by Titian, Velázquez, and Murillo—that King Joseph left behind as he fled the battlefield.

After Vitoria, the British swept through northern Spain as the French retreated in great confusion and disorder. A few scattered garrisons and Marshal Suchet's command in Catalonia and Aragon were all that remained of the Napoleonic Kingdom of Spain. Although the French tried to relieve the besieged fortresses of San Sebastian and Pamplona, they were repelled at Sorauren (July 28–30) and San Marcial (August 31) and forced across the Pyrenees. To all intents and purposes, the Peninsular War was over. Wellington was now in a position to plan for the invasion of France itself. The situation in Spain lay heavily on Napoleon's mind. He understood the urgency of delivering a decisive blow to the coalition in Germany so that he could turn his attention to the Pyrenees.[50]

Now that he had rejected a peace settlement, the only alternative for Napoleon, as had been the case so often in the past, was rapid and ruthless military action. This time, though, he was facing a rather different enemy. The Allies had shown the ability to learn from their past mistakes, and perhaps nothing illustrates this point better than the councils of war they held at Trachenberg and Reichenbach during the armistice. Here they developed an attritional strategy that was designed to counteract Napoleon's military genius. The Allies pledged to deploy up to half a million men in three major armies: the Army of Bohemia, with some 230,000 men, under the command of Austrian field marshal Karl Fürst zu Schwarzenberg; the Army of North Germany, of more than 140,000 men, under the Swedish crown prince, Bernadotte; and the Army of Silesia, with 105,000 men, led by a Prussian general, Blücher.[51] These were multinational forces designed to constrain any coalition member's ability to act out of national self-interest, and to prevent Napoleon from defeating them piecemeal. These armies were to accept battle only if their superiority was undoubted; if attacked by Napoleon, an army was to fall back while other Allied armies would advance to increase pressure on his flanks and communications and, if possible, destroy any forces the French emperor had dispatched under his lieutenants on separate missions. Once Napoleon was sufficiently weakened, the Allies would be in a position to unite their armies for the decisive battle.[52]

Armed with the new strategy, the Allies soon seized the initiative and gained a series of early victories. On August 23 Marshal Oudinot, whom Napoleon again instructed to seize Berlin, was defeated by Bernadotte's Army of North Germany at Grossbeeren and pushed back from the Prussian capital.[53] This was an ominous preview of what would happen once Napoleon delegated authority to his subordinates. Two days later Blücher defeated France's Marshal Macdonald on the Katzbach River and expelled the French from Silesia.[54] Napoleon slightly tilted the balance in his favor when he exploited a mistake by Schwarzenberg and surprised the exposed Army of Bohemia at Dresden on August 26–27; despite being outnumbered almost two to one, the emperor outmaneuvered his opponent and won an impressive tactical victory that cost the Allies more than 30,000 men.[55] Had the victory been followed up with vigor, Dresden might have ranked as one of Napoleon's decisive victories. But the combination of a lack of cavalry, bad weather, and Napoleon's own lack of resolve meant that the battle ultimately proved pyrrhic. At least the Emperor could draw solace from the news that his longstanding rival General Jean Moreau, who had returned from exile to support the Allies, had been killed by a French cannonball. "That rascal Bonaparte is always lucky," Moreau wrote his wife shortly before his death.[56]

Moreau did not live long enough to see his rival's run of good luck expire. Two days after Dresden, General Dominique Vandamme, whom Napoleon had left in charge of the pursuit of Schwarzenberg, found himself surrounded at Kulm, where his entire command was captured. On September 6 it was Marshal Ney's turn. Dispatched by Napoleon to seize Berlin, Ney was defeated at Dennewitz. Meanwhile, following the Trachenberg plan, the Allied forces withdrew as soon as Napoleon confronted them, forcing him to march back and forth between the Elbe and Bober Rivers in a futile attempt to gain a decisive victory. All the while, Schwarzenberg advanced into Saxony.[57] The Allied plan was clearly working. In less than a month of campaigning, the French had suffered thousands of losses with no tangible gains to show for them. The remaining troops were exhausted by the incessant marching and fighting, as well as the heavy rain that all but sapped the supply lines. Encouraged by these successes, the Allies concluded the Treaties of Toeplitz, on September 9, which reinforced earlier coalition agreements and further outlined general principles upon which postwar settlement would be reached. The general terms called for the material restoration of Austria and Prussia to their pre-1805/1806 status, dissolution of the Confederation of the Rhine, the restoration of the states of northwestern Europe to their 1803 status, and the partition of the Grand Duchy of Warsaw along lines that would be determined later. All three governments vowed not to make a separate peace with Napoleon and each agreed to keep an army in the field until the end of the war.

After Dennewitz, Napoleon adjusted his strategy. He made one more chase at Blücher's Army of Silesia and Bernadotte's Army of North Germany, but both of them declined battle and retreated across the Saale River. This was one of the most vital moments in the entire campaign. Blücher and Bernadotte had all but abandoned Berlin, which was defended by a small Prussian garrison. Had Napoleon decided to leave Silesia and shift his forces northward, the campaign would have followed a completely different course. Until this point the French operations were centered on Dresden, which offered many advantages, not the least of which was its central location. But it was also an unfortified town that could be easily threatened by the Allies. By shifting operations to the north, Napoleon could have turned the fortresses of Magdeburg, Torgau, Wittenberg, Küstrin, and Stettin into his bases of operation while leaving the Allied armies in the despoiled Saxon countryside. Yet he chose a different strategy. After months of chasing an elusive enemy, he decided to hunker down in Leipzig, let the Allies come to him, and wait for the chance to strike separately at their converging armies.

The Allies slowly closed around Napoleon at Leipzig. On October 15, as Schwarzenberg approached the city from the south and Blücher from the north, the French emperor still would have had a real chance of success if he had acted with his old vigor.[58] But by the sixteenth it was too late. When the battle began that overcast October morning, the Allies already had more than 200,000 men against Napoleon's 170,000. It was a day of desperate and bloody fighting that ended with neither side prevailing. But Napoleon's army, with its fixed number, was now pitted against an enemy that kept receiving reinforcements; 40,000 Russians under Bennigsen were followed by some 60,000 men under Bernadotte, bringing the total strength of the Allied armies to some 380,000 men and 1,500 guns, while Napoleon could barely muster 200,000 men and 900 cannon. The French emperor waited irresolutely through the seventeenth, though he should have either attacked or retreated. He sent a letter to the Austrian emperor proposing an armistice and vaguely hinting at concessions. But his enemies knew that he was at last in their coils, and they had no interest in letting him out.

On October 18 the battle resumed, with the odds now clearly stacked against the French, especially after the Saxon and Württemberg contingents had crossed over to the Allies. Disputing every inch of ground, the French were steadily pushed back to the city. By nightfall Napoleon had ordered a general retreat, and all that night his troops were crowding back into the town and jamming the western gates of the city. Remarkably, Napoleon had made no special preparations for the withdrawal and no extra spans had been erected across the Pleisse and Elster Rivers. The mass of the French army was retreating across a single bridge that quickly became blocked. To crown this day of disasters, a corporal left behind to blow up the bridge over the Elster got alarmed by the approach of enemy troops and prematurely lit the fuse as the French troops were still crossing it. As the charges exploded, the air was filled with flying fragments of the bridge and transports, not to mention the unfortunate horses and men who happened to be on it.[59] Thousands of French soldiers were stranded in the city and were captured; some tried to swim to safety and, like Marshal Jozef Poniatowski, drowned in the process.[60] Darkness brought an end to the battle. The magnitude of the Allied victory had eclipsed all previous battles of the Napoleonic Wars, with the French suffering staggering losses of more than 60,000 killed, wounded, and captured; thirty-six French generals were among the prisoners; and a third of all cannons were lost. The Allies losses were equally sanguine, more than 50,000.

The Battle of the Nations, as the engagement at Leipzig came to be called, was a transformative event, one that shattered the legacy of Austerlitz and Jena. If before the battle there had still remained a flickering possibility of Napoleon emerging victorious from this war, Leipzig extinguished it. The whole fabric of the Napoleonic Empire came crumbling to the ground. This defeat left Napoleon's German allies with no other option than to join the Allies. The next month (November 18–24) Russia, Austria, and Prussia declared the Confederation of the Rhine dissolved and negotiated new agreements with German princes, who were tasked with providing troops and supplies as well as procuring vast amounts of money for the continued struggle against their former master. The contingent of each German state was rated at double what it had furnished to Napoleon, with Saxony and Hanover furnishing 20,000, Hesse and Württemberg 12,000, and Baden 10,000. Ultimately, the German states provided more than 100,000 regular troops and an equal number of Landwehr troops.[61]

More crucial is that these German states now found themselves part of a bitter power struggle between Russia, Prussia, and Austria. The Habsburg court succeeded in negotiating separate military conventions with some German states (i.e., Hesse-Darmstadt and Württemberg), raising the prospect of an Austria-dominated southern Germany, which both Prussia and Russia considered detrimental to their interests. Taking advantage of his dynastic ties to many German princes, Emperor Alexander forced his way into the Austro-Württemberg alliance on November 2, 1813, and insisted on his involvement in the Austro-Bavarian treaty as well. Furthermore, between November 20 and December 2, the Russian diplomats negotiated separate agreements with Baden, Schwarzburg-Sondershausen, and Hesse-Kassel and put forth claims to Saxony, Thuringia, Hesse-Darmstadt, and Nassau, where Russian governors were supposed to set up administrative districts. Equally grasping was Prussia, which demanded vast compensations in Saxony and continued to occupy the Grand Duchy of Berg even after the last French soldier had left its territory.[62]

One might have expected the elated Allies to invade France, rushing in to overthrow the man who had tormented them for so long. Instead, in the aftermath of Leipzig they halted their operations to regroup. After taking up positions along the Rhine River, the coalition representatives assembled at Frankfurt to discuss what to do next. They were all concerned about the prospects of invading France: the memories of the French *levée en masse* and popular rising of the 1790s were still fresh, and the Allies were disinclined to pay the high price in men and matériel that the invasion would exact. More important, the coalition's conflicting aims and wishes had reasserted themselves. Disagreements had been scarce while the coalition struggled for control over central Europe. But now that it had been accomplished and the Allies stood on the banks of the Rhine, their unity began to wane. Bernadotte, the crown prince of Sweden, had occasionally demonstrated lackluster commitment to the Allied cause and was against the idea of invading France. His opposition came about not because he had once been a Frenchman but rather because he had far greater ambitions to satisfy, including taking charge of France once Napoleon was overthrown; if that failed, he was keen on strengthening Sweden's positions in northern Europe.[63] These political motives, along with his dynastic concerns, shaped Bernadotte's performance during the entire war.[64] Indeed, no one knew better than Bernadotte himself that his Swedish throne depended entirely on his accomplishing his goal of acquiring Norway—hence his decision to join the Allies only on condition that they would help him secure this realm from Napoleon's ally Denmark. Throughout the campaign he often deliberately kept his Swedish troops out of action because he thought he might need them later for conquests in the north.

Austria, having played such a decisive role in the events of 1813, had effectively fulfilled its goals, removing French influence in Germany. The Viennese court had no interest in the complete overthrow of Napoleon, who was, after all, married to Emperor Francis's daughter. To continue the war meant further sacrifices of men and money, while its result would inevitably advance the interests of St. Petersburg and Berlin more than those of Vienna. For Metternich, reaching the Rhine signaled the time to negotiate a peace, one that would create a balance between the great powers by using France as a counterweight against Russia. Equally important for Austria was to frustrate Russo-Prussian designs on Poland and Saxony as well as any other plans they might have for Germany that would threaten the national interests of Austria.

So it was Emperor Alexander and the Prussian senior officers—King Frederick William was anything but bellicose—who clamored for a continuation of the war. For the Russian ruler, the advantages were obvious. Aside from the symbolic importance of entering his enemy's capital city, he knew that the more prominently he figured in the taming of the Revolution incarnate, the more his voice would carry in the final settlement. Alexander's grand vision for Russia's place in postwar Europe required an energetic execution of the war and the destruction of French power. A negotiated peace with Napoleon while the French emperor was still on the throne and with French armies in the field could not provide the leverage that Alexander needed to secure his objectives, including forcing France to surrender Alsace to Austria as compensation for Vienna's cession of Galicia to Russian-controlled Poland. Furthermore, continued friction with the Austrians also raised Russian doubts whether they could gain sufficient support from any party involved in the negotiations; even Prussian support was seen as wavering, raising questions about the viability of Alexander's fundamental demand, which was incorporating Prussian Poland into his Polish domain and compensating Berlin with Saxony.

Despite the demands of the war party, Metternich and the peace party prevailed. The Allies offered Napoleon what became known as the Frankfurt Proposals. Drafted under Metternich's close supervision, the terms would have ensured the survival of the Napoleonic monarchy in France in exchange for Napoleon's acceptance of augmented natural frontiers. Napoleon would surrender Holland, Germany, Italy, and Spain but still retain Belgium, the left bank of the Rhine, and Savoy in northwestern Italy—which is to say, the original conquests of the French Revolution. These were generous terms, if one considers that Napoleon had already lost control over Germany, Italy, and Spain, and agreeing to them simply would have confirmed the reality on the ground. France still would have emerged larger that it had been since Charlemagne, and the Napoleonic monarchy certainly would have survived beyond 1815. And that was the exact purpose of the proposals. They reflected Metternich's firm belief that Russia would be the future threat to Europe's equilibrium; Russian insistence on the war and regime change in France only unnerved the Austrians, who interpreted this as Alexander's attempt to turn France into a Russian satellite. With Prussia already playing the role of a Russian associate, this postwar arrangement would have ensured Russian dominance on the continent. Containing ambitious tsars required the preservation of France as a great power, and granting natural frontiers ensured that the French would have sufficient resources to deter Russian aggrandizement in Europe.

How sincerely the offer was meant has been long debated by historians, but given continued dissent between the powers, it is probable that Napoleon could have had peace on these terms had he accepted the offer at once. Instead, he dithered. He was prepared to surrender Spain and Germany but balked at giving away Italy, which, in his words, "could make a diversion to Austria," and Holland, which "afforded so many resources."[65] Equally important for him was the realization that the price the Allies were asking for French acceptance of these terms was not the cessation of hostilities but the start of negotiations, and the Allies specified that these negotiations would not suspend military operations. Thus, even after he had renounced his conquests, he would not have obtained the certainty of preserving France from invasion. Grumbling that the coalition considered "the lion dead," Napoleon agreed to negotiate, and he instructed his envoy to inform the coalition that he was accepting "the general and summary bases" for talks.[66] Throughout November 1813 the envoys shuttled back and forth, discussing preliminary terms for opening negotiations.

British intervention soon rendered these negotiations moot. By now Wellington was already in southern France, and his military presence, along with the vast subsidies that the Allies continued to receive from London, gave Britain considerable bargaining power. The news of the Frankfurt Proposals alarmed the British government because its representative, the Earl of Aberdeen, not only had accepted Metternich's vision of postwar equilibrium but had promised to restore captured French colonies, and he had neglected to protest against British maritime interests being brought into the discussion. It was decided that Lord Castlereagh, the foreign secretary, must immediately go to Allied headquarters. As a favored apprentice of Prime Minister Pitt, Castlereagh had been long actively involved in British foreign policy and shared Pitt's broad vision of a post-Napoleonic settlement: the return of France to its 1792 borders, restoration of sovereigns overthrown during the Napoleonic Wars, acceptance of Russian expansion as long as Austria and Prussia were compensated, the formation of a territorial buffer zone around France to prevent any future aggression, and the conclusion of a general agreement for the mutual protection and security of the great powers.[67] This was a general program that Castlereagh tried to realize in 1813–1815. His instructions also specified the independence of Holland, Spain, and Portugal and made clear that Aberdeen was to be adamantly against any settlement that would have left France in control of any part of the Low Countries (especially Antwerp), which could threaten the British Isles.[68] Crucial to British interests was the question of maritime rights, of course, for they underpinned British imperial interests around the world. Castlereagh had made it clear that British naval power was such that the Allies should not even broach it in their discussions.[69]

The Frankfurt Proposals alarmed the British because they made clear that Metternich was steering the coalition in a direction that would leave many of Britain's war aims unfulfilled. Austria, as a continental power, harbored little concern for the issues that most concerned the British, such as maritime trading rights or the Low Countries. On the other hand, British influence in southern Italy was deeply worrying to Vienna, which preferred to see the Italian peninsula under its authority. To achieve his goals of containing Russia, maintaining political equilibrium, and preventing future revolutions, Metternich sought to isolate the British and, if possible, exclude them from negotiations that would have kept Napoleon on the French throne and limited France to its natural frontiers. This was an unsettling prospect for Britain.

Upon arriving on the continent, Castlereagh found the Allies lacking military and diplomatic unity. The Russian emperor's refusal to identify his objectives suggested his intention to use the war to push Russian influence deep into central Europe. Relations between Alexander and Metternich had been embittered to such a degree that the Austrians threatened to halt further military cooperation unless the Russians scaled back their ambitions. Castlereagh immediately set about the task of reconciling their differences, binding the Allies closer together, and, most crucial of all, creating a mechanism by which the coalition could act in unison against Napoleon and reorganize the continent after a generation of warfare. Here lay one of Castlereagh's greatest contributions to the Napoleonic Wars. He was one the least insular of British statesmen and demonstrated both common sense and a good grasp of the issues at stake. He diligently worked to bridge the divides between the Allies, and his eventual success generated a veritable diplomatic revolution in international affairs.[70]

Castlereagh did not believe that any peace would last as long as Napoleon continued to wear the imperial crown. Britain and Austria thus appeared diametrically opposed on this issue, one that might have proven insuperable if not for a rift in Anglo-Russian relations that paved the way for an Anglo-Austrian rapprochement. To encourage the Allies to fight on, Castlereagh informed them of the British offer of £5 million and a willingness to establish a Grand Alliance in which Russia would take the lead role as Britain's partner. However, Alexander rebuffed any offer that did not guarantee his major objective, Poland. He then departed for the front on January 16, leaving Metternich behind in Basle. The Austrian cleverly exploited this window of opportunity to seek, in his words, "an identity of thought and feeling" with Castlereagh. As soon as the British secretary reached the Swiss town, the Austrian minister arranged for several private meetings with him and during them offered a deeper perspective on the coalition's problems. Metternich understood that, given British intervention, the Frankfurt terms were no longer viable. Though he mistrusted the British, he also needed their help against Russian intrigue, and so he presented himself as a flexible proponent of Anglo-Austrian entente, in direct contrast to the Russian recalcitrance. He persuaded Castlereagh that if Russia was unchecked, Russian hegemony would replace French.

During the negotiations, the British secretary insisted that the former Dutch territories be merged with Belgium to form the Kingdom of Netherlands, which would be entrusted to the House of Orange, while Spain and Portugal would be returned to their former rulers. In exchange for Austrian support on these issues, Britain was willing to help Vienna in Italy and reach a compromise settlement in Germany. Metternich had no objections to Britain's plans in the Low Countries or to its unwillingness to discuss maritime rights, and the two statesmen agreed that for a lasting peace in Europe it was important to maintain a strong France as a counterbalance to the Russian Empire. Castlereagh, for his part, contended that British public opinion demanded Napoleon's abdication. Metternich preferred to see Napoleon remain on the throne, which meant that the emperor's son (and Emperor Francis's grandson) would eventually inherit the crown. However, Metternich was also willing to compromise on this issue, one that Britain clearly considered vital to its interests. For Austria, the only alternative to keeping Napoleon was restoring the Bourbon Dynasty, which would ensure the revival of France's traditional position as a counterpoint to Russia.

These discussions shifted the balance within the coalition against Russia. Castlereagh came to share Metternich's view of the potential threat Russia posed to the European balance of power, and agreed with his half brother, Sir Charles Stewart (Britain's ambassador to Prussia), that Russia's vast human and natural resources had been augmented further during the Napoleonic Wars. "If we consider all these circumstances in all their bearings and dependencies," observed Charles William Vane, Marquis of Londonderry, "is there a serious and reasonable man in Europe that must not admit that the whole system of European politics ought, as its leading principle and feature, to maintain, as an axiom, the necessity of setting bounds to this [Russian] formidable and encroaching power?"[71]

By January 1814, France's military prospects looked grim. The great empire that once had stretched from the Douro to the Niemen had been dissolved in the course of a single year. Napoleon's resources and manpower had been strained to the extreme. More than 100,000 men were tied down in besieged fortresses beyond the Rhine, while some 50,000 men, under Eugène de Beauharnais, were stuck in northern Italy and along France's Alpine borders. All the minor German states had, more or less willingly, joined the Allies. In Italy, Marshal Joachim Murat, hoping to safeguard his Neapolitan crown and encouraged by his wife (and Napoleon's sister), Caroline, had defected to the Allies, issued a proclamation denouncing the "mad ambitions" of his former benefactor, and marched with 30,000 men to support the Austrian efforts to reclaim northern Italy.[72] Spain had been liberated, and Wellington's Anglo-Allied army had already established itself in an unassailable position near Bayonne, in southern France.[73] The Allies commenced an invasion of France with three armies—Schwarzenberg's Army of Bohemia (200,000 men) advancing from Switzerland, Blücher's Army of Silesia (more than 50,000 men) moving from Germany toward Metz, and Bernadotte's Army of North Germany (120,000 men) proceeding toward northwestern France, with some of its units invading the Low Countries.

To confront these threats, Napoleon decreed new levies that raised a force of almost 120,000 men, many of them mere boys who were nicknamed *marie-louises* after their young empress.[74] With almost 100,000 troops committed to contain the British in southern France and another 20,000 to 30,000 to defend the Alpine borders, Napoleon could devote only 75,000 to 80,000 men to the east and northeastern frontier, where the main Allied invasion was unfolding. He made some effort to revive the spirit of 1793—allowing public performances of "La Marseillaise" and sending out a new generation of commissaries to the departments—but rebuffed suggestions to resort to popular support because he feared social instability and chaos. In any case, the nation itself was not ready for a repetition of 1793. After a decade of almost continuous warfare, the country's economy in decline and its industry at a standstill, two great armies destroyed in as many years, and the country menaced by foreign invasion, the public desire for peace was passionate and universal. Napoleon could no longer count on a popular response to calls of "la patrie en danger." Reflecting this uncertain mood, the Senate and Legislative Corps showed their first signs of defiance, with the latter urging the emperor to come to terms with the Allies and demanding civil and political liberties.[75] Napoleon's response was, as expected, swift and imperious. He prorogued the legislature and delivered a blistering attack on his critics:

You call yourselves Representatives of the Nation. It is not true. . . . I alone am the true Representative of the Nation. Twice 24,000,000 French called me to this throne: who of you would undertake such a burden? . . . What, who are you? Nothing—all authority is in the throne; and what is the Throne? A few boards covered with velvet? No! I am the Throne! . . . Must I sacrifice pride to obtain peace? I am proud, because I am brave. I am proud because I have done great things for France. In a word, France has more need of me than I have need of France. In three months we shall have peace, or I shall be dead.[76]

During these critical days Napoleon once again demonstrated the duality of his character. On one hand, here was a man who despite his brilliance, incisiveness, and clarity of mind regularly rejected rational thought and acted out of pride and egotism. At moments Napoleon had recognized that the Continental System was "a chimera," that the Confederation of the Rhine was a "bad calculation," and even that the Grand Empire was a lost cause.[77] Yet he never did anything about this and, instead, denounced those who dared to wish "to descend from the height to which I have raised France, to become a simple monarchy again instead of a proud Empire."[78] He regularly raged against client states that had turned their backs on him. Discussing the defection of Bavaria, his eyes flashed with anger: "Munich must burn! And burn it shall!"[79] This intransigence of temper played a decisive role in his downfall. If not state interests, common sense should have required him to conclude a peace.

But beneath it all remained the young and brilliant general who had stunned Europe twenty years earlier. He was still that talented, pensive, and hardworking man who was less the favored child of fortune than its maker. There were still flashes of the old genius. Despite everything arrayed against him, the new campaign saw the return of the younger and more energetic Napoleon—"I have put on my Italian boots," he famously quipped, referring to his great Italian campaigns of 1796–1797. He hastened preparations for a campaign based on the strategy of safeguarding the heart of his empire, Paris. His defensive campaign in February of 1814 remains a classic example of how a small force, resourcefully handled, may inflict defeat on an enemy superior in numbers. Of course, Napoleon's task was greatly facilitated by the Allies' continued bickering over the outcome of war and Europe's future prospects. Having liberated central Europe, they had already made it clear that there was wide disagreement as to how they would deal with the problems raised by Napoleon's defeat. These political discords had been made more serious by personal friction between the Allied leaders. Thus, even as the invasion began, their headquarters still debated their ultimate object: to overthrow Napoleon completely or to compel him to accept a peace that might still leave him in charge of France? Military operations were therefore often conducted disjointedly and lackadaisically.

In the opening phase of the campaign of 1814, Napoleon used the advantage of his central position to attack the various Allied armies in turn and push them back. On January 29 he surprised Blücher's Army of Silesia at Brienne-le-Château (where Napoleon had studied as a schoolboy), inflicting 4,000 casualties and forcing the Prussian general to fall southward. Three days later Napoleon was attacked by Blücher at La Rothière. A severe snowstorm blinded both sides, and while Napoleon managed to hold ground until nightfall, he was eventually forced to retreat.[80] This setback seems to have jolted the emperor, who on February 4 gave Caulaincourt permission to treat with the Allies. Several factors made Caulaincourt's task impossible. Six days earlier, the four Allied powers (Russia, Britain, Austria, and Prussia) had signed a secret protocol at Langres in which they agreed to make all the major decisions concerning postwar European settlement themselves. The agreement affirmed a balance of power as the guiding principle and promised to develop "a system of real and permanent Balance of Power in Europe" at a congress that would be organized after the war.[81]

But the Allies still lacked unity. The Austrians, sensing the growing ambitions of the Russian ruler, attempted to slow the pace of Allied military operations. Alexander saw through the Austrian smokescreen and refused to allow any delay. After the Prussian success at La Rothière, he instructed his envoy to suspend negotiations, and he argued that he could march straight to Paris and dethrone Napoleon. He also refused to bind himself to any declaration of war aims, insisting that none should be identified until Napoleon had been defeated and declaring that all options regarding France's future dynasty should be considered. Castlereagh had some stormy meetings with the Russian ruler before the latter agreed to resume negotiations.[82]

This was one of the focal moments in the campaign. The Russian emperor had realized that he could not win without Austria's military support and British subsidies. Conversely, Metternich knew that as long as the Anglo-Austrian entente remained firm, he would be able to restrain Russian ambitions. Castlereagh shared this sentiment after he came to perceive Alexander "as an uncooperative and ungrateful ally."[83] On January 29, 1814, the Allies signed the Protocols of Langres, which reflected the discussions they had held over the previous four weeks. The protocol affirmed that the balance of power, not sovereign equality, was the idea of the moment, and it reserved all major decisions concerning postwar reconstruction to the great powers themselves. It was agreed that France should be restricted to its "ancient frontiers" (again, as of 1792) and that all other questions, except maritime rights, would be settled at a congress to be held at Vienna.[84]

At the peace conference at Châtillon-sur-Seine, which opened on February 5, Napoleon was surprised to learn that the Allied terms no longer involved the 1797 frontiers (as envisioned in the Frankfurt Proposals) and had substituted those of 1792.[85] He found this a hard pill to swallow, refusing to accept any terms that would have reduced France to the boundaries of the ancien régime. His intransience only increased when his repeated requests about the plans that the Allies had made for Germany and Italy were ignored. The Allies could hardly tell him what they were, since they had not yet agreed on the issues themselves, but their response that German and Italian matters were of no concern to France only served to embitter the French emperor.

The Châtillon-sur-Seine conference continues to serve as a classic example of how difficult it is to conduct diplomatic negotiations while a war rages. When he was losing, Napoleon was willing to get what he could; with any glimpse of winning, he would change his mind. Thus just hours after dispatching his envoy to negotiate at Châtillon-sur-Seine he was already stretched out on the floor, poring over his maps and sticking pins into them. The reason for this change of attitude was newly received reports that the Allies had split their forces and that while Schwarzenberg's Army of Bohemia was slogging along the southern route toward Paris, Blücher's Army of Silesia remained unsupported in the valley of the Marne to the north. Napoleon was tempted to destroy the Prussians, which, in his mind, would have strengthened his position at the ongoing negotiations with the Allies. After a quick dash from Troyes, Napoleon launched one of his most remarkable campaigns, winning a quick succession of victories over the Russo-Prussian forces at Champaubert, Montmirail, Château-Thierry, and Vauchamps in the five days between February 10 and 14. The French then turned to Schwarzenberg's Austrian army, which in the meantime had begun its leisurely advance, defeating it at Mormant, Montereau, and Méry between February 17 and February 21.[86]

These were amazing accomplishments, but their overall impact would actually make it impossible for Napoleon to win the war. Although the French pushed the Allies back to Bar-sur-Aube and inflicted greater casualties than they suffered, their losses were still significant in light of the limited resources they had at hand. Furthermore, these victories emboldened Napoleon to order his envoy at the Châtillon congress to accept nothing less than the previously offered (and rejected) Frankfurt Proposals.

His hopes that his six-day campaign would splinter the coalition would not come to fruition, however. Allied self-confidence was indeed dented, and new fissures threatened to undermine their war effort. Recriminations between Austria and Russia had reached new heights, with Alexander feeling betrayed by the lackluster Austrian performance. Each power suspected that the other was trying to preserve its forces in order to have greater leverage during postwar negotiations over the spoils. But Castlereagh's timely intervention once again saved the day. He pointed out to the Allies the strength of their position, allayed their mutual suspicions, and, in his most crucial contribution, warned that Britain would never restore its colonial conquests unless there was a peace on the continent such as it desired. "Nothing keeps either power firm but the consciousness that without Great Britain the peace cannot be made," Castlereagh reported in late February.[87]

Castlereagh's efforts soon rallied the quarrelling Allies and helped to them rediscover their joint purpose to fight Napoleon. They confirmed this commitment in the Treaty of Chaumont (March 1), which Castlereagh helped negotiate and that formed what became known as the Quadruple Alliance. The Allies agreed to let Napoleon retain his throne only if he was willing to accept the offer of the "ancient frontiers" of France in return for a cease-fire. The Allies pledged that if the terms were rejected, they would fight the war against France to a conclusion, with each of the powers committing 150,000 troops to victory. Britain promised to contribute a subsidy of £5 million to the effort. More significantly, each member of the alliance agreed not to seek a separate accommodation with Napoleon—thus eliminating any possibility of his breaking up the alliance—and to remain united for twenty years following the conclusion of hostilities in order to ensure France's observance of the peace terms. These terms included a confederated Germany, an independent Switzerland, an Italy divided into independent (but Austria-influenced) states, a free Spain under the Bourbons, and an enlarged Holland under the House of Orange.[88] Here was the origin of the alliance that was to dominate European politics for three decades. It was designed, in the words of its chief architect, "not only as a systematic pledge of persevering concert among the leading Powers, but a refuge under which all the minor States, especially those on the Rhine, may look forward to find their security upon the return of peace."[89]

Napoleon rejected the offer, still firmly believing that a military campaign could turn the tide of war and cause the coalition to collapse. This rejection confirmed what many members of the coalition had suspected—namely, that the French emperor had never had any intention of negotiating in good faith, and that the only way to deal with him was through brute force. In early March he again targeted Blücher's Army of Silesia, ordering Marshals Marmont and Mortier to pursue the Russo-Prussians while he made a flanking maneuver to cut off their line of retreat. Blücher was surrounded on all sides, and the only way out was through the French-held fortress of Soissons. Incredibly, the Allied officers managed to convince the French commander of Soissons, General Jean-Claude Moreau, to abandon the fortress, allowing Blücher's weary troops to escape across the Aisne River.[90]

The Allied capture of Soissons on March 3 had a critical impact—"incalculable harm," in the words of Napoleon—on the course of the 1814 campaign.[91] Without this fortress, Blücher's men would have been forced to fight with their backs against the river and could have suffered another defeat à la Friedland.[92] But the opportunity was lost and the fall of Soissons proved fortuitous for the Allies. Once the Army of Silesia was safely across the river, they left a strong garrison at Soissons, blocking French operations and compelling Napoleon to turn to Craonne, where he sought to cross the Aisne River in order to flank the Army of Silesia. After his cavalry scouts seized an intact bridge at Berry-au-Bac, Napoleon received intelligence of Allied forces concentrating on the plateau near Craonne. Assuming that Blücher was still trying to retreat, Napoleon concluded that this was probably a covering force for the Army of Silesia and decided to destroy it. Instead, he came across Blücher's entire army.

The Battle of Craonne on March 7 did not go as either side planned. Blücher could not get all his forces into action, while Napoleon did not yet appreciate how powerful his opponent was. After several hours of fighting, in which the troops of Russian general Mikhail Vorontsov particularly distinguished themselves, Blücher decided to break off the action and had the troops fall back to the main position at Laon, about six miles to the northwest. Although Napoleon could claim a victory at Craonne since he was left in possession of the field, his army suffered heavy losses that it could not afford. After the battle both sides remained very much in the dark as to each other's actual strength and intentions. Still believing that Blücher was in retreat, Napoleon sought another opportunity to destroy part of the Army of Silesia. This led to a two-day battle at Laon, where the Allies successfully repelled French attacks and forced Napoleon to fall back.[93]

Soon the French emperor's situation turned grim. Ill tidings appeared from every quarter. While Napoleon was fighting Blücher at Craonne and Laon, Schwarzenberg had kept moving closer to Paris. In southern France, Wellington had crossed the Pau River and defeated Marshal Soult at Orthez on February 27. By mid-March the flag of the Bourbons appeared in Bordeaux, and the city shortly surrendered to the British without a fight.[94] Searching for any bit of good news, Napoleon grasped at a timely piece of intelligence. The Allies, encouraged by their recent successes, had gotten careless and left a single Russian corps under the French émigré General Emmanuel Saint-Priest at the city of Rheims, seeking to maintain communications between Blücher and Schwarzenberg. Located at the junction of major routes to Paris, Rheims was also important symbolically as the ancient coronation site for French kings. Napoleon immediately saw that the Russian corps (with a small Prussian contingent) was isolated and unsupported by the Allied forces. Consequently, he diverted part of his army to reclaim Rheims and crush the Russians. The first of his columns reached the town after a bruising march of twenty hours. It was near nightfall on March 13, and Saint-Priest had no idea what he was facing. He initially marched out to confront the enemy force, but his troops were soon manhandled back into the town by the stronger French forces. The ensuing Battle of Rheims resulted in an Allied defeat and cost the coalition as many as 5,000 men, almost half of them killed, including Saint-Priest himself.[95]

The French victory at Rheims stunned the Allies, who had already written off Napoleon only to see him reincarnate and shatter another Allied corps. Furthermore, in one quick march Napoleon had placed himself between the Allied armies and was in position to threaten the rear of both. For a moment the Allies vacillated about their next moves. Their hand was forced by the new French offensive. Napoleon chose to exploit his success at Rheims by moving farther eastward with a striking force and linking up with the French garrisons near the Rhine that were blockaded by the Allies. This, combined with growing partisan activity in the eastern part of France, would sever the supply lines of the Allied armies. However, before this bold strategic move could be undertaken, Napoleon decided to first target Schwarzenberg's Army of Bohemia, which had gotten dangerously close to Paris. Leaving Marshals Marmont and Mortier to watch Blücher in the north, he marched south with the remaining forces. aiming at the rear end of the Army of Bohemia. Upon learning about the French movement, Schwarzenberg, uncharacteristically, decided to halt his retreat and fight the French. In the ensuing battle at Arcis-sur-Aube (March 20) the Allies proved victorious primarily because Napoleon underestimated their strength—Schwarzenberg began with just 20,000 on the first day but mustered four times as many troops by the end of the battle.[96]

To recover his position, Napoleon then resorted to his earlier plan of marching eastward and linking up with the garrisons to cut the Allied supply lines. This was a bold course indeed, and Napoleon thought it was the best one available. On March 23 he outlined his plan in a short letter to his wife, Marie-Louise. It was intercepted by Allied scouts. The letter offered crucial intelligence on the French emperor's plans, his intent, and even his initial line of march and allowed the Allies to shift their attention to the French capital, where, as additional captured dispatches revealed, the political situation was very unstable. Napoleon's ministers spoke of the alarming extent of subversive activity, as well as of the weak defenses of the city. Emperor Alexander now insisted that the Allied armies immediately march on to Paris. By noon on March 30 the Allies had reached the Buttes-Chaumont and, ascending a nearby hill, surveyed the French capital spreading in front of them in the distance. Only hours separated them from a triumphant entry into the capital of their greatest enemy.

Paris was defended by the battered corps of Marshals Marmont and Mortier. The Allies first targeted the north of the city, the aim being to take the heights of Montmartre, which would have offered them the dominant position. Although far outnumbering the French defenders, they began their attack on a broad front and quickly got tangled up in a series of uncoordinated assaults on the northern faubourgs. The fighting continued all day and was desperate and bloody, especially around the faubourg of Pantin. By nightfall the French prevented the Allied forces from getting into Paris proper. Nonetheless, it was clear that the fate of the city had already been decided. During the night Marmont and Mortier accepted coalition parleys and agreed on terms of surrender at two in the morning on March 31, 1814. At the same time, Talleyrand, who had played such a crucial role in Napoleon's rise to power, now played an equally important part in his downfall. The former foreign minister organized a virtual coup d'état, forming a provisional government that opened negotiations with the Allies. It was he and fellow renegade Joseph Fouché, the former minister of police, who convinced the Allied leaders to restore the Bourbon dynasty on the throne of France and had the Senate adopt a special proclamation deposing Napoleon on April 2, 1814.

Now holed up at Fontainebleau, Napoleon was still determined to fight. His marshals were not. Tired of defending what they had begun to consider a lost cause, Marshals Ney, Oudinot, Lefebvre, Moncey, and others called for an end to the war. The Allies already occupied much of northern France, and the British were making significant advances in the south.[97] The marshals were anxious to secure their own futures before it was too late. In early April a group of them confronted Napoleon, hoping that he would resign in favor of his son and thus ensure the survival of the Napoleonic regime, from which they all had benefited. Napoleon reluctantly agreed to sign a conditional abdication, provided that his son was first recognized as his successor. Caulaincourt and marshals took this offer to the Allies.

On April 4, while Caulaincourt pleaded with the Russian emperor and the marshals emphasized that the army would stand by Napoleon and fight if the offer was spurned, stunning news was brought to Alexander that negated all of their arguments. Marshal Marmont had surrendered his entire command to the Allies, who hereafter insisted on unconditional abdication. Napoleon signed the document of abdication on April 6.[98] Five days later, on April 11, his fate was settled formally by the terms of the Treaty of Fontainebleau: Napoleon renounced the throne of France and was, in turn, recognized as the sovereign of the island of Elba and granted an annual income of 2 million francs from France. For a man who had fought the Allies so bitterly and for so long, this was hardly a harsh settlement, but for Napoleon the fall was great;

the following day he attempted unsuccessfully to commit suicide by taking poison. On April 20, in a now-famous scene depicted by French painter Antoine Alphonse Montfort, Napoleon bid farewell to his Imperial Guard at the Fontainebleau palace and, escorted by the Allied troops, set off for Elba. The journey proved to be an ignominious one. Encountering public enmity and at one point pelted with stones, he was forced to briefly disguise himself in a Russian uniform and a round hat with a white Bourbon cockade.[99]

Thus ended the longest coalition campaign of the Napoleonic Wars. The Treaty of Paris, signed on May 30, 1814, formally ended the War of the Sixth Coalition and restored "perpetual peace and friendship" to the entire continent for the first time in twenty-two years.[100] In drafting this treaty the Allies considered three major questions: Should France be allowed to retain prewar territory and status, or should it be stripped of much of its territory in order to permanently break its power? Should the French, who had exploited the entire continent for the better part of a decade, be treated likewise and obliged to pay reparations? How could the Allies ensure that postwar Europe remained stable and peaceful?

Once again these negotiations revealed significant differences between the coalition partners. Prussia, and the German states, which had been subjected to French economic exploitation and felt vulnerable to French aggressions in the future, insisted on harsher conditions that would have seen France lose key frontier territories and pay a considerable indemnity. Russia, Austria, and Britain were more conciliatory, understanding that reducing their former nemesis to the status of second-rate power would have served no useful purpose and would only further undermine the fragile political stability reached on the continent. Of course, neither did the victors want to handicap the restored French government with overly harsh peace terms that might provoke another popular tumult. The moderates ultimately prevailed, and probably the most striking feature of the final treaty was how surprisingly lenient the Allies were toward the vanquished France. In a major concession, they agreed to evacuate French territory even before a final treaty was formally ratified. Furthermore, no restriction was placed on the future size of the French army, and France was assessed no indemnity nor asked to compensate for the immense sums that its troops had exacted in conquered and occupied areas of Europe. Surprisingly, the Allies did not even require France to give back the vast majority of art treasures that Napoleon had pilfered during his conquests.

France was forced to recognize the loss of the remainder of its conquests in Holland, Germany, Italy, and Switzerland, but it was allowed to retain the borders that it had held as of January 1, 1792.[101] This meant that the defeated nation, far from being forced to give up its own territory, actually retained parts of Savoy, the Austrian Netherlands (Belgium), the Rhineland, and the papal enclaves of Avignon and Comtat Venaissin. France was defeated but emerged from the war with a territory that was larger—by 150 square miles and 450,000 inhabitants—than the one it had held at the start of it.[102] The Allies also returned all of the French overseas colonies, with the notable exception of the islands of Tobago and St. Lucia in the West Indies, and Île de France (Mauritius), Rodrigues, and the Seychelles in the Indian Ocean. All of those Britain retained. The treaty with France was only first step toward the general reorganization of Europe, which the Allies hoped would create a system based on a "real and permanent balance of power in Europe."[103] Accordingly, the agreement stipulated that the Allied powers would convene a special congress to reach a general settlement.

Before venturing into the world of diplomatic intrigues in Vienna, we should briefly return to events in North America, where the war between Britain and the United States had entered its second year. After early setbacks in 1812, American fortunes soon recovered, as Britain remained preoccupied with the Napoleonic Wars. Tens of thousands of British troops remained committed in the Iberian Peninsula, while millions of pounds sterling were spent on sustaining coalitions in Germany. The Americans took advantage of this.

In the spring of 1813, Major General (and future president) William H. Harrison took charge of the Army of the Northwest and defeated the British at Fort Meigs, near Perrysburg, Ohio. In September, US Navy master commandant Oliver Hazard Perry, despite failing to develop a clear plan or provide proper direction to his subordinates, won a naval battle on Lake Erie, capturing all six British warships that opposed him and establishing American naval supremacy on the Great Lakes.[104] Supported by Perry's squadron, Harrison was now ready to resume the offensive with his 7,000 seasoned troops. He recaptured Detroit on September 29 and pushed the British and their Native American allies down the Thames River into the Upper Canada, where, on October 5, he scored a victory near Chatham, Ontario.[105] The Battle of the Thames (or Moraviantown), as this encounter became known, consolidated American control over the northwest frontier but could not affect the course of the war. In fact, the US War Department ordered Harrison's militia disbanded and sent home, while his regular troops were diverted to the Niagara front line. Enraged, Harrison resigned his commission and returned to civil life.

The defeat on the Thames, meanwhile, had a profound impact on Britain's key ally, the Native American tribal confederacy, which collapsed after its leader, the Shawnee chief Tecumseh, was killed during the battle. Even more disastrous was the turn of events for Britain's other Native American ally, the

"Red Stick" Creeks, who had found themselves caught between the growing United States, the last gasps of the Spanish Empire, and meddling British traders and agents. The Creek Nation was hard pressed to pick a side and was deeply divided about waging war. This was particularly apparent when, on the eve of the Anglo-American conflict, Tecumseh had approached the Creeks with an offer of a pan-Indian militancy, and some Creek chiefs had failed to rally to the anti-American cause. Although neither British nor Spanish governments officially aided the tribes, individual traders from each nation did, probably with tacit state approval. Britain had long-standing relations with the tribes in the Gulf borderlands and was naturally interested in exploiting them to divert American manpower and supplies from the main frontline in the north.[106]

In July 1813 Mississippi militiamen and settlers from the Tensaw area attacked the Red Stick warriors near Burnt Corn Creek in a vain attempt to keep them from resupplying their ammunition at Pensacola. A retaliatory strike against a fortified settlement owned by Samuel Mims, now called Fort Mims, was a Red Stick victory. It shocked contemporaries by the brutality of the assault, in which some 250 civilians were killed. The massacre outraged the American public, and "Remember Fort Mims" became a national rallying cry.[107] Since regular American troops were committed to the Canadian front lines, Tennessee, Georgia, and the Mississippi Territory mobilized their own militias, which were placed under command of Colonel Andrew Jackson.[108] In a year-long campaign Jackson inflicted a series of defeats on the Creeks—most notably at the Battle of Horseshoe Bend (near Dadeville, Alabama) on March 27, 1814—that all but destroyed them militarily before Britain could free itself from the Napoleonic wars and substantially resupply and rearm the Creek warriors. Instead, the trounced Creeks were forced to cede more than 21 million acres of land—half of Alabama and part of southern Georgia—to the United States by the Treaty of Fort Jackson (August 9, 1814).[109]

Victory over the Creeks came at an opportune moment, because any reprieve that Americans had in their war against Britain ended with Napoleon's defeat. The British were finally able to redeploy substantial naval and army resources across the Atlantic. Of the forty-four units dispatched, almost half were from Wellington's veteran regiments from the Peninsular Army.[110] Their arrival dramatically increased the size of the British forces in North America to over 50,000 (versus the US Army's 35,000 to 40,000 men) and facilitated swift escalation in military operations that involved an invasion of New York states from Lower Canada, ambitious operations in the Chesapeake Bay area, and an operation designed to threaten American interests in New Orleans, whose capture would have allowed the British to control the trade in the Mississippi estuary.[111]

The fighting in New York began in the summer of 1814. The US secretary of war, John Armstrong, had sought to secure a victory in Canada before British reinforcements arrived there. In the newly reorganized US Army of the North, Major General Jacob Brown was given command of the Left Division, with orders to threaten Kingston, the main British base on Lake Ontario. As a contingency, he was instructed to lead an attack across the Niagara. To attack Kingston, the Americans needed naval support, but Brown was unable to cooperate with Commodore Isaac Chauncey, who commanded the American naval squadron at Sackett's Harbor, New York, and refused to move until he had received additional warships. Brown, therefore, settled for the second plan of attack. In early July he led his men across the Niagara River, forced the surrender of Fort Erie, and defeated Major General Phineas Riall, who commanded the Right Division of the British Army in Upper Canada, at the Battle of Chippawa on July 5.[112] While this victory showed the much-improved fighting capabilities of the American troops, it failed to produce a breakthrough in the war. Nor did the Battle of Lundy's Lane—one of the bloodiest of the war—which was fought on July 25.[113]

For all their success, the Americans could not overcome British opposition, which was buttressed by the newly arriving troops from Europe. In fact, American victories required so many casualties that the US forces were ultimately forced to fall back, and the Niagara campaign, as a whole, swung the tide of war to the British side. George Prévost, British governor-general of Canada and commander in chief, received substantial reinforcements from Europe, including several thousand veterans of Wellington's Peninsular Army, which he intended to deploy along the coastline of Lake Champlain and into Upper New York.[114] His plan was to employ a newly constructed naval squadron to gain naval supremacy on Lake Champlain, while the land forces would take the town of Plattsburgh. By September 6 the British reached Plattsburgh, where they encountered American positions manned by only 1,700 regulars under the command of Brigadier General Alexander Macomb. Had the British attacked, they might have gained a victory. But Prévost delayed his ground assault in order to wait for his naval squadron under Captain George Downie, which was expected to defeat the American flotilla, led by Master Commandant Thomas Macdonough, and establish British control of Lake Champlain. Yet in the naval clash on September 11 the Americans outmaneuvered their British counterparts and emerged decisively victorious. Prévost was so discouraged by this setback that he abandoned the attack by land against Macomb's defenses and retreated to Canada, arguing that even if Plattsburgh was captured, his troops could not be supplied without control of the lake.[115]

Meanwhile, the British had carried out a major diversion in the Chesapeake area, hoping to draw off American forces facing Prévost. In a bold plan, Vice Admiral Sir Alexander Cochrane and Major General Robert Ross decided to capture Washington, D.C., whose location near the Chesapeake Bay made it vulnerable to an amphibious assault. Cochrane successfully cornered the American squadron of Commodore Joshua Barney in the Patuxent River and opened a path for Ross's ground invasion, which was fully under way by late August. The British defeated Americans at the Battle of Bladensburg and, on August 24, captured Washington, where they proceeded to burn public buildings in retaliation for the American destruction of Tork (Toronto) and Newark earlier in the war. The British departed the following day only to return several weeks later to seize Baltimore, a vital port and a privateer hub some forty miles northeast of Washington, though the land and naval assault on the city on September 13–14 failed.[116] The British bombardment of Fort McHenry accomplished little beyond inspiriting Francis Scott Key, an American negotiator who was detained on a British warship and, "by the dawn's early light," watched "the rocket's red glare, the bombs bursting in air," to write the poem that eventually became the American national anthem.

The American successes at Lake Champlain, Plattsburgh, and Baltimore halted British advances in the Mid-Atlantic states and denied the British negotiators at the newly opened peace discussions at Ghent (Belgium) leverage to demand any territorial claims against the United States on the basis of *uti possidetis*, that is, retaining territory they held at the end of hostilities. After the failure of the Baltimore attack, the British forces withdrew to the West Indies, there to regroup and await reinforcements. In the fall the British commenced a joint land and naval campaign against American targets in the Gulf Coast. The campaign sought to deprive the United States of access to the crucial areas around the Gulf and ultimately influence peace negotiations to safeguard British interests in the region. The principal focus of the campaign was the city of New Orleans, a large commercial hub that served as the main outlet of American goods in the Gulf region and, as noted earlier, controlled access to the Mississippi River basin. The British also hoped to exploit the fact of the recent incorporation of these areas into the United States and solicit support from the Spanish and French residents, as well as Native American tribes, against the Americans. As early as the spring of 1814 Cochrane had sought to incite the Seminoles, in Spanish Florida, to fight against the Americans.

In mid-August a small British detachment, led by Major Edward Nicolls of the Royal Maines, captured the naval anchorage at Pensacola Bay, West Florida, and received support from some local Indians. A month later Nicolls, supported by a Royal Navy squadron under the command of Captain

William H. Percy, marched against Fort Bowyer, at the mouth of Mobile Bay but was unable to overcome the American garrison, commanded by Major William Lawrence. Losing one ship and suffering dozens of casualties, the British were forced to withdraw in mid-September. The British assault soon provoked an American counterattack. In November the American commander along the Gulf Coast, Major General Andrew Jackson, recaptured the town of Pensacola, easily overcoming local opposition. Next he moved against the British-held forts, causing the British to evacuate Pensacola Bay. Jackson then proceeded on to New Orleans, where he arrived on December 1, just in time to supervise defensive preparations against the impending British attack.

The British fleet, consisting of seven ships-of-the-line and numerous frigates and smaller vessels, and an even larger number of transports, carrying an expeditionary force of some 6,500 British regular soldiers, 1,000 marines, and approximately 1,000 West Indian troops, had sailed from Jamaica under the command of Admiral Cochrane and anchored in the Gulf of Mexico to the east of Lake Pontchartrain. By mid-December the British expeditionary force began to march toward New Orleans, where a decisive battle took place on January 8, 1815. The British commander, Lieutenant General Edward Pakenham, launched a frontal attack on Jackson's strong positions, where American musket- and gunfire mowed down large numbers of the attackers, including Pakenham, who was killed. After several hours of fighting, the British were forced to withdraw, leaving behind some 40 percent of their men as casualties. The Americans lost just 13 dead and 58 wounded.[117]

The Battle of New Orleans was a grand American victory, but it did not determine who was going to control this important commercial hub in the postwar world. Britain gave no thought to retaining any conquered territory as long as the United States accepted the terms being discussed in Ghent. Far from coveting New Orleans, Prime Minister Lord Liverpool dismissed it as a settlement that was "one of the most unhealthy in any part of America."[118] Furthermore, the Battle of New Orleans, which is sometimes called the "Needless Battle," had no direct influence on the terms of the ongoing Anglo-American peace negotiations, which culminated in the signing of the Treaty of Ghent on December 24, 1814. Because the news had to cross the Atlantic Ocean by sailing ship, it did not reach the United States until February 1815.[119] Though "needless," the Battle of New Orleans was important because it compelled Britain to abide by the final peace terms and part with any further interest in acquiring New Orleans or in securing control over the Mississippi estuary and regional trade. Both sides agreed to restore the *status quo ante bellum*.[120]

The Anglo-American war thus ended in a draw but left an enduring legacy. For the United States, the war was hardly the resounding success that President

James Madison's administration made it out to be. Hardly any American war aims had been fulfilled, and the final treaty made no mention of the direct causes of the war, including impressment of American citizens and British maritime practices. But the war did reshape American politics. It contributed to the collapse of the Federalist Party and ushered in the so-called Era of Good Feelings, reflecting a new sense of national purpose and unity among Americans in the aftermath of the war. The conflict also spurred American industrialization and highlighted the need for economic and financial reforms, which would be hotly debated for decades to come. The one unambiguous American success of the war was the advent of the United States Navy as a potent force and the backbone of American national security. In this sense, the war completed what had been started in 1775, securing the hegemony of the United States in North America and facilitating its emergency as the first postcolonial power.

Similarly, the war was a pivotal moment in Canadian history. Canada defied contemporary expectations that parts of its territory, especially in Upper Canada, would fall into American hands. Instead, American invasions were defeated and Canada survived the conflict unscathed. But the notion of the Canadians uniting in their efforts and forging their nation in a struggle against their southern neighbors is a myth. For the vast majority of Canadians, the response to war was one of apathy, resistance to requisitioning, and desertion. It was only in the postwar years that the Canadian elites developed a propaganda narrative about "unshaken loyalty, fidelity and attachment" shown by the Canadian volunteers and militiamen in defeating the American invaders.[121]

As for Britain, the War of 1812 was a direct outgrowth of its struggle against Napoleonic France, and its conduct of the war was inherently connected to the events in Europe. This conflict never seriously threatened British standing in North America, but some observers were concerned that "we should be considered both in America and Europe as partly beaten and partly intimidated into pacification."[122] By late 1814 Britain had more troops in Canada than in Europe and had an opportunity to inflict a lot of punishment on its opponent. But it was too late. Earlier setbacks had sapped its will to fight this expensive and remote conflict. Many Britons, especially those residing in port towns suffering from the loss of American trade, opposed this war and harshly criticized their government for its failure to bring a quick end to it. "The happiness and tranquility of this country," proclaimed the *Leeds Mercury*, "are much more closely connected with this subject than with victories in Spain or the movements of contending armies in Russia."[123] The war served as a major distraction from British efforts to defeat Napoleon, sapping much-needed human and material resources and constraining British diplomatic efforts in Vienna, where the stage was set for the greatest diplomatic spectacle of modern times.

CHAPTER 23 | The War and Peace, 1814–1815

THE CONGRESS OF VIENNA was one of the most distinguished assemblages in European history. Its uniqueness derives from the fact that a peace with the defeated power had already been achieved in the Treaties of Paris, and the congress was convened to deal with a general settlement of Europe and not just the resolution of a particular conflict.

The Congress of Vienna was not, strictly speaking, a congress at all. The delegates never met in a plenary session. Rather, a select group of them, representing the most powerful states, operated on the sidelines, away from the vibrant and effervescent social life in the Austrian capital city. Emperors, kings, and princes had descended upon Vienna along with numerous courtiers and pleasure-seekers, and the Austrian court did its best to cater to their wishes. Despite emerging from the war with one foot in bankruptcy, the Austrian emperor, Francis, risked the remainder in hosting this meeting. He had approved the creation of a special committee whose task it was to come with new forms of amusement for the thousands of visitors while keeping in mind their varied tastes and preferences, not to mention rank protocol. Many crucial decisions regarding the future of Europe were achieved at social events, where statesmen ate, drank, and engaged in dalliances. The Austrian government used an intricate system of espionage that employed countless housemaids, porters, coachmen, and other servants to procure every bit of information that might give it an advantage in diplomatic negotiations.[1]

Each of the Allied powers that had joined the struggle against Napoleon had done so at the time that seemed best suited to its own interests. Over the course of the 1813 campaigns, they had entered into separate treaties with each other to coordinate war efforts and to cement commitments. Despite all the efforts directed to fighting Napoleon, little attention had been given to precisely what would happen after his overthrow. The Allies had discussed some political, territorial, and economic concessions—for example, Russia's claims to Poland, Sweden's to Norway, and the restoration of Prussia and Austria to their prewar status—that member states deemed essential to their interests, but they had provided no mechanism by which to pursue such aims. In this sense, the signing of the Treaty of Chaumont in 1814 had far-reaching consequences. The Allies not only clarified their war aims and reaffirmed commitments not to make separate peace with France but agreed on broad provisions for a future European settlement: independence of Spain and Switzerland, restoration and enlargement of Holland, the establishment of a confederated Germany, the division of Italy, and so forth. The view that the treaty was to be integral to the reconstruction (and maintenance) of the postwar European order was acknowledged by its architects, who argued that it was intended "not only as a systematic pledge of preserving concert among the leading powers, but a refuge under which all the minor States, especially those on the Rhine, may look forward to find their security upon the return of peace relieved of the necessity of seeking a compromise with France."[2]

Yet Chaumont suffered from several drawbacks, chief among them being that it contained no provisions for matters that had been discussed in earlier agreements. Thus Prussia's aspiration to Saxony was not covered in the treaty; Russia's pledges to support a restoration of Austrian and Prussian prewar status were mentioned but not the exact prewar configurations. The treaty, further, did not reflect territorial arrangements that the Allies had already considered in Scandinavia, where Emperor Alexander had promised to compensate Sweden for the loss of Finland by supporting Swedish claims to Norway. Finally, the greatest beneficiary of the treaty was Britain, which had successfully excluded the question of maritime rights from any discussions. This meant that the British, who had seized vast overseas territories, alone could decide their future status and interpret maritime regulations.

The provisions of the Treaty of Chaumont set the cornerstone for the European alliance system and were further elaborated in the Peace of Paris, which also called for the convening of a "general congress" to discuss and complete the postwar settlement of Europe. Invitations were extended to "All the Powers engaged on either side in the present war," but in the secret provisions of the Treaty of Paris the Allied powers also agreed to reserve the de facto decision-making process to themselves so that they could decide upon "a system of real and permanent balance of power in Europe."[3] Minor powers were unaware of this arrangement and remained under the impression that they would be given a chance to contribute to the new European order.

Delegates began to arrive in Vienna toward the end of September 1814. They included representatives from Spain, the Papal States, Portugal, Sweden, Hanover, Bavaria, Württemberg, and dozens of other minor states. Two delegations came from Naples, one of them charged with the interests of King Joachim Murat, the other acting on behalf of the Bourbon dynasty. Spain was represented by Don Pedro Gómez de Labrador, while its neighbor Portugal, whose government was still in Brazil, sent Pedro de Sousa Holstein, Count of Palmela, to defend its interests.

French foreign minister Prince Charles-Maurice de Talleyrand was sent on behalf of the French Bourbon monarchy. He faced perhaps the most formidable task of all: reviving the fortunes of a defeated country. While he hoped to retain the French eastern frontier and to minimize any further losses overseas, by far his most important task was to safeguard France's status as a great power. Talleyrand thus considered Prussian aggrandizement as a direct threat to France and preferred some version of balance of power, a thought that squared well with Castlereagh and Metternich's own ideas about the future political settlement. A master pragmatist, Talleyrand had begun his career as a Catholic bishop before the revolution and had served every French government in a course of his fifty-year career. To his admirers, he was a statesman who nobly served the interests of France. To his detractors, he was driven by self-interest. Both sides agree that he was fond of money and used his political access to amass an immense personal fortune. The great revolutionary orator Honoré Mirabeau observed that Talleyrand "would sell his soul for money; and he would be right, for he would be exchanging dung for gold."[4] Even with the challenges he faced, the self-assured and witty Talleyrand thrived in the circumstances of 1814–1815, and his talent as a diplomat never shone brighter than during the nine-month-long conference in Vienna.[5]

The four great powers were represented by the same statesmen who had long transacted business together. Although Emperor Francis of Austria hosted the congress, he delegated diplomatic responsibilities to his minister, Metternich, who was assisted by a knowledgeable cadre of officials, including his deputy, Johann Philipp Freiherr von Wessenberg, and his personal secretary, Friedrich von Gentz, whose vivid letters and diaries remain a rich source of information about the period.[6] In addition, Freiherr von Binder advised on Italian issues and Johann Graf Radetzky von Radetz on military matters.

Metternich was a talented and experienced diplomat who, by his own admission, was "bad at skirmishes...but good at campaigns."[7] A supreme opportunist, he based his policies on a certain set of "principles," none of greater value than that of "equilibrium," which he had consistently applied in his domestic and foreign policy. Metternich believed that European

Map 28: Europe in 1815 after the Congress of Vienna

societies rested in a kind of balance that had been upset by the French Revolution and the Napoleonic conquests. Bringing Europe back to stability, therefore, had to involve returning "legitimate" rulers to their thrones and reversing some, if not all, of the changes that Napoleon had brought. Political equilibrium also informed Metternich's goal of defending Austria's position in Europe by constraining France in the west and preventing Russian dominance in the east. Austria could not accept exclusion from Poland (as Russia insisted on) and could not sanction the appropriation of Saxony (as Prussia desired) because these threatened the balance of power in central Europe. To prevent this, Metternich would use every expedient to detach German states from Russian and Prussian influence and was open to rapprochement with other powers, even France, to achieve these goals.[8]

The Russian delegation included Emperor Alexander I and his advisors, among them Karl Nesselrode, Count Giovanni Antonio Capo d'Istria, and Charles André (Carlo Andreo) Pozzo di Borgo.[9] Alexander was the only ruler who personally participated in the negotiations, and he revealed himself as a figure of intelligence and imagination, with a keen eye for finding ways of strengthening Russian positions in Europe. The great successes of 1812–1813 had also stoked the Russian sovereign's vanity and religious mysticism, making his actions sometimes hard to predict. Alexander believed that guns spoke louder than words and that Russia, having played the decisive role in the defeat of Napoleon, was entitled to a dominant role in the postwar settlement.

The Prussian mission was led by Karl von Hardenberg, the Prussian chancellor, who acted on behalf of King Frederick William III. The king was also present in Vienna but mostly abstained from direct diplomatic negotiations. Other principal Prussian delegates were Wilhelm von Humboldt (probably the most distinguished intellectual figure among the peacemakers), General Karl Friedrich von dem Knesebeck, Johann Gottfried Hoffman (one of the best statisticians in Europe), and Heinrich Freiherr vom und zum Stein. The Prussians expected a fit reward for the sacrifice of thousands of Prussian soldiers and the martial leadership of Blücher, nicknamed "Marschall Vorwärts" (Marshal Forward) for his indomitability. Although the Prussian delegation produced more memoranda than any other power, its role in the diplomatic deliberations failed to reflect its technical proficiency. The Prussians were still perceived as junior partners in the Russo-Prussian alliance; the Prussian king not only deferred to Russia on the issue of Poland but showed himself ready to follow Russian dictates on other matters of policy as well. Meanwhile, the Prussian generals, especially Blücher and the talented chief of staff, August Wilhelm Antonius Neidhardt von Gneisenau, had views and objects of their own, generally more belligerent than those of their sovereign and centered on an undying abhorrence of France, one that no concession could fully assuage.

Britain's delegation was initially led by Foreign Secretary Castlereagh (relieved by the Duke of Wellington in February 1815), who was assisted by his half-brother, Charles Stewart and Richard Le Poer Trench, Second Earl of Clancarty. One of the chief architects of the last coalition against Napoleon, Castlereagh was a talented but deeply solitary individual whose background, character, and accomplishments divided his contemporaries.[10] Throughout 1814 and 1815 he was determined to see that Britain played a leading role in the territorial settlements of Vienna. Because of Britain's unique position as an island nation and a naval superpower, it had no territorial ambitions on the continent (a position that was buttressed by its decision to restore almost all captured colonial possessions) and could play the role of a disinterested mediator—as long as its maritime and commercial interests were safe-guarded. On the other hand, at the start of the congress Britain had the dis-advantage of being the only Allied power still engaged in a major war, as the Anglo-American conflict had entered its second year.

The first meetings of the representatives of the four major powers—Metternich, Castlereagh, Hardenberg, and Nesselrode—took place on September 15, 1814, and led to the adoption of procedural rules for the congress, which officially opened on October 1.[11] This was a key step in con-figuring the conference, as there were no precedents to use as a model. The "Big Four," as Austria, Britain, Prussia, and Russia might be described, rejected the idea of summoning a plenary session of all representatives because this would have involved too many actors, most of whom were "without pre-vious concert in all the preliminary questions of difficulty," as Castlereagh put it in a letter to the prime minister, and would have therefore complicated the negotiating process.[12] One key outcome of these early deliberations was drawing a distinction between "great" and "small" powers, with the four victorious Allies constituting the former group while the rest of the European states fell into the latter category. On September 22, at Prussian insistence, the great powers adopted a special protocol to deny France any participation in their discussions. Castlereagh voiced his opposition at such harsh treat-ment of France now that it was under friendly Bourbon rulers. He insisted on adding a special declaration calling for relations with France and Spain to be conducted, based on amicable dispositions.[13] In practice this meant forming a directing committee of six powers (Britain, Russia, Austria, Prussia, France, and Spain), while actual decision-making would be still restricted to an inner committee of the first four.[14]

Talleyrand, who arrived in Vienna on September 23, denounced the Allied agreement of September 22 as both illegal and improper. He declared that France intended to defend the small powers and act on the understanding that all states should be represented at the congress and therefore to partici-pate in discussions. His actions were designed to drive a wedge between the Allied powers and to enhance France's bargaining power. On September 30 he and the Spanish representative, Labrador, received an invitation to a pre-liminary meeting of the plenipotentiaries, where the proposals made by the four great powers were presented. Talleyrand challenged them at once. He questioned his solitary representation of the French delegation. In response he was told that only the heads of each cabinet had been invited. Talleyrand retorted that Humboldt, who had accompanied Hardenberg, headed no cabinet. When informed that Humboldt was present because of Hardenberg's deafness, Talleyrand, who suffered from a bad leg, quipped, "We all have our infirmities and can exploit them when necessary."[15] Talleyrand thus made the Allied powers agree that each country could be represented by two delegates at the meetings. This was a seemingly minor concession. He then attacked the reference to "Allies" in the protocol. Inquiring whom the powers were allying against, given that that Napoleon had been defeated, he was told that the term was used for the sake of brevity. "Brevity," he replied, "should not be purchased at the price of accuracy." He argued that the Quadruple Alliance had become obsolete after the signing of the Treaty of Paris, and that any power that had taken part in the Napoleonic Wars had the right to participate in the congress's proceedings. The four Allies had no legal or moral justification for their actions. He refused to recognize their authority to discuss issues without the full congress.[16]

Talleyrand's challenges were welcomed and supported by the minor powers, forcing the Big Four to withdraw their proposals. The French foreign minister then contended that a directing body of the eight powers signatory to the Treaty of Paris had to be established and that the whole congress must confirm its authority in a plenary session. He thus succeeded in reducing the control that Austria, Prussia, Russia, and Britain had arrogated to themselves and ensured the inclusion of France, Spain, Sweden, and Portugal in major deliberations. Furthermore, Talleyrand demanded that all discussions and procedures of the congress be based upon the principles of legitimacy and public law. In his characteristic fashion, Talleyrand, having succeeded in getting France into the group of major players in January 1815, then abandoned the minor states and concentrated on his next objectives.

Two separate bodies directed the congress. The Council of Ministers of eight powers (France, Britain, Austria, Prussia, Spain, Portugal, Sweden, and Russia) organized ten separate committees to deal with specific issues. The committees varied in their composition and status: the German Committee, the Slave Trade Committee (or Conference), the Swiss Committee, the Committee on International Rivers, the Committee on Diplomatic Precedence, the Statistical Committee, the Drafting Committee, the Committees on Tuscany, the Committee on Sardinia and Genoa, and the Committee on the Duchy of Bouillon. At the same time, the Allied sovereigns held their daily meetings, in which they often discussed and agreed on issues in ways contrary to instructions given to their negotiators. These inconsistencies understandably led to unexpected difficulties.

The first major crisis was over the Polish-Saxon issue. As noted, after Napoleon had established the Duchy of Warsaw in 1807, Russia had felt threated by the prospects of a revived Polish state, one that could reclaim territories Russia had seized in the Polish partitions. In 1810 Alexander had tried unsuccessfully to secure French promises that Poland would never be restored. Napoleon's monumental failure in 1812 provided Alexander the opportunity to negate this threat once and forever. He intended to secure the larger part of the Polish lands under his control, thereby safeguarding Russia's western provinces as well as projecting its power deeper into Europe. Alexander knew the ramifications his plans would have in Europe, particularly given that the other powers, especially Austria and Prussia, would undoubtedly object. "Making public my intentions on Poland will certainly drive Austria and Prussia into the arms of France," he noted on January 13, 1813.[17]

Despite almost universal opposition from his own advisers, Alexander pushed for the creation of a larger Kingdom of Poland under Russian control. This raised two fundamental questions: how far would Poland's autonomy extend, and what would be the extent of Poland's new borders? The Russian intention to form a constitutional Polish kingdom challenged Austria's national security objectives of limiting Prussia's influence in Germany and restraining Russian expansion in central Europe. Metternich worried that the new Polish state would encourage political unrest in the Austrian-controlled Polish territories. At a meeting on September 19, before the congress was convened, he objected to the very use of the term "Poland" out of fear that it would serve as a rallying point for the Austrian Poles and destabilize Galicia.[18] Neither was Vienna or Berlin thrilled by the prospect of having a constitutional polity next to their borders, which could encourage their own subjects to demand similar concessions. Ultimately, it was the question of territory and political equilibrium, with attendant military and strategic considerations, that caused the great powers to oppose Russia's proposal. Alexander might have claimed that Polish restoration under Russian suzerainty would mean a separate administration and a representative constitution for the Poles, but other powers saw the plan as a barely concealed attempt at Russian expansionism. Austria, Britain, and France were not entirely opposed to the restoration of a Polish state but wanted to see it independent of Russia.[19]

Emperor Alexander thus found himself nearly isolated, with only Frederick William III willing to consider ceding territories that Prussia had acquired in the Polish Partitions so long as Prussia was compensated with lands elsewhere, preferably in Saxony, whose king had supported Napoleon and therefore, in Prussian eyes, had to be penalized.[20] Realizing how politically sensitive this project was, Emperor Alexander refused to make an open statement of his intentions with respect to Poland and repeatedly changed his position, promising British envoys that he would not press his claims on Prussian Poland while proposing to Austria that it cede the whole of Galicia in exchange for Russian support of the Austrian takeover of Alsace from France.[21] All this only served to deepen suspicions on the part of Britain and Austria, both of which were dubious about Russian reassurances that the Poles would retain their freedom. Both Castlereagh and Metternich saw the entire project as a scheme to extend Russian influence into central Europe and place Russian forces within striking distance of Berlin and Vienna. For the British, there was the additional concern of Prussian expansion in the Rhineland, leading them to greater ambitions in the Low Countries, which they considered crucial to Britain's national security.

The Allies' failure to come to an agreement over the status of Poland and Saxony in early 1814 meant that these issues became one of the core problems facing the Congress of Vienna. In October and November 1814 Castlereagh tried his best to convince Alexander to scale back his demands and to arrange some sort of compromise, but he failed. Russia insisted on Polish lands and Prussian compensation in Saxony; "the right of conquest is a legal title for the acquisition of sovereignty over a conquered country," stated a Russian memorandum.[22] Ever mindful of the need to keep a political equilibrium in central Europe, Austria pursued a more duplicitous route. Metternich first assured Alexander that Austria would support his Polish claim if he prevented Prussia from expanding into Saxony. The Austrian minister, meanwhile, approached the Prussian representative, Hardenberg, promising to support the Prussian claim in Saxony if Prussia in turn opposed Russian designs in Poland. However, the Prussians ignored the offer—Saxony was already under Russian occupation, and Berlin was certain of getting something out of its earlier treaties with the Russians.[23]

As tensions mounted, Talleyrand took advantage of it to play the great powers off one another. Citing the principle of legitimacy, he argued that Russia and Prussia had no authority to deprive the lawful king of Saxony of his territory and throne. "To recognize such a disposition as legitimate, one would have to hold it true that kings can be judged," he wrote. "That they can be judged by those who wish to and can seized their possessions... that sovereignty can be lost and gained by the single fact of conquest... in a word, that all is legitimate for him who is the strongest."[24] By posing as a defender of legitimacy, Talleyrand effectively turned France from a defeated nation into a crucial partner for anyone seeking to constrain the aggressive behavior of Russia. This was, naturally, very welcome news for the British and the Austrians.[25] British prime minister Lord Liverpool had already reconsidered his position vis-à-vis the nation his government had fought for so long. "The more I hear and see of the different courts of Europe," he observed, "the more convinced I am that the King of France is, amongst the great Powers, the only Sovereign in whom we can have any real confidence."[26]

As the year drew to an end, meetings of the great powers became ever more contentious. On December 30, exasperated by the British and Austrian refusal to compromise, the Prussian envoy, Hardenberg, threatened to consider any further delays in acknowledging Prussia's claims to Saxony as a declaration of war; Castlereagh countered that if such ill tempers prevailed, it would be better to end the congress at once.[27] This was an alarming turn of events, and some expressed the concern that a war might erupt between the former allies. Tensions mounted rapidly. By late December, the Danish envoy was startled when Castlereagh asked him how many men Denmark could deploy in case of war. The Prussian ambassador was increasingly convinced that "a second war is necessary, and it must take place sooner or later."[28] Talleyrand had already threatened to deploy as many as 300,000 men to support Saxon sovereignty, while the Austrians were taking stock of their armed forces and preparing plans for a possible mobilization. With the great powers rattling swords, the minor powers joined the fray as well. The Bavarians stood by their Saxon neighbors, and Prince Wrede, who represented Bavaria and commanded its army, assured the French delegation that some 40,000 Bavarian troops were ready to come to Saxony's aid. Meanwhile, the Danes were encouraged by the prospects of a new war against Prussia and Russia, hoping it would lead to their recovery of Norway and the containment of Sweden and Russia.[29]

The situation changed dramatically at the start of the new year. The first week of January brought unexpected news that Britain and the United States had ended their war. "The news of the American peace came like a shot here," wrote a British observer in Vienna. "Nobody expected it." Talleyrand quickly understood the massive implications of this event, calling it "la paix sterling."[30] Indeed, "released from the millstone of an American war," as Castlereagh put it, Britain could now make the necessary financial and military commitments in Europe.[31] The impact was immediate and sweeping. To contain the Russo-Prussian ambitions, Talleyrand, Metternich, and Castlereagh agreed on a secret alliance to be directed against the former coalition members. Rather than submit to the Russo-Prussian demands, they would show the resolve to fight. The agreement, signed on January 3, 1815, created a secret military alliance with France, Britain, and Austria, in which each pledged mutual support in the event any one of them became involved in a war. France and Austria promised to deploy 150,000 men, while Britain would supply them with money and consider any attack on Hanover or the

Low Countries as a casus belli. Thus, less than a year after being defeated, France succeeded in assuming a major role at the congress, exploited divisions among the great powers, and created a new axis of political alliances. This was a remarkable achievement. "The Coalition is dissolved," the jubilant Talleyrand wrote to Louis XVIII. "France is no longer isolated in Europe."[32]

The secret treaty mentioned previously was, however, a colossal bluff. Talleyrand knew that France was in no position to wage another war less than a year after Napoleon's defeat. Castlereagh acted against the instructions of his government in signing the agreement; Liverpool had warned him that "it would be quite impossible to embark this country in a war at present," and there could be no doubt that the British parliament would have refused to give its consent to a new conflict in Europe while fighting an old one in North America.[33] Austria's financial difficulties and its preoccupation with Italian affairs made it doubtful that Vienna would be capable of mounting a major military effort against Russia. But the ploy worked. Although the details of the alliance were kept secret, the news of its formation was carefully leaked, much to the surprise of the Russian and Prussian delegations. Facing the prospect of a general European war, neither Emperor Alexander nor King Frederick William was prepared to risk his gains, and both chose, as the proverb goes, a bird in hand to two in the bush.[34]

The crisis was effectively over by February. Austria submitted the proposal that served as the basis for the final settlement of the Polish-Saxon question. The great powers agreed that Poland would be turned into an ostensibly independent kingdom but a Russian protectorate. This was a greatly reduced version of the state—some 49,000 square miles with a population of some 3.2 million people—that Emperor Alexander had hoped for, since Prussia surrendered Warsaw but retained Posen and Thorn, while Austria kept the province of Galicia; Kraków was declared a free city under the joint Austro-Prussian-Russian protection. A similar compromise was struck in Saxony, where Prussia received two-fifths of the state (with a population of some 900,000 people) but the rest of Saxon territory was left under its legitimate ruler, King Frederick Augustus I. The Prussian senior officers were clearly disappointed by this arrangement and shared Blücher's sense of frustration and anger at exchanging Prussian territories for "300,000 Poles and just as many Saxons, who hate us and could never replace these faithful and self-sacrificing brothers."[35] The Polish-Saxon question required more energy, emotion, and negotiation than any other issue discussed at the congress. Once it was resolved, however, the delegations made considerable progress on other topics—until their work was interrupted by a sudden and improbable event.

In March 1815, Napoleon stunned Europe by daring to return to France. During his ten months of active government over the miniature kingdom on Elba, the emperor was well supplied with information from the mainland of Europe. He was therefore aware of the widespread discontent and knew that he retained considerable popularity in France. He undoubtedly took pleasure in observing the Allies' troubles and especially those of the French Bourbons. The monarchy of King Louis XVIII, who had spent the past quarter of a century in exile, was neither tyrannical nor malevolent, aspiring to restore peace and stability to the people, who desired both. But it struggled to reconcile some of its supporters' unilateral tendencies with the reality of the transformed French society. Louis XVIII returned to France with a strong desire to heal the country's wounds and to achieve, as he stated, "the fusion of the two peoples into one." France was indeed a nation divided against itself. If a good number of people welcomed the return of a king, equally as many remained supportive of Napoleon; furthermore, the newly returning die-hard emigrés (or Ultras, as they became known) hoped for a wholesale reversal of the social and political changes that the Revolution had unleashed in France. Yet the king agreed to grant the Charter of 1814 in order to calm popular sentiment as well as to satisfy the wishes of the Allies. This was a liberal constitution, one that retained the Revolution's social changes and Napoleon's administrative organization, promising representative government, ministerial responsibility, and protections for civil rights and freedoms.[36] It declared that "all justice emanates from the king" but also preserved the Napoleonic codes and other legal reforms, ensuring that when it came to social organization and equality of opportunity, France would remain a splendid exception on the continent, which was dominated by conservative ideology.[37]

Yet while experiencing intense relief at the end of a seemingly unending war, the French also became disillusioned with the new government. In practice the Bourbons had revealed that, as a wit said, "they had learned nothing and forgotten nothing." The Ultras, though small in number, were vocal about their ambitions to see their former power and property restored. Their insistence on holding ceremonies honoring those who had fought against the Revolution raised serious questions about the prejudices of the new government. Many disapproved of the change of the national flag from the tricolor to the white flag of the Bourbon dynasty and resented the presence of Allied agents meddling in French affairs. Although the king refused to satisfy all the Ultras' demands, his decision to restore property still in the hands of the state alarmed many French citizens who had purchased church or noble property in the previous quarter century; rumors that the land settlements of the Revolution would be reversed and that feudal obligations and church taxes would be revived were rife among the peasants.

The Bourbon monarchy, already lacking national support, further aggravated the situation through a series of unpopular if unavoidable decisions. The decision to grant the charter also backfired, as the Republicans and Bonapartists exploited their civil freedoms to openly criticize the government. When the crown imposed censorship, it provoked loud protests, even from the former anti-Napoleon intellectuals. Furthermore, it was inevitable that the Bourbons would start increasing taxes and dismantling the imperial war machine, both necessitated by financial crisis, the end of war, loss of empire, and France's peaceful stance toward the rest of the continent. The dismissal of thousands of troops and the placing of officers on half pay, along with the appointment of Ultras to high positions in the government and army, were bound to stir angry feelings. Disgruntled officials and soldiers soon scattered all over France, sowing hatred against the Bourbon government and laying the foundation for the Napoleonic legend. Against an out-of-touch monarchy led by an elderly invalid, Napoleon shone out again as the great man of action. The failures of the imperial regime were soon overlooked, and instead popular focus shifted to past glories. For soldiers, there was solace in remembering victorious campaigns; peasants remembered that, despite its many drawbacks, the Napoleonic regime never would have required them to relinquish lands that had previously belonged to the church and nobility. Though in practice it would have been impossible for the Ultras to reclaim their former lands and privileged status, public perception mattered more than practicality. Even the description of the charter as a "gift" from the king to the people posed a problem. Many feared that while it might be safe under the childless Louis XVIII, it could be endangered by his brother and heir, Charles, comte d'Artois, who was far more conservative and narrow-minded.[38]

From his palace in Portoferraio on Elba, Napoleon closely followed these developments in France as well as the bitter disputes over the spoils of war between the victorious Allies in Vienna.[39] By late February 1815 he had decided to return to France, reasoning that now that the French had endured twelve months of a mediocre government, they would be ready to take him back, and that the Allies, already at each other's throats, would be unwilling to risk another general war just to keep Louis XVIII on the throne. "There is no historic example that induces me to venture on this bold enterprise," he told a companion. "But I have taken into account the surprise that will seize on men, the state of public feeling, the resentment against the allies, the love of my soldiers, in fine, all the Napoleonic elements that still germinate in our beautiful France."[40] On February 26, accompanied by his staff and about 1,000 soldiers, he left Elba and set sail for France.

What happened next—popularly called the *vol d'aigle* (flight of the eagle)—was undoubtedly one of the most audacious and breathtaking ventures in history. "The eagle will fly from belfry to belfry until it reaches the towers of Notre Dame," Napoleon promised in a proclamation published upon his landing on the shores of the Gulf of Juan on March 1, 1815.[41] So it proved. As he marched toward the capital, Napoleon used the bitter memories of the previous year to navigate the more conservative areas, such as Provence, and make his way toward more sympathetic regions, such as Dauphine, where he was greeted with jubilation by both peasants and urbanites who genuinely dreaded the prospects of the restoration of the ancien régime. The army also considered him far more preferable to the Bourbons; when generals tried to rally troops to the king's side, they were told by their officers, "When you cry 'Long Live the King!' our men, and we, will answer 'Long Live the Emperor!'"[42] An entire royal detachment sent to arrest Napoleon switched sides in a thrilling and emotional encounter at the village of Laffrey. As Napoleon approached the troops blocking the path, a royalist officer ordered his troops to open fire, but no one obeyed. Instead, Napoleon, stepping toward soldiers with muskets leveled at him, cried, "Soldiers! I am your Emperor. Do you not recognize me? If there is one among you who would kill his general, here I am!" Shouts of "Vive l'empereur!" were the response, with the troops rushing to embrace Napoleon.[43]

Heartened by the outpouring of support, Napoleon made rapid progress toward the capital. What began as a perilous march turned into a triumphal procession. At Grenoble, a crowd greeted him on the outskirts of the city and, since the local governor had fled with the keys to the city, tore down the main gates and presented them to the emperor. On March 10 he was in Lyon, where he began issuing imperial decrees and welcomed the defection of additional royal forces, including those led by Marshal Michel Ney, who had earlier promised the king to bring Napoleon "in an iron cage" but now publicly declared that "the cause of the Bourbons is lost forever."[44] Ten days later, on March 20, Napoleon entered Paris, where a jubilant crowd carried him up the grand staircase into the Tuileries Palace, which King Louis XVIII and his court had abandoned just hours earlier on their way to Belgium. To many contemporaries, the "flight of the eagle" appeared nothing short of miraculous. "This was the greatest miracle made by God," exclaimed Honoré de Balzac, sixteen years old when Napoleon made his comeback. "Before him did ever a man gain an empire simply by showing his hat?"[45] Despite being defeated by the combined forces of Europe, Napoleon had reclaimed the crown in just three weeks, against all odds and by sheer force of will. The house of cards that the Allies had so hastily erected in France collapsed.

Once in Paris, however, cold reality set in, forcing him to look beyond the passion inspired by his return. Napoleon knew how capricious public support could be, noting that "the people have let me come, just as they let others go."[46] He understood that he could not restore the imperial regime as it had existed before. The situation demanded something different. He was surprised to see that the Bourbon misrule had rejuvenated the vigor of the revolutionary ideals, and he moved quickly to exploit this powerful force.[47] Napoleon assumed the mantle of defender of the Revolution and tailored his rhetoric to the character of his audience, pledging to shield the peasants from feudal and clerical reaction and to defend the gains that the bourgeois had made during his rule.[48] He presented himself as a ruler who had made some mistakes, but these had been occasioned by the exigencies of war. He assured his compatriots that he had changed and would no longer harbor grand ambitions. "Can one be as fat as I am, and still have ambition?" he joked, patting his stomach with both hands.[49]

Just two days after his arrival in Paris, Napoleon reconstituted his government, calling upon his old officials to return. He formed a French version of the Ministry of All Talents that included professional men like Martin-Michel-Charles Gaudin (finance), Caulaincourt (foreign affairs), and Marshal Davout (ministry of war), alongside the seasoned veteran Joseph Fouché (ministry of police) and republicans like Lazare Carnot (ministry of interior). "I have renounced the ideas of the Grand Empire," he proclaimed, "which during the last fifteen years I had only begun to found. Henceforth the happiness and consolidation of the French Empire will be the objects of my thoughts." He promised more representative government and asked one of the leading liberals (and a longtime critic), Benjamin Constant, to draft the Additional Act to the Imperial Constitution, which, once approved in a plebiscite, created a two-chamber freely elected parliament to govern alongside the emperor. The constitutional changes also introduced ministerial responsibility, ended censorship, and protected freedoms of press and expression.[50] To underscore his newly discovered revolutionary credentials, Napoleon supported popular assembly at the Champ de Mars, the scene of the great festival of federation twenty-five years earlier, and allowed the creation of a federative movement (fédérés) that was modeled after the one of 1789–1791.[51]

It is hard not to view Napoleon's latter-day conversion with skepticism. Eager as he was to exploit the popular fervor, he was not pleased to see the revival of the revolutionary spirit, with its focus on republicanism. Later, when exiled in St. Helena, he seemed to admit that he regretted accepting the Additional Act and probably genuinely intended to suspend it and dismiss the chambers in the event of a victorious campaign. A liberal parliament could never durably coexist with Napoleon, who believed that "a deliberative body is a fearful thing to deal with."[52] And the first signs from the revived chambers were not encouraging. In early June, the lower house rejected the emperor's nominee for its presidency and proceeded to elect an ex-Girondin revolutionary with a long history of opposing Napoleon. By June 11 the Emperor was already warning the chambers, "Let us not imitate the example of the later [Roman] Empire, which, invaded on all sides by the barbarians, made itself the laughingstock of posterity by discussing abstract questions when the battering-rams were breaking down the city gates."[53]

Neither should we assume that support for Napoleon was everywhere. The duc d'Angoulême was able to gather some 10,000 troops in southern France and march on Lyons before being defeated by the imperial forces. By mid-May, open revolts broke out in Brittany and the Vendée. More worrisome was the fact that in many regions of southern and western France—Flanders, Artois, Normandy, Brittany, Vendée, Languedoc, and Provence—the local notables largely refused to rally to Napoleon's cause. Interior Minister Carnot was forced to dismiss a number of local officials and replace them with loyal cadres, but the new appointees did not inspire much confidence on the ground and only further added to public discontent. And yet what makes the Hundred Days such a remarkable moment in the Napoleonic saga is that Napoleon was ultimately brought down not by domestic opposition or a revolt but by foreign intervention. If not for a war, the Napoleonic regime would have survived the immediate challenges of the restoration. Though hundreds of thousands of Frenchmen showed indifference to the restored Napoleonic government, there was also a powerful national expression of revolutionary élan, bellicose nationalism, and popular Bonapartism that would have carried the new regime forward.[54] By rallying behind Napoleon, many believed they were defending the revolutionary legacy, which was, in turn, a matter of mixed self-interest and principle.

As extraordinary as Napoleon's return was, it would have been better for France had he stayed on Elba. It is rather surprising that Napoleon ever seriously entertained hopes that the Allied powers, having spent more than a decade in a hugely costly effort to defeat him, would simply acquiesce to his return. The coalition members may have suffered from internal divisions, some of them very deep-seated indeed, but nothing could make them forget what it had meant to deal with the Napoleonic Empire. On receiving the news of Napoleon's escape at half past seven in the morning of March 7, Metternich immediately informed Emperor Francis, who instructed him to convey the news to Emperor Alexander and King Frederick William. By half past eight the minister had met both Allied leaders, who agreed to start mobilizing their forces. In the words of Metternich, "Thus the war was decided on in less than an hour."[55]

Napoleon tried to assure the Allies of his peaceful intentions but, unsurprisingly, found all diplomatic channels closed and none of the great powers willing to consider his offers. Instead, the news of his return galvanized the Allies. The plenipotentiaries of eight leading powers in Vienna declared their support for Louis XVIII and denounced Napoleon as "Enemy and Disturber of the Tranquility of the World" who, by breaking the Treaty of Paris of 1814, had turned himself into an outlaw. Much of the rest of Europe supported the Allies, although Marshal Joachim Murat, who was still hoping to reclaim his Neapolitan crown, declared for him. Murat's actions were significant because any expectation Napoleon might have had of altering the Austrian position was dispelled when Murat invaded the Papal States and called upon the Italians to revolt and accept him as a new king.[56]

By March 25, five days after Napoleon's entry into Paris, these powers were resolving practical matters to form the Seventh Coalition. Each of them pledged to furnish an army and to not lay down arms until Napoleon had been decisively defeated and, in the words of the coalition treaty, "rendered absolutely incapable of stirring up further troubles." The Allied plans called for a Prussian army of almost 120,000 men (led by Blücher) and an Anglo-Allied army of about 100,000 (under the Duke of Wellington) to invade Belgium and threaten northwestern France, while an Austrian army of more than 200,000 troops (under Schwarzenberg) would take up a position on the Upper Rhine. Meanwhile, Russian field marshal Barclay de Tolly would lead 150,000 troops to the Middle Rhine, and an Austro-Italian army of 75,000 men (led by General Johann Frimont) would cross France's southeastern border. Britain, ever the anti-Napoleon bank, pledged to place £5 million at the disposal of the coalition.

In light of the last campaign, waiting until the Allied armies had crossed the frontier would have been militarily and politically disastrous for Napoleon. With the nation divided and apprehensive, and the enemy expected to deploy more than 700,000 men, Napoleon's only chance was a quick and resounding victory that might rally the French population behind him and cause the coalition to splinter. In the three months after his return the emperor raised an army of more than 250,000 men, but after the necessary deductions had been made to suppress royalist revolts and to defend the southern and southeastern frontiers, he had no more than 130,000 men to face the Allied invasion on the Rhine. In contrast with 1814, he now had plenty of hardened veterans (including returned prisoners of war) who were eager to fight once more under the imperial eagle. But the choice of available officers, especially generals, was critically limited. The greater number of former generals rallied to Napoleon; still, a good number remained aloof or refused to come. Marshals Masséna and

Macdonald were offered commands but declined them while four others—Victor, Marmont, Augereau, and Berthier—were struck off the marshals' list for departing with Louis XVIII; Napoleon had hoped that the indispensable Berthier, would come back but the marshal, exhausted and disillusioned, fell to his death from a window of his home in Bamberg on June 1. Of the remaining marshals, Suchet was given command in the Alps, while Davout, perhaps the most capable of the marshals, was asked to stay in Paris as minister of war, a decision that many Napoleonophiles still lament. Instead, as he marched to war, Napoleon was accompanied by Marshal Nicolas Soult, who had no experience as a chief of staff; Marshal Michel Ney, who had struggled to recover from the physical and psychological strains of the last three years of campaigning; and the newly promoted Marshal Emmanuel Grouchy, a good cavalry commander but entirely untried in independent command.

The strategic situation at the outbreak of hostilities was that Napoleon had 128,000 men, concentrated in the area of Beaumont, in northern France.[57] He knew that the Austrian and Russian armies would not reach France's eastern frontiers before July. His immediate opponent was the Prussian army—of which Blücher was the head but Gneisenau the brain—which was deployed in the southeastern Netherlands, with General Wieprecht Graf von Zieten's 1st Prussian Corps (30,000 men) holding position at Charleroi, next to the French border. To the northwest, Wellington, with a mixed force of 100,000 British, Dutch, Belgian, and German troops, held the area around Brussels. Napoleon's operational plan involved getting between the Prussian and Anglo-Allied armies and, using this central position, forcing the enemy forces apart and then defeating them piecemeal. The concentration of the French army was effectively conceived and executed, such that neither Blücher nor Wellington was aware of the start of the French offensive on June 14. The French army was divided into two wings (commanded by Ney and Grouchy) and a reserve (the Imperial Guard under Napoleon himself), a formation that was perfectly suitable to Napoleon's strategic and operational goals but required effective and timely staff work to coordinate both wings and, more important, a clear grasp of his intentions by wing commanders.[58]

By June 15 the strategic situation clearly favored the French; their opponents proved to be slow in reacting. Wellington was still at Brussels, attending the Duchess of Richmond's famous ball, when he was surprised by the news of the French offensive. Shocked by the speed of the enemy concentration and advance, he supposedly exclaimed, "Napoleon has humbugged me, by God!"[59] Meanwhile, Blücher decided to concentrate his forces around Ligny, offering the French a chance to destroy the Prussians before the Anglo-Allied army could come. Accordingly, Napoleon led the Army of the North into

Belgium and defeated Blücher at Ligny on June 16. This victory cost the Prussians one-fifth of their 80,000 men and almost claimed Blücher's life.[60] Yet Ligny fell far short of Napoleon's original intention and remains a prime example of a tactical victory that leads to a strategic defeat. The Prussians may have been "damnably mauled," as Wellington observed, but they still remained an organized force led by officers who had shown themselves more than capable of executing a compact and orderly retreat. Furthermore, Ligny revealed crucial weaknesses on the French side. As he engaged the Prussians in battle, Napoleon instructed Ney to march northwest and overcome any enemy troops at the crucial road junction at the small village of Quatre Bras, then envelop the Prussian right flank. Napoleon intended to move his reserves first to support his left wing against the Prussians and then swing westward to join Ney and march toward Brussels, where the Anglo-Allied army would have been defeated. If properly implemented, the plan probably would have resulted in the defeat of both Allied armies within the first week of the war.

But it went awry. Soult's failure to establish a proper staff and the opacity of the orders he sent out was outstripped only by Ney's inability to grasp the overall strategy. He advanced along the Brussels road with unneeded caution and might have carried the Quatre Bras position even as late as eleven in the morning had he pressed hard. Instead he postponed operations till the afternoon, allowing the surprised Wellington to rush his reinforcements to support the small German brigade from the Dutch-Belgian division that held the road junction.[61] When the French attacked, they found the enemy positions too strong to carry. Exasperated, Ney diverted the corps of General Jean-Baptiste Drouet, comte d'Erlon, which originally had been allotted to the left wing but was recalled by Napoleon to complete the Prussian defeat at Ligny. When the marshal learned that d'Erlon had inexplicably turned around, he sent him urgent orders to retrace his way to Quatre Bras. These countermanding orders meant that d'Erlon spent much of the day marching between Quatre Bras and Ligny without participating in either battle, depriving the French of a decisive victory.

Still, the possibilities for the following few days looked propitious. Given the strength of his reserves, Napoleon could either complete the rout of the Prussians or turn his attention to Wellington, whose forces were stretched between Brussels and Quatre Bras. Over the next twelve-hour period, however, Napoleon showed himself uncharacteristically indecisive, failing to organize the pursuit and losing contact with the Prussians by the following morning. Quite unlike the disciplined man of the earlier years, he slept late and wasted the advantage of the early morning hours.[62] It was not till noon on June 17 that Napoleon ordered Grouchy, with 33,000 men, to pursue the

Prussians, while Ney was entirely ignored and received no new instructions to renew his attacks to pin down Wellington, who could have been easily defeated by Napoleon. Hence, by the time the emperor joined Ney at Quatre Bras, the Anglo-Allied army had already disengaged and retreated toward the villages of Mont Saint-Jean and Waterloo, where Wellington decided to fight upon receiving Blücher's assurance that at least one Prussian corps would come to his help. Napoleon followed the retreating British army, but the pursuit was not particularly vigorous. Heavy rains during the night of June 17–18 did not make the going easy.

On June 18, 1815, some 140,000 men converged on sleepy hamlets of Mont St. Jean, Belle Alliance, Hougomont, Placenoit, and Waterloo in what is today Belgium.[63] The future of the French Empire, if not the entire European continent, was at stake. The peculiarity of the subsequent battle was its narrow compass, with tens of thousands of men crammed into just three square miles at the start of the battle; the front was less than two miles wide, compared to six miles at Austerlitz or Borodino. Wellington, a superb defensive commander, had chosen his favorite position: on a rise where the reverse slopes offered protection to his infantry from enemy artillery fire. He took great care in deploying his troops, distributing his sturdy British divisions to stiffen the less-experienced Dutch-Belgian units.

Napoleon, on the other hand, underestimated his opponent and ignored the warnings of his Peninsular War veterans about the British commander and the firepower of his infantry, responding with bravado that "Wellington is a bad general, that the English are bad troops, and that this affair is nothing more serious than eating one's breakfast."[64] Instead of attempting to turn an enemy flank, Napoleon, just as he had at Borodino, chose a frontal assault designed to smash through the Allies' army. Because torrential rains had made the ground too sodden to admit of the easy movement of troops or artillery bombardment, he delayed the French attack until half past eleven, even as the news arrived of Prussian troops appearing on his right flank. Napoleon had earlier dismissed the Prussians as incapable of doing anything for at least another day and hoped that Grouchy would be able to fulfill his mission of preventing Blücher from reaching the battlefield. Much ink has been spilled blaming Grouchy for not marching "to the sound of the cannon," and Napoleon himself left a contemptuous assessment of the marshal. But Grouchy's lack of initiative, for which he compensated through literal obedience to orders at a time when improvisation would have been more suitable, was compounded by Napoleon's own errors and imprecise orders.[65]

Starting in the afternoon, the French launched repeated assaults to break the enemy front line. The British and their Dutch, Belgian, and German allies held their ground and repulsed the assaults with a combination of steely resolve and a massive concentration of firepower. Napoleon's own performance was unimposing and his decision to leave the tactical handling of the battle to Ney resulted in the latter's misreading the enemy movements and launching an impressive but utterly impractical cavalry charge against the British infantry, which formed squares and wore down the charging enemy horsemen. Equally ineffective was Napoleon's handling of the fighting at Hougoumont, where he originally intended to launch a diversionary attack to draw away the enemy reserves but eventually committed more than thirty battalions (some 14,000 men), who struggled to make headway against the British defenses. And yet by late afternoon the situation for Wellington was precarious, as the French capture of La Haye Sainte had threatened to pierce the center of the Anglo-Allied positions.

It was at this crucial moment that Prussians began to stream onto the battlefield. Leaving one corps at Wavre to pin down Grouchy, Blücher led the rest of his army, some 50,000 men in total, to support Wellington. The Prussian arrival boosted the morale of the battered Anglo-Allies and drew away Napoleon's reserves, which otherwise could have been used against Wellington's center. In a last, desperate attempt to turn the tide of battle, Napoleon sent his elite Imperial Guard up the ridge, but even these famed veterans could not break through Anglo-Allied lines and were met by with a hail of musketfire and grapeshot. As the Guard staggered and fell back, a cry went up through the rest of the French army, one unheard on European battlefields in some fifteen years of fighting: "La Garde recule!" (The Imperial Guard is falling back!).[66] All was lost for the French: a general panic set in, and thousands of French troops began to flee from the battlefront. As the darkness descended, some 65,000 men (two-thirds of them, Frenchmen) had been killed or wounded or were otherwise missing.

Waterloo was a comprehensive French defeat, both at the tactical level (where Napoleon had effectively conceded authority to his subordinates, especially Marshal Ney, who could do no better than launch frontal attacks) and at the operational level (where the failure was either compounded or caused, depending on one's point of view, by Grouchy's actions in the wake of Ligny). In this regard, the Battle of Waterloo is rightly celebrated as the end of French ascendancy in Europe. But upsetting as this might be to the British national pride, it was not the battle that forged a century. The fate of Europe had already been decided in the rolling hills of Leipzig and sealed amid the balls and festivities in Vienna. At the risk of sounding like a historical determinist, the argument here is that Napoleon had lost the war at the strategic level even before the first shot was fired. It is hard to envision any turn of events in which the Allied powers would have accepted his presence at the helm of France. Austria, the only power that Napoleon might have had a chance of wooing, was determined to see him ousted. Even as early as April 9, 1815, Metternich observed, "The Powers will not have Napoleon Bonaparte [and] will make war against him to the last."[67] By June 1815 the coalition ranged against France comprised Britain, Russia, Austria, Prussia, the Netherlands, Hanover, Portugal, Piedmont-Sardinia, the Two Sicilies, Sweden, Spain, the Swiss Confederation, and the Duchies of Nassau, Brunswick, and Tuscany. This was not a coalition that Napoleon could possibly defeat in battle. Even had the opening campaign been won, the emperor could not have changed the facts on the ground, which included the great powers' firm commitment to fight him. If not at Waterloo, he would have met his defeat at some other small hamlet in the Rhineland or northeastern France. Napoleon should have stayed on Elba; while it would have meant a less dramatic end to his remarkable life, France would have been better off. One cannot but feel sympathy for the French veterans who after the end of the war told "stories of his genius and execrated his government in the same breath. His officers cursed him as an Emperor and adored him [as a general] in the field....Everywhere Napoleon was called 'bon general, mais mauvais souverain.'"[68]

Despite the disaster at Waterloo, Napoleon still had some fight left in him. Returning to Paris on June 21, he believed that "all is not lost" and considered raising another army of some 300,000 men to continue the fight.[69] As irate as he might have been at Grouchy, he still welcomed the news of the general's successful retreat from Wavre, which preserved some 30,000 French troops. Napoleon's companions even urged him to seize power and declare himself a dictator. However, whatever plans he might have been formulating, he was thwarted by the actions of those who now fully understood that the war had been lost and that immediate action had to be taken to mitigate the impact of the defeat. Minister of Police Joseph Fouché emerged as a key leader in the behind-the-scenes intrigues that resulted in the formation of a special committee. This committee insisted that Napoleon give up the throne and that a provisional government take charge of the nation, a demand seconded by the legislative chambers.

On June 22, Napoleon abdicated once more in favor of his son, the four-year-old Napoleon II, the king of Rome. However, Fouché, who in the words of one contemporary had become "the regent de facto and the central point of every intrigue," insisted on the restoration of the Bourbon dynasty.[70] The disillusioned legislators, anxious to be rid of Napoleon, called up the National Guard to prevent any attempt at dissolving the chambers. With Wellington and Blücher advancing on Paris and Louis XVIII following "in the baggage train of the allies," it was increasingly becoming clear that Napoleon could no longer stay in France. On June 29 he traveled to the Atlantic coastline, arriving four days later at Rochefort, where he considered escaping to America. A British naval blockade made such a venture doubtful. Instead, after spending almost two weeks vacillating, the emperor surrendered to Captain Frederick Lewis Maitland of the HMS *Bellerophon* on July 15, writing his famous letter to the prince regent of Britain asking for asylum: "I have finished my political career, and I come, like Themistocles, to sit at the heart of the British people...the most powerful, constant and generous of my enemies."[71]

Napoleon seems to have had ambitions of settling down as an English country gentleman, but his appeal put the British government in an awkward position. It could not allow such a potent symbol of power and transformation to seek shelter on the British islands themselves. No one could imagine Napoleon simply retiring to private life. Allowing him any public involvement could pose significant risks, considering the radical undercurrents that had emerged in Britain at the end of the Napoleonic Wars. Furthermore, on August 2, the victorious Allies ruled that Napoleon was a prisoner of war and had to be confined to a place from which he would not be able to escape; they entrusted the British with the task of finding such a place. After careful deliberation, it was decided to send "Boney," as the British public came to call Napoleon during the war, to the bleak island of St. Helena in the South Atlantic, more than 1,500 miles from the nearest African coastline and some 4,500 miles from France.[72] As the Royal Navy controlled the Atlantic, escape from St. Helena was virtually impossible. Nonetheless, to further reduce the odds, the British deployed a small garrison on the island to watch Napoleon in his solitary, windswept house at Longwood. Surrounded by a small personal entourage, the fallen emperor spent the last six years of his life feuding with his British captors and waging his last and undoubtedly most successful campaign—that for posterity.

Imagining parallel histories is dangerous. Still, one cannot but speculate whether Europe would have been better off had the Napoleonic Wars ended differently. The Napoleonic conquests undoubtedly resulted in exploitation as well as in harsh repression. Yet the French armies also brought with them reforms that were built upon revolutionary ideals. They promised legal equality, personal freedom, and the inviolability of property; they proclaimed religious tolerance, reformed administrative and judicial systems, and standardized weights and measures. Whatever and however many his faults, Napoleon was a more enlightened figure than most autocratic rulers of Europe, and his defeat meant a setback for many of the ideals that underpin modern society.

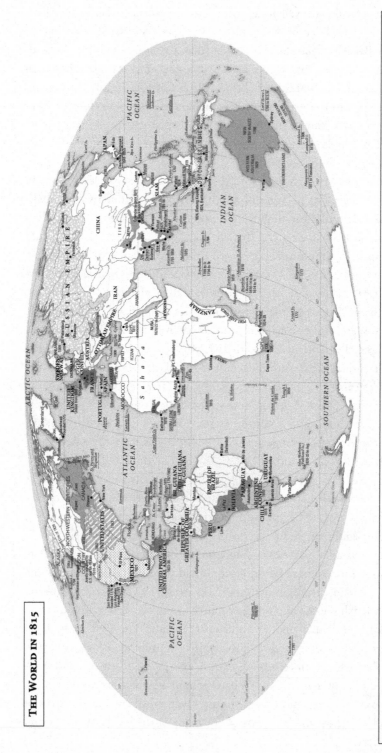

THE WORLD IN 1815

Spanish Possessions — British Possessions — Portuguese Possessions — French Possessions — Dutch Possessions — Danish Possessions — United States' Possessions — Russian Possessions

Map 29: The World in 1815

CHAPTER 24

The Aftermath of the Great War

T HE BATTLE OF WATERLOO marked the endpoint of what many contemporaries (especially in Britain) came to consider the "Great War." It heralded the start of a period of relative peace that would last for decades and help Europe recover from revolutionary turmoil and devastation. A decisive step toward this new era was taken just nine days before the Waterloo, when the Congress of Vienna adopted its Final Act, which completed its remapping of Europe and outlined significant changes to its political reorganization.[1]

The post-Napoleonic settlement reached at Vienna was based on four fundamental principles. First, the European powers sought to ensure an international equilibrium of political and military forces by discouraging the domination of Europe by any single state and encouraging a collaborative approach to the maintenance of peace. Although their interests were frequently in conflict, the great powers possessed enough mutual interest in safeguarding their own sovereignty from potential aggressor(s) to form the Concert of Europe, whose main purpose was to maintain peace and stability. This was not the balance of power in the traditional sense of the concept because the Napoleonic Wars left Europe rather unbalanced. In 1819 Dominique de Pradt, the French archbishop and a rather keen political observer, lamented the fact that "two giants have now established themselves in Europe, England and Russia. . . . It is true that in earlier times, before this new order arrived, dominant powers existed but they were never exclusively preeminent and never wielded such a disproportionate force vis-à-vis the other states." Pradt concluded that the new political reality in Europe could no longer be considered as based on the principle of the balance of power, but rather reflected the hegemony of Britain and Russia.[2] The archbishop's assessment echoed in the writings of many subsequent historians, including Enno Kraehe and Paul Schroeder, but the post-Napoleonic state of affairs requires a more nuanced approach.[3] As powerful as Britain and Russia were after the Napoleonic Wars, the European security regime was not necessarily bipolar, and it continued to be fluid and flexible, allowing other states to remain actively involved in it.[4] Self-interest and traditional ideas about political equipoise informed the Allies' decision not to weaken France unduly, so that it could serve as a counterweight to Russia, and to restore Austria and Prussia to their prewar status, so that they could serve as a bulwark against France. For nearly a century after the Congress of Vienna, the desire to maintain this equilibrium was an important component of international relations in Europe. It ensured that the first four decades after the end of the Napoleonic Wars were peaceful, while conflicts during the second half of the nineteenth century never morphed into a larger conflagration. Unlike the eighteenth century, which saw several lengthy conflicts involving virtually every European state, the post-Napoleonic conflicts in Europe tended to be events involving two or three nations and rarely lasting longer than two years.

Second was the principle of legitimacy, which was ostensibly aimed at restoring the legitimate monarchies and therefore preserving traditional institutions on the continent. Despite the many military victories of the French Revolution and under Napoleon, the older order of monarchical states, presided over by an established aristocracy, had survived and ultimately won the war. But the principal ideas of liberalism—individual freedoms, equality before the law, laissez-faire economics—were by no means defeated in 1815. In the post-Napoleonic period, as liberalism became identified with the middle class, many intellectuals and larger social groups felt that liberal ideology did not go far enough to satisfy their needs. The new generation of radicals desired to replace monarchical rule with republics and sought greater economic and social equality even if it entailed using violence to achieve those goals. These were very drastic ideas that even liberals found hard to support. In their struggles against conservative regimes, liberals and radicals did occasionally join their forces, but only up to a point.

The radical changes unleashed by the Revolution had their most profound impact on France and those areas of the Low Countries, Italy, and Germany that Napoleon had incorporated into his empire; economic liberalism, meanwhile, was embraced most enthusiastically in Britain. Their impact was milder to the east of the Rhine River, and they made only limited headway in the largely agricultural societies of eastern Europe. The Prussian progressive reforms stemmed not from French revolutionary influence but rather from within—the Prussian military and civil officials who were convinced the state needed to be modernized to defeat the French. In Prussia and Austria, not to mention smaller central European states, authority remained in the hands of an aristocratic class that was eager to combat subversion of the monarchical order by popular movements. It found in conservatism a political and social philosophy with which to contend against the wave of radicalism.

The foundation for the conservative philosophy had been laid in 1790 when British political theorist Edmund Burke published his *Reflections on the Revolution in France* and refined by later generations of conservative writers, who were terrified of the revolutionary excesses. These writers rejected any claim that society was based upon a "social contract" between people and government, one that could be redrafted as the need arose. They argued that society was an enduring partnership between the past, present, and future generations, or, in the words of Russian conservative writer Nikolai Karamzin, a living social organism that evolved over many hundreds of years and could not be cut off from its past if it was not to perish.[5] Like everything that lives, the state was God's creation, and no one generation had the right to destroy it; rather, it was their duty to pass it on. Hence, new rights and freedoms could not be based upon abstract concepts of natural law but had to be derived from preexisting rights and traditions.

After the end of the Napoleonic Wars, conservatives strove to revive pre-Napoleonic regimes, a process that included restoring "legitimate" rulers overthrown during the war and resurrecting systems based on contractual rights, services, and dependencies. None of the powers seriously contemplated returning all of the deposed rulers to their thrones or treating all rulers as legitimate. Therefore, the "restoration" of 1815 should not be considered as a return to Europe as it had been in 1789. For all their conservatism, the statesmen at Vienna were well aware of the unfeasibility of such an endeavor and understood the need to change and evolve gradually. In practice, they used the principle of legitimacy as a general guidepost to be respected in some instances and ignored in many others.

What lay behind this focus on collaboration and legitimacy was fear of revolution and upheaval that could once more set Europe on fire. Hence, closely related to the principle of legitimacy was the third pillar of post-Napoleonic settlement: intervention. The great powers agreed to protect each other and Europe in general against the infection of the revolutionary spirit. Whenever a state was threatened by turmoil, these powers, drawing on existing treaties and respecting current territorial arrangements, would intervene and uphold legitimate (read: conservative) order. When the powers collaborated in the 1820s and 1830s, they successfully put down liberal revolutions and maintained the conservative order of the day.

Finally, those three principles were tempered by the fourth: mutual compensation. In a general restructuring of Europe, the victors agreed that if one nation gave up territory or compromised on a certain interest, it would receive compensation in some shape or form. As we've seen, in the Polish-Saxon crisis, the great powers reached a compromise solution based on mutual compensation. A Polish state, better known as the Congress Poland, was resurrected within the Russian Empire and ostensibly granted a constitutional government that was far more liberal than that of the Russian patrimony. To form this new Polish entity, Russia convinced Prussia to surrender the Warsaw region (but without Posen) in exchange for being compensated with 40 percent of Saxony, the last remaining strip of the Swedish Pomerania on the Baltic, and all of the previous holdings in Westphalia, which were further augmented by a large tract of land on the left bank of the Rhine. Austria, meanwhile, gave up western Galicia and allowed Krakow to become a free city, but kept all the Polish lands that the Habsburgs had annexed south and east of the Vistula River and recovered those areas that Russia had claimed in 1809.[6]

Such compensations, however, flouted the very spirit of national self-determination that the Revolutionary and Napoleonic Wars had unleashed. Nationalism was a sentiment arising from an awareness of belonging to a community that shared bonds of common ethnicity, language, customs, religion, and cultural ties. It could only be stimulated and flourish in a society whose social and economic development allowed for a certain degree of political independence, popular education, and general participation in politics. Nationalism posed a great threat to states that had failed to develop national identities based on allegiance to common ideals, institutions, and shared political vision, so that citizenship became the criterion of nationality. France was the first nation fully to embrace these elements, and Napoleon's armies introduced them to other parts of Europe. Yet the powers that defeated Napoleon lacked these elements. This meant that a sense of nationality became intertwined with cultures and identities, which in the case of great European empires were rather diverse. Of course, subjects of the Austrian, Russian, and Ottoman Empires shared a bond to the sovereign and the allegiance to the empire as a whole but, as time progressed, they—whether Czechs, Poles, Hungarians, Bulgarians, Greeks, or others—became increasingly conscious of their own cultural uniqueness and of preserving it. This awareness of national individuality was the first step toward national self-determination, which threatened the integrity (if not the very existence) of the empires and endangered the European political order as set at the Congress of Vienna. For much of the nineteenth century, liberalism and nationalism represented twin forces of subversion, since the aspiration of national unity and independence did not appear possible without liberal transformation.

With the Final Act in hand, the European powers went about redrawing territorial boundaries and creating long-term stability on the continent. Napoleon's violation of the First Treaty of Paris and the wholehearted support he had received in many parts of France strengthened the arguments of those Allied leaders who had long advocated that leniency had to be replaced by firmer treatment. After Napoleon's second downfall, the Prussian representatives were particularly vocal in their argument that the French nation had forfeited every right to a generous peace. Prussia and others called for harsher conditions that would further constrain and weaken France. Castlereagh brushed aside the Prussian arguments, pointing out that imposing exacting demands on France would only undermine the Bourbons at home and might contribute to further political instability, which could, in turn, upset the delicate balance of power the Congress of Vienna sought to revive. "It is curious to observe," wrote Castlereagh in one of his letters, "the insatiable spirit of getting something without a thought of how it is to be preserved. There is not a Power, however feeble, that borders France from the Channel to the Mediterranean that is not pushing some acquisition under the plea of security and rectification of frontier."[7] After long negotiations, which continued well after the Congress of Vienna had completed its work in June 1815, the Allies signed the Second Treaty of Peace with France in Paris on November 20, 1815. The treaty consisted of several agreements dealing with key postwar issues, including indemnity, military occupation, deserters, territorial arrangements, private claims upon France, and the slave trade.

The most important of these agreements was the Definitive Treaty, signed in Paris on November 20, 1815, which outlined the final peace between France and the Allies. This agreement was considerably harsher than the one of 1814, forcing France to surrender additional frontier territory and fortresses and reducing French borders to those of 1790, rather than 1792. This meant the surrender of parts of Savoy, the Austrian Netherlands (Belgium), and the Rhineland that France had retained in 1814.[8] Furthermore, the treaty obliged France to pay a war indemnity of 700 million francs and bear the costs of an Allied army of occupation for up to five years, to maintain order and tranquility in the country in which, as the treaty noted, "the state of uneasiness and of fermentation...after so many violent convulsions, and particularly after the last catastrophe," was expected to endure.[9]

Disillusionment, anger, and a sense of national humiliation were widespread in France. The Allied Council, consisting of representatives of the victorious powers, set de-Bonapartization, demilitarization, and payment of reparations as its short-term goals. It largely fulfilled the first two goals within two years after the end of the Napoleonic Wars. Napoleon was exiled to St. Helena, while the Bonapartes were banned from France and closely monitored in the rest of Europe.[10] The French government and military were purged of Bonapartist officials and officers, many of them choosing to flee to North America.[11] King Louis XVIII demobilized Napoleon's Grande Armée, reducing its size from half a million to slightly over 200,000. The decision was necessary for the peace in Europe, as well as for balancing national finances, but it was bound to incite considerable anger among tens of thousands of Napoleonic veterans, who were condemned to lives of begging, poverty, petty crime, and institutional exploitation.

The question of reparations, however, hung heavily over France for several years. The Allies insisted that all money accounts arising out of the Definitive Treaty be settled before their forces of occupation withdrew. These reparations fell into two broad categories: war indemnities and claims made by private citizens against France. However, the Allies also expected the Bourbon monarchy to honor debts contracted by earlier French governments in territories occupied during the Napoleonic Wars, and to bear the costs of maintaining the forces of occupation. The total costs of reparations, therefore, would have been closer to 1.3 billion francs. As a whole, these reparations represented a new development in the history of conflict resolutions. Unlike earlier historical examples of reparations in which a victorious side compelled the losing one to pay particular costs of war, in 1815 the Allies wielded reparations as a punitive measure. In the words of economic historian Eugene N. White, "Reparations now became part of a tougher peace package, assessing a penalty for threatening the new European order and a deterrent against future [hostile] ventures. Payment of reparations was also an incentive, whose fulfillment would allow France to resume its role as a Great Power in the management of European affairs."[12] Another innovation was the use of the regime of military occupation to extract payments from the host country.

France's new prime minister, Armand-Emmanuel de Vignerot du Plessis, duc de Richelieu, was well placed to represent France in these difficult negotiations. A scion of a distinguished French aristocratic family, he emigrated from France during the Revolution and served in Russia, where Emperor Alexander came to appreciate his administrative skills and entrusted him with the governorship of a large province. Now back in France, Richelieu, with the support of French finance minister Louis Emmanuel Corvetto, took advantage of the fact that France had undergone a major financial restructuring, including bankruptcy during the Revolution, and that Napoleon had left behind little national debt.[13] With the help of a consortium of foreign banks led by Alexander Baring, Richelieu floated loans and obligations at low rates. By 1818, when the European powers met for a congress at

Aix-la-Chapelle, France had paid a total of 368 million francs. At that conference, Richelieu convinced the allies to accept a one-time payment of 280 million francs in lieu of the remaining reparations. The French government's ability to pay what constituted, in absolute terms, the biggest war reparations in modern history was of profound consequence. Reparations restored public credit in the French government and allowed the French state to entice new investments at lower rates. More crucial was that they served as a conduit for the transfer of capital from British bankers to continental governments that received French reparations and, hence, played a role in spurring recovery in postwar Europe.[14]

The Allies' longer-term aim in 1815 was achieving stability and permanence in international affairs. Mindful of France's historical penchant for territorial aspirations, they agreed to form defensive barriers around it. At the northern end was the new Kingdom of the Netherlands, which was formed by merging the former Austrian Netherlands with the Dutch provinces; the new polity was placed under the rule of the House of Orange.[15] Further along the northeastern boundary of France were a number of German states on the left bank of the Rhine, bolstered by Prussia's newly acquired territory there. Eastern approaches to France were guarded by the newly reorganized Switzerland. The specially formed Swiss Committee spent much time discussing the future of nineteen Swiss cantons, which were represented at the congress by separate delegations. Ultimately the committee agreed that an enlarged Switzerland of twenty-one cantons would be established under the rotating leadership of Zürich, Lucerne, and Berne; the five great powers then recognized the permanent neutrality of Switzerland.[16] Continuing along this defensive barrier down to the Mediterranean was the restored kingdom of Sardinia-Piedmont, which not only reclaimed its former possessions but was enlarged by the addition of Liguria (with Genoa), Nice, and a part of Savoy.[17] Finally, in the south of France, Spain was once again independent and under Bourbon rule, with Ferdinand VII joyfully greeted by his subjects in Madrid.

Farther to the east lay Prussia proper, Austria, and a confederation of the German states. The former, as we have seen, was restored to its pre-1806 status and power and was allowed to retain Posen and the port city of Danzig and annex portions of Saxony in return for giving up parts of Poland. Austria reclaimed all the territories it had lost since 1792 and was compensated for its loss of the Austrian Netherlands with Venetia and Lombardy in northern Italy. The Habsburgs were also pleased with the recovery of the Illyrian Provinces in the Adriatic, and Salzburg and the Tyrol, the last two having been lost to Bavaria in 1809.[18] One of the most important changes that the congress had made concerned the future of the minor German states. The

German Committee, formed to discuss the reorganization of the former Confederation of the Rhine, consisted of representatives of Austria, Prussia, Bavaria, Württemberg, and Hanover but was later enlarged to include Saxony, Hesse-Darmstadt, the Netherlands, and Denmark. It helped create the German Confederation (Deutscher Bund), a loose union of thirty-eight states and four free cities, whose mission was defined by the Vienna treaty as the "maintenance of the external and internal safety of Germany and of the independence and inviolability of the confederated states."[19] All members states pledged to defend not only "the whole of Germany" but each individual state of the union, and not to make war on each other.[20] The new confederation included individual German states such as Saxony, Württemberg, and Bavaria, as well as territories of the sovereign princes (the kings of Denmark, Britain, the Netherlands, Austria and Prussia) and the free towns of Germany. Excluded, however, were the Polish provinces of Prussia and those Habsburg-governed regions that lay outside the boundaries of the now-defunct Holy Roman Empire: Lombardy, Venetia, Hungary, and Polish Galicia. The German Confederation was administered through a federal Diet, under the presidency of Austria (whose emperor was still regarded as the traditional leader of Germany), that was established at Frankfurt to draft the laws and regulations of the Confederation.[21] Although the German Confederation encompassed almost all the German-speaking peoples of Europe and had the appearance of a national polity, it did not embrace the ideology of nationalism and was simply an expedient way of organizing and managing central European states.[22]

The Congress of Vienna also agreed upon major territorial adjustments outside central Europe. Sweden's involvement in the Sixth Coalition was, as we've seen, driven by the desire to acquire Norway, which Alexander had promised to Bernadotte at Abo in August 1812. To fulfill this transfer, the Allies forced King Frederick VI of Denmark to accept the Treaty of Kiel (January 1814), which ceded Heligoland to Britain and Norway to Sweden in exchange for Swedish Pomerania. However, the treaty was rejected by the Norwegians, who under the leadership of Prince Christian Frederick of Denmark, governor-general of Norway and heir presumptive to the thrones of Denmark and Norway, convened a constitutional assembly that proclaimed Norwegian independence and adopted a liberal constitution. Christian Frederick tried to gain support from the great powers, but none responded to his entreaties. Instead, they supported Bernadotte during the short Swedish-Norwegian War (July–August 1814), which saw unexpected Swedish defeats at Lier, Matrand, and Langnes before Swedish superiority in numbers made Norwegian defeat inevitable. The Congress of Vienna had thus confirmed the

Swedish acquisition of Norway and the loss of Finland to Russia. Pomerania, which under the Treaty of Kiel Sweden ceded to Denmark, was ultimately given to Prussia, which compensated Denmark with the small Duchy of Saxe-Lauenbourg.[23]

Italy was dealt with as a geographic rather than political entity, and its hopes for unity, revived under Napoleon, were soon quashed. Beyond the defensive barriers (Piedmont-Sardinia and Austrian-controlled Lombardy and Venetia), the congress restored a number of Italian rulers to their thrones. Pope Pius VII returned to the Papal States, while the Duchies of Parma, Piacenza, and Guastalla were awarded to Napoleon's wife, Empress Marie-Louise, for her lifetime. Naples and Sicily were once again reunited into the Bourbon-led Kingdom of the Two Sicilies, while the House of Habsburg-Lorraine returned to Tuscany and Modena.

Besides territorial divisions, the Final Act of the congress addressed other important issues. Britain, for instance, sought the total abolition of slavery. In early February 1815 the Slave Trade Committee adopted a declaration unanimously condemning the slave trade.[24] Although it was later included in the Final Act, the declaration had no binding provisions for signatory powers and did not prescribe when or how the trade should be abolished. Therefore, Britain eventually concluded separate agreements with states engaged in the slave trade. The Jewish community in Germany succeeded in lobbying the Prussian delegation to place the issue of Jewish rights on the agenda of the German Committee, which formally confirmed them in some German states and made a recommendation to extend them to others.

The Committee on International Rivers, established on December 14, 1814, discussed the question of navigation on the major rivers of Europe. It was agreed that navigation on key waterways, including the Rhine, Moselle, Neckar, and Meuse, would be free. The Rhine Commission was established to eliminate trade barriers and standardize navigational regulations, police ordinances, and emergency procedures on rivers.[25]

Another lasting achievement of the Congress of Vienna included settlements of diplomatic precedence and rank. It was agreed that the precedence of diplomatic representatives in a given country would be determined by the date of the official notification of their arrival at their mission. Diplomatic officials were organized into four classes: ambassadors and papal legates, ministers plenipotentiary, resident ministers, and chargés d'affaires. French was selected as the language of international diplomacy, confirming a state of affairs that had existed since the reign of Louis XIV.[26]

It can be safely argued that the state that gained most from the Napoleonic Wars was Britain, although its performance at the Congress of Vienna did not fully reflect the military, diplomatic, and financial efforts the wars had demanded of it. Britain voluntarily abandoned almost all of its colonial conquests, retaining the former Dutch colonies of Ceylon (Sri Lanka), Demerara (in Guiana, now Surinam), and the Cape Colony (on the southern coast of Africa). Britain had annexed nothing on the European continent. Furthermore, British negotiations had failed to secure an agreement to abolish the slave trade, and the Final Act contained only a brief declaration condemning in principle the traffic in slaves but leaving its actual suppression to future negotiations.

Such setbacks (if they can be termed such), however, belied some very considerable advantages that Britain had gained. During the Napoleonic Wars, the British took advantage of their naval supremacy to gain territory in virtually every part of the world and chose to retain those that offered strategic advantages. These included the island of Malta in the Mediterranean, which controlled the narrowest section of the Mediterranean Sea and ensured Britain's ability to control both sides of the Mediterranean basin; the island of Heligoland, in the North Sea, which sat at the estuaries of the two major German rivers (the Elbe and the Weser) and offered an excellent position to control trade in northwestern Germany; and, as we've seen, the Cape Colony, in southern Africa, which was a crucial waypoint on the only sea-lane connecting Europe to India and East Asia, and the island of Ceylon, which secured British control of trade routes around the southern tip of India. At the same time, the islands of St. Lucia, Tobago, and Trinidad in the Caribbean and Mauritius, the Seychelles, and Rodrigues in the Indian Ocean served as strategic bases for projecting British power and protecting its economic interests on both sides of the world. Most crucial, the British delegation managed to restore a semblance of European balance of power; it was not precisely the one Castlereagh and his colleagues had hoped for at the start of the congress, but, flawed as it was, the new international system offered the promise of keeping Europe at peace and of ensuring that Britain would not have to face alone another hegemonic power in Europe.

Not part of the congress but directly stemming from it was an agreement among the sovereigns of Austria, Prussia, and Russia to employ Christian principles in administering their nations and guiding their relations with other states. This idea for what became known as the Holy Alliance (Sainte Alliance) was suggested by Emperor Alexander as a means to maintain the conservative order. Some congress participants downplayed its relevance, with Castlereagh describing it as "a piece of sublime mysticism and nonsense" and Metternich famously calling it a "loud-sounding nothing."[27] Nevertheless, the idea was supported by European sovereigns, and a formal treaty was signed on September 26, 1815. Emperor Francis I, King Frederick William III, and Alexander I all agreed to take as their political guides "the precepts of that Holy Religion, namely, the precepts of Justice, Christian Charity, and Peace, which, far from being applicable only to private concerns, must have an immediate influence on the councils of Princes, and guide all their steps."[28] The contracting monarchs then pledged to join in "bonds of a true and indissoluble fraternity," to administer Europe with a sense of "Religion, Peace, and Justice" that was deeply rooted in Christianity, and to "lend each other aid and assistance" in case of need. Almost all the ruling princes of Europe eventually joined the alliance, except for the prince regent of Britain (who decried its reactionary spirit), Pope Pius VII (who felt no need to join a treaty to ensure that he acted according to Christian principles), and the Ottoman sultan.

In practical terms, a far more important treaty was signed on November 20, when the representatives of Austria, Britain, Prussia, and Russia agreed to renew their wartime coalition. This Quadruple Alliance had its antecedent in the Treaty of Chaumont (March 1814), when the powers pledged not to seek any separate peace with France and to maintain their military coalition until Napoleon had surrendered. Threatened by the diplomatic crisis over Poland and Saxony, this agreement returned to life during the Hundred Days and was now validated once more. The new treaty, approved on the same day of the signing of the second Treaty of Paris, formalized the alliance, with the powers pledging to secure Europe through a collective effort and committing them for twenty years to contribute tens of thousands of troops should the French attempt to overturn the Vienna settlement.

But the agreement went beyond military assurances. The post-Napoleonic Europe was fearful that the revolution would reappear in new forms and sought to take measures to prevent this. In Article VI of the treaty, the Allies agreed to hold "meetings at fixed periods...for the purpose of consulting upon their common interests." By agreeing to periodic conferences, the Allies could also use joint diplomacy, in concert with combined military measures, to ensure the execution of the political settlement made in Vienna. This arrangement represented a pioneering approach to establishing a new international security system that was designed to maintain peace, stability and order on the continent. This security came at a high price, however. For years to come European government demonstrated a growing obsession with the threat of radical conspiracies, a menace often exaggerated by self-serving agents and spies as well as high administrators eager for greater procurements. This was in many ways a "phantom terror," as historian Adam Zamoyski points out, but one that affected not just conservative states but the most liberal regimes as well, with Britain expanding repressive state powers and limiting civil liberties in the post-Napoleonic period. The new European security system entailed creation of a host of new control mechanisms, including larger state security bureaucracies, new passport controls, improved communication systems, and transnational police systems to track fugitive "terrorists." European states invoked a circular logic that treated their populations as objects of suspicion and justified surveillance and repression, which in turn engendered popular resistance, which then demanded more surveillance and repression. This paranoia drove European governments to centralize their administrative controls, expand policing to previously unprecedented levels, and stifle reform movements. The modern national security state was thus born.[29]

—◇◇◇※◇◇◇—

The Napoleonic Wars were perhaps the most powerful agents of social change between the Reformation and World War I. They fundamentally transformed the nature of sovereignty in Europe and demonstrated the growing ability of European states to achieve levels of social-military mobilization and economic production that allowed them to engage in prolonged and destructive conflicts. For the generations born at the end of the eighteenth century, the Napoleonic Wars were the defining event. Their cost in human lives seems incalculable in every sense, since documents on military casualties are either missing or suspect, as governments usually were (and still are) reluctant to let the public to learn about the full extent of sacrifices. Even more challenging is accounting for civilian losses. Hence, any discussion of the cost of the war inevitably requires some broad assessment.[30]

Overall, the Napoleonic Wars probably claimed about two million soldiers' lives in Europe; hundreds of thousands troops were wounded, and perhaps 15 to 20 percent of them were disabled for life. This number would increase if we account for civilian losses as well as military casualties from the French Revolutionary Wars. A rough estimate is that as many as 4 million people perished in Europe between 1792 and 1815—more than 2.5 percent of the estimated 150 million people living there. Of these, about 1.5 million Frenchmen died during military action, whether of wounds, diseases, accidents, starvation or other causes, during the entire period, including almost a million men lost under the First Empire. Well over a third of the generation of Frenchmen born between 1786 and 1795 died on the Napoleonic battlefields.[31] The Napoleonic Wars left deep scars on French society that took years to recover from. France "has bled at every pore and appears a vast mourning family," observed a visiting Englishman in the summer of 1815. "Three people out of five that one meets are habited in black." At every step one could see traces of the war; in Paris, "there was scarcely a driver of a fiacre, a waiter at a cafe, or a man in middle life, who had not been in a battle, served a campaign, or been wounded by a shot." Visitors to France were struck by the national mood: people "spoke of war as a thing of course, of its horrors as '*le sort de la guerre*' as if the miseries of war were as much a constituent part of the existence of continental nations as their climate. There was an apathy, a notion of dark destiny about the thing, as though the bloody turmoil the rising generation had lived in had utterly destroyed their perceptions of right."[32]

Other continental powers were hard hit too. Russian losses exceeded 500,000 people. Prussian, German, and Austrian casualties reached half a million, while Polish and Italian losses numbered as high as 200,000. Despite being relatively insulated from the continental struggles, Britain lost some 300,000 men, with the heaviest losses falling during the concluding years of the war, when the British army alone lost around 25,000 men each year. In fact, in its struggles against Napoleon, Britain lost as many men, as a proportion of its overall population, as it would in its conflict with Germany a hundred years later, although this loss of life took place over a much longer period of time. Between 1805 and 1813 the British army suffered nearly 200,000 casualties due to combat, disease, or accident.[33] The Royal Navy lost close to 100,000 men, with the vast majority of deaths attributed to disease; shipwrecks and fires accounted for another 13,000 lives (including the fateful night of December 23, 1811, when a storm claimed more than 2,000 men), while just 6,000 sailors were killed in combat.[34]

More British men died of disease and accident in the West and East Indies than during the entirety of the Peninsular War, which claimed a higher proportion of lives than any other Napoleonic conflict.[35] France, Spain, and Portugal bore the brunt of the losses in the Peninsula, with the war claiming an estimated 200,000 Frenchmen, more than 200,000 Portuguese, and at least 500,000 Spaniards; contemporary Spanish estimates suggested overall war casualties of 1 million people, which would have amounted to about 5 percent of the Spanish population and represented more than double the loss of the devastating Spanish Civil War of 1936–1939. The Peninsular War remains the bloodiest war in Spain's modern history. While the British battle losses during this war amounted to 8,178 killed and 37,765 wounded (with another 6,000 missing), death in battle did not represent the only cause of loss; in fact, far more British soldiers died of sickness, and a recent study suggests that two-thirds of the more than 55,000 British deaths (from eleven theaters of war) were not combat-related.[36]

Napoleon's invasion of Russia in 1812 and the subsequent campaigns in Germany and France were steeped in blood. The six-month Russian campaign claimed more than half a million lives, with the Grande Armée accounting for much of them; the total casualties at Borodino were as high as 70,000 men, or a staggering rate of 108 men each minute during the ten-hour battle. In the Mozhaisk district alone, local authorities gathered more than 52,000 human and more than 41,000 horse cadavers that had to be quickly interred in mass burials out of fear of the spread of contagion. Russia lost about 200,000 troops during this campaign, though to get a complete picture of the Russian losses we must also account for thousands of civilian losses, both from military actions and from disease and malnutrition. The work on gathering and burning cadavers continued for months after the fighting ended. Losses during the last year and half of the Napoleonic Wars were no less sanguinary. Just three battles—Lützen, Bautzen, and Leipzig—collectively claimed more than 150,000 casualties, and although many of the sick and lightly wounded ultimately returned to their units, the dead would have accounted for about a quarter of that number while thousands more would have been maimed and disabled. The massive Battle of the Nations at Leipzig in October 1813 was the largest Napoleonic battle, with over 80,000 killed and wounded. Further complicating an exact assessment, tens of thousands of civilians suffered from disease and malnutrition; an estimated 250,000 civilians—about 1 percent of the German population—died from the vicious typhoid epidemic that raged in central Europe in 1813–1814.[37] Meanwhile, bubonic plague claimed thousands of lives in the Balkan Peninsula before reaching southern Russia in 1812, when almost 10 percent of the population of Odessa perished, and Italy in 1815, when the town of Noja, on the Adriatic coastline, lost one in seven of its population; the town was promptly sealed off and the progress of the epidemic halted.

These numbers do not reflect losses from conflicts in the Balkans and Danubian Principalities, the Caucasus, the Middle East, India, North America, and Spanish America. As we have seen, these struggles are directly linked to the Revolutionary and Napoleonic Wars and left hundreds of thousands more killed, wounded, or disabled, so the global human costs of the Revolutionary and Napoleonic Era are most probably over 6 million lives. In Saint-Domingue alone, the twelve-year rebellion saw some of the most vicious fighting of the entire period, reducing its population by approximately 150,000–200,000 lives, with many others permanently scarred and crippled. The Anglo-American conflict in 1812–1815 saw the deaths of more than 20,000 soldiers, the vast majority from sickness rather than combat. The civilian toll of the war remains uncertain but undoubtedly no less severe.

And on it goes. The Serbian Revolt of 1804–1813 resulted in the loss of about a quarter million lives. Egypt and Arabia saw their populations significantly reduced as the result of the continued turmoil that raged in the wake of the French invasion of 1798. Russo-Ottoman military operations in the Danubian Principalities and the Caucasus probably claimed more than 100,000 lives—the failed Russian assault on the Ottoman fortress of Braila alone cost almost 5,000 casualties (half of them killed) on May 1, 1809, and caused profound hardship for local populations. By 1810 Wallachia, formerly one of the most fertile regions in southeastern Europe, was in such a state of disorder that entire communities suffered from famine and local authorities could no longer satisfy the Russian army's demands.[38] Far more destructive was the unremitting violence that began in Spanish America after Napoleon's takeover of Spain in 1808 and continued for seventeen years. Although precise statistics are hard to come by, we would not be mistaken to estimate that close to 1 million people perished during this conflict; in New Spain (Mexico) alone, over a quarter of a million people died between 1810 and 1821, while Venezuela lost as many as 200,000 people—a third of its total population.[39] In neighboring New Granada, as many as 250,000 people were killed achieving Gran Colombia's independence.[40]

Next to the loss of life were the immense material costs. Military expenses consumed a lion's share of states' resources, forcing governments to cut expenses elsewhere and find ways to extract additional resources. Many parts of Europe suffered because of the greater tendency of armies to live off the land and to be employed for prolonged occupation of countries. In Portugal and Spain the war had devastated a great number of towns and villages, as the repeated rampages by armies and guerrillas stripped the fields of their supplies and the pastures of their livestock. The Spanish province of Extremadura lost nearly 15 percent of its population. The town of Puerto Real, occupied by the French during their long siege of Cadiz in 1810–1812, lost 40 percent of its buildings and half of its population; less than half of its former farmland could be cultivated after the siege, and only one-quarter of its olive tree were still standing. The invasion route of the Grande Armée in Russia was marked by the smoldering ruins of dozens of villages and towns, including the great city of Moscow, which was completely devastated, with 6,350 houses (out of just over 9,000) destroyed, along with hundreds of taverns, shops, inns, and markets. Germany, where the fate of the Napoleonic Empire was decided in 1813, witnessed hundreds of thousands of French and Allied troops denuding towns and countrysides of grain, forage, and livestock. In 1814–1815, thousands of foreign troops occupied French regions, causing economic hardship to already impoverished areas. One Russian officer was astonished to find the French countryside "extremely poor...the people are deprived of most necessities."[41]

Nature only further complicated the process of post-Napoleonic recovery. In April 1815, the massive eruption of Mount Tambora, on the island of Sumbawa (in modern Indonesia), spewed a vast cloud of dust and ash that spread across the globe and altered weather patterns in many parts of the world; the eruption's effect was compounded by earlier volcanic activity that contributed to a global cooling.[42] A year after the eruption, the Paris Observatory recorded summer temperatures more than five degrees Fahrenheit below the mean. "Melancholy accounts have been received from all parts of the continent of the unusual wetness of the season," reported the *Norfolk Chronicle* in late July 1816. "In several provinces of Holland, the rich grasslands are all under water, and scarcity and high prices are naturally apprehended and dreaded. In France, the interior of the country has suffered greatly from the floods and rains." In Hungary brown-colored snow fell during the winter of 1816, while in northern Italy the snow remained on the ground till the end of spring. The changing weather affected crop yields and caused food shortages across Europe, which in turn led to social unrest, misery, and death. England, France, and parts of Germany and Switzerland witnessed riots and disturbances in 1816–1817 while a famine (and a typhus epidemic that accompanied it) claimed thousands of lives in already impoverished Ireland; in 1817, celebration of the second anniversary of the battle of Waterloo turned out to be an occasion for extensive food rioting in Brussels.[43] In the remote Croatian village of Zminj, the parish priest bemoaned the "fatal year" of 1816, which, because of frequent rain and other bad weather, turned out "so sterile that many citizens could not prepare enough cereals to last them for half a year, and some not even for two months." The following year was even worse; by March, "people began to be affected by Black Famine; yet they supported each other as long as they had anything to eat....But it was of short duration...Reduced to the uttermost misery they were walking around and falling dead, some at home, some along roads, some in the forests etc."[44] This natural calamity struck just as Europe and many parts of the world were recovering from the disruptions of the Napoleonic Wars. Poor harvests resulted in skyrocketing prices for food, especially grain, and complicated postwar reconstruction.

For more than two decades, European powers resorted to mercantilist practices to safeguard their interests and undermine rival economies; they also took measures against neutral shipping that could have transported enemy goods. As a result, international trade suffered from repeated disruptions and volatility, especially during the period 1806–1812, when France instituted the Continental System while Britain maintained its own blockade through orders-in-council. Wartime freight, insurance, and licensing dramatically increased the costs of doing business; in 1812, for example, they accounted for up to 40 percent of British wheat prices.[45] And yet the British economy continued its growth despite war and blockade. Development of a more efficient transportation network featuring coastal shipping, canals, and turnpike roads resulted in the integration of British domestic markets and more efficient specialization between different regions. Sound public finance and the growth of the banking sector further sustained British manufacturing growth. However, British rents rose considerably toward the end of the Napoleonic Wars, garnering handsome profits for landowners, who were reluctant to lose them once the war ended. The result was political lobbying for what became the Corn Law of 1815, which closed the British domestic market to foreign grain; the law was fiercely opposed by the rising class of industrialists who wished to maximize their profits by reducing wages that were already insufficient to feed workers.

The war cut swaths of devastation across western Russia, northern France, Germany, Spain, and Portugal. Industries linked with the Atlantic trade suffered a steep decline during the Continental System (although import-substituting industries saw some growth), and traditional centers of international trade waned as colonial empires collapsed. France came out of war without Louisiana and Saint-Domingue. The Spanish presence in the New World had been reduced to Cuba and Puerto Rico, while there was a growing rift between Portugal and Brazil, which ultimately led to the latter's independence in 1822. The Dutch lost South Africa, Ceylon, and the West Indies; in fact, Amsterdam saw its standing as a key center of international trade irreversibly undermined through the combined effects of French occupation, the Continental System, and the British blockade. On the other hand, by the war's end, Britain had firmly secured the position of the world's dominant economic power, and the extent of its immediate postwar hegemony can be gleaned from the share of world shipping that it had garnered: it jumped from 25 percent in 1780 to over 40 percent in 1820.[46] The fact that Britain enjoyed naval dominance served as a crucial precondition for the development of a broadly liberal international economy during the rest of the nineteenth century.[47]

The trade effects of the war extended well beyond European shorelines. The War of 1812 caused significant disruptions in North American trade, but these paled in comparison to the economic downturn in Latin America. Indeed, one of the most profound impacts of the Napoleonic Wars was the virtual collapse of European empires in the Western Hemisphere and the emergence of independent states that pursued their own, mostly competing, commercial policies. Former Spanish colonies adopted mercantilist policies to protect their economies, policies that had a huge effect on regional trade and commerce. A crucial feature of the emerging economic reality in South America was bilateral trade between newly independent states and Britain; before the war Latin America accounted for only 0.06 percent of British manufactured exports, but its share steadily increased to 3.3 percent in 1804–1806, more than 6 percent in 1814–1815, and some 15 percent by the 1820s.[48] Mexican silver output was also distressed by war blockades and political disorder in the Spanish colonies. It had averaged more than 20 million piasters between 1792 and 1806 before rapidly declining to just 16 million in 1807–1813, 11 million in 1814, and less than 9 million in later years. The shortage of Mexican silver had consequences for global trade. Britain's trade with India and China relied less on silver shipments and more on exports of merchandise, constituting an important change in the nature of economic relations between these states. The only region of the world that bucked the trend, and in fact experienced economic growth, was Southeast Asia, which was relatively unaffected by the Napoleonic Wars. While exports to Europe declined, Chinese and American merchants exploited this opportunity to profit in the spice trade, acquiring cloves, pepper, sugar, and coffee and shipping them to their home markets.[49]

Discussion of international trade would be incomplete without mentioning the wars' impact on Europe's traditional mercantilist practices in Asia. The Napoleonic Wars marked the end of the era of great European trading monopolies. The Dutch East India Company, which was still recovering from the impact of the Anglo-Dutch War of 1780–1784, ceased to exist in December 1799, and most of its possessions were subsequently occupied by Great Britain during the Napoleonic Wars. Meanwhile, the British East India Company also felt the effect of wartime conditions and lost its monopoly on trade with India in 1813.[50]

Neither should we forget that the Napoleonic Wars disrupted the Atlantic slave trade. With the Caribbean and Latin America in turmoil, it became increasingly more challenging to deliver slaves to colonies in those areas. Moreover, in February 1807, the British Parliament abolished the slave trade between Africa and British colonies and henceforth worked steadfastly to ensure that other countries followed suit. The Royal Navy's West Africa Squadron, established in 1808, regularly patrolled the African coastline, while British diplomats frequently used the lure of British subsidies to convince nations to end the slave trade. In 1810 an Anglo-Portuguese treaty compelled Portugal to restrict slavery, while the Anglo-Swedish treaty of 1813 did the same for Sweden. In 1814, by the Treaty of Paris, France agreed with Britain that the slave trade was "repugnant to the principles of natural justice" and agreed to abolish it in five years. That same year an Anglo-Netherlands treaty ended Dutch slaving. The United States put an end to the slave trade in 1807 but not to slavery itself, which survived until the Emancipation Proclamation in 1863.[51]

For the Allied powers, the maintenance of a stable political and international order was the paramount goal in the post-Napoleonic era. Peacetime nevertheless proved no less disruptive than wartime. During a quarter of a century of revolutionary turmoil and conquests Europe had experienced major political and economic reconstruction, and many elements of what constituted the ancien régime had been dissolved. Old social, political, and economic bonds had been loosened (in some cases completely severed), and a new society was in the process of formation. The downfall of the Napoleonic Empire, therefore, marked an abrupt reversal in this process, as the governing classes of the ancien régime had reclaimed their power. The victorious powers were genuinely concerned with the preservation of conservative regimes in Europe, an aspiration that was bolstered, at least in the short term, by the general exhaustion and war-weariness on the continent. In the streets of Paris in 1815 the cries of "Vive la paix!" reflected the general mood of the French public far better than "Vive les Bourbons!" The same can be said of the public in the rest of Europe, which suffered from war fatigue and economic chaos. For many Europeans, peace and order were worth having at any price.

The memories of the Revolution filled European leaders with a fear of popular ideologies and political movements that threatened to undermine the Viennese settlement. But they also came under immense pressure from the forces of economic and social change: industrialization, agricultural improvements, and the greater sophistication of economic enterprise, as well as improvements in transportation, communication and other areas, were transforming European societies and compelled political leaders to act. Therefore, we should not perceive them as myopic reactionaries who stubbornly refused to adjust. Even conservative governments in Austria and Russia understood the inevitability of change and in fact advocated reforms to remedy existing weaknesses in their own systems of government. However, they believed, in the words of a Russian emperor, that any and all changes should come from above rather than below. The process of reform had to be carried out in an orderly manner within the existing political and social framework. In practice, all governments struggled to reconcile their understanding of the need for change with a fear that changes might unleash popular forces that they would be unable to control, as happened in France in the 1790s.

Their efforts were complicated by the fact that the end of the Napoleonic Wars did not usher in a period of economic growth and prosperity. To the contrary, peace brought a postwar depression with a precipitous drop in the demand for manufactured goods and provisions, while the global climatic calamity caused some of the worst harvests in more than a century and resulted in food prices rising precipitously. The end of the Continental System was not followed by any serious attempt to revive open trade. Instead, a narrow economic nationalism triumphed, and European agriculture and industry suffered from the new tariff walls raised by European states. Prussia and Russia, for example, found their exports of grain and timber hindered by Britain's protective tariffs, including the Corn Law of 1815, which forbade the importation of cheaper foreign wheat. Meanwhile, prohibitive Russian and Austrian tariffs seriously affected the linen industry in Silesia, one of the chief manufacturing centers of Prussia. Napoleon's efforts to integrate manufacturing areas of the Rhineland and Westphalia within France's economic system meant that after the war local industries declined as France turned inward and imposed tariffs on imports.

———⚬⚬⚮⚬⚬———

The agricultural and manufacturing downturn in the post-Napoleonic era meant that there was little employment for the returning thousands of soldiers, while the condition of the poor remained near the point of desperation in most European countries. Unsurprisingly, these circumstances contributed to further agitation for individual freedom and written guarantees of rights, and forms of socialism that espoused democratic representation and equitable distribution of wealth. The post-Napoleonic unrest, therefore, was a manifestation of a larger struggle between forces of changes and tradition that helped create a modern Europe.

The political turmoil that the Napoleonic Wars unleashed continued to reverberate for decades to come. Major revolutions in 1820–1821, 1830, and 1848 were interspersed with numerous examples of smaller upheavals in 1819, 1822, 1825, 1832, 1834, 1839, and 1844, to mention just a few. In confronting these threats, European governments benefited from one important legacy of the Napoleonic Era: the war had swept aside many old administrative flaws and irregularities, so European governments now had more control over bureaucracy, law enforcement, and taxation. They thus were furnished with the apparatus with which to maintain power and initiate repressive measures. In 1819 the onset of political repression in much of Europe forced German governments, alarmed by the spread of liberalism, to impose the Carlsbad Decrees, which stifled political freedom. In Britain, abandonment of wartime taxes, continued industrialization (with its greater reliance on machines that contributed to high unemployment), and the general postwar economic downturn in Europe created one of the most volatile periods in the nation's history. Climatic calamity contributed to widespread unrest, which affected much of the country. In August 1819 this dissent reached its height when tens of thousands of demonstrators converged on St. Peter's Field outside Manchester, demanding not just bread but political reforms as well. The British government, like its continental counterparts, denounced such radical activity as unpatriotic and inspired by French "Jacobinism." It resorted to forceful action to suppress it. A peaceful demonstration at Manchester was violently dispersed, a move that the ruling elite welcomed as a victory against extremism but radicals denounced as the "Peterloo Massacre," a caustic reference to the British victory over Napoleon five years earlier. Following the example of continental powers, the British government suppressed radicalism throughout the 1820s, but uneven economic growth and prosperity continued to pose major challenges for years to come.[52]

The conservative ascendancy further gained momentum in 1820, when popular revolts threatened the Spanish and Neapolitan monarchies. European powers convened three congresses—Troppau (1820), Laibach (1821), and Verona (1822)—to confront these revolutionary challenges and relied upon the principles laid out at the Congress of Vienna to deal with them. Russia and Prussia supported Austrian interference in Naples and Piedmont, while France assisted the reactionary Bourbon monarchy in reclaiming its power in Spain. In 1825 it was Russia's turn to experience political unrest when a group of army officers exploited the death of Emperor Alexander to seek limited constitutional changes. The Decembrist Revolt lasted just a day before being crushed by Emperor Nicholas I's military. In France, Louis XVIII demonstrated pragmatism and intelligence in dealing with the revolutionary legacy and postwar challenges. Assisted by capable statesmen—Eli-Louis, duc de Decazes, and Armand-Emmanuel du Plessis de Richelieu, to name just a couple—he steered a middle course between ideological extremes, averting national bankruptcy and paying off a vast war indemnity. The fact this was accomplished while France was still occupied by a coalition force of 150,000 men may seem all the more astonishing, but the occupation left the French monarchy no choice except to undertake much-needed reforms to meet its financial obligations. The occupation played a crucial role in the post-Napoleonic economic and political reconstruction of France, which, needless to say, was achieved only after considerable public outcry from all the groups that had been affected by fiscal rigor and reform.[53] Louis XVIII's death and the ascent of his brother Charles X tilted the scales in favor of the reactionary party, whose missteps ultimately resulted in the revolution of 1830.

Of the post-Napoleonic revolutions, only those in Greece and South America proved to be successful, though for different reasons. The Greek Revolution was part of a succession of revolts by native ethnic peoples (largely

Slavic and Greek Orthodox) against Ottoman rule, but its causes, timing, and outcome were dependent as much on internal social and political factors within the Ottoman Empire as they were on broader developments in Europe. The French Revolution and the Napoleonic Wars shaped the intellectual and political context and contributed to the dissemination of the idea of national liberation and struggle against ancien régime monarchies. Unlike other anti-Ottoman uprisings, the Greek cause aroused widespread sympathy and support from European elites—including Lord Byron—who were inspired by classical Greek culture and history and eager to extend a helping hand. At the same time, the leaders of the European great powers were concerned by the implications of a revolt that violated the principles of legitimacy and balance as upheld at the Congress of Vienna. Rival powers felt tempted to intervene in Greece to protect their own interests. In the post-Napoleonic climate of conservatism and reaction, the great powers were initially loath to support the rebels' bid to topple legitimate Ottoman authority. However, in part because of their suspicion of each other's motives and in part because of their own motives, they became involved in the conflict on the side of the Greeks in 1827 and ensured the establishment of a completely autonomous Greek state in 1830. Russia was instrumental in this. In addition to long-standing ties with Christian populations of the Balkan peninsula, Russia had long desired to have freer access to the Mediterranean Sea. As historian Matthew Anderson pointed out, Russia's interest in the fate of the Ottoman Empire increased dramatically after the Napoleonic Wars. "The settlement and development of the fertile lands of the Black Sea steppe was bringing with it a spectacular growth in grain exports to western Europe. Odessa, by far the greatest center of this trade, was in the second decade of the nineteenth century the most rapidly growing port in the world. All this increased sharply for Russia the importance of free movement of her merchant ships through the Straits." By 1815 Russia had achieved the Ottoman concession of free passage for Russian merchant ships, which within five years resulted in a dramatic increase in Russian grain exports through the Black Sea ports. However, the Ottoman decision in the 1820s to restrict Russian movements through the straits caused considerable anxiety in Russian political and economic circles. Russia's early attempts at industrialization had resulted in the establishment of several thousand factories that, as Peter Hopkirk explained, "were becoming desperate for new markets."[54]

The Greek crisis marked the first major change in the map of Europe since the end of the Napoleonic Wars. It severely tested the Congress of Vienna settlement because it represented both a threat and an opportunity for European powers. The major powers did not want to be seen as supporting rebellion but also understood that there was an opportunity to project more power into the region. They took a more active role in the conflict and used Greek factions, explicitly aligned with one or another foreign side, to protect their own interests. The aftermath of the war hardly allayed such mutual jealousies, for in the end the Kingdom of Greece had a Bavarian monarch, French military advisors, and British administrators at the helm of government. As for Russia, the Treaties of Adrianople (1829) and Hünkar Iskelesi (1833) explicitly reaffirmed Russian privileges in the Danubian principalities and gave Russian merchant ships free navigation in the Ottoman Empire. The Greek Revolution exposed the weakness of the Ottoman Empire and set a precedent of great power intervention, protection, and guarantee of fledgling Balkan states; in 1829, with Russia defeating the sultan's forces, the European capitals were anticipating the collapse of the Ottoman Empire, and French foreign minister Jules de Polignac even approached Russia to discuss the partition of Ottoman territory. The Ottoman defeat thus aroused the ambitions of other ethnic groups, who relied on the historical-cultural justifications used for Greek secession as a template for their own national movements.[55]

Even more significant were events in South America, where, as we have seen, the first phase of the wars of independence ended in 1815. It had produced mixed results. All of the independence movements had been effectively stifled except those in Buenos Aires and Paraguay. Nevertheless, there were clear signs that Spanish royal authority was tottering. The downfall of the Napoleonic France did not mean an immediate end to the insurrections, despite what Spanish royalists had hoped. José Fernando de Abascal, the viceroy of Peru, complained in the fall of 1815 that despite the Allied victory over the "Misanthrope of Corsica," there still remained an acute threat to Spanish royal authority from "the harmful and false news [*falsas noticias*] with which [Napoleon's] vile henchmen attempt to transform the world."[56] At the helm of the largest political jurisdiction in South America, Abascal was well aware that the return of King Ferdinand VII of Spain and his insistence on restoration of the royal prerogatives that had been constrained by the Constitution of 1812 had exacerbated tensions between the royal metropole and its American colonies. Having experienced representative government, even if on a rather limited scale, creoles from Mexico to Chile had little interest in returning to absolute rule. In his effort to maintain "unity" between the colonies and Spain, Abascal resorted to a wide range of measures, from crushing insurgencies to running an effective propaganda campaign to counter Napoleonic "False news."[57] The revolutionary spirit, however, festered for years to come. The history of the Spanish colonies in the post-Napoleonic era is one of internal turmoil, bloodshed, and repression. The road to independence was long and difficult. In New Spain, the royalists had gained the upper hand, though two main guerrilla groups, led by Guadalupe Victoria in Puebla and Vicente Guerrero in Oaxaca, continued to operate beyond 1815. A congress of *criollos* declared their independence in September 1821 and formed the First Mexican Empire under Agustín de Iturbide the following year. This was the first independent postcolonial state in Mexico and the only Spanish colony to establish a monarchy after independence. However, the empire proved to be short-lived. In 1823 Mexico became a republic and embraced the right of self-determination, paving the way for the formation of the United Provinces of Central America, a federal republic modeled after the United States that brought together the states of Guatemala, Honduras, El Salvador, Costa Rica, and Nicaragua between 1823 and 1840. In New Granada and Venezuela, the republican patriots, under Simón Bolívar, Francisco de Paula Santander, Santiago Mariño, and others, lingered in the vast Orinoco River basin and along the Caribbean coast, often with material aid coming from Haiti. After several unsuccessful attempts to regain Caracas, Bolívar crossed the Andes to liberate Colombia before proceeding to Venezuela. The republicans defeated Spanish royalists at the Battle of Boyacá (August 7, 1819) and soon thereafter captured the Colombian capital, Bogotá. With Colombia secured, Bolívar moved on to defeat the royalists at the Battle of Carabobo in June 1821 and declared the independence of the Republic of Gran Colombia, which united Venezuela and Colombia. Bolívar supported republicans in Ecuador, where the royalists suffered a major setback at the Battle of Pichincha (May 24, 1822). On July 13, 1822, Ecuador was incorporated into Gran Colombia, which survived for another eight years. The royalists exercised strong authority in Chile, but across the Andes the Patriots remained in control of the United Provinces in the Río de La Plata (modern Argentina).

Few expected the independence movement to recover from the heavy blows it had sustained in 1812–1815. Yet in one of the greatest feats of the wars of independence, San Martín's Argentinian army crossed the Andes, joined the Chilean *criollos* under Bernardo O'Higgins, and defeated the royalists at the Battle of Chacabuco on February 12, 1817. A year later O'Higgins declared Chilean independence, while San Martín, aided by thousands of Chilean troops and a large contingent of British soldiers who had joined the revolution after the end of the Napoleonic Wars, continued his campaign northward to liberate Peru. Although Peruvian independence was proclaimed in December 1820, it would be another six years before the last royalist stronghold fell and the republicans consolidated their power.

Compared to Spanish America, Brazil's road to independence was relatively uneventful. King João VI, who had fled Portugal in 1807, stayed in Brazil for six years after the end of Napoleonic Wars. In 1816 he elevated the colony to the level of a kingdom and granted it considerable concessions. When João VI returned to Europe in July 1821 to deal with a liberal revolution in Lisbon, his son, Dom Pedro, stayed in Brazil as regent. Relations between the metropole and colony quickly deteriorated as the Portuguese Cortes (representative assembly) sought to restore Brazil's original colonial status. Pedro, who had spent much of his life in Rio de Janeiro, refused the Cortes's demand that he return to Portugal and instead declared Brazil's independence on September 7, 1822. In his famous "Grito do Ipiranga" (Cry of Ipiranga), Pedro removed Portuguese insignia from his uniform and declared, "Independence or death!" The resulting war between the newly established Brazilian army, which was supported by British veterans of the Napoleonic Wars, and Portuguese forces resulted in the former's victory and compelled Portugal to formally recognize Brazil's independence in 1825.

The turmoil in Latin America illuminated a crucial issue of the post-Vienna era—namely, the European powers' ability to intervene in colonial affairs and reverse the outcome of ongoing rebellions across the Atlantic. Considering the distances involved and its naval power, Britain played a vital role in this process. The British government was dismayed by the reactionary policies in Europe, where progressives were persecuted and imprisoned; in Spain, many of them were executed in gruesome fashion. Little surprise then that Britain refused to participate in such practices and increasingly distanced itself from continental powers. In 1825 Britain recognized the independence of several American republics: Mexico, Colombia, and Argentina. Eager to stress the morality and political soundness of his policy, Britain's new foreign secretary, George Canning, famously claimed that he "called the New World into existence to redress the balance of the Old."[58] But he also understood that if Spanish America was allowed to become a possession of the Bourbon crown, British trading opportunities would inevitably be limited and restricted.

When it came to the Western Hemisphere, the policy of the United States was, in general, quite similar to that of Britain, meaning aimed at promoting American economic interests and preventing European meddling in the region. Such aspirations were bolstered by improving Anglo-American relations. After the War of 1812, John Quincy Adams, the US secretary of state from 1817 to 1825, made the most of Britain's desire to seek friendlier relations with the US and gain access to American cotton and other supplies in exchange for manufactured goods and investment capital. In a sign of greater

Anglo-American cooperation, the Rush-Bagot Agreement of 1817 limited naval armaments on the Great Lakes and effectively demilitarized the US-Canada border. The subsequent Anglo-American Accords of 1818 resolved several issues left hanging after the War of 1812, with Britain recognizing American fishing rights off the Canadian coastlines, agreeing to the joint occupation of the Oregon Territory, and setting the boundary of the Louisiana Territory abutting Canada at the 49th parallel.

The northern borderlands secured, the United States flexed its muscles in the south. Given that Spain was still struggling to recover from the impact of the Napoleonic Wars and entangled in the independence movements in South America, many in the United States thought that the time was ripe for the US expansion in Florida and on the Pacific. Men such as General Andrew Jackson believed that Spanish control of Florida posed an unacceptable threat to the security of the southern US regions and insisted on preemptive occupation of Spanish territory. In the spring of 1818 Jackson led an invasion of Spanish Florida, ostensibly to destroy the encampments of the Native American tribes (the Seminoles) who straddled the Spanish-American border and occasionally raided neighboring Georgia. Jackson also viewed invasion as an opportunity to advance American claims to Florida. "Let it be signified to me through any channel," he wrote to President Monroe, "that the possession of the Floridas would be desirable to the United States, and in sixty days it will be accomplished."[59] Although President Monroe censured Jackson for exceeding his orders and had the expedition recalled, Secretary of State Adams exploited the new reality on the grounds. The invasion of Florida made it apparent that Spain, weakened by the Napoleonic Wars, did not have the means to retaliate against the United States. So Adams threatened and cajoled the Spanish officials into making concessions. In the Adams–Onís Treaty of 1819, Spain yielded to American threats, recognizing the prior American seizures of West Florida and ceding East Florida. Furthermore, Adams secured American control over the vast territory in the west, as the treaty drew the new boundary between the Louisiana Territory and the Spanish Southwest and had Spain relinquishing all of its claims to the Pacific Northwest.[60]

Encouraged by these achievements, the US government looked beyond its immediate borders. Central to the American success was Britain's refusal to intervene or support Spain in its confrontation with the Americans; even Jackson's decision to execute two British subjects during the occupation of Florida made no dent in official British policy, which was focused on retaining close economic ties with the United States. Moreover, Britain and the United States agreed that Spain's reconquest of colonies would have been detrimental to their economic and political interests and that it was of far greater advantage for them to have a multiplicity of fledgling republics instead of a single domain in the hands of a European power. Recognizing this common interest, the British foreign secretary, Canning, proposed in August 1823 that the two countries issue a joint statement opposing any European attempt to restore colonial authority in the Western Hemisphere. The Monroe administration rejected the offer because it came with a string attached: a pledge not to annex any former Spanish territory. Instead, in December 1823 President Monroe delivered his annual State of the Union message, which contained a memorable passage on the American territorial interests in the Western Hemisphere.

Better known as the Monroe Doctrine, this document made two broad and bold claims. First, it challenged Russian expansion along the Pacific Coast from Alaska to California and asserted that the "American continents...are henceforth not be considered as subject to future colonization by any European power." The second claim dealt with European interventions in Western hemisphere. Referring to the possibility of European powers acting against the new Spanish American republics, Monroe issued a warning. "We owe it...to candor, and to amicable relations existing between the United States and those powers, to declare that we should consider any attempt on their part to extend their political system to any portion of this hemisphere as dangerous to our peace and security."[61] The United States had assumed a special position as the guardian of the New World liberties, although it was the threat of British sea power rather than the words of an American president that prevented European interventions in Latin America.

———◦◦◦❈◦◦◦———

The Napoleonic Wars cast a long shadow over the nineteenth century. They had shaken the traditional way of life and the legitimacy of institutions such as monarchy, aristocracy, and slavery. They also left many issues unsolved. Hence, succeeding generations struggled over the legacies of conservatism and liberalism, centralization and modernization, republicanism and monarchism, industrialization and radicalism. In his exile on St. Helena, Napoleon nurtured a political legend that quickly evolved into a powerful myth of a benevolent emperor who was celebrated and idealized by the descendants of the very people who fought against him.[62] "During his life," remarked French writer François-René de Chateaubriand about the fallen emperor, "the world slipped from his grasp, but in death he possesses it." The Napoleonic heritage and Bonapartism—the political ideology centered on a strong popular national leader—were of vital importance in molding contemporary France as well as Europe.

The Napoleonic Wars were above all a European conflict, but they shaped Europe's relationship with the rest of the world. This conflict both compelled and encouraged European states to undergo a painful process of reform and modernization, which changed the balance of forces between different parts of the globe. For much of its history Europe lagged behind the more advanced and sophisticated civilizations in China and the Islamic world. And yet by the end of the Napoleonic Wars, European superiority in military matters, industrial development, and technological strength over the rest of the world was pronounced. This was the start of the Great Divergence, and the magnitude of this transformation would become ever clearer as the nineteenth century progressed.

NOTES

Prelim

1. Henry Dundas to Richard Wellesley, October 31, 1799, in "Contents of Mr. Dundas's Letters to the Marquis Wellesley...Governor-General of India, 1798–1800," NLS, MS.1062, 53.
2. Charles J. Esdaile, *Napoleon's Wars: An International History, 1803–1815* (New York: Viking, 2008), xiv–xv.
3. "After long and careful thought and study," observed one eminent British historian, "I have come to the conclusion that the West Indian campaigns [alone], both to Windward and Leeward [in 1794–1801], cost England in army and navy little fewer than 100,000 men, about one half of them dead, the remainder permanently unfit for service." John William Fortescue, *A History of the British Army* (London: Macmillan, 1906), IV, part I, 565.
4. Owen Connelly, *The French Revolution and Napoleonic Era* (Orlando, FL: Harcourt, 2000), 361.

Chapter 1

1. Budget Speech of February 17, 1792, in *The Speeches of the Right Honourable William Pitt in the House of Commons* (London: Longman, Hurst, Rees and Orne, 1806), II:36.
2. For classic works on the Atlantic revolutions, see Robert R. Palmer, *The Age of the Democratic Revolution: A Political History of Europe and America, 1760–1800*, 2 vols. (Princeton, NJ: Princeton University Press, 1959–1964); Jacques Léon Godechot, *La Grande Nation: L'expansion révolutionnaire de la France dans le monde de 1789 à 1799* (Paris: Aubier, 1956). Also see Pierre Serna, "Introduction—L'Europe une idée nouvelle à la fin du XVIIIe siècle?" in "Dire et faire l'Europe à la fin du XVIIIe siècle," ed. Pierre Serna, special issue, *La Révolution française* 2011, no. 4 (2011), available at http://lrf.revues.org/252.

3. See Jeremy Adelman, "An Age of Imperial Revolutions," *American Historical Review* 113 (2008): 319–40; David Ermitage and Sanjay Subrahmanyam, eds., *The Age of Revolutions in Global Context, c. 1760–1840* (New York: Palgrave Macmillan, 2010); Alan Forrest and Matthias Middell, eds., *The Routledge Companion to the French Revolution in World History* (London: Routledge, 2016); Wim Klooster, *Revolutions in the Atlantic World: A Comparative History* (New York: New York University Press, 2009); Christopher Bayly, "The 'Revolutionary Age' in the Wider World, c. 1790–1830," in *War, Empire, and Slavery, 1770–1830*, ed. Richard Bessel, Nicholas Guyatt, and Jane Rendall (Basingstoke: Palgrave Macmillan, 2010), 21–43.

4. See Bailey Stone, *The Genesis of the French Revolution: A Global-Historical Interpretation* (Cambridge: Cambridge University Press, 1994); Christopher Bayly, *The Birth of the Modern World, 1780–1914: Global Connections and Comparisons* (Malden, MA: Wiley-Blackwell, 2004); Lynn Hunt, "The French Revolution in Global Context," in *The Age of Revolutions in Global Context, c. 1760–1840*, ed. David Ermitage and Sanjay Subrahmanyam (New York: Palgrave Macmillan, 2010), 20–36.

5. The Trans-Atlantic Slave Trade Database, https://www.slavevoyages.org/assessment/estimates (accessed July 30, 2019).

6. Philippe Haudrère, *La compagnie française des Indes au XVIIIe siècle 1719–1795* (Paris: Librairie de l'Inde, 1989), 4:1, 215.

7. Richard Drayton, "The Globalization of France: Provincial Cities and French Expansion, c. 1500–1800," *History of European Ideas* 34 (2008): 424–30; Paul Butel, "France, the Antilles, and Europe in the Seventeenth and Eighteenth Centuries," in *The Rise of Merchant Empires: Long Distance Trade in the Early Modern World, 1350–1750*, ed. James D. Tracy (Cambridge: Cambridge University Press, 1993), 153–73.

8. See Louis Dermigny, "Circuits de l'argent et milieux d'affaires au XVIII siècle," *Revue historique* 212 (1954): 239–78; Louis Dermigny, "La France à la fin de l'ancien régime: Une carte monétaire," *Annales: Économies, sociétés, civilizations* 10, no. 4 (December 1955): 480–93; Stanley J. Stein and Barbara H. Stein, *Silver, Trade, and War: Spain and America in the Making of Early Modern Europe* (Baltimore: John Hopkins University Press, 2000), 52–53, 130–31, 143; Carlos Marichal, *Bankruptcy of Empire: Mexican Silver and the Wars Between Spain, Britain, and France, 1760–1810* (New York: Cambridge University Press, 2007).

9. Stanley J. Stein and Barbara H. Stein, *Apogee of Empire: Spain and New Spain in the Age of Charles III, 1759–1789* (Baltimore: John Hopkins University Press, 2003), 305–37; Guillaume Daudin, *Commerce et prospérité: La France au XVIIIe siècle* (Paris: Presses l'université Paris-Sorbonne, 2005), 235–37.

10. For a recent discussion, see Charles Walton, "The Fall from Eden: The Free Trade Origins of the French Revolution," in *The French Revolution in Global*

Perspective, ed. Suzanne Desan, Lynn Hunt, and William Max Nelson (Ithaca, NY: Cornell University Press, 2013), 44–56. Also see Marie Donaghay, "The Ghosts of Ruined Ships: The Commercial Treaty of 1786 and the Lessons of the Past," *CRE* 10 (1981): 111–18.

11. See Jules Conan, *La dernière compagnie française des Indes, 1715–75* (Paris: Marcel Rivière, 1942).

12. See Marc Vigié and Muriel Vigié, *L'herbe à nicot: Amateurs de tabac, Fermiers généraux et contrebandiers sous l'Ancien Régime* (Paris: Fayard, 1989); Jacob Price, *France and the Chesapeake: A History of the French Tobacco Monopoly, 1764–1791, and of Its Relationship to the British and American Tobacco Trades*, 2 vols. (Ann Arbor: University of Michigan Press, 1973); Edward Depitre, *La toile peinte en France au XVIIe et au XVIIIe siècles: Industrie, commerce, prohibitions* (Paris: M. Rivière, 1912).

13. Gary B. McCollim, *Louis XIV's Assault on Privilege: Nicolas Desmaretz and the Tax on Wealth* (Rochester, NY: University of Rochester Press, 2012), 14–49.

14. Michael Kwass, "The First War on Drugs: Tobacco Trafficking, Criminality, and the Fiscal State in Eighteenth-Century France," in *The Hidden History of Crime, Corruption, and States*, ed. Renate Bridenthal (Oxford: Berghahn Books, 2013), 76–97.

15. See Jean Nicolas, *La rébellion française: Mouvements populaires et conscience sociale, 1661–89* (Paris: Seuil, 2002); Michael Kwass, "The Global Underground: Smuggling, Rebellion, and the Origins of the French Revolution," in *The French Revolution in Global Perspective*, ed. Suzanne Desan, Lynn Hunt, and William Max Nelson (Ithaca, NY: Cornell University Press, 2013), 22.

16. For more details, see Joël Félix, "The Economy," in *Old Regime France, 1648–88*, ed. William Doyle (Oxford: Oxford University Press, 2001), 33–35; Michael Kwass, *Privilege and the Politics of Taxation in Eighteenth-Century France: Liberté, Égalité, Fiscalité* (Cambridge: Cambridge University Press, 2000).

17. Jan deVries, *The Economy of Europe in an Age of Crisis, 1600–50* (Cambridge: Cambridge University Press, 1976), 203; Richard Dale, *The First Crash: Lessons from the South Sea Bubble* (Princeton, NJ: Princeton University Press, 2004), 56.

18. Frank W. Brecher, *Losing a Continent: France's North American Policy, 1753–63* (Westport, CT: Greenwood, 1998), 44–50.

19. For a concise discussion, see Félix, "The Economy," 31–39.

20. Michel Morineau, "Budgets de l'État et gestion des finances royales en France au dix-huitième siècle," in *Revue historique* 536 (1980): 289–36; Félix, "The Economy," 36–41; Claude H. Van Tyne, "French Aid Before the Alliance of 1778," *American Historical Review* 31 (1925): 20–40; James C. Riley, "French Finances, 1727–1768," *Journal of Modern History* 59, no. 2 (June 1987): 209–43.

21. Guillaume Daudin, "Profitability of Slave and Long Distance Trading in Context: The Case of Eighteenth-Century France," *Journal of Economic History* 61, no. 1 (2004): 144–71.

22. François R. Velde and David R. Weir, "The Financial Market and Government Debt Policy in France, 1746–1793," *Journal of Economic History* 52, no. 1 (1992): 1–39.

23. George V. Taylor, "The Paris Bourse on the Eve of the Revolution, 1781–1789," *American Historical Review* 67, no. 4 (1962): 951–77.

24. J. Russell Major, *From Renaissance Monarchy to Absolute Monarchy: French Kings, Nobles, and Estates* (Baltimore: Johns Hopkins University Press, 1994); Donna Bohanan, *Crown and Nobility in Early Modern France* (New York: Palgrave, 2001); Julian Swann, *Provincial Power and Absolute Monarchy: The Estates General of Burgundy, 1661–90* (Cambridge: Cambridge University Press, 2003), 230–99. For details, see John J. Hurt, *Louis XIV and the Parlements: The Assertion of Royal Authority* (Manchester: Manchester University Press, 2004).

25. Julian Swann, *Politics and the Parlement of Paris Under Louis XV, 1754–74* (Cambridge: Cambridge University Press, 1995), 1–26, 45–86.

26. For details, see John McManners, *Church and Society in Eighteenth-Century France* (Oxford: Clarendon Press, 1998); Dale K. Van Kley, *The Religious Origins of the French Revolution: From Calvin to the Civil Constitution, 1560–91* (New Haven, CT: Yale University Press, 1996); Timothy Tackett, *Religion, Revolution, and Regional Culture in Eighteenth-Century France: The Ecclesiastical Oath of 1791* (Princeton, NJ: Princeton University Press, 1986); Guy Chaussinand-Nogaret, *The French Nobility in the Eighteenth Century: From Feudalism to Enlightenment* (Cambridge: Cambridge University Press, 1995); Jay M. Smith, *The French Nobility in the Eighteenth Century: Reassessments and New Approaches* (University Park: Pennsylvania State University Press, 2006).

27. William Doyle, *Origins of the French Revolution* (New York: Oxford University Press, 1980), 21.

28. George Rudé, *Revolutionary Europe, 1783–15* (New York: Harper Torchbooks, 1966), 74.

29. Jean-Jacques Rousseau, *The Social Contract* (New York: Hafner, 1947), 31.

30. For an excellent discussion, see Part Three, "The Products of the Press," in *Revolution in Print: The Press in France, 1775–1800*, ed. Robert Darnton and Daniel Roche (Berkeley: University of California Press, 1989), 141–90.

31. On the long- and short-term impacts of the American Revolution on France, see David Andress, "Atlantic Entanglements: Comparing the French and American Revolutions," in *The Routledge Companion to the French Revolution in World History*, ed. Alan Forrest and Matthias Middell (London: Routledge, 2016), 159–74.

32. For a good discussion, see Lynn Hunt, *Inventing Human Rights: A History* (London: W. W. Norton, 2007), 15–34.

33. For a concise discussion, see John Hardman, *French Politics, 1774–89: From the Accession of Louis XVI to the Fall of the Bastille* (London: Longman, 1995). A brief note should be made of the French royal family itself. King Louis XVI, who ascended the throne in 1774, was an intelligent, kindhearted, and generous

man, but he struggled to contain the political turmoil that demanded a man of firmer will and energy. His wife, Marie Antoinette, who exerted a strong influence over the king, was a beautiful and vivacious woman whose Austrian origin proved to be an important factor in shaping contemporary attitudes toward her. Although allied since 1756, France and Austria were historical enemies, and the French public was unsympathetic to the young Austrian archduchess when she wed the heir to the French throne. Her lavish lifestyle, exaggerated by pamphleteers, and unfounded rumors about her sexual escapades created a deeply negative impression of the queen and further damaged the prestige of the monarchy among the French public. For details, see John Hardman, *The Life of Louis XVI* (New Haven, CT: Yale University Press, 2016); Antonia Fraser, *Marie Antoinette: The Journey* (New York: Doubleday, 2001).

34. For details, see Donald Greer, *The Incidence of the Emigration During the French Revolution* (Cambridge, MA: Harvard University Press, 1951).

35. See Timothy Tacket, *When the King Took Flight* (Cambridge, MA: Harvard University Press, 2003).

36. "Réflexions du Prince Kaunitz sur les prétendus dangers de contagion, dont la nouvelle constitution française menace tous les autres États souverains de l'Europe," November 1791, in Alfred Ritter von Vivenot, ed., *Quellen zur Geschichte der deutschen Kaiserpolitik Österreichs während der französischen Revolution 1790–1801* (Vienna: Wilhelm Braumüller, 1879), I:285–86; Charles de Larivière, *Catherine la Grande d'après sa correspondance: Catherine II et la révolution française d'après de nouveaux documents* (Paris: H. Le Soudier, 1895), 363.

37. *Padua Circular*, July 5, 1791, accessed at http://chnm.gmu.edu/revolution/d/420.

38. Austro-Prussian Declaration, August 27, 1791, in Vivenot, ed., *Quellen zur Geschichte*, I:233–43, 255.

39. Paul W. Schroeder, *The Transformation of European Politics, 1763–48* (New York: Oxford University Press, 1994), 87–91. For a more in-depth look at the causes of war, see Timothy C. W. Blanning, *The Origins of the French Revolutionary Wars* (London: Longman, 1986); John Harold Clapham, *The Cause of the War of 1792* (Cambridge: Cambridge University Press, 1899).

40. For details, see Linda Frey and Marsha Frey, "'The Reign of Charlatans Is Over': The French Revolutionary Attack on Diplomatic Practice," *Journal of Modern History* 65 (1993): 706–44; Marc Bouloiseau, "L'organisation de l'Europe selon Brissot et les Girondins, à la fin de 1792," *Annales Historiques de la Révolution Française* 57 (1985): 290–94; Sylvia Neely, "The Uses of Power: Lafayette and Brissot in 1792," *Proceedings of the Western Society for French History* 34 (2006): 99–114.

41. Jacques-Pierre Brissot's speech of December 16, 1791, in Alphonse de Lamartine, *Histoire des Girondins* (Paris: Furne, 1847), II:58. Also see Hippolyte Adolphe Taine, *The French Revolution* (New York: Henry Holt, 1881), II:101;

Antonino de Francesco, "The American Origins of the French Revolutionary War," in *Republics at War, 1776–40: Revolutions, Conflicts, Geopolitics in Europe and the Atlantic World*, ed. Pierre Serna, Antonino de Francesco, and Judith A. Miller (New York: Palgrave Macmillan, 2013), 27–45.

42. *Le Patriote Français*, no. 857, December 15, 1791, 689. Digital version of the periodical accessible at http://gallica.bnf.fr/ark:/12148/cb32834106z/date.

43. Jacques-Pierre Brissot, *Second discours de J. P. Brissot, député, sur la néccéssite de faire la guerre aux princes allemands, prononcé à la société dans le séance du vendredi 30 December 1791* (Paris: Sociéte des Amis de la Constitution, 1791), http://books.google.com/books?id=EUtZAAAAcAAJ.

44. *Procès-Verbal de l'Assemblée nationale* (Paris: L'imprimerie nationale, 1792), VII:336. For an excellent discussion of the context in which this declaration was made, see William Doyle, *The Oxford History of the French Revolution* (Oxford: Oxford University Press, 1990), 159–84; Timothy C. W. Blanning, *The Origins of the French Revolutionary Wars* (Harlow: Longman, 1986): 97–99; John Hardman, "The Real and Imagined Conspiracies of Louis XVI," in *Conspiracy in the French Revolution*, ed. Peter Robert Campbell, Thomas E. Kaiser, and Marisa Linton (New York: Palgrave, 2007), 63–84.

45. Peter Paret, "Napoleon and the Revolution in War," in *Makers of Modern Strategy: From Machiavelli to the Nuclear Age*, ed. Peter Paret (Princeton, NJ: Princeton University Press, 1986), 124.

46. See Howard Rosen, "The Système Gribeauval: A Study of Technological Development and Institutional Change in Eighteenth Century France," Ph.D. dissertation, University of Chicago, 1981; Jonathan Abel, *Guibert: Father of Napoleon's Grande Armée* (Norman: University of Oklahoma Press, 2016).

47. Karl von Clausewitz, *On War*, ed. and trans. Michael Howard and Peter Paret (Princeton, NJ: Princeton University Press, 1976), 592, 609–10.

48. Annie Crépin, "The Army of the Republic: New Warfare and a New Army," in *Republics at War: Revolutions, Conflicts, Geopolitics in Europe and the Atlantic World*, ed. Pierre Serna, Antonino de Francesco, and Judith A. Miller (New York: Palgrave Macmillan, 2013), 131–48.

49. See speeches cited in Stephen M. Walt, *Revolution and War* (Ithaca, NY: Cornell University Press, 1997), 46–100.

Chapter 2

1. For a concise and insightful overview, see Jeremy Black, *European International Relations, 1648–1815* (New York: Palgrave, 2002).

2. See Stuart J. Kaufman, Richard Little, and William C. Wohlforth, *The Balance of Power in World History* (Basingstoke: Palgrave Macmillan, 2007).

3. Between 1700 and 1789 there were sixteen major conflicts involving European powers, with just thirty-three years of peace when no European power was at war on the continent.

4. George Liska, *Quest for Equilibrium: America and the Balance of Power on land and Sea* (Baltimore: John Hopkins University Press, 1977), 56.

5. Timothy C. W. Blanning, *The Origins of the French Revolutionary Wars* (London: Longman, 1986), 37.

6. There have been several attempts at classifying European states. In his seminal work on the revolutionary era, R. R. Palmer uses a different threefold classification: an eastern zone dominated by Russia, Austria, and the Ottomans; a middle zone with the smaller Italian and German states, as well as Switzerland; and to the north and west, an outer ring of nascent national states, including Sweden, Denmark, Prussia, Holland, Britain, France, Spain, and Portugal. See *The Age of the Democratic Revolution*, vol. 1, *The Challenge* (Princeton, NJ: Princeton University Press, 1959), 27–54. On the other hand, French historians Roland Mousnier and Ernest Labrousse placed European states into five groups: western (Britain, Holland, and France), southern (Spain, Portugal, and Italy), eastern (Russia, Poland, and the Ottoman Empire), central (Switzerland, the Holy Roman Empire, Austria, and Prussia), and northern (Denmark-Norway and Sweden). See *Le XVIIIe siècle; révolution intellectuelle technique et politique (1715–15)* (Paris: Presses universitaires de France, 1953).

7. During the Seven Years' War (1756–63) Prussia fought one of the greatest coalitions ever seen in Europe—Austria, France, Russia, Sweden, and most of the German states of the Holy Roman Empire—and survived intact.

8. For details, see Christopher M. Clark, *Iron Kingdom: The Rise and Downfall of Prussia, 1600–47* (Cambridge, MA: Belknap Press of Harvard University Press, 2006), ch. 9; Willy Real, *Von Potsdam nach Basel; Studien zur Geschichte der Beziehungen Preussens zu den europäischen Mächten vom Regierungsantritt Friedrich Wilhelms II. bis zum Abschluss des Friedens von Basel, 1786–95* (Basel: Helbing & Lichtenhahn, 1958).

9. For a concise survey, see Charles W. Ingrao, *The Habsburg Monarchy, 1618–15* (Cambridge: Cambridge University Press, 2000), 105–77.

10. Ernst Wangermann, "Preussen und die revolutionären Bewegungen in Ungarn und den österreichischen Niederlanden zur Zeit der französischen Revolution," in *Preussen und die revolutionäre Herausforderung seit 1789*, ed. Otto Büsch and Monika Neugebauer-Wölk (Berlin: Walter de Gruyter, 1991), 22–85.

11. "Much as I had read and heard of the commerce, wealth and magnificence of [Bordeaux]," wrote British traveler Arthur Young, "they greatly surpassed my expectations." See *Travels in France During the Years 1787, 1788 and 1789* (Cambridge: Cambridge University Press, 1929), 58.

12. For challenges Spain faced in the late eighteenth century, see Stanley J. Stein and Barbara H. Stein, *Apogee of Empire: Spain and New Spain in the Age of Charles III, 1759–89* (Baltimore, MD: Johns Hopkins University Press, 2003).

13. For a good overview of France in the eighteenth century, see Colin Jones, *The Great Nation: France from Louis XV to Napoleon* (New York: Penguin Books, 2003).

14. James S. Pritchard, *In Search of Empire: The French in the Americas, 1670–30* (Cambridge: Cambridge University Press, 2004).

15. Orville Theodore Murphy, *The Diplomatic Retreat of France and Public Opinion on the Eve of the French Revolution, 1783–89* (Washington, DC: Catholic University of America Press, 1998). For a concise and insightful discussion, see Jeremy Black, *France from Louis XIV to Napoleon: The Fate of Great Empire* (London: University College London Press, 1999), 128–48; Hamish M. Scott, *The Birth of a Great Power System, 1740–15* (London: Pearson Longman, 2006), 143–236.

16. Henri Legohérel, *Les trésoriers généraux de la Marine, 1517–88* (Paris: Éditions Cujas, 1965), 350–55.

17. For an interesting discussion of the notion of "British empire," see Eliga H. Gould, "The Empire That Britain Kept," in *The Oxford Handbook of the American Revolution*, ed. Edward G. Gray and Jane Kamensky (Oxford: Oxford University Press, 2013), 465–82.

18. For an excellent overview, see P. J. Marshall, ed., *Oxford History of the British Empire*, vol. 2, *The Eighteenth Century* (Oxford: Oxford University Press, 1998). For a revisionist take on the role of coal, see Gregory Clark and David Jacks, "Coal and the Industrial Revolution, 1700–1869," *European Review of Economic History* 11 (2007): 39–72. I am grateful to Prof. Michael Leggiere for turning my attention to this study.

19. Nicholas Riasanovsky and Mark D. Steinberg, *A History of Russia* (Oxford: Oxford University Press, 2011), 262–63, 305–6.

20. John A. Garraty and Peter Gay, *The Columbia History of the World* (New York: Harper & Row, 1972), 785.

21. For an overview of the Holy Roman Empire and its institutions, see Peter H. Wilson, *The Holy Roman Empire, 1495–1806* (New York: St. Martin's Press, 1999); John Gagliardo, *Reich and Nation: The Holy Roman Empire as Idea and Reality, 1763–1806* (Bloomington: Indiana University Press, 1980).

22. Voltaire, *Essai sur l'histoire generale et sur les moeurs et l'esprit des nations*, ed. M. Beuchot (Paris: Lefèvre, 1829), II:238.

23. For details, see Peter Wilson, *Heart of Europe: A History of the Holy Roman Empire* (Cambridge, MA: Belknap Press of Harvard University Press, 2016).

24. For example, there was a considerable Swiss presence in the French army, where the Swiss numbered between 10,000 and 20,000 men for much of the eighteenth century. Some 10,000 Swiss troops served in the Spanish army in the 1790s. There were also mercenary Swiss units serving under the British banners. See René Chartrand, *Louis XV's Army: Foreign Troops* (Oxford: Osprey, 1998); René Chartrand, *Spanish Army of the Napoleonic Wars*, vol. 1, *1793–1808* (Oxford: Osprey, 1998); René Chartrand, *Émigré and Foreign Troops in British Service*, vol. 2, *1803–15* (Oxford: Osprey, 2000); John McCormack, *One Million Mercenaries: Swiss Soldiers in the Armies of the World* (London: Leo Cooper, 1993), 125–61.

25. Jeremy Black, *Britain as a Military Power, 1688–15* (London: Routledge, 1999), 221.

26. Theda Skocpol, *States and Social Revolutions: A Comparative Analysis of France, Russia, and China* (Cambridge: Cambridge University Press, 1979), 60–61.

27. For an insightful discussion, see Virginia H. Aksan, *Ottoman Wars, 1700–70: An Empire Besieged* (New York: Pearson, 2007); Stanford J. Shaw, *History of the Ottoman Empire and Modern Turkey* (Cambridge: Cambridge University Press, 1976), I:217–76; Brian Davies, *Empire and Military Revolution in Eastern Europe; Russia's Turkish Wars in the Eighteenth Century* (London: Continuum, 2011), esp. 180–84. For the Ottoman role in the Seven Years' War, see Virginia H. Aksan, "The Ottoman Absence from the Battlefield of the Seven Years' War," in *The Seven Years' War: Global Views*, ed. Mark Danley and Patrick Speelman (Leiden: Brill, 2012), 165–90.

28. Isabel de Madariaga, "The Secret Austro-Russian Treaty of 1781," *Slavonic and East European Review* 38, no. 90 (1959): 114–45. The secret treaty came about as the result of an exchange of letters written in their own hands by Joseph II and Catherine. See *Joseph II und Katharina von Russland*, ed. Alfred Ritter von Arneth (Vienna: W. Braumuller, 1869).

29. See Alan F. Fisher, *The Russian Annexation of the Crimea, 1772–83* (Cambridge: Cambridge University Press, 1970).

30. Hugh Ragsdale, "Evaluating the Traditions of Russian Aggression: Catherine II and the Greek Project," *Slavonic and East European Review* 66, no. 1 (1988): 91–117.

31. For Austrian involvement in this war, see Matthew Z. Mayer, "Joseph II and the Campaign of 1788 Against the Ottoman Turks," MA thesis, McGill University, 1997; Matthew Z. Mayer, "The Price for Austria's Security: Part I. Joseph II, the Russian Alliance, and the Ottoman War, 1787–1789," *International History Review* 26, no. 2 (2004): 257–99; Michael Hochedlinger, *Austria's Wars of Emergence: War, State and Society in the Habsburg Monarchy, 1683–97* (London: Longman, 2003).

32. For details, see Aksan, *Ottoman Wars 1700–1870*, 129–79, esp. 147–50.

33. For an interesting discussion of the negotiations of the treaties of Jassy and Sistova (Ziştovi) that ended the Russo-Austrian-Ottoman War, see Câbî Ömer Efendi, *Câbî Târîhi—Târîhi Sultân Selim-i Sâlis ve Mahmûd-ı Sânî—Tahlîl ve Tenkidli Metin I,* ed. Mehmet Ali Beyan (Ankara: Türk Tarih Kurumu, 2003), 28–31.

34. Munro Price, "The Dutch Affairs and the Fall of the Ancien Régime, 1787–1787," in *Historical Journal* 38, no. 4 (1995): 875–905; Orville T. Murphy, *The Diplomatic Retreat of France and Public Opinion on the Eve of the French Revolution* (Washington, DC: Catholic University of America Press, 1998), 459–72.

35. Robert Nisbet Bain, *The Pupils of Peter the Great: A History of the Russian Court and Empire* (Wesminster: A. Constable, 1897), 6.

36. For Russia's motives, see Herbert H. Kaplan, *The First Partition of Poland* (New York: Columbia University Press, 1962); Robert E. Jones, "Runaway Peasants and Russian Motives for the Partitions of Poland," in *Imperial Russian Foreign*

Policy, ed. Hugh Ragsdale and V. Ponomarev (Cambridge: Cambridge University Press, 1993), 103–18. For a discussion of Russian domestic politics and their role in the Second Partition, see Jerzy Lojek, "Catherine's Armed Intervention in Poland: Origins of the Political Decisions at the Russian Court in 1791–1792," *Canadian-American Slavic Studies* 4 (1970): 570–93.

37. Russia obtained Byelorussia and Latvian Lithuania to the Dvina and Dnieper Rivers with some 1.3 million inhabitants. Austria received the province of Galicia, with a total population of 2.6 million. Prussia took the so-called Royal, or Polish, West Prussia, except Gdansk (Danzig) and Torun (Thorn).

38. Catherine's contempt for the Prussian king, the "stupid lout" she dubbed "Gu" (after Frédéric-Guillaume), was only matched by her scorn for the English king George III, the "marchand drapier" she dubbed "Ge." After their cooperation in the Dutch Republic in 1787 they were amalgamated into a single object of derision: "Gegu." Blanning, *The Origins of the French Revolutionary Wars*, 59.

39. For a good discussion, with Ottoman documentation, see Kemal Beydilli, *1790 Osmanlı-Prusya ittifâkı* (Istanbul: İstanbul Üniversitesi Yayınları, 1984).

40. For details, see Jerzy Kowecki, ed., *Sejm czteroletni i jego tradycje* (Warsaw: Państwowe Wydawnictwo Naukowe, 1991); Jerzy Kowecki and Bogusław Leśnodorski, *Konstytucja 3 maja 1791, statut Zgromadzenia Przyjaciół Konstytucji* (Warsaw: Państwowe Wydawnictwo Naukowe, 1981).

41. For details, see Robert H. Lord, *The Second Partition of Poland: A Study in Diplomatic History* (Cambridge MA: Harvard University Press, 1915); Adam Zamoyski, *The Last King of Poland* (London: Jonathan Cape, 1992), Jerzy T. Lukowski, *The Partitions of Poland, 1772, 1793, 1795* (Harlow: Longman Higher Education, 1998); Norman Davies, *God's Playground: A History of Poland* (New York: Columbia University Press, 1982), I:409–12, 511–46.

42. Wenzel Anton, prince of Kaunitz-Rietberg, the great Austrian diplomat and architect of anti-Prussian policy, saw his influence ebb away and be replaced by that of Baron Anton von Spielmann and Count Karl Johann Philipp Cobenzl, who rapidly gained influence under the new emperor. In the summer of 1792 Kaunitz resigned from his post as chancellor of Austria.

43. Russia gained the vast area of Byelorussia and Volhynia, including Minsk, Zytomier, and Kamieniec, while Prussia received an area nearly twice the size of its First Partition gains. For details on the Second Polish Partition, see Robert Howard Lord, *The Second Partition of Poland: A Study in Diplomatic History* (Cambridge: Harvard University Press, 1915); Jerzy Lukowski, *The Partitions of Poland: 1772, 1793, 1795* (London: Longman, 1999).

44. Nathaniel Jarret, "Britain and the Polish Question," paper presented at the annual meeting of the Consortium on the Revolutionary Era, February 2015. I am grateful to the author for sending me the full version of the paper.

45. There was also a significant presence of other European states. Russia was slowly expanding into Alaska, while Denmark controlled Greenland and the

Danish West Indies (islands of Sankt Thomas, Sankt Jan, and Sankt Croix) in the Caribbean. The Dutch held colonies in the Guianas (Berbice, Essequibo, Demerara, Pomeroon, Surinam), Curaçao, St. Eustatius, and dependencies. The Swedish held sway on the island of St. Barthélemy.

46. For details, see Warren L. Cook, *Floodtide of Empire: Spain and the Pacific Northwest, 1548–19* (New Haven, CT: Yale University Press, 1973); F. W. Howay, "The Spanish Settlement at Nootka," *Washington Historical Quarterly* VIII, no. 3 (1917): 163–71.

47. O. W. Frost, *Bering: The Russian Discovery of America* (New Haven, CT: Yale University Press, 2003).The strait was first discovered by Semyon Dezhnyov in 1648. The first visit of Russian navigators to the American coast was made in 1732 by the geodesist Mikhail Gvozdev, who reached Bolshaya Zemlya (close to Cape Prince of Wales).

48. For concise discussions, see A. Sokol, "Russian Expansion and Exploration in the Pacific," *American Slavic and East European Review* 11, no. 2 (1952): 85–105; Theodore S. Farrelly, "Early Russian Contact with Alaska," *Pacific Affairs* 7, no. 2 (1934): 193–97; N. Nozikov, *Russian Voyages Round the World* (London: Hutchinson, 1945). On the development of the Russian fur trade in the eighteenth century, see Raisa Makarova, *Russians on the Pacific, 1743–1799*, trans. and ed. Richard Pierce and Alton Donnelly (Kingston, ON: Limestone Press, 1975).

49. "The English in Kamchatka, 1779," *Geographical Journal* 84, no. 5 (1934): 417–19.

50. Seeking to contain encroachments by three European powers on what Russia considered its sphere of influence, Billings was instructed to pay special attention to "little-frequented and quite unknown islands lying to the leeward of the North American coast," and to make every effort to bring the new encountered peoples under the Russian scepter's sway. The expedition was required to maintain secrecy over its overall objectives, and Billings' instructions specified that "never, under any pretext whatsoever, are you to reveal to anyone the end or operations of this venture." Bad weather and changing political circumstances back in Europe delayed Billings's expedition, but he eventually reached the Aleutians in 1790 and stayed in the region for two years. For details, see "Instructions from Catherine II and the Admiralty College to Captain Lieutenant Joseph Billings for His Expedition to Northern Russia and the North Pacific Ocean," in Basil Dmytryshyn, ed., *Russian Penetration of the North Pacific Ocean, 1700–97* (Oregon: Oregon Historical Society Press, 1988), II:269–90.

51. For an excellent discussion, see Glynn Barratt, *Russia in Pacific Waters, 1715–25* (Vancouver: University of British Columbia Press, 1981),76–96.

52. "A Memorandum from Count Alexander Vorontsov and Count Alexander Bezborodko Concerning Russia's Rights to the Islands and Coasts of North America Which Were Discovered by Russian Seafarers," in Dmytryshyn, ed., *Russian Penetration of the North Pacific Ocean*, II:321–24.

53. They reported, for example, Catherine's intention to declare Russian sovereignty over North America from Mount St. Elias on the Pacific to the shores of Hudson's Bay. See Cook, *Floodtide of Empire*, 115–17; Herbert Ingram Priestley, *José de Gálvez: Visitor-General of New Spain (1765–71)* (Berkeley: University of California Press, 1916), 300.

54. The most thorough and balanced accounts of the Nootka Sound Crisis are Christian de Parrel, "Pitt et l'Espagne," *Revue d'histoire diplomatique* 64 (1950): 58–98, and William Ray Manning, "The Nootka Sound Controversy," *Annual Report of the American Historical Association for the Year 1904* (Washington, DC: AHA, 1905). Lennox Mills, "The Real Significance of the Nootka Sound Incident," *Canadian Historical Review* 6 (1925): 110–22, offers interesting interpretation centered on "irreconcilable British and Spanish principles of colonial sovereignty." John M. Norris, "Policy of the British Cabinet in the Nootka Crisis," *English Historical Review* 70 (1955): 562–80, focuses more on economic interests.

55. Samuel Flagg Bemis, *A Diplomatic History of the United States* (New York; Holt, Rinehart and Winston, 1965), 89.

56. See Francois Crouzet, *La guerre économique franco-anglaise au XVIIIe siècle* (Paris: Fayard, 2008).

57. For details, see Paul Butel, *L'Economie française au XVIIIe siècle* (Paris: SEDES, 1993).

58. Guillaume de Lamardelle, "Eloge du Comte d'Ennery et réforme judiciaire à Saint-Domingue," April 2, 1788, cited in Frédéric Régent, "Revolutions in France, Revolutions in the Caribbean," in *The Routledge Companion to the French Revolution in World History*, ed. Alan Forrest and Matthias Middell (London: Routledge, 2016), 61.

59. Paul Butel, *Histoire des Antilles francaises* (Paris: Perrin, 2007), 184; James Pritchard, *In Search of Empire: The French in the Americas, 1670–30* (Cambridge: Cambridge University Press, 2004), 424. For comparison, there were 700,000 slaves in all of the United States.

60. By 1789, the annual earnings from a slave exceeded 200 livres tournois. Compare it to 196.98 for a Frenchman in France and 157.25 for an Englishman. For details, see Vertus Saint-Louis, *Mer et liberté Haïti (1492–94)* (Port-au-Prince: Bibliothèque nationale d'Haiti, 2008).

61. See Laurent Dubois, *Avengers of the New World: The Story of the Haitian Revolution* (Cambridge, MA: Harvard University Press, 2004).

62. Régent, "Revolutions in France, Revolutions in the Caribbean," 63–69. Also see the introduction and ch. 1 in François Blancpain, *La colonie française de Saint-Domingue: De l'esclavage à l'indépendance* (Paris: Karthala, 2004).

63. *Courier de Provence*, August 20–21, 1789.

64. Yves Bénot, "The Chain of Slave Insurrections in the Caribbean, 1789–1791," in *The Abolitions of Slavery: From Léger Félicité Sonthonax to Victor Schoelcher, 1793, 1794, 1848*, ed. Marcel Dorigny (Paris: Éditions UNESCO, 1995), 147–54.

65. For an interesting discussion of the ceremony supposedly held by the insurrectionary leader Boukman Dutty at Bois Caiman to launch the August 1791 slave uprising see David Geggus, "The Bois Caiman Ceremony," in his *Haitian Revolutionary Studies* (Bloomington: Indiana University Press, 2002), 81–92.

66. Jeremy D. Popkin, *A Concise History of the Haitian Revolution* (Oxford: Blackwell, 2012), 30–46.

67. Frédéric Régent, "From Individual to Collective Emancipation: War and the Republic in the Caribbean During the French Revolution," in *Republics at War, 1776–40: Revolutions, Conflicts, Geopolitics in Europe and the Atlantic World*, ed. Pierre Serna, Antonino de Francesco, and Judith A. Miller (New York: Palgrave Macmillan, 2013), 165, 167.

68. David Geggus, "Jamaica and the Saint Domingue Slave Revolt, 1791–1793," *The Americas* 38 (October 1981): 223.

69. For an excellent discussion, see Laurent Dubois, *A Colony of Citizens: Revolution and Slave Emancipation in the French Caribbean, 1787–1804* (Chapel Hill: University of North Carolina Press, 2004).

Chapter 3

1. See Jonathan A. Abel, *Guibert: Father of Napoleon's Grande Armée* (Norman: University of Oklahoma Press, 2016), esp. 156–93.

2. *Décret de la Convention nationale, du 19 novembre 1792, l'an Ier de la république françoise: Par lequel la Convention déclare qu'elle accordera fraternité & secours à tous les peuples qui voudront recouvrer leur liberté* (Rennes: Imprimerie Nationale du Département d'Ille et Vilaine, 1792); Albert Goodwin, *The Friends of Liberty: The English Democratic Movement in the Age of the French Revolution* (London: Hutchinson, 1979), 236–51.

3. Albert Mathiez, *La révolution et les étrangers: cosmopolitisme et défense nationale* (Paris: La Renaissance du Livre, 1918), 84.

4. Marita Gilli, ed., *Un révolutionnaire allemand, Georg Forster (1754–94)* (Paris: Éditions du CTHS, 2005), 440.

5. Speech of June 7, 1799, in *The War Speeches of William Pitt the Younger*, ed. R. Coupland (Oxford: Clarendon Press, 1915), 244. "They will not accept, under the name of liberty, any model of government, but that which is conformable to their own opinions and ideas," declared British Prime Minister William Pitt. "And all men must learn from the mouth of their cannon the propagation of their system in every part of the world." Speech of December 1, 1793, in *The War Speeches*, 37. Also see Debate in the House of Commons, February 3, 1800, in *Parliamentary Register or History of the Proceedings and Debates of the Houses of Lords and Commons* (London: Wilson, 1800), X:319–24.

6. Debates of May 22, 1790, in *Archives Parlementaires de 1787 à 1860* (Paris: Paul Dupont, 1883), XV:662. Also see Hamish Scott, "Diplomacy," in *The Oxford Handbook of the Ancien Régime*, ed. William Doyle (Oxford: Oxford University Press, 2012), 50.

7. Edmund Burke, *The Works of the Right Honorable Edmund Burke* (London: Rivington, 1801), VIII:204.

8. In March 1793 the French did, however, occupy a large part of the Bishopric of Basel and absorbed it into France as the Department of Doubs. This had removed a key element in the Swiss defense, since the Jura defense line was lost. This opened a pathway for the French expansion into Switzerland, where France, which had been subject to an economic blockade, could procure important commodities, including grain, cattle, and saltpeter, from Swiss merchants and wartime speculators. For an interesting discussion of the importance of Swiss neutrality and trade to revolutionary France, see Edgar Bonjour, *Geschichte der schweizerischen Neutralität: vier Jahrhunderte eidgenössischer Aussenpolitik* (Basel: Helbing & Lichtenhahn, 1965), vol. 1.

9. J. Holland Rose and Alexander M. Broadley, *Dumouriez and the Defence of England Against Napoleon* (London: J. Lane, 1909), 145–86.

10. See J. Holland Rose, *Lord Hood and the Defence of Toulon* (Cambridge: Cambridge University Press, 1922); Robert Forczyk, *Toulon 1793: Napoleon's First Great Victory* (Oxford: Osprey, 2005).

11. Thomas Hippler, *Citizens, Soldiers and National Armies: Military Service in France and Germany, 1789–1830* (London: Routledge, 2008), 81–82.

12. For a recent discussion, see Jean-Joël Bregeon and Gérard Guicheteau, *Nouvelle histoire des guerres de Vendée* (Paris: Perrin, 2017).

13. Desmond Gregory, *The Ungovernable Rock: A History of the Anglo-Corsican Kingdom and Its Role in Britain's Mediterranean Strategy During the Revolutionary War, 1793–97* (Rutherford, NJ: Fairleigh Dickinson University Press, 1985).

14. See Sam Willis, *The Glorious First of June* (London: Quercus, 2011); Michael Duffy and Roger Morriss, eds., *The Glorious First of June 1794: A Naval Battle and Its Aftermath* (Exeter: University of Exeter Press, 2001).

15. For details, see R. B. Rose, *Gracchus Babeuf: The First Revolutionary Communist* (Stanford, CA: Stanford University Press, 1978).

16. Albert Sorel, *L'Europe et la Révolution française* (Paris: Plon Nourrit, 1903), V:20.

17. For a lengthy discussion of the War in the Pyrenees, see Antonio Canovas del Castillo, *Historia General de Espana* (Madrid: El progreso editorial, 1891–93), vols. XVI–XVIII.

18. Cited in Francois Guizot, *France* (New York: P. F. Colllier & Son, 1902), 318.

19. Geoffrey Bruun, *Europe and the French Imperium, 1799–14* (New York: Harper & Row, 1965), 116; Frederick C. Schneid, *Napoleon's Conquest of Europe: The War of the Third Coalition* (Westport, CT: Praeger, 2005), 39.

20. For an in-depth discussion, see Kenneth Gregory Johnson, "Louis-Thomas Villaret de Joyeuse: Admiral and Colonial Administrator (1747–1812)," PhD diss., Florida State University, 2006, 103–44.

21. Laurent, marquis de Gouvion Saint-Cyr, *Mémoires sur les campagnes des armées du Rhin et de Rhin-et-Moselle de 1792 jusqu'à la paix de Campo Formio* (Paris: Anselin, 1829), III:4.

22. Archduke Charles was supported by the 80,000 men of Dagobert Sigismund, Count von Wurmser, but Wurmser was soon ordered to lead part of his troops to Italy while the rest of his forces were garrisoned at key cities. Wurmser's departure was, in fact a blessing in disguise since it gave Archduke Charles greater flexibility to operate.

23. The failure of the French offensive on the Rhine in 1796 was the result of several key factors, most notably profound logistical challenges and the treason of General Jean Pichegru. For details on the latter, see Georges Caudrillier, *La trahison de Pichegru et les intrigues royalistes dans l'Est avant Fructidor* (Paris: Alcan, 1908). For the campaign in general, see Steven T. Ross, *Quest for Victory: French Military Strategy, 1792–99* (New York: Barnes, 1973); H. Bordeau, *Les armées du Rhin au début du Directoire* (Paris, 1909); Ramsay Weston Phipps, *The Armies of the First French Republic and the Rise of the Marshals of Napoleon I* (London: Oxford University Press, 1926), vol. 2; Timothy C. W. Blanning, *The French Revolution in Germany: Occupation and Resistance in the Rhineland, 1792–1802* (New York: Oxford University Press, 1983). For the Austrian side, see Archduke Charles, *Archduke Charles' 1796 Campaign in Germany*, trans. George F. Nafziger (West Chester, OH: Nafziger Collection, 2004); Gunther E. Rothenberg, *Napoleon's Great Adversaries: Archduke Charles and the Austrian Army, 1792–1814* (Bloomington: Indiana University Press, 1992); Lee W. Eysturlid, *The Formative Influences, Theories, and Campaigns of the Archduke Carl of Austria* (Westport CT: Greenwood Press, 2000).

24. Martin Boycott-Brown, *The Road to Rivoli: Napoleon's First Campaign* (London: Cassell, 2001); David Chandler, *The Campaigns of Napoleon* (New York: Macmillan, 1966), 53–87; Ramsay Weston Phipps, *The Armies of the First French Republic* (Oxford: Oxford University Press, 1931), vol. 3. For a broad overview of the war in the Piedmont before Bonaparte's appointment, see Léonce Krebs and Henri Moris, *Les campagnes dans les Alpes pendant la Révolution, 1794, 1795, 1796* (Paris: Plon, 1895); Ciro Paoletti, *La guerra delle Alpi (1792–96)* (Rome: USSME, 2000).

25. See Treaty of Paris, April 29, 1796, AN AF/IV/1702/4/2; Treaty of Turin, May 15, 1796, AN AF/IV/1702/4/3; Domenico Carutti, *Le Corte di Savoia durante le rivoluzione e l'impero francese* (Turin: L. Roux, 1888), vol. I. For a broad discussion of Piedmont's position before and during the Revolutionary Wars, see Ciro Paoletti, *Dal ducato all'unità: Tre secoli e mezzo di storia militare piemontese* (Rome: USSME, 2011).

26. See Chandler, *The Campaigns of Napoleon*, 88–112; Jean Thiry, *Bonaparte en Italie, 1796–97* (Paris: Berger-Levrault, 1973); Guglielmo Ferrero, *The Gamble: Bonaparte in Italy, 1796–97* (New York: Walker, 1961).

27. Phillip R. Cuccia, *Napoleon in Italy: The Sieges of Mantua, 1796–99* (Norman: University of Oklahoma Press, 2014).

28. For an in-depth discussion, see Raymond Kubben, *Regeneration and Hegemony: Franco-Batavian Relations in the Revolutionary Era, 1795–1803* (Leiden: Martinus Nijhoff, 2011), 501–66.

29. See Articles 3, 7, 8 and Secret Article 1 of the Treaty of Campo Formio, 1797, AN AF/III/59/235/1.

30. Article 6 and Secret Article 4 of the Treaty of Campo Formio, AN AF/III/59/235/1. Also see George B. McClellan, *Venice and Bonaparte* (Princeton, NJ: Princeton University Press, 1931).

31. Michel Kerautret, *Les grands traités du Consulat, 1799–1804. Documents diplomatiques du Consulat et de l'Empire* (Paris: Nouveau Monde Editions, 2002), I:93.

32. John Jervis St. Vincent, *Memoirs of Admiral the Right Hon. the Earl of St. Vincent, G.C.B., &c.*, ed. Jedediah Stephens Tucker (London: Richard Bentley, 1844), I:255.

33. William James, *Naval History of Great Britain* (London: Richard Bentley, 1837), II:29–53; John D. Harbron, *Trafalgar and the Spanish Navy* (Annapolis, MD: Naval Institute Press, 1988), 118–20; Claude Farrère, *Histoire de la marine française* (Paris: Flammarion, 1934); Noel Mostert, *The Line upon a Wind: The Greatest War Fought at Sea Under Sail 1793–1815* (London: Vintage, 2008).

34. James, *Naval History of Great Britain*, II:68–78; Christopher Lloyd, *St. Vincent and Camperdown* (New York: Macmillan, 1963); Sam Willis, *In the Hour of Victory: The Royal Navy at War in the Age of Nelson* (New York: W. W. Norton, 2014).

35. Horace Walpole to Sir Horace Mann, April 27, 1773, in *Letters of Horace Walpole, Earl of Orford* (London: Richard Bentley, 1843), II:237. Walpole spoke à propos the First Partition of Poland, but the statement reflected the limited nature of British power on the continent.

36. B. Collins, *War and Empire: The Expansion of Britain, 1790–1830: The Projection of British Power, 1775–1830* (London: Longman, 2010); M. Duffy, "World-Wide War and British Expansion, 1793–1815," in *The Oxford History of the British Empire*, vol. 2, *The Eighteenth Century*, ed. P. J. Marshall (Oxford: Oxford University Press, 2001).

37. See Robin Blackburn, "Haiti, Slavery, and the Age of the Democratic Revolution," *William and Mary Quarterly* 63 (2006): 643–73.

38. Pierre Pluchon, *Histoire des Antilles et de la Guyane* (Toulouse: Privat, 1982), 304–305; *Révolutions aux colonies* (Paris: Publication des Annales historiques de la Révolution française, 1993), 55–60.

39. The British attack on the Spanish possessions prompted a Spanish response. In 1798, a Spanish flotilla with some 2,000 men attacked the British settlement in the Bay of Honduras; after several small and unsuccessful engagements with the British forces, it was forced to withdraw in confusion.

40. Michael Duffy, *Soldiers, Sugar and Seapower: The British Expeditions to West Indies and the War Against Revolutionary France* (Oxford: Clarendon, Press, 1987), 291. Also see Michael Duffy, "The Caribbean Campaigns of the British Army, 1793–1815," in *The Road to Waterloo: The British Army and the Struggle Against Revolutionary and Napoleonic France, 1793–1815* (London: National Army Museum, 1990), 23–31.

41. Jeremy D. Popkin, *A Concise History of the Haitian Revolution* (Oxford: Blackwell, 2012), 48–61.

42. For a biography of Louverture, see George Tyson, ed., *Toussaint L'Ouverture* (Englewood Cliffs, NJ: Prentice Hall, 1973); Pierre Pluchon, *Toussaint Louverture: Un révolutionnaire noir d'Ancien Régime* (Paris: Fayard, 1989).

43. For an excellent discussion, see Sabine Manigat, "Les fondements sociaux de l'État louverturien," in *La Révolution francaise et Haiti: Filiations, ruptures, nouvelles dimensions*, ed. Michel Hector (Port-au-Prince: Sociéte haitienne d'histoire et de géographie, 1995), I:130–42.

44. W. James, *The Naval History of Great Britain from the Declaration of War by France in 1793 to the Accession of George IV* (London: Macmillan, 1837), I:118–20.

45. Lennox Algernon Mills, *Ceylon Under British Rule 1795–1832* (London: Milford, 1933), 9–15.

46. Graham Irwin, "Governor Couperus and the Surrender of Malacca, 1795," in *Journal of the Malayan Branch of the Royal Asiatic Society* 29, no. 3 (1956): 86–113.

47. See Wim Klooster and Geert Oostindie, eds., *Curaçao in the Age of Revolutions, 1795–1800* (Leiden: KITLV Press, 2011).

48. Francis Baring to Henry Dundas, January 12, 1795, in George M. Theal, ed., *Records of the Cape Colony* (London: Government of the Cape Colony, 1897), I:22.

49. Captain John Blankett to Under-Secretary Sir Evan Nepean, January 25, 1795, in Theal, ed., *Records of the Cape Colony*, 26.

50. President George Washington's Farewell Address, September 11, 1796, http://avalon.law.yale.edu/18th_century/washing.asp.

51. For an interesting discussion, see John Lamberton Harper, *American Machiavelli: Alexander Hamilton and the Origins of the U.S. Foreign Policy* (Cambridge: Cambridge University Press, 2004), 65–102.

52. Ron Chernow, *Alexander Hamilton* (New York: Penguin, 2004), 389–408.

53. "Proclamation 4—Neutrality of the United States in the War Involving Austria, Prussia, Sardinia, Great Britain, and the United Netherlands Against France," April 22, 1793, American Presidency Project, http://www.presidency.ucsb.edu/ws/index.php?pid=65475&st=&st1=. For an old but still useful study, see C. M. Thomas, *American Neutrality in 1793: A Study in Cabinet Government* (New York: Columbia University Press, 1931).

54. *American State Papers: Documents, Legislative and Executive, of the Congress of the United States*, ed. Walter Lowrie and Matthew St. Clair Clarke (Washington, DC: Gales and Seaton, 1833), I:240.

55. *American State Papers,* I:430.

56. In June 1794 the US Congress once again stressed American neutrality in European conflicts by passing the Neutrality Act, which made it illegal for an American to enlist in the service of a foreign power and prohibited the

"providing or preparing the means for any military expedition or enterprise...against the territory or dominions of any foreign prince or state of
whom the United States was at peace." The Neutrality Act, June 5, 1794, in
United States Statutes at Large, 3rd Cong., Sess. I., 381–84.

57. The Jay Treaty, 1794, and Associated Documents, Yale Law School, The
Avalon Project, http://avalon.law.yale.edu/subject_menus/jaymenu.asp.

58. Joseph Ellis, *Founding Brothers: The Revolutionary Generation* (New York:
Vintage Books, 2000), 136–37.

59. "American Affairs," in *Report on the Manuscripts of J. B. Fortescue, Esq. Preserved
at Dropmore* (London: HMSO, 1899), III:526.

60. Treaty of Friendship, Limits, and Navigation Between Spain and the United
States, October 27, 1795, http://avalon.law.yale.edu/18th_century/sp1795.asp.

61. Eric Robert Papenfuse, *The Evils of Necessity: Robert Goodloe Harper and the
Moral Dilemma of Slavery* (Philadelphia: American Philosophical Society,
1997), 27–28.

62. For details, see George C. Daughan, *If by Sea: The Forging of the American Navy
from the Revolution to the War of 1812* (New York: Basic Books, 2008), 325–45.

63. Convention Between the French Republic and the United States of America,
September 30, 1800, http://avalon.law.yale.edu/19th_century/fr1800.asp.

Chapter 4

1. French historian Marc Belissa, for example, draws an apt comparison with the
fall of the Berlin Wall in 1988. See his *Repenser l'ordre européen (1795–1802): De
la société des rois aux droits des nations* (Paris: Éditions Klimé, 2006).

2. Bernard Gainot, "Révolution, Liberté = Europe des nations? Sororité conflictuelle," in *Mélanges Michel Vovelle sur la Révolution, approaches plurielles*, ed. Jean
Paul Bertaud (Paris: Société des études robespierristes, 1997), 457–68.

3. For discussion related to Italy, see Anna Maria Rao, "Les républicains democrats italiens et le Directoire," in *La République directoriale*, ed. Philippe Bourdin
and Bernard Gainot (Paris: Société des Études Robespierristes, 1998), II:
1070–76; Antonio de Francesco, "Aux origins du movement démocratique
italien: quelques perspectives de recherché d'après l'exemple de la période
révolutionnaire 1796–1801," *Annales historiques de la Révolution Française* 308
(1997): 333–48.

4. For an interesting discussion of this concept, see Peter Sahlins, "Natural Frontiers
Revisited: France's Boundaries Since the Seventeenth Century," *American
Historical Review* 95, no. 5 (December 1990): 1423–51; Norman J. Pounds, "The
Origin of the Idea of Natural Frontiers in France," *Annals of the Association of
American Geographers* 41, no. 2 (June 1951): 146–57.

5. Jeremy Black, *France from Louis XIV to Napoleon: The Fate of Great Empire*
(London: University College London Press, 1999), 173.

6. In Italy alone, the French established a dozen republics that were merged,
expanded, or outright abolished over the next several years: Republic of Alba

(1796), Ligurian Republic (1796), Cispadane Republic (1796), Bolognese Republic (1796), Republic of Bergamo (1797), Republic of Crema (1797), Republic of Brescia (1797), Republic of Pescara (1797), Republic of Ancona (1797), Tiberina Republic (1798), Parthenopaean Republic (1799), Subalpine Republic (1800). In addition, there was the Batavian Republic (1795) in the Low Countries, the Cisrhenian Republic (1797) on the left bank of the Rhine, and the Helvetic Republic (1798) in Switzerland. See Michel Vovelle, *Les Républiques Soeurs sous le regard de la Grande Nation* (Paris: L'Harmattan, 2007).

7. Louis Charles Antoine Desaix de Veygoux, *Journal de voyage du general Desaix, Suisse et Italie (1797)*, ed. Arthur Chuquet (Paris: Plon-Nourrit, 1907), 256.

8. *Gazette Nationale, ou Le Moniteur Universel*, no. 123, 3 Pluviôse An 8, 487; Niall Ferguson, *Empire: The Rise and Demise of the British World Order and the Lessons for Global Power* (New York: Basic Books, 2004), 49.

9. "Declaration and Resolutions of the Society of United Irishmen of Belfast," in Theobald Wolfe Tone, *Life of Theobald Wolfe Tone: Memoirs, Journals and Political Writings, Compiled and Arranged by William T. W. Tone* (Dublin: Lilliput Press, 1998 [1826]), 298–99.

10. Richard Hayes, *Ireland and Irishmen in the French Revolution* (London: Ernest Benn, 1932). For political demands, see "The United Irishmen's Plan of Parliamentary Reform," in Edmond Curtis and R. B. McDowell, eds., *Irish Historical Documents 1172–1922* (New York: Barnes & Noble, 1968), 237–38.

11. "The Organization of the United Irishmen, 1797" in Curtis and McDowell, *Irish Historical Documents*, 240–41. Also see W. Benjamin Kennedy, "Conspiracy Tinged with Blarney: Wolfe Tone and Other Irish Emissaries to Revolutionary France," *CRE* 1978, 48–57.

12. For details, see Cathal Poirteir, ed. *The Great Irish Rebellion of 1798* (Dublin: Mercier Press, 1998); Thomas Bartlett, ed., *1798: A Bicentenary Perspective* (Dublin: Four Courts, 2003); Patrick Geoghegan, *The Irish Act of Union: A Study in High Politics, 1798–1801* (Dublin: Gill and Macmillan, 1999); Stephen Small, *Political Thought in Ireland, 1776–1798: Republicanism, Patriotism, and Radicalism* (Oxford: Clarendon Press, 2002); Jim Smyth, ed., *Revolution, Counter-revolution, and Union: Ireland in the 1790s* (Cambridge: Cambridge University Press, 2000).

13. Joseph Stock, *A Narrative of What Passed at Killalla in the County of Mayo and the Parts Adjacent During the French Invasion in the Summer of 1798* (London: J. Wright, 1800), 23–24.

14. For example, in 1769, the French foreign ministry proposed conquering Egypt to compensate for the loss of French colonies in the Americas. Francois-Charles Roux, *Les origines de l'expédition d' Egypte* (Paris: Plon-Nourrit, 1910), 294–95.

15. See Raoul Clément, *Les Français d'Égypte aux XVIIe et XVIIIe siècles* (Cairo: Impr. de l'Institut français d'archéologie orientale, 1960); Paul Masson, *Histoire du commerce français dans le Levant au XVIIe siècle* (Paris, Hachette, 1911).

16. Clément, *Les Français d'Égypte aux XVIIe et XVIIIe siècles*, 274.

17. Roux, *Les origines de l'expédition d'Egypte*, 246.

18. In March 1789 Ismael Bey sought French assistance against his political rivals. Yet the political crisis of 1789 prevented the Bourbon monarchy from acting on this request.

19. Daniel Crecelius and Gotcha Djaparidze, "Relations of the Georgian Mamluks of Egypt with Their Homeland in the Last Decades of the Eighteenth Century," *Journal of the Economic and Social History of the Orient* 45 (2002): 320–411.

20. Guillaume-Antoine Olivier, *Voyage dans l'Empire Othoman, l'Egypte et la Perse...* (Paris: H. Agasse, 1801), III:202–3.

21. Olivier, *Voyage dans l'Empire Othoman*, III:209. Also see Roux, *Les origines de l'expédition d'Egypte*, 248.

22. For details on Magallon's plan and Talleyrand's revisions to it, see Roux, *Les origines de l'expédition d'Egypte*, 323–29. Also see Henry Laurens et al., *L'Expedition d'Egypte, 1798–1801* (Paris: Armand Colin, 1989), 28.

23. Clément de La Jonquière, *L'expédition d'Égypte, 1798–1801* (Paris: H. Charles-Lavauzelle, 1899), I:169.

24. Napoleon, *Correspondance générale*, ed. Thierry Lentz (Paris: Fayard, 2004), I:1118.

25. See Talleyrand's lengthy report of February 14, 1798, in La Jonquière, *L'expédition d'Égypte, 1798–1801*, I:154–68. Not the least of the advantage was the Directory's calculation to neutralize General Bonaparte, an extremely popular general who might pose a political threat. As one British historian aptly put it, the Directors sent Bonaparte to Egypt "partly to get rid of him, partly to gratify him, and partly to dazzle and delight that portion of Parisian society who...had considerable influence on public opinion." Henry Richard Vassall-Fox, *Lord Holland's Foreign Reminiscences* (New York: Harper & Brothers, 1851), 158.

26. For details, see Henry Laurens, *Les origines intellectuelles de l'expédition d'Égypte: l'Orientalisme Islamisant en France (1698–1798)* (Paris: Éditions Isis, 1987).

27. Arrêtes du Directoire, 23 Germinal an VI (April 12, 1798), in *Correspondance de Napoleon*, IV:50–54.

28. The campaign discussion draws on Christopher Herold, *Bonaparte in Egypt* (London: Hamish Hamilton, 1962); Irene Bierman, *Napoleon in Egypt* (Los Angeles: Gustave E. von Grunebaum Center for Near Eastern Studies, 2003); Juan Ricardo Cole, *Napoleon's Egypt: Invading the Middle East* (New York: Palgrave Macmillan, 2008); Paul Strathern, *Napoleon in Egypt* (New York: Bantam Books, 2008); Nathan Schur, *Napoleon in the Holy Land* (London: Greenhill Books, 1999). For an Egyptian perspective, see 'Abd al-Raḥmān Jabarti, *Napoleon in Egypt: Al-Jabarti's Chronicle of the French Occupation, 1798* (Princeton, NJ: Markus Wiener, 2004); Abdullah Browne, *Bonaparte in Egypt: The French Campaign of 1798–1801 from the Egyptian Perspective* (London: Leonaur, 2012).

29. Jonquière, *L' expédition d'Égypte, 1798–1801*, I:518–27.

30. See Desmond Gregory, *Malta, Britain and the European Powers, 1793–1815* (Madison, NJ: Farleigh Dickinson University Press, 1996); William Hardman, *A History of Malta During the Period of the French and British Occupations, 1798–1815* (London: Longmans, Green, 1909).

31. See various orders in *Correspondance de Napoléon*, IV:143–76.

32. Jonquière, *L' expédition d'Égypte, 1798–1801,* I:644. Also see Ernle Bradford, *The Shield and the Sword: The Knights of St. John of Jerusalem, Rhodes and Malta* (New York: Dutton, 1973), 215–16.

33. Pierre Marie Louis de Boisgelin de Kerdu, *Ancient and Modern Malta* (London: R. Phillips, 1805), II:98–99. For documents on the French occupation, see Hannibal Publius Scicluna, *Documents Relating to the French Occupation of Malta in 1798–1800* (Valletta: Empire Press, 1923).

34. For good insights into the causes of the revolt, see Jean de Bosredon de Ransijat, *Journal du siège et blocus de Malte* (Paris: Valade, 1801), 278–86.

35. See Roderick McGrew, "Paul I and the Knights of Malta," in *Paul I: A Reassessment of His Life and Reign*, ed. Hugh Ragsdale (Pittsburgh: University Center for International Studies, 1979), 50; Norman E. Saul, *Russia and the Mediterranean, 1797–1807* (Chicago: University of Chicago Press, 1970), 35–39, 64–65. Bonaparte decreed that any contacts between Malta's Greek population and Russia would be punishable by death: "All Greek vessels navigating under the Russian flag, whenever captured by French ships, will be sunk." Order, 17 June 1798, in *Correspondance de Napoléon*, IV:168–69.

36. The Mamluks rose to power after overthrowing the Ayyubid dynasty in 1250, and over the next five centuries, two dynasties ruled Egypt: the Bahriyya (Bahri) Mamluks (1250–1382), mostly of Turkish origin, and the Burji (Burgite) Mamluks (1382–1517, though they retained a great deal of influence until 1811), mostly of Caucasian descent (Georgians, Circassians, Armenians). See Thomas Philipp and Ulrich Haarmann, *The Mamluks in Egyptian Politics and Society* (Cambridge: Cambridge University Press, 1998); Jane Hathaway, *The Politics of Households in Ottoman Egypt: The Rise of the Qazdaglis* (Cambridge: Cambridge University Press, 1997); Daniel Crecelius and Gotcha Djaparidze, "Georgians in the Military Establishment in Egypt in the Seventeenth and Eighteenth Centuries," *Annales Islamologiques* 42 (2008): 313–37; Daniel Crecelius and Gotcha Djaparidze, "Relations of the Georgian Mamluks of Egypt with Their Homeland in the Last Decades of the Eighteenth Century," *Journal of the Economic and Social History of the Orient* 45, no. 3 (2002): 320–41.

37. For Franco-Ottoman relations before and during the Egyptian expedition, see İsmail Soysal, *Fransız İhtilali ve Türk-Fransız Diplomasi Münasebetleri (1789–1802)* (Ankara: Türk Tarih Kurumu, 1999).

38. Ian Coller, "Egypt in the French Revolution," in *The French Revolution in Global Perspective*, ed. Suzanne Desan, Lynn Hunt, and William Max Nelson (Ithaca, NY: Cornell University Press, 2013), 131.

39. See Edward W. Said, *Orientalism* (New York: Vintage Books, 1979), 79–88.

40. See Eugene Tarle, *Admiral Ushakov na Sredizemnom more, 1798–1800* (Moscow: Voennoe Izdat. Ministerstva Oborony SSSR, 1948); Desmond Gregory, *Malta, Britain and the European Powers, 1793–1815* (Madison, NJ: Fairleigh Dickinson University Press, 1996).

41. See Alexander Mikhailovskii-Danilevskii and Dmitrii Miliutin, *Istoriya voiny Rossii s Frantsiei v tsarstvovanie imperatora Pavla I v 1799 g.*, 5 vols. (St. Petersburg: Tip. Shtaba voenno-uchebnykh zavedenii, 1852–57); Édouard Gachot, *Souvarow en Italie* (Paris: Perrin, 1903); Carl von Clausewitz, *La Campagne de 1799 en Italie et en Suisse* (Paris: Champ libre, 1979); Christopher Duffy, *Eagles over the Alps: Suvorov in Italy and Switzerland, 1799* (Chicago: Emperor's Press, 1999).

42. In his instructions to Semen Vorontsov, Russia's ambassador to London, Paul outlined his reasons for the break with Austria. Russian and British forces alone were not strong enough to defeat France, so instead Paul desired an alliance with Prussia to prevent Vienna "from executing its intention of seizing Piedmont, Genoa, and the Three Legations, in lieu of restoring these lands to those to whom they belong by right." If the king of Prussia would agree to an alliance, Paul was prepared to send him aid "in order to deliver Italy from the rapacity and boundless ambition of the House of Austria." In such a case, neither Russia nor Britain should object to the king making some acquisitions on the Rhine. Paul envisioned an alliance of Russia, Britain, Prussia, the Porte, Sweden, and Denmark that would put Austria in its place and was "capable of giving the law to all of Europe." Emperor Paul to Semen Vorontsov, October 15, 1799, *Dropmore Papers*, VI:32–34.

43. Emperor Paul I to Emperor Francis, October 22, 1799, in Mikhailovskii-Danilevskii and Miliutin, *Istoriya voiny Rossii s Frantsiei*, III:332. The British ambassador to Austria, Gilbert Elliot, Earl of Minto, warned his government that Austria's primary goal was to take control of the Italian conquests of France and it was willing to take extreme measures to accomplish this. The Austrian government "would probably make it the pivot on which their system would hereafter turn and...they would in the choice of their Allies, choose that Power, or those Powers, which should concur or acquiesce in this view. It seems to me as if a determine opposition on the part of Great Britain...might probably throw Austria once more into a connection with the French Republic, and become a motive...for a separate peace on that condition." *Life and Letters of Sir Hilbert Elliot, First Earl of Minto*, ed. the Countess of Minto (London: Longmans, Green, 1874), III:95.

44. Gaspar Jean Marie René de Cugnac, *Campagne de L'Armée de Réserve en 1800* (Paris: Libr. Military R. Chapelot, 1900); David Chandler, *The Campaigns of Napoleon* (New York: Macmillan, 1966), 264–97.

45. See Alexandre de Clercq, ed., *Recueil des Traités de la France* (Paris: A. Durand et Pedone-Lauriel, 1880), I:395–96. In six days of negotiations, the Austrian envoy, Count de Saint-Julien, was outwitted by the French foreign minister, Talleyrand, and despite lacking authority to do so, he signed preliminaries on

terms that were disadvantageous to Austria. Vienna disowned Saint-Julian and refused to ratify the agreement.

46. Paul W. Schroeder, *The Transformation of European Politics, 1763–1848* (New York: Oxford University Press, 1994), 209.

47. See Debate in the Commons on the Subsidies to the Emperor of Germany, July 18, 1800, in *The Parliamentary History of England from the Earliest Period to the Year 1803* (London: T. C. Hansard, 1820), XXXV:431–54. Volume 6 of the *Dropmore Papers*, featuring letters of Willian W. Grenville, provides important insights into the Anglo-Austrian relations in 1800.

Chapter 5

1. John F. Richards, *The New Cambridge History of India. Volume 1.5: The Mughal Empire* (Cambridge: Cambridge University Press, 1995), 253–81; C. A. Bayly, *The New Cambridge History of India. Volume 2.1: Indian Society and the Making of the British Empire* (Cambridge: Cambridge University Press, 1988), 7–44.

2. Among these leaders were the *peshwa* of Poona, the Gaekwads of Baroda, the Holkars of Indore and Malwa, the Sindhia (Scindias) of Gwalior and Ujjain, the Bhonsales of Nagpur, and the rajah of Berar. For details see Stewart Gordon, *The New Cambridge History of India*, vol. 2.4, *The Marathas, 1600–1818* (Cambridge: Cambridge University Press, 1993), 154–74. Also see V. G. Hatalkar, *Relations Between the French and the Marathas* (Bombay: T. V. Chidambaran, 1958); Umesh Ashokrao Kadam, *History of the Marathas: French-Maratha Relations, 1668–1818* (New Delhi: Sundeep Prakashan, 2008).

3. On Hyderabad, see Sunil Chander, "From a Pre-Colonial Order to a Princely State: Hyderabad in Transition, c. 1748–1865," Ph.D. diss., University of Cambridge, 1987, 71–88.

4. Under the terms of the treaty, Mysore ceded almost half of its territories. The *peshwa* acquired territory up to the Tungabhadra River; the *nizam* was awarded land from the Krishna to the Penner River and the forts of Cuddapah and Gandikota on the south bank of the Penner. The BEIC received a large portion of Mysore's Malabar coastal territories between the Kingdom of Travancore and the Kali River, as well as the Baramahal and Dindigul districts. Mysore also granted the rajah of Coorg his independence, although Coorg effectively became a BEIC dependency.

5. For a biography of Richard Wellesley, see Iris Butler, *The Eldest Brother: The Marquess Wellesley, the Duke of Wellington's Eldest Brother* (London: Hodder and Stoughton, 1973). For the Wellesley brothers in India, see John Severn, *Architects of Empire: The Duke of Wellington and His Brothers* (Norman: University of Oklahoma Press, 2007), 65–194.

6. Wellesley to Henry Dundas, February 28, 1798, in Henry Dundas and Richard Wellesley, *Two Views of British India: The Private Correspondence of Mr. Dundas and Lord Wellesley, 1798–1801*, ed. Edward Ingram (Bath: Adams & Dart, 1970), 28.

7. For details, see documents in "Contents of Mr. Dundas's letters to the Marquis Wellesley...Governor-General of India, 1798–1800," NLS, MS.1062; Arthur Wellesley, *A Selection from the Despatches, Treaties, and Other Papers of the Marquess Wellesley*, ed. Sidney Owen (Oxford: Clarendon Press, 1877); Dundas and Wellesley, *Two Views of British India.*

8. "Memorandum on Marquess Wellesley's Government in India," in Wellesley, *A Selection from the Despatches, Treaties, and Other Papers*, lxxv.

9. Dundas to Wellesley, 18 March 1799, "Contents of Mr. Dundas's Letters to the Marquis Wellesley...Governor-General of India, 1798–1800," NLS, MS.1062, p. 7.

10. In a letter to Dundas, Wellesley inquired as to what number of French troops in Tippu's service could be considered as a cause for hostilities. Dundas replied that in light of the circumstances, any number should be considered as such. Dundas to Wellesley, March 18, 1799, "Contents of Mr. Dundas's Letters to the Marquis Wellesley...Governor-General of India, 1798–1800," NLS, MS.1062, pp. 7–8.

11. Percival Spear, *The Oxford History of Modern India, 1740–1947* (Oxford: Oxford University Press, 1965), Part III, 111.

12. Stewart Gordon, *The New Cambridge History of India*, vol. 2, part 4, *The Marathas, 1600–1818* (Cambridge: Cambridge University Press, 1993), 166–72; Kaushik Roy, *War, Culture and Society in Early Modern South Asia, 1740–1849* (New York: Routledge, 2011), 109–17; Radhey Shyam Chaurasia, *History of the Marathas* (New Delhi: Atlantic, 2004), 21–65.

13. The full text of the Treaty of Bassein (1802) is in *Treaties and Engagements with Native Princes and States in India, Concluded for the Most Part in the Years 1817 and 1818*, BL, India Office Records, IOR/A/2/21, ix–xii; Richard Wellesley, *The Despatches, Minutes, and Correspondence of the Marquess Wellesley*, ed. Montgomery Martin (London: W. H. Allen, 1837), III:627–31.

14. For events leading up to the Anglo-Maratha War, see Govind S. Sardesai, *New History of the Marathas*, vol. 3, *Sunset over Maharashtra, 1772–1848* (New Delhi: Munshiram Manoharlal, 1986), 333–79; Pratul Chandra Gupta, *Baji Rao II and the East India Company, 1796–1818* (Bombay: Allied, 1964), 27–39; Rory Muir, *Wellington: The Path to Victory, 1769–1814* (New Haven, CT: Yale University Press, 2013), 106–25.

15. Arthur Wellesley, *The Despatches of Field Marshal the Duke of Wellington, During His Various Campaigns...*, ed. John Gurwood (London: John Murray, 1834), I:398.

16. Muir, *Wellington*, 130–47; Randolf G. S. Cooper, *The Anglo-Maratha Campaigns and the Contest for India: The Struggle for Control of the South Asian Military Economy* (Cambridge: Cambridge University Press, 2003), 82–212; K. G. Pietre, *The Second Anglo-Maratha War, 1802–05* (Poona: Dastane Ramchandra, 1990), 134–35.

17. *Treaties and Engagements with Native Princes and States in India*, xv–xviii; Wellesley, *The Despatches, Minutes, and Correspondence of the Marquess Wellesley*, III:634–36.

18. The Treaty of The Hague, signed on May 16, 1795, established a defensive alliance between France and the Batavian Republic. The latter, however, was clearly in a subservient position, for it was compelled to cede the territories of Maastricht, Venlo, and Flanders to France, pay a heavy war indemnity of 100 million guilders, support a French army of occupation, and provide cheap loans to the French republic.

19. AE Correspondance consulaire et commercial, "Alexandrie," 16. Excerpts from the memorandum are published in Francois Charles-Roux, *Les origines de l'expedition de l'Egypte* (Paris: Plon-Nourrit, 1910), 273.

20. AE Correspondance politique, "Perse," 8.

21. Georges Cuvier, "Eloge historique de Guill.-Ante. Olivier," and "Extrait d'une notice biographique sur Bruguières," in *Recueil des eloges historiques lus dans les séances publiques de l'Institut royal de France* (Paris, 1819), II:235–65, 425–42. Olivier returned to France alone in 1798 because Bruguière, never in good health, died in Italy in 1798. For an account of their travels, see G. A. Olivier, *Voyage dans l'Empire Othoman, l'Égypte et la Perse*, 6 vols. (Paris: Agasse, 1801–1807).

22. Paul Barras, *Mémoires de Barras, membre du Directoire*, ed. George Duruy (Paris: Hachette, 1896), III:161. The French foreign minister, Talleyrand, reinforced such sentiments in a February 1798 memorandum in which he argued that "having occupied and fortified Egypt, we shall send a corps of 15,000 men from Suez to India to join the forces of Tippu Sahib and drive away the English."

23. Glenville to Eden, January 16, 1798, FO, 7/51. For an interesting discussion of the debate between Grenville and Dundas over British strategy in 1799–1801, see Edward Ingram, "A Preview of the Great Game in Asia, III: The Origins of the British Expedition to Egypt in 1801," *Middle Eastern Studies* 9, no. 3 (1973): 296–314.

24. See Dundas to Wellesley, October 31, 1799, in Dundas and Wellesley, *Two Views of British India*, 206.

25. Secret Committee to the Governor General at Bengal, East India House, June 18, 1798, and H. Douglas to Governor General, Bengal, November 27, 1798, cited in Mubarak Al-Otabi, "The Qawasim and British Control of the Arabian Gulf," Ph.D. diss., University of Salford, 1989, 65. It is noteworthy that the British East India Company itself was rife with divisions and struggles between the City, Indian and private trade, and shipping interests, which frequently shaped British policies in Asia. For details, see C. H. Philips, *The East India Company, 1784–1834* (Manchester: Manchester University Press, 1961); Philip Lawson, *The East India Company: A History* (London: Longman, 1993).

26. Patricia Risso, *Oman and Muscat: An Early Modern History* (New York: St. Martin's Press, 1986); Jeremy Jones and Nicholas P. Ridout, *Oman: Culture and Diplomacy* (Edinburgh: Edinburgh University Press, 2012). For French relations with Muscat, see A. Auzouz, "La France et Muscate aux dix-huitième et dix-neuvième siècles," *Revue d'histoire diplomatique* XXIII (1909): 518–40.

27. Anglo-Omani Treaty (October 12, 1798), in Sir Charles U. Aitchison, ed., *A Collection of Treaties, Engagements and Sunnuds Relating to India and Neighboring Countries* (Calcutta: O. T. Cutter, 1865), VII:208–10; J. B. Kelly, *Britain and the Persian Gulf, 1795–1880* (Oxford: Clarendon Press, 1968), 65–67. The sultan also allowed the British East India Company to establish the first trading station in the Persian Gulf, and a British consul was posted to Muscat. A supplementary Anglo-Omani treaty was negotiated by John Malcolm in January 1800, specifying that an English political agent should reside at Muscat. Aitchison, *A Collection of Treaties, Engagements and Sunnuds*, VII:210–11.

28. The expedition consisted of 1,000 men and 14 cannon, supported by a small naval squadron. Edward Ingram, "A Preview of the Great Game in Asia, I: The British Occupation of Perim and Aden in 1799," *Middle Eastern Studies* 9, no. 1 (1973): 3–18.

29. Ingram, "A Preview of the Great Game in Asia, I," 10.

30. For example, British policy in Asia was subject to discussions by the Departments of War and Foreign Affairs, the Board of Control, and the BEIC government of India. In the case of the Near East, the British viewed it as comprising two distinct areas: the Mediterranean basin was in the purview of the Levant Company, while Arabia and the Persian Gulf was in that of the East India Company, with each side bitterly resenting any intrusion into its domain.

31. In November 1799 he lamented "the total forgetfulness we seem to labour under" with regard to the French presence in Egypt, which, he argued, represented a menace to India. "While there is [even] one thousand French troops anywhere in Egypt, I cannot concur in viewing the question in that light." Dundas to William Pitt, November 25, 1799, *Dropmore Papers*, VI:39. Also see Dundas to Grenville, November 24, 1799, *Dropmore Papers*, VI:37–38.

32. Dundas to Lord Grenville, June 13, 1798, in Wellesley, *The Despatches, Minutes, and Correspondence of the Marquess Wellesley*, I:689–91; Dundas to Lord Grenville, September 2, 1800, in *Dropmore Papers*, VI:312–13. For a broader discussion, see Edward Ingram, *Commitment to Empire: Prophecies of the Great Game in Asia, 1797–1800* (Oxford: Clarendon Press, 1981), 47–48; Piers Mackesy, *Statesmen at War: The Strategy of Overthrow, 1798–1799* (London: Longman, 1974), 7.

33. Dundas to Wellesley, September 27–November 1, 1799, in Dundas and Wellesley, *Two Views of British India*, 180, 203.

34. In October 1799, Wellesley did negotiate an agreement with the Portuguese to place a British garrison in Goa to preclude a possible French invasion.

35. For details see Piers Mackesy, *War Without Victory; The Downfall of Pitt, 1799–1802* (Oxford: Clarendon Press, 1984), 142–62; E. Ingram, "A Preview of the Great Game in Asia, III," 303–10.

36. Dundas favored focusing on operations in and around Egypt, calling for direct invasion of Egypt from the Mediterranean and Red Seas. But neither Grenville nor Wellesley had any interest in the Near East. Like Dundas, Wellesley was concerned about the French threat to India but thought that it would come by

a more traditional route around the Cape of Good Hope and utilizing the island of Mauritius as a base of operations. In late 1800, therefore, Wellesley focused his efforts on launching an expedition to Mauritius, only to face refusal of the British East Indies squadron commander to support it.

37. This British expeditionary force under Sir Ralph Abercromby had idled away much of the previous year between Italy, Minorca, Cadiz, and Malta, causing much discontent in British military circles. "What a disgraceful and what an expensive campaign we have made! Twenty-two thousand men, a large proportion not soldiers, floating round the greater part of Europe, the scorn and laughing stock of friends and foes," lamented one senior British official. Charles Cornwallis to Major General Ross, November 6, 1800, in *Correspondence of Charles, First Marquis Cornwallis*, ed. Charles Ross (London: John Murray, 1859), III:300–301.

38. For details, see Georges Rigault, *Le général Abdallah Menou et la dernière phase de l'expédition d'Egypte (1799–1801)* (Paris: Plon-Nourrit, 1911); Muḥammad Shafiq Ghurbāl, *Beginnings of the Egyptian Question and the Rise of Mehemet Ali* (New York: AMS Press, 1977).

39. For an interesting discussion, see Abbas Amanat and Farzin Vejdani, eds., *Iran Facing Others: Identity Boundaries in a Historical Perspective* (New York: Palgrave, 2012).

40. Petrus Bedik, *Cehil sutun, seu explicatio utriusque celeberrimi, ac pretiosissimi theatri quadraginta columnarum in Perside orientis, cum adjecta fusiori narratione de religione, moribus* (Vienna: Universitatis Typogr., 1678), 387–88.

41. This diplomatic overture was conducted by the BEIC's talented and versatile Iranian employee, Mahdi Ali Khan, who was appointed as the resident at Bushire. When in 1799 Fath Ali Shah sent some of his cavalry forces to Herat on his own accord, the British considered it within the context of their diplomatic efforts and wrongly attributed it to Mahdi Ali Khan's measures.

42. Malcolm initially visited Muscat, where he was able to negotiate a new agreement with the local sultan on January 18, 1800. He then proceeded to Persia, where, as Malcolm noted, his mission was threefold: "To relieve India from the annual alarm of Zaman Shah's invasion, which is always attended with serious expense to the Company, by occasioning a diversion upon his Persian provinces; to counteract the possible attempts of those villainous but active democrats the French; to restore to some part of its former prosperity a trade which has been in a great degree lost, are the leading objects of my journey." John William Kaye, *The Life and Correspondence of Major-General Sir John Malcolm* (London: Smith, Elder, 1856), I:89–90.

43. Kaye, *The Life and Correspondence of Major-General Sir John Malcolm*, I:111.

44. Kaye, *The Life and Correspondence of Major-General Sir John Malcolm*, I:116.

45. Treaty of Tehran (1801), in Aitchison, *A Collection of Treaties, Engagements and Sunnuds*, VII:112–17; Kelly, *Britain and the Persian Gulf*, 70–73; Denis Wright, *The English Amongst the Persians: Imperial Lives in Nineteenth Century Iran* (London: I. B. Tauris, 2001), 4–5. In addition, the treaty secured British

commercial interests in Persia, stipulating that English iron, lead, steel, and broadcloth should be admitted free of duty.

46. Percy M. Sykes, *History of Persia* (London: Macmillan, 1915), II:300–302; Birendra Varma, *From Delhi to Teheran: A Study of British Diplomatic Moves in North-Western India, Afghanistan and Persia, 1772–1803* (Patna: Janaki Prakashan, 1980), 186–92. Also see Malcolm Yapp, *Strategies of British India: Britain, Iran, and Afghanistan, 1798–1850* (Oxford: Clarendon Press, 1980); Robert Gleave, "The Clergy and the British: Perceptions of Religion and the Ulama in Early Qajar Iran," in *Anglo-Iranian Relations Since 1800*, ed. Vanessa Martin (New York: Routledge, 2005), 40–41.

47. Lindsey Hughes, *Peter the Great: A Biography* (New Haven, CT: Yale University Press, 2004), 174–75; Paul Bushkovitch, *Peter the Great* (London: Rowman & Littlefield, 2001), 137–38. By the Treaty of St. Petersburg (1723), Russia gained control of western coastal areas of the Caspian Sea and the Iranian provinces of Gilan, Mazandaran, and Astrabad.

48. Janet Martin, *Medieval Russia, 980–1584* (Cambridge: Cambridge University Press, 2003), 195–97, 261–35.

49. For a good overview, see Nikolas K. Gvosdev, *Imperial Policies and Perspectives Towards Georgia, 1760–1819* (New York: St. Martin's Press, 2000), 14–62.

50. See Giorgi Paichadze, *Georgievskii traktat* (Tbilisi: Metsniereba, 1983); A. Surguladze, *1783 tslis georgievskis traktati da misi istoriuli mnishvneloba* (Tbilisi: Tsodna, 1982); Zurab Avalov, *Prisoedinenie gruzii k Rossii* (St. Petersburg: Montvid, 1906). The treaty's text can be accessed at www.amsi.ge/istoria/sab/georgievski.html.

51. See David M. Lang, *The Last Years of the Georgian Monarchy, 1658–1832* (New York: Columbia University Press, 1957), 209–12.

52. See Marie F. Brosset, *Histoire de la Géorgie: depuis l'antiquité jusqu'au XIXe siècle* (St. Petersburg: Impr. de l'Académie impériale des sciences, 1849), vol. II.

53. Catherine to Zubov, February 19 (March 1), 1796, and Imperial Manifesto to the Iranian Peoples, March 27 (April 7), 1796, in Nikolai Dubrovin, *Istoriya voiny i vladychestva russkikh na Kavkaze* (St. Petersburg: Tip. Skorokhodova, 1886), III:70–80, 125–29; V. Potto, "Persidskii pokhod Zubova," in *Kavkazaskaya voina v otdelnykh ocherkakh, epizodakh, legendakh i biografiyakh* (St. Petersburg: Tip. E. Evdokimova, 1888), I:285–96; Muriel Atkin, *Russia and Iran, 1780–1828* (Minneapolis: University of Minnesota Press, 1980), 40–42.

54. For an insightful discussion, see Muriel Atkin, "The Pragmatic Diplomacy of Paul I: Russia's Relations with Asia, 1796–1801," *Slavic Review* 38, no. 1 (March 1979): 60–74.

55. The prominent British historian David Lang aptly noted that "by withdrawing her troops in 1787, failing to send them in time against Agha Muhammad in 1795, and again evacuating Georgia in 1797, Russia had undeniably forfeited any juridical right to demand Georgia's continued adherence to the Treaty of Georgievsk." Lang, *The Last Years of the Georgian Monarchy*, 173.

56. For details, see Gvosdev, *Imperial Policies and Perspectives Towards Georgia*, 77–98; Nikolai Dubrovin, *Georgii XII: Poslednii tsar Gruzii i prisoedinenie eia k Rossii* (St. Petersburg: Tip. Departamenta udelov, 1867); Laurens H. Rhinelander, "The Incorporation of the Caucasus into the Russian Empire: The Case of Georgia," Ph.D. diss., Columbia University, 1972; Zurab Avalov (Avalishvili), *Prisoedinenie Gruzii k Rossii* (St. Petersburg: Montvid, 1906).

57. Karl Roider, *Baron Thugut and Austria's Response to the French Revolution* (Princeton, NJ: Princeton University Press, 1987), 86.

58. *Décret de la Convention nationale, du 19 novembre 1792, l'an Ier de la république françoise: Par lequel la Convention déclare qu'elle accordera fraternité & secours à tous les peuples qui voudront recouvrer leur liberté* (Rennes: Imprimerie Nationale du Département d'Ille et Vilaine, 1792).

59. *Archives parlementaires de 1787 à 1860: recueil complet des débats législatifs et politiques des chambres françaises* (Paris: Librairie administrative Paul Dupont, 1909), LXIV, 231. Also see Virginie Martin, "In Search of the 'Glorious Peace'? Republican Diplomats at War, 1792–1799," in *Republics at War, 1776–1840: Revolutions, Conflicts, Geopolitics in Europe and the Atlantic World*, ed. Pierre Serna, Antonino de Francesco, and Judith A. Miller (New York: Palgrave Macmillan, 2013), 46–64.

60. Jacques Godechot, "Les variations de la politique française à l'égard des pays occupés de 1792 à 1815," in *Occupants, Occupés 1792–1815. Colloque de Bruxelles, 29 et 30 janvier 1968* (Brussels: Université libre de Bruxelles, Centre d'histoire économique et sociale, 1969), 27.

61. Cited in Jacques Godechot, *La grande nation: l'expansion révolutionnaire de la France dans le monde de 1789 à 1799* (Paris: Aubier, 1956), II:660.

62. Francois Furet, *Interpreting the French Revolution* (Cambridge: Cambridge University Press, 1981), 127.

Chapter 6

1. See Georges Lefebvre, *The Thermidorians and the Directory: Two Phases of the French Revolution* (New York: Random House, 1964), 387–45; William Doyle, *The Oxford History of the French Revolution* (Oxford: Oxford University Press, 1990), 318–68; Martyn Lyons, *France Under the Directory* (Cambridge: Cambridge University Press, 1975); Denis Woronoff, *The Thermidorean Regime and the Directory, 1794–1799* (Cambridge: Cambridge University Press, 1984). For insights into contemporaries' perceptions, see Paul Thiébault, *The Memoirs of Barton Thiébault*, trans. and ed. Arthurt Butler (New York: Macmillan, 1896), II:13–14; Antoine-Marie Chamans, *The Memoirs of Count Lavallette* (Philadelphia: Thomas T. Ash, 1832), 71–72.

2. The quote is from Napoleon's conversation with General Marmont, cited in J. Holland Rose, *The Life of Napoleon I* (London: George Bell and Sons, 1907), I:218.

3. For an in-depth discussion, see Malcolm Cook, *Napoleon Comes to Power: Democracy and Dictatorship in Revolutionary France, 1795–1804* (Cardiff: University of

Wales Press, 1998). For concise treatments see Andrew Roberts, *Napoleon: A Life* (New York: Viking, 2014), 215–27; Michael Broers, *Napoleon: Soldier of Destiny* (New York: Pegasus Books, 2014), 203–29; Robert B. Asprey, *The Rise of Napoleon Bonaparte* (New York: Basic Books, 2000), 327–39.

4. Thierry Lentz, *La France et l'Europe de Napoléon, 1804–1814* (Paris: Fayard, 2007), 107–46.

5. For discussion of the Consulate, see Thierry Lentz, *Le grand Consulat: 1799–1804* (Paris: Fayard, 1999); Jean Tulard, *Le Directoire et le Consulat* (Paris: Presses universitaires de France, 1991); Lefebvre, *Napoleon from Brumaire to Tilsit*, 71–92, 122–59.

6. Lentz, *La France et l'Europe de Napoléon*, 151–94.

7. For discussion of the electoral system, see Lentz, *La France et l'Europe de Napoléon*, 98–106.

8. Lentz, *La France et l'Europe de Napoléon,* 97; Isser Woloch, *Napoleon and His Collaborators: The Making of a Dictatorship* (New York: W. W. Norton, 2001), 94–96.

9. The 1800 plebiscite saw about 80 percent of voters abstaining, and the number of "yes" votes was in fact close to 1,5 million. For an excellent discussion, see Malcolm Crook, "Confidence from Below? Collaboration and Resistance in the Napoleonic Plebiscites," in *Collaboration and Resistance in Napoleonic Europe: State Formation in an Age of Upheaval, 1800–1815*, ed. Michael Rose (New York: Palgrave Macmillan, 2003), 19–36. For a local view of Lucien's falsifications, see Bernard Gainor, "Réflexions sur le plebiscite de l'an VIII à partit de l'exemple de la Saône-et-Loire," in *Le Bonheaur est une idéee neuve: Mélanges en l'honneur du Professeur Jean Bart*, ed. Jean Jacques Clère (Dijon: Presses universitaires de Dijon, 2000). The abstention rate remained high. For example, in Marseille, a city of 100,000 people, only 1,200 votes were cast. See Claude Langlois, "Le plébiscite de l'an VIII ou le coup d'Etat du 18 Pluviôse an VIII," *Annales historiques de la Révolution française*, 1972, 43–65, 231–46, 396–415; Claude Langlois, "Napoléon Bonaparte plebiscite?" in *L'Election du chef d'Etat en France: De Hugues Capet à nos jours*, ed. Leo Hamon and Guy Lobrichon (Paris: Beauchesne, 1988), 81–93.

10. Langlois, "'Le plébiscite de l'an VIII,'" 414.

11. Crook, "Confidence from Below?," 31; Jeff Horn, "Building the New Regime: Founding the Bonapartist State in the Department of the Aube," *French Historical Studies* 25, no. 2 (2002): 241.

12. Lentz, *La France et l'Europe de Napoléon*, 391–42.

13. Joseph N. Moody, *French Education Since Napoleon* (Syracuse: Syracuse University Press, 1978); Stewart McCain, *The Language Question Under Napoleon* (New York: Palgrave Macmillan, 2018), 117–50.

14. For a concise overview of Napoleon's reforms, see Robert B. Holtman, *The Napoleonic Revolution* (Baton Rouge: Louisiana State University Press, 1967).

15. Patrick M. Geoghegan, *The Irish Act of Union: A Study in High Politics, 1798–1801* (New York: St. Martin's Press, 1999); Daire Keogh and Kevin

Whelan, eds., *Acts of Union: The Causes, Contexts, and Consequences of the Act of Union* (Dublin: Four Courts Press, 2001); Hilary Larkin, *A History of Ireland, 1800–1922* (London: Anthem Press, 2014), 9–26.

16. William Pitt's speech of January 31, 1799, in *The Speeches of the Right Honourable William Pitt in the House of Commons* (London: Longman, 1808), III:29.

17. For historiographical discussion, see Liam Kennedy and David S. Johnson, "The Union of Ireland and Britain, 1801–1921," in *The Making of Modern Irish History: Revisionism and the Revisionist Controversy*, ed. D. George Boyce and Alan O'Day (New York: Routledge, 2006), 34–49.

18. For the start of Franco-Austrian negotiations, see August Fournier, "Die Mission des Grafen Saint-Julien im Jahre 1800," *Historische Studien und Skizzen* 1 (1885): 179–210.

19. "Everything gets confused more and more, and we fall into an inextricable incoherence," lamented Austrian foreign minister Johann Amadeus Franz de Paula Thugut on October 19, 1800, as he described the Austrian position at Lunéville and the prospect of Franco-Russian rapprochement. See his letters from October-November 1800 in Franz de Paula Thugut, *Vertrauliche Briefe des Freiherrn von Thugut* (Vienna: Wilhelm Braumüller, 1872), vol. 2, esp. 317–18, 321–22, 352–53. For an interesting discussion of Austrian internal politics, see Harold C. Deutsch, *The Genesis of Napoleonic Imperialism* (Cambridge, MA: Harvard University Press, 1938), 7–13.

20. The text of the treaty is in Alexandre de Clercq, ed., *Recueil des traités de la France* (Paris: A. Durand et Pedone-Lauriel, 1880), I:424–29; Georg Friedrich Martens, *Recueil des principaux traités d'alliance, de paix, de trève, de neuralité, de commerce, de limites, d'échange, etc.* (Gottingue: Librairie de Dieterich, 1801), VII:538–44.

21. See Karl Roider, *Baron Thugut and Austria's Response to the French Revolution* (Princeton: Princeton University Press, 1987), 371–73.

22. Bonaparte to the Senate, February 13, 1801, in *A Selection from the Letters and Despatches of the First Napoleon*, ed. D. Bingham (London: Chapman and Hall, 1884), I:341.

23. Clercq, *Recueil des traités de la France*, I:431–32.

24. Joseph Élisabeth Roger, comte de Damas d'Antigny, *Memoirs of the Comte Roger de Damas, 1787–1806*, ed. Jacques Rambaud (London: Chapman and Hall, 1913), 298–99.

25. Clercq, *Recueil des traités de la France*, I:432–34.

26. The treaty was not ratified and was published only nine months later, once Bonaparte ensured that there would be no opposition to this treaty in the legislative bodies.

27. For a good summary of negotiations, see M. Barbara, "Napoleon Bonaparte and the Restoration of Catholicism in France," *Catholic Historical Review* 12, no. 2 (1926): 241–57.

28. The text of the treaty can be seen at www.napoleon.org/fr/salle_lecture/articles/files/Concordat_18011.asp.

29. Louis Pierre Édouard Bignon, *Histoire de France, depuis le 18 brumaire, novembre 1799, jusqu'à la paix de Tilsit (Juillet 1807)* (Brussels: J. P. Meline, 1836), 173.

30. See Claude Langlois, "La fin des guerres de religion: La disparition de la violence religieuse en France au 19e siècle," *French Historical Studies* 21, no. 1 (1998): 3–25.

31. In an effort to minimize the damage, the Russian ambassador in London, Semen Vorontsov, described the Russian emperor as an infantile person and pleaded with the British cabinet members that "one should not be angry with infants." Vorontsov to Lord Grenville, July 2, 1800, in *Dropmore Papers*, VI:259, 261.

32. One Russian historian, Aleksandr Kornilov, called Paul a "crowned psychopath" and characterized his reign as "a sudden incursion, an unexpected squall, which fell in from without, confused everything, turned everything topsy-turvy, but was unable for long to interrupt or to profoundly alter the natural course of the ongoing process." Aleksandr Kornilov, *Kurs istorii Rossii XIX veka* (The Hague: Mouton, 1969), 58. For a more judicious and insightful discussion, see Ole Feldbaek, "The Foreign Policy of Tsar Paul I, 1800–1801: An Interpretation," *Jahrbücher für Geschichte Osteuropas* XXX (1982): 16–36; Hugh Ragsdale, "The Origins of Bonaparte's Russian Policy," *Slavic Review* 27, no. 1 (1968): 85–90; Hugh Ragsdale, *Détente in the Napoleonic Era: Bonaparte and the Russians* (Lawrence: University of Kansas Press, 1980).

33. Robert Meynadier, "Un plan de l'Empereur Paul de Russie," *La Revue de Paris* 6 (November-December 1920): 193–94; Sergey Tatishchev, "Paul 1er et Bonaparte," *Nouvelle revue* XLIX (1889): 260; Alexander Mikhailovskii-Danilevskii and Dmitrii Miliutin, *Istoriya voiny Rossii s Frantsiei v tsarstvovanie imperatora Pavla I v 1799 g.* (St. Petersburg: Tip. Shtaba voenno-uchebnykh zavedenii, 1852–57), V:494.

34. Bonaparte to Talleyrand, June 4 and July 4, 1800, in Napoleon Bonaparte, *Correspondance Générale*, ed. Thierry Lentz, Michel Kerautret, François Houdecek, et al. (Paris: Fayard, 2006), III: 280, 326.

35. For contemporary coverage, see *Monthly Visitor* XVI (January 1802): 11–15.

36. See Franco-Russian diplomatic correspondence in Alexander Trachevskii, "Diplomaticheskie snosheniya Frantsii i Rossii v epokhu Napoleona I, 1800–1802," *SIRIO* LXX (1890): 1–10; F. Martens, *Recueil des traités et conventions conclus par la Russie avec les puissances étrangères* (St. Petersburg: A. Böhnke, 1902), XIII:250–70.

37. In response, Britain ordered its commanders not to admit the Russians to Malta for fear that they would close the port of Valletta to the British navy.

38. Diplomatic Note, October 8, 1800, in Trachevskii, "Diplomaticheskie snosheniya," 10–11.

39. According to the memorandum, "Greece with all the islands of the Archipelago will be established after the example of the Venetian islands as a republic, under the protection of the four powers.... But for now, the Greeks themselves will come under the scepter of Russia."

40. Emperor Paul scribbled on the margins, "Maybe too much!?" Rostopchin argued the Austrian "emperor and his ministers would be as satisfied with the partition of Turkey as would be a ruined man who has just gained the grand prize at the lottery."

41. See "Zapiska grafa F.V. Rostopchina o politicheskikh otnosheniyakh Rossii v poslednie mesyatsy Pavlovskago tsarstvovaniya," *Russkii arkhiv*, 1878, I:109–10. For the French version, see Duc de Broglie, "La Politique de la Russie en 1800 d'apres un document inédit," *Révue d'histoire diplomatique* 3 (1889): 1–12.

42. Mark McKinley Lee, "Paul I and the Indian Expedition of 1801: Myth and Reality," MA thesis, Texas Tech University, 1984, 74–219. Also see V. T. Lebedev, *V Indiyu, voyeno-statisticheskiy i strategicheskiv ocherk* (St. Petersburg: Tipografiy a A. A. Porokhovskchikova, 1898); Alex Zotov, "The Failed Franco-Russian Expedition to India, 1801," http://history-gatchina.ru/paul/india/index.htm.

43. Gottfried Wilhelm Leibniz, *Mémoire de Leibnitz à Louis XIV sur la conquête de l'Égypte* (Paris: Edouard Garnot, 1840), 37–51; Curt Bogislaus Ludvig Kristoffer von Stedingk, *Mémoires posthumes du feldmaréchal comte de Stedingk: rédigés sur des lettres, dépêches et autres pièces authentiques laissées à sa famille*, ed. Magnus Fredrik Ferdinand Björnstjerna (Paris: A. Bertrand, 1845), II:6–9. Also see P. Karatygin, "Proekt Russko-frantsuzskoi ekspeditsii v Indiyu 1800 g.," *Russkaya starina* 8 (1873): 401–9.

44. In his *Napoleon's Wars: An International History* (88–89), Charles Esdaile rightly downplays the importance of this expedition but incorrectly ties it to "a quite separate crisis" in Georgia that suffered from a Persian invasion for its pursuit of closer relations with Russia. Esdaile implies that the Cossack expedition was a response to the 1795 invasion of Georgia by Agha Muhammad Khan of Persia. But such a connection is disputable. Russia, in fact, responded to the Persian invasion of Georgia the very next year (1796) when Catherine II dispatched a Russian corps, under command of Count Valerian Zubov, to southern Caucasus. Zubov successfully attacked Persian interests in what is today Daghestan and Azerbaijan, capturing Baku in June 1796. It was Emperor Paul who, upon his accession to the throne, stopped the Russian invasion of Iran and recalled troops back home.

45. Paul to Orlov, January 12/24, 1801, in Nikolai Shilder, *Imperator Pavel I* (St. Petersburg, 1801), 417.

46. Lord Grenville believed that for Britain, the right to search convoys was a "question of little less than its independence, affecting all its sources of greatness, and shaking the very foundations of its naval power." Cited in Piers Mackesy, *War Without Victory: The Downfall of Pitt, 1799–1802* (Oxford: Clarendon Press, 1984), 134.

47. T. K. Derry, "Scandinavia," in *The New Cambridge Modern History*, ed. C. W. Crawley (Cambridge: Cambridge University Press, 1975), 484.

48. Philip G. Dwyer, "Prussia and the Armed Neutrality: The Invasion of Hanover in 1801," *International History Review* 15, no. 4 (1993): 662–64.

49. For details, see Alfred Mahan, *The Influence of Sea Power upon the French Revolution and Empire, 1793–1812* (Boston: Little, Brown, 1918), II:41–45; Ole Feldbaek, *Danmark og Det væbnede neutralitetsforbund 1800–1801: småstatspolitik i en verdenskrig* (Copenhagen: Institut for økonomisk historie ved Københavns universitet, 1980).

50. Hugh Ragsdale, "A Continental System in 1801: Paul I and Bonaparte," *Journal of Modern History* 42, no. 1 (March 1970): 70–89. Also see his "Russia, Prussia, and Europe in the Policy of Paul V," *Jahrbücher für Geschichte Osteuropas* XXXI (1983): 81–118.

51. David Macmillan, "Paul's Retributive Measures of 1800 Against Britain: The Final Turning-Point in British Commercial Attitudes Towards Russia," *Canadian-American Slavic Studies* VI, no. 1 (1973): 72–77.

52. Originaltraktater med främmande makter (traktater), August 31, 1805, Riksarkivet, SE/RA/25.3/2/39/A-B; Russian Imperial Declaration (August 27, 1800), Convention Between Russia, Sweden, and Denmark-Norway (December 16, 1800), and Convention Between Russia and Prussia (December 18, 1800) in August James Brown Scott, ed., *The Armed Neutralities of 1780 and 1800: A Collection of Official Documents* (New York: Oxford University Press, 1918), 489–92, 531–49.

53. Hanover was joined to the British crown by personal union and was an important commercial emporium in northern Germany, an obvious target for any state wishing to apply diplomatic pressure to Britain.

54. Paul W. Schroeder, *The Transformation of European Politics, 1763–48* (New York: Oxford University Press, 1994), 220.

55. Declaration of the King of Prussia, in Scott, *The Armed Neutralities of 1780 and 1800*, 592–94. For more details, see Paul Bailleur, ed., *Preussen und Frankreich von 1795 bis 1807: Diplomatische correspondenzen*, vol. 2 (Leipzig: S. Hirzel, 1881–1887). Also see Dwyer, "Prussia and the Armed Neutrality," 661–87; Guy Stanton Ford, *Hanover and Prussia, 1795–1803: A Study in Neutrality* (New York: Columbia University Press, 1903), 192–268.

56. See the excellent discussion in Eugene Tarle, *Kontinentalnaya blokada* (Moscow: Zadruga, 1913); William F. Galpin, *The Grain Supply of England During the Napoleonic Period* (New York: Macmillan, 1925); Robert G. Albion, *Forests and Sea Power: The Timber Problem of the Royal Navy, 1652–1862* (Cambridge MA: Harvard University Press, 1927).

57. For a broader discussion of the British strategy in 1800–1801, see Mackesy, *War Without Victory*, 95–201.

58. William Laird Clowes, *The Royal Navy: A History from the Earliest Times to the Present* (London: Sampson Loaw, Marston, 1899), IV:470–71; *The Naval Chronicle*, ed. James Stanier Clarke (London: Bunney & Gold, 1801) V:162, 444–45; VI:148; Neville A. T. Hall, *Slave Society in the Danish West Indies: St. Thomas, St. John and St. Croix*, ed. B. W. Higman (Kingston: University of the West Indies Press, 1994), 26.

59. See Ole Feldbæk, *The Battle of Copenhagen 1801: Nelson and the Danes* (Barnsley: Leo Cooper, 2002).

60. Some Russian contemporaries believed that the British government was involved in the assassination and that the English gold helped finance the conspiracy. For contemporary testimonies see *Tsarubiistvo 11 marta 1801 goda: Zapiski uchastnikov i sovremennikov* (St. Petersburg, 1907); *Arkhiv kniazya Vorontsova* (Moscow, 1870–1895), X:113–14, XIV:146–48. Also see James J. Kenney, "Lord Whitworth and the Conspiracy Against Tsar Paul I: The New Evidence of the Kent Archive," *Slavic Review* 36, no. 2 (June 1977): 205–19.

61. Luccesini's report of April 17, 1801, in Paul Bailleu, ed. *Preussen und Frankreich von 1795 bis 1807: Diplomatische correspondenzen* (Leipzig: S. Hirzel, 1887), II:38.

62. Dwyer, "Prussia and the Armed Neutrality," 86.

63. See Ford, *Hanover and Prussia*, 271–90.

64. For correspondence between Bonaparte and Mustafa Pasha, see *Pièces curieuses ou Alger en 1802* (Paris: Palais Royal, 1830), 5–16.

65. *A Selection from the Letters and Despatches of the First Napoleon*, ed. Bingham, I:397, 398–99, 401.

66. The text of the act is available in *A Century of Lawmaking for a New Nation: U.S. Congressional Documents and Debates, 1774–1875*, http://memory.loc. gov/cgi-bin/ampage?collId=llsl&fileName=001/llsl001.db&recNum =473.

67. Treaty of Peace and Amity, September 5, 1795, Yale University, The Avalon Project, http://avalon.law.yale.edu/18th_century/bar1795t.asp. Also see Martha Elena Rojas, "'Insults Unpunished': Barbary Captives, American Slaves, and the Negotiation of Liberty," *Early American Studies: An Interdisciplinary Journal* 1, no. 2 (2003): 159–86.

68. Treaties with Tripoli (November 4, 1796), Algiers (January 3, 1797), and Tunis (August 28, 1797), Yale University, The Avalon Project, http://avalon. law.yale.edu/subject_menus/barmenu.asp.

69. Joseph Whelan, *Jefferson's War: America's First War on Terror, 1801–1805* (New York: Carroll and Graf, 2003); Michael L. S. Kitzen, *Tripoli and the United States at War: A History of American Relations with the Barbary States, 1785–1805* (Jefferson, NC: McFarland, 1993).

70. Spencer C. Tucker, *Stephen Decatur: A Life Most Bold and Daring* (Annapolis, MD: Naval Institute Press, 2004).

71. Richard Zacks, *The Pirate Coast: Thomas Jefferson, the First Marines, and the Secret Mission of 1805* (New York: Hyperion, 2005); Richard Parker, *Uncle Sam in Barbary: A Diplomatic History* (Tallahassee: University Press of Florida, 2004).

72. Joshua London, *Victory in Tripoli: How America's War with the Barbary Pirates Established the U.S. Navy and Shaped a Nation* (Hoboken, NJ: John Wiley, 2005).

Chapter 7

1. For an excellent discussion, see John D. Grainger, *The Amiens Truce: Britain and Bonaparte, 1801–03* (Rochester, NY: Boydell Press, 2004). Also see James Raymond Weinlader, "The Peace of Amiens, 1801–02: Its Justification in Relation to Empire," Ph.D. diss., University of Wisconsin, 1977.

2. Bonaparte to George III, December 25, 1799, in Napoleon, *Correspondance générale*, ed. Thierry Lentz (Paris: Fayard, 2004), II:1115.

3. George III to Lord Grenville, September 4, 1792, in *The Letters of King George III*, ed. Bonamy Dobree (London: Cassell, 1935), 215.

4. George III to Lord Grenville, August 2, 1792, in *The Letters of King George III*:218–19; George III, *The Later Correspondence of George III*, ed. Arthur Aspinall (Cambridge: Cambridge University Press, 1963), II:73.

5. George III to Lord Grenville, January 1, 1800, in *The Later Correspondence of George III*, III:308.

6. Earl Philip Henry Stanhope, *Life of the Right Honourable William Pitt* (London: John Murray, 1867), III:215–16. Also see Robert Bisset, *The History of the Reign of George III to the Termination of the Late War* (London: A. Strahan, 1803), VI:350–51.

7. Otto to Grenville, August 24, 1800, in *The Parliamentary History of England, from the Earliest Period to the Year 1803* (London: T. C. Hansard, 1820), XXXV:540–41.

8. The first force that Bonaparte had in mind was that in Egypt. The men of the army that Bonaparte led to the shores of North Africa had been greatly reduced in number by disease and casualties, but they still maintained effective control over significant territory in Egypt. Yet Admiral Nelson's naval triumph at Aboukir Bay (1798) had severed their connections with France, and it was clear that unless something decisive was done, the French army would gradually waste away. Bonaparte understood this well and was keen on extricating his troops. The second force on Bonaparte's mind was that on the island of Malta, where the French garrison of Valetta had been under siege by coalition forces for the best part of two years. For Malta, see William Hardman, *A History of Malta During the Period of the French and British Occupations, 1798–1815* (London: Longmans, Green, 1909), 107–35.

9. Carysfort to Grenville, November 12, 1800, *Dropmore Papers*, VI:374–76. Carysfort's letter contained two of Gentz's *mémoires* describing European sentiment.

10. For detailed discussion of Pitt's resignation and its impact, see John Ehrman, *The Younger Pitt: The Consuming Struggle* (Stanford, CA: Stanford University Press, 1996), 495–533. Some French historians argue that the resignation of William Pitt's government, which included notable hawks, had been made as a "strategic ploy" to avoid both the humiliation of being forced to negotiate peace with France and to have hands free in case of a future return to power.

See Edouard Driault, *Napoléon et l'Europe. The Politique Extérieure du Premier Consul (1800–03)* (Paris: Felix Alcan, 1910), 162–64.

11. Bonaparte to Talleyrand, July 28, 1800 (no. 5034), September 30, 1800 (no. 5120), January 27, 1801 (no. 5327), February 13, 1801 (no. 5365), and March 2, 1801 (no. 5426); Bonaparte to the King of Spain, November 8, 1800 (no. 5165), in *CN*, VI:426–27, 469, 499, 590–92; VII:22–23, 54–55; Traité préliminaire d'alliance signé ã Madrid, January 29, 1801; Ratification du Premier Consul…sur le traité préliminaire d'alliance signé à Madrid, February 17, 1801, in Alexandre de Clercq, ed., *Recueil des traités de la France* (Paris: A. Durand et Pedone-Lauriel, 1880), I:420–24.

12. Angelo Pereira, *D. João VI principe e rei* (Lisbon: Empresa Nacional de Publicidade, 1953), I:70; Valentim Alexandre, *Os sentidos do Império: questão nacional e questão colonial na crise do Antigo Regime português* (Porto: Edições Afrontamento, 1993), 102–3, 115–16, 121–26; Albert Silbert, *Do Portugal de antigo regime ao Portugal oitocentista* (Lisbon: Livros Horizonte, 1981), 49–52. For treaties of Badajoz and Madrid, see Georg Friedrich Martens, *Recueil des principaux traités d'alliance, de paix, de trève, de neuralité, de commerce, de limites, d'échange, etc.* (Gottingen: Librairie de Dieterich, 1801), VII:348–51; 373–76.

13. Frederick C. Schneid, *Napoleon's Conquest of Europe: The War of the Third Coalition* (Westport, CT: Praeger, 2005), 23.

14. For effects of the War of Oranges outside Europe, see Mark A. Frakes, "Governor Ribera and the War of Oranges on Paraguay's Frontiers," *The Americas* 45, no. 4 (1989): 489–508; Barbara Anne Ganson, *The Guarani Under Spanish Rule in the Rio de la Plata* (Stanford, CA: Stanford University Press, 2003), 155–56.

15. See Desmond Gregory, *The Beneficent Usurpers: A History of the British in Madeira* (London: Associated University Presses, 1988), 47–64.

16. The final treaty was also signed by José Nicolás de Azar for Spain and Rutger Jan Schimmelpenninck for the Batavian Republic.

17. There was a separate Franco-Dutch agreement of August 1801 that required the removal of French troops from Holland when the general peace was signed. Also, the Treaty of Lunéville had a separate provision for recognizing the independence of the Batavian, Helvetic, Cisalpine, and Ligurian Republics.

18. Treaty of Amiens, March 25, 1802, Fondation Napoléon, https://www.napoleon.org/histoire-des-2-empires/articles/le-traite-de-la-paix-damiens.

19. The return of the captured colonies was an important concession, and it made it abundantly manifest that Britain had not waged war with the sole view of enlarging its colonial empire.

20. *Diaries and Correspondence of James Harris, First Earl of Malmesbury* (London: Richard Bentley, 1845), IV:69.

21. William Eden Baron Auckland, *The Journal and Correspondence of William, Lord Auckland* (London: Richard Bentley, 1862), IV:143–44.

22. Lord Grenville to William Pitt, October 6, 1801, *Dropmore Papers*, VII:50–51. Also see *Duke of Buckingham and Chandos, Memoirs of the Court and Cabinets of George the Third* (London: Hurst and Blackett, 1855), III:178.

23. Auckland, *Journal and Correspondence*, IV:143–44.

24. William Woodfall, ed., *The Parliamentary Register, or an Impartial Report of the Debates that Occur in the Two Houses of Parliament* (London: John Stockdale, 1802), I:64.

25. Schroeder correctly notes that the Amiens treaty was a testament to "France's skill and persistence in negotiations, the Addington government's distraction and weakness, and Cornwallis's inexperience as a negotiator." Paul W. Schroeder, *The Transformation of European Politics, 1763–1848* (New York: Oxford University Press, 1994), 227.

26. Piers Mackesy, *War Without Victory; The Downfall of Pitt, 1799–1802* (Oxford: Clarendon Press, 1984), 215–16. It must be noted that the British ministers, all honorable but not very experienced men, were willing to accept agreement because they believed that British interests in India and the Caribbean had been safeguarded by the retention of Ceylon and Trinidad, which could serve as important staging grounds.

27. For example, Conrad Gill condemns them for framing "the provisions with the confidence of inexperience and with the joy of restoring peace to Europe. In their pacific enthusiasm the ministers made terms which Pitt and his colleagues would have rejected without a second thought." "The Relations Between England and France in 1802," *English Historical Review* XXIV, no. 93 (1909): 61.

28. For an interesting discussion, see Michael Duffy, "British Diplomacy and the French Wars, 1789–1815," in *Britain and the French Revolution, 1789–1815*, ed. H. T. Dickinson (New York: St. Martin's Press, 1989), 127–45; Piers Mackesy, "Strategic Problems of the British War Effort," in *Britain and the French Revolution, 1789–1815*, ed. H. T. Dickinson (New York: St. Martin's Press, 1989), 147–64; Paul Schroeder, "The Collapse of the Second Coalition," *Journal of Modern History* LIX (1987): 244–90.

29. Charles Creighton, *A History of Epidemics in Britain* (Cambridge: Cambridge University Press, 1894), II:159–60. The price of wheat was 61s 8d per quarter in the spring of 1799, 94 s 2d. in December 1799, 134 s. 5d. in June 1800, and 180s in late summer 1801. It fell back to 57–60s. in 1802 (II:162).

30. Auckland, *Journal and Correspondence*, IV:144.

31. Auckland, *Journal and Correspondence*, IV:144.

32. Admiral Viscount Keith, *The Keith Papers: Selected from the Papers of Admiral Viscount Keith*, ed. Christopher Lloyd (London: Navy Records Society, 1950), II:376.

33. Edmund Burke, "Letters on a Regicide Peace," in *The Works of the Right Hon. Edmund Burke*, ed. Henry Rogers (London: Henry G. Bohn, 1841), II:334.

34. Carl Ludwig Lokke, "French Designs on Paraguay in 1803," *Hispanic American Historical Review* 8, no. 3 (August 1928): 392–405.

35. Pierre-Alexandre-Laurent Forfait's memorandum, 12 Germinal An X (1802), cited in Henri Prentout, *L'Ile de France sous Decaen, 1803–10* (Paris: Librairie Hachette, 1901), 14.

36. Bonaparte to General Berthier, July 18, 1802; Bonaparte to Admiral Decrès, January 15, 1803, in *CN*, no. 6189, VII:524; no. 6544, VIII:176–78.

37. Prentout, *L'Ile de France sous Decaen*, xiv-xxii, 1–4, 16–31. Only thirty-four years old, Decaen was largely unknown and unconnected with any previous colonial ventures, and seemed unlikely to cause any trouble: writing in January 1803, British ambassador Whitworth observed that Decaen "is a young man, and bears a very fair character in private life, but possesses no very shining talents either as a general or a statesman. We may therefore conclude that, as far as he is concerned, it is intended rather to improve what possessions they [the French] already have in India than to extend them by conquest or intrigue." Oscar Browning, *England and Napoleon in 1803, Being the Despatches of Lord Whitworth and Others* (London: Longmans, Green, 1887), 45. For some historians, Bonaparte's decision to select Decaen, "an avowed fire-eating Anglophobe," served as yet another example of his "scarcely concealed contempt" for peace with Britain. W. M. Sloane, "Napoleon's Plans for a Colonial System," *American Historical Review* 4, no. 3 (April 1899): 441.

38. George McCall Theal, *History of South Africa* (London: Swan Sonnenschein, 1908), I:93–108.

39. Also see reports of English residents at the Cape in J. Holland Rose, "The French East-Indian Expedition at the Cape in 1803," *English Historical Review* 15, no. 57 (1900): 129–32.

40. Prentout, *L'Ile de France sous Decaen*, 31–60.

41. Journaux du capitaine de vaisseau Nicolas Baudin, commandant de l'expédition, 1800–1803, AN MAR/5JJ/35-MAR/5JJ/40/D; Nicole Starbuck, "Constructing the 'Perfect' Voyage: Nicolas Baudin at Port Jackson, 1802," Ph.D. diss., University of Adelaide, 2009; Serge M. Rivière and Kumari R. Issur, eds., *Baudin-Flinders dans l'océan indien: Voyages, découvertes, rencontre* (Paris: L'Harmattan, 2006), Ernest Scott, *Terre Napoléon: A History of French Explorations and Projects in Australia* (London: Methuen, 1910).

42. For instructions, see Ernest Scott, "Baudin's Voyage of Exploration to Australia," *English Historical Review* 28, no. 110 (April 1913): 341–46. For documents related to the expedition, see Nicolas Baudin, *Mon voyage aux terres australes: journal personnel du commandant Baudin* (Paris: Imprimerie nationale éditions, 2000).

43. See François Péron, *French Designs on Colonial New South Wales: François Péron's Memoir on the English Settlements in New Holland, Van Diemen's Land and the Archipelagos of the Great Pacific Ocean*, ed. Jean Fornasiero and John West-Sooby (Adelaide: Friends of the State Library of South Australia, 2014). Some modern scholars still argue that "in spite of almost total absence of documents, [they] still persist in believing in the political character of the Baudin expedition."

Jean-Paul Faivre, "Preface," in Nicolas Baudin, *The Journal of Post Captain Nicolas Baudin, Commander-in-Chief of the Corvettes Géographe and Naturaliste,* ed. and trans. Christine Cornell (Adelaide: Libraries Board of South Australia, 1974), xiii. For a countering view, see Scott, *Terre Napoléon,* 122–89, 262–82.

44. For a succinct discussion of Toussaint's motives, see Jeremy D. Popkin, *A Concise History of the Haitian Revolution* (Oxford: Blackwell, 2012), 111–13.

45. Constitution du 22 frimaire an VIII (December 13, 1799), AN AE/I/29/4.

46. Laurent Dubois, *A Colony of Citizens: Revolution and Slave Emancipation in the French Caribbean, 1787–1804* (Chapel Hill: University of North Carolina Press, 2004), 288–89, 326–27, 351.

47. See C. L. R. James, *The Black Jacobins; Toussaint L'Ouverture and the San Domingo Revolution* (New York: Vintage Books, 1989), 270, 275, 294; Claude Wanquet, *La France et la première abolition de l'esclavage, 1794–1802: le cas des colonies orientales, Ile de France (Maurice) et la Réunion* (Paris: Karthala, 1998), 636. Napoleon's own reminiscences provided sufficient fodder for such claims. See his statements on Saint-Domingue in Emmanuel de Las Cases, *Mémorial de Sainte Hélène* (Paris: Gallimard–La Pléiade, 1956), 769; Barry O'Meara, *Napoleon in Exile: or, A Voice from St. Helena* (New York: William Gowans, 1853), II:199.

48. For an excellent discussion of racism in early modern Europe, see Miriam Eliav-Feldon, Benjamin Isaac, and Joseph Ziegler, *The Origins of Racism in the West* (Cambridge: Cambridge University Press, 2009).

49. "Aux citoyens de Saint-Domingue," December 25, 1799, in *CN*, no. 4455, VI:42.

50. Arrête of December 25, 1799, in *CN*, VI:43. Also see Pierre Pluchon, *Toussaint Louverture* (Paris: Fayard, 1989), 447–48.

51. Pierre-Louis Roederer, *Mémoires sur la Révolution, le Consulat, et l'Empire* (Paris: Plon, 1942), 131.

52. "Notes sur Saint Domingue," in *CN*, XXX:529. For Bonaparte's decision to launch the expedition, see Popkin, *A Concise History of the Haitian Revolution,* 116–19; Philippe R. Girard, *The Slaves Who Defeated Napoleon: Toussaint Louverture and the Haitian War of Independence, 1801–1804* (Tuscaloosa: University of Alabama Press, 2011), 33–49. Also Pierre Branda and Thierry Lentz, *Napoléon, l'esclavage et les colonies* (Paris: Fayard, 2006); Marcel Dorigny, *Rétablissement de l'esclavage dans les colonies françaises 1802: Ruptures et continuités de la politique colonial française* (Paris: Maisonneuve-Larose, 2003). On the last two years of Toussaint's life, see Philippe Girard, *Toussaint Louverture: A Revolutionary Life* (New York: Basic Books, 2016), 217–52.

53. "Notes pour server aux instructions à donner au capitaine general Leclerc," October 31, 1801, in Charles Leclerc, *Lettres du Général Leclerc,* ed. Paul Roussier (Paris: Société de l'histoire des colonies françaises, 1937), 263–74.

54. See Michel-Étienne Descourtilz's memoirs in Jeremy D. Popkin, ed., *Facing Racial Revolution: Eyewitness Accounts of the Haitian Insurrection* (Chicago: University of Chicago Press, 2007), 306.

55. Restoration of slavery in Guiana was the work of French colonial administrator Jean-Baptiste Victor Hugues, who had vocally championed emancipation of slaves during the Revolution only to gradually revive it in 1802–1803.

56. For details, see Claude Ribbe, *Le crime de Napoléon* (Paris: Cherche Midi, 2013); Laurent Dubois, *Avengers of the New World: The Story of the Haitian Revolution* (Cambridge, MA: Harvard University Press, 2004), 293; Adam Hochschild, *Bury the Chains: Prophets and Rebels in the Fight to Free an Empire's Slaves* (New York: Houghton Mifflin, 2006), 293–94.

57. Leclerc to Bonaparte, October 7, 1802, in *Lettres du Général Leclerc*, 256.

58. See Girard, *The Slaves Who Defeated Napoleon*, 159–247, 291–312.

59. Between 1791 and 1803 some 100,000 people perished in the revolutionary turmoil, the vast majority of them being blacks.

60. For Dessalines, see Timoleon C. Brutus, *L'homme d'Airain, étude monographique sur Jean-Jacques Dessalines, fondateur de la nation haïtienne*, 2 vols. (Port-au-Prince: N. A. Theodore, 1946–1947); Henock Trouillot, *Dessalines: ou, La tragédie post-coloniale* (Port-au-Prince: Editions Panorama, 1966).

61. For an illuminating study, see Ada Ferrer, *Freedom's Mirror: Cuba and Haiti in the Age of Revolution* (Cambridge: Cambridge University Press, 2014).

62. For details, see *Life and Correspondence of Rufus King*, ed. Charles R. King (New York: G. P. Putnam's Sons, 1896), III:61.

63. Treaty of San Ildefonso, October 1, 1800, www.napoleon-series.org/research/government/diplomatic/ c_ildefonso.html.

64. William Cobbett, "Cession of Louisiana" (editorial), in *Cobbett's Annual Register* (London: Cox and Baylis, 1802), I:46. For a concise and insightful discussion of Britain's position, see Bradford Perkins, "England and the Louisiana Question," *Huntington Library Quarterly* 18, no. 3 (May 1955): 279–95.

65. James Madison to Robert Livingston and James Monroe, March 2, 1803, in *The Papers of James Madison: Secretary of State Series*, ed. Mary A . Hackett (Charlottesville: University Press of Virginia, 1984), IV:364–78.

66. Jefferson to Pierre S. du Pont de Nemours, April 25, 1802, in *The Writings of Thomas Jefferson*, ed. Andrew A. Lipscomb (Washington, DC: Thomas Jefferson Memorial Association, 1903), X317. In a long letter to Robert Livingston, American minister to France, Jefferson explained that "the day that France takes possession of New Orleans fixes her sentence which is to restrain her forever her low water mark . . . From that moment we must marry ourselves to the British fleet and nation." Jefferson to Livingston, April 18, 1802 in *Memoir, Correspondence and Miscellanies from the Papers of Thomas Jefferson*, ed. Thomas Jefferson Randolph (Boston: Gray and Bowen, 1830), III:492.

67. Convention entre la République française et les Etats-Unis d'Amérique réglant l'application du traité de cession de la Louisiane aux Etats-Unis d'Amérique, AN AF/IV/1704/6/12. Also see "The Louisiana Purchase" collection of documents at The Napoleon Series, www.napoleon-series.org/research/government/diplomatic/c_louisiana.html; Monroe and Livingston to James Madison,

May 12–13, 1803, in *The Papers of James Madison,* ed. William T. Hutchinson et al. (Chicago: University of Chicago Press, 1965), IV:590–94, 601. Also see Robert D. Bush, *The Louisiana Purchase: A Global Context* (New York: Routledge, 2014), 69–96.

68. Under the agreement, the two banks promised to provide for an exchange of stock for specie (mainly from Britain) in three installments, paying a total of 53 million francs for securities that had a face value of 60 million, keeping the difference as a fee. The US Treasury redeemed all bonds between 1812 and 1823, with banks and bondholders earning over $8 million in interest. For details (and relevant documents), see James E. Winston and R. W. Colomb, "How the Louisiana Purchase Was Financed," *Louisiana Historical Quarterly* XII (1929): 189–237.

69. Henry Adams, *History of the United States of America During the First Administration of Thomas Jefferson* (New York: Charles Scribner's Sons, 1889), II:49.

70. "From 1804 to 1808, traders flooded Charleston with 39,075 African slaves, over one-tenth of the total number of slaves brought into all of British North America over the previous two hundred years—probably the strongest surge in the history of the global slave trade." Jed Handelsman Shugerman, "The Louisiana Purchase and South Carolina's Reopening of the Slave Trade in 1803," *Journal of the Early Republic* 22, no. 2 (Summer, 2002): 263–90.

71. For details, see Sean M. Theriault, "Party Politics During the Louisiana Purchase," *Social Science History* 30, no. 2 (Summer 2006): 293–324; Joyce Appleby, "Jefferson's Resolute Leadership and Drive Toward Empire," in *Major Problems in American Foreign Relations*, ed. Dennis Merrill and Thomas G. Paterson (Boston: Houghton Mifflin, 2005), I:99–103; Charles A. Cerami, *Jefferson's Great Gamble: The Remarkable Story of Jefferson, Napoleon, and the Men Behind the Louisiana Purchase* (Naperville, IL: Sourcebooks, 2003); Jon Kukla, *A Wilderness So Immense: The Louisiana Purchase and the Destiny of America* (New York: Knopf, 2003); Peter Kastor and Francois Weil. *Empires of the Imagination: Transatlantic Histories of the Louisiana Purchase* (Charlottesville: University of Virginia Press, 2008); Patrick G. Williams, S. Charles Bolton, and Jeanne M. Whayne. *A Whole Country in Commotion: The Louisiana Purchase and the American Southwest* (Fayetteville: University of Arkansas Press, 2005).

72. Jeremy D. Bailey, *Thomas Jefferson and Executive Power* (Cambridge: Cambridge University Press, 2010), 171–94.

73. J. A. van Houtte, "The Low Countries and Scandinavia," and Anton Guilland, "France and Her Tributaries (1801–1803)," both in *The Cambridge Modern History*, ed. A. Ward et al. (New York: Macmillan, 1906), 88–91, 469–70.

74. In August 1801 Bonaparte signed a Franco-Dutch convention pledging to reduce French occupying forces to 10,000 men. In return, the Dutch were forced to pay a vast indemnity of 5 million florins. See George de Martens, *Recueil des principaux traités d'alliance, de paix, de trève, de neuralité, de commerce, de limites, d'échange, etc.*, 2nd ed. (Gottingen: Librairie de Dieterich, 1831), VII:368–73.

75. I base my discussion on Holger Böning, *Der Traum von Freiheit und Gleichheit. Helvetische Revolution und Republik (1798–1803). Die Schweiz auf dem Weg zur bürgerlichen Demokratie* (Zurich: Orell Füssli Verlag, 1998); Andreas Grünewald, *Die Helvetische Republik 1798–1803* (Reinach: Multipress-Verl., 2001); Clive H. Church and Randolph C. Head. *A Concise History of Switzerland* (Cambridge: Cambridge University Press, 2013); James M. Luck, *A History of Switzerland* (Palo Alto, CA: Society for the Promotion of Science and Scholarship, 1985). For excellent analysis of Swiss political culture during the revolutionary era, see Marc H. Lerner, *A Laboratory of Liberty: The Transformation of Political Culture in Republican Switzerland, 1750–1848* (Leiden: Brill, 2012), 10–136.

76. See Bonaparte's proclamation of September 30, 1802, in Johannes Strickler, ed., *Actensammlung aus der Zeit der Helvetischen Republik (1798–1803)* (Bern: Buchdruckerei Stämpfli, 1902), VIII:1437.

77. Bonaparte's Proclamation of September 30, 1802, in *CN*, no. 6352, VIII: 53–55. Also see Clive H. Church and Randolph C. Head, *A Concise History of Switzerland* (Cambridge: Cambridge University Press, 2013), 138–42. The Act of Mediation, the constitutions of the nineteen cantons and the Constitution of the Confederation are available in *Repertorium der Abschiede der eidgenössischen Tagsatzungen vom Jahr 1803 bis Ende des Jahrs 1813* (Bern: Rätzer, 1843).

78. Bonaparte secured strategically important areas, including the Simplon and its approaches, and forced the Swiss to surrender the Valais region so France could build a military road connecting it to northern Italy. When in 1804 the Swiss tried to introduce military reforms, Bonaparte promptly forbade them. For an interesting discussion, see Gabrielle B. Clemens, "The Swiss Case in the Napoleonic Empire," in *The Napoleonic Empire and the New European Political Culture*, ed. Michael Broers, Peter Hicks, and Agustin Guimera (New York: Palgrave, 2012), 132–42.

79. Note of October 9, 1802, in Arthur Paget, *The Paget Papers: Diplomatic and Other Correspondence of the Right Honorable Sir Arthur Paget, G.C.B. (1794–1807)*, ed. Augustus Paget (London: William Heinemann, 1896), II:62–63. Bonaparte was "audaciously interfering to deprive the gallant Swiss of the right of establishing their liberties," railed Sir John Wrottesley in the House of Commons. *Parliamentary History of England*, XXXVI:950.

80. *The New Annual Register, or General Repository of History, Politics, and Literature for the Year 1803* (London: G. and J. Robinson, 1804), 238.

81. Bonaparte to Talleyrand, November 4, 1802, in *CN*, no. 6,414, VIII:90.

82. "Message to the Chambers," in Napoleon, *A Selection from the Letters and Despatches of the First Napoleon*, ed. D. Bingham (London: Chapman and Hall, 1884), II:5. See Arrêté, April 12 (backdated to April 2), 1801, in *CN*, no. 5526, VII:117–19.

83. See Bonaparte's acceptance speech, January 26, 1802, in *CN*, no. 5934, VII:371–73. For a broad overview, see Alexander Grab, *Napoleon and the*

Transformation of Europe (New York: Palgrave Macmillan, 2003), 159–65. The *consulta*'s first choice as the president of the Italian Republic was a prominent Italian republican, Francesco Melzi d'Eril. But the notables were told that they could make a better choice and, taking a hint, offered the position to Bonaparte.

84. Anton Guilland, "France and Her Tributaries (1801–1803)," in *The Cambridge Modern History*, ed. A. Ward et al. (New York: Macmillan, 1906), IX:88.

85. See Arrêté, April 12 (backdated to April 2), 1801, in *CN*, no. 5526, VII:117–19.

86. In 1796 France negotiated treaties with the princes of Baden and Wurttemberg that also called for compensation for lost territories. See de Clerq, *Recueil des Traités*, I:283–87, 292–99. For an interesting discussion, see Sydney Biro, *The German Policy of Revolutionary France: A Study in French Diplomacy During the War of the First Coalition, 1792–1797* (Cambridge, MA: Harvard University Press, 1957), vol. 2.

87. Grab, *Napoleon and the Transformation of Europe*, 88.

88. For pertinent documents, see "The Reorganization of Germany," www.napoleon-series.org/research/government/diplomatic/c_germany.html.

89. Bonaparte to Talleyrand, April 3, 1802, in *Correspondance générale*, III:948.

90. Bonaparte to Joseph Bonaparte, January 20, 1801, in *The Confidential Correspondence of Napoleon Bonaparte with His Brother Joseph* (New York: D. Appleton and Company, 1856), I:53. Also see Bonaparte's instructions to Talleyrand asking to clarify Russia's position on German matters, Bonaparte to Talleyrand, April 3, 1802, in *Correspondance générale*, III:944–48.

91. See treaty's text in Du Clercq, *Recueil des traités de la France*, I:583–87.

92. See Harold C. Deutsch, *The Genesis of Napoleonic Imperialism* (Cambridge, MA: Harvard University Press, 1938), 38–55.

93. Bonaparte to Maximillian Joseph of Bavaria, October 11, 1801, in *CN*, no. 5796, VII:285.

94. Hajo Holborn, *A History of Modern Germany, 1648–1840* (New York: Alfred A. Knopf, 1967), 367–68; Grab, *Napoleon and the Transformation of Europe*, 88–89.

Chapter 8

1. My understanding of Napoleonic sea power has been shaped by long discussions with Dr. Kenneth G. Johnson of the Air University, who has shined much new light on this subject. Until the publication of Johnson's opus on Napoleon's use of seapower, the most concise treatment of this subject is his long essay "Napoleon's War at Sea," in *Napoleon and the Operational Art of War*, ed. Michael V. Leggiere (Leiden: Brill, 2016), 387–475.

2. Notes pour le Ministre de la Marine, February 19, 1802, *CN*, no. 5968, VII:395–96.

3. As Talleyrand explained in 1806, Napoleon "does not imagine that any particular article of the Treaty of Amiens produced the war. He is convinced that the true cause was [his] refusal to make a treaty of commerce, which would necessarily have been prejudicial to the manufactures and industry of this country." Cited

in Conrad Gill, "The Relations Between England and France in 1802," *English Historical review* 24, no. 93 (1909): 78.

4. *Life and Letters of Sir Gilbert Elliot, First Earl of Minto*, ed. Countess of Minto (London: Longmans, Green, 1874), III:209.

5. The agreement ended the British blockade of the ships of France and its client states, but it did nothing about the French prohibition of British shipping within four leagues of the French coast. Consequently, a number of British ships had been seized and confiscated by the French authorities, who, in response to British protests, declared that they were only carrying out existing laws, just as the British had done with regard to their newspapers.

6. See the data in Jedidiah Morse, *The American Geography, or A View of the Present State of All the Kingdoms, States and Colonies* (Boston: Thomes & Andrews, 1812), II:72; Willian Cunningham, *The Growth of English Industry and Commerce in Modern Times* (London: Frank Cass, 1968), appendix F, 933.

7. Cited in Harold C. Deutsch, *The Genesis of Napoleonic Imperialism* (Cambridge, MA: Harvard University Press, 1938), 100.

8. See Charles Walton, "The Free-Trade Origins of the French Revolution," in *The French Revolution in Global Perspective*, ed. Suzanne Desan, Lynn Hunt, and William Max Nelson (Ithaca, NY: Cornell University Press, 2013), 44–56.

9. The Methuen Treaty of 1793 stipulated that Portuguese wines imported into England would be subject to a third less duty than wines imported from France. A. D. Francis, "John Methuen and the Anglo-Portuguese Treaties of 1703," *Historical Journal* 3, no. 2 (1960): 103–24.

10. In the meantime, the British government refused to recognize commercial agents that France had sent, arguing that a commercial treaty had to be concluded first. For French complaints, see AE "Angleterre," 600.

11. Bonaparte was a mercantilist by inclination and believed that he could direct commerce much the way he could the military. For interesting insights into his views on commerce, see Jean-Antoine Chaptal, *Mes souvenirs sur Napoléon* (Paris: E. Plon, Nourrit, 1893), 274–76, 281–83. "A prohibition imposed to such a degree had the character of a real blockade against England, and its object was to make her perish of want in the midst of her riches," argued one French historian. "This has been regarded [by Britain] as a deliberately hostile act by Napoleon," counters a modern British historian. "But no state is required to enter into a commercial treaty she knows would work to her disadvantage." Pierre Lanfrey, *Histoire de Napoleon Ier* (Paris: Charpentier, 1869), II:454; Andrew Roberts, *Napoleon: A Life* (New York: Viking, 2014), 308.

12. "Lord Elgin's Report on Levantine Affairs and Malta," February 28, 1803, *English Historical Review* 36, no. 142 (1921): 236.

13. Treaty of Amiens, www.napoleon-series.org/research/government/diplomatic/c_amiens.html.

14. See Desmond Gregory, *Malta, Britain and the European Powers, 1793–1815* (Madison, NJ: Farleigh Dickinson University Press, 1996), ch. 8.

15. Bonaparte to Alexander I of Russia, 11 March 1803, *SIRIO*, LXXVII (1891): 55.

16. Preface, in *A Description of Malta, with a Sketch of Its History and That of Its Fortifications, tr. from the Ital., with Notes, by an Officer Resident on the Island* (Malta, 1801), iv.

17. Britain had also failed to evacuate entirely its garrison from Egypt, and some of its troops remained in Alexandria after Egypt was formally restored to the Ottomans. It was not until France issued a demand for its complete withdrawal that Britain satisfied the conditions of the treaty on this point.

18. Hawkesbury to Lord Whitworth, November 14, 1802, in Charles Duke Yonge, *The Life and Administration of Robert Banks, Second Earl of Liverpool, K.G.* (London: Macmillan, 1868), I:97.

19. For the scope and purpose of Sebastiani's mission, see Bonaparte to Talleyrand (August 29, 1802) and Bonaparte to Sebastiani (September 5, 1802), *CN*, VIII:9–10, 25–26. For details on Sebastiani's visit to Tripoli, see André Auzoux, "La mission de Sébastiani à Tripoli en l'an X (1802)," in *Revue des études napoléoniennes* XVI (1919): 225–36.

20. AE "Angleterre," 600. Steven Englund raises other possibilities: "Was the publication in *Le Moniteur* intended as a diversion from the rout that the French had suffered in the Antilles? It was certainly a trait of Bonaparte's to try to cover a retreat with a diversion, but it was equally true that Napoleon was obsessed with a 'return' of Egypt both to vindicate his personal honor and as a stepping-stone to his 'Alexandrian' dream of an Eastern empire. Then, too, maybe Sebastiani's piece was also 'payment' for the favorable review that the *London Times* (a semi-official newspaper) accorded to a book that teemed with libels about Bonaparte's Egyptian campaign." Steven Englund, *Napoleon: A Political Life* (New York: Scribner, 2004), 259.

21. It is noteworthy that Bonaparte personally edited Sebastiani's report and, clearly anticipating British response, tried to mitigate its tone by replacing words or cutting sentences. For details see Deutsch, *The Genesis of Napoleonic Imperialism*, 117–20.

22. Bonaparte instructed his foreign minister to meet Lord Whitworth, "denying any the smallest intention of the First Consul's again interfering in the affairs of Egypt [and] that he was heartily tired of Egypt." Lord Whitworth's report of February 7, 1803, in Oscar Browning, *England and Napoleon in 1803, Being the Despatches of Lord Whitworth and Others* (London: Longmans, Green, 1887), 63.

23. William Miles to Stephen Rolleston, June 10, 1803, in *The Correspondence of William Augustus Miles on the French Revolution, 1789–1817* (London: Longmans, Green, 1890), II:333.

24. It was already too late to halt the British evacuation of Egypt, since the orders had left London in November and preparations were under way just as Sebastiani's report appeared. The evacuation was duly completed on March 11, 1803.

25. Even as he disclaimed any designs on Egypt, in the very same sentence Bonaparte also suggested that "sooner or later Egypt would belong to France, either by falling to pieces of the Turkish Empire, or by some arrangement with the Porte." Lord Whitworth's report of February 21, 1803, in Browning, *England and Napoleon in 1803*, 79–80. And Napoleon's minister in London underscored the French position on Britain's adherence to all of the treaty's provisions by invoking the formula "either all of the treaty or none of the treaty," to which the British foreign secretary replied, "Either the state of the continent as it was or none at all." Talleyrand to Bonaparte, November 3, 1802, in *Lettres inédites de Talleyrand à Napoléon, 1800–1809*, ed. Pierre Bertrand (Paris: Perrin, 1889), 23–24.

26. "Exposé de la situation de la République," February 20, 1803, in *CN*, no. 6591, VIII:219.

27. Instructions for Ambassador Andréossy, February 19, 1803, AE "Angleterre," 600. Also see Andreossy's report of March 1, 1803, in the same source, 600.

28. George III, George III, *The Later Correspondence of George III*, ed. A. Aspinall (Cambridge: Cambridge University Press, 1968) IV:83. The royal statement seems to have incorporated (verbatim) parts of Addington's letter to the king of March 6, 1803, IV:82.

29. Deutsch, *The Genesis of Napoleonic Imperialism*, 128.

30. See Andreossy's report of March 8, 1803, AE "Angleterre," 600.

31. Talleyrand to Andreossy, March 12, 1803, AE "Angleterre," 600; Lord Whitworth's reports of March 12 and 17, 1803, in Browning, *England and Napoleon in 1803*, 110–12, 127.

32. Bonaparte to Alexander I, March 11, 1803, *SIRIO*, LXXVII (1891): 55; *CN*, no. 6625, VIII:236–37.

33. Lord Whitworth's report of March 14, 1803, in Browning, *England and Napoleon in 1803*, 115–17; Markov's report of March 16, in *SIRIO*, LXXVII (1891): 63–67.

34. Hortense Beauharnais, *Mémoires de la reine Hortense*, ed. Jean Hanoteau (Paris: Plon, 1927), I:146–47; Lord Whitworth's report of March 14, 1803, in Browning, *England and Napoleon in 1803*, 126.

35. Lord Whitworth's report of March 17, 1803, in Browning, *England and Napoleon in 1803*, 128.

36. Lord Whitworth's report of March 18, 1803, in Browning, *England and Napoleon in 1803*, 129. Hawkesbury's letter and Bonaparte's memo are both in AE "Angleterre," 600.

37. See Minister of Marine Decrès's report to Bonaparte, March 31, 1803 (Archives Nationales, IV 1190), cited in unpublished paper, Kenneth Johnson, "Bayou to the Baltic: Napoleon's Campaigns of 1803–1804."

38. "Notes of an Arrangement to be Concluded by Treaty or Convention Between His Majesty and the French Government," April 3, 1803, in Browning, *England and Napoleon in 1803*, 151.

39. Lord Whitworth's report of April 9, 1803, in Browning, *England and Napoleon in 1803*, 162–67; Talleyrand to Andreossy, April 9, 1803, AE "Angleterre," 600.

40. Talleyrand noted, "Here we have, without doubt, the first verbal ultimatum of which the history of modern negotiations has any record, and when one thinks in what circumstances this procedure is employed, it is difficult to avoid the painful idea that the English government is planning to bring about a rupture." Talleyrand to Andreossy, April 29, 1803, AE "Angleterre," 600.

41. Lord Hawkesbury to Lord Whitworth, April 23, 1803, in Browning, *England and Napoleon in 1803*, 182–83.

42. In light of the British behavior, "no consideration on earth should induce him to consent to a concession in perpetuity of Malta in any shape whatever," Bonaparte declared. Lord Whitworth's report of April 23, 1803, in Browning, *England and Napoleon in 1803*, 183.

43. Talleyrand to Whitworth, May 2, 1803; Lord Whitworth to Hawkesbury, May 4, 1803, in Browning, *England and Napoleon in 1803*, 218–22. Also see Talleyrand to Andreossy, May 3, 1803, AE "Angleterre," 600.

44. Talleyrand to Andreossy, May 3, 1803, AE "Angleterre," 600.

45. Lord Whitworth's report of May 4, 1803, in Browning, *England and Napoleon in 1803*, 220.

46. Lord Hawkesbury to Lord Whitworth, May 7, 1803, in Browning, *England and Napoleon in 1803*, 224.

47. Alexander to Bonaparte, Alexander to Markov, and Vorontsov to Markov, all April 22, 1803, in *SIRIO*, LXXVII (1891), 100–112; Lord Whitworth's report of May 12, 1803, in Browning, *England and Napoleon in 1803*, 236.

48. Lord Whitworth's report (May 14) and the French memo are in Browning, *England and Napoleon in 1803*, 242–43. The French ambassador's instructions of May 13, 1803, authorized him to conclude a formal convention on these terms. See correspondence between Talleyrand and Andreossy, May 13–20, 1803, AE "Angleterre," 600.

49. The declaration of the war listed a number of factors contributing to the British decision to resume hostilities. It first complained about France's failure to accept a treaty of commerce with Britain and open its market to the British commerce. Next came protests against France's continued military presence in Holland, intervention in Switzerland, and annexations of Piedmont, Parma, Placentia, and Elba. The British government argued that in light of France's actions, it could not fulfill its obligation to evacuate Malta. It justified its action by noting that some provisions of Article X had not been yet fulfilled: a grand master had not been elected and Austria, Russia, and Prussia had failed to provide guarantees for the protection of the island. Furthermore, Britain argued that the order of the Maltese knights itself had undergone changes that were deep enough to make it unable to survive on Malta. Out of five *langues* that existed in 1802, two (Aragon and Castile) had been abolished by Spain, one (Italy) had disappeared after the French annexation of Piedmont,

and the property of the fourth one was about to be sequestered by Bavaria. The British government accused France of masterminding these changes in an effort to emasculate the order so as to make it "incapable of maintaining independence." These changes, therefore, constituted a breach of the treaty. The declaration of war also argued that despite pledging to guarantee the integrity of the Ottoman Empire, France still entertained views hostile to the Turks. Therefore, Britain could not be "justified in evacuating the island of Malta without receiving some other security." Finally the declaration mentioned Bonaparte's ill-treatment of the British ambassador, demands for expulsion of French émigrés from Britain, and coercion of the Hamburg newspapers to publish anti-British articles as further examples of French indignities toward Britain. "Declaration of War Against France," May 18, 1803, in *The Annual Register... for the Year 1803* (London: W. Otridge and Son, 1805), 734–42.

50. For details, see J. E. Cookson, *The Friends of Peace: Anti-War Liberalism in England, 1793–1815* (Cambridge: Cambridge University Press, 1982).

51. Jenny Uglow, *In These Times: Living in Britain Through Napoleon's Wars, 1793–1815* (New York: Macmillan, 2014), 342. Also see Kevin Linch, "A Geography of Loyalism? The Local Military Forces of the West Riding of Yorkshire, 1794–1814," *War and Society* 19 (May 2001): 1–21; J. W. Fortescue, *The County Lieutenancies and the Army, 1803–1814* (London: Macmillan, 1909), 26–48, 64–69.

52. Otto Brandt, *England und die Napoleonische Weltpolitik, 1800–1803* (Heidelberg: C. Winter, 1916), 210.

53. For Duroc's reports, see AE "Russie," 140, 168–215.

54. Alexandre de Clercq, ed., *Recueil des Traités de la France* (Paris: A. Durand et Pedone-Lauriel, 1880), I:467–68, 474–75.

55. *VPR*, I:442–45, 463–66; Frederick W. Kagan, *The End of the Old Order: Napoleon and Europe, 1801–05* (New York: Da Capo Press, 2006), 60–66.

56. Vorontsov to Markov, February 10, 1802, in *SIRIO* LXX (1890): 332–33.

57. As Hawkesbury explained in his letter to the British ambassador in Vienna, peace with France would be inherently of a fragile nature, and "we ought never to forget that is possible we may have no choice, and that we may be reduced to the necessity of trying again the chances of war; and, even if peace could be concluded, the power of France on the Continent of Europe [has] become so formidable, that it is of the utmost importance that a good understanding should subsist amongst the other great powers of Europe." Hawkesbury to Minto, April 24, 1801, FO 7/63.

58. Hawkesbury to St. Helens, April 30, 1801, FO 65/48.

59. See *The Parliamentary History of England, from the Earliest Period to the Year 1803* (London: T.C. Hansard, 1820), XXXVI:18–25.

60. For details, see Hawkesbury's letters from March to June 1801 at FO 65/48 and 65/51. In his instructions (May 19, 1801) to St. Helens, Hawkesbury underscored that Russia must be informed that Britain is "actuated by now

views of ambition and aggrandizement, but solely by a desire of restoring peace to Europe, on terms which may insure its duration"; FO 65/48.

61. Alexander I to Semen Vorontsov, November 12, 1801, *Arkhiv knyazya Vorontsova* (Moscow: Tip. Gracheva, 1876), X:300.

62. See the memorandum "Du système politique de l'empire de Russie," 28 July 1801, *VPR*, I:63–66.

63. Panin to S. Vorontsov, September 14, 1801, *Arkhiv knyazya Vorontsova*, XI, 155. For British letters, see FO 65/48. The Russian government was certainly pleased to hear from Hawkesbury that "of the three powers, Turkey, Naples and Sardinia for whom the [Russian] emperor has [expressed] a peculiar interest, the first two have been effectually provided for in the preliminaries." Hawkesbury to St. Helens, October 16, 1801, FO 65/49.

64. St. Helens to Hawkesbury, September 10, 1801, FO 65/49.

65. See treaty's text in Du Clercq, *Recueil des traités de la France*, I:583–87.

66. Hawkesbury to Vorontsov, January 8, 1802, FO 65/50. Interestingly, the British continued to defer to the Russian court, sharing key details of their negotiations with France.

67. For details, see H. Beeley, "A Project of Alliance with Russia in 1802," *English Historical Review* 49, no. 195 (1934): 497–502.

68. See Hawkesbury's letters of September 11, 1802, FO 65/51.

69. Hawkesbury to Warren, October 27, 1802, FO 65/51.

70. Alexander I to S. Vorontsov, January 20, 1803, *Arkhiv khyazya Vorontsova*, X:304–6. Also see Alexander I to S. Vorontsov, November 18, 1802, *VPR*, I:327; Alexander Vorontsov to Markov, January 5, 1803, *SIRIO* (1890), LXX:616.

71. F. de Martens, *Recueil des traités et conventions conclus par la Russie avec les puissances étrangères* (St. Petersburg: A. Böhnke, 1895), XI:68.

72. Traité de paix entre la République française et la Sublime Porte ottomane. Paris, le 6 messidor an X, AN AE/III/53.

73. "Lord Elgin's Report on Levantine Affairs and Malta," February 28, 1803, *English Historical Review* 36, no. 142 (1921): 234–36.

74. Bonaparte to Duroc, April 24, 1801, in *CN*, VII:134.

75. Albert Vandal, *Napoléon et Alexandre Ier, l'alliance russe sous le premier Empire* (Paris: 1896), I:3.

76. Vorontsov to Markov, January 5, 1803, in *SIRIO* LXX (1890): 619. Almost a month later, Vorontsov again explained that Alexander was "satisfied with the lot which providence has assigned him and does not plan aggrandizement in any direction. He expects that no one should aggrandize himself at the expense of Turkey." Vorontsov to Markov, February 1, 1803, *SIRIO*, LXXVII (1891): 20.

77. Vorontsov to Markov, January 5, 1803, *SIRIO*, LXX (1890): 616.

78. Hawkesbury to St. Helens, October 3, 1801, FO 65/49.

79. See Kurakin's letter of August 13, 1802, in Martens, *Recueil des traités et conventions conclus par la Russie*, XI:67.

80. For details, see Warren's reports of December 10, 1802–20 January 1803, FO 65/51.

81. Hawkesbury to Lord Whitworth, February 9, 1803, in Browning, *England and Napoleon in 1803*, 65–68.

82. Lord Whitworth to Hawkesbury, February 14, 1803, in Browning, *England and Napoleon in 1803*, 70.

83. A. Vorontsov to Warren, March 21, 1803; S. Vorontsov to Alexander I, March 25, 1803, *VPR*, I:393, 399. Also see A. Vorontsov to Markov, 5 January 1803, *SIRIO*, LXX (1890): 616.

84. British statesmen complained about the erratic nature of Russian promises. As Lord Malmesbury wrote, "Russia was now what she has ever been since she had held...a place among the greater powers of Europe—cajoling them all and courting flattery from them all, but certainly never meaning to take an active part on behalf of any of them.... I fear we here rely too much on Russia: she will give us advice, but not assistance." *Diaries and Correspondence of James Harris First Earl of Malmesbury* (London: Richard Bentley, 1844), IV:252.

85. Bonaparte to Alexander I, March 11, 1803, *SIRIO*, LXXVII (1891): 55; *CN*, no. 6625, VIII:236–37.

86. "It has sufficed that you should have expressed the wish for it," Talleyrand assured the Russian ambassador, "that the First Consul has inserted in this publication a phrase of such a nature as to reassure the Ottoman Porte on all the evil rumors which may have reached her." Talleyrand to Markov, February 21, 1803, in *SIRIO*, LXXVII (1891): 42.

87. Markov to Alexander, March 16, 1803, in *SIRIO*, LXXVII (1891): 61; Whitworth to Hawkesbury, May 4, 1803, in Browning, *England and Napoleon in 1803*, 223.

88. Lord Hawkesbury supposedly made this remark upon receiving the offer. See *The Diaries and Correspondence of the Right Hon. George Rose*, edited by Rev. Leveson Vernon Harcourt (London: Richard Bentley, 1860), II:43n.

89. *Diaries and Correspondence of James Harris First Earl of Malmesbury*, IV:259. In fact, Addington went as far as to conceal its existence during his speech to Parliament, when he claimed that "if the interposition of Russia had been offered, due regard would have been paid it." This statement drew a vociferous response from the Russian embassy that accused the prime minister of misleading the public. See Vorontsov's account in *The Diaries and Correspondence of the Right Hon. George Rose*, II:43–44.

90. Alan Schom, *Napoleon Bonaparte* (New York: HarperCollins, 1997), 307. French historian Pierre Coquelle argued that Bonaparte desired war to establish an empire; *Napoléon et l'Angleterre, 1803–1813* (Paris: Plon-Nourrit, 1904), 80.

91. John D. Grainger, *The Amiens Truce: Britain and Bonaparte, 1801–1803* (Rochester, NY: Boydell Press, 2004), 211.

92. Paul W. Schroeder, *The Transformation of European Politics, 1763–1848* (New York: Oxford University Press, 1994), 230. "It is difficult not to conclude that

it was thanks to [Bonaparte] that all chance of a lasting peace was lost," argues British historian Charles Esdaile, but he is also careful to observe that "this is not say that Napoleon deliberately sought a rupture of the Treaty of Amiens. Indeed, though he may have believed that war with Britain and the other powers was inevitable in the end, he had no desire for the breathing space he had obtained in Europe to come to an end after only one year." Charles Esdaile, *Napoleon's Wars: An International History* (New York: Penguin, 2008) 132–33, 153.

93. Bonaparte's Anglophobia manifested itself in many areas, some rather trivial. Thus in September 1802 he complained that the Louvre had on public display a Gobelins tapestry showing the 1346 English siege of Calais. "Such subjects should not be available for public viewing in Paris," he observed. Napoleon, *Correspondance Générale*, ed. Thierry Lentz (Paris: Fayard, 2004), III:1104–5. But it must be also noted that there was strong anti-British feeling in French society as a whole and especially in the trading classes, which faced British competition. On behalf of the Committee of Public Safety Betrand Barère famously insisted that "young French republicans must suck in hatred of the name of Englishman with their mother's milk." For an interesting discussion, see Frances Acomb, *Anglophobia in France, 1763–1789: An Essay in the History of Constitutionalism and Nationalism* (Durham, NC: Duke University Press, 1950); Albert Sorel, *L'Europe et la revolution Française* (Paris: Plon-Nourrit, 1904), VI:262–63.

94. For the most recent reassessment of the role of "natural frontiers" in French foreign policy, see Jordan R. Hayworth, *Revolutionary France's War of Conquest in the Rhineland: Conquering the Natural Frontier, 1792–1797* (Cambridge: Cambridge University Press, 2019).

95. Hermann Stegemann, *Der Kampf um den Rhein. Das Stromgebiet des Rheins im Rahmen der großen Politik und im Wandel der Kriegsgeschichte* (Stuttgart: Deutsche Verlags-Anstalt, 1924), 464.

96. Paul Kennedy, *Rise and Fall of British Naval Mastery* (London: Ashfield, 1976), 97–98, 106–20. Also see Paul Kennedy, *The Rise and Fall of the Great Powers* (New York: Random House, 1987), 148–49.

97. Englund, *Napoleon*, 261.

98. *The Diaries and Letters of Sir George Jackson, KCH, from the Peace of Amiens to the Battle of Talavera* (London: Richard Bentley and Son, 1872), I:56.

99. One French historian acerbically notes, "Britain's justification [for war] was the preservation of the European balance of power but this grave concern did not extend to the seas, since in her eyes God had created the oceans for the English." Georges Lefebvre, *Napoleon: From 18 Brumaire to Tilsit, 1799–1807* (New York: Columbia University Press, 1969), 179.

100. See Frederick Kagan, "The View from a Rogue State: What Napoleon Can Tell Us About Dealing with Iran," C-SPAN, July 20, 2006, https://www.c-span.org/video/?193520-1/the-end-order.

101. Vorontsov to Markov, February 10, 1802, in *SIRIO* LXX (1890): 332–33. Also see Martens, *Recueil des traités et conventions conclus par la Russie*, IX, 67.

102. Henry Dundas submitted this memorandum to the government's consideration in late March 1800. Correctly noting that commerce and naval power were "essential to the permanent interest and prosperity of the British Empire." Dundas believed that decisive victory over France was unattainable and the government must do everything to seize and defend new markets for the British industry and commercial enterprise; if Britain did not act, France would exploits its military successes to seize the markets for herself. To prevent this, Dundas advocated forceful penetration of the Spanish colonies, including seizing the island of Tenerife, New Orleans, the mouths of the Orinoco River and the river Plate, and La Concepcion on the Chilean coastline. In the fall of 1800, Dundas secured a qualified approval from the cabinet to pursue his plans for the capture of Cuba and other Spanish possessions. See Dundas's memorandum of March 31, 1800, in "Papers of Henry Dundas, First Viscount Melville, 1779–1813," David M. Rubenstein Rare Book and Manuscript Library, Duke University.

103. For example, Tim Blanning claims that France violated the terms of the 1802 Peace of Amiens by not evacuating troops from the Batavian Republic, annexing Piedmont, occupying Parma, and intervening in Switzerland. However, none of these events constituted a breach of the actual provisions of the Treaty of Amiens. In fact, France honored its obligations by discussing the fate of prisoners of war (Article II), recognizing the republic of the Seven Islands (Article IX), and evacuating from Naples and the Roman State (as required by Article XI). The rest of the treaty dealt with Spanish (Articles IV, VII), Dutch (Article V, VI), and, most important, British obligations (Articles III, VI, VIII, IX, X, XV). Blanning, *The Pursuit of Glory: Europe 1648–1815* (New York: Viking, 2007), 654.

104. It must be noted that Britain was actively trying to stir up turmoil in Switzerland. For British efforts to use "pecuniary assistance," see *The New Annual Register, or General Repository of History, Politics, and Literature for the Year 1803* (London: G. and J. Robinson, 1804), 238.

105. Nicomede Bianchi, *Storia della monarchia piemontese dal 1773 sino al 1861* (Turin: Fratelli Bocca, 1879), III:419–20. Russia did try to uphold Sardinian interests, and the Russian envoy to Paris raised this question in conversations with Bonaparte.

106. In Article XI of the treaty, Austria and France pledged to "mutually guaranty the independence of the Batavian, Helvetic, Cisalpine, and Ligurian republics, and the right of the people who inhabit them to adopt what form of government they please." Traité de paix entre la République française et S.M. l'Empereur, et le corps germanique signé à Lunéville, in Leopold Neumann, ed., *Recueil des traités et conventions conclus par l'Autriche avec les puissances étrangères depuis 1763 jusqu'à nos jours* (Leipzig: F. A. Brockhaus, 1856), II:1–6. The treaty

was signed on February 9 and ratified by Austria on March 9 and by France on March 11, 1801.

107. Michel Franceschi and Ben Weider, *The Wars Against Napoleon: Debunking the Myth of the Napoleonic Wars* (New York: Savas Beatie, 2008), 11. In 1902 Arthur-Lévy asserted that "during the whole of his reign, Napoleon's sole aim was to arrive at a just and lasting peace which would ensure to France that status to which she is entitled." Arthur-Lévy, *Napoléon et la Paix* (Paris: Nelson, 1902), 15.

108. Carl von Clausewitz, *On War*, trans. Michael Howard and Peter Paret (Oxford: Oxford University Press, 2007), 28.

109. As Peter Englund aptly put it, "Bonaparte did not *have* to drive England to war, but in view of what he did, England *had* to declare it." Englund, *Napoleon*, 262.

110. Bonaparte's letter of January 15, 1803, to Decaen shows that he anticipated the peace would survive for at least another year and a half. *Correspondance Générale*, no. 7425, III:30.

111. *Morning Post*, February 1, 1803.

112. Joseph Pelet de la Lozère, *Napoleon in Council or the Opinions Delivered by Bonaparte in the Council of State* (London: Whittaker, 1837), 308.

113. Grainger, *The Amiens Truce*, 147–48.

114. One of them, Jean-Gabriel Peltier, was eventually tried for criminal libel and found guilty in February 1803. The start of the war, however, meant that he was never imprisoned. Hélène Maspéro-Clerc, "Un journaliste émigré jugé à Londres pour diffamation envers le Premier Consul," *Revue d'histoire moderne et contemporaine* 18, no. 2 (1971): 261–81.

115. Michael Durey, "Lord Grenville and the 'Smoking Gun': The Plot to Assassinate the French Directory in 1798–1799 Reconsidered," *Historical Journal* 45, no. 3 (2002): 547–68.

116. Furthermore, Britain's suspension of habeas corpus allowed the arrest and imprisonment of persons "on suspicion," without requiring charges or a trial.

117. Frank McLynn, *Napoleon: A Biography* (New York: Arcade, 2002), 269.

118. Martens, *Recueil des traités et conventions conclus par la Russie*, IX, 70. "The real cause of the rupture," states the eminent British historian J. Holland Rose, "was an essential divergence of view on Oriental policy, in which the future of India, Egypt, and Malta stood in vital relation." But Charles Esdaile, one of the best British historians of the Napoleonic Era, believes that "what it came down to was that Napoleon could not accept the notion that there should be curbs on his freedom of action. At the same time, however, Britain had no means of imposing those curbs except through war. With neither Britain nor France prepared to make fundamental concessions, there could be in the end be but one outcome." A counterpoint is offered by Harold Deutsch: "Britain had allowed herself to be inveigled into a bargain which she later felt herself incapable of living up to, for the peace she signed was the utter negation of every principle for which her traditions commanded her to fight to the bitter

end. Not only was the balance of power on the Continent overthrown, but all the axioms of this doctrine were equally strained. In addition to this, the great French colonial empire, which the cherished peace of 1763 was thought to have abolished for all time, seemed on the point of being re-established." Rose in Thomas Ussher, *Napoleon's Last Voyages, Being the Diaries of Sir Thomas Ussher*, ed. J. Holland Rose (New York; Charles Scribner's Sons, 1906), 51n.; Esdaile, *Napoleon's Wars*, 153; Deutsch, *The Genesis of Napoleonic Imperialism*, 96.

119. Talleyrand to Hédouville, August 29, 1803, AE "Russie," 142.

120. Bonaparte to Talleyrand (letter with two annexes), August 23, 1803, *CN*, VIII: 490–91; Lord Grenville to the Marquis of Buckingham, March 22, 1803, in *Memoirs of the Court and Cabinets of George the Third* (London: Hurst and Blackett, 1855), III:267.

121. Note of October 9, 1802 in Arthur Paget, *The Paget Papers: Diplomatic and Other Correspondence of the Right Honorable Sir Arthur Paget, G.C.B. (1794–1807)*, ed. Augustus Paget (London: William Heinemann, 1896), II, 62–63; *Diaries and Correspondence of James Harris, First Earl of Malmesbury*, IV:279.

122. British ambassador Lord Whitworth's reports often exaggerated domestic problems in France and claimed that "nine people out of ten" opposed Bonaparte's government and that every year "weakens the Consular Government, unsupported as it stand by confidence or affection" and strengthens those whose "object and interest it is to overturn it." See his report of December 1, 1802, in Browning, *England and Napoleon in 1803*, 18.

123. Deutsch, *The Genesis of Napoleonic Imperialism*, 141–44.

124. Schroeder, *The Transformation of European Politics*, 243.

125. For Alexander's position, see his instructions of September 1801 in Martens, *Recueil des traités et conventions conclus par Russie*, II:374–75.

Chapter 9

1. For an interesting discussion, see Daniel A. Baugh, "Great Britain's 'Blue-Water' Policy, 1689–1815," *International History Review* 10, no. 1 (1998): 33–58; Jeremy Black and Philip Woodfine, eds., *The British Navy and the Use of Naval Power in the Eighteenth Century* (Leicester: Leicester University Press, 1988).

2. *Morning Post*, August 25, 1804.

3. For an in-depth discussion based on the Dutch archival sources, see Martijn Wink, "Een militair debacle? Bataafse militaire inzet in West-Indië 1802–1804," BA thesis, University of Leiden, 2018. I am grateful to Martijn Wink for sharing his work with me.

4. Martin A. Klein, "Slaves, Gum, and Peanuts: Adaptation to the End of the Slave Trade in Senegal, 1817–48," *William and Mary Quarterly*, 66, no. 4 (2009), 895–914.

5. Walter Frewen Lord, "Goree: A Lost Possession of England," *Transactions of the Royal Historical Society* 11 (1897): 139–52; J. M. Gray, *A History of the Gambia* (Cambridge: Cambridge University Press, 2015), 284–86.

6. Napoleon to Decrès, June 17, 1803, in Édouard Desbrière, *1793–1805: projets et tentatives de débarquement aux îles Britanniques* (Paris: R. Chapelot, 1902), III:84.

7. See Desbrière, *1793–1805*, III:107–109, 355–56, 380, 411.

8. Franco-Dutch Convention, June 25, 1803 in Georg Friedrich Martens, *Recueil des principaux traités d'alliance, de paix, de trève, de neuralité, de commerce, de limites, d'échange, etc.* (Gottingue: Librairie de Dieterich, 1801), VII:702–706.

9. Franco-Suisse Conventions, September 27, 1803, in Martens, *Recueil des principaux traités*, VIII:132–39.

10. Charles Auriol, *La France, l'Angleterre et Naples de 1803 á 1806* (Paris: Plon-Nourrity, 1904), I:352–447.

11. On the role of Hanover in British policies of the revolutionary era, see Torsten Riotte, *Hannover in der Britischen politik (1792–1815)* (Münster: Lit, 2005), esp. 61–162.

12. Bonaparte to Frederick William of Prussia, March 11, 1803, and Bonaparte to Duroc, March 12, 1803, *CN*, no. 6629, VIII:243–46.

13. For details, see Brendan Simms, *The Impact of Napoleon: Prussian High Politics, Foreign Policy, and the Crisis of the Executive, 1797–1806* (Cambridge: Cambridge University Press, 1997), 67–148.

14. F. de Martens, *Recueil des traités et conventions conclus par la Russie avec les puissances étrangères* (St. Petersburg: A. Böhnke, 1895), VI:310.

15. Frederick William to Bonaparte, March 25, 1803, Archives du Ministère des Affaires Étrangères, "Prusse," 227.

16. For details, see Paul Bailleur, ed., *Preussen und Frankreich von 1795 bis 1807: Diplomatische correspondenzen* (Leipzig: S. Hirzel, 1887), II:95–102; Philip G. Dwyer, "Two Definitions of Neutrality: Prussia, the European States-System, and the French Invasion of Hanover in 1803," *International History Review* 19, no. 3 (1997): 525–28.

17. Talleyrand to Laforest, May 17, 1803, in Bailleu, *Preussen und Frankreich*, II:142–45.

18. For better insights into Russian foreign policy, see Patricia Grimsted, "Czartoryski's System for Russian Foreign Policy, 1803," in *California Slavic Studies*, ed. Nicholas V. Riasanovsky and Gleb Struve (Berkeley: University of California Press, 1970), V:19–92.

19. A Prussian envoy reported that senior Russian officials, including Chancellor Vorontsov, believed that by offering to occupy Prussia, Prussia had become "the executor of Bonaparte's will [*volonté*]." Heinrich Ulmann, *Russisch-preussische politik unter Alexander I. und Friedrich Wilhelm III. bis 1806* (Leipzig: Duncker und Humblot, 1899), 61–62. For interesting insights, see Uta Krüger-Löwenstein, *Russland, Frankreich und das Reich 1801–1803; zur Vorgeschichte der 3. Koalition* (Wiesbaden: Steiner, 1972), 43–63, 104–25.

20. See Haugwitz to Frederick William III, October 26, 1803, and Haugwitz's Memorandum of November 3, 1803, in Bailleu, *Preussen und Frankreich*, II:209–13.

21. Louis Pierre Bignon, *Histoire de France depuis 1793 jusu'en 1812* (Paris: Charles Bechet, 1830), III:128–30; Adolphus William Ward, *Great Britain and Hanover* (Oxford: Clarendon Press, 1899), 202–8; Friedrich von Ompteda, *Die Ueberwdltigung Hannovers durch die Franzosen* (Hanover: Helwing, 1862), 126–27.

22. Harold C. Deutsch, *The Genesis of Napoleonic Imperialism* (Cambridge, MA: Harvard University Press, 1938), 169.

23. See "Projet de concert à établir entre sa majesté l'empereur de toutes les Russies et sa majesté le roi de Prusse," *VPR,* I:442–44, 463–65. Also Alopeus to Haugwitz, May 19, 1803, *VPR,* I:434; Vorontsov to Alopeus, May 24, 1803, in Martens, *Recueil des traités conclus par la Russie,* VI:314.

24. For discussion of Russian motives, see Ulmann, *Russisch-preussische politik,* 69; W. H. Zawadzki, "Prince Adam Czartoryski and Napoleonic France, 1801–1805: A Study in Political Attitudes," *Historical Journal* 18, no. 2 (1975): 248–49. For Bonaparte's overtures see Bailleu, *Preussen und Frankreich,* II:148–51, and Johann von Lombard's report on his negotiations with Bonaparte, 183–89; Deutsch, *The Genesis of Napoleonic Imperialism,* 165–68.

25. *The Works of William Shakespeare: The Tragedy of Julius Caesar,* edited by Michael MacMillan (London: Methuen, 1902), 132.

26. Haugwitz to Frederick William III, and Frederick William III to Haugwitz, June 4–9, 1803, in Bailleu, *Preussen und Frankreich,* II:152–54, 159–61.

27. For details, see letters by Lucchesini and Talleyrand, November–December 1803, in Bailleu, *Preussen und Frankreich,* II:215–20, 223–32.

28. Cobenzl to Colloredo, July 6, 1802, in Deutsch, *The Genesis of Napoleonic Imperialism,* 58.

29. Article II, Anglo-Russian Treaty, April 11, 1805, in J. Holland Rose, ed., *Select Despatches from the British Foreign Office Archives Relating to the Formation of the Third Coalition Against France, 1804–1805* (London: Royal Historical Society, 1904), 266.

30. Andrés Muriel, *Historia de Carlos IV* (Madrid: Imp. de Manuel Tello, 1894), XXXIV:82–87.

31. Armstrong to Monroe, May 4, 1805, cited in Clifford L. Egan, "The United States, France, and West Florida, 1803–1807," *Florida Historical Quarterly* 47, no. 3 (1969): 234.

32. Frederick C. Schneid, *Napoleon's Conquest of Europe: The War of the Third Coalition* (Westport, CT: Praeger, 2005), 24.

33. For details, see Salvador Bermúdez de Castro y O'Lawlor, marqués de Lema, *Antecedentes políticos y diplomáticos de los sucesos de 1808; Estudio histórico-crítico escrito con la presencia de documentos inéditos del Archivo Reservado de Fernando VII, del Histórico-nacional y otros* (Madrid: F. Beltrán, 1912), esp. 231–32.

34. Javier Cuenca Esteban, "Statistics of Spain's Colonial Trade, 1792–1820: Consular Duties, Cargo Inventories and Balances of Trade," *Hispanic American Historical Review* 61, no. 3 (1981): 409.

35. See André Fugier, *Napoléon et l'Espagne, 1799–1808* (Paris: F. Alcan, 1930), I:185–89; Jacques Chastenet, *Godoy: Master of Spain, 1792–1808* (London: Batchworth Press, 1953), 118.

36. Ana María Schop Soler, *Las relaciones entre España y Rusia en la época de Carlos IV* (Barcelona: Universidad de Barcelona, Cátedra de Historia General de España, 1971), 88.

37. Schop Soler, *Las relaciones entre España y Rusia*, 116–17.

38. Spain was also given an "option" of declaring war on Britain, which would then require a Spanish contribution of two corps, one to invade Portugal and another to blockade Gibraltar.

39. Napoleon to Talleyrand, August 14–16, 1803, in *CN*, nos. 7,007–7,008, VIII:458–63.

40. Fugier, *Napoleon et l'Espagne,* I:220–22.

41. Bonaparte to Charles IV, September 18, 1803, *CN*, no. 7113, VIII:680–81.

42. Michael W. Jones, "Fear and Domination: Pierre Riel, the Marquis de Beurnonville at the Spanish Court and Napoleon Bonaparte's Spanish Policy, 1802–05," Ph.D. diss., Florida State University, 2004, 80.

43. Frederick H. Black, "Diplomatic Struggles: British Support in Spain and Portugal, 1800–1810," Ph.D. diss., Florida State University, 2005, 47–72.

44. Alexandre de Clercq, ed., *Recueil des Traités de la France* (Paris: A. Durand et Pedone-Lauriel, 1880), II:83–84. In December, Portugal signed a similar agreement with France, buying its neutrality for a price of 16 million francs and the opening of Portuguese markets to French commerce.

45. Charles-Alexandre Geoffroy de Grandmaison, *L'Espagne et Napoléon, 1804–1809* (Paris: Plon-Nourrit, 1908), I:1–5; André Fugier, *Napoléon et l'Espagne, 1799–1808* (Paris: F. Alcan, 1930), I:186–97, 204–47, 294–313.

46. See Desbrière, *1793–1805*, vol. I for preparations in 1794–1797 and volume II for 1798–1801.

47. See instructions and reports in Desbrière, *1793–1805*, vols. III–IV, and in Napoleon, *Correspondance Générale*, ed. Thierry Lentz (Paris: Fayard, 2004), vols. 4–5. Well over a third of Napoleon's correspondence for the years 1803 and 1804 relates to the planning of the invasion of Britain. Also see H. F. B. Wheeler, *Napoleon and the Invasion of England: The Story of the Great Terror* (London: John Lane, 1908), vol. 2.

48. See documents in SHD MV BB1, 26.

49. Probably the best study on the national flotilla remains Jacques Blanc, "La flottille nationale, 1803–1805," MA thesis, Université Paris IV, 2007.

50. Peter Lloyd, *The French Are Coming! 1805: The Invasion Scare of 1803–1805* (Kent, UK: Spellmount, 1991), 24–25, 29–30.

51. Spending costs estimated based on data in Desbrière, *1793–1805*, III:90–92, 97, 111–12, 149, 152, 174, 350, 358, 384–85, 389, 452, 463, 538. Documents preserved in the French archives also provide wealth of data on this point. In August 1803, a report to the Minister of the Navy showed that prices

for gunboats and transports ranged between 6,000 francs for a caique (small fishing boat) to 140,000 francs for a flat-bottomed transport. See documents in SHD MV BB1, 28 and AN Archives du Consulat et de la Secrétairerie d'État impériale AF/IV/1195, 1203–205.

52. Martin van Creveld, *Command in War* (Cambridge, MA: Harvard University Press, 1985), 65–78, provides a good summary of Napoleon's headquarters and staff system. For the unheralded but crucial figure of Intendant General Pierre Daru, see Bernard Bergerot, *Daru, Intendant-Général de la Grande Armée* (Paris: Tallandier, 1991).

53. Berthier to Ney, January 18, 1807, in Jean Baptiste Modeste Eugene Vachée, *Napoleon at Work* (London: Adam and Charles Black, 1914), 24; Gunther Rothenberg, *The Art of Warfare in the Age of Napoleon* (Bloomington: Indiana University Press, 1978), 129.

54. Napoleon established six camps along the Atlantic coastline. Soult took command of the camps around Boulogne, called "camp de Boulogne et de Saint-Omer"; Ney commanded "camp de Montreuil," established near Étaples; Davout was in charge of camps in the north, near Bruges and Ambleteuse. The locations of some of these camps are particularly noteworthy, since they allowed Napoleon to draw on resources from outside France. Thus, the Bayonne camp, commanded by Marshal Pierre Augereu, was located on the border with Spain, and its presence (with the implied threat to Spain) compelled the Spanish court to buy its neutrality with a large financial subsidy. Desbrière, *1793–1805*, III:68–77; Fréderic Lemaire, "Les camps napoléoniens d'Étaples-sur-Mer (camp de Montreuil, 1803–1805). Recherches en cours," in *Revue du Nord*, 2010, 39–49 n. 388. For French threats against Spain, see Bonaparte to Talleyrand, August 14, 1803, *CN*, no. 7007, VIII:458–61.

55. Jean Roch Coignet, *Les Cahiers du capitaine Coignet* (Paris: Hachette, 1883), 161–62. For discussion of officers and soldiers of the Grande Armée, see Michael J. Hughes, *Forging Napoleon's Grande Armee: Motivation, Military Culture, and Masculinity in the French Army, 1800–1808* (New York: New York University Press, 2012); Jean-Claude Damamme, *Les soldats de la Grande Armée* (Paris: Perrin, 1998); John Robert Elting, *Swords Around a Throne: Napoleon's Grande Armée* (New York: Free Press, 1988).

56. "Note pour le Bureau de l'Organization, 8 fructidor an XIII" (August 26, 1805), in Paul Claude Alombert-Goget and Jean Lambert Alphonse Colin, *La Campagne de 1805 en Allemagne* (Paris: R. Chapelot, 1902), I:330–32; see also "Composition of the Grande Armée as of 30 September 1805," II:158–68.

57. Napoleon to Eugène de Beauharnais, June 7, 1809, in *CN*, no. 15310, XIX:81.

58. "War is the province of uncertainty: three-fourths of those things upon which action in War must be calculated, are hidden more or less in the clouds of great uncertainty. Here, then, above all a fine and penetrating mind is called for, to search out the truth by the tact of its judgment." Carl von Clausewitz, *On War*, trans. J. J. Graham (London: Kegan Paul, Trench, Trubner, 1908), I:48–49.

59. David Chandler, *The Campaigns of Napoleon* (New York: Scribner, 1966), 185.

60. For a long term impact of this scare on the British public, see Eve Darian-Smith, *Bridging Divides: The Channel Tunnel and English Legal Identity in the New Europe* (Berkeley: University of California Press, 1999), 71–93.

61. Cited in Donald Graves, *Dragon Rampant: The Royal Welch Fusiliers at War, 1793–1815* (Barnsley, UK: Frontline Books, 2010), 51.

Chapter 10

1. See Louis Georges de Cadoudal, *Georges Cadoudal et la chouannerie* (Paris: E. Plon, 1887), 292–317; G. Lenotre, *Georges Cadoudal* (Paris: B. Grasset, 1929); Patrick Huchet, *Georges Cadoudal et les chouans* (Rennes: Éditions Ouest-France, 1998); Jean François Chiappe, *Georges Cadoudal ou la liberté* (Paris: Librairie académique Perrin, 1971); Jean de La Varende, *Cadoudal* (Paris: Éditions françaises d'Amsterdam, 1952).

2. Anne Jean Marie René Savary, *Memoirs of the Duke of Rovigo* (London: Henry Colburn, 1828), I:287. On Bernadotte's involvement in these intrigues, see Dunbar Plunket Barton, *Bernadotte and Napoleon, 1763–1810* (London: John Murray, 1921), 47–65.

3. Anne-Louise-Germaine de Staël, *Ten Years' Exile* (London: Treuttel and Wurtz, 1821), 68–69.

4. John R. Hall, *General Pichegru's Treason* (London: Smith, Elder, 1915), 349–51. For Pichegru's earlier intrigues, see G. Caudrillier, *Le Trahison de Pichegru et les intrigues royalistes dans l'Est avant Fructidor* (Paris: Félix Alcan, 1908).

5. Frances Montgomery, "General Moreau and the Conspiracy Against Napoleon in 1804: The Verdict of the Court and of History," *Proceedings of the Consortium on Revolutionary Europe*, 1988, 165–87; Ernest Picard, *Bonaparte et Moreau* (Paris: Plon-Nourrit, 1905), 352–405. Also see Pierre Savinel, *Moreau, rival républicain de Bonaparte* (Rennes: Ouest-France, 1986); Soizik Moreau, *Jean-Victor Moreau: l'adversaire de Napoléon* (Paris: Punctum, 2005).

6. Jean-Paul Bertaud, *Bonaparte et le duc d'Enghien: le duel des deux France* (Paris: R. Laffront, 1972); Henri Welschinger, *Le duc d'Enghien* (Paris: E. Plon, Nourrit, 1888). The duke had commanded royalist troops during the Revolutionary Wars and sworn opposition to the revolutionary government.

7. Henri Welschinger, *Le duc d'Enghien. L'enlèvement d'Ettenheim et l'exécution de Vincennes* (Paris: Plon-Nourrit, 1913); Andréa Davy-Rousseau, "Autour de la mort du duc d'Enghien," *Revue du souvenir Napoléonien* 334 (1984): 2–15; Jacques Godechot, *The Counter-Revolution: Doctrine and Action, 1789–1804* (Princeton, NJ: Princeton University Press, 1981), 376–81.

8. André François Miot de Mélito, *Memoirs of Count Miot de Mélito, Minister, Ambassador, Councillor of State and Member of the Institute of France, Between the Years 1788 and 1815*, ed. Wilhelm August Fleischmann (New York: Scribner, 1881), 311.

9. Miot de Mélito, *Memoirs*, 310.

10. Miot de Mélito, *Memoirs*, 312–14; Vincent Cronin, *Napoleon Bonaparte: An Intimate Biography* (New York ; Morrow, 1972), 244.

11. "Récit de Le Couteulx de Canteleu," in *Correspondance du duc d'Enghien (1801–1804) et documents sur son enlèvement et sa mort* (Paris: A. Picard, 1908), II:443.

12. Henri Welschinger, "L'Europe et l'exécution du duc d'Enghien," in *Revue de la Société des études historiques* 8 (1890): 1–19, 73–94.

13. Cited in Harold C. Deutsch, *The Genesis of Napoleonic Imperialism* (Cambridge, MA: Harvard University Press, 1938), 193.

14. Welschinger, "L'Europe et l'exécution du duc d'Enghien," 84.

15. When told that his conduct was not reflecting the wishes of his sovereign, Markov replied, "The emperor may have his opinion, but the Russians have their own." Talleyrand to Laforest, October 4, 1803, in Paul Bailleur, ed., *Preussen und Frankreich von 1795 bis 1807: Diplomatische correspondenzen*, vol. 2 (Leipzig: S. Hirzel, 1881–1887), II:205.

16. See Jacques Godechot, *Le comte d'Antraigues: Un espion dans l'Europe des émigrés* (Paris: Fayard, 1986); Léonce Pingaud, *Un agent secret sous la révolution et l'empire: le comte d'Antraigues* (Paris, E. Plon Nourrit, 1894).

17. The Russian foreign minister noted in his memoirs: "The seizure of the Duc d'Enghien by a French detachment in an independent country with which France was at peace, and his trial and execution which immediately followed, produced a general feeling of stupor and indignation which those who did not witness it could not easily realize." Adam Czartoryski, *Memoirs of Prince Adam Czartoryski and His Correspondence with Alexander I,* ed. Adam Gielgud (London: Remington, 1888), II:14.

18. Edouard Driault, *Napoléon et l'Europe. Austerlitz, la fin du Saint-empire (1804–1806)* (Paris: F. Alcan, 1912), 53–64; Deutsch, *The Genesis of Napoleonic Imperialism*, 200–204.

19. Czartoryski, *Memoirs*, II:15; Albert Sorel, *L'Europe et la Révolution française* (Paris: Plon Nourrit, 1903), VI:361.

20. For the Russian overtures to Austria, see *VPR*, I:216, 222–23, 236, 246, 251 and 295. For the Austrian side, see Adolf Beer, *Zehn jahre österreichischer politik, 1801–1810* (Leipzig: F.A. Brockhaus, 1877), 73–77.

21. The Berlin Declaration, May 24, 1804, in F. de Martens, *Recueil des traités et conventions conclus par la Russie avec les puissances étrangères* (St. Petersburg: A. Böhnke, 1895), VI:337–45. For a broad discussion, see Deutsch, *The Genesis of Napoleonic Imperialism*, 160–71; Schroeder, *The Transformation of European Politics*, 253–55.

22. Miot de Mélito, *Memoirs*, 248; Lucchesini's report of July 20, 1802, in Bailleur, *Preussen und Frankreich*, II:106; Markov's report of June 5, 1802, in *SIRIO* (1890) LXX:427.

23. Joseph Bonaparte argued this point in one of his letters: "The conspiracy of Georges and Moreau decided the declaration of a hereditary title. With Napoleon as Consul for a period, a *coup de main* might overthrow him; as

Consul for life, the blow of a murderer would have been required. He assumed hereditary rank as a shield. It would then no longer suffice to kill him; the whole State would have had to be overthrown. The truth is that the nature of things tended towards the hereditary principle: it was a matter of necessity." Cited in Claude-Francois Méneval, *Mémoires pour servir à histoire de Napoléon Ier depuis 1802 jusqu'à 1815* (Paris: E. Dentu, 1893), I:330.

24. Henri Welschinger, *Le Pape et l'Empereur, 1804–1815* (Paris: Librairie Plon-Nourrit, 1905), 15.

25. Constitution de l'an XII: senatus-consulte du 28 floréal an XII conférant le titre d'empereur héréditaire des Français à Napoléon Bonaparte, AN' AE/II/1512. For details, see Thierry Lentz, ed., *La proclamation du Premier Empire* (Paris: Fondation Napoléon, 2002).

26. Lentz, *La France et l'Europe de Napoléon*, 97. The results show that 60 percent of some 8.9 million voters had abstained.

27. Louis Madelin, *The Consulate and the Empire* (New York: AMS Press, 1967), I:212.

28. The date itself was a compromise between Napoleon's demand for November 9 (the fifth anniversary of the Eighteenth of Brumaire coup) and the pope's desire to have the coronation coincide with Christmas (the 804th anniversary of Charlemagne's coronation). For details, see Thierry Lentz, Émilie Barthet, et al., *Le sacre de Napoléon, 2 décembre 1804* (Paris: Nouveau Monde, 2003).

29. Lentz, *La France et l'Europe de Napoléon*, 27–84; Irene Collins, *Napoleon and His Parliaments, 1800–1815* (New York: St. Martin's Press, 1979).

30. In July 1804, with Austrian delaying the recognition, Napoleon threatened to take action. In July the Russian envoy reported a conversation Napoleon had with his aides-de-camp where he threatened that "if [Austria] continued to prevaricate, he would fix a term for her to make a decision and then, if she let that term pass without sending new letters of accreditation to her ambassador, he would change the face of Europe." Oubril to Czartoryski, July 6, 1804, *SIRIO*, LXXVII (1891): 659.

31. Czartoryski to Razumovskii, June 19, 1804, *VPR*, II:31.

32. Napoleon to Francis of Austria, to Charles IV of Spain, and to Ferdinand of Naples, January 1–2, 1805, in *CN*, X:98–99, 101–3.

33. Napoleon to George III, January 2, 1805, in *CN*, X:100–101.

34. Adam Jerzy Czartoryski, *Mémoires du Prince Adam Czartoryski et Correspondance avec l'Empereur Alexandre Ier* (Paris: E. Plon, Nourrit, 1887), I:388.

35. Deutsch, *The Genesis of Napoleonic Imperialism*, 257–332; Schroeder, *Transformation of European Politics*, 258–72; Frederick W. Kagan, *The End of the Old Order: Napoleon and Europe 1801–1805* (New York: Da Capo, 2006), 83–228.

36. For details, see the Russo-Swedish Convention, January 14, 1805, and the Russian Declaration of Guarantee of the Anglo-Swedish Convention, August 31, 1805, in Originaltraktater med främmande makter (traktater), Riksarkivet, SE/RA/25.3/2/42/A-H, SE/RA/25.3/2/43/A-B. Also see Convention Between

Russia and Kingdom of Both Sicilies, September 10, 1805, *VPR*, II:570–77; Russo-Turkish Treaty, September 23, 1805, *VPR*, II:584–94; Article I, St. Petersburg Convention, April 11, 1805, *VPR*, II:356.

37. Article 2 in Martens, *Recueil des Traités*, II:435.

38. Separate Article 6, Martens, *Recueil des Traités*, II:443.

39. Kagan, *The End of the Old Order*, 234; Moritz Edler von Angeli, "Ulm und Austerlitz. Studie auf Grund archivalischer Quellen über den Feldzug 1805 in Deutschland," *Mittheilungen des Kaiserlichen und Koniglichen Kriegsarchivs* (Vienna, 1877), 398–400; in Paul Claude Alombert-Goget and Jean Lambert Alphonse Colin, *La Campagne de 1805 en Allemagne* (Paris: R. Chapelot, 1902), I:39–69; David Chandler, *The Campaigns of Napoleon* (New York: Scribner, 1966), 382–83.

40. As war loomed between France and Austria, Napoleon sought allies from among the larger German states, some of which had territory to gain and greater autonomy to acquire by siding against the Habsburgs. Bavaria was the first to throw in its lot with France, signing a treaty of alliance on September 23, 1805, followed by Baden and Württemberg on October 1 and 8, respectively.

41. Alfred Krauss, *Beilagen zu 1805 der Feldzug von Ulm* (Vienna: Seidel und Sohn, 1912), Beilage III:1–6.

42. Much has been made in English-language studies of the difference of twelve days between the Gregorian and Julian calendars used, respectively, in Austria and Russia. However, archival documentation, including original correspondence between Russian and Austrian high commands, does not support such claims. In fact, Russian letters carried dates under both calendars.

43. François Nicolas Mollien, *Mémoires d'un ministre du trésor public: 1780–1815* (Paris: Félix Alcan, 1898) I:408–9.

44. Miot de Mélito, *Memoirs*, II:142–43.

45. For a concise but insightful discussion of the Grande Armée's march to the Rhine, see Frederic L. Huidekoper, "Napoleon's Concentration on the Rhine and Main in 1805," *Journal of the Military Service Institution of the United States* XLI (1907): 207–20.

46. Eric Arnold, "Fouche Versus Savary: French Military Intelligence in the Ulm-Austerlitz Campaign," in *Proceedings of the Consortium on Revolutionary Europe*, 1976, 55–67. Also see Jean Savant, *Les espions de Napoléon* (Paris: Hachette, 1957), 123–45; Paul Müller, *L'Espionnage militaire sous Napoleon 1er Ch. Schulmeister* (Paris: Berger-Levrault, 1896); Abel Douay and Gérard Hertault, *Schulmeister: dans les coulisses de la Grande Armée* (Paris: Nouveau Monde Éditions, 2002).

47. Two Austrian detachments, however, did break out of the encirclement, only to surrender later: the Archduke Ferdinand, with 13,000 cavalry, eventually capitulated at Trochtelfingen, while another 12,000 men wound up laying down their arms at Neustadt.

48. Elsewhere the minor Allied operations failed as well. The British and Swedes had achieved little in Hanover, while the Russian expeditionary corps was

turned back by a storm. In southern Italy, the French defeated the British-supported Neapolitans and chased them from the mainland to Sicily.

49. On October 2, Major General Peter Bagration, who commanded the Russian advance guard, reported: "I made forced marches on [September' 27–28], the first march lasting continuously for almost 24 hours, and the second one even longer than that." Bagration to Kutuzov, October 2, 1805, in *Dokumenti shtaba M. I. Kutuzova, 1805–1806*, ed. A. Karvyalis and V. Soloveyev (Vilnius: Gos. izdatelstvo polit literatury, 1951), 59–60. Kutuzov complained that the Russian soldiers were given rest only after four days of forced marches. Consequently, the number of sick greatly increased while "the healthy soldiers are so exhausted that they are barely standing on their feet. Furthermore, due to damp weather, most of our troops have already worn down their boots and are forced to walk bare-footed and suffer so grievously from marching on paved roads that they can no longer remain in ranks." Kutuzov to Strauch, October 1, 1805, in *M. I. Kutuzov: Sbornik dokumentov*, ed. Liubomir Beskrovnyi (Moscow: Voennoe izdatelstvo Voennogo Ministerstva Soyuza SSR, 1954), II:68–69.

50. Murat to Napoleon, November 13, 1805, in Paul Le Brethon, ed. *Lettres et Documents pour servir a l'histoire de Joachim Murat, 1767–1815* (Paris: Librarie Plon, 1910), IV:146–48.

51. For an excellent discussion of this incident, see Frederic L. Huidekoper, "The Surprise of the Tabor Bridge at Vienna by Prince Murat and Marshal Lannes, November 13, 1805," in *Journal of the Military Service Institution of the United States* XXXVI (1905): 275–93, 513–30.

52. Napoleon to Murat, November 16, 1805, in Napoleon, *Correspondance générale*, ed. Thierry Lentz (Paris: Fayard, 2008), V:856.

53. Russo-Prussian Convention, November 3, 1805, *VPR*, II:613–19.

54. However, the relations between the Russian and Austrian officers remained tense—the former loathed the latter, who, they claimed, had lost every battle in the campaign and now wanted the Russians to do the heavy work. These sentiments were reinforced by Russian accusations that some Austrian officers were spying for the French. Kutuzov to Liechtenstein, November 24, 1805, *Dokumenty shtaba M.I. Kutuzova, 1805–1806*, ed. V. Karvyalis and A. Solovyeov (Vilna, 1951), 199–200.

55. Alexander later observed, "I was young and inexperienced; Kutuzov told me that we had to act differently, but he should have been more persistent in his arguments." Nikolai Shilder, *Imperator Aleksandr Pervyi, ego zhizn' i tsarstvovanie* (St. Petersburg: A. S. Suvorin, 1897), II:134.

56. Weyrother was among a few Austrian officers who had influence over Alexander. Prince Adam Czartoryski, the Russian emperor's trusted confidant, recalled that Weyrother was "an officer of great bravery and military knowledge, but, like General Mack, he trusted too much in his combinations, which were often complicated, and did not admit that they might be foiled by the skill of the

enemy." Czartoryski, *Memoirs*, 102. Similar characterization of Weyrother in W. Rüstow, *Der krieg von 1805 in Deutschland und Italien* (Zürich: Meyer & Zeller, 1859), 325.

57. Christopher Duffy, *Austerlitz 1805* (London: Seeley Service, 1977), 75.

58. *The Czar's General: The Memoirs of a Russian General in the Napoleonic Wars*, trans. and ed. Alexander Mikaberidze (Welwyn Garden City, UK: Ravenhall Books, 2005), 56. Alexey Yermolov, one of the most distinguished Russian generals of the early nineteenth century, commanded a horse artillery company in the Russian advance (and later rear) guards.

59. Shilder, *Alexander*, 135; Alexander Mikhailovsky-Danilevsky, *Opisanie pervoi voiny imperatora Aleksandra s Napoleonom v 1805-m godu* (St. Petersburg: Tip. Shtaba otd. korpusa vnutrennei strazhi, 1844), 142; Czartoryski, *Memoirs*, 104; Alexander-Andrault Langeron, "Journal inédit de la campagne de 1805," in *Relations et rapports officiels de la bataille d'Austerlitz, 1805*, ed. Jacques Garnier (Paris: La Vouivre, 1998), 31.

60. "Disposition for Offensive to Menitz and Sokolnitz Against the Enemy Right Flank on December 1, 1805," n.d. (ca. November 30, 1805), RGVIA, f. 846 op. 16, d. 3117/1, ll. 47.

61. Czartoryski, *Memoirs*, II:105.

62. Langeron, *Journal inedit de la campagne de 1805*, 31. Major General Stutterheim observed, "The Allies flattered themselves that [Napoleon] would not risk the fate of a battle in front of Brünn. After [the action at Wischau] this *hope* became the prevailing *opinion* at the headquarters." Stutterheim, *La Bataille d'Austerlitz, par un militaire témoin de la journée du 2 décembre 1805* (Paris, 1806), 44.

63. "Additional Bulletin, December 31, 1805, Correspondence of Olry, *Istoricheskii Vestnik* 147 (1917): 458–59.

64. Dolgorukov to Alexander, November 25, 1805, in Mikhailovsky-Danilevsky, *Opisanie*, 144. Listening to Dolgorukov's overbearing remarks, Napoleon lost his temper: "Away with you! Go and tell your emperor that I am not in the habit of tolerating insults of this kind. Be gone immediately!" Paul-Philippe Ségur, *Histoire et mémoires* (Paris: Librairie de Firmin-Didot, 1877), II:448. Also see Jean Lambert Alphonse Colin, "Campagne de 1805," *Revue Historique* 77 (1907): 284–90; Anne Jean Marie René Savary, *Memoirs du duc de Rovigo* (London: H. Colburn, 1828), II:198–99.

65. Langeron, *Journal inedit de la campagne de 1805*, 30; Mikhailovsky-Danilevsky, *Opisanie*, 145.

66. "Additional Bulletin, December 31, 1805, Correspondence of Olry, in *Istoricheskii Vestnik* 147 (1917): 460–61.

67. Duffy, *Austerlitz*, 81; Rüstow, *Der Krieg von 1805*, 356–57; Dokhturov was near Hostjeradek and Kinmeyer's detachment was at Augezo. General Langeron's column was on Dokhturov's right flank. Przybyszewsky was at Pratzen. Kollowrath stopped behind him and Liechtenstein was even further behind the third and fourth columns.

68. "Deployment of Troops, December 1, 1805," in Mikhailovsky-Danilevsky, *Opisanie*, 145–48; Langeron, *Journal inedit de la campagne de 1805*, 41; Jean Lambert Alphonse Colin, "Campagne de 1805," *Revue Historique* 77 (1907): 291; Michel de Lombarès, "Devant Austerlitz," *Revue historique de l'armée* 3 (1947): 47.

69. Joseph de Maistre, *Peterburgskie pisma* (St. Petersburg, 1995), 61. Similar information in Correspondence of Olry, in *Istoricheskii Vestnik*, 147 (1917): 433.

70. *Diaries and Correspondence of James Harris, First Earl of Malmesbury* (London: Richard Bentley, 1845), IV:339.

71. General Dmitri Dokhturov's letters to his wife, *Russkii arkhiv* 12, no. 1 (1874): 1091–2.

72. Peter Goodwin, *The Ships of Trafalgar: The British, French and Spanish Fleets, 21 October 1805* (London: Conway Maritime, 2005); Robert Mackenzie, *The Trafalgar Roll: The Officers, the Men, the Ships* (London: Chatham, 2004); Brian Lavery, *Nelson's Fleet at Trafalgar* (Annapolis, MD: Naval Institute Press, 2004).

73. See Roger Knight, *Pursuit of Victory: The Life and Achievemnt of Horatio Nelson* (London: Allen Lane, 2005), 502–8; Adam Nicolson, *Men of Honour: Trafalgar and the Making of the English Hero* (London: HarperCollins, 2005).

74. Nelson to Rose, October 6, 1805, in *The Dispatches and Letters of Vice Admiral Lord Viscount Nelson*, ed. Nicholas H. Nicholas (Cambridge: Cambridge University Press, 2011), VII:80; also see his October 9, 1805, letter to Collingwood.

75. Captain Pierre Servaux's account in Edward Fraser, *The Enemy at Trafalgar: An Account of the Battle from Eye-Witness Narratives and Letters and Despatches from the French and Spanish Fleets* (London: Hodder & Stoughton, 1906), 214.

76. For a discussion of the battle, see Alan Schom, *Trafalgar: Countdown to Battle, 1803–1805* (London: Penguin, 1992); John Harbron, *Trafalgar and the Spanish Navy: The Spanish Experience of Sea Power* (London: Conway Maritime, 2004); John Terraine, *Trafalgar* (London: Wordsworth, 1998); René Maine, *Trafalgar: Napoleon's Naval Waterloo* (London: Thames and Hudson, 1957); Gregory Fremont-Barnes, *Trafalgar 1805: Nelson's Crowning Victory* (Oxford: Osprey, 2005).

77. For example, Ian Christie, *Wars and Revolutions: Britain, 1760–1815* (Cambridge, MA: Harvard University Press, 1982), 266; J. Steven Watson, *The Oxford History of England*, vol. XII, *The Reign of George III, 1760–1815* (Oxford: Clarendon Press, 1960), 433; Roy Adkins, *Trafalgar: The Biography of a Battle* (London: Little, Brown, 2005), 277–78; David Andress, *The Savage Storm: Britain on the Brink in the Age of Napoleon* (London: Little, Brown, 2012), 124. Also see Arthur Bryant, *Years of Victory, 1802–1812* (New York: Harper & Bros. 1945); C. Northcote Parkinson, *Britannia Rules: The Classic Age of Naval History 1793–1815* (London: Weidenfeld & Nicolson, 1977).

78. Piers Mackesy lamented that fact that "the struggle at sea has generally been written as thought it ended at Trafalgar before the war had run a quarter of its course." Piers Mackesy, *The War in the Mediterranean 1803–1810* (Cambrdge,

MA: Harvard University Press, 1957), vii. For a recent discussion, see James Davey's excellent study, *In Nelson's Wake: The Navy and the Napoleonic Wars* (New Haven, CT: Yale University Press, 2015).

79. Michael Broers, *The Napoleonic Empire in Italy, 1796–1814: Cultural Imperialism in a European Context?* (New York: Palgrave Macmillan, 2005), 190–92; Charles McKay, "French Mismanagement and the Revolt of Parma, 1806," *Proceedings of the Consortium on Revolutionary Europe*, 1995, 445–52.

80. Napoleon to Junot, February 7, 1806, in *CN*, XII:18–19.

81. Henri Welschinger, *Le pape et l'empereur, 1804–1815* (Paris: Plon-Nourrit, 1905), 46–62; E. Hales, *Napoleon and the Pope: The Story of Napoleon and Pius VII* (London: Eyre & Spottiswoode, 1961), 178–79, 184–89. Also see Margaret M. O'Dwyer, *The Papacy in the Age of Napoleon and the Restoration: Pius VII, 1800–1823* (Lanham, MD: University Press of America, 1985); Carla Nardi, *Napoleone e Roma: la politica della consulta romana* (Rome: Ecole française de Rome, 1989).

82. John A. Davis, *Naples and Napoleon: Southern Italy and the European Revolutions (1780–1860)* (Oxford: Oxford University Press, 2006); 130–34; Harold Acton, *The Bourbons of Naples, 1734–1825* (London: Methuen, 1956), 520–40.

83. Frederick C. Schneid, *Napoleon's Italian Campaigns: 1805–1815* (Westport, CT: Praeger, 2002), 3–46.

84. See William Henry Flayhart, *Counterpoint to Trafalgar: The Anglo-Russian invasion of Naples, 1805–1806* (Gainesville: University Press of Florida, 2004); Piers Mackesy, *The War in the Mediterranean, 1803–1810* (Cambridge, MA: Harvard University Press, 1957), 78–84.

85. Napoleon to Queen Caroline of Naples, January 2, 1805, in *CN*, X:103–4.

86. Robert Matteson Johnston, *The Napoleonic Empire in Southern Italy and the Rise of the Secret Societies* (New York: Macmillan, 1904), 88–96.

87. Schneid, *Napoleon's Italian Campaigns*, 51.

88. For details, see Richard Hopton, *The Battle of Maida 1806: Fifteen Minutes of Glory* (London: Leo Cooper, 2002).

89. See James R. Arnold, "A Reappraisal of Column Versus Line in the Peninsular War," *Journal of Military History* 68, no. 2 (April 2004): 535–52.

90. Stuart to Windham, July 6, 1806, cited in Milton C. Finley, "The Most Monstrous of Wars: Suppression of Calabrian Brigandage, 1806–1811," *Proceedings of the Consortium on Revolutionary Europe*, 1989, II:254.

91. For an in-depth discussion, see Nicolas Cadet, *Honneur et violences de guerre au temps de Napoléon: La campagne de Calabre* (Paris: Éditions Vendémiaire, 2015); Milton Finley, *The Most Monstrous of Wars: The Napoleonic Guerrilla War in Southern Italy, 1806–1811* (Columbia: University of South Carolina Press, 1994).

92. John Ehrman, *The Younger Pitt: The Consuming Struggle* (Stanford, CA: Stanford University Press, 1996), 822–23.

93. Bavaria received the Margravate of Burgau; the Principality of Eichstadt; the Tyrol, Vorarlburg, Hohenems, Königsegg-Rothenfels, Tettnang, and Argen; and

the City of Lindau. Württemberg gained the cities of Ehingen, Munderkingen, Riedlingen, Mengen, and Sulgen; the County of Hohenberg; the Landgravate of Nellenbourg; and the Prefecture of Altorf. The Electorate of Baden, elevated to a grand duchy, received part of the Brisgau, the Ortenau, the City of Constance, and the Commandery of Meinau. As a small form of compensation, Austria was allowed to annex Salzburg, Berchtesgaden, and the Estates of the Teutonic Order.

94. See Peter H. Wilson, "Bolstering the Prestige of the Habsburgs: The End of the Holy Roman Empire in 1806," *International History Review* 28, no. 4 (December 2006): 709–36. Sixteen states joined the Rheinbund on July 12, 1806: Bavaria, Württemberg, Aschaffenburg/Regensburg, Baden, Berg, Arenberg, Nassau-Usingen, Nassau-Weilburg, Hohenzollern-Hechingen, Hohenzollern-Sigmaringen, Salm-Salm, Salm-Kyrburg, Isenburg, Leyen, Liechtenstein, and Hesse-Darmstadt. Grand Duchy of· Wützburg joined on September 25 and Saxony on December 11. Four days later the Confederation enlarged to include Saxe-Coburg, Saxe-Gotha, Saxe-Hildburghausen, Saxe-Meiningen, and Saxe-Weimar-Eisenach. The next major expansion occurred in April 1807, when twelve more states joined.

95. Sam A. Mustafa, *Germany in the Modern World: A New History* (New York: Rowman & Littlefield, 2011), 94.

96. For great insights into Prussian government, society, and culture, see Peter Paret's *The Cognitive Challenge of War: Prussia 1806* (Princeton: Princeton University Press, 2009).

97. Michael V. Leggiere, *Blucher: Scourge of Napoleon* (Norman: University of Oklahoma Press, 2014), 91; Simms, *Prussian High Politics*, 269–96.

98. The original booklet was reprinted on its centennial anniversary in 1906, and its authorship has been credited to Philipp Christian Gottlieb Yelin. See *Deutschland in seiner tiefen Erniedrigung* (Stuttgart: Lehmann, 1906), https://books.google.com/books?id=gAgSAAAAYAAJ. The booklet's title, "Germany in its Deepest Humiliation," would feature as a prominent refrain on the pages of Adolf Hitler's *Mein Kampf*.

99. "The abominable crime of Braunau has electrified everyone," one Austrian statesman noted in late September. A Nassau diplomat, Hans Christoph von Gagern, was more forceful in his condemnation: "The time will come when this national injury will be bathed in blood," he told the French foreign minister. "It will never be forgotten." Friedrich von Gentz to Metternich, September 23, 1806, in *Briefe von und an Friedrich von Gentz*, ed. Friedrich Carl Wittichen (Munich: R. Oldenbourg, 1913), III:59–60; Hellmuth Rössler, *Zwischen Revolution und Reaktion; ein Lebensbild des Reichsfreiherrn Hans Christoph von Gagern, 1766–1852* (Göttingen: Musterschmidt-Verlag, 1958), 108–9. In his most recent study, French historian Michel Kerautret referred to the Palm affair as a "state crime." See *Un Crime d'État sous l'empire: L'Affaire Palm* (Paris: Vendémiaire Editions, 2015).

100. Cited in Brendan Simms, *The Impact of Napoleon: Prussian High Politics, Foreign Policy, and the Crisis of the Executive, 1797–1806* (Cambridge: Cambridge University Press, 1997), 279.

101. Simms, *Prussian High Politics*, 296–300.

102. Schroeder, *Transformation of European Politics*, 304. "In short, the simple desire for survival, not the fear of losing territorial gains, motivated Prussia's stand in 1806," argues Brendan Simms. Simms, *Prussian High Politics*, 298.

103. Jean-Baptiste Antoine Marcellin Marbot, *The Memoirs of Baron de Marbot* (London: Longmans, Green, 1903), I:173.

104. Cited in Karen Hagemann, *Revisiting Prussia's War Against Napoleon: History, Culture and Memory* (Cambridge: Cambridge University Press, 2015), 34.

105. Dennis Showalter, "Reform and Stability: Prussia's Military Dialectic from Hubertusberg to Waterloo," in *The Projection and Limitations of Imperial Powers, 1618–1850*, ed. Frederick C. Schneid (Leiden: Brill, 2012), 89–97; Olaf Jessen, "Eingeschlafen auf den Lorbeeren Friedrichs des Großen?," in *1806: Jena, Auerstedt und die Kapitulation von Magdeburg: Schande oder Chance?*, ed. Mathias Tullner and Sascha Möbius (Halle: Landesheimatbund Sachsen-Anhalt, 2007), 110–29.

106. Carl von Clausewitz, *On War*, ed. Michael Howard and Peter Paret (Princeton, NJ: Princeton University Press, 1976), 155.

107. See Friedrich Eduard Alexander von Höpfner, *Der Krieg von 1806 und 1807 {i.e. achtzehnhundertsechs und achtzehnhundertsieben}: ein Beitrag zur Geschichte der Preussischen Armee nach den Quellen des Kriegs-Archivs bearbeitet* (Berlin: Schropp, 1850), I, chs. 1–7.

108. Höpfner, *Der Krieg von 1806 und 1807*, I:265–300; David G. Chandler, "Napoleon, Operational Art, and the Jena Campaign," in *Historical Perspectives of the Operational Art*, ed. Michael D. Krause and R. Cody Philips (Washington, DC: Center for Military History, 2007), 39–44.

109. See Gerd Fesser, *1806, die Doppelschlacht bei Jena und Auerstedt* (Jena: Bussert und Stadeler, 2006); Gerhard Bauer and Karl-Heinz Lutz, *Jena 1806: Vorgeschichte und Rezeption* (Potsdam: Militärgeschichtliches Forschungsamt, 2009).

110. The Prussians lost around 10,000 killed and wounded at Jena, along with 15,000 prisoners, 34 colors, and 120 guns, against a loss to Napoleon of around 5,000 men. At Auerstädt, the Prussian casualties amounted to some 10,000 dead and wounded, 3,000 prisoners, and 115 guns, while the French lost 7,000 dead and wounded, 25 percent of Davout's entire force. For discussion of the campaign, see Chandler, *Campaigns of Napoleon*, 452–506; Oscar von Lettow-Vorbeck, *Der Krieg von 1806–1907*, vol. I, *Jena und Auerstedt* (Berlin: Mittler und Sohn, 1896); F. N. Maude, *The Jena Campaign* (New York: Macmillan, 1909); F. Loraine Petre, *Napoleon's Conquest of Prussia—1806* (London: John Lane, 1907); Paul Jean Foucart, *Campagne de Prusse, 1806: d'après les archives de la guerre* (Paris: Berger-Levrault, 1887); Henri Bonnal, *La manoeuvre de Iéna* (Paris: Chapelot, 1904).

111. For current German historiographical debate on the fortress capitulations and their impact, see Mathias Tullner and Sascha Möbius, eds., *1806: Jena, Auerstedt und die Kapitulation von Magdeburg: Schande oder Chance?* (Halle: Landesheimatbund Sachsen-Anhalt, 2007). The most notable articles are Mathias Tullner, "Die preußische Niederlage bei Jena und Auerstedt (Hassenhausen) und die Kapitulation von Magdeburg" (130–39); Wilfried Lübeck, "8. November 1806—die Kapitulation von Magdeburg, die feige Tat des Gouverneurs v. Kleist?" (140–52); and Bernhard Mai, "Die Belagerungen von Magdeburg, Kolberg und Breslau 1806/07" (153–72).

112. Petre, *Napoleon's Conquest of Prussia—1806*, 236–55.

113. Leggiere, *Blucher*, 108–12.

114. Dennis E. Showalter, "Hubertusberg to Auerstedt: The Prussian Army in Decline?," *German History* 12 (1994): 308–33.

115. Napoleon then took the great Prussian king's sword as a personal trophy.

116. Alexander Mikhailovsky-Danilevsky, *Opisanie vtoroi voini Imperatora Aleksandra s Napoleonom v 1806–1807 godakh* (St. Petersburg, 1846), 47–53.

117. Bennigsen commanded some 70,000 men with 276 guns. Buxhöwden had 55,000 men with 216 guns. In addition, General Essen's corp of 37,000 men with 132 guns was marching from the Dniestr. Order of Battle of Bennigsen's, Buxhöwden's and Essen's Corps, Mikhailovsky-Danilevsky, *Opisanie vtoroi voini Imperatora Aleksandra* (1846), 63n., 69n. Also see Army Rosters, RGVIA, f. 846, op. 16, d. 3164, ll. 25–33.

118. Alexander to Tolstoy, n.d., in Mikhailovsky-Danilevsky, *Opisanie vtoroi voini Imperatora Aleksandra* (1846), 72–73. General Mikhail Kutuzov, one of a few able Russian commanders, was disgraced after the defeat at Austerlitz.

119. Jean-Roch Coignet, *The Narrative of Captain Coignet, Soldier of the Empire, 1776–1850* (New York: Thomas Y. Crowell, 1890), 138. For the Russian perspective, see Alexander Mikaberidze, ed., *The Russian Eyewitness Accounts of the Campaign of 1807* (London: Pen & Sword, 2015), 27–108.

120. For discussion of the operations in late 1806, see Höpfner, *Der Krieg von 1806 und 1807*, III:1–157; Mathieu Dumas, *Précis des événements militaires, ou, Essais historiques sur les campagnes de 1799 à 1814* (Paris: Treuttel et Wurtz, 1826), XVII:99–205; Karl Ritter von Landmann, *Der Krieg von 1806 und 1807: auf Grund urkundlichen Materials sowie der neuesten Forschungen und Quellen* (Berlin: Voss, 1909), 300–327; Carl von Plotho, *Tagebuch während des Krieges zwischen Russland und Preussen einerseits, und Frankreich andrerseits, in den Jahren 1806 und 1807* (Berlin: F. Braunes, 1811), 1–43; F. Lorain Petre, *Napoleon's Campaign in Poland, 1806–7* (London: Sampson Low, Marston, 1901), 59–118.

121. His appointment was a big mistake. Kamensky was sixty-nine years old and had not commanded an army in over a decade. He was already in such bad health that upon reaching Vilna in late November, he complained that "I almost completely lost my vision. I am not able to find any locations on the map and had to ask other to find them. I suffer from [excruciating] pains in the

eyes and head and cannot ride the horse....I am signing [orders] without even knowing what they prescribe." Kamensky to Alexander, December 22, 1807, in Mikhailovsky-Danilevsky, *Opisanie vtoroi voini Imperatora Aleksandra* (1846), 76.

122. Höpfner, *Der Krieg von 1806 und 1807*, III:193–94; E. Grenier, *Étude sur 1807: Manoeuvres d'Eylau et Friedland* (Paris, 1911), 51–53; Oscar von Lettow-Vorbeck, *Der krieg von 1806 und 1807* (Berlin, 1896), IV:31–49; Colmar von der Goltz, *From Jena to Eylau: The Disgrace and the Redemption of the Old-Prussian Army: A Study in Military History* (London, 1913), 197–203.

123. Denis Davydov, "Vospominaniya o srazhenii pri Preussisch-Eylau 1807 goda yanvarya 26-go i 27-go," in *Russkaya voennaya proza XIX veka* (Leningrad: Lenizdatm, 1989), http://www.museum.ru/1812/Library/Davidov7/index.html.

124. Antoine Jomini, *Vie politique et militaire de Napoleon, racontée par lui même* (Paris, 1827), II:355.

125. See James R. Arnold and Ralph R. Reinertsen, *Crisis in the Snows: Russia Confronts Napoleon: The Eylau Campaign 1806–1807* (Lexington, VA: Napoleon Books, 2007).

126. For the battle of Eylau, see Chandler, *The Campaigns of Napoleon*, 535–51; Petre, *Napoleon's Campaign in Poland*, 158–208; Mikhailovsky-Danilevsky, *Opisanie vtoroi voini Imperatora Aleksandra* (1846), 161–217; Höpfner, *Der Krieg von 1806 und 1807*, III:201–58.

127. Jean-Baptiste Barrès, *Memoirs of a Napoleonic Officer* (London: G. Allen & Unwin, 1925), 101.

128. À l'Armee; Napoleon to Berthier, 60th–61st Bulletins, February 16–19, 1807, in *CN*, XIV, nos. 11,816, 11,820, 11,822, 11,827, 11,830, 11,832, 381–91; Mikhailovsky-Danilevsky, *Opisanie vtoroi voini Imperatora Aleksandra* (1846), 233–34; Petre, *Napoleon's Campaign in Poland*, 215–37.

129. Bennigsen, "Memoirs," *Russkaya starina* 100 (December 1899): 700; Robert Wilson, *Brief Remarks on the Character and Composition of the Russian Army and a Sketch of the Campaigns in Poland in the Years 1806 and 1807* (London: C. Roworth, 1810), 128–29; *Ob uchastii gvardii v kampaniu 1807 g.*, RGVIA, f. 846, op. 16, d. 3163, ll. 1–13.

130. Hardenberg's Notes on Alexander's Meeting with Friedrich-Wilhelm III, in *VPR*, III:546; Landmann, *Der Krieg von 1806 und 1807*, 388–89; Bennigsen, "Memoirs," *Russkaya starina* 100 (October 1899): 226–28; 100 (December 1899): 697–700.

131. In a letter to Alexander, Bennigsen accused General Sacken of insubordination and held him responsible for the failure of the maneuver at Guttstadt. Sacken was eventually subjected to a court-martial and justified his actions by referring to Bennigsen's confusing orders. The hearings on Sacken's case continued for over three years. The court found him guilty but did not impose any punishment because of Sacken's distinguished career. Bennigsen, "Memoirs," *Russkaya starina* 101 (January 1901): 272; Mikhailovsky-Danilevsky, *Opisanie*

vtoroi voini Imperatora Aleksandra (1846), 298–302; Höpfner, *Der Krieg von 1806 und 1807*, III:583.

132. "Relation de la Bataille de Heilsberg le 10 Juin 1807," RGVIA, f. 846, op. 16, d. 3204, ll. 9–10; Mikhailovsky-Danilevsky, *Opisanie vtoroi voini Imperatora Aleksandra* (1846), 307–8; Höpfner, *Der Krieg von 1806 und 1807*, III:602–22; Landmann, *Der Krieg von 1806 und 1807*, 412–15.

133. Petre, *Napoleon's Campaign in Poland*, 304–9; Höpfner, *Der Krieg von 1806 und 1807*, III:652–53; Plotho, *Tagebuch während des Krieges*, 163. For the most recent English-language account, see James R. Arnold and Ralph R. Reinertsen, *Napoleon's Triumph: La Grande Armée Versus the Tsar's Army: The Friedland Campaign, 1807* (Lexington, VA: Napoleon Books, 2011).

134. Harold T. Parker, *Three Napoleonic Battles* (Durham, NC: Duke University Press, 1983), 17–18.

135. Maurice Girod de L'Ain, *Grands artilleurs: Drouot—Sénarmont—Eblé* (Paris: Berger-Levrault, 1895), 180–81, 224–26.

136. Leveson-Gower to Canning, June 17, 1807, cited in Herbert Butterfield, *The Peace Tactics of Napoleon, 1806–1808* (Cambridge: Cambridge University Press, 1959), 197–98.

137. As overheard by one of British commissioner Robert Wilson's contacts. Michael Glover, *A Very Slippery Fellow: The Life of Sir Robert Wilson, 1777–1849* (Oxford: Oxford University Press, 1978), 40. For an alternative version in which Alexander's first words were "I will be your second against England," see Napoleon to Alexander, July 1, 1812, in *Correspondance générale*, XII:787. Also see Louis Pierre Bignon, *Histoire de France depuis le 18 Brumaire jusqu'a la Paix de Tilsit* (Paris: Charles Béchet, 1830), VI:316; Armand Lefebvre, *Histoire des cabinets de l'Europe pendant le Consulat et l'Empire* (Paris: Pagnerre, 1847), III:102.

138. Russia also agreed to cede the port town of Cattaro (now Kotor, Montenegro) and the Ionian Islands to France, strengthening Napoleon's presence in the Adriatic Sea.

139. Treaty of Tilsit, July 7, 1807, Fondation Napoléon, https://www.napoleon.org/histoire-des-2-empires/articles/traite-de-tilsit-avec-la-russie-7-juillet-1807.

140. Lefebvre, *Napoleon*, 249. Another eminent French scholar, Jean Tulard, agrees: "The notion of the Grand Empire succeeded, starting from 1805, that of the Grand Nation." See Jean Tulard, ed., *Dictionnaire Napoléon* (Paris: Fayard, 1987), 833.

141. Claire Élisabeth Rémusat, *Mémoires de Madame de Rémusat 1802–1808* (Paris: Calmann-Lévy, 1880), III:202–5.

142. "Discours de S. M. L'Empereur et Roi à l'ouverture du Corps Législatif," August 16, 1807, in *CN*, XV:498–500.

143. At home, Napoleon further augmented his power by abolishing the Tribunate. Senatus Consultum, August 19, 1807, www.napoleon-series.org/research/government/legislation/c_tribunate.html.

144. See Reinhart Koselleck, "Über die Theoriebedürftigkeit der Geschichtswissenschaft," in *Theorie der Geschichtswissenschaft und Praxis des Geschichtsunterrichts*, ed. Werner Conze (Stuttgart: Klett, 1972), 10–28; Niklas Olsen, *History in the Plural: An Introduction to the Work of Reinhart Koselleck* (New York: Berghahn Books, 2014), 167–202.

Chapter 11

1. Wars involving Britain and France since 1697 included the War of the Spanish Succession (1701–1714), War of the Austrian Succession (1740–1748), Seven Years' War (1756–1763), American Revolutionary War (1775–1783), and French Revolutionary Wars (1793–1802). Britain and France were allied on just one occasion, during the War of the Quadruple Alliance (1718–1720).

2. Eli F. Heckscher, *The Continental System: An Economic Interpretation* (Oxford: Clarendon Press, 1922), 18–27, 42–43, 47, 77, 91; J. Holland Rose, "Napoleon and English Commerce," *English Historical Review* 8 (1893): 704–25. On the question of neutral powers, see W. Allison Phillips and Arthur H. Reede, *Neutrality: Its History, Economic, and Law*, vol. 2, *The Napoleonic Period* (New York: Columbia University Press, 1936).

3. In June 1793 Britain prohibited all food imports into France but rescinded this decision a few months later.

4. Heckscher, *The Continental System: An Economic Interpretation*, 81–83. Also see Frank Edgar Melvin, *Napoleon's Navigation System: A Study of Trade Control During the Continental Blockade* (New York: University of Pennsylvania, 1919), ch. 1.

5. The last hundred years had seen the appearance of a number of studies (mostly unpublished theses and dissertations) on the general nature of the Continental System and its effect on European states. The topic is long overdue for a fresh reassessment, with Heckscher's *The Continental System: An Economic Interpretation* remaining the only global survey. Recent valuable additions to the historiography include Katherine Aaslestad and Johan Joor, eds., *Revisiting Napoleon's Continental System: Local, Regional and European Experiences* (New York: Palgrave Macmillan, 2014) and Francois Crouzet, "The Continental System: After Eighty Years," in *Eli Heckscher, International Trade, and Economic History*, ed. Ronald Findlay, Rolf G. H. Henriksson, Hakan Lindgren, and Mats Lundahl (Cambridge, MA: MIT Press, 2006), 323–42. My discussion of the Continental System is based on additional readings of Geoffrey James Ellis, *Napoleon's Continental Blockade: The Case of Alsace* (New York: Oxford University Press, 1981); Harley Farris Anton, "The Continental Study: A Study of Its Operation and Feasibility," MA thesis, Louisiana State University, 1976; Merritt P. Whitten, "France and the Continental System of the Berlin Decree," M.S thesis, University of Wisconsin–Madison, 1964; François Crouzet, *L'économie britannique et le blocus continental, 1806–1813* (Paris: Presses universitaires de France, 1958); Albert John Daeley, "The Continental System in France as Illustrated by American Trade," PhD diss., University of Wisconsin–Madison,

1949; John Baugham Harrison, "The Continental System in Italy as Revealed by American Commerce," PhD diss., University of Wisconsin–Madison, 1937; Leah Julia Fritz, "Napoleon's Continental System in the North German States," MA thesis, University of Wisconsin–Madison, 1937; Andrew Wellington Tuholski, "The Continental System of Napoleon," MA thesis, Columbia University, 1919.

6. Napoleon to Eugène de Beauharnais, August 23, 1810, *Correspondance de Napoléon*, XXI:60.

7. Berlin Decree, November 21, 1806, in *Correspondance de Napoléon*, XIII:555.

8. British Order-in-Council, November 11, 1807, in *American State Papers: Documents Legislative and Executive of the Congress of the United States*, ed. Walter Lowrie and Matthew St. Clair Clarke (Washington: Gales and Seaton, 1832), III:269–70.

9. Milan Decree, December 17, 1807, in Napoleon, *Correspondance Générale*, ed. Thierry Lentz (Paris: Fayard, 2004), VII:1361.

10. A distinction between these two terms has long been maintained by French historians Marcel Dunan and Roger Dufraisse. See Marcel Dunan, "Le système continental," *Revue des études Napoléoniennes* 3 (1913): 115–46; Dunan, "L'Italie et le système continental," *Revue de l'Institut Napoléon* 96 (1965): 176–92; Roger Dufraisse, "Régime douanier, blocus, système continental: essai de mise au point," *Revue d'histoire économique et sociale* 44 (1966): 518–34; Dufraisse, "Napoléon pour ou contre l'Europe," *Revue du souvenir Napoléonien* 402 (1995): 4–25.

11. Napoleon to Eugène de Beauharnais, August 23, 1810, *Correspondance de Napoléon*, XXI:60.

12. In the words of Eli Hecksher, this was "the French continental market design," an assessment echoed by another great scholar, G. Ellis, who described it "a one way common-market." See A. Chabert, *Essai sur les mouvements des revenus et de l'activité économique en France de 1789 à 1820* (Paris: Librairie de Médicis, 1949).

13. For example, in 1810, a new tariff disallowed the Italian kingdom from importing any but French linen, gauze, cotton cloth, and wool cloth. Owen Connelly, *Napoleon's Satellite Kingdoms* (New York: Free Press, 1965), 48.

14. Napoleon to Louis Napoleon, December 15, 1806, in *Lettres inédites de Napoléon 1er* (an VIII–1809), ed. Leon Lecestre (Paris: Librairie Plon, 1897), I:82.

15. See P. K. O'Brien, "Public Finance," in *The Rise of Financial Capitalism: International Capital Markets in the Age of Reason*, ed. Larry Neal (Cambridge: Cambridge University Press, 1990), 201–22; O'Brien, "Public Finance in the Wars with France, 1793–1815," in *Britain and the French Revolution, 1789–1815*, ed. H. T. Dickinson (New York: St. Martin's, 1989), 165–87.

16. Napoleon to Louis Napoleon, April 3, 1808, in *Correspondance de Napoléon*, XVI:473. When Scottish peer Alexander, marquess of Douglas and Clydesdale, offered Jacques Louis David the enormous sum of 1,000 guineas for a portrait

of the emperor, Napoleon gave his consent provided the portrait (the celebrated *Napoleon in His Study*) was paid for in cash. For details, see Philippe Bordes, *Jacques-Louis David: Empire to Exile* (New Haven, CT: Yale University Press, 2005), 113–21.

17. B. R. Mitchell and Phyllis Deane, *Abstract of British Historical Statistics* (Cambridge: Cambridge University Press, 1962), 441–43.

18. See Roger Knight, *Britain Against Napoleon: The Organization of Victory, 1793–1815* (London: Allen Lane, 2013). For a discussion of whether France could have starved out Britain, see William Freeman Galpin, *The Grain Supply of England during the Napoleonic Period* (New York: Macmillan, 1925), 109–22, 168–201.

19. Heckscher, *The Continental System: An Economic Interpretation,* 93.

20. For an in-depth look, see Eugene Tarle, *Kontinental'naya blokada* (Moscow: Zadruga, 1913); Carlo Zaghi, *L'Italia di Napoleon dalla Cisalpina al Regno* (Turin: UTET, 1986). For a more concise discussion, see Alexander Grab, "The Kingdom of Italy and Napoleon's Continental Blockade," in *Revisiting Napoleon's Continental System: Local, Regional and European Experiences,* ed. Katherine Aasletad and Johan Joor (New York: Palgrave Macmillan, 2014), 98–111; Grab, "The Politics of Finance in Napoleonic Italy (1802–1814)," *Journal of Modern Italian Studies* 3, no. 2 (1998): 127–43.

21. Alexandre Chabert, *Essai sur les mouvements des revenus et de l'activité economique en France de 1798 à 1820* (Paris: Librairie de Médicis, 1949), 368–69; François Crouzet, "Wars, Blockade, and Economic Change in Europe, 1792–1815," *Journal of Economic History* 24, no. 4 (1964): 575–77.

22. See Louis Bergeron, *Banquiers, négociants et manufacturiers parisiens du Directoire à l'Empire* (Paris: Éditions de l'EHESS, 2000), chs. 10–11.

23. See Agusti Nieto-Galan, *Colouring Textiles: A History of Natural Dyestuffs in Industrial Europe* (Boston: Kluwer Academic, 2001), ch. 3.

24. Bergeron, *France Under Napoleon,* 159–60, 162–67, 172–84; Heckscher, *The Continental System: An Economic Interpretation,* 286–94; François Crouzet, "Wars, Blockade, and Economic Change in Europe, 1792–1815," *Journal of Economic History* 24, no. 4 (1964): 567–88. Soda ash (sodium carbonate) and potash (potassium carbonate) are vital chemicals in the glass, textile, soap, and paper industries. In 1791 Nicolas Leblanc patented a new process of producing these alkalis from sea salt, but his success was interrupted by the French Revolution, when the revolutionary governments confiscated Leblanc's plant and publicized his methods. Napoleon restored the plant to Leblanc, but Leblanc struggled to compete against rival companies that exploited his invention.

25. House of Lords, Orders of Council, February 15, 1808, in *The Parliamentary Register* (London: John Stockdale, 1808), I:365.

26. B. H. Tolley, "The Liverpool Campaign Against the Order in Council and the War of 1812," in *Liverpool and Merseyside: Essays in the Economic and Social History of the Port and Its Hinterland,* ed. J. R. Harris (New York: Augustus M. Kelley,

1969), 98–145; D. J. Moss, "Birmingham and the Campaign Against the Orders-in-Council and the East India Company Charter, 1812–13," *Canadian Journal of History* 11 (1976): 173–88; Antonette L. McDaniel, "'Thus Has the People Gloriously Triumphed': Petitioning, Political Mobilization and the Orders-in-Council Repeal Campaign, 1808–1812," PhD diss., University of Tennessee, Knoxville, 1992.

27. *The Bank—The Stock Exchange—The Bankers—The Bankers' Clearing House—The Minister and the Public* (London: E. Wilson, 1821), 75. The West End banks sprang up in and around Westminster and the Strand to serve British elite, i.e., the gentry, nobility, and mercantile elite. See Eric Kerridge, *Trade and Banking in Early Modern England* (Manchester: Manchester University Press, 1988), 76–84.

28. Mina Ishizu, "Boom and Crisis in Financing British Transatlantic Trade: A Case Study of the Bankrupcy of John Leigh & Company in 1811," in *The History of Bankruptcy: Economic, Social and Cultural Implications in Early Modern Europe*, ed. Thomas M. Safley (New York: Routledge, 2013), 144–54.

29. B. R. Mitchell, *British Historical Statistics* (Cambridge: Cambridge University Press, 1988), 495. On British efforts in northern Europe, see A. N. Ryan, "The Defence of British Trade in the Baltic, 1808–1813," *English Historical Review* 74, no. 292 (1959): 443–66.

30. For an interesting discussion, see Knight, *Britain Against Napoleon*, 386–416.

31. R. P. Dunn-Pattison, *Napoleon's Marshals* (London: Methuen, 1909), 60–61.

32. Knight, *Britain Against Napoleon*, 403.

33. For an interesting discussion, see essays by Silvia Marzagalli ("The Continental System: A View from the Sea"), Jann M. Witt ("Smuggling and Blockade-Running During the Anglo-Danish War from 1807 to 1814"), and Michael Rowe ("Economic Warfare, Organize Crime and the Collapse of Napoleon's Empire") in *Revisiting Napoleon's Continental System*, ed. Aaslestad and Joor, 90–93, 153–69, 196–99. Also see Gavin Daily, "Napoleon and the 'City of Smugglers,' 1810–1814," *Historical Journal* 50, no. 2 (2007): 333–52; Daily, "English Smugglers, the Channel, and the Napoleonic Wars, 1800–1814," *Journal of British Studies* 46, no. 1 (2007): 30–46.

34. For an interesting discussion of French industrial development during the French Revolution and Empire, see Jeff Horn, *The Path Not Taken: French Industrialization in the Age of Revolution, 1750–1830* (Cambridge, MA: MIT Press, 2006), chs. 5–7. Horn argues (quite provocatively) that the main reason for France's failure to adopt the "liberal" industrial policies of the British was not Napoleon's failure to comprehend them but rather the legacy of the French Revolution, most notably the fear of worker revolt. If British industrialists could count on the British state to keep workers in their place, French industrialists lived in the shadow of the great revolutionary turmoil and could not similarly count on the French state.

35. Cited in Melvin, *Napoleon's Navigation System*, 48.

36. François Crouzet, "Wars, Blockade, and Economic Change in Europe, 1792–1815," *Journal of Economic History* 24, no. 4 (1964): 571.

37. Melvin, *Napoleon's Navigation System*, 114–17, 120, 124, 128–29, 135–37, 173–78, 300–307. For an in-depth study, see Silvia Marzagalli, *Les boulevards de la fraude: La négoce maritime et le Blocus continental 1806–1813, Bordeaux, Hambourg, Livourne* (Villeneuve-d'Ascq: Presses universitaires du Septentrion, 1999); Marzagalli, *Bordeaux et les États-Unis, 1776–1815: politique et stratégies négociantes dans la genèse d'un réseau commercial* (Geneva: Droz, 2014); Daeley, "The Continental System in France as Illustrated by American Trade."

38. Heckscher, *The Continental System: An Economic Interpretation*, 258, 272–77.

39. F. Evrard, "Le commerce des laines d'Espagne sous le Premier Empire," *Revue d'histoire moderne et contemporaine* 4 (1937): 212–18.

40. Jean Labasse, *Le Commerce des soies à Lyon sous Napoléon et la crise de 1811* (Paris: Presses universitaires de France, 1957), 70–83.

41. See Richard J. Barker, "The Conseil General des Manufactures Under Napoleon (1810–1814)," *French Historical Studies* 6, no. 2 (1969): 198–213.

42. For insights, see François Crouzet, "Les consequences économiques de la Révolution: à propos d'un inédit de Sir Francis d'Ivernois," *Annales historiques de la Révolution francaise* XXXIV (1962): 182–217.

43. David Landes points out that "the 1850s and 1860s were the years when western Europe caught up with Britain. Not in a quantitative sense; that was to come later, and then only in certain areas. Nor even qualitatively, whether in scale and efficiency of production of given industries, or in degree of industrialization of the economy as a whole." David S. Landes, *The Unbound Prometheus: Technological Change and Industrial Development in Western Europe from 1750 to the Present* (Cambridge: Cambridge University Press, 2003), 41–230 (quoted from 228–29). Also see François Crouzet, "Wars, Blockade, and Economic Change in Europe, 1792–1815," *Journal of Economic History* 24, no. 4 (1964): 578, 585.

44. August Wilhelm von Schlegel, *The Continental System, and Its Relations with Sweden* (London: J. J. Stockdale, 1813), 86–87.

Chapter 12

1. H. V. Livermore, *A New History of Portugal* (Cambridge: Cambridge University Press, 1966), 213–38; António Henrique R. de Oliveira Marques, *History of Portugal* (New York: Columbia University Press, 1972), I:407–17, 421–25.

2. Stanley J. Stein and Barbara H. Stein, *The Colonial Heritage of Latin America: Essays on Economic Dependence in Perspective* (New York: Oxford University Press, 1970), 113.

3. Kenneth R. Maxwell, "The Generation of the 1790s and the Idea of the Luso-Brazilian Empire," in *Colonial Roots of Modern Brazil*, ed. D. Alden (Berkeley: University of California Press, 1973), 118–21.

4. For an excellent overview, see Kenneth R. Maxwell, *Conflicts and Conspiracies: Brazil and Portugal, 1750–1808* (Cambridge: Cambridge University Press, 1973).

5. Though Spain and Portugal fought several conflicts—in 1735–1737, 1761–1763, and 1776–1777—in the eighteenth century they involved colonial holdings in South America.

6. For details on the historical relationship between Britan and Portugal, see Davis Francis, *Portugal, 1715–1808: Joanine, Pombaline and Rococo Portugal as Seen by British Diplomats and Traders* (London: Tamesis Books, 1985), 197–202, 237–43; A. B. Wallis Chapman, "The Commercial Relations of England and Portugal, 1487–1807," *Transactions of the Royal Historical Society* 1 (1907): 174–79; Harold Edward Stephen Fisher, *The Portugal Trade: A Study of Anglo-Portuguese Commerce, 1700–1770* (London: Methuen, 1971). On Portuguese neutrality and the declaration of Lisbon as a free port, see George Friedrich Martens, *Recueil des Principaux Traités...conclus par les Puissances de l'Europe* (Gottingen: Jean Chrétien Dieterich, 1800), VI:606–8; VII:140. Some Portuguese ministers, most notably Antonio d'Araujo e Azevedo, sought closer ties with France and even concluded a secret treaty (1797) with France pledging to close the ports of Portugal to British vessels. But London demanded Lisbon disavow it and the treaty was not ratified. See Martens, *Recueil*, VII:201; *Dropmore Papers*, III:282, 355, 359, 373.

7. Valentim Alexandre, *Os sentidos do Império: questão nacional e questão colonial na crise do Antigo Regime português* (Porto: Edições Afrontamento, 1993), 100–104.

8. Napoleon, *Correspondance générale*, ed. Thierry Lentz (Paris: Fayard, 2004), III:438.

9. Margaret Scott Chrisawn, *The Emperor's Friend: Marshal Jean Lannes* (Westport, CT: Greenwood Press, 2001), 87.

10. Chrisawn, *The Emperor's Friend*, 93.

11. Ángelo Pereira, *D. João VI principe e rei* (Lisbon: Empresa Nacional de Publicidade, 1953), I:106–7; Alexandre, *Os sentidos do Império*, 129–35.

12. Charles de Mouy, "L'ambassade du général Junot à Lisbonne d'après des documents inédits," in *Revue des deux mondes* CXXI (1894): 144–45; Charles Hugh Mackay, "The Tempest: The Life and Career of Jean-Andoche Junot, 1771–1813," Ph.D. diss., Florida State University, 1995, 89–100.

13. Napoleon to King Charles IV, Sep'tember 7, 1807, *Correspondance générale*, VII:1106.

14. Kenneth G. Johnson, "Napoleon's War at Sea," in *Napoleon and the Operational Art of War*, ed. Michael V. Leggiere (Leiden: Brill, 2016), 440. For examples of Napoleon's demands, see his letters to Junot in *CN*, XVI:128–30, 147–48, 156. The recently published volume VIII (1808) of *Correspondance générale* shows how much time Napoleon devoted to the rebuilding of the French navy. Out of 3,021 letters included in the volume, well over 200 were sent to Decrès, Napoleon's naval minister, containing technical details and plans for a naval buildup and various maritime expeditions.

15. Napoleon to Talleyrand, July 19, 1807, *CN*, XV:433. Also see Alphonse Louis Grasset, *La Guerre d'Espagne, 1807–1813* (Paris: Berger-Levrault, 1914), I:94–121.

16. For further details, see Hauterive to Rayneval, July 30, 1807; Rayneval to Talleyrand, August 12, 1807, AE "Portugal," 126.

17. See Araujo to Rayneval, August 21, 1807, AE "Portugal," 126.

18. Rayneval to Champagny, October 2, 1807, AE "Portugal," 126.

19. Alan K. Manchester, *British Preeminence in Brazil, Its Rise and Decline: A Study in European Expansion* (Chapel Hill: University of North Carolina Press, 1933), 54. Also see Livermore, *A New History of Portugal*, 248.

20. Oliveira Marques, *History of Portugal*, I:425. To one British historian, Dom João was "alternately swayed by fear and indolence, a miserable example of helpless folly." William Napier, *History of the War in the Peninsula and in the South of France* (London: John Murray, 1828), I:143.

21. Manchester, *British Preeminence in Brazil*, 58–63. Gordon Teffeteller, "England and Brazil: Strangford and Joao VI," *Proceedings of the Consortiium on Revolutionary Europe*, 1990, 203–5.

22. André Fugier, *Napoléon et l'Espagne, 1799–1808* (Paris: F. Alcan, 1930), II:347–48.

23. Extract from "Official Declaration of the Blockade of the Mouth of the Tagus," cited in Donald D. Howard, "Portugal and the Anglo-Russian Naval Crisis (1808)," *Naval War College Review* 34 (1981): 49–50.

24. Convention secrète et Convention relative à l'occupation du Portugal, October 27, 1807, in *CN*, XVI:118–21. The treaty called for a French army of 25,000 infantry and 3,000 cavalry to march across Spain to Lisbon. A Spanish force of 8,000 infantry and 3,000 cavalry, under French control, would join the French in Lisbon. Another 10,000 Spanish troops would seize Oporto, while some 6,000 men would occupy Portuguese Algarve. In case of a British attack, France had the right to send 40,000 more troops to Portugal.

25. Etruria was formally ruled by Charles Louis but, due to his age (he was just four years old when he inherited the crown in 1803), his mother, Maria Luisa of Spain, served as the regent. In August 1807 French troops invaded the kingdom on the grounds that it had become a center of smuggling and espionage.

26. Mackay, *The Tempest*, 122–27.

27. After the French troops passed Salamanca, there were instances of pillage committed by the French soldiers, some of whom were murdered by Spanish peasants. Adolphe Thiers, *Histoire du Consulat et de l'Empire* (Paris: Paulin, 1849), VIII:329–30. For challenges the French troops faced, see Mackay, *The Tempest*, 138–46. Also see David Buttery, *Wellington Against Junot: The First Invasion of Portugal, 1807–1808* (Barnsley: Pen & Sword Military, 2011), chs. 3–4. For a Spanish perspective on the French march, see Pedro Agustín Girón, *Recuerdos (1778–1837)*, ed. Ana María Berazaluce (Pamplona: Ed. Univ. de Navarra, 1978).

28. On November 12 Napoleon sent Junot a set of instructions for the occupation of Portugal. Junot was ordered to seize the Portuguese fleet, disarm the

Portuguese army, and send some 6,000 of its soldiers to France; the prince regent was to be convinced to go "willingly" to France, while the French troops were to confiscate British goods and detain British subjects. The French general was told to "set an example of absolute incorruptibility." *CN*, XVI:156–57.

29. Manuel de Oliveira Lima, *Dom João VI no Brazil: 1808–1821* (Rio de Janeiro: Journal do Commercio, 1908) I:45–55. Also see Sir Sidney Smith's letters and other documents in John Barrow, *The Life and Correspondence of Admiral Sir William Sidney Smith* (London: Richard Bentley, 1848), II:261–69; Charles Oman, *A History of the Peninsular War* (Oxford: Clarendon Press, 1902), I:30.

30. Manchester, *British Preeminence in Brazil*, 65–68. For details on the embarkation, see Thomas O'Neill, *A Concise and Accurate Account of the Proceedings of the Squadron Under the Command of Rear Admiral Sir Will. Sidney Smith, K.G., in Effecting the Escape and Escorting the Royal Family of Portugal to the Brazils on the 29th of November 1807* (London: R. Edwards, 1809).

31. Oman, *A History of the Peninsular War*, I:30–31. This was just a ragged vanguard of some 1,500 men (out of 25,000) who had undertaken a forced march to get to Lisbon in time. In the rugged terrain of the border districts near Almeida, the French suffered terribly from the lack of supplies and torrential rains. As one French participant recalled, "The state we were in when we entered Lisbon is hardly credible. Our clothing had lost all shape and colour…[soldiers were] fagged out, unwashed, ghastly objects…no longer [with] strength to march even to the sound of the drum." Paul Charles Thiebault, *The Memoirs of Baron Thiebault* (London: Smith, Elder & Co., 1896), II:199.

32. Oman, *A History of the Peninsular War*, I:31.

33. Napoleon to Junot, October 17–31, 1807, in *CN*, XVI:98–99, 130; Napoleon to Clarke, October 28, 1807, in *New Letters of Napoleon I Omitted from the Edition Published Under the Auspices of Napoleon III*, ed. Mary Loyd (New York: D. Appleton, 1897), 53.

34. Lord Russel of Liverpool, *Knight of the Sword: The Life and Letters of Admiral Sir William Sidney Smith* (London: Victor Gollancz, 1964), 168–69; Paul C Krajeski, *In the Shadow of Nelson: The Naval Leadership of Admiral Sir Charles Cotton, 1753–1812* (Westport, CT: Greenwood Press, 2000), 56–58.

35. Fugier, *Napoléon et l'Espagne*, II:352–54.

36. Napoleon to Junot, December 23, 1807, in *CN*, XVI:214–16.

37. Georges Lefebvre, *Napoleon* (London: Routledge & Kegan Paul, 1969), II:15.

38. Oliveira Marques, *History of Portugal*, I:429.

39. Allan J. Kuethe and Kenneth J. Adrien, *The Spanish Atlantic World in the Eighteenth Century: War and the Bourbon Reforms, 1713–1796* (Cambridge: Cambridge University Press, 2014), 133–66, 231–33, 271–73, 280–84, 350–53.

40. John R. Fisher, *Commercial Relations Between Spain and Spanish America in the Era off Free Trade, 1778–1796* (Liverpool: Centre for Latin American Studies, University of Liverpool, 1985), 9–19.

41. John R. Fisher, *The Economic Aspects of Spanish Imperialism in America, 1492–1810* (Liverpool: Liverpool University Press, 1997), 197–216; Adrian J. Pearce, *British Trade with Spanish America, 1763 to 2008* (Liverpool: Liverpool University Press, 2007), 161–229. In 1799 Charles IV revoked the decree on free trade, but colonial officials continued to trade with "neutrals," arguing that this was essential to raising sufficient revenues to defend the colonies, as well as to ensure the loyalty of the colonists, who benefited from the relaxation of trade restrictions.

42. Gabriel H. Lovett, *Napoleon and the Birth of Modern Spain* (New York: New York University Press, 1965), I:1–46. Also see Scott Eastman, *Preaching Spanish Nationalism Across the Hispanic Atlantic, 1759–1823* (Baton Rouge: Louisiana State University, 2012), 1–44.

43. Vicente Pérez Moreda, "Spain's Demographic Modernization, 1800–1930," in *The Economic Modernization of Spain, 1830–1930,* ed. Nicolás Sánchez-Albornoz (New York: New York University Press, 1987), 34.

44. Elizabeth Vassall Fox Holland, *The Spanish Journal of Elizabeth, Lady Holland,* ed. Giles Stephen Holland Fox-Strangways (London: Longmans, 1910), II:85–86, 123–24.

45. Proclamation of Godoy, October 5, 1806, in Oman, *A History of the Peninsular War,* I:603.

46. Napoleon's disdain for Godoy was quite well known. When in 1801 Godoy asked Lucien Bonaparte to send him a portrait of the First Consul, Napoleon forbade it. "I shall never send my portrait to a man who keeps his predecessor in a dungeon [the Count of Aranda, Godoy's predecessor, was imprisoned] and who adopts the customs of the Inquisition. I may make use of him, but I owe him nothing but contempt." Napoleon, *A Selection from the Letters and Despatches of the First Napoleon,* edited by D. Bingham (London: Chapman and Hall, 1884), I:349. And as early as 1805, Napoleon had told a confidant that "a Bourbon on the throne of Spain makes for a dangerous neighbor." Jean-Baptiste Jourdan, *Mémoires militaires du Maréchal Jourdan (guerre d'Espagne)* (Paris: Flammarion, 1899), 9. Also see Robert B. Mowat, *The Diplomacy of Napoleon* (New York: Longmans, Green, 1924), 208–9.

47. This discussion is mainly based on Fugier, *Napoléon et L'Espagne,* I:22–395; II:85–211; Geoffroy de Grandmaison, *L'Espagne et Napoléon* (Paris: Plon-Nourrit, 1908), I:72–169.

48. Copia de un real decreto por el que se comunica haber evitado una conjura para destronar a Carlos IV, October 31, 1807; Copia de una circular expedida para que todos los pueblos solemnicen acción de gracias por haber evitado una conjura para destronar a Carlos IV, November 3, 1807, Archivo de la Real Chancillería de Valladolid, Cédulas y Pragmáticas, Caja 30.41, 30.42.

49. Grandmaison, *L'Espagne et Napoléon,* I:99–114. For a more detailed discussion see Fugier, *Napoléon et L'Espagne,* II:216–345.

50. Pieter Geyl, *Napoleon: For and Against* (New York: Penguin Books, 1982), 92. For a French diplomatic report on the situation in Spain, including characteristics

of the Bourbon royalty and Godoy, see Tournon to Napoleon, December 20, 1807, AN, AF IV 1680.

51. Conde de Toreno, *Historia del Levantamiento, Guerra y Revolución de España*, ed. Joaquín Varela Suanzes-Carpegna (Madrid: Centro de Estudios Políticos y Constitucionales, 2008), 4.

52. Michel Morineau, *Incroyables gazettes et fabuleux métaux: les retours des trésors américains d'après les gazettes hollandaises (XVIe–XVIIIe siècles)* (Cambridge: Cambridge University Press, 1985), 454. Also see Carlos Marichal, *La bancarrota del virreinato, Nueva España y las finanzas del imperio español, 1780–1810* (México: El Colegio de México, Fideicomiso Historia de las Américas, Fondo de Cultura Económica, 1999), 173; Javier Cuenca, "Statistics of Spain's Colonial Trade, 1792–1820: Consular Duties, Cargo Inventories and Balance of Trade," *Hispanic American Historical Review* 61, no. 3 (1981): 381–428. Also see Barbara H. Stein and Stanley J. Stein, *Edge of Crisis: War and Trade in the Spanish Atlantic, 1789–1808* (Baltimore: John Hopkins University Press, 2009).

53. Richard Herr, *Rural Change and Royal Finances in Spain at the End of the Old Regime* (Berkeley: University of California Press, 1989), 137–38.

54. Francis Baring, head of the highly influential Barings Company, secured the support of the British government to ship the Mexican silver. For a detailed discussion, see Adrian J. Pearce, "The Hope-Barings Contract: Finance and Trade Between Europe and the Americas, 1805–1808," *English Historical Review* 124, no. 511 (2009): 1324–52; John A Jackson, "The Mexican Silver Scheme: Finance and Profiteering in the Napoleonic Era, 1796–1811," Ph.D. diss., University of North Carolina, 1978; Carlos Marichal, *Bankruptcy of Empire: Mexican Silver and the Wars Between Spain, Britain and France, 1760–1810* (Cambridge: Cambridge University Press, 2007), ch. 5.

55. *A Selection from the Letters and Despatches of the First Napoleon*, II:352.

56. Paul Schroeder is correct in noting that Napoleon undertook "the Spanish venture, like many others, for varied reasons—anti-British, familial and dynastic, economic, military, and personal. It is useless to debate which was decisive and wrong to suppose that a venture which had such profound effect must have had equally profound causes." Paul W. Schroeder, *The Transformation of European Politics, 1763–1848* (New York: Oxford University Press, 1994), 341.

57. Napoleon to Junot, October 17, 1807, in *Correspondance générale*, VII:1204.

58. Oman, *A History of the Peninsular War*, I:36–37.

59. Nick Lipscombe, *The Peninsular War Atlas* (Oxford: Osprey, 2014), 30–32.

60. Napoleon to Champagny, March 9, 1808, in *Correspondance générale*, VIII:237.

61. See Napoleon's instructions in *CN*, XVI, nos. 13626, 13632, 13652, 13656, 13675, 13682. For an interesting study on Murat in Spain in 1808, see Joachim Murat, *Murat, lieutenant de l'empereur en Espagne 1808: d'après sa correspondance inédite et des documents originaux* (Paris: E. Plon, 1897).

62. Royal Decrees of March 16–21, 1808, in Biblioteca Histórica Municipal (Madrid), C 34363. On April 8, 1808, another royal decree declared the Spanish king's avid desire to "consolidate the bonds of friendship and the intimate alliance" between France and Spain.

63. Simon Barton, *A History of Spain* (New York: Palgrave Macmillan, 2009), 165–66; José Joaquín de Mora, *Mémoires historiques sur Ferdinand VII, roi des Espagnes* (Paris: Librairie Universelle, 1824), 35–45, 334–37; Manuel Godoy, *Memorias* (Gerona: Libreria de Vicente Oliva, 1841), VI:1–62.

64. See Royal Proclamation of March 19, 1808, in "Expediente sobre la abdicación de Carlos IV a favor de su hijo Fernando VII, la confirmación en sus puestos de todos los ministros de los tribunales, y sobre la llegada del nuevo monarca a Madrid," Archivo Histórico Nacional (Madrid), Consejos, 5511, Exp.2. Also see Royal Decree of March 18–19, 1808, on the events at Aranjuez and the arrest of Godoy, in Biblioteca Histórica Municipal, C 34363.

65. Grandmaison, *L'Espagne et Napoléon,* I:99–114; Fugier, *Napoléon et L'Espagne,* II:383–93; Richard Herr, "The Constitution of 1812 and the Spanish Road to Parliamentary Monarchy," in *Revolution and the Meanings of Freedom in the Nineteenth Century,* ed. Isser Woloch (Stanford, CA: Stanford University Press, 1996), 70–71.

66. Napoleon's recently published correspondence for the year 1808 contains numerous letters announcing his intention to oversee Spanish matters in person, yet he did not leave Paris, ultimately informing Murat that "circumstances have forced me to delay my departure." He blamed this delay on Russia's declaration of war on Sweden, but in reality he was already preoccupied with a secret dynastic project that would have overthrown the Bourbons and replaced Charles IV with Louis Bonaparte. The project failed when Louis refused the crown. See Napoleon's letters of March 23–27, 1808, *Correspondance générale,* VIII, nos. 17,462, 17,510.

67. Godoy was rescued from captivity and transported to France, where he spent the next few years living in exile, first at Fontainebleau, then at Compiègne, and finally Aix-en-Provence. After the fall of Napoleon, Godoy was denied return to Spain and lived for many years in Italy. He was allowed to return to Spain only in 1844 but remained in France, where he died in Paris in 1851.

68. Schroeder, *The Transformation of European Politics,* 343.

69. José Canga Argüelles, *Observaciones sobre la historia de la guerra de España* (London: D. M. Calero, 1829), I:37–39.

70. Tournon to Napoleon, March 13, 1808, cited in Francisco Martí Gilabert, *El motín de Aranjuez* (Pamplona: Universidad de Navarra, 1972), 106.

71. Anne Jean Marie René Savary, *Mémoires du duc de Rovigo: pour servir à l'histoire de l'empereur Napoléon* (Paris: A. Bossange, 1828), III:358.

72. Juan Pérez de Guzmán, *El dos de mayo de 1808 en Madrid* (Madrid: Establecimiento tipográfico sucesores de Rivadeneyra, 1908), 361–417; on the

impact of the Madrid revolt, see 465–540. For the French side, see *Murat, lieutenant de l'empereur en Espagne 1808,* 314–45.

73. Louis Bonaparte declined the Spanish crown, and Jérôme was equally unenthusiastic about it.

74. For details, see Jean-Paul Coujou, "Political Thought and Legal Theory in Suárez," in *A Companion to Francisco Suárez,* ed. Victor M. Salas and Robert L. Fastiggi (Leiden: Brill, 2014), 29–71; Brian Hamnett, "The Meieva Roots of Spanish Constitutionalism," in *The Rise of Constitutional Government in the Iberian Atlantic World: The Impact of the Cádiz Constitution of 1812,* ed. Natalia Sobrevilla Perea and Scott Eastman (Tuscaloosa: University of Alabama Press, 2015), 19–41; Richard Hocquellet, *Résistance et revolution durant l'occupation napoléonienne en Espagne, 1808–1812* (Paris: La boutique de l'histoire, 2001), 140–54.

75. In some juntas, revolutionaries took the lead and constituted the majority, while in other cases people of prominence before the upheavals retained their positions. Charles J. Esdaile, *Spain in the Liberal Age: From Constitution to Civil War, 1808–1939* (Oxford: Blackwell, 2000), 17.

76. Manuel Ardit Lucas, *Revolucion liberal y revuelta campesina: un ensayo sobre la desintegracion del regimen feudal en el Pais Valenciano (1793/1840)* (Barcelona: Editorial Ariel, 1977), 139–40; Lovett, *Napoleon and the Birth of Modern Spain,* I:166.

77. See Joaquín Varela Suanzes-Carpegna, *La teoría del Estado en las Cortes de Cádiz: orígenes del constitucionalismo hispánico* (Madrid: Centro de Estudios Políticos y Constitucionales, 2011). On the emerging notions of Spanish nationalism, see Scott Eastman, *Preaching Spanish Nationalism Across the Hispanic Atlantic, 1759–1823* (Baton Rouge: Louisiana State University Press, 2012).

78. Despite Napoleon's efforts, most of the leading Spanish notables refused to participate in the assembly, which ultimately comprised fewer than a hundred members, mostly from the nobility and the Bourbon bureaucracy; it was far from being regarded as a genuine national institution. The assembly was convened on May 24, began its sessions on June 15, and finished its work on July 7, 1808.

79. The text of the statute is available at https://es.wikisource.org/wiki/Constituci% C3%B3n_de_Bayona_de_1808.

80. Louis François Joseph Bausset-Roquefort, *Private Memoirs of the Court of Napoleon and of Some Public Events of the Imperial Reign, from 1805 to the First of May 1814, to Serve as a Contribution to the History of Napoleon* (Philadelphia: Carey, Lea & Carey, 1828), 188–89.

81. Lipscombe, *The Peninsular War Atlas,* 44–46.

82. Owen Connelly, *The Gentle Bonaparte: A Biography of Joseph, Napoleon's Elder Brother* (New York: Macmillan, 1968), 99–116.

83. See Eugène Titeux, *Le Général Dupont: une erreur historique* (Puteaux-sur-Seine: Prieur et Dubois et Cie, 1903), vol. 3; Francisco Vela, *La batalla de Bailén,*

1808: el águila derrotada (Madrid: Almena Ediciones, 2007); Dominique Vedel, *Relations de la campagne d'Andalousie, 1808* (Paris: La Vouivre, 1999); Charles Clerc, *Guerre d'Espagne: Capitulation de Baylen* (Paris: Ancienne Libraire Thorin et Fils Albert Fontemoing, 1903).

84. Upon his return to France, Dupont was court-martialed, cashiered, and imprisoned at Fort de Joux; other commanding officers also bore the brunt of imperial anger. Meanwhile, the French rank and file spent six long years in captivity. The prisoners were placed aboard prison hulks in Cadiz, where they suffered from abuse, malnutrition, overcrowding and bad weather. In later years, they were transferred to the island of Cabrera, where, largely abandoned by the Spanish authorities, they endured indescribable hardship. Fewer than half survived in captivity. For documents relating to the enquiry that Napoleon organized in 1812 to investigate circumstances of the French surrender, see Susan Howard, "The Bailen Enquiry," *The Napoleon Series*, http://www.napoleon-series.org/military/battles/1808/Peninsula/Bailen/BailenEnquiry/c_bailen Enquiry.html. See Théophile Geisendorf-Des Gouttes, *Les prisonniers de guerre au temps du Ier empire. La déportation aux Baléares et aux Canaries (les archipels enchanteurs et farouches) des soldats de Baylen et des marins de Trafalgar (1809–1814)* (Geneva: Éditions Labor, 1936); Pierre Pellissier and Jérôme Phelipeau, *Les grognards de Cabrera: 1809–1814* (Paris: Hachette littérature, 1979); Denis Smith, *The Prisoners of Cabrera: Napoleon's Forgotten Soldiers, 1809–1814* (New York: Four Walls Eight Windows, 2001).

85. Connelly, *The Gentle Bonaparte*, 117–18.

86. Formed in September 1808 at Aranjuez, the Supreme Central Governing Junta, led by the aged conde de Floridablanca, Spain's former secretary of state (1776–1792), consisted of members of each of the provincial juntas. Ultimately driven to the southern port city of Cadiz, it presided over the governance and prosecution of the war for the next two years. Esdaile, *Spain in the Liberal Age*, 22.

87. Mildred Fryman, "Charles Stuart and the Common Cause: Anglo-Portuguese Diplomatic Relations, 1810–1814," *Proceedings of the Consortium on Revolutionary Europe*, 1977, 105–15.

88. Oman, *Peninsular War*, I:210–12; Jac Weller, *Wellington in the Peninsula, 1808–1814* (London: Nicolas Vane, 1962), 30–31; Lipscombe, *The Peninsular War Atlas*, 60–65.

89. For an example of public response, see Lord Byron's satirical poem in *The Gentleman's Magazine* (January 1809), 62: "And ever since that martial synod met, Britannia sickens, / Cintra! at thy name." *The Complete Works of Lord Byron*, ed. Henry Lytton Bulwer (London: A. and W. Galignani, 1841), 74. For a full account of the British public reaction to the convention, see Michael Glover, *Britannia Sickens: Sir Arthur Wellesley and the Convention of Cintra* (London, Leo Cooper, 1970).

90. John Joseph Stockdale, *The Proceedings on the Enquiry into the Armistice and Convention of Cintra, and into the Conduct of the Officers Concerned* (London: Stockdale,

1809). For Wellesley's involvement in the convention, see Rory Muir, *Wellington: The Path to Victory, 1769–1814* (New Haven, CT: Yale University Press, 2013), 264–82.

91. See Stephen Summerfield and Susan Law, *Sir John Moore and the Universal Soldier*, vol. 1, *The Man, the Commander and the Shorncliffe System of Training* (London: Ken Trotman, 2015).

92. Oman, *A History of Peninsular War*, I:368–75.

93. D. W. Davies, *Sir John Moore's Peninsular Campaign 1808–1809* (The Hague: Martinus Nijhoff, 1974), 63–65; Christopher Summerville, *March of Death: Sir John Moore's Retreat to Corunna, 1808–1809* (London: Greenhill Books, 2003), 23.

94. Treaty of Tilsit, July 7, 1807, Fondation Napoléon, https://www.napoleon.org/histoire-des-2-empires/articles/traite-de-tilsit-avec-la-russie-7-juillet-1807.

95. Albert Vandal, *Napoléon et Alexandre 1er: l'alliance russe sous le 1er Empire* (Paris, 1894–97), I:165–77, 182–87, 190–203; Vernon J. Puryear, *Napoleon and the Dardanelles* (Berkeley: University of California Press, 1951), 234–35, 248–49. See also *SIRIO* LXXXIII (1892) and LXXXIX (1893) for documents related to General Anne Jean Marie Rene Savary's mission to St. Petersburg in late 1807 and General Tolstoy's embassy to Paris.

96. For examples of Russian disillusionment see *SIRIO* LXXXIX (1893):194–95, 366–68, 407–11, 476–79. Also see E. Driault, *Napoléon et l'Europe: Tilsit. France et Russie sous le premier empire. La Question de Pologne (1806–1809)* (Paris: F. Alcan, 1917), 272–91.

97. Pierre Lanfrey, *The History of Napoleon the First* (New York: Macmillan, 1894), III:487.

98. Johann Wilhelm von Goethe, *Mélanges par Goethe*, ed. Jacques Porchat (Paris: Hachette, 1863), 307–9. King Maximilian Joseph of Bavaria was not initially invited, reflecting certain tensions that emerged between Napoleon and this Bavarian ruler. In the end, the latter still came to Erfurt. For an interesting discussion, see Matthias Stickler, "Erfurt als Wende—Bayern und Württemberg und das Scheitern der Pläne Napoleons I. für einen Ausbau der Rheinbundverfassung," in *Der Erfurter Fürstenkongreß 1808: Hintergründe, Ablauf, Wirkung*, ed. Rudolf Benl (Erfurt: Stadtarchiv, 2008), 266–300.

99. Charles-Maurice de Talleyrand, *Mémoires (1754–1815)* (Paris: Plon, 1982), 439. Also see *Mémoires, documents et écrits divers laissés par le prince de Metternich* (Paris: Plon, 1881), II:227.

100. See Gustav Brünnert, *Napoleons Aufenthalt in Erfurt im Jahre 1808* (Erfurt: Druck von Fr. Bartholomäus, 1899).

101. For insights, see *Mémoires d'Aimée de Coigny*, ed. Etienne Lamy (Paris: Calmann-Lévy, 1902), 193, 209–12, 239.

102. For discussion of Talleyrand's intentions, see Emile Dard, *Napoléon et Talleyrand* (Paris: Plon, 1935), 203–17; Georges Lacour-Gayet, *Talleyrand, 1754–1838* (Paris: Payot, 1930), II:238–54; Georges Bordonove, *Talleyrand* (Paris: Pygmalion,

2007); Emmanuel Waresquiel, *Talleyrand: Le prince immobile* (Paris: Fayard, 2006). There is sufficient evidence to suggest that Talleyrand was in the pay of Austria from 1809. See E. Dard, "La Vengeance de Talleyrand," *Revue des deux mondes* XX (1934): 215–29.

103. The quote is as reported by Metternich after the conversation with Talleyrand. *Mémoires de Metternich*, II:248.

104. Armand-Augustin-Louis de Caulaincourt, *Memoirs* (London: Cassell, 1935), I:540.

105. Eugene Tarle, *Talleyrand* (Moscow: Urait, 2017), 96. Also see Émile Dard, "La vengeance de Talleyrand (1809)," *Revue des Deux Mondes* 20, no. 1 (1934): 215–29. After Erfurt, the Russian government dispatched the young Count Karl von Nesselrode, officially as an advisor to the Russian ambassador, to serve as a personal liaison between Emperor Alexander and Talleyrand.

106. "Posolstvo grafa P.A. Tolstogo v Parizhe v 1807 i 1808 gg," *SIRIO* LXXXIX (1893): esp. 689–94.

107. See Articles 8 through 11, Convention of Erfurt, October 12, 1808, www.napoleon-series.org/research/government/diplomatic/c_erfurt.html. In Article 11, France and Russia pledged to "maintain the integrity of the other possessions of the Ottoman Empire, not wishing to undertake themselves or suffer that there should be undertaken any enterprise against any part of that Empire, unless they should be previously informed of it."

108. Equally decisive were French operations in Catalonia, where they routed Spaniards at Cardedeu (December 16) and Molins de Rei (December 21). Lipscombe, *The Peninsular War Atlas,* 70–87.

109. Neil Campbell, *Napoleon on Elba: Diary of an Eyewitness to Exile*, ed. Jonathan North (Welwyn, UK: Ravenhall, 2004), 50.

110. Napoleon, *Correspondance générale*, VIII:489.

111. Proclamation of December 7, 1808, in Grandmaison, *L'Espagne et Napoléon*, I:402.

112. John H. Gill, *1809: Thunder on the Danube: Napoleon's Defeat of the Habsburgs* (Barnsley, UK: Frontline Books, 2008), I:14–15.

113. Napier, *History of the War in the Peninsula*, I:425–49; Davies, *Sir John Moore's Peninsular Campaign,* 114–53; Lipscombe, *The Peninsular War Atlas,* 80, 88.

114. Bausset, *Private Memoirs*, 238.

115. Aymar-Olivier Le Harivel de Gonneville, *Recollections of Colonel de Gonneville* (London: Hurst and Blackett, 1875), I:189–90; Bausset, *Private Memoirs*, 239.

116. Davies, *Sir John Moore's Peninsular Campaign,* 178–238; Napier, *History of the War in the Peninsula*, I:473–97; Summerville, *March of Death,* 131–78, 180. For a more concise treatment, see Philip Haythornthwaite, *Corunna 1809: Sir John Moore's Fighting Retreat* (Oxford: Osprey, 2001).

117. Lipscombe, *The Peninsular War Atlas,* 89–96.

118. Cited in Christopher Hibbert, *Corunna* (London: Batsford, 1961), 188.

119. Charles Esdaile, *The Peninsular War: A New History* (New York: Palgrave Macmillan, 2003), 151–56.

120. After a six-day dash across northern Spain and most of France, Napoleon reached Paris in the morning of January 23. Five days later, the imperial fury rained down on Talleyrand, who was sacked from the Office of the Grand Chamberlain. Fouché was spared, but was instructed in no uncertain terms to concern himself only with affairs relating to his ministry.

121. Oman, *A History of the Peninsular War*, II:90–143; Jacques Belmas, *Journaux des sièges faits ou soutenus par les Français dans la Péninsule de 1807 à 1814* (Paris: Firmin Didot Frères, 1836), vol. II; Raymond Rudorff, *War to the Death: The Sieges of Saragossa, 1808–1809* (New York: Macmillan, 1974).

122. André François Miot de Melito, *Memoirs of Count Miot de Melito, Minister, Ambassador, Councillor of State and Member of the Institute of France, Between the Years 1788 and 1815*, ed. Wilhelm August Fleischmann (New York: Scribner, 1881), 557.

123. Schroeder, *The Transformation of European Politics*, 343.

124. For a good example of the sheer effort required for convoying, see Rafael Farias, ed., *Memorias de la Guerra de la Independencia: escritas por soldados franceses* (Madrid: Hispano-Africana, 1919), 269–87.

125. Fernando Diaz Plaja, *La historia de España en sus documentos. El siglo XIX* (Madrid: Instituto de Estudios Políticos, 1954), 74–76.

126. "Instrucción que su Majestad se ha dignado aprobar para el corso terrestre contra los ejércitos franceses," April 17, 1809, Archivo Histórico Nacional (Madrid), Estado, 11, A, http://pares.mcu.es/GuerraIndependencia/catalog/show/2728028.

127. See Charles J. Esdaile, *Fighting Napoleon: Guerrillas, Bandits and Adventurers in Spain, 1808–1814* (New Haven, CT: Yale University Press, 2004); Esdaile, *The Peninsular War: A New History* (New York: Palgrave Macmillan, 2003). For a more traditional interpretation of *la guerrilla*, see Ronald Fraser, *Napoleon's Cursed War: Popular Resistance in the Spanish Peninsular War* (London: Verso, 2008); John Tone, *The Fatal Knot: The Guerrilla War in Navarre and the Defeat of Napoleon in Spain* (Chapel Hill: University of North Carolina Press, 1994).

128. For a concise discussion, see Don Alexander, "The Impact of Guerrilla Warfare in Spain on French Combat Strength," *Proceedings of the Consortium on Revolutionary Europe*, 1975, 91–103.

129. Antoine René Charles Mathurin de La Forest, *Correspondance du comte de la Forest, ambassadeur de France en Espagne 1808–1813* (Paris: A. Picard et Fils, 1905), IV:31; also see IV:49, 98, 204; V:209, 304. Napoleon did establish a special corps of French gendarmerie to provide protection against the guerrillas. See Oman, *A History of the Peninsular War*, III:203–204; Grandmaison, *L'Espagne et Napoléon: 1804–1809*, III, 251–52.

130. Denis Charles Parquin, *Souvenirs et campagnes d'un vieux soldat de l'empire (1803–1814)* (Paris: Berger-Levrault, 1903), 254.

131. Muir, *Wellington: The Path to Victory*, 283–98.

132. Among the many biographies of Wellington of particular importance are Rory Muir's two-volume magnum opus *Wellington: The Path to Victory, 1769–1814* (New Haven, CT: Yale University Press, 2013) and *Wellington: Waterloo and the Fortunes of Peace* (New Haven, CT: Yale University Press, 2015), and Huw Davies's *Wellington's War: The Making of a Military Genius* (New Haven, CT: Yale University Press, 2014).

133. See Andrew Field, *Talavera: Wellington's First Victory in Spain* (Barnsley: Pen & Sword, 2006); Rene Chartrand, *Talavera 1809: Wellington's Lighting Strike into Spain* (Oxford: Osprey, 2013).

134. Donald D. Horward, "Wellington's Peninsular Strategy, Portugal and the Lines of Torres Vedras," *Portuguese Studies Review* 2 (1993): 46–59; Ian Fletcher, *The Lines of Torres Vedras 1809–11* (Oxford: Osprey, 2003); John Grehan, *The Lines of Torres Vedras: The Cornerstone of Wellington's Strategy in the Peninsular War 1809–1812* (Staplehurst: Spellmount, 2000). On Beresford and the reorganization of the Portuguese army, see Samuel Edison Vichness, "Marshal of Portugal: The Military Career of William Carr Beresford, 1785–1814," Ph.D. diss., Florida State University, 1976, 218–381; Malyn Newitt and Martin Robson, *Lord Beresford and British Intervention in Portugal, 1807–1820* (Lisbon: Impr. de Ciências Sociais, 2004).

135. Brian de Toy, "Wellington's Lifeline: Naval Logistics in the Peninsula," *Proceedings of the Consortium on Revolutionary Europe*, 1995, 361; Donald D. Horward, "Admiral Berkeley and the Duke of Wellington: The Winning Combination in the Peninsula," in *New Interpretations in Naval History*, ed. William B. Cogar (Annapolis MD: Naval Institute Press, 1989), 105–20; Horward, "Wellington, Berkeley, and the Royal Navy: Sea Power and the Defense of Portugal (1908–1812)," *British Historical Society of Portugal Annual Report and Review* 18 (1991): 85–104; Horward, "British Sea Power and Its Influence upon the Peninsular War (1808–1814)," *Naval War College Review* 31, no. 2 (1978): 54–71. Also see Brian de Toy, "Wellington's Admiral: The Life and Career of George Berkeley, 1753–1818," Ph.D. diss., Florida State University, 1997, 492–565. For a book-length treatment of the role of the navy during the Peninsular War, see Christopher Hall, *Wellington's Navy: Seapower and the Peninsular War 1807–1814* (London, 2004). For an in-depth discussion of British logistics, see T. M. D. Redgrave, "Wellington's Logistical Arrangements in the Peninsular War, 1809–1814," Ph.D. diss., King's College London, 1979.

136. Donald D. Horward, "Logistics and Strategy in the Peninsula," *Proceedings of the Consortium on Revolutionary Europe*, 1999, 357–59; De Toy, "Wellington's Lifeline," 361; Hall, *Wellington's Navy*, 95.

137. Rear Admiral Martin to Lord Keith, September 21, 1813, in *Letters and Papers of Admiral of the Fleet Sir Thos. Byam Martin*, ed. Richard Vesey Hamilton (London: Navy Records Society, 1898), II:409.

138. Don W. Alexander, *Rod of Iron: French Counterinsurgency Policy in Aragon During the Peninsular War* (Wilmington: Scholarly Resources, 1985); Mark A. Reeves, "Iberian Leech: Napoleon's Counterinsurgency Operations in the Peninsular, 1807–1810," MMAS thesis, US Army Command and General Staff College, 2005, 81–84; Philippe H. Gennequin, "'The Centurions vs. the Hydra': French Counterinsurgency in the Peninsular War (1808–1812)," MMAS thesis, US Army Command and General Staff College, 2011, 44–76. Also see John L. Tone, *The Fatal Knot: The Guerrilla War in Navarre and the Defeat of Napoleon in Spain* (Chapel Hill: University of North Carolina Press, 1994); Jean-Yves Puyo, "Les expériences de Suchet à l'armée d'Aragon," *Revue du souvenir Napoléonien* 439 (2002): 8–15; David J. Lemelin, "Marshal Suchet in Aragon," *Military Review* 78 (1998): 86–90.

139. Lipscombe, *The Peninsular War Atlas*, 148–51; Oman, *A History of the Peninsular War*, III:9–66.

140. In late January 1810, the Supreme Central Governing Junta dissolved itself and handed power to a five-man Council of Regency that was to serve on behalf of the still-captive Bourbon monarchs.

141. For details, see François Crouzet, *L'économie britannique et le blocus continental (1806–1813)* (Paris: Presses universitaires de France, 1958), I:284–403; John Severn, *A Wellesley Affair: Richard Marquess Wellesley and the Conduct of Anglo-Spanish Diplomacy, 1809–1812* (Tallahassee: University Presses of Florida, 1981), 46–131; Muir, *Wellington: The Path to Victory*, 319, 327, 346–47.

142. But the question remains whether the French could have ended war at this junction. For some historians, the answer is yes. "Had the invasion of Portugal proved successful, there would have been no power of resistance left in Galicia, in Cadiz, in Valencia, or even in Catalonia; and the war would have ere long flickered out," notes Charles Oman. His conclusion is echoed in the works of another great British scholar, Charles Esdaile, who believes that had Napoleon provided a constant supply of reinforcements, the French "could have crushed resistance in Spain and then marched against Portugal in such overwhelming force that even Wellington could not have overcome them." It must be noted however that the French continued to face profound logistical challenges in Spain's rugged environment and struggled to maintain control of some areas. Marshal Pierre Augereau, who had replaced Saint-Cyr in Catalonia, continued to face an uphill struggle against the enterprising and obstinate Catalans, while Suchet was checked at Valencia and faced fresh disturbances in Aragon in 1810. Charles Oman, "The Peninsular War, 1808–1814," in *The Cambridge Modern History*, ed. A. W. Ward et al. (Cambridge: Cambridge University Press, 1969), IX:458; Esdaile, *Napoleon's Wars: An International History*, 351.

143. For an excellent eyewitness account, see Jean Jacques Pelet, *The French Campaign in Portugal, 1810–1811: An Account by Jean Jacques Pelet*, trans. Donald D. Horward (Minneapolis: University of Minnesota Press, 1972).

144. See Donald D. Horward, *The Battle of Bussaco: Masséna vs. Wellington* (Tallahassee: Florida State University Press, 1965); René Chartrand, *Bussaco, 1810: Wellington Defeats Napoleon's Marshals* (Oxford: Osprey, 2001).

145. Maurice Girod de l'Ain, *Vie militaire du Général Foy* (Paris, E. Plon, Nourrit, 1900), 343. For an in-depth discussion, see John Grehan, *The Lines of Torres Vedras: The Cornerstone of Wellington's Strategy in the Peninsular War, 1809–1812* (London: Spellmount, 2000).

146. Pelet, *The French Campaign in Portugal*, 273.

147. Wellington to the Earl of Liverpool, December 21, 1810, in *The Dispatches of Field Marshal the Duke of Wellington During His Various Campaigns in India, Denmark, Portugal, Spain, the Low Countries, and France from 1799 to 1818*, ed. Lt. Colonel Gurwood (London: John Murrat, 1837), VII:54. Also see Muir, *Wellington: The Path to Victory*, 399–406.

148. Esdaile, *Peninsular War*, 328.

149. Grenville to Grey, November 1, 1819, *Dropmore Papers*, X:61–62.

150. Muir, *Wellington: The Path to Victory*, 402–3.

151. Donald D. Horward, "Wellington and the Defense of Portugal, 1808–1813," *Proceedings of the Consortium on Revolutionary Europe*, 1987, 101; Muir, *Wellington: The Path to Victory*, 399–400.

152. See Guy Dempsey, *Albuera 1811: The Bloodiest Battle of the Peninsular War* (London: Frontline Books, 2008); Mark S. Thompson, *The Fatal Hill: The Allied Campaign Under Beresford in Southern Spain in 1811* (Chapelgarth, UK: n.p., 2002). The French lost 7,000–8,000 men, about a third of their total force.

153. Gates, *The Spanish Ulcer*, 343–50.

154. The best account of this battle is in Rory Muir, *Salamanca 1812* (New Haven, CT: Yale University Press, 2001). For a more concise treatment, see Ian Fletcher, *Salamanca 1812: Wellington Crushes Marmont* (Oxford: Osprey, 2004).

155. Girod de l'Ain, *Vie militaire du Général Foy*, 178.

156. Napier, *History of the War in the Peninsula*, III:130.

157. Gates, *The Spanish Ulcer*, 372–73.

158. Few of these deputies had been elected directly because of the ongoing war in Spain. Deputies from Spanish America had been selected by the oligarchic *cabildos* (city councils).

159. Luis Palacios Bañuelos, Ignacio Ruiz Rodríguez, and Fernando Bermejo Batanero, eds., *Cádiz 1812: origen del constitucionalismo español* (Madrid: Dykinson, 2013), 117–66; Burton Laverne Showers, "The Constitutional Debates on the Spanish Constitution of 1812," M.A. thesis, University of Wisconsin–Madison, 1950.

160. The text was drafted by a special commission of fifteen deputies throughout 1811. It was then debated by the Cortes and approved on March 18, 1812.

161. See Arnold R. Verduin, "The Spanish Constitution of 1812 and the Influence of the French Revolution Thereon," M.A. thesis, University of Wisconsin–Madison, 1930. The text of the Constitution of 1812 can be found at Biblioteca

Virtual Miguel de Cervantes, www.cervantesvirtual.com/servlet/SirveObras/
c1812/12159396448091522976624/index.htm.

162. Charles R. Berry, "The Election of the Mexican Deputies to the Spanish Cortes,
1810–1822," in *Mexico and the Spanish Cortes, 1810–1822*, ed. N. L. Benson
(Austin: University of Texas Press, 1966), 22–31; John R. Fisher, *Government
and Society in Colonial Peru: The Intendant System, 1784–1814* (London: Athlone
Press, 1970), 217–18.

163. Natalia Sobrevilla Perea and Scott Eastman, eds., *The Rise of Constitutional
Government in the Iberian Atlantic World: The Impact of the Cádiz Constitution of
1812* (Tuscaloosa: University of Alabama Press, 2015), 264.

164. On Peru, see Natalia Sobrevilla Perea, "Loyalism and Liberalism in Peru,
1810–1824," in *The Rise of Constitutional Government in the Iberian Atlantic
World*, ed. Natalia Sobrevilla Perea and Scott Eastman (Tuscaloosa: University
of Alabama Press, 2015), 111–32. On the formation of political leaders, see
Adam Sharman and Stephen G. H. Roberts, eds., *1812 Echoes: The Cadiz
Constitution in Hispanic History, Culture and Politics* (Newcastle upon Tyne:
Cambridge Scholars Publishing, 2013).

Chapter 13

1. Thomas Nipperday, *Germany from Napoleon to Bismarck 1800–1866*, trans.
Daniel Nolan (Dublin: Gill & Macmillan, 1996), 1.

2. Louis Bergeron, *France Under Napoleon* (Princeton, NJ: Princeton University
Press, 1981), xiv.

3. Nipperday, *Germany from Napoleon to Bismarck*, 1.

4. Alexander Grab, *Napoleon and the Transformation of Europe* (New York: Palgrave
Macmillan, 2003), 19.

5. James J. Sheehan, "State and Nationality in the Napoleonic Period," in *The
State of Germany: The National Idea in the Making, Unmaking, and Remaking of a
Modern Nation-State*, ed. John Breuilly (Harlow: Longman, 1992), 47–59.

6. Napoleon to Jérôme, November 15, 1807, in Napoleon, *Correspondance générale*,
ed. Thierry Lentz (Paris: Fayard, 2004), VII:1321.

7. Louis Madelin, *La Rome de Napoléon; la domination français à Rome de 1809 à
1814* (Paris: Plon-Nourrit, 1906), 3.

8. See Herbert Fisher, *Studies in Napoleonic Statesmanship: Germany* (Oxford:
Clarendon Press, 1903), 173–223, 312–32; Charles Schmidt, *Le grand-duché de
Berg (1806–13); étude sur la domination française en Allemagne sous Napoléon 1er*
(Paris: F. Alcan, 1905).

9. Allen Cronenberg, "Montgelas and the Reorganization of Napoleonic Bavaria,"
Proceedings of the Consortium on Revolutionary Europe, 1989, 712–19; Daniel
Michael Klang, "Bavaria and the Age of Napoleon," Ph.D. diss., Princeton
University, 1963; Chester Penn Higby, *The Religious Policy of the Bavarian
Government During the Napoleonic Period* (New York: Columbia University
Press, 1919).

10. See Dominique de Villepin, *Les Cent-Jours, ou, L'esprit de sacrifice* (Paris: Perrin, 2001); Michel Franceschi and Ben Weider, *The Wars Against Napoleon: Debunking the Myth of the Napoleonic Wars* (New York: Savas Beatie, 2008), 80–81; Don Dombowsky, *Nietzsche and Napoleon: The Dionysian Conspiracy* (Cardiff: University of Wales Press, 2014), sec. 3.12.

11. Geoffrey Ellis, "The Continental System Revisited," in *Revisiting Napoleon's Continental System: Local, Regional and European Experiences*, ed. Katherine B. Aalestad and Johan Joor (London: Palgrave Macmillan, 2015), 33.

12. In addition to the previously cited works on the Continental System, see Pierre Branda, ed., *L'economie selon Napoléon: monnaie, banque, crises et commerce sous le Premier Empire* (Paris: Éditions Vendémiaire, 2016).

13. In his insightful study of the Napoleonic empire, British historian Michael Broers suggests distinguishing between the "inner empire," which included the lands acquired prior to 1807, an "outer empire" that was gained in 1808–12, and various "intermediate zones," all of which had experienced varied levels of efficacy of the Napoleonic regime. See Broers, *Europe Under Napoleon 1799–1815* (New York: Edward Arnold, 1996).

14. See Rafał Kowalczyk, *Polityka gospodarcza i finansowa Księstwa Warszawskiego w latach 1807–12* (Łódź: Wydawn. Uniwersytet Łódzkiego, 2010); Henryk Grossmann, *Struktura społeczna i gospodarcza Księstwa Warszawskiego: na podstawie spisów ludności, 1808–10* (Warsaw: Nakł. Gł. Urzędu Statystycznego, 1925). Also see Monika Senkowska-Gluck, "Les majorats français dans le duché de Varsovie (1807–1813)," *Annales historiques de la Révolution française* 36 (1964): 373–86; Senkowska-Gluck, *Donacje napoleońskie w Księstwie Warszawskim; studium historycyno-prawne* (Wrocław: Zakład Narodowy im. Ossolińskich, 1968).

15. See Elisabeth Fehrenbach, *Traditionale Gesellschaft und revolutionäres Recht: die Einführung des Code Napoléon in den Rheinbundstaaten* (Göttingen: Vandenhoeck & Ruprecht, 1974); Fehrenbach, *Der Kampf um die Einführung des Code Napoléon in den Rheinbundstaaten* (Wiesbaden: Steiner, 1973); Helmut Berding, *Napoleonische Herrschafts- und Gesellschaftspolitik im Königreich Westfalen: 1807–13* (Göttingen: Vandenhoeck und Ruprecht, 1973). See Isabel Hull, *Sexuality, State, and Civil Society in Germany, 1700–1815* (Ithaca, NY: Cornell University Press, 1996).

16. Hull, *Sexuality, State, and Civil Society in Germany.*

17. Marshal Eduard Mortier's Proclamation of November 1, 1806, Hessisches Staatsarchiv Marburg, www.digam.net.

18. For an excellent overview, see Sam A. Mustafa, *Napoleon's Paper Kingdom: The Life and Death of Westphalia, 1807–13* (New York: Rowman & Littlefield, 2017).

19. See Roger Darquenne, *La conscription dans le département de Jemappes (1798–1813)* (Mons: Cercle archéologique de Mons, 1970).

20. Fisher, *Studies in Napoleonic Statesmanship*, 181, 214–215, 300–301. See also Jean-Camille-Abel-Fleuri Sauzey, *Les Allemands sous les aigles françaises; essai sur*

les troupes de la Confédération du Rhin, 1806–14. Tome I: Le régiment de Francfort (Paris: R. Chapelot, 1902).

21. Alexander Grab, "Army, State, and Society: Conscription and Desertion in Napoleonic Italy (1802–1814)," *Journal of Modern History* 67, no. 1 (1995): 28.

22. Cited in Grab, "Army, State, and Society," 25.

23. On the impact of conscription on various parts of Europe, see Isser Woloch, "Napoleonic Conscription: State Power and Civil Society," *Past and Present* 111 (1986): 101–29; Grab, "Army, State, and Society"; Alan Forrest, *Conscripts and Deserters: The Army and the French Society During the Revolution and Empire* (New York, 1989); Darquenne, *La conscription dans le département de Jemappes*.

24. For an excellent discussion, see Woloch, "Napoleonic Conscription." Also see Woloch, *The New Regime: Transformations of the French Civic Order, 1789–1820s* (New York: W. W. Norton, 1995), 380–426.

25. Alexander Grab, "State, Society and Tax Policy in Napoleonic Europe," in *Napoleon and Europe*, ed. Philip Dwyer (London: Pearson, 2001), 169.

26. For an excellent discussion, see Marcel Marion, *Histoire financière de la France depuis 1715. Tome IV: 1797–18. La fin de la Révolution, le Consulat et l'Empire. La liberation du territoire* (Paris: Librairie Arthur Rousseau, 1925).

27. Napoleon to Eugène de Beauharnais, August 23, 1810, in *Correspondance de Napoléon*, XX:61.

28. Napoleon to Soult, July 14, 1810, in *Napoléon raconté par l'écrit: Livres anciens, manuscrits, documents imprimés et autographes, iconographie* (Paris: Teissèdre, 2004), 56–57. Also see Bruno Colson, *Napoleon on War* (New York: Oxford University Press, 2015), 245–46.

29. Marion, *Histoire financière de la France depuis 1715*, IV:318; Grab, "State, Society and Tax Policy in Napoleonic Europe," 185.

30. Mustafa, *Napoleon's Paper Kingdom*, 79–106.

31. For details, see Pierre Branda, *Le prix de la gloire. Napoléon et l'argent* (Paris: Fayard, 2007); Branda, "La guerre a-t-elle payée la guerre?" in *Napoléon et l'Europe*, ed. Thierry Lenz (Paris: Fayard, 2005), 258–73.

32. Michel Bruguière, "Domaine extraordinaire," in *Dictionnaire Napoléon*, ed. Jean Tulard (Paris, 1989), 608.

33. Nicola Todorov, "Finances et fiscalité dans le royaume de Westphalie," in *La revue de l'Institut Napoléon* 189 (2004): 7–46. Also see Helmut Berding, "Le Royaume de Westphalie, état-modèle," *Francia: Forschungen zur westeuropäischen Geschichte* 10 (1982): 345–58.

34. John A. Davis, "The Napoleonic Era in Southern Italy: An Ambiguous Legacy?," *Proceedings of the British Academy* 80 (1993): 133–48. Also see Pasquale Villani, *Mezzogiorno tra riforme e rivoluzione* (Bari: Laterza, 1962).

35. Stuart Woolf, *Napoleon's Integration of Europe* (London: Routledge, 1991), 184. Also see Geoffrey Ellis, "The Nature of Napoleonic Imperialism," in *Napoleon and Europe*, ed. Philip Dwyer (London: Pearson, 2001), 97–117.

36. Napoleon continues, "They will esteem you only to the degree to which they fear you, and they will fear you only to the degree to which they are aware that their duplicity and treacherous character are known to you." Napoleon to Talleyrand, October 7, 1797, no. 2292; Napoleon to Eugène de Beauharnais, July 27, 1805, in *CN*, no. 9028, III:369; XI:48.

37. Part of the Papal States, the region is located on the Adriatic coastline in the central area of the peninsula, bordered by Emilia-Romagna to the north, Tuscany to the west, Umbria to the southwest, and Abruzzo and Lazio.

38. For a good overview of French religious policy, see Michael Broers, *The Politics of Religion in Napoleonic Italy: The War Against God, 1801–14* (New York: Routledge, 2002). For the French occupation of Rome, see Susan Vandiver Nicassio, *Imperial City: Rome Under Napoleon* (Chicago: University of Chicago Press, 2009); Louis Madelin, *La Rome de Napoléon; la domination français à Rome de 1809 à 1814* (Paris, Plon-Nourrit, 1906).

39. This discussion is based on Alexander Grab, "From the French Revolution to Napoleon," in *Italy in the Nineteenth Century: 1796–1900*, ed. John A. Davis (Oxford: Oxford University Press, 2000), 25–48; Nicassio, *Imperial City: Rome Under Napoleon*, 151–94; Michael Broers, *The Napoleonic Empire in Italy, 1796–14: Cultural Imperialism in a European Context?* (New York: Palgrave Macmillan, 2005), 123–74; Desmond Gregory, *Napoleon's Italy* (Madison: Fairleigh Dickinson University Press, 2001), 119–32; Owen Connelly, *Napoleon's Satellite Kingdoms* (New York: Free Press, 1965), 19–126.

40. For a good discussion of the wars' impact on Italy, see Frederick C. Schneid, *Soldiers of Napoleon's Kingdom of Italy: Army, State, and Society, 1800–15* (Boulder, CO: Westview Press, 1995); Paolo Coturri, *Partire partirò, partir bisogna: Firenze e la Toscana nelle campagne napoleoniche, 1793–15* (Florence: Sarnus, 2009); Virgilio Ilari et. al. *Il regno di Sardegna nelle guerre napoleoniche e le legioni anglo-italiane, 1799–1815* (Novara: Widerholdt Frères, 2008); Vittorio Scotti Douglas, ed., *Gli Italiani in Spagna nella guerra napoleonica, 1807–13: i fatti, i testimoni, l'eredità: atti del IV Convegno internazionale di "Spagna contemporanea," Novi Ligure, 22–24 ottobre 2004* (Alessandria: Edizioni dell'Orso, 2006).

41. Alexander Grab, "The Kingdom of Italy and Napoleon's Continental Blockade," *Proceedings of the Consortium on Revolutionary Europe*, 1988, 587–604.

42. Davis, *Naples and Napoleon*, 163–208.

43. Luigi de Rosa, "Property Rights, Institutional Change and Economic Growth in Southern Italy in the XVIIIth and XIXth Centuries," *Journal of European Economic History* 8, no. 3(1979): 531–51.

44. Joseph Bonaparte introduced a conscription by lottery in 1807 but as the system failed to provide sufficient recruits, it was replaced with quotas in 1808. Oftentimes quotas were met by sending detained brigands and convicts to the military depots. For details, see Nino Cortese, "L'esercito napoletano nelle guerre napoleoniche," *Archivio storico per le province napoletane* 51 (1926): 319–21.

45. For an in-depth discussion, see Maria Christina Ermice, *Le origini del Gran Libro del debito pubblico e l'emergere di nuovi gruppi sociali (1806–15)* (Naples: Arte Tipografica Editrice, 2005).

46. Davis, *Naples and Napoleon*, 180.

47. Napoleon to Clarke, October 13, 1810, in *Correspondance de Napoléon*, XXI:216–17; Albert Espitalier, *Napoleon and King Murat* (London: John Lane, 1912), 66–88.

48. For an interesting discussion, see Desmond Gregory, *Sicily: The Insecure Base: A History of the British Occupation of Sicily, 1806–15* (Rutherford, NJ: Fairleigh Dickinson University Press, 1988), 15–57. For the most recent account of the Franco-British struggle in the Mediterranean, see Gareth Glover, *The Forgotten War Against Napoleon: Conflict in the Mediterranean, 1793–15* (Barnsley: Pen & Sword, 2017).

49. Under the Sicilian tradition, there were only four instances—an enemy invasion, an insurrection, the captivity of the king, and a royal marriage—when the power of the assembly could be dispensed with in raising new revenues.

50. Joseph Alexander von Helfert, *Königin Karolina von Neapel und Sicilien im Kampfe gegen die französische Weltherrschaft, 1790–1814: mit Benützung von Schriftstücken des K.K. Haus-, Hof- und Staats-Archivs* (Vienna: Braumüller, 1878), 432–34.

51. Oscar Browning, "Queen Caroline of Naples," *English Historical Review* 2, no. 7 (July 1887): 488.

52. John Rosselli, *Lord William Bentinck: The Making of a Liberal Imperialist, 1774–39* (Berkeley: University of California Press, 1974), 147. For more details, see Browning, "Queen Caroline of Naples," 490–91.

53. Browning, "Queen Caroline of Naples," 492–97; Rosselli, *Lord William Bentinck*, 152ff.

54. C. W. Crawley, "England and the Sicilian Constitution of 1812," *English Historical Review* 55, no. 218 (1940): 251–74; Rosselli, *Lord William Bentinck*, 157–60.

55. Edward Blaquiere, *Letters from the Mediterranean...* (London: Henry Colt, 1813), I:405.

56. Paolo Balsamo's quote in Moses I. Finley, *A History of Sicily* (New York: Viking, 1987), 150.

57. Rosselli, *Lord William Bentinck*, 151.

58. Browning, "Queen Caroline of Naples," 499–513.

59. For insights, see Eckart Kehr, Hanna Schissler, and Hans-Ulrich Wehler, *Preussische Finanzpolitik, 1806–1810: Quellen zur Verwaltung der Ministerien Stein und Altenstein* (Göttingen: Vandenhoeck & Ruprecht, 1984).

60. Johann Fichte, *Fichte: Addresses to the German Nation*, ed. Gregory Moore (Cambridge: Cambridge University Press, 2008).

61. James J. Sheehan, *German History, 1770–1866* (Oxford: Clarendon Press, 2008), 295–310; Marion Gray, "Bureaucratic Transition and Accommodation

of the Aristocracy in the Prussian Reform Year 1808," *Proceedings of the Consortium on Revolutionary Europe* (1981), 86–92.

62. For details, see Charles Edward White, *The Enlightened Soldier: Scharnhorst and the Militärische Gesellschaft in Berlin, 1801–05* (Westport, CT: Praeger, 1989); Michael Schoy, "General Gerhard von Scharnhorst: Mentor of Clausewitz and Father of the Prussian-German General Staff," Canadian Defense Forces Publication, https://www.cfc.forces.gc.ca/259/181/82_schoy.pdf.

63. See Peter Josephson, Thomas Karlsohn, and Johan Östling, *The Humboldtian Tradition: Origins and Legacies* (Leiden: Brill, 2014).

64. The Order of Cabinet, June 30, 1808, cited in John R. Seeley, *Life and Times of Stein: Germany and Prussia in the Napoleonic Age* (Boston: Roberts Brothers, 1879), I:387.

Chapter 14

1. Cited in James J. Sheehan, *German History, 1770–1866* (Oxford: Clarendon Press, 2008), 285.

2. Hruby to Stadion, July 31, 1808, in Adolf Beer, *Zehn jahre österreichischer politik, 1801–1810* (Leipzig: F. A. Brockhaus, 1877), 352–53. Also see Stadion's memoranda (December 1808) in Beer, *Zehn jahre*, 516–25; Metternich to Stadion, September 24 and October 30, 1808, in Clemens Wenzel Lothar Fürst von Metternich, *Memoirs of Prince Metternich, 1773–1815*, ed. Richard Metternich, trans. Robina Napier (London: Richard Bentley, 1880), II:283–88.

3. See Gunther E. Rothenberg, *Napoleon's Great Adversaries: The Archduke Charles and the Austrian Army, 1792–1814* (Bloomington: Indiana University Press, 1982); Lee W. Eysturlid, *The Formative Influences, Theories and Campaigns of the Archduke Carl of Austria* (Westport, CT: Greenwood, 2000).

4. Opposition primarily came from Archduke Charles and Gentz. See Enno E. Kraehe, *Metternich's German Policy* (Princeton, NJ: Princeton University Press, 1983), I:74–75.

5. Metternich to Stadion, April 3, 1809, in Metternich, *Memoirs*, II:347.

6. Canning's reply to the Austrian government, December 24, 1808, cited in John M. Sherwig, *Guineas and Gunpowder: British Foreign Aid in the Wars with France, 1793–1815* (Cambridge, MA: Harvard University Press, 1969), 208–9.

7. Scherwig, *Guineas*, 208–9, 212–13.

8. Rory Muir, *Britain and the Defeat of Napoleon, 1807–1815* (New Haven: Yale University Press, 1996), 89–90; Christopher Hall, *British Strategy in the Napoleonic Wars, 1803–1815* (Manchester: Manchester University Press, 1992), 177.

9. Cited in John H. Gill, *1809: Thunder on the Danube: Napoleon's Defeat of the Habsburgs* (Barnsley, UK: Frontline Books, 2008), I:20.

10. Gill, *1809*, I:379–80.

11. Article X of the Convention d'Alliance signed at Erfurt on October 12, 1808, in F. de Martens, *Recueil des traités et conventions conclus par la Russie avec les puissances étrangères* (St. Petersburg: A. Böhnke, 1895).

12. Rumyantsev to Alexander, January 24, 1809, *VPR*, IV:465–66.

13. Kurakin to Alexander I, January 30, 1809, *VPR*, IV:468–69.

14. Rumyantsev to Alexander, February 11, 1809, *VPR*, IV:468–69. Napoleon's sentiments seem to have rubbed off on Alexander, who found "the blindness of Austria inexplicable. Perhaps it is produced by England." Alexander to Napoleon, January 27, 1809, in Sergei Tatishev, *Alexandre 1er et Napoléon: d'après leur correspondence inédite, 1801–12* (Paris, 1891), 468–69. Russian minister of war Alexei Arakcheyev was convinced that Austria was "driven by England" toward war and that "Russia will be duty bound to honor its treaties with France." Arakcheyev to Prozorovskii, January 12, 1809, *VPR*, IV:461.

15. Schwarzenberg to Princess Schwarzenberg, March 21, 1809, in *Karl Philipp zu Schwarzenberg, Briefe des Feldmarschalls Fursten Schwarzenberg an seine Frau 1799–16* (Vienna, 1913), 165–67. "In all of Russia," one court nobleman confided to a police informant, "there are only five prominent people who are not against the current alliance [with France] and we know quite well who they are and whenever they enter the society, everyone whispers, 'This is one of the five.' This expression is so well known that as soon as one of the five enters the room, all conversations cease at once." Fogel to Balashov, June 10, 1809, *VPR*, V:69. Also see Nikolay Dubrovin, "Russkaya zhizn v nachale XIX veka," *Russkaya starina* 12 (1898): 508; Schwarzenberg to Stadion, March 2, 1809, in Tatishev, *Alexandre 1er et Napoléon*, 465; Kazimierz Waliszewski, *La Russie il y a cent ans: Le regne d'Alexandre 1er* (Paris, 1923), I:283.

16. Secret agent Fogel reported in the spring of 1809 that Bagration bluntly told the French ambassador that he would never command an army against Austrian Archduke Carl; *VPR*, IV:66. For contemporary views, see "Pisma A. Bulgakova k ego bratu iz Peterburga v Venu 1808–1809," *Russkii arkhiv* 9 (1899): 82.

17. Russian diplomat Alexander Butenev, who served under Rumyantsev, commented in his memoirs that "in Rumyantsev's opinion, only Napoleon was capable of restraining revolutionary movements in Europe, and when Napoleon fell in 1815, [Rumyantsev] predicted the rise of such movements." "Vospominania russkogo diplomata A. P. Buteneva," *Russkii arkhiv* 3 (1881): 58–59.

18. Vel. Kn. Nikolay Mikhailovich, *Diplomaticheskie snoshenia Rossii i Frantsii po doneseniyam poslov Imperatorov Aleksandra i Napoleona, 1808–1812 (St. Petersburg: Ekspeditsia zagotovleniya gosudarstvennykh bumag, 1905)*, I:xxvi–xxviii.

19. Frederick William III to Alexander, Alexander to Frederick William III, May 2–19, in *Correspondance inédite du roi Frédéric-Guillaume III et de la reine Louise avec l'empereur Alexandre Ier d'après les originaux des archives de Berlin et de Saint Petersbourg*, ed. Paul Bailleu (Leipzig, 1900), 184–91.

20. Llewellyn D. Cook, "Prince Schwarzenberg's Mission to St. Petersburg, 1809," *Proceedings of the Consortium on Revolutionary Europe*, 1998, 399–410.

21. See Stadion's instructions to Lieutenant Wagner (January 28, 1809) and Wessenberg (February 20, 1809), in Wladislaw Fedorowicz, *1809. Campagne de Pologne, depuis le commencement jusqu'à l'occupation de Varsovie* (Paris: Plon-Nourrit, 1911), 67–73, 95. Also Hellmuth Rössler, *Graf Johann Philipp Stadion, Napoleons deutscher Gegenspieler* (Vienna: Herold, 1966), I:318–19.

22. Alexander to Rumyantsev, February 14, 1809, *VPR*, IV:493–95.

23. Alexander to Rumyantsev, February 14, 1809, *VPR*, IV:494.

24. Schwarzenberg to Franz, April 21, 1809, in Gustav Just, *Politik oder Strategie? Kritische Studien über den Warschauer Feldzug Österreichs und die Haltung Russlands 1809* (Vienna, 1909), 69–70.

25. Moritz Edler v. Angeli, *Erzherzog Karl von Osterreich als Feldherr und Heeresorganisator* (Vienna: K. u. K. Hof-universitäts-Buchhändler, 1896–1898), IV:33–55.

26. Schneid, *Napoleon's Italian Campaigns*, 59–84; Gill, *1809*, II:201–45.

27. Cited in Rothenberg, *Napoleon's Great Adversaries*, 146.

28. Louis Francois Lejeune, *Memoirs of Baron Lejeune*, ed. A. Bell (London, 1897), I:215–16.

29. For a definitive account, see Gill, *1809*, vol. I. Also see Henri Bonnal, *La manœuvre de Landshut: étude sur la stratégie de Napoléon et sa psychologie militaire depuis le milieu de l'anée 1808 jusqu'au 30 avril 1809* (Paris: R. Chapelot, 1905); Charles Gaspard Louis Saski, *Campagne de 1809 en Allemagne et en Autriche* (Paris Berger-Levrault, 1899), II:255–265, 276–99.

30. Gill, *1809*, I:223–303; Angeli, *Erzherzog Karl von Osterreich als Feldherr und Heeresorganisator,* IV:75–187; Saski, *Campagne de 1809*, II:332–75.

31. Sheehan, *German History*, 287; Oscar Criste, *Erzherzog Carl von Österreich* (Vienna: W. Braumüller, 1912), III:79–80.

32. Angeli, *Erzherzog Karl von Osterreich als Feldherr und Heeresorganisator,* IV:315–28.

33. Gill, *1809*, II:129–98; Robert M. Epstein, *Napoleon's Last Victory and the Emergence of Modern War* (Lawrence: University Press of Kansas, 1994), 104–18. Also see F. Loraine Petre, *Napoleon and the Archduke Charles* (London: John Lane, 1909).

34. Angeli, *Erzherzog Karl von Osterreich als Feldherr und Heeresorganisator,* IV:335–51.

35. Gill, *1809*, II:196.

36. Frederick C. Schneid, *Napoleon's Italian Campaigns: 1805–1815* (Westport, CT: Praeger, 2002), 85–102; Gill, *1809*, II:246–97; Petre, *Napoleon and the Archduke Charles,* 314–16.

37. For the most recent English study of the revolts of Katte, Dörnberg, and Schill, see Sam A. Mustafa, *The Long Ride of Major von Schill: A Journey Through German History and Memory* (Lanham, MD: Rowman & Littlefield, 2008).

38. Ultimately, Brunswick understood that the French victory at Wagram had turned the tide of the war, and he conceived a daring plan of escaping out of Saxony to the estuary of the Wesser River, where he could be rescued by the British navy. Starting on July 20, the duke's "Black Brunswickers," though threatened on all sides, fought their way to the lower Weser, where they

boarded the British ships at Elsfleth; the survivors were carried to Spain, where they served with distinction under the Duke of Wellington. Fred Mentzel, "Der Vertrag Herzog Friedrich Wilhelms von Braunschweig mit der britischen Regierung über die Verwendung des Schwarzen Korps (1809)," *Braunschweigisches Jahrbuch* 55 (1974): 230–39.

39. See Marcus Junkelman, *Napoleon und Bayern den Anfängen des Königreiches* (Regensburg: F. Pustet, 1985); Karl Paulin, *Andreas Hofer und der Tiroler Freiheitskampf 1809* (Vienna: Tosa-Verl, 1996).

40. Alexander Grab, "State Power, Brigandage and Rural Resistance in Napoleonic Italy," *European History Quarterly* 25 (1995): 39–70; Mario Leonardi, "L'insorgenza del 1809 nel regno d'Italia," *Annunario dell'Istituto per l'Età Moderna e Contemporanea* 31, no. 2 (1980): 435–37. For a broader discussion of the heavy-handed nature of the French regime in Italy, see Michael Broers, *The Napoleonic Empire in Italy, 1796–1814: Cultural Imperialism in a European Context?* (New York: Palgrave Macmillan, 2005), 123–59.

41. For definitive treatments of the Wagram campaign see Gill, *1809*, vol. III; Gunther E. Rothenberg, *The Emperor's Last Victory: Napoleon and the Battle of Wagram* (London: Weidenfeld and Nicolson, 2004). For more concise discussions, see Epstein, *Napoleon's Last Victory*, 129–70; Ian Castle, *Aspern and Wagram 1809: Mighty Clash of Empires* (London: Osprey, 1994); Sławomir Leśniewski, *Wagram 1809* (Warsaw: Bellona, 2003); Jean Thiry, *Wagram* (Paris: Berger-Levrault, 1966).

42. This changing nature of the war constituted what one historian has described as "the emergence of modern war." Epstein, *Napoleon's Last Victory*, 171.

43. For an in-depth discussion see Milton Finley, *The Most Monstrous of Wars: The Napoleonic Guerrilla War in Southern Italy, 1806–1811* (Columbia: University of South Carolina Press, 1994), 114–25.

44. Beer, *Zehn jahre österreichischer politik*, 335–41; Sherwig, *Guineas and Gunpowder*, 208–13; Hellmuth Rössler, *Graf Johann Philipp Stadion, Napoleons deutscher* (Vienna: Herold, 1966), 318–19.

45. Though one may argue that Foreign Secretary Canning was also keen to clear his name in the wake of the British setbacks in Spain—that is, the Convention of Cintra and the French escape from Portugal.

46. Castlereagh envisioned an expedition to Walcheren as early as 1797. See his letter of December 25, 1797, in Robert Stewart, Viscount Castlereagh, *Correspondence, Despatches and Other Papers of Viscount Castlereagh* (London: William Shoberl, 1851), VI:245–47.

47. John Bew, *Castlereagh: A Life* (Oxford: Oxford University Press, 2012), 250.

48. Gordon C. Bond, *The Grand Expedition: The British Invasion of Holland in 1809* (Athens: University of Georgia Press, 1979), 10–12.

49. See memorandums by Castlereagh, Lieutenant Colonel Gordon, and Major General Alexander Hope in Castlereagh, *Correspondence, Despatches and Other Papers*, VI:247–65.

50. William Jerdan, *Autobiography* (London: Arthur Hall, 1852), I:115.

51. For details, see Victor Enthoven, *Een haven te ver: de Britse expeditie naar de Schelde van 1809* (Nijmegen: Vantilt, 2009); T. van Gent, *De Engelse invasie van Walcheren in 1809* (Amsterdam: De Bataafsche Leeuw, 2001); Théo Fleischman, *L'expedition anglaise sur le continent en 1809, conquête de l'île de Walcheren et menace sur Anvers* (Brussels: La Renaissance du livre, 1973).

52. Bond, *The Grand Expedition*, 90–113. Also see Martin R. Howard, *Walcheren 1809: The Scandalous Destruction of a British Army* (Barnsley: Pen & Sword Military, 2012).

53. See Gordon Bond, "Walcheren Fever: The Curse of the British Army, 1809–1814," *Proceedings of the Consortium on Revolutionary Europe*, 1989, 579–85; T. H. McGuffie, "The Walcheren Expedition and the Walcheren Fever," *English Historical Review* 62, no. 243 (1947): 191–202. Napoleon was aware of Walcheren's insalubrious climate and certainly expected that the British would suffer from it. Napoleon to Clarke, August 22, 1809, *Correspondence de Napoléon*, no. 15,698, XIX:382–384.

54. Bond, *The Grand Expedition*, 126–32.

55. For Napoleon's assessment, see Barry Edward O'Meara, *A Voice from St. Helena* (London: Simpkin and Marshall, 1822), I:255–56.

56. Bond, *The Grand Expedition*, 142–43.

57. Giles Hunt, *The Duel: Castlereagh, Canning and Deadly Cabinet Rivalry* (London: I. B. Tauris, 2008); George Canning, *Memoirs of the Life of the Right Honourable George Canning* (London: Thomas Tegg, 1828), II:185–91; W. Alison Phillips, *George Canning* (New York: E. P. Dutton, 1903), 77–79; Bew, *Castlereagh*, 257–67.

58. Albert Vandal, *Napoléon et Alexandre 1er: l'alliance russe sous le 1er Empire* (Paris, 1894–97), II:72.

59. Alexander to Golitsyn, April 21, 1809, RGVIA, f. VUA, d. 3369, l. 3–4.

60. Champagny to Caulaincourt, 2 June, 1809, in Vandal, *Napoléon et Alexandre 1er*, II:94.

61. Alexander to Golitsyn, 18 May, 1809, RGVIA, f. VUA, d. 3369, l. 11–13b.

62. Journal of Military Operations of the Russian Army in Galicia in 1809, RGVIA, f. VUA, d. 3365; Alexander Mikhailovskii-Danilevskii, *Opisanie voiny protiv Avstrii v 1809 godu*, RGVIA, f. VUA, d. 3360.

63. Ferdinand to Franz, June 6, 1809, in Bronislaw Pawlowski, *Historja Wojny Polsko–Austrajackiej 1809 Roku* (Warsaw, 1935), 362–63.

64. Cited in Roman Soltyk, *Relation des Opérations de l'Armée aux orders du Prince Joseph Poniatowski* (Paris, 1841), 278; Mikhailovskii-Danilevskii, "Opisanie voiny protiv Avstrii," RGVIA, f. VUA, d. 3360, l.119b. On one occasion when a bridge was thrown over the river at Radomysl and it was time to launch a joint Russo-Polish operation, the Russian commander "found various pretexts to delay the operation. It was 'Monday,' which he alleged was an inauspicious day and one on which the Russians abstained from combat. The following day

he found he had lost his Cross of St. George, which he took as an ill omen." Soltyk, *Relation des opérations*, 282–83.

65. Archduke Ferdinand to Golitsyn, Golitsyn to Archduke Ferdinand, April 30–May 4, 1809, in Modest Bogdanovich, *Istoriya tsarstvovaniya imperatora Aleksandra I i Rossii v ego vremya* (St. Petersburg, 1869), II:64; Just, *Politik oder Strategie?*, 79–82.

66. Champagny to Caulaincourt, June 2, 1809, in Vandal, *Napoléon et Alexandre 1er*, II:95.

67. Alexander to Golitsyn, May 29, 1809, RGVIA, f. VUA, d. 3369, l. 15–16b. Documents related to Gorchakov's court-martial were also printed in *Zhurnal imperatorskogo Russkago Voenno-Istoricheskogo Obshestva* 2 (1911): 1–10.

68. For details, see Alexander Mikaberidze, "Non-Belligerent Belligerent Russia and the Franco-Austrian War of 1809," *Napoleonica. La Revue* 10 (2011): 15–18.

69. Napoleon to Frederick, April 2, 1811, in *CN*, no. 17553, XXII:17.

70. Mikhailovskii-Danilevskii, *Opisanie voiny protiv Avstrii*, RGVIA, f. VUA, d. 3360, l.118–118b.

71. Golitsyn to Alexander, July 5, August 23, 1809, *VPR*, V:89–90. Golitsyn's letter included his correspondence with Poniatowski.

72. For a Polish view of the events, see Poniatowski's letter to Napoleon in Soltyk, *Relation des opérations*, 319–20. Russian sources deny that Austrians intentionally surrendered the city to the Russians and point to two killed and several wounded Russian soldiers as evidence that the Russians took the city by force. See Bogdanovich, *Istoria tsarstvovania imperatora Aleksandra I*, II:449.

73. Golitsyn to Alexander, July 17, 1809, in Bogdanovich, *Istoria tsarstvovania imperatora Aleksandra I*, II:447–48. Golitsyn's letter to General Suvorov spoke of Polish "tavern crowds [*traktirnye skopisha*] that incited meaningless quibbles." Golitsyn to Suvorov, August 22, 1809, RGVIA, f. VUA, d. 3375, l. 6–7b. The Russians returned the favor in kind. General Adjutant Gagarin told Alexander that in Krakow he observed "our officials engaged in a behavior that was contrary to the spirit of reciprocity and acquiescence, making numerous cavils in petty and unworthy affairs." Arakcheyev to Golitsyn, August 15, 1809, RGVIA, f. VUA, d. 3371, l. 18–18b.

74. Golitsyn to Poniatowski, August 2, 1809, in Bogdanovich, *Istoria tsarstvovania imperatora Aleksandra I*, II:450; Golitsyn to Alexander, August 7, 1809, *VPR*, V:122. "There is not a single Pole who does not dream about the restoration of his fatherland, which is quite natural since who would not desire that the land where he was born should be under a single authority that was recognized by your ancestors." Golitsyn to Alexander, June 16, 1809, *VPR*, V:76–77.

75. Emperor Francis was concerned that Russia sought "to take possession of the greater part of Galicia without any effort whatsoever." Franz to Ferdinand, June 23, 1809, in Pawlowski, *Historja Wojny Polsko–Austrajackiej 1809 Roku*, 444.

76. Rumyantsev to Golitsyn, June 27, 1809, *VPR*, V:85–86. French version, albeit an abridged one, is in Vandal, *Napoléon et Alexandre 1er*, II:547–48.

77. Caulaincourt to Napoleon, August 3, 1809, in Vandal, *Napoléon et Alexandre Ier*, II:112–13.

78. The letter, written by Rumyantsev, complained about "the forces of the Duchy of Warsaw playing a duplicitous role in Galicia. They acted not just as troops of the Saxon army, but also called themselves the Poles; they published proclamations in the name of their fatherland; they spoke about the restoration of Poland; they recruited soldiers even [outside the Duchy of Warsaw], appealing to them with patriotic petitions. Some subjects of [the Russian] emperor, who have peacefully lived under his authority since the complete destruction of the polish kingdom, were enticed by such appeals.... The coat of arms of the former Polish states has appeared once against on the borders of the [Russian] empire. Is this done so that everyone can see whose territory it is?... The idea of restoring the Polish kingdom is on the mind of the people residing in the Duchy of Warsaw. This is not a secret intention, but rather an openly professed hope." Rumyantsev to Caulauincourt, July 27, 1809, *VPR*, V:116–17.

79. "Convention non ratifiée par l'Empereur Napoléon Ier," in *CN*, XX:148–49.

80. Napoleon instructed Champagny on February 6, 1810, to draft his response and counterproposal (see *CN*, no. 16178, XX:149–50), but Russians rejected the French draft as well. Alexander instead sent a new draft (March 17) that essentially demanded the same thing.

81. Napoleon to Caulaincourt, July 1, 1810, in *CN*, no. 16181, XX:158–59.

82. Rumyantsev to Bethmann, June 20, 1809, *VPR*, V:78–79.

83. Alexander to Rumyantsev, August 16, 1809, *VPR*, V:130–31.

84. Phillip Vigel, *Vospominaniya F.F. Vigelya* (Moscow: Katkov i K., 1864), III, 61–62; Caulaincourt to Napoleon, August 2 and August 19, 1809, in Nikolay Mikhailovich, *Diplomaticheskie snoshenia Rossii i Frantsii, IV:34, 52;* Vandal, *Napoléon et Alexandre Ier*, II:112–13.

85. Prozorovsky to Golitsyn, August 4, 1809, in *Russkii arkhiv* 2 (1876): 157–59. It is worth noting that Prozorovsky derisively referred to the imperial dynasty as the "House of Holstein" to underscore its German, and therefore alien, character.

Chapter 15

1. See Michael Roberts, *The Swedish Imperial Experience, 1650–18* (Cambridge: Cambridge University Press, 1979). For a broad overview of the Baltic region, see Michael North, *The Baltic: A History* (Cambridge, MA: Harvard University Press, 2015), 117–82.

2. Hildor A. Barton, *Scandinavia in the Revolutionary Era* (Minneapolis: University of Minnesota Press, 1986), 181.

3. See Sten Carl Oscar Carlsson, *Gustaf IV Adolf, en biografi* (Stockholm: Wahlström & Widstrand, 1946); Matti Klinge, *Napoleonin varjo: Euroopan ja Suomen murros 1795–15* (Helsinki: Otava, 2009).

4. On the importance of Pomerania to Sweden, see Jens E. Olesen, "Schwedisch-Pommern in der schwedischen Politik nach 1806," in *Das Ende des Alten Reiches*

im Ostseeraum: Wahrnehmungen und Transformationen, ed. Michael North and Robert Riemer (Köln: Böhlau, 2008), 274–92.

5. Prince Royal of Denmark to Prince Christian August, November 21, 1806, in *Meddelelser fra krigsarkiverne udgine af Generalstaben* (Copenhagen: F. Hegel & Son, 1885), II:347–48.

6. Gustaf Björlin, *Sveriges krig i tyskland åren 1805–07* (Stockholm: Militärlitteratúr-Föreningens förlag, 1882), 100, 144–54, 162–72, 174–87.

7. Christer Jorgensen, *The Anglo-Swedish Alliance Against Napoleonic France* (New York: Palgrave, 2004), 75–80.

8. Christophe Guillaume de Koch and Frédéric Schoell, *Histoire abrégée des Traités de paix entre les puissances de l'Europe depuis la Paix de Westphalie* (Brussels: Meline, Cans, 1838), III:45–46.

9. Koch and Schoell, *Histoire abrégée*, 47–48. Yet, as with other coalition partners, Sweden complained about British failure to send adequate military support fast enough. Jorgensen points out that British "procrastination" resulted from the fact that Britain only had 16,000 troops available for continental service and was also hampered in terms of available tonnage to launch an expedition. More important, "The British refused... to act before they knew exactly what Gustavus IV's plans were and how many troops they would be called upon to subsidize." Jorgensen, *The Anglo-Swedish Alliance*, 80–89.

10. Björlin, *Sveriges krig i tyskland åren 1805–1807*, 214–26. For the French side, see Vigier de Saint-Junien, *Brune's 1807 Campaign in Swedish Pomerania*, trans. and ed. George Nafziger (West Chester, OH: Nafziger Collection, 2001).

11. Prince Royal of Denmark to Prince Christian August, November 21, 1806, in *Meddelelser fra krigsarkiverne udgine af Generalstaben* (Copenhagen: F. Hegel & Son, 1885), II:347–48.

12. For reports of the Danish officials and border commanders, see *Meddelelser fra krigsarkiverne udgine af Generalstaben*, II:310ff. Murat's response of November 8 is at II:325.

13. See *Hansard's Parliamentary Debates*, "Papers Relative to the Expedition to Copenhagen," X:765–67, 775–76. Also see Rasmus Glenthøj and Morten Nordhagen Ottosen, *Experiences of War and Nationality in Denmark and Norway, 1807–15* (New York: Palgrave Macmillan, 2014), 30.

14. Canning to Lord Granville Leveson Gower, July 21 (postscript dated July 22), in A. N. Ryan, "Documents Relating to the Copenhagen Operation, 1807," *Publications of the Navy Record Society* 125, no. 5 (1984): 307–8.

15. See *Hansard's Parliamentary Debates*, X:13, 18, 30, 59, 68, 69, 72–73, 74–75, 86–87, 92, 94, 252–66. The debates of February 1–3, 1808, are partly available online at http://hansard.millbanksystems.com/volumes/1/10.

16. Oscar Browning, "A British Agent at Tilsit," *English Historical Review* 17, no. 65 (1902): 110; Thomas Munch-Petersen, "Colin Alexander Mackenzie: A British Agent at Tilsit," *Northern Studies* 37 (2003): 9–16; J. Holland Rose, "A British Agent at Tilsit," *English Historical Review* 16, no. 64 (1901): 712–18;

J. Holland Rose, "Canning and the Secret Intelligence from Tilsit (July 16–23, 1807)," *Transactions of the Royal Historical Society* (n.s.) 20 (1906): 61–77.

17. Thomas Munch-Petersen, "The Secret Intelligence from Tilsit: New Light on the Events Surrounding the British Bombardment of Copenhagen in 1807," *Historisk Tidsskrift* 102, no. 1 (2002): 55–96.

18. For an excellent discussion, see Robert G. Albion, *Forests and Sea Power: The Timber Problem of the Royal Navy, 1652–1862* (Cambridge, MA: Harvard University Press), esp. 20–32.

19. George Louis Beer, *British Colonial Policy, 1754–1765* (New York: Macmillan, 1907), 215–17. Also see *Remarks on the Probable Conduct of Russia and France Towards This Country, Also on the Necessity of Great Britain Becoming Independent of the Northern Powers for Her Maritime Supplies* (London, 1805), 93–95; Joshua Jepson Oddy, *European Commerce: Shewing New and Secure Channels of Trade with the Continent of Europe* (London, 1805).

20. Data taken from Oddy, *European Commerce*, 398.

21. Writing to Admiral James Gambier in September 1807, Henry Phipps Lord Mulgrave, the foreign secretary under William Pitt the Younger in 1805–1806, was particularly concerned about the French occupation of the island of Zealand, which could allow Napoleon to close the Baltic. Mulgrave considered the recapture of the island as "a consideration of the utmost magnitude" since it would ensure British access to the Baltic and might drive a wedge into the Franco-Russian alliance. Lord Mulgrave to Gambier, in *Memorials, Personal and Historical of Lord Gambier*, ed. Georgiana Chatterton (London: Hurst and Blackett, 1861), II:43.

22. In May 1807 Lord Pembroke, newly appointed British ambassador to Vienna, was traveling on the frigate *Astrea*, commanded by Captain Dunbar, via Copenhagen, where he claimed to have observed Danes hastily outfitting their ships. Pembroke's report was bolstered by Captain Dunbar's more detailed account of the alleged Danish preparations. "What Lord Pembroke actually saw was and remains a mystery," note modern-day Danish historians. "The only ship that had been fitted out was a ship of the line being prepared to take a Russian princess to St. Petersburg." Glenthøj and Ottosen, *Experiences of War and Nationality in Denmark and Norway,* 31. See also A. N. Ryan, "The Causes of the British Attack upon Copenhagen in 1807," *English Historical Review* 63, no. 266 (1953): 43ff.

23. Carl J. Kulsrud, "The Seizure of the Danish Fleet in 1807," *American Journal of International Law* 32, no. 2 (1938): 280–311. For a more critical view, see Eric Moller, "England og Danmark-Norge 1807," *Dansk Historisk Tidsskrift* 8, no. 3 (1912): 310–21.

24. Glenthøj and Ottosen, *Experiences of War and Nationality in Denmark and Norway,* 32.

25. Napoleon to Talleyrand, July 31, 1807, in CN, XV:459–60. He expressed the same desire two days later, writing to his governor of the Hanseatic cities:

"Either Denmark declares war on England, or I will declare war on Denmark." Napoleon to Bernadotte, August 2, 1807, in *CN*, XV:467.

26. Glenthøj and Ottosen, *Experiences of War and Nationality in Denmark and Norway*, 30–31. Also see H. Arnold Barton, *Scandinavia in the Revolutionary Era, 1760–1815* (Minneapolis: University of Minnesota Press, 1986), 277–78.

27. John D. Grainger, *The British Navy in the Baltic* (Woodbridge: Boydell Press, 2014), 167–71; Ryan, "The Causes of the British Attack upon Copenhagen in 1807," 51–52.

28. Glenthøj and Ottosen, *Experiences of War and Nationality in Denmark and Norway*, 29–31.

29. J. Bernstorff to Prince Regent, August 3, 1807, in *Historisk Tidsskrift* 6, no. 1 (1887–88): 38.

30. See Glenthøj and Ottosen, *Experiences of War and Nationality in Denmark and Norway*, 42–45.

31. Grainger, *The British Navy in the Baltic*, 173.

32. Sir Arthur Paget, *The Paget Papers: Diplomatic and Other Correspondence of the Right Hon. Sir Arthur Paget, G.C.B., 1794–1807*, ed. Augustus Berkeley Paget (London: W. Heinemann, 1896), II:376.

33. Avgustina Stanislavskaya, *Russko-angliiskie otnosheniya i problemy Sredizemnomorya, 1798–07* (Moscow: USSR Academy of Sciences, 1962), 482.

34. Declaration on the Rupture of the Peace with England, November 5, 1807, in *PSZ*, XXIX:1306–8.

35. Public memory of the British attack lasted for a long time, sustained by the visible scars of the attacks that Copenhagen bore well into the 1830s.

36. The French military presence in northern Germany, of course, played a key role in ensuring that the Danish government had no other viable option apart from surrendering Holstein, Schleswig, or other parts of their realm.

37. In total, the Danes and Norwegians seized some 2,000 British merchant vessels during the war, occasionally battling (with some success) British warships too.

38. T. K. Derry, *History of Scandinavia* (Minneapolis: University of Minnesota Press, 1979), 204–5.

39. Jón Rúnar Sveinsson, *Society, Urbanity and Housing in Iceland* (Gävle, Sweden: Meyers, 2000), 43. The total population of Iceland was slightly over 47,000 people. Richard Tomasson, *Iceland: The First New Society* (Minneapolis: University of Minnesota Press, 1980), 58.

40. Anna Agnarsdottir, "Scottish Plans for the Annexation of Iceland, 1785–1813," *Northern Studies* 29 (1992): 83–91.

41. For details, see Anna Agnarsdottir, "The Imperial Atlantic System: Iceland and Britain During the Napoleonic Wars," in *Atlantic History: History of the Atlantic System 1580–1830*, ed. Horst Pietschmann (Gottingen: Vandenhoeck & Ruprecht, 2002), 497–512; Agnarsdottir, "The Challenge of War on Maritime Trade in the North Atlantic: The Case of the British Trade to Iceland during the Napoleonic Wars," in *Merchant Organization and Maritime Trade in*

the North Atlantic, 1660–1815, ed. Olaf Uwe Jansen (St. John's, Newfoundland: International Maritime Economic History Association, 1998), 221–58. On Joseph Banks and Iceland, see Anna Agnarsdóttir, ed., *Sir Joseph Banks, Iceland and the North Atlantic 1772–1820: Journals, Letters and Documents* (London: Hakluyt Society, 2016).

42. Samuel Phelps, *Observations on the Importance of Extending the British Fisheries Etc.* (London: W. Simpkin, 1817), 58.

43. Gunnar Karlsson, *The History of Iceland* (Minneapolis: University of Minnesota Press, 2000), 195–96.

44. For a biographical study, see Sarah Bakewell, *The English Dane: From King of Iceland to Tasmanian Convict* (New York: Random House, 2011).

45. Jørgen Jørgensen, *The Convict King, Being the Life and Adventures of Jorgen Jorgenson* (London: Ward & Downey, 1891), 69–70.

46. Jørgensen spent two years in prison. After his release he led a peripatetic life, traveling in Europe and Australia.

47. Anna Agnarsdóttir, "Iceland Under British Protection During the Napoleonic Wars," in *Scandinavia in the Age of Revolution: Nordic Political Cultures, 1740–1820*, ed. Pasi Ihalainen, Karin Sennefelt, Michael Bregnsbo, and Patrik Winton (Burlington, VT: Ashgate, 2011), 255–66.

48. Jorgensen, *The Anglo-Swedish Alliance*, 100–125.

49. Russia received additional territories in Finland, including the cities of Friedrichsham, Wilmanstrandt (Lappeenrantd), and Neschlodt (Savonlinna).

50. Sam Clason, *Gustaf IV Adolf och den europeiska krisen under Napoleon: Historiska uppsatser* (Stockholm: Geber, 1913), 102–3. The diplomat in question was Curt Bogislaus Ludvig Kristoffer von Stedingk, Sweden's ambassador to Russia, who had submitted a report on his conversation with the Russian Chancellor Nikolai Rumyantsev. Stedingk to Gustavus IV, December 5, 1807, in *Mémoires posthumes du Feld-Maréchal Comte de Stedingk* (Paris: Arthus-Bertrand, 1845), II:398.

51. Clason, *Gustaf IV Adolf*, 104.

52. For Russo-Swedish negotiations, see Clason, *Gustaf IV Adolf*, 104–15; Carl Henrik von Platen, *Stedingk: Curt von Stedingk (1746–1837): kosmopolit, krigare och diplomat hos Ludvig XVI, Gustavus III och Katarina den stora* (Stockholm: Atlantis, 1995), 241–44.

53. Henry Crabb Robinson, *Diary, Reminiscences and Correspondence*, ed. Thomas Sadler (Boston: Fields, Osgood, 1870), I:167.

54. "Declaration on Imposing Embargo on the English Vessels," November 9, 1807, *PSZ*, XXIX:1316. On the eve of the declaration, the Russian government sent out secret instructions to port authorities to detain British ships, but the news soon spread, causing dozens of British ships to hastily depart from the Russian ports. At Kronstadt and Riga alone, more than sixty British vessels, fully laden with goods, weighed anchor and escaped. M. Zlotnikov, *Kontinentalnaya blokada i Rossiya* (Moscow: Nauka, 1966), 136–37.

55. The Russian diplomats provided a steady stream of intelligence reports on the Swedish military installations and armed forced. See Clason, *Gustaf IV Adolf*, 124–29.

56. Alexander Mikhailovsky-Danilevsky, *Opisanie Finlyandskoi Voiny v 1808 i 1809 godakh* (St. Petersburg, 1841), 7–9; G. Zakharov, *Russko-Shvedskaya Voina 1808–09 gg.* (Moscow, 1940), 10; *Narrative of the Conquest of Finland by the Russians in the Years 1808–09: From an Unpublished Work by a Russian Officer of Rank,* ed. Gen. Monteith (London, 1854), 1–2. The latter source is an English translation of a study by General Paul Suchtelen, who participated in the campaign.

57. *Narrative of the Conquest of Finland*, 3–4. What was more, the Danish envoy to St. Petersburg, Otto von Blome, had also told Stedingk that Russia intended to attack Sweden soon and that Denmark would be obliged to support this war effort. This information was ignored in Stockholm and the Swedish government learned of Denmark's commitments to Russia only on March 7, 1808, two weeks after the Russian invasion of Finland had commenced, and even then only after a Russian diplomatic courier was seized north of Stockholm and his documents confiscated. I am grateful to Morten Nordhagen Ottosen for bringing this information to my attention.

58. The Swedes were able to mobilize some 50,000 men, but of these only 19,000 (14,984 regular troops and 4,000 militia [*vargering*]) were under the command of General Carl Nathanael Klercker in Finland. A strong garrison of 7,000 men protected the fortress of Sveaborg, known as the Gibraltar of the North, on the coast of the Gulf of Finland. Erik Hornborg, *När Riket Sprängdes: Fälttågen i Finland och Västerbotten 1808–09* (Stockholm, 1955), 24; Johan Gustaf Björlin, *Finska Kriget 1808 och 1809* (Stockholm, 1905), 16.

59. Raymond Carr, "Gustavus IV and the British Government 1804–9," *English Historical Review* 60, no. 236 (January 1945): 58–61.

60. Gustavus to Klingspor, February 5, 1808, in Mikhailovsky-Danilevsky, *Opisanie Finlyandskoi voiny,* 16.

61. Clason, *Gustaf IV Adolf*, 130–34. The Russians even withheld Ambassador Stedingk's passports for some time and then rerouted him repeatedly to make sure that he would not arrive back in Sweden in time to warn of the impending attack.

62. "Proclamation of February 28," "Address to Local Population," "Address to Finnish Soldiers," February 22–28, 1808, *VPR*, IV:170, 176.

63. Generalstabens krigshistoriska afdelning, *Sveriges krig åren 1808 och 1809* (Stockholm: Kongl. boktryckeriet P. A. Norstedt & söner, 1890), II:101–76.

64. The Swedish War Council supported Field Marshal Mauritz Klingspor's plan to remain on the defensive and withdraw his forces to western Finland. See Generalstabens krigshistoriska afdelning, *Sveriges krig åren 1808 och 1809,* II:86–97; Hornborg, *När Riket Sprängdes,* 6, 13–14, 20–26, 31–36, 47–50; Anders Persson, *1808: Gerillakriget i Finland* (Stockholm, 1986), 19–20; Allan

Sandström, *Sveriges sista krig: de dramatiska åren 1808–09* (Örebro: Bokförlaget Libris, 1994), 16–17; Björlin, *Finska Kriget 1808 och 1809*, 18–24. Also see Martin Hårdstedt, *Finska kriget 1808–09* (Stockholm: Prisma, 2006).

65. Generalstabens krigshistoriska afdelning, *Sveriges krig åren 1808 och 1809*, II:159–65; Hornborg, *När Riket Sprängdes*, 87–99; Zakharov, *Russko-Schvedskaya voina*, 30–33; Mikhailovsky-Danilevsky, *Opisanie Finlyandskoi voiny*, 80–91; Petrus Nordman, *Krigsman och krigsminnen* (Helsingfors: Schildt, 1918), 120–22.

66. Alexander Bulgakov to Constantine Bulgakov, May 11, 1808, *Russkii arkhiv* 37, no. 3 (1899): 55; *Polnoe sobranie zakonov Rossiiskoi imperii*, XXX, no. 22,881.

67. Jacob von Ræder, *Danmarks Krigs- og Politiske Historie fra Krigens udbrud 1807 til freden til Jönkjöping den 10de december* (Copenhagen: Reitzel, 1847), II:98–102. The Danish declaration of war had been written on February 29, but its proclamation was deliberately delayed for two weeks because the Danes hoped the Russian invasion would force Sweden to seek a negotiated settlement and that the Danes would not have to fight.

68. Denmark was forced to make major territorial concessions as the result of the 1645 Treaty of Brömsebro (Norwegian provinces of Jämtland, Härjedalen, and Idre and Särna, as well as the Danish Baltic Sea islands of Gotland and Ösel) and the 1658 Treaty of Roskilde (Danish provinces of Scania, Blegkinge, Halland, and Bornholm and the Norwegian provinces of Bohuslän [Båhuslen] and Trøndelag). For details, see Michael Roberts, *The Swedish Imperial Experience, 1560–1718* (Cambridge: Cambridge University Press, 1979), 7–8; Robert Frost, *The Northern Wars: War, State and Society in Northeastern Europe 1558–1721* (New York: Longman, 2000), 135–41, 180–82.

69. For Danish diplomatic and military efforts on the eve of the war, see Ræder, *Danmarks Krigs- og Politiske Historie*, II:78–105, 158–66.

70. Ehrenheim to Wetterstedt, March 4, 1808, in *Handlingar ur v. Brinkman'ska archivet på Trolle-Ljungby*, ed. Gustaf Andersson (Ürebro: N. M. Lindh, 1865), II:211. Also see Carl Gustaf von Brinkman to Essen, March 9, 1808, in Hilma Borelius, *Carl Gustaf von Brinkman* (Stockholm: A. Bonnier, 1918), II:230–31. Carl Gustaf von Brinkman was deputy chancellor and Swedish ambassador to London.

71. Wetterstedt to Adlerberg, March 17, 1808, cited in Christer Jorgensen, "The Common Cause: The Life and Death of the Anglo-Swedish Alliance Against France, 1805–1809," Ph.D. diss., University College London, 1999, 144–45.

72. See Sven G. Trulsson, "Canning, den hemliga kanalen till förhandlingerna i Tilsit och invasionsföretaget mot Köpenhamn 1807," *Scandia* 29 (1963): 320–59.

73. Karen Larsen, *History of Norway* (Princeton, NJ: Princeton University Press, 1950), 366.

74. Elof Tegnér, *Gustaf Mauritz Armfelt* (Stockholm: Beijer, 1887), III:145–52.

75. Carl Fredrik Meijer, *Kriget emellan Sverige och Danmark, åren 1808 och 1809* (Stockholm: O. L. Lamm, 1867), 71–108; Ernst von Vegesack, *Svenska arméens*

fälttåg uti Tyskland och Norrige åren 1805, 1806, 1807 och 1808 (Stockholm: L. J. Hjerta, 1840), 102–10.

76. Hornborg, *När Riket Sprängdes*, 87–105; Björlin, *Finska Kriget 1808 och 1809*, 91–107, 248–60, 269–73.

77. For the Finnish guerrilla war, see Persson, *1808*; Jussi T. Lappalainen, Lars Ericson Wolke, and Ali Pylkkänen, *Sota Suomesta: Suomen sota 1808–09* (Hämeenlinna: Suomalaisen Kirjallisuuden Seura, 2007).

78. See Persson, *1808*, 125–43, 145–65.

79. Imperial Manifesto of June 17, 1808, and Imperial Decree of February 1, 1809, in D. G. Kirby, ed., *Finland and Russia, 1808–20: From Autonomy to Independence: A Selection of Documents* (London: Macmillan, 1975), 12–14.

80. Eino Jutikkala and Kauko Pirinen, *A History of Finland* (New York: Praeger, 1962), 147–50, 159–71, 176–77; Fred Singleton (with A. F. Upton), *A Short History of Finland* (Cambridge: Cambridge University Press, 2003), 58–60.

81. See Andreas Kappeler, *The Russian Empire: A Multiethnic History* (London: Longman, 2001), 60–212 (on Finland, 94–98). Also see Jyrki Paaskoski, "Venäjän keisarikunta ja Suomen suuriruhtinaskunnan synty 1808–20," in *Venäjän keisarikunta ja Suomen suuriruhtinaskunnan synty 1808–20* (Helsinki: Kansallisarkisto, 2009), 42–46; Max Engman, *Pitkät jäähyväiset: Suomi Ruotsin ja Venäjän välissä vuoden 1809 jälkeen* (Helsinki: Werner Söderström Osakeyhtiö, 2009).

82. Mulgrave to Saumarez, February 20, 1808, in James Saumarez, *The Saumarez Papers: Selections from the Baltic Correspondence of Vice-Admiral Sir James Saumarez, 1808–12*, ed. A. N. Ryan (London: Navy Records Society, 1968), 7. The squadron comprised *Victory* (100), *Centaur, Superb, Implacable, Brunswick, Mars, Orion, Goliath, Vanguard* (74s), *Dictator* and *Africa* (64s), and five frigates. See also Tom Voelcker, *Admiral Saumarez Versus Napoleon: The Baltic, 1807–12* (Woodbridge: Boydell Press, 2008), 34–38.

83. Admiralty to Saumarez, April 16–22, 1808, in *The Saumarez Papers*, 11–14. Also see Castlereagh to the King, April 17, 1808, in George III, *The Later Correspondence of George III*, ed. A. Aspinall (Cambridge: Cambridge University Press, 1970), V:65–66; Christopher Hall, *British Strategy in the Napoleonic Wars, 1803–1815* (Manchester: Manchester University Press, 1992), 163–64; Rory Muir, *Britain and the Defeat of Napoleon, 1807–1815* (New Haven: Yale University Press, 1996), 26.

84. Voelcker, *Admiral Saumarez Versus Napoleon*, 38–41. This problem stemmed from the Swedish minister in London who far exceeded in his instructions in the assurances he gave the British government.

85. Cited in D. W. Davies, *Sir John Moore's Peninsular Campaign 1808–1809* (The Hague: Martinus Nijhoff, 1974), 35.

86. See Jorgensen, *The Anglo-Swedish Alliance*, 145–52.

87. Voelcker, *Admiral Saumarez versus Napoleon*, 38–42; Hall, *British Strategy*, 165.

88. Charles Oman, *A History of the Peninsular War* (1902; rpt., Oxford: Clarendon Press, 2004), I:369–70.

89. In fact, as early as April 1808, George Canning expressed interest in helping Romana's division to escape from Denmark.

90. See James Robertson, *Narrative of a Secret Mission to the Danish Islands in 1808* (London: Longman, Roberts, and Green, 1863), 1–83.

91. See Paul Louis Hippolyte Boppe, *Les Espagnols à la Grande-Armée: le corps de la Romana, 1807–08; le régiment Joseph-Napoléon, 1809–13* (Paris: C. Terana, 1986).

92. Nikolai Dubrovin, "Russkaya zhizn' v nachale XIX veka," *Russkaya starina* 107, no. 9 (1901): 449.

93. It is worth noting that during the Russo-Persian War of 1804–13, British officers who accompanied Sir John Malcolm's 1809 embassy provided training to the reforming Persian army and accompanied it on an unsuccessful campaign in Georgia; one of these officers, William Monteith, later commanded a frontier force and the garrison of Erivan. See Chapter 16.

94. Among the first acts of the war, the British authorities detained Russian vesels in British ports, including the 44-gun Russian frigate *Speshnyy*, carrying the payroll for Vice Admiral Dmitry Senyavin's squadron in the Mediterranean, in Portsmouth, and the sloop *Diana*, sailing under command of Vasilii Golovin on a scientific expedition to the Pacific Ocean, in Simon's Town in South Africa.

95. For details, see Donald D. Howard, "Portugal and the Anglo-Russian Naval Crisis (1808)," *Naval War College Review* 34 (1981): 48–74; N. Skritskii, *Admiral Senyavin* (Moscow: Veche, 2013).

96. James Saumarez, *Memoirs and Correspondence of Admiral Lord de Saumarez*, ed. James Ross (London: Richard Bentley, 1838), II:98–101.

97. Voelcker, *Admiral Saumarez Versus Napoleon*, 55–56.

98. *Times*, July 29, 1809; *London Gazette*, August 22, 1809, July 9, 1811, February 24, 1810.

99. See Treaty of Örebro, July 18, 1812, in *British and Foreign State Papers, 1812–14* (London: James Rigway and Sons, 1841), I, pt. 1, 13–15.

100. Ehrenheim to Adlerberg, July 7, 1808, cited in Jorgensen, *The Anglo-Swedish Alliance*.

101. Jorgensen, *The Anglo-Swedish Alliance*, 140–52.

102. Anthony Merry to Canning, February 24, 1809, FO 73/54.

103. Anders Grade, *Sverige och Tilsitalliansen (1807–10)* (Lund: Gleerupska univ.-bokhandeln, 1913), 265–79.

104. Björlin, *Finska Kriget 1808 och 1809*, 216–31, 234–47; Alexander Mikaberidze, "'The Lion of the Russian Army': Life and Military Career of General Prince Peter Bagration 1765–1812," Florida State University, Ph.D. diss., 2003, 458–60.

105. I. I. Kiaiviarianen, *Mezhdunarodnie otnoshenia na severe Evropi v nachale XIX veka i prisoedinenie Finlandii k Rossii v 1809 godu* (Petrozavodsk: Karelskoe knizhnoe izd-vo, 1965), 36–41, 146–53, 172–93, 211–25.

106. Singleton, *A Short History of Finland*, 63–66.

107. Meijer, *Kriget emellan Sverige och Danmark*, 124–55.

108. Gustavus demoted three guard regiments and prosecuted more than a hundred officers for cowardice and desertion during the failed September 1808 landings in Finland.

109. For an in-depth discussion, see Sten Carl Oscar Carlsson, *Gustaf IV Adolfs fall: krisen i riksstyrelsen, konspirationerna och statsvälvningen (1807–09)* (Lund: C. Bloms boktryckeri, 1944).

110. See Merry to Canning, March 12, 1809, FO, 73/55.

111. The Swedes convened the Riksdag (national legislature) on May 1 to discuss Sweden's political future. The Riksdag drafted and approved a new constitution— it survived until 1975—that limited the power of the Swedish monarchy by delegating more power to the legislative body and to the Royal Council. Duke Karl of Sudermania was then elected king as Karl XIII (Charles XIII, 1809–1818) on June 5. Franklin D. Scott, *Sweden: The Nation's History* (Carbondale: Southern Illinois University Press, 1988), 295–96; H. Arnold Barton, "The Swedish Succession Crises of 1809–1810 and the Question of Scandinavian Union," in *Essays on Scandinavian History* (Carbondale: Southern Illinois University Press, 2009), 136–60; Allan Sandström, *Sveriges Sista Krig: De Dramatiska Åren 1808–09* (Örebro: Bokförlaget Libris, 1994), 127–59; Walter Sandelius, "Dictatorship and Irresponsible Parliamentarism—A Study in the Government of Sweden," *Political Science Quarterly* 49, no. 3 (1934): 347–71. King Gustaf Adolf remained in detention for nine months before being released. He left Sweden in December 1809, divorced his wife in 1812, and spent almost thirty years living in great loneliness and indigence in Switzerland, where he died in 1837.

112. For a historiographic overview, see Åke Sandström, "Sveriges 1809: föreställn-ingar om finska kriget under 200 år," in *Fänrikens marknadsminne: Finska kriget 1808–09 och dess följder i eftervärldens ögon*, ed. Max Engman (Jyväskylä: SLS Atlantis, 2009), 28–54.

113. H. Arnold Barton, "Late Gustavian Autocracy in Sweden: Gustaf Iv Adolf and His Opponents, 1792–1809," in *Essays on Scandinavian History* (Carbondale: Southern Illinois University Press, 2009), 118–20; Mikael Alm, "Dynasty in the Making: A New King and His 'Old' Men in Royal Ceremonies 1810–44," in *Scripts of Kingship: Essays on Bernadotte and Dynastic Formation in an Age of Revolution,* ed. Mikael Alm and Britt-Inger Johansson (Uppsala: Opuscula Historica Upsaliensia, 2008), 23–48; Pasi Ihalainen and Anders Sundin, "Continuity and Change in the Language of Politics at the Swedish Diet, 1769–10," in *Scandinavia in the Age of Revolution: Nordic Political Cultures, 1740–1820*, ed. Pasi Ihalainen, Michael Bregnsbo, Karin Sennefelt, and Patrik Winton (Farnham: Ashgate, 2011), 169–92.

114. Merry to Canning, March 14–19, 1809, FO 73/55.

115. Napoleon to Karl, April 12, 1809, in Peter A. Granberg, *Historisk tafla af F.D. Konung Gustaf IV Adolfs sednaste regerings-år* (Stockholm: C. Delén, 1811), II:151–52.

116. The British envoy had refused it, noting his government had no interest in getting involved in Sweden's internal affairs, especially when it involved bringing the uncooperative Gustavus back into power. Merry to Canning, April 21–25, 1809, FO 73/55.

117. Mikaberidze, "The Lion of the Russian Army," 467–77; Mikhailovsky-Danilevsky, *Opisanie Finliandskoi Voini v 1808 i 1809 godakh*, 396–408; K. Ordin, *Pokorenie Finlandii: opit opisanie po neizdannim istochnikam* (St. Petersburg, 1889), I:419–20; H. Algren, "Furst Barclay de Tollys tåg öfver Bottniska viken 1809. (Ur ryska generalen von Bergs efterlämnade papper)," *Svensk Militär Tidskrift*, 1914, 195–99.

118. Algren, "Furst Barclay de Tollys tåg öfver Bottniska viken 1809," 196–97. Also see Ordin, *Pokorenie Finlandii*, 421.

119. Mikhail Borodkin, *Istoriia Finliandii: vremia Imperatora Aleksandra I* (St. Petersburg, 1909), 198; Mikhailovsky-Danilevsky, *Opisanie Finliandskoi Voini v 1808 i 1809 godakh*, 404–8.

120. Karl to Alexander I, March 18, 1809, in Granberg, *Historisk tafla af F.D. Konung Gustaf IV Adolfs sednaste regerings-år*, II:145–46. Karl also wrote to the Danish king and Napoleon (II:147–48).

121. Ordin, *Pokorenie Finlandii*, 426. One of the participants, General Paul Suchtelen, observed, "Knorring was alarmed for the safety of his army: he was a talented and experienced general, but he was rather wanting in an adventurous spirit, without which success in war never can be complete. He tended to calculate risks to such a degree that it made him afraid of trusting anything to chance. Thus, he gave up on this glorious undertaking too easily, though not without a very reasonable motive." *Narrative of the Conquest of Finland by the Russians in the Years 1808–09: From an Unpublished Work by a Russian Officer of Rank*, ed. Gen. Monteith (London, 1854), 194. Hearing about Knorring's decision to withdraw to Finland, Swedish General Cronstedt remarked, "I cannot believe Knorring would act so imprudently." Borodkin, *Istoriia Finliandii*, 198.

122. Knorring to Barclay de Tolly, Knorring to Kulnev, Stroganov to Schultzenheim, Armistice Treaty (between Barclay de Tolly and Cronsdedt), Armistice Treaty (between Gripenberg and Shuvalov) 20–March 25, 1809, *VPR*, IV:539–41, 546–49, 693–94, 698–99. Alexey Arakcheyev, the Russian minister of war, shares responsibility for this decision. With the Russian forces about to invade the Swedish mainland, he realized the grave consequences any setbacks might have for the army and, more important, for himself. Therefore, he ordered a halt to the Russian offensive and requested additional instructions from Emperor Alexander, even though the emperor had already given him "unlimited authority throughout Finland." Considering the distance and time necessary to receive those instructions, Arakcheyev's actions simply wasted precious time that the Russians needed for invasion. Alexander to Arakcheyev, March 7/19, 1809, in Nikolai Shilder, *Imperator Aleksandr Pervyi, ego zhizn' i tsarstvovanie* (St. Petersburg: A. S. Suvorin, 1897), II:238; Ordin, *Pokorenie Finlandii*,

421; Mikhailovsky-Danilevsky, *Opisanie Finliandskoi Voini v 1808 i 1809 godakh*, 388–89; Borodkin, *Istoriia Finliandii*, 195, 199–200.

123. Voelcker, *Admiral Saumarez Versus Napoleon*, 90–92.

124. Ordin, *Pokorenie Finlandii*, 430–31; Borodkin, *Istoriia Finliandii*, 200.

125. For insights, see Lee Sather, *The Prince of Scandinavia: Prince Christian August and the Scandinavian Crisis of 1807–10* (Oslo: Försvaretsmuseet, 2015). I am grateful to Morten Nordhagen Ottosen for bringing this crucial work to my attention.

126. Meijer, *Kriget emellan Sverige och Danmark*, 189–98.

127. Erik Hamnström, *Freden i Fredrikshamn* (Uppsala: Wretmans tryckeri, 1902), 83–87, 91.

128. Hamnström, *Freden i Fredrikshamn,* 104.

129. Originaltraktater med främmande makter (traktater), 17 September 1809, Riksarkivet (Swedish National Archives), SE/RA/25.3/2/44/A (1809).

130. Although for some Swedes this was a moment of "national trauma," overall Swedish public response to the loss of the "proud Finnish nation" was in fact rather muted. It was only in the second half of the nineteenth century that the writings of nationalist Swedish historians began to describe the events of 1808–1809 as a "national catastrophe." See Henrik Edgren, "Traumakonstruktionen: Svensk historieskrivning om rikssprängningen 1809," *Scandia* 76, no. 1 (2010): 9–39.

131. Petri Karonen, *Pohjoinen suurvalta: Ruotsi ja Suomi 1521–1809* (Helsinki: WS Bookwell, 2008), 434–36.

132. Oswald Kuylenstierna, *Karl Johan och Napoleon 1797–1814* (Stockholm: Geber, 1914), 172–77.

133. Hans Klaeber, *Marskalk Bernadotte: Kronprins af Sverige* (Stockholm: Norstedt, 1913), 250–58.

134. Napoleon to Bernadotte, September 10, 1810, in *CN*, XXI:100.

135. Dunbar Plunket Barton, *Bernadotte and Napoleon, 1763–1810* (London: John Murray, 1921), 307.

Chapter 16

1. For a more in-depth treatment, see Suraiya N. Faroqhi, ed., *The Cambridge History of Turkey*, vol. 3, *The Later Ottoman Empire, 1603–1839* (Cambridge: Cambridge University Press, 2006), 135–225.

2. For an interesting overview of the Ottoman Empire in the eighteenth century, see Ali Yaycioglu, *Partners of the Empire: The Crisis of the Ottoman Order in the Age of Revolutions* (Stanford, CA: Stanford University Press, 2016), 17–156. For a more in-depth look at challenges the Ottomans faced even at their capital city, see Betül Başaran, *Selim III: Social Control and Policing in Constantinople at the End of the Eighteenth Century: Between Crisis and Order* (Boston: Brill, 2014), 13–105; Betül Başaran and Cengiz Kirli, "Some Observations on Constantinople's Artisans During the Reign of Selim III (1789–1808)," in *Bread from the Lion's*

Mouth: Artisans Struggling for a Livelihood in Ottoman Cities, ed. Suraiya Faroqhi (New York: Berghahn Books, 2015), 259–77.

3. For a good overview of the Ottoman military ups and downs, see Virginia H. Aksan, "War and Peace," in *The Cambridge History of Turkey*, vol. 3, *The Later Ottoman Empire, 1603–1839*, ed. Suraiya N. Faroqhi (Cambridge: Cambridge University Press, 2006), 81–118.

4. Virginia H. Aksan has shown that the influence of the French technical specialists, while important, has been exaggerated in the casting of artillery and in the recruiting and training of new units of field artillery. See her "Breaking the Spell of the Baron de Tott: Reframing the Question of Military Reform in the Ottoman Empire, 1760–1830," *International History Review* 24, no. 2 (2002): 258–63.

5. For an in-depth discussion of the Ottoman naval reforms, see Tuncay Zorlu, *Innovation and Empire in Turkey: Sultan Selim III and the Modernisation of the Ottoman Navy* (London: Tauris Academic Studies, 2008).

6. As Virginia Aksan has argued, Selim's military reforms must be placed with the context of "the climate and articulation of reform within Ottoman society." For Selim, the military changes were intricately involved with the reformulating of dynastic and religious ideology, incorporation of new elites into the center of power and the reforms of bureaucracy. See Virginia H. Aksan, *Ottoman Wars, 1700–1870: An Empire Besieged* (New York: Pearson, 2007), 180–81.

7. Aksan, *Ottoman Wars*, 192–97; Stanford J. Shaw, "The Origins of Ottoman Military Reform: The Nizam-I Cedid Army of Sultan Selim III," *Journal of Modern History* 37 (1965): 291–305. Also see Niyazi Berkes, *The Development of Secularism in Turkey* (Montreal: McGill University Press, 1964), 72–81; Gabor Agoston, "Military Transformation in the Ottoman Empire and Russia, 1500–1800," *Kritika: Explorations in Russian and Eurasian History* 12 (2011): 281–319.

8. See Zorlu, *Innovation and Empire in Turkey*, 15–76.

9. Enver Ziya Karal, *Selim III'ün hatt-i hümayunları: Nizam-i Cedit: 1789–1807* (Ankara: Türk Tarih Kurumu Basımevı, 1946), 81–93; Osman Özkul, *Gelenek ve modernite arasında Osmanlı ulemâsı* (İstanbul: Birharf Yayınları, 2005), 316ff.

10. Karal, *Selim III'ün hatt-i hümayunları*, 43–81.

11. For discussion of the expanded role of the *ulama* in government and diplomacy in the eighteenth century, see Madeline C. Zilfi, "The Ottoman Ulama," in *The Cambridge History of Turkey*, vol. 3, *The Later Ottoman Empire, 1603–1839*, ed. Suraiya N. Faroqhi (Cambridge: Cambridge University Press, 2006), 223–25; Uriel Heyd, "The Ottoman Ulama and Westernization at the Time of Selim IIII and Mahmud II," in *Studies in Islamic History and Civilization* (Jerusalem: Magnes Press, Hebrew University, 1961), 63–96.

12. Virginia Aksan, "Locating the Ottomans in Napoleon's World," in *Napoleon's Empire: European Politics in Global Perspective*, ed. Ute Planert (London: Palgrave, 2015), 283.

13. For an in-depth discussion, see Dušan Pantelić, *Beogradski pašaluk: posle svištovskog mira, 1791–1794* (Belgrade: Grafički zavod "Makarije," 1927).

14. Robert Zens, "Pasvanoglu Osman Pasa and the Pasalik of Belgrade, 1791–1807," *International Journal of Turkish Studies* 8, nos. 1–2 (2002): 89–104. Also see the sultan's orders and other documents in D. Ikhchiev, ed., *Turski dŭrzhavni dokumenti za Osman pazvantoglu Vidinski* (Sofia: Dŭrzhavna pechatnitsa, 1908), XXIV:1–128.

15. Vera Mutafčieva, *Kărdžalijsko vreme* (Sofia: Bălgarskata Akademija na Naukite, 1993), 143–83.

16. Ikhchiev, *Turski dŭrzhavni dokumenti*, 122.

17. Zens, "Pasvanoglu Osman Pasa and the Pasalik of Belgrade," 100–102.

18. See Sessions of the State Council, April 11–15 and August 8, 1801; Report of A. Vorontsov and V. Kochubei, July 6, 1801, in *Arkhiv Gosudarstvennogo Soveta*, III, part ii, 1189–90, 1191–4, 1197–8, 1200–1206.

19. Session of the State Council, August 8, 1801, *Arkhiv Gosudarstvennogo Soveta*, III, part ii, 1196–7.

20. Alexander to Knorring, September 12, 1801, April 23, 1802, *Akty sobrannye kavkazskoiu arkheograficheskoiu kommissieiu*, I:436, 689. Alexander instructed Paul Tsitsianov to " endeavor to gain for the Russian government the trust, not only of Georgia but of various neighboring states where they are accustomed to see only the cruelty of Persian power. They will regard every act of a strong state founded on justice and strength as, so to speak, supernatural. [In doing this you] ought to win their favor to it [Russian rule] quickly." Alexander to Tsitsianov, September 26, 1802, II:7–8.

21. The imperial manifesto was accompanied by instructions on the new system of administration in eastern Georgia. The realm was divided into five districts (*uezds*, three in Kartli and two in Kakheti) on the Russian model, with administrative centers at Tbilisi, Gori, Dusheti, Telavi, and Sighnaghi. With the Georgian royal family removed from power, the commander in chief on Russia's Caucasian front assumed to the leadership of the central government in Tbilisi and received the title of *pravitel* or administrator of Georgia. For details, see Nikolas K. Gvosdev, *Imperial Policies and Perspectives Towards Georgia, 1760–1819* (New York: St. Martin's Press, 2000); Laurens H. Rhinelander, "The Incorporation of the Caucasus into the Russian Empire: The Case of Georgia," Ph.D. diss., Columbia University, 1972; Zurab Avalov (Avalishvili), *Prisoedinenie Gruzii k Rossii* (St. Petersburg: Montvid, 1906); Nikolay Dubrovin, *Giorgii XII: Poslednii tsar Gruzii i prisoedinenie eia k Rossii* (St. Petersburg, 1897).

22. Meeting of the Secret Committee, March 31, 1802, in Grand Duke Nikolai Mikhailovich, *Graf Pavel Aleksandrovich Stroganov* (St. Petersburg, 1903), II:205.

23. The Austrian Habsburgs facilitated the migration of many Serbian families from Ottoman Serbia into southern Hungary (under Austrian control since

1686), while the Habsburg occupation of Belgrade (1719–39) brought Austrian authority to many Serbs south of the Danube. See Miroslav Đorđević, *Politička istorija Srbije XIX i XX veka*, vol. I, *1804–1813* (Belgrade: Prosveta, 1956), 25–54; Dusan Pantelic, *Beogradski Pašaluk posle svistovskog mira, 1791–1794* (Belgrade: Grafički zavod "Makarije," 1927).

24. For details, see Harvey L. Dyck, "New Serbia and the Origins of the Eastern Question, 1751–55: A Habsburg Perspective," *Russian Review* 40 (1981): 1–19; Lawrence P. Meriage, "The First Serbian Uprising (1804–1813) and the Nineteenth-Century Origins of the Eastern Question," *Slavic Review* 37 (1978): 422–23; Stanford Shaw, "The Ottoman Empire and the Serbian Uprising 1804–1807," in *The First Serbian Uprising, 1804–1813*, ed. W. S. Vucinich (New York: Brooklyn College Press, 1982), 71–94.

25. See relevant Serbian and Austrian correspondence in Aleksa Ivić, ed., *Spisi bečkih arhiva o prvom srpskom ustanku* (Belgrade: Srpska kraljevska akademija, 1935), I:34, 56, 69, 85–86, 154–60. For discussion of the Austrian response, see Adolf Beer, *Die orientalische Politik Österreichs seit 1774* (Prague: F. Tempsky, 1883), 183–85, 187–90, 196.

26. While rebuffing the Serbs, Russia strengthened ties with Montenegro, whose territory it hoped to use as a base for the Russian Mediterranean squadron. Norman E. Saul, *Russia and the Mediterranean 1797–1807* (Chicago: University of Chicago Press, 1970), 196–202.

27. For an interesting discussion, see Ercüment Kuran, *Avrupa'da Osmanlı İkâmet Elçiliklerinin Kuruluşu ve İlk Elçilerin Siyasî Faaliyetleri, 1793–1821* (Ankara: Türk Kültürünü Araştırma Enstitüsü Yayımı, 1968), 15–22; *Salnâme-i Nezaret-i Hariciyye* (Constantinople, 1884), 178–92; Carter V. Findley, "The Legacy of Tradition to Reform: Origins of the Ottoman Foreign Ministry," *International Journal of Middle East Studies* 4 (1970): 334–57; Carter V. Findley, "The Foundation of the Ottoman Foreign Ministry: The Beginnings of Bureaucratic Reform under Selim III and Mahmud II," *International Journal of Middle East Studies* 3 (1972): 388–416; J. C. Hurewitz, "Ottoman Diplomacy and the European State System," *Middle East Journal* 15 (1961): 141–52.

28. For broad surveys of the topic, see J. A. R. Marriott, *The Eastern Question: An Historical Study in European Diplomacy* (Oxford: Clarendon Press, 1940); M. S. Anderson, *The Eastern Question, 1774–1923: A Study in International Relations* (New York: St. Martin's Press, 1966); A. L. Macfie, *The Eastern Question, 1774–1923* (London: Longman, 1996); Lucien Frary and Mara Kozelsky, eds., *Russian-Ottoman Borderlands: The Eastern Question Reconsidered* (Madison: University of Wisconsin Press, 2014).

29. Baki Tezcan, *The Second Ottoman Empire: Political and Social Transformation in the Early Modern World* (Cambridge: Cambridge University Press, 2010), 9–10; Karen Barkey, *The Empire of Difference: The Ottomans in Comparative Perspective* (Cambridge: Cambridge University Press, 2008), 197–262; Donald Quataert, *The Ottoman Empire, 1700–1922* (Cambridge: Cambridge University Press,

2000), 37–53. On the Ottoman place in early modern history, see Palmira Brummett, "Imagining the Early Modern Ottoman Space from World History to Piri Reis," in *The Early Modern Ottomans: Remapping the Empire*, ed. Virginia H. Aksan and Daniel Goffman (Cambridge: Cambridge University Press, 2007), 17–58.

30. Cited in S. Solovyev, "Vostochnyi vopros 50 let nazad," *Drevniaia i novaia Rossiia* 2 (1876): 129. Also see V. P. Grachev, "Plany sozdaniya slavyano-serbskogo gosudarstva na Balkanakh v nachale XIX v. i otnoshenie k nim pravitel'stva Rossii," in *Rossiia i Balkany: Iz istorii obschestvenno-politicheskikh i kulturnykh svyazei (XVIII v.–1878 g.)*, ed. I. Dostyan (Moscow: Institut slavya-novedeniya i balkanistiki RAN, 1995), 8–9.

31. Fatih Yeşil, "Looking at the French Revolution Through Ottoman Eyes: Ebubekir Ratib Efendi's Observations," *Bulletin of SOAS* 70 (2007): 283–304.

32. Allan Cunningham, "The Ochakov Debate," in *Anglo-Ottoman Encounters in the Age of Revolution*, ed. Edward Ingram (London: F. Cass, 1993), 1–31; Nathaniel Jarrett, "The Specter of Ochakov: Public Diplomacy in Britain, 1791–1792," in *Selected Papers of the Consortium on the Revolutionary Era* (2014), 55–77.

33. See Mehmet Alaaddin Yalçınkaya, *The First Permanent Ottoman Embassy in Europe: The Embassy of Yusuf Agah Efendi to London (1793–1797)* (Constantinople: Isis Press, 2010).

34. See Katherine E. Fleming, *The Muslim Bonaparte: Diplomacy and Orientalism in Ali Pasha's Greece* (Princeton, NJ: Princeton University Press, 1999).

35. For an interesting discussion, see Virginia H. Aksan, "Ottoman-French Relations 1739–1768," in *Studies on Ottoman Diplomatic History*, ed. Sinan Kuneralp (Constantinople: Isis Press, 1987), 41–58.

36. The Ottoman government knew of the French preparations and was informed by the Russians that the French expedition could target Ottoman territory. Aware of the French involvement in Albania and the Ionian Islands, the Ottomans initially expected the French expedition to sail there but sought to clarify the situation with the French government. In July Ottoman ambassador Seyyid Mehmed Emin Vahid Efendi met French foreign minister Talleyrand, who assured him that France cherished its longtime ally and had no hostile intentions toward it. For details, see İsmail Soysal, *Fransız İhtilali ve Türk-Fransız Diplomasi Münasebetleri (1789–1802)* (Ankara: Türk Tarih Kurumu, 1999), 204–5; Ercüment Kuran, *Avrupa'da Osmanlı İkamet Elçiliklerinin Kuruluşu ve İlk Elçilerin Siyasi Faaliyetleri, 1793–1821* (Ankara: Türk Kültürünü Araştırma Enstitüsü Yayınları, 1988), 30; Azmi Süslü, "Ambassadeurs Turcs envoyés en France et Vahîd Pacha," in *Tarih Araştırmaları Dergisi*, no. 60 (2016):195–211.

37. See Ie. Metaxa, *Zapiski flota kapitan-leitenanta Iegora Metaksy, zakliuchayushchiie v sebe povestvovaniie o voiennykh podvigakh Rossiiskoi eskadry, pokorivshei pod nachal'stvom admiral Fiodora Fiodorovicha Ushakova Ionicheskiie ostrova pri sodeist-vii Porty Ottomanskoi v 1798 i 1799 godakh* (Petrograd, 1915), 12–14; Henri

Dehérain, "La rupture du gouvernement Ottoman avec la France en l'an VI," *Revue d'histoire diplomatique* 39 (1925): 9–43.

38. P. Pisani, "L'expédition Russo-Turque aux îles ioniennes en 1789–1799," *Revue d'Histoire diplomatique* 2 (1888): 190–222; James L. McKnight, "Admiral Ushakov and the Ionian Republic: The Genesis of Russia's First Balkan Satellite," Ph.D. diss., University of Wisconsin, 1965, 32–35; Saul, *Russia and the Mediterranean 1797–1807*, 59–69, 73–74.

39. Hutchinson to Elgin, April 25, 1801, FO Turkey 32; Hutchinson to Dundas, April 20, 1801; Hutchinson to Hobart, June 2 and 29, 1801, WO 1, 345.

40. James Philip Morier was private secretary to Thomas Bruce, Earl of Elgin, Britain's ambassador to the Ottoman Empire. He left an interesting account of the British invasion: *Memoir of a Campaign with the Ottoman Army in Egypt, from February to July 1800* (London: J. Debrett, 1801).

41. Morier's Memorandum, July 7, 1801, FO Turkey 32.

42. William Hamilton, *Remarks on Several Parts of Turkey. Part I. Ægyptiaca, or, Some Account of the Ancient and Modern State of Egypt, as Obtained in the Years 1801, 1802* (London: T. Payne, 1809), 6–8; Louis Pantaléon Jude Amédée Noé, *Mémoires relatifs à l'expédition anglaise: partie du Bengale en 1800 pour aller combattre en Égypte l'armée d'orient* (Paris: Imprimerie royale, 1826), 216–42.

43. Elgin to Hawkesbury, January 15, 1803, FO Turkey 38.

44. Napoleon to Talleyrand, August 29, 1802; Napoleon to Sebastiani, September 5, 1802, in *Correspondance de Napoléon*, VIII:9–10, 25–26.

45. Elgin to Hawkesbury, November 14, 1802, FO Turkey 36.

46. Hamilton, *Remarks on Several Parts of Turkey*, viii–ix.

47. Much of this discussion relies on AE "Turquie," 204. For the Ottoman accession to the Treaty of Amiens, see Act of Accession of May 13, 1802, in Gabriel Noradounghian, ed., *Recueil d'actes internationaux de l'Empire ottoman* (Paris: F. Pichon, 1900), II:50–52.

48. For the text of this treaty, see Definitive Treaty of Peace Between the French Republic and the Sublime Ottoman Porte, http://www.napoleon-series.org/research/government/diplomatic/c_ottoman.html. Article 6 of the treaty called for "the restorations and indemnifications which are due to the agents of the two powers, or to their citizens and subjects, whose effects have been confiscated or sequestrated during the war." During negotiations Napoleon drove a hard bargain, insisting on indemnifying only civilian losses. At the same time, he refused to consider losses sustained by the Ottoman civilians in Egypt but demanded Ottoman compensation for more than 1,800 French civilians who had been arrested (and their property seized) during the war. Considering that no Ottoman civilians had been detained in France, the Turks were clearly at a disadvantage. Ultimately, after more than a year and a half of negotiations, the sides had failed to reach a general settlement.

49. For details, see reports by E. Gandin (secretary at the French embassy in Constantinople), A. Raubaud (French agent in Smyrna), and V. Fourçade

(former vice consul at Crete), AE "Turquie," 204; AE Mémoires et Documents, "Turquie," 14, 64.

50. Markov to Vorontsov, March 17, 1803, in *SIRIO* (1891), LXXVII:69. Also see Emperor Alexander to Semen Vorontsov, January 20, 1803, in *Arkhiv Vorontsova*, X:304–5.

51. Albert Vandal, *Napoléon et Alexandre 1er: l'alliance russe sous le 1er Empire* (Paris: Plon-Nourrit, 1894), I:4.

52. Hawkesbury to Warren, February 1, 1803; Russian note of March 12, 1803, FO Russia 52.

53. Francis to Cobenzl, March 31, 1801, in Beer, *Die orientalische politik Oesterreichs seit 1774*, 771–72. In Francis's words, the Ottoman provinces that Austria was likely to receive were all mountainous and populated by "fanatical and rabid" populations that would resist any outside interferences.

54. AE "Turquie," 205.

55. AE "Turquie," 205. On Ali Pasha's anti-French activities, see Frédéric François Guillaume Vaudoncourt, *Memoirs on the Ionian Islands* (London: Baldwin, Cradock, and Joy, 1816), 240–53; Auguste Boppe, *L'Albanie et Napoléon, 1797–1814* (Paris: Hachette, 1914), 19–43.

56. Declaration of Neutrality, September 20, 1803, in Noradounghian, *Recueil d'actes internationaux de l'Empire ottoman*, 69–70.

57. See Czartoryski's memorandum, February 29, 1804, in *SIRIO*, 77:486–98.

58. Garlike to Warren, January 3, 1804; Warren to Hawkesbury, February 3, 1804, FO Russia 54; Vorontsov to Czartoryski, June 29, 1804, in *Arkhiv Vorontsova*, XV:230–33.

59. The Constantinople Convention, April 2, in *PSZ*, no. 19336, XXVI:88–92.

60. Kahraman Sakul, "Ottoman Attempts to Control the Adriatic Frontier in the Napoleonic Wars," in *Proceedings of the British Academy* 156 (2009): 253–70.

61. In August 1797 General Bonaparte informed the Directory that the Ionian Islands were of greater interest to France than the entire Italian Peninsula because they would enable France to directly intervene in Ottoman affairs. *Correspondance de Napoléon*, III:235.

62. For details, see A. M. Stanislavskaia, *Rossiia i Gretsiia v kontse XVIII–nachale XIX veka: Poltika Rossii v Ionicheskoi respublike, 1798–1807 g.g* (Moscow: Nauka 1976); J. L. McKnight, "Russia and the Ionian Islands, 1798–1807: The Conquest of the Islands and Their Role in Russian Diplomacy," MA thesis, University of Wisconsin, 1962.

63. Alexander to V. S. Tomara, January 14 and February 27, 1802; Alexander to G. D. Mocenigo. March 12, 1802, in *VPR*, I:167–68, 175–76, 182–83. For discussions of the French threat, see Russian diplomatic correspondence in *SIRIO*, 77:410–17; *Arkhiv Vorontsova*, XX:292–94; *VPR*, I:433, 513–17, 530–31, 557.

64. Czartoryski to G. D. Mocenigo, August 12, 1804, *VPR*, II:111.

65. "Article pour l'arrangement des affaires de l'Europe a la suite d'une guerre heureuse (1804)" in Czartoryski, *Mémoires*, II:65–66. Czartoryski warned that

"when the Ottoman body becomes rotten and gangrene set in its vital elements, we will not suffer to see its fate decided in any way contrary to the major interests of Russia." Czartoryski to Semen Vorontsov, October 25, 1804, in *Arkhiv Vorontsova*, XV:277–79. Also see "Imperial Instructions to N. Novosiltsev," September 23, 1804, in *VPR*, II:138–46.

66. Record of the Meeting of N. N. Novosiltsev with Prime Minister Pitt, December 25, 1804, in *VPR*, II:226–27.

67. F. de Martens, *Recueil des traités et conventions conclus par la Russie avec les puissances étrangères* (St. Petersburg: A. Böhnke, 1895), XI:98–99.

68. Instructions to Gower, October 10, 1804, FO Russia 56.

69. Declaration of Alliance, November 6, 1804, *VPR*, II:175–76.

70. Czartoryski to Alexander Vorontsov, December 2, 1804, in Czartoryski, *Mémoires*, II:58. Signed in 1799, the treaty of alliance was supposed to last six years, but in January 1803 the sultan requested its renewal with Britain's accession to it. Russia initially refused to commit to the renewal. When the terms of the treaty of alliance were communicated to the British government, Czartoryski made sure to note that the Russian government "understands Eastern policies infinitely better because we are closer to the region that the court of St. James. We ask you, therefore, to listen to our advice, to follow our directions, not to interfere we with our operation or do anything without prior agreement with us." Czartoryski to Semen Vorontsov, May 15, 1805, *Arkhiv Vorontsova*, XV:301.

71. Czartoryski to Vorontsov, August 30, 1804, in *VPR*, II:120.

72. Draft text of the treaty in *VPR*, II:677–78; Armand Goşu, *La troisième coalition antinapoléonienne et la Sublime Porte 1805* (Constantinople: Isis, 2003), 129–33.

73. See correspondence between Charles Arbuthnot, Britain's ambassador in Constantinople, and Henry Phipps, Lord Mulgrave, Secretary for Foreign Affairs, in September 1805, FO Turkey 46.

74. Arbuthnot to Mulgrave, September 10, 1805, FO Turkey 46.

75. Goşu, *La troisième coalition antinapoléonienne et la Sublime Porte*, 25–42; E. Verbitskii, "Peregovory Rossii i Osmanskoi imperii o vozobnovlienii soyuznogo dogovora 1798 (1799) g.," in *Rossiia i Iugo-Vostochnaia Evropa*, ed. A. Narochnitskii (Kishinev: Shtiintsa, 1984), 60–67.

76. See text of the treaty in Noradounghian, *Recueil d'actes internationaux de l'Empire ottoman*, II:70–77.

77. AE "Turquie," 207.

78. Napoleon to Brune, March 14, 1804, in Ignace de Testa, ed., *Recueil des traités de la Porte Ottomane, avec les puissances étrangères* (Paris: Amyot, 1864), II:255.

79. AE "Turquie," 208.

80. Brune to Napoleon, May 22, 1804; Selim III to Napoleon, May 18, 1804, in Testa, *Recueil des traités de la Porte Ottomane*, II:256–69.

81. AE "Turquie," 206.

82. For details, see Edouard Driault, *Napoléon et l'Europe: Austerlitz, la fin du Saint-empire (1804–1806)* (Paris: F. Alcan, 1912), 80–90.

83. See Russian and British notes in Testa, ed., *Recueil des traités de la Porte Ottomane*, II:346–47.

84. See correspondence on this matter in Testa, ed., *Recueil des traités de la Porte Ottomane*, II:339–52. Also see Enver Ziya Karal, *Halet efendinin Paris Büyük elçiliği (1802–1806)* (İstanbul: Kanaat Basımevi, 1940), 68–74.

85. P. Coquelle, "L'ambassade du maréchal Brune à Constantinople (1803–1805)," in *Revue d'histoire diplomatique* 18 (1904): 71; Italinskii to the Ottoman government, October 8 and December 15, 1804, in *VPR*, II:156–58, 204–6.

86. Brune's explanatory letter in Testa, ed., *Recueil des traités de la Porte Ottomane*, II:349–50.

87. Napoleon to Selim III, January 30, 1805, in *CN*, no. 8298, X:130. Napoleon also complained of the Ottoman failure to do something about continued Russian military movements through the straits to the Ionian islands and Corfu. Napoleon to Brune, July 27, 1807, in Testa, ed., *Recueil des traités de la Porte Ottomane*, II:270–71. Determined to meet the perceived Ottoman menace with menace, Napoleon also contemplated a possibility of partitioning the Porte as the "best way to deliver a crushing blow to Russia and to Austria"; one of the memorandums prepared by the French foreign ministry envisioned inciting a Greek uprising and dispatching a French force to European Turkey with a goal of restoring the "Eastern Greek Empire," which would serve as an "insurmountable barrier" for other powers. AE "Turquie," 210.

88. Arbuthnot to Mulgrave, February 6, 1806, FO Turkey 49.

89. For Ruffin's reports, see AE "Turquie," 210, 211.

90. Enver Ziya Karal, *Selim III. ün Hatt-i Humayunlari* (Ankara: Türk Tarih Kurumu basımevi, 1942), 91.

91. See Italiinskii's note to the Porte in *VPR*, III:37–38. Also see Arbuthnot to Mulgrave (with enclosed note of February 4), February 6, 1806, FO Turkey 49.

92. Nihat Karaer, "Abdürrahim Muhib Efendi'nin Paris Büyükelçiliği (1806–1811) ve Döneminde Osmanlı Fransız Diplomasi Ðlişkileri," *Osmanlı Tarihi Araştırma ve Uygulama Merkezi Dergisi*, no. 30 (2011): 4–5. Anticipating a change, Talleyrand in fact sent his trusted secretary on a special mission to Constantinople in order to assure the Ottomans of Napoleon's good intentions and to urge Kethüda Ibrahim Nesim Efendi, who was considered pro-French and had good relations with the French chargé d'affaires Pierre Ruffin, to influence Ottoman policy in France's favor. The office of *kethüda* was the second most important in the Porte, granting its holder, who was a deputy to the grand vizier, immense authority in home and military affairs.

93. Driault, *Napoléon et l'Europe: Austerlitz*, 404–5; Vernon J. Puryear, *Napoleon and the Dardanelles* (Berkeley: University of California Press, 1951), 58–59. As part of his efforts to woo the Ottomans, Napoleon had his famed bulletins and other propaganda pieces translated into Turkish and sent to Constantinople. Napoleon to Cambaceres, December 11, 1806, in *CN*, XIV:64.

94. Napoleon to Selim III, June 20, 1806, in *CN*, XII:474.

95. Italiinskii to Czartory, March 14, 1806, *VPR*, III:82–83; Selim's letter to Alexander is enclosed in Arbuthnot's report of March 21, in FO Turkey 49.

96. Karadjordje to Emperor Francis I, January 24, 1806; Francis I to Selim III, March 12, 1806; Selim III to Francis I, April 25, 1806, in *Spisi bečkih arhiva o prvom srpskom ustanku*, III:16–19, 69–71, 120–21; Beer, *Die orientalische Politik Österreichs seit 1774*, 193–95.

97. Notes of the January 1806 Meeting of the State Council, in *SIRIO* (1892), LXXXII:240.

98. For French consular reports see AE Correspondance consulaire et commerciale, "Jassy," 1; "Bucarest," 2. Some of the Bucarest reports, especially post-1809, have been printed in *Documente privitoare la Istoria Românilor. Corespondentă diplomatica și rapoarte consulare franceze: (1603–1824)* (Bucharest: Acad. Rom. și Ministerul Cultelor și Instrucțiunii Publice, 1912), XVI:652ff.

99. Italiinskii to Czartoryski, April 12, 1806, *VPR*, III:110–14.

100. Gower to Mulgrave, March 2, 1806, FO Russia 62.

101. Memorandum of early January 1806, in *VPR*, III:11.

102. Memorandum of January 23, 1806 (no. 76), in *SIRIO* (1892), LXXXII:254. See also Czartoryski's other memorandums in *SIRIO* (1892), LXXXII:265–75, 315–16, 322–24.

103. Memorandum of January 23, 1806 (no. 77), in *SIRIO*, 82:265.

104. Paul Pisani, *La Dalmatie de 1797 à 1815* (Paris: A. Picard et fils, 1893), 160–65.

105. Grand Duke Nikolai Mikhailovich, *Graf Pavel Aleksandrovich Stroganov (1774–1817)* (St. Petersburg: Eksp. Zag. Gos. Bumag, 1903), III:1–3.

106. Czartoryski to Stroganov, February 6, 1806, in Nikolai Mikhailovich, *Graf Pavel Aleksandrovich Stroganov*, III:9–12; Semen Vorontsov to Czartoryski, March 31, 1806, in *Arkhiv Vorontsova*, XV:389–95.

107. Fox to Gower, April 29, 1806, FO Russia 62.

108. Arbuthnot to Mulgrave, January 20 and February 15, 1806, F.O. Turkey 49. Also see Czartoryski's memorandum of May 25, 1806, in Mikhailovich, *Graf Pavel Aleksandrovich Stroganov*, III:18–22.

109. After the setback in Britain, the Russian government adopted a different approach, considering making a deal with Napoleon whereby Russia would tolerate the latter's influence in Italy, on condition that France renounce any intention of encroaching upon the Ottoman Empire or of acquiring a preponderant influence there. Memorandum of March 7, 1806 (no. 85), in *SIRIO* (1892), LXXXII:320–21.

110. Nihat Karaer, "Abdürrahim Muhib Efendi'nin Paris Büyükelçiliği (1806–1811) ve Döneminde Osmanlı-Fransız Diplomasi Ilişkileri," *Osmanlı Tarihi Araştırma ve Uygulama Merkezi Dergisi*, no. 30 (2011): 4–6.

111. Ruffin to Talleyrand, March 27, 1806, *Documente privitoare la Istoria Românilor* (Bucharest: I. V. Socecŭ, 1885), II:334–35. Also see Bekir Günay, *Paris'te bir Osmanlı: Seyyid Abdurrahim Muhib Efendi'nin Paris sefirliği ve Büyük Sefaretnamesi* (İstanbul: Kitabevi, 2009).

112. For an interesting discussion of capitulations and the role of foreign trade, see Mehmet Bulut, *Ottoman-Dutch Economic Relations in the Early Modern Period* (Hilversum: Verloren, 2001), 54–59.

113. P. Coquelle, "Sébastiani, ambassadeur à Constantinople, 1806–1808," *Revue d'histoire diplomatique*, 18 (1904): 579–80, 594. Coquelle argues that the French agreed to this in return for the deposition of the *hospodars*.

114. Czartoryski to Italiinskii, June 13, 1806, in *VPR*, III:189–91. Also see instructions to Pierre d'Oubril, Russia's plenipotentiary to France, May 12, 1806, in *VPR*, III:134–36. D'Oubril was specifically cautioned against accepting any conditions that would limit or abrogate Russia's rights in the Ottoman Empire.

115. See the treaty text in *The Annual Register... for the Year 1806* (London, 1808), 796–97.

116. See relevant correspondence in *VPR*, III:42, 45, 58–61.

117. Full text of the declaration is available in *VPR*, III:231–33.

118. P. Coquelle, "Sébastiani, ambassadeur à Constantinople, 1806–1808," *Revue d'histoire diplomatique*, 18 (1904): 576–78; Nihat Karaer, "Abdürrahim Muhib Efendi'nin Paris Büyükelçiliği (1806–1811) ve Döneminde Osmanlı-Fransız Diplomasi Ilişkileri," *Osmanlı Tarihi Araştırma ve Uygulama Merkezi Dergisi*, no. 30 (2011): 7–8.

119. A *hospodar* was a local prince in Wallachia and Moldova. *Hospodars* usually belonged to Phanariotes, a small caste of Greek and Hellenized Romanian and Albanian families who took their collective name from the Phanar or Lighthouse quarter of Constantinople. For a detailed discussion of local politics in Bessarabia, Wallachia, and Moldavia, see George Jewsbury, "Russian Administrative Policies Toward Bessarabia, 1806–1828," Ph.D. diss., University of Washington, 1970. For a comparative study, see Keith Hitchins, "Small Powers: Wallachia and Georgia Confront the Eastern Question, 1768–1802," in *The Balkans and Caucasus: Parallel Processes on the Opposite Sides of the Black Sea*, ed. I. Biliarsky, O. Cristea, and A. Oroveanu (Cambridge: Cambridge Scholars, 2012), 12–28.

120. Instructions to Italiinskii, May 28 and July 30, 1806, in *VPR*, III:180, 252–53. Also see Italiinskii's reports of August 23–30 in *VPR*, III:263–66, 284–87.

121. Although the Hatt-i Şerif of 1802 was in the form of a sultan's decree, it was regarded as a binding convention. The Ottomans tried to argue that because the decree emanated from the Porte, it could be annulled by it as well, but the Russians rejected such explanations. See the text of the decree in Noradounghian, ed., *Recueil d'actes internationaux de l'Empire ottoman*, II:55–67.

122. Alexander to Italiinskii, March 8, 1806; Budberg's memorandum, c. December 1806, in *SIRIO* (1892), LXXXII:325–28, 488–94.

123. Czartoryski to Emperor Alexander, March 7, 1806, in *SIRIO* (1892), LXXXII:315–19.

124. In a note presented on August 28, the Russian ambassador outlined a long list of grievances that required redress: obstacles to Russian trade and suppression of the *berats*; the non-observance of the tariff; the Porte's failure to implement

the Convention of 1800 regarding the Septinsular Republic; the abuses of the Ottoman notables on the Danube; the Porte's stated desire to restrict the passage of Russian warships through the straits. *VPR*, III:273–76.

125. A detailed account of the Ottoman deliberations is available in Arbuthnot's dispatches (FO Turkey 51), which also contain reports from a British diplomat, William Wellesley Pole, who was allowed to attend the Ottoman council meetings on October 12–13.

126. Alexander to Michelson, October 27–28 and November 4, 1806, in A. Petrov, *Voina Rossii s Turtsiei, 1806–1812* (St. Petersburg: Voenn. Tip., 1885), I:375–81. The sultan declared war on Russia on January 3, 1807. See Circular to Foreign Missions, in Noradounghian, *Recueil d'actes internationaux de l'Empire ottoman*, II:79–80.

127. See Alexander I to Kamensky, December 27, 1806; Budberg to Italiinskii, November 27, 1806, in *VPR*, III:381–84, 387–88, 439–41.

128. Petrov, *Voina Rossii s Turtsiei*, 54–121.

129. On December 23, 1806, the Ottoman General Council made the decision to declare war, and two days later confirmed that decision. The war was formally declared on December 27 and the news officially communicated on January 3, 1807. See Circular to Foreign Missions, in Noradounghian, ed., *Recueil d'actes internationaux de l'Empire ottoman*, II:79–80.

130. Napoleon to Fouche, December 31, 1806, in *New Letters of Napoleon I*, ed. Mary Lloyd (New York: D. Appleton, 1897), 35–36.

131. Napoleon to Selim III, January 1, 1807, in *CN*, XIV:128. See a similar letter of January 20 in XIV:220.

132. Napoleon to Sebastiani, January 20, 1807; Napoleon to Marmont, January 29, 1807, in Testa ed., *Recueil des traités de la Porte Ottomane*, II:290–93. Also see Nihat Karaer, "Abdürrahim Muhib Efendi'nin Paris Büyükelçiliği (1806–1811) ve Döneminde OsmanlıFransız Diplomasi Đlişkileri," *Osmanlı Tarihi Araştırma ve Uygulama Merkezi Dergisi*, no. 30 (2011), 6.

133. Alexander Mikhailovsky-Danilevsky, *The Russo-Turkish War of 1806–1812*, trans. and ed. Alexander Mikaberidze (West Chester, OH: Nafziger Collection, 2002), I:26–48.

134. Karal, *Selim III'ün hatt-i hümayunları*, 97–98.

135. William Clark Russell, *The Life of Admiral Lord Collingwood* (London: Methuen, 1901), 202–18; Max Adams, *Trafalgar's Lost Hero: Admiral Lord Collingwood and the Defeat of Napoleon* (Hoboken, NJ: John Wiley & Sons, 2005), 230–40.

136. Grenville to the Marquis of Buckingham, November 25, 1806, in *Memoirs of the Court and Cabinets of George III* (London: Hurst and Blackett, 1855), IV:101.

137. Lord Collingwood to Duckworth, January 13, 1807, in Robert Stewart, *Correspondence, Despatches, and Other Papers... of Viscount Castlereagh* (London: William Shoberl, 1848–1853), VI:151–53.

138. Nicholas Tracy, ed., *The Naval Chronicle: The Contemporary Record of the Royal Navy at War* (London: Stackpole Books, 1999), IV:12–35.

139. Sebstiani's report of January 27 and 30, cited in Talleyrand to Napoleon, March 4, 1807, in *Lettres inédites de Talleyrand à Napoléon*, ed. Pierre Betrand (Paris: Perrin, 1889), 321–23. On January 29, British ambassador Arbuthnot invited the British residents for a dinner on board a British ship, which, amid toasts and conversations, quietly raised sail and slipped out of Constantinople, with all guests still aboard it.

140. Henry Richard Vassall Holland, *Memoirs of the Whig Party During My Time* (London: Longman, Brown, Green, and Longmans, 1854), II:106.

141. Henry Blackwood to Lord Castlereagh, March 6, 1807, in *Memoirs and Correspondence of Viscount Castlereagh*, VI:165–66.

142. See French reports in AE "Turquie," 213. Sebastiani's reports show that the Spanish envoy and his staff also participated in the preparation of the defenses.

143. Henry Blackwood to Lord Castlereagh, March 6, 1807, in *Memoirs and Correspondence of Viscount Castlereagh*, VI:165–66; AE "Turquie," 213.

144. David Blackmore, *Warfare on the Mediterranean in the Age of Sail* (Jefferson, NC: McFarland, 2011), 258; John William Fortescue, *A History of the British Army* (London: Macmillan, 1910), VI:6–7.

145. Lord Burghersh to his father, March 6, 1807, in *Correspondence of Lord Burghersh, Afterwards Eleventh Earl of Westmorland, 1808–1840* (London: J. Murray, 1912), 8.

146. For details, see Georges Douin, *L'Angleterre et l'Égypte. La campagne de 1807* (Cairo: Institut français d'archéologie orientale du Caire, 1928), i–xxi; Fatih Yeşil, *Trajik Zafer Büyük Güçlerin Doğu Akdeniz'deki Siyasi ve Askeri Mücadelesi (1806–1807)* (İstanbul: Türkiye İş Bankası Kültür yayınları, 2017).

147. See relevant correspondence in Georges Douin, *L'Égypte de 1802 à 1804: Correspondance des Consuls de France en Égypte* (Cairo: Institut français d'archéologie orientale du Caire, 1925), 40–54.

148. For an interesting discussion on the French and British agents in Egypt, see Maya Jasanoff, *Edge of Empire: Lives, Culture and Conquest in the East, 1750–1850* (New York: Vintage Books, 2005), 226–29.

149. See *Gentleman's Magazine*, October 7, 1803; *Morning Herald*, October 8–November 1, 1803; London *Times*, October 10–December 17, 1803; *Morning Post*, October 17–November 9, 1803.

150. Afaf Lutfi Sayyid-Marsot, *Egypt in the Reign of Muhammad Ali* (Cambridge: Cambridge University Press, 1984), 38–41.

151. Cited in Sayyid-Marsot, *Egypt in the Reign of Muhammad Ali*, 46.

152. Henry Dodwell, *The Founder of Modern Egypt: A Study of Muhammad 'Ali* (Cambridge: Cambridge University Press, 1931), 17–19; Khaled Fahmy, *Mehmet Ali: From Ottoman Governor to Ruler of Egypt* (Oxford: Oneworld, 2009), 22–26, 29–31.

153. Sayyid-Marsot, *Egypt in the Reign of Muhammad Ali*, 42–74; a good description of Mehmet Ali's character is at 24–35.

154. Selim III tried removing Mehmet Ali just a year later. In June 1806 the sultan sent Musa Pasha, the *wali* of Salonika, with orders to trade places with the

Egyptian governor. Upon his arrival in Cairo, Musa Pasha realized that he lacked sufficient military force to enforce the sultanic edict.

155. For details, see Douin, *L'Angleterre et l'Égypte. La campagne de 1807*, 1–115; Fortescue, *A History of the British Army*, VI:8–28.

156. For French consul Drovetti's involvement, see Édouard Driault, *Mohamed Aly et Napoléon (1807–1814): Correspondance des consuls de France en Égypte* (Cairo: Institut française d'archéologie orientale, 1925), 65–66.

157. For the role of the British agent Misset in these setbacks, see Muḥammad Shafiq Ghurbal, *The Beginnings of the Egyptian Question and the Rise of Mehemet Ali* (London: George Routledge & Sons, 1928), 248–51.

158. Fortescue, *A History of the British Army*, VI:28. Also see John Marlow, *Perfidious Albion: The Origins of Anglo-French Rivalry in the Levant* (London: Elek Books, 1971), 121.

159. For an interesting discussion, see Kenneth M. Cuno, *The Pasha's Peasants: Land, Society, and Economy in Lower Egypt, 1740–1858* (Cambridge: Cambridge University Press, 1991); Khaled Fahmy, *All the Pasha's Men: Mehmet Ali, His Army, and the Making of Modern Egypt* (Cairo: American University in Cairo Press, 2002); Edouard Driault, *La formation de l'empire de Mohamed Aly de l'Arabie au Soudan (1814–1823): correspondance des consuls de France en Égypte* (Cairo: Institut français d'archéologie orientale du Caire, 1927).

160. Aksan, *Ottoman Wars*, 246ff.; Yaycioglu, *Partners of the Empire*, 157ff. For the Janissary rebel leader, see Ahmet Refik and Enfel Doğan, *Kabakçı Mustafa* (İstanbul: Heyamola Yayınları, 2005).

161. Stanford J. Shaw, *History of the Ottoman Empire and Modern Turkey* (Cambridge: Cambridge University Press, 1977), II:1–2; Yaycioglu, *Partners of the Empire*, 189–90.

162. Yaycioglu, *Partners of the Empire*, 203–4, 219–22; Mehrdad Kia, *The Ottoman Empire* (Westport CT: Greenwood, 2008), 104; Shaw, *History of the Ottoman Empire*, II:2–3.

163. Shaw, *History of the Ottoman Empire*, II:4–5.

164. Savary to Napoleon, November 4, 1807, in *SIRIO* (1892), LXXXIII:184.

165. For the text of the Treaty of Tilsit, see www.napoleon-series.org/research/government/diplomatic/c_tilsit.html.

166. Savary to Napoleon, September 23, October 9, and November 15, 1807; Guilleminot to Savary, September 28, 1807; Alexander to Napoleon, November 15, 1807, in *SIRIO* (1892), LXXXIII:78–82, 85, 122–23, 192–94, 220–34, 294–95; Rumyantsev to Tolstoy, November 6, 1807, in *SIRIO* (1893), LXXXIX:218–19. Also see Nihat Karaer, "Abdürrahim Muhib Efendi'nin Paris Büyükelçiliği (1806–1811) ve Döneminde Osmanlı-Fransız Diplomasi İlişkileri," *Osmanlı Tarihi Araştırma ve Uygulama Merkezi Dergisi*, no. 30 (2011): 11–12.

167. Savary to Napoleon, November 4, 1807, in *SIRIO* (1892), LXXXIII:180.

168. Instructions to Count Tolstoy, September 26, 1807, in *SIRIO* (1893), LXXXIX:106–12.

169. Napoleon to Savary, October 6, 1807, in *Correspondance de Napoléon*, XVI:74. Also see Champagny to Caulaincourt, April 2, 1808, in *SIRIO* (1893), LXXXVIII:594.

170. See transcripts of conversations between Emperor Alexander, Rumyantsev, and French ambassador Caulaincourt in Serge Tatistcheff, *Alexandre I et Napoléon: d'après leur correspondance inédite 1801–1812* (Paris: Perrin, 1891), 303–78.

171. See Articles 8, 9, and 11 of the Erfurt Convention, http://www.napoleon-series.org/research/government/diplomatic/c_erfurt.html.

172. See correspondence in AE "Turquie," 217. Also see Karaer, "Abdürrahim Muhib Efendi'nin Paris Büyükelçiliği," 15–16.

173. Herbert Randolph, *Life of General Sir Robert Wilson...from Autobiographical Memoirs, Journals, Narratives, Correspondence, Etc.* (London: J. Murray, 1862), II:436–37.

174. See text of the treaty in Noradounghian, ed., *Recueil d'actes internationaux de l'Empire ottoman*, II:81–85. For details on negotiations, see Robert Adair, *The Negotiations for the Peace of the Dardanelles in 1808–9, with Dispatches and Official Documents* (London: Longman, Brown, Green, and Longman, 1845), 2 vols. The text of the treaty is in I:118–23.

175. Adair to Canning, March 19, 1809, in Adair, *The Negotiations for the Peace of the Dardanelles in 1808–9*, 151.

176. "Discours a l'ouverture de la session du Corps Législatif," December 3, 1809, in *Correspondance de Napoléon*, XX:50.

177. Metternich to Stadion, August 17, 1808, in *Mémoires, documents et écrits divers laissés par le prince de Metternich* (Paris: Plon, 1881), II:197.

178. French writer Alphonse de Lamartine acquired al-Sayegh's manuscript and translated it into French in 1835. For an English translation, see *Narrative of the Residence of Fatalla Sayeghir: Among the Wandering Arabs of the Great Desert* (Philadelphia: Carey, Lea, and Blanchard, 1836). For a critical edition, see *Le desert et la gloire: les memoires d'un agent syrien de Napoleon*, trans. and ed. Joseph Chelhod (Paris: Gallimard, 1991).

179. For a critical review, see George M. Haddad, "Fathallah al-Sayegh and His Account of a Napoleonic Mission Among the Arab Nomads: History or Fiction?," *Studia Islamica* 24 (1966): 107–23.

180. Napoleon to Champagny, October 13, 1810, *Correspondance de Napoléon*, XXI:213–14. Napoleon repeated his order to the consuls on December 6, 1810, XXI:303.

181. Miroslav R. Đorđević, *Oslobodilački rat srpskih ustanika, 1804–1806* (Belgrade: Vojnoizdavački zavod, 1967), 372–75.

182. See correspondence in *VPR*, IV:367–68, 439–40, 456–58.

183. One Russian military historian aptly observed that Prozorovsky "still practiced the tactics of the 1769 campaign." A. Petrov, *Vlianie Turetskikh voin s polovini proshlogo stoletia na razvitie Russkago voennago iskusstva* (St. Petersburg, 1894), 227.

184. Petrov, *Voina Rossii s Turtsiei*, II:218–28. For details, see Alexander Langeron, "Zapiski Grafa Langerona. Voina s Turtsiei v 1806–1812 gg.," in *Russkaya starina* 132 (1907): 153–66; 133 (1908): 711–26; 134 (1908): 225–40. The Russians lost 2,229 killed and 2,550 wounded; some Russian regiments suffered almost 90 percent casualties—the 13th Jager Regiment lost 900 out of 1,100 men. A contemporary recalled that, seeing the assault gone wrong, "Prince Prozorovsky was in despair; he cried, fell to his knees, and tore his hair. Kutuzov was standing nearby, with his usual composure. To comfort the field marshal, he told him, 'Sometimes even worse happens; I lost the Battle of Austerlitz that decided the fate of Europe, and still I did not cry.'" Concerned about his position after this defeat, Prozorovsky perceived Kutuzov as a threat to himself and blamed him and other senior Russian officers for the failure. Kutuzov was recalled from the army and later served as a governor of Vilna.

185. It seems Prozorovsky's age prevented him from understanding the situation correctly. On July 1, he informed the Serbs that Russia had promised them only diplomatic and material support, and so the Russian army would not defend Serbia. Instead, Prozorovsky advised them "to wait for the advance of the Russian army across the Danube." Yet Isaev's detachment had been already cooperating with the Serbs for the past two years. In addition, Prozorovsky's suggestion to wait for the Russian advance was cynical considering the Turks were advancing toward Belgrade. Prozorovsky to the Serbian State Council, July 1, 1809, in Petrov, *Voina Rossii s Turtsiei*, II:275.

186. *Spisi bečkih archiva o Prvom sprskom ustanku* (Belgrade, 1936–1973), VI:294, 301–5; Grgur Jaksic, *Evropa i vaskrs Srbije, 1804–1834* (Belgrade: Narodna misao, 1927), 129–33; Petrov, *Voina Rossii s Turtsiei*, II:216, 274–75, 289–300; Dragoslav Jankovic, *Fracuska štampa o prvom srpskom ustanku* (Belgrade: Naučno delo, 1959), 292–303. Both sides fought with a remarkable ferocity. On one occasion, the Turkish commander decapitated several hundred Serbs and embedded their skulls into a "Tower of Skulls" at Nis. The remains of this tower could still be seen in the 1970s. Lawrence Meriage, "Russia and the First Serbian Revolution," Ph.D. diss., Indiana University, 1975, 193n.; Wayne Vucinich, "The Serbian Insurgents and the Russo-Turkish War of 1809–1812," in *The First Serbian Uprising, 1804–1813*, ed. Wayne Vucinich (New York: Brooklyn College, 1982), 141.

187. Vigel, *Vospominaniya F.F. Vigelya*, III:90.

188. Karadjordje to Isaev, September 16, 1809, *Voennyi sbornik* 11 (1864): 267–68. Bagration instructed Rodofinikin to respond to this letter. See Rodofinikin to Karadjorje, October 5, 1809, *VPR*, V:238–39; *Voennyi sbornik* 11 (1864): 268–70.

189. Rodofinikin to Karadjordje, October 5, 1809, *VPR*, V:238–39; Lazar Arsenijevic-Batalaka, *Istorija Prvog Srpskog Ustanka* (Belgrade, 1898–99), 702–3. Also see Karadjordje to Isaev, September 16, 1809, *Voennyi sbornik* 11 (1864): 266–72.

190. Bagration to Rodofinikin, December 18, 1809, *VPR*, V:684; Nikolay Dubrovin, "Materials for the History of Reign of Alexander," *Voennyi sbornik* 2 (1865): 223–24.

191. Rodofinikin to Bagration, October 24, 1809, *VPR*, V:225. Dubrovin noted that Karadjordje tended to exaggerate the threats, and he misunderstood Russian actions in 1808–1809. During their negotiations with the French, the Serbian delegates complained that Russia failed to fulfill its promises. Meriage to Champagny, February 21, 1810, in Ogis Bop [Auguste Boppe], ed., "Karadjordje i Francuska. Dokumenti o dogadjajima Srbije sa Napoleonom I (1809–1814)," *Otadžbina*, XIX (1888): 336–38.

192. Karadjordje to Ledoulx, August 16, 1809, in Bop, ed., "Karadjordje i Francuska," 118–20.

193. See relevant letters in Bop, ed., "Karadjordje i Francuska," 122–24, 336–38.

194. For details on Metternich's Eastern policies, see Vasilj Popović, *Meternihova politika na Bliskom Istoku* (Belgrade: Srpska kraljevska akademija, 1931).

195. Metternich to Emperor Francis, July 9, 1810, in *Mémoires, documents et écrits divers laissés par le prince de Metternich*, II:361; also see his report of July 28, II:369–80.

196. Metternich to Emperor Francis, July 28, 1810, in *Mémoires, documents et écrits divers laissés par le prince de Metternich*, II:369–71.

197. Martens, *Recueil des traités et conventions conclus par la Russie*, III:73–77.

198. Meriage, *Russia and the First Serbian Revolution*, 197–98; Vucinich, "The Serbian Insurgents and the Russo-Turkish War of 1809–1812," 146–51; Miroslav Djordjevic, *Politička istorija Srbije XIX i XX veka* (Belgrade: Prosveta, 1956), 263–65.

199. Canning to Wellesley, October 4, 1810, in Čeda Mijatović, ed., "Prepisi iz zvaničnih I poverljivih izveštaja engleske ambasade u Carigradu od 1804–1814," *Spomenik* 52 (1922): 80.

200. Mijatović, ed., "Prepisi iz zvaničnih," 81.

201. Grgur Jakšić and Vojislav Vučković, *Francuski dokumenti o prvom i drugom ustanku (1804–1830)* (Belgrade: Naučno delo, 1957), 71–72.

202. Canning to Wellesley, October 4, 1810, in Mijatović, ed. "Prepisi iz zvaničnih," 81.

203. Karadjordje to Stevan Jevtić, September 21, 1810, in *Josef Freiherr von Simbschen und die Stellung Österreichs zur serbischen Frage (1807–1810)*, ed. Franz Xaver Krones (Vienna: In Commission bei F. Tempsky, 1890), 128–31.

204. Bagration to Rodofinikin, December 1, 1809; Rofodinikin to Bagration, December 12, 1809, Bagration to Rumyantsev, December 25, 1809, January 10, 1810, *VPR*, V:313, 325–26, 343, 682; Arsenijevic-Batalaka, *Istorija Prvog Srpskog Ustanka*, 786–87; Djordjevic, *Politička istorija Srbije*, 265–71.

205. Hurshid Pasha to Karadjordje, November 21, 1809, *Voennyi sbornik* 2 (1865): 261–62.

206. Arsenijevic-Batalaka, *Istorija Prvog Srpskog Ustanka*, 716–22; Djordjevic, *Politička istorija Srbije*, 270–72.

207. Bagration to Rumyantsev, January 10, 1810, *VPR*, V:344. Also, *Voennyi sbornik* 2 (1865): 233. Archimandrite Melentje was presented with a diamond ring worth 900 rubles, Milan Obrenovic and Petar Dobrnjac were given gold swords with inscriptions for courage, and the secretaries and other members of the delegation received substantial sums of money. Metropolitan Leontije, an influential Serbian cleric, was appeased with embroidered vestments and a golden cross. Dubrovin, "Materials for the History of Reign of Alexander," 233–34; Bagration to Rumyantsev, January 10, 1810, *VPR*, V:344–45.

208. Bagration to Rodofinikin, January 5, 1810, *VPR*, V:335. There was also an earlier instruction dated November 24, 1809, but it is not preserved at the archives. However, Bagration repeated part of it in his next message to Rodofinikin.

209. Petrov, *Voina Rossii s Turtsiei*, II:475–76.

210. Bagration to Rodofinikin, January 5, 1810, *VPR*, V:336.

211. Vigel, *Vospominaniya F.F. Vigelya*, III:91.

212. Mikhailovsky-Danilevsky, *Russo-Turkish War of 1806–1812*, II:9–59.

213. Otto to Maret, March 6, 1811, in Jakšić and Vučković, *Francuski dokumenti o prvom i drugom ustanku*, 72–73; Beer, *Die orientalische Politik Österreichs seit 1774*, 253.

214. See details of General Radetzky's memorandum in Beer, *Die orientalische Politik Österreichs seit 1774*, 254.

215. Beer, *Die orientalische Politik Österreichs seit 1774*, 225–29.

216. P. Shuvalov to Rumyantsev, February 9, 1811, *VPR*, VI:44–48.

217. Martens, *Recueil des traités et conventions conclus par la Russie*, III:77.

218. Martens, *Recueil de traités et conventions conclus par la Russie*, III:78.

219. *VPR*, VI:48–50, 692–93.

220. Petrov, *Voina Rossii s Turtsiei*, III:249–77.

221. Text of the treaty in Noradounghian, ed., *Recueil d'actes internationaux de l'Empire ottoman*, II:86–92; *VPR*, VI:406–17.

Chapter 17

1. Jacob Coleman Hurewitz, *Diplomacy in the Near and Middle East: A Documentary Record* (Princeton, NJ: Van Nostrand, 1956), I:68–70. Also see R. Greaves, "Iranian Relations with Great Britain and British India," *Cambridge History of Iran* VII:375–79; M. Igamberdyev, *Iran v mezhdunarodnykh otnosheniyakh pervoi treti XIX veka* (Samarkand: Izd-vo Samarkandskogo Gos. Univ., 1961).

2. Malcolm Yapp, *Strategies of British India: Britain, Iran and Afghanistan, 1798–1850* (Oxford: Clarendon Press, 1980), 36–38.

3. See Donald Rayfield, *Edge of Empires: A History of Georgia* (London: Reaktion, 2012), 250–64; Ronald Grigor Suny, *The Making of the Georgian Nation* (Bloomington: Indiana University Press, 1994), 59–69; V. Togonidze, *Kartlis mtianetis glekhta ajanyeba (1804 ts.)* (Tbilisi: Sakhelgami, 1951).

4. Alexander to Tsitsianov, September 20, 1802, in *Akty*, II:3–4. Alexander believed that the Russian annexation of Georgia would allow for introduction

of the principles of the Enlightenment and modernity to what he considered a backward people. See Imperial Instructions to the Legal Commission, May 27, 1802, in *Akty*, VI, pt. 1, 78.

5. For a good overview, see Nikolas Gvosdev, *Imperial Policies and Perspectives Towards Georgia, 1760–1819* (London: Palgrave Macmillan, 2000), 99–116.

6. See Nikolai Dubrovin, *Istoriia voiny i vladychestva russkikh na Kavkaze* (St. Petersburg: Typ. I. N. Skorokhodov, 1886), IV:1–25, 339–60, 491–528; Gvosdev, *Imperial Policies and Perspectives Towards Georgia*, 102–6; Vladimir Lapin, *Tsitsianov* (Moscow: Molodaya gvardiya, 2011).

7. See documents in *Akty*, I:413–508.

8. "Since the time when the globe divided into four parts, [Georgia] was included in the Iranian state," noted Fath Ali Shah's chief vizier, Hajji Ibrahim. "In the time of previous Iranian shahs the inhabitants [of Georgia] always adhered by service and obediences to their [shah's] decrees but were never part of the Russian realm." Hajji Ibrahim to Kovalenskii, n.d. [1800] in *Akty*, I:97.

9. For example, Agha Muhammad Khan did not claim the title of shah until after his campaign in Georgia in 1795, which had provided him with grounds to claim that he had recovered formerly vassal territories of Georgia and neighboring territories. He was formally declared a shah in March 1796. See Gavin Humbly, "Agha Muhammad Khan and the Establishment of the Qajar Dynasty," in *The Cambridge History of Iran: From Nadir Shah to the Islamic Republic*, ed. Peter Avery et al. (Cambridge: Cambridge University Press, 1991), VII:129, 146–47; J. R. Perry, "Āḡā Moḥammad Khan Qājār," *Encyclopaedia Iranica* (online ed., 1982), available at www.iranicaonline.org/articles/aga-mohammad-khan. For an interesting discussion on the political reality of incorporating territories into the Qajar monarchy, see Firoozeh Kashani-Sabet, *Frontier Fictions: Shaping the Iranian Nation, 1804–46* (Princeton NJ: Princeton University Press, 1999). On the evolving notion of the "Guarded Domains of Iran" since the thirteenth century, see Ahmad Ashraf, "Iranian Identity. III: Medieval Islamic Period," in *Encyclopaedia Iranica* (online ed., 1982), available at www.iranicaonline.org/articles/iranian-identity-iii-medieval-islamic-period.

10. Edward Ingram, *Britain's Persia Connection, 1798–1828: Prelude to the Great Game* (Oxford: Clarendon Press, 1992), 80–82. "The British aversion to commitments in peacetime," notes Ingram, "may have been strengthened by their resentment of the demands made on them by the Qajar regime in Persia in the twenty-five years following the Napoleonic Wars....Like many similar arrangements between the British and foreigners, its legacy was bitterness and disappointment. Expecting to be offered help, the British resented being asked for it. They expected to fight Napoleon to the last Austrian and to defend India to the last Persian" (2).

11. See Tsitsianov to Kochubei, October 12, 1804; Tsitsianov to Czartoryski, June 29 and August 25, 1805, in *Akty*, II:812–13, 831, 847.

12. Z. Grigoryan, *Prisoedinenie Vostochnoi Armenii k Rossii v nachale XIX veka* (Moscow: Izd-vo sotsialno-ekonomicheskoi lt-ry, 1959), 66–76.

13. Dubrovin, *Istoriia voiny i vladychestva russkikh na Kavkaze*, IV:339–69, 392–400, 419–31, 466–77; Kh. Ibragimbeili, *Rossiya i Azerbaijan v pervoi treti XIX veka* (Moscow: Nauka, 1969), 64–65; Günal Teymurova, "1806–1812 Osmanli-Rusya Savaşi ve Azerbaycan," *Journal of Ottoman Civilization Studies*, no. 2 (2016): 48–49. Also see A. Ionnisian, *Prisoedinenie Zakavkaziya k Rossii i mezhdunarodnye otnosheniya v nachale XIX stoletiya* (Yerevan: Izd-vo AN Armyanskoi SSR, 1958); Vasilii Potto, *Kavkazskaia voina* (St. Petersburg: Tip. E. Evdokimova, 1887), volume 1; Y. Mahmudov and K. Şükürov, *Azerbaycan: Beynelhalq Münasibetler VeDiplomatiya Tarihi. 1639–1828* (Baku: 2009), I:356–63.

14. Dubrovin, *Istoriia voiny i vladychestva russkikh na Kavkaze*, IV:489–90.

15. "He was also endowed with administrative ability of a high order, coupled with an aggressive, over-bearing spirit, that served him admirably in his dealings with the native rulers, Christian as well as Mussulman though probably enough it contributed both to his own tragic fate and to that of one of his most valued subordinates.... [His wit] made him powerful enemies, yet taken with his soldierly qualities and care for those who served him well, secured him the love, the adoration almost of the army." J. Baddeley, *The Russian Conquest of the Caucasus* (London: Longmans, Green, 1908), 61–62. For a good discussion, see Muriel Atkin, *Russia and Iran, 1780–1828* (Minneapolis: University of Minnesota Press, 1980), 71–81; Gvosdev, *Imperial Policies and Perspectives Towards Georgia*, 103–16.

16. Dubrovin, *Istoriia voiny i vladychestva russkikh na Kavkaze*, V:61–83.

17. Gudovich to Alexander, September 27, 1807; Gudovich to Rumiantsev, September 27, 1807; Tormasov to Barclay de Tolly, January 28, 1811, in *Akty*, III:100, 707, IV:187–89; N. Beliavskii and Vasilii Potto, *Utverzhdenie Russkago vladychestva na Kavkaze* (Tiflis, 1901), I:197, II:270–71; Dubrovin, *Istoriia voiny i vladychestva russkikh na Kavkaze*, IV:436–37, V:19, 228–29, 234. For discussion of the quality of the Russian troops in the Caucasus, see Atkin, *Russia and Iran*, 104–7.

18. See Tsitsianov to Admiral Pavel Chichagov; Tsitsianov to Pevtsov, February 10, 1805, in *Akty*, II:735–37.

19. Caulaincourt to Napoleon, August 12, 1808, in Vel. Kn. Nikolay Mikhailovich, *Diplomaticheskie snoshenia Rossii i Frantsii po doneseniyam poslov Imperatorov Aleksandra i Napoleona, 1808–1812* (St. Petersburg: Ekspeditsia zagotovleniya gosudarstvennykh bumag, 1905), II:280. Also see the Russian memorandum on negotiations with Fath Ali Shah in *VPR*, III:726–27.

20. The Russian memorandum on negotiations with Fath Ali Shah (1806) is in *VPR*, III:726–27.

21. Arbuthnot to Adair, August 16, 1806, cited in Ingram, *Britain's Persian Connection*, 82.

22. Alexander to Gudovich, October 16, 1806, in *Akty*, III:420–21.

23. *Akty*, III:435.

24. *Akty*, III:437–38.

25. Alfred de Gardane, *La mission du Général Gardane en Perse sous le premier Empire* (Paris: Librarie de Ad. Laine, 1865), 24. Gardanne incorrectly identifies the Russian envoy as "Istifanow." In reality his name was Stepanov and he was one of Gudovich's aides-de-camp. Delayed in Tabriz for twenty days, Stepanov met Crown Prince Abbas Mirza only on January 4, 1807, just as the Iranian envoy was negotiating with the French in Poland. After another three-week delay, he was allowed to proceed to Tehran, where he was kept for almost six months without ever meeting the shah.

26. See AE "Turquie," 207; Napoleon to Talleyrand, September 28, 1803, in *CN*, IX:4.

27. Henri Dehérain, *La vie de Pierre Ruffin, Orientaliste et diplomate, 1742–1824* (Paris: P.Geuthner, 1930), II:25ff; Napoleon to Talleyrand, May 21, 1804, March 20, 1805, in *CN*, IX:357, X:238.

28. Napoleon to Talleyrand, June 9, 1806, in *CN*, XII:449–50.

29. Napoleon to Talleyrand, March 19 and April 7, 1805, in *CN*, X:237, 292–93.

30. N. Gotteri, "Antoine-Alexandre Romieu (1764–1805), général et diplomate," *Revue dromoise* 88, no. 468 (1993): 411–56; 88, no. 469 (1993): 476–564; Iradj Amini, *Napoleon and Persia: Franco-Persian Relations Under the First Empire* (Richmond, Surrey: Curzon, 1999), 65–75; Ch. de Voogd, "Les Français en Perse (1805–1809)," *Studia Iranica* 10, no. 2 (1981): 249.

31. Dehérain, *La vie de Pierre Ruffin*, II:30–31.

32. Alexander Stratton to Harford Jones, June 14, 1805, in *Correspondence, Despatches, and Other Papers of Viscount Castlereagh, Second Marquess of Londonderry*, ed. Charles William Vane (London: William Shoberl, 1851), V:420.

33. Napoleon to Fath Ali Shah, February 16, 1806, in *CN*, X:148–49.

34. B. Balayan, *Diplomaticheskaya istoriya Russko-iranskikh voin i prisoedineniya Vostochnoi Armenii k Rossii* (Yerevan: Izd.-vo AN Armyanskoi SSR, 1988), 45–46; Vernon J. Puryear, *Napoleon and the Dardanelles* (Berkeley: University of California Press, 1951), 57.

35. Romieu's report is at AE Correspondance Politique, "Perse," IX. A condensed version of the report is cited in Amini, *Napoleon and Persia*, 72ff. Romieu's report was later incorporated in Jean Rousseau's more influential *Tableau general de la Perse modern*, a lengthy manuscript that provided Napoleon with detailed information on Iranian history, geography, politics, traditions, etc., and thus helped shape French policies in Iran. For an in-depth discussion, see Irene Natchkebia, "Unrealized Project: Rousseau's Plan of Franco-Persian Trade in the Context of the Indian Expedition (1807)," in *Studies on Iran and the Caucasus*, ed. Uwe Bläsing et. al. (Leiden: Brill, 2015), 115–25.

36. Pierre-Amédée Jaubert, *Voyage en Arménie et en Perse: fait dans les années 1805 et 1806* (Paris: Pelicier, 1821), 17–68; Puryear, *Napoleon and the Dardanelles*, 46–52, 55–56, 155–57. Armenian historian Balayan claims that the British

agents had convinced Mahmud Pasha of Bayazid to detain the French envoy. Balayan, *Diplomaticheskaya istoriya Russko-iranskikh voin,* 47.

37. Fath Ali Shah to Napoleon, December 1806, AN AE/III/215; Amini, *Napoleon and Persia,* 76–89.

38. Napoleon to Talleyrand, March 13, 1807, in *CN,* XIV:437.

39. For related documents, see Treaty of Defensive Alliance, May 4, 1807, AN AE/III/54/a; Napoleon to Fath Ali Shah, January 17 and April 3, 1807; Napoleon to Talleyrand, April 27, 1807, in *CN,* XIV:207, XV:15, 152.

40. Napoleon to Fath Ali Shah, January 17, 1807, in *CN,* XIV:207.

41. Treaty of Defensive Alliance, May 4, 1807, AN AE/III/54/b; Edouard Driault, *La politique orientale de Napoleon: Sébastiani et Gardane, 1806–1808* (Paris: Alcan, 1904), 170ff.; Amini, *Napoleon and Persia,* 205–8.

42. Gardane was the grandson of Ange de Gardane, Louis XIV's envoy to the Safavid court at the start of the eighteenth century. Between Jaubert's departure and the arrival of Gardane, several other French envoys—Joseph-Marie Jouannin, Auguste de Bontemps-Lefort, Jean-Baptiste-Louis-Jacques Rousseau, and Xavier de La Blanche—visited Iran, reflecting the scope of Napoleon's interest in this realm.

43. Instructions pour le Général Gardane, May 10, 1807, *CN,* XV:210–14; Gardane, *La mission du Général Gardane en Perse,* 27–29, 81–99. See also Napoleon to Fath Ali Shah, April 20 and May 5, 1807, in *CN,* XV:119–20, 191.

44. The French legation comprised about three dozen people, including six interpreters, one physician, three missionaries, and thirteen military men (four engineer captains, one infantry captain, one cavalry captain, two artillery lieutenants, two engineer-geographer lieutenants, and three sergeants major). Gardane, *La mission du Général Gardane,* 103–5; de Voogd, "Les Français en Perse (1805–1809)," 253; Amini, *Napoleon and Persia,* 104–5.

45. Dubrovin, *Istoriia voiny i vladychestva russkikh na Kavkaze,* V:127–79. Also see Nikoloz Kortua, *Sakartvelo 1806–12 tslebis Ruset-Turketis omshi: rusi da kartveli xalxebis sabrdzolo tanamegobrobis istoriidan* (Tbilisi: Tsodna, 1964).

46. See Abbas Mirza's letter in *Akty,* III:436–37.

47. See Gardane, *La mission du Général Gardane en Perse,* 106–9; Henri Dehérain, "Lettres inédites de membres de la mission Gardane en Perse (1807–9)," *Revue de l'histoire des colonies françaises* XVI (1923): 249–82.

48. AE "Perse," IX. Also see Gardane, *La mission du Général Gardane en Perse,* 106–7.

49. Harford Jones, *An Account of the Transactions of His Majesty's Mission to the Court of Persia in the Years 1807–11* (London: James Bohn, 1834), I:256. Also see Steven R. Ward, *Immortal: A Military History of Iran and Its Armed Forces* (Washington, DC: Georgetown University Press, 2009), 74–75.

50. Fath Ali Shah to Napoleon, n.d. [ca. 1806], cited in Atkin, *Russia and Iran,* 126. Also see Convention Between France and Iran Signed on January 21, 1808, on the Delivery of Muskets from France to Iran, AE/III/55.

51. Amini, *Napoleon et la Perse*, 195f.

52. Article 4 of the treaty; Amini, *Napoleon and Persia*, 206.

53. AE, "Perse," IX.

54. For details, see AE "Perse," IX and X, containing Gardane's report about audience with the shah and his reports to the Ministry of Foreign Affairs. Also see Gardane, *La mission du Général Gardane en Perse*, 167–70, 275–77. For an in-depth discussion, see Driault, *La politique orientale de Napoleon*, 126, 135, 142–48, 152.

55. Caulaincourt to Napoleon, August 12, 1808, in Grand Duke Nikolai Mikhailovich, *Diplomaticheskie snosheniya Rossii i Frantsii*, II:280.

56. See Gudovich to Budberg, September 29, 1806 (with a letter from a senior Qajar official); Alexander to Gudovich, October 16, 1806, in *Akty*, III:419–21.

57. See Gudovich's correspondence with Emperor Alexander, Chancellor Rumyantsev, and other senior officials in *Akty*, III:425–26, 429–30, 433–46, 449–51, 456–64, 485–86.

58. Lord Minto to Colonel Barry Close, October 11, 1807, in Gilbert Elliot-Murray-Kynynmound, Earl of Minto, *Lord Minto in India: Life and Letters of G. Elliot from 1807 to 1814* (London: Longmans, Green, 1880), 51.

59. Minto, *Lord Minto in India*, 110–11. For Minto's fears of the French invasion, see 101–10.

60. John William Kaye, *The Life and Correspondence of Major-General Sir John Malcolm, Late Envoy to Persia and Governor of Bombay* (London: Smith, Taylor, 1856), I:420–21.

61. Amini, *Napoleon and Persia*, 140–46.

62. AE "Perse," X.

63. AE "Perse," X.

64. AE "Perse," X.

65. For a concise discussion of Lajard's mission, see Amini, *Napoleon and Persia*, 153–56.

66. Journal of the Russian Operations, in RGVIA, f. VUA, d. 4265, ll. 41–102; Dubrovin, *Istoriia voiny i vladychestva russkikh na Kavkaze*, V:200–227.

67. "O deistviyakh frantsuzskoi missii v Persii," November 23, 1808; RGVIA, f. VUA, d. 4265, ll. 41–43; Rumyantsev to Alexander I, December 1808, RGVIA, f. VUA, d. 4265, ll. 44–54b.

68. Gudovich to Major-General Akhverdov, November 6, 1808; Gudovich to Alexander, December 23, 1808 in *Akty*, III:241, 252–64; Nikolay Beliavskii and Vasilii Potto, *Utverzhdenie Russkago vladychestva na Kavkaze* (Tiflis: Izd. Voenno-istoricheskago otd. Pri Shtabe Kavkaz. Voen. Okruga, 1901), I:251–57, 303–8. Also see Caulaincourt to Napoleon, February 22, 1809, in Grand Duke Nikolai Mikhailovich, *Les Relations diplomatiques de la Russie et de la France d'apres les rapports des ambassadeurs d'Alexandre et de Napoleon, 1808–12* (St. Petersburg, 1905–1914), III:100–101.

69. See reports by Gardane, Felix Lajard (third secretary in Gardane's mission), and Joseph Jouannin (French consul in Iran) in AE "Perse," X.

70. Gardane, *La mission du Général Gardane en Perse,* 234; Amini, *Napoleon and Persia,* 157–59.

71. Gardane, *La mission du Général Gardane en Perse,* 235–36.

72. AE "Perse," X.

73. Amini, *Napoleon and Persia,* 170–79.

74. AE "Perse," XI.

75. Charles Umpherston Aitchison, *A Collection of Treaties, Engagements, and Sunnuds Relating to India and Neighbouring Countries* (Calcutta: O. T. Cutter, 1865), VII:117–20. The preliminary treaty was formalized into the Treaty of Friendship and Alliance in March 1812. See Aitchison, *A Collection of Treaties,* VII:122–26. Also see Jones, *An Account of the Transactions of His Majesty's Mission,* I:185–200; R. M. Savory, "British and French Diplomacy in Persia, 1801–1810," *Iran* 10 (1972): 34–40.

76. Jones, *An Account of the Transactions of His Majesty's Mission,* I:200ff.

77. Tormasdov to A. Prozorovskii, April 17, 1809, in *Akty,* IV:631–32.

78. See Tormasov to Rumyantsev, June 10, 1809, RGVIA, f. VUA, d. 6184, ll. 38–45; Tormasov to Arakcheyev, September 22, 1809, RGVIA, f. VUA, d. 4267, ll. 1–8b; Tormasov to Rumyantsev, September 22, 1809 in *Akty,* IV:693–96. Also see Günal Teymurova, "1806–1812 Osmanli-Rusya Savaşi ve Azerbaycan," *Journal of Ottoman Civilization Studies,* no. 2 (2016): 51–54.

79. Tormasov to Arakcheyev, September 22, 1809, RGVIA, f. VUA, d. 4267, ll. 1–8b; Tormasov to Rumyantsev, September 22, 1809 in *Akty,* IV:693-96. Also see Nikoloz Kortua, *Sakartvelo 1806–12 tslebis Ruset-Turketis omshi: rusi da kartveli xalxebis sabrdzolo tanamegobrobis istoriidan* (Tbilisi: Tsodna, 1964).

80. N. Berdzenishvili, *Sakartvelos istoria* (Tbilisi, 1958), I:407–8; G.V. Khachapuridze, *K istorii Gruzii pervoi poloviny XIX veka* (Tbilisi, 1950), 98–99. Also see Petr Butkov, *Materially dlia novoi istorii Kavkaza s 1722 po 1803 god* (St. Petersburg: Tip. Imp. Akademii nauk, 1869), III:392–93; Nikolay Dubrovin, *Istoriia voiny i vladychestva russkikh na Kavkaze* (St. Petersburg: Tip. Departamenta udelov, 1887), V, 252–318.

81. AE "Perse," t. XIII, 1810, f. 322.

82. A. Villemain, *Souvenirs contemporains d'histoire et de littérature* (Paris: Didier, 1854), I:175–80. For a broad view of Franco-Georgian diplomacy, see Ilia Tabagoua, "La Géorgie dans les plans de Napoléon," *Bedi Kartlisa: Revue de Kartvélologie* XXIX (1972): 106–18; Ilia Tabagoua, *Sakartvelo-safrangetis urtiertobis istoriidan (XVIII s. mitsuruli–XIX s. dasatskisi)* (Tbilisi: Metsniereba, 1974); Nebi Gümüş, "Son Gürcü Krali II. Solomon'un Ruslara Karşi Mücadelesi ve Osmanli Devleti İle İlişkileri," *Necmettin Erbakan Üniversitesi İlahiyat Fakültesi Dergisi,* no. 22 (2006): 105–18; Alexander Mikaberidze, "Franco-Georgian Diplomatic Relations, 1810–1811," The Napoleon Series, http://napoleon-series.com/research/government/diplomatic/c_georgia1.html.

83. Tormasov to Barclay de Tolly, May 26, 1810, RGVIA, f. VUA, d. 6186, ll. 19–24.

84. Beliavskii and Potto, *Utverzhdenie Russkago vladychestva*, II:191–206, 243–68; A. Petrov, *Voina Rossii s Turtsiei, 1806–1812* (St. Petersburg: Voenn. Tip., 1885), III:207–29; Günal Teymurova, "1806–1812 Osmanli-Rusya Savaşi ve Azerbaycan," *Journal of Ottoman Civilization Studies*, no. 2 (2016): 54–55.

85. Tormasov to Barclay de Tolly, September 12, 1811, RGVIA, f. VUA, d. 6192, ll. 96–102.

86. Beliavskii and Potto, *Utverzhdenie Russkago vladychestva*, II:269–86.

87. Paulucci to Barclay de Tolly, November 7, 1811, RGVIA, f. VUA, d. 6192, ll. 116–19; Paulucci to Alexander, April 8, 1812; Paulucci to Barclay de Tolly, March 15, 1812 in *Akty*, V:177–80, 191–92; Dubrovin, *Istoriia voiny i vladychestva russkikh na Kavkaze*, V:435–37; Beliavskii and Potto, *Utverzhdenie Russkago vladychestva*, II:287–315.

88. Ingram, *Britain's Persian Connection*, 164–67.

89. Russia offered to recognize Talysh Khanate as a neutral territory that would serve as a buffer between the two empires. But this would still have required Tehran to accept the loss of Georgia and much of eastern Caucasia. See relevant correspondence in *Akty*, V:662–70.

90. See complaints from the residents of Gareji, Machkhaani, Kakabeti, Vejini, Zegani, and other villages, March 1812, in Shota Khantadze, ed., *Dokumentebi kakhetis 1812 tslis ajankebis istoriisatvis* (Tbilisi: Tbilisi University Press, 1999); 30, 41–42, 47, 54, 57–58, 67, 84, 89, 103–4. For a discussion of the problems with the Russian civilian government, see V. Ivanenko, *Grazhdanskoe upravlenie Zakavkaziem ot prisoedineniya Gruzii do namestnichestva Velikago Kniazya Mikhaila Nikolayevicha* (Tiflis: Tip. Kantselyarii Glavnonachalstvuyuschego grazhdanskoi chastyu na Kavkaze, 1901), 76ff.

91. See Akaki Gelashvili, *Kakhetis 1812 tslis ajankeba* (Tbilisis: Artanuji, 2010); Durmishkhan Tsintsadze, *Dokumentebi kakhetis 1812 tslis ajankebis istoriisatvis* (Tbilisi: Tbilisi State University Press, 1999).

92. Beliavskii and Potto, *Utverzhdenie Russkago vladychestva*, II:304–8.

93. Rtischev to Alexander, November 12, 1812, in *Akty*, V:684–86; Beliavskii and Potto, *Utverzhdenie Russkago vladychestva*, II:459–70; V. Sollogub, *Biografiya generala Kotlyarosvkogo* (St. Petersburg: Tip. K. Kraya, 1836), 116–22; Baddeley, *The Russian Conquest of the Caucasus*, 88–89.

94. Dubrovin, *Istoriia voiny i vladychestva russkikh na Kavkaze*, VI:39–100. Also see *Akty*, V:697–700, 702–3, 710–11.

95. Ouseley to Castlereagh, July 10, 1813, cited in Atkin, *Russia and Iran*, 141.

96. Rtischev to Rumyantsev, December 1, 1813, in *Akty*, V:739–47.

97. See the treaty's text in Hurewitz, *The Middle East and North Africa in World Politics*, I:197–99.

98. Mansoureh Ettehadieh Nezam-Mafi, "Qajar Iran (1795–1921)," in *The Oxford Handbook of Iranian History*, ed. Touraj Daryaee (Oxford: Oxford University Press, 2012), 323.

99. In the this new *bunichah* system, Abbas Mirza put in place a form of conscription under which each province was called upon to provide a specific number of recruits, with a quota calculated on the basis of the amount of land under cultivation, supplemented by voluntary enlistment and incorporation of small tribal contingents.

Chapter 18

1. Based on tonnage of sailing vessels larger than 500 tons. See data in J. Glete, *Navies and Nations: Warships, Navies and State Building in Europe and America, 1500–1860* (Stockholm: Almqvist & Wiksell International, 1993), app. 2, II:553–695.

2. Leonard Monteath Thompson, *A History of South Africa* (New Haven, CT: Yale University Press, 1990), 35–36; Richard Elphick and Hermann Giliomee, eds., *The Shaping of South African Society, 1652–1840* (Middletown, CT: Wesleyan University Press, 1979), 93–100, 136–38.

3. Ben Hughes, *The British Invasion of the River Plate 1806–1807: How the Redcoats Were Humbled and a Nation Was Born* (Barnsley, UK: Pen & Sword Military, 2013), 12–21.

4. Thompson, *A History of South Africa,* 54–56. Also see William M. Freund, "The Cape Under the Transitional Governments, 1795–1814," in *The Shaping of South African Society 1652–1840,* ed. Richard Elphick and Hermann Giliomee (Middletown, CT: Wesleyan University Press, 1979), 329–30.

5. See John Rydjord, *Foreign Interest in the Independence of New Spain* (New York: Octagon Books, 1972), 154, 202–3. For an earlier period, see William Kaufmann, *British Policy and the Independence of Latin America, 1804–1828* (New Haven CT: Yale University Press, 1951), 1–17.

6. William Spence Robertson, *The Life of Miranda* (Chapel Hill: University of North Carolina Press, 1929), I:282–83.

7. Rydjord, *Foreign Interest in the Independence of New Spain,* 235.

8. Robertson, *The Life of Miranda,* I:293–327; Karen Racine, *Francisco de Miranda: A Transatlantic Life in the Age of Revolution* (Wilmington, DE: Scholarly Resources, 2003), ch. 5.

9. On Popham, see Hugh Popham, *A Damned Cunning Fellow: The Eventful Life of Sir Home Popham* (Tywardreath, UK: Old Ferry, 1991).

10. Popham to Secretary of the Admiralty Marsden, April 30, 1806, in Theodore Edward Hook, *The Life of General, the Right Honourable, Sir David Baird* (London: Richard Bentley, 1832), II:142–43. Popham later recorded that in 1805 he "had a long conversation with [Prime Minister Pitt] on the original project of the expedition to South America, in the course of which Mr. Pitt informed me, that from the then state of Europe, and the confederation in part formed, and forming against France, there was a great anxiety to endeavor, by friendly negotiation, to detach Spain from its connection with that power, and, until the result of such an attempt should be known, it was desirable to suspend

all hostile operations in South America; but, in case of failure in this object, it was his intention to enter on the original project." *Minutes of a Court Martial, Holden on Board His Majesty's Ship Gladiator in Portsmouth Harbor...*(London: Longman, 1807), 80.

11. Alexander Gillespie, *Gleanings and Remarks Collected During Many Months of Residence at Buenos Ayres and Within the Upper Country* (Leeds: B. Dewhirst, 1818), 28–29. For a good overview of the expedition see Hughes, *The British Invasion of the River Plate 1806–1807,* 24–25; James Davey, "The Atlantic Empire, European War and the Naval Expeditions to South America, 1806–1807," in *The Royal Navy and the British Atlantic World, 1750–1820,* ed. John McAleer and Christer Petley (Basingstoke: Palgrave Macmillan, 2016), 147–72.

12. Popham to the Mayor and Corporation of Birmingham, July 1, 1806, in *The British Trident, or Register of Naval Actions,* ed. Archibald Duncan (London: James, Cundee, 1806), V:349; *The Naval Chronicle for 1806* (London: Joyce Gold, 1806), XVI:373–74. Also see Popham's letter of July 20, 1806, to Miranda in Robertson, *The Life of Miranda,* 323–24.

13. For an interesting discussion of economic conditions in Buenos Aires, see Lyman L. Johnson, *Workshop of Revolution: Plebeian Buenos Aires and the Atlantic World, 1776–1810* (Durham, NC: Duke University Press, 2011).

14. *A la reconquista de la capital de Bueno Aires por las tropas de mar y tierra, á las órdenes del capitan de Navio, Don Santiago Liniers, el 12 de agosto de 1806* (Buenos Aires: Niños Expósitós, 1806). For English-language studies, see Hughes, *The British Invasion of the River Plate 1806–1807;* Ian Fletcher, *The Waters of Oblivion: The British Invasion of the Rio de la Plata, 1806–07* (Staplehurst, UK: Spellmount, 1991); John D. Grainger, *British Campaigns in the South Atlantic 1805–1807* (Barnsley, UK: Pen & Sword Military, 2015); John D. Grainger, *The Royal Navy in the River Plate, 1806–1807* (Aldershot: Scolar Press, 1996).

15. See Alberto Mario Salas, *Diario de Bueno Aires, 1806–1807* (Buenos Aires: Editorial Sudamericana, 1981), 476–510; Francisco Saguí, *Los últimos cuatro años de la dominación española en el antiguo vireinato del Rio de la Plata desde 26 de junio de 1806 hasta 25 de mayo 1810: memoria histórica familiar* (Buenos Aires: Imprenta Americana, 1874), 65–88, 484–512; José Juan Biedma, *Documentos referents de la Guerra de la indepencia de América a emancipación politica de la República Argentina y de otras secciones de América a qye cooperó desde 1810 a 1828,* tome 2, *Antecedentes popoliticos, económicos y administrativos de la revolución de Mayo de 1810* (Buenos Aires: Archivo General de la Nación Argentina, 1914), 611–23; Bernardo Lozier Almazán, *Liniers y su tiempo* (Buenos Aires: Emcé Editores, 1990), 150–61.

16. See document 464 in *1806–1807 Invasiones Inglesas al Río de la Plata: aporte documental* (Buenos Aires: Inst. Histórico de la Ciudad de Buenos Aires, 2006), 50–51.

17. For details, see Carlos Pueyrredón, *1810. La revolución de Mayo segun amplica documentación de la época* (Buenos Aires: Ediciones Peusar, 1953), 35–36; Salas,

Diario de Bueno Aires, 371–72; Biedma, *Documentos referents de la Guerra de la indepencia,* II, 440–50; Instituto de Estudios Historicos, *La reconquista y defensa de Buenos Aires, 1806–1807* (Buenos Aires: Editores Peuser, 1947), 476.

18. Johnson, *Workshop of Revolution,* 262–71.

19. The government approved "the judicious, able, and spirited conduct" of British troops but disapproved of the attack itself because it had been undertaken without the government's approval. *Minutes of a Court Martial,* 54–56, 69–70.

20. Grenville to Lord Auckland, June 5, 1806, in *Dropmore Papers,* VIII:179.

21. Auckland to Grenville, September 1 and 14, November 25, 1806, *Dropmore Papers,* VIII:302, 332, 441–42.

22. Howick to Morpeth, September 24, 1806, cited in George M. Trevelyan, *Lord Grey of the Reform Bill* (London: Longmans, Green, 1920), 151.

23. Windham to Grenville, September 11, 1806, *Dropmore Papers,* VIII:321.

24. For details, see Grenville to Buckingham, October 3, 1806, *Memoirs of the Court and Cabinets of George III,* IV:79–80; Arthur Wellesley's Memoranda, November 2–21, 1806, *Dropmore Papers,* IX:481–92. Also see *Dropmore Papers,* VIII:386–87, 418–20; *Supplementary Despatches and Memoranda of Field Marshal Arthur, Duke of Wellington* (London: John Murray, 1860), VI:35–39, 40–55.

25. Wellesley's Memorandum, November 20, 1806, *Supplementary Despatches and Memoranda,* VI:50.

26. My discussion of events in the West Indies and the Atlantic is mainly based on Kenneth Johnson, "Napoleon's War at Sea," in *Napoleon and the Operational Art of War,* ed. Michael V. Leggiere (Leiden: Brill, 2016), 387–475; William Laird Clowes et al., *The Royal Navy: A History from the Earliest Times to 1900* (London: Chatham, 1997), vol. 5; Louis Edouard Chevalier, *Histoire de la marine française sous le consulat et l'empire* (Paris: L. Hachette, 1886); Robert Gardiner, *The Campaign of Trafalgar* (London: Caxton Editions, 2001); Robert Gardiner, *The Victory of Seapower: Winning the Napoleonic War, 1806–1814* (London: Caxton Editions, 1998); William James, *The Naval History of Great Britain* (London: Conway Maritime Press, 2002), vols. 3–5.

27. WO 1/146 West Indies and South America, ix, Surinam, Volume I (Governor's dispatches, 1801–1802; dispatches on recapture in 1804). I am very grateful to Martijn Wink for sharing details (and copies of documents) of his research on the fall of Surinam in 1804.

28. Cited in Kevin D. McCranie, "Britain's Royal Navy and the Defeat of Napoleon," in *Napoleon and the Operational Art of War,* ed. Leggiere, 476.

29. Eluding British efforts to intercept him, Allemand captured one British warship, three smaller vessels, and more than forty merchant ships before triumphantly returning to Rochefort in November 1805. Chevalier, *Histoire de la marine française sous le consulat et l'empire,* 240–41.

30. Chevalier, *Histoire de la marine française sous le consulat et l'empire,* 260–63.

31. Johnson, *Napoleon's War at Sea,* 430.

32. Chevalier, *Histoire de la marine française sous le consulat et l'empire,* 264–66.

33. James, *The Naval History of Great Britain*, IV:190–203; Chevalier, *Histoire de la marine française sous le consulat et l'empire*, 251–55.

34. Napoleon to Berthier, March 31, 1806, in *CN*, XII:246–47.

35. Johnson, *Napoleon's War at Sea*, 434. In total these cruises cost France seven ships, six frigates, and seven brigs or corvettes, as well as 1,700 men killed or wounded and 4,800 men captured.

36. Johnson, *Napoleon's War at Sea*, 437.

37. Piers Mackesy, *The War in the Mediterranean, 1803-1810* (London: Longmans, Green, 1957), 249–54.

38. Robert Castlereagh, *Correspondence, Despatches, and Other Papers of Viscount Castlereagh*, ed. Charles Vane (London: William Shorberl, 1851), VIII:87.

39. On Curaçao, see P. A. Euwens, "Een Engelsch gourveneur van Curaçao," *De West-Indische Gids*, 1924–1925, 461–64; P. A. Euwens, "De eerste dagen van het Engelsche bewind op Curaçao in 1807," *De West-Indische Gids*, 1924–1925, 575–81; B. De Gaay Fortman, "De Kolonie Curaçao Onder Engelsch Bestuur Van 1807 Tot 1816," *De West-Indische Gids*, 1944–1945, 229–46. For the impact of the British invasion on St. Thomas, St. John, and St. Croix, see N. A. T. Hall, *Slave Society in the Danish West Indies: St. Thomas, St. John and St Croix* (Mona, Jamaica: University of the West Indies Press, 1992).

40. James Lucas Yeo to the Admiralty, January 15, 1809, *The Naval Chronicle*, XXI, 337–41; James, *The Naval History of Great Britain*, V:209–13.

41. Kenneth Gregory Johnson, "Louis-Thomas Villaret de Joyeuse: Admiral and Colonial Administrator (1747–1812)," Ph.D. diss., Florida State University, 2006, 246–65. During the siege of Fort Desaix, the British had fired more than 8,000 bombs, 2,000 shells, and 4,000 cannonballs, almost entirely destroying the fort and its vicinity.

42. Alan Burns, *History of the British West Indies* (London: George Allen & Unwin, 1965), 586–87.

43. The French kept churning out vessels with such efficiency that one British naval commander spoke of "another navy, as if by magic, [springing] forth from the forests to the seashore." Edward P. Brenton, *The Naval History of Great Britain from the Year 1783 to 1836* (London: H. Coburn, 1837), II:112.

44. *The Monthly Magazine or British Register* XXXII (1811), part II, 73. Also see *The Naval Chronicle*, XXVI, 158; Richard Glover, "The French Fleet, 1807–1814: Britain's Problem and Madison's Opportunity," *Journal of Modern History* 39, no. 3 (1967): 233–52.

45. For an interesting discussion, see Janet Macdonald, *The British Navy's Victualling Board, 1793–1815* (Woodbridge: Boydell Press, 2010); James Davey, *In Nelson's Wake: The Navy and the Napoleonic Wars* (New Haven, CT: Yale University Press, 2015), 160–206.

46. See Robert G. Albion, *Forests and Sea Power: The Timber Problem of the Royal Navy, 1652–1852* (Cambridge, MA: Harvard University Press, 1926), 20–32; James Davey, *The Transformation of British Naval Strategy: Seapower and Supply*

in Northern Europe, 1808–1812 (Woodbridge: Boydell Press, 2012), 55–73, 173–92; J. Ross Dancy, *The Myth of the Press Gang: Volunteers, Impressment and the Naval Manpower in the Late Eighteenth Century* (Woodbridge: Boydell Press, 2015), 28–29; Clowes et al., *The Royal Navy: A History*, V:10. The number of ships-of-the-line had risen from 111 in 1803 to 120 in 1806 and 127 in 1809 but then fell to 118 in 1814.

47. Most of these successes date from 1809, when a British attack with fireships at the Basque Roads (also known as Aix Roads) destroyed three ships-of-the-line; in the West Indies, the French ship-of-the-line *d'Haupoult* was captured in April 1809, while in the Mediterranean, Admiral George Martin was able to destroy two ships-of-the-line in October 1809. Three years later, the French also lost the 74-gun *Rivoli* on its maiden voyage in the northern Adriatic in February 1812.

48. Thomas Barnes Cochrane Dundonald and H. R. Fox Bourne, *The Life of Thomas, Lord Cochrane, Tenth Earl of Dundonald* (London, R. Bentley, 1869), I:12.

49. David Cordingly, *Cochrane: The Real Master and Commander* (New York: Bloomsbury, 2007).

50. Cochrane Dundonald and Fox Bourne, *The Life of Thomas, Lord Cochrane,* 16.

51. Cochrane urged Gambier to continue the attack but was instead instructed to depart for Britain with dispatches detailing the action. In London, Cochrane was hailed as a hero and knighted, but he publicly vented his frustration with Gambier's failure to annihilate the French. This all but ended his professional career, since he was no longer given a command and was prevented from returning to sea.

52. Noel Mostert, *The Line upon a Wind: The Great War at Sea, 1793–1815* (New York: W. W. Norton, 207), 569.

53. For details, see Jahleel Brenton, *Memoir of the Life and Services of Vice Admiral Sir Jahleel Brenton*, ed. Henry Raikes (London: Hatchard, 1846), 319–72.

54. Edward Osler, *The Life of Admiral Viscount Exmouth* (London: Geo. Routledge, 1854), 173.

55. "The highest estimate of the relative value of a three-decker [100 guns and more] and a two-decker [80–64 guns] is that of [Admiral] Jervis, who wrote after the battle of Cape Saint Vincent that he considered the two captured Spanish first-rates to be worth more than six French two-deckers." Mackesy, *The War in the Mediterranean*, xiii.

Chapter 19

1. There is a vast literature on British imperialism in India. In my discussions I rely primarily on P. J. Marshall, ed., *The Oxford History of the British Empire*, vol. 2, *The Eighteenth Century* (Oxford: Oxford University Press, 1998); H. V. Bowen, *The Business of Empire: The East India Company and Imperial Britain, 1756–1833* (Cambridge: Cambridge University Press, 2006); Ian Watson, *Foundation for Empire: English Private Trade in India, 1659–1760* (New Delhi: Vikas, 1980);

C. A. Bayly, *Indian Society and the Making of the British Empire* (Cambridge: Cambridge University Press, 1988); K. N. Chaudhuri, *The Trading World of Asia and the East India Company, 1660–1760* (Cambridge: Cambridge University Press, 1978).

2. John Robert Seeley, *The Expansion of England: Two Courses of Lectures* (1883; repr., Cambridge: Cambridge University Press, 2010), 8.

3. On the mainsprings of imperial expansion, see Bernard Porter, *The Absent-Minded Imperialists: Empire, Society, and Culture in Britain* (Oxford: Oxford University Press, 2004); Timothy H. Parsons, *The Rule of Empires: Those Who Built Them, Those Who Endured Them, and Why They Always Fall* (Oxford: Oxford University Press, 2010); Piers Brendon, *The Decline and Fall of the British Empire, 1781–1797* (New York: Alfred A. Knopf, 2007).

4. For a general history of the BEIC, see Antony Wild, *The East India Company: Trade and Conquest from 1600* (New York: Lyons Press, 2000).

5. Parsons, *The Rule of Empires*, 173.

6. See Anthony Webster, *The Twilight of the East India Company: The Evolution of Anglo-Asian Commerce and Politics, 1790–1860* (Woodbridge: Boydell Press, 2009); Sudipta Sen, *Empire of Free Trade: The East India Company and the Making of the Colonial Marketplace* (Philadelphia: University of Pennsylvania Press, 1998); Philip Lawson, *The East India Company: A History* (London: Longman, 1993).

7. Peter A. Ward, *British Naval Power in the East, 1794–1805: The Command of Admiral Peter Rainier* (Oxford: Boydell Press, 2013), 2.

8. See P. J. Marshall, *The New Cambridge History of India*, vol. II, part 2, *Bengal: The British Bridgehead* (Cambridge: Cambridge University Press, 1987), 77–92; Daniel Baugh, *The Global Seven Years' War, 1754–1763: Britain and France in a Great Power Contest* (London: Longman, 2011), 282–97; P. J. Marshall, *East Indian Fortunes: The British in Bengal in the Eighteenth Century* (Oxford: Oxford University Press, 1976).

9. Holden Furber, "The East India Directors in 1784," *Journal of Modern History* 5, no. 4 (1933): 479–95; C. H. Philips, "The East India Company 'Interest' and the English Government, 1783–4," *Transactions of the Royal Historical Society (Fourth Series)* 20 (1937): 83–101.

10. *The Parliamentary Register or History of the Proceedings and Debates of the House of Commons* (London: J. Debrett, 1788), XXIII:301; *Cobbett's Parliamentary History of England* (London: T. C. Hansard, 1815), XXIV:1094. The Board of Control consisted of six members, including Britain's secretary of state and the Chancellor of the Exchequer. The Secret Committee consisted of just three members. William Foster, "The India Board (1784–1858)," *Transactions of the Royal Historical Society (Third Series)* 11 (1917): 61–85; C. H. Philips, "The Secret Committee of the East India Company, 1784–1858," in *Bulletin of the School of Oriental and African Studies* 10, no. 3 (1940): 699–700.

11. See Nicholas B. Dirks, *The Scandal of Empire: India and the Creation of Imperial Britain* (Cambridge, MA: Belknap Press, 2006); H. V. Bowen, *The Business of*

Empire: The East India Company and Imperial Britain, 1756–1833 (Cambridge: Cambridge University Press, 2006).

12. C. A. Bayly, *The Birth of the Modern World, 1780–1914: Global Connections and Comparisons* (Malden, MA: Blackwell, 2004).

13. According to Geoffrey Parker, Indian efforts to catch up to the Western powers by adopting their military tactics and weaponry were a case of too little too late. R. G. S. Cooper argues that the Indian defeat was largely the result of their poor command structure and the lack of an institutionalized officer corps. Geoffrey Parker, *The Military Revolution: Military Innovation and the Rise of the West, 1500–1800* (Cambridge: Cambridge University Press, 1988), 136; Randolf G. S. Cooper, "Wellington and the Marathas in 1803," *International History Review* 11 (1989): 38.

14. For details see Maistre de La Touche, *The History of Hyder Shah, Alias Hyder Ali Khan Bahadur* (Calcutta: Sanders, Cones, 1848); Praxy Fernandes, *The Tigers of Mysore: A Biography of Hyder Ali and Tipu Sultan* (New Delhi: Viking, 1991).

15. K. G. Pitre, *The Second Anglo-Maratha War, 1802–1805: A Study in Military History* (Poona: Dastane Ramchandra, 1990), 135. As British historian P. J. Marshall observed, "The future Duke of Wellington's victory at Assaye in 1803 was no more an easy triumph for superior western technology and organization than had been Francisco de Almeida's at Diu in 1509." P. J. Marshall, "Western Arms in Maritime Asia in the Early Phases of Expansion," in *Warfare, Expansion and Resistance*, ed. Patrick Tick (London: Routledge, 2001), V:133.

16. Jeremy Black, *Britain as a Military Power, 1688–1815* (London: University College London Press, 1999), 132. Also see Black, *The British Seaborne Empire* (New Haven, CT: Yale University Press, 2004), 139–40; Black, *European Warfare 1660–1815* (London: University College London Press, 1994).

17. See chapters 1–3 in Nicholas B. Dirks, *The Scandal of Empire: India and the Creation of Imperial Britain* (Cambridge, MA: Harvard University Press, 2006).

18. For details, see Dharma Kumar and Meghnad Desai, *The Cambridge Economic History of India*, vol. 2, *c. 1757–c. 1970* (Cambridge: Cambridge University Press, 1983), 3–35, 242–352.

19. Wellesley "found the East India Company a trading body, but left it an imperial power." *Encyclopedia Britannica*, 11th ed. (1910–1911), XXVIII:506.

20. Only the formidable Ranjit Singh (r. 1801–1839) of the Sikh Empire (northwest India) was capable of keeping the British at bay for another two generations. J. S. Grewal, *The New Cambridge History of India*, vol. II, part 3, *The Sikhs of the Punjab* (Cambridge: Cambridge University Press, 1998), 99–127. Also see Pradeep Barua, "Military Developments in India, 1750–1850," *Journal of Military History*, 58, no. 4 (1994): 610–13.

21. Michael Duffy, "World Wide War, 1793–1815," in *The Oxford History of the British Empire: The Eighteenth Century*, ed. P. J. Marshall (Oxford: Oxford University Press, 1998), II:202.

22. For an excellent discussion, see Peter A. Ward, *British Naval Power in the East, 1794–1805: The Command of Admiral Peter Rainier* (Oxford: Boydell Press, 2013).

23. Castlereagh to Wellesley, March 16, 1803, in *The Despatches, Minutes, and Correspondance, of the Marquess Wellesley During His Administration in India*, ed. Montgomery Martin (London: W. Allen, 1837), III:290.

24. Thomas George Percival Spear, *The Oxford History of Modern India, 1790–1975* (Delhi: Oxford University Press, 1978), 114. The British regular army establishment in India doubled from 10,700 in 1796 to over 26,000 in 1801. John William Fortescue, *A History of the British Army* (London: Macmillan, 1910), IV:719–20, 938–39.

25. James W. Hoover, *Men Without Hats: Dialogue, Discipline, and Discontent in the Madras Army 1806–1807* (New Delhi: Manohar, 2007); P. Chinnian, *The Vellore Mutiny, 1806: The First Uprising Against the British* (Madras: n.p., 1982); Maya Gupta, *Lord William Bentinck in Madras and the Vellore Mutiny, 1803–7* (New Delhi: Capital, 1986).

26. Mountstuart Elphinstone, *An Account of the Kingdom of Caubul, and Its Dependencies in Persia, Tartary, and India* (London: Longman, 1815), 1. A similar sentiment was reflected by Henry Dundas, who wanted to "exclude the French from all such connections and possessions in Asia…as might facilitated to them the means…of directing the efforts of any considerable body of troops against our Indian territories." Cited in Edward Ingram, *In Defense of British India: Great Britain in the Middle East, 1775–1842* (London: Frank Cass, 1984), 132.

27. For an excellent discussion of Minto's foreign policy, see Amita Das, *Defending British India Against Napoleon: The Foreign Policy of Governor-General Lord Minto, 1807–1813*, ed. Aditya Das (London: Boydell and Brewer, 2016).

28. Ingram, *In Defense of British India*, 130–49; T. E. Colebrook, *Life of the Honourable Mounstuart Elphinstone* (London: John Murray, 1884), I:187–229; Robert D. Crews, *Afghan Modern: The History of a Global Nation* (Cambridge, MA: Harvard University Press, 2015), 58–59.

29. For insights, see K. N. Chaudhuri, *Trade and Civilisation in the Indian Ocean: An Economic History from the Rise of Islam to 1750* (Cambridge: Cambridge University Press, 1985); Pedro Machado, *Ocean of Trade: South Asian Merchants, Africa and the Indian Ocean, c. 1750–1850* (Cambridge: Cambridge University Press, 2014).

30. See Yasuko Suzuki, *Japan-Netherlands Trade 1600–1800: The Dutch East India Company and Beyond* (Kyoto: Kyoto University Press, 2012).

31. W. G. Beasley, "The Foreign Threat and the Opening of the Ports," in *The Cambridge History of Japan*, vol. 5, *The Nineteenth Century*, ed. Marius B. Jansen (Cambridge: Cambridge University Press, 1989), 261.

32. For interesting details, see Hendrik Doeff, *Herinneringen uit Japan* (Haarlem: Francois Bohn, 1833). Doeff was the chief Dutch resident in Japan from 1804 to 1817.

33. W. G. Aston, "H.M.S. 'Phaeton' at Nagasaki in 1808," *Transactions of the Asiatic Society of Japan* 7, no. 1 (February 1879): 329.

34. Doeff, *Herinneringen uit Japan,* 161–64; Aston, "H.M.S. 'Phaeton' at Nagasaki in 1808," 330–40; Noell Wilson, "Tokugawa Defense Redux: Organizational Failure in the 'Phaeton' Incident of 1808," *Journal of Japanese Studies* 36, no. 1 (2010): 15–16. Also see W. G. Beasley, *Great Britain and the Opening of Japan, 1834–1858* (London: Luzac, 1951), 5–7.

35. Stamford Raffles, "Extract from the Secret Report of Mr. Henry Doeff Concerning the Occurrences with the English Frigate the Phaeton in the Bay of Nangasacky...," in *Report on Japan to the Secret Committee of the English East India Company, 1812–1816,* ed. Montague Paske-Smith (Kobe: Thompson, 1929), 142–43.

36. Wilson, "Tokugawa Defense Redux," 1–32.

37. The first major test of this law was the *Morrison* incident (Morison-gō Jiken), involving an American merchant ship, *Morrison,* that entered Japanese coastal waters and was fired upon by Japanese coastal defenses in 1837.

38. Masayoshi Sugimoto and David L. Swain, *Science and Culture in Traditional Japan* (Tokyo: Charles E. Tuttle, 1989), 332–33.

39. George Alexander Lensen, "Early Russo-Japanese Relations," *Far Eastern Quarterly* 10, no. 1 (1950): 3–9.

40. "A Memorandum from Count Alexander Vorontsov and Count Alexander Bezborodko Concerning Russia's Rights to the Islands and Coasts of North America Which Were Discovered by Russian Seafarers," in Basil Dmytryshyn, *Russian Penetration of the North Pacific Ocean, 1700–1797* (Portland: Oregon Historical Society, 1988), II:321–24.

41. Gertrude Atherton, "Nicolai Petrovich Rezanov," *North American Review* 189, no. 642 (1909): 651–57; William McOmie, "With All Due Respect: Reconsidering the Rezanov Mission to Japan," *Proceedings of the Japan Society,* 148 (2011): 71–154.

42. A. Sgibnev, "Popytki russkikh k zavedeniu torgovykh snoshenii s Iaponieiu (v XVIII i nachale XIX stoletii)," *Morskoi sbornik uchenago otdelenia morskogo tekhnicheskago komiteta,* 1869, 58.

43. Glynn Barratt, *Russia in Pacific Waters, 1715–1825* (Vancouver: University of British Columbia Press, 1981), 143–46; George Alexander Lensen, *The Russian Push Toward Japan: Russo-Japanese Relations, 1697–1875* (Princeton, NJ: Princeton University Press, 1959), 161–69; W. G. Aston, "Russian Descents in Saghalin and Itorup in the Years 1806 and 1807," *Transactions of the Asiatic Society of Japan* 1 (1874): 86–95.

44. L. M. Cullen, *A History of Japan, 1582–1941: Internal and External Worlds* (Cambridge: Cambridge University Press, 2003), 147–48.

45. Wilson, "Tokugawa Defense Redux," 27.

46. Supercargoes were merchants who held a commission from the BEIC to conduct trade with their Chinese counterparts.

47. Pei-kai Cheng and M. Lestz, with J. Spence, eds., *The Search for Modern China: A Documentary History* (New York: W. W. Norton, 1999), 106.

48. Hosea Ballou Morse, *The Chronicles of the East India Company Trading to China, 1635–1834* (Oxford: Oxford University Press, 1926), II:68. For a discussion of

the Portuguese in Macao see A. M. Martins do Vale, *Os Portugueses em Macau (1750–1800)* (Lisbon: Instituto Português do Oriente, 1997); Shantha Hariharan, "Macao and the English East India Company in the Early Nineteenth Century: Resistance and Confrontation," *Portuguese Studies* 23, no. 2 (2007): 135–52.

49. Shantha Hariharan, "Luso-British Cooperation in India: A Portuguese Frigate in the Service of a British Expedition," *South Asia Research* 26, no. 2 (2006): 133–43.

50. Shantha Hariharan, "Relations Between Macao and Britain During the Napoleonic Wars: Attempt to Land British Troops in Macao, 1802," *South Asia Research* 30, 2 (2010): 193.

51. M. C. B. Maybon, "Les Anglais à Macao en 1802 et en 1808," in *Bulletin de l'École française d'Extrême-Orient* 6 (1906): 302; Wensheng Wang, *White Lotus Rebels and South China Pirates* (Cambridge, MA: Harvard University Press, 2014), 235–36; Fei Chengkang, *Macao 400 Years* (Shanghai: Shanghai Academy of Social Sciences, 1996), 179–80.

52. Wellesley to James Drummond, November 20, 1801, in *The Despatches, Minutes, and Correspondence, of the Marquess Wellesley*, II:611–14; Wellesley to the Viceroy of Goa, January 17, 1802, in *Journal of the Bombay Branch of the Royal Asiatic Society* XIII (1877): 118–19; Shantha Hariharan, "Relations Between Macao and Britain During the Napoleonic Wars: Attempt to Land British Troops in Macao, 1802," *South Asia Research* 30, no. 2 (2010): 185–96; Austin Coates, *Macao and the British, 1637–1842: Prelude to Hong Kong* (Hong Kong: Hong Kong University Press, 2009), 92.

53. Maybon, "Les Anglais à Macao," 305–6.

54. Maybon, "Les Anglais à Macao," 307–9; Frederic Wakeman, "Drury's Occupation of Macau and China's Response to Early Modern Imperialism," *East Asian History*, no. 28 (2004): 28–29.

55. Peter A. Ward, *British Naval Power in the East, 1794–1805: The Command of Admiral Peter Rainier* (Oxford: Boydell Press, 2013), 82–83.

56. Hosea Ballou Morse, *The Chronicles of the East India Company, Trading to China 1635–1834* (Oxford: Clarendon Press, 1926), III:85–88; Wang, *White Lotus Rebels and South China Pirates*, 237–40.

57. The gist of the British thinking can be seen in the title of collection preserved at the India Office Records, British Library: "Papers regarding the combined Naval and Military Expedition sent from India to Macao in September 1808 to forestall a possible French occupation," IOR/F/4/307/7025.

58. Select Committee's report to the Secret Committee, March 30, 1809, in Morse, *The Chronicles of the East India Company*, III:96. The main function of the Select Committee, whose membership consisted of supercargoes, was to facilitate the arrival of ships from Britain and India at the start of the trade season, to sell British merchandise, to buy return cargoes of Chinese goods, and to arrange for the ships' return at the end of the season.

59. Select Committee's report to the Secret Committee, August 16, 1808, in Morse, *The Chronicles of the East India Company*, III:87.

60. Viceroy Francisco Antonio da Veiga Cabral left India in 1806 and was replaced by Bernardo José Maria de Lorraine and Silveira, whose hands were tied by the presence of a strong British force in Goa; the British occupation was imposed upon Cabral by Wellesley under the pretext of protecting it from the French.

61. Cited in Cyril N. Parkinson, *War in the Eastern Seas, 1793–1815* (London: G. Allen and Unwin, 1954), 321–22.

62. For details see "Papers regarding the combined Naval and Military Expedition sent from India to Macao in September 1808 to forestall a possible French occupation," IOR/F/4/307/7025.

63. Christopher Goscha, *Vietnam: A New History* (New York: Basic Books, 2016), 41–46; David Joel Steinberg, ed., *In Search of Southeast Asia* (Honolulu: University of Hawaii Press, 1987), 128; Maybon, "Les Anglais à Macao," 313–15; Alastair Lamb, *The Mandarin Road to Old Hué: Narratives of Anglo-Vietnamese Diplomacy from the 17th Century to the Eve of the French Conquest* (London: Chatto & Windus, 1970), 175, 189–95. For an interesting comparative approach, see Victor Lieberman, *Strange Parallels: Southeast Asia in Global Context, c. 800– 1830* (Cambridge: Cambridge University Press, 2003), 25, 60, 352.

64. Maybon, "Les Anglais à Macao," 313–15; Zeeman and Bletterman to Felix de St. Croix, February 25, 1809, AE MD Asie XX (Indes Orintales, Chine, Cochinchine); Antonio Da Silva Rego, *O Ultramar português no século XVIII (1700–1833)* (Lisbon: Agência Geral do Ultramar, 1970), 336–37; Magalhäes, "As tentativas de Recuperação Asiática," 58; Coates, *Macao and the British*, 97–98; Also see Shantha Hariharan and P. S. Hariharan, "The Expedition to Garrison Portuguese Macao with British Troops: Temporary Occupation and Re-Embarkation, 1808," *International Journal of Maritime History* 25, no. 2 (2013): 90–92.

65. Hariharan and Hariharan, "The Expedition to Garrison Portuguese Macao with British Troops," 91–92; Zeeman and Bletterman to Felix de St. Croix, February 25, 1809, AE Mémoires et Documents, Asie XX (Indes Orintales, Chine, Cochinchine). The Portuguese remained in charge of the Macao administration, and movement of British ships and troops required Portuguese approval. The British presence had to be approved by the Portuguese crown within two years or by the Portuguese viceroy within a year.

66. Henry Beveridge, *A Comprehensive History of India, Civil, Military, Social, from the First Landing of the English to the Suppression of the Sepoy Rebellion* (London: Blackie & Son, 1862), II:846. For the Portuguese view, see Joaquim Magalhäes, "As tentativas de Recuperação Asiática," in *História da expansão portuguesa*, ed. Francisco Bethencourt and K. Chaudhuri (Lisbon: Círculo de Leitores, 1999), II:58.

67. Drury to Chinese governor general, October 14, 1808, cited in Hariharan and Hariharan, "The Expedition to Garrison Portuguese Macao with British Troops," 95.

68. Wang, *White Lotus Rebels and South China Rebels*, 242; Morse, *The Chronicles of the East India Company*, III:87–88; Maybon, "Les Anglais à Macao," 316.

69. Select Committee to Drury, October 23, 1808, cited in Hariharan and Hariharan, "The Expedition to Garrison Portuguese Macao with British Troops," 95.

70. Zeeman and Bletterman to Felix de St. Croix, February 25, 1809, AE MD Asie XX (Indes Orintales, Chine, Cochinchine). Also see Parkinson, *War in the Eastern Seas*, 328–30.

71. Morse, *The Chronicles of the East India Company*, III:89–90.

72. Lo-Shu Fu, ed., *A Documentary Chronicle of Sino-Western Relations (1644–1820)* (Tucson: University of Arizona Press, 1967), 369–70. Also see Wang, *White Lotus Rebels and South China Rebels*, 243–44; Maybon, "Les Anglais à Macao," 317; Morse, *Chronicles of the East India Company*, III:87–91.

73. Describing the events of September–December 1808, the Dutch merchants in Macao spoke of "the ridiculous English expedition." Zeeman and Bletterman to Felix de St. Croix, February 25, 1809, AE MD Asie XX (Indes Orintales, Chine, Cochinchine).

74. Cited in Hariharan and Hariharan, "The Expedition to Garrison Portuguese Macao with British Troops," 108–9.

75. Maybon, "Les Anglais à Macao," 325.

76. For an interesting discussion, see K. N. Chaudhuri, *The Trading World of Asia and the English East India Company: 1660–1760* (Cambridge: Cambridge University Press, 1978), 1–40, 79–130.

77. See Javier Cuenca Esteban, "The British Balance of Payments, 1772–1820: India Transfers and War Finance," *Economic History Review* 54, no. 1 (2001): 58–86.

78. Henri Prentout, *L'Île de France sous Decaen, 1803–1810* (Paris: Hachette, 1901), 61–267.

79. Beatrice Nicolini, *Makran, Oman, and Zanzibar: Three-Terminal Cultural Corridor in the Western Indian Ocean (1799–1856)* (Leiden: Brill, 2004), 94; J. B. Kelly, *Britain and the Persian Gulf, 1795–1880* (Oxford: Clarendon Press, 1991), 75; Prentout, *L'Île de France sous Decaen*, 332–34.

80. Jerome A. Saldanha, *The Persian Gulf Précis: Précis of Correspondence Regarding the Affairs of the Persian Gulf, 1801–1853* (Gerrards Cross: Archive Editions, 1986), 29.

81. André Auzoux, "La France et Mascate aux XVIIIe et XIXe siècles," *Revue d'histoire diplomatique*, 1910, 234–55; Prentout, *L'Île de France sous Decaen*, 335–40.

82. While dealing with Muscat, Decaen had also directed his attention to Yemen after envoys from Mocha, one of the principal Yemeni ports, had visited him in 1804. The French general used this opportunity to learn a great deal about political and economic situation in the southwestern corner of Arabia. He was informed, for example, of the problems British had faced during their brief occupation of the island of Perrim. Prentout, *L'Île de France sous Decaen*, 342–43.

83. Kelly, *Britain and the Persian Gulf*, 77.

84. Parkinson, *War in the Eastern Seas*, 221–35.

85. William Laird Clowes et al., *The Royal Navy: A History from the Earliest Times to 1900* (London: Chatham, 1997), V:339.

86. Parkinson, *War in the Eastern Seas*, 236–75.

87. Parkinson, *War in the Eastern Seas*, 277.

88. Out of just six ships that Linois had at his disposal, one was ordered to return to France in 1804, another was detached to the Dutch colonies, a third was was wrecked in 1805, and a fourth was detached for service in the Pacific, leaving the admiral with just two ships by late 1805.

89. Kenneth Johnson, "Napoleon's War at Sea," in *Napoleon and the Operational Art of War*, ed. Michael V. Leggiere (Leiden: Brill, 2016), 459.

90. Cited in Ingram, *In Defense of British India*, 124.

91. Cited in Ingram, *In Defense of British India*, 125.

92. Minto to Pellew, May 4, 1808, cited in Ingram, *In Defense of British India*, 127.

93. For the 1807–1808 period, see Parkinson, *War in the Eastern Seas*, 276–319.

94. Jean-Paul Faivre, *Le contre-amiral Hamelin et la Marine française* (Paris: Nouvelles éditions latines, 1962), 80–86; Parkinson, *War in the Eastern Seas*, 364–82; Stephen Taylor, *Storm and Conquest: The Clash of Empires in the Eastern Seas, 1809* (New York: W. W. Norton, 2008), 251–55.

95. Robert Gardiner, *The Victory of Seapower: Winning the Napoleonic War, 1806–1814* (London: Caxton Editions, 1998), 92–96; William James, *The Naval History of Great Britain* (London: Conway Maritime Press, 2002), V:197–98, 271–73.

96. Parkinson, *War in the Eastern Seas*, 383–96; Prentout, *L'Île de France sous Decaen*, 558–79; Taylor, *Storm and Conquest*, 279–300.

97. Widely celebrated in France, it remains the only naval battle commemorated on the Arc de Triomphe.

98. James, *The Naval History of Great Britain*, V:428.

99. Prentout, *L'Île de France sous Decaen*, 592–614; Parkinson, *War in the Eastern Seas*, 397–410; Gardiner, *The Victory of Seapower*, 96–97; Clowes et al., *The Royal Navy*, V:294–95; James, *The Naval History of Great Britain*, V:325–26.

100. For details on Napoleon's efforts to support Decaen in 1810, see *CN*, XX:403, 439; XXI:4–5, 83–85, 244–46, 421–22.

101. Gardiner, *The Victory of Seapower*, 98–99.

102. Johnson, "Napoleon's War at Sea," 461.

103. Bernard Vlekke, *Nusantara: A History of the East Indian Archipelago* (Cambridge, MA: Harvard University Press, 1943), 105–213.

104. For the charter's text and related documents, see Pieter Mijer, ed., *Verzameling van instructien, ordonnancien en reglementen voor de regering van Nederlandsch Indië* (Batavia: Ter Lands-Drukkerij, 1848), 119–344.

105. Instructions in Mijer, *Verzameling van instruction*, 345–68.

106. Board of Control to Lord Minto, August 31, 1810, in *Het Nederlandsch gezag over Java en onderhoorigheden sedert 1811. Verzameling van onuitgegeven stukken uit*

de koloniale en andere arhieven, ed. Marinus Lodewijk van Deventer (S'Gravenhage: M. Nijhoff, 1891), I:4 n.1.

107. Fortescue, *A History of the British Army*, VII:605–6.

108. The expedition was initially under the command of Vice Admiral William O'Bryen Drury, but he died in March 1811.

109. *Lord Minto in India: Life and Letters of Gilbert Elliot, First Earl of Minto, from 1807 to 1814* (London: Longmans, Green, 1880), 291.

110. For details on the campaign, see Janssens's report in Johan Karel Jacob De Jonge, ed., *De opkomst van het Nederlandsch gezag in Oost-Indië* ('S Gravenhage: M. Nijhoff, 1888), XIII:545–49; Parkinson, *War in the Eastern Seas*, 414–17; Bernhard, Duke of Saxe-Weimar-Eisenach, *Précis de la campagne de Java en 1811* (La Haye: T. Lejeune, 1834); G. B. Hooijer, *De krijgsgeschiedenis van Nederlandsch-Indië van 1811 tot 1894* (Batavia: G. Kolff, 1895), I:9–31.

111. Minto to the Earl of Liverpool, September 2, 1811, in William Thorn, *Memoir of the Conquest of Java, with the Subsequent Operations of the British Forces in the Oriental Archipelago* (London: T. Egerton, 1815), 88–89.

Chapter 20

1. In the early eighteenth century Spanish kings, following a French example, also introduced the system of intendants to Spain's New World territories. These royal officials possessed broad military, administrative, and financial authority within their intendancies, smaller divisions within each viceroyalty, and were responsible not to the viceroy but to the monarchy in Madrid. John Lynch, *Bourbon Spain, 1700–1808* (Oxford: Basil Blackwell, 1989), 169, 329–40; David R. Ringrose, *Spain, Europe and the "Spanish Miracle," 1700–1900* (Cambridge: Cambridge University Press, 1997), 257–58; Matthew Restall and Kris E. Lane, *Latin America in Colonial Times* (Cambridge: Cambridge University Press, 2011), 129–232, 255–74. On the level of autonomy of the *cabildos*, see Jordana Dym, *From Sovereign Villages to National States: City, State and Federation in Central America, 1759–39* (Albuquerque: University of New Mexico Press, 2006), 33–64.

2. Lynch, *Bourbon Spain*, 348–50.

3. On the Enlightenment in Latin America, see Brian Hamnett, *The Enlightenment in Iberia and Ibero-America* (Cardiff: University of Wales Press, 2017); Owen A. Aldridge, ed., *The Ibero American Enlightenment* (Urbana: University of Illinois Press, 1971); Arthur P. Whitaker, ed., *Latin America and the Enlightenment* (Ithaca, NY: Great Seal Books, 1958).

4. By comparison, the total population of British North America in 1770 was 2.3 million, of whom 1.8 were white and 467,000 black; although there are no contemporary statistics for Native Americans, it is estimated the number of those residing east of the Mississippi hovered around 150,000. John McCusker and Russell Menard, *The Economy of British America* (Chapel Hill: University of North Carolina Press, 2014), 54.

5. For a concise discussion, see Mark A. Burkholder, *Spaniards in the Colonial Empire: Creoles vs. Peninsulars?* (Malden, MA: John Wiley & Sons, 2013); John Lynch, *The Spanish-American Revolutions, 1808–1826* (New York: Norton, 1973), 18ff. For population data, see Richard Morse, "Urban Development of Colonial Spanish America," in *The Cambridge History of Latin America*, ed. Leslie Bethell (Cambridge: Cambridge University Press, 1984), II:89.

6. Michael Zeuske, "The French Revolution in Spanish America," in *The Routledge Companion to the French Revolution in World History*, ed. Alan Forrest and Matthias Middell (London: Routledge, 2016), 77–96.

7. Brissot to Miranda, October 13, 1792, in Arístides Rojas, ed., *Miranda dans la révolution française. Recueil de documents authentiques relatifs à l'histoire du général Francisco de Miranda, pendant son séjour en France de 1792 à 1798* (Caracas: Impr. et lith. du Gouvernement national, 1889), 8.

8. Albert Sorel, *L'Europe et la Révolution française* (Paris: Plon Nourrit, 1903), II:422–423.

9. Dumouriez to Lebrun, November 30, 1792, in Sorel, *L'Europe et la révolution française*, III:175. See the 1792 plan for revolution in Louisiana, and Gilbert Imlay's memorandum, in *Annual Report of the American Historical Association*, 1896, I:945–54. Also see "Documents on the Relations of France to Louisiana, 1792–1795," *American Historical Review* 3 (1898): 491–10.

10. Records of the Meeting of the Committee of General Defense, January 25, 1793, in François-Alphonse Aulard, *Recueil des actes du Comité de salut public* (Paris: Imprimerie nationale, 1889), II:10. The committee again discussed this issue during its meeting on April 5. Aulard, *Recueil*, III:82.

11. Instructions of December 1792, in *Annual Report of the American Historical Association*, 1896, I:957–63.

12. Clark to Genêt, February 5, 1793, in *Annual Report of the American Historical Association*, 1896, I:967–71.

13. William Hayden English, *Conquest of the Country Northwest of the River Ohio, 1778–1783, and Life of Gen. George Rogers Clark* (Indianapolis: Bowen-Merrill, 1896), II:817–18.

14. For an interesting contemporary assessment, see French Minister to Philadelphia P. A. Adet's report of February 9, 1796, in *Annual Report of the American Historical Association* (1903), II:826–31.

15. R. King to Secretary of State, March 29 and June 1, 1801, in *The Life and Correspondence of Rufus King*, ed. Charles R. King (New York: G. P. Putnam's Sons, 1896), III:414–15; 469; *American State Papers: Documents, Legislative and Executive, of the Congress of the United States*, ed. Walter Lowrie and Matthew St. Clair Clarke (Washington, DC: Gales and Seaton, 1832), II:509–10. For an old but still highly useful discussion, see Frederick J. Turner, "The Diplomatic Contest for the Mississippi Valley," *Atlantic Monthly* XCIII (1904): 676–91, 807–17.

16. J. Leitch Wright, *William Augustus Bowles: Director General of the Creek Nation* (Athens: University of Georgia Press, 2010), 96–98; Thomas Perkins

Abernethy, *The South in the New Nation, 1789–1819* (Baton Rouge: Louisiana State University Press, 1961), 169–91.

17. King to Secretary of State, April 2, 1803, in *The Life and Correspondence of Rufus King,* IV:241.

18. King to Secretary of State, June 1, 1801, and April 2, 1803, in *The Life and Correspondence of Rufus King,* III:469, IV:241.

19. Thornton to Hawkesbury, May 30, 1803, in James A. Robertson, ed., *Louisiana Under the Rule of Spain, France, and the United States, 1785–1807* (Cleveland: Arthur H. Clark, 1911), II:20–21.

20. King to Secretary of State, April 2, 1803, in *The Life and Correspondence of Rufus King,* IV:241.

21. Lord Hawkesbury to King, May 19, 1803, in *The Life and Correspondence of Rufus King,* IV:26263.

22. For the conspiracy of Aaron Burr, see documents related to his trial in Thomas Jefferson Papers at the Library of Congress, https://www.loc.gov/collections/thomas-jefferson-papers; Walter Flavius McCaleb, *The Aaron Burr Conspiracy* (New York: Wilson-Erickson, 1936); Thomas Perkins Abernethy, *The Burr Conspiracy* (New York: Oxford University Press, 1954).

23. Wilkinson to Jefferson, March 12, 1807, cited in Isaac J. Cox, "The Pan-American Policy of Jefferson and Wilkinson," *Mississippi Valley Historical Review* 1, no. 2 (1914): 215.

24. Cox, "The Pan-American Policy of Jefferson and Wilkinson," 215.

25. Jefferson to Bowdoin, April 2, 1807, in *The Works of Thomas Jefferson* (New York: G. P. Putnam's Sons, 1905), X:381–82. The entire set of Jefferson's works is available at http://oll.libertyfund.org/titles/jefferson-the-works-of-thomas-jefferson-12-vols.

26. *Politicheskii, statisticheskii i geograficheskii zhurnal,* January 1808.

27. In 1808–1809 one of the leading merchants in St. Petersburg, Ivan Kremer, submitted a project for an expedition to South America. Discussing political and economic realities in Europe, Kremer noted that, given the Continental Blockade, Britain could not supply Spanish and Portuguese colonies in America with basic supplies and raw materials, which were usually acquired in Russia. Therefore, Russia stood to derive considerable benefits from entering American markets, where it could sell necessary raw materials and buy sorely needed colonial produce. The Russian government approved this project and Kremer outfitted two vessels for the long journey to the Americas. The Russian merchants were not alone in their hopes to establish direct trade in the New World. Their Portuguese colleagues also hoped to exploit lucrative trade with the northern power. In 1811–1812 Dionizio Pedro Lopes, one of the most successful Portuguese merchants, undertook an arduous fourteen-month journey from Russia to Brazil, where he promoted commercial ties and offered his services to local merchants needing credit lines to trade with Russia. Russell H. Bartley,

Imperial Russia and the Struggle for Latin American Independence, 1808–28 (Austin: University of Texas at Austin, 1978), 38–40.

28. Bartley, *Imperial Russia and the Struggle for Latin American Independence*, 42.

29. In September 1811 Rumyantsev submitted a new memorandum on relations between Russia and Spanish America. "There can be no doubt," he observed, "about the extent to which our commerce would benefit from this extension of direct relations to a region overflowing with all manner of products and even the most precious of metals, yet wanting for our surpluses of goods."

30. J. Holland Rose, *The Life of Napoleon I* (London: George Bell and Sons, 1907), I:154.

31. José M. Portillo Valdés, *Crisis atlántica: Autonomía e independencia en la crisis de la monarquía Española* (Madrid: Marcial pons, 2006), 56ff.; Antonio Moliner Prada, "El movimiento juntero en la España de 1808," in *1808: La eclosión juntera en el mundo hispano,* ed. Manuel Chust (Mexico City: Fondo de Cultura Económica, 2007), 51–79.

32. See Champagny's and Azanza's letters to colonial officials (including Azanza's May 13 memorandum on "the New Government of Spain") in Archives du Ministère des Affaires Étrangères, Correspondance politique, "Espagne," 674. These documents are also discussed in William S. Robertson, *France and Latin-American Independence* (New York: Octagon Books, 1967), 41–44.

33. Among these was Claude Henri Étienne Marquis de Sassenay, whom Napoleon selected as his agent in South America. Claude Henri Étienne Sassenay, *Napoléon Ier et la fondation de la République Argentine; Jacques de Liniers, comte de Buenos-Ayres, vice-roi de La Plata, et le marquis de Sassenay (1808–10)* (Paris: E. Plon, Nourrit, 1892), 128–84; for an example of Napoleon's instructions to his emissaries, see 131–34.

34. Champagny to Sassenay, May 29, 1808, in Sassenay, *Napoléon Ier et la fondation de la République Argentine*, 132. Dispatches to specific colonial administrators, including Viceroy Liniers of Río de La Plata, are preserved at Archives du Ministère des Affaires Étrangères, "Espagne," 674–75. For further details on French outreach to the Spanish colonial officials, see Robertson, *France and Latin-American Independence,* 49ff.

35. Rapport de M. de Sassenay, May 23, 1810, in Sassenay, *Napoléon Ier et la fondation de la République Argentine*, 251–52. For responses in various parts of Spanish America, see Robertson, *France and Latin-American Independence,* 57–60.

36. "Manifesto Addressed to All Nations by the Supreme Director of Chile, on the Motives Which Justify the Revolution of the Country, and the Declaration of Its Independence," in *American State Papers: Documents, Legislative and Executive of the Congress of the United States* (Washington, DC: Gales and Seaton, 1834), IV:322.

37. Brian R. Hamnett, "Mexico's Royalist Coalition: The Response to Revolution 1808–1821," *Journal of Latin American Studies* 12, no. 1 (1980): 57–62. For events in Venezuela, see documents in José Félix Blanco, ed., *Documentos para*

la historia de la vida publica del Libertador de Colombia, Peru y Bolivia (Caracas: Imprenta de "La Opinion Nacional," 1875), II:160–62.

38. *Justa reclamacion: que los representantes de la casa Real de España doña Carlota Juaquina de Bourbon Princesa de Portugal y Brazil, y Don Pedro Carlos de Bourbon y Braganza, Infante de España, hacen á su alteza Real el Principe Regente de Portugal* (1808), https://archive.org/details/justareclamacionoocarl; *Respuesta de S.A.R. el Principe Regente de Portugal, á la reclamacion hecha por SS. AA. RR. La Princesa del Brazil, y el Infante de España don Pedro Carlos,: implorando su proteccion y auxilios para sostener sus derechos, conservando los del Rey de España, y demas miembros de la Real Familia, arrancada y conducida con violencia á lo interior del Imperio Frances* (1808), https://archive.org/details/respuestadesarelooport; *Manifiesto dirigido á los fieles vasallos de su Magestad Católica el Rey de las Españas é Indias* (1808), https://archive.org/details/manifiesto dirigioocarl.

39. Julián María Rubio, *La infanta Carlota Joaquina y la política de España en América (1808–12)* (Madrid: Impr. de E. Maestre, 1920), 42–73; R. A. Humphreys, *Liberation in South America, 1806–27: The Career of James Paroissien* (London: Athlone Press, 1952), 21–36.

40. William Kaufmann, *British Policy and the Independence of Latin America, 1804–1828* (New Haven, CT: Yale University Press, 1951), 58. Also see John Street, "Lord Strangford and Rio de la Plata, 1808–1815," in *Hispanic American Historical Review* 33, no. 4 (1953): 477–86.

41. The name, coined by Thomas Carlyle in 1858, stems from the incident that sparked the conflict. Robert Jenkins, a captain of a British merchant ship and acknowledged smuggler, was caught by a Spanish warship while engaging in contraband and had his ear cut off by Julio León Fandiño, Spanish commanding officer. The severed ear was subsequently exhibited before the British Parliament, which denounced Spanish "depredations upon the British subjects" and considered the incident as an insult and a *casus belli*. Harold W. V. Temperley, "The Causes of the War of Jenkins' Ear, 1739," *Transactions of the Royal Historical Society* 3 (1909): 197–36; Edward W. Lawson, "What Became of the Man Who Cut off Jenkins' Ear?," *Florida Historical Quarterly* 37, no. 1 (1958): 33–41.

42. Kaufmann, *British Policy and the Independence of Latin America*, 18–37.

43. Castlereagh's memorandum, May 1, 1807, in Robert Stewart, Viscount Castlereagh, *Correspondence, Despatches and Other Papers of Viscount Castlereagh* (London: William Shoberl, 1851), VII:321. His undated memorandum starts with "the liberation of South America must be accomplished through the wishes and exertions of the inhabitants," but then proceeds to outline plans for British intervention. Also see projects by the Duke of Orleans ("Memoir on Spanish America and the Viceroyalty of Mexico in particular"), General Dumouriez ("On the Establishment of Naval Stations and Survey of the States of America"), and Miranda's continued appeals for British intervention into Spanish America, which Castlereagh considered and discussed in 1807. *Correspondence, Despatches and Other Papers of Castlereagh*, VII:332–90.

44. Sheridan's speech of June 15, 1808, in *Hansard's Parliamentary Debates*, XI:887–88; *Morning Chronicle*, June 9, 1808.

45. Castlereagh to the Duke of Manchester, June 4, 1808, in *Correspondence, Despatches and Other Papers of Castlereagh*, VI:365.

46. Kaufmann, *British Policy and the Independence of Latin America*, 53.

47. Canning to Strangford, April 17, 1808, cited in Alan K. Manchester, *British Preeminence in Brazil, Its Rise and Decline: A Study in European Expansion* (Chapel Hill: University of North Carolina Press, 1933), 78.

48. *Le Moniteur Universal*, December 14, 1809.

49. For details, see Robertson, *France and Latin-American Independence*, 62–104; John Rydjord, *Foreign Interest in the Independence of New Spain: An Introduction to the War for Independence* (Durham, NC: Duke University Press, 1935), 259–62, 290–308. Also see Caracciolo Parra-Perez, *Bayona y la politica de Napoleon en America* (Caracas: Tipografía americana, 1939).

50. In contrast, the islands of Cuba and Puerto Rico, as well as the regions of Santo Domingo and Central America, remained firmly royalist due to several factors, including the presence of strong garrisons and fear of slave uprisings.

51. For an interesting discussion of the meaning of royalism in the Spanish America, see Marcela Echeverri, "Popular Royalists, Empire and Politics in Southwestern New Granada," *Hispanic American Historical Review* 91, no. 2 (2011): 237–69.

52. For a discussion of wars of Latin American independence as a transatlantic civil war between Spaniards, see Jaime E. Rodríguez O., *The Independence of Spanish America* (Cambridge: Cambridge University Press, 1998).

53. Rydjord, *Foreign Interest in the Independence of New Spain*, 272–85; Hugh M. Hamill, "'An 'Absurd Insurrection'? Creole Insecurity, Pro-Spanish Propaganda, and the Hidalgo Revolt," in *The Birth of Modern Mexico, 1780–1824*, ed. Christon I. Archer (Lanham MD: Rowman & Littlefield, 2003), 71–72; Brian R. Hamnett, "Mexico's Royalist Coalition: The Response to Revolution 1808–1821," *Journal of Latin American Studies* 12, no. 1 (1980): 57–62; Francisco A. Eissa-Barroso, "The Illusion of Disloyalty: Rumours, Distrust, and Antagonism, and the Charges Brought Against the Viceroy of New Spain in the Autumn of 1808," *Hispanic Research Journal* 11, no. 1 (2010): 25–36.

54. See Timothy E. Anna, *The Fall of the Royal Government in Mexico City* (Lincoln: University of Nebraska Press, 1978), 35–54.

55. See Eric van Young, *The Other Rebellion: Popular Violence, Ideology, and the Mexican Struggle for Independence, 1810–21* (Stanford, CA: Stanford University Press, 2001).

56. For details, see Timothy J. Henderson, *The Mexican Wars of Independence* (New York: Hill and Wang, 2009), 90–92; Hugh M. Hamill, *The Hidalgo Revolt: Prelude to Mexican Independence* (Gainesville: University of Florida Press, 1966).

57. See Wilbert H. Timmons, *Morelos: Priest, Soldier, Statesman of Mexico* (El Paso, TX: Western College Press, 1963).

58. Jaime E. Rodríguez, *"We Are Now the True Spaniards"*: *Sovereignty, Revolution, Independence, and the Emergence of the Federal Republic of Mexico, 1808–24* (Stanford, CA: Stanford University Press, 2012), 221–31; Jaime Salazar Adame and Smirna Romero Garibay, *El Congreso de Chilpancingo: 200 años* (Guerrero, Mexico: Consejo de la Crónica del Estado de Guerrero, 2015).

59. Anthony McFarlane, *War and Independence in Spanish America* (New York: Routledge, 2014), 219–82.

60. Fabrício Prado, *Edge of Empire: Atlantic Networks and Revolution in Bourbon Río de la Plata* (Berkeley: University of California Press, 2015), esp. 155.

61. For details, see Arturo Bentancur, *El puerto colonial de Montevideo* (Montevideo: Universidade de la República; FHCE, 1997), II:15–17.

62. *Documentos relativos a la Junta Montevideana de Gobierno de 1808* (Montevideo: Museo Histórico Nacional A. Monteverde, 1958), I:210–18; Miguel Angel Cárcano, *La Politica Internacional en la Historia Argentina* (Buenos Aires: Editorial Universitaria de Buenos Aires, 1972), I:270; Alfredo Avila and Pedro Pérez Herrero, *Las experiencias de 1808 en iberoamérica* (Mexico City: Universidad Nacional Autónoma de México, Instituto de Investigaciones Históricas, 2008), 543.

63. For details, see documents in Ricardo Rodolfo Caillet-Bois, *Mayo documental* (Buenos Aires: Universidad de Buenos Aires, 1961), IX:150–70.

64. See the excellent discussion in Bernardo Lozier Almazán, *Martín de Alzaga: historia de una trágica ambición* (Buenos Aires: Ediciones Ciudad, 1998), esp. 194ff.; Jeremy Adelman, *Sovereignty and Revolution in the Iberian Atlantic* (Princeton, NJ: Princeton University Press, 2009), 208–10; Carlos Alberto Pueyrredón, *1810. La revolución de Mayo* (Buenos Aires: Ediciones Peuser, 1953), 247–49, 278–80.

65. For an excellent overview, see McFarlane, *War and Independence in Spanish America*, 145–80.

66. Luis Herreros de Tejada, *El teniente general D. Jose Manuel de Goyeneche, primer conde de Guaqui* (Barcelona: Oliva de Vilanova, 1923), 263–84.

67. Prado, *Edge of Empire*, 159–62.

68. Kaufmann, *British Policy and the Independence of Latin America*, 59–60.

69. Pablo Camogli and Luciano de Privitellio, *Batallas por la libertad: todos los combates de la guerra de la independencia* (Buenos Aires: Aguilar, 2005), 166–68.

70. McFarlane, *War and Independence in Spanish America*, 205–7.

71. John Hoyt Williams, *The Rise and Fall of the Paraguayan Republic, 1800–70* (Austin: Institute of Latin American Studies, University of Texas at Austin, 1979), ch. 1.

72. Robert L. Gilmore, "The Imperial Crisis, Rebellion and the Viceroy: Nueva Granada in 1809," *Hispanic American Historical Review* 40, no. 1 (1960): 2–24.

73. David Bethell, "The Independence of Spanish South America," in *The Cambridge History of Latin America*, ed. Leslie Bethell (Cambridge: Cambridge University Press, 1985), III:113.

74. This captaincy general was technically part of the Viceroyalty of New Granada but was autonomously administered.

75. Kaufmann, *British Policy and the Independence of Latin America*, 49–52.

76. McFarlane, *War and Independence in Spanish America*, 111–44.

Chapter 21

1. Friedrich Meinecke, *The Age of German Liberation, 1795–1815*, ed. Peter Paret (Berkeley: University of California Press, 1977), 102. Also see James Elstone Dow, *A Good German Conscience: The Life and Time of Ernst Moritz Arndt* (Lanham, MD: University Press of America, 1995); Jon Vanden Heuvel, *A German Life in the Age of Revolution: Joseph Görres, 1776–1848* (Washington, DC: Catholic University of America Press, 2001), chs. 6–7.

2. Martin P. Schennach, "'We Are Constituted as a Nation': Austria in the Era of Napoleon," in *Napoleon's Empire: European Politics in Global Perspective*, ed. Ute Planert (New York: Palgrave Macmillan, 2016), 245–46.

3. Some may also cite the popular uprising in Spain as a particularly striking example of nationalist reaction against Napoleon and the French, but in the motivation triad of "God, king, and nation" the latter was frequently negated by Spanish parochialism and tradition. See E. Goodman, "Spanish Nationalism in the Struggle Against Napoleon," *Review of Politics* 20, no. 3 (July 1958): 330–46; Charles J. Esdaile, *Outpost of Empire: The Napoleonic Occupation of Andalucia, 1810–12* (Norman: University of Oklahoma Press, 2012).

4. For details on the Franco-Russian relations, see Albert Vandal, *Napoléon et Alexandre Ier, l'alliance russe sous le premier Empire* (Paris: 1896), III:1–455; Dominic Lieven, *Russia Against Napoleon* (London: Penguin, 2010), chs. 3–4; Michael Adams, *Napoleon and Russia* (London: Hambledon Continuum, 2006), chs. 12–14.

5. Eugene Tarle, *Sochineniya*, vol. 3, *Kontinentalnaya blokada* (Moscow, 1958), 342–43. In June 1807, just weeks before the Treaty of Tilsit, the English merchants were responsible for almost half of the goods traded in St. Petersburg and delivered goods for a total value of 2.1 billion rubles, far ahead of any other European country and second only to the 2.6 billion rubles' worth of goods traded by Russian merchants. Just two months later, the share of goods traded by the British merchants dramatically fell to only 0.5 million rubles in July and none in September, while the total value of goods traded in the Russian capital fell from 4.9 billion (June) to 2.7 billion (July) to 1.5 billion in September. Based on data in *St. Petersburgskie Vedomosti* of August–November 1807. For an in-depth discussion, see Mikhail Zlotnikov, *Kontinentalnaya blokada i Rossiya* (Moscow: Nauka, 1966). Zlotnikov's study remains one of the best analyses of the Continental Blockade's effect on Russia. The author wrote his manuscript before World War II and made extensive use of archival materials, some of which were later destroyed during the war. So far there is no other study that can approach this book in its level of detail or scope.

6. See Caulaincourt to Napoleon, April 5, 1808, in *SIRIO*, 138:637; Zlotnikov, *Kontinentalnaya blokada i Rossiya*. 142. For a broader discussion, see Saulius Antanas Girnius, "Russia and the Continental Blockade," PhD diss., University of Chicago, 1981.

7. For an interesting discussion of the French effort to mitigate the Russian economic crisis, see the French diplomatic correspondence in *SIRIO*, vol. 138.

8. A large component in this deficit increase was military expenditures, which grew throughout the period 1805–1811. In 1808–1811, Russia, after ending the war with France, waged simultaneous wars against Sweden and Ottoman Empire, while being nominally at war with Britain (the Anglo-Russian conflict was limited to a few naval actions in the Baltic Sea).

9. The growing annual deficit was covered by new issues of paper currency. In 1801 the government had 214 million rubles' worth of paper money in circulation and gradually increased that number to offset economic problems. In 1807 the government issued 63 million new paper rubles; in 1808, 95 million (the highest during the Napoleonic Wars); in 1809, 55.8 million; and in 1810, another 46.2 million. Ivan Bliokh, *Finansy Rossii XIX stoletiya*. (St. Petersburg: M. M. Stasyulevich, 1882), I:84.

10. The Russian government did take measures to avoid the catastrophe. It restricted the amount of money printed, and it pledged to consider paper rubles as a state debt that would be redeemed at all cost. Taxes were raised, superfluous spending cut, and import of luxury items restricted through prohibitive tariffs. Finally Russia began to allow neutral ships to trade in Russian ports, which effectively undermined the Continental System.

11. Napoleon to Champagny, Champagny to Kurakin, November 4–December 2, 1810, in *CN*, nos. 17,099 and 17,179, XXI:252–53, 297–98; for similar sentiments, see also nos. 17,041, 17,071, 17,099, 17,831, and 17,917. Also see Caulaincourt to Champagny, July 16, 1808; Caulaincourt to Champagny, April 18, 1810, Caulaincourt to Champagny, April 30, 1810, Vel. Kn. Nikolay Mikhailovich, *Diplomaticheskie snoshenia Rossii i Frantsii po doneseniyam poslov Imperatorov Aleksandra i Napoleona, 1808–1812* (St. Petersburg: Ekspeditsia zagotovleniya gosudarstvennykh bumag, 1905), II:231; IV:359–66.

12. Napoleon's memorandum, in Vandal, *Napoléon et Alexandre*, III:222.

13. Nicola Todorov has recently argued that Napoleon's territorial annexations in 1810–1812 were in fact part of a larger (and secret) plan to invade Britain. For details see his *La Grande Armée à la conquête de l'Angleterre: Le plan secret de Napoléon* (Paris: Éditions Vendémiaire, 2016).

14. This report, dated March 16, 1810, is reproduced in full (in French) in Nikolai Shilder, *Imperator Aleksandr Pervyi* (St. Petersburg, 1898), III:471–83. A month later, Napoleon approved Champagny's proposal for the creation of an alliance between France, Sweden, Denmark, and the Grand Duchy of Warsaw, which, however, did not materialize due to Swedish and Danish reluctance to participate. *CN*, XX:305. Champagny wrote to the French envoy to Denmark,

Charles-François-Luce Didelot, that "Sweden already fears Russia. Does Denmark feel the same fear? Common interests must force Sweden, Denmark, and the Duchy of Warsaw to unite in a secret alliance, which can absolutely and really be guaranteed by France." Denmark eventually agreed to a treaty with France. On March 7, 1812, Napoleon shored up his northern territories by inducing the Danish king, Frederick VI, to mobilize 10,000 troops on the Holstein and Schleswig frontier to deter a possible landing there by British, Swedish, and/or Russian troops. The Military Convention between France and Denmark of March 7, 1812 can be found in Jules de Clercq, ed., *Recueil des traités de la France* (Paris, 1864), II:363–65.

15. Throughout 1810 and 1811, the Prussian court was haunted by the dread that Napoleon might attempt to carry out his oft-repeated threat to dispossess the Hohenzollern dynasty. Consequently, King Frederick William III pursued a dual policy of appeasing France in public while secretly seeking help against Napoleon. In this, he was influenced by his chancellor, Karl August von Hardenberg, and the head of the Prussian General Staff, General Gerhard Johann David Waitz von Scharnhorst. On October 18, 1811, Russian foreign minister Nikolai Petrovich Rumyantsev and Scharnhorst actually signed a treaty of mutual support in the event of a war with France. But the Prussian king refused to ratify that deal unless Austria joined the effort as well—a step that the Austrian emperor, Francis I, was not yet willing to make.

16. The Franco-Prussian Treaty of Paris of February 24, 1812, can be found in Clercq, *Recueil des traités de la France*, II:356–63. Also see Llewellyn Cook, "Prince Schwarzenberg's Crisis in 1812: In The Service Of Two Emperors," *CRE* (1995), 351–58; Llewellyn Cook, "Prince Schwarzenberg's Mission to St. Petersburg, 1809," *CRE* (1998), 399–410.

17. The Franco-Austrian treaty of March 14, 1812, can be found in Clercq, *Recueil des traités de la France*, II:369–72. Also see Cook, "Prince Schwarzenberg's Crisis in 1812" and "Prince Schwarzenberg's Mission to St. Petersburg."

18. *VPR*, VI:318–28. The Treaty of St. Petersburg was augmented with additional conventions signed in Vilna on June 3 and Åbo on August 30.

19. Russia received Bessarabia and most of western Georgia but surrendered Moldavia and Wallachia, which its armies had occupied since 1807. For the text of the treaty, see *VPR*, VI:406–17.

20. On December 19, 1811, Napoleon's private secretary, Claude François de Méneval, informed the emperor's librarian, Antoine-Alexandre Barbier: "I request that you send me for His Majesty a few good books, most suitable for studying the nature of the soil of Russia, and especially of Lithuania, with respect to its marshes, rivers, forests, and roads. His Majesty also desires to obtain works that describe, in detail, the campaign of Charles XII in Poland and Russia. In addition, send any books on military operations in this region that might be useful." *CN*, XXIII:95. A month later Méneval again asked for books concerning the "history of Courland, as well as all that can be obtained

regarding the history, geography, and topography of Riga, Livonia, etc." *CN*, XXIII:162.

21. *CN*, XXIII:143, 432.

22. Major French garrisons in North Germany included Hamburg (6,375 men), Magdeburg (8,851), Danzig (20,464), and Stettin (8,491). For Napoleon's preparations see *Correspondance de Napoléon*, vols. 21–23; Louis Joseph Margueron, ed., *Campagne de Russie: préliminaires de la Campagne de Russie, ses causes, sa préparation, organisation de l'armée du 1 Janvier 1810 au 31 Janvier 1812*, 2 vols. (Paris: Lavauzelle 1899).

23. See Décret du 21 décembre 1811, in Margueron, *Campagne de Russie*, III:427–30.

24. The army consisted of about 492,000 infantry, 96,000 cavalry, and some 20,000 auxiliary forces. On March 3, Napoleon settled the organization of the Grand Armée, which consisted of eight army corps (four French and four foreign) and four cavalry corps. *CN*, no. 18544, XXIII:277–78.

25. The term "Vilna Maneuver" is rarely used in Anglophone studies, but it has a long history in Russian and French historiography. See H. Bonnal, *La manoevre de Vilna* (Paris: Chapelot, 1905); B. Kuznetsov, *Kratkii ocherk podgotovki i razvertyvanie storon v 1812 g. Vilenskaya operatsiya* (Moscow, 1932); V. Kharkevich, *Voina 1812 g. ot Nemana do Smolenska* (Vilna, 1901), 96–158.

26. Napoleon to Berthier, July 2, 1812, in *CN*, XXIV:7.

27. Berthier to Davout, 8:00 p.m., June 24, 1812, in Gabriel Fabry, *Campagne de Russie, 1812* (Paris: Lucien Gougy, 1900), I:4.

28. Napoleon to Berthier, 5:00 a.m., June 25, 1812, in Fabry, *Campagne de Russie*, I:9.

29. For the Anglo-Russian treaty's text, see *PSZ*, XXXII:389–90; F. Martens, *Recueil des traités et conventions conclus par la Russie avec les puissances étrangères* (St. Petersburg: A. Böhnke, 1902), XI:162–65.

30. Treaty of Velikie Luki, July 20, 1812, *VPR*, VI:495–97.

31. For details, see V. Roginskii, *Shvetsiya i Rossiya: Soyuz 1812 goda* (Moscow: Nauka, 1978), 118, 158–59.

32. The British merchants demanded 25 rubles for each musket and 29 rubles per *pud* of gunpowder, a significant markup considering that muskets cost less than 15 rubles before the war. See P. Schukin, ed., *Bumagi otnosyaschiesya do Otechestvennoi voiny 1812 goda* (Moscow: Tip. A. Mamontova, 1903), VII:181–82.

33. The British weapons were retrofitted at the Sestroretskii Arms Manufacturing facility and placed at the St. Pegtersburg Arsenal. In December, some 30,000 British muskets were delivered to Nizhegorod Province to equip the newly raised reserve units, while more than 7,700 muskets were sent to the 6th and 21st Divisions; the remaining 12,240 weapons were kept at the aarsenal and were later distributed to the militias. For criticism of British arms supplies, see the works of Soviet historians including Pavel Zhilin, *Kontranastuplenie Kutuzova v 1812 g.* (Moscow: Voennoe izd-vo, 1950), 119–20; L. Zak, Angliya

i germanskaya problema. Iz Diplomaticheskoi istorii napoleonovskikh voin (Moscow: Izd-vo Instituta Mezhd. Otnoshenii, 1963), 55–56. For most recent (and judicious) discussion, see A. Orlov, *Soyuz Peterburga i Londona: Rossiisko-Britanskie otnosheniya v epokhu napoleonovskikh voina* (Moscow: Progress-Traditsiya, 2005), 226–29.

34. Martens, *Recueil des traités et conventions conclus par la Russie,* XI:166. The British envoy to St. Petersburg, William, Earl Cathcart, was given some £500,000 to support Sweden and Russia, but the sum was clearly insufficient for Russia's military needs. John M. Sherwig, *Guineas and Gunpowder: British Foreign Aid in the Wars with France, 1793–1815* (Cambridge, MA: Harvard University Press, 1969), 277–81. For discussion of the British government's position, see *Hansard's Parliamentary Debates* (London: T. C. Hansard, 1812), XXIV:50–66. It is noteworthy that when the British Parliament debated providing £200,000 in specie and goods to help the inhabitants of devastated Moscow, senior Russian officials wanted to decline the sum because it was perceived as rather negligible—Moscow's devastation was estimated at some £25 million—and humiliating to accept and because they feared that "behind this offer might be concealed [British] intention to instill new habits [onto the Russians] and to spread among the common folk dependence on foreign indulgences that only the English themselves can satisfy." Emperor Alexander rejected these arguments. Rumyantsev to Emperor Alexander; Alexander to Rumyantsev, January 15, 1813, in *Russkaya Starina* 1 (1870): 474–76. The British government also declined to help Russia with regard to the foreign debt it owed to the Dutch bankers.

35. See Adrian Randall, *Riotous Assemblies: Popular Protest in Hanoverian England* (Oxford: Oxford University Press, 2006), 271–331; John Stevenson, *Popular Disturbances in England, 1700–1870* (London: Longman, 1979), 155–61.

36. For details, see Stephan Talty's *The Illustrious Dead: The Terrifying Story of How Typhus Killed Napoleon's Greatest Army* (New York: Random House, 2009), although it tends to exaggerate the role of disease in shaping the outcome of the campaign.

37. Heinrich von Roos, *Avec Napoléon en Russie. Souvenirs d'un médecin de la Grande Armée* (Paris, 1913), 51–53.

38. Anton Gijsbert van Dedem de Gelder, *Un général hollandais sous le premier empire. Mémoires du général Bon de Dedem de Gelder* (Paris: Plon Nourrit, 1900), 225–27.

39. For an in-depth discussion, see Alexander Mikaberidze, *Napoleon Versus Kutuzov: The Battle of Borodino* (London: Pen & Sword, 2007); Christopher Duffy, *Borodino and the War of 1812* (New York: Scribner, 1972); A. Popov and V. Zemtsov, *Borodino: yuzhnyi flang* (Moscow: Kniga, 2009); A. Popov, *Borodino: severnyi flang* (Moscow: Kniga, 2008).

40. See Alexander M. Martin, *Enlightened Metropolis: Constructing Imperial Moscow, 1762–1855* (Oxford: Oxford University Press, 2013).

41. For details, see Alexander Mikaberidze, *Napoleon's Trial by Fire: The Burning of Moscow* (London: Pen & Sword, 2014) and Vladimir Zemtsov, *1812 god: Pozhar Moskvy* (Moscow: Kniga, 2010).

42. Mathieu Dumas, *Souvenirs de lieutenant général comte Mathieu Dumas, de 1770–1836* (Paris: Gosselin, 1839), III:454–55.

43. Lieven, *Russia Against Napoleon*, 251.

44. Philippe-Paul Ségur, *History of the Expedition to Russia Undertaken by the Emperor Napoleon in the Year 1812* (London, 1825), 77.

45. Grand Duchess Catherine to Emperor Alexander, September 18, 1812, in *Correspondance de l'Empereur Alexandre Ier avec sa soeur la Grande-Duchess Catherine* (St. Petersburg: Manufacture des papiers de l'État, 1910), letter XXXIII.

46. Jean-Pierre Barrau, "Jean-Pierre Armand Barrau, Quartier-Maitre au IVe Corps de la Grande Armée, sur la Campagne de Russie," *Rivista Italiana di Studi Napoleonici* 1 (1979): 91.

47. For details see Iv. Bezsonov, *Bitva v Maloyaroslavtse, 12 oktyabrya 1812 goda* (Kaluga: Tip. Gubernskogo pravleniya, 1912); Aleksei Vasiliev, "Srazhenie za Maloyaroslavets, 12 oktyabrya 1812 goda," in *Yubileinyj sbornik. K 190-letiyu Maloyarslavetskogo srazheniya*, http://www.museum.ru/1812/library/Mmnk/2002_9.html.

48. Thierry Lentz, *La conspiration du général Malet, 23 octobre 1812: premier ébranlement du trône de Napoléon* (Paris: Perrin, 2012).

49. For in-depth discussion see Alexander Mikaberidze, *Napoleon's Great Escape: The Battle of the Berezina* (London: Pen & Sword, 2010).

50. For an excellent discussion of French leadership at this period, see Frederick C. Schneid, "The Dynamics of Defeat: French Army Leadership, December 1812–March 1813," *Journal of Military History* 63, no. 1 (1999): 7–28. By late December, the last remnants of the Grande Armée, including the corps of Macdonald and Schwarzenberg, crossed the Niemen. Macdonald received his orders to retreat on December 18 and started the next day in two columns. He moved largely unimpeded by the Russians, who focused on Napoleon's main body. On reaching Tauroggen along the Russo-Prussian border, Prussian general Hans David Ludwig von Yorck concluded the famous convention by which the Prussians were declared neutral. On learning of the catastrophe of the Grande Armée, Schwarzenberg retreated to Bielostok between December 14 and 18; General Jean Louis Ebénézer Reynier's Saxon corps followed him behind the Bug. The Austrian corps eventually reached its own territory, while Reynier moved into Saxony. Poniatowski's Polish corps was interned by the Austrians until the summer armistice of 1813.

51. Robert Wilson, *Narrative of Events During the Invasion of Russia by Napoleon Bonaparte* (London: John Murray, 1869), 368.

52. See Alexander Mikaberidze, "Napoleon's Lost Legions: The Grande Armée Prisoners of War in Russia," *Napoleonica: La Revue* 3, no. 21 (2014): 35–44, http://www.cairn.info/revue-napoleonica-la-revue-2014-3-page-35.htm.

53. Robert Wilson, *Narrative of Events During the Invasion of Russia by Napoleon Bonaparte* (London: John Murray, 1860), 234. Arguing with Bennigsen over strategy, Kutuzov repeatedly argued against unnecessary losses that might weaken Russia's positions in Europe. "We will never come to an agreement; you are only thinking of the benefit for England while to me, even if that island sinks to the bottom of the sea, I would not sigh." A. Voyeikov, "General Graf Leontii Leontievich Bennigsen," *Russkii Arkhiv* 59 (1868): 1857.

54. Eugène of Württemberg, "Vospominania o kampanii 1812 g v Rossii," *Voennii zhurnal* 3 (1849): 131.

55. See Donald R. Hickey, *The War of 1812: A Forgotten Conflict* (Urbana: University of Illinois Press, 2012), 1–3.

56. Turreau to Talleyrand, July 9, 1805, in Archives du Ministère des Affaires Étrangères, Correspondance politique, "Etats-Unis," 58.

57. See discussion of American causes in Troy Bickham, *The Weight of Vengeance: The United States, the British Empire and the War of 1812* (Oxford: Oxford University Press, 2012), ch. 1.

58. Confidential Message, June 1, 1812, in *The Addresses and Messages of the Presidents of the United States to Congress* (New York: Charles Lohman, 1837), 120–24. For a more in-depth discussion, see J. C. A. Stagg, *The War of 1812: Conflict for a Continent* (Cambridge: Cambrudge University Press, 2012), 1–47; Reginald Horsman, *The Causes of the War of 1812* (Philadelphia: University of Pennsylvania Press, 1962); Bradford Perkins, *Prologue to War England and the United States, 1805–12* (Berkeley: University of California Press, 1961).

59. Thomas Jefferson to James Madison, June 6, 1812, in *The Writings of Thomas Jefferson* (Washington, DC: Taylor & Maury, 1854), VI:58.

60. See Gregory Evans Dowd, *A Spirited Resistance: The North American Indian Struggle for Unity, 1745–1815* (Baltimore: Johns Hopkins University Press, 1992); Timothy D. Willig, *Restoring the Chain of Friendship: British Policy and the Indians of the Great Lakes, 1783–1815* (Lincoln: University of Nebraska Press, 2008); Robert M. Owens, *Mr. Jefferson's Hammer: William Henry Harrison and the Origins of American Indian Policy* (Norman: University of Oklahoma Press, 2007).

61. Matthew S. Seligmann, *Rum, Sodomy, Prayers and the Lash Revisited: Winston Churchill and Social Reform in the Royal Navy, 1900–1915* (Oxford: Oxford University Press, 2018), 1.

62. For a critical reassessment of press gangs and impressment in Britain, see J. Ross Dancy, *The Myth of the Press Gang: Volunteers, Impressment and the Naval Manpower Problem in the Late Eighteenth Century* (Rochester, NY: Boydell Press, 2015). This book is one of the first statistical studies of the Royal Navy manning in the eighteenth and early nineteenth centuries, based on exhaustive analysis of muster books from over eighty warships. Also see Nicholas Rogers, *The Press Gang: Naval Impressment and its Opponents in Georgian Britain* (London: Continuum, 2007); Brian DeToy, "The Impressment of American Seamen

during the Napoleonic Wars," *CRE* (1998), 492–501; Keith Mercer, "Northern Exposure: Resistance to Naval Impressment in British North America, 1775–1815," *Canadian Historical Review* 91, no. 2 (June 2010): 199–232; Hickey, *The War of 1812*, 11.

63. For a more critical view see Donald R. Adams Jr., "American Neutrality and Prosperity, 1793–1808: A Reconsideration," *Journal of Economic History* 40, no. 4 (1980): 713–37.

64. Spencer Tucker and Frank Reuter, *Injured Honor: The* Chesapeake-Leopard *Affairs, June 22, 1807* (Annapolis, MD: Naval Institute Press, 1996).

65. John Lambert, *Travels Through Lower Canada and the United States of North America in the Years of 1806, 1807 and 1808* (London: Richard Phillips, 1810), II:157.

66. Bradford Perkins, *Prologue to War: England and the United States, 1805–12* (Berkeley: University of California Press, 1961), 210–20.

67. W. Freeman Galpin, "The American Grain Trade to the Spanish Peninsula, 1810–1814," *American Historical Review* XXVIII (1923): 24–25. For an interesting insight into the Anglo-American commerce as exemplified by W. G. & J. Strutt Company, see R. S. Fitton, "Overseas Trade during the Napoleonic Wars, as Illustrated by the Records of W. G. & J. Strutt," *Economica* 20, no. 77 (1953): 58–69.

68. Henry Adams, *History of the United States of America* (New York: C. Scribner's Sons, 1921), V:252–58.

69. Adams, *History of the United States of America*, V:262–315. For a broad discussion on non-importation see Herbert Heaton, "Non-Importation, 1806–1812," *Journal of Economic History* 1, no. 2 (1941): 178–98.

70. David Milne's report of April 9, 1812, *Report on the Manuscripts of Colonel David Milne Home* (London: His Majesty's Stationery Office, 1902), 155. For data on American ships, see G. E. Watson, "The United States and the Peninsular War, 1808–1812," *Historical Journal* 19, no. 4 (1976): 870–71.

71. Wellington to Stuart, March 1, 1811, in *The Dispatches of Field Marshal, the Duke of Wellington*, ed. John Gurwood (London: John Murray, 1838), VII:324.

72. See interesting discussion in Leland R. Johnson, "The Suspense Was Hell: The Senate Vote for War in 1812," *Indiana Magazine of History* 65 (December 1969): 247–67.

73. For discussion of supply routes, see Philip Lord Jr., "The Mohawk/Oneida Corridor: The Geography of the Inland Navigation Across New York," in *The Sixty Years' War for the Great Lakes, 1754–1814*, ed. David Curtis Skaggs and Larry L. Nelson (East Lansing: Michigan State University Press, 2001), 275–90.

74. Cited in Bickham, *The Weight of Vengeance*.

75. John K. Mahon, "British Command Decisions in the Northern Campaigns of the War of 1812," *Canadian Historical Review* 46 (September 1965): 219–37.

76. For the discussion of war aims, see Reginald Horsman, "Western War Aims, 1811–1812," *Indiana Magazine of History* 53 (March 1957): 1–18. For the role

of "war hawks," a group of congressmen who led the nation into the war, see Harry W. Fritz, "The War Hawks of 1812," *Capitol Studies* 5 (Spring 1977): 25–42. On Tenskwatawa and Tecumseh, see R. David Edmunds, "Tecumseh, the Shawnee Prophet, and American History: A Reassessment," *Western Historical Quarterly* 14 (July 1983): 261–76; Alfred A. Cave, "The Shawnee Prophet, Tecumseh, and Tippecanoe: A Case Study of Historical Myth-Making," *Journal of the Early Republic* 22 (Winter 2002): 637–73.

77. Cited in Robert V. Remini, Henry Clay, *Statesman for the Union* (New York: W. W. Norton, 1991), 60.

78. Jefferson to William Duane, August 4, 1812, in *The Writings of Thomas Jefferson*, XIII:180–81. Also see Pierre Berton, *The Invasion of Canada, 1812–13* (Toronto: Anchor Books, 1980), 15, 99–100; Donald R. Hickey, *The War of 1812: A Short History* (Urbana: University of Illinois Press, 1995), 9–14.

79. Jeffrey Kimball, "The Fog and Friction of Frontier War: The Role of Logistics in American Offensive Failure During the War of 1812," *Old Northwest* 5 (Winter 1979): 323–43.

80. Robert B. McAfee, *History of the Late War in the Western Country* (Bowling Green, OH: Historical Publications, 1919), 121.

81. Jon Latimer, *1812: War with America* (Cambridge, MA: Belknap Press, 2007), 76–83; Theodore J. Crackel, "The Battle of Queenston Heights, 13 October, 1812," in *America's First Battles, 1776–1965*, ed. Charles E. Heller and William A. Sofft (Lawrence: University Press of Kansas, 1986); 33–56.

82. John Robert Elting, *Amateurs, to Arms! A Military History of the War of 1812* (Chapel Hill, NC: Algonquin Books of Chapel Hill, 1991), 50–51. In a separate development, General William Henry Harrison, governor of the Indiana Territory, was able to rebuild US forces in the area, and in November he launched a major offensive against the Miami Indians who had attacked Fort Wayne and Fort Harrison in the Indiana Territory. This campaign culminated in the engagement at Mississinewa (present-day Alabama), where the US force captured a couple of settlements and defeated a Native American counterattack on December 18 before losses and cold weather forced them to withdraw. Still, the expedition secured Harrison's flank from further interference by the Native American tribes.

83. On problems that plagued the British navy, see Barry J. Lohnes, "British Naval Problems at Halifax during the War of 1812," *Mariner's Mirror* 59 (August 1973): 317–33.

84. For a detailed discussion, see Kevin D. McCranie, *Utmost Gallantry: The U.S. and Royal Navies at Sea in the War of 1812* (Annapolis, MD: Naval Institute Press, 2011).

85. For an excellent discussion, see Brian Arthur, *How Britain Won the War of 1812: The Royal Navy's Blockades of the United States, 1812–15* (Rochester, NY: Boydell Press, 2011); Wade Dudley, *Splintering the Wooden Wall: The British Blockade of the United States, 1812–15* (Annapolis, MD: Naval Institute Press, 2003).

86. In September, just as Napoleon was to occupy Moscow, the Russian government asked John Quincy Adams, American minister at St. Petersburg, whether the United States would be open to the offer of Russian mediation with Britain. Adams quickly conveyed the news to President Madison, who accepted it in early 1813 and appointed two commissioners (Albert Gallatin, secretary of the treasury, and James Bayard, a senator from Delaware) to negotiate peace with the help of Russian mediators. This mission produced no results because the British government rejected Russian mediation on the grounds that its disputes with the United States involved internal issues that were not subject to foreign meddling. But the real cause for British apprehension lay in Russian support for the American conception of maritime law, one that assumed a narrow view of belligerent rights and provided a broader interpretation of neutral rights. Britain expected American negotiators to bring up these issues during postwar negotiations, and Russian mediation could have provided them with much-needed support. *State Papers and Public Documents of the United States* (Boston: T. B. Wait and Sons, 1817), IX:358.

87. Wellington to Lt. Gen. Sir T. Graham, May 8, 1812, in *The Dispatches of Field Marshal, the Duke of Wellington*, IX:129–30.

88. Wellington to Stuart, May 3, 1812, in *The Dispatches of Field Marshal, the Duke of Wellington*, X:342–45. Wellington explored several other possible sources of supplies, including Barbary States, "British settlements in North America," "Western Islands," and Mexico, which "ought to be able to supply some." Writing to his brother Henry, he expressed his irritation at the Americans, noting, "It would be capital to turn the tables upon these cunning Americans, and not to allow them to have any intercourse with those ports [Cadiz and Lisbon]." Wellington to Sir Henry Wellesley, May 10, 1812, in *The Dispatches of Field Marshal, the Duke of Wellington*, IX:132–33.

89. For example, see documents, including a license from Admiral Herbert Sawyer, in the *Julia, Luce, Master* case of 1814, in *Report of Cases Argued and Decided in the Supreme Court of the United States* (Rochester, NY: Lawyers Cooperative Publishing, 1910), 3:181.

Chapter 22

1. F. Martens, *Recueil des traités et conventions conclus par la Russie avec les puissances étrangères* (St. Petersburg: A. Böhnke, 1902), VII:60–62. Napoleon's heavy-handed treatment only further drove the Prussians into the Russian embrace. In one of the many mistakes he had committed in 1813, the emperor rejected the Prussian king's request for certain territorial restitutions and the payment of debts France owed Berlin for war supplies as the price for Prussia's continued allegiance to the alliance with France.

2. Jean D'Ussel, *Études sur l'année 1813. La défection de la Prusse (décembre 1812–mars 1813)* (Paris: Plon-Nourrit, 1907), 1–150; Martens, *Recueil des traités et conventions*, VII:57–62. Another Prussian General, von Bülow, declined

to sign a convention with the Russians but allowed them to advance towards the Oder River. See Michael V. Leggiere, "The Life, Letters and Campaigns of Friedrich Wilhelm Graf Bülow von Dennewitz, 1755–1816," PhD diss., Florida State University, 1997, 190–220.

3. Martens, *Recueil des traités et conventions*, VII:62–86; Philipp Anton Guido von Meyer, *Corpus iuris Confoederationis Germanicae oder Staatsacten für Geschichte und öffentliches Recht des Deutschen Bundes* (Frankfurt am Main: Brönner, 1858), I:135–39.

4. Kutuzov to Wintzingerode, Kalisch, April 5, 1813, RGVIA, f. VUA, op. 16, d. 3921, ll.133b–134b. For discussion, see Michael V. Leggiere, *Napoleon and the Struggle for Germany: The Franco-Prussian War of 1813* (Cambridge: Cambridge University Press, 2015), I:127–32; Dominic Lieven, *Russia Against Napoleon* (London: Penguin, 2010), 290–91.

5. Meyer, *Corpus iuris Confoederationis Germanicae*, I:139.

6. Ibid., I:146–47.

7. Thomas Nipperday aptly observes that Metternich knew that "Austria's whole existence rested on the sanctity of treaties." *Germany from Napoleon to Bismarck 1800–1866*, trans. Daniel Nolan (Dublin: Gill & Macmillan, 1996), 70.

8. Martens, *Recueil des traités et conventions*, III:89–91.

9. For a full account of Lord Walpole's mission to Vienna, see Charles Buckland, *Metternich and the British Government from 1809 to 1813* (London: Macmillan, 1932), 407–38. Also see Francis Peter Werry, *Personal Memoirs and Letters of Francis Peter Werry, Attaché to the British Embassies at St. Petersburgh and Vienna in 1812–15* (London: Charles J. Skeet, 1861), 163–73.

10. For a detailed discussion see Jean D'Ussel, *Études sur l'année 1813: L'intervention de l'Autriche (décembre 1812–mai 1813)* (Paris: Plon-Nourrit, 1912), 172–289, 329–59.

11. *Correspondance de Napoléon*, XXIV:342.

12. Napoleon to Frederick VI of Denmark and Norway, January 5, 1813, in *Correspondance de Napoléon*, XXIV:369.

13. Napoleon to Eugene, January 29, 1813, in *Correspondance de Napoléon*, XXIV:468.

14. Michael V. Leggiere, "Prometheus Chained, 1813–1815," in *Napoleon and the Operational Art of War*, ed. Michael V. Leggiere (Leiden: Brill, 2016), 320–21.

15. Napoleon to King Frederick of Württemberg, April 24, 1813, in *Correspondance de Napoléon*, XXV:226.

16. See Leggiere, *Napoleon and the Struggle for Germany*, I:70–119.

17. August von Gneisenau's report cited in Leggiere, *Napoleon and the Struggle for Germany*, I:262.

18. For the role of Berlin in Napoleon's strategy, see Michael V. Leggiere, *Napoleon and Berlin: The Franco-Prussian War in North Germany, 1813* (Norman: University of Oklahoma Press, 2002).

19. Leggiere, *Napoleon and the Struggle for Germany*, I:298–377; on Ney's action, see I:347–49.

20. Leggiere, *Napoleon and the Struggle for Germany*, I:382–422.

21. Leggiere, *Napoleon and the Struggle for Germany*, I:142.

22. London *Gazette*, March 30, 1813, in *The Royal Military Chronicle or British Officers' Monthly Register*, 1813, VI:248–49. Russian officer Waldemar Lowernstern notes in his memoirs that almost as soon as his detachment occupied the small town of Blankenese on the outskirts of Hamburg, he was approached by a British consul, Mitchell, who urged him to allow British commerce onto the continent. See *Mémoires du général-major russe baron de Löwenstern (1776–1858)* (Paris: A. Fontemoing, 1903), II:268–69.

23. See text of the armistice in Agathon Jean François Fain, *Manuscrit de 1813, contenant le précis des évènemens de cette année* (Paris: Delaunay, 1825), I:484–89.

24. Napoleon to General Clarke, June 2, 1813, in *Correspondance de Napoléon*, XXV:346–47.

25. Fain, *Manuscrit de 1813*, I:430.

26. Paul W. Schroeder, *The Transformation of European Politics, 1763–1848* (New York: Oxford University Press, 1994), 461–63.

27. Britain's diplomatic efforts in April–November 1813 had been hampered by the fact that its representatives were not men of sufficient weight to gain a commanding influence at the Allied headquarters. Viscount Cathcart and Sir Charles Stewart (Castlereagh's half brother), attached to the Russian and Prussian headquarters, respectively, were good soldiers but could hardly compete with the more experienced diplomats. The Earl of Aberdeen, who was dispatched to Austria, was too young and inexperienced to contend with men like Metternich; the Frankfurt Proposals of November 1813 had made this abundantly clear. Throughout the 1813 campaign the treaties between the Allied powers were drawn up and generally signed before the British representatives were fully informed; agreements with Britain tended to be confined to subsidies and the conduct of the war rather than much more important issues of postwar settlement.

28. Castlereagh to Cathcart, January 15, 1813, in Robert Stewart, Viscount Castlereagh, *Correspondence, Despatches and Other Papers of Viscount Castlereagh* (London: William Shoberl, 1851), VIII:304; John M. Sherwig, *Guineas and Gunpowder: British Foreign Aid in the Wars with France, 1793–1815* (Cambridge, MA: Harvard University Press, 1969), 283–84.

29. Protocol of the Meeting of the Secret Financial Committee, December 21, 1812, and Alexander to Lieven, February 1, 1813, in *VPR*, VI:629; VII:37–39, 709. Also see Charles Stewart to Castlereagh, May 18, 1813, in *Memoirs and Correspondence of Viscount Castlereagh*, IX:15–16.

30. Martens, *Recueil des traités et conventions*, XI:179. Russia and Britain ultimately settled on arranging payments in both subsidies and the "federative paper," specially guaranteed paper money. In late March 1813 Britain agreed to provide £1,333,334 in silver and £3,333,334 in "federative papers"; £500,000 in silver were set aside for the needs of Dmitri Senyavin's squadron, which was

still detained in Britain. These arrangements were formalized in an Anglo-Russian Convention at Reichenbach on June 15, 1813; a separate convention on the "federative papers" was signed in London on September 30, 1813. Yet little of this money found its way to Russia, which received only slightly more than £1 million by the end of the 1813 campaign. See the March Agreement in *VPR*, VII:136–37; the September Convention in Martens, *Recueil des traités et conventions*, XI:189–95. For a general discussion, see Sherwig, *Guineas and Gunpowder*, 289–92; A. Orlov, *Soyuz Peterburga i Londona: rossiisko-britanskie otnosheniya v epokhu napoleonovskikh voin* (Moscow: Progress-Traditsia, 2005), 255–59, 263–65.

31. For details see Rory Muir, *Britain and the Defeat of Napoleon, 1807–1815* (New Haven: Yale University Press, 1996), 243–61, 280–98; Muriel E. Chamberlain, *"Pax Britannica"? British Foreign Policy, 1789–1914* (London: Routledge, 1999), 41–59; R. W. Seton-Watson, *Britain in Europe, 1789–1914* (New York: Howard Fertig, 1968), 31–37; Adolphus W. Ward and George P. Gooch, *The Cambridge History of British Foreign Policy, 1783–1919*, vol. 1, *1783–1815* (Cambridge: Cambridge University Press, 1922), 392–428.

32. For the text see Wilhelm Oncken, *Oesterreich und Preussen im Befreiungskriege: urkundliche Aufschlüsse über die politische Geschichte des Jahres 1813* (Berlin: G. Grote, 1879), II:636–37.

33. "Une paix continentale bonne," in Oncken, *Oesterreich und Preussen im Befreiungskriege*, II:644.

34. "Le Minimum des pretentions" in Oncken, *Oesterreich und Preussen im Befreiungskriege*, II:644.

35. *Mémoires, documents and écrits divers... de Prince de Metternich*, I:135–54; Enno E. Kraehe, *Metternich's German Policy* (Princeton, NJ: Princeton University Press, 1983), I:176–78; Schroeder, *The Transformation of European Politics*, 470–72; Martens, *Recueil des traités et conventions*, III:92–100; *VPR*, VII:237–38, 259–63, 275–76, 733–37; Oncken, *Oesterreich und Preussen im Befreiungskriege*, II:649–79.

36. *Mémoires, documents and écrits divers... de Prince de Metternich*, I:147; Fain, *Manuscrit de 1813*, II:34–44.

37. The Reichenbach Protocol called for the end of French control over the Grand Duchy of Warsaw and its partition; Prussia's restoration and expansion eastward; the return of the Adriatic coast (Illyria) to Austria; and the independence of the Hanseatic cities in northern Germany. Should Napoleon refuse these terms, Austria would join the Sixth Coalition with at least 150,000 men and fight for the harsher, maximum program as formulated by Hardenberg and Nesselrode.

38. The BEIC Secret Committee to the Governor General at Bengal, East India House, June 18, 1798, cited in Mubarak Al-Otabi, "The Qawasim and British Control of the Arabian Gulf," PhD diss., University of Salford, 1989, 65.

39. Schroeder, *Transformation of European Politics*, 460, 472.

40. Karl Nesselrode, "Zapiski grafa K.V. Nesselrode," in *Russkii vestnik* 59 (1865), 559. Also see Napoleon to Ney, August 4, 1813, in *Correspondance de Napoléon*, XXVI:2–3; Adam Zamoyski, *Rites of Peace: The Fall of Napoleon and the Congress of Vienna* (London: Harper Perennial, 2007), 82; Albert Sorel, *L'Europe et la revolution Française* (Paris: Plon-Nourrit, 1904), VIII:154. For more in-depth discussion, see Martens, *Recueil des traités et conventions*, III:110–15; *VPR*, VII:283–92, 299, 324–30, 343–45, 740–43, 746–47, 748, 754.

41. In his memoirs, Metternich portrays himself as luring Napoleon to destruction by a subtle and farsighted diplomacy; according to this version, Austrian peace negotiations were not genuine and only intended to gain time to complete the Austrian mobilization and brand Napoleon as the warmonger. But the Austrian diplomatic correspondence in the spring and summer of 1813 shows that Metternich was genuinely trying to reach a negotiated peace that would have perpetuated a Napoleonic regime in France, albeit within certain constraints.

42. One of the reasons Napoleon delayed responses to the Allied offers was his ten-day (July 25–August 4) visit to Mainz to see Empress Marie-Louise. The purpose of the visit was, as he explained to Caulaincourt, "give the Empress another child." Remarkable as it is to see Napoleon leaving crucial negotiations to get intimate with his wife, there was an important political purpose to this rendezvous. "A second male heir would have strengthened his diplomatic position. Napoleon's real aim was at once to assert his independence from the negotiations, and to pile the pressure on the other Powers for last-minute concessions." Munro Price, *Napoleon: The End of Glory* (Oxford: Oxford University Press, 2014), 98.

43. Andrew Roberts, *Napoleon: A Life* (New York: Viking, 2014), 659.

44. For details, see Price, *Napoleon*, 93–94, 109–10.

45. The Duchy of Warsaw was to be dissolved and divided between Russia, Austria, and Prussia, with Prussia receiving Danzig. Hamburg and Lübeck would become independent cities, and the rest of France's north German conquests would be returned at the conclusion of a general peace. France would renounce the protectorate of the Rhine Confederation, Prussia would be enlarged with a defensible frontier on the Elbe, Austria would regain Illyria, and all the European states, large and small, would sign a guarantee of mutual security. Sorel, *L'Europe et la Révolution française*, VIII:171–72.

46. From Napoleon's conversation with Caulaincourt as they traveled from Smorgoni to Paris in December 1812. General Armand de Caulaincourt, *With Napoleon in Russia* (New York: William Morrow, 1935), 298.

47. The armistice terms allowed for another week after the expiration of the truce on the tenth for the armies to prepare for the war. Napoleon believed that the Allies would be willing to consider his response during this timeframe. Metternich was informed of the French response on August 10, but he concealed it from the Allied representatives until Napoleon's formal reply arrived on the following day.

48. Kraehe, *Metternich's German Policy*, I:183–84.

49. Austrian Declaration of War, August 12, 1813, in *British and Foreign State Papers* (London: James Ridgway and Sons, 1841) I, part 1, 810–22.

50. See Charles Oman, *A History of the Peninsular War*, vol. 6, *September 1, 1812–August 5, 1813* (Oxford: Clarendon Press); José Gregorio Cayuela Fernández and José Ángel Gallego Palomares, *La Guerra de la independencia: historia bélica, pueblo y nación en España (1808–1814)* (Salamanca: Universidad de Salamanca, 2008), 471–92; Rory Muir, *Wellington: The Path to Victory, 1769–1814* (New Haven, CT: Yale University Press, 2013): 517–32, 537–65.

51. The fourth Allied army, the Army of Poland (57,000 men) under General Bennigsen, was still being formed but was expected to join the campaign in September.

52. For the Trachenberg plan, see Leggiere, *Napoleon and the Struggle for Germany*, II:23–60; Alan Sked, *Radetzky: Imperial Victor and Military Genius* (London: I. B. Tauris, 2011), 40–43; F. Loraine Petre, *Napoleon's Last Campaign in Germany, 1813* (London: John Lane, 1912), 181–84; E. Glaise von Horstenau, *La campagne de Dresde, Geschichte der Kämpfe Österreichs. Kriege unter der Regierung des Kaisers Franz. Befreiungskrieg 1813 und 1814* (Vienna: L. W. Seidel und Sohn, 1913), III:3–6.

53. Leggiere, *Napoleon and Berlin*, 160–76; Kyle O. Eidahl, "The Military Career of Nicolas Charles Oudinot (1767–1847)," PhD diss., Florida State University, 1990, 349–56; Eidahl, "Napoleon's Faulty Strategy: Oudinot's Operations against Berlin, 1813," *CRE* (1995), 395–403.

54. Leggiere, *Napoleon and the Struggle for Germany*, II:235–86.

55. David Chandler, *The Campaigns of Napoleon* (New York: Macmillan, 1966), 904–11.

56. Moreau to his wife, n.d., in *A Selection from the Letters and Despatches of the First Napoleon*, ed. D. Bingham (London: Chapman and Hall, 1884), III:266.

57. Leggiere, *Napoleon and Berlin*, 189–211; Chandler, *The Campaigns of Napoleon*, 911–15; Modest Bogdanovich, *Istoriya voiny 1813 goda za nezavisimost Germanii* (St. Petersburg: Tip. Shtaba voenno-uchebnykh zavedenii, 1863), II:195–279.

58. Leggiere, *Napoleon and the Struggle for Germany*, II:605–18.

59. Leggiere, *Napoleon and Berlin*, 275.

60. For an in-depth account of the battle, see Bruno Colson, *Leipzig: La Bataille des Nations, 16–19 Octobre 1813* (Paris: Perrin, 2013); Leggiere, *Napoleon and the Struggle for Germany*, II:624–58. For a more concise look, see Stéphane Calvet, *Leipzig, 1813: La guerre des peuples* (Paris: Vendémiaire, 2015); F. Maude, *The Leipzig Campaign* (New York: Macmillan, 1908), 254–64; Peter Hofschröer, *Leipzig, 1813: The Battle of the Nations* (Oxford: Osprey, 1993); Digby Smith, *1813, Leipzig: Napoleon and the Battle of the Nations* (London: Greenhill, 2001). Amid the commotion of retreat, French general Chateau noticed "a man of peculiar dress and with only a small retinue; he was whistling the air of *Marlbrough s'en va-t-en guerre* [a popular French folk song] but was deeply lost

in thought. Chateau thought he was a *bourgeois* and was about to approach him to ask a question.... But it was the Emperor himself, who, with his usual composure seemed to be completely detached from the scenes of destruction that surrounded him." Henri de Jomini, *Précis politique et militaire des campagnes de 1812 à 1814* (Lausanne: B. Benda, 1886), II:207n.

61. The agreement specified that one-half of the contingent was to consist of troops of the line, and the other half of Landwehr, or militia. In addition to this, corps of volunteers were allowed to be raised, and the Landsturm was organized in all countries that seemed to require such extraordinary precautions. For details, see *VPR*, VII:453–66; Martens, *Recueil des traités et conventions*, VII:136–37, 140–52.

62. Kraehe, *Metternich's German Policy*, 219–49; Schroeder, *Transformation of European Politics*, 478–84; *VPR*, VII:452–66, 483, 486–91; Martens, *Recueil des traités et conventions*, VII:115–36.

63. "Bonaparte is a rascal; he has to be killed," Bernadotte supposedly stated on one occasion. "As long as he lives, he will be the curse of the world. There must be no emperors, this is not a French title; France needs a king, but a soldier-kind. The Bourbon dynasty is exhausted and will never return. Who could suit the French more than me?" Sorel, *L'Europe et la Révolution française*, VIII:190. Also see L. Pingaud, *Bernadotte, Napoléon et les Bourbons, 1797, 1844* (Paris: L. Plon, 1901), 220–303.

64. See Leggiere, *Napoleon and Berlin*, 293–94.

65. Agathon Jean François Fain, *Memoirs of the Invasion of France by the Allied Armies and of the Last Six Months of the Reign of Napoleon* (London: H. Colburn, 1834), 7.

66. Anne-Jean-Marie-René Savary, duc de Rovigo, *Mémoires du Duc de Rovigo: pour servir à l'histoire de l'empereur Napoléon* (Paris: A. Bossange, 1828), VI:239. Napoleon tried a couple of diplomatic ruses of his own. In November 1813 he unexpectedly announced the restoration of Ferdinand VII to the throne of Spain but on condition that the Spanish Cortes, which controlled the country, would stay out of the war. In December Napoleon also released Pope Pius VII, hoping that his return to Italy would sow discord and complicate Austrian plans for reclaiming the peninsula. Neither ploy worked, however.

67. See Official Communication to the Russian Ambassador at London, January 19, 1805, in Charles K. Webster, *British Diplomacy, 1813–1815* (London: G. Bell and Sons, 1921), 389–94.

68. Cabinet Memorandum, December 26, 1813, in W. Alison Phillips, *The Confederation of Europe: A Study of the European Alliance, 1813–1823* (London: Longmans, Green, 1914), 65–66.

69. "I cannot omit again impressing upon your Lordship the importance of awakening the [Russian] Emperor's mind to the necessity, for his own interests as well as ours, of peremptorily excluding from the general negotiations every maritime question. If he does not, he will risk a similar misunderstanding between those Powers on whose union the safety of Europe now rests. Great Britain may be

driven out of a Congress, but not out of its maritime rights, and, if the Continental Powers know their own interests, they will not hazard this." Castlereagh to Cathcart, July 14, 1813, in Webster, *British Diplomacy, 1813–1815*, 14.

70. For insights, see Castlereagh's correspondence in Webster, *British Diplomacy, 1813–1815*, and analysis in Bew, *Castlereagh*, 319–51; Paul W. Schroeder, "An Unnatural 'Natural Alliance': Castlereagh, Metternich and Aberdeen in 1813," *International History Review* 10, no. 4 (1988): 522–40.

71. For a full quote, see Charles William Vane Marquis of Londonderry, *Narrative of the War in Germany and France in 1813 and 1814* (London: Henry Colburn and Richard Bentley, 1830), 255–56.

72. Napoleon was naturally maddened by the news. "The conduct of the King of Naples is infamous and there is no name for that of the Queen [Caroline]. I hope to live long enough to be able to revenge myself and France for such an insult and for such fearful ingratitude," Napoleon to Fouché, February 13, 1814, in *Correspondance de Napoléon*, XXVII:157.

73. Michael V. Leggiere, *The Fall of Napoleon*, vol. 1, *The Allied Invasion of France, 1813–1814* (Cambridge: Cambridge University Press, 2017), 269–333; Maurice Henri Weil, *La Campagne de 1814* (Paris: Librairie Militaire de L. Baudoin, 1891), I:33–341; Muir, *Wellington: The Path to Victory*, 552–65; Alexandre Benckendorf, "The Liberation of the Netherlands (November–December 1813): From the Mémoires du comte Alexandre Benckendorf," ed. and trans. Alexander Mikaberidze, in The Napoleon Series, http://www.napoleon-series.org/research/russianarchives/c_netherlands.html.

74. For an exalting view of *marie-louises*, see Henry Houssaye, *Napoleon and the Campaign of 1814* (London: Hugh Rees, 1914), 24. For a critical assessment of Houssaye's view, see Charles J. Esdaile, *Napoleon, France and Waterloo: The Eagle Rejected* (Barnsley: Pen & Sword, 2016), 83–84.

75. Étienne-Denis Pasquier, *Histoire de mon temps. Mémoires du chancelier Pasquier* (Paris: E. Plon, Nourrit, 1893), II:117–29.

76. Cited in Leggiere, *The Fall of Napoleon*, I:82. Parts of this speech also appear in other sources—Christopher Herold, *The Age of Napoleon* (New York: Houghton Mifflin, 2003), 375; Felix Markham, *Napoleon* (New York: Mentor, 1963), 209; Ralph Ashby, *Napoleon Against Great Odds: The Emperor and the Defenders of France, 1814* (Santa Barbara CA: Praeger, 2010), 30—but the specific wording varies slightly in these renditions.

77. From Napoleon's conversation with the German banker Bethmann, cited in August Fournier, *Napoleon I: A Biography* (New York: H. Holt, 1911), 330.

78. Cited in Fournier, *Napoleon I*, 331.

79. Pasquier, *Histoire de mon temps*, II:99. A slightly different version is in Alphone de Beauchamp, *Histoire des campagnes de 1814 et de 1815* (Paris: Le Normant, 1816), I:43.

80. Michael V. Leggiere, *Blücher: Scourge of Napoleon* (Norman: University of Oklahoma Press, 2014), 324–25; Weil, *La campagne de 1814*, I:342–425, 458–507.

81. Webster, *The Foreign Policy of Castlereagh*, 206; Leggiere, *The Fall of Napoleon*, I:534–54.

82. See *SIRIO* 31 (1880): 369–71; Castlereagh to Liverpool, February 18, 1814 (enclosing Lieven's letter to Nesselrode); Castlereagh to Clancarty, February 20, 1814, in *Memoirs and correspondence of Viscount Castlereagh*, IX:266–73, 284–85; "Extrait des Mémoires de la Princesse Lieven," in Grand Duke Nikolai Mikhailovich, ed., *Correspondance de l'empereur Alexandre Ier avec sa soeur la grande-duchesse Catherine, princesse d'Oldenbourg, puis reine de Wurtemberg, 1805–18* (St. Petersburg: Manufacture de Papiers de l'Etat, 1910), 225–27.

83. Kraehe, *Metternich's German Policy*, 288–94.

84. Leggiere, *The Fall of Napoleon*, 534–54.

85. Wilhelm Oncken, "*Die Krisis der letzten Friedensverhandlung mit Napoleon I: Februar 1814*," in *Historisches Taschenbuch* (Leipzig: F.A. Brockhaus, 1886), VI:5–19.

86. Henry Houssaye, *1814* (Paris: Librairie Académique Didier, 1895), 59–86; Modest Bogdanovich, *Istoriya voiny 1814 goda fo Frantsii i nizlozheniya Napoleona I* (St. Petersburg, 1865), I:176–255; Weil, *La campagne de 1814*, II:139–221, 274–346.

87. Castlereagh to Liverpool, February 26, 1814, in Webster, *British Diplomacy, 1813–1815*, 160–61.

88. The treaty's text is in the Napoleon Series, http://www.napoleon-series.org/research/government/ diplomatic/c_chaumont.html. For discussion, see August Fournier, *Der Congress von Châtillon. Die Politik im Kriege von 1814. Eine historische Studie* (Vienna: F. Tempsky, 1900), 105–25.

89. Castlereagh to Liverpool, March 10, 1814, cited in Webster, *The Congress of Vienna, 1814–1815*, 32.

90. Henry Houssaye, "La Capitulation de Soissons en 1814, d'après les documents originaux," *Revue des Deux Mondes* 70 (1885): 553–88; Bogdanovich, *Istoriya voiny 1814 goda*, I:289–308; Alexander Mikaberidze, ed., *The Russian Eyewitness Accounts of the Campaign of 1814* (London: Frontline Books, 2013), 128–44.

91. Napoleon to King Joseph, March 5, 1814, in *Correspondance de Napoléon*, XXVII:288. Writing to his minister of war, the French emperor demanded, "Let this wretch [the commandant of Soissons] be arrested, as well as all the members of his war council; let him be impeached before a military commission composed of generals, and for God's sake act so that they may be all shot within twenty-four hours on the Place de Grève. It is time to make examples. Let the cause of the sentence be fully explained, printed, and distributed in every direction." Moreau was fortunate that the war ended before he could be court-martialed, and he was able to enjoy a peaceful retirement after the war. Napoleon to Clarke, March 5, 1814, in A. Thiers, *Histoire du Consulat et de l'Empire* (Bruxelles: Librairie de J. B. Tarride, 1860), X:35.

92. One French historian goes as far as to claim that next to the Battle of Waterloo, the capitulation of Soissons was the most disastrous event of

French history! Thiers, *Histoire du Consulat et de l'Empire*, XVIII:42. Clausewitz downplayed the event, arguing against "the exaggerated importance that is always attributed to the capture of this place [Soissons]." Carl von Clausewitz, *La Campagne de 1813 et la Campagne de 1814* (Paris: Librairie Militaire R. Chapelot, 1900), 175.

93. Bogdanovich, *Istoriya voiny 1814 goda*, I:330–50; Houssaye, *1814*, 167–232; Weil, *La Campagne de 1814*, III:148–245; Mikaberidze, *The Russian Eyewitness Accounts*, 145–60.

94. Muir, *Wellington*, I:566–76.

95. Bogdanovich, *Istoriya voiny 1814 goda*, I:351–64; Mikaberidze, *The Russian Eyewitness Accounts*, 161–99; Weil, *La Campagne de 1814*, III:263–71.

96. Weil, *La Campagne de 1814*, III:424–47.

97. Wellington defeated the French at Toulouse on April 10, 1814. Muir, *Wellington*, I:578–84; Francisco Vela Santiago, *Toulouse 1814: la última batalla de la Guerra de Independencia española* (Madrid: Almena, 2014).

98. For an excellent discussion, see Thierry Lentz, *Les vingt jours de Fontainebleau: la première abdication de Napoléon, 31 mars–20 avril 1814* (Paris: Perrin, 2014). In the often-repeated traditional account, the marshals, led by Ney, Lefebvre, and Moncey, confronted Napoleon and in a stormy conversation rejected his suggestion to continue fighting, telling him bluntly that "the army will obey its chiefs." Napoleon supposedly then grabbed a sheet of paper and wrote a statement consenting to abdicate. Lentz has shown much of this to be untrue.

99. Neil Campbell, *Napoleon at Fontainebleau and Elba, Being a Journal of Occurrences in 1814–15* (London: John Murray, 1869), 190–91; F. L. von Waldburg-Truchsess, *Nouvelle relation de l'itinéraire de Napoléon de Fontainebleau à l'Ile d'Elbe* (Paris: C.-L.-F. Panckoucke, 1815), 24–25.

100. Article 1, Constitutional Statute, May 30, 1814, in the Napoleon Series, http://www.napoleon-series.org/research/government/diplomatic/c_paris1.html.

101. Article 2, Constitutional Statute, May 30, 1814.

102. To strengthen France's neighbors, Holland was enlarged through the annexation of Belgium, Luxembourg, and a strip of land along the left bank of the Rhine. The Swiss confederate organization was recognized and Piedmont-Sardinia was restored in its "ancient dominions" but forced to give Savoy to France; as a compensation, the Sardinian king received Genoa.

103. Article 1, Separate and Secret Articles between France and Great Britain, Austria, Prussia, and Russia, May 30, 1814.

104. Jon Latimer, *1812: War with America* (Cambridge MA: Belknap Press of Harvard University Press, 2007), 177–84; Donald R. Hickey, *The War of 1812: A Forgotten Conflict* (Champaign: University of Illinois Press, 2012), 128–31; Michael A. Palmer, "A Failure of Command, Control, and Communications: Oliver Hazard Perry and the Battle of Lake Erie," *Journal of Erie Studies* 17 (Fall 1988): 7–26.

105. Latimer, *1812: War with America*, 184–92.

106. Frank L. Owsley, "The Role of the South in the British Grand Strategy in the War of 1812," *Tennessee Historical Quarterly* 31 (Spring 1972): 22–38.

107. For a recent discussion, see the introduction and essays by Robert G. Thrower, Gregory E. Dowd, Robert P. Collins, Kathryn E. Holland Braund, and Gregory Waselkov in *Tohopeka: Rethinking the Creek War and the War of 1812*, ed. Kathryn E. Holland Braund (Tuscaloosa: University of Alabama Press, 2012).

108. For details, see Henry S. Halbert and T. H. Ball, *The Creek War of 1813 and 1814* (Tuscaloosa: University of Alabama Press, 1995); Frank L. Owsley, *Struggle for the Gulf Borderlands: The Creek War and the Battle of New Orleans* (Tuscaloosa: University of Alabama Press, 2000); Tom Kanon, *Tennesseans at War, 1812–15: Andrew Jackson, the Creek War, and the Battle of New Orleans* (Tuscaloosa: University of Alabama Press, 2014), 56–119.

109. Another 1.9 million acres were transferred to the Cherokee Nation, which was allied with the Americans during the war.

110. Donald E. Graves, "The Redcoats Are Coming! British Troop Movements to North America in 1814," *Journal of the War of 1812* 6, no. 3 (2001): 12–18.

111. During the war the United States called up some 10,110 volunteers in federal service, 3,049 rangers, and 458,463 militiamen, almost half of them (197,653) in 1814 alone. See Graves, "The Redcoats Are Coming!," 17–18; J. C. A. Stagg, "Enlisted Men in the United States Army, 1812–1815: A Preliminary Survey," *William and Mary Quarterly* 43 (October 1986): 615–45.

112. Latimer, *1812: War with America*, 282–86; Jeffrey Kimball, "The Battle of Chippawa: Infantry Tactics in the War of 1812," *Military Affairs* 31 (Winter 1967–68): 169–86.

113. See Donald E. Graves, *"Where Right and Glory Lead!": The Battle of Lundy's Lane, 1814* (Toronto: Robin Brass, 2014).

114. For details, see Donald E. Graves, "'The Finest Army Britain Ever Sent to North America': The Composition, Strength, and Losses of British Land Forces During the Plattsburgh Campaign, September 1814," *Journal of the War of 1812* 7, no. 4 (Fall/Winter 2003): 6–12.

115. Latimer, *1812: War with America*, 345–68; Walter R. Borneman, *1812: The War That Forged a Nation* (New York: Harper Collins, 2007), 199–215. Also see Allan S. Everest, *The War of 1812 in the Champlain Valley* (Syracuse, NY: Syracuse University Press, 1981). Asked to comment about the North American theater, Wellington argued that "The defence of Canada...depends upon the navigation of the lakes....Any offensive operation founded upon Canada must be preceded by the establishment of naval superiority on the lakes." Wellington to Earl Bathurst, February 22, 1814, in Arthur Wellesley, *The Dispatches of Field Marshal the Duke of Wellington, During His Various Campaigns*, ed. John Gurwood (London: John Murray, 1834), XI:525.

116. Borneman, *1812: The War That Forged a Nation*, 216–48.

117. For details, see Donald R. Hickey, *Glorious Victory: Andrew Jackson and the Battle of New Orleans* (Baltimore: John Hopkins University Press, 2015); Robert V. Remini, *The Battle of New Orleans: Andrew Jackson and America's First Military Victory* (London: Pimlico, 2001); Robin Reilly, *The British at the Gates: The New Orleans Campaign in the War of 1812* (New York: Putnam, 1974).

118. James A. Carr, "The Battle of New Orleans and the Treaty of Ghent," *Diplomatic History* 3 (Summer 1979): 273–82.

119. Contrary to popular perceptions, the Peace of Ghent did not end the war upon its signing on December 24. Article I of the treaty stipulated that all hostilities would be suspended only after the treaty had been ratified by both parties. Britain ratified the treaty three days later, but it was not until February 16, 1815, or five weeks after the battle, that the Congress consented to it.

120. The United States did acquire Mobile and a stretch of West Florida that extended from the Pearl to the Perdido River south of the 31st parallel, about 6,000 square miles in total.

121. *The Report of the Loyal and Patriotic Society of Upper Canada* (Montreal: William Gray, 1817), 353.

122. London *Times*, December 28, 1812.

123. *Leeds Mercury*, August 8, 1812.

Chapter 23

1. On the festivities and social setting, see David King, *Vienna, 1814: How the Conquerors of Napoleon Made Love, War, and Peace at the Congress of Vienna* (New York: Harmony Books, 2008); Adam Zamoyski, *Rites of Peace: The Fall of Napoleon and the Congress of Vienna* (New York: HarperCollins Publishers, 2007); Gregor Dallas, *1815: The Roads to Waterloo* (London: Richard Cohen, 1996); Charles-Otto Zieseniss, *Le Congrès de Vienne et l'Europe des princes* (Paris: Belfond, 1984); Wolf D. Gruner, *Der Wiener Kongress, 1814/15* (Stuttgart: Philipp Reclam, 2014); Harold Nicolson, *The Congress of Vienna: A Study in Allied Unity: 1812–1822* (New York: HBJ Books, 1974), 159–60. For original police reports and other documents, see Maurice-Henri Weil, *Les dessous du Congrès de Vienne: d'après les documents originaux des archives du Ministère impérial et royal de l'intérieur à Vienne* (Paris: Librairie Payot, 1917), vol. 1; August Fournier, ed., *Die Geheimpolizei auf dem Wiener Kongress. Eine Auswahl aus ihren Papieren* (Vienna: F. Tempsky, 1913).

2. Castlereagh to Liverpool, March 10, 1814, in Charles Webster, *The Congress of Vienna, 1814–1815* (London: Oxford University Press, 1919), 51.

3. Treaty of Paris, May 30, 1814, in The Napoleon Series, http://www.napoleon-series.org/research/government/diplomatic/c_paris1.html.

4. Cited in Duff Cooper, *Talleyrand* (New York: Grove Press, 2001), 28.

5. For most recent and judicious discussion of the diplomat, see Emmanuel de Waresquiel, *Talleyrand: le prince immobile* (Paris: Fayard, 2003); For a more

in-depth treatment, see Georges Lacour-Gayet's four-volume study *Talleyrand,*
1754–1838 (Paris: Payot, 1930).

6. For Gentz's biography, see Paul R. Sweet, *Friedrich von Gentz: Defender of the Old*
Order (Westport, CT: Greenwood Press, 1970).

7. Nicolson, *The Congress of Vienna*, 38.

8. For a historical assessment of Metternich, see Alan Sked, *Metternich and Austria:*
An Evaluation (New York: Palgrave Macmillan, 2008).

9. It is noteworthy that almost none of Alexander's senior advisors were Russian,
but rather Germans (Stein, Stakelberg, and Nesselrode), Poles (Czartoryski),
Swiss (Laharpe), and natives of Corfu (Capo d'Istria) and Corsica (Pozzo di
Borgo).

10. See John Bew, *Castlereagh: A Life* (Oxford: Oxford University Press, 2012),
558ff. After Castlereagh committed suicide in 1822, Lord Byron wrote a dis-
paraging epigram about him: "Posterity will ne'er survey / A nobler grave
than this: / Here lie the bones of Castlereagh: / Stop, traveler, and piss." *The*
Works of Lord Byron, ed. Rowland E. Prothero (London: John Murray, 1904),
IV:394.

11. Unless otherwise noted, my discussion of the congress is based on Nicolson, *The*
Congress of Vienna; Brian E. Vick, *The Congress of Vienna: Power and Politics After*
Napoleon (Cambridge MA: Harvard University Press, 2014); Enno E. Kraehe,
Metternich's German Policy, vol. 2, *The Congress of Vienna* (Princeton, NJ: Princeton
University Press, 1983); Thierry Lentz, *Le Congrès de Vienne: Une refondation de*
l'Europe 1814–1815 (Paris: Perrin, 2013); Mark Jarrett, *The Congress of Vienna*
and Its Legacy: War and Great Power Diplomacy After Napoleon (London: I. B. Tauris,
2013); Jacques-Alain de Sédouy, *Le Congrès de Vienne: L'Europe contre la France*
1812–1815 (Paris: Perrin, 2003); Henry Kissinger, *A World Restored: Metternich,*
Castlereagh and the Problem of Peace 1812–1822 (London: Phoenix, 2000 [1957]).

12. Castlereagh to Liverpool, September 24, 1814, in Webster, *The Congress of*
Vienna, 1814–1815, Appendix I, 150.

13. Protocols of the Conference of Plenipotentiaries, September 22, 1814, in
British and Foreign State Papers (London: James Ridgway and Sons, 1839),
II:554–57.

14. For details, see memorandums in Webster, *The Congress of Vienna, 1814–1815*,
appendices II–V, 151–64.

15. Nicolson, *The Congress of Vienna*, 141.

16. Talleyrand to King Louis XVIII, October 4, 1814, in *Correspondance inédite du*
prince de Talleyrand et du roi Louis XVIII pendant le Congrès de Vienne, ed. Georges
Pallain (Paris: E. Plon, 1881), 10–24; Talleyrand's memo of October 1, 1814,
in *British and Foreign State Papers*, II:559–60.

17. Alexander to Czartoryski, January 13, 1813, in *Mémoires du prince Adam*
Czartoryski et correspondance avec l'Empereur Alexandre Ier, ed. Charles de Mazade
(Paris: Plon, 1887), II:302–3.

18. *VPR*, VIII:103–5.

19. On the Polish-Saxon crisis see Vick, *The Congress of Vienna*, 278–320; Jarrett, *The Congress of Vienna and Its Legacy*, 98–119; C. K. Webster, "England and the Polish-Saxon Problem at the Congress of Vienna," *Transactions of the Royal Historical Society* 7 (1913): 49–101.

20. The Russo-Prussian alliance treaties, signed in early 1813, were based on the plan of exchanging Prussia's Polish territories (seized in 1792–1795) for all of Saxony.

21. Cathcart to Castlereagh, January 16, 1814, in Robert Stewart, Viscount Castlereagh, *Correspondence, Despatches and Other Papers of Viscount Castlereagh* (London: William Shoberl, 1851), IX:171; Münster to the Prince Regent, February 23–25, in August Fournier, *Der Congress von Châtillon Die politik im kriege von 1814. Eine historische studie* (Vienna: F. Tempsky, 1900), 302–3. Also see "Zur Vorgeschichte des Wiener Kongresses," in August Fournier, *Historische Studien und Skizzen* (Vienna: Wilhelm Braumüller, 1908), II:295–98.

22. Memorandum of December 20, 1814, in Leonard Chodzko Angeberg, *Le Congrès de Vienne et les Traités de 1815* (Paris: Amyot, 1864), I:553.

23. Enno E. Kraehe, *Metternich's Germany Policy*, vol. II, *The Congress of Vienna, 1814–1815* (Princeton, NJ: Princeton University Press, 1983), 241–63.

24. Talleyrand to Metternich, December 19, 1814, in Angeberg, *Le Congrès de Vienne*, I:540–44.

25. Castlereagh to Liverpool, December 25, 1814, in *Supplementary Despatches and Memoranda of Field Marshal Arthur, Duke of Wellington* (London: John Murray, 1860), IX:511; Talleyrand to King Louis XVIII, December 28, 1814, in *Correspondance inédite du prince de Talleyrand et du roi Louis XVIII*, 198.

26. Liverpool to Wellington, December 23, 1814, in *Supplementary Despatches, Correspondence and Memoranda of Field Marshal Duke of Wellington*, IX:494.

27. Castlereagh to Liverpool, January 1, 1815, in Webster, "England and the Polish-Saxon Problem at the Congress of Vienna," 88–89.

28. Niels Rosenkrantz, *Journal du Congrès de Vienne, 1814–1815*, ed. Georg Nørregård (Copenhagen: G. E. C. Gad, 1953), 114; Wilhelm von Humboldt, *Wilhelm und Caroline von Humboldt in ihren Briefen* (Berlin, 1910), IV:441.

29. Talleyrand to King, September 25, 1814, in *Correspondance inédite du prince de Talleyrand et du roi Louis XVIII*, 3; Rosenkrantz, *Journal du Congrès de Vienne*, 125–26.

30. Lord Apsley to Earl Bathurst, January 5, 1815 in *Report on the Manuscripts of Earl Bathurst Preserved at Cirencester Park* (London: Her Majesty's Stationery Office, 1923), 320.

31. Castlereagh to Liverpool, January 2, 1815, in *Supplementary Despatches, Correspondence and Memoranda of Field Marshal Duke of Wellington*, IX:523.

32. Talleyrand to Louis XVIII, January 4, 1814, in *Correspondance inédite du prince de Talleyrand et du roi Louis XVIII*, 209.

33. Liverpool to Castlereagh, December 23, 1814, in *Supplementary Despatches, Correspondence and Memoranda of Field Marshal Duke of Wellington*, IX:498.

34. Vick, *The Congress of Vienna*, 278–320; Jarrett, *The Congress of Vienna and Its Legacy*, 94–130; Zamoyski, *Rites of Peace*, 385–419. Also see Cooke to Liverpool, January 2, 1815, in *Supplementary Despatches and Memoranda of Field Marshal Arthur Duke of Wellington*, IX:521.

35. Cited in Michael V. Leggiere, *Blücher: Scourge of Napoleon* (Norman: University of Oklahoma Press, 2014), 372.

36. "Le Charte de 1814," in Léon Cahen and Albert Mathiez, *Les lois française de 1815 à nos jours: accompagnées des documents politiques les plus importants* (Paris: Alcan, 1919), 11–19.

37. Article 57, in "Le Charte de 1814," 18.

38. For an interesting discussion of the Bourbon missteps, see André Jardin and André Jean Tudesq, *La France des notables. L'évolution générale: 1815–1848* (Paris: Éditions du Seuil, 1973), 24–26.

39. A recent study is Mark Braude, *The Invisible Emperor: Napoleon on Elba from Exile to Escape* (New York: Penguin, 2018).

40. Guillaume Joseph Roux Peyrusse, *Mémorial et archives de m. le baron Peyrusse, trésorier général de la couronne pendant les centjours, Vienne—Moscou—Île d'Elbe* (Carcassonne: P. Labau 1869), 277–78.

41. "À l'Armée," March 1, 1815, in *CN*, XXVIII:4. Also see proclamations to the French people and to the Imperial Guard in *CN*, XXVIII:1–3, 5–7. For details, see Norman MacKenzie, *The Escape from Elba: The Fall and Flight of Napoleon, 1814–1815* (New York: Oxford University Press, 1982), 71–216; Henri Houssay, *1815. Le Retour de l'Ile d'Elbe* (Paris: Perrin, 1901), 200–269.

42. See for example, Nicolas Charles Oudinot, *Memoirs of Marshal Oudinot, duc de Reggio*, ed. Gaston Stiegler (London: H. Henry, 1896), 295–96; Etienne-Jacques-Joseph-Alexandre Macdonald, *Recollections of Marshal Macdonald, Duke of Tarentum*, ed. Camille Rousset (London: R. Bentley and Son, 1892), II:232–85.

43. Accounts differ as to Napoleon's exact words; the present citation is enshrined on the local commemorative plaque in Laffray. Napoleon knew that he had little to fear from the soldiers of the 5th Line Regiment, who had already been engaged in discussions to switch sides and revealed sympathies to the imperial cause. For details, see Paul Britten Austin, *1815: The Return of Napoleon* (London: Greenhill Books, 2002), 135–60; Houssay, *1815. Le Retour de l'Ile d'Elbe*, 239–46.

44. Order of the Day, March 13, 1815, in *Trial of Marshal Ney, Prince of Moskwa, for High Treason...* (London: E. Cox and Son, 1816), 45.

45. Honoré de Balzac, "Le Medecin de Campagne," in *Œuvres complètes de M. de Balzac*, ed. Jean A. Ducourneau (Paris: Furne, 1845), XIII:446.

46. François Nicolas Mollien, *Mémoires d'un ministre du trésor public 1780–1815* (Paris: Guillaumin, 1898), III:419.

47. Louis-Mathieu Molé, *Le comte Molé, 1781–1855: sa vie, ses mémoires*, ed. Helie Guillaume Hubert Noailles (Paris: E. Champion, 1922), I:208–9.

48. In fact, one of Napoleon's first proclamations, to the inhabitants of the Alpine departments on March 6, already talks about his intention to redress "all inequalities," restore equality of "all classes," and guarantee all property possessions. See *CN*, XXVIII:7.

49. Jean Rapp, *Mémoires*...(Paris: Didot, 1823), 282.

50. Napoleon's Speech at the Council of State, March 26, 1815, in *CN*, XXVIII:36; Acte additionnel aux constitutions du Premier Empire, AN AE/II/1577.

51. See the excellent discussion in R. S. Alexander, *Bonapartism and Revolutionary Tradition in France: The Fédérés of 1815* (Cambridge: Cambridge University Press, 1991).

52. Gaspard Gourgaud, *Talks of Napoleon at St. Helena*...(Chicago: A. C. McClurg, 1904), 192.

53. Napoleon's Speech to the Chambers, June 11, 1815, in *CN*, XXVIII:312–13.

54. On popular Bonapartism in 1815, see Frédéric Bluche, *Le Bonapartisme: aux origines de la droite autoritaire (1800–1850)* (Paris: Nouvelles éditions Latines, 1980), 95–122.

55. *Memoirs of Prince Metternich*, ed. Richard Metternich, trans. Robina Napier (New York: Charles Scribner's Sons, 1880), I:255.

56. Murat rashly marched northward and was routed by the Austrians at Tolentino on May 3; when he arrived in the south of France as a refugee, Napoleon refused to see or employ him.

57. Ordre du Jour, June 13, 1815, in *CN*, no. 22049, XXVIII:320–22.

58. Napoleon to Ney, June 16, 1815, in *CN*, no. 22058, XXVIII:335.

59. Captain Bowles to Lord Fitzharris, June 19, 1815, in *A Series of Letters: Of the First Earl of Malmesbury, His Family and Friends from 1745 to 1820*, ed. James Harris (London: Richard Bentley, 1870), II:445–46.

60. Leggiere, *Blucher*, 388–404; Peter Hofschröer, *Waterloo, 1815: Quatre Bras and Ligny* (Barnsley: Pen & Sword, 2005), 73–91; Andrew Uffindell, *The Eagle's Last Triumph: Napoleon's Victory at Ligny, June 1815* (London: Greenhill Books, 1994).

61. For an excellent discussion based on British and Dutch sources, see Erwin Muilwijk, *Quatre Bras, Perponcher's Gamble: 16th June 1815* (Bleiswijk, Netherlands: Sovereign House Books, 2013). For the French side, see Paul L. Dawson, *Marshal Ney at Quatre Bras* (Barnsley: Frontline Books, 2017).

62. Archibald Frank Becke, *Napoleon and Waterloo: The Emperor's Campaign with the Armée du Nord, 1815* (London: Greenhill Books, 1995), 134.

63. More has been written on Waterloo than any other battle of the Napoleonic war. I found the following studies useful: Charles J. Esdaile, *The Eagle Rejected: Napoleon, France and Waterloo* (Barnsley: Frontline Books, 2016); Paul L. Dawson, *Waterloo: The Truth at Last: Why Napoleon Lost the Great Battle* (Barnsley: Frontline Books, 2018); Andrew Field, *Waterloo: The French Perspective* (Barnsley: Pen & Sword, 2017); Alan Forrest, *Waterloo* (Oxford: Oxford University Press, 2015), Mark Adkin, *The Waterloo Companion* (London: Aurum

Press, 2001); Jac Weller, *Wellington at Waterloo* (London: Greenhill, 1992); Henry Houssaye, *1815* (Paris: Perrin, 1909). For a micro-study of the battle, see Brendan Simms, *The Longest Afternoon: The 400 Men Who Decided the Battle of Waterloo* (New York: Basic Books, 2015). For eyewitness accounts, Gareth Glover's multi-volume *The Waterloo Archive* (London: Frontline Books, 2010–2014) is indispensable. Equally useful is Glover's concise but insightful *Waterloo: Myth and Reality* (Barnsley: Pen & Sword, 2014). For the usually over-looked Dutch and Belgian contributions, see Erwin Muilwijk, *Standing Firm at Waterloo: 17 & 18 June* (Bleiswijk, Netherlands: Sovereign House Books, 2014). For how the battle was remembered, see Timothy Fitzpatrick, *The Long Shadow of Waterloo: Myths, Memories and Debates* (Oxford: Casemate, 2019).

64. Cited in Rory Muir, *Wellington: Waterloo and the Fortunes of Peace* (New Haven, CT: Yale University Press, 2015), 63.

65. For a recent discussion, see Paul L. Dawson, *Napoleon and Grouchy: The Last Great Waterloo Mystery Unravelled* (Barnsley: Frontline Books, 2017).

66. For the most recent discussion of General Pierre Jacques Étienne Cambronne and the famous story of the last stand of the Imperial Guard, see Stéphane Calvet's revisionist study, *Cambronne: La Légende de Waterloo* (Paris: Vendémiaire, 2015).

67. *Memoirs of Prince Metternich*, II:602.

68. Benjamin Robert Haydon, *Life of Benjamin Robert Haydon, Historical Painter, from His Autobiography and Journals*, ed. Tom Taylor (London: Longman, Brown, Green, and Longmans, 1853), I:239.

69. Napoleon to Joseph, June 19, 1815, in *Lettres Inédites de Napoléon Ier (An VIII, 1815)* (Paris: Plon, 1897), II:357–58.

70. Armand Augustin Louis de Caulaincourt, *Napoleon and His Times* (Philadelphia: E. L. Carey & A. Hart, 1838), II:173.

71. Napoleon to the Prince Recent of Britain, July 14, 1815, in *CN*, XXVIII:348. See Charles-Éloi Vial, *Le dernier voyage de l'empereur: Paris–Île d'Aix, 1815* (Paris: Éditions Vendémiaire, 2015); J. David Markham, *The Road to St. Helena: Napoleon After Waterloo* (Barnsley: Pen & Sword, 2008), 101–23.

72. See Michal J. Thornton, *Napoleon After Waterloo: England and the St. Helena Decision* (Stanford, CA: Stanford University Press, 1968), esp. 124–60; Paul Brunyee, *Napoleon's Britons and the St. Helena Decision* (Stroud: History Press, 2009).

Chapter 24

1. For the text of the Final Act, see *The Parliamentary Debates from the Year 1803 to the Present Time* (London: T. C. Hansard, 1816), XXXII:71ff.

2. Dominique de Pradt, *L'Europe après le Congrès d'Aix-la-Chapelle* (Paris: Béchet Ainé, 1819), 236.

3. Enno Kraehe, "A Bipolar Balance of Power," *American Historical Review* 97 (1992): 707–15. In addition to his magnum opus, *The Transformation of*

European Politics, 1763–1848 (Oxford: Oxford Clarendon Press, 1994), see Schroeder's articles "Did the Vienna Settlement Rest on a Balance of Power?," *American Historical Review* 97 (1992): 683–706, and "Alliances, 1815–1945: Weapons of Power and Tools of Management,"\ in *Historical Dimensions of National Security Problems*, ed. Klaus Knorr (Lawrence: University Press of Kansas, 1975), 218–28. For the most recent reassessment of the Congress System, see Beatrice de Graaf, Ido de Haan, and Brian E. Vick, eds., *Securing Europe After Napoleon: 1815 and the New European Security Culture* (Cambridge: Cambridge University Press, 2019).

4. Wolf Gruner has done much work highlighting the role of the German middle states in the post-Napoleonic international relations. See his *Der Deutsche Bund 1815–1866* (Munich: Beck, 2012) and *Der Wiener Kongress 1814/1815* (Stuttgart: Reclam Verlag, 2014). Also see his revisionist approach to the Congress of Vienna in "Was There a Reformed Balance of Power System or Cooperative Great Power Hegemony," *American Historical Review* 97 (1992): 725–32.

5. For details, see Joseph L. Black, *Nicholas Karamzin and Russian Society in the Nineteenth Century* (Toronto: University of Toronto Press, 1975).

6. On the Polish settlement, see Articles 1 to 12, and on the Saxon/Prussian compromise, see Articles 15–25 of the Final Act.

7. Cited in Walter Alison Phillips, *The Confederation of Europe: A Study of the European Alliance, 1813–1823* (London: Longmans, Green, 1920), 138–39.

8. Article 1, Definitive Treaty Between Great Britain, Austria, Prussia and Russia, and France, November 20, 1815, in *Britain and Foreign State Papers* (London: James Ridgway and Sons, 1839), III:284–87.

9. See Article 4 of the Treaty of Paris, and Convention between Britain, Austria, Prussia and Russia, and France, Relative to the Pecuniary Indemnity to be Paid by France to the Allied Powers, November 20, 1815, in *Britain and Foreign State Papers*, III:293–98; Convention Between Britain, Austria, Prussia and Russia, and France, Relative to the Occupation of a Military Line in France by an Allied Army, November 20, 1815, in *Britain and Foreign State Papers*, III:298–305. For in-depth discussion of the Allied occupation of France, see Christine Haynes, *Our Friends the Enemies: The Occupation of France After Napoleon* (Cambridge MA: Harvard University Press, 2018).

10. On the Bonapartes after Napoleon, see Pierre Branda, *La Saga des Bonaparte* (Paris: Perrin, 2018); David Stackton, *The Bonapartes* (London: Hodder and Soughton, 1967).

11. See Rafe Blaufarb, *Bonapartists in the Borderlands: French Exiles and Refugees on the Gulf Coast, 1815–1835* (Tuscaloosa: University of Alabama Press, 2005); Eric Saugera, *Reborn in America: French Exiles and Refugees in the United States and the Vine and Olive Adventure, 1815–1865* (Tuscaloosa: University of Alabama Press, 2011).

12. Eugene N. White, "Making the French Pay: The Costs and Consequences of the Napoleonic Reparations," *European Review of Economic History* 5, no. 3 (2001): 339.

13. One British historian pointed out that after the Napoleonic Wars Britain "found herself, the victor, in the curious position of being far more heavily burdened with debt that France, who had lost." J. H. Clapham, "The Economic Condition of Europe After the Napoleonic War," *Scientific Monthly* 11, no. 4 (1920): 321; Clapham, *The Economic Development of France and Germany, 1815–1914* (Cambridge: Cambridge University Press, 1968), 121–22. For comparison of British and French finances (and debt), see Michael D. Bordo and Eugene N. White. "A Tale of Two Currencies: British and French Finance During the Napoleonic Wars," *Journal of Economic History* 51, no. 2 (1991): 303–16.

14. Thomas Dwight Veve, *The Duke of Wellington and the British Army of Occupation in France, 1815–1818* (Westport, CT: Greenwood Press, 1992), 138–40; Haynes, *Our Friends the Enemies*, 219–24.

15. Act 10, "Treaty between the King of the Netherlands, Prussia, England, Austria and Russia," May 31, 1815, in *The Parliamentary Debates from the Year 1803 to the Present Time*, XXXII: 175–80. Also see Articles 65–73 of the Final Act of the Congress of Vienna.

16. Act 11, Declaration of the Powers on the Affairs of the Helvetic Confederacy, March 20, 1815; Act of Accession of the Swiss Diet, May 27, 1815, in *The Parliamentary Debates from the Year 1803 to the Present Time*, XXXII:182–88. Also see Articles 74–84 of the Final Act of the Congress of Vienna.

17. Acts 12, 13 and 14, in *The Parliamentary Debates from the Year 1803 to the Present Time*, XXXII:188–200. Also see Articles 85–91 of the Final Act of the Congress of Vienna.

18. Articles 65–73 of the Final Act of the Congress of Vienna.

19. Act 9, Article 2, "Federative Constitution of Germany," June 8, 1815, *The Parliamentary Debates from the Year 1803 to the Present Time*, XXXII:168. Also see Article 63, The Final Act of the Congress of Vienna: "The Act was initially signed by 38 plenipotentiaries from 34 principalities and four free cities; the 39th state, Hesse-Homburg, was added in 1817."

20. Act 9, Article 11, "Federative Constitution of Germany," June 8, 1815, *The Parliamentary Debates from the Year 1803 to the Present Time*, XXXII:170.

21. See Articles 53–64 of the Final Act of the Congress of Vienna.

22. See Wolf Gruner, *Der Deutsche Bund 1815–1866* (Munich: Beck, 2012); David G. Williamson, *Germany Since 1815: A Nation Forged and Renewed* (New York: Palgrave Macmillan, 2005), 17–39; Frank B. Tipton, *A History of Modern Germany Since 1815* (Berkeley: University of California Press, 2003), 1–58.

23. T. K. Derry, *History of Scandinavia: Norway, Sweden, Denmark, Finland, and Iceland* (Minneapolis: University of Minnesota Press, 1979), 211–15.

24. Act 15, "Declaration of the Powers on the Abolition of the Slave Trade," February 8, 1815, in *The Parliamentary Debates from the Year 1803 to the Present Time*, XXXII:200–201.

25. Act 16, "Regulations for the Free Navigation of Rivers," in *The Parliamentary Debates from the Year 1803 to the Present Time*, XXXII:202–14.

26. Act 17, "Regulations Concerning the Precedence of Diplomatic Agents," in *The Parliamentary Debates from the Year 1803 to the Present Time*, XXXII:214–15.

27. Viscount Castlereagh to Lord Liverpool, September 28, 1815, in *The Life and Administration of Robert Banks, Second Earl of Liverpool*, ed. Charles Yonge (London: Macmillan, 1868), II:229; Clemens Wenzel Lothar Fürst von Metternich, *Memoirs of Prince Metternich, 1773–1815*, ed. Richard Metternich, trans. Robina Napier (London: Richard Bentley, 1880), I:165.

28. The Treaty of the Holy Alliance, September 26, 1815, in *Britain and Foreign State Papers*, III:211.

29. See the excellent discussion in de Graaf, de Haan, and Vick, *Securing Europe After Napoleon*; Beatrice de Graaf, *Tegen de terreur. Hoe Europa veilig werd na Napoleon* (Amsterdam: Prometheus, 2018); Adam Zamoyski, *Phantom Terror: Political Paranoia and the Creation of the Modern State, 1789–1848* (New York: Basic Books, 2015).

30. The most recent discussion of the aftermath and costs of war is Alan Forrest, Karen Hagemann, and Michael Rowe, eds., *War, Demobilization and Memory: The Legacy of War in the Era of Atlantic Revolutions* (New York: Palgrave Macmillan, 2016).

31. For an in-depth discussion of historiography and data, see Jacques Houdaille, "Pertes de l'armée de terre sous le premier Empire, d'après les registres matricules," in *Population* 27, no. 1 (1972): 27–50. For a concise discussion, see David Rouanet, "Bilan humain des guerres de l'Empire," in *Napoléon et l'Europe*, ed. Émile Robbe and François Lagrange (Paris: Musée de l'Armée, 2013), 56–59.

32. Haydon, *Life of Benjamin Robert Haydon*, I, 238–39; William Dorset Fellowes, *Paris: During the Interesting Month of July, 1815. A Series of Letters Addressed to a Friend in London* (London: Gales and Fenner, 1815), 22.

33. This number includes both British and foreign casualties. See J. W. Fortescue, *The County Lieutenancies and the Army, 1803–1814* (London: Macmillan, 1909), 291; William B. Hodge, "On the Mortality Arising from Military Operations," *Journal of the Statistical Society of London* XIX (1856): 264–65.

34. Martin Robson, *A History of the Royal Navy: The Napoleonic Wars* (London: I. B. Tauris, 2014), 156.

35. John William Fortescue, *A History of the British Army* (London: Macmillan, 1910), IV, part 1, 565; Michael Duffy, *Soldiers, Sugar and Seapower: The British Expeditions to the West Indies and the War against Revolutionary France* (Oxford: Clarendon Press, 1987).

36. Robert Burnham and Ron McGuigan, *The British Army Against Napoleon: Facts, Lists and Trivia, 1805–1815* (Havertown, MD: Frontline Books, 2010), 213–14; Andrew Bamford, *Sickness, Suffering, and the Sword: The British*

Regiment on Campaign (Norman: University of Oklahoma Press, 2014), 220–22, 303–4.

37. M. R. Smallman-Raynor and A. D. Cliff, *War Epidemics: An Historical Geography of Infectious Diseases in Military Conflict and Civil Strife, 1850–2000* (Oxford: Oxford University Press, 2004), 107–9.

38. Bagration to the Noble Estate of Wallachia, February 8, 1810, in *Bagration v Dunaiskikh kniazhestvakh: Sbornik Dokumentov* (Chişinău, 1949), 76.

39. Anthony McFarlane, *War and Independence in Spanish America* (New York: Routledge, 2014), 293.

40. Robert Harvey, *Liberators: South America's Savage Wars of Freedom, 1810–1830* (London: Robinson, 2002), 192.

41. Pavel Pushin, *Diaries of the 1812–1814 Campaigns*, trans. and ed. A. Mikaberidze (Tbilisi: NSG, 2011), 151, 154.

42. The other major eruptions included the 1808–1809 eruption in the southwestern Pacific Ocean, 1812 eruptions by La Soufrière on St. Vincent in the Caribbean and Awu in the Sangihe Islands (Dutch East Indies), the 1813 eruption in Suwanosejima in the Ryukyu Islands, (Japan), and the 1814 one in Mayon in the Philippines. For a detailed discussion of the Tambora eruption, see Gillen D'Arcy Wood, *Tambora: The Eruption That Changed the World* (Princeton, NJ: Princeton University Press, 2015).

43. See John Dexter Post, *The Last Great Subsistence Crisis in the Western World* (Baltimore: John Hopkins University Press, 1977), 77.

44. Kresimir Kuzic, "The Impact of Two Volcano Eruptions on the Croatian Lands at the Beginning of the 19th Century," *Croatian Meteorological Journal* 42 (2007): 17–18.

45. Glenn Hueckel, "War and the British Economy, 1793–1815: A General Equilibrium Analysis," *Explorations in Economic History* 10 (1973): 369. Also see A. Gayer, W. Rostow and A. Schwartz, *The Growth and Fluctuations of the British Economy, 1790–1850* (Oxford: Clarendon Press, 1953).

46. Angus Maddison, *The World Economy: A Millennial Perspective* (Paris: OECD, 2001), 95.

47. Patrick O'Brien, "The Impact of the Revolutionary and Napoleonic Wars, 1793–1815, on the Long-Run Growth of the British Economy," *Review (Fernand Braudel Center)* XII (1989): 383.

48. See Victor Bulmer-Thomas, *The Economic History of Latin America Since Independence* (Cambridge: Cambridge University Press, 2003); Ralph Davis, *The Industrial Revolution and British Overseas Trade* (Leicester: Leicester University Press, 1979).

49. See D. Bulbeck et al., *Southeast Asian Exports since the 14th Century: Cloves, Pepper, Coffee and Sugar* (Leiden: KITLV Press, 1998).

50. A. Webster, "The Political Economy of Trade Liberalization: The East India Company Charter of 1813," *Economic History Review* (n.s.) 43 (1990): 404–19.

51. See D. Eltis and J. Walvin, eds., *The Abolition of the Atlantic Slave Trade: Origins and Effects in Europe, Africa and the Americas* (Madison: University of Wisconsin Press, 1981).

52. For example, in 1830, Britain experienced the Swing Riots, a widespread rural uprising that opposed the process of enclosure and mechanized agriculture and sought to reverse progressive impoverishment and dispossession of the English agricultural workforce; in its scale, this rural uprising very nearly matched France's "Great Fear" rioting of 1789. For details, see John E. Archer, *Social Unrest and Popular Protest in England, 1780–1840* (Cambridge: Cambridge University Press, 2000), ch. 2.

53. See Haynes, *Our Friends the Enemies.*

54. Matthew Anderson, "Russia and the Eastern Question, 1821–1941," in *Europe's Balance of Power 1815–1848,* ed. Alan Sked (London: Macmillan, 1979), 82; Artur Attman, "The Russian Market in World Trade, 1500–1860," *Scandinavian Economic History Review* XXIX, no. 3 (1981): 196–97; Peter Hopkirk, *The Great Game: On Secret Service in High Asia* (Oxford: Oxford University Press, 1990), 102.

55. See David Brewer, *The Flame of Freedom: The Greek War of Independence, 1821–1833* (London: John Murray, 2001); Nikiforos Diamandouros, ed., *Hellenism and the First Greek War of Liberation (1821–1830): Continuity and Change* (Thessaloniki, Greece: Institute for Balkan Studies, 1976); George Finlay, *History of the Greek Revolution* (London: Zeno, 1971).

56. José Fernando de Abascal, Viceroy of Peru, to Miguel de Lardizabal, Secretary of Indies in Madrid, October 12, 1815, Archivo General de Indias, Lima, Peru, 749, N. 76, p. 678.

57. For details, see B. R. Hamnett, *La política contrarevolucionaria del Virrey Abascal: Peru, 1806–1816* (Lima: IEP, 2000); V. Peralta Ruiz, *En defense de la autoridad: política y cultura bajo el gobierno del virrey Abascal: Perú 1806–1816* (Madrid: Consejo Superior de Investigaciones Científicas, 2002).

58. Harold Temperley, *The Foreign Policy of Canning, 1822–1827: England, the Neo-Holy Alliance and the New World* (New York: Frank Cass, 1966), 584.

59. Jackson to Monroe, January 6, 1818, in *The Papers of Andrew Jackson,* ed. Harold D. Moser, David R. Hoth and George H. Hoemann (Knoxville: University of Tennessee Press, 1994), IV:167.

60. Treaty of Amity, Settlement, and Limits Between the United States of America and His Catholic Majesty, 1819, available at the Avalon Project, Yale Law School, http://avalon.law.yale.edu/19th_century/sp1819.asp.

61. See Jay Sexton, *The Monroe Doctrine: Empire and Nation in Nineteenth-Century America* (New York: Hill and Wang, 2011); Dexter Perkins, *A History of the Monroe Doctrine* (Boston: Little, Brown, 1963).

62. See Sudhir Hazareesingh, *The Legend of Napoleon* (London: Granta Books, 2004); Hazareesingh, *The Saint-Napoleon: Celebrating Sovereignty in Nineteenth-Century France* (Cambridge: MA: Harvard University Press, 2004).

SELECT BIBLIOGRAPHY

Abbreviations

AE	Archives du Ministère des Affaires Etrangères, Paris, France.
AN	Archives Nationales, Paris.
BL	British Library.
CN	Napoleon Bonaparte, *Correspondance de Napoleon Ier, publ. par ordre de l'Empereur Napoléon III,* 32 vols (Paris: Imprimerie Impériale, 1858–69).
CRE	*Proceedings of the Consortium on Revolutionary Europe. Dropmore Papers: The Manuscripts of J. B. Fortescue, Esq., Preserved at Dropmore* (London: Historical Manuscripts Commission, 1908).
FO	Foreign Office, National Archives (formerly Public Records Office), Kew, Great Britain.
NLS	National Library of Scotland.
PSZ	*Polnoe sobranie zakonov Rossiiskoi imperii.*
RGVIA	Russian State Military Historical Archive.
Riksarkivet	Swedish National Archives, Stockholm.
SHD	Service historique de la Défense
SIRIO	*Sbornik Imperatorskago Russkago Istoricheskago Obschestva.*
VPR	*Vneshnaya politika Rossii XIX i nachala XX veka: dokumenti Rossiiskogo Ministerstva Inostrannikh del* (Moscow, 1961).
WO	War Office, The National Archives (formerly The Public Records Office), Kew, Great Britain.

Archives

Archives du Ministère des Affaires Etrangères, Paris, FranceArchives Nationale, Paris, France
Archivo Histórico Nacional, Madrid, Spain
Archivo General de Indias, Sevilla, Spain
Archivo de la Real Chancillería de Valladolid, Spain
Biblioteca Histórica Municipal, Madrid, Spain
Central Historical Archive of Moscow
Centre des Archives diplomatiques de La Courneuve, Paris, France
India Office Records and Private Papers, British Library, London, Great Britain
Kriegsarchiv, Vienna, Austria
National Library of Scotland, Edinburgh, Scotland
Riksarkivet, Swedish National Archives, Stockholm, Sweden.
Russian State Military Historical Archive, Moscow, Russia
Service Historique de l'Armée de Terre, Paris France
The National Archives (formerly The Public Records Office), Kew, Great Britain

Periodicals

American Historical Review
Cobbett's Annual Register
The English Historical Review
Gazette Nationale, ou Le Moniteur Universel
Gentleman's Magazine
The International History Review
Istoricheskii Vestnik
Le patriote français
London Gazette
The Monthly Visitor
Morning Chronicle
The New Annual Register
Revue d'histoire diplomatique
Revue de l'Institut Napoléon
Revue des études napoléoniennes
Revue d'histoire moderne et contemporaine
Revue du souvenir napoléonien
Revue historique
Royal Military Chronicle
Russkaya starina
Russkii arkhiv
Sankt Petersburgskie vedomosti
Sbornik Imperatorskago russkago istoricheskago obshchestva
Slavic Review

The Times (London)
Voennyi sbornik

Primary Sources

Abbot, Charles. *The Diary and Correspondence of Charles Abbot, Lord Colchester, Speaker of the House of Commons, 1802–1817*. London: J. Murray, 1861.

Aitchison, Sir Charles U., ed. *A Collection of Treaties, Engagements and Sunnuds Relating to India and Neighboring Countries*. 7 vols. Calcutta: O. T. Cutter, 1862–1866.

Akty sobrannye kavkazskoiu arkheograficheskoiu kommissieiu. Edited by A. Berzhe. 12 vols. Tiflis, 1866–1904.

American State Papers: Documents, Legislative and Executive, of the Congress of the United States. Edited by Walter Lowrie and Matthew St. Clair Clarke. Washington, DC: Gales and Seaton, 1833.

Archduke Charles. *Archduke Charles' 1796 Campaign in Germany*. Translated by George F. Nafziger. West Chester, OH: Nafziger Collection, 2004.

Archives parlementaires de 1787 à 1860: recueil complet des débats législatifs et politiques des chambres françaises. 82 vols. Paris: Librairie Administrative Paul Dupont, 1862–1913.

Arkhiv Gosudarstvennogo Soveta. St. Petersburg: Sobstvennoi E. I. V. Kantseliarii, 1869–1904.

Arkhiv kniazya Vorontsova. 40 vols. Moscow: Tip. A. I. Mamontova; Tip. Gracheva, 1870–1895.

Arneth, Alfred Ritter von. *Joseph II und Katharina von Russland*. Vienna: W. Braumuller, 1869.

Auckland, William Eden. *The Journal and Correspondence of William, Lord Auckland*. London: Richard Bentley, 1862.

Bailleur, Paul, ed. *Preussen und Frankreich von 1795 bis 1807: Diplomatische correspondenzen*. 2 vols. Leipzig: S. Hirzel, 1881–1887.

Banks, Joseph. *Sir Joseph Banks, Iceland and the North Atlantic 1772–1820: Journals, Letters and Documents*. Edited by Anna Agnarsdottir. London: Hakluyt Society, 2016.

Barras, Paul. *Mémoires de Barras, membre du Directoire*. Edited by George Duruy. 3 vols. Paris: Hachette, 1896.

Barrès, Jean Baptiste. *Memoirs of a Napoleonic Officer*. London: G. Allen & Unwin, 1925.

Bathurst, Seymour Henry. *Historical Manuscripts Commission Report on the Manuscripts of Earl Bathurst Preserved at Cirencester Park*. Edited by Francis B. Bickley. London: Stat. Office, 1923.

Baudin, Nicolas. *Mon voyage aux terres australes: journal personnel du commandant Baudin*. Paris: Imprimerie nationale, 2000.

Bausset-Roquefort, Louis François Joseph. *Private Memoirs of the Court of Napoleon and of Some Public Events of the Imperial Reign, from 1805 to the First of May 1814, to*

Serve as a Contribution to the History of Napoleon. Philadelphia: Carey, Lea & Carey, 1828.

Beauharnais, Eugène de. *Mémoires et correspondance politique et militaire du Prince Eugène*. Edited by A. Du Casse. 10 vols. Paris: Lévy, 1858–1860.

Beauharnais, Hortense de. *Mémoires de la reine Hortense*. Edited by Jean Hanoteau. Paris: Plon, 1927.

Biedma, José Juan, ed. *Documentos referents de la guerra de la indepencia de América a emancipación politica de la República Argentina y de otras secciones de América a qye cooperó desde 1810 a 1828*, vol. 2, *Antecedentes popoliticos, económicos y administrativos de la revolución de Mayo de 1810*. Buenos Aires: Archivo General de la Nación Argentina, 1914.

Bonaparte, Joseph. *Mémoires et correspondance politique et militaire du roi Joseph*. Edited by A. Du Casse. 10 vols. Paris, 1854–1856.

Bonaparte, Napoleon. *The Confidential Correspondence of Napoleon Bonaparte with His Brother Joseph*. New York: D. Appleton, 1856.

Bonaparte, Napoleon. *Correspondance de Napoleon Ier, publ. par ordre de l'Empereur Napoléon III*. 32 vols. Paris: Imprimerie Impériale, 1858–69.

Bonaparte, Napoleon. *Correspondance générale*. Edited by Thierry Lentz, Michel Kerautret, François Houdecek, et al. 15 vols. Paris: Fayard, 2004–2018.

Bonaparte, Napoleon. *Dernières lettres inédites de Napoléon*. Edited by Léonce de Brotonne. Paris: Champion, 1903.

Bonaparte, Napoleon. *Lettres inédites de Napoléon 1er (an VIII—1809)*. Edited by Leon Lecestre. Paris: Librairie Plon, 1897.

Bonaparte, Napoleon. *New Letters of Napoleon I Omitted from the Edition Published Under the Auspices of Napoleon III*. Edited by Lady Mary Loyd. New York: D. Appleton, 1897.

Bonaparte, Napoleon. *Ordres et apostilles de Napoléon, 1799–1815*. Edited by Athur Chuquet. Paris: Champion, 1911.

Bonaparte, Napoleon. *A Selection from the Letters and Despatches of the First Napoleon*. Edited by D. Bingham. 3 vols. London: Chapman and Hall, 1884.

Bosredon de Ransijat, Jean de. *Journal du siége et blocus de Malte*. Paris: Imprimerie de Valade, 1801.

Brissot, Jacques-Pierre. *Second discours de J. P. Brissot, député, sur la nécéssite de faire la guerre aux princes allemands, prononcé à la société dans le séance du vendredi 30 December 1791*. Paris: Sociéte des Amis de la Constitution, 1791.

British and Foreign State Papers, 1812–1814. London: James Rigway and Sons, 1841.

Browning, Oscar. *England and Napoleon in 1803, being the Despatches of Lord Witworth and Others, Now First Printed...Edited for the Royal Historical Society*. London: Longmans, Green, 1887.

Burke, Edmund. *The Works of the Right Honorable Edmund Burke*. London: Rivington, 1801.

Caillet-Bois, Ricardo Rodolfo, ed. *Mayo documental*. Buenos Aires: Universidad de Buenos Aires, 1961.

Campbell, Neil. *Napoleon on Elba: Diary of an Eyewitness to Exile.* Edited by Jonathan North. Welwyn Garden City, UK: Ravenhall, 2004.

Canning, George. *Memoirs of the Life of the Right Honourable George Canning.* London: Thomas Tegg, 1828.

Caulaincourt, Armand-Augustin-Louis de. *Memoirs.* London: Cassell, 1935.

Chatterton, Lady Georgiana. *Memorials, Personal and Historical of Lord Gambier.* London: Hurst and Blackett, 1861.

Cheng, Pei-kai, and M. Lestz, with J. Spence, eds. *The Search for Modern China: A Documentary History.* New York: W. W. Norton, 1999.

Chuquet, Arthur, ed. *Journal de voyage du général Desaix, Suisse et Italie (1797).* Paris: Plon-Nourrit, 1907.

Clausewitz, Karl von. *La campagne de 1799 en Italie et en Suisse.* Paris: Champ libre, 1979.

Clausewitz, Karl von. *On War.* Edited and translated by Michael Howard and Peter Paret. Princeton, NJ: Princeton University Press, 1976.

Clercq, Alexandre de, ed. *Recueil des traités de la France.* 3 vols. Paris: A. Durand et Pedone-Lauriel, 1880–1882.

Coignet, Jean Roch. *Les cahiers du capitaine Coignet.* Paris: Hachette, 1883.

Cornwallis, Charles. *Correspondence of Charles, First Marquis Cornwallis.* Edited by Charles Ross. 3 vols. London: John Murray, 1859.

Curtis, Edmond, and R. B. McDowell, eds. *Irish Historical Documents 1172–1922.* New York: Barnes & Noble, 1968.

Czartoryski, Adam Jerzy. *Mémoires du Prince Adam Czartoryski et correspondance avec l'Empereur Alexandre Ier.* Paris: E. Plon, Nourrit, 1887.

Damas, Roger. *Memoirs of the Comte Roger de Damas, 1787–1806.* London: Chapman and Hall, 1913.

Deventer, Marinus Lodewijk van, ed. *Het Nederlandsch gezag over Java en onderhoorigheden sedert 1811. Verzameling van onuitgegeven stukken uit de koloniale en andere arhieven.* S'Gravenhage: M. Nijhoff, 1891.

Documente privitoare la Istoria Românilor. Corespondentă diplomatică și rapoarte consulare franceze (1603–1824). Edited by Eudoxiu Hurmuzaki et al. Bucharest: Acad. Rom. și Ministerul Cultelor și Instrucțiunii Publice, 1912.

Documente privitoare la Istoria Românilor. Edited by Ioan Bogdan et al. Bucharest: I. V. Socecŭ, 1885.

Documente privitoare la Istoria Românilor. Rapoarte consulare prusiene din Iași și București (1763–1844). Edited by Nicolae Iorga. Bucharest: Acad. Rom. și Ministerul Cultelor și Instrucțiunii Publice, 1897.

Douin, Georges, ed. *L'Égypte de 1802 à 1804: correspondance des consuls de France en Égypte.* Cairo: Institut français d'archéologie orientale du Caire, 1925.

Driault, Édouard. *Mohamed Aly et Napoléon (1807–1814): correspondance des consuls de France en Égypte.* Cairo: Institut française d'archéologie orientale, 1925.

Dundas, Henry. "Papers of Henry Dundas, First Viscount Melville, 1779–1813." David M. Rubenstein Rare Book and Manuscript Library, Duke University.

Elphinstone, George Keith. *The Keith Papers: Selected from the Papers of Admiral Viscount Keith*. Edited by Christopher Lloyd. London: Navy Records Society, 1950.

Elphinstone, Mountstuart. *An Account of the Kingdom of Caubul, and Its Dependencies in Persia, Tartary, and India*. London: Longman, 1815.

Enghien, duc de. *Correspondance du duc d'Enghien (1801–1804) et documents sur son enlèvement et sa mort*. Paris: A. Picard, 1908.

Fain, Agathon Jean François. *Manuscrit de 1813, contenant le précis des évènemens de cette année*. Paris: Delaunay, 1825.

Fain, Agathon Jean François. *Memoirs of the Invasion of France by the Allied Armies and of the Last Six Months of the Reign of Napoleon*. London: H. Colburn, 1834.

Fitzpatrick, Walter, ed. *Report on the Manuscripts of J. B. Fortescue, Esq. Preserved at Dropmore*. 10 vols. London: Her Majesty's Stationery Office, 1892–1927.

Fournier, August, ed. *Die Geheimpolizei auf dem Wiener Kongress. Eine Auswahl aus ihren Papieren* Vienna: F. Tempsky, 1913.

Fraser, Edward, ed. *The Enemy at Trafalgar: An Account of the Battle from Eye-Witness Narratives and Letters and Despatches from the French and Spanish Fleets*. London: Hodder & Stoughton, 1906.

Garnier, Jacques, ed. *Relations et rapports officiels de la bataille d'Austerlitz, 1805*. Paris: La Vouivre, 1998.

George III. *The Later Correspondence of George III*. Edited by Arthur Aspinall. Cambridge: Cambridge University Press, 1963.

George III. *The Letters of King George III*. Edited by Dobree Bonamy. London: Cassell, 1935.

Godoy, Manuel. *Memorias . . .* Gerona: Libreria de Vicente Oliva, 1841.

Gorchkoff, Dimitri, ed. *Moskva i Otechestvennaya voina 1812 goda*. Moscow: Izdatelstvo Glavnogo arkhivnogo upravleniya goroda Moskvy, 2011–2012, 2 volumes.

Gower, Graville Leveson. *Lord Granville Leveson Gower, First Earl Granville: Private Correspondence, 1781 to 1821*. Edited by Lady Granville. New York: E. P. Dutton, 1916.

Holland, Henry Richard Vassall. *Memoirs of the Whig Party During My Time*. London: Longman, Brown, Green, and Longmans, 1854.

Holland, Lady Elizabeth Vassall Fox. *The Spanish Journal of Elizabeth, Lady Holland*. Edited by Giles Stephen Holland Fox-Strangways. London: Longmans, 1910.

Ikhchiev, D., ed. *Turski dŭrzhavni dokumenti za Osman pazvantoglu Vidinski*. Sofia: Dŭrzhavna pechatnitsa, 1908.

Ingram, Edward, ed. *Two Views of British India: The Private Correspondence of Mr. Dundas and Lord Wellesley, 1798–1801*. Bath: Adams & Dart, 1970.

Ivić, Aleksa, ed. *Spisi bečkih arhiva o prvom srpskom ustanku*. Belgrade: Srpska kraljevska akademija, 1935.

Jabarti, 'Abd al-Raḥmān al-. *Napoleon in Egypt: Al-Jabarti's chronicle of the French occupation, 1798*. Princeton, NJ: Markus Wiener, 2004.

Jackson, George. *The Diaries and Letters of Sir George Jackson, KCH, From the Peace of Amiens to the Battle of Talavera*. London: Richard Bentley and Son, 1872.

Jakšić, Grgur, and Vojislav Vučković, ed. *Francuski dokumenti o prvom i drugom ustanku (1804–1830)*. Belgrade: Naučno delo, 1957.

Jaubert, Pierre-Amédée. *Voyage en Arménie et en Perse: fait dans les années 1805 et 1806*. Paris: Pelicier, 1821.

Jefferson, Thomas. *Memoir, Correspondence and Miscellanies from the Papers of Thomas Jefferson*. Edited by Thomas Jefferson Randolph. Boston: Gray and Bowen, 1830.

Jefferson, Thomas. *The Writings of Thomas Jefferson*. Edited by Andrew A. Lipscomb. Washington, DC: Thomas Jefferson Memorial Association, 1903.

Jones, Harford. *An Account of the Transactions of His Majesty's Mission to the Court of Persia in the Years 1807–11*. London: James Bohn, 1834.

Jourdan, Jean-Baptiste. *Mémoires militaires du Maréchal Jourdan (guerre d'Espagne)*. Paris: Flammarion, 1899.

Karvyalis, A., and V. Soloveyev, eds. *Dokumenty shtaba M. I. Kutuzova, 1805–1806*. Vilnius: Gos. izdatelstvo polit literatury, 1951.

Kerautret, Michel, ed. *Les grands traités du Consulat, 1799–1804. Documents diplomatiques du Consulat et de l'Empire*. Paris: Nouveau Monde, 2002.

Khantadze, Shota, ed. *Dokumentebi kakhetis 1812 tslis ajankebis istoriisatvis*. Tbilisi: Tbilisi University Press, 1999.

Kutuzov, Mikhail. *M. I. Kutuzov: Sbornik dokumentov*. Edited by Liubomir Beskrovnyi. 5 vols. Moscow: Voennoe izdatelstvo Voennogo Ministerstva Soyuza SSR, 1954.

La Forest, Antoine René Charles Mathurin de. *Correspondance du comte de la Forest, ambassadeur de France en Espagne 1808–1813*. Paris: A. Picard et fils, 1905.

La Jonquière, Clément de Taffanel. *L' expédition d'Égypte, 1798–1801*. 5 vols. Paris: H. Charles-Lavauzelle, 1899–1907.

Larivière, Charles de. *Catherine II et la Révolution française d'après de nouveaux documents*. Paris: H. Le Soudier, 1895.

Las Cases, Emmanuel de. *Mémorial de Sainte Hélène*. Paris: Gallimard–La Pléiade, 1956.

Leclerc, Charles. *Lettres du Général Leclerc*. Edited by Paul Roussier. Paris: Société de l'histoire des colonies françaises, 1937.

Murat, Joachim. *Lettres et documents pour servir à l'histoire de Joachim Murat*. Edited by Paul Le Brethon. 8 vols. Paris: Librarie Plon, 1908–1914.

Löwenstern, Waldemar. *Mémoires du général-major russe baron de Löwenstern (1776–1858)*. Paris: A. Fontemoing, 1903.

Madison, James. *The Papers of James Madison: Secretary of State Series*. Charlottesville: University Press of Virginia, 1984.

Malmesbury, James Harris. *Diaries and Correspondence of James Harris, First Earl of Malmesbury*. London: Richard Bentley, 1845.

Marbot, Jean-Baptiste Antoine Marcellin. *The Memoirs of Baron de Marbot*. London: Longmans, Green, 1903.

Martens, Fedor F. *Recueil des traités et conventions conclus par la Russie avec les puissances étrangères*. 15 vols. St. Petersburg: A. Böhnke, 1874–1909.

Martens, Georg Friedrich. *Recueil des principaux traités d'alliance, de paix, de trève, de neuralité, de commerce, de limites, d'échange, etc.* 10 vols. Göttingen: Librairie de Dieterich, 1801–1828.

Meddelelser fra krigsarkiverne udgivne af Generalstaben. 8 vols. Copenhagen: F. Hegel & Son, 1883–1900.

Méneval, Claude-Francois. *Mémoires pour servir a histoire de Napoléon Ier depuis 1802 jusqu'à 1815.* Paris: E. Dentu, 1893.

Metternich, Klemens Wenzel Lothar Fürst von. *Mémoires, documents et écrits divers laissés par le prince de Metternich.* Edited by A. de Klinkowstroem. Paris: Plon, 1881–1883.

Metternich, Klemens Wenzel Lothar Fürst von. *Memoirs of Prince Metternich, 1773–1815.* Edited by Prince Richard Metternich. Translated by Alexander Napier. London: Richard Bentley, 1880.

Meyer, Philipp Anton Guido von, ed. *Corpus iuris Confoederationis Germanicae oder Staatsacten für Geschichte und öffentliches Recht des Deutschen Bundes.* Frankfurt: Brönner, 1858.

Mijer, Pieter, ed. *Verzameling van instructien, ordonnancien en reglementen voor de regering van Nederlandsch Indië.* Batavia: Ter Lands-Drukkerij, 1848.

Mikaberidze, Alexander, ed. *The Russian Eyewitness Accounts of the Campaign of 1807.* London: Pen & Sword, 2015.

Mikaberidze, Alexander, ed. *The Russian Eyewitness Accounts of the Campaign of 1812.* London: Pen & Sword, 2012.

Mikaberidze, Alexander, ed. *The Russian Eyewitness Accounts of the Campaign of 1814.* London: Pen & Sword, 2014.

Miles, William. *The Correspondence of William Augustus Miles on the French Revolution, 1789–1817.* London: Longmans, Green, 1890.

Minto, Gilbert Elliot. *Life and Letters of Sir Hilbert Elliot, First Earl of Minto.* Edited by the Countess of Minto. 3 vols. London: Longmans, Green, 1874.

Miot de Mélito, André François. *Memoirs of Count Miot de Mélito, Minister, Ambassador, Councillor of State and Member of the Institute of France, Between the Years 1788 and 1815.* Edited by Wilhelm August Fleischmann. New York: Scribner, 1881.

Mollien, François Nicolas. *Mémoires d'un ministre du trésor public: 1780–1815.* Paris: Félix Alcan, 1898.

Mora, José Joaquín de. *Mémoires historiques sur Ferdinand VII, roi des Espagnes.* Paris: Librairie Universelle, 1824.

Murat, Joachim. *Murat, lieutenant de l'empereur en Espagne 1808: d'après sa correspondance inédite et des documents originaux.* Paris: E. Plon, 1897.

Nelson, Horatio. *The Dispatches and Letters of Vice Admiral Lord Viscount Nelson.* edited by Nicholas H. Nicholas. Cambridge: Cambridge University Press, 2011.

Noradounghian, Gabriel, ed. *Recueil d'actes internationaux de l'Empire ottoman.* Paris: F. Pichon, 1900.

O'Meara, Barry. *Napoleon in exile: or, A voice from St. Helena.* New York: William Gowans, 1853.

Paget, Sir Arthur. *The Paget Papers: Diplomatic and Other Correspondence of the Right Hon. Sir Arthur Paget, G.C.B., 1794–1807*. Edited by Augustus Berkeley Paget. London: W. Heinemann, 1896.

The Parliamentary Register or History of the Proceedings and Debates of the Houses of Lords and Commons. London: Wilson/Debrett, 1797–1802. 18 vols.

Parquin, Denis Charles. *Souvenirs et campagnes d'un vieux soldat de l'empire (1803–1814)*. Paris: Berger-Levrault, 1903.

Pelet de la Lozèere, Joseph. *Napoleon in Council or the Opinions Delivered by Bonaparte in the Council of State*. London: Whittaker, 1837.

Pelet, Jean Jacques. *The French Campaign in Portugal, 1810–1811: An Account by Jean Jacques Pelet*. Translated and edited by Donald D. Horward. Minneapolis: University of Minnesota Press, 1972.

Péron, François. *French Designs on Colonial New South Wales: François Péron's Memoir on the English Settlements in New Holland, Van Diemen's Land and the Archipelagos of the Great Pacific Ocean*. Edited by Jean Fornasiero and John West-Sooby. Adelaide: Friends of the State Library of South Australia, 2014.

Pitt, William. *The Speeches of the Right Honourable William Pitt in the House of Commons*. London: Longman, Hurst, Rees and Orne, 1806.

Pitt, William. *The War Speeches of William Pitt the Younger*. Edited by R. Coupland. Oxford: Clarendon Press, 1915.

Plaja, Fernando Diaz. *La historia de España en sus documentos. El siglo XIX*. Madrid: Instituto de Estudios Políticos, 1954.

Popkin, Jeremy D., ed. *Facing Racial Revolution: Eyewitness Accounts of the Haitian Insurrection*. Chicago: University of Chicago Press, 2007.

Procès-verbal de l'Assemblée nationale. Paris: Imprimerie mationale, 1792.

Rémusat, Claire Élisabeth. *Mémoires de Madame de Rémusat, 1802–1808*. 3 vols. Paris: Calmann-Lévy, 1879–1880.

Roederer, Pierre-Louis. *Mémoires sur la Révolution, le Consulat, et l'Empire*. Paris: Plon, 1942.

Rose, J. Holland, ed. *Select Despatches from the British Foreign Office Archives Relating to the Formation of the Third Coalition Against France, 1804–1805*. London: Royal Historical Society, 1904.

Rosenkrantz, Niels. *Journal du Congrès de Vienne, 1814–1815*. Edited by Georg Nørregård. Copenhagen: G. E. C. Gad, 1953.

Saint-Cyr, Laurent. *Mémoires sur les campagnes des armées du Rhin et de Rhin-et-Moselle de 1792 jusqu'à la paix de Campo Formio*. Paris: Anselin, 1829.

Saumarez, James. *The Saumarez Papers: Selections from the Baltic Correspondence of Vice-Admiral Sir James Saumarez, 1808–1812*. Edited by A. Ryan. London: Navy Records Society, 1968.

Savary, Anne-Jean-Marie-René. *Mémoires du Duc de Rovigo: pour servir à l'histoire de l'empereur Napoléon*. Paris: A. Bossange, 1828.

Scicluna, Hannibal Publius. *Documents Relating to the French Occupation of Malta in 1798–1800*. Valletta, Malta: Empire Press, 1923.

Scott, August James Brown, ed. *The Armed Neutralities of 1780 and 1800: A Collection of Official Documents*. New York: Oxford University Press, 1918.

Ségur, Paul-Philippe. *Histoire et mémoires*. Paris: Librairie de Firmin-Didot, 1877.

Staël, Anne-Louise-Germaine de. *Ten Years' Exile*. London: Treuttel and Wurtz, 1821.

Stein, Friedrich vom. *Briefe von und an Friedrich von Gentz*. Edited by Friedrich Carl Wittichen. Munich: R. Oldenbourg, 1913.

Stewart, Robert. *Correspondence, Despatches and other Papers of Viscount Castlereagh*. Edited by the Marquess of Londonderry. London: William Shoberl, 1848–1853.

Strickler, Johannes, ed. *Actensammlung aus der Zeit der Helvetischen Republik (1798–1803)*. Bern: Buchdruckerei Stämpfli, 1902.

Talleyrand, Charles-Maurice de. *Correspondance inédite du prince de Talleyrand et du roi Louis XVIII pendant le Congrès de Vienne*. Edited by Georges Pallain. Paris: E. Plon, 1881.

Talleyrand, Charles-Maurice de. *Lettres inédites de Talleyrand à Napoléon, 1800–1809*. Edited by Pierre Bertrand. Paris: Perrin, 1889.

Talleyrand, Charles-Maurice de. *Mémoires (1754–1815)*. Paris: Plon, 1982.

Tatistcheff, Serge. *Alexandre I et Napoléon: d'après leur correspondance inédite 1801–1812*. Paris: Perrin, 1891.

Testa, Ignace de, ed. *Recueil des traités de la Porte Ottomane, avec les puissances étrangères*. Paris: Amyot, 1864.

Theal, George M., ed. *Records of the Cape Colony*. London: Government of the Cape Colony, 1897.

Thiebault, Paul Charles. *The Memoirs of Baron Thiebault*. London: Smith, Elder, 1896.

Thugut, Franz de Paula. *Vertrauliche Briefe des Freiherrn von Thugut*. Vienna: Wilhelm Braumüller, 1872.

Tone, Theobald Wolfe. *Life of Theobald Wolfe Tone: Memoirs, Journals and Political Writings*. Compiled by William T. W. Tone. Dublin: Lilliput Press, 1998.

Trachevskii, Alexander, ed. "Diplomaticheskie snosheniya Frantsii i Rossii v epokhu Napoleona I, 1800–1802." *Sbornik Imperatorskago Russkago Istoricheskago Obschestva* LXX (1890).

Tucker, Jedediah Stephens, ed. *Memoirs of Admiral the Right Hon the Earl of St Vincent GCB Etc*. London: Richard Bentley, 1844.

Ussher, Thomas. *Napoleon's Last Voyages, Being the Diaries of Sir Thomas Ussher*. Edited by J. Holland Rose. New York: Charles Scribner's Sons, 1906.

Villiers, George. *Memoirs of the Court and Cabinets of George the Third*. London: Hurst and Blackett, 1855.

Vivenot, Alfred Ritter von, ed. *Quellen zur Geschichte der deutschen Kaiserpolitik Österreichs während der französischen Revolution 1790–1801*. Vienna: Wilhelm Braumüller, 1879.

Vneshnaya politika Rossii XIX i nachala XX veka: dokumenti Rossiiskogo Ministerstva Inostrannikh del. 15 vols. Moscow: Gos. izd-vo polit. lit-ry, 1960–1995.

Walpole, Horace. *Letters of Horace Walpole, Earl of Orford.* London: Richard Bentley, 1843.

Weil, Maurice-Henri. *Les dessous du Congrés de Vienne: d'après les documents originaux des archives du Ministère impérial et royal de l'intérieur à Vienne.* Paris: Librairie Payot, 1917.

Wellington, Arthur. *The Dispatches of Field Marshal the Duke of Wellington, During His Various Campaigns...* Edited by John Gurwood. 13 vols. London: John Murray, 1834–1839.

Wellesley, Richard. *The Despatches, Minutes, and Correspondence of the Marquess Wellesley.* 5 vols. Edited by Montgomery Martin. London: W. H. Allen, 1837–1840.

Wellesley, Richard. *A Selection from the Despatches, Treaties, and Other Papers of the Marquess Wellesley.* Edited by Sidney Owen. Oxford: Clarendon Press, 1877.

Wellesley, Richard. *The Wellesley Papers. The Life and Correspondence of Richard Colley Wellesley, Marquess Wellesley, 1760–1842.* Edited by the Earl of Rosebery. London: H. Jenkins, 1914.

Wilson, Robert. *Brief Remarks on the Character and Composition of the Russian Army and a Sketch of the Campaigns in Poland in the Years 1806 and 1807.* London: C. Roworth, 1810.

Wilson, Robert. *Life of General Sir Robert Wilson.* 2 vols. Edited by Herbert Randolph. London: john Murray, 1862.

Windham, William. *The Diary of the Right Hon. William Windham, 1784 to 1810.* Edited by H. Baring. London: Longmans, 1866.

Windham, William. *The Windham Papers: The Life and Correspondence of the Rt. Hon. William Windham, 1750–1810.* Edited by the Earl of Rosebery. London: H. Jenkins, 1913.

Woodfall, William, ed. *The Parliamentary Register, or an Impartial Report of the Debates that Occur in the Two Houses of Parliament.* London: John Stockdale, 1802.

Yermolov, Alexey. *The Czar's General: The Memoirs of a Russian General in the Napoleonic Wars.* Translated and edited by Alexander Mikaberidze. Welwyn Garden City, UK: Ravenhall Books, 2005.

Secondary Sources

Aaslestad, Katherine, and Johan Joor, eds. *Revisiting Napoleon's Continental System: Local, Regional and European Experiences.* New York: Palgrave Macmillan, 2014.

Abel, Jonathan. *Guibert: Father of Napoleon's Grande Armée.* Norman: University of Oklahoma Press, 2016.

Acomb, Frances. *Anglophobia in France, 1763–1789: An Essay in the History of Constitutionalism and Nationalism.* Durham, NC: Duke University Press, 1950.

Acton, Harold. *The Bourbons of Naples, 1734–1825.* London: Methuen, 1956.

Adair, Robert. *The Negotiations for the Peace of the Dardanelles in 1808–9, with Dispatches and Official Documents.* 2 vols. London: Longman, Brown, Green, and Longman, 1845.

Adams, Henry. *History of the United States of America During the First Administration of Thomas Jefferson.* New York: Charles Scribner's Sons, 1889.

Adams, Max. *Trafalgar's Lost Hero: Admiral Lord Collingwood and the Defeat of Napoleon.* Hoboken, NJ: John Wiley & Sons, 2005.

Adams, Michael. *Napoleon and Russia.* London: Hambledon Continuum, 2006.

Adelman, Jeremy. "An Age of Imperial Revolutions." *American Historical Review* 113 (2008): 319–40.

Adelman, Jeremy. *Sovereignty and Revolution in the Iberian Atlantic.* Princeton, NJ: Princeton University Press, 2009.

Agnarsdottir, Anna. "The Challenge of War on Maritime Trade in the North Atlantic: The Case of the British Trade to Iceland During the Napoleonic Wars." In *Merchant Organization and Maritime Trade in the North Atlantic, 1660–1815,* ed. Olaf Uwe Jansen, 221–58. St. John's, Newfoundland: International Maritime Economic History Association, 1998.

Agnarsdottir, Anna. "The Imperial Atlantic System: Iceland and Britain During the Napoleonic Wars." In *Atlantic History: History of the Atlantic System 1580–1830,* edited by Horst Pietschmann, 497–512. Göttingen: Vandenhoeck & Ruprecht, 2002.

Agnarsdottir, Anna. "Scottish Plans for the Annexation of Iceland, 1785–1813." *Northern Studies* 29 (1992): 83–91.

Agoston, Gabor. "Military Transformation in the Ottoman Empire and Russia, 1500–1800." *Kritika: Explorations in Russian and Eurasian History* 12 (2011): 281–319.

Aksan, Virginia H., and Daniel Goffman, eds. "Breaking the Spell of the Baron de Tott. Reframing the Question of Military Reform in the Ottoman Empire, 1760–1830." *International History Review* 24, no. 2 (2002): 258–63.

Aksan, Virginia H., and Daniel Goffman, eds. *The Early Modern Ottomans: Remapping the Empire.* Cambridge: Cambridge University Press, 2007.

Aksan, Virginia H., and Daniel Goffman, eds. *Ottoman Wars, 1700–1870: An Empire Besieged.* New York: Pearson, 2007.

Albion, Robert G. *Forests and Sea Power: The Timber Problem of the Royal Navy, 1652–1862.* Cambridge, MA: Harvard University Press, 1927.

Alexander, Don W. *Rod of Iron: French Counterinsurgency Policy in Aragon During the Peninsular War.* Wilmington, DE: Scholarly Resources, 1985.

Alexandre, Valentim. *Os sentidos do Império: questão nacional e questão colonial na crise do Antigo Regime português.* Porto: Edições Afrontamento, 1993.

Almazán, Bernardo Lozier. *Liniers y su tiempo.* Buenos Aires: Emcé, 1990.

Alombert-Goget, Paul Claude, and Jean Lambert Alphonse Colin. *La Campagne de 1805 en Allemagne.* Paris: R. Chapelot, 1902.

Al-Otabi, Mubarak. "The Qawasim and British Control of the Arabian Gulf." PhD dissertation, University of Salford, 1989.

Amanat, Abbas, and Farzin Vejdani, eds. *Iran Facing Others: Identity Boundaries in a Historical Perspective.* New York: Palgrave, 2012.

Amini, Iradj. *Napoleon and Persia: Franco-Persian Relations Under the First Empire.* Richmond, Surrey: Curzon, 1999.

Anderson, M. S. *The Eastern Question, 1774–1923: A Study in International Relations.* New York: St. Martin's Press, 1966.

Andress, David. *The Savage Storm: Britain on the Brink in the Age of Napoleon.* London: Little, Brown, 2012.

Angeli, Moritz Edler von. "Ulm und Austerlitz. Studie auf Grund archivalischer Quellen über den Feldzug 1805 in Deutschland." *Mittheilungen des Kaiserlichen und Koniglichen Kriegsarchivs,* 1877.

Angeli, Moritz Edler von. *Erzherzog Karl von Osterreich als Feldherr und Heeresorganisator.* Vienna: K. u. K. Hof-universitäts-Buchhändler, 1896–1898.

Anna, Timothy E. *The Fall of the Royal Government in Mexico City.* Lincoln: University of Nebraska Press, 1978.

Argüelles, José Canga. *Observaciones sobre la Historia de la Guerra de España.* London: D. M. Calero, 1829.

Arnold, Eric. "Fouché Versus Savary: French Military Intelligence in the Ulm-Austerlitz Campaign." *Proceedings of the Consortium on Revolutionary Europe,* 1976, 55–67.

Arnold, James R. "A Reappraisal of Column Versus Line in the Peninsular War." *Journal of Military History* 68, no. 2 (April 2004): 535–52.

Arnold, James R., and Ralph R. Reinertsen. *Crisis in the Snows: Russia Confronts Napoleon: The Eylau Campaign 1806–1807.* Lexington, VA: Napoleon Books, 2007.

Arnold, James R., and Ralph R. Reinertsen. *Napoleon's Triumph: La Grande Armée Versus the Tsar's Army: The Friedland Campaign, 1807.* Lexington, VA: Napoleon Books, 2011.

Arthur, Brian. *How Britain Won the War of 1812: The Royal Navy's Blockades of the United States, 1812–1815.* Rochester, NY: Boydell Press, 2011.

Asprey, Robert B. *The Rise of Napoleon Bonaparte.* New York: Basic Books, 2000.

Atkin, Muriel. *Russia and Iran, 1780–1828.* Minneapolis: University of Minnesota Press, 1980.

Auriol, Charles. *La France, l'Angleterre et Naples de 1803 á 1806.* Paris: Plon-Nourrity, 1904.

Auzoux, André. "La France et Muscate aux dis-huitième et dix-neuvième siècles." *Revue d'histoire diplomatique* XXIII (1909): 518–40.

Auzoux, André. "La mission de Sébastiani a Tripoli en l'an X (1802)." *Revue des études napoléoniennes* XVI (1919): 225–36.

Avalov (Avalishvili), Zurab. *Prisoedinenie gruzii k Rossii.* St. Petersburg: Montvid, 1906.

Avery, Peter, et al., eds. *The Cambridge History of Iran: From Nadir Shah to the Islamic Republic.* Cambridge: Cambridge University Press, 1991.

Baddeley, J. *The Russian Conquest of the Caucasus.* London: Longmans, Green, 1908.

Bailey, Jeremy D. *Thomas Jefferson and Executive Power.* Cambridge: Cambridge University Press, 2010.

Balayan, B. *Diplomaticheskaya istoriya Russko-iranskikh voin i prisoedineniya Vostochnoi Armenii k Rossii.* Yerevan: Izd.-vo AN Armyanskoi SSR, 1988.

Bañuelos, Luis Palacios, Ignacio Ruiz Rodríguez, Fernando Bermejo Batanero, eds. *Cádiz 1812: origen del constitucionalismo español.* Madrid: Dykinson, 2013.

Barbara, M. "Napoleon Bonaparte and the Restoration of Catholicism in France." *Catholic Historical Review* 12, no. 2 (July 1926): 241–57.

Barker, Richard J. "The Conseil General des Manufactures Under Napoleon (1810–1814)." *French Historical Studies* 6, no. 2 (1969): 198–213.

Barkey, Karen. *The Empire of Difference: The Ottomans in Comparative Perspective.* Cambridge: Cambridge University Press, 2008.

Barratt, Glynn. *Russia in Pacific Waters, 1715–1825.* Vancouver: University of British Columbia Press, 1981.

Bartlett, Thomas, ed. *1798: A Bicentenary Perspective.* Dublin: Four Courts, 2003.

Bartley, Russell H. *Imperial Russia and the Struggle for Latin American Independence, 1808–1828.* Austin: University of Texas Press, 1978.

Barton, Dunbar Plunket. *Bernadotte and Napoleon, 1763–1810.* London: John Murray, 1921.

Barton, H. Arnold. *Essays on Scandinavian History.* Carbondale: Southern Illinois University Press, 2009.

Barton, H. Arnold. *Scandinavia in the Revolutionary Era.* Minneapolis: University of Minnesota Press, 1986.

Başaran, Betül. *Selim III, Social Control, and Policing in Constantinople at the End of the Eighteenth Century: Between Crisis and Order.* Leiden: Brill, 2014.

Bauer, Gerhard, and Karl-Heinz Lutz. *Jena 1806: Vorgeschichte und Rezeption.* Potsdam: Militärgeschichtliches Forschungsamt, 2009.

Baugh, Daniel. *The Global Seven Years' War, 1754–1763: Britain and France in a Great Power Contest.* London: Longman, 2011.

Baugh, Daniel A. "Great Britain's 'Blue-Water' Policy, 1689–1815." *International History Review* 10, no. 1 (1998): 33–58.

Bayly, Christopher A. *The Birth of the Modern World, 1780–1914: Global Connections and Comparisons.* Malden, MA: Wiley-Blackwell, 2004.

Bayly, Christopher A. *Indian Society and the Making of the British Empire.* Cambridge: Cambridge University Press, 1988.

Beeley, H. "A Project of Alliance with Russia in 1802." *English Historical Review* 49, no. 195 (1934): 497–502.

Beer, Adolf. *Die orientalische Politik Österreichs seit 1774.* Prague: F. Tempsky, 1883.

Beer, Adolf. *Zehn jahre österreichischer politik, 1801–1810.* Leipzig: F. A. Brockhaus, 1877.

Beliavskii, N., and Vasilii Potto. *Utverzhdenie Russkago vladychestva na Kavkaze.* Tiflis, 1901.

Belissa, Marc. *Repenser l'ordre européen (1795–1802): De la société des rois aux droits des nations.* Paris: Éditions Klimé, 2006.

Berding, Helmut. *Napoleonische Herrschafts- und Gesellschaftspolitik im Königreich Westfalen: 1807–1813.* Göttingen: Vandenhoeck und Ruprecht, 1973.

Berding, Helmut. "Le Royaume de Westphalie, Etat-modèle." *Francia: Forschungen zur westeuropäischen Geschichte* 10 (1982): 345–58.

Berdzenishvili, N. *Sakartvelos istoria*. Tbilisi, 1958.

Bergeron, Louis. *Banquiers, négociants et manufacturiers parisiens du Directoire à l'Empire*. Paris: Éditions de l'EHESS, 2000.

Bergeron, Louis. *France Under Napoleon*. Princeton, NJ: Princeton University Press, 1981.

Bergerot, Bernard. *Daru, Intendant-Général de la Grande Armée*. Paris: Tallandier, 1991.

Bertaud, Jean-Paul. *Bonaparte et le duc d'Enghien: le duel des deux France*. Paris: R. Laffront, 1972.

Berton, Pierre. *The Invasion of Canada, 1812–1813*. Toronto: Anchor Books, 1980.

Bessel, Richard, Nicholas Guyatt, and Jane Rendall, eds. *War, Empire, and Slavery, 1770–1830*. Basingstoke, UK: Palgrave Macmillan, 2010.

Bethell, Leslie, ed. *The Cambridge History of Latin America*. Cambridge: Cambridge University Press, 1984.

Bethencourt, Francisco, and K. Chaudhuri, eds. *História da expansão portuguesa*. Lisbon: Círculo de Leitores, 1999.

Bew, John. *Castlereagh: A Life*. Oxford: Oxford University Press, 2012.

Beydilli, Kemal. *1790 Osmanlı-Prusya ittifâkı*. Istanbul: İstanbul Üniversitesi Yayınları, 1984.

Bezotosnyi, Viktor. *Napoleonovskie voiny*. Moscow: Veche, 2010.

Bianchi, Nicomede. *Storia della monarchia piemontese dal 1773 sino al 1861*. Turin: Fratelli Bocca, 1879.

Bickham, Troy. *The Weight of Vengeance: The United States, the British Empire and the War of 1812*. Oxford: Oxford University Press, 2012.

Bierman, Irene. *Napoleon in Egypt*. Los Angeles: Gustave E. von Grunebaum Center for Near Eastern Studies, 2003.

Bignon, Louis Pierre Édouard. *Histoire de France, depuis le 18 brumaire, novembre 1799, jusqu'à la paix de Tilsit (Juillet 1807)*. Brussels: J. P. Meline, 1836.

Bignon, Louis Pierre Édouard. *Histoire de France depuis 1793 jusu'en 1812*. Paris: Charles Bechet, 1830.

Biro, Sydney. *The German Policy of Revolutionary France: A Study in French Diplomacy During the War of the First Coalition, 1792–1797*. Cambridge, MA: Harvard University Press, 1957.

Björlin, Gustaf. *Sveriges krig i tyskland åren 1805–1807*. Stockholm: Militärlitteratúr-Föreningens förlag, 1882.

Black, Frederick H. "Diplomatic Struggles: British Support in Spain and Portugal, 1800–1810." PhD dissertation, Florida State University, 2005.

Black, Jeremy. *Britain as a Military Power, 1688–1815*. London: Routledge, 1999.

Black, Jeremy. *British Foreign Policy in an Age of Revolutions, 1783–1793*. Cambridge: Cambridge University Press, 1994.

Black, Jeremy. *European International Relations, 1648–1815*. New York: Palgrave, 2002.

Black, Jeremy. *France from Louis XIV to Napoleon: The Fate of Great Empire*. London: University College London Press, 1999.

Black, Jeremy, and Philip Woodfine, eds. *The British Navy and the Use of Naval Power in the Eighteenth Century*. Leicester: Leicester University Press, 1988.

Blackburn, Robin. "Haiti, Slavery, and the Age of the Democratic Revolution." *William and Mary Quarterly* 63 (2006): 643–73.

Blanc, Jacques. "La flottille nationale, 1803–1805." MA thesis, Université Paris IV, 2007.

Blancpain, François. *La colonie française de Saint-Domingue: De l'esclavage à l'indépendance*. Paris: Karthala, 2004.

Blanning, Timothy. *The French Revolution in Germany. Occupation and Resistance in the Rhineland, 1792–1802*. New York: Oxford University Press, 1983.

Blanning, Timothy. *The Origins of the French Revolutionary Wars*. London: Longman, 1986.

Blanning, Timothy. *The Pursuit of Glory: Europe 1648–1815*. New York: Viking, 2007.

Blaufarb, Rafe. *Bonapartists in the Borderlands: French Exiles and Refugees on the Gulf Coast, 1815–1835*. Tuscaloosa: University of Alabama Press, 2005.

Bogdanovich, Modest. *Istoriya tsarstvovaniya imperatora Aleksandra I i Rossii v ego vremya*. St. Petersburg, 1869.

Bogdanovich, Modest. *Istoriya voiny 1813 goda za nezavisimost Germanii*. St. Petersburg: Tip. Shtaba voenno-uchebnykh zavedenii, 1863.

Bogdanovich, Modest. *Istoriya voiny 1814 goda fo Frantsii i nizlozheniya Napoleona I*. St. Petersburg, 1865.

Bond, Gordon C. *The Grand Expedition: The British Invasion of Holland in 1809*. Athens: University of Georgia Press, 1979.

Böning, Holger. *Der Traum von Freiheit und Gleichheit. Helvetische Revolution und Republik (1798–1803). Die Schweiz auf dem Weg zur bürgerlichen Demokratie*. Zurich: Orell Füssli Verlag, 1998.

Bonjour, Edgar. *Geschichte der schweizerischen Neutralität: vier Jahrhunderte eidgenössischer Aussenpolitik*. Basel: Helbing & Lichtenhahn, 1965.

Boppe, Auguste. *L'Albanie et Napoléon, 1797–1814*. Paris: Hachette, 1914.

Boppe, Paul Louis Hippolyte. *Les Espagnols à la Grande-Armée: le corps de la Romana, 1807–1808; le régiment Joseph-Napoléon, 1809–1813*. Paris: C. Terana, 1986.

Borodkin, Mikhail. *Istoriia Finliandii: vremia Imperatora Aleksandra I*. St. Petersburg, 1909.

Bourdin, Philippe, and Bernard Gainot, eds. *La République directoriale*. Paris: Société des études robespierristes, 1998.

Bowen, H. V. *The Business of Empire: The East India Company and Imperial Britain, 1756–1833*. Cambridge: Cambridge University Press, 2006.

Boyce, D. George, and Alan O'Day, eds. *The Making of Modern Irish History: Revisionism and the Revisionist Controversy*. New York: Routledge, 2006.

Boycott-Brown, Martin. *The Road to Rivoli: Napoleon's First Campaign*. London: Cassell, 2001.

Branda, Pierre, ed. *L'économie selon Napoléon: monnaie, banque, crises et commerce sous le Premier Empire*. Paris: Vendémiaire, 2016.

Branda, Pierre, ed. *La saga des Bonaparte*. Paris: Perrin, 2018.

Branda, Pierre, ed. *Le prix de la gloire. Napoléon et l'argent*. Paris: Fayard, 2007.

Branda, Pierre, and Thierry Lentz. *Napoléon, l'esclavage et les colonies*. Paris: Fayard, 2006.

Brandt, Otto. *England und die Napoleonische Weltpolitik, 1800–1803*. Heidelberg: C. Winter, 1916.

Braude, Mark. *The Invisible Emperor: Napoleon on Elba from Exile to Escape*. New York: Penguin, 2018.

Brecher, Frank W. *Losing a Continent: France's North American Policy, 1753–1763*. Westport, CT: Greenwood, 1998.

Bregeon, Jean-Joël, and Gérard Guicheteau. *Nouvelle histoire des guerres de Vendée*. Paris: Perrin, 2017.

Brendon, Piers. *The Decline and Fall of the British Empire, 1781–1797*. New York: Alfred A. Knopf, 2007.

Brenton, Edward P. *The Naval History of Great Britain from the Year 1783 to 1836*. London: H. Coburn, 1837.

Broers, Michael. *Europe Under Napoleon 1799–1815*. New York: Edward Arnold, 1996.

Broers, Michael. *Napoleon: Soldier of Destiny*. New York: Pegasus Books, 2014.

Broers, Michael. *The Napoleonic Empire in Italy, 1796–1814: Cultural Imperialism in a European Context?* New York: Palgrave Macmillan, 2005.

Broers, Michael. *The Politics of Religion in Napoleonic Italy: The War Against God, 1801–1814*. New York: Routledge, 2002.

Broers, Michael, Peter Hicks, and Agustin Guimera, eds. *The Napoleonic Empire and the New European Political Culture*. New York: Palgrave, 2012.

Browne, Abdullah. *Bonaparte in Egypt: The French Campaign of 1798–1801 from the Egyptian Perspective*. London: Leonaur, 2012.

Brünnert, Gustav. *Napoleons Aufenthalt in Erfurt im Jahre 1808*. Erfurt: Druck von Fr. Bartholomäus, 1899.

Brutus, Timoleon C. *L'homme d'Airain, étude monographique sur Jean-Jacques Dessalines, fondateur de la nation haïtienne*. 2 vols. Port-au-Prince: N. A. Theodore, 1946–1947.

Bruun, Geoffrey. *Europe and the French Imperium, 1799–1814*. New York: Harper & Row, 1965.

Burns, Alan. *History of the British West Indies*. London: George Allen & Unwin, 1965.

Büsch, Otto, and Monika Neugebauer-Wölk, eds. *Preussen und die revolutionäre Herausforderung seit 1789*. Berlin: Walter de Gruyter, 1991.

Bush, Robert D. *The Louisiana Purchase: A Global Context*. New York: Routledge, 2014.

Butel, Paul. *L'économie française au XVIIIe siècle.* Paris: SEDES, 1993.

Butel, Paul. *Histoire des Antilles francaises.* Paris: Perrin, 2007.

Butler, Iris. *The Eldest Brother: The Marquess Wellesley, the Duke of Wellington's Eldest Brother.* London: Hodder and Stoughton, 1973.

Butterfield, Herbert. *The Peace Tactics of Napoleon, 1806–1808.* Cambridge: Cambridge University Press, 1959.

Buttery, David. *Wellington Against Junot: The First Invasion of Portugal, 1807–1808.* Barnsley: Pen & Sword Military, 2011.

Cadet, Nicolas. *Honneur et violences de guerre au temps de Napoléon: La campagne de Calabre.* Paris: Vendémiaire, 2015.

Cadoudal, Louis Georges de. *Georges Cadoudal et la chouannerie.* Paris: E. Plon, 1887.

Camogli, Pablo, and Luciano de Privitellio. *Batallas por la libertad: todos los combates de la guerra de la independencia.* Buenos Aires: Aguilar, 2005.

Campbell, Peter Robert, Thomas E. Kaiser, and Marisa Linton, eds. *Conspiracy in the French Revolution.* New York: Palgrave, 2007.

Canovas del Castillo, Antonio. *Historia general de España.* Madrid: El progreso editorial, 1891–1893.

Carlsson, Sten Carl Oscar. *Gustaf IV Adolf, en biografi.* Stockholm: Wahlström & Widstrand, 1946.

Carlsson, Sten Carl Oscar. *Gustaf IV Adolfs fall: krisen i riksstyrelsen, konspirationerna och statsvälvningen (1807–1809).* Lund: C. Bloms boktryckeri, 1944.

Carr, Raymond. "Gustavus IV and the British Government 1804–9." *English Historical Review* 60, no. 236 (1945): 58–61.

Carutti, Domenico. *Le Corte di Savoia durante le rivoluzione e l'impero francese.* Turin: L. Roux, 1888.

Castro y O'Lawlor, Salvador Bermúdez de, marqués de Lema, *Antecedentes políticos y diplomáticos de los sucesos de 1808; Estudio histórico-crítico escrito con la presencia de documentos inéditos del Archivo Reservado de Fernando VII, del Histórico-nacional y otros.* Madrid, F. Beltrán, 1912.

Cerami, Charles A. *Jefferson's Great Gamble: The Remarkable Story of Jefferson, Napoleon, and the Men Behind the Louisiana Purchase.* Naperville, IL: Sourcebooks, 2003.

Chabert, A. *Essai sur les mouvements des revenus et de l'activité économique en France de 1789 à 1820.* Paris: Librairie de Médicis, 1949.

Chandler, David. *The Campaigns of Napoleon.* New York: Macmillan, 1966.

Chaptal, Jean-Antoine. *Mes souvenirs sur Napoléon.* Paris: E. Plon, Nourrit, 1893.

Chastenet, Jacques. *Godoy: Master of Spain, 1792–1808.* London: Batchworth Press, 1953.

Chaudhuri, K. N. *The Trading World of Asia and the East India Company, 1660–1760.* Cambridge: Cambridge University Press, 1978.

Chaurasia, Radhey Shyam. *History of the Marathas.* New Delhi: Atlantic, 2004.

Chaussinand-Nogaret, Guy. *The French Nobility in the Eighteenth Century: From Feudalism to Enlightenment.* Cambridge: Cambridge University Press, 1995.

Chevalier, Louis Edouard. *Histoire de la marine française sous le Consulat et l'Empire*. Paris: L. Hachette, 1886.

Chiappe, Jean François. *Georges Cadoudal ou La liberté*. Paris: Librairie académique Perrin, 1971.

Chrisawn, Margaret Scott. *The Emperor's Friend: Marshal Jean Lannes*. Westport, CT: Greenwood Press, 2001.

Church, Clive H., and Randolph C. Head. *A Concise History of Switzerland*. Cambridge: Cambridge University Press, 2013.

Chust, Manuel, ed. *1808: La eclosión juntera en el mundo hispano*. Mexico City: Fondo de Cultura Económica, 2007.

Clapham, John Harold. *The Cause of the War of 1792*. Cambridge: Cambridge University Press, 1899.

Clark, Christopher M. *Iron Kingdom: The Rise and Downfall of Prussia, 1600–1947*. Cambridge, MA: Belknap Press, 2006.

Clason, Sam. *Gustaf IV Adolf och den europeiska krisen under Napoleon: Historiska uppsatser*. Stockholm: Geber, 1913.

Clément, Raoul. *Les français d'Égypte aux XVIIe et XVIIIe siècles*. Cairo: Institut français d'archéologie orientale, 1960.

Coates, Austin. *Macao and the British, 1637–1842: Prelude to Hong Kong*. Hong Kong: Hong Kong University Press, 2009.

Cole, Juan Ricardo. *Napoleon's Egypt: Invading the Middle East*. New York: Palgrave Macmillan, 2008.

Collins, Bruce. *War and Empire: The Expansion of Britain, 1790–1830: The Projection of British Power, 1775–1830*. London: Longman, 2010.

Collins, Irene. *Napoleon and His Parliaments, 1800–1815*. New York: St. Martin's Press, 1979.

Colson, Bruno. *Leipzig: La Bataille des Nations, 16–19 Octobre 1813*. Paris: Perrin, 2013.

Conan, Jules. *La dernière compagnie française des Indes, 1715–1875*. Paris: Marcel Rivière, 1942.

Connelly, Owen. *The French Revolution and Napoleonic Era*. Orlando, FL: Harcourt, 2000.

Connelly, Owen. *The Gentle Bonaparte: A Biography of Joseph, Napoleon's Elder Brother*. New York: Macmillan, 1968.

Connelly, Owen. *Napoleon's Satellite Kingdoms*. New York: Free Press, 1965.

Cook, Malcolm. *Napoleon Comes to Power: Democracy and Dictatorship in Revolutionary France, 1795–1804*. Cardiff: University of Wales Press, 1998.

Cook, Warren L. *Floodtide of Empire: Spain and the Pacific Northwest, 1548–1819*. New Haven, CT: Yale University Press, 1973.

Cookson, J. E. *The Friends of Peace: Anti-War Liberalism in England, 1793–1815*. Cambridge: Cambridge University Press, 1982.

Cooper, Randolf G. S. *The Anglo-Maratha Campaigns and the Contest for India: The Struggle for Control of the South Asian Military Economy*. Cambridge: Cambridge University Press, 2003.

Coquelle, Pierre. *Napoléon et l'Angleterre, 1803–1813*. Paris: Plon-Nourrit, 1904.

Coturri, Paolo. *Partire partirò, partir bisogna: Firenze e la Toscana nelle campagne napole-oniche, 1793–1815*. Florence: Sarnus, 2009.

Coujou, Jean-Paul. "Political Thought and Legal Theory in Suárez." In *A Companion to Francisco Suárez*, edited by Victor M. Salas and Robert L. Fastiggi, 29–71. Leiden: Brill, 2014.

Crawley, C. W., ed. *The New Cambridge Modern History*. Cambridge: Cambridge University Press, 1975.

Crecelius, Daniel, and Gotcha Djaparidze. "Georgians in the Military Establishment in Egypt in the Seventeenth and Eighteenth Centuries." *Annales Islamologiques* 42 (2008): 313–37.

Crecelius, Daniel, and Gotcha Djaparidze. "Relations of the Georgian Mamluks of Egypt with Their Homeland in the Last Decades of the Eighteenth Century." *Journal of the Economic and Social History of the Orient* 45 (2002): 320–41.

Creveld, Martin van. *Command in War.* Cambridge, MA: Harvard University Press, 1985.

Crews, Robert D. *Afghan Modern: The History of a Global Nation.* Cambridge, MA: Harvard University Press, 2015.

Crouzet, François. *L'économie britannique et le blocus continental, 1806–1813*. Paris: Presses universitaires de France, 1958.

Crouzet, François. *La guerre économique franco-anglaise au XVIIIe siècle*. Paris: Fayard, 2008.

Cuccia, Phillip R. *Napoleon in Italy: The Sieges of Mantua, 1796–1799*. Norman: University of Oklahoma Press, 2014.

Cugnac, Gaspar Jean Marie René de. *Campagne de l'Armée de réserve en 1800*. Paris: Libr. Military R. Chapelot, 1900.

Cullen, L. M. *A History of Japan, 1582–1941: Internal and External Worlds*. Cambridge: Cambridge University Press, 2003.

Cuno, Kenneth M. *The Pasha's Peasants: Land, Society, and Economy in Lower Egypt, 1740–1858*. Cambridge: Cambridge University Press, 1991.

Daeley, Albert John. "The Continental System in France as Illustrated by American Trade." PhD dissertation, University of Wisconsin-Madison, 1949.

Dale, Richard. *The First Crash: Lessons from the South Sea Bubble*. Princeton, NJ: Princeton University Press, 2004.

Damamme, Jean-Claude. *Les soldats de la Grande Armée*. Paris: Perrin, 1998.

Dancy, J. Ross. *The Myth of the Press Gang: Volunteers, Impressment and the Naval Manpower in the Late Eighteenth Century*. Woodbridge: Boydell Press, 2015.

Das, Amita. *Defending British India Against Napoleon: The Foreign Policy of Governor-General Lord Minto, 1807–1813*. Edited by Aditya Das. London: Boydell and Brewer, 2016.

Daudin, Guillaume. *Commerce et prospérité: la France au XVIIIe siècle*. Paris: Presses l'université Paris-Sorbonne, 2005.

Daughan, George C. *If by Sea: The Forging of the American Navy from the Revolution to the War of 1812*. New York: Basic Books, 2008.

Davey, James. *In Nelson's Wake: The Navy and the Napoleonic Wars*. New Haven, CT: Yale University Press, 2015.

Davey, James. *The Transformation of British Naval Strategy: Seapower and Supply in Northern Europe, 1808–1812.* Woodbridge: Boydell Press, 2012.

Davies, Brian. *Empire and Military Revolution in Eastern Europe: Russia's Turkish Wars in the Eighteenth Century.* London: Continuum, 2011.

Davies, D. W. *Sir John Moore's Peninsular Campaign 1808–1809.* The Hague: Martinus Nijhoff, 1974.

Davies, Norman. *God's Playground: A History of Poland.* New York: Columbia University Press, 1982.

Davis, John A. *Naples and Napoleon: Southern Italy and the European Revolutions (1780–1860).* Oxford: Oxford University Press, 2006.

Davy-Rousseau, Andréa. "Autour de la mort du duc d'Enghien." *Revue du souvenir napoléonien* 334 (1984): 2–15.

Dawson, Paul L. *Napoleon and Grouchy: The Last Great Waterloo Mystery Unravelled.* Barnsley, UK: Frontline Books, 2017.

Dawson, Paul L. *Waterloo, the Truth at Last: Why Napoleon Lost the Great Battle.* Barnsley, UK: Frontline Books, 2018.

Dehérain, Henri. "Lettres inédites de membres de la mission Gardane en Perse (1807–9)." *Revue de l'histoire des colonies françaises* XVI (1923): 249–82.

Dempsey, Guy. *Albuera 1811: The Bloodiest Battle of the Peninsular War.* London: Frontline Books, 2008.

Dermigny, Louis. "Circuits de l'argent et milieux d'affaires au XVIII siècle." *Revue historique* 212 (1954): 239–78.

Dermigny, Louis. "La France à la fin de l'ancien régime: Une carte monétaire." *Annales: économies, sociétés, civilizations* 10, no. 4 (December 1955): 480–93.

Desan, Suzanne, Lynn Hunt, and William Max Nelson, eds. *The French Revolution in Global Perspective.* Ithaca, NY: Cornell University Press, 2013.

Desbrière, Édouard. *1793–1805: projets et tentatives de débarquement aux Îles britanniques.* Paris: R. Chapelot, 1902.

DeToy, Brian. "Wellington's Admiral: The Life and Career of George Berkeley, 1753–1818." PhD dissertation, Florida State University, 1997.

Deutsch, Harold C. *The Genesis of Napoleonic Imperialism.* Cambridge, MA: Harvard University Press, 1938.

Dickinson, H. T, ed. *Britain and the French Revolution, 1789–1815.* New York: St. Martin's Press, 1989.

Dirks, Nicholas B. *The Scandal of Empire: India and the Creation of Imperial Britain.* Cambridge, MA: Belknap Press, 2006.

Dmytryshyn, Basil, ed. *Russian Penetration of the North Pacific Ocean, 1700–1797.* Portland: Oregon Historical Society Press, 1988.

Dodwell, Henry. *The Founder of Modern Egypt: A Study of Muhammad 'Ali.* Cambridge: Cambridge University Press, 1931.

Đorđević, Miroslav R. *Oslobodilački rat srpskih ustanika, 1804–1806.* Belgrade: Vojnoizdavački zavod, 1967.

Đorđević, Miroslav R. *Politička istorija Srbije XIX i XX veka,* vol. I, *1804–1813.* Belgrade: Prosveta, 1956.

Dorigny, Marcel, ed. *The Abolitions of Slavery: From Léger Félicité Sonthonax to Victor Schoelcher, 1793, 1794, 1848*. Paris: Editions UNESCO, 1995.

Dorigny, Marcel, ed. *Rétablissement de l'esclavage dans les colonies françaises 1802: Ruptures et continuités de la politique colonial française*. Paris: Maisonneuve-Larose, 2003.

Douay, Abel, and Gérard Hertault. *Schulmeister: dans les coulisses de la Grande Armée*. Paris: Nouveau Monde, 2002.

Douin, Georges. *L'Angleterre et l'Égypte. La campagne de 1807*. Cairo: Institut français d'archéologie orientale du Caire, 1928.

Doyle, William. *Old Regime France, 1648–1788*. Oxford: Oxford University Press, 2001.

Doyle, William. *Origins of the French Revolution*. New York: Oxford University Press, 1980.

Doyle, William, ed. *The Oxford Handbook of the Ancien Régime*. Oxford: Oxford University Press, 2012.

Doyle, William. *The Oxford History of the French Revolution*. Oxford: Oxford University Press, 1990.

Drayton, Richard. "The Globalization of France: Provincial Cities and French Expansion, c. 1500–1800." *History of European Ideas* 34 (2008): 424–30.

Driault, Édouard. *Napoléon et l'Europe: Tilsit. France et Russie sous le Premier Empire. La question de Pologne (1806–1809)*. Paris: F. Alcan, 1917.

Driault, Édouard. *La formation de l'empire de Mohamed Aly de l'Arabie au Soudan (1814–1823): correspondance des consuls de France en Égypte*. Cairo: Institut français d'archéologie orientale du Caire, 1927.

Driault, Édouard. *Napoléon et l'Europe. Austerlitz, la fin du Saint-empire (1804–1806)*. Paris: F. Alcan, 1912.

Driault, Édouard. *Napoléon et l'Europe. La politique extérieure du Premier Consul (1800–1803)*. Paris: Felix Alcan, 1910.

Dubois, Laurent. *Avengers of the New World: The Story of the Haitian Revolution*. Cambridge, MA: Harvard University Press, 2004.

Dubois, Laurent. *A Colony of Citizens: Revolution and Slave Emancipation in the French Caribbean, 1787–1804*. Chapel Hill: University of North Carolina Press, 2004.

Dubrovin, Nikolai. *Georgii XII: Poslednii tsar Gruzii i prisoedinenie eia k Rossii*. St. Petersburg: Tip. Departamenta udelov, 1867.

Dubrovin, Nikolai. *Istoriya voiny i vladychestva russkikh na Kavkaze*. 6 vols. St. Petersburg: Tip. Skorokhodova, 1871–1888.

Duffy, Michael. *Soldiers, Sugar and Seapower: The British Expeditions to West Indies and the War Against Revolutionary France*. Oxford: Clarendon, Press, 1987.

Durey, Michael. "Lord Grenville and the 'Smoking Gun': The Plot to Assassinate the French Directory in 1798–1799 Reconsidered." *Historical Journal* 45, no. 3 (2002): 547–68.

D'Ussel, Jean. *Études sur l'année 1813: l'intervention de l'Autriche (décembre 1812–mai 1813)*. Paris: Plon-Nourrit, 1912.

Dwyer, Philip, ed. *Napoleon and Europe*. London: Pearson, 2001.

Dyck, Harvey L. "New Serbia and the Origins of the Eastern Question, 1751–55: A Habsburg Perspective." *Russian Review* 40 (1981): 1–19.

Dym, Jordana. *From Sovereign Villages to National States: City, State and Federation in Central America, 1759–1839*. Albuquerque: University of New Mexico Press, 2006.

Eastman, Scott. *Preaching Spanish Nationalism Across the Hispanic Atlantic, 1759–1823*. Baton Rouge: Louisiana State University Press, 2012.

Ehrman, John. *The Younger Pitt: The Consuming Struggle*. Stanford, CA: Stanford University Press, 1996.

Eidahl, Kyle O. "The Military Career of Nicolas Charles Oudinot (1767–1847)." PhD dissertation, Florida State University, 1990.

Ellis, Geoffrey James. *Napoleon's Continental Blockade: The Case of Alsace*. New York: Oxford University Press, 1981.

Elphick, Richard, and Hermann Giliomee, eds. *The Shaping of South African Society, 1652–1840*. Middletown, CT: Wesleyan University Press, 1979.

Elting, John Robert. *Swords Around a Throne: Napoleon's Grande Armée*. New York: Free Press, 1988.

Englund, Steven. *Napoleon: A Political Life*. New York: Scribner, 2004.

Enthoven, Victor. *Een haven te ver: de Britse expeditie naar de Schelde van 1809*. Nijmegen: Vantilt, 2009.

Epstein, Robert M. *Napoleon's Last Victory and the Emergence of Modern War*. Lawrence: University Press of Kansas, 1994.

Ermice, Maria Christina. *Le origini del Gran Libro del debito pubblico e l'emergere di nuovi gruppi sociali (1806–1815)*. Naples: Arte Tipografica Editrice, 2005.

Ermitage, David, and Sanjay Subrahmanyam, eds. *The Age of Revolutions in Global Context, c. 1760–1840*. New York: Palgrave Macmillan, 2010.

Esdaile, Charles J. *Fighting Napoleon: Guerrillas, Bandits and Adventurers in Spain, 1808–1814*. New Haven, CT: Yale University Press, 2004.

Esdaile, Charles J. *Napoleon, France and Waterloo: The Eagle Rejected*. Barnsley: Pen & Sword, 2016.

Esdaile, Charles J. *Napoleon's Wars: An International History, 1803–1815*. New York: Viking, 2008.

Esdaile, Charles J. *Outpost of Empire: The Napoleonic Occupation of Andalucia, 1810–1812*. Norman: University of Oklahoma Press, 2012.

Esdaile, Charles J. *The Peninsular War: A New History*. New York: Palgrave Macmillan, 2003.

Esdaile, Charles J. *Spain in the Liberal Age: From Constitution to Civil War, 1808–1939*. Oxford: Blackwell, 2000.

Eysturlid, Lee W. *The Formative Influences, Theories and Campaigns of the Archduke Carl of Austria*. Westport, CT: Greenwood, 2000.

Fahmy, Khaled. *All the Pasha's Men: Mehmet Ali, His Army, and the Making of Modern Egypt*. Cairo: American University in Cairo Press, 2002.

Fahmy, Khaled. *Mehmet Ali: From Ottoman Governor to Ruler of Egypt*. Oxford: Oneworld, 2009.

Faivre, Jean-Paul. *Le contre-amiral Hamelin et la Marine française*. Paris: Nouvelles Éditions latines, 1962.

Faroqhi, Suraiya N., ed. *The Cambridge History of Turkey*, vol. 3, *The Later Ottoman Empire, 1603–1839*. Cambridge: Cambridge University Press, 2006.

Farrère, Claude. *Histoire de la marine française*. Paris: Flammarion, 1934.

Fehrenbach, Elisabeth. *Der Kampf um die Einführung des Code Napoléon in den Rheinbundstaaten*. Wiesbaden: Steiner, 1973.

Fehrenbach, Elisabeth. *Traditionale Gesellschaft und revolutionäres Recht: die Einführung des Code Napoléon in den Rheinbundstaaten*. Göttingen: Vandenhoeck & Ruprecht, 1974.

Feldbaek, Ole. *The Battle of Copenhagen 1801: Nelson and the Danes*. Barnsley: Leo Cooper, 2002.

Feldbaek, Ole. *Danmark og Det væbnede neutralitetsforbund 1800–1801: småstatspolitik i en verdenskrig*. Copenhagen: Institut for økonomisk historie ved Københavns universitet, 1980.

Feldbaek, Ole. "The Foreign Policy of Tsar Paul I, 18 00–1801: An Interpretation." *Jahrbücher für Geschichte Östeuropas* XXX (1982): 16–36.

Ferguson, Niall. *Empire: The Rise and Demise of the British World Order and the Lessons for Global Power*. New York: Basic Books, 2004.

Ferrer, Ada. *Freedom's Mirror: Cuba and Haiti in the Age of Revolution*. Cambridge: Cambridge University Press, 2014.

Ferrero, Guglielmo. *The Gamble: Bonaparte in Italy, 1796–1797*. New York: Walker, 1961.

Fesser, Gerd. *1806, die Doppelschlacht bei Jena und Auerstedt*. Jena: Bussert und Stadeler, 2006.

Field, Andrew. *Talavera: Wellington's First Victory in Spain*. Barnsley: Pen & Sword, 2006.

Field, Andrew. *Waterloo: The French Perspective*. Barsnley: Pen & Sword, 2017.

Finley, Milton. *The Most Monstrous of Wars: The Napoleonic Guerrilla War in Southern Italy, 1806–1811*. Columbia: University of South Carolina Press, 1994.

Fisher, Alan F. *The Russian Annexation of the Crimea, 1772–1783*. Cambridge: Cambridge University Press, 1970.

Fisher, Harold Edward Stephen. *The Portugal Trade: A Study of Anglo-Portuguese Commerce, 1700–1770*. London: Methuen, 1971.

Fisher, Herbert. *Studies in Napoleonic Statesmanship: Germany*. Oxford: Clarendon Press, 1903.

Fisher, John R. *Commercial Relations Between Spain and Spanish America in the Era of Free Trade, 1778–1796*. Liverpool: Centre for Latin American Studies, University of Liverpool, 1985.

Fisher, John R. *The Economic Aspects of Spanish Imperialism in America, 1492–1810*. Liverpool: Liverpool University Press, 1997.

Fisher, John R. *Government and Society in Colonial Peru: The Intendant System, 1784–1814.* London: The Athlone Press, 1970.

Flayhart, William Henry. *Counterpoint to Trafalgar: The Anglo-Russian Invasion of Naples, 1805–06.* Gainesville: University Press of Florida, 2004.

Fleischman, Théo. *L'expedition anglaise sur le continent en 1809, conquête de l'île de Walcheren et menace sur Anvers.* Brussels: La Renaissance du livre, 1973.

Fleming, Katherine E. *The Muslim Bonaparte: Diplomacy and Orientalism in Ali Pasha's Greece.* Princeton, NJ: Princeton University Press, 1999.

Fletcher, Ian. *The Lines of Torres Vedras 1809–11.* Oxford: Osprey, 2003.

Fletcher, Ian. *The Waters of Oblivion: The British Invasion of the Río de la Plata, 1806–07.* Staplehurst, UK: Spellmount, 1991.

Ford, Guy Stanton. *Hanover and Prussia, 1795–1803. A Study in Neutrality.* New York: Columbia University Press, 1903.

Forrest, Alan. *Conscripts and Deserters: The Army and the French Society During the Revolution and Empire.* New York: Oxford University Press, 1989.

Forrest, Alan, Karen Hagemann, and Michael Rowe, eds. *War, Demobilization and Memory: The Legacy of War in the Era of Atlantic Revolutions.* New York: Palgrave Macmillan, 2016.

Forrest, Alan, and Matthias Middell, eds. *The Routledge Companion to the French Revolution in World History.* London: Routledge, 2016.

Fortescue, J. W. *The County Lieutenancies and the Army, 1803–1814.* London: Macmillan, 1909.

Fortescue, John William. *A History of the British Army.* 6 vols. London: Macmillan, 1906–1930.

Foucart, Paul Jean. *Campagne de Prusse, 1806: d'après les archives de la guerre.* Paris: Berger-Levrault, 1887.

Francis, Davis. *Portugal, 1715–1808: Joanine, Pombaline and Rococo Portugal as Seen by British Diplomats and Traders.* London: Tamesis Books, 1985.

Frary, Lucien, and Mara Kozelsky, eds. *Russian-Ottoman Borderlands: The Eastern Question Reconsidered.* Madison: University of Wisconsin Press, 2014.

Fraser, Ronald. *Napoleon's Cursed War: Popular Resistance in the Spanish Peninsular War.* London: Verso, 2008.

Fugier, André. *Napoléon et l'Espagne, 1799–1808.* Paris: F. Alcan, 1930.

Furet, François. *Interpreting the French Revolution.* Cambridge: Cambridge University Press, 1981.

Gachot, Edouard. *Souvarow en Italie.* Paris: Perrin, 1903.

Gagliardo, John. *Reich and Nation: The Holy Roman Empire as Idea and Reality, 1763–1806.* Bloomington: Indiana University Press, 1980.

Gainot, Bernard. "Révolution, liberté = Europe des nations? Sororité conflictuelle." In *Mélanges Michel Vovelle sur la Révolution, approaches plurielles,* edited by Jean Paul Bertaud, 457–68. Paris: Société des études robespierristes, 1997.

Galpin, William Freeman. *The Grain Supply of England During the Napoleonic Period.* New York: Macmillan, 1925.

Ganson, Barbara Anne. *The Guarani Under Spanish Rule in the Río de la Plata*. Stanford: Stanford University Press, 2003.

Gardane, Alfred de. *La mission du Général Gardane en Perse sous le premier Empire*. Paris: Librarie de Ad. Laine, 1865.

Gardiner, Robert. *The Campaign of Trafalgar*. London: Caxton Editions, 2001.

Gardiner, Robert. *The Victory of Seapower: Winning the Napoleonic War, 1806–1814*. London: Caxton Editions, 1998.

Geggus, David. *Haitian Revolutionary Studies*. Bloomington: Indiana University Press, 2002.

Geisendorf–Des Gouttes, Théophile. *Les prisonniers de guerre au temps du Ier empire. La déportation aux Baléares et aux Canaries (les archipels enchanteurs et farouches) des soldats de Baylen et des marins de Trafalgar (1809–1814)*. Genève: Éditions Labor, 1936.

Gelashvili, Akaki. *Kakhetis 1812 tslis ajankeba*. Tbilisi: Artanuji, 2010.

Generalstabens krigshistoriska afdelning, Sveriges krig åren 1808 och 1809. Stockholm: Kongl. boktryckeriet P. A. Norstedt & söner, 1890.

Gent, T. van. *De Engelse invasie van Walcheren in 1809*. Amsterdam: De Bataafsche Leeuw, 2001.

Geoghegan, Patrick. *The Irish Act of Union: A Study in High Politics, 1798–1801*. Dublin: Gill and Macmillan, 1999.

Ghurbal, Muḥammad Shafīq. *The Beginnings of the Egyptian Question and the Rise of Mehemet Ali*. London: George Routledge & Sons, 1928.

Gill, John H. *1809. Thunder on the Danube*. 3 vols. Barnsley, UK: Frontline Books, 2008.

Girard, Philippe R. *The Slaves Who Defeated Napoleon: Toussaint Louverture and the Haitian War of Independence, 1801–1804*. Tuscaloosa: University of Alabama Press, 2011.

Girnius, Saulius Antanas. "Russia and the Continental Blockade." PhD dissertation. University of Chicago, 1981.

Glenthøj, Rasmus, and Morten Nordhagen Ottosen, *Experiences of War and Nationality in Denmark and Norway, 1807–1815*. New York: Palgrave Macmillan, 2014.

Glover, Gareth. *The Forgotten War Against Napoleon: Conflict in the Mediterranean, 1793–1815*. Barnsley: Pen & Sword, 2017.

Glover, Gareth. *Waterloo: Myth and Reality*. Barnsley: Pen and Sword, 2014.

Glover, Michael. *A Very Slippery Fellow: The Life of Sir Robert Wilson, 1777–1849*. Oxford: Oxford University Press, 1978.

Godechot, Jacques Léon. *Le Comte d'Antraigues: Un espion dans l'Europe des émigrés*. Paris: Fayard, 1986.

Godechot, Jacques Léon. *The Counter-Revolution: Doctrine and Action, 1789–1804*. Princeton, NJ: Princeton University Press, 1981.

Godechot, Jacques Léon. *La Grande Nation: L'expansion révolutionnaire de la France dans le monde de 1789 à 1799*. Paris: Aubier, 1956.

Gonneville, Aymar-Olivier Le Harivel de. *Recollections of Colonel de Gonneville*. London: Hurst and Blackett, 1875.

Goodwin, Albert. *The Friends of Liberty: The English Democratic Movement in the Age of the French Revolution*. London: Hutchinson, 1979.

Gordon, Stewart. *The New Cambridge History of India*, vol. 2, part 4, *The Marathas, 1600–1818*. Cambridge: Cambridge University Press, 1993.

Graaf, Beatrice de, Ido de Haan, and Brian E. Vick, eds. *Securing Europe After Napoleon: 1815 and the New European Security Culture*. Cambridge: Cambridge University Press, 2019.

Graaf, Beatrice de. *Tegen de terreur. Hoe Europa veilig werd na Napoleon*. Amsterdam: Prometheus, 2018.

Grab, Alexander. "Army, State, and Society: Conscription and Desertion in Napoleonic Italy (1802–1814)." *Journal of Modern History* 67, no. 1 (1995): 25–54.

Grab, Alexander. "From the French Revolution to Napoleon." In *Italy in the Nineteenth Century: 1796–1900*, edited by John A. Davis, 25–48. Oxford: Oxford University Press, 2000.

Grab, Alexander. *Napoleon and the Transformation of Europe*. New York: Palgrave Macmillan, 2003.

Grab, Alexander. "The Politics of Finance in Napoleonic Italy (1802–1814)." *Journal of Modern Italian Studies* 3, no. 2 (1998): 127–43.

Grab, Alexander. "State Power, Brigandage and Rural Resistance in Napoleonic Italy." *European History Quarterly* 25 (1995): 39–70.

Grade, Anders. *Sverige och Tilsitalliansen (1807–1810)*. Lund: Gleerupska univ.-bokhandeln, 1913.

Grainger, John D. *The Amiens Truce: Britain and Bonaparte, 1801–1803*. Rochester, NY: Boydell Press, 2004.

Grainger, John D. *British Campaigns in the South Atlantic 1805–1807*. Barnsley, UK: Pen & Sword Military, 2015.

Grainger, John D. *The British Navy in the Baltic*. Woodbridge: Boydell Press, 2014.

Grandmaison, Charles-Alexandre Geoffroy de. *L'Espagne et Napoléon, 1804–1809*. Paris: Plon-Nourrit, 1908.

Grasset, Alphonse Louis. *La Guerre d'Espagne, 1807–1813*. Paris: Berger-Levrault, 1914.

Graves, Donald. *Dragon Rampant: The Royal Welch Fusiliers at War, 1793–1815*. Barnsley, UK: Frontline Books, 2010.

Gray, J. M. *A History of the Gambia*. Cambridge: Cambridge University Press, 2015.

Greer, Donald. *The Incidence of the Emigration During the French Revolution*. Cambridge, MA: Harvard University Press, 1951.

Gregory, Desmond. *The Beneficent Usurpers: A History of the British in Madeira*. London: Associated University Presses, 1988.

Gregory, Desmond. *Malta, Britain and the European Powers, 1793–1815*. Madison, NJ: Farleigh Dickinson University Press, 1996.

Gregory, Desmond. *Napoleon's Italy*. Madison, NJ: Fairleigh Dickinson University Press, 2001.

Gregory, Desmond. *Sicily: The Insecure Base: A History of the British Occupation of Sicily, 1806–1815.* Rutherford, NJ: Fairleigh Dickinson University Press, 1988.

Gregory, Desmond. *The Ungovernable Rock: A History of the Anglo-Corsican Kingdom and its Role in Britain's Mediterranean Strategy During the Revolutionary War, 1793–1797.* Rutherford, NJ: Fairleigh Dickinson University Press, 1985.

Grehan, John. *The Lines of Torres Vedras: The Cornerstone of Wellington's Strategy in the Peninsular War, 1809–1812.* London: Spellmount, 2000.

Grewal, J. S. *The New Cambridge History of India*, vol. 2, part 3, *The Sikhs of the Punjab*. Cambridge: Cambridge University Press, 1998.

Grigoryan, Z. *Prisoedinenie Vostochnoi Armenii k Rossii v nachale XIX veka.* Moscow: Izd-vo sotsialno-ekonomicheskoi lt-ry, 1959.

Grimsted, Patricia. "Czartoryski's System for Russian Foreign Policy, 1803." *California Slavic Studies* V (1970): 19–92.

Grossmann, Henryk. *Struktura społeczna i gospodarcza Księstwa Warszawskiego: na podstawie spisów ludności, 1808–1810.* Warsaw: Nakł. Gł. Urzędu Statystycznego, 1925.

Gruner, Wolf D. *Der Deutsche Bund 1815–1866.* Munich: Beck, 2012.

Der Wiener Kongress, 1814/15. Stuttgart: Philipp Reclam, 2014.

Gupta, Pratul Chandra. *Baji Rao II and the East India Company, 1796–1818.* Bombay: Allied, 1964.

Guzmán, Juan Pérez de. *El dos de mayo de 1808 en Madrid.* Madrid: Establecimiento Tipográfico Sucesores de Rivadeneyra, 1908.

Gvosdev, Nikolas K. *Imperial Policies and Perspectives Towards Georgia, 1760–1819.* New York: St. Martin's Press, 2000.

Hagemann, Karen. *Revisiting Prussia's War Against Napoleon: History, Culture and Memory.* Cambridge: Cambridge University Press, 2015.

Hales, E. *Napoleon and the Pope: The Story of Napoleon and Pius VII.* London: Eyre & Spottiswoode, 1961.

Hall, Christopher. *Wellington's Navy: Seapower and the Peninsular War 1807–1814.* London: Chatham, 2004.

Hall, John R. *General Pichegru's Treason.* London: Smith, Elder, 1915.

Hamill, Hugh M. *The Hidalgo Revolt: Prelude to Mexican Independence.* Gainesville: University of Florida Press, 1966.

Hamnett, Brian. "The Meieva Roots of Spanish Constitutionalism." In *The Rise of Constitutional Government in the Iberian Atlantic World: The Impact of the Cádiz Constitution of 1812*, edited by Natalia Sobrevilla Perea and Scott Eastman, 19–41. Tuscaloosa: University of Alabama Press, 2015.

Harbron, John. *Trafalgar and the Spanish Navy: The Spanish Experience of Sea Power.* London: Conway Maritime, 2004.

Hardman, John. *French Politics, 1774–1789: From the Accession of Louis XVI to the Fall of the Bastille.* London: Longman, 1995.

Hardman, John. *The Life of Louis XVI.* New Haven, CT: Yale University Press, 2016.

Hardman, William. *A History of Malta During the Period of the French and British Occupations, 1798–1815.* London: Longmans, Green, 1909.

Hariharan, Shantha. "Luso-British Cooperation in India: A Portuguese Frigate in the Service of a British Expedition." *South Asia Research* 26, no. 2 (2006): 133–43.

Hariharan, Shantha. "Macao and the English East India Company in the Early Nineteenth Century: Resistance and Confrontation." *Portuguese Studies* 23, no. 2 (2007): 135–52.

Hariharan, Shantha, and P. S. Hariharan. "The Expedition to Garrison Portuguese Macao with British Troops: Temporary Occupation and Re-Embarkation, 1808." *International Journal of Maritime History* 25, no. 2 (2013): 85–116.

Harper, John Lamberton. *American Machiavelli: Alexander Hamilton and the Origins of the U.S. Foreign Policy.* Cambridge: Cambridge University Press, 2004.

Harvey, Robert. *Liberators: South America's Savage Wars of Freedom, 1810–1830.* London: Robinson, 2002.

Hatalkar, V. G. *Relations Between the French and the Marathas.* Bombay: T. V. Chidambaran, 1958.

Hathaway, Jane. *The Politics of Households in Ottoman Egypt: The Rise of the Qazdaglis.* Cambridge: Cambridge University Press, 1997.

Haudrère, Philippe. *La compagnie française des Indes au XVIIIe siècle 1719–1795.* Paris: Librairie de l'Inde, 1989.

Haynes, Christine. *Our Friends the Enemies: The Occupation of France After Napoleon.* Cambridge, MA: Harvard University Press, 2018.

Hayworth, Jordan R. *Revolutionary France's War of Conquest in the Rhineland: Conquering the Natural Frontier, 1792–1797.* Cambridge: Cambridge University Press, 2019.

Hazareesingh, Sudhir. *The Legend of Napoleon.* London: Granta Books, 2004.

Hazareesingh, Sudhir. *The Saint-Napoleon. Celebrating Sovereignty in Nineteenth-Century France.* Cambridge, MA: Harvard University Press, 2004.

Heckscher, Eli F. *The Continental System: An Economic Interpretation.* Oxford: Clarendon Press, 1922.

Hector, Michel, ed. *La Révolution francaise et Haiti: Filiations, ruptures, nouvelles dimensions.* Port-au-Prince: Sociéte Haitienne d'histoire et de géographie, 1995.

Helfert, Joseph Alexander von. *Königin Karolina von Neapel und Sicilien im Kampfe gegen die französische Weltherrschaft, 1790–1814: mit Benützung von Schriftstücken des K.K. Haus-, Hof- und Staats-Archivs.* Vienna: Braumüller, 1878.

Herold, Christopher. *Bonaparte in Egypt.* London: Hamish Hamilton, 1962.

Herr, Richard. *Rural Change and Royal Finances in Spain at the End of the Old Regime.* Berkeley: University of California Press, 1989.

Heyd, Uriel. "The Ottoman Ulama and Westernization at the Time of Selim IIII and Mahmud II." In *Studies in Islamic History and Civilization,* 63–96. Jerusalem: Magnes Press, Hebrew University, 1961.

Hickey, Donald R. *Glorious Victory: Andrew Jackson and the Battle of New Orleans.* Baltimore: John Hopkins University Press, 2015.

Hickey, Donald R. *The War of 1812: A Short History*. Urbana: University of Illinois Press, 1995.

Higby, Chester Penn. *The Religious Policy of the Bavarian Government During the Napoleonic Period*. New York: Columbia University, 1919.

Hippler, Thomas. *Citizens, Soldiers and National Armies: Military Service in France and Germany, 1789–1830*. London: Routledge, 2008.

Hochedlinger, Michael. *Austria's Wars of Emergence: War, State and Society in the Habsburg Monarchy, 1683–1797*. London: Longman, 2003.

Hochschild, Adam. *Bury the Chains: Prophets and Rebels in the Fight to Free an Empire's Slaves*. New York: Houghton Mifflin, 2006.

Hocquellet, Richard. *Résistance et revolution durant l'occupation napoléonienne en Espagne, 1808–1812*. Paris: La Boutique de l'histoire éd., 2001.

Holborn, Hajo. *A History of Modern Germany, 1648–1840*. New York: Alfred A. Knopf, 1967.

Holtman, Robert B. *The Napoleonic Revolution*. Baton Rouge: Louisiana State University Press, 1967.

Höpfner, Friedrich Eduard Alexander von. *Der Krieg von 1806 und 1807 (i.e. achtzehn-hundertsechs und achtzehnhundertsieben): ein Beitrag zur Geschichte der Preussischen Armee nach den Quellen des Kriegs-Archivs bearbeitet*. Berlin: Schropp, 1850.

Hopton, Richard. *The Battle of Maida 1806: Fifteen Minutes of Glory*. London: Leo Cooper, 2002.

Horn, Jeff. *The PathNnot Taken: French Industrialization in the Age of Revolution, 1750–1830*. Cambridge, MA: MIT Press, 2006.

Horsman, Reginald. *The Causes of the War of 1812*. Philadelphia: University of Pennsylvania Press, 1962.

Horward, Donald D. *The Battle of Bussaco: Masséna vs. Wellington*. Tallahassee: Florida State University Press, 1965.

Houssaye, Henry. *Napoleon and the Campaign of 1814*. London: Hugh Rees, 1914.

Howard, Martin R. *Walcheren 1809: The Scandalous Destruction of a British Army*. Barnsley, UK: Pen & Sword Military, 2012.

Huchet, Patrick. *Georges Cadoudal et les chouans*. Rennes: Editions Ouest-France, 1998.

Hughes, Ben. *The British Invasion of the River Plate 1806–1807: How the Redcoats Were Humbled and a Nation Was Born*. Barnsley, UK: Pen & Sword Military, 2013.

Hughes, Michael J. *Forging Napoleon's Grande Armee: Motivation, Military Culture, and Masculinity in the French Army, 1800–1808*. New York: New York University Press, 2012.

Hull, Isabel. *Sexuality, State, and Civil Society in Germany, 1700–1815*. Ithaca: Cornell University Press, 1996.

Hunt, Lynn. *Inventing Human Rights: A History*. London: W. W. Norton, 2007.

Ibragimbeili, Kh. *Rossiya i Azerbaijan v pervoi treti XIX veka*. Moscow: Nauka, 1969.

Igamberdyev, M. *Iran v mezhdunarodnykh otnosheniyakh pervoi treti XIX veka*. Samarkand: Izd-vo Samarkandskogo gos. univ., 1961.

Ihalainen, Pasi, Karin Sennefelt, Michael Bregnsbo, and Patrik Winton, eds. *Scandinavia in the Age of Revolution: Nordic Political Cultures, 1740–1820.* Burlington, VT: Ashgate, 2011.

Ilari, Virgilio, et al. *Il regno di Sardegna nelle guerre napoleoniche e le legioni anglo-italiane, 1799–1815.* Novara: Widerholdt Frères, 2008.

Ingram, Edward. *Britain's Persia Connection, 1798–1828: Prelude to the Great Game.* Oxford: Clarendon Press, 1992.

Ingram, Edward. *Commitment to Empire: Prophecies of the Great Game in Asia, 1797–1800.* Oxford: Clarendon Press, 1981.

Ingrao, Charles W. *The Habsburg Monarchy, 1618–1815.* Cambridge: Cambridge University Press, 2000.

Ionnisian, A. *Prisoedinenie Zakavkaziya k Rossii i mezhdunarodnye otnosheniya v nachale XIX stoletiya.* Yerevan: Izd-vo AN Armyanskoi SSR, 1958.

Jackson, John A. "The Mexican Silver Scheme: Finance and Profiteering in the Napoleonic Era, 1796–1811." PhD dissertation, University of North Carolina, 1978.

James, C. L. R. *The Black Jacobins: Toussaint L'Ouverture and the San Domingo Revolution.* New York: Vintage Books, 1989.

James, William. *The Naval History of Great Britain.* 6 vols. London: Conway Maritime Press, 2002.

Jansen, Marius B., ed. *The Cambridge History of Japan*, vol. 5, *The Nineteenth Century.* Cambridge: Cambridge University Press, 1989.

Jarrett, Mark. *The Congress of Vienna and its Legacy: War and Great Power Diplomacy After Napoleon.* London: I. B. Tauris, 2013.

Jasanoff, Maya. *Edge of Empire: Lives, Culture and Conquest in the East, 1750–1850.* New York: Vintage Books, 2005.

Jewsbury, George. "Russian Administrative Policies Toward Bessarabia, 1806–1828." PhD dissertation, University of Washington, 1970.

Johnson, Kenneth G. "Louis-Thomas Villaret de Joyeuse: Admiral and Colonial Administrator (1747–1812)." PhD dissertation, Florida State University, 2006.

Johnson, Kenneth G. "Napoleon's War at Sea." In *Napoleon and the Operational Art of War*, edited by Michael V. Leggiere, 387–475. Leiden: Brill, 2016.

Johnson, Lyman L. *Workshop of Revolution: Plebeian Buenos Aires and the Atlantic World, 1776–1810.* Durham, NC: Duke University Press, 2011.

Johnston, Robert Matteson. *The Napoleonic Empire in Southern Italy and the Rise of the Secret Societies.* New York: Macmillan, 1904.

Jones, Colin. *The Great Nation: France from Louis XV to Napoleon.* New York: Penguin Books, 2003.

Jones, Jeremy, and Nicholas P. Ridout. *Oman: Culture and Diplomacy.* Edinburgh: Edinburgh University Press, 2012.

Jones, Michael W. "Fear and Domination: Pierre Riel, the Marquis de Beurnonville at the Spanish Court and Napoleon Bonaparte's Spanish Policy, 1802–05." PhD dissertation, Florida State University, 2004.

Jorgensen, Christer. *The Anglo-Swedish Alliance Against Napoleonic France.* New York: Palgrave, 2004.

Judson, Pieter M. *The Habsburg Empire: A New History.* Cambridge, MA: Belknap Press, 2016.

Junkelman, Marcus. *Napoleon und Bayern den Anfängen des Königreiches.* Regensburg: F. Pustet, 1985.

Just, Gustav. *Politik oder Strategie? Kritische Studien über den Warschauer Feldzug Österreichs und die Haltung Russlands 1809.* Vienna: Seidel & Sohn, 1909.

Kadam, Umesh Ashokrao. *History of the Marathas: French-Maratha Relations, 1668–1818.* New Delhi: Sundeep Prakashan, 2008.

Kagan, Frederick W. *The End of the Old Order: Napoleon and Europe, 1801–1805.* New York: Da Capo Press, 2006.

Kaplan, Herbert H. *The First Partition of Poland.* New York: Columbia University Press, 1962.

Karal, Enver Ziya. *Selim III'ün hatt-i hümayunları: Nizam-i Cedit: 1789–1807.* Ankara: Türk Tarih Kurumu Basımevı, 1946.

Karlsson, Gunnar. *The History of Iceland.* Minneapolis: University of Minnesota Press, 2000.

Karonen, Petri. *Pohjoinen suurvalta: Ruotsi ja Suomi 1521–1809.* Helsinki: WS Bookwell, 2008.

Kashani-Sabet, Firoozeh. *Frontier Fictions: Shaping the Iranian Nation, 1804–1946.* Princeton, NJ: Princeton University Press, 1999.

Kastor, Peter, and François Weil. *Empires of the Imagination: Transatlantic Histories of the Louisiana Purchase.* Charlottesville: University of Virginia Press, 2008.

Kaufmann, William. *British Policy and the Independence of Latin America, 1804–1828.* New Haven, CT: Yale University Press, 1951.

Kaye, John William, *The Life and Correspondence of Major-General Sir John Malcolm.* London: Smith, Elder, 1856.

Kelly, J. B. *Britain and the Persian Gulf, 1795–1880.* Oxford: Clarendon Press, 1968.

Kennedy, James J. "Lord Whitworth and the Conspiracy Against Tsar Paul I: The New Evidence of the Kent Archive." *Slavic Review* 36, no. 2 (June 1977): 205–19.

Kerautret, Michel. *Un crime d'état sous l'empire: l'affaire Palm.* Paris: Vendémiaire, 2015.

Kiaiviarianen, I. I. *Mezhdunarodnie otnoshenia na severe Evropi v nachale XIX veka i prisoedinenie Finlandii k Rossii v 1809 godu.* Petrozavodsk: Karelskoe knizhnoe izd-vo, 1965.

King, David. *Vienna, 1814: How the Conquerors of Napoleon Made Love, War, and Peace at the Congress of Vienna.* New York: Harmony Books, 2008.

Kissinger, Henry. *A World Restored: Metternich, Castlereagh and the Problem of Peace 1812–1822.* London: Phoenix, 2000.

Kitzen, Michael L. S. *Tripoli and the United States at War: A History of American Relations with the Barbary States, 1785–1805.* Jefferson, NC: McFarland, 1993.

Klang, Daniel Michael. "Bavaria and the Age of Napoleon." PhD dissertation, Princeton University, 1963.

Klinge, Matti. *Napoleonin varjo: Euroopan ja Suomen murros 1795–1815.* Helsinki: Otava, 2009.

Klooster, Wim. *Revolutions in the Atlantic World: A Comparative History.* New York: New York University Press, 2009.

Klooster, Wim, and Geert Oostindie, eds. *Curaçao in the Age of Revolutions, 1795–1800.* Leiden: KITLV Press, 2011.

Knight, Roger. *Britain Against Napoleon: The Organization of Victory, 1793–1815.* London: Allen Lane, 2013.

Knight, Roger. *Pursuit of Victory: The Life and Achievemnt of Horatio Nelson.* London: Allen Lane, 2005.

Kortua, Nikoloz. *Sakartvelo 1806–1812 tslebis Ruset-Turketis omshi: rusi da kartveli xalxebis sabrdzolo tanamegobrobis istoriidan.* Tbilisi: Tsodna, 1964.

Kowalczyk, Rafał. *Polityka gospodarcza i finansowa Księstwa Warszawskiego w latach 1807–1812.* Łódź: Wydawn. Uniwersytet Łódzkiego, 2010.

Kowecki, Jerzy, ed. *Sejm czteroletni i jego tradycje.* Warsaw: Państwowe Wydawnictwo Naukowe, 1991.

Kowecki, Jerzy, and Bogusław Leśnodorski, *Konstytucja 3 maja 1791, statut Zgromadzenia Przyjaciół Konstytucji.* Warsaw: Państwowe Wydawnictwo Naukowe, 1981.

Kraehe, Enno E. *Metternich's German Policy.* 2 vols. Princeton, NJ: Princeton University Press, 1983.

Krajeski, Paul C. *In the Shadow of Nelson: The Naval Leadership of Admiral Sir Charles Cotton, 1753–1812.* Westport, CT: Greenwood Press, 2000.

Krauss, Alfred. *Beilagen zu 1805 der Feldzug von Ulm.* Vienna: Seidel und Sohn, 1912.

Krebs, Léonce, and Henri Moris. *Les campagnes dans les Alpes pendant la Révolution, 1794, 1795, 1796.* Paris: Plon, 1895.

Krüger-Löwenstein, Uta. Russland, *Frankreich und das Reich 1801–1803; zur Vorgeschichte der 3. Koalition.* Wiesbaden: Steiner, 1972.

Kubben, Raymond. *Regeneration and Hegemony: Franco-Batavian Relations in the Revolutionary Era, 1795–1803.* Leiden: Martinus Nijhoff, 2011.

Kuethe, Allan J., and Kenneth J. Adrien, *The Spanish Atlantic World in the Eighteenth Century: War and the Bourbon Reforms, 1713–1796.* Cambridge: Cambridge University Press, 2014.

Kukla, Jon. *A Wilderness So Immense: The Louisiana Purchase and the Destiny of America.* New York: Knopf, 2003.

Kumar, Dharma, and Meghnad Desai, ed. *The Cambridge Economic History of India,* vol. 2, *c. 1757–c. 1970.* Cambridge: Cambridge University Press, 1983.

Kuran, Ercüment. *Avrupa'da Osmanlı İkamet Elçiliklerinin Kuruluşu ve İlk Elçilerin Siyasi Faaliyetleri, 1793–1821.* Ankara: Türk Kültürünü Araştırma Enstitüsü Yayınları, 1988.

Kwass, Michael. *Privilege and the Politics of Taxation in Eighteenth-Century France: Liberté, Égalité, Fiscalité.* Cambridge: Cambridge University Press, 2000.

Labasse, Jean. *Le commerce des soies à Lyon sous Napoleon et la crise de 1811*. Paris: Presses universitaires de France, 1957.

Lamartine, Alphonse de. *Histoire des Girondins*. Paris: Furne, 1847.

Landes, David S. *The Unbound Prometheus: Technological Change and Industrial Development in Western Europe from 1750 to the Present*. Cambridge: Cambridge University Press, 2003.

Lanfrey, Pierre. *Histoire de Napoleon Ier*. Paris: Charpentier, 1869.

Lang, David M. *The Last Years of the Georgian Monarchy, 1658–1832*. New York: Columbia University Press, 1957.

Lappalainen, Jussi T., Lars Ericson Wolke and Ali Pylkkänen, *Sota Suomesta: Suomen sota 1808–1809*. Hämeenlinna: Suomalaisen Kirjallisuuden Seura, 2007.

Larkin, Hilary. *A History of Ireland, 1800–1922*. London: Anthem Press, 2014.

Laurens, Henry. *Les origines intellectuelles de l'expédition d'Égypte: L'Orientalisme Islamisant en France (1698–1798)*. Paris: Isis, 1987.

Laurens, Henry, et al. *L'Expedition d'Egypte, 1798–1801*. Paris: Armand Colin, 1989.

Lavery, Brian. *Nelson's Fleet at Trafalgar*. Annapolis, MD: Naval Institute Press, 2004.

Lawson, Philip. *The East India Company: A History*. London: Longman, 1993.

Lebedev, V. T. *V Indiyu, voyeno-statisticheskiy i strategicheskiv ocherk*. St. Petersburg: Tip ografiya A. A. Porokhovskchikova, 1898.

Lee, Mark McKinley. "Paul I and the Indian Expedition of 1801: Myth and Reality." MA thesis, Texas Tech University, 1984.

Lefebvre, Armand. *Histoire des cabinets de l'Europe pendant le Consulat et l'Empire*. Paris: Pagnerre, 1847.

Lefebvre, Georges. *Napoleon*. 2 vols. London: Routledge & Kegan Paul, 1969.

Lefebvre, Georges. *The Thermidorians and the Directory: Two Phases of the French Revolution*. New York: Random House, 1964.

Leggiere, Michael V. *Blücher: Scourge of Napoleon*. Norman: University of Oklahoma Press, 2014.

Leggiere, Michael V. *The Fall of Napoleon: The Allied Invasion of France, 1813–1814*. Cambridge: Cambridge University Press, 2007.

Leggiere, Michael V. "The Life, Letters and Campaigns of Friedrich Wilhelm Graf Bülow von Dennewitz, 1755–1816." PhD dissertation, Florida State University, 1997.

Leggiere, Michael V. *Napoleon and Berlin: The Franco-Prussian War in North Germany, 1813*. Norman: University of Oklahoma Press, 2002.

Leggiere, Michael V. *Napoleon and the Struggle for Germany*. 2 vols. Cambridge: Cambridge University Press, 2015.

Legohérel, Henri. *Les trésoriers généraux de la Marine, 1517–1788*. Paris: Cujas, 1965.

Lenotre, G. *Georges Cadoudal*. Paris: B. Grasset, 1929.

Lensen, George Alexander. *The Russian Push Toward Japan: Russo-Japanese Relations, 1697–1875*. Princeton, NJ: Princeton University Press, 1959.

Lentz, Thierry. *Le congrès de Vienne: Une refondation de l'Europe 1814–1815*. Paris: Perrin, 2013.

Lentz, Thierry. *La France et l'Europe de Napoléon, 1804–1814*. Paris: Fayard, 2007.

Lentz, Thierry. *Le grand Consulat: 1799–1804*. Paris: Fayard, 1999.

Lentz, Thierry, ed. *Napoléon et l'Europe*. Paris: Fayard, 2005.

Lentz, Thierry. *La proclamation du Premier Empire*. Paris: Fondation Napoléon, 2002.

Lentz, Thierry. *Les vingt jours de Fontainebleau: la première abdication de Napoléon, 31 mars-20 avril 1814*. Paris: Perrin, 2014.

Lentz, Thierry, Émilie Barthet, et al. *Le sacre de Napoléon, 2 décembre 1804*. Paris: Nouveau Monde, 2003.

Lettow-Vorbeck, Oscar von. *Der Krieg von 1806–1907*, vol. I, *Jena und Auerstedt*. Berlin: Mittler und Sohn, 1896.

Lieven, Dominic. *Russia Against Napoleon*. London: Penguin, 2010.

Lipscombe, Nick. *The Peninsular War Atlas*. Oxford: Osprey, 2014.

Livermore, H. V. *A New History of Portugal*. Cambridge: Cambridge University Press, 1966.

Lloyd, Peter. *The French Are Coming! 1805: The Invasion Scare of 1803–1805*. Kent, UK: Spellmount, 1991.

Lojek, Jerzy. "Catherine's Armed Intervention in Poland: Origins of the Political Decisions at the Russian Court in 1791–1792." *Canadian-American Slavic Studies* 4 (1970): 570–93.

Lokke, Carl Ludwig. "French Designs on Paraguay in 1803." *Hispanic American Historical Review* 8, no. 3 (August 1928): 392–405.

London, Joshua. *Victory in Tripoli: How America's War with the Barbary Pirates Established the U.S. Navy and Shaped a Nation*. Hoboken, NJ: John Wiley, 2005.

Lord, Robert H. *The Second Partition of Poland: A Study in Diplomatic History*. Cambridge, MA: Harvard University Press, 1915.

Lovett, Gabriel H. *Napoleon and the Birth of Modern Spain*. 2 vols. New York: New York University Press, 1965.

Lucas, Manuel Ardit. *Revolucion liberal y revuelta campesina: un ensayo sobre la desintegracion del regimen feudal en el Pais Valenciano (1793/1840)*. Barcelona: Ariel, 1977.

Luck, James M. *A History of Switzerland*. Palo Alto, CA: Society for the Promotion of Science and Scholarship, 1985.

Lukowski, Jerzy T. *The Partitions of Poland, 1772, 1793, 1795*. Harlow: Longman Higher Education, 1998.

Lynch, John. *Bourbon Spain, 1700–1808*. Oxford: Basil Blackwell, 1989.

Lynch, John. *The Spanish-American Revolutions, 1808–1826*. New York: Norton, 1973.

Lyons, Martyn. *France Under the Directory*. Cambridge: Cambridge University Press, 1975.

Maybon, M. C. B. "Les Anglais à Macao en 1802 et en 1808." *Bulletin de l'École française d'Extrême-Orient* 6 (1906): 301–25. Electronic version available at http://www.persee.fr/doc/befeo_0336-1519_1906_num_6_1_4261.

Mackay, Charles Hugh. "The Tempest: The Life and Career of Jean-Andoche Junot, 1771–1813." PhD dissertation, Florida State University, 1995.

MacKenzie, Norman. *The Escape from Elba: The Fall and Flight of Napoleon, 1814–1815*. New York: Oxford University Press, 1982.

Mackenzie, Robert. *The Trafalgar Roll: The Officers, the Men, the Ships.* London: Chatham, 2004.

Mackesy, Piers. *Statesmen at War: The Strategy of Overthrow, 1798–1799.* London: Longman, 1974.

Mackesy, Piers. *The War in the Mediterranean 1803–1810.* Cambridge, MA: Harvard University Press, 1957.

Mackesy, Piers. *War Without Victory: The Downfall of Pitt, 1799–1802.* Oxford: Clarendon Press, 1984.

Macmillan, David. "Paul's Retributive Measures of 1800 Against Britain: The Final Turning-Point in British Commercial Attitudes Towards Russia." *Canadian-American Slavic Studies* VI, no. 1 (1973): 68–77.

Madariaga, Isabel de. "The Secret Austro-Russian Treaty of 1781." *Slavonic and East European Review* 38, no. 90 (1959): 114–45.

Madelin, Louis. *The Consulate and the Empire.* New York: AMS Press, 1967.

Madelin, Louis. *La Rome de Napoléon: la domination français à Rome de 1809 à 1814.* Paris: Plon-Nourrit, 1906.

Mahan, Alfred. *The Influence of Sea Power upon the French Revolution and Empire, 1793–1812.* Boston: Little, Brown, 1918.

Manchester, Alan K. *British Preeminence in Brazil, Its Rise and Decline: A Study in European Expansion.* Chapel Hill: University of North Carolina Press, 1933.

Manning, William Ray. "The Nootka Sound Controversy." *Annual Report of the American Historical Association for the Year 1904.* Washington, DC, 1905.

Marichal, Carlos. *Bankruptcy of Empire: Mexican Silver and the Wars Between Spain, Britain, and France, 1760–1810.* New York: Cambridge University Press, 2007.

Marion, Marcel. *Histoire financière de la France depuis 1715,* vol. IV, *1797–1818. La fin de la Révolution, le Consulat et l'Empire. La liberation du territoire.* Paris: Librairie Arthur Rousseau, 1925.

Markham, J. David. *Napoleon's Road to Glory: Triumphs, Defeats and Immortality.* London: Brassey's, 2003.

Markham, J. David. *The Road to St. Helena: Napoleon After Waterloo.* Barnsley, UK: Pen & Sword, 2008.

Marriott, J. A. R. *The Eastern Question: An Historical Study in European Diplomacy.* Oxford: Clarendon Press, 1940.

Marshall, P. J. *East Indian Fortunes: The British in Bengal in the Eighteenth Century.* Oxford: Oxford University Press, 1976.

Marshall, P. J., ed. *The New Cambridge History of India,* vol. 2, part 2, *Bengal: The British Bridgehead.* Cambridge: Cambridge University Press, 1987.

Marshall, P. J., ed. *Oxford History of the British Empire,* vol. 2, *The Eighteenth Century.* Oxford: Oxford University Press, 1998.

Martin, Alexander M. *Enlightened Metropolis: Constructing Imperial Moscow, 1762–1855.* Oxford: Oxford University Press, 2013.

Martin, Vanessa, ed., *Anglo-Iranian Relations Since 1800.* New York: Routledge, 2005.

Martins do Vale, A. M. *Os Portugueses em Macau (1750–1800)*. Lisbon: Instituto Português do Oriente, 1997.

Marzagalli, Silvia. *Bordeaux et les États-Unis, 1776–1815: politique et stratégies négociantes dans la genèse d'un réseau commercial*. Geneva: Droz, 2014.

Marzagalli, Silvia. *Les boulevards de la fraude: La négoce maritime et le Blocus continental 1806–1813, Bordeaux, Hambourg, Livourne*. Villeneuve-d'Ascq: Presses universitaires du Septentrion, 1999.

Maspéro-Clerc, Hélène. "Un journaliste émigré jugé a Londres pour diffamation envers le Premier Consul." *Revue d'histoire moderne et contemporaine* 18, no. 2 (1971): 261–81.

Masson, Paul. *Histoire du commerce français dans le Levant au XVIIe siècle*. Paris, Hachette, 1911.

Mathiez, Albert. *La révolution et les étrangers: cosmopolitisme et défense nationale*. Paris: La Renaissance du Livre, 1918.

Maude, F. N. *The Jena Campaign*. New York: Macmillan, 1909.

Maxwell, Kenneth R. *Conflicts and Conspiracies: Brazil and Portugal, 1750–1808*. Cambridge: Cambridge University Press, 1973.

Mayer, Matthew Z. "Joseph II and the Campaign of 1788 Against the Ottoman Turks." MA thesis, McGill University, 1997.

McCain, Stewart. *The Language Question Under Napoleon*. New York: Palgrave Macmillan, 2018.

McClellan, George B. *Venice and Bonaparte*. Princeton, NJ: Princeton University Press, 1931.

McCollim, Gary B. *Louis XIV's Assault on Privilege: Nicolas Desmaretz and the Tax on Wealth*. Rochester, NY: University of Rochester Press, 2012.

McCranie, Kevin D. *Utmost Gallantry: The U.S. and Royal Navies at Sea in the War of 1812*. Annapolis, MD: Naval Institute Press, 2011.

McFarlane, Anthony. *War and Independence in Spanish America*. New York: Routledge, 2014.

McKnight, James L. "Admiral Ushakov and the Ionian Republic: The Genesis of Russia's First Balkan Satellite." PhD dissertation, University of Wisconsin, 1965.

McLynn, Frank. *Napoleon: A Biography*. New York: Arcade, 2002.

McManners, John. *Church and Society in Eighteenth-Century France*. Oxford: Clarendon Press, 1998.

Melvin, Frank Edgar. *Napoleon's Navigation System: A Study of Trade Control During the Continental Blockade*. New York: D. Appleton, 1919.

Meriage, Lawrence P. "The First Serbian Uprising (1804–1813) and the Nineteenth-Century Origins of the Eastern Question." *Slavic Review* 37 (1978): 422–23.

Mikaberidze, Alexander. *Napoleon versus Kutuzov: The Battle of Borodino*. London: Pen & Sword, 2007.

Mikaberidze, Alexander. *Napoleon's Great Escape: The Battle of the Berezina*. London: Pen & Sword, 2010.

Mikaberidze, Alexander. *Napoleon's Trial by Fire: The Burning of Moscow.* London: Pen & Sword, 2014.

Mikaberidze, Alexander. "Non-Belligerent Belligerent Russia and the Franco-Austrian War of 1809." *Napoleonica. La Revue* 10 (2011): 4–22.

Mikhailovskii-Danilevskii, Alexander, and Dmitrii Miliutin, *Istoriya voiny Rossii s Frantsiei v tsarstvovanie imperatora Pavla I v 1799 g.* 5 vols. St. Petersburg: Tip. Shtaba voenno-uchebnykh zavedenii, 1852–1857.

Mikhailovsky-Danilevsky, Alexander. *Opisanie Finlyandskoi Voiny v 1808 i 1809 godakh.* St. Petersburg: Tip. Shtaba otd. korpusa vnutrennei strazhi, 1841.

Mikhailovsky-Danilevsky, Alexander. *Opisanie pervoi voiny imperatora Aleksandra s Napoleonom v 1805–m godu.* St. Petersburg: Tip. Shtaba otd. korpusa vnutrennei strazhi, 1844.

Mikhailovsky-Danilevsky, Alexander. *Opisanie vtoroi voini Imperatora Aleksandra s Napoleonom v 1806–1807 godakh.* St. Petersburg. 1846.

Mills, Lennox Algernon. *Ceylon Under British Rule 1795–1932.* London: Milford, 1933.

Moody, Joseph N. *French Education Since Napoleon.* Syracuse: Syracuse University Press, 1978.

Moreau, Soizik. *Jean-Victor Moreau: l'adversaire de Napoléon.* Paris: Punctum, 2005.

Morineau, Michel. "Budgets de l'état et gestion des finances royales en France au dix-huitième siècle." *Revue historique* 536 (1980): 289–336.

Morse, Hosea Ballou. *The Chronicles of the East India Company, Trading to China 1635–1834.* Oxford: Clarendon Press, 1926.

Mostert, Noel. *The Line upon a Wind: The Greatest War Fought at Sea Under Sail 1793–1815.* London: Vintage, 2008.

Mousnier, Roland, and Ernest Labrousse. *Le XVIIIe siècle; révolution intellectuelle technique et politique (1715–1815).* Paris: Presses universitaires de France, 1953.

Muilwijk, Erwin. *Standing Firm at Waterloo: 17 & 18 June.* Bleiswijk, Netherlands: Sovereign House Books, 2014.

Muir, Rory. *Salamanca 1812.* New Haven, CT: Yale University Press, 2001.

Muir, Rory. *Wellington: The Path to Victory, 1769–1814.* New Haven, CT: Yale University Press, 2013.

Müller, Paul. *L'espionnage militaire sous Napoleon 1er Ch. Schulmeister.* Paris: Berger-Levrault, 1896.

Muriel, Andrés. *Historia de Carlos IV.* Madrid: Imp. de Manuel Tello, 1894.

Murphy, Orville Theodore. *The Diplomatic Retreat of France and Public Opinion on the Eve of the French Revolution, 1783–1789.* Washington, DC: Catholic University of America Press, 1998.

Mustafa, Sam A. *The Long Ride of Major von Schill: A Journey Through German History and Memory.* Lanham, MD: Rowman & Littlefield, 2008.

Mustafa, Sam A. *Napoleon's Paper Kingdom: The Life and Death of Westphalia, 1807–1813.* New York: Rowman & Littlefield, 2017.

Mutafčieva, Vera. *Kărdžalijsko vreme.* Sofia: Bălgarskata Akademija na Naukite, 1993.

Napier, William Francis Patrick. *History of the War in the Peninsula and in the South of France*. 5 vols. Cambridge: Cambridge University Press, 2010–2011.

Nardi, Carla. *Napoleone e Roma: la politica della consulta romana*. Rome: École française de Rome, 1989.

Narochnitskii, A., ed. *Rossiia i Iugo-Vostochnaia Evropa*. Kishinev: Shtiintsa, 1984.

Natchkebia, Irene. "Unrealized Project: Rousseaus' Plan of Franco-Persian Trade in the Context of the Indian Expedition (1807)." In *Studies on Iran and the Caucasus*, edited by Uwe Bläsing et al., 115–25. Leiden: Brill, 2015.

Neal, Larry, ed. *The Rise of Financial Capitalism: International Capital Markets in the Age of Reason*. Cambridge: Cambridge University Press, 1990.

Newitt, Malyn, and Martin Robson. *Lord Beresford and British Intervention in Portugal, 1807–1820*. Lisbon: Impr. de Ciências Sociais, 2004.

Nicassio, Susan Vandiver. *Imperial City: Rome Under Napoleon*. Chicago: University of Chicago Press, 2009.

Nicolas, Jean. *La rébellion française: Mouvements populaires et conscience sociale, 1661–1789*. Paris: Seuil, 2002.

Nicolini, Beatrice. *Makran, Oman, and Zanzibar: Three-Terminal Cultural Corridor in the Western Indian Ocean (1799–1856)*. Leiden: Brill, 2004.

Nicolson, Adam. *Men of Honour: Trafalgar and the Making of the English Hero*. London: HarperCollins, 2005.

Nicolson, Harold. *The Congress of Vienna: A Study in Allied Unity: 1812–1822*. New York: HBJ Books, 1974.

Nikolai Mikhailovich, Grand Duke. *Diplomaticheskie snoshenia Rossii i Frantsii po doneseniyam poslov Imperatorov Aleksandra i Napoleona, 1808–1812*. 6 vols. St. Petersburg: Ekspeditsia zagotovleniya gosudarstvennykh bumag, 1905–1908.

Nipperday, Thomas. *Germany from Napoleon to Bismarck 1800–1866*. Translated by Daniel Nolan. Dublin: Gill & Macmillan, 1996.

Olesen, Jens E. "Schwedisch-Pommern in der schwedischen Politik nach 1806." In *Das Ende des Alten Reiches im Ostseeraum: ahrnehmungen und Transformationen*, edited by Michael North and Robert Riemer, 274–92. Köln: Böhlau, 2008.

Oliveira Lima, Manuel de. *Dom João VI no Brazil: 1808–1821*. Rio de Janeiro: Journal do Commercio, 1908.

Oliveira Marques, António Henrique R. de. *History of Portugal*. New York: Columbia University Press, 1972.

Oman, Charles. *A History of the Peninsular War*. 7 vols. 1902; reprint, London: Greenhill, 2004.

Ompteda, Friedrich von. *Die Ueberwdltigung Hannovers durch die Franzosen*. Hanover: Helwing, 1862.

Oncken, Wilhelm. *Oesterreich und Preussen im Befreiungskriege: urkundliche Aufschlüsse über die politische Geschichte des Jahres 1813*. Berlin: G. Grote, 1879.

Ordin, K. *Pokorenie Finlandii: opit opisanie po neizdannim istochnikam*. 2 vols. St. Petersburg, 1889.

Orlov, A. *Soyuz Peterburga i Londona: Rossiisko-Britanskie otnosheniya v epokhu napoleonovskikh voina.* Moscow: Progress-Traditsiya, 2005.

Özkul, Osman. *Gelenek ve modernite arasında Osmanlı ulemâsı.* İstanbul: Birharf Yayınları, 2005.

Paichadze, Giorgi. *Georgievskii traktat.* Tbilisi: Metsniereba, 1983.

Palmer, Robert R. *The Age of the Democratic Revolution: A Political History of Europe and America, 1760–1800.* 2 vols. Princeton, NJ: Princeton University Press, 1959–1964.

Pantelic, Dusan. *Beogradski Pašaluk posle svistovskog mira, 1791–1794.* Belgrade: Grafički zavod Makarije, 1927.

Pantelić, Dušan. *Beogradski pašaluk: posle svištovskog mira, 1791–1794.* Belgrade: Grafički zavod Makarije, 1927.

Paoletti, Ciro. *Dal Ducato all'Unità: Tre secoli e mezzo di storia militare piemontese.* Rome: USSME, 2011.

Paoletti, Ciro. *La Guerra delle Alpi (1792–1796).* Rome: USSME, 2000.

Paret, Peter. *The Cognitive Challenge of War: Prussia 1806.* Princeton, NJ: Princeton University Press, 2009.

Paret, Peter. *Makers of Modern Strategy: from Machiavelli to the Nuclear Age.* Princeton NJ: Princeton University Press, 1986.

Parker, Harold T. *Three Napoleonic Battles.* Durham, NC: Duke University Press, 1983.

Parker, Richard. *Uncle Sam in Barbary: A Diplomatic History.* Tallahassee: University Press of Florida, 2004.

The Parliamentary History of England from the Earliest Period to the Year 1803. London: T. C. Hansard, 1820.

Parrel, Christian de. "Pitt et l'Espagne." *Revue d'histoire diplomatique* 64 (1950): 58–98.

Parsons, Timothy H. *The Rule of Empires: Those Who Built Them, Those Who Endured Them, and Why They Always Fall.* Oxford: Oxford University Press, 2010.

Paulin, Karl. *Andreas Hofer und der Tiroler Freiheitskampf 1809.* Vienna: Tosa-Verl, 1996.

Pearce, Adrian J. *British Trade with Spanish America, 1763 to 2008.* Liverpool: Liverpool University Press, 2007.

Pellissier, Pierre, and Jérôme Phelipeau. *Les grognards de Cabrera: 1809–1814.* Paris: Hachette littérature, 1979.

Pereira, Angelo. *D. João VI príncipe e rei.* Lisboa: Empresa Nacional de Publicidade, 1953.

Perkins, Bradford. "England and the Louisiana Question." *Huntington Library Quarterly* 18, no. 3 (May 1955): 279–95.

Perkins, Bradford. *Prologue to War England and the United States, 1805–1812.* Berkeley, University of California Press, 1961.

Persson, Anders. *1808: gerillakriget i Finland.* Stockholm: Ordfront, 1986.

Petre, F. Loraine. *Napoleon and the Archduke Charles.* London: John Lane, 1909.

Petre, F. Loraine. *Napoleon's Conquest of Prussia—1806.* London: John Lane, 1907.

Petrov, A. *Voina Rossii s Turtsiei, 1806–1812.* 3 vols. St. Petersburg, 1887.

Philipp, Thomas, and Ulrich Haarmann. *The Mamluks in Egyptian Politics and Society.* Cambridge: Cambridge University Press, 1998.

Philips, C. H. *The East India Company, 1784–1834.* Manchester: Manchester University Press, 1961.

Phillips, W. Alison. *George Canning.* New York: E. P. Dutton, 1903.

Phillips, W. Alison, and Arthur H. Reede. *Neutrality: Its History, Economic, and Law,* vol. 2, *The Napoleonic Period.* New York: Columbia University Press, 1936.

Phipps, Ramsay Weston. *The Armies of the First French Republic and the Rise of the Marshals of Napoleon I.* 5 vols. London: Oxford University Press, 1926–1939.

Picard, Ernest. *Bonaparte et Moreau.* Paris: Plon-Nourrit, 1905.

Pièces curieuses ou Alger en 1802. Paris: Palais Royal, 1830.

Pietre, K. G. *The Second Anglo-Maratha War, 1802–1805.* Poona: Dastane Ramchandra, 1990.

Pingaud, Léonce. *Un agent secret sous la révolution et l'empire: le comte d'Antraigues.* Paris: E. Plon Nourrit, 1894.

Pisani, Paul. *La Dalmatie de 1797 à 1815.* Paris: A. Picard et fils, 1893.

Planert, Ute, ed. *Napoleon's Empire: European Politics in Global Perspective.* New York: Palgrave Macmillan, 2016.

Platen, Carl Henrik von. *Stedingk: Curt von Stedingk (1746–1837): kosmopolit, krigare och diplomat hos Ludvig XVI, Gustavus III och Katarina den stora.* Stockholm: Atlantis, 1995.

Pluchon, Pierre. *Histoire des Antilles et de la Guyane.* Toulouse: Privat, 1982.

Pluchon, Pierre. *Toussaint Louverture: Un révolutionnaire noir d'Ancien Régime.* Paris: Fayard, 1989.

Poirteir, Cathal, ed. *The Great Irish Rebellion of 1798.* Dublin: Mercier Press, 1998.

Popkin, Jeremy D. *A Concise History of the Haitian Revolution.* Oxford: Blackwel, 2012.

Popov, A. I. *Smolenskie bitvy.* 2 vols, Moscow: Knizhnoe izdatelstvo, 2012.

Popov, A. I. *Voina 1812 goda: boevye deistviya na yuzhnom flange.* 3 vols, Moscow: Knizhnoe izdatelstvo, 2016.

Popov, A. I. *Vtoroe nastuplenie Velikoi armii v Russkoi kampanii.* 2 vols, Moscow: Knizhnoe izdatelstvo, 2017.

Porter, Bernard. *The Absent-Minded Imperialists: Empire, Society, and Culture in Britain.* Oxford: Oxford University Press, 2004.

Potto, Vasilii. *Kavkazskaia voina.* St. Petersburg: Tip. E. Evdokimova, 1887.

Pounds, Norman J. "The Origin of the Idea of Natural Frontiers in France." *Annals of the Association of American Geographers* 41, no. 2 (June 1951): 146–57.

Prado, Fabrício. *Edge of Empire: Atlantic Networks and Revolution in Bourbon Río de la Plata.* Berkeley: University of California Press, 2015.

Prentout, Henri. *L'Ile de France sous Decaen, 1803–1810.* Paris: Librairie Hachette, 1901.

Price, Jacob. *France and the Chesapeake: A History of the French Tobacco Monopoly, 1764–1791, and of Its Relationship to the British and American Tobacco Trades.* 2 vols. Ann Arbor: University of Michigan Press, 1973.

Price, Munro. *Napoleon: The End of Glory*. Oxford: Oxford University Press, 2014.

Pritchard, James S. *In Search of Empire: The French in the Americas, 1670–1730*. Cambridge: Cambridge University Press, 2004.

Pueyrredón, Carlos. *1810. La revolución de Mayo segun amplica documentación de la época*. Buenos Aires: Peusar, 1953.

Puryear, Vernon J. *Napoleon and the Dardanelles*. Berkeley: University of California Press, 1951.

Quataert, Donald. *The Ottoman Empire, 1700–1922*. Cambridge: Cambridge University Press, 2000.

Ragsdale, Hugh. "A Continental System in 1801: Paul I and Bonaparte." *Journal of Modern History* 42, no. 1 (March 1970): 70–89.

Ragsdale, Hugh. *Détente in the Napoleonic Era: Bonaparte and the Russians*. Lawrence: University of Kansas Press, 1980.

Ragsdale, Hugh. "Evaluating the Traditions of Russian Aggression: Catherine II and the Greek Project."*The Slavonic and East European Review* 66, no. 1 (1988): 91–117.

Ragsdale, Hugh. "The Origins of Bonaparte's Russian Policy." *Slavic Review* 27, no. 1 (March 1968): 85–90.

Ragdale, Hugh. *Paul I: A Reassessment of His Life and Reign*. Pittsburg: University Center for International Studies, 1979.

Ragsdale, Hugh. "Russia, Prussia, and Europe in the Policy of Paul I." *Jahrbücher für Geschichte Östeuropas* XXXI (1983): 81–118.

Ragsdale, Hugh, and V. Ponomarev, eds. *Imperial Russian Foreign Policy*. Cambridge: Cambridge University Press, 1993.

Randolph, Herbert. *Life of General Sir Robert Wilson... from Autobiographical Memoirs, Journals, Narratives, Correspondence, Etc.* London: J. Murray, 1862.

Rayfield, Donald. *Edge of Empires: A History of Georgia*. London: Reaktion, 2012.

Real, Willy. *Von Potsdam nach Basel; Studien zur Geschichte der Beziehungen Preussens zu den europäischen Mächten vom Regierungsantritt Friedrich Wilhelms II. bis zum Abschluss des Friedens von Basel, 1786–1795*. Basel: Helbing & Lichtenhahn, 1958.

Redgrave, T. M. D. "Wellington's Logistical Arrangements in the Peninsular War, 1809–1814." PhD dissertation, King's College London, 1979.

Restall, Matthew, and Kris E. Lane. *Latin America in Colonial Times*. Cambridge: Cambridge University Press, 2011.

Rhinelander, Laurens H. "The Incorporation of the Caucasus into the Russian Empire: The Case of Georgia." PhD dissertation, Columbia University, 1972.

Riasanovsky, Nicholas, and Mark D. Steinberg. *A History of Russia*. Oxford: Oxford University Press, 2011.

Ribbe, Claude. *Le crime de Napoléon*. Paris: Cherche-midi, 2013.

Rigault, Georges. *Le général Abdallah Menou et la dernière phase de l'expédition d'Egypte (1799–1801)*. Paris: Plon-Nourrit, 1911.

Riley, James C. "French Finances, 1727–1768." *Journal of Modern History* 59, no. 2 (1987): 209–43.

Ringrose, David R. *Spain, Europe and the "Spanish Miracle," 1700–1900*. Cambridge: Cambridge University Press, 1997.

Riotte, Torsten. *Hannover in der Britischen politik (1792–1815)*. Münster: Lit, 2005.

Risso, Patricia. *Oman & Muscat: An Early Modern History*. New York: St. Martin's Press, 1986.

Rivière, Serge M., and Kumari R. Issur, eds. *Baudin—Flinders dans l'océan indien: Voyages, découvertes, rencontre*. Paris: L'Harmattan, 2006.

Roberts, Andrew. *Napoleon: A Life*. New York: Penguin Books, 2014.

Roberts, Michael. *The Swedish Imperial Experience, 1650–1718*. Cambridge: Cambridge University Press, 1979.

Robertson, James A., ed. *Louisiana Under the Rule of Spain, France, and the United States, 1785–1807*. Cleveland: Arthur H. Clark, 1911.

Robertson, William S. *France and Latin-American Independence*. New York: octagon Books, 1967.

Rodríguez, Jaime E. *"We Are Now the True Spaniards": Sovereignty, Revolution, Independence, and the Emergence of the Federal Republic of Mexico, 1808–1824*. Stanford, CA: Stanford University Press, 2012.

Rogers, Nicholas. *The Press Gang: Naval Impressment and its Opponents in Georgian Britain*. London: Continuum, 2007.

Roider, Karl. *Baron Thugut and Austria's Response to the French Revolution*. Princeton, NJ: Princeton University Press, 1987.

Rojas, Martha Elena. "'Insults Unpunished': Barbary Captives, American Slaves, and the Negotiation of Liberty." *Early American Studies: An Interdisciplinary Journal* 1, no. 2 (2003): 159–86.

Rose, J. Holland. "The French East-Indian Expedition at the Cape in 1803." *English Historical Review* 15, no. 57 (January 1900): 129–32.

Rose, J. Holland. *The Life of Napoleon I*. London: George Bell and Sons, 1907.

Rose, J. Holland. *Lord Hood and the Defence of Toulon*. Cambridge: Cambridge University Press, 1922.

Rose, J. Holland, and Alexander M. Broadley. *Dumouriez and the Defence of England Against Napoleon*. London: J. Lane, 1909.

Rose, Michael, ed. *Collaboration and Resistance in Napoleonic Europe: State Formation in an Age of Upheaval, 1800–1815*. New York: Palgrave Macmillan, 2003.

Ross, Steven T. *Quest for Victory: French Military Strategy, 1792–1799*. New York: Barnes, 1973.

Rosselli, John. *Lord William Bentinck: The Making of a Liberal Imperialist, 1774–1839*. Berkeley: University of California Press, 1974.

Rössler, Hellmuth. *Graf Johann Philipp Stadion, Napoleons deutscher Gegenspieler*. Vienna: Herold, 1966.

Rothenberg, Gunther E. *The Art of Warfare in the Age of Napoleon*. Bloomington: Indiana University Press, 1978.

Rothenberg, Gunther E. *The Emperor's Last Victory: Napoleon and the Battle of Wagram*. London: Weidenfeld and Nicolson, 2004.

Rothenberg, Gunther E. *Napoleon's Great Adversaries: Archduke Charles and the Austrian Army, 1792–1814.* Bloomington: Indiana University Press, 1992.

Roux, Francois-Charles. *Les origines de l'expédition d' Egypte.* Paris: Plon-Nourrit, 1910.

Roy, Kaushik. *War, Culture and Society in Early Modern South Asia, 1740–1849.* New York: Routledge, 2011.

Rudé, George. *Revolutionary Europe, 1783–1815.* New York: Harper Torchbooks, 1966.

Rudorff, Raymond. *War to the Death: The Sieges of Saragossa, 1808–1809.* New York: Macmillan, 1974.

Rüstow, W. *Der krieg von 1805 in Deutschland und Italien.* Zurich: Meyer & Zeller, 1859.

Ryan, A. N. "The Defence of British Trade in the Baltic, 1808–1813." *English Historical Review* 74, no. 292 (1959): 443–66.

Rydjord, John. *Foreign Interest in the Independence of New Spain.* New York: Octagon Books, 1972.

Sahlins, Peter. "Natural Frontiers Revisited: France's Boundaries Since the Seventeenth Century." *American Historical Review* 95, no. 5 (December 1990): 1423–51.

Saint-Junien, Vigier de. *Brune's 1807 Campaign in Swedish Pomerania.* Translated and edited by George Nafziger. West Chester, OH: Nafziger Collection, 2001.

Saint-Louis, Vertus. *Mer et liberté Haïti (1492–1794).* Port-au-Prince: Bibliothèque nationale d'Haiti, 2008.

Sánchez-Albornoz, Nicolás, ed. *The Economic Modernization of Spain, 1830–1930.* New York: New York University Press, 1987.

Sandström, Allan. *Sveriges Sista Krig: De Dramatiska Åren 1808–1809.* Örebro: Bokförlaget Libris, 1994.

Sardesai, Govind S. *New History of the Marathas,* vol. 3, *Sunset over Maharashtra, 1772–1848.* New Delhi: Munshiram Manoharlal, 1986.

Saski, Charles Gaspard Louis. *Campagne de 1809 en Allemagne et en Autriche.* Paris: Berger-Levrault, 1899.

Sather, Lee. *The Prince of Scandinavia: Prince Christian August and the Scandinavian Crisis of 1807–1810.* Oslo: Forsvarsmuseet 2015.

Saugera, Eric. *Reborn in America: French Exiles and Refugees in the United States and the Vine and Olive Adventure, 1815–1865.* Tuscaloosa: University of Alabama Press, 2011.

Saul, Norman E. *Russia and the Mediterranean 1797–1807.* Chicago: University of Chicago Press, 1970.

Sauzey, Jean-Camille-Abel-Fleuri. *Les Allemands sous les aigles françaises; essai sur les troupes de la Confédération du Rhin, 1806–1814.* 6 vols. Paris: R. Chapelot, 1902–1912.

Savant, Jean. *Les espions de Napoléon.* Paris: Hachette, 1957.

Savinel, Pierre. *Moreau, rival républicain de Bonaparte.* Rennes: Ouest-France, 1986.

Sayyid-Marsot, Afaf Lutfi. *Egypt in the Reign of Muhammad Ali*. Cambridge: Cambridge University Press, 1984.

Schlegel, August Wilhelm von. *The Continental System, and Its Relations with Sweden*. London: J. J. Stockdale, 1813.

Schmidt, Charles. *Le grand-duché de Berg (1806–1813); étude sur la domination française en Allemagne sous Napoléon ler*. Paris: F. Alcan, 1905.

Schneid, Frederick C. *European Armies of the French Revolution, 1789–1802*. Norman: University of Oklahoma Press, 2015.

Schneid, Frederick C. *Napoleon's Conquest of Europe: The War of the Third Coalition*. Westport, CT: Praeger, 2005.

Schneid, Frederick C. *Napoleon's Italian Campaigns: 1805–1815*. Westport, CT: Praeger, 2002.

Schneid, Frederick C. *Soldiers of Napoleon's Kingdom of Italy: Army, State, and Society, 1800–1815*. Boulder, CO: Westview Press, 1995.

Schneid, Frederick C. *Warfare in Europe, 1792–1815*. Aldershot: Ashgate, 2007.

Schom, Alan. *Napoleon Bonaparte*. New York: HarperCollins, 1997.

Schop Soler, Ana María. *Las relaciones entre España y Rusia en la época de Carlos IV*. Barcelona: Universidad de Barcelona, Cátedra de Historia General de España, 1971.

Schroeder, Paul W. *The Transformation of European Politics, 1763–1848*. New York: Oxford University Press, 1994.

Schur, Nathan. *Napoleon in the Holy Land*. London: Greenhill Books, 1999.

Scott, Ernest. *Terre Napoléon: A History of French Explorations and Projects in Australia*. London: Methuen, 1910.

Scott, Hamish M. *The Birth of a Great Power System, 1740–1815*. London: Pearson Longman, 2006.

Sédouy, Jacques-Alain de. *Le Congrès de Vienne: l'Europe contre la France 1812–1815*. Paris: Perrin, 2003.

Seeley, John R. *Life and Times of Stein: Germany and Prussia in the Napoleonic Age*. Boston: Roberts Brothers, 1879.

Sen, Sudipta. *Empire of Free Trade: The East India Company and the Making of the Colonial Marketplace*. Philadelphia: University of Pennsylvania Press, 1998.

Senkowska-Gluck, Monika. "Les majorats français dans le duché de Varsovie (1807–1813)." *Annales historiques de la Révolution française* 36 (1964): 373–86.

Senkowska-Gluck, Monika. *Donacje napoleońskie w Księstwie Warszawskim; studium historycyno-prawne*. Wrocław: Zakład Narodowy im. Ossolińskich, 1968.

Serna, Pierre, Antonino de Francesco, and Judith A. Miller, eds. *Republics at War, 1776–1840: Revolutions, Conflicts, Geopolitics in Europe and the Atlantic World*. New York: Palgrave Macmillan, 2013.

Serna, Pierre. "Introduction—L'Europe une idée nouvelle à la fin du XVIIIe siècle?" *La Révolution française* 4 (2011).

Severn, John. *Architects of Empire. The Duke of Wellington and His Brothers*. Norman: University of Oklahoma Press, 2007.

Severn, John. *A Wellesley Affair: Richard Marquess Wellesley and the Conduct of Anglo-Spanish Diplomacy, 1809–1812*. Tallahassee: University Presses of Florida, 1981.

Sharman, Adam, and Stephen G. H. Roberts, eds. *1812 Echoes: The Cadiz Constitution in Hispanic History, Culture and Politics* (Newcastle upon Tyne: Cambridge Scholars Publishing, 2013).

Shaw, Stanford J. *History of the Ottoman Empire and Modern Turkey*. Cambridge: Cambridge University Press, 1976.

Sheehan, James J. *German History, 1770–1866*. Oxford: Clarendon Press, 2008.

Sheehan, James J. "State and Nationality in the Napoleonic Period." In *The State of Germany: The National Idea in the Making, Unmaking, and Remaking of a Modern Nation-State*, edited by John Breuilly, 47–59. Harlow: Longman, 1992.

Sherwig, John M. *Guineas and Gunpowder: British Foreign Aid in the Wars with France, 1793—1815*. Cambridge MA: Harvard University Press, 1969.

Shilder, Nikolai. *Imperator Aleksandr Pervyi, ego zhizn' i tsarstvovanie*. 3 vols. St. Petersburg: A. S. Suvorin, 1897.

Shilder, Nikolai. *Imperator Pavel I*. St. Petersburg: Izd. A. S. Suvorina, 1901.

Showalter, Dennis. "Reform and Stability: Prussia's Military Dialectic from Hubertusberg to Waterloo." In *The Projection and Limitations of Imperial Powers, 1618–1850*, edited by Frederick C. Schneid, 89–97. Leiden: Brill, 2012.

Shugerman, Jed Handelsman. "The Louisiana Purchase and South Carolina's Reopening of the Slave Trade in 1803." *Journal of the Early Republic* 22, no. 2 (2002): 263–90.

Silbert, Albert. *Do Portugal de antigo regime ao Portugal oitocentista*. Lisboa: Livros Horizonte, 1981.

Simms, Brendan. *The Impact of Napoleon: Prussian High Politics, Foreign Policy, and the Crisis of the Executive, 1797–1806*. Cambridge: Cambridge University Press, 1997.

Sked, Alan. *Metternich and Austria: An Evaluation*. New York: Palgrave Macmillan, 2008.

Sked, Alan. *Radetzky: Imperial Victor and Military Genius*. London: I. B. Tauris, 2011.

Small, Stephen. *Political Thought in Ireland, 1776–1798: Republicanism, Patriotism, and Radicalism*. Oxford: Clarendon Press, 2002.

Smith, Denis. *The Prisoners of Cabrera: Napoleon's Forgotten Soldiers, 1809–1814*. New York: Four Walls Eight Windows, 2001.

Smith, Jay M. *The French Nobility in the Eighteenth Century: Reassessments and New Approaches*. University Park: Pennsylvania State University Press, 2006.

Smyth, Jim, ed. *Revolution, Counter-revolution, and Union: Ireland in the 1790s*. Cambridge: Cambridge University Press, 2000.

Sokol, A. "Russian Expansion and Exploration in the Pacific." *American Slavic and East European Review* 11, no. 2 (April 1952): 85–105.

Sokolov, Oleg. *Austerlitz. Napoleon, Rossiya i Evropa, 1799–1805*. 2 vols. Moscow: Imperia Istorii, 2006.

Sokolov, Oleg. *Bitva dvukh imperii, 1805–1812*. St. Petersburg: Astrel, 2012.

Sorel, Albert. *L'Europe et la Révolution Française.* 8 vols. Paris: Plon Nourrit, 1887–1904.

Soysal, İsmail. *Fransız İhtilali ve Türk-Fransız Diplomasi Münasebetleri (1789–1802).* Ankara: Türk Tarih Kurumu, 1999.

Spear, Percival. *The Oxford History of Modern India, 1740–1947.* Oxford: Oxford University Press, 1965.

Stagg, J. C. A. *The War of 1812: Conflict for a Continent.* Cambridge: Cambridge University Press, 2012.

Stanhope, Philip Henry. *Life of the Right Honourable William Pitt.* London: John Murray, 1867.

Stanislavskaia, Avgustine. *Rossiia i Gretsiia v kontse XVIII–nachale XIX veka: Poltika Rossii v Ionicheskoi respublike, 1798–1807 g.g.* Moscow: Nauka 1976.

Stanislavskaia, Avgustine. *Russko-angliiskie otnosheniya i problemy Sredizemnomorya, 1798–1807.* Moscow: USSR Academy of Sciences, 1962.

Starbuck, Nicole. "Constructing the 'Perfect' Voyage: Nicolas Baudin at Port Jackson, 1802." PhD dissertation, University of Adelaide, 2009.

Stegemann, Hermann. *Der Kampf um den Rhein. Das Stromgebiet des Rheins im Rahmen der großen Politik und im Wandel der Kriegsgeschichte.* Stuttgart: Deutsche Verlags-Anstalt, 1924.

Stein, Stanley J., and Barbara H. Stein. *Apogee of Empire: Spain and New Spain in the Age of Charles III, 1759–1789.* Baltimore: John Hopkins University Press, 2003.

Stein, Stanley J., and Barbara H. Stein. *The Colonial Heritage of Latin America: Essays on Economic Dependence in Perspective.* New York: Oxford University Press, 1970.

Stein, Stanley J., and Barbara H. Stein. *Silver, Trade, and War: Spain and America in the Making of Early Modern Europe.* Baltimore: John Hopkins University Press, 2000.

Stickler, Matthias. "Erfurt als Wende—Bayern und Württemberg und das Scheitern der Pläne Napoleons I. für einen Ausbau der Rheinbundverfassung." In *Der Erfurter Fürstenkongreß 1808: Hintergründe, Ablauf, Wirkung,* edited by Rudolf Benl, 266–300. Erfurt: Stadtarchiv, 2008.

Stone, Bailey. *The Genesis of the French Revolution: A Global-Historical Interpretation.* Cambridge: Cambridge University Press, 1994.

Strathern, Paul. *Napoleon in Egypt.* New York: Bantam Books, 2008.

Street, John. *Artigas and the Emancipation of Uruguay.* Cambridge: Cambridge University Press, 1959.

Suanzes-Carpegna, Joaquín Varela. *La teoría del Estado en las Cortes de Cádiz: orígenes del constitucionalismo hispánico.* Madrid: Centro de Estudios Políticos y Constitucionales, 2011.

Summerfield, Stephen, and Susan Law. *Sir John Moore and the Universal Soldier,* vol. 1, *The Man, the Commander and the Shorncliffe System of Training.* London: Ken Trotman, 2015.

Suny, Ronald Grigor. *The Making of the Georgian Nation.* Bloomington: Indiana University Press, 1994.

Surguladze, A. *1783 tslis georgievskis traktati da misi istoriuli mnishvneloba.* Tbilisi: Tsodna, 1982.

Suzuki, Yasuko. *Japan-Netherlands Trade 1600–1800: The Dutch East India Company and Beyond.* Kyoto: Kyoto University Press, 2012.

Sveinsson, Jón Rúnar. *Society, Urbanity and Housing in Iceland.* Gävle, Sweden: Meyers, 2000.

Sykes, Percy M. *History of Persia.* London: Macmillan, 1915.

Tackett, Timothy. *Religion, Revolution, and Regional Culture in Eighteenth-Century France: The Ecclesiastical Oath of 1791.* Princeton, NJ: Princeton University Press, 1986.

Tackett, Timothy. *When the King Took Flight.* Cambridge, MA: Harvard University Press, 2003.

Taine, Hippolyte Adolphe. *The French Revolution.* New York: Henry Holt, 1881.

Tarle, Eugene. *Admiral Ushakov na Sredizemnom more, 1798–1800.* Moscow: Voennoe Izdat. Ministerstva Oborony SSSR, 1948.

Tarle, Eugene. *Kontinentalnaya blokada.* Moscow: Zadruga, 1913.

Tarle, Eugene. *Sochineniya.* 12 vols. Moscow: Izd-vo Akademii nauk SSSR, 1957–1962.

Taylor, George V. "The Paris Bourse on the Eve of the Revolution, 1781–1789." *American Historical Review* 67, no. 4 (1962): 951–77.

Taylor, Stephen. *Storm and Conquest: The Clash of Empires in the Eastern Seas, 1809.* New York: W. W. Norton, 2008.

Tezcan, Baki. *The Second Ottoman Empire: Political and Social Transformation in the Early Modern World.* Cambridge: Cambridge University Press, 2010.

Thiry, Jean. *Bonaparte en Italie, 1796–1797.* Paris: Berger-Levrault, 1973.

Thompson, Leonard Monteath. *A History of South Africa.* New Haven, CT: Yale University Press, 1990.

Thornton, Michal J. *Napoleon After Waterloo: England and the St. Helena Decision.* Stanford, CA: Stanford University Press, 1968.

Todorov, Nicola. "Finances et fiscalité dans le royaume de Westphalie." *La revue de l'Institut Napoléon* 2004, no. 11 (2005): 7–46.

Tomasson, Richard. *Iceland: The First New Society.* Minneapolis: University of Minnesota Press, 1980.

Tone, John. *The Fatal Knot: The Guerrilla War in Navarre and the Defeat of Napoleon in Spain.* Chapel Hill: University of North Carolina Press, 1994.

Toreno, Conde de. *Historia del levantamiento, guerra y revolución de España.* Edited by Joaquín Varela Suanzes-Carpegna. Madrid: Centro de Estudios Políticos y Constitucionales, 2008.

Tracy, James D., ed. *The Rise of Merchant Empires: Long Distance Trade in the Early Modern World, 1350–1750.* Cambridge: Cambridge University Press, 1993.

Trouillot, Henock. *Dessalines: ou, La tragédie post-coloniale.* Port-au-Prince: Panorama, 1966.

Tucker, Spencer C. *Stephen Decatur: A Life Most Bold and Daring.* Annapolis, MD: Naval Institute Press, 2004.

Tulard, Jean. *Le Directoire et le Consulat.* Paris: Presses universitaires de France, 1991.

Tullner, Mathias, and Sascha Möbius, eds. *1806: Jena, Auerstedt und die Kapitulation von Magdeburg: Schande oder Chance?* Halle: Landesheimatbund Sachsen-Anhalt, 2007.

Tyson, George, ed. *Toussaint L'Ouverture.* Englewood Cliffs, NJ: Prentice Hall, 1973.

Uglow, Jenny. *In These Times: Living in Britain Through Napoleon's Wars, 1793–1815.* New York: Macmillan, 2014.

Ulmann, Heinrich. *Russisch-preussische politik unter Alexander I. und Friedrich Wilhelm III. bis 1806.* Leipzig: Duncker und Humblot, 1899.

Vachée, Jean Baptiste Modeste Eugene. *Napoleon at Work.* London: Adam and Charles Black, 1914.

Valdés, José M. Portillo. *Crisis atlántica: Autonomía e independencia en la crisis de la monarquía Española.* Madrid: Marcial pons, 2006.

Van Kley, Dale K. *The Religious Origins of the French Revolution: From Calvin to the Civil Constitution, 1560–1791.* New Haven, CT: Yale University Press, 1996.

Vandal, Albert. *Napoléon et Alexandre 1er: l'alliance russe sous le 1er Empire.* 3 vols. Paris: Plon-Nourrit, 1894–1897.

Varma, Birendra. *From Delhi to Teheran: A Study of British Diplomatic Moves in North-Western India, Afghanistan and Persia, 1772–1803.* Patna: Janaki Prakashan, 1980.

Vedel, Dominique. *Relations de la campagne d'Andalousie, 1808.* Paris: La Vouivre, 1999.

Vela, Francisco. *La batalla de Bailén, 1808: el águila derrotada.* Madrid: Almena Ediciones, 2007.

Velde, François R., and David R. Weir. "The Financial Market and Government Debt Policy in France, 1746–1793." *Journal of Economic History* 52, no. 1 (1992): 1–39.

Veve, Thomas Dwight. *The Duke of Wellington and the British Army of Occupation in France, 1815–1818.* Westport CT: Greenwood Press, 1992.

Vichness, Samuel Edison. "Marshal of Portugal: The Military Career of William Carr Beresford, 1785–1814." PhD dissertation, Florida State University, 1976.

Vick, Brian E. *The Congress of Vienna: Power and Politics After Napoleon.* Cambridge, MA: Harvard University Press, 2014.

Vigié, Marc, and Muriel Vigié. *L'herbe à nicot: amateurs de tabac, fermiers généraux et contrebandiers sous l'Ancien Régime.* Paris: Fayard, 1989.

Villani, Pasquale. *Mezzogiorno tra riforme e rivoluzione.* Bari: Laterza, 1962.

Vlekke, Bernard. *Nusantara: A History of the East Indian Archipelago.* Cambridge, MA: Harvard University Press, 1943.

Voelcker, Tom. *Admiral Saumarez Versus Napoleon: The Baltic, 1807–1812.* Woodbridge: Boydell Press, 2008.

Vovelle, Michel. *Les républiques soeurs sous le regard de la Grande Nation.* Paris: L'Harmattan, 2007.

Vries, Jan de. *The Economy of Europe in an Age of Crisis, 1600–1750.* Cambridge: Cambridge University Press, 1976.

Vucinich, W. S., ed. *The First Serbian Uprising, 1804–1813*. New York: Brooklyn College Press, 1982.

Wanquet, Claude. *La France et la première abolition de l'esclavage, 1794–1802: le cas des colonies orientales, Île de France (Maurice) et la Réunion*. Paris: Karthala, 1998.

Ward, Adolphus W. *Great Britain and Hanover*. Oxford: Clarendon Press, 1899.

Ward, Adolphus W., and George P. Gooch. *The Cambridge History of British Foreign Policy, 1783–1919*, vol. 1, *1783–1815*. Cambridge: Cambridge University Press, 1922.

Ward, Peter A. *British Naval Power in the East, 1794–1805: The Command of Admiral Peter Rainier*. Oxford: Boydell Press, 2013.

Waresquiel, Emmanuel. *Talleyrand: le prince immobile*. Paris: Fayard, 2006.

Watson, Ian. *Foundation for Empire: English Private Trade in India, 1659–1760*. New Delhi: Vikas, 1980.

Webster, Anthony. *The Twilight of the East India Company: The Evolution of Anglo-Asian Commerce and Politics, 1790–1860*. Woodbridge: Boydell Press, 2009.

Weil, Maurice Henri. *La Campagne de 1814*. Paris: Librairie Militaire de L. Baudoin, 1891.

Weinlader, James Raymond. "The Peace of Amiens, 1801–1802: Its Justification in Relation to Empire." PhD dissertation, University of Wisconsin, 1977.

Weller, Jac. *Wellington in the Peninsula, 1808–1814*. London: Nicolas Vane, 1962.

Welschinger, Henri. *Le duc d'Enghien*. Paris: E. Plon, Nourrit, 1888.

Welschinger, Henri. *Le duc d'Enghien. L'enlèvement d'Ettenheim et l'exécution de Vincennes*. Paris: Plon-Nourrit, 1913.

Welschinger, Henri. "L'Europe et l'exécution du duc d'Enghien." *Revue de la Société des études historiques* 8 (1890): 1–19, 73–94.

Welschinger, Henri. *Le pape et l'empereur, 1804–1815*. Paris, Librairie Plon-Nourrit, 1905.

Wheeler, H. F. B. *Napoleon and the Invasion of England: The Story of the Great Terror*. London: John Lane, 1908.

Whelan, Joseph. *Jefferson's War: America's First War on Terror, 1801–1805*. New York: Carroll and Graf, 2003.

White, Charles Edward. *The Enlightened Soldier: Scharnhorst and the Militarische Gesellschaft in Berlin, 1801–1805*. Westport, CT: Praeger, 1989.

Wild, Antony. *The East India Company: Trade and Conquest from 1600*. New York: Lyons Press, 2000.

Williams, John Hoyt. *The Rise and Fall of the Paraguayan Republic, 1800–1870*. Austin: Institute of Latin American Studies, University of Texas at Austin, 1979.

Williams, Patrick G., S. Charles Bolton, and Jeanne M. Whayne. *A Whole Country in Commotion: The Louisiana Purchase and the American Southwest*. Fayetteville: University of Arkansas Press, 2005.

Willis, Sam. *In the Hour of Victory: The Royal Navy at War in the Age of Nelson*. New York: W. W. Norton, 2014.

Wilson, Peter H. *Heart of Europe: A History of the Holy Roman Empire*. Cambridge, MA: Belknap Press, 2016.

Wilson, Peter H. *The Holy Roman Empire, 1495–1806.* New York: St. Martin's Press, 1999.

Wink, Martijn. "Een militair debacle? Bataafse militaire inzet in West-Indië 1802–1804." BA thesis, University of Leiden, 2018.

Winston, James E., and R. W. Colomb. "How the Louisiana Purchase Was Financed." *Louisiana Historical Quarterly* XII (1929): 189–237.

Woloch, Isser. *Napoleon and His Collaborators: The Making of a Dictatorship.* New York: W. W. Norton, 2001.

Woloch, Isser. "Napoleonic Conscription: State Power and Civil Society." *Past and Present* 111 (1986): 101–29.

Woloch, Isser. *The New Regime: Transformations of the French Civic Order, 1789–1820s.* New York: W. W. Norton, 1995.

Woolf, Stuart. *Napoleon's Integration of Europe.* London: Routledge, 1991.

Woronoff, Denis. *The Thermidorean Regime and the Directory, 1794–1799.* Cambridge: Cambridge University Press, 1984.

Wright, Denis. *The English Amongst the Persians: Imperial Lives in Nineteenth Century Iran.* London: I. B. Tauris, 2001.

Yalçınkaya, Mehmet Alaaddin. *The First Permanent Ottoman Embassy in Europe: The Embassy of Yusuf Agah Efendi to London (1793–1797).* Istanbul: Isis Press, 2010.

Yapp, Malcolm. *Strategies of British India: Britain, Iran, and Afghanistan, 1798–1850.* Oxford: Clarendon Press, 1980.

Yaycioglu, Ali. *Partners of the Empire: The Crisis of the Ottoman Order in the Age of Revolutions.* Stanford: Stanford University Press, 2016.

Yonge, Charles Duke. *The Life and Administration of Robert Banks, Second Earl of Liverpool, K.G.* London: Macmillan, 1868.

Young, Eric van. *The Other Rebellion: Popular Violence, Ideology, and the Mexican Struggle for Independence, 1810–1821.* Stanford: Stanford University Press, 2001.

Zacks, Richard. *The Pirate Coast: Thomas Jefferson, the First Marines, and the Secret Mission of 1805.* New York: Hyperion, 2005.

Zaghi, Carlo. *L'Italia di Napoleon dalla Cisalpina al Regno.* Turin: UTET, 1986.

Zamoyski, Adam. *Moscow 1812: Napoleon's Fatal March.* New York: Harper Perennial, 2005.

Zamoyski, Adam. *Phantom Terror: Political Paranoia and the Creation of the Modern State, 1789–1848.* New York: Basic Books, 2015.

Zamoyski, Adam. *Rites of Peace: The Fall of Napoleon and the Congress of Vienna.* London: Harper Perennial, 2007.

Zawadzki, W. H. "Prince Adam Czartoryski and Napoleonic France, 1801–1805: A Study in Political Attitudes." *Historical Journal* 18, no. 2 (1975): 248–49.

Zemtsov, Vladimir. *1812 god: Pozhar Moskvy.* Moscow: Kniga, 2010.

Zlotnikov, M. *Kontinentalnaya blokada i Rossiya.* Moscow: Nauka, 1966.

Zorlu, Tuncay. *Innovation and Empire in Turkey: Sultan Selim III and the Modernisation of the Ottoman Navy.* London: Tauris Academic Studies, 2008.

INDEX